RUSSIA

MONGOLIA

N-ND
ESTONIA
LATVIA
LITHUANIA
ELARUS
UKRAINE
IA
MOLDOVA
BULGARIA
TURKEY
CY.
SYRIA
LB.
IS.
JR.
IRAQ
EGYPT
KUWAIT
SAUDI
ARABIA
BA.
U.A.E.
OMAN
ERITREA
YEMEN
DJIBOUTI
SUDAN
ETHIOPIA
EP.
JGANDA
RWANDA
BURUNDI
NGO
(Kinshasa)
KENYA
TANZANIA
SOMALIA
ZAMBIA
ZIM-
BABWE
BOT-
WANA
MALAWI
UTH
RICA
LESOTHO
SWAZILAND
MOZAMBIQUE
MADAGASCAR

GA.
AZ.
AR.
KAZAKSTAN
UZBEKI-
STAN
TK.
KY.
TJ.
AFGHANI-
STAN
IRAN
PAKI-
STAN
NEPAL
BHUTAN
INDIA
BANG-
LADESH
MYAN-
MAR
LAOS
THAILAND
SRI LANKA
CAMBODIA
MALAYSIA
VIETNAM
BRUNEI

CHINA

N. KOREA
S. KOREA
JAPAN

TAIWAN

PHILIPPINES

PACIFIC
OCEAN

INDONESIA

PAPUA
NEW GUINEA
SOLOMON IS.

INDIAN OCEAN

AUSTRALIA

NEW
ZEALAND

THE WORLD - August 2002

FOURTH EDITION

International Business Law

Text, Cases, and Readings

Ray August

Professor of Business Law
College of Business and Economics
Washington State University
J.D., University of Texas at Austin
LL.M. in International Law, University of Cambridge
Ph.D. in American Legal History, University of Idaho

PEARSON

Prentice Hall

Upper Saddle River, New Jersey 07458

Library of Congress Cataloging-in-Publication Data

August, Ray
   International business law : text, cases, and readings / Ray August.—4th ed.
      p.   cm.
   Includes bibliographical references and index.
   ISBN 0-13-101410-2
   1. Commercial law.   2. International business enterprises—Law and legislation.   3.
Foreign trade regulation.   I. Title.

K1005 .I58   2003
341.7′53—dc21

              2002035502

Acquisitions Editor: David Parker
Editor-in-Chief: Jeff Shelstad
Assistant Editor: Ashley Keim
Editorial Assistant: Melissa Yu
Marketing Manager: Debbie Clare
Marketing Assistant: Amanda Fisher
Managing Editor: John Roberts
Production Editor: Renata Butera
Production Assistant: Joe DeProspero
Permissions Coordinator: Suzanne Grappi
Associate Director, Manufacturing: Vincent Scelta
Production Manager: Arnold Vila
Manufacturing Buyer: Michelle Klein
Cover Design: Bruce Kenselaar
Cover Illustration/Photo: The Studio Dog
Composition: BookMasters, Inc.
Full-Service Project Management: Jennifer Welsch, BookMasters, Inc.
Printer/Binder: Courier/Kendallville
Cover Printer: Phoenix Color Corp.

Credits and acknowledgments borrowed from other sources and reproduced, with permission, in this textbook appear on appropriate page within the text.

Pearson Education LTD.
Pearson Education Australia PTY, Limited
Pearson Education Singapore, Pte. Ltd
Pearson Education North Asia Ltd
Pearson Education, Canada, Ltd
Pearson Educatión de México, S.A. de C.V.
Pearson Education–Japan
Pearson Education Malaysia, Pte. Ltd

10 9 8 7 6 5 4
ISBN 0-13-101410-2

To my love, Diana

Brief Contents

Contents

Preface

Business today is truly international. Worldwide, approximately half of all business transactions are done across national borders. An enterprise, therefore, that chooses to ignore all but the laws and legal procedures of its own country is choosing to work half blind.

Lawyers and businesspeople have to have a basic understanding of legal systems other than their own. The consequence of failing to do so is nowhere more forcefully stated than in an opinion of Philippine Supreme Court Justice Cruz:

> The petitioners' counsel have submitted a memorandum replete with citations of American cases, as if they were arguing before a court of the United States. The Court is bemused by such attitude. While these decisions do have persuasive effect upon us, they can at best be invoked only to support our own jurisprudence, which we have developed and enriched on the basis of our own persuasions as a people, particularly since we became independent. . . .
>
> We appreciate the assistance foreign decisions offer us. . . . But we should not place undue and fawning reliance upon them and regard them as indispensable mental crutches without which we cannot come to our own decision through the employment of our own endowments. We live in a different ambiance and must decide our own problems in the light of our own interests and needs, and of our qualities and even idiosyncrasies as a people, and always with our own concept of law and justice.
>
> *Sanders v. Veridiano.*
> Philippine Supreme Court.
> *Supreme Court Reports Annotated, Second Series,* vol. 162, p. 88 (1988).

The goal of this book is to show how firms doing business between the more than 185 countries of the world are governed and regulated. No single legal system is emphasized; rather, cases and materials from many countries are collected to show both the diversity and the similarity of businesses and of the law.

International organizations play a large role in regulating international business, and they too are examined, along with the treaties, conventions, and agreements that created them and the treaties, conventions, and rules that they administer.

SPECIAL FEATURES

This is a book of text, cases, and readings. Depending on the teaching style of the instructor, as well as the backgrounds of students, either the text or the cases and readings can be emphasized.

As much as possible, sexist language in the text has been avoided. Unfortunately, many (if not most) international statutory and case materials use only the masculine gender (i.e., he, him, his) when speaking of a person. Unfortunately, as well, the English language does not have a neuter pronoun that can be readily substituted for these words. To be consistent, and to avoid the clumsiness of phrases such as "he or she," or "he/she," or "s/he," the masculine gender is also used in the text when general reference is made to an individual.

Plain Language Citations

Standard law abbreviations, such as [1961] 3 W.I.REP. 198, would be all but meaningless to most readers (even most lawyers with access to domestic citation dictionaries) because the cases and materials are taken from many uncommon sources. As a consequence, all citations are given in the following form: name, volume, part (if appropriate), series (if appropriate), page, court, and year. For example: *West Indian Reports,* vol. 3, p. 198 (Br. Guiana Supreme Ct., 1961).

In addition, when case materials are available on the Internet, the World Wide Web address for those materials is provided in a footnote. These addresses are also listed on the "links" page of the textbook's Web site at IntBusLaw.com.

Margin Notes

Key words and phrases are defined in margin notes for ready reference and easy review.

Chapter Questions and Review Problem

Each chapter concludes with a series of questions that highlight the major topics of the chapter. For instructors (or students) who prefer to have a single unifying problem tying all of the elements of each chapter (and the book) together, an "applicational" review problem is also provided.

SUPPORTING MATERIALS

Web Site

Supporting materials for this textbook are available on the Internet at IntBusLaw.com and www.prenhall.com/august. These include update information and errata, model syllabi for both undergraduate and graduate courses, and links to case materials and other supporting materials.

Full Cases Online

Cases in this edition marked with the mouse ( ) icon are available online at IntBusLaw. com and www.prenhall.com/august in their full length and in their original unedited format.

Student Guide

A guide for students containing summaries of the text; practice true-or-false, multiple choice, and essay questions; and lists of key words and phrases for each chapter is available on the Internet at IntBusLaw.com and www.prenhall.com/august.

International Law Dictionary and Directory

A dictionary of international legal and business terms, plus links to key international organizations and resources on the World Wide Web, is available on the Internet at IntBusLaw.com and www.prenhall.com/august.

Online Lectures

Audiovisual lectures covering the entire textbook are available on the Internet at IntBusLaw. com and www.prenhall.com/august. These lectures contain both outlines and narration by an animated cartoon character. They can be viewed—even with low-speed Internet connections— using free downloadable software available at the Web site just mentioned.

CHANGES IN THE FOURTH EDITION

The fourth edition contains new cases, new readings, and new and updated text. There are 19 new cases—approximately one-fifth of all the cases in the book. As in the previous editions, they are taken from a wide range of jurisdictions. New jurisdictions represented include Canada, Spain, and the International Tribunal for the Law of Seas. Among the more interesting new cases are those dealing with the Bhopal incident, the U.S. Antiterrorism Act, and the Unocal—human rights of workers—suit.

There are 10 new readings dealing with a wide variety of controversial issues, especially issues related to international business ethics. Among these are a reading on cultural differences ("The Clash of Civilizations?"), a report on the U.S. view on the Kyoto Protocol, a report on the 1999 WTO meeting in Seattle ("The Battle for Seattle"), an examination of the use of compulsory patents by Third World countries to combat AIDS, an article on the pros and cons of countertrade, and a defense of the practice of reincorporating in tax havens to avoid paying high taxes.

There are updated materials in Chapter 1 describing the structure and organization of the European Union and new materials in Chapter 2 on climate control and the Kyoto Protocol. The materials on criminal jurisdiction in Chapter 3 have been updated and new materials have been added on the exercise of extraterritorial jurisdiction. The discussion of the organization of multinational enterprises and the European Union's anticompetitive behavior rules in Chapter 4 have been updated (reflecting structural changes in the E.U.'s treaties, such as the renumbering of old Articles 85 and 86 as Articles 81 and 82). Chapter 5 now includes a discussion, in connection with the Bhopal Case, of the rules that apply to companies whose subsidiaries cause tort injuries. The discussion in Chapter 7 of the IMF's facilities is updated. There are new materials in Chapter 9 describing the WIPO Arbitration and Mediation Center's role in resolving Internet domain name disputes. The Incoterms discussed in Chapter 11 have been updated to the 2000 edition of those terms. Chapter 12 has new materials dealing with countertrade. The tax tables in Chapter 13 have been completely updated. Finally, readers will notice the addition of a number of new photographs, illustrations, and cartoons.

ACKNOWLEDGMENTS: FIRST EDITION

It would have been impossible to produce this book without the help of a great many people. I want to thank my wife, Diana Pace, who drew all of the maps, who proofread the manuscript more times than either one of us cares to remember, and who helped me in so many ways. Diana's mother, Genny Pace, also kindly and carefully proofread the manuscript. Mary Arndt, Gerald D'Souza, Otis Henderson, Meredith Kinzer, Katie Leid, Sandie Meyers, Kristi Nelson, Rae Ann Pugliese, and Kelly Rice all helped with typing.

I am especially grateful to the individuals who reviewed the early drafts of the book and who provided invaluable suggestions for its improvement: Teresa Brady of Holy Family College in Philadelphia, Robert Chatov of the State University of New York at Buffalo, John L. Ewing-Smith of Burlington County College in New Jersey, Andy Khan of Athabasca University in Alberta, Roger Pitchford of Massey University in New Zealand, Bruce L. Rockwood of Bloomsburg University in Pennsylvania, Clyde D. Stoltenberg of the University of Kansas, and Alfred E. Sutherland of Boston College. Finally, Joe Heider, Don Hull, Brian Hatch, Wendy Goldner, and Henry Pils of Prentice Hall made important contributions in getting the book to market.

ACKNOWLEDGMENTS: SECOND EDITION

Much of the work that went into completing the Second Edition was done while I was on sabbatical from Washington State University. I want to thank Dean Gale Sullenberger and former Dean Rom Markin of the College of Business and Economics and Prof. Glenn L. Johnson, Chairman of the Department of Accounting and Business Law, not only for allowing me to take a leave but also for providing me with help and encouragement to complete the book. While I was on sabbatical, I was a Visiting Scholar at the School of Law at the University of Washington. My thanks to Dean Wallace D. Loh, Emily Swanson, the faculty, and especially the librarians for opening up their resources to me. My thanks as well to the librarians at Washington State University, the University of Idaho, and the University of Idaho College of Law, all of whom were most helpful.

The editorial staff at Prentice Hall was, as always, hard working, professional, and most supportive. My thanks to Don Hull, John Larkin, Andrea Cuperman, Anne Graydon, and Nancy Marcello.

Finally, a special thanks to Diana Pace, my wife, who gave so much of her time to read, reread, critique, edit, and improve this book; and to draw and redraw its maps and other exhibits. The book was always a work of love for me, but it was just plain hard work for her. Thank you, sweetheart.

ACKNOWLEDGMENTS: THIRD EDITION

I want to thank those individuals who sent letters and e-mail messages offering advice and updates about the materials in the Second Edition, much of which I have posted on the Internet on the textbook's Web site. These include Craig Barkacs of the University of San Diego, Paul Eden of the University of Leeds, and Albert Pucciarelli of Fordham University.

I want to thank Dean Glenn Johnson and former Dean Gale Sullenberger, of the College of Business and Economics at Washington State University, both of whom provided support and encouragement for the revision of this textbook. Again, I greatly appreciate the help of the librarians at Washington State University, the University of Washington, the University of Idaho, and the University of Texas at Austin, all of whom helped me identify and locate materials on international business law.

I am grateful to the individuals who reviewed the Second Edition and provided helpful suggestions for improving the Third Edition: Mark Blodgett, Suffolk University; Mary Smidt, University of Phoenix; Paul Frantz, California State University, Long Beach; and David Austil, Union University.

The editorial staff at Prentice Hall, as always, was very supportive and helpful in getting this textbook into production and out into the market. My thanks to Natalie Anderson, Linda Schreiber, Jessica Sabloff, Debbie Clare, and Linda Albelli. My special thanks goes to my local Prentice Hall sales representative, Larry Armstrong, for his help in getting copies of the textbook and the instructor's manual to instructors both locally and around the world.

I want to thank Impressions Book and Journal Services, Inc., who did an excellent job copyediting, typesetting, and proofreading the text.

As always, I could not have written this textbook without the help, support, and encouragement of my wife, Diana Pace. Thank you, my darling.

ACKNOWLEDGMENTS: FOURTH EDITION

My thanks to those individuals who reviewed the Third Edition and provided very helpful suggestions for improving this edition: Wendy Gelman, Florida International University; Kenneth B. Goldsmith, American Intercontinental University; Tayyab Mahmud, Cleveland-Marshall College of Law, Cleveland State University; Lamar Odom, Our Lady of the Lake University; John W. Palmer, Center for Academic Integrity; Bruce L. Rockwood, Suffolk University; Kurt M. Saunders, California State University Northridge; and W. Ray Williams, Rutgers University.

I want to thank Dean Len Jessup and former Dean Glenn Johnson of the College of Business and Economics at Washington State University, and Director Bob Greenberg of the School of Accounting, Information Systems and Business Law at Washington State University, all of whom provided support and encouragement for the revision of this textbook. I greatly appreciate the help of the librarians at Washington State University, the University of Washington, and the University of Idaho all of whom helped me identify and locate materials on international business law.

As always, the editorial staff at Prentice Hall did an outstanding job in getting this textbook into production and out into the market. My thanks to Jeff Shelstad, Alana Bradley, David Parker, Ashley Keim, Elena Picnic, Debbie Clare, Renata Butera, Sam Goffinet and Melissa Yu. Thanks also to Larry Armstrong, to my local Prentice Hall sales representative, who continues to do an outstanding job getting copies of the textbook and the instructor's manual to instructors both locally and around the world.

My thanks to Keri Jean Miksza for her excellent work copyediting the text and to BookMasters, Inc., which did an excellent job with the composition of my book.

Of course, this book could not have been written without the help, support, and encouragement of my wife, Diana Pace. Thank you, sweetheart.

—Ray August
ray@august1.com
September 2, 2002

CHAPTER

Introduction to International and Comparative Law

1

A. WHAT IS INTERNATIONAL LAW?

international law: The body of legal rules and norms that regulates activities carried on beyond the legal boundaries of a single state.

public international law: That division of international law that deals primarily with the rights and duties of states and intergovernmental organizations as between themselves.

private international law: That division of international law that deals primarily with the rights and duties of individuals and nongovernmental organizations in their international affairs.

comity: (From Latin *comitas:* "courteousness.") The practice or courtesy existing between states of treating each other with goodwill and civility.

International law is the body of rules and norms that regulates activities carried on outside the legal boundaries of states. In particular, it regulates three international relationships: (1) those between states and states, (2) those between states and persons, and (3) those between persons and persons.

The subject matter of international law has changed dramatically in recent years. Traditionally, this area of law dealt only with conduct between states and was called the law of nations. Later, it came to be called **public international law**, in part to distinguish it from private international law. **Private international law** is the name given to the rules that regulate the affairs of private persons internationally. Examples of public and private international law are shown in Exhibit 1-1.

Contemporary international law now regulates organizations and individuals as well as nations, and the division between public and private law has become blurred. Today, the term *international law* applies to any conduct outside the boundaries of states, whether of a public or a private nature.

Because there is no world government, some have questioned if international law is really law. It is law, quite simply, because states and individuals regard it as such. This becomes clear when international law is compared with international comity.

Comity is the practice, or courtesy, between states of treating each other with goodwill and civility. It is not law, however, because states do not regard it as something they are required to respect. For example, until it became a matter of legal obligation under the 1961 Vienna Convention on Diplomatic Relations,[1] it was long considered to be a customary courtesy to allow foreign diplomats the privilege of importing goods they intended for their own private use free of customs duties. The privilege was not a legal right guaranteed by international law, however, because states did not feel compelled to grant the privilege except as a courtesy.[2]

---

[1] Article 36.

[2] Another example of comity is set out in Republic of the Philippines v. Westinghouse Elec. Corp., *Federal Reporter, Third Series,* vol. 43, p. 65 (3rd Circuit Ct. of Appeals 1994). In this case, the appellate court overturned the U.S. trial

Public International Law	Private International Law
Sources of international law	Noncommercial
Scope of international law	Torts
International personality	Inheritances
State territory	Nationality
State succession	Marriage and divorce
State responsibility to aliens	Commercial
Law of the sea	Contracts and sales
International dispute settlement	Transportation
Law of war	Money and banking
	Financing
	Securities regulations
	Intellectual property
	Antitrust
	Antifraud
	Taxation

EXHIBIT 1-1 Examples of Public and Private International Law

B. THE MAKING OF INTERNATIONAL LAW

Within nations, law is made by legislatures, courts, and other agencies of government. On the international level, by comparison, no formal machinery for making law exists. There is no world government. Nonetheless, in working together, the different states function in the roles of both lobbyists and legislators.

state practice: The conduct and practices of states in their dealings with each other.

As a basic principle, international law comes into effect only when states consent to it. The general consent of the international community can be found in **state practice**, that is, in the conduct and practices of states in their dealings with each other. Statements or evidence of general consent can be found in the decisions of the International Court of Justice (ICJ) (or its predecessor, the Permanent Court of International Justice), in resolutions passed by the General Assembly of the United Nations, in "law-making" **multilateral treaties**, and in the conclusions of international conferences. Sometimes, when a provision is repeated over and over in **bilateral treaties**, courts and law writers will regard the provision as having the general consent of the international community. Legal writers often cite unratified treaties and reports of international agencies, such as those of the International Law Commission, as indicating a trend toward general consent.

multilateral treaty: Treaty between more than two states.

arbitration: (From Latin *arbitrari:* "to give judgment.") The process by which parties to a dispute submit their differences to the judgment of an impartial third person or group selected by mutual consent.

The particular consent of a state to be bound by an international law can be found in the declarations of its government, in its domestic legislation, in its court decisions, and in the treaties (both bilateral and multilateral) to which it is a party.

bilateral treaty: Formal binding agreement between two states.

Recently, the widespread use of **arbitration** tribunals to resolve disputes between private parties has also led to the creation of an international **case law** that is independent of state action. Because lawyers representing states in international tribunals are willing to point to this case law as precedent for resolving disputes between states, and because international tribunals are willing to recognize it in such proceedings, one can conclude that the states of the world have given their general consent to its use.

case law: Law based on judicial decision or precedent rather than statutes.

C. SOURCES OF INTERNATIONAL LAW

The sources, or evidences, of international law are what international tribunals rely on in determining the content of international law. Article 38(1) of the Statute of the International Court of Justice lists the sources that the Court is permitted to use. Most writers regard this

court's order requiring the Philippine government to cease harassing witnesses in the Philippines. The appellate court held that the trial court could request compliance by a foreign sovereign as a matter of comity, but that it could not order compliance as a matter of law.

list as being reasonably complete and one that other international courts should use as well. Article 38(1) provides:

> The Court, whose function is to decide in accordance with international law such disputes as are submitted to it, shall apply:
>
> (a) international conventions, whether general or particular, establishing rules expressly recognized by the contesting states;
> (b) international custom, as evidence of a general practice accepted as law;
> (c) the general principles of law recognized by civilized nations;
> (d) subject to the provisions of Article 59, judicial decisions and the teachings of the most highly qualified publicists of the various nations, as subsidiary means for the determination of rules of law.

hierarchy: A group arranged according to rank or authority.

This listing implies a **hierarchy**, or order, in which these sources are to be relied on. That is, treaties or conventions are to be turned to before custom, custom before general principles of law, and general principles before judicial decisions or publicists' writings. Strictly speaking, Article 38(1) does not set up a hierarchy; but in practice, the ICJ and other tribunals turn first to treaties. This is appropriate because treaties (especially those ratified by the states parties involved in a dispute) are clear-cut statements of the rules the court should apply. Also, customary law, which is based on practice, is more appropriate than general principles, which are usually found inductively by legal writers who have examined the long-standing practices of states. Finally, all of these are considered more reliable than either court decisions or lawyers' writings because the latter are used only to apply or interpret the former.

Treaties and Conventions

treaty: (From Latin *tractare:* "to treat.") Legally binding agreement between two or more states.

In international law the equivalents of legislation are treaties and conventions. **Treaties** are legally binding agreements between two or more states. **Conventions** are legally binding agreements between states sponsored by international organizations, such as the United Nations. Both are binding upon states because of a shared sense of commitment and because one state fears that if it does not respect its promises, other states will not respect their promises.

convention: (From Latin *convenire:* "to come together.") Legally binding agreement between states sponsored by an international organization.

Today, most of the customary rules that once governed treaties are contained in the Vienna Convention on the Law of Treaties,[3] which came into force in 1980.[4] It only applies to treaties adopted after a party ratifies the agreement; nevertheless, its wide acceptance by states and its codification of customary rules has made it the *de facto*[5] standard for interpretation.

Article 2(1)(a) of the Vienna Convention states that "'Treaty' means an international agreement concluded between states in written form and governed by international law, whether embodied in a single instrument or two or more related instruments and whatever its particular designation." To avoid complexity, this definition excludes certain agreements, including oral promises, unilateral promises,[6] agreements relating to international organizations, agreements governed by municipal law, and agreements that were not intended to create a legal relationship. Because these agreements are excluded in the Convention's definition, however, does not mean that international tribunals will ignore them or that they do not have effect.

---

[3]The text of the Vienna Convention is posted at www.un.org/law/ilc/texts/treaties.htm.

[4]Currently, there are 90 states parties, including most of the developed world other than France and the United States. United Nations, *Multilateral Treaties Deposited with the Secretary-General, Status as at 5 August 2002,* posted at www.un.org/Depts/Treaty/final/ts2/newfiles/part_boo/xxiiiboo/xxiii_1.html.

[5]Latin: "from the fact" or "in fact"; in effect although not formally recognized.

[6]*See* Nuclear Tests Cases, *International Court of Justice Reports,* vol. 1974, p. 253 (1974). In 1963, the Nuclear Test Ban Treaty was concluded, forbidding atmospheric tests of nuclear bombs. France did not sign the treaty and conducted tests in the South Pacific in 1972 and 1973. Australia and New Zealand brought suits in the ICJ against France. The cases were taken off the Court's list without a decision on the merits when France declared that it would discontinue testing after 1973. The judgment of the Court stated: "It is well recognized that declarations made by way of unilateral acts, concerning legal or factual situations, may have the effect of creating legal obligations. . . . The objects of the statements [by France] are clear and they were addressed to the international community as a whole, and the Court holds that they constitute an undertaking possessing legal effect." (Note: In 1981, France resumed testing.)

The principle recognized in the Nuclear Tests Cases was later applied by the ICJ in the Case Concerning Military and Paramilitary Activities in and against Nicaragua (Nicaragua v. United States), *International Court of Justice Reports,* vol. 1986, p. 14 at p. 132 (1986) and in the Case Concerning the Frontier Dispute (Burkina Faso v. Mali), *International Court of Justice Reports,* vol. 1986, p. 554 at pp. 573–574 (1986).

The effect of an authorized oral commitment made by a government official of one state to a government official of another state is discussed in Case 1–1.

Case 1–1 Legal Status of Eastern Greenland
Denmark v. Norway

Permanent Court of International Justice, 1933.
Permanent Court of International Justice Reports, vol. 1933, Series A/B, No. 53 (1933).

In discussions held on July 14, 1919, the Danish ambassador to Norway suggested to Monsieur Ihlen, the Norwegian foreign minister, that Denmark would raise no objection at the Paris Peace Conference to Norway's claim to Spitzbergen if Norway would agree not to oppose Denmark's claim to the whole of Greenland at the same conference. On July 22, 1919, in the course of additional discussions with the Danish ambassador, M[onsieur] Ihlen announced that "the Norwegian Government would not make any difficulty" concerning the Danish claim. Later, in the suit between the two countries over which had sovereignty over Greenland, Denmark argued that this declaration was binding upon Norway.

JUDGMENT OF THE COURT:

This declaration of M[onsieur] Ihlen has been relied on by Counsel for Denmark as a recognition of an existing Danish sovereignty in Greenland. The Court is unable to accept this point of view. A careful examination of the words used and of the circumstances in which they were used, as well as of the subsequent developments, shows that M[onsieur] Ihlen cannot have meant to be giving then and there a definite recognition of Danish sovereignty over Greenland, and shows also that he cannot have been understood by the Danish Government at the time as having done so. In the text of M[onsieur] Ihlen's minute[s], submitted by the Norwegian Government, which has not been disputed by the Danish Government, the phrase used by M[onsieur] Ihlen is couched in the future tense: "*ne fera pas de difficultes*"; he had been informed that it was at the Peace Conference that the Danish Government intended to bring up the question: and two years later—when assurances had been received from the Principal Allied Powers—the Danish Government made a further application to the Norwegian Government to obtain the recognition which they desired of Danish sovereignty over all Greenland.

Nevertheless, the point which must now be considered is whether the Ihlen declaration—even if not constituting a definitive recognition of Danish sovereignty—did not constitute an engagement obliging Norway to refrain from occupying any part of Greenland.

. . . It is clear from the relevant Danish documents which preceded the Danish Minister's démarche[7] at Christiana on July 14th, 1919, that the Danish attitude in the Spitzbergen question and the Norwegian attitude in the Greenland question were regarded in Denmark as interdependent, and this interdependence appears to be reflected also in M[onsieur] Ihlen's minute[s] of the interview. Even if this interdependence—which, in view of the affirmative reply of the Norwegian Government, in whose name the Minister for Foreign Affairs was speaking, would have created a bilateral engagement—is not held to have been established, it can hardly be denied that what Denmark was asking of Norway ("not to make any difficulties in the settlement of the [Greenland] question") was equivalent to what she was indicating [was] her readiness to concede in the Spitzbergen question (to refrain from opposing "the wishes of Norway in regard to the settlement of this question.") What Denmark desired to obtain from Norway was that the latter should do nothing to obstruct the Danish plans in regard to Greenland. The declaration which the Minister for Foreign Affairs gave on July 22, 1919, on behalf of the Norwegian Government, was definitely affirmative: "I told the Danish Minister today that the Norwegian Government would not make any difficulty in the settlement of this question."

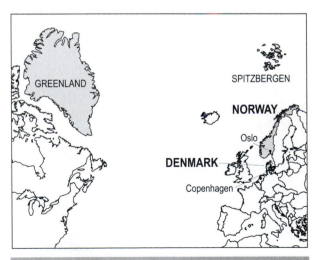

MAP 1-1 Greenland and Spitzbergen (1919)

[7French: "course of action."]

The Court considers it beyond all dispute that a reply of this nature given by the Minister of Foreign Affairs on behalf of his Government in response to [a] request by the diplomatic representative of a foreign Power, in regard to a question falling within his province, is binding upon the country to which the Minister belongs. . . .

It follows that, as a result of the undertaking involved in the Ihlen declaration of July 22nd, 1919, Norway is under an obligation to refrain from contesting Danish sovereignty over Greenland as a whole, and *a fortiori*[8] to refrain from occupying a part of Greenland.

SEPARATE OPINION OF JUDGE ANZILOTTI:

No arbitral or judicial decision relating to the international competence of a Minister for Foreign Affairs has been brought to the knowledge of the Court; nor has this question been exhaustively treated by legal authorities. It is my opinion, it must be recognized that the constant and general practice of states has been to invest the Minister for Foreign Affairs—the direct agent of the chief of the state—with authority to make statements on current affairs to foreign diplomatic representatives, and in particular to inform them as to the attitude which the government, in whose name he speaks, will adopt in a given question. Declarations of this kind are binding upon the state.

As regards the question whether Norwegian constitutional law authorized the Minister for Foreign Affairs to make the declaration, that is a point which, in my opinion, does not concern the Danish Government: it was M[onsieur] Ihlen's duty to refrain from giving his reply until he had obtained any assent that might be requisite under the Norwegian laws. ■

[8Latin: "more conclusively" or "with stronger reason."]

Custom

custom: A long-established tradition or usage that becomes customary law if it is (a) consistently and regularly observed and (b) recognized by those states observing it as a practice that they must obligatorily follow.

Some rules have simply been around for such a long time or are so generally accepted that they are described as **customary** laws. International customary law, however, is not fixed. Simply because certain practices were once followed in the international community does not mean that they are still followed today. Indeed, the development and evolution of customary international law is in a continual state of flux. For example, rules that govern the "art" of war are revised at the end of practically every major conflict to reflect the circumstances of a changed world. The present rule that requires a soldier to fight only with "combatants" is rather outdated in today's world of terrorism and guerrilla warfare and will likely be changed in the near future. In the arena of international commercial law, the rate of change is just as fast. Much of this reflects developments in modern technology. Laws governing the flow of data across international borders (such as messages sent by satellite or transoceanic cable) are presently in a state that might best be described as "confused." Many countries want to regulate the movement of such information, others demand free and undisturbed movement, and still others want guarantees against invasions of privacy. At present, the regulation is left up to each government, and little "common" law exists.

usus: (Latin: "usage.") A consistent and recurring practice.

To show that a customary practice has become customary law, two elements must be established—one behavioral and one psychological. The first—called **usus** in Latin—requires consistent and recurring action (or lack of action if the custom is one of noninvolvement) by states. Evidence of such action can be found in the official statements of governments, including diplomatic correspondence, policy statements and press releases, the opinions of legal advisors, executive decrees, orders to military or naval forces, comments on draft treaties, national court decisions,[9] and even legislation of a subordinate government.[10]

Consistent and recurring practice does not mean lengthy (as in "since time immemorial," which is sometimes given as the rule in municipal practice), nor does it mean that it must be followed by all states. On the other hand, it must be accepted by a reasonably large number of major states for a period long enough to be recognized by the courts as establishing constant and uniform conduct.

---

[9]The basis for the concept of the "historic bay," which is now part of the international law of the sea, was first adopted by the U.S. Supreme Court in 1969 in Louisiana v. United States, *United States Reports,* vol. 394, p. 11 (Supreme Ct., 1969).

[10]The use of American state legislation as being indicative of a customary international practice was relied upon by the U.S. Supreme Court in the case of *The Scotia, id.,* vol. 81, p. 170 (Supreme Ct., 1871).

opinio juris sive neces-
sitatis: (Latin: "of the
opinion that it is a nec-
essary law.") Maxim
requiring a state to
observe a customary
practice only if it is one
that international law
requires the state to
observe.

The psychological element in showing that a customary practice has become law is the requirement that states observing the custom must regard it as binding. That is, they must recognize the custom as being a practice that they must obligatorily follow as compared with one that they follow out of courtesy (i.e., comity) to other states. This is often referred to by the Latin phrase ***opinio juris sive necessitatis***. The Permanent Court of International Justice (PCIJ) discussed this requirement in 1927 in the case of *The Lotus*. The case involved a collision on the high seas between a French steamer and a Turkish collier in which some Turkish crew members and passengers lost their lives. When the French ship docked in a Turkish port, the Turkish government began criminal proceedings against the French officers on watch at the time of the collision. The French appealed to the PCIJ arguing that Turkey had violated international law, because, France said, only the flag state has jurisdiction over criminal incidents on the high seas. The PCIJ said that the few cases France cited for this proposition "merely show that states had often, in practice, abstained from instituting criminal proceedings, and not that they recognized themselves as being obliged to do so; for only if such abstentions were based on their being conscious of a duty to abstain would it be possible to speak of an international custom."[11] Turkey was allowed to continue with its criminal prosecution.

persistent objection:
Active rejection of a
customary practice
from its first observance
by other states.

Even if the international community follows a practice and recognizes it as binding customary law, under some circumstances the rule will not apply to a particular state. This happens when a state **persistently objects** to a practice during its formative stages and thus never becomes a party to it.[12] This can also happen after a customary rule has become generally accepted, if a state is allowed by the international community to deviate from the general practice. In the *Anglo-Norwegian Fisheries Case*,[13] the United Kingdom sued Norway in the International Court of Justice because Norway was not allowing British fishing vessels to enter what Norway claimed were its territorial waters and the British claimed were high seas. Norway was using a special rule for connecting rocks and islands in drawing its territorial boundaries that was contrary to the general rule followed by most countries. The ICJ endorsed Norway's action because Norway had been claiming the disputed waters since 1812 and because most countries of the world had never objected. Thus, by the acquiescence of other countries, Norway was excused from following a generally accepted customary rule of international law.

The exception that excuses a state from the application of a customary rule because the state refuses from the outset to recognize the rule is the topic considered in Case 1–2.

---

[11]*Permanent Court of International Justice Reports,* vol. 1927, Series A, No. 10, p. 28 (1927).
[12]This view is succinctly set out in the concurring opinion of Judge Gross in the Nuclear Tests Cases, *International Court of Justice Reports,* vol. 1974, p. 286 (1974).
[13]*Id.,* vol. 1951, p. 116 (1951).

Case 1–2   The Asylum Case
Colombia v. Peru

International Court of Justice, 1950.
International Court of Justice Reports, vol. 1950, p. 266 (1950).

Colombia granted political asylum in its embassy in Lima, Peru, to Señor Haya de la Torre, a Peruvian politician who had participated in an unsuccessful rebellion in Peru in 1948. Colombia asked Peru for the safe conduct of Haya de la Torre from Lima to the Colombian border. Peru refused. Colombia then sued Peru in the ICJ and asked the Court to determine, among other things, that "Colombia, as the state granting asylum, is competent to qualify the offense [as political or not] for the purpose of the said asylum." Columbia argued for such a determination on the basis of both treaty provisions and "American international law in general." The ICJ considered the last point in the following extract.

MAP 1-2 Columbia and Peru (1948)

usage practiced by the states in question, and that this usage is the expression of a right appertaining to the state granting asylum and a duty incumbent on the territorial state. This follows from Article 38 of the Statute of the Court, which refers to international custom "as evidence of a general practice accepted as law."

. . . [T]he Colombian government has referred to a large number of cases in which diplomatic asylum was in fact granted and respected. But it has not shown that the alleged rule of unilateral and definitive qualification was invoked or . . . that it was, apart from conventional stipulations, exercised by the states granting asylum as a right appertaining to them and respected by the territorial state as a duty incumbent on them. . . . The facts brought to the knowledge of the Court disclose so much uncertainty and contradiction, so much fluctuation and discrepancy in the exercise of diplomatic asylum and in the official views expressed on various occasions, there has been so much inconsistency in the rapid succession of conventions on asylum, ratified by some states and rejected by others, and the practice has been so much influenced by considerations of political expediency in the various cases, that it is not possible to discern in all this any constant and uniform usage, accepted as law, with regard to the alleged rule. . . .

The Court cannot therefore find that the Colombian government has proved the existence of such a custom. But even if it could be supposed that such a custom existed between certain Latin-American states only, it could not be invoked against Peru which, far from having by its attitude adhered to it, has, on the contrary, repudiated it by refraining from ratifying the Montevideo Conventions of 1933 and 1939, which were the first to include a rule concerning the qualification of the offense in matters of diplomatic asylum.

Peru was under no obligation to give Señor Haya de la Torre safe passage out of the country. ◼

JUDGMENT OF THE COURT:

. . . The Colombian government has finally invoked "American international law in general." In addition to the rules arising from agreements which have already been considered, it has relied on an alleged regional or local custom peculiar to Latin-American states.

The party which relies on a custom of this kind must prove that this custom is established in such a manner that it has become binding on the other party. The Colombian government must prove that the rule invoked by it is in accordance with a constant and uniform

General Principles

general principles:
Principles of law common to the world's legal systems.

When courts are required to decide international disputes, they frequently rely on the **general principles** of law that are common to the legal systems of the world. Indeed, although there are more than 200 states in the world today, there are, in practical terms, only two major legal systems: the Anglo-American common law system and the Romano-Germanic civil law system; and the two are remarkably similar in their basic procedures and substantive rules. It is this similarity that provides courts with the "general principles" they can use in deciding many problems that arise in international disputes.

D. THE SCOPE OF INTERNATIONAL LAW IN ACTUAL PRACTICE

The Practice in International Tribunals

subservient: (From Latin *subservire:* "to serve under.") Subordinate in capacity or function.

In actual practice, international tribunals generally regard municipal law as **subservient** to international law. For example, in the *Greco-Bulgarian Communities Case,* the Permanent Court of International Justice said that "it is a generally accepted principle of international law that in the relations between [states] who are contracting parties to a treaty, the provisions of their municipal law cannot prevail over those of the treaty."[14]

And in the *Polish Nationals in Danzig Case*, the same court said: "It should . . . be observed . . . that a state cannot adduce as against another state its own Constitution with a view to evading obligations incumbent upon it under international law or treaties in force."[15]

Not only do international tribunals treat international law as the superior law, but they also regard states as having a general obligation to bring their municipal law into compliance with international norms. In the *Exchange of Greek and Turkish Populations Case*, the Permanent Court of International Justice was asked to interpret a clause in the 1923 Treaty of Lausanne that required the parties to modify their municipal law to ensure that the treaty would be carried out. It said: "This clause . . . merely lays stress on a principle which is self-evident according to which a state which has contracted valid international obligations is bound to make in its legislation such modification as may be necessary to ensure the fulfillment of the obligations undertaken."[16]

Procedurally, international tribunals treat municipal law as "mere fact." For example, in the *Certain German Interests in Polish Upper Silesia Case*, the PCIJ observed:

> It might be asked whether a difficulty does not arise from the fact that the Court would have to deal with the Polish law of July 14th, 1920. This, however, does not appear to be the case. From the standpoint of International Law and of the Court which is its organ, municipal laws are mere facts which express the will and constitute the activities of states, in the same manner as do legal decisions or administrative measures. The Court is certainly not called upon to interpret the Polish law as such; but there is nothing to prevent the Courts giving judgment on the question whether or not, in applying the law, Poland is acting in conformity with its obligations toward Germany under the Geneva Convention.[17]

Several consequences of treating municipal law as a fact are significant—such as the requirement that states parties must prove what the law is, that municipal laws will not be interpreted by an international tribunal, and that an international tribunal will not declare such law either void or valid.

The Practice in Municipal Courts

correlative: A reciprocal or complementary relationship.

In municipal courts, international law is generally treated as **correlative**. That is, once a court determines that a particular rule of international law is applicable in a particular case, the law will be treated as law and not as a fact. The major question for the court then is whether the international law has been received into the local jurisprudence. How the court will answer this question depends on whether the law is based on customary practice or is contained in a treaty.

doctrine of incorporation: Customary international law is part of domestic law to the extent it is not inconsistent.

In most countries, customary international law is received in accordance with the **doctrine of incorporation**. That is, customary international law is treated as adopted to the extent that it is not inconsistent with prior municipal legislation or judicial decisions of final authority.[18] A minority of courts (i.e., some courts in the United Kingdom and the British Commonwealth) apply the **doctrine of transformation**. This holds that customary international law is not applicable until clearly adopted by legislative action, judicial decision, or established local usage.[19]

doctrine of transformation: Customary international law is applicable domestically only after it is adopted by legislation, court decision, or local usage.

The reception rules found in treaties depend on two factors. One is the nature of the treaty, and the other is the constitutional structure of the ratifying state.

self-executing treaty: A treaty containing a term that says it is directly effective within the signatory states upon ratification.

As to the nature of treaties, they may be either self-executing or non-self-executing. A **self-executing treaty** is one that contains a provision that says the treaty will apply to the parties without their having to adopt any domestic enabling legislation; a **non-self-executing treaty** has no such provision. Case 1–3 examines this difference.

non-self-executing treaty: A treaty that requires state parties to enact enabling legislation before it becomes effective domestically.

---

[14]*Permanent Court of International Justice Reports,* vol. 1930, Series B, No. 17, p. 32 (1930).

[15]*Id.,* vol. 1931, Series A/B, No. 44, p. 24 (1931).

[16]*Id.,* vol. 1925, Series B, No. 10, p. 20 (1925).

[17]*Id.,* vol. 1926, Series A, No. 20, p. 41 (1926).

[18]In Triquet v. Bath in *Burrow's Reports,* vol. 1764, pt. 3, p. 1478 (King's Bench, 1764), Lord Mansfield stated: "I remember in a case before Lord Talbot . . . [that he] declared a clear opinion: 'That the law of nations, in its full extent was part of the law of England.' . . . I remember, too, Lord Hardiwickes declaring his opinion to the same effect; and denying that Lord Chief Justice Holt ever had any doubt as to the law of nations being part of the law of England. . . ."

[19]In Chung Chi Cheung v. Rex, *Law Reports, Appeal Cases,* vol. 1939, p. 160 (1939), Lord Atkin said: "[S]o far, at any rate, as the Courts of this country are concerned, international law has no validity save insofar as its principles are accepted and adopted by our own domestic law."

As to the structure of states, their constitutions may assign to one or more state organs (or branches) the responsibility for entering into treaties. Thus, in many countries, responsibility for adopting treaties is shared by the executive and the legislature. For example, in the United States, the federal Constitution gives the President responsibility for negotiating treaties and the Senate responsibility for ratifying them (i.e., for giving its "advice and consent" to their adoption). Over the years, however, this cumbersome arrangement[20] has led the United States to develop two kinds of treaties: **constitutional treaties** and **executive agreements**. The first are made according to the Constitution's provisions (i.e., they are negotiated by the President and ratified by the Senate); the second are agreements made solely by the President (i.e., without the "advice and consent" of the Senate). As to external matters, both of these have the same effect (i.e., they are commitments that impose binding international obligations on the United States); but as to internal matters, they are different. Constitutional treaties that are self-executing are effective domestically; nothing more needs to be done to implement them. Executive agreements—and constitutional treaties that are non-self-executing—have no effect domestically; to obtain effect, implementing legislation must be adopted.[21]

constitutional treaty: A treaty adopted according to the constitutional provisions of the ratifying state.

executive agreement: A treaty or international agreement entered into by a state's executive with-out following the state's constitutionally required ratification procedure. It is not effective domestically.

---

[20]It is cumbersome because often a political party in opposition to the President controls the Senate, and the two may not share the same view of international relations.
[21]Examples of American executive agreements that have no domestic effect are the many overseas military-basing agreements made by the U.S. government during the cold war era of 1945 to 1990. An important example of a U.S. executive agreement that was given domestic effect through the adoption of implementing legislation was the General Agreement on Tariffs and Trade 1947 (GATT 1947).

Case 1–3   Sei Fujii v. State
Colombia v. Peru

United States, Supreme Court of California, 1952. *California Reports, Second Series*, vol. 38, p. 718 (1952).

Mr. Sei Fujii, a Japanese alien, purchased real estate in California shortly after World War II. Because he was ineligible for citizenship under U.S. naturalization laws, a trial court held that his ownership of the land violated California's alien land law and that the land escheated to the state. Mr. Sei Fujii appealed and an intermediate appellate court held that the alien land law violated the United Nations Charter's human rights provisions and it reversed the decision of the trial court. The state of California appealed to the state Supreme Court.

CHIEF JUSTICE GIBSON:

Plaintiff, an alien Japanese who is ineligible to citizenship under our naturalization laws, appeals from a judgment declaring that certain land purchased by him in 1948 had escheated to the state. There is no treaty between this country and Japan which confers upon plaintiff the right to own land, and the sole question presented on this appeal is the validity of the California alien land law.[22]

United Nations Charter

It is first contended that the land law has been invalidated and superseded by the provisions of the United Nations Charter pledging the member nations to promote the observance of human rights and fundamental freedoms without distinction as to race. Plaintiff relies on statements in the preamble and in Articles 1, 55 and 56 of the Charter. . . .

It is not disputed that the Charter is a treaty, and our federal Constitution provides that treaties made under the authority of the United States are part of the supreme law of the land and that the judges in every state are bound thereby.[23] A treaty, however, does not automatically supersede local laws which are inconsistent with it unless the

---

[22]The pertinent portions of the alien land law . . . (1945) . . . are as follows: . . . "§ 7 Any real property hereafter acquired in fee in violation of the provisions of this act by [an alien ineligible for citizenship under the laws of the United States or ineligible to own land in the United States because no treaty between the United States and his or her country provides for such a right] . . . shall escheat as of the date of such acquiring, to, and become and remain the property of the State of California."
[23]United States Constitution, Article VI.

treaty provisions are self-executing. In the words of Chief Justice Marshall: A treaty is "to be regarded in the courts of justice as equivalent to an act of the Legislature, whenever it operates of itself, without the aid of any legislative provision. But when the terms of the stipulation import a contract—when either of the parties engages to perform a particular act, the treaty addresses itself to the political, not the judicial department; and the Legislature must execute the contract, before it can become a rule for the court."[24]

In determining whether a treaty is self-executing, courts look to the intent of the signatory parties as manifested by the language of the instrument, and, if the instrument is uncertain, recourse may be had to the circumstances surrounding its execution. . . . In order for a treaty provision to be operative without the aid of implementing legislation and to have the force and effect of a statute, it must appear that the framers of the treaty intended to prescribe a rule that, standing alone, would be enforceable in the courts. . . .

It is clear that the provisions of the preamble and of Article 1 of the Charter which are claimed to be in conflict with the alien land law are not self-executing. They state general purposes and objectives of the United Nations Organization and do not purport to impose legal obligations on the individual member nations or to create rights in private persons. It is equally clear that none of the other provisions relied on by plaintiff is self-executing. Article 55 declares that the United Nations "shall promote . . . universal respect for all without distinction as to race, sex, language, or religion," and in Article 56, the member nations "pledge themselves to take joint and separate action in cooperation with the Organization for the achievement of the purposes set forth in Article 55." Although the member nations have obligated themselves to cooperate with the international organization in promoting respect for, and observance of, human rights, it is plain that it was contemplated that future legislative action by the several nations would be required to accomplish the declared objectives, and there is nothing to indicate that these provisions were intended to become rules of law for the courts of this country upon the ratification of the Charter.

The language used in Articles 55 and 56 is not of the type customarily employed in treaties which have been held to be self-executing and to create rights and duties in individuals. For example, [in many cases considered by the U.S. Supreme Court] . . . treaty provisions were enforced without implementing legislation where they prescribed in detail the rules governing rights and obligations of individuals or specifically provided that citizens of one nation shall have the same rights while in the other country as are enjoyed by that country's own citizens. . . .

It is significant to note that when the framers of the Charter intended to make certain provisions effective with-

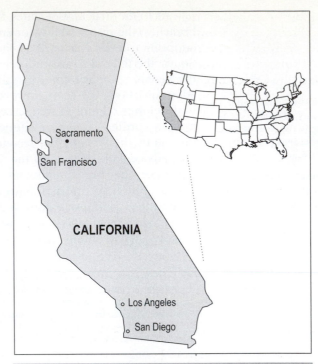

MAP 1-3   California (1952)

out the aid of implementing legislation they employed language which is clear and definite and manifests that intention. For example, Article 104 provides: "The organization shall enjoy in the territory of each of its members such legal capacity as may be necessary for the exercise of its functions and the fulfillment of its purposes. Article 105 provides: "1. The organization shall enjoy in the territory of each of its members such privileges and immunities as are necessary for the fulfillment of its purposes. 2. Representatives of the members of the United Nations and officials of the organization shall similarly enjoy such privileges and immunities as are necessary for the independent exercise of their functions in connection with the organization." In *Curran v. City of New York*,[25] these articles were treated as being self-executory. . . .

The provisions in the Charter pledging cooperation in promoting observance of fundamental freedoms lack the mandatory quality and definiteness which would indicate an intent to create justiciable rights in private persons immediately upon ratification. Instead, they are framed as a promise of future action by the member nations. Secretary of State Stettinius, Chairman of the United States delegation at the San Francisco Conference where the Charter was drafted, stated in his report to President Truman that Article 56 "pledges the various countries to cooperate with the organization by joint and separate action in the achievement of the economic and social objectives of the organization without

---

[24]Foster v. Neilson [*United States Reports*, vol. 27, p. 253 (Supreme Ct., 1829)].
[25]*New York Supplement, Second Series*, vol. 77, p. 206 at p. 212 (1947).

infringing upon their right to order their national affairs according to their own best ability, in their own way, and in accordance with their own political and economic institutions and processes."[26] The same view was repeatedly expressed by delegates of other nations in the debates attending the drafting of Article 56. . . .

The humane and enlightened objectives of the United Nations Charter are, of course, entitled to respectful consideration by the courts and Legislatures of every member nation, since that document expresses the universal desire of thinking men for peace and for equality of rights and opportunities. The Charter represents a moral commitment of foremost importance, and we must not permit the spirit of our pledge to be compromised or disparaged in either our domestic or foreign affairs. We are satisfied, however, that the Charter provisions relied on by plaintiff were not intended to supersede existing domestic legislation, and we cannot hold that they operate to invalidate the alien land law.

Fourteenth Amendment of the Federal Constitution

The next question is whether the alien land law violates the due process and equal protection clauses of the Fourteenth Amendment [of the United States Constitution]. . . .

. . . The California alien land law is obviously designed and administered as an instrument for effectuating racial discrimination, and the most searching examination discloses no circumstances justifying classification on that basis. There is nothing to indicate that those alien residents who are racially ineligible for citizenship possess characteristics which are dangerous to the legitimate interests of the state, or that they, as a class, might use the land for purposes injurious to public morals, safety or welfare. Accordingly, we hold that the alien land law is invalid as in violation of the Fourteenth Amendment.

The judgment of the intermediate appellate court was reversed in part and affirmed in part. Although the United Nations Charter established no rights that applied directly to the plaintiff, the due process and equal protection clauses of the Fourteenth Amendment of the U.S. Constitution forbade racial discrimination of the kind contained in the California alien land law. ■

---

[26]*Report to the President of the Results of the San Francisco Conference . . . ,* Department of State Publication 2349, Conference Series 71, p. 115.

Although the power to make treaties is shared by the executive and the legislature in the great majority of states, this is not the only model. In some countries—notably Britain and the British Commonwealth countries—only the executive (i.e., the crown or government) is able to make treaties. In these countries, moreover, only the executive is regarded as bound by the treaty, because only the executive was a party to it. Even if a treaty is self-executing, it is only self-executing as to the executive. Neither the parliament nor the courts nor the citizens of the state are directly affected by the treaty (that is, they have neither rights granted nor obligations imposed) until domestic enabling legislation is adopted.[27]

E. INTERNATIONAL PERSONS

state: A political entity comprising a territory, a population, a government capable of entering into international relations, and a government capable of controlling its territory and peoples.

The personalities of international law are states and their subdivisions, international organizations, businesses, and individuals.

States

States are political entities that have a territory, a population, a government capable of entering into international relations, and a government capable of controlling its territory and peoples. Included in this definition are three kinds of states: independent states, dependent states, and inchoate states.

independent state: A state that is sovereign; one that operates independently internationally.

dependent state: A state that has surrendered its rights to conduct international affairs to another state.

Independent states are free from the political control of other states and free to enter into agreements with other international persons. **Dependent states** have formally surrendered some aspect of their political and governmental functions to another state.

---

[27]This rule does not apply in the United Kingdom to European Union legislation. EU legislation is treated in U.K. courts as being directly effective even though there is no U.K. implementing legislation.

inchoate: (From Latin *inchoare:* "to start work on.") Begun, but not completed; imperfectly formed or developed.

recognition: Formal acknowledgment or acceptance by a government of the independence and sovereignty of a newly created state or of a newly established government in another state, especially one established by revolution.

declaratory doctrine: The legal existence of a state or government happens automatically by operation of law.

constitutive doctrine: The legal existence of a state or government is dependent on recognition by other states.

Inchoate states lack some attribute required to be treated as a fully independent state; most commonly they lack territory or population.

Recognition

For a state to exist in the international community it must be recognized by other states. **Recognition** comes about by a unilateral declaration, and it can be either explicit (express) or implicit (tacit). Once given, it implies that the recognized state or government is entitled to the rights and privileges granted by international law.

The recognition of a government is different from the recognition of a state. A state is recognized when an identifiable government, people, and territory first come into existence. If the government later changes, it may not be recognized even though recognition of the state continues.

Two theories have been suggested as guidelines for when a government should be recognized: the **declaratory doctrine** and the **constitutive doctrine**. The first holds that the legal existence of a government happens automatically by operation of law whenever a government is capable of controlling a territory and its people. The second states that a government does not truly come into existence until such time as it is recognized by other states and participates in the international arena. Which of these two theories ought to be applied in an American court was the issue in Case 1–4.

Case 1–4 Matimak Trading Co. v. Khalily and D.A.Y. Kids Sportswear Inc. ☞

United States, Second Circuit Court of Appeals, 1997. *Federal Reporter, Third Series*, vol. 118, p. 76 (1997).[28]

CIRCUIT JUDGE MCLAUGHLIN:

Plaintiff appeals from an order entered August 19, 1996, in the United States District Court for the Southern District of New York (Judge Wood) dismissing plaintiff's claims for lack of subject matter jurisdiction. We review de novo the grant of the dismissal motion. The principal issue is whether a Hong Kong corporation is either a "citizen or subject" of a "foreign state" for purposes of alienage jurisdiction.[29] More precisely the issue is whether Hong Kong may be regarded as a "foreign state." We hold that it may not and, accordingly, affirm the district court.

BACKGROUND

Plaintiff Matimak Trading Co. Ltd. is a corporation organized under the laws of Hong Kong, with its principal place of business in Hong Kong. It seeks to sue Albert Khalily and D.A.Y. Kids Sportswear Inc., two New York corporations, in the Southern District of New York for breach of contract. Matimak invoked the court's diversity jurisdiction under *United States Code*, title 28, § 1332(a)(2), which provides jurisdiction over any civil action arising between "citizens of a state and citizens or subjects of a foreign state."

In June 1996, the district court *sua sponte*[30] raised the issue of the court's subject matter jurisdiction. In August 1996, after allowing the parties to brief the issue, the district court dismissed the complaint for lack of subject matter jurisdiction. The court concluded that Hong Kong is not a "foreign state" under the diversity statute, and, consequently, Matimak is not a "citizen or subject" of a "foreign state."

DISCUSSION

This is not the first time we have had to navigate what we have earlier described as a "shoalstrewn area of the law."[31] Article III of the Constitution extends the federal judicial power to "all Cases . . . between a state, or citi-

---

[28]The text of the opinion is posted on the FindLaw Internet Web site at laws.findlaw.com/2nd/969117a.html.
[29]*See* United States Constitution, art. III, § 2, clause 1; *United States Code*, title 28, § 1332(a)(2).
[30]Latin: "on its own initiative."]
[31]National Petrochemical Co. of Iran v. M/T Stolt Sheaf, *Federal Reporter, Second Series,* vol. 860, 551 at p. 552 (2d Circuit Ct. of Appeals, 1988).

zens thereof, and foreign states, Citizens or Subjects." The United States Judicial Code tracks the constitutional language by providing diversity jurisdiction over any civil action arising between "citizens of a state and citizens or subjects of a foreign state."[32] This judicial power is referred to as "alienage jurisdiction."

MAP 1-4   *Hong Kong (1997)*

British sovereignty over Hong Kong ceases on July 1, 1997, when Hong Kong becomes a special administrative region of the People's Republic of China. Diversity of citizenship, however, is determined as of the commencement of an action.

Given these building blocks, we must address three principal questions: (1) whether Hong Kong is a "foreign state," such that Matimak is a "citizen or subject" of a "foreign state"; (2) whether Matimak is a "citizen or subject" of the United Kingdom, by virtue of Hong Kong's relationship with the United Kingdom when it brought suit; and (3) whether any and all non-citizens of the United States may *ipso facto* invoke alienage jurisdiction against a United States citizen. Although not addressed by the parties, this last question is the focus of the dissent, and thus merits serious consideration.

I. IS HONG KONG A "FOREIGN STATE"?

A. Well-Established Principles in This Court

Neither the Constitution nor § 1332(a)(2) [of the Judicial Code] defines "foreign state." However, "[i]t has

generally been held that a foreign state is one formally recognized by the executive branch of the United States government."[33] For purposes of diversity jurisdiction, a corporation is a "citizen" or "subject" of the entity under whose sovereignty it is created.[34]

The Supreme Court has never addressed the issue before us. This Court, however, has applied these general rules in addressing alienage jurisdiction on several occasions.

In *Iran Handicraft and Carpet Export Center v. Marjan International Corp.*[35] an Iranian corporation sued a New York corporation in the Southern District of New York for breach of contract. When the complaint was filed, Iran was undergoing a revolutionary change of government. The issue was whether the court was required to find that the United States formally recognized the new government of Iran to permit the plaintiff to invoke alienage jurisdiction. The court noted the general rule that a "foreign state" in § 1332(a)(2) is one "formally recognized by the executive branch." The court explained:

> Because the Constitution empowers only the President to "receive Ambassadors and other public Ministers," the courts have deferred to the executive branch when determining what entities shall be considered foreign states. The recognition of foreign states and of foreign governments, therefore, is wholly a prerogative of the executive branch. Thus, it is outside the competence of the judiciary to pass judgment upon executive branch decisions regarding recognition.

The court surveyed the case law, concluding that "[i]n cases involving parties claiming to be citizens of a foreign state, . . . courts have focused on whether the foreign state was recognized by the United States as 'a free and independent sovereign.'" This description is consistent with the accepted definition of a "state" in international law, which requires that the entity have a "'defined territory'" and be "'under the control of its own government.'"[36] Relying on the State Department's clarification of Iran's diplomatic status, the *Iran Handicraft* court concluded that "it is beyond doubt that the United States continues to recognize Iran as an independent sovereign nation."

The parties here agree that the United States has not formally recognized Hong Kong as a foreign state. Invoking the jurisprudence of this Court and others, however, Matimak contends that Hong Kong has received "*de facto*" recognition as a foreign state by the United States, and thus its citizens may invoke alienage jurisdiction.

---

[32]*United States Code,* title 28, § 1332(a)(2).

[33]C. Wright, A. Miller & E. Cooper, *Federal Practice & Procedure,* vol. 13B, § 3604 (1984).

[34]*See* National Steamship Co. v. Tugman, *United States Reports,* vol. 106, p. 118 at p. 121 (Supreme Ct., 1882); *Restatement (Second) of the Foreign Relations Law of the United States* § 26 (1965).

[35]*Federal Supplement,* vol. 655, p. 1275 (District Ct. for S. District of N.Y.), affirmed, *Federal Reporter, Second Series,* vol. 868, p. 1267 (2d Circuit Ct. of Appeals, 1988).

[36]National Petrochemical Co. of Iran v. M/T Stolt Sheaf, *Federal Reporter, Second Series,* vol. 860, p. 551 at p. 553 (2d Circuit Ct. of Appeals, 1988) (quoting *Restatement (Third) of the Foreign Relations Law of the United States* § 201 (1987)).

Matimak points to the United States' diplomatic and economic ties with Hong Kong as evidence of this recognition.

This Court established the doctrine of *de facto* recognition in *Murarka v. Bachrack Brothers, Inc.*[37] In that case a partnership doing business in New Delhi, India sued a New York corporation. The court ruled that it had alienage jurisdiction despite the fact that the complaint was filed thirty days before the United States formally recognized India as a foreign state. The court explained:

> True, as of July 14, 1947, our Government had not yet given India *de jure*[38] recognition, but its exchange of ambassadors in February and April 1947 certainly amounted at least to *de facto* recognition, if not more. To all intents and purposes, these acts constituted a full recognition of the Interim Government of India at a time when India's ties with Great Britain were in the process of withering away, which was followed a month later, when partition took place between India and Pakistan, by the final severance of India's status as a part of the British Empire. . . . Unless form rather than substance is to govern, we think that in every substantial sense by the time this complaint was filed India had become an independent international entity and was so recognized by the United States.

This analysis might reasonably be regarded as nothing more than an acknowledgment of the United States' imminent formal recognition of a sovereign state. The analogy of Hong Kong to India is inapt. India, which had been a colony of Great Britain, was about to become an independent sovereign nation. Not so for Hong Kong, which is about to be absorbed into China. Hong Kong is merely changing fealty.

Matimak, of course, argues for a more flexible interpretation of the *de facto* test. At the very least, however, as *Iran Handicraft* noted, the *de facto* test depends heavily on whether the Executive Branch regards the entity as an "independent sovereign nation."[39] It is beyond cavil that "[w]ho is the sovereign, *de jure* or *de facto*, of a territory, is not a judicial, but a political, question, the determination of which by the legislative and executive departments of any government conclusively binds the judges, as well as all other officers, citizens, and subjects of that government."[40]

The deference to the Executive Branch exhibited in *Iran Handicraft* and *Murarka* was similarly crucial in *Calderone v. Naviera Vacuba S/A*,[41] where we sustained alienage jurisdiction in a suit between a Cuban corporation and an American company. The court explained:

> Considerations of both international relations and judicial administration lead us to conclude that the onus is on the Department of State, or some other department of the Executive Branch, to bring to the attention of the courts its decision that permitting nationalized Cuban corporations to sue is contrary to the national interest. Since silence on the question may be highly desirable, it would not be wise for the court unnecessarily to force the Government's hand. However, in this case we need not merely rely on the maintenance of the status quo, because the Executive Branch has made its wishes known. . . . [T]he Department of Justice has urged that nationalized Cuban corporations have access to our courts with the protection of the act of state doctrine.

Courts have consistently required such deference for purposes of alienage jurisdiction.[42]

When Matimak brought this suit in August 1995, Hong Kong was a "British Dependent Territory" and was ruled by a governor appointed by the United Kingdom. As such, it maintained some independence in its international economic and diplomatic relationships, but in matters of defense and foreign affairs remained dependent on the United Kingdom.

Hong Kong is the United States' twelfth-largest trading partner, with direct United States financial investment of almost twelve billion dollars.[43] Hong Kong's relationship with the United States was most recently manifested in the United States–Hong Kong Policy Act of 1992,[44] which makes clear that Congress desires United States–Hong Kong relations to continue after July 1, 1997, when Hong Kong becomes a special administrative region of China. The Act states that "Hong Kong plays an important role in today's regional and world economy. This role is reflected in strong economic, cultural, and other ties with the United States that give the United States a strong interest in the continued vitality, prosperity, and stability of Hong Kong."

The Policy Act makes equally clear, however, that the United States does not regard Hong Kong as an independent, sovereign political entity. The Act provides that Hong Kong "will continue to enjoy a high degree of autonomy on all matters other than defense and foreign

---

[37]*Id.,* vol. 215, 547 (2d Circuit Ct. of Appeals, 1954).

[38 Latin: "by right" or "by law"; according to law.]

[39]*Federal Supplement,* vol. 655 at p. 1278.

[40]Jones v. United States, *United States Reports,* vol. 137, p. 202 at p. 212 (Supreme Ct., 1890). . . .

[41]*Federal Reporter, Second Series,* vol. 325, p. 76 (1963), modified on other grounds, *id.,* vol. 328, p. (2d Circuit Ct. of Appeals, 1964) (per curiam).

[42]*See,* e.g., Abu-Zeineh v. Federal Labs., Inc., No. 91–2148, at pp. 3-5 (District Ct. for W. District of Pennsylvania, Dec. 7, 1994) (holding that Palestine is not a foreign state for purposes of alienage jurisdiction, as Palestine had not been recognized by the United States as an independent, sovereign nation). . . .

[43]*See* Letter from Jim Hergen, Assistant Legal Advisor for East Asian and Pacific Affairs, U.S. Department of State, to Marshall T. Potashner, Attorney for Matimak, of June 21, 1996, at p. 3.

[44]*United States Code,* title 22, §§ 5701–32 (West Supplement, 1996).

affairs" and emphasizes that only "with respect to economic and trade matters" shall the United States "continue to treat Hong Kong as a territory which is fully autonomous from the United Kingdom." The Act points to the need to safeguard human rights during the "transition in the exercise of sovereignty over Hong Kong."

The United States has embraced the same position on this appeal. Having originally stated that "Hong Kong should . . . be treated in the courts of the United States as a *de facto* 'foreign state' " for purposes of alienage jurisdiction,[45] the United States reversed course. In its *amicus*[46] brief, the Justice Department notes that "[t]he State Department no longer urges treatment of Hong Kong as a *de facto* foreign state and withdraws any reliance on this contention."[47]

Although we need not resolve this issue here, we note that the State Department's unexplained change in stance following the district court's opinion might under different circumstances require further inquiry into its ulterior motives. No reason is apparent, and none is suggested, for refusing to defer to the State Department in this case.

The State Department's stance on appeal confirms what is already clear from the United States' dealings with Hong Kong, as evidenced in the Policy Act: it does not regard Hong Kong as an independent sovereign entity.

For these reasons, it is clear that the United States does not recognize Hong Kong as a sovereign and independent international entity. Accordingly, consistent with this Court's precedent, Matimak cannot invoke alienage jurisdiction as a "citizen or subject" of Hong Kong.

* * *

II. IS MATIMAK A "CITIZEN OR SUBJECT" OF THE UNITED KINGDOM?

Well-established principles—both in this Circuit and elsewhere—furnish the analytical scaffolding for determining whether Matimak is a citizen or subject of the United Kingdom. There is no question, of course, that the United States formally recognizes the United Kingdom as a sovereign international entity.

We begin with the truism that a foreign state is entitled to define who are its citizens or subjects. It is another accepted precept that a corporation, for purposes of diversity jurisdiction, is a "citizen" or "subject" of the entity under whose sovereignty it is created.

* * *

The Justice Department, as *amicus*, argues that as a Hong Kong corporation, Matimak is governed by the Hong Kong *Companies Ordinance*, which is modeled on the *British Companies Act* 1948. The Justice Department concludes that because the ultimate sovereign authority over the plaintiff is the British Crown, Matimak should be treated as a subject of United Kingdom sovereignty for purposes of § 1332. Hong Kong corporations, however, are no more "subjects" than "citizens."

The fact that the Hong Kong *Companies Ordinance* may be "ultimately traceable" to the British Crown is too attenuated a connection. Matimak was incorporated under Hong Kong law, the *Companies Ordinance* 1984 of Hong Kong, and is entitled to the protections of Hong Kong law only.

Matimak is not a "citizen or subject" of a foreign state. It is thus stateless. And a stateless person—the proverbial man without a country—cannot sue a United States citizen under alienage jurisdiction.

III. DOES "CITIZEN OR SUBJECT" IN § 1332(A)(2) DESCRIBE ANY AND ALL PERSONS WHO ARE NOT CITIZENS OF THE UNITED STATES?

It has recently been suggested that the Founding Fathers intended to confer alienage jurisdiction over suits between a United States citizen and any other person in the world who is not a United States citizen.[48] The dissent makes the same argument, substantially adopting the analysis set forth in this commentary and arguing that the Judiciary Act, prior to its amendment in 1875, evidenced the intent of the drafters.

Even beyond its obvious rejection of well-established precedent, this argument is flawed in several respects.

* * *

During the Constitutional Convention of 1787, the drafters of the Constitution used the phrase "citizen or subject of a foreign state" as frequently as "alien" or "foreigner." As the dissent stresses, a basic assumption of the drafters was that anyone who was not a citizen of the United States must by definition have been subject to the power of a foreign government or sovereign. The "idea of statelessness" was simply not in their "contemplation."

---

[45]Letter from Hergen to Potashner, *supra*, at p. 2.

[[46]Abbreviated form of *amicus curiae*. Latin: "friend of the court." One not a party to a suit who is permitted by the court to advise it in respect to some matter of law that directly affects the case in question.]

[47]The Justice Department chose to inform the Court of this crucial fact in a footnote. This Court frowns on raising such important points in footnotes, either before the district court or on appeal. "The enormous volume of briefs and arguments pressed on each panel of this court at every sitting precludes our scouring through footnotes in search of some possibly meritorious point that counsel did not consider of sufficient importance to include as part of the argument." United States v. Restrepo, *Federal Reporter, Second Series,* vol. 986, p. 1462 at p. 1463 (2d Circuit Ct. of Appeals, 1993).

[48]*See* Christine Biancheria, "Restoring the Right to Have Rights: Statelessness and Alienage Jurisdiction in Light of Abu-Zeineh v. Federal Laboratories, Inc., *American University Journal of International Law & Policy,* vol. 11, p. 195 (1996).

... [However], the dissent's conclusion that the drafters in the late-eighteenth century intended that all "foreigners," including stateless persons, be entitled to invoke alienage jurisdiction over a United States citizen ignores the fact that the term in 1787 did not include stateless persons—a category of people unknown to the drafters of the Constitution.

The dissent also appears to agree that the overriding rationale of alienage jurisdiction was to accord foreign citizens a neutral forum rather than a state court that might be perceived by a foreigner as biased in favor of its own citizens. This would avoid entanglements with foreign states and sovereigns. According alienage jurisdiction to "stateless" persons does not serve this rationale: there is no danger of foreign entanglements, as there is no sovereign with whom the United State could become entangled.

* * *

It might occasionally seem incongruous not to allow a stateless person to bring suit in federal court; but this does not make it inconsistent with the idea of alienage jurisdiction. The drafters' worry that foreigners not suffer prejudice in state courts reflected their concern that such prejudice might harm foreign relations; avoiding prejudice to the individual foreigners themselves was not an independent concern. At any rate, stateless persons are not totally denied an American forum; they may choose to sue in a state court.[49]

* * *

CONCLUSION

Matimak is not a "citizen or subject of a foreign state," under *United States Code*, title 28, § 1332(a)(2), and there is no other basis for jurisdiction over Matimak's suit. The district court properly dismissed Matimak's suit for lack of subject matter jurisdiction. Accordingly, the order of the district court is *affirmed*.

CIRCUIT JUDGE ALTIMARI, DISSENTING:

* * *

... [O]ur jurisprudence has heretofore barred stateless persons from access to our federal courts. Today, the majority bars stateless corporations as well.

A stateless corporation is an oxymoron. In the United States, a corporation cannot be created without the imprimatur of the state. This is also true in Great Britain and Hong Kong. ... [Nevertheless, the majority has decided that] a Hong Kong corporation, such as Matimak, is denied access to our federal courts under alienage diversity jurisdiction because it is not a British corporation. Is it thus so easy to disavow a person or a corporate entity?

* * *

The majority emphasizes the importance of affording deference to the Executive Branch. In fact, it extensively quotes from *Calderone* [*v. Naviera Vacuba S/A*] in which this Court sustained alienage diversity jurisdiction because the Executive Branch made its wishes known.[50] In this case, the Department of State and the Department of Justice unequivocally made their wishes known—they withdrew support of *de facto* recognition of Hong Kong and urged this Court to recognize Hong Kong as a "citizen or subject" of the United Kingdom. ∎

* * *

---

[49]*See* Romanella v. Hayward, No. 96-9222, at p. 1 (2d Circuit Ct. of Appeals, May 23, 1997); Blair Holdings Corp. v. Rubinstein, *Federal Supplement,* vol. 133, p. 496 at p. 501 (District Ct. S. District of N.Y., 1955).
[50]*Federal Reporter, Second Series,* vol. 325 at p. 77.

Estrada Doctrine:
Doctrine that foreign governments will not be explicitly recognized.

It is important for a government to be recognized because recognition implies that the recognizing government wishes to have normal relations. And recognized governments are entitled, among other things, to diplomatic protection and sovereign immunity. To avoid any possible connotation that recognition also means approval, many governments have adopted a policy of never formally recognizing other governments. This policy is known as the **Estrada Doctrine**, after the Mexican foreign minister who first stated it.

Territorial Sovereignty

territorial sovereignty:
The right of a government to exclusively exercise its powers within a particular territory.

For a state to exist, it must have **territorial sovereignty**. Sovereignty is the right to exercise the functions of a state within a territory.[51] This right, however, may not be absolute. Other

---

[51]Island of Palmas Case (The Netherlands v. United States), Permanent Court of Arbitration, 1928, *United Nations Reports of International Arbitral Awards,* vol. 2, p. 829 (1928).

servitude: (From Latin *servitudo:* "slavery.") A right to the use of another's property.

states may obtain **servitudes**, either by treaty or practice, to a limited use of certain territory. Commonly this is the exercise of rights-of-way, such as the rights of the ships of all nations to use the Suez and Panama canals.[52]

Servitudes can also be negative. That is, they may prevent one state from doing something within its territory that causes injury to a second state. Case 1–5 provides an example of a negative servitude.

---

[52]The 1888 Convention Respecting Free Navigation of the Suez Canal, also known as the Convention of Constantinople, declared the Suez Canal open to ships of all nations. *American Journal of International Law,* vol. 3, p. 123 (1909). The 1977 Panama Canal Treaty states that the canal "shall remain . . . open to peaceful transit by the vessels of all nations on terms of entire equality." *Id.,* vol. 72, p. 238 (1978). Servitudes are usually created by treaty but they can be created by custom as well, as the ICJ pointed out in the Right of Passage over Indian Territories (Portugal v. India) Case. *International Court of Justice Reports,* vol. 1960, p. 6 (1960).

Case 1–5   The Trail Smelter Arbitration
United States v. Canada

American-Canadian Joint Commission, Arbitral Tribunal, 1938 and 1941.
United Nations Reports of International Arbitral Awards, vol. 3, p. 1905.

At the beginning of this century, a Canadian company built a lead and zinc smelting plant at Trail, British Columbia, about 10 miles north of the state of Washington border. Beginning in the 1920s, production was increased and by 1930 more than 300 tons of sulfur, including large quantities of sulfur dioxide, were being emitted daily. Some of the emissions were being carried down the Columbia River Valley and allegedly causing damage to land and other property in Washington. After negotiations between the United States and Canada, the latter agreed in 1928 to refer the matter to the American–Canadian Joint Commission that the two countries had established in the Boundary Waters Treaty of 1909. In 1931, the Commission's Arbitral Tribunal reported that damage had occurred in the amount of $350,000. Canada did not dispute its liability and agreed to pay this amount. The smelter continued to operate, however, and continued to emit pollutants into the air over Washington. In 1938, the United States claimed $2 million in damages for the years 1931 to 1937. The Tribunal allowed the claim only in part, awarding damages of just $78,000. In 1941, the United States sought to have the operation of the smelter enjoined. The following question was submitted to the Tribunal: "whether the Trail Smelter should be required to refrain from causing damage in the state of Washington in the future and, if so, to what extent?"

1941 REPORT OF THE TRIBUNAL:

The first problem which arises is whether the question should be answered on the basis of the law followed in the United States or on the basis of international law. The Tribunal, however, finds that this problem need not be solved here as the law followed in the United States in dealing with quasi-sovereign rights of the states of the Union, in the matter of air pollution, whilst more definite, is in conformity with the general rules of international law.

Particularly in reaching its conclusions as regards this question . . . , the Tribunal has given consideration to the desire of the high contracting parties "to reach a solution just to all parties concerned." As Professor Eagleton puts it: "A state owes at all times a duty to protect other states against injurious acts by individuals from within its jurisdiction."[53] A great number of such general pronouncements by leading authorities concerning the duty of a state to respect other states and their territory have been presented to the Tribunal. . . . But the real difficulty often arises rather when it comes to determine what, *pro subjecta materie,*[54] is deemed to constitute an injurious act.

A case concerning, as the present one does, territorial relations, decided by the Federal Court of Switzerland between the Cantons of Soleure and Argovia, may serve to illustrate the relativity of the rule. Soleure brought a suit against her sister state to enjoin use of a shooting establishment which endangered her territory. The court, in granting the injunction, said: "This right (sovereignty) excludes . . . not only the usurpation and exercise of sovereign rights (of another state) . . . but also an actual encroachment which might prejudice the natural use of the territory and the free

---

[53]*Responsibility of States in International Law,* p. 80 (1928).
[[54]Latin: "for the subject matter"; concerning the subject matter at hand.]

MAP 1-5 British Columbia and Washington (1941)

movement of its inhabitants." As a result of the decision, Argovia made plans for the improvement of the existing installations. These, however, were considered as insufficient protection by Soleure. The Canton of Argovia then moved the Federal Court to decree that the shooting be again permitted after completion of the projected improvements. This motion was granted. "The demand of the government of Soleure," said the court, "that all endangerment be absolutely abolished apparently goes too far." The court found that all risk whatever had not been eliminated, as the region was flat and absolutely safe shooting ranges were only found in mountain valleys; that there was a federal duty for the communes to provide facilities for military target practice and that "no more precautions may be demanded for shooting ranges near the boundaries of two Cantons than are required for shooting ranges in the interior of a Canton." . . .

No case of air pollution dealt with by an international tribunal has been brought to the attention of the Tribunal nor does the Tribunal know of any such case. The nearest analogy is that of water pollution. But, here

also, no decision of an international tribunal has been cited or has been found.

There are, however, as regards both air pollution and water pollution, certain decisions of the Supreme Court of the United States which may legitimately be taken as a guide in this field in international law, for it is reasonable to follow by analogy, in international cases, precedents established by that court in dealing with controversies between states of the Union or with other controversies concerning the quasi-sovereign rights of such states, where no contrary rule prevails in international law and no reason for rejecting such precedents can be adduced from the limitations of sovereignty inherent in the Constitution of the United States. . . .

The Tribunal, therefore, finds that the above decisions, taken as a whole, constitute an adequate basis for its conclusions, namely that, under the principles of international law, as well as the law of the United States, no state has the right to use or permit the use of its territory in such a manner as to cause injury by fumes in or to the territory of another or the properties or persons therein, when the case is of serious consequences and the injury is established by clear and convincing evidence.

The decisions of the Supreme Court of the United States which are the basis of these conclusions are decisions in equity and a solution inspired by them, together with the régime hereinafter prescribed, will, in the opinion of the Tribunal, be "just to all parties concerned," as long, at least, as the present conditions in the Columbia River Valley continue to prevail.

Considering the circumstances of the case, the Tribunal holds that the Dominion of Canada is responsible in international law for the conduct of the Trail Smelter. Apart from the undertakings in the Convention, it is, therefore, the duty of the government of the Dominion of Canada to see to it that this conduct should be in conformity with the obligation of the Dominion under international law as herein determined.

The Tribunal, therefore, answers [the question submitted] as follows: . . . So long as the present conditions in the Colombia River Valley prevail, the Trail Smelter shall be required from causing any damage through fumes in the state of Washington; the damage herein referred to and its extent being such as would be recoverable under the decisions of the courts of the United States in suits between private individuals. The indemnity for such damage should be fixed in such manner as the governments, acting under Article XI of the Convention, should agree upon. ■

To have territorial sovereignty, a state must first acquire territory. This is done in two ways: (1) by the occupation of land not claimed by another sovereign and (2) by the transfer of territory from one sovereign to another. Once territory is acquired, a state's title is affirmed either by the formal recognition of other states or by a process of estoppel.

estoppel: (From Old French *estoupail:* "stopper" or "bung.") Legal rule that one cannot make an allegation or denial of fact that is contrary to one's previous actions or words.

Estoppel arises when a state fails to speak up and object to another's exercise of sovereignty when it would be reasonable to do so. By failing to object, a state is tacitly recognizing the new status quo. This has the evidentiary effect of making it difficult (but not impossible) for a state to change its position. To establish estoppel, some authorities (but not all) say that detrimental reliance must be shown. That is, the state claiming the territory must have made some improvement there (such as building roadways) that would be lost to it if recognition were denied.

Changes in Territorial Sovereignty

When there is a change in sovereignty over territory, several legal consequences arise. As to treaty rights and obligations, successor states must observe treaties that implement general rules of international law, and they are bound by **dispositive treaties**—that is, treaties concerned with rights over territory, such as boundaries and servitudes.

dispositive treaty: A treaty concerned with rights over territory, such as boundaries and servitudes.

The obligation of a successor state to observe other treaty commitments depends on whether it acquires a territory by a merger, partial absorption, or complete absorption or whether a seceding territory attains its independence through decolonization or dissolution. The **Merger Rule** governs the first of these cases. This rule presumes that when two states merge to form a new state (i.e., State A and State B merge and become State C), then the preexisting treaties remain in force in the territories where they previously applied (i.e., State A treaties remain in force in the former territory of State A, and State B treaties remain in force in the former territory of State B). For example, when Egypt and Syria merged to form the United Arab Republic (1958–1961), the new republic declared that

Merger Rule: Legal rule that the treaties in effect in a former state remain in effect in its territory when it becomes part of a new state.

> . . . the Union is a single member of the United Nations, bound by the provisions of the Charter, and that all international treaties and agreements concluded by Egypt or Syria with other countries will remain valid within the regional limits prescribed on their conclusion and in accordance with the principles of international law.[55]

There are, however, two exceptions to the Merger Rule. First, the new successor state and other states parties to a treaty with one of the predecessor states can agree to either terminate the treaty or extend it to the whole territory of the new state. (E.g., when Tanganyika and Zanzibar merged in 1964, Zanzibar's treaties were given force throughout the new state of Tanzania.[56]) Second, a treaty will terminate if its object and purpose can no longer be accomplished or if the conditions necessary to accomplish its object and purpose have radically changed. (E.g., after the formation of the United Netherlands in 1815, the Dutch argued the new state was so different from its predecessors that a treaty with the United States had to be terminated.[57])

Moving Boundaries Rule: Legal rule that the treaties of a state absorbing new territory become effective within the absorbed territory.

If territory from one state shifts to another (i.e., a province in State A becomes a province in State B), the law of state succession applies the **Moving Boundaries Rule**. This holds that the treaties of the absorbing state displace the treaties of the receding state in the territory where sovereignty has changed. Thus, for example, when France took over Alsace-Lorraine after World War I, France's treaties displaced those of Germany in the annexed territory.[58] Similarly, the Federal Republic of Germany's treaties displaced those of France when it regained control of the Saarland in 1957;[59] and in 1969, when the Netherlands transferred West New Guinea to Indonesia, Indonesia's treaties were extended over its new territory.[60]

---

[55]*United Nations Juridical Yearbook,* vol. 2, p. 113 (UN Doc. A/CN.4/150, 1962).

[56]Report of the International Law Commission to the General Assembly, *Yearbook of the International Law Commission,* vol. 2, pt. 1, p. 258 (UN Doc. A/9610/Rev. 1, 1974).

[57]John B. Moore, *A Digest of International Law,* vol. 5, p. 344 (1906).

[58]*See* Société Lebrun v. Dussy & Lucas, *Annual Digest of Public International Law Cases,* vol. 3, p. 86 (Belgian Court of Appeals, 1926).

[59]Daniel P. O'Connell, *State Succession in Municipal Law and International Law,* 41 (1967).

[60]Report of the International Law Commission to the General Assembly, *Yearbook of the International Law Commission,* vol. 2, pt. 1, p. 209 (UN Doc. A/9610/Rev. 1, 1974).

Clean Slate Doctrine:
Doctrine that a new
state coming into exis-
tence through decolo-
nization is under no
obligation to succeed to
the treaties of its former
colonial power.

When a new state comes into being through decolonization, its obligation to observe the treaties made by its colonial parent state are determined by the so-called **Clean Slate Doctrine**. That is, the ex-colony starts with no obligation to succeed to the treaties of its former colonial power.[61] Nevertheless, it is common practice for a newly independent ex-colony to announce its intention to continue to be bound by existing treaties.[62]

When two states come into existence following the disintegration of a predecessor, the Clean Slate Doctrine does not apply. Rather, both are bound by the predecessor's treaties to the extent they are applicable within each of their territories.[63] For example, when the Soviet Union broke up into 12 republics in 1991, the international community insisted that each of the republics acknowledge its obligation to observe the existing treaties of the Soviet Union, including arms control and human rights treaties, before they would be recognized. The United States, Great Britain, France, and China—the four remaining permanent members of the United Nations Security Council—relied on the same rule in announcing that Russia would automatically succeed to the Soviet seat on the Council.[64]

The nationals of a territory that is acquired by a successor state will keep the nationality of the predecessor state unless a different result is agreed to in a treaty of cession or by municipal legislation.

Public property located within a territory becomes the property of the successor state, while property located in a third state belongs to whichever government the third state recognizes. If a third state recognizes both states, however, the property will belong to whichever state is in actual possession, as Case 1–6 points out.

---

[61]Vienna Convention on the Succession of States in Respect of Treaties, Article 16. The Clean Slate Doctrine does not, however, affect the general rule that successor states are bound by dispositive treaties and treaties acknowledging a general rule of international law. Report of the International Law Commission to the General Assembly, *Yearbook of the International Law Commission*, vol. 2, pt. 1, p. 214 (UN Doc. A/9610/Rev. 1, 1974).

[62]In re Commissioner of Correctional Services, ex parte Fitz Henry, *Jamaica Law Reports*, vol. 14, p. 288, *International Law Reports*, vol. 72, p. 63 (1987), a Jamaican national awaiting extradition to the United States applied for a writ of *habeas corpus* claiming that the extradition treaty in question had been concluded before Jamaica became independent in 1962 and, therefore, according to the Clean Slate Doctrine was not in force in Jamaica. The Ministry of Foreign Affairs, however, produced evidence showing that Jamaica's Prime Minister had affirmed the extradition treaty after independence and, furthermore, that several extradition orders subsequently had been made pursuant to the treaty. The court did not grant the writ.

[63]Vienna Convention on the Succession of States in Respect of Treaties, Article 34.

[64]Cable News Network, December 26, 1991.

Case 1–6 *Arab Republic of Syria v. Arab Republic of Egypt*

Brazil, Supreme Court, 1982.
Revista Trimestral de Jurisprudencia, vol. 104, p. 889 (1983); *International Law Reports*, vol. 91, p. 289 (1993).

In 1951, the government of Syria purchased property in Rio de Janeiro, Brazil, for its embassy. In 1958, when Syria and Egypt merged to form the United Arab Republic (UAR), the property was turned over to the UAR. The UAR was represented by a single ambassador to Brazil. In 1961, the UAR was dissolved and Syria and Egypt again became separate independent sovereign states. Syria then sought to reclaim its embassy, but the property was being occupied at that time by an Egyptian diplomat (who had been the UAR's last ambassador) and he refused to return the property to Syria. Subsequently,

the property was used as the Egyptian embassy and later (following the move of the Brazilian capital from Rio de Janeiro to Brasilia) as an Egyptian consulate.

In 1981, the Syrian Ambassador to Brazil brought suit in the Brazilian Supreme Court against the Egyptian Ambassador to Brazil and the Egyptian Consul in Rio de Janeiro seeking to reclaim possession of the property. Neither the Egyptian Ambassador nor Consul nor the Egyptian government formally appeared to answer the suit. The Egyptian Ambassador informed the Brazilian Ministry of Foreign Affairs by diplomatic correspondence that Egypt regarded itself as possessing jurisdictional immunity and that the Brazilian courts were not competent to hear a dispute between two sovereign foreign states.

MAP 1-6   Brazil (1983)

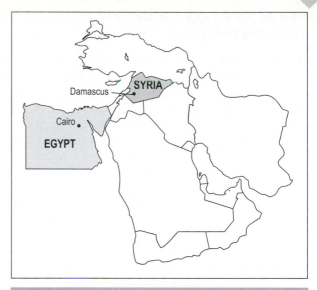

MAP 1-7   Syria and Egypt (1983)

The Court considered whether Egypt's contentions were valid.

JUDGE CLOVIS RAMALHETE:

. . . I believe, on the basis of the submissions made, that state succession occurred twice in relation to the parties. First, when the constituent states gave the UAR in its constitution the authority to act in their place internationally, and, second, when the UAR was dissolved by the decision of its constituent states.

That this truly is a case of state succession can be seen from the fact that the constituent states granted the United Arab Republic the authority to exercise the powers they had previously exercised in their dealings with other states, and that because of this the UAR was endowed with its own legal personality and the right to establish diplomatic missions in place of its constituent states.

In the case before us, ownership of the property in question was automatically transferred at the moment that sovereignty (with respect to the carrying on of foreign relations) was transferred. . . .

In light of the above considerations, it is clear that the dispute which gave rise to the dissolution of the United Arab Republic . . . was an international dispute between two states. . . . It is also clear that this is not a

private dispute over which a foreign state may exercise jurisdiction and in which the parties to the dispute may be compelled to appear before the courts of that state. Indeed, the manner in which the Ambassador of Syria and the Ambassador of Egypt have formulated their jurisdictional arguments clearly demonstrates that this is a dispute between states and not a case of private litigation between two ambassadors concerning property located in Brazil.

In sum, the case before this Court is concerned with . . . the scope and the limits of state succession in a dispute between two sovereign states. In such a case, no judicial decision can be made. Accordingly, I believe that the complaint should be annulled and the suit vacated.[65]

To reiterate, I am of the opinion that Brazilian courts may not consider disputes arising out of questions relating to state succession that affect foreign states. In particular, the principle of equality of states denies to a court in a third state the competency to decide a dispute between two states which arose out of actions taken by them in the exercise of their sovereign powers and which they failed to resolve at the time that they dissolved their Union.

. . . This does not mean that all judicial recourse is denied to the parties. They are, of course, at liberty to utilize other peaceful means to resolve their dispute, such as mediation, arbitration, or the lodging of a claim before an international tribunal. . . .

In conclusion, I vote in favor of the annulment of this suit.

DECISION OF THE COURT

. . . [T]he suit is annulled and the case is dismissed. . . .

---

[65][Brazil, Federal] Code of Civil Procedure, § 267(vi).

JUDGE NERI DA SILVEIRA [DISSENTING]: . . .

In deference to Brazil's sovereignty and its duty to guarantee the property rights set out in its Constitution and laws, it is my belief that Brazil must not allow its courts to tolerate any infringement of those rights, even when the infringement is alleged in a complaint brought by one foreign state against another. Indeed, given that the property in question is located in Brazil, a holding that the Brazilian courts lack competence to hear such a matter would mean that title to this property could never be adequately safeguarded because no foreign court would have jurisdiction and any judgment it might render would be unenforceable within Brazil. . . .

If the plaintiff were a private person and was denied the right to bring a claim before the Brazilian courts that was based on the same grounds and facts as the claim brought by the Arab Republic of Syria . . . we would hold that such a denial would violate Article 8 of the Universal Declaration of Human Rights,[66] which provides:

Everyone has the right to an effective remedy by the competent national tribunals for acts violating the fundamental rights granted him by the Constitution or by law.

As a direct consequence of this public international law rule, the municipal courts are obliged to guarantee the basic human rights granted by the Constitution and the laws of their state. . . .

Viewing the issue involved in this case in light of the above . . . one has to admit that there is at least one exception . . . to the principle of absolute sovereign immunity (which provides that one state may not exercise jurisdiction over another because of the rule of *par in parem non habet jurisdictionem*)[67] and that that exception allows a foreign state to be sued in proceedings concerning a right in property whose title is registered in Brazil.[68]

I therefore consider that this Court is competent to examine the claim brought by the Arab Republic of Syria pursuant to Article 119(1)(c) of the Constitution and also to make a decision on the merits of the case. . . . ■

---

[66]Adopted by the General Assembly of the United Nations on December 10, 1948.
[[67]Latin: "an equal has no jurisdiction over an equal."]
[68]*Revista Trimestral de Jurisprudencia,* vol. 24, p. 45.

The private property rights of individuals do not lapse because of a change in government. A government, however, is always entitled to expropriate the property of its own nationals, so private property rights may well be adversely affected by a change in government. Similarly, a successor state is, as a general proposition, bound by the private contractual obligations of its predecessors; and to the extent a successor acquires part or all of a territory, it is proportionately responsible for that territory's national debt.

International Organizations

According to the Charter of the United Nations, there are two kinds of international organizations: (1) public or intergovernmental organizations (IGOs) and (2) private or nongovernmental organizations (NGOs).[69]

Intergovernmental Organizations

intergovernmental organization (IGO): A permanent organization set up by two or more states to carry on activities of common interest.

Intergovernmental organizations are permanent organizations set up by two or more states to carry on activities of common interest.[70] Modern IGOs evolved from the European practice of convening conferences at the end of wars to draw new boundaries and sign peace treaties. Beginning in the nineteenth century, these conferences turned to sponsoring multilateral treaties and the setting up of organizations both to maintain the peace[71] and to carry on a vari-

---

[69]United Nations Charter, Article 71. The terminology used in the United Nations Charter assumes that the organizations are *international* and not domestic or municipal IGOs and NGOs. That same assumption is made here.

[70]Clive Archer defines an intergovernmental organization as "a formal continuous structure established by agreement between members (governmental and/or nongovernmental) from two or more sovereign states with the aim of pursuing the common interest of the membership." *International Organizations,* p. 35 (1983).

[71]The peace in nineteenth-century Europe was maintained informally through an arrangement known as the Concert of Europe. This arrangement involved regular consultations between the major powers (Austria, France, Great Britain, Prussia, and Russia) who acted together to recognize new states and to put down military uprisings in others.

ety of other international activities of common interest, such as the delivery of mail[72] and the protection of industrial and literary property.[73]

Following World War I, the League of Nations was founded as the first organization that was both general in scope and universal in its intended membership. After World War II, the activities of the League were taken over and greatly expanded by the United Nations.

Since World War II, the number of intergovernmental organizations has increased dramatically. Today there are some 400 IGOs. Most significantly, IGOs have evolved from the simple meeting or conference of states to entities that have permanent structures and staffs, carry on a variety of activities, and, at least in the case of one IGO, have supranational powers.

charter: A document outlining the principles, functions, and organization of a juridical entity.

Unlike states, an IGO is created much in the fashion of a corporation. Its aims and objectives, internal structure, resources, and express powers are set out in a "constituent instrument," or **charter**, which is drafted and adopted by the organization's member states. The United Nations Charter, for example, gives the organization its name,[74] sets out its purposes and principles,[75] defines its membership,[76] names its structural elements or "organs,"[77] describes the makeup and powers of those organs,[78] sets out the rights and duties of its members,[79] endows the organization with international personality,[80] and describes the procedures for the Charter's ratification and amendment.[81]

legal capacity: Qualification or authority, such as the qualification or authority to carry on international relations.

For an IGO to have the **legal capacity** to deal with other international persons—including the capacity to carry on diplomatic relations with a state or to sue or be sued in an international or municipal court—it must be recognized. With respect to its own state members, most authorities regard recognition as being implicit. In other words, by becoming a member in an IGO, a state automatically recognizes the IGO's international personality. This is not, however, the uniform rule. In the United Kingdom, the fact that the executive becomes a member in an intergovernmental organization does not imply any internal recognition. Thus, the U.K. courts will not recognize the capacity of an IGO to bring suit or be sued in the United Kingdom unless the U.K. government specifically certifies that the IGO has such capacity.

As for establishing the legal capacity of an IGO vis-à-vis its nonmember states, recognition is also required. In some states, such as the United States, an IGO is essentially regarded as an agency of its members and recognition of the IGO will be implied if its member states are recognized.[82] In other countries, including the United Kingdom, recognition requires specific certification from the government.

Case 1–7 explores why the courts in the United Kingdom need certification from the executive before they will recognize the capacity of IGOs.

---

[72]The Universal Postal Union was established in 1874. The Union's Internet Web site is at www.upu.int/.

[73]The International Bureau of Industrial Property was set up in 1883 and the International Bureau of Literary Property in 1886.

[74]United Nations Charter, Preamble. The text of the Charter is posted on the Internet at www.un.org/aboutun/charter/.

[75]*Id.,* Chapter I.

[76]*Id.,* Chapter II.

[77]*Id.,* Chapter III.

[78]*Id.,* Chapters IV, V, VI, VII, X, XIII, XIV, and XV.

[79]*Id.,* Chapters I, VI, VIII, IX, XI, and XII.

[80]*Id.,* Chapter XVI.

[81]*Id.,* Chapters XVII, XVIII, and XIX.

[82]*See* International Tin Council v. Amalgamet, Inc., *New York Supplement,* Second Series, vol. 524, p. 971 (Supreme Ct. of New York, 1988).

Case 1-7   Arab Monetary Fund v. Hashim and Others (No. 3)

England, High Court, Chancery Division, 1989.
Weekly Law Reports, vol. 1990, pt. 3, p. 139 (1990);
International Law Reports, vol. 83, p. 244 (1990).

The Arab Monetary Fund (AMF) was an organization created by a group of 20 Arab states and the Palestine Liberation Organization in 1976. The charter of the organization, the Arab Monetary Fund Agreement (Agreement), provided that the AMF was to have an "independent juridical personality and . . . in particular the right to own, contract, and litigate." A federal decree issued by the President of the United Arab Emirates (UAE) gave the Agreement the force of law throughout the UAE, including the emirate of Abu Dhabi, where the AMF had its headquarters.

The AMF brought suit in the English courts against Dr. Hashim, its former Director-General, and various other defendants, alleging that they had misappropriated AMF funds. The defendants asked to have the suit dismissed, arguing that the AMF had no legal personality in the United Kingdom and, therefore, could not bring this suit. The United Kingdom was not a member of the AMF nor had it formally recognized the AMF under the provisions of the United Kingdom's International Organizations Act of 1968.

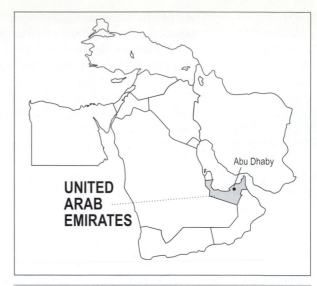

MAP 1-8 United Arab Emirates (1990)

JUDGE HOFFMANN:

. . . Mr. Pollock, who appeared for AMF, advanced two grounds on which the fund's existence should be recognized. The first was that the English conflict of laws recognizes the existence of legal entities constituted under international law just as it recognizes those constituted under foreign systems of domestic law. The second was that the AMF had been constituted under a system of domestic law, namely, that of its headquarters state of Abu Dhabi, and should therefore be recognized as an ordinary foreign juridical entity.

For reasons which I shall explain, I was more attracted by Mr. Pollock's first answer than by his second. But the motion was argued when the judgment of the House of Lords in *J. H. Rayner (Mincing Lane), Ltd. v. Department of Trade and Industry*,[83] (which I shall call "the *Tin Case*") was known to be imminent and I reserved my judgment until after it had been given. I then heard further submissions from counsel. Mr. Pollock now concedes that the *Tin* judgments make his first submission untenable. I agree. But I need to say why it originally appealed to me in order to explain certain difficulties I had with Mr. Pollock's second submission, which I have nevertheless decided to accept.

Until the *Tin Case*, there was no authority for or against Mr. Pollock's first submission, although it had the support of distinguished writers on international law. The absence of authority is not surprising in view of the relatively recent growth of international trading and banking organizations and the statutory provisions,

which have existed since 1944, for conferring capacity in domestic law on those constituted under treaties to which the United Kingdom is a party.[84] In 1945, however, Dr. C. W. Jenks expressed the view that in this respect the statute was only declaratory of the common law.[85] Dr. F. A. Mann wrote in similar terms in 1967,[86] but added the rider that an international organization, like a foreign state, could be accorded legal capacity in the courts only if it was recognized by the executive. This qualification has not been universally accepted by other writers,[87] but seems to be logical. The recognition of an international organization at the level of international law must be a matter for the executive and it would be rather odd if the English courts recognized the existence in domestic law of an international organization which Her Majesty's government declined to recognize in international law.

Extending our conflict rule to international organizations seems to me to be sensible and practical. The rule as it applies to entities created by foreign domestic laws is based on the inconvenience of having legal entities which exist in one country but not in another. International organizations set up by foreign states do exist in fairly substantial numbers, trade with this country, and bank in the City of London. They are invariably recognized as juridical entities by the domestic systems of the parties to the treaty as well as many other countries. The evidence in this case was that the fund would be recognized in Switzerland and, as Lord Justice Kerr pointed out in the *Tin Case* in the Court of Appeal,[88] the New York courts

[83]*Weekly Law Reports,* vol. 1989, pt. 3, p. 969 (1989).
[84]*See* Diplomatic Privileges (Extension) Act, 1944.
[85]*See* "The Legal Personality of International Organizations," *British Year Book of International Law,* pp. 267–275 (1945).
[86]*See* "International Corporations and National Law," *British Year Book of International Law,* pp. 145–174 (1967).
[87]*See* J. C. Collier, "The Status of an International Corporation," *Multum Non Multa: Festschrift für Kurt Lipstein,* pp. 21–29 (Karlsruhe, 1980).
[88]*Law Reports, Chancery,* vol. 1989, p. 72 at p. 172 (1989).

appeared to have no difficulty about recognizing the existence of the International Tin Council, even though the United States was not a party to the treaty. It is difficult to see why an entity created by treaty between two or more foreign states should be less entitled to recognition than an entity created under the sovereign authority of a single foreign state within its domestic system. I shall however briefly list some of the objections advanced by Mr. Sumption, who appeared for the banks.

(1) The United Kingdom is not obliged to recognize an entity created by a treaty to which it was not a party. . . .

(2) United Kingdom legislation since the Diplomatic Privileges (Extension) Act 1944 is inconsistent with the existence of a common law conflicts rule for the recognition of international organizations. . . .

(3) Recognition of an entity created by international treaty would offend the rule that the legal consequences of treaties are not justiciable in domestic courts. . . .

(4) The fund has not been accorded recognition by Her Majesty's government. . . . That brings me to the *Tin Case.*[89] The International Tin Council was created by a treaty to which the United Kingdom was a party, had its headquarters in London and was accorded the legal capacities of a body corporate in English domestic law by statutory instrument. The AMF, on the other hand, was created by a treaty to which the United Kingdom was not a party and is not the subject of a statutory instrument or any other United Kingdom legislation. The *Tin Case* raised, as Lord Templeman said,[90] "a short question of construction of the plain words of a statutory instrument," whereas the question in this case is the scope of the common law conflicts rule. Nevertheless, the reasoning of their Lordships is inconsistent with Mr. Pollock's first submission.

Lord Templeman found it unnecessary to speculate about what the status of the International Tin Council [ITC] would have been absent an Order in Council.[91] But Lord Oliver of Aylmerton, with whom the others of their Lordships agreed, made some pertinent observations. The effect of the Order in Council, he said,[92] was "to create the

ITC (which, as an international legal *persona*,[93] had no status under the laws of the United Kingdom) a legal person in its own right. . . ." Speaking of the status of the ITC as an international entity, he said:[94]

> Let it be assumed for the moment, that the international entity known as the ITC is, by the treaty, one for the engagements of which the member states become liable in international law, that entity is not the entity which entered into the contract relevant to these appeals. Those contracts were effected by the separate *persona ficta*[95] which was created by the Order in Council.

and again:[96]

> Whilst it is, of course, not inaccurate to describe Article 4 of the Order as one which "recognizes" the ITC as an international organization, such "recognition" is of no consequence in domestic law unless and until it is accompanied by the *creation* of a legal *persona.* Without the Order in Council the ITC had no legal existence in the law of the United Kingdom and no significance save as the name of an international body created by a treaty between sovereign states which was not justiciable by municipal courts.

These passages destroy the possibility of a common law conflict rule under which the courts can recognize the existence of an international organization as such.

I therefore turn to Mr. Pollock's second submission, which was that the AMF should be recognized as an entity constituted under Abu Dhabi domestic law. This route did not at first attract me because the AMF is not an Abu Dhabi entity. It is an international entity which has been accorded legal personality under Abu Dhabi law and I regarded the argument over whether such legal personality was "recognized" or "constituted" and whether it was by local statute or local conflict rules as somewhat barren. If the domestic Abu Dhabi entity was something different from the international organization, the same fund would have a separate existence under the laws of each of the member states which accorded it legal personality and one of these *personae fictae* would presumably be able to sue another in an English court. That seemed an unappetizing conclusion.

But the inconvenience of the *Tin Case,* as I see it, is that I ignore the treaty and regard the AMF as constituted under the Abu Dhabi law as a separate *persona ficta.* As such, it is entitled to recognition as a domestic

---

[89]*Weekly Law Reports,* vol. 1989, pt. 3, p. 969 (1989).
[90]*Id.,* p. 980.
[91]*I.e.,* a formal order of recognition issued pursuant to the International Organizations Act.]
[92][*Weekly Law Reports,* vol. 1989, pt. 3,] p. 1008 [(1989)].
[93]Latin: "personality."]
[94][*Weekly Law Reports,* vol. 1989, pt. 3,] at p. 1011 [(1989)].
[95]Latin: "fictional person."]
[96][*Weekly Law Reports,* vol. 1989, pt. 3,] at p. 1012 [(1989)].

entity under ordinary conflict rules.[97] I am able to reach this conclusion because the United Arab Emirates happen to have passed legislation conferring juridical personality on the AMF. It may not have been open to me if there had been no legislation because the personality of the AMF was recognized under the conflict rules of all member states. This would have been unfortunate because the challenge to the AMF's existence is not a mere procedural objection which could be met by reconstituting the action with (say) the United Arab Emirates as plaintiff suing on behalf of itself and all other members. The new plaintiffs would have to show that they have a cause of action under the law of the place where the alleged fraud was committed and may not be able to do so because by the law of Abu Dhabi the money belonged to the AMF and not to the individual members.

Mr. Sumpton met Mr. Pollock's submission by saying that in the case of an international organization, the legislation conferring personality under the law of a member state should be regarded as purely territorial in scope. Its purpose was solely to give effect to the treaty obligation to accord personality in its domestic law and not to create a separate entity capable of recognition abroad. Otherwise an international organization would fragment into at least as many separate entities as there were members. If I could regard the international organization as, for our purposes, identical in law with the Abu Dhabi entity, I think Mr. Sumpton's argument would be entirely correct. But since the international entity has no existence, I do not see how I can take it into account as a ground for refusing recognition to what is plainly a legal entity under the law of Abu Dhabi. I accept that a logical consequence is the existence of other emanations of the fund under the laws of other member states. This raises questions of trinitarian subtlety into which I am grateful that I need not enter.

I therefore find that the AMF exists in English law and dismiss the first set of motions.

The Court of Appeal overruled Judge Hoffmann's decision in this case.[98] *The House of Lords, however, reversed the Court of Appeal, reinstating Judge Hoffmann's opinion and adopting his reasoning.*[99] ■

---

[97]*Compare* Chaff and Hay Requisition Committee v. J. A. Hemphill and Sons (Pty.), Ltd., *Commonwealth Law Reports,* vol. 74, p. 375 (1947).
[98]*All England Law Reports,* vol. 1990, pt. 2, p. 769 (1990).
[99]*Id.,* vol. 1991, pt. 1, p. 871 (1991).

The United Nations The most important of the intergovernmental organizations is the United Nations.[100] Its Charter, a multilateral treaty, came into force on October 24, 1945. (See Exhibit 1-2.)Its goals are the maintenance of peace and security in the world, the promotion of economic and social cooperation, and the protection of human rights. The philosophical basis the drafters of the UN Charter relied on to achieve these goals was their belief in the rule of law. Corollaries of this philosophy are the several principles that are written into the Charter. In particular, members are sovereign equals, disputes must be settled peacefully, and all members are obliged to fulfill their international obligations in good faith.

organ: (From Greek *organon:* "tool" or "instrument.") An agency that carries on specific functions within a larger organization.

The **organs** of the UN are the General Assembly, the Security Council, the Secretariat, the International Court of Justice, the Trusteeship Council, and the Economic and Social Council. The General Assembly is a quasi-legislative body made up of representatives of all member states. Its function is to discuss any question or matter within the scope of the Charter. The Security Council is made up of representatives of 15 member states, 5 of which are permanent member states. It is responsible for maintaining international peace and security, and it is the only UN organ with the authority to use armed force. A Secretary-General elected by the General Assembly heads up the UN's Secretariat. The Secretariat is the UN's administrative arm, responsible for making reports and recommendations to the General Assembly and the Security Council.

The International Court of Justice is the UN's principal judicial body. The Trusteeship Council, which no longer has a function, was set up at the end of World War II to supervise the world's non-self-governing territories. Finally, the Economic and Social Council, which comprises 54 member states elected by the General Assembly, is responsible for promoting economic, social, health, cultural, and educational progress as well as respect for human rights.

United Nations System: A group of autonomous organizations affiliated with the United Nations.

The **United Nations System** is the name given to various autonomous agencies (themselves IGOs) concerned with a wide range of economic and social problems that have entered into

---

[100]The United Nations Internet Web site is at www.un.org/.

EXHIBIT 1-2

The United Nations

From August through October of 1944, representatives of China, the Soviet Union, the United Kingdom, and the United States met at Dumbarton Oaks, a mansion in Georgetown, near Washington, D.C., to draft proposals for a United Nations Charter. In April of the next year, delegates from 50 countries met in San Francisco at the United Nations Conference on International Organization to debate and refine the proposals. A final Charter was adopted unanimously on June 25, 1946, and signed the next day by the representatives of all 50 countries. Poland, which was not represented at the Conference, signed it later and became one of the original 51 United Nations member states.

The inaugural meeting of the Conference on Security Organization for Peace in Post-War World (the Dumbarton Oaks Conference), August 21, 1945. (UN/DPI Photo)

The United Nations officially came into existence on October 24, 1945, when the Charter had been ratified by China, France, the Soviet Union, the United Kingdom, the United States and by a majority of the other signatories. October 24 is now celebrated each year as United Nations Day.

European Union: An intergovernmental organization that has as its goals the elimination of internal frontiers and the establishment of a political, economic, and monetary union.

agreements with the United Nations to become UN Specialized Agencies (see Exhibit 1-3). Additionally, two other organizations—the World Trade Organization (WTO) and the International Atomic Energy Agency (IAEA)—although not Specialized Agencies, have entered into similar relationships with the UN.

The European Union   Another important intergovernmental organization is the **European Union** (EU).[101] Founded in 1951 by 6 states (Belgium, France, Germany, Italy, Luxembourg, and the Netherlands), its member states increased to 9 in 1973 (with the addition of Denmark,

---

EXHIBIT 1-3   The Specialized Agencies of the United Nations

Nonbanking Agencies		World Bank Group	
FAO	Food and Agriculture Organization	IBRD	International Bank for Reconstruction and Development
ICAO	International Civil Aviation Organization		
IFAD	International Fund for Agricultural Development	IDA	International Development Agency
ILO	International Labor Organization	IFC	International Finance Corporation
IMF	International Monetary Fund	MIGA	Multilateral Investment Guarantee Agency
IMO	International Maritime Organization	ICSID	International Center for the Settlement of Investment Disputes
ITU	International Telecommunications Union		
UNESCO	United Nations Educational, Scientific and Cultural Organization		
UNIDO	United Nations International Development Organization		
UPU	Universal Postal Union		
WHO	World Health Organization		
WIPO	World Intellectual Property Organization		
WMO	World Meteorological Organization		

---

[101]The European Union's Internet Web site is at europa.eu.int/index.htm.

Ireland, and the United Kingdom), to 10 in 1981 (when Greece joined), to 12 in 1986 (when Portugal and Spain became members), and most recently to 15 in 1995 (when Austria, Finland, and Sweden were admitted).

The founding states created the European Union in order to integrate their economies and political institutions. The process of integration began with the adoption of the European Coal and Steel Community (ECSC) Treaty,[102] which the founding states signed in Paris in 1951. Although no longer in force—it expired in 2002—the ECSC, created a common market for coal and steel and intergovernmental institutions to oversee this original "community." Building on the experience of the ECSC, the original member states adopted the Treaty Establishing the European Community (EC Treaty)[103] and the European Atomic Energy Community (EAEC or Euratom) Treaty,[104] which they signed in Rome in 1957. Ten years later, the Merger Treaty, signed in Brussels in 1967, consolidated the separate institutional organizations that oversaw the three separate communities into a single structure. In 1992, in Maastricht, the member states signed the European Union (EU) Treaty.[105] The EU Treaty established a political union,[106] common citizenship for nationals of the member states, a Social Charter,[107] a monetary union, a Central Bank, and a common currency (the euro).[108] Then in 1997, the Treaty of Amsterdam eliminated all internal borders,[109] established a larger role for the European Parliament,[110] renamed the EEC Treaty as the Treaty Establishing the European Community (the EC Treaty), and consolidated and renumbered the articles of the EC and the EU treaties. Most recently, in anticipation of the accession of new member states from Eastern and Southern Europe,[111] the Treaty of Nice,[112] signed in 2001, made changes—effective in 2005—to the makeup of and the voting mechanisms of the principal EU institutions.

Supranational Powers. Unlike most other intergovernmental organizations, the European Union is endowed with **supranational powers**. That is, EU law within its scope of applicability is superior to the laws of the member states. This "supremacy principle" has two consequences: one, the member states are required to bring their internal laws into compliance with EU law and, two, EU law is directly effective within the member states.

supranational powers: Powers surrendered by member states to an intergovernmental organization. Such powers are superior to and preempt the laws and regulations of its member states. In exercising these powers, the organization may grant rights and privileges to the nationals of its member states, which those individuals may directly invoke.

An example of the obligation of member states to bring their internal laws into compliance with the EU legal order is provided by the case of *Commission v. Belgium.* Taxes imposed by Belgium discriminated against lumber produced in other member states contrary to Article 90[113] of the EC Treaty. In defending itself before the European Court of Justice in an action brought by the European Commission under Article 226,[114] the government of Belgium said that it had introduced draft legislation in the Belgian Chamber of Representatives two years earlier but the legislation had not been passed. The government explained that the principle of separation of powers that applied in Belgium prevented the government from doing anything more. This excuse did not impress the Court of Justice. It said: "The obligations arising under Article 90 of the Treaty devolve upon states as such and the liability of a member state under Article 226 arises whatever the agency of the state whose action or inaction is the cause of the failure to fulfill its obligations, even in the case of a constitutionally independent institution."[115]

---

[102]The text of the treaty is posted at europa.eu.int/abc/obj/treaties/en/entoc29.htm.

[103]The treaty is posted at europa.eu.int/eur-lex/en/treaties/dat/ec_cons_treaty_en.pdf.

[104]The treaty is posted at europa.eu.int/abc/obj/treaties/en/entoc38.htm.

[105]The treaty is posted at europa.eu.int/eur-lex/en/treaties/dat/eu_cons_treaty_en.pdf. The EU Treaty changed the names of the principal institutions of the EU to European Commission, European Council (formerly the Council of Ministers), European Parliament, European Court of Justice, European Economic and Social Committee, and European Court of Auditors.

[106]The EU's Commission (see the following discussion) is authorized to discuss both foreign policy and security issues.

[107]The Social Charter establishes uniform minimum social and economic standards for individuals.

[108]The United Kingdom, which objected to most of the changes in the Maastricht Treaty, obtained a special concession that allows it to avoid participating in the monetary union and that excuses it from the requirements of the Social Charter.

[109]Great Britain and Ireland will be temporarily exempted from this requirement.

[110]The treaty is posted at ue.eu.int/Amsterdam/en/amsteroc/en/treaty/treaty.htm.

[111]As of June 2002, twelve countries were applicants for admission to the EU: Bulgaria, Cyprus, Czech Republic, Estonia, Hungary, Latvia, Lithuania, Malta, Poland, Romania, Slovakia, and Slovenia.

[112]The treaty is posted at europa.eu.int/eur-lex/en/treaties/dat/nice_treaty_en.pdf.

[113]Formerly Article 95.

[114]Formerly Article 169.

[115]Case 77/69, *European Court Reports,* vol. 1970, p. 237 at p. 243 (1970).

The direct applicability of the supremacy principle is illustrated by the case of *Costa v. ENEL*. That case involved a challenge to Italy's decision in 1962 to nationalize its private electric generating companies. Mr. Costa, a shareholder in one of those companies, refused to pay his electric bill; and when he was sued by the National Electric Board (*ENEL*), he defended himself by arguing that the nationalization decree violated the European Community Treaty (then known as the European Economic Community Treaty). The trial court referred the matter to the European Court of Justice. There, *ENEL* argued that the Court of Justice's decision would be irrelevant because the trial court, being an Italian court, was obliged by Italian law to apply Italian law. The Court disagreed, pointing out that some provisions of the EEC Treaty are directly effective and bestow rights on individuals that the agencies of the member states are obliged to respect. The Court stated:

> By contrast with ordinary international treaties, the EEC Treaty has created its own legal system which, on the entry into force of the Treaty, became an integral part of the legal systems of the member states and which their courts are bound to apply.
>
> By creating a Community of unlimited duration, having its own institutions, its own personality, its own legal capacity and capacity of representation on the international plane, and, more particularly, real powers stemming from a limitation of sovereignty, or a transfer of powers from the states to the Community, the member states have limited their sovereign rights, albeit within limited fields, and have thus created a body of law which binds both their nationals and themselves.[116]

Thus, not only Mr. Costa but any other individual is entitled to directly invoke the EC Treaty in the courts of the EU member states.

Case 1–8 examines both the obligation of member states to bring their laws into accord with the EU treaties (in particular the European Community Treaty—then known as the European Economic Community Treaty) and the direct effect of those treaties.

---

[116]Case 6/64, *European Court Reports*, vol. 1964, p. 585 at p. 593 (1964).

Case 1–8   *Eunomia di Porro & Co. v. Italian Ministry of Public Education*

European Communities, Court of Justice, 1971.
Case 18/71, *Recueil de la jurisprudence de la Cour*, vol. 17, p. 811 (1971); *International Law Reports*, vol. 47, p. 14 (1974).

In March of 1970, the firm of Eunomia di Porro exported a painting valued at 500,000 lire from Italy to Germany through the Italian customs post at Domodossola. The customs post collected a tax of 108,750 lire. Citing a 1968 decision of the Court of Justice of the European Communities that had held that Italy was in default of its obligation to abolish duties on exports to other member states under Article 16 of the European Economic Community Treaty (now the European Community Treaty), because it was continuing to levy taxes on the export of art works,[117] Eunomia di Porro brought suit in the District Court of Turin (Tribunale de Torino) *asking that the tax it had paid be returned. The District Court referred the matter to the Court of Justice of the European Communities, asking the latter if Article 16 of the EEC Treaty was directly effective in Italy and whether it conferred on private individuals rights that had to be protected by the Italian courts.*

The history of the direct effect of EEC Treaty provisions was reviewed by one of the Court of Justice's Advocate-Generals[118] in his argument to the Court. The Court, following the reasoning of the Advocate-General, held that

---

[117]Re Export Tax on Art Treasures (EC Commission v. Italy), Case 7/68, *Recueil de la jurisprudence de la Cour,* vol. 14, p. 617 (1969).

[118]An Advocate-General is an official, commonly found in civil law countries, who prepares a detailed brief analyzing the arguments of the parties and suggesting how the court should decide the case. Unlike courts in common law countries, the opinions of civil law courts generally do not engage in extensive analysis of the issues; rather, they state a conclusion and a concise reason for their conclusion. Often, but not always, the court will adopt the reasoning of the Advocate-General.

Article 16 did produce direct effects on the relationships between member states of the European Economic Community and their citizens.

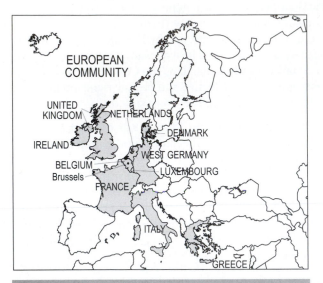

MAP 1-9 European Communities (1971)

SUBMISSIONS OF THE ADVOCATE-GENERAL:

. . . Certainly there already exists an extensive case law built up by this Court on the problem of the direct applicability of Treaty provisions. The parties have duly cited it, and it suffices merely to recall it in the present case.

This line of cases begins with Case 26/62.[119] In that case the Court laid down the fundamental proposition that:

the Community constitutes a new legal order in international law . . . a legal order, whose subjects are not only member states, but also individuals.

Community law confers rights on individuals not only where the Treaty provides for this explicitly, but also on the basis of unequivocal obligations which the Treaty imposes on individuals as well as on the member states and the Community institutions. [As to] Article 12 of the EEC Treaty, the provision then in question (whereby "member states shall refrain from introducing as between themselves any new customs duties on imports or exports or any taxes having equivalent effect and from increasing those which they already levy in their trade with each other"), the Court laid down that this was "a clear and unconditional prohibition," an obligation which was "not restricted by any reservation on the part of states seeking to make its fulfillment

dependent on an act of domestic law," a provision whose effectiveness required "no intervention by the national legislator." This provision could therefore be interpreted so as "to produce direct effects and create individual rights which national courts must respect." In Case 57/65[120] this case law was further developed in connection with Article 95 of the EEC Treaty, which prohibits member states from imposing "directly or indirectly on the products of other member states any internal taxation of any kind in excess of that imposed directly or indirectly on similar domestic products," and particularly the provision in the first paragraph of Article 95 whereby member states:

shall, not later than at the beginning of the second stage,[121] eliminate or amend any provisions existing when this Treaty comes into force which conflict with the above rules.

This admittedly involved an obligation on the member states to take action, and to apply provisions of domestic law; but because no latitude was allowed to the states as regards timing, the third paragraph of Article 95 having to be applied by 31 December 1961 at the latest, and because the first paragraph of Article 95 contains "a clear and unconditional obligation," which requires "no measures . . . on the part of the member states," the Article amounts to a "complete, legally perfect" rule of law, which took full effect on expiry of the period mentioned in the third paragraph, and is apt "to produce direct effects on the legal relationships between member states and persons subject to their law." Case 13/68[122] belongs to the same line of cases. It concerned the prohibition in Articles 31 and 32 of the EEC Treaty against introducing "new quantitative restrictions or measures having equivalent effect," and the provision that member states, in their trade with one another:

shall refrain from making quotas and measures having equivalent effect, which were in existence when this Treaty came into force, more restrictive than they were.

This case established that Article 31 of the Treaty contains, for the period subsequent to the notification of lists of liberalized products, or at the latest after expiry of the notification period (even if the member states have not fulfilled their obligation to take action), a "clear prohibition," an obligation "which is not restricted by any reservation on the part of states seeking to make its fulfillment dependent on an act of domestic law or measure of the Community institutions." It is therefore

---

[119]N. V. Algemene Transport en Expedite Onderneming Van Gend en Loos v. Nederlandse Belastingadministratie, *Recueil de la jurisprudence de la Cour,* vol. 9, p. 1 (1963).

[120]Firma Alfons Lütticke GmbH v. Hauptzollamt Saarlouis, *Recueil de la jurisprudence de la Cour,* vol. 12, p. 294 (1966).

[121]The European Economic Community Treaty was phased in over a series of stages. During the first stage, which lasted from 1958 to 1968, member states were required, among other things, to eliminate or amend inconsistent domestic legislation.]

[122]Salgoil SpA v. Foreign Trade Ministry of the Italian Republic, *Recueil de la jurisprudence de la Cour,* vol. 14, p. 661 (1969).

"particularly apt to produce direct effects on the legal relationships between member states and persons subject to their law," and creates "individual rights which national courts must respect." Only in relation to the final sentence of the second paragraph of Article 32, and Article 33, did the Court hold that there was no direct effect, because they provided for a gradual removal of restrictions in the course of the transitional period, i.e. an obligation to take action, in the fulfillment of which the member states enjoyed a certain latitude. Hence, these provisions were too imprecise to be treated as having direct effect. Finally—without the list being exhaustive—we may mention Case 33/70.[123] Here again the question related to a Treaty obligation to take action, namely that arising from Article 13 of the EEC Treaty, which concerned the gradual abolition as between member states of taxes having equivalent effect to import duties. This abolition had to be effected during the transitional period in accordance with a timetable specified in the Commission's directives, in that case by 1 July 1968 at the latest. The Court, as you know, laid down that the directive in question had fixed a date by which the obligation arising from Article 13 had to be carried out. This amounted to a clear and unequivocal prohibition to which member states "had attached no reservation making its effectiveness dependent on a positive act of domestic law or an intervention of the Community institutions." It therefore had to be inferred that the relevant directive of the Commission, in conjunction with Articles 9 and 13(2) of the Treaty, had direct effect on the relationships between the member state to which the directive was addressed and its citizens, and had, from 1 July 1968, conferred rights on the latter "which domestic courts must respect."

From this line of cases, then, the correct solution of the present case may be deduced without any difficulty. We conclude that Article 16, with which we are now concerned, speaks of customs duties on export[s] and taxes having equivalent effect, and thus uses expressions comparable with those in Article 12. A time limit is fixed for the abolition, and this is laid down by the Treaty itself, not by any secondary source of Community law. There is no room for any latitude on the part of the states. Together with Article 9, whereby the foundation of the Community is a customs union, which involves "the prohibition as between member states of customs duties on imports and exports and of all taxes having equivalent effect," Article 16 of the EEC Treaty thus contains, since 1 January 1962, a clear, precise prohibition, unrestricted by any reservation or condition. The obligations thus imposed on member states are, to adopt the language of the cases already cited, complete and legally perfect. Hence, rights are created for individuals

which national courts must protect. In this connection—as will be remembered from Case 13/68—it is left to the national legal system to define the nature of these rights and to determine the form of judgment appropriate to protect them.

The questions of the President of the Tribunale di Torino should be answered in this sense. Further exposition would be superfluous.

JUDGMENT OF THE COURT OF JUSTICE OF THE EUROPEAN COMMUNITIES:

By Order dated 6 April 1971, lodged with the Registry of the Court on 15 April 1971, the President of the Tribunale de Torino has referred to the Court, under Article 177 of the Treaty establishing the European Economic Community, two questions relating to the interpretation of Article 16 of the said Treaty.

It appears from the Order referring the case that the judge doing so has to decide on an application for repayment of the export tax imposed on articles of artistic, historical, archaeological or ethnological value by Law No. 1089 of 1 June 1939, which is charged on the occasion of export of a work of art to another member state. This tax, as was declared by this Court in its judgment of 10 December 1968 (Case 7/68), is a tax having equivalent effect to a customs duty on exports, and falls under Article 16 of the Treaty.

By the first question, the Court is asked whether Article 16 amounts to a rule of law immediately applicable and directly effective in the Italian state from 1 January 1962. Should this question be answered in the affirmative, the Court is asked whether—from the said date—that rule has conferred on individuals, as against the Italian state, subjective rights which the courts must protect. Since the two questions are closely connected, it is convenient to consider them together.

By Article 9 of the EEC Treaty, the Community is based on a customs union, which implies, *inter alia*,[124] the prohibition as between member states of customs duties and any taxes having equivalent effect. By Article 16 of the Treaty, member states shall, as between themselves, abolish customs duties and taxes having equivalent effect, at the latest by the end of the first stage.

Articles 9 and 16, read in conjunction, contain a clear and precise prohibition, in relation to all taxes having equivalent effect to customs duties on export, and at the latest from the end of the first stage, against collecting such taxes, a prohibition whose effectiveness does not depend on any domestic legal measure nor on any intervention by the Community institutions. This prohibition is by its nature perfectly apt to produce

---

[123]SACE SpA v. Ministry of Finance of the Italian Republic, *Recueil de la jurisprudence de la Cour,* vol. 16, p. 1213 (1970).
[124Latin: "among other things."]

effects directly on the legal relationships between the member states and their subjects.

Consequently, from the end of the first stage (i.e., from 1 January 1962), these articles conferred on individuals rights which national courts must protect, and which must prevail over conflicting provisions of domestic law, even if the member state has not taken steps at the proper time to repeal such provisions. . . .

THE COURT

. . . concludes: From 1 January 1962, the date the first stage of the transitional period came to an end, Article 16 of the Treaty produces direct effects on the relationships between member states and their subjects and confers on the latter rights which national courts must protect. ■

The Institutions of the European Union. The main institutions of the European Union (see Exhibit 1-5 on page 33) are (1) the European Commission, (2) the Council of the European Union, (3) the European Parliament, (4) the European Economic and Social Committee, (5) the European Committee of Regions, (6) the European Court of First Instance, (7) the European Court of Justice, and (8) the European Central Bank.

European Commission: The administrative and executive arm of the European Union.

The European Commission The **European Commission** is the EU's executive.[125] That is, it drafts legislation for submission to the Council and the Parliament, and once the legislation is adopted it is responsible for its implementation. The Commission also is responsible for overseeing the implementation of the treaties that establish the EU. Additionally, it represents the EU internationally.

The Commission is currently composed of 20 individuals[126] appointed by Parliament for five year terms (see Exhibit 1-4). The President of the Commission is nominated by the European Council. The other 19 commissioners are nominated by the member states in consultation with the President. The large states—Germany, France, Italy, Spain, and the United Kingdom—nominate two commissioners each, and the small states, one each. All of the commissioners must act only in the interest of the EU, and they are forbidden to receive instructions from any national government. Parliament can force the Commission to resign by adopting a motion of censure.[127]

Commission decisions are made collegially, even though each commissioner is given responsibility for specific activities. The tasks of the Commission are to (1) ensure that EU rules are respected (to do this, the Commission has investigative powers and it can impose fines on individuals or companies it finds to be in breach of the rules; it can also take member states that

EXHIBIT 1-4 European Union Commission

European Union Commission, January 2001. Seated (l to r): Vice President Neil Kinnock, President Romano Prodi, Vice President Loyola de Palacio del Valle-Lersundi
(Photo: © Reuter Raymond/CORBIS SYGMA.)

---

[125]Information about the Commission is posted on the Internet at europa.eu.int/comm/index_en.htm.

[126]The number of commissioners will increase to a maximum of 27 with the addition of new member states.

[127]The Parliament had never censured the Commission, which requires the support of an absolute majority of members and two-thirds of the votes cast. In March 1999, however, following an investigation into allegations of mismanagement by a committee of independent experts mandated by Parliament, the Commission chose to resign rather than face censure by Parliament.

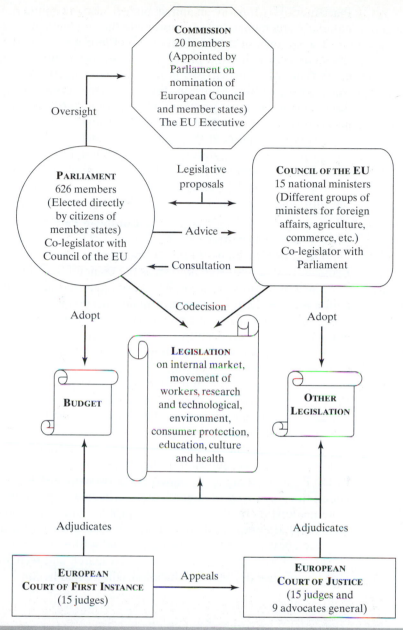

EXHIBIT 1-5   Powers of the European Union Institutions

fail to respect their obligations before the European Court of Justice), (2) propose to the European Council measures likely to advance the development of EU policies, (3) implement EU policies, and (4) manage the funds that make up most of the EU budget.

The Commission has an administrative staff of some 15,000 officials divided between 23 Directorates-General that are located primarily in Brussels and Luxembourg. Of these officials, more than one in five are employed as translators (a reflection of the EU's use of 11 equally authoritative languages to carry out its business).

Council of the European Union   The **Council of the European Union** is the member state governments' representative.[128] Its role is to: (1) adopt legislation[129] in conjunction with the

Council of the EU: Representative of the member state governments and the co-legislative body (with Parliament) of the European Union.

_____

[128] The Council's Internet Web site is at ue.eu.int/en/summ.htm.
[129] EU legislation is given various names. It is called a "regulation" when it applies directly; a "decision" when it is binding only on the member states, companies, or individuals to whom it is addressed; a "directive" when it lays down compulsory objectives but leaves it to the member states to translate these into national legislation; and a "recommendation" or "opinion" when it is not binding.

Parliament,[130] (2) adopt an annual budget, also in conjunction with Parliament, (3) adopt international agreements, and (4) coordinate the economic policies of the member states.

The Council of the EU is made up of ministers from the member state governments. Like the Commission, it has a presidency, which is rotated among the member state governments every 6 months. Participants in the Council's meetings change according to the agenda. For example, Agriculture Ministers discuss farm matters and Employment and Economic Ministers discuss unemployment problems. Foreign Ministers not only discuss foreign policy matters but also coordinate the work of the other ministers.

Every six months, at the beginning of each new presidency, the heads of state or government of the member states, along with their Foreign Ministers, meet with the European Commission President in an EU Summit that is known (somewhat confusingly) as the "European Council." Unlike the Council of the EU, which is responsible for EU rule making, the European Council focuses on establishing general policies and goals for the EU.[131]

European Parliament:
The co-legislative body (with the Council of the EU) and the main supervisory institution of the European Union.

The European Parliament   The **European Parliament** has 626 members elected every five years by universal suffrage.[132] It holds most of its plenary sessions (session attended by all of its members) in Strasbourg, France. Other plenary sessions and committee meetings are held in Brussels, Belgium. Its staff, known as the General Secretariat, is located in Luxembourg.

Since its first election in 1979, Parliament has acquired increased powers. At first only a deliberative body, it now has three main roles: (1) it has oversight authority over all EU institutions (2) it shares legislative power with the Council of the EU, and (3) it determines the EU's annual budget in conjunction with the Council.

Parliament's oversight authority extends beyond its power to appoint and censure the Commission (discussed earlier). Most importantly, it has limited oversight authority over the Council. Its members may ask the Council to respond to written and oral questions, and the President of the Council attends the plenary sessions and takes part in important debates.

EU legislation is made jointly by Parliament and the Council. Prior to the adoption of the 1992 EU Treaty, the Council could adopt legislation after consulting Parliament, regardless of Parliament's recommendations. Now, most legislation is adopted through a process known as "codecision." This requires draft legislation prepared by the Commission to be reviewed twice by the Parliament and the Council. If the two co-legislative bodies cannot agree, a "conciliation committee" made up of Council and Parliament representatives, with the participation of the Commission, attempts to reach a compromise draft. If a compromise draft is reached, it is submitted to Parliament and the Council for a third review for its final adoption.

The codecision process is used for adopting legislation governing the common internal market, the free movement of workers, research and technological development, the environment, consumer protection, education, culture and health.[133]

---

[130]The decisions of the Council of the EU may be made by simple majority, qualified majority, or unanimity, depending on the action it is taking. Most legislation is adopted by a qualified majority vote. Using this procedure, 62 votes out of a total of 87 votes are needed. France, Germany, Italy, and the United Kingdom each have 10 votes; Spain has 8; Belgium, Greece, the Netherlands, and Portugal have 5 each; Austria and Sweden have 4; Denmark., Finland, and Ireland have 3 each; and Luxembourg has 2 votes. The cases in which a qualified majority voting procedure may be used include decisions relating to the completion of the European internal market, to research and technology, to regional policy, and to improvement of the working environment.

[131]The original EU treaties did not envision meetings of the heads of state or government. Beginning in the 1960s, however, they began to meet on an occasional basis and by the mid-1970s their meetings took place semi-annually. The role of the European Council was finally recognized in 1992 in Article 4 of the European Union Treaty.

[132]The number of members elected by each state is as follows:

Germany	99	The Netherlands	31	Austria	21
France	87	Belgium	25	Denmark	16
Italy	87	Greece	25	Finland	16
United Kingdom	87	Portugal	25	Ireland	15
Spain	64	Sweden	22	Luxembourg	6

Members are grouped by political affiliation rather than nationality. Nearly 100 political parties are represented in the Parliament, ranging from far left to far right. These are organized in a limited number of political groups (presently eight).

[133]The codecision process is described in Article 251 of the Treaty Establishing the European Communities and it applies to non-discrimination on the basis of nationality (Article 12), right to move and reside (Article 18), freedom of movement for the workers (Article 40), social security for migrant workers (Article 42), right of establishment (Articles 44(1), 46(2), 47(1), and 47(2)), transport (Article 71(1)), transport (Article 80), internal market (Article 95)

For certain kinds of legislation, Parliament only has a veto right; it may not amend or modify a commission proposal. This power, known as "assent," applies to proposals for the accession of new members, to the adoption of certain international agreements, and to certain rules relating to the European Central Bank.[134] If Parliament does not give its assent, the legislation cannot be adopted. For other legislation, notably for tax matters and the review of farm price supports, the Parliament may only express an opinion.

The process by which the EU's annual budget is adopted is somewhat similar to the code-cision procedure. The Commission submits a draft budget to Parliament and the Council, each of which may review it twice. If they are unable to agree, the Council makes the final decision on so-called "compulsory expenditures" (mainly agricultural expenditures and expenditures related to international agreements with third countries). Parliament has the final say on "non-compulsory expenditures" and the final adoption of the budget in its entirety.

European Economic and Social Committee   Before the Council can adopt a proposal, opinions first must be obtained from the Parliament and, in many cases, from the Union's **Economic and Social Committee.**[135] In essence, this consultative body is an institutionalized lobby. Its 222 members represent a wide range of special interest groups, including employers, trade unions, consumers, farmers, and so on.

European Committee of Regions   The 1993 Maastricht Treaty on European Union created a second consultative body: the **Committee of Regions.**[136] The Committee, which consists of 222 representatives of local and regional governments, was established to ensure that the public authorities closest to the citizen—such as mayors, city and county councilors, and regional presidents—are consulted on EU proposals of direct interest to them. In particular, the Committee must be consulted on matters relating to trans-European networks, public health, education, youth, culture, and economic and social cohesion.

European Court of First Instance   The **Court of First Instance**[137] is the EU's trial court for cases brought by individuals to challenge legislation or actions taken by the EU institutions, to challenge an institution's failure to act,[138] and for deciding employment disputes between EU institutions and their employees. It is made up of 15 judges appointed by the common accord of the member states for renewable terms of 6 years. The Court sits in chambers of 3 or 5 judges to decide most disputes, but it may sit in plenary session to decide important cases.[139]

European Court of Justice   The EU's **Court of Justice**[140] is also made up of 15 judges selected in the same fashion and for the same term as judges of the Court of First Instance. It, too, sits in chambers of 3 or 5 judges or in plenary session.[141] The Court hears contentious cases and makes preliminary rulings. It hears four kinds of contentious cases: (1) appeals from the Court of First Instance; (2) complaints brought by the Commission or one member state against another member state for failure of the latter to meet its obligations under EU law; (3) complaints

---

Economic and Social Committee: A European Union consultative body made up of special interest groups.

Committee of Regions: A European Union consultative body made up of representatives of local and regional governments.

European Court of First Instance: The European Union's trial court with jurisdiction over (1) disputes brought by private persons against an EU institution and (2) employment disputes between EU institutions and their employees.

European Court of Justice: The supreme tribunal of the European Union.

---

employment (encouragement actions) (Article 129), customs cooperation (Article 135), fight against social exclusion (encouragement actions) (Article137(2)), equal opportunities and equal treatment (Article 141 (3)), implementing decisions relating to the European Social Fund (Article 148), education (encouragement actions) (Article 149(4)), vocational training (Article 150(4)), culture (except the recommendations) (Article 151(5)), health (encouragement actions) (Article 152(4)), consumers (Article 153(4), trans-European networks (guidelines) (Article 156), implementing decisions relating to the European Regional Development Fund (Article 162), research (framework program) (Article 166(1)), research (Article 172(2)), environment: general action programs (Articles 175(1) and 175(3)), transparency (Article 255), prevention of and fight against fraud (Article 280), statistics (Article 285), and creation of a consultative body for data protection (Article 286).

[134]Assent is required for specific missions of the European Central Bank (Treaty Establishing the European Communities, Article 105(6)), amendment of the statutes of the European System of Central Banks/European Central Bank (Article 107(5), structural funds and cohesion funds (Article 161), uniform electoral procedure (Article 190(4)), specified international agreements (Article 300(3)), accession of new Member States (EU Treaty, Article 49).

[135]The European Economic and Social Committee's Internet Web site is at www.ces.eu.int/en/org/fr_org_welcome.htm.

[136]The European Committee of Regions' Web site is at www.cor.eu.int/.

[137]The European Court of First Instance Web site is at www.europa.eu.int/cj/en/index.htm.

[138]Individuals may seek the annulment of a legal measure that is of direct and individual concern to them; they may bring actions to compel an EU institution to act; and they may seek damages for injuries caused by EU institutions or servants in the performance of their duties.

[139]European Union Treaty, Article 168A.

[140]The European Court of Justice can be found on the World Wide Web at www.europa.eu.int/cj/index.htm.

[141]European Union Treaty, Article 165. Every 3 years there is a partial replacement of judges. Seven and eight are replaced alternatively. *Id.,* Article 176.

European Court of
First Instance
(Photo: European
Community © 1999.)

European Court of
Justice
(Photo: European
Community © 1999.)

**European Central
Bank:** The central bank
of the European Union.

**European Court of
Auditors:** The institu-
tion responsible for
supervising the Euro-
pean Union's budget.

brought by a member state against an EU institution or its servants for failing to act or for injuries they may have caused; and (4) actions brought by a member state, the Council, the Commission, or the Parliament seeking the annulment of an EU legal measure.[142] Preliminary rulings come about when a national court is hearing a case involving an EU law and the national court is in doubt as to the interpretation or validity of that law. In such a case, the national court may, and in some cases must, request a preliminary ruling from the Court of Justice.[143]

Nine Advocates-General assist the judges of the Court of Justice in carrying out their duties.[144] An Advocate-General is an official, commonly found in courts in civil law countries, who prepares a detailed brief analyzing the arguments of the parties and suggesting how the court should decide the case. In many regards, an Advocate-General's brief is similar to an opinion prepared by a judge in a common law country. The reason for this is that the opinions handed down by civil law courts (including the European Court of Justice) generally do not engage in an extensive analysis of the issues; rather, they state a conclusion and a concise reason for their conclusion. Often, but not always, the court will adopt (sometimes in the fewest of words) the reasoning of the Advocate-General.

European Central Bank   The **European Central Bank** (ECB), which came into being on January 1, 1999, is responsible for carrying out the EU's monetary policy. The ECB's decision-making bodies are a Governing Council and an Executive Board. These oversee the European System of Central Banks (ESCB). The ESCB determines the amount of money in circulation, conducts foreign-exchange operations, holds and manages the member states' official foreign reserves, and ensures the smooth operation of payment systems.

European Court of Auditors   The EU budget, which is funded from customs duties and agricultural levies on external imports and from a portion of the value-added tax (VAT) collected in the member states, is supervised by a **Court of Auditors**[145] made up of 15 individuals appointed by mutual agreement of the European Council for six-year terms. The Court of Auditors has wide-ranging powers to examine the legality and regularity of EU receipts and expenditures and to ensure the sound financial management of the budget.

Other Intergovernmental Organizations

IGOs can be categorized into two basic groups: (1) general intergovernmental organizations that have competence in a wide variety of fields, including politics, security, culture, and economics, like the United Nations, and (2) specialized intergovernmental organizations that limit their activities to a particular field.

General Intergovernmental Organizations   Three prominent regional general IGOs are devoted to political cooperation, security, and the promotion of economic, social, and cultural development. They are the Council of Europe,[146] the African Union (AU),[147] and the Organization of American

---

[142]*Id.*, Articles 169 through 171 provide for actions for infringement against a member state for failing to observe an EU treaty or a law derived therefrom; Articles 173, 174, and 176 provide for an action to annul the acts taken by the Union's institutions in violation of the EU treaties; Articles 175 and 176 provide for action to compel an EU institution to take action; and Articles 178 and 215(2) provide for an action for damages arising from the non-contractual (i.e., tort) liability of the Union.

[143]*Id.*, Article 177. The Court will only hear requests (1) that involve a genuine issue as to Union law and (2) that the referring court regards as being necessary to its being able to give a judgment. *See* Costa v. ENEL, Case 6/64, *European Court Reports,* vol. 1964, p. 585 (1964), and Case 68/80, *European Court Reports,* vol. 1980, p. 771 (1980).

[144]European Union Treaty, Article 166. As with the judges, half of the Advocates-General are replaced every three years. *Id.,* Article 167. No Advocates-General serve in the Court of First Instance. In certain cases, one of the judges of the Court of First Instance will perform the functions of Advocate-General.

[145]The European Court of Auditors' Internet Web site is at www.eca.eu.int/.

[146]As of July 1999, the Council of Europe had 40 members: Albania, Andorra, Austria, Belgium, Bulgaria, Croatia, Cyprus, Czech Republic, Denmark, Estonia, Finland, France, Georgia, Germany, Greece, Hungary, Iceland, Ireland, Italy, Latvia, Liechtenstein, Lithuania, Luxembourg, Macedonia, Malta, Moldova, the Netherlands, Norway, Poland, Portugal, Romania, the Russian Federation, San Marino, Slovakia, Slovenia, Spain, Sweden, Switzerland, Turkey, Ukraine, and the United Kingdom. *See* the list of member states on the Council's Internet Web site at www.coe.fr/eng/std/states.htm.

[147]The AU has is goals the economic, political, and social integration and development of the African people. It is the successor to the Organization of African Union (OAU), which was founded in 1963 with the goals of eradicating all forms of colonialism in Africa and promoting the sovereignty, territorial integrity, and independence of its members. As of June 2000, the OAU had 53 members: Algeria, Angola, Benin, Botswana, Burkina Faso, Burundi, Cameroon, Cape Verde, Central African Republic, Chad, Comoros, Cote D'Ivoire, Democratic Republic of Congo,

States (OAS).[148] The oldest is the OAS, which was established in its present form in 1948. The Council of Europe was created in 1949 and the AU (which replaced the Organization of African Unity, founded in 1963) came into being in 2002. Each limits membership to states from their region. The Council of Europe further limits its membership to states committed to the rule of law and the enjoyment of human rights. Spain and Portugal, for example, were excluded from the Council until the mid-1970s because they did not have democratic regimes. The OAS admits any independent American state except those involved in territorial disputes. Belize and Guyana were not admitted until 1993 because of this requirement. Any independent sovereign African state is eligible for membership in the AU with the exception of countries ruled by white minority regimes.

The institutional structure of all three of these organizations is quite similar. The Council of Europe is different in one important respect, however. It has a Parliamentary Assembly whose representatives are elected by the national parliaments of the member states and whose numbers vary in proportion to the population of each member.[149] The representatives do not vote as a block representing their states, but individually or as part of political parties that have formed within the Assembly. This means that individuals influence the deliberations more than governments.[150]

All three organizations seek to promote cooperation between their members in a variety of fields. Because of differing circumstances, each, however, has emphasized a slightly different agenda. The Council of Europe has stressed legal, social, and cultural matters; the OAS has emphasized issues of peace and security; while the newly established AU is concentrating on political cooperation. Human rights are an important interest of all three. Individuals within member states of the Council of Europe may bring human rights cases directly to a European Court of Human Rights.[151] Within the OAS, individuals may submit complaints to an Inter-American Commission on Human Rights. The Commission, after carrying out an independent investigation, will either submit a report to the OAS's Council or, if the member state concerned has recognized the court's jurisdiction, forward the complaint to the Inter-American Court of Human Rights. In Africa, the AU has a Human Rights Commission with investigatory powers similar to those of the Inter-American Commission.[152]

In addition to these three regional general IGOs, there are three notable nonregional general IGOs: the Commonwealth of Nations,[153] the Arab League,[154] and the Commonwealth of

---

Djibouti, Egypt, Equatorial Guinea, Eritrea, Ethiopia, Gabon, Gambia, Ghana, Guinea, Guinea-Bissau, Kenya, Lesotho, Liberia, Libya, Madagascar, Malawi, Mali, Mauritania, Mauritius, Mozambique, Namibia, Niger, Nigeria, Rwanda, Saharawi Arab Democratic Republic, Sao Tome and Principe, Seychelles, Senegal, Sierra Leone, Somalia, South Africa, Sudan, Swaziland, Tanzania, Togo, Tunisia, Uganda, Zambia, and Zimbabwe. The AU homepage is at www.africa-union.org/. For the history and structure of the AU, *see* the AU Summit 2002 page maintain by the South African Department of Foreign Affairs at www.au2002.gov.za/.

[148]The Organization of American States has as its objectives "peace and justice, [and] promoting solidarity among the American states." It has 35 members: Antigua and Barbuda, Argentina, the Bahamas, Barbados, Belize, Bolivia, Brazil, Canada, Chile, Colombia, Costa Rica, Cuba (suspended from participating in OAS activities in 1962 but not from membership), Dominica, Dominican Republic, Ecuador, El Salvador, Grenada, Guatemala, Guyana, Haiti, Honduras, Jamaica, Mexico, Nicaragua, Panama, Paraguay, Peru, Saint Lucia, Saint Vincent and the Grenadines, Suriname, Saint Kitts and Nevis, Trinidad and Tobago, the United States of America, Uruguay, and Venezuela. *See* the list of member states on the OAS's Internet Web site at www.oas.org/en/ mstates/mstates.htm.

[149]*See* "About the Council of Europe" on the Council's Internet home page at www.coe.fr/eng/ present/about.htm.

[150]The African Union will have a Parliamentary Assembly once the Protocol creating the assembly is ratified by 35 member states. As of July 2002, only three states had ratified the Protocol. *See* www.au2002.gov.za/.

[151]*See* the Court's home page at www.dhcour.coe.fr/.

[152]The AU Charter calls for the creation of a Court of Justice, but the member states have yet to agree on the court's jurisdiction. *See* www.au2002.gov.za/.

[153]Established in 1931 to promote cooperation among states that were once part of the British Empire and that recognize the British Monarchy as their heads of state. The British Commonwealth of Nations has 54 members: Antigua and Barbuda, Australia, the Bahamas, Bangladesh, Barbados, Belize, Botswana, Brunei, Cameroon, Canada, Cyprus, Dominica, Fiji, The Gambia, Ghana, Grenada, Guyana, India, Jamaica, Kenya, Kiribati, Lesotho, Malawi, Malaysia, the Maldives, Malta, Mauritius, Mozambique, Namibia, Nauru, New Zealand, Nigeria (suspended in 1995), Pakistan, Papua New Guinea, Saint Kitts and Nevis, Saint Lucia, Saint Vincent and the Grenadines, Seychelles, Sierra Leone, Singapore, Solomon Islands, South Africa, Sri Lanka, Swaziland, Tanzania, Tonga, Trinidad and Tobago, Tuvalu, the United Kingdom, Uganda, Vanuatu, Western Samoa, Zambia, and Zimbabwe. The Republic of Ireland is associated with it for commercial purposes but is not a member. *See* the British Monarchy home page on the Internet at www.royal.gov.uk/today/qcw.htm. Also *see* the Commonwealth's home page at www.thecommonwealth.org/ and the Commonwealth OnLine page at www.tcol.co.uk/index.htm.

[154]Founded in 1945, the League of Arab States (Arab League) seeks to promote political, economic, cultural, and communication ties among its members and to mediate internal disputes. As of 1998 it had 22 members: Algeria, Bahrain, Comoros, Djibouti, Egypt, Iraq, Jordan, Kuwait, Lebanon, Libya, Mauritania, Morocco, Oman, Qatar, Saudi Arabia, Somalia, Sudan, Syria, Tunisia, the United Arab Emirates, Yemen, and the Palestine Liberation Organization. *See* the Central Intelligence Agency's *CIA Factbook* at www.odci.gov/cia/publications/factbook/appc.html.

Independent States.[155] The Commonwealth of Nations limits its membership to countries that were formerly part of the British Empire; the Arab League is open only to Arab nations; and the Commonwealth of Independent States is made up of former republics of the Soviet Union. Unlike other general IGOs, the Commonwealth of Nations has no charter (or, at least, no written charter) and, beyond a Secretariat, no organs other than a biennial meeting of heads of government, annual meetings of finance ministers, and regular meetings of other ministers (especially education, law, and health). The Arab League has a Council made up of representatives of each member state, several committees that assist the Council, and a Secretariat. In addition, Arab kings and presidents meet at regular Arab League summit conferences. The Commonwealth of Independent States was originally set up to provide for the orderly dissolution of the former Soviet Union. It now seeks to promote cooperation among the former Soviet republics. Each of these organizations encourages cooperation among its members, but, unlike the Council of Europe or the Organization of American States, which carry on many service functions, they are primarily forum organizations.

Specialized Intergovernmental Organizations   There is a whole range of specialized intergovernmental organizations that deal with a wide variety of areas of mutual interest to their members. Examples are the European Space Agency,[156] the International Coffee Organization,[157] the International Criminal Police Organization (INTERPOL),[158] the International Institute for the Unification of Private Law (*UNIDROIT*),[159] and the World Tourism Organization.[160]

One important group of specialized IGOs promotes economic cooperation and development. This group is made up of several types of organizations, the most developed of which are the common markets or **customs unions**, such as the European Union.[161] Customs unions are intended to eliminate trade barriers between their members and to establish common external tariffs. Aside from the EU, the success of other customs unions (see Exhibit 1-6) has been limited for several reasons. First, the economies of their member states—all developing countries—tend to compete with, rather than complement, each other. Second, many of the member states only recently gained independence and they are reluctant to surrender that independence to a central authority. Third, the economic gains made within these unions have often been unequal, prompting those states that have not shared fully to become discouraged and withdraw.

A second type of cooperative economic IGO is the **free trade area** (FTA). FTAs are set up to eliminate trade barriers between member states without establishing a common external tariff. Examples include the Association of Southeast Asian Nations Free Trade Area (ASEAN-FTA),[162] the Central European Free Trade Area (CEFTA),[163] the European Free Trade Association (EFTA),[164] the Southern Cone Common Market (*MERCOSUR*),[165] and the North American Free Trade Agreement (NAFTA).[166]

customs union: A group of states that have reduced or eliminated trade barriers between themselves and have established a common external tariff.

free trade area: A group of states that have reduced or eliminated trade barriers between themselves but that maintain their own individual tariffs as to other states.

---

[155]Established in 1991, its members are Armenia, Azerbaijan, Belarus, Georgia, Kazakhstan, Kyrgyzstan, Moldova, the Russian Federation, Tajikistan, Turkmenistan, Ukraine, and Uzbekistan. *See id.*

[156]Founded in 1975, it has 14 state members. *See* the European Space Agency's home page at www.esrin.esa.it/.

[157]Founded in 1963, it has 44 exporting state members and 18 importing state members. *See* the International Coffee Organization's home page at www.ico.org/.

[158]Founded in 1923, it has 177 state members. *See* INTERPOL's home page at www.kenpubs.co.uk/interpol-pr/ index.html.

[159]Founded in 1926, it has 57 state members. *See* UNIDROIT's home page at www.unidroit.org/.

[160]Founded in 1975, it has 138 state members and 350 affiliated tourism organizations. *See* the World Tourism Organization's home page at www.world-tourism.org/.

[161]Established in 1960 to bring about the economic union of Belgium, Luxembourg, and the Netherlands.

[162]Established in 1992 to facilitate the free exchange of goods in Southeast Asia within 15 years. Its members are Brunei, Indonesia, Laos, Malaysia, Myanmar, the Philippines, Singapore, Thailand, and Vietnam. *See* the Association of Southeast Asian Nations' Internet site at www.aseansec.org/.

[163]Established in 1993 to progressively create a free trade area by January 1, 2001. Its members are Bulgaria, the Czech Republic, Hungary, Poland, Romania, and the Slovak Republic.

[164]Established in 1960, the European Free Trade Association presently has only four members: Iceland, Liechtenstein, Norway, and Switzerland. In 1991, EFTA and the European Community (now the European Union) entered into a trade agreement (called the European Economic Area) that joined the EU and three of the EFTA states (Iceland, Liechtenstein, and Norway) into the world's largest free trade area. *See* EFTA's home page at www.efta.int/ structure/ main/index.html.

[165]The Mercado Común Sudamericano was established in 1991. Its members are Argentina, Brazil, Paraguay, and Uruguay. *See* the Uruguayan embassy Web site at www.embassy.org/uruguay/ for a description of MERCOSUR.

[166]Agreed to in 1993 by Canada, Mexico, and the United States, NAFTA came into effect January 1, 1994. *See* the U.S. Department of Commerce's NAFTA Web page at www.mac.doc.gov/nafta/nafta2.htm. *See* also the NAFTA Secretariat's home page at www.nafta-sec-alena.org/.

ANCOM	Andean Common Market. Established in 1992 to create a free trade zone. A common external tariff was adopted in 1993. Members are Bolivia, Colombia, Ecuador, Peru, and Venezuela.[167]
CACM	Central American Common Market. Established in 1997 to replace a common market of the same name that functioned from 1960 to 1969. Members are Costa Rica, El Salvador, Guatemala, Honduras, and Nicaragua.[168]
CARICOM	Caribbean Community. Established in 1973, it replaced the Caribbean Free Trade Association created in 1965. Its members are Antigua and Barbuda, the Bahamas, Barbados, Belize, Dominica, Grenada, Guyana, Jamaica, Montserrat, Saint Kitts and Nevis, Saint Lucia, Saint Vincent and the Grenadines, Suriname, and Trinidad and Tobago. In 1989, the Community agreed to create a Single Market and Economy (unofficially known as the Caribbean Common Market) by 1994.[169]
COMESA	Common Market for Eastern and Southern Africa (formerly Preferential Trade Area for Eastern and Southern African States). Established in 1981 to create a common market. Members are Angola, Burundi, Comoros, Democratic Republic of the Congo, Djibouti, Egypt, Eritrea, Ethiopia, Kenya, Madagascar, Malawi, Mauritius, Namibia, Rwanda, Seychelles, Sudan, Swaziland, Tanzania, Uganda, Zambia, and Zimbabwe.[170]
ECCAS	Economic Community of Central African States. Established in 1981 to gradually create a common market. Members are Burundi, Cameroon, Central African Republic, Chad, Democratic Republic of the Congo, Republic of the Congo, Equatorial Guinea, Gabon, Rwanda, and São Tomé and Príncipe.
ECOWAS	Economic Community of West African States. Established in 1975 to promote economic development and gradually create a common market. Members are Benin, Burkina Faso, Cape Verde, Gambia, Ghana, Guinea, Guinea-Bissau, Ivory Coast, Liberia, Mali, Mauritania, Niger, Nigeria, Senegal, Sierra Leone, and Togo.[171]
SACU	Southern African Customs Union. Established in 1969 to promote free trade and cooperation in customs matters. Members are Botswana, Lesotho, Namibia, South Africa, and Swaziland.[172]
SADC	Southern African Development Community. Established in 1979, it seeks to establish an economic union among its members: Angola, Botswana, Congo (Kinshasa), Lesotho, Malawi, Mauritius, Mozambique, Namibia, Seychelles, South Africa, Swaziland, Tanzania, Zambia, and Zimbabwe.[173]
UDEAC	Central African Customs and Economic Union. Established in 1964 to promote the gradual and progressive creation of a common market. Members are Cameroon, Central African Republic, Chad, Republic of the Congo, Equatorial Guinea, and Gabon.[174]

EXHIBIT 1-6   *Customs Unions in the Developing World*

economic consultative association: A group of states that exchanges information, coordinates economic policy, and promotes trade cooperation.

Finally, a third type of IGO involved in economic cooperation and development is the **economic consultative association.** The function of a consultative association is to gather and exchange statistics and information, to coordinate the economic policies of member states, and to promote mutual trade cooperation. Examples are the Organization for Economic Cooperation and Development (OECD),[175] (see Exhibit 1-7), the Colombo Plan for

---

[167]See the International Monetary Fund's *Directory of Economic, Commodity, and Development Organizations* entry on the Andean Community General Secretariat at www.imf.org/external/np/sec/decdo/acuerdo.htm.

[168]See id. on the Secretariat for Central American Economic Integration at www.imf.org/external/np/sec/decdo/sieca.htm.

[169]See id. on the Caribbean Community at www.imf.org/external/np/sec/decdo/caricom.htm.

[170]See the Common Market for Eastern and Southern Africa's home page at www.comesa.int/.

[171]See the International Monetary Fund's Directory of Economic, Commodity, and Development Organizations entry on the Economic Community of West African States at www.imf.org/external/np/sec/decdo/ecowas.htm.

[172]See the *Almanac of Politics and Government* at www.polisci.com/world/intorg/134.htm.

[173]See the Commonwealth of Nations' entry on the Southern African Development Community at www.tcol.co.uk/comorg/sadc.htm.

[174]See the Central African Customs and Economic Union's home page at www.socatel.intnet.cf/accueil1.htm.

[175]Established in 1961, the Organization for Economic Cooperation and Development has 29 members: Australia, Austria, Belgium, Canada, the Czech Republic, Denmark, Finland, France, Germany, Greece, Hungary, Iceland, Ireland, Italy, Japan, Korea, Luxembourg, Mexico, the Netherlands, New Zealand, Norway, Poland, Portugal, Spain,

Cooperative Economic and Social Development in Asia and the Pacific (Colombo Plan),[176] the Group of 77 (G-77),[177] and the Organization of Petroleum Exporting Countries (OPEC).[178]

Nongovernmental Organizations

nongovernmental orga-nization (NGO): An international organization made up of persons other than states.

nonprofit nongovern-mental organization: An international organization that draws its members from among individuals and domestic organizations (sometimes including local governments, such as municipalities) who reside in two or more states.

multinational enter-prise: Business firm operating branches, subsidiaries, or joint ventures in two or more states.

Nongovernmental organizations (NGOs) include nonprofit and for-profit NGOs. **Nonprofit NGOs** serve as coordinating agencies for private national groups in international affairs. Examples of nonprofit NGOs are the International Air Transport Association,[179] the International Bar Association,[180] Amnesty International,[181] and the International Committee of the Red Cross.[182]

For-profit NGOs, also known as transnational corporations or **multinational enterprises** (MNEs), are businesses operating branches or subsidiaries or joint ventures in two or more countries. The organizational structures of MNEs are as diverse as any national business. They may invest in other businesses abroad; they may establish physical plants with management, labor and financing overseas; they may have a single central headquarters; or they may be loosely coordinated through contractual agreements.

States perceive MNEs both as necessities and as threats, and they have tried to work together to adopt international regulations both to control and to promote them. The International Chamber of Commerce, the Organization for Economic Cooperation and Development, the International Labor Organization, and the United Nations Commission on Transnational Corporations have each produced codes of conduct for MNEs. These codes' influence, however, has been limited since they are only suggested guidelines.[183]

In particular, the MNEs have acquired the authority to enter into international agreements with states and to sue states in at least one international tribunal. The right to sue a state is granted in the Convention on the Settlement of International Disputes between States and Nationals of Other States adopted in 1965. This Convention, sponsored by the World Bank,[184] is meant to encourage investment in underdeveloped countries. To do this, it allows MNEs to enter into agreements with developing countries, and it requires both the MNEs and the coun-

---

Sweden, Switzerland, Turkey, the United Kingdom, and the United States. The goals of the OECD are to help "member countries promote economic growth, employment and improved standards of living through the coordination of policy" and to encourage "the sound and harmonious development of the world economy and improve the lot of developing countries, particularly the poorest." *See* the OECD home page at www.oecd.org/.

[176]Established in 1959, the Colombo Plan for Cooperative Economic and Social Development in Asia and the Pacific seeks to aid the economic development of its Asian members. There are 26 members: Afghanistan, Australia, Bangladesh, Bhutan, Burma, Canada, Fiji, India, Indonesia, Iran, Japan, Kampuchea, Laos, Malaysia, the Maldives, Nepal, New Zealand, Pakistan, Papua New Guinea, the Philippines, South Korea, Singapore, Sri Lanka, Thailand, the United Kingdom, and the United States. *See* the Commonwealth of Nations Internet page describing the Colombo Plan at www.thecommonwealth.org/htm/info/links/colombo.htm.

[177]Established in 1967 following the first meeting of the UN Conference on Trade and Development (UNCTAD). Originally an *ad hoc* group of 77 developing countries who sought to coordinate their negotiating positions within UNCTAD, the Group of 77 now functions as a Third World "negotiating block" in its dealings with the developed world. The G-77 promotes mutual cooperation and the establishment of a "New Economic Order" (to give international negotiating power to the Third World). At present there are 132 members. *See* the Group of 77's home page at www.g77.org/.

[178]Established in 1960, the Organization of Petroleum Exporting Countries attempts to set world oil prices by coordinating the oil production of its member states. There are 11 OPEC members: Algeria, Indonesia, Iran, Iraq, Kuwait, Libya, Nigeria, Qatar, Saudi Arabia, the United Arab Emirates, and Venezuela. Ecuador was a member from 1973 to 1992 and Gabon from 1975 to 1994. *See* the OPEC home page at www.opec.org/.

[179]Founded in 1945, the International Air Transport Association represents 259 airlines in promoting an economically viable international air transport industry. *See* the IATA home page at www.iata.org/.

[180]Founded in 1947, the International Bar Association promotes the exchange of information, the discussion of legal issues, and the independence of the profession. It represents 173 member organizations and 18,000 individual members in 183 countries. *See* its home page at www.ibanet.org/.

[181]Founded in 1961, Amnesty International undertakes campaigns to free prisoners of conscience, ensure fair and prompt trials for political prisoners, abolish cruel and unusual punishments, and end extrajudicial executions. It is made up of 4,300 local groups and approximately 1 million members and supporters in 100 countries. *See* its home page at www.amnesty.org/.

[182]Founded in 1863, the International Committee of the Red Cross seeks to help all victims of war and internal violence by coordinating the activities of 175 national Red Cross and Red Crescent societies. *See* the ICRC home page at www.icrc.org/.

[183]Ruth Cummings and Paul Bierly, "The Moral Uncertainty of International Business," *Proceedings of the Eastern Academy of Management* (1996), posted on Paul Bierly's Internet Web site at blue.temple.edu/~eastern/bierly.html.

[184]The World Bank Internet Web site is at www.worldbank.org/.

EXHIBIT 1-7

Organization for Economic Cooperation and Development

The Organization for Economic Cooperation and Development (OECD) is a forum organization for developed countries, whose members discuss, develop, and perfect common economic and social policies. It is sometimes referred to as the "rich countries club" because its members produce two-thirds of the world's goods and services.

In October 1947, Western European heads of state met to discuss the Marshall Plan, the U.S. sponsored plan for post-World War II European economic recovery, at Chateau de la Muette ini Paris. This meeting led to the creation of the Organization for European Economic Cooperation in April 1948, which became the Organization for Economic Cooperation and Development in September 1961, with the addition of United States and Canada as members. (Photo: © Hulton-Deutsch Collection/CORBIS.)

tries to resolve any disputes about their agreements by a mandatory mechanism of conciliation and arbitration. Currently, 126 states are parties to the Convention.[185]

F. THE RIGHTS OF INDIVIDUALS UNDER INTERNATIONAL LAW

International law looks upon individuals in two different ways: (1) it ignores them or (2) it treats them as its subjects. The traditional view is to ignore them. This is based on the idea that international law (or, more particularly, "the law of nations") applies only to states. Some writers still believe that this is the only proper way for international law to treat individuals. For example, the Chinese international law writer K'ung Meng has this to say:

> [A]ccording to the fundamental characteristics of international law (it is the law among states), individuals can only be subjects of municipal law and cannot be subjects of international law. In international relations, individuals are represented by their own countries and if rights and interests (such as entry, residence, employment, and property) are violated in a foreign country, individuals should negotiate with the state concerned through the organs of their home country. Only their home country enjoys the rights of diplomatic protection in international law.[186]

Even though individuals have no direct rights according to this traditional view, they do have derivative rights. That is, as K'ung Meng points out in the excerpt, the state of which an individual is a national can seek redress on behalf of that individual from any foreign state that causes the individual injury. The rationale for allowing such action by the individual's state of nationality is based on the notion that an injury to a national is an injury to the state.

---

[185]World Bank, "An Overview of ICSID," posted on the World Bank's Internet Web site at www.worldbank.org/html/extdr/icsid.html.

[186]K'ung Meng, "A Criticism of the Theories of Bourgeois International Law Concerning the Subjects of International Law and Recognition of States," *Kuo-chi wen-t'i yen-chiu,* no. 2, p. 44 (1960), translated in Jerome Cohen and Hungdah Chiu, *People's China and International Law: A Documentary Study,* vol. 1, p. 97 (1974).

	Law of State Responsibility	International Human Rights Law
Basis of a claim	Any loss of property or personal injury	Injuries defined by treaty
Claimant	The state of which the injured individual is a national	The injured individual
Defendant	A foreign state	Any state

EXHIBIT 1-8   Comparison of the Law of State Responsibility and International Human Rights Law

state responsibility: Liability of a state for the injuries that it causes to foreign persons.

The traditional international law concept that allows a state to seek compensation from other states for injuries done to its nationals is known as the law of **state responsibility**. Although it protects individuals from virtually any kind of mistreatment by foreign states, the law of state responsibility gives individuals few rights. In particular, it does not give them the right to pursue their own claims or the right to protest the actions of their own national state. (The law of state responsibility is discussed more fully in Chapter 2.)

The second way in which international law looks upon individuals is to treat them as its subjects. This view—one developed only over the last half-century—regards individuals as having basic **human rights** and, significantly, the right to assert claims on their own behalf against states, including the state of their nationality.[187] In comparison with the law of state responsibility, however, the kinds of claims that individuals can raise are limited. That is, they can only be based on rights granted in treaties or in widely recognized international declarations.

human rights: Basic rights intended to protect all people from cruel and inhumane treatment, threats to their lives, and persecution.

Exhibit 1-8 compares the scope and nature of the law of state responsibility with that of international human rights law.

Case 1-9 examines the differences between the traditional law of state responsibility and international human rights law.

---

[187] *See,* for example, Alvarez-Machain v. United States, *Federal Reporter, Third Series,* vol. 266, p. 1045 (9th Circuit Ct. of Appeals 2001) in which a Mexican national successfully sued the United States for kidnapping him and forcefully abducting him from Mexico to stand trial—a trial in which he was acquitted—in the United States.

Case 1–9   De Sanchez v. Banco Central De Nicaragua

United States, Court of Appeals, Fifth Circuit, 1985.
Federal Reporter, Second Series, vol. 770, p. 1385 (1985);
International Law Reports, vol. 88, p. 76 (1992).

CIRCUIT JUDGE GOLDBERG: . . .

In July 1979, the Nicaraguan government of General Anastasio Somoza fell to the Sandinista revolutionaries. As usually occurs, members of the old regime fled the country to escape the reach of "revolutionary justice." But where defeated aristocracies once emigrated to London or Paris, now they seem to wind up in Miami. One of the emigres—Mrs. Josefina Navarro de Sanchez, the wife of President Somoza's former Minister of Defense—brought the present suit to collect on a check for $150,000 issued to her by the Nicaraguan Central Bank (Banco Central de Nicaragua) shortly before Somoza's fall. Mrs. Sanchez was unable to cash this check after the new government assumed power and placed a stop-payment order on it.

[Mrs. Sanchez then brought suit against the Banco Central in a United States court seeking an order to make it honor the check (which was drawn on a U.S. bank). The trial court instead granted Banco Central's motion for a summary judgment and dismissed the suit. Mrs. Sanchez appealed. The central issue on appeal was whether an individual (Mrs. Sanchez) who is a national of a state (Nicaragua) can sue an agency of that state (the Banco Central) in another state's courts for an alleged contractual breach.] . . .

International law, as its name suggests, deals with relations between sovereign states, not between states and individuals. Nations, not individuals have been its traditional subjects. Injuries to individuals have been cognizable only where they implicate two or more different nations: if one state injures the national of another state, then this can give rise to a violation of international law since the individual's injury is viewed as an injury to his state. As long as a nation

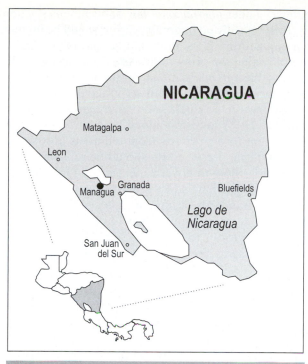

MAP 1-10 Nicaragua (1985)

injures only its own nationals, however, then no other state's interest is involved; the injury is a purely domestic affair, to be resolved within the confines of the nation itself.[188]

Recently, this traditional dichotomy between injuries to states and to individuals—and between injuries to homegrown and to alien individuals—has begun to erode. The international human rights movement is premised on the belief that international law sets a minimum standard not only for the treatment of aliens but also for the treatment of human beings generally. Nevertheless, the standards of human rights that have been generally accepted—and hence incorporated into the law of nations—are still limited. They encompass only such basic rights as the right not to be murdered, tortured, or otherwise subjected to cruel, inhuman, or degrading punishment; the right not to be a slave; and the right not to be arbitrarily detained.[189] At present, the taking by a state of its national's property does not contravene the international law of minimum human rights.[190] This has been held to be true in much more egregious situations than the present, including cases where the plaintiff had had his property taken pursuant to Nazi racial decrees.[191] It is

---

[188]Potentially, an injury by a state to its own nationals might implicate international law if the injury occurred within another state's territory. In that event, the state where the injury occurred might have an interest if the injury affected its territorial sovereignty. International law would become involved not because of the status of the injured party but because of the location of the injury.

In the present case, Mrs. Sanchez claims that her injury occurred in the United States, since that is where Banco Central's check was made payable. We need not decide here whether Banco Central's contractual obligations were "located" in the United States. Even if they were, the breach of these obligations was not of such a nature as to affront the territorial sovereignty of the United States. The situation might be different if Nicaragua had attempted to expropriate a piece of real property owned by Mrs. Sanchez in the United States. Then, Nicaragua's actions could be seen as literally challenging the authority of the United States over its own territory. We decide here only that takings of *intangible* property rights—including breaches of contract—do not violate international law where the injured party is national of the acting state, regardless of the property's location.

See Dreyfus v. Von Finck, *Federal Reporter, Second Series,* vol. 534, p. 24 at p. 31 (Second Circuit Ct. of Appeals, 1976): "[V]iolations of international law do not occur when the aggrieved parties are nationals of the acting state." In Filartiga v. Pena-Irala, *Federal Reporter, Second Series,* vol. 630, p. 876 (Second Circuit Ct. of Appeals, 1980), the court criticized this statement in Dreyfus as being "clearly out of tune with the current usage and practice of international law." *Id.* at p. 884. The Filartiga court found instead that "international law confers fundamental rights upon all people vis-à-vis their own governments" and that "the right to be free from torture is now among them." *Id.,* at p. 885. However, when read together with the later Second Circuit opinion in Verlinden, B.V. v. Central Bank of Nigeria, *Federal Reporter, Second Series,* vol. 647, p. 320 (Second Circuit Ct. of Appeals, 1981), reversed on other grounds, *United States Reports,* vol. 461, p. 480 (Supreme Ct., 1983), it is clear that this criticism was made only in relation to the international law of human rights, and was not intended to call into question the principle enumerated in Dreyfus as it applies to expropriations of property. In Verlinden, Judge Kaufman, the author of Filartiga, cited Dreyfus with approval in holding that "commercial violations, such as those here alleged, do not constitute breaches of international law." *Federal Reporter, Second Series,* vol. 647, p. 320 at p. 325 n. 16 (Second Circuit Ct. of Appeals, 1981).

R. Swift, *International Law: Current and Classic,* p. 324 (1969): "Traditionally, states have been free under international law to treat their nationals as they wished."

[189]*See* Filartiga v. Pena-Irala, *Federal Reporter, Second Series,* vol. 630, p. 876 at pp. 884–85 (Second Circuit Ct. of Appeals, 1980): "[O]fficial torture violates international law even if practiced on state's own citizens"; *Restatement (Revised) of Foreign Relations Law of the United States,* § 702 (Tentative Draft No. 6, 1985).

[190]Verlinden, B. V. v. Central Bank of Nigeria, *Federal Reporter, Second Series,* vol. 647, p. 320 at p. 325 n. 16 (Second Circuit Ct. of Appeals, 1981); Dreyfus v. Von Finck, *Federal Reporter, Second Series,* vol. 534, p. 24 at pp. 30-31 (Second Circuit Ct. of Appeals, 1976); IIT v. Vencap, Ltd., Federal Reporter, Second Series, vol. 519, p. 1001 at p. 1015 (Second Circuit Ct. of Appeals, 1975): "We cannot subscribe to plaintiff's view that the Eighth Commandment 'Thou shalt not steal' is part of the law of nations"; Jafari v. Islamic Republic of Iran, *Federal Supplement,* vol. 539, p. 209 at p. 215 (District Ct. for N. District of Illinois, 1982); *confirm* United States v. Belmont, *United States Reports,* vol. 301, p. 324 at p. 332 (Supreme Ct., 1937): "What another country has done in the way of taking over property of its nationals . . . is not a matter for judicial consideration here. Such nationals must look to their own government for any redress to which they may be entitled"; F. Palacio y Compañia, S.A. v. Brush, *Federal Supplement,* vol. 256, p. 481 at p. 487 (District Ct. for S. District of New York, 1966): "[C]onfiscations by a state of the property of its own nationals, no matter how flagrant and regardless of whether compensation has been provided, do not constitute violations of international law," affirmed in a memorandum decision, *Federal Reporter, Second Series,* vol. 375, p. 1011 (Second Circuit Ct. of Appeals), *certiorari* denied, *United States Reports,* vol. 389, p. 830 (Supreme Ct., 1967); Salimoff & Co. v. Standard Oil Co., *New York Reports,* vol. 262, p. 220 at p. 227 (Ct. of Appeals, 1933): "According to the law of nations, [the Soviet Union] did no legal wrong when it confiscated the oil of its own nationals and sold it in Russia to the defendants"; *Restatement (Revised) of Foreign Relations Law of the United States,* § 702 comment a (Tentative Draft No. 6, 1985).

[191]Dreyfus v. Von Finck, *Federal Reporter, Second Series,* vol. 534, p. 24 at pp. 30–31 (Second Circuit Ct. of Appeals, 1976).

certainly true here. As the court noted in *Jafari v. Islamic Republic of Iran*:[192]

> It may be foreign to our way of life and thought, but the fact is that governmental expropriation is not so universally abhorred that its prohibition commands the "general assent of civilized nations" ... — a prerequisite to incorporation in the "law of nations." ... We cannot elevate our American-centered view of governmental taking of property without compensation into a rule that binds all "civilized nations."[193]

The doctrine that international law does not generally govern disputes between a state and its own nationals rests on fundamental principles. At base, it is what makes individuals subjects of one state rather than of the international community generally. If we could inquire into the legitimacy under *international law* of Nicaragua's actions here, then virtually no internal measure would be immune from our scrutiny. Concomitantly, actions of the United States affecting the property of American citizens would become subject to international norms and hence reviewable by the courts of other nations. In the field of international law, where no single sovereign reigns supreme, the Golden Rule[194] takes on added poignancy. Just as we would resent foreign courts from telling us how we can and cannot rule ourselves, we should be reluctant to tell other nations how to govern themselves. Only where a state has engaged in conduct against its citizens that outrages basic standards of human rights or that calls into question the territorial sovereignty of the United States is it appropriate for us to interfere. Since this is not such a case, we decline to apply international law to Nicaragua's conduct. ...

Affirmed. ■

---

[192]*Federal Supplement*, vol. 539, p. 209 (District Ct. for N. District of Illinois, 1982).
[193]*Id.*, at p. 215. ...
[[194]The Golden Rule is "Do to others as you would have them do to you." It is not, as Judge Goldberg seems to suggest, "Leave others alone out of fear that they might not leave you alone." *Ed.*]

G. COMPARISON OF MUNICIPAL LEGAL SYSTEMS

comparative law: The study, analysis, and comparison of the world's municipal law systems.

There are more than 200 nations in the world today, and each has a different set of laws that govern its people and its relations with the rest of the world. Whereas international law governs relations between states, institutions, and individuals across national boundaries, municipal law governs these same persons (including the private or commercial conduct of foreign states) within the boundaries of a particular state. Although it would be impossible to describe the legal system of every nation, it is possible to describe the basic systems or "family groupings." The study, analysis, and comparison of the different municipal law systems is known as **comparative law**.

Comparative lawyers classify countries into legal families. The two most widely distributed families are the Romano-Germanic Civil Law and the Anglo-American Common Law. Another family that has become important internationally in recent years is Islamic Law.

Of course, each of these families has many subfamilies; for example, within the Romano-Germanic family one finds the Romanist, Germanic, and Latin American subfamilies. In addition, many legal systems are hybrids. The Japanese and the South African legal systems thus have elements of both the civil and the common law. Finally, some legal practices are truly unique to a particular country. This is especially so in some African countries that use tribal customary law to varying degrees. Drawing a "family tree," as a consequence, can become very complicated and the map in Exhibit 1-9 should be considered as only a generalization.

It is important to understand that the legal system in one country can vary greatly from that in another country, even if both belong to one of the major legal families. This is because the values underlying a legal system can vary greatly among countries, depending on a country's history, language, religion, ethics, and other cultural factors. The importance of cultural differences, the way those differences affect the community of nations, and the affect they can have on international law, is discussed in Reading 1–1.

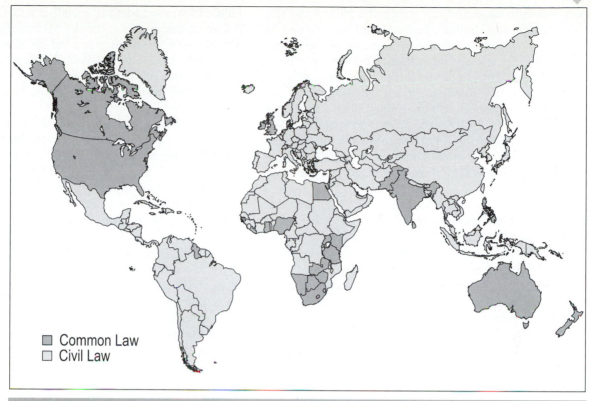

EXHIBIT 1-9   The World's Legal Systems

Common Law
Civil Law

Reading 1–1   The Clash of Civilizations?

Samuel P. Huntington, "The Clash of Civilizations?" *Foreign Affairs* (Summer 1993).

THE NEXT PATTERN OF CONFLICT

World politics is entering a new phase, and intellectuals have not hesitated to proliferate visions of what it will be—the end of history, the return of traditional rivalries between nation states, and the decline of the nation state from the conflicting pulls of tribalism and globalism, among others. Each of these visions catches aspects of the emerging reality. Yet they all miss a crucial, indeed a central, aspect of what global politics is likely to be in the coming years.

It is my hypothesis that the fundamental source of conflict in this new world will not be primarily ideological or primarily economic. The great divisions among humankind and the dominating source of conflict will be cultural. Nation states will remain the most powerful actors in world affairs, but the principal conflicts of global politics will occur between nations and groups of different civilizations. The clash of civilizations will domi-

nate global politics. The fault lines between civilizations will be the battle lines of the future.

* * *

WHY CIVILIZATIONS WILL CLASH

Civilization identity will be increasingly important in the future, and the world will be shaped in large measure by the interactions among seven or eight major civilizations. These include Western, Confucian, Japanese, Islamic, Hindu, Slavic-Orthodox, Latin American and possibly African civilization. The most important conflicts of the future will occur along the cultural fault lines separating these civilizations from one another.

Why Will This Be the Case?

First, differences among civilizations are not only real; they are basic. Civilizations are differentiated from each other by history, language, culture, tradition and, most important, religion. The people of different civilizations have different views on the relations between God and man, the individual and the group, the citizen and the state, parents and children, husband and wife, as well as differing views of the relative importance of rights and responsibilities, liberty and authority, equality and hierarchy. These differences are the product of centuries. They will not soon disappear. They are far more fundamental than differences among political ideologies and political regimes. Differences do not necessarily mean conflict, and conflict does not necessarily mean violence. Over the centuries, however, differences among civilizations have generated the most prolonged and the most violent conflicts.

Second, the world is becoming a smaller place. The interactions between peoples of different civilizations are increasing; these increasing interactions intensify civilization consciousness and awareness of differences between civilizations and commonalities within civilizations. North African immigration to France generates hostility among Frenchmen and at the same time increased receptivity to immigration by "good" European Catholic Poles. Americans react far more negatively to Japanese investment than to larger investments from Canada and European countries. Similarly, as Donald Horowitz has pointed out, "An Ibo may be . . . an Owerri Ibo or an Onitsha Ibo in what was the Eastern region of Nigeria. In Lagos, he is simply an Ibo. In London, he is a Nigerian. In New York, he is an African." The interactions among peoples of different civilizations enhance the civilization-consciousness of people that, in turn, invigorates differences and animosities stretching or thought to stretch back deep into history.

Third, the processes of economic modernization and social change throughout the world are separating people from long-standing local identities. They also weaken the nation state as a source of identity. In much of the world, religion has moved in to fill this gap, often in the form of movements that are labeled "fundamentalist." Such movements are found in Western Christianity, Judaism, Buddhism and Hinduism, as well as in Islam. In most countries and most religions the people active in fundamentalist movements are young, college-educated, middle-class technicians, professionals and business persons. The "unsecularization of the world," George Weigel has remarked, "is one of the dominant social facts of life in the late twentieth century." The revival of religion, "*la revanche de Dieu*," as Gilles Kepel labeled it, provides a basis for identity and commitment that transcends national boundaries and unites civilizations.

Fourth, the growth of civilization-consciousness is enhanced by the dual role of the West. On the one hand, the West is at a peak of power. At the same time, however, and perhaps as a result, a return to the roots phenomenon is occurring among non-Western civilizations. Increasingly one hears references to trends toward a turning inward and "Asianization" in Japan, the end of the Nehru legacy and the "Hinduization" of India, the

failure of Western ideas of socialism and nationalism and hence "re-Islamization" of the Middle East, and now a debate over Westernization versus Russianization in Boris Yeltsin's country. A West at the peak of its power confronts non-Wests that increasingly have the desire, the will and the resources to shape the world in non-Western ways.

In the past, the elites of non-Western societies were usually the people who were most involved with the West, had been educated at Oxford, the Sorbonne or Sandhurst, and had absorbed Western attitudes and values. At the same time, the populace in non-Western countries often remained deeply imbued with the indigenous culture. Now, however, these relationships are being reversed. A de-Westernization and indigenization of elites is occurring in many non-Western countries at the same time that Western, usually American, cultures, styles and habits become more popular among the mass of the people.

Fifth, cultural characteristics and differences are less mutable, and hence less easily compromised and resolved, than political and economic ones. In the former Soviet Union, communists can become democrats, the rich can become poor and the poor rich, but Russians cannot become Estonians and Azeris cannot become Armenians. In class and ideological conflicts, the key question was "Which side are you on?" and people could and did choose sides and change sides. In conflicts between civilizations, the question is "What are you?" That is a given that cannot be changed. And as we know, from Bosnia to the Caucasus to the Sudan, the wrong answer to that question can mean a bullet in the head. Even more than ethnicity, religion discriminates sharply and exclusively among people. A person can be half-French and half-Arab and simultaneously even a citizen of two countries. It is more difficult to be half-Catholic and half-Muslim.

Finally, economic regionalism is increasing. The proportions of total trade that were intraregional rose between 1980 and 1989 from 51 percent to 59 percent in Europe, 33 percent to 37 percent in East Asia, and 32 percent to 36 percent in North America. The importance of regional economic blocs is likely to continue to increase in the future. On the one hand, successful economic regionalism will reinforce civilization-consciousness. On the other hand, economic regionalism may succeed only when it is rooted in a common civilization. The European Community rests on the shared foundation of European culture and Western Christianity. The success of the North American Free Trade Area depends on the convergence now underway of Mexican, Canadian and American cultures. Japan, in contrast, faces difficulties in creating a comparable economic entity in East Asia because Japan is a society and civilization unique to itself. However strong the trade and investment links Japan may develop with other East

Asian countries, its cultural differences with those countries inhibit and perhaps preclude its promoting regional economic integration like that in Europe and North America.

Common culture, in contrast, is clearly facilitating the rapid expansion of the economic relations between the People's Republic of China and Hong Kong, Taiwan, Singapore and the overseas Chinese communities in other Asian countries. With the Cold War over, cultural commonalities increasingly overcome ideological differences, and mainland China and Taiwan move closer together. If cultural commonality is a prerequisite for economic integration, the principal East Asian economic bloc of the future is likely to be centered on China. This bloc is, in fact, already coming into existence. As Murray Weidenbaum has observed,

Despite the current Japanese dominance of the region, the Chinese-based economy of Asia is rapidly emerging as a new epicenter for industry, commerce and finance. This strategic area contains substantial amounts of technology and manufacturing capability (Taiwan), outstanding entrepreneurial, marketing and services acumen (Hong Kong), a fine communications network (Singapore), a tremendous pool of financial capital (all three), and very large endowments of land, resources and labor (mainland China).... From Guangzhou to Singapore, from Kuala Lumpur to Manila, this influential network — often based on extensions of the traditional clans — has been described as the backbone of the East Asian economy.[195]

Culture and religion also form the basis of the Economic Cooperation Organization, which brings together ten non-Arab Muslim countries: Iran, Pakistan, Turkey, Azerbaijan, Kazakhstan, Kyrgyzstan, Turkmenistan, Tadjikistan, Uzbekistan and Afghanistan. One impetus to the revival and expansion of this organization, founded originally in the 1960s by Turkey, Pakistan and Iran, is the realization by the leaders of several of these countries that they had no chance of admission to the European Community. Similarly, CARICOM, the Central American Common Market and MERCOSUR rest on common cultural foundations. Efforts to build a broader Caribbean-Central American economic entity bridging the Anglo-Latin divide, however, have to date failed.

As people define their identity in ethnic and religious terms, they are likely to see an "us" versus "them" relation existing between themselves and people of different ethnicity or religion. The end of ideologically defined states in Eastern Europe and the former Soviet Union permits traditional ethnic identities and animosities to come to the fore. Differences in culture and religion create differences over policy issues, ranging from human rights to immigration to trade and commerce to the environment. Geographical propinquity gives rise to conflicting territorial claims from Bosnia to Mindanao. Most important, the efforts of the West to promote its values of democracy and liberalism as universal values, to maintain its military predominance, and to advance its economic interests engender countering responses from other civilizations. Decreasingly able to mobilize support and form coalitions on the basis of ideology, governments and groups will increasingly attempt to mobilize support by appealing to common religion and civilization identity.

* * *

THE WEST VERSUS THE REST

The West is now at an extraordinary peak of power in relation to other civilizations. Its superpower opponent has disappeared from the map. Military conflict among Western states is unthinkable, and Western military power is unrivaled. Apart from Japan, the West faces no economic challenge. It dominates international political and security institutions and, with Japan, international economic institutions. Global political and security issues are effectively settled by a directorate of the United States, Britain and France, world economic issues by a directorate of the United States, Germany and Japan, all of which maintain extraordinarily close relations with each other to the exclusion of lesser and largely non-Western countries. Decisions made at the UN Security Council or in the International Monetary Fund that reflect the interests of the West are presented to the word as reflecting the desires of the world community. The very phrase "the world community" has become the euphemistic collective noun (replacing "the Free World") to give global legitimacy to actions reflecting the interests of the United States and other Western powers.[196] Through the IMF and other international economic institutions, the West promotes its economic interests and imposes on other nations the economic policies it thinks appropriate. In any poll of non-Western peoples, the IMF undoubtedly would win the support of finance ministers and a few others, but get an overwhelmingly unfavorable rating from just about everyone else, who would agree with Georgy Arbatov's characterization of IMF officials as "neo-Bolsheviks who love

---

[195]Murray Weidenbaum, "Greater China: The Next Economic Superpower," *Contemporary Issues* (St. Louis: Washington University Center for the Study of American Business, February 1993), Series 57, pp. 2–3.

[196]Almost invariably Western leaders claim they are acting on behalf of "the world community." One minor lapse occurred during the run-up to the Gulf War. In an interview on "Good Morning America," December 21, 1990, British Prime Minister John Major referred to the actions "the West" was taking against Saddam Hussein. He quickly corrected himself and subsequently referred to "the world community." He was, however, right when he erred.

expropriating other people's money, imposing undemocratic and alien rules of economic and political conduct and stifling economic freedom."

Western domination of the UN Security Council and its decisions, tempered only by occasional abstention by China, produced UN legitimation of the West's use of force to drive Iraq out of Kuwait and its elimination of Iraq's sophisticated weapons and capacity to produce such weapons. It also produced the quite unprecedented action by the United States, Britain and France in getting the Security Council to demand that Libya hand over the Pan Am 103 bombing suspects and then to impose sanctions when Libya refused. After defeating the largest Arab army, the West did not hesitate to throw its weight around in the Arab world. The West in effect is using international institutions, military power and economic resources to run the world in ways that will maintain Western predominance, protect Western interests and promote Western political and economic values.

That at least is the way in which non-Westerners see the new world, and there is a significant element of truth in their view. Differences in power and struggles for military, economic and institutional power are thus one source of conflict between the West and other civilizations. Differences in culture, that is basic values and beliefs, are a second source of conflict. V. S. Naipaul has argued that Western civilization is the "universal civilization" that "fits all men." At a superficial level much of Western culture has indeed permeated the rest of the world. At a more basic level, however, Western concepts differ fundamentally from those prevalent in other civilizations. Western ideas of individualism, liberalism, constitutionalism, human rights, equality, liberty, the rule of law, democracy, free markets, the separation of church and state, often have little resonance in Islamic, Confucian, Japanese, Hindu, Buddhist or Orthodox cultures. Western efforts to propagate such ideas produce instead a reaction against "human rights imperialism" and a reaffirmation of indigenous values, as can be seen in the support for religious fundamentalism by the younger generation in non-Western cultures. The very notion that there could be a "universal civilization" is a Western idea, directly at odds with the particularism of most Asian societies and their emphasis on what distinguishes one people from another. Indeed, the author of a review of 100 comparative studies of values in different societies concluded that "the values that are most important in the West are least important worldwide."[197] In the political realm, of course, these differences are most manifest in the efforts of the United States and other Western powers to induce other peoples to adopt Western ideas concerning democracy and human rights. Modern democratic government originated in the West.

When it has developed in non-Western societies it has usually been the product of Western colonialism or imposition.

* * *

IMPLICATIONS FOR THE WEST

This article does not argue that civilization identities will replace all other identities, that nation states will disappear, that each civilization will become a single coherent political entity, that groups within a civilization will not conflict with and even fight each other. This paper does set forth the hypotheses that differences between civilizations are real and important; civilization-consciousness is increasing; conflict between civilizations will supplant ideological and other forms of conflict as the dominant global form of conflict; international relations, historically a game played out within Western civilization, will increasingly be de-Westernized and become a game in which non-Western civilizations are actors and not simply objects; successful political, security and economic international institutions are more likely to develop within civilizations than across civilizations; conflicts between groups in different civilizations will be more frequent, more sustained and more violent than conflicts between groups in the same civilization; violent conflicts between groups in different civilizations are the most likely and most dangerous source of escalation that could lead to global wars; the paramount axis of world politics will be the relations between "the West and the Rest"; the elites in some torn non-Western countries will try to make their countries part of the West, but in most cases face major obstacles to accomplishing this; a central focus of conflict for the immediate future will be between the West and several Islamic-Confucian states.

This is not to advocate the desirability of conflicts between civilizations. It is to set forth descriptive hypotheses as to what the future may be like. If these are plausible hypotheses, however, it is necessary to consider their implications for Western policy. These implications should be divided between short-term advantage and long-term accommodation. In the short term it is clearly in the interest of the West to promote greater cooperation and unity within its own civilization, particularly between its European and North American components; to incorporate into the West societies in Eastern Europe and Latin America whose cultures are close to those of the West; to promote and maintain cooperative relations with Russia and Japan; to prevent escalation of local inter-civilization conflicts into major inter-civilization wars; to limit the expansion of the military strength of Confucian and Islamic states; to moderate the reduction of Western mili-

---

[197]Harry C. Triandis, *New York Times,* December 25, 1990, p. 41, and "Cross-Cultural Studies of Individualism and Collectivism," *Nebraska Symposium on Motivation,* vol. 37, 1980, pp. 41–133.

tary capabilities and maintain military superiority in East and Southwest Asia; to exploit differences and conflicts among Confucian and Islamic states; to support in other civilizations groups sympathetic to Western values and interests; to strengthen international institutions that reflect and legitimate Western interests and values and to promote the involvement of non-Western states in those institutions.

In the longer term other measures would be called for. Western civilization is both Western and modern. Non-Western civilizations have attempted to become modern without becoming Western. To date, only Japan has fully succeeded in this quest. Non-Western civilizations will continue to attempt to acquire the wealth, technology, skills, machines and weapons that are part of being modern. They will also attempt to reconcile this modernity with their traditional culture and values. Their

economic and military strength relative to the West will increase. Hence the West will increasingly have to accommodate these non-Western modern civilizations whose power approaches that of the West but whose values and interests differ significantly from those of the West. This will require the West to maintain the economic and military power necessary to protect its interests in relation to these civilizations. It will. also, however, require the West to develop a more profound understanding of the basic religious and philosophical assumptions underlying other civilizations and the ways in which people in those civilizations see their interests. It will require an effort to identify elements of commonality between Western and other civilizations. For the relevant future, there will be no universal civilization, but instead a world of different civilizations, each of which will have to learn to coexist with the others. ■

The Romano-Germanic Civil Law System

civil law: (1) The legal system derived from Roman and Germanic practice and set out in national law codes. (2) As distinguished from public law, the body of law dealing with the rights of private citizens.

Corpus Juris Civilis: (Latin: "body of civil law.") Codification of Roman law completed about 534 A.D. at the order of Emperor Justinian, that selected, arranged, and condensed the ancient laws.

glossator: One who makes a textual gloss or glossary (i.e., a brief note or explanation in the margins or between lines of a text as to the meaning of a difficult or obscure word or expression).

commentator: One who provides a systematic series of explanations or interpretations.

jus commune: (Latin: "the common right.") Law based on Roman law, canon law, and the interpretations of glossators and commentators, and common to Europe at the beginning of the Renaissance.

The oldest and most influential of the legal families is the Romano-Germanic legal system, commonly called the **civil law**. The civil law dates to 450 B.C., the traditional date when Rome adopted its Twelve Tables (a code of laws applicable to Romans). The most significant event in the historical development of the civil law, however, was the compilation and codification (that is, the selection, arrangement, and simplification) of all Roman law done under the direction of Byzantine Emperor Justinian (483–565 A.D.). This code, known as the **Corpus Juris Civilis**, was compiled between 528 and 534 A.D. It was important because it preserved in written form the ancient legal system. The Roman law was displaced to some extent by the rules of the Germanic tribes when they overran the Western Empire. Germanic tribal law, however, recognized the principle of personal (as opposed to territorial) law, so the former Roman subjects and their descendants were allowed to follow the Roman law. The medieval Roman Catholic Church also played an important role in preserving the ancient law. Canon law, the law used in the Church's courts, was based on Roman law.

With the revival of interest in classical culture in Western Europe in the eleventh and twelfth centuries, accompanied by the discovery of a copy of the long lost *Corpus Juris Civilis*, active study of the ancient Roman law began in earnest. At universities in northern Italy— especially Bologna—the *Corpus Juris Civilis* was systematically analyzed, first by **glossators** (who added notes—annotations—explaining its meaning) and later by **commentators** (who attempted to adapt it to the needs of their time). Students from throughout Europe, who traveled to Italy to study, returned to their own countries to become the new profession of lawyers. Not only did they set up new universities—in Paris, Oxford, Prague, Heidelburg, Kraków, and Copenhagen—but they also found work both in the Church and as advisors to princes and municipalities. Their common background led to the creation of a new civil law, one based on the Roman law, canon law, and the huge body of writings created by the glossators and commentators. This was called the *jus commune*, or the common law of Europe.

At the same time, Europe was emerging from a long period of economic stagnation. The newly founded towns gave rise to markets, fairs, and banks, and the rapid development of maritime and overland trade eventually led to large commercial centers that had a need for laws to govern their business transactions. The Germanic law, which at first had been adequate for the general needs of a rural, agrarian society, did not contain legal concepts that suited the needs of the commercial community. Nor did the Roman law, which presumed the presence of an extensive imperial government that no longer existed. The guilds and merchants' associations began to follow their own practices and they set up their own courts (called *pepoudrous* courts, or literally "dusty feet" courts, but euphemistically referred to in English as "piepowder" courts).

These courts worked out rules and procedures based on the customs of the merchants that were practical and fair. Soon these same rules were being applied both in governmental and church courts, and eventually the ***lex mercatoria*** (law merchant) became an international body of generally accepted commercial rules that transcended national boundaries. It proved to be more influential than even the civil law, spreading to England where the legal community resisted the Roman law tradition. Today, many of the concepts contained in the law merchant are incorporated in modern commercial law codes, such as the United Nations Convention on Contracts for the International Sale of Goods.

In the sixteenth and seventeenth centuries, the centers of European legal scholarship moved to France and Holland. The new study of the *jus commune* was carried on by French Humanists and Dutch Naturalists. Using historical analysis and philology (i.e., the tracing out of the development of the usage of words), the Humanists came to believe that the *jus commune* was only a product of history and that the *Corpus Juris Civilis* was merely an ancient text (rather than a holy encapsulation of the "living law"). This desanctification of Roman law was continued by the Dutch Naturalists, who developed the theory that law was based on a universal law of nature, and not on the contents of an ancient sacred book.

Along with the development of a theory of law, other events would eventually lead to the disappearance of the *jus commune* as the common law of Europe. The appearance of national states, with national literatures written in national languages (rather than Latin as had been the case before), led to aspirations for systems of national law. In many of the states of continental Europe, legal nationalism found its embodiment in national codes. The first such codes appeared in Scandinavia in the seventeenth century. In the eighteenth century, the codes of France, Prussia, and Austria were the products of "enlightened" monarchs like Frederick the Great of Prussia (1712–1786) and Joseph II of Austria (1741–1790). As such, they attempted not only to bring about legal unity within a single kingdom, but also to express the political and philosophical ideals of the time.

Two national codes have had such widespread and lasting influence that they are now regarded as the very basis of the modern civil law. Both the French Civil Code of 1804 and the German Civil Code of 1896 were models for most of the other contemporary civil codes. The French Code is now followed in the Netherlands, Belgium, Poland, Spain, Portugal, Latin America, sub-Saharan Africa, Indochina, and Indonesia; the German in Austria, Czechoslovakia, Greece, Hungary, Switzerland, Yugoslavia, Turkey, Japan, and South Korea.

The **French Civil Code** is often referred to as the *Code Napoléon*, because of the extensive involvement of Napoléon Bonaparte (1769–1821) in its writing. Jean Jacques Cambacérès (1753–1824), second consul under Napoléon, and a commission of four jurists were the principal drafters. Most scholars rightfully regard it as the first modern code. Although organized structurally in much the same fashion as the *Corpus Juris Civilis*, it was not merely a restatement of prior law. It incorporated the principal ideas of the French Revolution, including the right to possess private property, the freedom to contract, and the autonomy of the patriarchal family. With regard to private property, the Code's authors consciously attempted to break up the old feudal estates of the aristocracy by prohibiting restraints on the sale of land as well as restraints on its transfer in a will.

The Code, nevertheless, preserved much of the past. Because it was written in a remarkably short period of time—at the insistence of Napoléon—its authors relied heavily on the *jus commune*, French royal ordinances, academic writings, and customary law (especially the influential Custom of Paris, which had been transcribed in the sixteenth century). Like the authors of other seventeenth- and eighteenth-century codes, the draftsmen of the *Code Napoléon* looked on their work as putting all of the prior French law through a "sieve of reasons." Unlike the German Code, however, the style and form of the French Code are straightforward, easy to read, and understandable to everyone—in many respects, it reminds one of the United States Constitution. Also, like the U.S. Constitution, the authors of the French Code realized that they could not foresee every possible legal eventuality, so they set out flexible general rules rather than detailed provisions. Jean Portalis (1746–1807), one of the authors, said:

> We have equally avoided the dangerous ambition to regulate and foresee everything.... The function of law is to fix in broad outline the general maxims of justice, to

---

lex mercatoria: (Latin: "law merchant.") Common commercial rules and procedures used throughout Europe in the Renaissance.

French Civil Code: Law code promulgated in 1804 by Napoléon that collected, arranged, and simplified French law.

establish principles rich in implications, and not to descend into the details of the questions that can arise in each subject.

German Civil Code:
Law code promulgated in 1896 that is based primarily on the *Corpus Juris Civilis* and that is characterized by its detailed structure and its technical precision.

The **German Civil Code** (*Bürgerliches Gesetzbuch*) was enacted almost a century later, partly because Germany first had to take shape as a nation and partly because of the influence of a group of German scholars known as **Pandectists**. The leader of the Pandectists, Friedrich Karl von Savigny (1779–1861), argued that a German code could not be adopted until extensive study of Germany's legal institutions had been made. Rather than studying German legal materials, however, the Pandectists concentrated on the text of the *Corpus Juris Civilis*, with the aim of discovering its "latent" or underlying principles and organization. From these studies a highly structured and technically precise system was eventually devised for use in Germany.

Pandectists: (From Latin *pandect:* "all receiving.") Scholars who attempted to prepare a pandect, or complete and comprehensive treatise or digest of the law.

The drafting project itself was enormous, taking more than 20 years to complete. Issued finally in 1896, the German Code's organization and form is incredibly precise and technical. Special terminology was devised. Legal concepts were defined and then used in the same way throughout the entire Code. Sentence structure indicates which party has the burden of proof. Elaborate cross-references keep the Code reasonably brief and make it a logical and unified system. Unlike the French Code, which was intended to be a handbook for the citizen, the German Code was meant for the use of trained experts.

Although the French and German codes are different in style and tone, they are more similar than dissimilar. Both are based on the *jus commune*, especially in their approach to the law of obligations and in their overall structure. They also rely on many of the same political and philosophical ideals, notably laissez-faire economics and the autonomous rights of individuals.

public law:
Constitutional and administrative law. It is not included in civil law codes.

Separate and apart from the movement for codification of civil or private law was the development of **public law**. Civil law (*droit civil, Zivilrecht*) is, for civilian lawyers, only the law contained in the codes and its auxiliary statutes (that is, the law of persons, family law, property law, the law of succession, the law of obligations, commercial law, and labor law). Opposed to this is public law (that is, constitutional and administrative), which has been treated in a variety of ways in the civil law countries. Germany established a branch of administrative courts to review the acts of its government agencies, and France created a Council of State to protect individual rights and supervise the administrative processes of government (technically, however, the Council is not a court). Austria has created a Constitutional Court to ensure that its legislation complies with the guidelines established in its Constitution, and similar courts have been established in many other countries. The civil law countries, however, have no consistent approach to public law, and many civilian lawyers still regard constitutional law as a form of political science.

In the twentieth century, especially in the years since World War II, changes in France and Germany—as well as the other civil law countries—have had profound effects on the civil law. For one, there has been a movement away from relying only on the civil code. Special legislation and judicial interpretations have become more influential. There has also been some revision of the codes themselves, especially in Germany. Also, with the advent of the European Union, there is now a move toward harmonizing the laws of the Union's member states.

Case 1–10 describes some of the basic characteristics of French law and points out some of the factors that distinguish it from the common law system of England.

Case 1–10   Raulin v. Fischer

England, King's Bench, 1911.
Law Reports, King's Bench Division, vol. 1911, pt. 2, p. 93 (1911).

Miss Fischer, an American, recklessly rode a horse in the Avenue du Bois de Boulogne in Paris and ran into

Monsieur Raulin, a French officer, seriously injuring him. The Procureur de la Republique prosecuted Fischer for criminal negligence in the Civil Court of First Instance of the Department of the Seine, which was then sitting as a correctional tribunal pursuant to Article 320 of the French Penal Code.

By the provisions of the French Code d'Instruction Criminelle, a person who is injured by a criminal act may intervene in the prosecution (action publique) *and make a claim for damages. In such a case, the injured individual's claim* (action civile) *is tried along with the action publique and one judgment is pronounced for both. Raulin intervened in the prosecution of Fischer and claimed damages.*

At a hearing held in 1909, Fischer, who did not appear, was convicted and sentenced to one month's imprisonment and a fine of 100 francs. Because the Court did not have sufficient evidence before it to decide how extensive the injury was that Raulin had suffered, it entered a provisional award of 5,000 francs for damages and ordered him to be examined by an expert. Following the expert's report to the Court, the award was changed to 15,000 francs for damages and 917 francs for costs.

Later, Raulin sought to recover the sum of 636 pounds, 13 shillings, and 6 pence in an English court, that being the equivalent in English money of the 15,917 francs that the French court had ordered Fischer to pay him.

JUDGE HAMILTON:

On the judgment of the French Court the plaintiff is in my opinion entitled to recover the English equivalent of 15,000 francs that have been awarded him as damages. It was not disputed by the defendant's counsel that he would be so entitled but for the rule of private international law that a penal judgment of a court in one country cannot be enforced by action in another country. The point raised for the defendant was that the judgment sued on was in truth a penal judgment within that rule, and that though part of it might be more or less civil in its character there was no power in this court to dissect the judgment and enforce here that part which was enforceable by action though the judgment as a whole was not enforceable.

Although the French courts might refuse to distinguish between the parts of a judgment which may be called principal and the parts which may be called accessory, the parts which are by way of punishment and the parts which are by way of civil remedy, it does not follow that the English courts in dealing with a French judgment should take the same course. The rule which governs such a question is that laid down by the Privy Council in *Huntington v. Attrill.*[198] It was there held that, a judgment having been given by a New York court against the respondent under a New York statute which imposed a liability for false representation, and an action having been brought in an Ontario court upon that judgment, it was the duty of the Ontario court to determine for itself whether the judgment sued on was a penal one

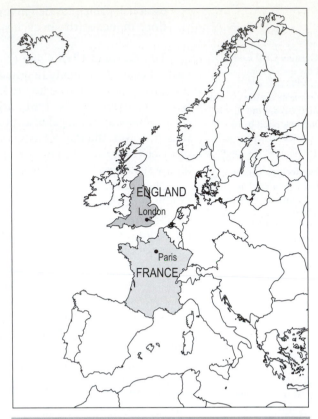

MAP 1-11 France and England (1911)

or not, and that it was not bound by the interpretation put upon the statute by the New York courts. . . . I have therefore to inquire first of all whether this judgment insofar as it concerns the present plaintiff is one for the satisfaction of a private wrong or for the punishment of an infraction of public law; and secondly whether, if it be as regards him only for the satisfaction of a private wrong, it is one which can be separated from the rest of the judgment, so that he may sue upon the judgment in spite of the fact that a considerable part of its relates to purely criminal proceedings.

Certain French expert witnesses were called before me, and the effect of their evidence was this. In various respects that remedy in the form in which it was pursued differs from the form in which it might have been pursued. The result of Monsieur Raulin having pursued his remedy for compensation by intervention in the prosecution instead of bringing a separate civil action was that he came before a court especially assigned to criminal business. That court decided both in the prosecution and in the civil intervention, and to that extent the plaintiff obtained his judgment from a correctional tribunal. But in other respects it does not appear to me that his remedy differed in its character from the remedy which he might have pursued by a separate civil action. The prosecution

---

[198]*Law Reports, Appeal Cases*, vol. 1893, p. 150 (1893).

abates with the death of the accused. The civil remedy does not. The liability to imprisonment in order to enforce payment of the damages is in law an incident both of the intervention in the *action publique* and of the separate civil action. The course of procedure differs because, instead of the whole conduct of the action on the intervener's side resting with the plaintiff as it would have done in civil proceedings, he has to adapt himself to the control of the proceedings by the Procurator of the Republic. But the issues remain unchanged. The issue between the Procurator and the accused was whether she had broken the law against driving negligently contained in Art. 320 of the Penal Code. On that issue the contributory negligence of the plaintiff would have afforded no defense, but the contributory negligence of the plaintiff would have been material to the question of damages claimed by him as an intervening party, and that issue, if the facts justified it, would be raised just as much in the civil intervention in the action publique as it could in a separate action civile. It seems to me that there is no doubt that the public prosecution and private suit are two quite separate and distinct proceedings although they are for the purposes of procedure combined in one. The judgment for the 15,000 francs is not in any respect a judgment in a proceeding "in favor of the state whose law has been infringed." It is a judgment in what is substantially a civil suit for the compensation of a person who has sustained a private wrong.

The other question is whether it is practicable to distinguish the portion of the adjudication which was not part of the criminal suit from that portion of it which

was. In this connection certain decisions of French courts were cited to me, but not much assistance is to be gained from them, especially in view of the evidence that according to the jurisprudence of France the decisions of the courts are not binding even upon the courts of inferior jurisdiction unless they are pronounced in the same cause or matter, and, consequently, though the decisions of the courts are constantly cited, they are cited by way of edification only and not as authority.

In any case, according to the judgment of the Privy Council, this is not a matter in which I am bound by the view of the French Courts. It is one in which I must determine for myself whether the enforcement of the plaintiff's rights would either directly or indirectly involve the execution of the penal law of another state. In my opinion it would not. Moreover here the decision awarding the final damages was not even pronounced at the same time as the decision inflicting the fine. It was given at a time when the only issue being contested was of a private and civil character, and one with which the state had nothing whatever to do. I think the decision must be for the plaintiff. I am fortified in this view by . . . Sir Francis Piggott's work on Foreign Judgments[199] in which he deals with this very provision of the French law, that civil proceedings for a tort are allowed to be tacked on to criminal proceedings for the offense and damages may be awarded to the person injured, and suggests that the award of damages in such case is a civil judgment recognizable in England in the usual way.

Judgment for plaintiff. ■

---

[199] *Piggott on Foreign Judgments,* part I, p. 90 (3rd ed.).

The Anglo-American Common Law System

common law: The legal system of England and countries that were once English colonies. It is based primarily on court-made rules or precedent.

The origins of the Anglo-American **common law** system can be traced back to the year 1066, when the Normans conquered England and William the Conqueror began to centralize the governmental administration of his new kingdom. The name "common law" is derived from the theory that the King's courts represented the common custom of the realm, as opposed to the local customary law practiced in the county and manorial courts.

Development of the enduring principles of the common law was largely the product of three courts created by Henry II (1133–1189). The Court of Exchequer settled tax disputes; the Court of Common Pleas dealt with matters that did not involve a direct interest of the King, such as title to land, enforcement of promises, and payment of debts; and the Court of King's Bench handled cases of a direct royal interest, such as the issuance of "writs" (written decrees) to control unruly public officials. Eventually, the jurisdiction of the King's Bench was used to control abuses of power by the King himself, establishing a fundamental doctrine of the common law: the **supremacy of the law**. (Today, the doctrine of supremacy means not only that the King is subject to the law but that the acts of ordinary government agencies can be reviewed in the courts.) Also, when the Court of Common Pleas began to charge large fees to hear cases, much of its jurisdiction was taken over by the King's Bench. The judges of the King's Bench did this by broadly interpreting the writ of trespass so that it took in virtually every kind

supremacy of the law: Doctrine that all persons, including the sovereign, are subordinate to the rule of law.

of tort, and by expanding the meaning of the writ of assumpsit so that it applied to most forms of contracts.

An important aspect of the common law is the idea that it is based on the customary practice of the courts, and the term itself is often used to describe that part of English law that is not based on statutory law or legislation. In its narrow sense, the "common law" must also be distinguished from the law that evolved out of **equity** (principles of justice developed by the King's Chaplain, or Chancellor, to provide parties with a remedy when none was available in the King's courts) and out of **admiralty** (the law and court with jurisdiction over marine affairs in general), and from other specialized jurisdictions. The common law's basis in court decisions, or **precedent**, is also the principal factor distinguishing it from the Romano-Germanic civil law, where the grounds for deciding cases are found in codes, statutes, and prescribed texts.

One limitation of early common law practice was its inflexibility. In 1285, the Statute of Westminster curtailed the creation of new writs that, until that time, the courts had been devising in an attempt to expand their jurisdiction. As a consequence, the courts soon could hear only cases that fit precisely within the parameters of the traditional writs. Also, as the scope of the courts' jurisdiction narrowed, the procedural rules they followed became more complex. Finally, with the exception of a few kinds of suits that involved the recovery of real or personal property, the only remedy the courts could give was money for damages actually done. In part, the courts of equity—which had the power to order an injunction, restitution, or specific performance—were created to overcome these limitations.

Until the nineteenth century there continued to be a sharp division between the common law and equity. Then New York enacted a code of civil procedure in 1848, drafted by David Dudley Field (1805–1894), that merged law and equity into one jurisdiction. This "Field Code" required law suits to be tried in a single class of courts, using a single procedure. It was soon adopted by most of the American states, by the American federal government, and eventually by England in the Judicature Acts of 1873 and 1875, and in many British colonies.

The way in which the common law spread around the world is different from the way in which the civil law was distributed. In each of the principal nations in which the common law developed—Australia, Canada, India, Ireland, New Zealand, and the United States—there was a direct political linkage to England. Although there was a linkage of sorts with Rome for the European and Latin American civil law countries, the connection with other civil law countries is more tenuous. Also, the civil law is the easier of the two legal traditions to be received. The civil law is encapsulated in convenient codes and it deals primarily with private law that is of little threat to the local political system. Common law, on the other hand, is a matrix of case law and statutes; it uses the jury system and the doctrine of supremacy to limit the actions of the government; and it encompasses a complex terminology. See Exhibit 1-10.

The Islamic Law System

Today, one person in four is a Muslim. Most live in states in the Middle East, North Africa, and Southern Asia. Islam is the principal religion of Saudi Arabia, Qatar, the United Arab Emirates, Oman, Yemen, Syria, Jordan, Kuwait, Kazakhstan, Uzbekistan, Kyrgyzstan, Tajikistan, Turkmenistan, Azerbaijan, Iran, Iraq, Afghanistan, Pakistan, Armenia, Turkey, Egypt, Sudan, Somalia, Libya, Algeria, Tunisia, Niger, Mali, Morocco, Mauritania, Bangladesh, Malaysia, and Indonesia. Islamic law is the principal source of law in Saudi Arabia, and it is followed, at least to some extent, in all of the others.

The Islamic legal system is known as **_Shari'a_**. It is derived from the following sources, in the order of their importance: (1) the _Koran_, (2) the _Sunna_ or traditional teachings and practices of the Prophet Muhammad (570–632 A.D.), (3) the writings of Islamic scholars who derived rules by analogy from the principles established in the _Koran_ and the _Sunna_, and (4) the consensus of the legal community.

In the tenth century A.D., three centuries after the founding of Islam, the legal community decided that further improvement of the scholars' analysis of divine law was impossible. They decided at that time to "close the door of _ijtihad_ (independent reasoning)," freezing the evolution of Islamic law. As a consequence, _Shari'a_ judges and scholars may only apply the law as it was set down by the early writers. They may not change, modify, or extend that law.

---

equity: (From Latin _æquitas:_ "even" or "fair.") Being just, impartial, and fair. Justice applied in circumstances not covered by rules of law.

admiralty: The law and court with jurisdiction over maritime affairs in general.

precedent: (From Latin _præcedens:_ "going before in time.") An act or instance that may be used as a model for later similar cases.

Shari'a: (Arabic: "jurisprudence.") The Islamic legal system. It is based upon principles found in the _Koran_ and related writings.

	Civil Law	**Common Law**
Ideological basis	Positive law; laissez-faire economics	Natural law
Status of law	Independent of government	Superior to government
Legal rules	Based on general principles	Based on specific circumstances
Content	Private law	Private law; public law
Basic source	Codes	Case law
Most influenced by	Law writers	Judges
Reasoning	Deductive	Inductive
Procedure	Inquisitorial	Adversarial
Fact finder	Judge	Jury
Use of case law as precedent	Respected	Required
Constitutional review by	Special agency or category of courts	Regular courts (no written constitution in England)
Review of government agencies	Special agency or category of courts	Regular courts

EXHIBIT 1-10　General Characteristics of the World's Two Major Legal Systems

The closing of the door of *ijtihad* has produced a legal system that is often at odds with the modern world. Many important figures in the Islamic world (including Saudi Arabia's King Fahd [1922–]) have recently advocated reopening the door of *ijtihad*, but this step has been vehemently opposed by traditionalists (including Iran's late Ayatollah Khomeini [1900–1989]). It is important to note that the *Shari'a* is primarily a moral code, more concerned with ethics than with the promotion of commerce or of international relations. Nonetheless, many principles of the *Shari'a* are not unlike the principles found in the civil law and the common law. Case 1–11 points out the many similarities between the *Shari'a* and the secular legal systems.

Case 1–11　Libyan American Oil Company (LIAMCO) v. Government of the Libyan Arab Republic

Dr. Sobhi Mahmassani, Sole Arbitrator, 1977.
International Legal Materials, vol. 20, p. 1 (1981);
International Law Reports, vol. 62, p. 140 (1982).

In 1955, the Libyan American Oil Company (LIAMCO), a Delaware corporation, acquired three concessions (Nos. 16, 17, and 20) from the Libyan Ministry of Petroleum. The concessions, which followed a model set out in the Libyan Petroleum Law of 1955, gave LIAMCO the exclusive right for 50 years to search for, extract, and sell petroleum from designated areas of Libya. On several occasions between 1955 and 1968, the concessions were amended with LIAMCO's consent. In their final form, each concession provides that

the contractual rights expressly created by this concession shall not be altered, except by mutual consent of the parties (Clause 16).

Clause 28 of each of the concessions also provided for the settlement of disputes by arbitration and stated that the concession

shall be governed by and interpreted in accordance with the principles of the law of Libya common to the principles of international law and, in the absence of such common principles, then by and in accordance with the general principles of law, including such of those principles as may have been applied by international tribunals.

In 1969, a military coup led by Colonel Muammar Gadhafi deposed the Libyan monarchy and established the Libyan Arab Republic. Between 1970 and 1973, the new government negotiated changes in the economic provisions of the LIAMCO concessions. Then, in September 1973, the Libyan Revolutionary Command Council promulgated Law No. 66, nationalizing 51 percent of LIAMCO's concession rights. In February 1974, LIAMCO's remaining rights were also nationalized. Both laws included provision for compensation. A press statement issued by the Libyan government promised that LIAMCO would receive the net book value of each concession as compensation. No compensation was actually offered to LIAMCO.

LIAMCO asked for the matter to be referred to arbitration in accordance with Article 28 of the concessions. Libya rejected the request and refused to nominate an arbitrator. LIAMCO then asked the President of the International Court of Justice to appoint a Sole Arbitrator in accordance with the arbitration clause. The ICJ President nominated Dr. Sobhi Mahmassani, a well-known authority on Islamic law. Libya did not take part in the arbitration proceedings. LIAMCO asked the Sole Arbitrator to declare that:

(1) *the nationalization laws constituted a fundamental breach of the concessions;*
(2) *the nationalization laws were ineffective to transfer rights under the concession and neither the purported transfer of these rights nor the title of Libya to oil extracted from the concession areas was entitled to international recognition;*
(3) *in the event of LIAMCO not being restored to its concession rights, it should be entitled to damages.*

DR. SOBHI MAHMASSANI: . . .

Analysis of the Choice of Law Clause

The proper law governing LIAMCO's Concession Agreements, as set forth in the amended version and said Clause 28, para. 7, is in the first place the law of Libya when consistent with international law, and subsidiarily the general principles of law.

Hence, the principal proper law of the contract in said Concessions is Libyan domestic law. But it is specified in the Agreements that this covers only "the principles of law of Libya common to the principles of international law." Thus, it excludes any part of Libyan law which is in conflict with the principles of international law.

To decide the meaning of "the principles of international law," it is useful to refer to those of its sources that are accepted by the International Court of Justice. Article 38 of its Statute provides as follows:

1. The Court, whose function is to decide in accordance with international law such disputes as are submitted to it, shall apply:
  (a) international conventions, whether general or particular, establishing rules expressly recognized by the contesting states;

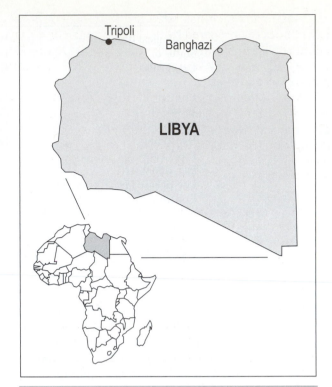

MAP 1-12 Libya (1979)

  (b) international custom, as evidence of a general practice accepted as law;
  (c) the general principles of law recognized by civilized nations;
  (d) subject to the provisions of Article 59 (concerning the relative effects of judgments), judicial decisions and the teachings of the most highly qualified publicists of the various nations, as subsidiary means for the determination of rules of law.

2. This provision shall not prejudice the power of the Court to decide a case *ex aequo it bono*,[200] if the parties agree thereto.

As to the meaning of "the principles of the law of Libya" in this connection, it is relevant to point out that this comprises any legislative enactment consistent with international legal principles. It includes, *inter alia*,[201] all Petroleum concessions laws, all consistent relevant sections of any private or public Libyan legislation, including the Civil Code.

In particular, Article 1, para. 2, of the Libyan Civil Code, promulgated on 28 November 1953, provides that:

(2) If there is no legal text to be applied the judge will adjudicate in accordance with the principles of Islamic law, failing which in accordance with custom, and failing that in accordance with natural law and the rules of equity.

---

[200]Latin: "according to what is just and good."]
[201]Latin: "among other things."]

This text, which has been inserted in other Arab Civil Codes (all prepared by the late Egyptian jurist, Dr. Abdulrazzak Sanhoury), adds to Libyan statutory law two complementary sources, namely Islamic law and natural law and equity.

Apart from that specific reference to Islamic law, this law deserves special mention in connection with Libya. It has always been the common law governing family matters in Libya as well as in all Arab and most Islamic countries. Libya adopts in this field the teachings of the Maliki School of Jurisprudence, which is one of the four Sunni Schools.

Moreover, the Revolutionary government underscores the importance of this source of law in its new legislation. Pursuant to this policy, the Revolutionary Command Council, by Decree dated 28 October 1971 (9 Ramadan 1391 H.), provided that Islamic law shall be the principal source of Libyan legislation, and appointed special commissions to review existing laws and to amend them according to dictates of Islamic *Shari'a.* Typical examples of such amended laws are the Statute on *Wakfs* No. 124 of 1972, the Larceny Statute No. 148 of 1972, and the Adultery Statute No. 70 of 1973.

It is relevant to note that the other subsidiary legal sources mentioned in said Article 1 of the Libyan Civil Code, namely custom and natural law and equity, are also in harmony with the Islamic legal system itself. As a matter of fact, in the absence of a contrary legal text based on the Holy Koran or the Traditions of the Prophet [i.e., the Sunna], Islamic law considers custom as a source of law and as complementary to and explanatory of the contents of contracts, especially in commercial transactions. This is illustrated by many Islamic legal maxims, of which the following may be quoted:[202]

- Custom is authoritative.

"العادة المحكمة"

- Public usage is conclusive and action may be taken in accordance therewith.

"استعمال الناس حجه يجب العمل بها"

- What is customary is deemed as if stipulated by agreement.

"المعروف عرفا كالمشروط شرطا"

- What is customary amongst merchants is deemed as if agreed upon between them.

"المعروف بين التجار كالمشروط بينهم"

- A matter established by custom is like a matter established by law.

"التعيين بالعرف كالتعيين بالنص"

Similarly, equity (*Istihsan*) is considered as an auxiliary source of law, especially by the Maliki and Hanafi Schools. Further, all Islamic rules of law are based on and influenced by religious and moral precepts of Islam.[203]

It is very relevant in this connection to point out that Islamic law treats international law (the Law of *Siyar*) as an imperative compendium forming part of the general positive law, and that the principles of that part are very similar to those adopted by modern international legal theory.[204]

Thus, it has been pointed out that Libyan law in general and Islamic law in particular have common rules and principles with international law, and provide for the application of custom and equity as subsidiary sources. Consequently, these provisions are, in general consistent and in harmony with the contents of the proper law of the contract chosen and agreed upon in Clause 28, para. 7, of LIAMCO's Concession Agreements, in which it is provided, as already explained, that said Agreements are governed primarily by those principles of the law of Libya as are common to the principles of international law.

Moreover, in the absence of that primary law of the contract, the same Paragraph provides as a secondary choice to apply subsidiarily "the general principles of law as may have been applied by international tribunals." These general principles are usually embodied in most recognized legal systems, and particularly in Libyan legislation, including its modern codes and Islamic law. They are applied by municipal courts and are mainly referred to in international and arbitral case law. They, thus, form a compendium of legal precepts and maxims, universally accepted in theory and practice. Instances of such precepts are, *inter alia,* the principle of the sanctity of property and contracts, the respect of acquired vested rights, the prohibition of unjust enrichment, the obligation of compensation in cases of expropriation and wrongful damage, etc.

The Arbitration Clause and Its Validity

* * *

It has been contended by the Libyan government, in its Circular letter of 8 December 1973, addressed to all oil companies . . . that it rejects arbitration as contrary to the heart of its sovereignty. Such argument cannot be retained against said international practice, which was also

---

[202]Articles 36, 37, 43–45 of the Ottoman *Hajallah Code. Vis* our book *The Philosophy of Jurisprudence in Islam,* pp. 266-7 (4th Arabic edition, Beirut, 1975), and its English translation, pp. 132–133, (Leyden, 1961).

[203]*Id.,* Arabic text p. 190 et seq., English translation p. 85 et seq.; and our book *The Moral Bases of Islamic Jurisprudence,* pp. 367–75, (Arabic, Beirut, 1973).

[204]*Vis* our lectures in the Academy of International Law entitled "General Principles of International Law in the Light of Islamic Doctrine," *Recueil des cours de l'Académie de droit international* (1966), and our book on *International Law and Relations in Islam* (Arabic, Beirut, 1972).

confirmed in many international conventions and resolutions. For instance, the Convention of 1966 on the Settlement of Investment Disputes between States and Nationals of other States provides, in its Article 25, that whenever the parties have agreed to arbitrate no party may withdraw its consent unilaterally. More generally, Resolution No. 1803 (XVII) of the United Nations General Assembly, dated 21 December 1962, while proclaiming the permanent sovereignty of peoples and nations over their natural resources, confirms the obligation of the state to respect arbitration agreements (Section 1, paras. 1 and 4).

Therefore, a state may always validly waive its so-called sovereign rights by signing an arbitration agreement and then by staying bound to it.

Moreover, that ruling is in harmony with Islamic law and practice, which is officially adopted by Libya. This is evidenced by many historical precedents. For in-stance, Prophet Muhammad was appointed as an arbitrator before Islam by the Meccans, and after Islam by the Treaty of Medina. He was confirmed by the Holy Koran[205] as the natural arbitrator in all disputes relating to Muslims. He himself resorted to arbitration in his conflict with the Tribe of Banu Qurayza. Muslim rulers followed this practice in many instances, the most famous of which was the arbitration agreement concluded in the year 659 A.D. (37 H.) between Caliph 'Ali Mu'awiya after the battle of Siffin.[206] . . .

Sanctity of Contracts

The right to conclude contracts is one of the primordial civil rights acknowledged since olden times. It was the essence of *commercium*[207] or *jus commercii*[208] of the Roman *jus civile*[209] whose scope was enlarged and extended by *jus gentium*.[210] Then it was always and constantly considered as security for economic transactions, and was even extended to the field of international relations.

This fundamental right is protected and characterized by two important propositions couched respectively in the expression that "the contract is the law of the parties," and in the Latin maxim that *pacta sunt servanda* (pacts are to be observed).

The first proposition means that the contracting parties are free to arrange their contractual relationship as they mutually intend. The second means that a freely and validly concluded contract is binding upon the parties in their mutual relationship.

In fact, the principle of the sanctity of contracts, in its two characteristic propositions, has always constituted an integral part of most legal systems. These include those systems that are based on Roman law, the Napoleonic Code (e.g. Article 1134) and other European civil codes, as well as Anglo-Saxon Common Law and Islamic Jurisprudence (*Shari'a*).

Libya adopted and incorporated this legal principle in its Article 147 of the Civil Code (same in Article 147 of the Egyptian code, Article 146 of the Iraqi and Kuwaiti codes, Article 148 of the Syrian code, and Article 221 of the Lebanese Code of Obligations and Contracts), whose paragraph 1 reads as follows:

> The contract is the law of the parties. It cannot be cancelled or amended except by their mutual consent or for reasons admitted by the Law.

The binding force of the contract is expressed in Article 148, para. 1, of the same Code:

> A contract shall be performed according to its contents and in the manner which accords with good faith.

Moreover, Islamic law, which as we have seen forms a complementary part of the law of Libya (Article 1 of its Civil Code) underscores the binding nature of contractual relations and of all terms and conditions of a contract that are not contrary to a text of law. This is expressed in the legal maxim:

> A stipulation is to be complied with as far as possible.[211]

"يلزم مراعاة الشرط بقدر الامكان" (المادة ٨٣ مجلة)

This maxim is corroborated by the various sources of Islamic law. For instance, a Koranic Verse ordains:

> Oh, you who believe, perform the contracts.[212]

"ياايهاالذين آمنوا بالعقود" (المائدة، ١)

In the same sense, a Tradition of the Prophet reads:

> Muslims are bound by their stipulations.[213]

"المسلمون على شروطهم"

(الجامع الصغير للسيوطي ج ٢ رقم ٩٢١٣)

Muslim commentators and jurists expounded this binding force of contracts in detail. In particular, the Learned Ibn Al-Kayyem elaborated this principle in his great treatise *I'lâm Al-Muwaq'een*.[214]

---

[205]*Sura* (Chapter) IV, Verse 65.

[206]*Vis* our lectures on international law, "General Principles of International Law in the Light of Islamic Doctrine," *Recueil des cours de l'Acadèmie de droit international*, pp. 272–273 (1966), and in *International Law and Relations in Islam*, pp. 160–163 (Arabic, Beirut, 1972).

[207]Latin: "commerce."]

[208]Latin: "commercial law."]

[209]Latin: "civil law."]

[210]Latin: "the law of nations."]

[211]The Ottoman *Majallah* Code, Article 83. *Vis* our book *The General Theory [of Obligations and Contracts under Islamic Law]*, vol. II, pp. 335 and 462 [(in Arabic)].

[212]*Koran, sura* (chapter) V, verse 1.

[213]*Al-Jami' As-Sagheer*, vol. II, No. 9213.

[214]Cairo, vol. I, p. 299, and vol. III, pp. 337–340.

Further, and as a corollary to the binding force of the contract, its repeal or alteration requires a contrary mutual consent (*contrarius consensus*) of the contracting parties. This is well underscored in said paragraph 1 of Article 147 of the Libyan Civil Code, as well as in most legal systems mentioned above.

Consequently, one of the parties cannot unilaterally cancel or modify the contents of the agreement, unless it is so authorized by the law, by a special provision of the agreement, or by its nature which implies such presumed intention of the parties.

Likewise, the same rule is recognized in Islamic law, in which cancellation of a contract is not valid except by mutual consent (*alikâlah*).[215]

Furthermore, some contracts explicitly emphasize the already mentioned principles and corollaries in a special provision, as in Clause 16 of LIAMCO's Concession Agreements, wherein it is provided that the:

contractual rights expressly created by this Concession shall not be altered except by mutual consent of the parties.

The said Libyan law, whether in the text of the civil code or in the complementary Islamic Jurisprudence appears clearly consistent with international law in this connection, as exemplified by international statutes and custom.

In the first place, it is relevant to recall here what has been provided in the above mentioned United Nations Resolutions in relation to the subject matter.

Resolution No. 626 of 21 December 1952, while asserting the right of states to exploit freely their natural wealth and resources stresses "the need for maintaining the flow of capital in conditions of security, mutual confidence and economic cooperation among nations."

Resolution No. 1803 of 14 December 1962 declares in Paragraph I, 8, that:

Agreements relative to foreign investments freely concluded by sovereign states or between such states shall be respected in good faith.

Resolution No. 3281 of 12 December 1974, called the Charter of Economic Rights and Duties of States, recites among the fundamentals of international relations: the fulfillment in good faith of international obligations and the respect for human rights and fundamental freedoms (Chap. i, j, and k).

International custom and case law had always sustained the proposition of *pacta sunt servanda*. It has been upheld in many arbitration awards, such as *Aramco–Saudi Arabia Arbitration of 1958*,[216] and *Sapphire International Petroleum, Ltd. v. National Iranian Oil of 1963*.[217]

This principle is also upheld by most international publicists, who maintain that the sovereign right of nationalization is limited by the respect due for contractual rights.[218] Professor Lapradelle, as rapporteur of the 1950 meeting of the *Institut de droit international*, recorded that:

Nationalization, as a unilateral act of sovereignty, shall respect validly concluded agreements, whether by treaty or contract.[219]

The principle of the respect for agreements is thus applicable to ordinary contracts and concession agreements. It is binding on individuals as well as governments. The same is admitted in Islamic law, as is evidenced by many historical precedents. For instance, no less than the Great Caliphs Omar Ibn Al-Khattab and Imam 'Ali accepted to abide by their agreements and to appear before the *Cadis* (Judges) as ordinary litigants without feeling that this conduct was against their sovereign dignity.[220]

Libya was held to be bound by its arbitration agreement and to have breached its concession contracts with LIAMCO. LIAMCO was awarded U.S. $80,085,677 in damages. ∎

---

[215]*Vis* Articles 163 and 190 of the Ottoman Majallah Code. *Vis* our book *The General Theory [of Obligations and Contracts under Islamic Law]*, vol. II, p. 486 [(In Arabic)].
[216]*International Law Reports*, vol. 27, p. 117.]
[217][*Id.*, vol. 35, p. 136.]
[218]*Vis* Wehberg, "*Pacta sunt servanda*," in *American Journal of International Law*, vol. 1959, p. 786 (1959); and [S.] Friedman, *Expropriation in International Law*, pp. 220–221 [(London, 1953)].
[219]*Annuaire de l'Institut*, vol. 1, p. 67 (1950).
[220]*Vis* our article on "The Judiciary and Al-Mawerdi," *Al-Mawerdi Millenium* (Arabic, Cairo, November 1975).

Chapter Questions

1. Define law.
2. The Harvester Company entered into a contract with Country R to harvest lumber on government land in Country R for a period of 20 years. The contract provided that if there were any disputes, the matter was to be resolved by arbitration with the International Chamber of Commerce appointing the arbitrator, and the arbitrator applying the rules of

international law, the general principles of law, and equity. Two years later, Country R told Harvester to cease operations and leave the country. Country R made no effort to recompense Harvester for the country's breach of the contract. Harvester has now initiated an arbitration proceeding. Country R claims that contracts between a state and a private person can be broken at any time by the state because to do otherwise would be to deny the state its sovereignty. Discuss.

3. What is the difference between public and private international law? Is this a legitimate way to classify international law?

4. Several years ago, a multilateral treaty came into effect among some 45 countries, including most of the major developed countries of the world. The treaty, known as the "Outer Space Treaty," forbids any member state from claiming "any planet, satellite, asteroid, or other celestial body" as part of the territory of the member state. State X, which is not a party to the treaty, recently sent a spacecraft to the earth's moon. The crew members of the craft unfurled the flag of State X and claimed a 1,000 square kilometer surface area of the moon to be part of the territory of State X. Several small buildings were constructed, including a radio transponder and a landing guidance system.

   State Y, joined by the other member states of the Outer Space Treaty, has brought suit against State X in the International Court of Justice. They ask the Court to declare that State X's claim to the territorial annexation of part of the moon be declared void. They argue that the provisions of the Outer Space Treaty forbidding such annexations are part of customary international law and that the treaty itself is an expression of the world community's *opinio juris.* State X argues that even if there is an *opinio juris,* none of the members of the world community have acted to prevent the annexation of parts of the surface of the moon, and therefore there is no *usus.* How should the Court rule? Discuss.

5. The head of the national police of Country X, Commandant Doe, ordered a raid on the house of Jones, an outspoken opponent of the dictator of Country X. Jones was forcibly dragged from his home, brutalized, and then taken to the office of Doe, who personally executed Jones without any legal cause. Jones's body was then dumped on the steps of his home, terrifying his widow. Jones's widow fled to Country Y and took asylum. Several months later, Doe came to Country Y on a personal visit. While Doe was in Country Y, Jones's widow brought a wrongful death suit against him. Country Y has a statute that gives its courts jurisdiction over actions brought by a plaintiff either in delict or tort for a violation of international law. Will widow Jones succeed in her complaint? Discuss.

6. On July 20, 1974, Turkey invaded Cyprus to "protect" the minority Turkish population of Cyprus, occupying approximately the northern third of the island nation. On November 15, 1983, following a failure of the negotiations between Turkey and Cyprus, the area under the control of the Turkish Army declared itself the Turkish Republic of Northern Cyprus (TRNC). To this date, only Turkey has recognized the TRNC.

   Assume that a large cache of precious metals belonging to the treasury of Cyprus was captured by the Turkish Army during its invasion and subsequently turned over to the TRNC. The TRNC has now contracted to sell the cache to a private buyer in Western Europe. The Cyprus government, learning of this, brings suit in the state where delivery is to take place asking the Court to either (a) enjoin the sale and turn the metals over to Cyprus or (b) require the buyer to pay Cyprus for the metals once they are delivered by the TRNC. How should the Court rule? Discuss.

7. State A dumps its raw, unprocessed sewage into the sea thereby killing much of the marine life along its coastline and the coastlines of its neighbors, States B and C. The three States each have recognized the jurisdiction of the International Court of Justice (ICJ) to resolve disputes between them involving breaches of international law. States B and C, accordingly, have brought suit in the ICJ against State A. They have asked the Court to order State A to take immediate steps to stop dumping sewage into the ocean and to pay for their expenses in cleaning up their coastlines. What should the Court do? Discuss.

8. State A and State B share a common border. State A has ratified the UN Convention on the Prevention and Punishment of the Crime of Genocide, State B has not. State A has entered into a treaty establishing commercial relations with State X and extending Most Favored Nation status to State X, State B has not. State A has a treaty with State Y that

establishes the international border between State Y and State A's Western Province. Which of these treaties will continue to have effect in the changed territory if
(a) State A cedes its Western Province to State B?
(b) The Western Province obtains its independence?
(c) State A and State B merge and become new State C?

Review Problem

You are a finalist for a position in the United Nations Office of Legal Affairs. The Assistant Secretary-General for Legal Affairs, the head of that office, has invited you to her office for an interview. During the course of the interview, she asks you the following questions:

1. What is international law? How is it different from comity?
2. How is international law made?
3. What rules govern the making of international treaties?
4. What must one show to establish the existence of a customary rule of international law?
5. If a state ratifies an international human rights convention but refuses to implement the convention's provisions domestically, who may sue to compel the state to comply with its obligations?
6. A certain large country has recently broken up into several smaller countries. When should those countries be recognized? What are the legal consequences of extending recognition?
7. How are intergovernmental organizations different from nongovernmental organizations?
8. Does international law grant individuals any benefits, rights or duties?
9. What are the principal similarities of the common law, the civil law, and Islamic law, and what influence do those municipal law systems have on international law?

CHAPTER
State Responsibility and Environmental Regulation

2

Chapter Outline

Elihu Root U.S. Secretary of State (1905–1909), Nobel Laureate (Peace Prize 1912), U.S. Senator (1909–1915) (Photo: The Nobel Foundation.)

Introduction

For a long time, it has been a tenet of international law that a state that causes an injury to a foreign national is responsible to the national's state (but not to the national) for the harm done.[1] As U.S. Secretary of State Elihu Root said in 1909:

> Each country is bound to give the nationals of another country in its territory the benefit of the same laws, the same administration, the same protection, and same redress for injury which it gives to its own citizens, and neither more nor less: provided the protection which the country gives to its own citizens conforms to the established standards of civilization.
>
> There is a standard of justice, very simple, very fundamental, and of such general acceptance by all civilized countries as to form a part of the international law of the world. The condition upon which any country is entitled to measure the justice due from it to an alien by the justice which it accords to its own citizens is that its system of law and administration shall conform to this general standard. If any country's system of law and administration does not conform to that standard, although the people of the country may be content or compelled to live under it, no other country can be compelled to accept it as furnishing a satisfactory measure of treatment to its citizens.[2]

This notion of state responsibility will be examined in this chapter. We will consider when a state is responsible, what the standard of responsibility is, what defenses states have against allegations of mistreatment, and what steps aliens and foreign businesses can take to minimize potential losses. We will also examine the insurance programs that states and intergovernmental organizations have established to protect companies investing internationally.

---

[1]This responsibility is derived from the general responsibility of one state to another for the injuries it may cause. The rationale used in this particular instance is that an injury to a state's national is an injury to that state.
[2]*Proceedings of the American Society of International Law,* pp. 20–21 (1910).

Finally, we will examine the international legal obligations of states to protect the environment. In particular, we will look at the responsibilities states have to curtail pollution, protect natural resources, and fine polluters.

A. STATE RESPONSIBILITY

state responsibility: Liability of a state for the injuries that it causes to aliens and foreign businesses.

Two things must be shown to establish that a state is responsible for an injury to an alien or foreign business. There must be (1) "conduct consisting of an action or omission . . . attributable to the State under international law," and the conduct must (2) "constitute . . . a breach of an international obligation of the State."[3]

Doctrine of Imputability

impute: (From Latin *imputare:* "to charge.") To attribute something done by one person, such as an act or crime, to another.

A theory known as the doctrine of imputability says that a state is only responsible for actions that are **imputable** or attributable to it. The most commonly accepted interpretation of this says that the state is responsible for acts done by officials within their apparent authority. This includes (1) acts within the scope of an official's authority and (2) acts outside their scope of authority if the state provided the means or facilities to accomplish the act.[4] Thus, states are responsible both for mistaken actions[5] and even for actions done contrary to express orders, as Case 2–1 makes clear.

---

[3]Article 3, International Law Commission Draft Articles on State Responsibility, 1979, in *Yearbook of the International Law Commission,* vol. 2, pt. 2, p. 90 (1979).

[4]"The conduct of an organ of a State, a territorial governmental entity, empowered to exercise elements of the governmental authority, such organ having acted in that capacity, shall be considered as an act of the State under international law even if, in the particular case, the organ exceeded its competence according to international law or contravened instructions concerning its activity." *Id.,* Article 10.

There is, however, a contrary view supported by some old case law that says that a State is not responsible for acts of officials that are manifestly *ultra vires* (i.e., beyond their authorized powers). In the American Bible Society Case (1885), United States Secretary of State Thomas Bayard wrote: "It is a rule of international law that sovereigns are not liable . . . for damages to a foreigner when arising from the misconduct of agents acting out of the range not only of their real but their apparent authority." John B. Moore, *Digest of International Law,* vol. 6, p. 743 (1906).

[5]An example is provided by the Union Bridge Company Claim (1924). After the outbreak of the war between the Orange Free State and Great Britain in 1899, a British colonial government railway storekeeper was told to confiscate all bridge material destined for the Orange Free State. By mistake he confiscated material belonging to a neutral alien that was intended for road construction. The arbitrators held that Great Britain was liable. The judgment stated: "That liability is not affected either by the fact that he did so under a mistake as to the character and ownership of the material or that it was a time of pressure and confusion caused by war, or by the fact, which, on the evidence, must be admitted, that there was no intention on the part of the British authorities to appropriate the material in question. . . ." *United Nations Reports of International Arbitral Awards,* vol. 6, p. 138.

Case 2–1 Sandline International Inc. v. Papua New Guinea

International Arbitration under the UNCITRAL Rules (October 1998)
International Law Reports, vol. 117, p. 552 (2000)
Rt. Hon. Sir Edward Somers, Rt. Hon. Sir Michael Kerr, and Hon. Sir Daryl Dawson.

BACKGROUND

The Panguna Copper Mine is situated on the island of Bougainville, which is part of the Independent State of Papua New Guinea (PNG). When it was operating, the mine employed some 4,000 people and provided 17 percent of the revenue of PNG. Late in 1998, a dispute arose between the Government of PNG and Bougainville landowners whose land had been resumed for the development of the mine. The dispute escalated in the following year when the landowners blew up power pylons, cutting off power to the mine and forcing it to shut down. A revolutionary movement subsequently grew out of the conflict, which was no longer confined to landowners, seeking the independence of Bougainville from PNG or, possibly, the union of Bougainville with the Solomon

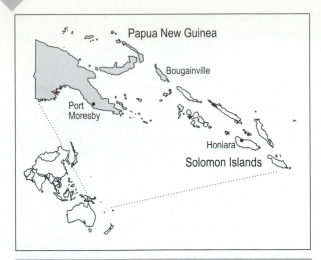

MAP 2-1   Papua New Guinea and Solomon Islands (1997)

Islands. An armed struggle took place between the PNG Defense Force and a local force which had emerged and became known as the Bougainville Revolutionary Army (BRA). A number of person, including civilians, were killed. The PNG Defense Force was unable to recover possession of the mine and the Government was forced to examine the military options for the resolution of the Bougainville problem. The PNG Defense Force lacked the necessary equipment, in particular, helicopter gunships, helicopter troop carriers and modern electronic warfare equipment. Consequently, the PNG Government looked for assistance outside PNG.

THE 1997 AGREEMENT

Negotiations took place between representatives of PNG and Sandline International Inc. (Sandline), a company incorporated in the Commonwealth of the Bahamas and carrying on business in the United Kingdom, which led to the conclusion of an Agreement dated 31 January 1997 between PNG and Sandline (hereinafter referred to as "the Agreement"). The nature of those negotiations is not material for present purposes, for it is not disputed that the Agreement was signed by Mr. Haiveta, the Deputy Prime Minister of PNG, on behalf of PNG, with the knowledge and approval of the Prime Minister and the Minister of Defense and pursuant to a resolution of the National Executive Council of PNG which "approved the use of PNG Special Forces Unit with Sandline International on operations in Bougainville" and "approved U.S. $36 million to engage Sandline International for the operations with the initial 50 percent [to] be paid and the remained to be settled once operations commence." Approval was given in identical terms by the PNG National Security Council.

Sandline was described in the Agreement as: a company specializing in rendering military and security services of an operational, training and support nature, particularly in situations of internal conflict only for and on behalf of recognized Government, in accord with international doctrines and in conformance with the Geneva Convention.

The Agreement recited that PNG was engulfed in a state of conflict with the BRA and required military assistance. It further recited that Sandline was contracted to provide personnel and related services and equipment to:

- train the State's Special Forces in tactical skills specific to the objective;
- gather intelligence to support effective deployment and operations;
- conduct offensive operations in Bougainville in conjunction with PNG defense forces to render the BRA military ineffective and repossess the Panguna mine; and
- provide follow-up operational support, to be further specified and agreed upon between the parties and is subject to separate service provision levels and fee negotiations.

For its part, PNG was to ensure full cooperation from within its organization and that of the PNG defense force.

Sandline's inclusive fee for the provision of personnel, equipment and services under the Agreement was specified as U.S. $36 million. U.S. $18 million was immediately due on the signing of the Agreement and was deemed "the initial payment." The balance of U.S. $18 million was payable within 30 days of the deployment by Sandline of a sixteen man Command, Administration and Training Team in PNG. The initial payment of U.S. $18 million was paid by PNG. Notwithstanding that the required Command, Administration and Training Team was deployed in the first week of the contract and that certain equipment was duly delivered, the balance of U.S. $18 million was not, and has not been, paid.

* * *

THE BREAKDOWN OF THE AGREEMENT

Until the evening of 16 March 1997, the parties were engaged in the performance of the Agreement in an apparently cooperative manner. On that evening, there was an insurrection or mutiny by members of the PNG Defense Force in Port Moresby, led by the Commander of the Force, General Singirok. The uprising was named "Operation Rausim Kwik." Sandline personnel were placed under arrest. The military forces involved were joined the next day by civilians and there outbreaks of rioting and looting and something in the nature of a siege of the Parliament building. On 21 March 1997 Sandline personnel were, with one exception, flown out of PNG, the remaining member being allowed to leave shortly thereafter.

The Prime Minister of PNG "suspended" the Agreement and announced a judicial inquiry to establish the facts concerning the origins of the Agreement. A Commission of Inquiry reported about 29 May 1997 without questioning Sandline's effective engagement under the Agreement. But on 3 June PNG alleged that the Agreement had been frustrated on the ground that its performance was impossible.

* * *

Pursuant to the arbitration clause in the agreement, Sandline claimed from PNG payment of the sum of U.S. $18 million, being the second payment referred to in the Agreement. . . .

* * *

. . . PNG . . . plead that under the laws of PNG the contract was unlawful and that those who had purported to enter into on behalf of PNG lacked the capacity to do so.

* * *

[PNG's answer to Sandline claim] was that the agreement with Sandline was null and void, being at all times illegal and unlawful both in its formation and performance. The illegality alleged was that the Agreement and its performance were in contravention of § 200 of the PNG Constitution. . . .

Sandline's reply [to PNG's answer] was twofold. First, it said that upon true construction of § 200 of the Constitution, neither the agreement nor its intended performance was contrary to its provisions nor the provisions of any of the other statutes relied upon by PNG. Alternatively, Sandline said that English law, by which the contract was governed, included international law and the under such law, PNG could not, in the events which happened, rely upon § 200 of the Constitution. . . .

* * *

THE FIRST ISSUE

. . . The proper construction of § 200 of the PNG Constitution and its application in the circumstances of this case were the subject of argument before the Tribunal. However, the Tribunal is of the view that it is neither necessary nor desirable to express any final opinion upon the scope of the section, it being possible to reach a conclusion for the purposes of this Interim Award by assuming, without deciding the illegality or unlawfulness under the section for which PNG contends. The scope and intent of § 200 is

better left to the courts of PNG where knowledge and understanding of the local conditions give them a better and more accurate assessment of its effect. . . .

* * *

INTERNATIONAL LAW

The rules of international law in this case are clearly established and their application causes no difficulty. PNG submits that they have no application because the agreement between it and Sandline, a private party, does not attract international law. However, it is incontrovertible that PNG is an independent sate and purported to contract in that capacity. An agreement between a private party and a state is an international, not a domestic, contract. This Tribunal is an international, not a domestic, arbitral tribunal and is bound to apply the rules of international law. Those rules are not excluded from, but form part of, English law, which is the law chosen by the parties to govern their contract. PNG cited no authority to support its submission and there is ample authority to the contrary.[6] The submission of PNG must be rejected.

In international law, in relation to contracts to which a state is a party and which are to be performed within the territory of that state . . . a state cannot rely upon its own internal laws as the basis for a plea that a contract concluded by it is illegal. It is a clearly established principle of international law that acts of a state will be regarded as such even if they are *ultra vires* or unlawful under the internal law of the state. Of course, a state is a juristic person and can only act through its institutions, officials or employees (commonly referred to in international law as organs). But the acts or omission when the purport to act in their capacity as organs of the state are regarded internationally as those of the state even though they contravene the internal law of the state. The Report of the International Law Commission of the United Nations[7] expressed the principle as follows:

The characterization of certain conduct of organs as acts of the state for the purpose of determining its international responsibility is completely independent of the characterization of the same conduct as acts of the state liable to incur administrative responsibility under internal law.

In *Southern Pacific Properties (Middle East) Ltd. v. Arab Republic of Egypt,*[8] the respondent submitted that it

---

[6]*See* e.g., George W. Hopkins (US) v. United Mexican States, [*Annual Digest of Public International Law Cases,* vol. 3, p. 228]; Setenave v. Settebello, [*International Law Reports,* vol. 89, p. 313]; Southern Pacific Properties (Middle East) Ltd v. Arab Republic of Egypt [*id.,* vol. 106, p. 501]; Société Ouest Africaine des Bétons Industriels (SOABI) v. State of Senegal, *International Centre for Settlement of Investment Disputes Reports,* vol. 1988, pt. 2, p. 190; United States (on behalf of P. W. Shufeldt) v. Guatemala, *United Nations Reports of International Arbitral Awards,* vol. 1930, pt. 2, vol. 1079; In the Matter of Revere Copper and Brass Inc. and Overseas Private Investment Corporation (1978), *International Law Reports,* vol. 56, p. 258; AMOCO International Finance Corporation v. Iran (1987); *Iran-United Nations Claims Tribunal Reports,* vol. 15, p. 189; Fromatome v. Atomic Energy Commission of Iran (1983), *Yearbook of Commercial Arbitration,* vol. 8, p. 99; Phillips Petroleum Company Iran v. Iran (1989), *Iran-United Nations Claims Tribunal Reports,* vol. 21, p. 79.
[7]*Yearbook of the International Law Commission,* vol. 2, p. 61 (1975).
[8]*International Centre for Settlement of Investment Disputes Reports,* vol. 3, p. 102.

was not liable for certain acts of Egyptian official which it said were legally nonexistent or absolutely null and void according to Egyptian law. The Tribunal said of its award:[9]

The principle of international law which the Tribunal is bound to apply is that which establishes the international responsibility of the state when unauthorized or *ultra vires* acts of officials have been performed by state agents under cover of their official character. If such unauthorized or *ultra vires* acts could not be ascribed to the state, all state responsibility would be rendered illusory. For this reason . . . the practice of states has conclusively established their international responsibility for state organs, even if accomplished outside the limits of their competence and contrary to domestic law.

It is unnecessary to cite further authority for the principle, but other examples of its application are to be found in the cases referred to in [footnote 6].

The rules of international law referred to above are, of themselves, sufficient to dispose of the defense of illegality or unlawfulness raised by PNG. But there is the added rule that a party may not deny the validity of a contract entered into on its behalf by another if, by its conduct, it later consents to the contract. It is known as the doctrine of preclusion [or ratification] and, whether upon the concepts of acquiescence, estoppel or waiver, is well established in international law. In the end, the doctrine finds its justification in considerations of good faith and conscience which underlie the basic principle of international law: *pacta sunt servanda*.[10] An apposite example is the *Shufeldt Claim*.[11] In that case, the claimant entered into a contract with the Government of Guatemala for a chicle concession, the validity of which the government denied on the ground that it lacked the necessary approval of the legislature. The Tribunal said:[12]

In view of my finding that the contract was laid before the Legislature and approved by them, it is not necessary for me to deal with the second point raised by the United States, *viz.*, that the Guatemala Government having recognized the validity of the contract for six years and received all the benefits to which they were entitled under the contract and allowed Shufeldt to go on spending money on the concession, is precluded from denying its validity, even if the approval of the legislature had not been given.

I may however state on this point that in all the circumstances I have related and the whole case submitted to me, I have no doubt that this contention of the United States is sound and in keeping with the principles of international law and I so find.

APPLICATION OF INTERNATIONAL LAW

Upon the basis of the facts recited . . . above, there can be no doubt that in executing the agreement between Sandline and PNG, the Deputy Prime Minister, Mr. Haiveta, purported to act on behalf of the PNG. Not only did he purport to exercise the authority with which he was invested by his official position, but he did so after negotiations involving the Prime Minister and the Minister for Defense and with the approval of the National Executive Council. No question of illegality was raised with Sandline. In these circumstances, for the reasons given above, a valid contract was concluded between Sandline and PNG, notwithstanding any failure to observe the constitutional and other statutory provisions upon which PNG relies to establish the illegality or unlawfulness of the Agreement or lack of capacity to enter into it. Any such illegality or unlawfulness or lack of capacity arose, if it arose at all, under the internal laws of the PNG and not under international law which, for the purpose of determining the validity of a contract, disregards the internal laws of a contracting state. The agreement was not illegal or unlawful under international law or under any established principle of public policy. A political decision having been made by PNG to enter into it, its execution by a person with apparent authority to bind the state gave rise to a valid contract in the eyes of international law.

In addition, PNG participated in the performance of the contract before the events of 16 March 1997. It paid the first installment of U.S. $18 million due under the terms of the contract. It facilitated entry of Sandline personnel and equipment into PNG for the purpose of carrying out the contract. Even after the events of 16 March 1997, PNG affirmed rather than denied the existence of the contract by alleging that it had been frustrated by those and later events and counterclaiming on that basis. It was not until late in these proceedings that PNG abandoned the defense of frustration and raised the defense of illegality and unlawfulness. Although it is strictly unnecessary to do so . . . the Tribunal express the view that, in the events which occurred, PNG is precluded from denying the validity of its agreement with Sandline.

CONCLUSION

The Tribunal rejects the defense of illegality or unlawfulness raised by PNG. In the end that is the only defense raised, and it follows from its rejection that PNG is liable for its failure to perform the terms of the contract. ■

---

[9]*Id.* at ¶ 85.
[10]Latin: "The agreement shall be observed."]
[11]United States (on behalf of P. W. Shufeldt) v. Guatemala, *United Nations Reports of International Arbitral Awards,* vol. 1930, pt. 2, vol. 1079.
[12]*Id.* at p. 1094.

Nonimputable Acts

Because states are only responsible for actions taken by their officials, they are not responsible for the acts of private persons,[13] acts of officials of other states[14] or international organizations,[15] or acts of insurrectionaries.[16] This is explained in Case 2–2.

---

[13]International Law Commission Draft Articles on State Responsibility, 1979, *Year Book of the International Law Commission,* vol. 2, pt. 2, p. 90 (1979). Article 11(1) states: "The conduct of a person or a group of persons not acting on behalf of the State shall not be considered as an act of the State under international law."

[14]*Id.,* Article 12(1) provides: "The conduct of an organ of a State acting in that capacity, which takes place in the territory of another State or in any other territory under its jurisdiction, shall not be considered as an act of the latter State under international law."

[15]*Id.,* Article 13(1) says: "The conduct of an organ of an international organization acting in that capacity shall not be considered as an act of the State under international law by reason only of the fact that such conduct has taken place in the territory of that State or in any other territory under its jurisdiction."

[16]*Id.,* Article 14(1): "The conduct of an organ of an insurrectional movement, which is established in the territory of a State or in any other territory under its administration, shall not be considered as an act of that State under international law."

Case 2–2   Home Missionary Society Case

Home Frontier and Foreign Missionary Society of the United Brethren in Christ (United States v. Great Britain) Claim

American and British Claims Arbitration Tribunal, 1920. *United Nations Reports of International Arbitral Awards,* vol. 6, p. 42.

AWARD OF THE TRIBUNAL:

In 1898, the collection of a tax newly imposed [by Great Britain] on the natives of the Protectorate [of Sierra Leone] and known as the "hut tax" was the signal for a serious and widespread revolt in the Ronietta district. The revolt broke out on April 27 and lasted for several days. . . .

In the course of the rebellion all [the claimant's] . . . missions were attacked, and either destroyed or damaged, and some of the missionaries were murdered. . . .

The contention of the United States government before this Tribunal is that the revolt was the result of the imposition and attempted collection of the "hut tax"; that it was within the knowledge of the British government that this tax was the object of deep native resentment; that in the face of the native danger the British government wholly failed to take proper steps for the maintenance of order and the protection of life and property; that the loss of life and damage to property was the result of this neglect and failure of duty, and therefore that it is liable to pay compensation.

Now, even assuming that the "hut tax" was the effective cause of the native rebellion, it was in itself a fiscal measure in accordance not only with general usage in colonial administration, but also with the usual practice in African countries. . . .

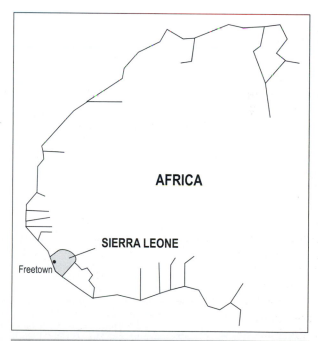

MAP 2-2   Sierra Leone (1898)

It was a measure to which the British government was perfectly entitled to resort in the legitimate exercise of sovereignty, if it was required. . . .

Further, though it may be true that some difficulty might have been foreseen, there was nothing to suggest that it would be more serious than is usual and inevitable in a semi-barbarous and only partially colonized protectorate, and certainly nothing to lead to any apprehension of widespread revolt.

It is a well-established principle of international law that no government can be held responsible for the act of rebellious bodies of men committed in violation of its authority, where it is itself guilty of no breach of good faith, or of no negligence in suppressing insurrection.[17]

The good faith of the British government cannot be questioned, and as to the conditions prevailing in the Protectorate there is no evidence to support the contention that it failed in its duty to afford adequate protection for life and property. . . . The Tribunal decides that this claim must be dismissed. ■

---

[17]Moore's *International Law Digest,* vol. 6, p. 956; vol. 7, p. 957; Moore's *Arbitrations,* pp. 2991–2992; British Answer, p. 1.

Terrorism

terrorism: (From Latin *terror:* "to frighten.") The sustained clandestine use of violence for a political purpose.

Terrorism is the sustained clandestine use of violence—murder, kidnapping, bombings—for a political purpose.[18]

Two important features characterize modern terrorism. One is the quest for spectacular and horrible incidents that attract media attention. Examples include the crashing of hijacked commercial aircraft into the World Trade Center towers on New York and into the Pentagon in Washington in 2001 allegedly ordered by Saudi millionaire Osama bin Laden; and the bombings of American embassies in Kenya and Tanzania in 1998, also allegedly ordered by bin Laden.[19] The second characteristic is state support and sometimes direct state action. In the 1970s and 1980s, Middle Eastern terrorists benefited greatly from the support, training, or refuge provided by pro-Soviet states like Bulgaria, Cuba, and East Germany, as well as Middle Eastern states like Algeria, Iran, Iraq, Libya, South Yemen, Tunisia, and Syria. Examples of this type of state assistance include the 1985 hijacking of the Italian cruise ship *Achille Lauro* by Palestinians, the murder of a U.S. passenger, and the subsequent release of one of the terrorists who was traveling under a diplomatic passport.[20] Attacks by Libyan-supported terrorists on airports in Rome and Vienna in 1985 and on a discotheque in Berlin in 1986 led to a raid by American fighter jets against terrorist training camps and air defense sites in Libya.[21] State terrorism can also include the clandestine kidnapping and murder of a state's own people by its government, as was the case in Nazi Germany in the 1930s and 1940s, in Argentina from 1972 to 1976 when a military junta was in power, and in many other countries since.[22]

Efforts to counter terrorism in recent years have led to the adoption of the Tokyo Convention of 1963[23] and the Montreal Convention of 1971 on the hijacking and sabotage of civilian aircraft;[24] to the 1973 Convention on crimes against diplomats[25] and the 1979 Hague Convention on hostage taking;[26] and most recently to the 1988 Convention for the Suppression of Unlawful Acts Against

---

[18]*See* Terrorism Research Center, "Definitions of Terrorism," posted at www.terrorism.com/terrorism/def.html. One must distinguish terrorism from the attacks by fanatics on individuals (such as the assassination of Abraham Lincoln) or on military personnel in a war zone (such as the bombings of the U.S. Marine and French Foreign Legion bunkers in Lebanon in 1983).

[19]CNN, "Sources: Bin Laden Charged with Inciting Violence against U.S. Citizens" (August 25, 1998), posted at cnn.com/US/9808/25/bin.laden.01/index.html.

[20]*See* Associated Press, "After U.S. Protests, Achille Lauro Hijacker Recaptured" (March 22, 1996), posted at www.nando.net/newsroom/ntn/world/032296/world4_23115.html.

[21]*See Seattle Times,* "Trial Begins in the 1986 Bombing of Berlin Disco" (November 18, 1997), posted at www.seattletimes.com/extra/browse/html97/altdisc_111897.html.

[22]*See* United Nations Commission on Human Rights, "Report of the Working Group on Enforced or Involuntary Disappearances," Doc. E/CN.4/1996/38 (January 15, 1996), posted at www1.umn.edu/humanrts/commission/thematic52/1996_38.htm.

[23]Tokyo Convention on Offenses and Certain Other Acts Committed on Board Aircraft, *American Journal of International Law,* vol. 58, p. 566 (1964).

[24]Montreal Convention for the Suppression of Unlawful Acts against the Safety of Civil Aviation, *International Legal Materials,* vol. 10, p. 1151 (1971). This convention is posted on the Fletcher School of Law & Diplomacy's Multilateral Project Web site at www.tufts.edu/fletcher/multi/texts/BH586.txt. A Protocol to the Convention entitled Suppression of Unlawful Acts of Violence at Airports Serving International Aviation was adopted in 1988.

[25]Convention on the Prevention and Punishment of Crimes against Internationally Protected Persons Including Diplomats, *International Legal Materials,* vol. 13, p. 42 (1974); *United Nations Treaty Series,* vol. 1035, p. 168, posted at www.un.org/Depts/Treaty/.

[26]Hague Convention against the Taking of Hostages, *International Legal Materials,* vol. 18, p. 1456 (1979); *United Nations Treaty Series,* vol. 1316, p. 206, posted at www.un.org/Depts/Treaty/.

the Safety of Maritime Navigation.[27] These conventions classify certain kinds of acts as "international crimes" that are punishable by any state regardless of the nationality of the criminal or the victim or the locality of the offense. They do not, however, impose liability on states that participate in state terrorism.

The extent to which states are held legally responsible internationally for terrorism is limited to helping other states bring terrorists to trial. For example, the United Nations Security Council adopted a resolution in 1992 demanding that Libya extradite to France, the United Kingdom, or the United States two alleged terrorists suspected of putting a bomb aboard the Pan American airliner that blew up over Lockerbie, Scotland, but it imposed no sanctions of Libya.[28] A second resolution imposed limited sanctions, but they were meant only to encourage Libya to turn over the alleged terrorists and not as a punishment of the country itself.[29]

Most domestic terrorism legislation similarly does not impose liability on states for terrorism. The United Kingdom Terrorism Act 2000,[30] for example, applies only to non-state organizations.[31] The United States Antiterrorism and Effective Death Penalty Act of 1996 is the exception.[32] The U.S. Act grants U.S. federal courts jurisdiction to hear suits against foreign states and their officials and creates a private cause of action for personal injuries and death resulting from state-sponsored terrorist attacks. The application of the Act is described in Case 2–3.

---

[27]International Maritime Organization Convention for the Suppression of Unlawful Acts against the Safety of Maritime Navigation, posted at sedac.ciesin.org/pidb/texts/acrc/unlawfulNav.txt.html.
[28]Security Council Resolution 731 (1992), posted at gopher://gopher.undp.org:70/00/undocs/scd/scouncil/s92/6.
[29]Security Council Resolution 748 (1992), posted at gopher://gopher.undp.org:70/00/undocs/scd/scouncil/s92/23. In 1998, following Libya's agreement to extradite the alleged terrorists to the Netherlands for trial, the Security Council promised to lift these sanctions once the extradition took place. Resolution 1192 (1998) posted at www.un.org/plweb-cgi/since.cgi?dbname=scres& foryear=1998.
[30]Terrorism Act 2000, chap. 11 (Eng.) posted at www.homeoffice.gov.uk/terrorism/index.htm.
[31]A list of proscribed organizations is set out in Schedule 2 of the Terrorism Act 2000, which is posted at www. legislation.hmso.gov.uk/acts/acts2000/00011-k.htm#sch2. Section 3 of the Terrorism Act authorizes the U.K. Secretary of State to update the list. The Secretary of State did so in March 2001 in the Terrorism Act 2000 (Proscribed Organizations) (Amendment) Order 2001, which is posted at www.homeoffice.gov.uk/terrorism/index.htm.
[32]*United States Statutes at Large*, title 110, § 1214. See *United States Code* title 8, § 241(a)(4)(B).

Case 2–3   *Flatow v. The Islamic Republic of Iran*

United States District Court for the District of Columbia. *Federal Supplement*, vol. 999, p. 1 (1998).

JUDGE ROYCE C. LAMBERTH:

This is an action for wrongful death resulting from an act of state-sponsored terrorism. Defendants have not entered an appearance in this matter. This Court entered Defendants' default on September 4, 1997. Notwithstanding indicia of Defendants' willful default, however, this Court is compelled to make further inquiry prior to entering a judgment by default against Defendants. As with actions against the federal government, the Foreign Sovereign Immunities Act ("FSIA") requires that a default judgment against a foreign state be entered only after plaintiff "establishes his claim or right to relief by evidence that is satisfactory to the Court."[33]

Plaintiff brings this action pursuant to two recently enacted amendments to the FSIA, which grant jurisdiction over foreign states and their officials, agents and employees, and create federal causes of action related to personal injury or death resulting from state-sponsored terrorist attacks. Given these novel enactments . . . this Court has engaged in a systematic review of dispositive legal issues prior to making its determination that Plaintiff has established his claim and right to relief to the satisfaction of this Court.

FINDINGS OF FACT

This matter came before the Court for an evidentiary hearing on March 2–3, 1998. The Plaintiff proceeded in the manner of a nonjury trial before the Court and the following findings of fact are based upon the sworn testimony and documents entered into evidence in accordance with the Federal Rules of Evidence. Plaintiff has "established his claim or right to relief by evidence that is satisfactory to the Court" as required by United States Code, title 28,

---

[33]*United States Code*, title 28, § 1608(e).

MAP 2-3 Iran and Israel (1997)

§ 1608(e). This Court finds the following facts to be established by clear and convincing evidence, which would have been sufficient to establish a prima facie case in a contested proceeding:

* * *

5. On April 9, 1995, decedent Alisa Michelle Flatow was a passenger on the number 36 Egged bus, which was traveling from Ashkelon, Israel, to a Mediterranean resort in the Gush Katif community. Testimony of Kesari Rusa.

6. At or about 12:05 P.M. local time, near Kfar Darom in the Gaza Strip, a suicide bomber drove a van loaded with explosives into the number 36 Egged bus, causing an explosion that destroyed the bus. Testimony of Kesari Rusa....

* * *

14. ... Alisa Michelle Flatow died at approximately 10:00 A.M. local time on April 10, 1995.... [T]estimony of Dr. Allan Fisher....

* * *

16. The Shaqaqi faction of Palestine Islamic Jihad claimed responsibility for and in fact perpetrated the terrorist act which caused the death of Alisa Michelle Flatow. Palestine Islamic Jihad is a series of loosely affiliated factions rather than a cohesive group. The Shaqaqi faction is a terrorist cell with a small core mem-

bership. Its sole purpose is to conduct terrorist activities in the Gaza region, and its sole source of funding is the Islamic Republic of Iran. Testimony of Dr. Reuven Paz; testimony of Dr. Patrick Clawson; testimony of former FBI Deputy Assistant Director for Counterterrorism Harry Brandon....

* * *

18. In July 1996, Plaintiff Stephen M. Flatow and his counsel met with Ambassador Philip Wilcox, who then served as the Department of State's Coordinator for Counterterrorism. During that meeting, he informed Mr. Flatow that the Department of State was satisfied that the group which had claimed responsibility for the bombing, the Shaqaqi faction of Palestine Islamic Jihad, had in fact perpetrated the bombing, and that the Islamic Republic of Iran provided approximately two million dollars to Palestine Islamic Jihad annually in support of its terrorist activities. Affidavit of Stephen M. Flatow....

19. Defendant the Islamic Republic of Iran is a foreign state and has been designated a state sponsor of terrorism pursuant to section 6(j) of the Export Administration Act of 1979[34] continuously since January 19, 1984. Defendant provides material support and resources to Palestine Islamic Jihad by supplying funds and training for the Shaqaqi faction's terrorist activities in the Gaza Strip region. Testimony of Dr. Reuven Paz, testimony of Dr. Patrick Clawson, testimony of former FBI Deputy Assistant Director for Counterterrorism Harry Brandon.

20. Defendant the Islamic Republic of Iran sponsors the Shaqaqi faction's terrorist activities within the meaning of United States Code, title 28, § 1605(a)(7) and § 1605 note by providing it with all of its funding. Testimony of Dr. Reuven Paz; testimony of Dr. Patrick Clawson; testimony of former FBI Deputy Assistant Director for Counterterrorism Harry Brandon.

* * *

I. CONCLUSIONS OF LAW WITH RESPECT TO JURISDICTION

A. The Foreign Sovereign Immunities Act Controls This Action.

As this action is brought against a foreign state, its intelligence service acting as its agent, and three of its officials, acting in their official capacity, the Foreign Sover-

---

[34]*Id.*, title 50, App. § 2405(j)).

eign Immunities Act of 1976[35] ("FSIA"), as amended, controls this action.

* * *

1. Recent Amendments to the Foreign Sovereign Immunities Act Create Subject Matter Jurisdiction and Federal Causes of Action for Certain Acts of State Sponsored Terrorism.   . . . In the Anti-terrorism and Effective Death Penalty Act of 1996, Congress [amended the FSIA and] lifted the immunity of foreign states for a certain category of sovereign acts which are repugnant to the United States and the international community—terrorism.[36] That Act created an exception to the immunity of those foreign states officially designated by the Department of State as terrorist states if the foreign state commits a terrorist act, or provides material support and resources to an individual or entity which commits such an act, which results in the death or personal injury of a United States citizen.

Although the Antiterrorism Act created a forum competent to adjudicate claims arising from offenses of this nature, serious issues remained, in particular, the causes of action available to plaintiffs. Congressman Jim Saxton sponsored [a second] amendment to [the FSIA] with the intent to clarify this and other issues. In Congressman Saxton's experience as Chairman of the House Task Force on Counterterrorism and Unconventional Warfare and member of the House National Security Committee, in order for the exception for immunity to have the desired deterrent effect, the potential civil liability for foreign states which commit and sponsor acts of terrorism would have to be substantial. Therefore, the [second] amendment . . . expressly provided, inter alia, that punitive damages were available in actions brought under the state sponsored terrorism exception to immunity.[37] This provision of law is commonly referred to as the "Flatow Amendment."

* * *

B. Subject Matter Jurisdiction

In order to establish subject matter jurisdiction pursuant to § 1605(a)(7) [of the FSIA], a claim must contain the following statutory elements:

(1) that personal injury or death resulted from an act of torture, extrajudicial killing, aircraft sabotage, or hostage taking; and

(2) the act was either perpetrated by the foreign state directly or by a non-state actor which receives material support or resources from the foreign state defendant; and

(3) the act or the provision of material support or resources is engaged in by an agent, official or employee of the foreign state while acting within the scope of his or her office, agency or employment; and

(4) that the foreign state be designated as a state sponsor of terrorism either at the time the incident complained of occurred or was later so designated as a result of such act; and

(5) if the incident complained of occurred with the foreign state defendant's territory, plaintiff has offered the defendants a reasonable opportunity to arbitrate the matter; and

(6) either the plaintiff or the victim was a United States national at the time of the incident; and

(7) similar conduct by United States agents, officials, or employees within the United States would be actionable.[38]

While elements (4)–(6) are pure questions of fact, elements (1)–(3) and (7) are mixed questions of law and fact, and, in the absence of settled precedent, require interpretation.

1. A Suicide Bombing Is an Act of Extrajudicial Killing. Plaintiff describes the cause of his daughter's death as an "extrajudicial killing" within the meaning of § 1605(a)(7) [of the FSIA]. The state-sponsored terrorism exception to immunity expressly adopts the definition of extrajudicial killing set forth in the Torture Victim Protection Act of 1991.[39] That Act defines an "extrajudicial killing" as

a deliberated killing not authorized by a previous judgment pronounced by a regularly constituted court affording all judicial guarantees which are recognized as indispensable by civilized peoples. Such term, however, does not include any such killing that, under international law, is lawfully carried out under the authority of a foreign nation. (Emphasis added).

Deliberate is defined as:

. . . Carried on coolly and steadily, especially according to a preconceived design; given to weighing facts and arguments with a view to a choice or decision; careful in considering the consequences of a step; . . .[40]

---

[35]*Id.*, title 28, §§ 1602–1611 *et seq.*
[36]*Id.*, § 1605 (hereinafter "state sponsored terrorism exception").
[37][Codified at] *id.* § 1605 note.
[38]*Id.* § 1605(a)(7).
[39]*Id.* § 1605(e)(1).
[40]*Black's Law Dictionary,* pp. 426–27 (6th ed. 1990).

Other courts have found that summary executions, for example, would be considered "extrajudicial killings"....[41] In actions brought under the Alien Tort Statute[42] and the Torture Victim Protection Act,[43] courts have suggested, in the context of command responsibility, that a course of indiscriminate brutality, known to result in deaths, rises to the level of "extrajudicial killings."[44]

* * *

As the state sponsored terrorism exception expressly incorporates a definition from the United States criminal code chapter on international terrorism, ... [a] definition from that chapter is ... apropos:

(1) the term "international terrorism" means activities that—

    A. involve violent acts or acts dangerous to human life that are a violation of the criminal laws of the United States or of any State, or that would be a criminal violation if committed within the jurisdiction of the United States or of any State;

    B. appear to be intended—

      i) to intimidate or coerce a civilian population;

      ii) to influence the policy of a government by intimidation or coercion;

      iii) to affect the conduct of a government by assassination or kidnapping;

and

    C. occur primarily outside the territorial jurisdiction of the United States, or transcend national boundaries in terms of the means by which they are accomplished, the persons they appear intended to intimidate or coerce, or the locale in which their perpetrators operate or seek asylum; ...[45]

Attempts to reach a fixed, universally accepted definition of international terrorism have been frustrated both by changes in terrorist methodology and the lack of any precise definition of the term "terrorism." Therefore, the United States characterizes rather than enumerates acts for the purposes of designating foreign state sponsors of terrorism and defining criminal terrorist offenses under federal law. Each of the acts listed in § 1605(a)(7) [of the FSIA] fully conform with the foregoing definitions and provisions.

This Court concludes that a suicide bombing conforms with each of the foregoing provisions and defini-

tions, and therefore is an act of "extrajudicial killing" within the meaning of United States Code, title 28, § 1605(a)(7).

2. The Routine Provision of Financial Assistance to a Terrorist Group in Support of Its Terrorist Activities Constitutes the Provision of Material Support or Resources Within the Meaning Of 28 U.S.C. § 1605(a)(7). The state-sponsored terrorism provision adopts the definition of "providing material support or resources" set forth in the federal criminal code. [As defined in the federal criminal code]:

    ... "material support or resources" means currency or other financial securities, financial services, lodging, training, safehouses, false documentation or identification, communications equipment, facilities, weapons, lethal substances, explosives, personnel, transportation, and other physical assets, but does not include humanitarian assistance to persons not directly involved in such violations.[46]

This Court concludes that the routine provision of financial assistance to a terrorist group in support of its terrorist activities constitutes "providing material support or resources" for a terrorist act within the meaning of § 1605(a)(7) [of the FSIA]. Furthermore, as nothing in [the preceding definition] indicates otherwise, this Court also concludes that a plaintiff need not establish that the material support or resources provided by a foreign state for a terrorist act contributed directly to the act from which his claim arises in order to satisfy § 1605(a)(7)'s statutory requirements for subject matter jurisdiction. Sponsorship of a terrorist group which causes the personal injury or death of a United States national alone is sufficient to invoke jurisdiction.

3. The Provision of Material Support and Resources to a Terrorist Group is an Act Within the Scope of a Foreign State's Agent's and High Officials' Agency and Offices. The law of *respondeat superior*[47] demonstrates that if a foreign state's agent, official or employee provides material support and resources to a terrorist organization, such provision will be considered an act within the scope of his or her agency, office or employment.

* * *

... This Court concludes that if a foreign state's heads of state, intelligence service, and minister of intelligence routinely provide material support or resources to a terrorist group, whose activities are consistent with

---

[41]*See* Lafontant v. Aristide, *Federal Supplement,* vol. 844, p. 128 (District Ct. for the E. District of New York 1994) (dicta).
[42]*United States Code,* title 28, § 1350.
[43]*Id.,* § 1605(e)(1).
[44]*See* Hilao v. Estate of Marcos, *Federal Reporter, Third Series,* vol. 103, 776 at pp. 776–77 (11th Circuit Ct. of Appeals 1996).
[45]*United States Code,* title 18, § 2331.
[46]*Id.,* § 2339A(a).
[[47]Latin: "The master is responsible."]

the foreign state's customs or policies, then that agent and those officials have acted squarely within the scope of their agency and offices within the meaning of § 1605(a)(7) and § 1605 note [of the FSIA].

4. United States Officials Would Be Liable for Providing Material Support or Resources to a Terrorist Group Within the United States.   The Flatow Amendment[48] clarifies that the liability of foreign states and their officials must be comparable to that of the United States and its agents, officials, and employees officials. This Court concludes that if officials of the United States, while acting in their official capacities, provide material support and resources to a terrorist group which executed a suicide bombing within the United States, those officials would not be immune from civil suits for wrongful death and personal injury.

* * *

CONCLUSION

This Court possess subject matter jurisdiction over this action. . . . Plaintiff has established to this Court's satisfaction, pursuant to 28 U.S.C. § 1608(e), and by clear and convincing evidence, that Defendants, the Islamic Republic of Iran, the Iranian Ministry of Information and Security, Ayatollah Ali Hoseini Khamenei, former President Ali Akbar Hashemi-Rafsanjani, and former Minister Ali Fallahian-Khuzestani, are jointly and severally liable for all damages awarded by this Court to Plaintiff Stephen M. Flatow, in his own right, as Administrator of the Estate of Alisa Michelle Flatow, and on behalf of decedent's heirs-at-law, for their provision of material support and resources to a terrorist group which caused the extrajudicial killing of Alisa Michelle Flatow. ∎

---

[48]*Id.,* title 28, § 1605 note.

Fault and Causation

culpa: (Latin: "fault or error.") Responsibility for wrongdoing.

The case law and most law writers suggest that a country is responsible for injuries regardless of fault. In other words, there is no requirement to show **culpa** (fault) by the country (either through knowledge or negligence).[49]

causation: (From Latin *causa:* "reason.") The act or agency that produces an effect, result, or consequence.

This rule reflects the difficulties of proving a lack of proper care by a state. Instead, courts look to **causation**. That is, did the state or its officials actually cause the injury? In the *Lighthouses* arbitration between France and Greece, a question arose about Greece's eviction of a French firm from its offices in Salonika and its responsibility for the loss of merchandise destroyed by a fire at the firm's temporary location. The Permanent Court of Arbitration said:

> Even if one were inclined . . . to hold that Greece is responsible for the consequences of that evacuation, one could not . . . admit a causal relationship between the damage caused by the fire, on the one part, and that following on the evacuation, on the other, so as to justify holding Greece liable for the disastrous effects of the fire. . . . The damage was neither a foreseeable nor a normal consequence of the evacuation, nor

---

[49]A different view was expressed by two dissenting judges in the Corfu Channel Case (United Kingdom v. Albania) (Merits), which involved a suit brought by the United Kingdom for injuries its warships suffered from striking mines in Albanian waters. The Majority opinion stated as follows: "The court must examine . . . whether it has been established by means of indirect evidence that Albania has knowledge of the minelaying in her territorial waters independently of any connivance on her part in this operation. The proof may be drawn from inferences of fact, provided that they leave no room for reasonable doubt. . . :

"In fact, Albania neither notified the existence of the minefield, nor warned the British warships of the danger they were approaching. . . .

"In fact, nothing was attempted by the Albanian authorities to prevent the disaster. These grave omissions involve the international responsibility of Albania. . . ."

Judge Krylov disagreed. In his dissent, he wrote: "Is it then possible to found the international responsibility of Albania on the notion of culpa? Can it be argued that Albania failed to exercise the diligence required of international law to prevent the laying of mines in the Corfu Channel? . . .

"In view of . . . the inadequacy of the evidence produced by the British, I am unable to reach the conclusion that Albania was responsible for the explosions. . . . One cannot condemn a State on the basis of probabilities. To establish international responsibility, one must have clear and indisputable facts. In the present case the facts are absent."

And Judge Azevedo added: "The notion of culpa is always changing and undergoing a slow process of evolution; moving away from the classical elements of imprudence and negligence, it tends to draw nearer to the system of objective responsibility; and this has led certain present-day authors to deny that culpa is definitely separate, in regard to a theory based solely on risk." *International Court of Justice Reports,* vol. 1949, p. 2 (1949).

attributable to any want of care on the part of Greece. All causal connection is lacking, and in those circumstances Claim No. 19 must be rejected.[50]

B. STANDARD OF CARE

Once it has been established that a state is connected to an action, one has to determine the criteria it is to be judged by. Two criteria have appeared in the case law: the "international standard" (or sometimes the "international minimum standard") and the "national standard."

The National Standard of Care

national standard of care: Doctrine that a state must treat aliens in the same way that it treats its own nationals.

Third World countries (especially the Latin American countries before World War II and the Afro-Asian countries since) have pressed for a **national standard of care**. That is, a state should treat an alien exactly as it treats its own nationals—no better, no worse. The critics point out, however, that this is not protection for aliens if the nationals are ill treated; and if the rule were carried to its extreme, it would mean that aliens should be given the same privileges (voting, health care, etc.) as nationals—both logical absurdities.

International support for the "national standard" or "equality of treatment" doctrine has fluctuated over the years.[51] Efforts by the Soviet Union to obtain support for a 1962 United Nations General Assembly resolution that would have established "the inalienable rights of peoples and nations to the unobstructed execution of nationalization, expropriation, and other measures" was defeated by a vote of 48 to 34, with 21 abstentions. Among those nations voting against the resolution were 16 Latin American states and 10 African and Asian states. Two Latin American and 19 African and Asian states were those that abstained. In the debate leading up to the vote, the representatives of many developing countries sought to reassure the capital-exporting states of Western Europe and North America that they had no intention of confiscating foreign investments.

The role that foreign capital plays in development and the fear of offending states that extend economic and other kinds of assistance—matters frankly admitted to in the debates—were important factors in defeating the Soviet proposal. On the other hand, the less developed countries generally have been unwilling to reject the "national treatment" doctrine and sign treaties obliging them to pay just compensation if they expropriate foreign investments. The United States, which for a long time was the principal source of private investment capital, has been able to get only a handful of states to sign such agreements. Moreover, those treaties seem to provide little protection because either party can terminate them without giving notice.

The operation of the national standard doctrine is illustrated by Case 2–4.

[50]*United Nations Reports of International Arbitral Awards*, vol. 12, pp. 217–218; *International Law Reports*, vol. 23, pp. 352–353, (1956).
[51]The 1930 Hague Conference for the Codification of International Law was unable to formulate a draft convention on the responsibility of states because a large minority of delegates (17 of 40) favored the "equality of treatment" doctrine rather than the "international standard" doctrine. This minority was composed of the seven Latin American states that took part in the vote, four Asian and African states, five Eastern European states, and Portugal. Had all the Latin American states and the Soviet Union attended the Conference, there probably would have been a majority in support of the national standard.

Case 2–4   Cantero Herrera v. Canevaro & Co.

Peru, Supreme Court, 1927.
Annual Digest and Reports of International Law Cases, vol. 4, p. 219 (1927).

Cantero Herrera, a Cuban national residing in Lima, Peru, filed suit on July 22, 1913, as agent for certain nonresident Cuban citizens against a Peruvian national *named Cesar Saco y Flores in the Civil Court of Lima for partition and distribution of an inheritance in the estate known as "Huayto." Later, on September 29, 1913, the Sociedad Canevaro & Cia., also of Lima, was made a codefendant as the purchaser of the estate from Saco y Flores, and the Court was asked to declare the sale to it void.*

The court of first instance, on January 10, 1919, decided against Cantero Herrera and co-plaintiffs on three grounds: (1) that they had shown no right to the distribution they had asked for, (2) that the sale by Saco y Flores to Canevaro & Cia. was valid, and (3) that the action was barred by the statute of limitations. The Superior Court affirmed this judgment on September 23, 1920, and the Supreme Court on August 21, 1921.

The plaintiffs did nothing further until January 28, 1927. On that date, the Cuban Envoy Extraordinary and Minister Plenipotentiary at Lima sent a Note to the Foreign Minister of Peru. The Note impugned these judgments, alleging that they were tantamount to a denial of justice to the plaintiffs because they were contrary to Peruvian law. The Cuban Envoy therefore called upon the government of Peru to acknowledge that there had been a denial of justice and to make due reparations. The Peruvian government referred the matter to the Supreme Court.

OPINION OF THE SUPREME COURT:

Between Peru and Cuba there is no treaty regarding foreigners; but the tenor of our laws and the principles generally accepted, especially those proclaimed in American international law, are sufficient to make the question raised by the diplomatic representative of Cuba doctrinally simple.

The condition of foreigners in Peru, from the point of view of private rights, is not left entirely to the provisions on international convenience, nor subordinated to the simple fact of reciprocity, since Articles 32 and 33 of our Civil Code provide that "civil rights are independent of the status of the citizen," and that "foreigners enjoy in Peru all rights concerning the security of their person and property and the free administration of the same."

Equality between natives and foreigners before the Civil Law implies their equality as to judicial competence and form of proceeding in the same subject matter; hence, foreigners enjoy in Peru the same rights, means, recourses and guarantees as nationals to sue for and defend their rights; the *cautio judicatum solvi*[52] (which, as a dilatory objection against the alien [complainant], transient or without known assets, was allowed under the Code abrogated in 1912) is no longer in force notwithstanding that it is still sanctioned by legislation of some countries, including that of Cuba. . . .

The diplomatic representative of Cuba agrees, as must be true, that the ordinary suit commenced by Cantero Herrera against Saco and Canevaro came to a close with the judgment of the Supreme Court, dated 11 August, 1921. As a result, that judgment has placed a final, absolute and definitive seal upon all questions of a

MAP 2-4   Cuba and Peru (1927)

legal and juridical character ventilated in the litigation between the said parties, in conformity with the precepts of the Constitution and the laws of Peru, from whose sovereignty the foreigner litigating in the national jurisdiction cannot abstract himself, and which merely gives positive expression to the old classic adage *res judicata pro veritate habetur.*[53] . . .

There is no doubt that nations reciprocally owe one another justice, and are bound to extend it to foreigners having recourse to their tribunals and to give them the opportunity to obtain it in the like measure with nationals; but the good understanding among them, harmonizing all interests, has raised to the category of international law the authority of the thing adjudged, and no self-respecting country will countenance that any other country should impeach the force and legality of an executed judgment, rendered regularly by its authorities, as an emanation of sovereignty.

It is on this account that, in keeping with our political Constitution, it belongs to the President of the Republic, who represents abroad the national sovereignty, "to enforce, obligatorily, the judgments and resolutions of the tribunals and courts" (Article 121, par. 10); and Article 30 of the same Constitution contains this important provision, which it is timely to mention with respect to a claim growing out of litigation over territorial property:

---

[52]Latin: "to be exempted from a judgment bond." A preliminary motion allowed in some civil law countries until the early twentieth century that allowed a defendant to object that an alien plaintiff should not be allowed to proceed until he posted a bond.]
[53]Latin: "a thing is adjudged which is truly adjudged."]

"foreigners are, as to their property, in the same condition as Peruvians, and cannot in any case invoke with regard thereto an exceptional situation, nor have recourse to diplomatic claims. . . ."

It is erroneous to suppose that the conclusion of a proceeding in which a foreigner has failed, marks the occasion for the transference of the issue to the diplomatic plane. If it were so, the passions accumulated around matters of an entirely private nature would constantly poison the best-cemented international relations.

In the relations of nation to nation, the rule is respect for the sovereignty of friendly powers, typified in the authority of its judges and of its [courts'] decisions. The exception is the claim based on the motive of denial of justice; but to make such claim comfortable with the principles and usages of international law, it is necessary that the case be one of the utmost seriousness, that the denial of justice be manifest or notorious, that is, that the hearing which the foreigner claims, or the recourse which he interposes, has been denied him, and in general that the exercise of his rights and rights of action is interfered with contrary to law, or is subjected to unwarranted delays; because all this involves and constitutes an odious exception, a legal infringement which he establishes objectively, without offending the jurisdiction of the country, and which compromises the responsibility of the State.

Cantero Herrera has not been denied a hearing by our tribunals, nor the interposition of any recourse or means of defense permitted by the law, nor has he been subjected to any objectionable treatment. Neither can he aver, as has been alleged in other cases, that he has been cited before a court lacking jurisdiction, or has been judged without being summoned; being the plaintiff, he has selected the court and the proceeding, and with the most absolute freedom has pleaded at every stage, by word of mouth and in writing, everything he has deemed necessary in support of his right. Of what, then, does he complain? Of not having won the action? It is not on that condition, nor on any other, that the portals of justice are thrown open to the public authorities, to foreigners, or to anyone else. . . .

The claim was denied. ■

The International Standard of Care

international standard of care: Doctrine that a state is responsible for injuring an alien when the state's conduct violates international norms.

The standard of care favored by major Western countries is known as the **international standard**. This standard says that although a country has no obligation to admit aliens to its territory, once it does, it must treat them in a civilized manner. In the *Neer Claim*, the arbitrator held that the mistreatment of an alien constitutes a "delinquency" (and thus a violation of the international standard) if it "should amount to an outrage, to bad faith, to willful neglect of duty or to an insufficiency of governmental action so far short of international standards that every reasonable and impartial man would readily recognize its insufficiency."[54]

Such delinquencies can be either crimes or torts. In its 1979 *Draft Articles on State Responsibility*, the International Law Commission suggested that state acts are international crimes if they seriously breach international peace, deny peoples the right of self-determination, or fail to safeguard human life and dignity (e.g., slavery, genocide, and apartheid). Other breaches, according to the *Draft Articles*, are international torts.[55] The most common international tort is the expropriation or nationalization of aliens' and foreign businesses' property. "Denial of justice" is also a common tort. We will look at both these torts in the materials that follow.[56]

---

[54]*United Nations Reports of International Arbitral Awards,* vol. 4, p. 60 (1920).

[55]"1. An act of State which constitutes a breach of an international obligation is an international wrongful act, regardless of the subject matter of the obligation breached. 2. An internationally wrongful act which results from the breach by a State of an international obligation so essential for the protection of fundamental interests of the international community that its breach is recognized as a crime by that community as a whole, constitutes an international crime. 3. Subject to paragraph 2, and on the basis of the rules of international law in force, an international crime may result, *inter alia,* from: (a) a serious breach of an international obligation of essential importance for maintenance of international peace and security, such as that prohibiting aggression; (b) a serious breach of an international obligation of essential importance for safeguarding the right of self-determination of peoples, such as that prohibiting the establishment or maintenance by force of colonial domination; (c) a serious breach on a widespread scale of an international obligation of essential importance for safeguarding the human being, such as those prohibiting slavery, genocide, apartheid; (d) a serious breach of an international obligation of essential importance for the safeguarding and preservation of the human environment, such as those prohibiting massive pollution of the atmosphere or of the seas. 4. Any international wrongful act which is not an international crime in accordance with paragraph 2, constitutes an international delict." Article 19, International Law Commission Draft Articles on State Responsibility, 1979, in *Yearbook of the International Law Commission,* vol. 2, pt. 2, p. 90 (1979).

[56]International crimes are examined in the next chapter and in Ray August, *Public International Law: Text, Cases, and Readings* (1995).

Expropriation

expropriation: (From Latin *expropriare:* "to take away one's own.") A taking of private property by a government.

Expropriation or nationalization is the taking or deprivation of the property of foreigners. The right of states to expropriate foreign property is universally recognized, as is its analogy in municipal law, the right of eminent domain. Western countries regard expropriation, much as they regard eminent domain, as proper so long as it is done for a legitimate public purpose and the state pays prompt, adequate, and effective compensation.

Some controversy exists over whether the public-purpose element is required. Some argue that it is,[57] others that it should be expressed only as a requirement not to discriminate against a particular class of foreigners. For example, in the *LIAMCO Case*, which involved the expropriation of an American oil company by Libya, the arbitrator stated:

> As to the contention that the said measures were politically motivated and not in pursuance of a legitimate public purpose, it is the general opinion in international theory that the public utility principle is not a necessary requisite for the legality of a nationalization. This principle was mentioned by Grotius and other later publicists, but now there is no international authority, from a judicial or any other source, to support its application to nationalization. . . .
>
> However, political motivation may take the shape of discrimination as a result of political retaliation . . . [and it] . . . is clear and undisputed that nondiscrimination is a requisite for the validity of a lawful nationalization. . . . Therefore, a purely discriminatory nationalization is illegal and wrongful."[58]

For practical considerations (i.e., given the difficulty of defining a public purpose), this is probably the best rule, and the one most likely to be applied by tribunals.

The meaning that the major Western industrial powers give to the phrase "prompt, adequate and effective compensation" was succinctly stated by the plaintiff in its pleadings in the *Anglo-Iranian Oil Co. (United Kingdom v. Iran) Case*. The case involved the expropriation of British-owned oil companies in Iran. The plaintiff, the United Kingdom, stated:

> . . . it is clear that the nationalization of the property of foreigners, even if not unlawful on any other ground, becomes an unlawful confiscation unless the provision is made for compensation which is adequate, prompt and effective. By "adequate" compensation is meant "the value of the undertaking at the moment of dispossession, plus interest to the day of judgment"—per the . . . *Chorzów Factory Case.*
>
> . . . [Second, the requirement for] prompt compensation means immediate payment in cash. . . .
>
> The third requirement is summed up in the word "effective" and means that the recipient of the compensation must be able to make use of it. . . . Monetary compensation which is in blocked currency is not effective. . . .[59]

The adequacy of compensation, the meaning of discrimination, and the question of whether a nationalization decree can be applied extraterritorially are considered in Case 2–5.

---

[57]In the BP Exploration Co. (Libya), Ltd. v. Libyan Arab Republic Case, Libya nationalized a British Petroleum subsidiary operating in Libya but did not nationalize property belonging to other foreign oil companies. Libya was seeking to retaliate against the United Kingdom (which then owned a substantial share of BP) for the United Kingdom's refusal to help a Libyan ally in the Persian Gulf prevent Iran from occupying certain islands the ally claimed. The arbitrator held as follows: "The BP Nationalization Law, and the actions taken thereunder by the Respondent, do constitute a fundamental breach of the BP Concession as they amount to a total repudiation of the agreement and the obligations of the Respondent thereunder, and, on the basis of rules of applicable systems of law too elementary and voluminous to require or permit citation, the Tribunal so holds. Further, the taking by the Respondent of the property, rights and interests of the Claimant clearly violates public international law as it was made for purely extraneous political reasons and was arbitrary and discriminatory in character. Nearly two years have now passed since the nationalization, and the fact that no offer of compensation has been made indicates that the taking was also confiscatory." *International Law Reports,* vol. 53. p. 297 (1974).

[58]Because "Libya's motive for nationalization was its desire to preserve the ownership of oil," the arbitrator concluded that the expropriation was not discriminatory. Libyan American Oil Co. (LIAMCO) v. Government of the Libyan Arab Republic, *International Legal Materials,* vol. 20, p. 1 at p. 58 (1981).

[59]*International Court of Justice Pleadings,* vol. 1952, p. 105 (1952).

Case 2–5   ACSYNGO v. Compagnie de Saint-Gobain (France), SA

Belgium, Commercial Court of Namur, 1986.
Revue pratique des sociétés, vol. 85 (1986); *International Legal Materials,* vol. 26, p. 1251 (1987); *International Law Reports,* vol. 82, p. 128 (1990).

By a law adopted on February 11, 1982, France nationalized various industrial concerns, banks, and financial institutions, including the French conglomerate Compagnie de Saint-Gobain. The nationalization decree transferred to the French state those shares in the nationalized firms that were held by private investors. Compensation was paid for the shares based on their average quoted price on the stock exchange during a reference period, adjusted to take into account inflation and lost dividends.

The Compagnie de Saint-Gobain owned, either directly or through its Dutch and Swiss subsidiaries, 50.04 percent of the stock of Glaceries de Saint-Roch, a Belgian company. In August 1981, the affected shareholders of the French company formed an association known as the Syndicate of Shareholders in the Compagnie de Saint-Gobain (ACSYNGO). In June 1982, ACSYNGO initiated proceedings in Belgium claiming that the former shareholders it represented were the real owners of the stock of Glaceries de Saint-Roch and that the Compagnie de Saint-Gobain and its subsidiaries should be divested of their controlling interest in the Belgian company. They argued that to allow the French company and its foreign subsidiaries to retain their ownership interest in the Belgian company would amount to giving extraterritorial effect to a foreign nationalization decree that was both expropriatory and discriminatory.

JUDGMENT: . . .

I. Requirements for Recognizing the Foreign Nationalization of Private Property

* * *

In order to satisfy international public policy, the nationalization of private property cannot be expropriatory nor discriminatory. These requirements have been recited frequently in Belgium, even though the Court of Cassation has yet to enshrine them in a decision *de principe.*[60]

(a) A Nationalization Decree May Not Be Expropriatory.
According to French legal doctrine, the nationalization of private property only amounts to an improper expropria-

MAP 2-5   France and Belgium (1986)

tion if the compensation offered the property's owners is inadequate.[61] According to the law of Belgium, property owners must be given compensation that is both fair and adequate. The method for compensating owners [of nationalized property] established by Articles 4 and 5 of the French Law of February 11, 1982, . . . makes use of the average quoted stock exchange price during a particular reference period and then adjusts this price upwards by 14 percent as an offset for inflation and lost dividends.

Using this method, the value of a share of Saint-Gobain stock was fixed at 174 French francs. For the six month period immediately preceding the French legislative elections of May 10, 1981, the highest stock exchange price for a share was 142 French francs. Except for a brief period in October 1978 when the quoted price reached 178 francs, one has to go back to 1973 in order to find a price of 175 francs or more.

According to Belgian law, international public policy does not demand that compensation be based on the full value of the particular assets being nationalized or that the

---

[60French: "of principle." A decision *de principe* made by the Court of Cassation, the highest appellate court in Belgium, is binding on lower courts.]
61Batiffol and Lagarde, *Droit international privé,* vol. 2, no. 523, and the references cited in note 38 *bis.*

value be determined according to particular accounting principles. In this case, where the value of a share was based on the average quoted stock exchange price adjusted for inflation and lost dividends, we cannot, from the point of view of public international law, say that the compensation paid shareholders was a violation of that policy. . . .

In this case, the compensation was both fair and adequate as those terms are defined by Belgian law. The nationalization of the shares of Saint-Gobain cannot be held to be confiscatory.

(b) A Nationalization Decree May Not Be Discriminatory. The principle of nondiscrimination does not prevent a State from enacting laws that treat persons differently in different situations. Put another way, different treatment is allowed when different persons are involved in different circumstances. This principle, which was adopted by the French Constitutional Council on January 17, 1979,[62] is also applicable in Belgium.

It is true that France did not nationalize those shares of the Compagnie de Saint-Gobain (approximately 40 percent of the total of all shares) that were already owned by public sector companies. However, since those shares were already indirectly owned by the public, it was pointless for France to do so.

The Law of February 11, 1982, does not discriminate on the basis of race, religion, or political preference. Even though it is directed at specific economic sectors, this is not an improper form of discrimination.

In sum, the rules governing the legality of a nationalization decree carried out by a foreign State within its own territory have not been violated.

Nevertheless, the fact that private property located within a State's territory has been nationalized in accordance with these rules does not legitimize an extraterritorial nationalization of property located outside the State's territory. We turn now to examine that problem.

II. Does the French Law of February 11, 1982, Have Extraterritorial Effect?

(a) The Problem. . . .   Both the case law and the commentators who have written on this subject, at least in the West, generally regard nationalization decrees as having a strictly territorial scope.

This territoriality rule means that a nationalization decree will have no effect on assets located outside the territory of the nationalizing State on the date the decree

is enacted.[63] This is because a State's sovereignty over assets located within its territory ends at its borders, and a State cannot enact decrees appropriating property when the property is beyond the reach of its sovereignty. . . .

The rule that "a nationalization decree can only have effect within the territory of the nationalizing State" has been adopted by the French Court of Cassation.[64] . . .

While this rule has been applied on a number of occasions in Belgium, it should be noted that in each instance the particular nationalization decree was held to have been illegal because it was confiscatory or because it involved ethnic discrimination. This was so in the cases involving the nationalization decrees adopted in the Union of Soviet Socialist Republics,[65] in Germany by the Nazi regime,[66] in Mexico,[67] in Hungary,[68] and finally in Czechoslovakia.[69] . . .

In light of the above, the problem facing us is best framed as follows: Does the rule of international law making the exercise of foreign sovereign acts within Belgium illegal mean that the French nationalization decree is illegal if it produces effects within Belgium?

The French Law [of February 11, 1982,] did not directly nationalize S.A. Glacieres de Saint-Roch [the Belgian subsidiary of the Compagnie de Saint-Gobain]. The Law did not directly transfer to the French State the majority of shares in the Belgian company. Rather, according to the claimants, it was through the intermediary of the Compagnie de Saint-Gobain and its other subsidiaries that the Belgian company was indirectly nationalized by France.

Strictly speaking, the French Parliament only mandated the transfer to the French State of the ownership assets legally situated in France. . . .

As a consequence, there has been no change in the identity of the shareholders of the Belgian subsidiary. According to French law, the French company and its Swiss and Dutch subsidiaries were and continue to be the owners of the majority of the shares of Glaceries de Saint-Roch. . . .

(b) The Arguments of the Parties.   The claimants argue that France has "indirectly nationalized" the [non-French] assets of the Compagnie de Saint-Gobain. With regard to the assets located in Belgium, the claimants contend that France's indirect acquisition of the majority of the shares in Glaceries de Saint-Roch is a State action that violates the sovereignty of Belgium. . . .

---

[62]*Journal Officiel de la République Française,* p. 173.

[63]Rigaux and Verhoeven, "Nationalisations et relations internationales," *Journal des tribunaux,* no. 13 (1982).

[64]Cassation of February 20, 1979, *Revue critique de droit international privé,* p. 803 (1979), with note by Batiffol; [*International Law Reports,* vol. 80, p. 428 (1989)].

[65]Decision of June 11, 1936, Appeals Court, Brussels, *Belgique judiciare,* vol. 1937, p. 590; Decision of June 25, 1947, Commercial Court, Brussels, *Revue pratique des sociétés,* vol. 1948, p. 67.

[66]Decision of June 9, 1938, Commercial Court, Brussels, *Belgique judiciare,* vol. 1939, p. 563.

[67]Decision of February 21, 1939, Civil Court, Antwerp, *Belgique judiciare,* vol. 1939, p. 372.

[68]Decision of May 24, 1951, Commercial Court, Brussels, *Revue pratique des sociétés,* vol. 1954, p. 90.

[69]Decision of March 17, 1959, Appeals Court, Brussels, *Pasicrisie Belge,* vol. 2, p. 148 (1960) and Cassation of June 2, 1960, *Revue critique de judiciare Belge,* vol. 1962, p. 446.

The defendants . . . argue that treating an indirect nationalization in the same way as a direct nationalization is a mistaken misapplication of a rule of international law that is only meant to apply to uncompensated expropriations of private property.

(c) The Difficulties Raised by the Claimants' Theory. According to the claimants, the consequence of France's illegal State action is that "the former shareholders of the French parent company are and continue to be the owners of the Belgian company of Glaceries de Saint-Roch and only those former shareholders can lawfully exercise the voting rights inherent in the shares of both the French parent company and its Swiss and Dutch subsidiaries." . . .

This theory of the claimants is similar to the German theory of the *"Spaltgesellschaft."*[70] The essence of this theory is that it is impossible to separate the assets of a company located outside the territory of a nationalizing State from the rights of the company's shareholders in those assets. Thus, if one State were to nationalize a company with assets in another State, a splinter or residual company would automatically come into existence in that other State, and its shareholders would be the shareholders of the original nationalized company.[71]

[This German theory, however, has an important exception. That is,] . . . a shareholder who receives full compensation for the nationalized assets of a foreign company would be acting improperly (i.e., in bad faith) if he invoked the theory in order to obtain recognition of his continuing title in that part of the nationalized assets located within Germany.[72] . . .

[Aside from this exception, there are other problems with the claimants' theory.] What happens when the some of the shareholders do not invoke their rights or invoke them late? Does [the splinter or residual] company continue to exist between the date [when the original company] is nationalized and the date when a court hands down a decision on a claim made by the former shareholders? Can a [splinter or residual] company receive payments in discharge of obligations owed to it during this time? How should an increase in capitalization be treated (as actually happened in this case when capital was increased by one billion Belgian francs in 1982)? How are the creditors of the different companies to be protected . . . ? Do shareholders implicitly renounce the right to make any further claims when they accept compensation under a nationalization decree? Finally, what happens in the event of reprivatization? . . .

III. Additional Grounds . . .

The problems raised by the present dispute are of considerable interest both with respect to determining the applicable law and with respect to the economic and social repercussions which the decision sought by the claimants might produce. . . . It appears that American law recognizes the extraterritorial effects of a nationalization decree so long as the decree is adopted in a democratic manner and it provides for appropriate compensation.[73] . . .

Swiss commentators, with some caution, have deduced [from decisions of the Swiss Supreme Court] that the territoriality rule should not be applied if the economic consequences would be inappropriate.[74]

We believe, similarly, that the appropriation of the . . . foreign assets [of a private person] is lawful if the appropriation does not violate the public policy (i.e., the public order and interest) of the State where the assets are located.

In sum, we will recognize that a foreign nationalization may lawfully have extraterritorial effects in Belgium if this is the only reasonable way to protect the Belgian interests involved. This is especially so in the case where the value of the assets located in Belgium are totally dependent on the value of the main assets located abroad. In this case, we take note of the fact that the economic, social, and financial value of the Belgian company (S.A. Glaceries de Saint-Roch) is very much dependent on its membership in the Compagnie de Saint-Gobain group.

In the glass sector alone, the net profit of the Saint-Gobain group increased from 31 million French francs in 1982 to 139 million in 1985. Overall, its net profit increased from 371 million French francs in 1982 to 753 million in 1985.[75] The profits for the first reporting period of 1986 are nearly double those for the same period in 1985.[76] Preserving these links [between the Belgian subsidiary and the French group] is, therefore, clearly in the best interest of Belgium.

For these reasons the Court . . . Holds that the action is unfounded. ■

---

[70]German: "split company."]

[71]Tribunal, District of Zurich, 1958, *Außenwirtschaftsdienst,* vol. 1958, p. 80.

[72]Prof. Seidl-Hohenveldren, Unpublished Paper No. 26, Symposium on the International Effects of Nationalizations at the Institut du droit et des pratiques internationales (Paris, February 18–19, 1982).

[73]Ira M. Millstein, Report to a Colloquium at the International Chamber of Commerce (Paris, February 18–19, 1982); *confirm* Matthias, *Recht der Internationalem Wirtschaft,* pp. 640–644 (1982); Goldman, "Décision du Conseil constitutionel relatives aux Nationalisations et Droit International," *Journal de droit international (Clunet),* vol. 1982, p. 316.

[74]Vannond, *Fragen des Internationalen Enteignungs-und Konfiskationsrechts,* p. 32, n. 23 (Thesis, Zurich, 1959); Vischer, *Droit international privé,* p. 11.

[75]"La Vie Economique," *Le Figaro,* p. 18 (October 7, 1986).

[76]*Le Monde,* p. 34 (October 8, 1986).

Many Third World countries object to the requirement of adequate compensation when, as the Western countries would have it, it is for full market value. They argue that factors (such as colonial domination) should be taken into consideration, and two United Nations General Assembly Resolutions have taken that viewpoint.[77] Western commentators, however, have interpreted the Resolutions as only setting out a long-term goal and not expressing the current status of customary international law.

Possibly the best statement of the Third World position is given in Case 2–6.

---

[77]UN General Assembly Resolution 1803 (XVII) on Permanent Sovereignty over Natural Resources, 1963, in *United Nations General Assembly Official Record*, 17th Sess., supp. 17, p. 15, states, in Article 4: "Nationalization, expropriation or requisitioning shall be based on grounds or reasons of public utility, security or the national interest which are recognized as overriding purely individual or private interests, both domestic and foreign. In such cases the owner shall be paid appropriate compensation *in accordance with the rules in force in the State* taking such measures in the exercise of its sovereignty and in accordance with international law. In any case where the question of compensation gives rise to a controversy, the national jurisdiction of the State taking such measures shall be exhausted. However, upon agreement by sovereign States and other parties concerned, settlement of the dispute should be made through arbitration or international adjudication." (Emphasis added.)

And the Charter of Economic Rights and Duties of States, 1974, UN General Assembly Resolution 3281 (XXIX), *International Legal Materials*, vol. 14, p. 251, provides in Article 2(2)(c): "Each State has the right . . . to nationalize, expropriate or transfer ownership of foreign property, in which case appropriate compensation should be paid by the State adopting such measures, taking into account its relevant laws and regulations and all circumstances that the State considers pertinent. . . ."

Case 2–6   Case Concerning Barcelona Traction, Light, and Power Company, Ltd. (Second Phase)

Belgium v. Spain

International Court of Justice, 1970.
International Court of Justice Reports, vol. 1970, p. 3 (1970).

Barcelona Traction, Light, and Power Company, Ltd. (Barcelona Traction) manufactured and supplied electricity in Spain. Although doing business in Spain, it was incorporated in Canada and maintained its headquarters in Toronto. The company issued corporate bonds to investors outside of Spain. During the Spanish Civil War (1936–1939), the government of Spain refused to allow Barcelona Traction to transfer currency from Spain to pay interest to the bondholders. The interest payments were never resumed.

In 1948, several Spaniards purchased some of the bonds and then brought suit in a Spanish court asking it to declare Barcelona Traction bankrupt because it had failed to pay the interest on the bonds. The court did so and, following several motions and appeals, all of the assets in Spain belonging to the company were finally sold by public auction in 1952. The proceeds from the sale were distributed to creditors and only a very small sum was to be paid to shareholders.

The shareholders then sought the assistance of their home states in seeking to obtain a larger settlement. Canada,

among other states, complained to Spain of denials of justice and of the violation of certain treaties it alleged were applicable. Canada, however, eventually agreed that Spain had acted properly in denying Barcelona Traction the right to transfer currency abroad and later in declaring the company bankrupt.

Belgium took an interest in the matter because Belgians owned 88 percent of the shares in Barcelona Traction. It disagreed that Spain had acted properly and after Spain became a member of the United Nations in 1955, Belgium filed a complaint before the International Court of Justice in 1958. The proceedings were suspended and then discontinued while representatives of the private interests concerned carried on negotiations. When the negotiations failed, Belgium submitted a new application to the Court in 1962.

Spain promptly objected that Belgium could not sponsor Barcelona Traction's or its shareholders' complaints because Barcelona Traction was a Canadian company.

JUDGMENT OF THE COURT: . . .

When a State admits into its territory foreign investments or foreign nationals, whether natural or juristic persons, it is bound to extend to them the protection of

MAP 2-6 Spain and Belgium (1948)

the law and assumes obligations concerning the treatment to be afforded them. . . .

SEPARATE OPINION OF JUDGE PADILLA NERVO [OF MEXICO]: . . .

The history of the responsibility of States in respect to the treatment of foreign nationals is the history of abuses, illegal interference in the domestic jurisdiction of weaker States, unjust claims, threats and even military aggression under the flag of exercising rights of protection, and the imposing of sanctions in order to oblige a government to make the reparations demanded.

Special agreements to establish arbitral tribunals were on many occasions concluded under pressure, by political, economic or military threats.

The protecting States, in many instances, are more concerned with obtaining financial settlements than with preserving principles. Against the pressure of diplomatic protection, weaker States could do no more than to preserve and defend a principle of international law, while giving way under the guise of accepting friendly settlements, either giving the compensation demanded or by establishing claims commissions which had as a point of departure the acceptance of responsibility for acts or omissions, where the government was, neither in fact nor in law, really responsible.

In the written and in the oral pleadings the Applicant has made reference, in support of his thesis, to arbitral decisions of claims commissions—among others those between Mexico and the United States, 1923.

These decisions do not necessarily give expression to rules of customary international law, as . . . the Commissions were authorized to decide these claims "in accordance with principles of international law, justice and equity," and, therefore, may have been influenced by other than strictly legal considerations.[78] . . .

Now the evolution of international law has other horizons and its progressive development is more promising, as Rosenne wrote:

There is prevalent in the world today a widespread questioning of the contemporary international law. This feeling is based on the view that for the greater part international law is the product of European imperialism and colonialism and does not take sufficient account of the completely changed pattern of international relations which now exists. . . .

Careful scrutiny of the record of the Court may lead to the conclusion that it has been remarkably perceptive of the changing currents of international thought. In this respect it has performed a major service to the international community as a whole, because the need to bring international law into line with present-day requirements and conditions is real and urgent.[79]

The law, in all its aspects, the jurisprudence and the practice of States change as the world and the everyday requirements of international life change, but those responsible for its progressive evolution should take care that their decisions do, in the long run, contribute to the maintenance of peace and security and the betterment of the majority of mankind.

In considering the needs and the good of the international community in our changing world, one must realize that there are more important aspects than those concerned with economic interests and profit making; other legitimate interests of a political and moral nature are at stake and should be considered in judging the behavior and operation of the complex international scope of modern commercial enterprises.

It is not the shareholders in those huge corporations who are in need of diplomatic protection; it is rather the poorer or weaker States, where the investments take place, who need to be protected against encroachment by powerful financial groups, or against unwarranted diplomatic pressure from governments who appear to be always ready to back at any rate their national shareholders, even when they are legally obliged to share the risk of their corporation and follow its fate, or even in

[78]Georg Schwarzenberger, *International Law,* vol. 1, p. 201 (1945).
[79]Shabtai Rosenne, *The Law and Practice of the International Court,* vol. 1, pp. 17–18 (1965).

case of shareholders who are not or have never been under the limited jurisdiction of the State *of residence* accused of having violated in respect of them certain fundamental rights concerning the treatment of foreigners. It can be said that, by the mere fact of the existence of certain rules concerning the treatment of foreigners, these have certain fundamental rights that the State *of residence* cannot violate without incurring international responsibility; but this is not the case of foreign shareholders as such, who may be scattered all over the world and have never been or need not be *residents* of the respondent State or under its jurisdiction.

In the case of the *Rosa Gelbtrunk* claim between Salvador and the United States, the President of the arbitration commission expressed a view which may summarize the position of foreigners in a country where they are resident. This view was expressed as follows:

> A citizen or subject of one nation who, in the pursuit of commercial enterprise, carries on trade within the territory and under the protection of the sovereignty of a nation other than his own, is to be considered *as having cast in his lot* with the subjects or citizens of the State in which he *resides* and carries on business. (Italics added.)

"In this case," Schwarzenberger remarks, "the rule was applied to the loss of foreign property in the course of a civil war. The decision touches, however, one aspect of a much wider problem: the existence of international minimum standards, by which, regarding foreigners, territorial jurisdiction is limited." . . .

Much has been said about the justification for not leaving the shareholders in those enterprises without protection.

Perhaps modern international business practice has a tendency to be soft and partial towards the powerful and the rich, but no rule of law could be built on such flimsy bases.

Investors who go abroad in search of profits take a risk and go there for better or for worse, not only for better. They should respect the institutions and abide by the national laws of the country where they chose to go. ■

Denial of Justice

A **denial of justice** is said to exist "when there is a denial, unwarranted delay or obstruction of access to courts, gross deficiency in the administration of judicial or remedial process, failure to provide those guarantees which are generally considered indispensable to the proper administration of justice, or a manifestly unjust judgment. An error of a national court which does not produce a manifest injustice is not a denial of justice."[80]

As with the expropriation cases, the states that advocate the application of a national standard emphasize that notions of justice are relative to each society and that whether or not there has been a denial of justice with respect to a particular case requires an understanding of the judicial system of the society where the case arose.

Both the international standard and the national standard are illustrated in Case 2–7.

---

[80]Harvard Draft Convention on the Responsibility of States for Damage Done in Their Territory to the Person or Property of Foreigners, 1929, Article 9.

Case 2–7   Chattin v. United Mexican States

Mexico–United States General Claims Commission, 1927. *United Nations Reports of International Arbitral Awards,* vol. 4, p. 282.

PRESIDING COMMISSIONER VAN VOLLENHOVEN:

This claim is made by the United States of America against the United Mexican States on behalf of B. E. Chattin, an American national. Chattin, who since 1908 was an employee (at first freight conductor, thereafter passenger conductor) of the Ferrocarril Sud-Pacifico de Mexico (Southern Pacific Railroad Company of Mexico) and who in the Summer of 1910 performed his duties in the State of Sinaloa, was on July 9, 1910, arrested at Mazatlán, Sinaloa, on a charge of embezzlement; was tried there in January 1911, convicted on February 6, 1911, and sentenced to two years imprisonment; but was released from the jail at Mazatlán in May or June 1911, as a consequence of disturbances caused by the Madero revolution. He then returned to the United States. It is alleged that the arrest, the trial, and the sentence were illegal, that the treatment in jail was inhuman, and that Chattin was damaged to the extent of $50,000, which amount Mexico should pay. . . .

. . . On or about July 8, 1910, one Cenobio Ramírez, a Mexican employee (brakeman) of the [Southern Pacific Railroad Company] . . . , was arrested at Mazatlán on a charge of fraudulent sale of railroad tickets of the said company, and in his appearance before the District Court in that town he accused the conductor Chattin—who since May 9, 1910, had charge of trains operating between Mazatlán and Acaponeta, Nayarit—as the principal in the crime which he, Ramírez was charged; whereupon Chattin also was arrested by the Mazatlán police, on July 9 (not 10), 1910. On August 3 (not 13), 1910, his case was consolidated not only with that of Ramírez, but also with that of three more American railway conductors (Haley, Englehart, and Parrish) and of four Mexicans. After many months of preparation and a trial at Mazatlán, during both of which Chattin, it is alleged, lacked proper information, legal assistance, assistance of an interpreter and confrontation with the witnesses, he was convicted on February 6, 1911, by the said District Court of Mazatlán as stated above. The case was carried on appeal to the Third Circuit Court at Mexico City, which court on July 3, 1911, affirmed the sentence. In the meantime (May or June, 1911) Chattin had been released by the population of Mazatlán which threw open the doors of the jail in the time elapsing between the departure of the representatives of the Diaz regime and the arrival of the Madero forces. . . .

MAP 2-7   Sinaloa and Nayarit, Mexico (1911)

IRREGULARITY OF COURT PROCEEDINGS

. . . For undue delay of the proceedings . . . , there is convincing evidence in more than one respect. The formal proceedings began on July 9, 1910. Chattin was not heard in court until more than one hundred days thereafter. The stubs and perhaps other pieces of evidence against Chattin were presented to the Court on August 3, 1910; Chattin, however, was not allowed to testify regarding them until October 28, 1910. Between the end of July and October 8, 1910, the judge merely waited. . . . Another remarkable proof of the measure of speed which the Judge deemed due to a man deprived of his liberty, is in that, whereas Chattin appealed from the decree of his formal imprisonment on July 11, 1910—an appeal which would seem to be of rather an urgent character—"the corresponding copy for the appeal" was not remitted to the appellate Court until September 12, 1910; this Court did not render judgment until October 27, 1910; and though its decision was forwarded to Mazatlán on October 31, 1910, its receipt was not established until November 12, 1910. . . .

The allegation . . . that the accused had not been duly informed regarding the charge brought against him is proven by the record, and to a painful extent. The real complainant in this case was the railroad company, acting through its general manager; this manager, an American, not only was allowed to make full statement to the Court . . . without ever being confronted with the accused and his colleagues, but he was even allowed to submit to the Court a series of anonymous written accusations. . . . Were they made known to the conductors? . . . [O]n August 3, 1910, they were ordered added to the court record; but that same day they were delivered to a translator; and they did not reappear on the court record until after January 16, 1911, when the investigations were over and Chattin's lawyer had filed his briefs. . . .

The allegations . . . that the accused lacked counsel and an interpreter are disproven by the records of the court proceedings. . . .

The allegation . . . that the witnesses were not sworn is irrelevant, as Mexican law does not require an "oath" (it is satisfied with a solemn promise, *protesta*, to tell the truth), nor do international standards of civilization. . . .

The allegation . . . that the hearings in open court lasted only some five minutes is proven by the record. This trial in open court was held on January 27, 1911. It was a pure formality, in which only confirmations were made of written documents, and in which not even the lawyer of the accused conductors took the trouble to say more than a word or two. . . .

CONVICTION ON INSUFFICIENT EVIDENCE

. . . From the record there is not convincing evidence that the proof against Chattin, scanty and weak though it may have been, was not such as to warrant a conviction. . . . The allegation that the Court in this matter was biased against American citizens would seem to be contradicted by the fact that, together with four Americans, five Mexicans were indicted as well, four of whom had been caught and have subsequently been convicted—that one of these Mexicans was punished as severely as the Americans were—and that the lower penalties imposed on the three others are explained by motives which, even if not shared, would seem reasonable. . . .

MISTREATMENT IN PRISON

The allegation of the claimant regarding mistreatment in the jail at Mazatlán refers to filthy and unsanitary conditions, bad food, and frequent compulsion to witness the shooting of prisoners. . . . The statement made in the Mexican reply brief that "a jail is a place of punishment, and not a place of pleasure" can have no bearing on the cases of Chattin and his colleagues, who were not convicts in prison, but persons in detention and presumed to be innocent until the Court held the contrary. On the record as it stands, however, inhuman treatment in jail is not proven.

CONCLUSION

Bringing the proceedings of Mexican authorities against Chattin to the test of international standards . . . , there can be no doubt of their being highly insufficient. Inquiring whether there is convincing evidence of these unjust proceedings . . . , the answer must be in the affirmative. Since this is a case of alleged responsibility of Mexico for injustice committed by its judiciary, it is necessary to inquire whether the treatment of Chattin amounts even to an outrage, to bad faith, to willful neglect of duty, or to an insufficiency of governmental action recognizable by every unbiased man . . . ; and the answer here again can only be in the affirmative.

An illegal arrest of Chattin is not proved. Irregularity of court proceedings is proven with reference to absence of proper investigations, insufficiency of confrontations, withholding from the accused the opportunity to know all of the charges brought against him, undue delay of the proceedings, making the hearings in open court a mere formality, and a continued absence of seriousness on the part of the Court. Insufficiency of evidence against Chattin is not convincingly proven; intentional severity of the punishment is proven, without

its being shown that the explanation is to be found in the unfairmindedness of the Judge. Mistreatment in prison is not proven. Taking into consideration, on the one hand, that this is a case of direct governmental responsibility, and on the other hand, that Chattin, because of his escape, has stayed in jail for eleven months instead of for two years, it would seem proper to allow in behalf of this claimant damages in the sum of $5,000 without interest.

DISSENTING OPINION OF COMMISSIONER FERNANDEZ MACGREGOR: . . .

. . . All the criticism which has been made of these proceedings, I regret to say, appears to arise from lack of knowledge of the judicial system and practice of Mexico, and, what is more dangerous, from the application thereto of tests belonging to foreign systems of law. For example, in some of the latter the investigation of a crime is made only by the police magistrates and the trial proper is conducted by the judge. Hence the reluctance in accepting that one same judge may have the two functions and that, therefore, he may have to receive in the preliminary investigation (*instrucción*) of the case all kinds of data, with the obligation, of course, of not taking them into account at the time of judgment, if they have no probative weight. It is certain that the secret report, so much discussed in this case, would have been received by the police of the countries which place the investigation exclusively in the hands of such branch. This same police would have been free to follow all the clues or to abandon them at its discretion; but the Judge is criticized here because he did not follow up completely the clue given by Ramírez with respect to Chattin. The same domestic test—to call it such—is used to understand what is a trial or open trial imagining at the same time that it must have the sacred forms of common law and without remembering that the same goal is reached by many roads. And the same can be said when speaking of the manner of taking testimony of witnesses, of cross-examination, of holding confrontations, etc.

In view of the above considerations, I am of the opinion that the claim should be disallowed. ∎

C. OBJECTIONS

States can raise several objections to complaints brought against them, including lack of standing, lack of nationality, lack of a genuine link, and failure to exhaust remedies.

lack of standing:
Objection that may be made to an international tribunal's exercise of jurisdiction when a plaintiff is not qualified to appear before the court.

Lack of Standing

A common objection states raise to being sued in international tribunals is **lack of standing**. That is, if a plaintiff is a person not qualified to appear before the particular court, the case must be dismissed. In most international tribunals, such as the International Court of Justice, only a *state* can file a complaint. If a private person or company were to appear as a plaintiff, the case would be dismissed for want of standing.[81] In these tribunals, the only way for the matter to be heard is for a state to sponsor the suit of its national.[82]

Lack of Nationality

lack of nationality of the claim: Objection that may be made to an international tribunal's exercise of jurisdiction when the state bringing suit is doing so on behalf of a person who is not a national of that state.

An objection related to lack of standing is **lack of nationality**. Although a state may bring a complaint in an international tribunal on behalf of one of its own nationals, it may not do so on behalf of any other person.

This rule is easily applied with respect to persons with a single nationality and to stateless persons (the first have a claim if they are sponsored by the state of their nationality; the second cannot be sponsored by any state). Its application becomes more complex, however, with dual nationals. The traditional rule is that either state can complain as to a third state; but between the two, neither can complain.[83] In the *Canevaro Case*, a person who had both Italian and Peruvian nationality sought the sponsorship of Italy in a complaint against Peru. The Permanent Court of Arbitration said:

> And whereas, as a matter of fact, Raphael Canevaro has on several occasions acted as a Peruvian citizen, both by running as a candidate for the Senate, where none are admitted except Peruvian citizens, and where he went to defend his election, and also especially by accepting the office of Consul General of the Netherlands, after soliciting the authorization of the Peruvian Government and then of the Peruvian Congress; And whereas, under these circumstances, whatever Raphael Canevaro's status may be in Italy with respect to his nationality, the Government of Peru has a right to consider him as a Peruvian citizen and to deny his status as an Italian claimant."[84]

Following World War II, however, a new rule evolved that allows the state of which the individual has the "master" nationality (i.e., the one with which he has the most links) to complain against the other. Thus, in the *Mergé Claim*, where the injured individual was both an Italian and an American citizen, the Italian–United States Conciliation Commission recognized that the United States had the right to sponsor a complaint against Italy. It stated:

> In view of the principles accepted, it is considered that the government of the United States of America shall be entitled to protect nationals before this Commission in cases of dual nationality, United States and Italian, whenever the United States nationality is the effective nationality. In order to establish the prevalence of the United States nationality in individual cases, habitual residence can be one of the criteria of evaluation, but not the only one. The conduct of the individual in his economic, social, political, civic and family life, as well as the closer and more effective bond with one of the two States must be considered.[85]

Effect of an Injured Person's Waiver of the Right of His National State to Bring Suit on His Behalf
Because the right to sue in most international tribunals belongs only to the state, the state has full control over the action. It can refuse to bring the complaint, it can abandon it, or it can settle it adversely to the interests of its national. But this being so, can the state bring the complaint over

---

[81]The lack of standing objection would obviously not apply in tribunals such as the International Center for the Settlement of Investment Disputes or the European Court of Human Rights, where the right of private persons to bring actions against a state is allowed.

[82]In the Mavrommatis Palestine Concessions Case, the Permanent Court said: "By taking up the case of one of its subjects and by resorting to diplomatic action or international judicial proceedings on his behalf, a State is in reality asserting its own rights—its right to ensure, in the person of its subjects, respect for the rules of international law." *Permanent Court of International Justice Reports,* Series A, No. 2, p. 12 (1924).

[83]The rule can be found in the 1930 Hague Convention on Certain Questions Relating to the Conflict of Nationality Laws, *League of Nations Treaty Series,* vol. 179, p. 189. Article 4 provides: "A State may not afford diplomatic protection to one of its own nationals against a State whose nationality such person also possesses."

[84]Award of the Permanent Court of Arbitration, 1912. An English translation is found in the *American Journal of International Law,* vol. 6, p. 746 (1912).

[85]After examining the facts of the case, the Commission found that the claimant could not satisfy the test. *International Law Reports,* vol. 22, p. 443 (1955). This test was subsequently adopted by the Iran-United States Claims Tribunal in the case of Esphahanian v. Bank Tejarat, *Iran-United States Claims Tribunal Reports,* vol. 2, p. 171 (1983); *International Law Reports,* vol. 72, p. 479 (1987).

Calvo Clause: A clause in an agreement between a host state and a foreign investor that says that the investor will not seek the diplomatic assistance of his, her, or its home state in resolving disputes with the host state.

the objection of its own national? This question comes up because of something known as the **Calvo Clause**. The Calvo Clause requires an investor who seeks to establish a business operation in a foreign country to agree, in advance, that he, she, or it will not ask for its home state to intervene in any dispute with the host state. In the *Barcelona Traction Case*, the International Court of Justice expressed the view that Calvo Clauses are ineffective. It said, "[A] claim belongs to a state and not to an individual; therefore, any attempt of waiver by the individual is ineffective."[86]

As a practical matter, however, Calvo Clauses do have some impact. The U.S. Department of State, for example, does take into consideration a waiver when it determines its willingness to espouse a claim and the effort it will expend in seeking compensation.[87]

Lack of a Genuine Link

lack of a genuine link: Objection that may be made to an international tribunal's exercise of jurisdiction when there is no real and bona fide relationship between the state bringing the suit and the person on whose behalf the suit is brought.

A person whose suit is being sponsored by a state in an international tribunal must be a real and bona fide national of that state. That is, the person's nationality must be genuine and not based on a token relationship. If it is based on a token or insignificant relationship, the opposing state can raise an objection of a **lack of a genuine link** to the sponsoring state. In the famous *Nottebohm Case*, the International Court of Justice held that an individual who went to Liechtenstein for 3 weeks to acquire that state's nationality, then returned abroad, did not establish a real or effective link that would justify Liechtenstein in bringing a complaint against another state for depriving that individual of his property.[88]

For companies, the ability of a state to sponsor a complaint depends on the particular company's nationality. States have a wide variety of national rules that define the nationality of a company. Regardless of these tests, international tribunals now require that a company have a genuine link with its sponsoring state.

Failure to Exhaust Remedies

failure to exhaust remedies: Objection that may be made to an international tribunal's exercise of jurisdiction when the private person on whose behalf the suit is brought, failed to seek relief from the defendant state.

Before an individual or business firm can seek the support of its home state in supporting a complaint of mistreatment by a foreign state, the individual or firm must exhaust all of the local remedies available to it within the foreign state.[89] **Failure to exhaust remedies** is thus an objection that the foreign state may raise in an international tribunal. As is the case in municipal law, the requirement that complainants must exhaust their local remedies serves to resolve problems at the lowest level and with the least use of a sovereign's time.

There are exceptions to the rule, of course. If an adequate remedy is clearly unavailable,[90] if the requirement to exhaust a person's remedies is waived by treaty, if the injury was done directly to a state (rather than to a private person), or if the defendant state has delayed excessively in granting a remedy, the requirement is excused. With regard to this last point—excessive delay—one has to recognize that ordinary court cases in many countries often take years to resolve, so this may well be an ineffective exception to the basic rule. For example, the *Interhandel Case* involved a situation where a Swiss firm had spent nine years in American courts attempting to recover assets the United States military had seized during World War II.

---

[86]Case Concerning Barcelona Traction, Light, and Power Company, Ltd. (Preliminary Objections), *International Court of Justice Reports,* vol. 1964, p. 6 (1964).

[87]Joseph Sweeny, Covey Oliver, and Noyes Leech, *The International Legal System,* pp. 1161–1163 (2nd ed., 1981).

[88]Nottebohm, a resident of Guatemala, realized in 1939 that his German citizenship might be a disadvantage if Guatemala entered World War II on the side of the Allies. He therefore went to Liechtenstein for a few weeks with his brother, acquired Liechtenstein citizenship, and automatically gave up his German citizenship. After Guatemala declared war on Germany, he was arrested, confined, and his property confiscated. Liechtenstein brought an action in 1951 seeking restitution. The ICJ held that there has to be a genuine link between the claimant state and its national and that no such link existed in this case. *International Court of Justice Reports,* vol. 1955, p. 4 (1955).

[89]In the Ambatielos Arbitration (1956), a Greek, who had contracted to buy ships from the British government, accused the British of breaking the contract and brought suit in the English High Court. He failed to call a key witness there and lost; and he lost for the same reason in the Court of Appeal. Greece then made a claim on his behalf. The arbitrators held that Ambatielos had failed to exhaust all local remedies by not calling the witness and by not appealing to the House of Lords. *International Law Reports,* vol. 23, p. 306 (1956).

[90]In the Robert E. Brown Case (1923), an arbitral tribunal found that Brown was not required to exhaust his local remedies in South Africa because "all three branches of the government conspired to ruin his enterprise. . . . The judiciary, at first recalcitrant, was at length reduced to submission and brought into line with a determined policy of the Executive. . . ." It said: "[I]n the frequently quoted language of an American Secretary of State: 'A claimant in a foreign State is not required to exhaust justice in such State where there is no justice to exhaust.' " *United Nations Reports of International Arbitral Awards,* vol. 6, pp. 120, 129.

The firm had lost at the trial court level, and its appeals had been denied. When the U.S. State Department advised Switzerland that the firm's chances of success in obtaining a new trial were nonexistent, the Swiss government lodged a complaint on the firm's behalf in the International Court of Justice. In the meantime, however, the U.S. Supreme Court ordered a new trial. The ICJ then dismissed the Swiss claim, stating that the firm's local remedies had not been exhausted.[91]

In Case 2–8, the defendant objected to an international tribunal's assumption of jurisdiction on the grounds that there was no genuine link, no exhaustion of remedies, and that the parties affected did not possess the nationality of the plaintiff state.

---

[91]Switzerland v. United States, *International Court of Justice Reports,* vol. 1959, p. 6 (1959).

Case 2–8   The M/V SAIGA Case (Merits)
Saint Vincent and the Grenadines v. Guinea

International Tribunal for the Law of the Sea
Case No. 2, 1999, posted at www.itlos.org

On October 27, 1997, the M/V Saiga, *an oil tanker, was engaged in selling "gas oil" to fishing and other vessels within Guinea's exclusive economic zone. The next day, the Guinean Navy boarded the* Saiga *just beyond Guinea's exclusive economic zone and the master, crew, and the ship were arrested. The government of Guinea charged the master with importing "without declaring it, merchandise that is taxable on entering national Guinean territory, in this case diesel oil" and brought criminal proceedings against him for "committing the crimes of contraband, fraud, and tax evasion."*

At the time of the arrest, the vessel was owned by Tabona Shipping Company Ltd. of Nicosia, Cyprus, managed by Seascot Shipmanagement Ltd. of Glasgow, Scotland, and under charter to Lemania Shipping Group Ltd. of Geneva, Switzerland. It had been provisionally registered in Saint Vincent and the Grenadines (SVG) on March 12, 1997. The master and crew of the ship were all of Ukrainian nationality. The owner of the cargo of gas oil on board was Addax BV of Geneva, Switzerland.

On November 13, 1997, the SVG submitted a request to the International Tribunal for the Law of the Sea (ITLOS) for an order that would direct Guinea to release the Saiga *and its crew. ITLOS issued an order on December 4 calling for Guinea to release the vessel and its crew upon the posting by SGV of a U.S. $400,000 letter of credit.*

On December 17, a Guinean trial court convicted the master of the Saiga *of the criminal charges that had been brought against him, and the Guinean Court of Appeal affirmed the conviction on February 3, 1998. The Court of Appeal imposed a suspended sentence of six months imprisonment, a fine of 15,354,040,000 Guinean francs, and ordered that all fees and expenses be at his expense. It*

MAP 2-8   Guinea (1997)

also ordered the confiscation of the cargo—4,941 metric tons of gas oil—and the seizure of the vessel as a guarantee for payment of the fine.

On December 22, 1997, SVG sent notice to Guinea that it was instituting arbitral proceedings before ITLOS in accordance with the UN Convention of the Law of the Sea, a treaty to which both states are parties. On January 13, 1998, SVG filed a copy of the notice with ITLOS and it asked for the Tribunal to prescribe provisional measures concerning the arrest and detention of the Saiga.

On February 20, 1998, Guinea agreed to submit to the proceedings before ITLOS and on February 28 it released the ship, the master, and those members of the crew had not previously been released.

On March 11, ITLOS issued a provisional measure calling on Guinea to refrain from taking or enforcing any measures against the Saiga, *or its master, crew, owners or operators. In June, both parties submitted memorials to ITLOS. SVG asked the Tribunal to declare that "the actions of Guinea (*inter alia *the attack on the M/V "Saiga" and her crew in the exclusive economic zone of Sierra Leone, its subsequent arrest, its detention and the removal of the cargo of gas oil, its filing of charges against St. Vincent and the Grenadines and its subsequently issuing a judgment against them) violate the right of St. Vincent and the Grenadines and vessels flying its flag to enjoy freedom of navigation and/or other internationally lawful uses of the sea related to the freedom of navigation." Guinea responded with a motion to dismiss the proceeding. Guinea contended, in part, that the proceeding ought to be dismissed because there was no genuine link between SVG and the* Saiga, *because the master had not exhausted all of his local remedies within Guinea, and because the master, the crew, and other interested persons were not nationals of SVG so that SVG could not being this action on their behalf.*

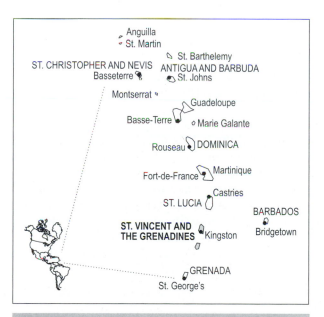

MAP 2-9   Saint Vincent and the Grenadines (1997)

THE TRIBUNAL . . . DELIVERS
THE FOLLOWING JUDGMENT:

* * *

The next objection to admissibility raised by Guinea is that there was no genuine link between the *Saiga* and Saint Vincent and the Grenadines. Guinea contends that "without a genuine link between Saint Vincent and the Grenadines and the M/V 'Saiga', Saint Vincent and the Grenadines' claim concerning a violation of its right of navigation and the status of the ship is not admissible

before the Tribunal vis-à-vis Guinea, because Guinea is not bound to recognize the Vincentian nationality of the M/V 'Saiga', which forms a prerequisite for the mentioned claim in international law".

Article 91, paragraph 1, of the [United Nations Convention on the Law of the Sea (the Convention)] provides: "There must exist a genuine link between the State and the ship." Two questions need to be addressed in this connection. The first is whether the absence of a genuine link between a flag State and a ship entitles another State to refuse to recognize the nationality of the ship. The second question is whether or not a genuine link existed between the *Saiga* and Saint Vincent and the Grenadines at the time of the incident.

With regard to the first question, the Tribunal notes that the provision in article 91, paragraph 1, of the Convention, requiring a genuine link between the State and the ship, does not provide the answer. Nor do articles 92 and 94 of the Convention, which together with article 91 constitute the context of the provision, provide the answer. The Tribunal, however, recalls that the International Law Commission, in article 29 of the Draft Articles on the Law of the Sea adopted by it in 1956, proposed the concept of a "genuine link" as a criterion not only for the attribution of nationality to a ship but also for the recognition by other States of such nationality. After providing that "ships have the nationality of the State whose flag they are entitled to fly", the draft article continued: "Nevertheless, for purposes of recognition of the national character of the ship by other States, there must exist a genuine link between the State and the ship". This sentence was not included in article 5, paragraph 1, of the Convention on the High Seas of 29 April 1958 (hereinafter "the 1958 Convention"), which reads, in part, as follows:

> There must exist a genuine link between the State and the ship; in particular, the State must effectively exercise its jurisdiction and control in administrative, technical and social matters over ships flying its flag.

Thus, while the obligation regarding a genuine link was maintained in the 1958 Convention, the proposal that the existence of a genuine link should be a basis for the recognition of nationality was not adopted.

The Convention follows the approach of the 1958 Convention. Article 91 retains the part of the third sentence of article 5, paragraph 1, of the 1958 Convention which provides that there must be a genuine link between the State and the ship. The other part of that sentence, stating that the flag State shall effectively exercise its jurisdiction and control in administrative, technical and social matters over ships flying its flag, is reflected in article 94 of the Convention, dealing with the duties of the flag State.

Paragraphs 2 to 5 of article 94 of the Convention outline the measures that a flag State is required to take to exercise effective jurisdiction as envisaged in paragraph 1. Paragraph 6 sets out the procedure to be followed where another State has "clear grounds to believe that proper jurisdiction and control with respect to a ship have not been exercised". That State is entitled to report the facts to the flag State which is then obliged to "investigate the matter and, if appropriate, take any action necessary to remedy the situation". There is nothing in article 94 to permit a State which discovers evidence indicating the absence of proper jurisdiction and control by a flag State over a ship to refuse to recognize the right of the ship to fly the flag of the flag State.

The conclusion of the Tribunal is that the purpose of the provisions of the Convention on the need for a genuine link between a ship and its flag State is to secure more effective implementation of the duties of the flag State, and not to establish criteria by reference to which the validity of the registration of ships in a flag State may be challenged by other States.

* * *

In the light of the above considerations, the Tribunal concludes that there is no legal basis for the claim of Guinea that it can refuse to recognize the right of the *Saiga* to fly the flag of Saint Vincent and the Grenadines on the ground that there was no genuine link between the ship and Saint Vincent and the Grenadines.

With regard to the second question, the Tribunal finds that, in any case, the evidence adduced by Guinea is not sufficient to justify its contention that there was no genuine link between the ship and Saint Vincent and the Grenadines at the material time.

For the above reasons, the Tribunal rejects the objection to admissibility based on the absence of a genuine link between the *Saiga* and Saint Vincent and the Grenadines.

Exhaustion of Local Remedies

Guinea further objects to the admissibility of certain claims advanced by Saint Vincent and the Grenadines in respect of damage suffered by natural and juridical persons as a result of the measures taken by Guinea against the *Saiga*. It contends that these claims are inadmissible because the persons concerned did not exhaust local remedies, as required by article 295 of the Convention.

In particular, Guinea claims that the Master did not exhaust the remedies available to him under Guinean law by failing to have recourse to the Supreme Court (*cour suprême*) against the Judgment of 3 February 1998 of the Criminal Chamber (*chambre correctionnelle*) of the Court of Appeal of Conakry. Similarly, the owners of the *Saiga*, as well as the owners of the confiscated cargo of gas oil, had the right to institute legal proceedings to challenge the seizure of the ship and the confiscation of the cargo, but neither of them exercised this right. . . .

Before dealing with the arguments of the parties, it is necessary to consider whether the rule that local remedies must be exhausted is applicable in the present case. Article 295 of the Convention reads as follows:

ARTICLE 295
EXHAUSTION OF LOCAL REMEDIES
Any dispute between States Parties concerning the interpretation or application of this Convention may be submitted to the procedures provided for in [section 2 of Part XV] only after local remedies have been exhausted where this is required by international law.

It follows that the question whether local remedies must be exhausted is answered by international law. The Tribunal must, therefore, refer to international law in order to ascertain the requirements for the application of this rule and to determine whether or not those requirements are satisfied in the present case.

* * *

As stated in article 22 of the Draft Articles on State Responsibility adopted on first reading by the International Law Commission, the rule that local remedies must be exhausted is applicable when "the conduct of a State has created a situation not in conformity with the result required of it by an international obligation concerning the treatment to be accorded to aliens . . . ." None of the violations of rights claimed by Saint Vincent and the Grenadines [including the right of freedom of navigation and the right not to be subjected to the customs and contraband laws of Guinea] can be described as breaches of obligations concerning the treatment to be accorded to aliens. They are all direct violations of the rights of Saint Vincent and the Grenadines. Damage to the persons involved in the operation of the ship arises from those violations. Accordingly, the claims in respect of such damage are not subject to the rule that local remedies must be exhausted.

* * *

The Tribunal, therefore, rejects the objection of Guinea to admissibility based on the non-exhaustion of local remedies.

Nationality of Claims

In its last objection to admissibility, Guinea argues that certain claims of Saint Vincent and the Grenadines cannot be entertained by the Tribunal because they relate to violations of the rights of persons who are not nationals of Saint Vincent and the Grenadines. According to Guinea, the claims of Saint Vincent and the Grenadines in respect of loss or damage sustained by the ship, its owners, the Master and other members of the crew and other persons, including the owners of the cargo, are clearly claims of diplomatic protection. In its view, Saint Vincent and the Grenadines is not competent to institute these claims on behalf of the persons concerned since none of them is a national of Saint Vincent and the Grenadines. During the oral proceedings, Guinea withdrew its objection as far as it relates to the shipowners, but maintained it in respect of the other persons.

In opposing this objection, Saint Vincent and the Grenadines maintains that the rule of international law that a State is entitled to claim protection only for its nationals does not apply to claims in respect of persons and things on board a ship flying its flag. In such cases, the flag State has the right to bring claims in respect of violations against the ship and all persons on board or interested in its operation. Saint Vincent and the Grenadines, therefore, asserts that it has the right to protect the ship flying its flag and those who serve on board, irrespective of their nationality.

In dealing with this question, the Tribunal finds sufficient guidance in the Convention. The Convention contains detailed provisions concerning the duties of flag States regarding ships flying their flag. Articles 94 and 217, in particular, set out the obligations of the flag State which can be discharged only through the exercise of appropriate jurisdiction and control over natural and juridical persons such as the Master and other members of the crew, the owners or operators and other persons involved in the activities of the ship. No distinction is made in these provisions between nationals and non-nationals of a flag State. Additionally, Articles 106, 110, paragraph 3, and 111, paragraph 8, of the Convention contain provisions applicable to cases in which measures have been taken by a State against a foreign ship. These measures are, respectively, seizure of a ship on suspicion of piracy, exercise of the right of visit on board the ship, and arrest of a ship in exercise of the right of hot pursuit. In these cases, the Convention provides that, if the measures are found not to be justified, the State taking the measures shall be obliged to pay compensation "for any loss or damage" sustained. In these cases, the Convention does not relate the right to compensation to the nationality of persons suffering loss or damage. Furthermore, in relation to proceedings for prompt release under Article 292 of the Convention, no significance is attached to the nationalities of persons involved in the operations of an arrested ship.

The provisions referred to in the preceding paragraph indicate that the Convention considers a ship as a unit, as regards the obligations of the flag State with respect to the ship and the right of a flag State to seek reparation for loss or damage caused to the ship by acts of other States and to institute proceedings under Article 292 of the Convention. Thus the ship, every thing on it, and every person involved or interested in its operations are treated as an entity linked to the flag State. The nationalities of these persons are not relevant.

* * *

In the light of the above considerations, the Tribunal rejects the objection to admissibility based on nationality of claims.

* * *

Reparation

It is a well-established rule of international law that a State which suffers damage as a result of an internationally wrongful act by another State is entitled to obtain reparation for the damage suffered from the State which committed the wrongful act and that "reparation must, as far as possible, wipe out all the consequences of the illegal act and reestablish the situation which would, in all probability, have existed if that act had not been committed"[92]

* * *

In the view of the Tribunal, Saint Vincent and the Grenadines is entitled to reparation for damage suffered directly by it as well as for damage or other loss suffered by the *Saiga,* including all persons involved or interested in its operation. . . . ■

---

[92]Factory at Chorzów, Merits, Judgment No.13, 1928, *Permanent Court of International Justice Reports,* Series A, No.17, p.47.

Other Objections

laches: (From Latin *laxus:* "loose" or "lax.") Negligent delay in asserting a right or a claim.

dirty hands: The plaintiff took inappropriate steps in attempting to recoup a loss prior to bringing a claim.

A defendant state may also argue that a claimant delayed too long in bringing a claim (this is called **laches**)[93] or that the complainant is tainted with **dirty hands**. For example, in the *I'm Alone Case*, a United States Coast Guard cutter sank a ship smuggling liquor into the United States in 1934. The ship was flying the British flag and its owners got Britain to assert a claim against the United States in an arbitration tribunal. The arbitrators held that the sinking was illegal, but they refused to award damages to the *I'm Alone*'s owners. They did so because the ship had been involved in smuggling and therefore had dirty hands. Even so, the tribunal

---

[93]Gentini's Claim (1903), *United Nations Reports of International Arbitral Awards,* vol. 10, pp. 552–555.

required the United States to apologize to the British government and to pay it $25,000 for the insult done to the British flag.[94]

D. RELIEF

restitution in kind: The item taken is to be returned.

satisfaction: The honor of the injured state is to be restored.

compensatory damages: Money is to be paid for the cost of the injury suffered.

Several kinds of relief can be obtained from states for injuring an alien. International tribunals have awarded **restitution in kind**,[95] **satisfaction**,[96] and **compensatory damages**. An award of relief is discussed in Case 2-9.

---

[94]*Id.,* vol. 3, p. 1609.

[95]In the Temple of Preah Vihear Case (Cambodia v. Thailand), Thailand was ordered to return religious objects it had illegally taken from a temple in Cambodia. *International Court of Justice Reports,* vol. 1962, p. 6 (1962).

[96]The Borchgrave Case involved an incident where a member of Belgium's Madrid embassy staff was found dead on a roadside in Spain in 1936. The PCIJ noted: "In consequence, proceeding on the principles of international law relating to the responsibility of States, the Belgian Government demanded as reparation: (1) an expression of the Spanish government's excuses and regrets; (2) transfer of the corpse to the port of embarkation with military honors; . . . and (4) punishment of the guilty." *Permanent Court of International Justice Reports,* Series A/B, No. 72, p. 165 (1937).

Case 2–9   Re Letelier and Moffitt

Chile–United States International Commission, 1992. *International Law Reports,* vol. 88, p. 727 (1992).

In 1976, Orlando Letelier, a former Foreign Minister of Chile, was killed by a car bomb in the city of Washington in the United States. The bomb also killed Ronni Moffitt and seriously injured her husband, Michael Moffitt, both of whom had been riding in the car with Señor Letelier. Moffitt, Letelier's estate and various relatives of the two persons killed then brought suit in the United States alleging that the government of Chile had been responsible for the killings. The U.S. trial court held that Chile was not entitled to sovereign immunity, and when Chile refused to participate in the proceeding, it awarded the plaintiffs a default judgment of approximately U.S. $5 million.

Because the plaintiffs were unsuccessful in executing the judgment against Chile, the U.S. government intervened on their behalf and made an international claim against the government of Chile. Later, the United States invoked the 1914 Treaty for the Settlement of Disputes That May Occur between the United States and Chile (popularly known as the Bryan-Suárez Mujica Treaty). Chile denied responsibility for the car bombing but it did express its willingness to make an ex gratia[97] payment to the U.S. government to be received on behalf of the victims' families. In 1990, the United States and Chile concluded a compromis[98] establishing a Commission pursuant to the 1914 Treaty and Chile agreed to make an ex gratia *payment in an amount to be determined by the Commission.*

AWARD OF THE COMMISSION: . . .

Before proceeding to a precise determination of the payments to be made to the members of the Letelier and Moffitt families . . . , the Commission believes it advisable to indicate the general criteria that it has taken into consideration in setting the amount of those payments.

It is necessary to remember, first of all, that according to . . . the *Compromis,* the Commission is to determine the amount of the *ex gratia* payment to be made by the government of Chile in conformity with the applicable principles of international law, as though liability were established.

In this regard, the judgment handed down by the Permanent Court of International Justice in the *Chorzów Factory Case*[99] cited by the United States and Chile in their respective written presentations, may be taken as enunciating a general rule. The pertinent portion of this judgment reads *verbatim* as follows:

[R]eperation must, as far as possible, wipe out all the consequences of the illegal act and reestablish the situation which would, in all probability, have existed if that act had not been committed.

---

[97]Latin: "out of grace" or "as a matter of grace." Used to indicate an action taken as a favor, in contrast to one taken *ex debito,* "as a matter of right."

[98]French: "a mutual promise" or "a compromise." An agreement to abide by the decision of an arbitrator.

[99]*Permanent Court of International Justice Reports,* Series A, No. 17, p. 46 (1927).

MAP 2-10   Washington, D.C. (1976)

The Commission has also kept in mind the need to apply the same rules to the members of the families of Orlando Letelier and of Ronni Moffitt, with no differentiation whatever by reason of their nationality.

It should be pointed out that the Commission has followed the same criteria in examining the situation of each of the beneficiaries of these payments. In each of these cases, the Commission has examined the loss of financial support and services and the material and moral damages suffered by each of the claimant family members. The Commission has also examined the appropriateness of the expenses in each case.

In respect of interest, the Commission has considered that since the compensation for the above elements has been expressed at present value it is unnecessary to provide for the payment of interest.

These general considerations having been presented, it is now appropriate to proceed to a precise determination of the amounts that in the judgment of the Commission should be paid by the government of Chile to the various claimants.

We will start with the Letelier family by first of all examining the amount of the compensation to be paid for the loss of financial support suffered by Mr. Letelier's widow and children.

In order to calculate the amount due under this item, the Commission has taken into account what it considers to be the most likely assumption about the remainder of Mr. Letelier's working life had it not been cut short by the assassination to which he fell victim.

The Commission examined various hypotheses. These included the possibility that Mr. Letelier would have continued at the Institute for Policy Studies (hereinafter referred to as "the IPS") for the remainder of his working life; that he would at some point, in view of his

previous experience, have switched to a career as an international banker; and that he would have returned to Chile in 1990, on the restoration of the democratic government there, and from then onwards have undertaken a career in Chilean public service in some such capacity as that of Minister of State, Ambassador, or Senator.

In reaching conclusions on this aspect the Commission took into account the salary and fringe benefits which Mr. Letelier would have received from 1976 until at least 1990 with the IPS and the sums he would have received in that period for continuing to teach courses at the American University. It also took into account the amounts which would have been paid him as salary and retirement pension for the remainder of his expectation of life (until 2007) had he returned to Chile in 1990 and worked in public service in one of the capacities referred to above. It did not include income from other sources such as conferences, lectures, or publications because it considered that there were insufficient bases on which to establish such income in this case. Nor did the Commission include an award for the provision by Mr. Letelier of household services, such as carpentry, because it considered such activities on his part to be more in the nature of an occasional pastime to which it was not in a position to attribute a pecuniary value.

Allowing for the uncertainties which must surround any attempt to predict the course which Mr. Letelier's life would have taken, the Commission decided in all the circumstances to award a sum of one million two hundred thousand dollars (U.S. $1,200,000) as compensation for loss of financial support suffered by Mrs. Isabel Morel de Letelier and her sons as the result of the murder of Orlando Letelier.

The Commission agreed on the payment of one hundred sixty thousand dollars (U.S. $160,000) in moral damages to Mrs. Isabel Morel de Letelier and eighty thousand dollars (U.S. $80,000) to each of the couple's four children: Christian, Francisco, Jose, and Juan Pablo. In setting this figure, the Commission took into account, by way of comparison, the amounts granted for moral damages by jurisdictional organs of the inter-American system and those ordered, also in recent years, by arbitration or judicial tribunals. Needless to say, in making these comparisons, the factual differences between the cases that served as a guide in setting these amounts were borne in mind.

Lastly, the Commission awarded Mrs. Isabel Morel de Letelier, as reimbursement of medical expenses for health problems resulting from the attack, the amount of sixteen thousand four hundred dollars (U.S. $16,400).

. . . [The Commission then made similar determinations with respect to the Moffitt family.] . . .

All the figures mentioned above amount to a total of two million six hundred and eleven thousand eight hundred and ninety two dollars (U.S. $2,611,892), which is the final amount of compensation to be paid by the State of Chile.

* * *

SEPARATE CONCURRING OPINION OF PROFESSOR FRANCISCO ORREGO VICUNA:

The undersigned Commissioner concurs in the decision reached unanimously by the Commission. . . . There are, however, a number of points of law and opinion which should be explained by means of this Separate Opinion in the light of the present State of international law. . . .

* * *

Punitive Damages Not Acceptable

The principles of international law applicable in the matter of compensation for damages arising from death or personal injury of individuals are fairly straightforward and have been greatly clarified as the result of important works of writers of international law, numerous decisions, and diplomatic practice.[100] This is not the occasion to explain such principles but to draw the attention to some salient issues of relevance for the adjudication of the present case.

It should firstly be reiterated that international law has not accepted as one of its principles the concept of punitive damages.[101] While this type of damage has not been claimed in th[is] instance, the issue is whether a claim of an excessive or disproportionate amount of compensation can result in a similar effect, that is in the punishment or repression of the defendant state. The Commissioner undersigned is of the opinion that this would be very much the case irrespectively of the claim being labeled punitive or not. It follows that a claim involving this result would be entirely unwarranted and contrary to the principles of international law. This Commissioner is pleased to concur in the decision of the Commission determining an amount of compensation which is not excessive or disproportionate.

Remoteness and Causal Consequences: A Basic Distinction

It should be noted next that international law, like domestic law, draws a basic distinction between the remoteness of damage and the proximity which is associated with the natural and causal consequences of an act.[102] . . .

There can be no doubt . . . that international law allows for compensation of reasonably foreseeable loss of income of the families of the victims, while . . . excluding remote damages. This in fact means that the lost income to be compensated is to be determined in the light of the specific activities which the victims had at the time of their death and the conditions and expectations reasonably deriving therefrom. Remote or speculative loss of income, which cannot be linked to such activities and conditions, ought to be excluded from the determination of compensation.

This . . . [consideration] is of particular relevance for the determination of the amount of compensation in the present case since it involves the need to exclude remote scenarios relating the career of one of the victims [i.e., Letelier] and retain such other activities which meet the standard of proximity. In view of the political activities which the victim carried out at the time of his death and of the prominence which a public personality of his position would no doubt have attained in Chile as a member of parliament, a cabinet minister, or some other high political office, it is only natural to consider that this type of work would have prevailed during his probable stay in the United States and later upon his return to Chilean political life. Different considerations apply of course to the prospective career of the other victim [i.e., Ronni Moffitt] in the line of clerical services in the United States.

* * *

The Compensation for Moral Damages

Compensation for moral damages is clearly [allowed for by] . . . international law. . . . This damage being by its very nature nonmaterial, the determination of the amount of compensation is a most difficult question requiring that both the standards of justice and reasonableness be met.

On this point it should be noted that the Chilean State has taken important steps to satisfy the moral dimension of the human rights situations with which it has had to deal. The facts of having the Head of State apologize to the families of the victims, of a nonjudicial inquiry having been ordered by . . . a National Commission on Truth and Reconciliation, of having requested Congress to enact legislation on compensation, and of having prosecuted before the Chilean courts those individuals having been charged criminally in the present case, are all indications that the Chilean State is not indifferent to the moral issues involved in the mat-

---

[100]*See* generally Marjorie M. Whiteman, *Damages in International Law,* pp. 637 *et seq.* (1937); George T. Yates, III, "State Responsibility for Non-wealth Injuries to Aliens in the Post War Era," in Richard B. Lillich (ed.), *International Law of State Responsibility for Injuries to Aliens* (1983).

[101]Clyde Eagleton, *The Responsibility of States in International Law,* pp. 185–197, particularly at pp. 190–191 (1928); Eduardo Jiménez de Aréchaga, "Responsabilidad internacional del Estado," in *Derecho Internacional Público,* vol. IV, capítulo III, pp. 33–89, particularly at pp. 64–65 (1989).

[102]Ian Brownlie, *System of the Law of Nations, State Responsibility,* Part I, pp. 224–225 (1983).

ter. This positive attitude has a bearing on the determination of compensation for moral damages.

In a number of cases adjudicated under international law, the decision itself has been considered a form of satisfaction. The situation here is somewhat different since the Commission is only empowered to determine the amount of compensation and not to establish any form of responsibility, which is usually the basis of that satisfaction. The fact of this compensation being associated with an *ex gratia* payment makes an important difference as to the effect of the decision on the question of satisfaction. Furthermore, the question of satisfaction arises not in relation to individuals but in relation to another State, which could have been offended by a wrongful act. This is not the case in th[is] instance since . . . the United States government is intervening on behalf of the families and not on behalf of its own interest. The fact that the Chilean government has agreed to make an *ex gratia* payment . . . , however, is relevant for the relationship vis-à-vis those families and it can be considered as the equivalent of a satisfaction in such other relationships. ■

E. INSURANCE

insurance: The contractual commitment by an insurer to indemnify an insured against specific contingencies and perils.

Insurance is the contractual commitment by an insurer to indemnify an insured against specific contingencies and perils. For multinational enterprises, the contingencies and perils of operating abroad include those common to domestic businesses—such as property losses, casualty losses, and losses suffered by employees—as well as special losses arising from political violence and political instability.

Both domestically and internationally, insurance is an important business tool that can either supplement or take the place of litigation. For example, should a court find a firm liable for an injury to a customer, supplier, investor, competitor, or a government agency for whatever reason, liability insurance can pay the award. Similarly, if a foreign government nationalizes a multinational firm's property and refuses to pay compensation or to honor an award in a domestic or international court, political risk insurance can cover the firm's loss.

A variety of insurance products for multinational enterprises are available from private insurers, governments, and intergovernmental agencies. These include international property insurance, international casualty insurance, coverage for overseas employees, and special coverages. Exhibit 2-1 describes the particular forms of these coverages.

Private Insurers

Private insurers who offer international insurance include the Exporters Insurance Company of Bermuda, the British Trade Indemnity Group, the Dutch and British Nederlandsche Credietverzekering Maatsschappij, the French Compagnie Française d'Assurance pour le Commerce Exterieur,[103] and the following U.S. firms: Foreign Credit Insurance Association,[104] American Credit Indemnity,[105] American International Group Global & Political Risk Insurance Co.,[106] and CNA Credit.[107] Most of these insurers provide the full range of insurance products listed in Exhibit 2-1. However, specialty coverage, especially political risk insurance, is often expensive or unavailable in designated high-risk countries.

National Investment Guarantee Programs

Because private international insurance is usually unavailable for companies doing business in high-risk countries, most government-sponsored insurance agencies concentrate on providing just such coverage. That is not to say that they provide coverage for all high-risk countries. Rather, they target their insurance offerings in order to promote domestic exports to certain favored countries.

---

[103]Internet home page: www.coface.fr.
[104]Internet home page: www.island-metro.com/trade/fcia.htm.
[105]Internet home page: www.aciins.com.
[106]Internet home page: www.aig.com.
[107]Internet home page: members.aol.com/jluftman/index.html.

International Property Insurance

- **Foreign Commercial Property Insurance** covers financial losses from damage to an insured's overseas buildings and their contents, damage to the facilities of an overseas supplier or customer, loss of property in the custody of a salesperson, and loss of income from foreign royalties.
- **Marine Cargo Insurance** protects goods in transit, whether by land, sea, or air.
- **Comprehensive Dishonesty, Disappearance, and Destruction Insurance** is a form of fidelity and commercial crime insurance that covers losses from employee dishonesty (such as the loss of money, securities, or other property because of an employee's fraudulent or dishonest acts); losses inside an insured's premises due to actual destruction, disappearance, or misappropriation; losses outside an insured's premises while property is being transported by a messenger or armored vehicle; losses from "good faith" acceptance of counterfeit paper currency or money orders; losses from the forgery or alteration of checks, bank drafts, promissory notes, credit cards, or similar financial instruments; and losses from computer fraud.

International Casualty Insurance

- **Foreign Commercial General Liability Insurance** protects against financial loss stemming from third-party lawsuits brought against an insured because of its overseas business activities. Third parties include customers, suppliers, investors, government agencies, and competitors who bring suits for such things as bodily injury, property damage, product liability, contractual liability, personal injury, and advertising injury.
- **Foreign Voluntary Workers' Compensation Insurance** protects employers from claims involving work-related injuries and endemic diseases incurred by overseas employees.
- **Employer's Liability Insurance** covers an employer for the legal costs resulting from bodily injury or death of overseas employees.
- **Excess Repatriation Expense Insurance** reimburses an employer for expenses in excess of normal transportation costs for the repatriation of injured, sick, or deceased employees.
- **Foreign Commercial Automobile Liability Insurance** provides coverage for an insured's overseas automobiles whether they are owned, hired, or borrowed.

Coverage for Overseas Employees

- **Foreign Accident and Health Insurance** covers employees and their family members traveling overseas.
- **Accident and Sickness (Medical) Insurance** covers employees in the event of accident, injury, or sickness abroad.
- **Accidental Death and Dismemberment Insurance** pays an employee involved in an accident resulting in dismemberment or the employee's dependents in the event of death.
- **Emergency Medical Evacuation Insurance** pays for an employee's transportation to a proper medical facility for treatment.
- **Repatriation of Remains Insurance** pays for the cost of repatriating an employee's remains to his home country.

Specialty Coverages

- **Kidnap, Ransom, and Extortion Insurance** covers losses resulting from kidnapping, wrongful detention, bodily injury extortion, property damage extortion, product contamination extortion, trade secret extortion, hijacking, and blackmail.
- **Sabotage and Terrorism Insurance** covers losses to an insured's overseas facilities and operations caused by saboteurs and terrorists.
- **Political Risk Insurance** covers losses from the unexpected, discriminatory, or arbitrary acts by foreign governments, such as confiscation, expropriation, or nationalization of assets; currency inconvertibility; war and political violence; contract repudiation; and the wrongful calling of "on demand" guarantees.

EXHIBIT 2-1 International Insurance Products[a]

[a]This list is based on descriptions in the American International Underwriters' *WORLDRISK Brochure* posted on the Internet at aiu.aig.com/aiu/aiu36.htm.

Nations with government agencies that offer international insurance include the United States, Canada, and most Western European and many Latin American countries.[108] An example of such an agency is the United States Overseas Private Investment Corporation.

---

[108]The International Trade Center (a UN agency operated jointly by UNCTAD and the WTO) lists the following countries as providing international insurance through state-run insurance agencies: Argentina, Australia, Austria, Bangladesh, Barbados, Belgium, Brazil, Cameroon, Canada, Chile, Colombia, Cyprus, the Czech Republic, Denmark, Ecuador, Egypt, Finland, France, Germany, Greece, Hong Kong, Hungary, India, Indonesia, Ireland, Israel, Italy, the Ivory Coast, Jamaica, Japan, Lesotho, Liberia, Luxembourg, Malaysia, Malta, Mexico, Morocco, the Netherlands, New Zealand, Nigeria, Norway, Pakistan, Peru, the Philippines, Poland, Portugal, Republic of Korea, Romania, Russia, Saudi Arabia, Senegal, Singapore, Slovakia, Slovenia, South Africa, Spain, Sri Lanka, Swaziland, Sweden, Switzerland, Taiwan, Thailand, Trinidad and Tobago, Tunisia, Turkey, the United Kingdom, the United States, Uruguay, Venezuela, Zambia, and Zimbabwe. *See* www.intracen.org/itc/services/ tfs/creditag.htm.

The United States Overseas Private Investment Corporation

American political risk investment insurance dates back to the 1948 Marshall Plan, which offered limited assistance to private American companies investing in war-ravaged Europe. In the 1950s, the focus of the U.S. overseas investment program shifted from Europe to less developed countries (LDCs) in Africa, Asia, and Latin America. At the same time, the investment guarantees were increased to protect against expropriation, transfer risks, and risks associated with political violence. This program was run by the Agency for International Development (AID) until 1969, when Congress created the Overseas Private Investment Corporation (OPIC) as an independent government agency in corporate form. OPIC began doing business in 1971.[109]

OPIC's mission is to "mobilize and facilitate the participation of United States private capital and skills in the economic and social development of less developed friendly countries and areas, thereby complementing the development assistance objectives of the United States. . . ."[110] To that end, OPIC runs two basic programs: a political risk insurance program and a finance program. The discussion here focuses on the first (and by far the largest) of these. It is important, nevertheless, to note that OPIC functions as a bank as well as an insurer.[111]

The political risk insurance program covers the political risk of expropriation, currency inconvertibility, and various kinds of risks associated with political violence.

Expropriation   In OPIC's early years, expropriation coverage (or coverage against nationalization or other noncompensated taking by a foreign government) was the primary insurance sought by American companies investing overseas. This is no longer the case. Expropriation claims have declined significantly, with the last notable series of claims spawned by the Iranian Revolution of the mid-1970s. Demands for expropriation coverage have correspondingly declined.

creeping expropriation:
A series of administrative acts that in combination result in depriving persons of their property.

Few of the recent expropriation claims have been for outright confiscation or nationalization. Instead, most claims are now for **creeping expropriation**—that is, expropriation through a series of acts that individually might be seen as administrative actions or general health, safety, or welfare measures undertaken by the host government.

This trend is attributable to at least three factors. First, most LDC governments need to attract foreign investment and they are reluctant to take any action that might discourage investment in their countries. Second, LDC governments have become much more sophisticated. Instead of using outright nationalization with all of its undesirable repercussions, they achieve the same political or economic objectives through other means (e.g., creeping expropriation). Third, international transactions no longer consist mainly of agreements with a host government for the extraction of minerals or other resources. Instead, international investments typically take the form of a joint venture or some other form of cooperative dealing that involves both the host country government and private host country nationals.

Claims for creeping expropriation, in contrast to overt nationalization, present OPIC with a significant problem: defining *de facto*,[112] or creeping, expropriation. OPIC has defined it "as any act, or series of acts, for which the State is responsible, which are illegal under domestic or international law, and which have a *substantial enough* adverse effect on either the enterprise or the investor's rights under the enterprise."[113]

This definition, of course, leads to the question of how much is "substantial enough." In general, OPIC answers by looking at what happened to the entire investment. OPIC does not insure against partial expropriation or for some diminishment in the value of an investment. Thus, unless an investor is willing to give up all claims to its entire investment, OPIC does not regard the expropriation as being substantial enough.[114] Case 2-10 explains this concept.

---

[109]*See* OPIC's Internet home page at www.opic.gov/.
[110]Foreign Assistance Act, *United States Code,* Title 22, § 2191 (1982).
[111]OPIC's finance program is designed to let OPIC participate as a medium- to long-term project lender. For small businesses involved in small projects, OPIC can participate as a direct lender. For larger investors involved in larger projects, OPIC can facilitate commercial lending by providing investment guarantees for commercial bank loans.
[112]Latin: "from the fact" or "in fact"; in effect although not formally recognized.
[113]*See* Robert Shanks, "Insuring Investment and Loans Against Currency Inconvertibility, Expropriation and Political Violence," *Hastings International and Comparative Law Review,* vol. 9, p. 425 (1986).
[114]*See* OPIC Form Contract 234 KGT 12–85 ("plain language contract"). Articles IV, V, reprinted in *United States Federal Register,* Title 51, ¶ 17, 3438 (1986).

Case 2–10 In the Matter of Revere Copper and Brass, Inc. and Overseas Private Investment Corporation

Arbitration Tribunal, 1978.
International Law Reports, vol. 56, p. 258 (1980).

Between 1967 and 1975, Revere Copper and Brass, Inc., (Revere) made substantial investments in a bauxite-aluminum plant, opened and operated by Revere's wholly owned subsidiary, Revere Jamaica Alumina, Ltd., (RJA), in Jamaica. The plant was established in 1967, pursuant to an agreement (the 1967 Agreement) between RJA and the Jamaican government. The 1967 Agreement prescribed the amount of taxes and royalties RJA was to pay to the government and provided, in Clause 12, that no further taxes or financial burdens would be imposed on RJA and that the government would do nothing to derogate from RJA's rights concerning the project. The 1967 Agreement was to remain in force for 25 years for the purpose of taxation and royalties, and it stated that it had been concluded in order to give RJA reasonable, long-term safeguards for its investments in Jamaica. In accordance with the 1967 Agreement, the government granted RJA a 25-year bauxite mining lease and RJA set up a bauxite-aluminum plant.

In 1972, there was a change of government in Jamaica. On January 3, 1974, the Prime Minister of Jamaica announced that the government was no longer bound by the contracts with the several foreign bauxite and aluminum companies then operating in Jamaica, including RJA. Attempts by the government to force RJA to renegotiate the 1967 Agreement failed. In June 1974, the Jamaican Parliament passed the Bauxite (Production Levy) Act, which greatly increased the tax on bauxite payable by all companies, including RJA. RJA's claim that it was not liable to pay the increased levy because of the 1967 Agreement was rejected by the Supreme Court of Jamaica. In addition, the Jamaican Mining Law was amended in June 1974 and royalties on bauxite were increased. As a result, the RJA plant began to suffer considerable losses and ceased operation in August 1975.

Under the United States foreign investment guarantee program, Revere's investment in the RJA plant had been insured with the Overseas Private Investment Corporation. The guarantee contract provided in Section 1.15 for compensation for loss resulting from "expropriatory action" of a kind contrary to the principles of international law and including action that prevented the investor "from exercising effective control over the use or disposition of a substantial portion of its property." Revere contended that the increased levy and royalties amounted to a repudiation of the 1967 Agreement by the Jamaican government, that this repudia-

tion was contrary to international law, and that its effect was to deprive Revere of effective control of its investment. OPIC argued that because Jamaican law governed the 1967 Agreement, the Agreement had not been repudiated, and that in any event, there was no deprivation of effective control.

MAP 2-11 Jamaica (1978)

AWARD: . . .

(c) Did the Acts of June 1974 Constitute Breaches of the Agreement? . . .

The magnitude of the Bauxite Levy was admittedly substantial. For two years, 1974 and 1975, Revere paid $9,494,000. By OPIC's analysis this was equivalent to a gross production tax, for 1974, at the rate of about 20 percent, which would have been about 34 percent if Revere had not received a substantial subvention in exchange for incurring the expense of a feasibility study as to a proposed expansion of the plant. For 1975, OPIC estimates the rate at 35.9 percent on the actual production and at a hypothetical rate of about 30 percent if the plant had not shut down in August and had produced in 1975 the tonnage that was produced in 1974.

The effect of the Levy on the aluminum companies in general and on Revere in particular is clouded by the extent to which it may have been passed through to consumers by price increases. There was no legal impediment against a pass through except to the extent that price controls in the United States may have prevented it during the brief period when controls were in effect. All costs, particularly oil and labor, were rising rapidly and so were prices after controls were removed. In our view of the case we are not obliged to make any precise findings on this subject and we could not do so with confidence in any event on the record before us as to the period when Revere was in operation. In any event, we agree with OPIC that the Levy was not confiscatory and that it did not prevent RJA "from exercising effective control over the use or disposition of a substantial portion of its property." In our view, however, the important question is whether the Levy constituted a breach of the 1967 Agreement.

The Supreme Court of Jamaica in the action brought there by RJA held that under Jamaican law the 1967 Agreement "did not create any rights in RJA as against future taxes and that, therefore, the enactment of the bauxite production levy was not a breach of RJA's 1967 Agreement." We emphatically do not suggest that Chief Justice Smith did not properly state and apply Jamaican law or that RJA was not afforded full "due process" in the Jamaican court.

Chief Justice Smith did not address himself to the question whether the government was bound in international law to observe the good faith commitments made by it in contracts with foreign nationals. When he ruled that the provisions of Clause 12 were "void *ab initio*"[115] because Ministers could not fetter the sovereign power of Parliament to legislate with respect to taxation, he applied principles of domestic law and not principles of international law.

If the parties had intended to preserve the government's legislative freedom without the consequences under international law of violating its commitments, they could have done so in the Agreements entered into with the aluminum companies in 1957, 1966, and 1967. They did not do so. The 1957 commitments were allowed to stand unaltered for seventeen years, to be renewed and amplified in 1966 and 1967, and the latter to remain in effect for eight and seven years respectively. . . .

Admittedly Parliament could at any time legislate with respect to taxes and thus override contracts with private parties. It could not, however, deprive such parties of compensation if the circumstances justified the payment of compensation under international law principles. In our view, such circumstances existed in this case.

We find that the commitments made by the government were internationally binding. . . . Action contrary to them . . . constituted a breach.

(d) Did the Government Repudiate Its Obligations Under the Agreement?

Revere argues that the Prime Minister's declarations and other acts by the government constituted a repudia-

tion of the Agreement as a whole. To the contrary, OPIC says there were many instances where the continued existence of the Agreement was recognized. These included the Heads of Agreement of December 20, 1974, which provided for an amendment of the "existing Agreement" and various statements in the course of negotiations. RJA, they also say, still has all the rights needed for mining bauxite and producing alumina.

In Section 274 of . . . the American Law Institute Restatement of the Law Contracts (Second ed., 1974), headed "When a Statement or an Act is a Repudiation," the term "repudiation" is said to be: . . .

> (b) a voluntary affirmative act which renders [the obligator] unable or apparently unable to perform without a breach.

In the comment to (b), it is said that the language "must be sufficiently positive to be reasonably interpreted to mean that the party will not or cannot perform." It is also said:

> Language that is accompanied by a breach of nonperformance may amount to a repudiation even though, standing alone, it would not be sufficiently positive. . . .

The law of England and the United States is largely similar on this point.[116]

Numerous official statements during the first half of 1974 made clear the government's intentions and determination to replace the existing contracts with new arrangements. These, coupled with the legislative Acts of June 1974, appear to us to meet the requirements of repudiation.

Thus, on January 3, 1974, the Prime Minister publicly announced that "the government of Jamaica cannot be bound" by its agreements with the aluminum companies "any longer." On March 15, 1974, negotiating proposals were submitted, some of which were stated as negotiating proposals, but many were put in terms of contract changes that had been or were being made. For example, the revenue proposals stated:

> ". . . special arrangements relating to income tax rates under previous Agreements *will cease*"; "A production levy *will be introduced* effective and payable 1st January 1974"; "The present royalty rates *will be replaced* . . . effective and payable from 1st January 1974"; depletion allowances "*will discontinue* effective 1st January 1974"; . . . "the government *will not grant* any exemption from the payment of withholding taxes"; "The production levy and the royalties *will be subject to review* at the end of two years . . . and thereafter every two years"; OPIC premia "*will not be allowed* as a deductible expense"; "government *reserves the right to grant* to other companies terms and conditions different from those granted to your

---

[115]Latin: "from the beginning."]
[116]*Corbin on Contracts*, vol. 4, § 959, etc.

company"; . . . "all of the foreign exchange proceeds . . . *must be sold* to an authorized depository; . . . All overseas payments *must be made* from a Jamaican bank account and *must be subject* to the approval of the Bank of Jamaica in accordance with the Exchange Control Law"; "exports of bauxite and alumina *will be regulated.*" (Emphasis added.) . . .

. . . [A] May 15, 1974 government press release stated:

The renegotiation of contracts with aluminum companies is not only a necessity and the right of a sovereign nation, but an obligation to the people. These considerations outweigh the sanctity of contractual arrangements.

It is clear from these statements and from the action taken by Parliament on June 8 and 17 and Ministerial actions thereafter, pursuant to these enactments, that the government had decided to establish a new relationship with the aluminum companies and that it would not revert to the earlier agreements. It is impossible to conclude that the government was prepared to continue on the 1967 terms. This is confirmed by a U.S. Embassy cable of May 21, 1974, in which it was said:

It is now obvious that the govt. meant pretty much what it said in its Mar. 15 list of demands . . . and that its notion of negotiations is a joint determination over how its objectives are to be achieved, and not an exchange of concessions leading to a general compromise. . . .

The legislative Acts of June 1974, the earlier and related statements of the Prime Minister, the elected Chief of State, the peremptory nature of the negotiating proposals of March 15, and actions subsequent to the June 1974 legislation in total evidenced repudiation by the government by June 30, 1974, of its obligations under the Agreement with RJA. . . .

(e) Did Repudiation of the Agreement Constitute Expropriatory Action Under Section 1.15?

This is not a claim against the government of Jamaica for damages for breach or repudiation of the Agreement on the ground that such action constituted a violation of international law. The sole question for decision here is whether the government actions repudiating the Agreement directly prevented RJA from exercising effective control over the use or disposition of a substantial portion of its property or from operating the property. The answer to this question requires an analysis of the Agreement and its relation to the use, operation and disposition of the plant and other facilities. . . .

In our view the effects of the Jamaican government's actions in repudiating its long-term commitments to RJA have substantially the same impact on effective control over use and operation as if the properties were themselves conceded by a concession contract that was repudiated. In reaching this conclusion we are mindful that government

action impact must be on the *exercise* of control, and that the control referred to must be "effective"; that is, it must be practical and not merely theoretical control. This is not a legalistic but a practical problem. OPIC argues that RJA still has all the rights and property that it had before the events of 1974; it is in possession of the plant and other facilities; it has a Mining Lease; it can operate as it did before. This may be true in a formal sense, but for the reasons stated below we do not regard RJA's "control" of the use and operation of its properties as any longer "effective" in view of the destruction by government action of its contract rights.

Control in a large industrial enterprise, such as that conducted by RJA in Jamaica, is exercised by a continuous stream of decisions. It is this decision-making process that must be examined before deciding whether effective control exists and can be exercised in the absence of a stabilization agreement with the government.

We heard testimony about the possible need for new and perhaps different boilers and also about problems of the mud flats, both of which called for some action, some decision. We mention these matters simply as examples of the continuous need for decisions in any large enterprise. In analyzing the control of the RJA enterprise the focus should be on decision making and on what happens to it when the contract disappears on which the entire structure was built, for we have no doubt that this structure was built on the contract and would not have been built without it.

Without putting too fine a point on it, such factors as present cost, probable life of the facility, financing, probable impact on total operation, anticipated return, all leading to a cost-benefit analysis, are some of the factors at the heart of the day-to-day decision making in small matters as well as large ones. Rational decisions require some continuity of the enterprise. In a large enterprise like the present one, with the contract gone, decisions simply become gambles. Risks are inherent in all such decision making, but without the contract the odds cannot be calculated. There is no way in which rational decisions can be made. What the government did yesterday it can do tomorrow or next week or next month. If it did one thing yesterday, it can do something else tomorrow or next week or next month. This is the antithesis of the rational decision making that lies at the heart of control. Here "effective control" not only of the contract but of the entire operation has been lost, due directly to the action of the government. Webster defines "directly" as "in a direct way; without anything intervening." Nothing intervened here between the government actions and the loss of effective control. . . .

If this analysis is not valid, if physical impact on a substantial portion or all of the property or on the operation of the enterprise is needed to trigger Subsection 1.15(d), one must ask at what point, if ever, in a complex industrial operation such as we have here, involving large investments, will the cumulative impact of the inability to make rational decisions in fact trigger this subsection?

Must one wait until there has occurred something akin to the troops coming in, little by little or all at once, in a nineteenth century sense? Must there be some physical impact? In our view such narrow interpretation of the contract of insurance does not fit the realities of today and was not intended by the framers of Subsection 1.15. . . .

On the issue of liability, therefore, we find on the merits for Revere and award accordingly.

The Tribunal awarded Revere $1,131,144 plus interest.

Mr. Bergan, one of the three arbitrators, wrote a minority opinion. He held that even if the Jamaican government's actions had been contrary to international law, it had not amounted to "expropriatory action" as defined by Section 1.15 of the insurance contract. The increased bauxite levy and royalties had financially embarrassed RJA and Revere, but they had not deprived them of the effective control of the plant, which remained in RJA's possession and subject to its directions. ◼

Currency Inconvertibility   OPIC offers insurance that guarantees that an investor will be able to convert local currency into dollars, an important guarantee because most American investors have to pay their obligations (e.g., loans, dividends, etc.) in dollars. OPIC's coverage, however, only insures an existing legal right to convert. In the absence of such a right, as in China, OPIC cannot offer this form of coverage. If there is a legal right to convert, however, OPIC will insure that right against an outright denial or an adverse change in conditions (such as a change in banking procedures) making convertibility effectively impossible.

Political Violence   Finally, OPIC offers insurance against losses due to political violence. Political violence is a euphemism for various kinds of risks associated with wars, revolutions, civil strife, and terrorism. This coverage is different from OPIC's expropriation or inconvertibility coverage because the risk is different. Unlike the other risks, this one is generally beyond the control of the host government. In addition, when there is a claim, OPIC's ability to salvage its losses are much weaker. As with the other kinds of expropriation, OPIC has subrogation rights against the host government (i.e., it can bring a claim to recover the money it pays out to the firms it insures). Subrogation rights are of little practical value, however, against a government that is unable to control insurgent violence.

OPIC protects itself both by charging higher insurance rates for countries that are more susceptible to political violence and by requiring investors to take actions to manage perceived risks. Of course, OPIC will decline to insure a project that it perceives is a bad risk. OPIC also limits its exposure in any one country to no more than 10 percent of its total risk.

In contrast to its political risk coverage, OPIC generally does not vary its rates for expropriation or inconvertibility insurance significantly from one country to another. It does this because (1) OPIC is an incentive program and (2) its policies commonly extend for as long as 20 years, making any evaluation of host government conduct difficult.

Multilateral Investment Guaranty Programs

Many writers long believed that "schemes for general multilateral conventions guaranteeing foreign investments against confiscation are highly unlikely to attract the support of a significant number of less developed countries"[117] and that investors would have to rely solely on national programs, such as OPIC. Newly independent states, the writers reasoned, "would be loath in many cases to limit their freedom of action with respect to property acquired during the colonial period."[118]

Despite these inauspicious auguries, the World Bank[119] created a multilateral investment guarantee program in the mid-1980s. Known as the Multilateral Investment Guaranty Agency (MIGA),[120] it opened for business in 1987. In most respects it functions similarly to national programs, such as OPIC, with the important exception that it operates under the political oversight of both capital-exporting and capital-importing states.

---

[117]Oliver J. Lissitzyn, "International Law in a Divided World," *International Conciliation,* No. 543 (March 1963).
[118]*Id.*
[119]The World Bank's Internet home page is at www.worldbank.org/.
[120]MIGA's Internet home page is at www.miga.org/.

F. ENVIRONMENTAL PROTECTION

Contemporary efforts to comprehensively protect the environment date back only to 1968, when the United Nations adopted Resolution 2398 convening the Stockholm Conference on the Human Environment. In 1972, the Conference issued the **Stockholm Declaration**,[121] adopting a list of principles that define both new human rights and new state responsibilities. Two of these are especially noteworthy. Principle 1 proclaims:

> Man has the fundamental right to freedom, equality, and adequate conditions of life, in an environment of a quality that permits a life of dignity and well-being.

And Principle 21 provides:

> States have, in accordance with the Charter of the United Nations and the principles of international law, the sovereign right to exploit their own resources pursuant to their own environmental policies, and the responsibility to ensure that activities within their jurisdiction or control do not cause damage to the environment of other states or of areas beyond the limits of national jurisdiction.

Among the recommendations of the Stockholm Conference was a proposal that the UN General Assembly create a United Nations Environment Program (UNEP).[122] This the Assembly did in December 1972.[123] Since its beginning, UNEP has been active in monitoring the earth's environment, drafting international and regional treaties, and adopting recommended principles and guidelines.[124]

Twenty years after the Stockholm Convention, the United Nations Conference on the Environment and Development (UNCED) convened in Rio de Janeiro in June 1992. The **Rio Declaration** reaffirmed the principles set forth in the Stockholm Declaration.[125] In addition, it linked protection of the environment and development as related goals (a concept that had been hotly debated in 1972).[126] Principle 4 of the Rio Declaration provides as follows:

> In order to achieve sustainable development, environmental protection shall constitute an integral part of the development process and cannot be considered in isolation from it.

Many other new principles were agreed to as well, such as (1) the recognition of a "right of development,"[127] (2) an assertion that "each individual shall have appropriate access to information concerning the environment that is held by public authorities,"[128] (3) the promotion of a "supportive and open international economic system . . . to better address the problems of

---

[121]Formally the "Declaration of the United Nations Conference on the Human Environment (1972)." The text of the declaration is posted on the Internet at www.tufts.edu/fletcher/multi/texts/ STOCKHOLM-DECL.txt.

[122]UNEP's Internet home page is at www.unep.org/.

[123]Resolution 2997 (XXVII), United Nations, General Assembly Official Records, 27th Session, Supp. no. 30, p. 43 (December 15, 1972).

[124]UNEP consists of a Governing Council composed of 58 member states elected by the UN General Assembly. Its Secretariat is headquartered in Nairobi and headed by an Under Secretary-General of the UN who serves as UNEP's executive director. As part of its monitoring activities, it runs Earthwatch, which assesses the state of the earth's environment through its Global Environment Monitoring System, its International Environmental Information System, and its International Register of Potentially Toxic Chemicals. Other activities of UNEP include (1) implementation of the World Plan of Action on the Ozone Layer, (2) climate research and assessment, (3) development of rules to control the international movement of hazardous wastes, (4) implementation of a marine environment action plan, (5) the management of water resources, (6) coordination of an action plan to combat desertification, (7) assessment of the world's forests, (8) maintenance of biological diversity, (9) encouraging cleaner industrial production through better technology, (10) assessment of the impact of the use of energy on the environment, (11) preparation of environmental guidelines for urban development, (12) the protection of human health and well-being, (13) assessing and combating threats to the lithosphere, (14) determination of the risks of specific chemicals to the environment, (15) maintenance of an international register of environmental treaties, (16) development of educational programs on the environment, and (17) assisting environmental planners and policy makers to prepare long-range environmental plans.

[125]Rio Declaration on Environment and Development, UNCED Doc. A/CONF.151/5 Rev.1 (June 13, 1992), reprinted in *International Legal Materials,* vol. 31, p. 874 (1992). The text of the Rio Declaration is posted on UNEP's Internet Web site at www.unep.org/unep/rio.htm. Another copy of the Rio Declaration as well as related materials is available on Information Habitat's Web site at www.infohabitat.org/agenda21.

[126]Edith Brown Weiss, "Introductory Note to United Nations Conference on Environment and Development," *International Legal Materials,* vol. 31, p. 814 at p. 816 (1992).

[127]Rio Declaration on Environment and Development, Principle 3.

[128]*Id.,* Principle 10.

precautionary approach: Maxim that states should not delay in taking action to correct a threat of serious or irreversible damage to the environment merely because there is a lack of scientific certainty that injury will result.

Agenda 21: A schedule of developmental and environmental goals for the period leading up to the year 2000 and beyond. These include the promotion of sustainable and environmentally friendly growth, the elimination and prevention of pollution, and the protection and conservation of the earth's natural resources.

environmental degradation,"[129] (4) adoption of the **precautionary approach** to protecting the environment (i.e., where there are "threats of serious or irreversible damage," action to correct the problem should not be delayed merely because there is a "lack of scientific certainty" that injury will result),[130] and (5) a statement that all states have an obligation to prepare an "environmental impact assessment" whenever activities are proposed by a governmental agency that "are likely to have a significant adverse impact on the environment."[131]

UNCED also adopted a statement designating objectives and priority actions for the international community for the years leading up to the year 2000 and beyond (called **Agenda 21**).[132] This Agenda includes both developmental and environmental goals. The former are to promote sustainable and environmentally friendly growth.[133] The latter are, in essence, to prevent pollution and to conserve and protect the earth's natural resources.

The environmental goals are not new. They have been the main objectives of the international community since the Stockholm Conference. To implement them, states have become parties to various multilateral, regional, and bilateral treaties.[134] In the materials that follow, we will look at some of the more important multilateral arrangements that exist today.

Regulation of Pollution

Efforts to minimize pollution have taken two approaches: a sectoral approach regulating particular sectors of the environment and a product approach regulating particular pollutants.

Sectoral Regulations

The main environmental sectors subject to international regulations are the marine environment and the atmosphere.

Marine Pollution   The 1982 United Nations Convention on the Law of the Sea (UNCLOS)[135] imposes on all states the obligation "to protect and preserve the marine environment."[136] Article 194(1) provides as follows:

> States shall take, individually or jointly as appropriate, all measures consistent with this Convention that are necessary to prevent, reduce, and control pollution of the

---

[129]*Id.*, Principle 12.

[130]*Id.*, Principle 15.

[131]*Id.*, Principle 17.

[132]The name, in part, honors Principle 21 of the Stockholm Declaration. To monitor and review the development goals of Agenda 21, the states that participated in UNCED agreed to establish a new UN Commission for Sustainable Development (as a companion agency to the existing UN Environment Program). This will be an intergovernmental body reporting to the UN Economic and Social Council. *See* General Assembly Resolution 47/191 of December 22, 1992, *International Legal Materials*, vol. 32, p. 254 (1993). The text of the resolution is posted on the UN gopher at gopher://gopher.un.org:70/ 00/ga/recs/47/191. For information about the Commission, *see* the UN Web site at www.un.org/ esa/sustdev/csd.htm.

[133]For a thorough review of the preliminary negotiations and preparatory meetings leading up to the adoption of Agenda 21 and to the UNCED meeting in Rio, *see* Nicholas A. Robinson, ed., *Agenda 21 & the UNCED Proceedings* (3 vols., 1992), and Shanna L. Halpern, *The United Nations Conference on Environment and Development: Process and Documentation* (1992), which is posted on the Consortium for International Earth Science Information Network Web site at infoserver.ciesin.org/ docs/008–585/unced-home.html.

[134]For the texts of most of these treaties *see* the Environmental Treaties and Resource Indicators (ENTRI) Web site on the Internet at sedac.ciesin.org/pidb/texts-home.html.

[135]Members of the Convention as of May 30, 2002, were Algeria, Angola, Antigua and Barbuda, Argentina, Australia, Austria, Bahamas, Bahrain, Bangladesh, Barbados, Belgium, Belize, Benin, Bolivia, Bosnia and Herzegovina, Botswana, Brazil, Brunei Darussalam, Bulgaria, Cameroon, Cape Verde, Chile, China, Comoros, Cook Islands, Costa Rica, Côte d'Ivoire, Croatia, Cuba, Cyprus, Czech Republic, Democratic Republic of the Congo, Djibouti, Dominica, Egypt, Equatorial Guinea, European Union, Fiji, Finland, France, Gabon, Gambia, Georgia, Germany, Ghana, Greece, Grenada, Guatemala, Guinea, Guinea-Bissau, Guyana, Haiti, Honduras, Hungary, Iceland, India, Indonesia, Iraq, Ireland, Italy, Jamaica, Japan, Jordan, Kenya, Kuwait, Laos, Lebanon, Luxembourg, Macedonia, Madagascar, Malaysia, Maldives, Mali, Malta, Marshall Islands, Mauritania, Mauritius, Mexico, Micronesia, Monaco, Mongolia, Mozambique, Myanmar, Namibia, Nauru, Nepal, Netherlands, New Zealand, Nicaragua, Nigeria, Norway, Oman, Pakistan, Palau, Panama, Papua New Guinea, Paraguay, Philippines, Poland, Portugal, Republic of Korea, Romania, Russia, Saint Kitts and Nevis, Saint Lucia, Saint Vincent and the Grenadines, Samoa, Sao Tome and Principe, Saudi Arabia, Senegal, Seychelles, Sierra Leone, Singapore, Slovakia, Slovenia, Solomon Islands, Somalia, South Africa, Spain, Sri Lanka, Sudan, Suriname, Sweden, Tanzania, Togo, Tonga, Trinidad and Tobago, Tunisia, Uganda, Ukraine, United Kingdom, Uruguay, Vanuatu, Vietnam, Yemen, Yugoslavia, Zambia, and Zimbabwe. *See* UN Web site at www.un.org/Depts/los/convention_agreements/convention_agreements.htm.

[136]United Nations Convention on the Law of the Sea, Article 193 (1982). The text of the convention is posted on the Internet at www.tufts.edu/departments/fletcher/multi/sea.html. Currently there are 130 states parties. *Multilateral*

marine environment from any source, using for this purpose the best practicable means at their disposal and in accordance with their capabilities, and they shall endeavor to harmonize their policies in this connection.

In particular, states are to take measures to minimize to the fullest possible extent (1) the release of toxic, harmful, or noxious substances from land-based sources, (2) pollution from vessels, (3) pollution from the installations and devices used in the exploration or exploitation of the seabed and its subsoil, and (4) pollution from other installations and devices operating in the marine environment.[137]

Other duties incumbent on states are (1) not to pollute the environment of neighboring states,[138] (2) not to transfer damage or hazards from one area to another or to transform them from one type of pollution to another,[139] (3) not to intentionally or accidentally introduce alien or new species into the marine environment,[140] (4) to notify other affected states when the marine environment is in imminent danger of being damaged or has been damaged by pollution,[141] and (5) to monitor and assess the risks and effects of pollution and to publish the results of those studies.[142]

To carry out these duties, states are required to "adopt laws and regulations" and "take other measures" to "prevent, reduce, and control pollution."[143] Once adopted, these rules may be enforced by (1) flag states with regard to vessels flying their flag,[144] (2) port states as to vessels voluntarily within their ports,[145] and (3) coastal states as to vessels navigating within their territorial sea or exclusive economic zone[146] or vessels that are found to be dumping materials onto their continental shelf.[147]

UNCLOS provides that disputes between states are to be resolved by negotiation or mediation. If no resolution is possible by these means, then either party may submit the dispute to the International Tribunal for the Law of the Sea, a tribunal established by the convention, or to the International Court of Justice or to a mutually agreeable arbitration tribunal.[148]

In Case 2–11, the International Tribunal for the Law of the Sea was asked to apply provisional measures (restraining orders pending a decision on the merits) in a case of an alleged violation of the UNCLOS.

Treaties Deposited with the Secretary-General: Status as at 15 December 1998, posted on the UN Web site at www.un.org/Depts/Treaty/final/ts2/newfiles/ part_boo/xxi_boo/xxi_6.html.

[137]*Id.,* Article 194(3).
[138]*Id.,* Article 193(2).
[139]*Id.,* Article 195.
[140]*Id.,* Article 196.
[141]*Id.,* Article 198.
[142]*Id.,* Articles 204, 205, and 206.
[143]*Id.,* Articles 207–212.
[144]*Id.,* Article 217.
[145]*Id.,* Article 218.
[146]*Id.,* Article 220.
[147]*Id.,* Article 216.
[148]*Id.,* Article 287. The first application submitted to ITLOS to resolve a dispute was received by the tribunal on November 11, 1997. The dispute was between Saint Vincent and the Grenadines and Guinea. *See* the M/V *Saiga* Case (Case 2–8).

Case 2–11   Southern Bluefin Tuna Cases: Provisional Measures

New Zealand v. Japan; Australia v. Japan (Case Nos. 3 and 4) 1999.
International Tribunal for the Law of the Sea
Posted at www.itlos.org

On August 27, 1999, Australia and New Zealand initiated proceeding in the International for the Law of the Sea against Japan alleging that a unilateral experimental fishing program undertaken by Japan was contrary to the United

Nations Convention on the Law of the Sea (UNCLOS), the 1993 Convention for the Conservation of Southern Bluefin Tuna (CCSBT) and customary international law. Australia and New Zealand simultaneously sought provisional measures (that is, restraining orders pending a decision on the merits) under UNCLOS Article 290(5).

THE TRIBUNAL:

* * *

63. *Considering that*, in accordance with article 290 of the [United Nations] Convention [on the Law of the Sea], the Tribunal may prescribe provisional measures to preserve the respective rights of the parties to the dispute or to prevent serious harm to the marine environment;

* * *

70. *Considering that* the conservation of the living resources of the sea is an element in the protection and preservation of the marine environment;

71. *Considering that* there is no disagreement between the parties that the stock of southern bluefin tuna is severely depleted and is at its historically lowest levels and that this is a cause for serious biological concern;

* * *

73. *Considering that*, in the view of the Tribunal, the parties should in the circumstances act with prudence and caution to ensure that effective conservation measures are taken to prevent serious harm to the stock of southern bluefin tuna;

* * *

80. *Considering that*, although the Tribunal cannot conclusively assess the scientific evidence presented by the parties, it finds that measures should be taken as a matter of urgency to preserve the rights of the parties and to avert further deterioration of the southern bluefin tuna stock;

* * *

90. *For these reasons*, THE TRIBUNAL,

1. Prescribes, pending a decision of the arbitral tribunal, the following measures:

   (a) Australia, Japan and New Zealand shall each ensure that no action is taken which might aggravate or extend the disputes submitted to the arbitral tribunal;

* * *

   (d) Australia, Japan, and New Zealand shall each refrain from conducting an experimental fishing program involving the taking of a catch of southern bluefin tuna, except with the agreement of the other parties or unless the experimental catch is counted against its annual national allocation. . . .

SEPARATE OPINION OF JUDGE AD HOC SHEARER

* * *

The ineluctable fact proved before the Tribunal is that Japan, for the past two years, has been conducting an experimental fishing program without the consent of the other two parties to the CCSBT in excess of its annual quota as last agreed by the Commission. "Experimental fishing" is not a concept recognized, as such, either by the CCSBT or by the United Nations Convention on the Law of the Sea. The expression is not a term of art. It can be characterized, in theory, as one of a number of means of testing the recovery of fish stocks in various places and at various stages of their growth. To that extent it

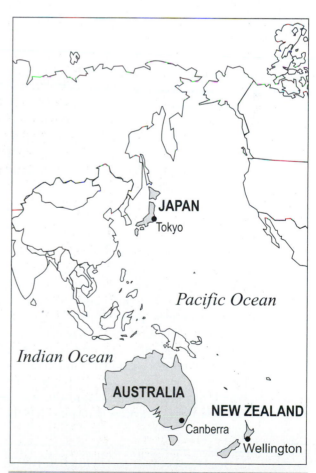

MAP 2-12 Australia, Japan and New Zealand (1999)

was within the powers of the Commission established under the CCSBT to approve an experimental fishing program as part of its scientific studies aimed at obtaining more accurate data concerning southern bluefin tuna stocks. But agreement on experimental fishing in 1998 and 1999 was not forthcoming in view of the failure of the parties to agree upon a change to the previously agreed total annual catch (TAC) and the catches for experimental fishing that would be allowed in addition to the annual national allocations of the TAC.

* * *

. . . Since the Commission under the CCSBT was established in 1994, Australia and New Zealand have taken a precautionary approach and have been unwilling to increase the TAC, despite Japan's arguments that the scientific evidence supported the sustainability of an increase. Because the Commission operates on the unanimity principle, no change in the TAC or national allocations could be effected. There is thus stalemate in the Commission on this issue.

* * *

The Precautionary Principle/Approach

The difficulties of applying the precautionary principle to fisheries management have been well explained in a recent work of persuasive authority.[149] There is a considerable literature devoted to the emergence of the precautionary principle in international law generally,[150] but whether that principle can of itself be a mandate for action, or provide definitive answers to all questions of environmental policy, must be doubted.[151] As Professor Orrego Vicuna has remarked, "Scientific uncertainty is normally the rule in fisheries management and a straightforward application of the precautionary principle would have resulted in the impossibility of proceeding with any activity relating to marine fisheries."[152] Hence, there is a preference by some to use the word "approach" rather than "principle". That this is so, particularly in the case of fisheries management, is confirmed by the wording of Article 6 of the Agreement for the Implementation of the Provisions of the United Nations Convention on the Law of the Sea Relating to the Conservation and Management of Straddling Fish Stocks and Highly Migratory Fish Stocks, December 4, 1995, which obliges states parties to apply "the precautionary approach." Annex II to the Agreement lays down "guidelines" for the application of the precautionary approach. This Agreement, which has not yet entered into force, was signed by all three parties to the present dispute. It is thus

an instrument of important reference to the parties in view of its probable future application to them, and in the meantime, at least, as a set of standards and approaches commanding broad international acceptance.

The Tribunal has not found it necessary to enter into a discussion of the precautionary principle/approach. However, I believe that the measures ordered by the Tribunal are rightly based upon considerations deriving from a precautionary approach.

* * *

SEPARATE OPINION BY JUDGE LAING

* * *

The Tribunal's Order does not refer to the "precautionary principle." Instead, in the recitals it chronicles the opposing views of the Applicants and Respondents about the condition of the stock in view of the allegations about the impact thereon of utilization. It also recites that "the parties should in the circumstances act with "prudence and caution" to ensure that effective conservation measures are taken to prevent serious harm to the stock." It further notes the scientific disagreement about appropriate measures to conserve the stock and the non-agreement of the parties about whether the measures actually taken have led to improvement. This aspect of the recitals states the Tribunal's conclusion about the need for article 290-type of measures despite the Tribunal's inability conclusively to assess the scientific evidence. In my view, these statements are pregnant with meaning. . . .

Background on Environmental Precaution

The notion of environmental precaution largely stems from diplomatic practice and treaty-making in the spheres, originally, of international marine pollution and, now, of biodiversity, climate change, pollution generally and, broadly, the environment. Its main thesis is that, in the face of serious risk to or grounds (as appropriately qualified) for concern about the environment, scientific uncertainty or the absence of complete proof should not stand in the way of positive action to minimize risks or take actions of a conservatory, preventative or curative nature. In addition to scientific uncertainty, the most frequently articulated conditions or circumstances are concerns of an intergenerational nature and forensic or proof difficulties, generally in the context of rapid change and perceived high risks. The thrust of the notion is vesting a broad dispensation to policy makers, seeking to provide guidance to administrative and other decision-makers and shifting the burden of proof to the State in

---

[149]Francisco Orrego Vicuna, *The Changing International Law of High Seas Fisheries* (1999).
[150]*See,* for example, David Freestone and Ellen Hay (eds.), *The Precautionary Principle and International Law: The Challenge of Implementation* (1996).
[151]*See* Philippe Sands, *Principles of Environmental Law,* vol. 1, pp. 211–213 (1995).
[152]*The Changing International Law of High Seas Fisheries,* p. 157 (1999).

control of the territory from which the harm might emanate or to the responsible actor. The notion has been rapidly adopted in most recent instruments and policy documents on the protection and preservation of the environment.[153]

Even as questioning of the acceptability of the precautionary notion diminishes, challenges increase regarding such specifics as: the wide potential ambit of its coverage; the clarity of operational criteria; the monetary costs of environmental regulation; possible public health risks associated with the very remedies improvised to avoid risk; diversity and vagueness of articulations of the notion; uncertainties about attendant obligations, and the imprecision and subjectivity of such a value-laden notion.[154] Nevertheless, the notion has been "broadly accepted for international action, even if the consequence of its application in a given situation remains open to interpretation."[155]

Nevertheless, it is not possible, on the basis of the materials available and arguments presented on this application for provisional measures, to determine whether, as [Australia and New Zealand] contend, customary international law recognizes a precautionary principle.

Precaution in Marine Living Resource Management

However, it cannot be denied that UNCLOS adopts a precautionary approach. This may be gleaned, *inter alia*, from preambular paragraph 4, identifying as an aspect of the "legal order for the seas and oceans" "the conservation of their living resources . . . " Several provisions in Part V of the Convention, e.g. Articles 63–66, on conservation and utilization of a number of species in the exclusive economic zone, identify conservation as a crucial value. So do Article 61, specifically dealing with conservation in general and Article 64, dealing with conservation and optimum utilization of highly migratory species (such as tuna). Article 116, on the right to fish on the high seas, *inter alia* reiterates the conservation obligation on nationals of non-coastal/distant fishing States while fishing in the exclusive economic zone of other States. Article 117 explicitly articulates the duty of all States "to take, or to co-operate with other States in taking, measures for their respective nationals as may be necessary for" conservation of living resources in the

high seas. Article 118 requires inter-State cooperation in the conservation and management of high seas living resources. Such cooperation is to extend to negotiations leading to the establishment of subregional or regional fisheries organizations. And article 119, entitled "conservation of the living resources of the high seas", deals with the allocation of allowable catches and "establishing other conservation measures." Although paragraph 1(a) refers to measures, based on the best scientific evidence, for production of the maximum sustainable yield, the conservatory thrust of this article is vigorously reaffirmed by the treatment, in paragraph (b), of the effects of management measures on associated or dependent species the populations of which should be maintained or restored "above levels at which their reproduction may become seriously threatened." Article 116, in association with the Part V articles mentioned above, has been stated to point to the precautionary "principle" of fisheries management, while Article 119 has been said to reflect a precautionary "approach" "when scientific data is not available or is inadequate to enable comprehensive decision-making."[156] Most of these are the very provisions before this Tribunal today. Strikingly, also, Article 290:1's reference to serious harm to the marine environment as a basis for provisional measures also underscores the salience of the approach.

* * *

My conclusions . . . are bolstered by such recent precedents as paragraph 17.21 of Agenda 21. It is also reinforced by various provisions in articles 6 and 7 of the Code of Conduct for Responsible Fisheries of the Food and Agriculture Organization and articles 5(c) and 6 of the Straddling Stocks Agreement, with detailed requirements for the application of the precautionary approach. In the present context, it matters little that the former is a voluntary Code and the latter is not yet in force. With some cogency, these developments were judicially presaged by the International Court of Justice in 1974:

[E]ven if the Court holds that Iceland's extension of its fishery limits is not opposable to the Applicant, this does not mean that the Applicant is under no obligation to Iceland with respect to fishing in disputed waters in the 12-mile to 50-mile zone. On the contrary, both States have an obligation to take full

---

[153]Of note is ¶ 17.21 of Agenda 21, adopted at the 1992 Rio Conference on the Environment and Development. Paragraph 17.1 also calls for "new approaches to the marine and coastal area management and development, at the national, regional and global levels, approaches that are integrated in context and are precautionary and anticipatory in ambit . . ." Paragraph 15 of the Rio Declaration, adopted at the same Conference, provides that "In order to protect the environment, the precautionary approach shall be widely applied by States according to their capabilities. Where there are threats of serious or irreversible damage, lack of full scientific certainty shall not be used as a reason for postponing cost-effective measures to prevent environmental degradation." . . .

[154]Philippe Sands in *The Precautionary Principle and International Law: The Challenge of Implementation*, p. 134 (D. Freestone and E. Hey, eds., 1996); F. Cross, *Washington & Lee Law Review*, vol. 53, pp. 851–925 (1996); J. Hickey and V. Walker, *Virginia Environmental Law Journal*, vol. 14, pp. 423–454 (1995); J. Macdonald, *26 O.D.I.L.* 255–86 (1995).

[155]A. D'Amato and K. Engel, *International Environmental Law Anthology*, p. 22 (1996).

[156]*United Nations Convention on the Law of the Sea 1982: A Commentary* (hereafter *Virginia Commentary*), vol. 4, pp. 288, 310 (Shabtai Rosenne and Louis B. Sohn, eds. 1989).

account of each other's rights and of any fishery waters. It is one of the advances in maritime international law, resulting from the intensification of fishing, that the former *laissez-faire* treatment of the living resources of the sea in the high seas has been replaced by a recognition of a duty to have due regard to the rights of other States and the needs of conservation for the benefit of all. Consequently, both Parties have the obligation to keep under review the fishery re-

sources in the disputed waters and to examine together, in the light of scientific and other available information, the measures required for the conservation and development, and equitable exploitation, of those resources, taking into account any international agreement in force between them . . .[157] ∎

* * *

---

[157]Fisheries Jurisdiction case, *International Court of Justice Reports,* vol. 1974, p. 3, p. 31, ¶ 72 (1974).

In addition to the 1982 UN Convention, several other international conventions and instruments deal with more particular problems of ocean pollution. Among these are the 1954 Convention for the Prevention of Pollution of the Sea by Oil;[158] the 1969 Convention Relating to Intervention on the High Seas in Case of Oil Pollution Casualties;[159] the 1972 Convention on the Prevention of Marine Pollution by Dumping of Wastes and Other Matter;[160] the 1973 Convention for the Prevention of Pollution from Ships;[161] the 1974 Convention on the Prevention of Marine Pollution from Land-Based Sources;[162] the 1989 Convention on Salvage;[163] and the 1990 Convention on Oil Pollution Preparedness, Response, and Cooperation.[164]

Climate and Air Pollution   The principal international treaty dealing with the problem of global warming is the **United Nations Framework Convention on Climate** (UNFCC).[165] Adopted in 1992 at the UN Conference on the Environment and Development in Rio de Janeiro and in force since 1994, the Convention establishes objectives and principles, commitments for different groups of countries, and a set of institutions to enable its member states to monitor the convention's implementation and to continue discussions on how best to deal with the problem.

The ultimate objective of the UNFCC is the "stabilization of atmospheric concentrations of greenhouse gases at levels that would prevent dangerous anthropogenic[166] interference with the climate system. . . ."[167] Although the Convention does not define "dangerous," it does state that ecosystems should be allowed to adapt naturally, the food supply should not be threatened, and economic development should be able to proceed in a sustainable manner.[168]

United Nations Framework Convention on Climate: Multilateral convention adopted in 1992 and in force since 1994. It seeks to stabilize and diminish greenhouses gases in the atmosphere.

---

[158]*United Nations Treaty Series,* vol. 327, p. 3. The text is also posted on the Internet at www.tufts.edu/departments/fletcher/multi/texts/tre-0130.txt.

[159]*Id.,* vol. 970, p. 211. The text is also available online at sedac.ciesin.org/pidb/texts/intervention.high.seas.casualties.1969.html.

[160]*Id.,* vol. 1046, p. 120. The text is also online at sedac.ciesin.org/pidb/texts/marine. pollution.dumping.of.wastes.1972.html.

[161]The convention is in *International Legal Materials,* vol. 12, p. 1319 (1973), and its 1978 Protocol is in *id.* at vol. 17, p. 546 (1978). The texts of both are posted on the Internet at sedac.ciesin.org/pidb/texts/pollution.from.ships.1973.html and at sedac.ciesin.org/pidb/ texts/acrc/marpolp.txt.html.

[162]The text of the convention is posted on the Internet at sedac.ciesin.org/pidb/texts/marine.pollution.land.based.sources.1974.html. Its 1990 Protocol is at sedac.ciesin.org/pidb/texts/acrc/kuwaitprot.txt.html.

[163]*International Environmental Law, Multilateral Treaties,* vol. 989, p. 32 (W. E. Burhenne, ed.) and on the Internet at www.jus.uio.no/lm/imo.salvage.convention.1989/doc.html.

[164]*International Legal Materials,* vol. 30, p. 735 (1991), and at sedac.ciesin.org/pidb/texts/oil.pollution.preparedness.1990.html.

    Other regional conventions are posted on the Internet on the Center for International Earth Science Information Network's Web site at sedac.ciesin.org/pidb/texts-subject.html#Oceans. For an analysis and explanation of these conventions *see* "Research Paper No. 27," in *Agenda 21 & the UNCED Proceedings,* pp. 1207–1341 (Nicholas A. Robinson, ed., 3 vols., 1992).

[165]The convention's Secretariat maintains a home page at unfccc.int/.

[166]Man made.

[167]UN Framework Convention on Climate Control, Article 2. The text of the convention is posted online at unfccc.int/resource/conv/conv_004.html.

[168]UNFCC, Article 2.

The principles adopted by the Convention are meant to address two main political problems: (1) how to distribute the burden of reducing emissions among different countries and (2) how to deal with scientific uncertainty. The principles of "equity" and "common but differentiated responsibilities"[169] address the first of these. In other words, the Convention recognizes that industrialized countries have historically been the main source of the problem and have more resources to address it, and that the developing countries are more vulnerable to its adverse effects and have the least resources to address the problem. It therefore requires industrialized countries to take the lead in modifying long-term emission trends and it calls on the richest countries to provide financial and technological resources to help developing countries stabilize their greenhouse gas emissions.

To deal with second political problem, of scientific uncertainty, the convention adopts the "precautionary principle." This principle, also incorporated in the Rio Declaration, responds to the dilemma that, while there are many uncertainties still surrounding climate change, waiting for full scientific certainty before taking action is almost certain to be too late to avert its worst impacts. The Convention, accordingly, calls for member states to adopt "precautionary measures" to combat climate change, stating that, "where there are threats of serious or irreversible damage, lack of full scientific certainty should not be used as a reason for postponing such measures."[170]

The Convention divides it member countries into two main groups. Developed countries—currently 40 are members[171]—are known as Annex I countries (because they are listed in the convention's Annex I). Other member countries are known as non-Annex I countries.

Both groups of member countries have general obligations. These include the obligations to: (1) promote programs to address greenhouse gas emissions, (2) protect so-called carbon "sinks" and "reservoirs" (forests and other natural systems that remove carbon from the atmosphere), (3) assess the environmental impact of their social and economic policies, (4) develop and share climate-friendly technologies and practices, (5) promote education, training and public awareness of climate change, and (6) submit reports (known as "national communications") on the actions they are taking to implement the convention.[172] In addition, Annex I countries have an obligation to adopt climate change policies and measures with the "aim" of returning their greenhouse gas emissions to 1990 levels.[173] This "aim" was supposed to have been achieved by the year 2000, but it proved to be too ambitious, especially as it was "non-legally binding" commitment.

The institutional structure set up by the convention consists of a Conference of the Parties, two subsidiary bodies (the Subsidiary Body for Scientific and Technological Advice and the Subsidiary Body for Implementation), and a secretariat. The Conference of the Parties meets annually to review the "national communications" and to negotiate substantive new commitments;[174] the two subsidiary bodies carry out preparatory work for the Conference of the Parties;[175] and the secretariat, with a staff of 150, provides support.[176]

At the Conference of Parties meeting at Kyoto, Japan in 1997, the member countries drafted a Protocol[177] to the Convention which would legally bind the developed Annex I countries to reduce the amount of their greenhouse gas emissions by 5.2 percent below 1990 levels during the five-year period between 2008 and 2012.[178] In order for the **Kyoto Protocol** to come into force it must be ratified or acceded to by: (1) 55 percent of all member countries and

Kyoto Protocol:
Supplemental agreement to UN Framework Convention on Climate Control drafted in 1997. It would require developed member countries of the Convention to reduce greenhouse gas emissions by 5.2 percent below 1990 levels.

---

[169]*Id.*, Article 3(1).

[170]*Id.*, Article 3(3).

[171]The developed Annex I member countries are: Australia, Austria, Belarus, Belgium, Bulgaria, Canada, Croatia, Czech Republic, Denmark, Estonia, the European Community, Finland, France, Germany, Greece, Hungary, Iceland, Ireland, Italy, Japan, Latvia, Liechtenstein, Lithuania, Luxembourg, Monaco, Netherlands, New Zealand, Norway, Poland, Portugal, Romania, Russia, Slovakia, Slovenia, Spain, Sweden, Switzerland, Turkey, Ukraine, the United Kingdom, and the United States.

[172]UNFCC, Article 4.

[173]*Id.*, Article 4(2)(b).

[174]*Id.*, Article 7.

[175]*Id.*, Articles 9 and 10.

[176]*Id.*, Article 8.

[177]The text of the Kyoto Protocol is posted at unfccc.int/resource/docs/convkp/kpeng.html.

[178]The target decreases vary by country. The agreed targets are an 8 percent reduction for the European Union, Bulgaria, Czech Republic, Estonia, Latvia, Liechtenstein, Lithuania, Monaco, Romania, Slovakia, Slovenia, and Switzerland; a 7 percent reduction for the United States; a 6 percent reduction for Canada, Hungary, Japan, and Poland; a 5 percent reduction for Croatia; a 0 percent reduction for New Zealand, Russia, and Ukraine; a 1 percent increase for Norway; an 8 percent increase for Australia; and a 10 percent increase for Iceland. Kyoto Protocol, Annex B.

(2) Annex I Parties accounting for 55 percent of that group's carbon dioxide emissions in 1990.[179] The first of these requirements has already been met[180] and it is likely the second will be met prior to 2003.[181]

The only developed Annex I country to indicate that it will not be a party to the Kyoto Protocol is the United States. The reasons for the United States' refusal to participate are described in Reading 2–1.

---

[179]Kyoto Protocol, Article 25.

[180]As of June 4, 2002, 84 countries were parties to the Protocol. *See* status of the Protocol at unfccc.int/resource/convkp.html.

[181]Annex I countries—including the European Union member states and Japan—accounting for 35 percent of that groups' 1990 emissions were parties as of June 4, 2002. *Id.* If Russia and Canada ratify the Protocol, which they are expected to do, the Protocol will be in force.

Reading 2–1   The U.S. View: Kyoto Protocol Is Fundamentally Flawed

Remarks by U.S. President George W. Bush on Global Climate Change in the White House Rose Garden, June 11, 2001.
Posted on State Department Web site at www.state.gov/g/oes/rls/rm/4149.htm

PRESIDENT BUSH:

Good morning. I've just met with senior members of my administration who are working to develop an effective and science-based approach to addressing the important issues of global climate change.

* * *

The issue of climate change respects no border. Its effects cannot be reined in by an army nor advanced by any ideology. Climate change, with its potential to impact every corner of the world, is an issue that must be addressed by the world.

The Kyoto Protocol was fatally flawed in fundamental ways. But the process used to bring nations together to discuss our joint response to climate change is an important one. That is why I am today committing the United States of America to work within the United Nations framework and elsewhere to develop with our friends and allies and nations throughout the world an effective and science-based response to the issue of global warming.

* * *

There are only two ways to stabilize concentration of greenhouse gases. One is to avoid emitting them in the first place; the other is to try to capture them after they're created. And there are problems with both approaches. We're making great progress through technology, but have not yet developed cost-effective ways to capture carbon emissions at their source; although there is some promising work that is being done.

And a growing population requires more energy to heat and cool our homes, more gas to drive our cars. Even though we're making progress on conservation and energy efficiency and have significantly reduced the amount of carbon emissions per unit of GDP.

Our country, the United States is the world's largest emitter of manmade greenhouse gases. We account for almost 20 percent of the world's man-made greenhouse emissions. We also account for about one-quarter of the world's economic output. We recognize the responsibility to reduce our emissions. We also recognize the other part of the story—that the rest of the world emits 80 percent of all greenhouse gases. And many of those emissions come from developing countries.

This is a challenge that requires a 100 percent effort; ours, and the rest of the world's. The world's second-largest emitter of greenhouse gases is China. Yet, China was entirely exempted from the requirements of the Kyoto Protocol.

India and Germany are among the top emitters. Yet, India was also exempt from Kyoto. These and other developing countries that are experiencing rapid growth face challenges in reducing their emissions without harming their economies. We want to work coopera-

U.S. President George W. Bush and U.S. Environmental Protection Agency Administrator Christine Todd Whitman in the White House Rose Garden. (Photo: AFP Photo/Joyce Naltchayan © AFP/CORBIS.)

tively with these countries in their efforts to reduce greenhouse emissions and maintain economic growth.

Kyoto also failed to address two major pollutants that have an impact on warming: black soot and tropospheric ozone. Both are proven health hazards. Reducing both would not only address climate change, but also dramatically improve people's health.

Kyoto is, in many ways, unrealistic. Many countries cannot meet their Kyoto targets. The targets themselves were arbitrary and not based upon science. For America, complying with those mandates would have a negative economic impact, with layoffs of workers and price increases for consumers. And when you evaluate all these flaws, most reasonable people will understand that it's not sound public policy.

That's why 95 members of the United States Senate expressed a reluctance to endorse such an approach. Yet, America's unwillingness to embrace a flawed treaty should not be read by our friends and allies as any abdication of responsibility. To the contrary, my administration is committed to a leadership role on the issue of climate change.

We recognize our responsibility and will meet it—at home, in our hemisphere, and in the world. My Cabinet-level working group on climate change is recommending a number of initial steps, and will continue to work on additional ideas. The working group proposes the United States help lead the way by advancing the science on climate change, advancing the technology to monitor and reduce greenhouse gases, and creating partnerships within our hemisphere and beyond to monitor and measure and mitigate emissions.

* * *

So we're creating the National Climate Change Technology Initiative to strengthen research at universities and national labs, to enhance partnerships in applied research, to develop improved technology for measuring and monitoring gross and net greenhouse gas emissions, and to fund demonstration projects for cutting-edge technologies, such as bio-reactors and fuel cells.

Even with the best science, even with the best technology, we all know the United States cannot solve this global problem alone. We're building partnerships within the Western Hemisphere and with other like-minded countries. Last week, Secretary Powell signed a new CONCAUSA Declaration with the countries of Central America, calling for cooperative efforts on science research, monitoring and measuring of emissions, technology development, and investment in forest conservation.

We will work with the Inter-American Institute for Global Change Research and other institutions to better understand regional impacts of climate change. We will establish a partnership to monitor and mitigate emissions. And at home, I call on Congress to work with my administration on the initiatives to enhance conservation and energy efficiency outlined in my energy plan, to implement the increased use of renewables, natural gas and hydropower that are outlined in the plan, and to increase the generation of safe and clean nuclear power.

By increasing conservation and energy efficiency and aggressively using these clean energy technologies, we can reduce our greenhouse gas emissions by significant amounts in the coming years. We can make great progress in reducing emissions, and we will. Yet, even that isn't enough.

I've asked my advisors to consider approaches to reduce greenhouse gas emissions, including those that tap the power of markets, help realize the promise of technology and ensure the widest-possible global participation. As we analyze the possibilities, we will be guided by several basic principles. Our approach must be consistent with the long-term goal of stabilizing greenhouse gas concentrations in the atmosphere. Our actions should be measured as we learn more from science and build on it.

Our approach must be flexible to adjust to new information and take advantage of new technology. We must always act to ensure continued economic growth and prosperity for our citizens and for citizens throughout the world. We should pursue market-based incentives and spur technological innovation.

And, finally, our approach must be based on global participation, including that of developing countries whose net greenhouse gas emissions now exceed those in the developed countries. ■

Other international treaties dealing with the climate and air pollution are the 1979 Geneva Convention on Long-Range Transboundary Air Pollution,[182] the 1985 Vienna Convention for

---

[182]The text of this convention is posted on the Internet at sedac.ciesin.org/pidb/texts/ transboundary.air.pollution. 1979.html. This is a European regional convention that was drafted under the auspices of the UN Economic Commission. As of December 1998, 42 states and the European Union were parties. *Multilateral Treaties Deposited with the Secretary-General: Status as at 15 December 1998,* posted on the UN Web site at www.un.org/ Depts/Treaty/. Its objectives, set out in Article 2, are "to limit and, as far as possible, gradually reduce and prevent air pollution including long-range transboundary pollution." To accomplish this, Article 6 requires states parties "to develop the best policies and strategies, including air quality management systems, . . . compatible with balanced development. . . ."

the Protection of the Ozone Layer with[183] its 1987 Montreal Protocol on Substances that Deplete the Ozone Layer,[184] and Annex 16 on Environmental Protection to the 1944 Chicago Convention on International Civil Aviation.[185]

Product Regulations

The principal product areas subject to international environmental regulation are toxic waste and nuclear materials.

Toxic Waste Toxic and other wastes are regulated by the 1989 Basel Convention on the Control of Transboundary Movements of Hazardous Wastes and Their Disposal, which came into force in 1992.[186] The Convention forbids the export of "hazardous wastes and other wastes" to non–states parties and to states parties unwilling or incapable of safely accepting them;[187] and it forbids states parties to import wastes unless they can safely manage them.[188] It also requires states parties to take appropriate actions to minimize their own production of hazardous wastes.[189]

International Atomic Energy Agency:
Intergovernmental organization responsible for supervising the use of fissionable material, developing safety standards, and promoting the peaceful use of atomic energy.

Nuclear Materials The **International Atomic Energy Agency** (IAEA) is the primary intergovernmental organization responsible for supervising the use of fissionable materials.[190] Its Statute (a multilateral convention that came into force in 1957)[191] makes the IAEA responsible for setting up safety standards for the protection of health and to minimize injury to life and property.[192]

---

[183]The text of the Vienna Convention is at sedac.ciesin.org/pidb/texts/vienna.ozone.layer. protection.1985.html. As of December 1998, 168 states and the European Union were parties. *Id.* It seeks "to protect human health and the environment against adverse effects resulting or likely to result from human activities which modify or are likely to modify the ozone layer." Article 2. States parties are required to cooperate in scientific research and to exchange information relating to science, technology, and the legal implementation of the Convention's goals. Articles 3 and 4.

[184]The text of the Montreal Protocol is at sedac.ciesin.org/pidb/texts/montreal.protocol.ozone. 1987.html. As of December 1998, 167 states and the European Union were parties to the Montreal Protocol. *Id.* The Protocol expands the goals of the 1985 Vienna Convention, requiring states parties "to protect the ozone layer by taking precautionary measures to control equitably total global emissions of substances that deplete it, with the ultimate objective of their elimination. . . ." Preamble. As currently amended, the Protocol requires the staged phaseout of a list of chlorofluorocarbons and halons, and of carbon tertrachloride, by the year 2000, and a phaseout of methyl choloroform by 2005. Articles 2A-2H.

[185]The text of the Chicago Convention is at www.iasl.mcgill.ca/airlaw/public/chicago/ chicago1944a.pdf. As of December 1998, there were 181 states parties to the Chicago Convention. Annals of Air and Space Law, vol. XVIII, pt. 2 (1998). Annex 16 is described in the *Yearbook of International Cooperation on Environment and Development 1988/1999* at www.ext.grida.no/ggynet/agree/atmosphe/annex16.htm. Annex 16 establishes standardized international emissions limits for aircraft noise and gaseous pollutants and a uniform certification system to enforce them. Its goal is to reconcile air transport needs with environmental concerns, especially in locales close to airports.

[186]The text is in *International Legal Materials,* vol. 28, p. 649 (1989). It is also posted on the Internet at sedac.ciesin.org/pidb/texts/basel.transboundary.hazardous.wastes.1989.html. As of August 2002, 134 states had become parties. *Multilateral Treaties Deposited with the Secretary-General: Status as at 31 August 2002,* posted on the UN Web site at www.un.org/Depts/Treaty/final/ ts2/newfiles/part_boo/xxviiboo/xxvii_3.html.

[187]Convention on the Control of Transboundary Movements of Hazardous Wastes and Their Disposal, Articles 4(1) and 4(5). Article 6 forbids the export of wastes to Antarctica.

[188]*Id.,* Article 4(2)(g). Article 9 also forbids the import of waste unless it is required as a raw material for a recycling or recovery industry or if the exporting state does not have the capacity to properly dispose of it.

[189]*Id.,* Article 4(2)(a). Article 4(3) requires states parties to treat the illegal traffic in hazardous wastes as criminal conduct.

[190]The IAEA's Internet home page is at www.iaea.org/.

[191]Statute of the International Atomic Energy Agency, adopted in October 1956, in force July 1957. The text is in *United Nations Treaty Series,* vol. 276, p. 3, and on the Internet at www.iaea.OR.at/worldatom/documents/statute.html. As of August 2002, there were 134 states parties. *See* membership listing at www.iaea.or.at/worldatom/about/.

    The IAEA is an agency within the United Nations system. It consists of a General Conference of all states parties that meets annually. A Board of Governors (made up of 35 states members, 22 of which are elected by the General Conference and 12 of which are designated by the Board itself) meets about six times a year to carry out the functions of the Agency. A Director-General, who heads up the Agency's Secretariat, assists the Board. *See id.*

[192]Article III. *See* Mohamed Elbaradei, Edwin Nwogugu, and John Rames, *International Law and Nuclear Energy: Overview of the Legal Framework,* at www.iaea.or.at/worldatom/periodicals/bulletin/bull373/rames.html.

    In its role as an overseer of the environment, the IAEA has sponsored several treaties relating to nuclear safety. The 1986 Convention on Early Notification of a Nuclear Accident (text in *International Legal Materials,* vol. 25, p. 1377 [1986], and on the Internet at www.iaea.or.at/worldatom/documents/Legal/; 87 states parties as of February 2002, *id.*) and the 1986 Convention on Assistance in the Case of a Nuclear Accident or Radiological Emergency (text on the Internet at *id.,* 84 states parties as of August 2002, *id.*) were both adopted following the nuclear accident at Chernobyl, Ukraine, on April 25, 1986. The 1979 Convention on the Physical Protection of Nuclear Material (text at *id.,* 78 states parties as of August 2002, *id.*) establishes guidelines for transporting nuclear materials. The 1994 Convention on Nuclear Safety (text at *id.,* 54 states parties as of August 2002, *id.*) sets out nonbinding recommendations for siting, design, construction, operation, providing adequate financial and human resources, and assessing and verifying safety, quality assurance, and emergency preparedness of nuclear facilities.

It also gives the IAEA responsibility for promoting the peaceful use of atomic energy, for ensuring that its own nuclear materials and assistance are not misused, and for overseeing the nuclear devices and materials of certain "non-nuclear weapons" states to ensure that they are not diverted to military uses.[193]

One of the IAEA's main functions is to oversee compliance with the 1968 Treaty on the Non-Proliferation of Nuclear Weapons.[194] In doing so, the IAEA carries out inspections at nuclear facilities in some 60 non-nuclear weapons states.[195] In July 1991, the IAEA determined that Iraq had not been submitting nuclear materials and certain of its facilities to inspection, and it adopted a resolution of noncompliance that it forwarded to the UN Security Council. Following the Gulf War and Iraq's expulsion from Kuwait, Iraq agreed to allow the IAEA to conduct special inspections of its nuclear materials and facilities, including an examination of documents showing how and from whom it had obtained equipment that it had intended to use for the production of nuclear weapons.[196] In mid-1994, North Korea similarly refused to allow IAEA inspectors to examine its nuclear facilities. At one point, North Korea announced that it was withdrawing from the Non-Proliferation Treaty, but it later said that it would continue its membership after the United States and South Korea agreed to high-level negotiations over the normalization of relations between the three countries.[197]

Protection of Natural Resources

World Charter for Nature: UN General Assembly Resolution 37/7, adopted October 28, 1982. It states that all states have a duty to respect the essential processes of nature and not to impair them.

In October 1982, the United Nations General Assembly adopted the **World Charter for Nature**.[198] The Charter declares, simply, that "[n]ature shall be respected and its essential processes shall not be impaired."[199] In this regard, the Charter states that "living resources shall not be utilized in excess of their natural capacity for regeneration"[200] and that all "ecosystems and organisms, as well as the land, marine, and atmospheric resources that are utilized by man, shall be managed to achieve and maintain optimum sustainable productivity . . . [without endangering] those other ecosystems or species with which they coexist."[201]

The World Charter for Nature also declares that states need to establish procedures to control "activities which might have an impact on nature."[202] In particular, it calls upon states to (1) avoid activities that are likely to cause irreversible damage to nature,[203] (2) conduct "exhaustive" examinations to demonstrate that the expected benefits outweigh the potential damage to nature before proceeding with activities that are likely to pose a significant risk,[204] and (3) prepare environmental

---

[193]Article II. *See* Mohamed Elbaradei, Edwin Nwogugu, and John Rames, *International Law and Nuclear Energy: Overview of the Legal Framework,* at www.iaea.or.at/worldatom/periodical/bulletin/bull373/rames.html.

[194]The text is on the UN Web site at disarmament.un.org/treatystatus.nsf. As of March 2002, there were 187 states parties.

  Other treaties that regulate and limit the use of nuclear weapons are the 1959 Antarctic Treaty (text at *id.,* 44 states parties as of March 2002), the 1963 Treaty Banning Nuclear Weapons Tests in the Atmosphere, in Outer Space, and Under Water (text at *id.,* 124 states parties as of March 1997); and the 1967 Treaty on Principles Governing the Activities of States in the Exploration and Use of Outer Space Including the Moon and Other Celestial Bodies (the Outer Space Treaty, text at *id.,* 96 states parties as of March 2002). The Outer Space Treaty prohibits nuclear weapons and other weapons of mass destruction from being put into orbit or installed and/or launched from the moon or other celestial bodies.

  In 1997, the UN General Assembly adopted a Comprehensive Nuclear Test Ban Treaty. The text is posted at *id.* As of March 2002, there were 94 states parties (but the treaty will not come into force until ratified by the 46 states listed in Annex 2). The treaty provides for on-site inspections and a system for dispute resolutions.

[195]Article III(1).

[196]The special inspection program was required by Security Council Resolution 687.

[197]Cable News Network, June 22, 1994.

[198]Resolution 37/7 (XXXVII). U.N. Doc. A/37/L4 and Add. 1 (1982). The text is in *International Legal Materials,* vol. 22, p. 455 (1983); and on the Internet at www.tufts.edu/departments/ fletcher/multi/texts/UNGARES37-7.txt.

  The International Union for Conservation of Nature and Natural Resources (IUCN), a non-governmental organization, was mainly responsible for the drafting of the World Charter for Nature. The Charter was adopted by the General Assembly by a vote of 111 in favor to 1 against (the United States), with 18 abstentions. *See* Michel Prieur, "Protection of the Environment," in *International Law: Achievements and Prospects,* p. 1017 at pp. 1031–1032 (Mohammed Bedjaoui, ed., 1991).

[199]World Charter for Nature, Principle 1.

[200]*Id.,* Principle 10(a).

[201]*Id.,* Principle 4.

[202]*Id.,* Principle 11.

[203]*Id.,* Principle 11(a).

[204]*Id.,* Principle 11(b).

impact studies that include plans for minimizing potential adverse effects before undertaking activities that may disturb nature.[205]

Over the years, a variety of conventions have been adopted that seek to protect both terrestrial living resources[206] and marine living resources[207] and, in effect, to carry out the objectives of the World Charter for Nature.[208] Recently, at the 1992 Rio Conference, a new wide-reaching conservation convention was signed: the Convention on Biological Diversity.[209] This Convention calls for states parties to identify and monitor biological diversity,[210] develop strategies, plans, and programs for conserving biological diversity,[211] and undertake environmental impact assessments of activities that adversely affect biological diversity.[212]

The Rio Conference's Declaration on Environment and Development attempted to reconcile the different and sometimes antagonistic needs of protecting the environment and promoting development. It called upon states parties, and the international community as a whole, to make environmental protection "an integral part of the development process" and not to consider the two in isolation from each other.[213]

Liability for Environmental Damage

There are a few conventions that impose liability on persons who cause damage to the environment. These conventions, in general, define the nature of the liability, the persons who are liable, and the extent of their liability. Thus, with respect to damage resulting from the use of nuclear materials, the operators of nuclear installations are made "absolutely and exclusively" liable for any damage they cause.[214] This includes continuing liability for damage that occurs while nuclear materials are being transported by ship from one installation to another.[215]

---

[205]*Id.,* Principle 11(c).

[206]Among the international conventions protecting terrestrial living resources are the 1950 International Convention for the Protection of Birds (text at sedac.ciesin.org/pidb/texts/protection.of.birds. 1950.html, 10 states parties as of July 2002); the 1971 Convention on Wetlands of International Importance Especially as Waterfowl Habitat (text at sedac.ciesin.org/pidb/texts/ramsar.wetlands.waterfowl. habitat.1971.html, 61 states parties as of July 2002); the 1972 Convention for the Protection of Antarctic Seals (text at sedac.ciesin.org/pidb/texts/antarctic.seals.1972.html; 16 states parties as of July 2002); the 1972 Convention Concerning the Protection of the World Cultural and Natural Heritage (text at whc.unesco.org/nwhc/pages/doc/dc_f15.htm, 172 states parties as of July 2002); the 1973 Convention on International Trade in Endangered Species of Wild Fauna and Flora (text at sedac.ciesin.org/pidb/ texts/cites.trade.endangered.species.1973.html, 158 states parties as of July 2002); the 1976 Agreement on the Conservation of Polar Bears (text at sedac.ciesin.org/pidb/ texts/polar.bears.1973.html, five states parties as of July 2002); the 1979 Convention on the Conservation of Migratory Species of Wild Animals (text at sedac.ciesin. org/pidb/texts/migratory.wild.animals. 1979.html, 39 states parties as of July 2002); the 1980 Convention on the Conservation of Antarctic Marine Living Resources (text at sedac.ciesin.org/pidb/texts/antarctic.marine.resources. 1980.html, 26 states parties as of July 2002; and the 1983 International Tropical Timber Agreement (text at sedac. ciesin.org/pidb/texts/tropical.timber.1983.html, 42 states parties as of July 2002).

[207]The principal international convention protecting marine living resources is the 1946 International Convention for the Regulation of Whaling (text at www.iwcoffice.org/Convention.htm, 48 states parties as of July 2002). A significant number of regional conventions regulate fisheries in most of the world's oceans. *See* "Survey of International Agreements and Instruments," in *Agenda 21 & the UNCED Proceedings,* p. 763 at pp. 790–796 (Nicholas A. Robinson, ed., 3 vols., 1992).

[208]Links to international nature and biodiversity treaties and conventions are available on the Pace University School of Law Web site at www.law.pace.edu/env/naturebio.html.

[209]Text at www.biodiv.org/convention/articles.asp. There were 183 states parties as of July 2002. The Secretariat for the Convention maintains a Web site at www.biodiv.org/.

In January 2000, the Conference of the Parties to the Convention on Biological Diversity adopted a supplementary agreement to the Convention known as the Cartagena Protocol on Biosafety. The Protocol seeks to protect biological diversity from the risks posed by genetically modified organisms. To do so, it establishes an advance informed agreement (AIA) procedure for so that countries are provided with the information necessary to make informed decisions before agreeing to the import of such organisms into their territory. The text of the Protocol is at www.biodiv.org/biosafety/protocol.asp. There were 21 state parties as of July 2002.

[210]Convention on Biological Diversity, Article 7.

The term "biological diversity" is defined as "the variability among living organisms from all sources including, inter alia, terrestrial, marine and other aquatic ecosystems, and the ecological complexes of which they are part; this includes diversity within species, between species, and of ecosystems." Article 2.

[211]*Id.,* Article 6.

[212]*Id.,* Article 14.

[213]Principle 4.

[214]1963 Convention on Civil Liability for Nuclear Damage (text at www.iaea.or.at/worldatom/glance/legal/inf500.html, 23 states parties as of July 2002), Articles II and IV.

[215]1971 Convention Relating to Civil Liability in the Field of Maritime Carriage of Nuclear Material (text at sedac.ciesin.org/pidb/texts/maritime.carriage.nuclear.material.1971.html, 14 states parties as of July 2002).

States parties are allowed to set liability limits, but these can be no less than 5 million U.S. gold-based dollars.[216]

Similar rules apply to marine oil pollution. The operators of oil tankers or other ships that pollute the ocean with oil are liable "regardless of fault or negligence" up to a maximum limit of 59.7 million Special Drawing Rights (about U.S. $76.5 million) depending on the tonnage of the ship.[217] Victims who suffer damages exceeding this amount can seek additional compensation from an International Fund for Compensation of Oil Pollution Damage. The Fund provides compensation of up to 950 million gold-based French francs for a single incident.[218]

---

[216]Convention on Civil Liability for Nuclear Damage, Article V. States can also provide for a limitation period in which an injured party can apply for compensation, but this period can be no less than 10 years.

[217]1992 International Convention on Civil Liability for Oil Pollution Damage (text at drakon.uio.no/lm/imo.civil. liability.oil.pollution.damage.protocol.1992/doc.html, 86 state parties as of June 2002), Article V. This convention amended and is in the process of replacing the 1969 International Convention on Civil Liability for Oil Pollution Damage (text in sedac.ciesin.org/pidb/texts/civil.liability.oil.pollution.damage.1969.html, 50 remaining states parties as of June 2002).

[218]1971 International Convention on the Establishment of an International Fund for Compensation of Oil Pollution Damage (sedac.ciesin.org/entri/texts/intl.fund.oil.pollution.damage.1971. html, 45 states parties as of July 2002), Article V.

Chapter Questions

1. Cue Co., a large multinational enterprise incorporated and headquartered in Country Q, owns and operates a banana plantation in Chiquitaland, a small less developed country. Rebels, with whom the Chiquitaland government has been engaged in a civil war for several years, made a raid on the plantation destroying most of its banana plants, all of its buildings, and killing the manager, a citizen of Country Q. Q and Chiquitaland State are parties to an Arbitration Treaty and they agree to submit the dispute to arbitration. Is Chiquitaland liable for the injuries to Cue Co.'s plantation and for the death of the manager? Discuss.

2. M, a member of the intelligence bureau of the Fanatical Republic of Quirkydom, defects to Country A. M discloses that Quirkydom had planned and financed several terrorists attacks inside Country A over the past 10 years, including the kidnapping and murder of the Chief Executive Officer of the largest business firm in Country A. M's disclosures include original documents, tape recordings, and videotapes that contain incriminating statements made by the terrorists, members of Quirkydom's intelligence bureau, its Prime Minister, and several Cabinet members. After the daughter of the deceased CEO demanded that Country A sue Quirkydom in the International Court of Justice (ICJ), Country A did so. Both Quirkydom and Country A have recognized the jurisdiction of the ICJ to hear their international disputes. Is Quirkydom liable for the acts of these terrorists? How should the ICJ rule? Discuss.

3. Mr. A was a national of Country U. Mr. A worked in Country X as a consultant for the Country X National Railroad (XNRR) from 1980 to 1990. Country X's government is a radical military dictatorship. While Mr. A was riding on an XNRR train, the train was attacked by a group of terrorists (who like to be called "The Good Guys"). The Good Guys took control of the train, and Mr. A was trapped on board. Rather than attempting to rescue the passengers of the train—including Mr. A—the government strafed the train with military aircraft. The train was destroyed and everyone on board was killed. After receiving a series of complaints from Country U on behalf of the heirs of Mr. A, Country X has agreed that an international tribunal will determine if it (Country X) is liable for Mr. A's death. How will the tribunal hold? Discuss.

4. The Big Co. is incorporated and headquartered in Country K, but the majority of shares are owned by shareholders who are nationals of Country M. In 1980, the Big Co. obtained an oil concession in Ruraltania that was valid for 40 years. The concession contained a "stabilization" clause that provided that the concession could not be altered except by the consent of both parties. To exploit the concession, Big Co. set up a local subsidiary, Little Co., that was incorporated in Ruraltania but wholly owned by Big Co. Two years ago, a major political

change occurred in Ruraltania. A new government terminated all foreign-owned concessions including that of Big Co. but excluded one Japanese offshore oil concession. By decree, the new Minister for Oil was authorized to fix the compensation—if any—due to foreign companies. The ordinary courts were abolished and replaced by revolutionary tribunals.

The manager of Little Co., himself a national of Country K, criticized the new policy in a television interview, and the next day a group of university students took over Little Co.'s offices, burning and destroying files and other property, and injuring the manager. It took nearly 2 weeks for the Ruraltanian authorities to evict the students. Country K and Ruraltania are parties to an Arbitration Treaty and they agree to submit the dispute to arbitration. Country K files a claim for the following: (a) the reinstatement of the concession, or (b) compensation to cover the full cost of all assets and installations, lost profits for the next 20 years, interest on the above effective from the date when the concession was terminated, and, in either case, (c) compensation to cover the property damages to Little Co. and the injuries suffered by the manager. How should the arbitration tribunal rule? Discuss.

5. In the preceding question, assume that Country K decides not to assert any claims on behalf of either Big Co. or Little Co. May Country M do so? Discuss.

6. How is the national standard doctrine different from the international standard doctrine? Which is the fairer rule?

7. MNF, Inc., a large multinational firm incorporated and headquartered in Country C, entered into an investment agreement with Needyland, a small less developed country. MNF agreed to set up a mine to extract copper ore, a refinery, and a plant to manufacture electrical wiring. Needyland agreed to give MNF a 20-year tax holiday (i.e., MNF would not have to pay any local taxes for a period of 20 years). Finally, MNF agreed that "MNF, Inc. will not seek the diplomatic assistance of Country C in resolving any dispute it may have with Needyland." After MNF completed construction on the mine, refinery, and plant, and just as it began to make a profit on its investment, the government of Needyland changed. The new government enacted a statute that imposed a "nontax operating fee" of 30 percent on the annual earnings of all businesses involved in the mining, refining, or processing of copper. MNF was the only such firm. MNF complained to the new government with no result that this "fee" violated its investment agreement. The local courts dismissed MNF's request for an injunction as baseless. MNF then sought the diplomatic assistance of Country C.

Country C and Needyland are parties to an Arbitration Treaty and they agree to submit the dispute to arbitration. Needyland argues that MNF had no right to seek the diplomatic assistance of Country C and, therefore, Country C has no right to seek compensation from Needyland on behalf of MNF. Is Needyland correct? Discuss.

8. Assume in the preceding case that MNF, Inc. had purchased political risk insurance from an agency of Country C. Assume, as well, that the Country C insurance program is identical to that offered by the United States Overseas Private Investment Corporation (OPIC). Has the MNF operation in Needyland been ruined by creeping expropriation? Must the Country C insurance program pay MNF for its losses? Discuss.

9. A Crocodonian business firm chartered an airplane owned by the Republic of Crocodonia to fly cargo to Country U. The cargo was a load of crocodile skins that are legal to own and sell in Crocodonia but that are considered contraband in Country U. The business firm, knowing this, mislabeled the cargo as cowhides. When the plane landed in Country U, Country U's Contraband Enforcement Agency seized both the plane and its cargo. The cargo was destroyed and the plane was sold in accordance with a Country U antiracketeering statute. The government of Crocodonia was incensed. It sent a diplomatic message to Country U protesting that its national honor had been sullied by Country U's actions. Crocodonia and Country U are parties to an Arbitration Treaty and they agree to submit the dispute to arbitration. Crocodonia seeks compensation for the airplane and, on behalf of the Crocodonian business firm, compensation for the destroyed cargo. What will the arbitration tribunal decide? Discuss.

10. The *S.S. Rustbucket,* an oil tanker flying the flag of State V, a small and very poor developing country, had a terrible leak. As the tanker steamed across the high seas near State W, it

discharged some 20,000 barrels of crude oil into a very rich fishing area, killing huge quantities of fish and other aquatic animals. A warship from State W detained the *Rustbucket* until barges could be brought alongside and all of the oil on the tanker pumped off. The *Rustbucket* has brought suit in a State W court to recover damages for the loss of its cargo, the loss of the profits it was to earn, and for being improperly detained on the high seas by a State W warship. The *Rustbucket* has proven to the court that it was in full compliance with the pollution control regulations of State V. Will the *Rustbucket* be successful?

11. State X licensed the Glowing Power Co. to operate several nuclear power plants within its territory. Despite all due care, an accident occurred at one of these plants and a large cloud of radioactive dust escaped into the atmosphere. The cloud floated into the airspace above State Y before it began settling. It then caused extensive damage to the population and the natural environment of State Y. Is State X liable? Is the Glowing Power Co. liable?

Review Problem

You have been hired as an Assistant in the law department of MegaBranch Industries (MBI), a multinational enterprise that has branches in countries around the world. You are responsible for overseeing the legal affairs of MBI branches in eight countries.

1. In Country A, a Branch Manager has been kidnapped by either rebels, terrorists, or thugs (the reports are unclear) and she may be dead. What international legal responsibilities does Country A have to help the manager or to compensate her heirs for her loss of life?

2. Country B has just announced that it is expropriating MBI's local branch and that it will pay compensation for the expropriation only after collecting the following from MBI: (a) the taxes MBI did not pay because it had doctored its books, (b) the fees MBI did not pay because it had bribed local officials to avoid paying the full amount due, and (c) the cost of cleaning up the toxic pollution that MBI's branch generated. Can Country B do this?

3. MBI is planning on setting up a new branch in Country C. The government of Country C insists that MBI agree that it will not seek the diplomatic assistance of any other country in resolving any dispute it might have in the future with Country C. Should MBI agree to this condition?

4. MBI has its headquarters in Country X, it is incorporated in Country Y, and most of its shareholders are nationals of Country Z. In the event that MBI has difficulties in dealing with Country D, which country (X, Y, or Z) should it look to for diplomatic protection and assistance?

5. Country E has imposed new regulations on the local MBI branch. What must MBI do before asking its national country to seek relief on its behalf in an international tribunal?

6. Country F has passed several new environmental regulations—in violation of the investment agreement it signed several years ago with MBI—that make the operation of the local branch there unprofitable. MBI has political risk insurance with Country U that is identical to the political risk insurance offered by the United States Overseas Private Investment Corporation (OPIC). Can MBI collect on its policy?

7. Country G's currency is not convertible and it is regularly devalued. Moreover, inflation in Country G is running in excess of 1,000 percent per year. MBI is considering the establishment of a branch that will receive all of its earnings in Country G currency. What can MBI do to get its profits out of Country G?

8. MBI has not had much luck in getting its home country to provide diplomatic assistance when it has had foreign branches expropriated by local states. It wants to make an investment in Country H (which very much needs the investment). Is there anything that MBI can do to ensure that MBI itself can arbitrate a settlement with Country H in the event of a dispute?

9. MBI's has a branch in Country I, a developed Annex I country that has yet to ratify the Kyoto Protocol. Should MBI encourage the Country I government to support or oppose ratification of the Protocol?

10. MBI's Chief Operating Officer believes that large profits are to be made in collecting nuclear, chemical, and biological wastes in developed countries and processing and dumping the wastes in the oceans or in developing countries. He has asked you to outline the legal constraints MBI would face if it decides to enter this business. You have agreed to do so.

CHAPTER

Dispute Settlement

3

A. SETTLEMENT OF DISPUTES THROUGH DIPLOMACY

diplomacy: A form of international dispute settlement that attempts to reconcile parties to a disagreement by use of negotiation, mediation, or inquiry.

negotiation: (From Latin *negotiari:* "to carry on business.") The process of reaching an agreement by conferring or discussing.

Diplomacy is the process of reconciling the parties to a disagreement by negotiation, mediation, or inquiry. Although diplomacy is formally applied only to disputes between states, it is informally applied to disputes involving institutions and individuals as well.[1]

Negotiation

Negotiation, as its name implies, is the process of reaching an agreement by discussion.[2] Despite its simplicity, negotiation is an important tool in the process of dispute settlement, and undoubtedly the one most commonly relied on. It is used not merely to resolve disputes but to prevent them from arising in the first place and to lay the groundwork for other forms of dispute settlement.

---

[1]In disputes involving institutions and/or persons, diplomacy is commonly referred to as "alternative dispute resolution."

[2]Negotiation should be distinguished from debates in international organizations. For example, in the South-West Africa Cases (Preliminary Objections) in *International Court of Justice Reports,* vol. 1962, p. 319 (1962), South Africa argued that any dispute between itself and the petitioners, Ethiopia and Liberia, was not ripe for a decision by the ICJ because the petitioners had not shown that the case could not be settled by negotiation, a jurisdictional requirement imposed by Article 7 of the South-West Africa Mandate. The Court rejected the argument on the ground that extensive negotiations in the UN had ended in deadlock. Judges Spender and Fitzmaurice disagreed; their dissenting opinion stated: "[A] 'negotiation' confined to the floor of an International Assembly, consisting of allegations of members, resolutions of the Assembly pursuant thereto, denial of allegations, refusal to comply with resolutions or to respond to action taken thereunder, cannot be enough to justify the Court in holding that the dispute 'cannot' be settled by negotiations, when no direct diplomatic interchanges have ever taken place between the parties, and therefore no attempt at settlement has ever been made at the state and diplomatic level."

Negotiations between states are most commonly conducted on an *ad hoc*[3] basis, but sometimes the procedure is more formal. In such cases, states negotiate through normal diplomatic channels, through the use of competent authorities, through the establishment of mixed or joint commissions, or even through summit meetings. Summit meetings have been popular in recent years because they are an effective way to bypass the official bureaucracy of the participating states. On the other hand, they are often arranged to gain political capital out of an agreement already finalized through ordinary negotiations.

Mediation

mediation: (From Latin *mediates:* "to be in the middle.") Bringing about a peaceful settlement or compromise between parties to a dispute through the benevolent intervention of an impartial third party.

good offices: A third party who provides the means by which two disputing parties may communicate with each other.

conciliation: (From Latin *conciliare:* "to call or bring together.") The process by which an impartial third party makes an independent investigation and suggests a solution to a dispute.

inquiry: (From Latin *inquirere:* "to seek after" or "to search for.") The process by which an impartial third party makes an investigation to determine the facts underlying a dispute without resolving the dispute itself.

Mediation involves the use of a third party who transmits and interprets the proposals of the principal parties and sometimes advances independent proposals. When mediators provide a channel of communications only, it is said that they are offering their **good offices**. When they make a formal investigation and present a formal proposal, they are involved in a **conciliation**.[4]

The process of mediation can start with a request from one or more of the parties, but not infrequently an outsider offers to serve as a mediator. For example, during the 1982 Falklands War between Argentina and the United Kingdom, both U.S. Secretary of State Alexander Haig and UN Secretary-General Javier Pérez de Cuellar tendered their good offices. And in a dispute between Pakistan and India over the Kashmir in 1965, the U.S.S.R., a major Asiatic power, helped obtain a cease-fire between these two Asiatic countries.

Mediation can occur only if all the parties to a dispute consent to it. Thus, South Africa's policy of apartheid[5] could not be mediated because South Africa regarded it as an internal matter. And during Nigeria's war with the secessionist state of Biafra (1967–1970), Nigeria refused all offers of mediation because it regarded the war as an internal affair.

The mediator, in particular, must be acceptable to both parties. In the Falklands War, Argentina objected to Secretary Haig because the United States was a NATO ally of the United Kingdom and was providing logistical support for the British task force. (In fact, Secretary Haig's offer of mediation antagonized the Argentines.) Because Secretary-General Pérez de Cuellar had remained impartial, he was acceptable to both sides.

Inquiry

An **inquiry** is a process used to determine a disputed fact or facts. Unlike a mediation, which tries to resolve an entire dispute, an inquiry focuses only on a particular incident. The Hague Convention for the Pacific Settlement of International Disputes of 1899 called for the use of commissions of inquiry to determine factual questions of an international nature. However, fearing that commissions of inquiry might threaten national sovereignty, the Convention limited the use of inquiries to disputes "involving neither honor nor essential interests" of the parties. The limitation proved unnecessary, however, as the 1904 *Dogger Bank Inquiry* made clear. That commission, made up of representatives from Russia, Britain, France, Austro-Hungary, and the United States, was asked to determine whether a Russian fleet on its way to the Orient during the Russo-Japanese War had cause for opening fire on a group of British trawlers fishing on the Dogger Bank. The Russian admiral in charge of the fleet had said that he feared attack by Japanese torpedo boats. The commission found that there had been no torpedo boats in the area and the Russian admiral was not, therefore, justified in opening fire. It diplomatically added, however, that these findings were not "of a nature to cast any discredit upon the military qualities or the humanity of Admiral Rojdestvensky or the personnel of his squadron." Both parties accepted the report and Russia paid Britain £65,000 in damages.[6]

In 1907, a second Hague Convention for the Pacific Settlement of International Disputes devised more extensive and less limiting rules for commissions of inquiry. For instance, it said

[3]Latin: "for this." Something done for a specific purpose, circumstance, or case.

[4]Article 1 of the Institute of International Law's model Regulation on the Procedure of International Conciliation defines conciliation as "a method for the settlement of international disputes of any nature, according to which a Commission is set up by the parties, either on a permanent basis or an ad hoc basis to deal with the dispute, proceeds to the impartial examination of the dispute and attempts to define the terms of a settlement susceptible of being accepted by them, or of affording the parties, with a view to its settlement, such aid as they may have requested."

[5]Afrikäans (South African Dutch): *apart* "apart" and *heid* "hood." Racial discrimination against blacks and others of non-Caucasian descent.

[6]*The Hague Court Reports,* p. 410 (James B. Scott, ed., 1916).

that parties could agree in advance to be bound by the decision of the commission. This happened in the *Tubantia Incident* of 1916, in which Germany was held responsible for the sinking of a neutral Dutch ship during World War I.[7]

Several treaties setting up commissions of inquiry were signed and ratified during the 1910s and 1920s, most notably the Taft Treaties negotiated by the United States, the United Kingdom, and France, and the Bryan Treaties between the United States and several Latin American countries. Despite these treaties, only one inquiry has been conducted since 1922.[8] Matters that inquiries might have considered have been resolved instead by negotiation, mediation, or investigations conducted by independent international organizations. For example, the staff of the International Civil Aviation Organization investigated the Soviet downing of a Korean Air Lines jet in 1983.

B. SETTLEMENT OF DISPUTES IN INTERNATIONAL TRIBUNALS

An international dispute is settled in much the same way that a domestic dispute is settled. Parties usually try diplomacy first. If diplomacy fails, it is normal to turn to the courts. If a dispute is between states or intergovernmental organizations (IGOs), they may be able to take their case to an international tribunal, such as the International Court of Justice or a dispute resolution panel of the World Trade Organization, or, barring this, to arbitration. If a dispute is between private persons or between a private person and a state or between a private person and an IGO, the dispute will normally end up in arbitration or in a municipal court. Arbitration between private persons and states, and between persons and persons, is commonly arranged through a permanent arbitration tribunal (or "facility") such as the International Center for the Settlement of Investment Disputes.[9]

International Court of Justice

The International Court of Justice (ICJ) was created in 1945 as one of the organs of the United Nations. See Exhibit 3-1 on page 123. It was modeled on the Permanent Court of International Justice (PCIJ), which functioned as an organ of the League of Nations from 1920 to 1939.

The United Nations Charter declares that all the member states of the UN are automatically parties to the Statute of the International Court of Justice, which is included as an annex to the Charter. Nonmembers may adhere to the Statute, but to do so they must agree to respect the Court's decisions and to help cover the Court's expenses.[10]

The ICJ has the **jurisdiction**—or power—to hear two kinds of cases:[11] (1) those between states (based on the Court's "contentious" jurisdiction)[12] and (2) those requested by organs or specialized agencies of the United Nations (based on the Court's "advisory" jurisdiction).[13] The ICJ has no authority to hear cases involving individuals or entities other than those just mentioned.[14]

jurisdiction: (From Latin *jurisdictio:* "administration of the law.") The authority or power of a court or tribunal to hear a particular case or dispute.

---

[7]*Id.,* Second Series, p. 135 (James B. Scott, ed., 1932).

[8]Red Crusader Incident (1962), *International Law Reports,* vol. 35, p. 485 (1963).

[9]This dispute settlement process is outlined in Article 33(1) of the United Nations Charter as follows: "The parties to any dispute, the continuance of which is likely to endanger the maintenance of international peace and security, shall, first of all, seek a solution by negotiation, inquiry, mediation, conciliation, arbitration, judicial settlement, resort to regional agencies or arrangements, or other peaceful means of their own choice." The UN Charter is posted on the UN Web site at www.un.org/aboutun/charter/.

[10]Security Council Resolution 9 (October 15, 1946) provides: "The International Court of Justice shall be open to a state which is not a party to the Statute of the International Court of Justice, upon the following condition, namely, that such state shall previously have deposited with the Registrar of the Court a declaration by which it accepts the jurisdiction of the Court in accordance with the Charter of the United Nations and with the terms and subject to the conditions of the Statute and the Rules of the Court, and undertakes to comply in good faith with the decision or decisions of the Court and to accept all the obligations of a member of the United Nations under Article 94 of the Charter."

The only non-UN member is the Vatican.

[11]The opinions of all of the Court's decisions are posted on the Internet at www.icj-cij.org/icjwww/idecisions.htm.

[12]Statute of the International Court of Justice, Articles 34 and 36. The Statute is posted on the ICJ's Web site at www.icj-cij.org/icjwww/ibasicdocuments/Basetext/istatute.htm.

[13]*Id.,* Article 65(1); United Nations Charter, Article 96.

[14]Before West Germany became a member of the United Nations and while its status as a state was still at issue, it was allowed to participate in the North Sea Continental Shelf Cases, *International Court of Justice Reports,* vol. 1969, p. 3 (1969), under a declaration accepting the Court's jurisdiction. The parties did not raise its status as a state, nor did the Court consider it.

Contentious Jurisdiction

Before the ICJ can hear a contentious case, all of the states parties to the proceeding must have recognized the Court's **contentious jurisdiction**. This is most commonly done on an *ad hoc* basis; that is, parties to an existing dispute negotiate a special agreement to let the ICJ decide the case.[15] Sometimes these agreements are made permanent by being included in a bilateral treaty.[16] A less common and more controversial means by which the Court can acquire jurisdiction is through unilateral declarations made by each of the parties.

contentious jurisdiction: The power of a court to hear a matter that involves a dispute between two or more parties.

Optional Clause jurisdiction: A unilateral grant of jurisdiction by a state to the International Court of Justice that allows the Court to resolve disputes involving that state.

Optional Clause Jurisdiction   Article 36(2) of the Statute of the Court—known as the Optional Clause—allows states to make a unilateral declaration recognizing "as compulsory *ipso facto*[17] and without special agreement, in relation to any other state accepting the same obligation, the jurisdiction of the Court in all legal disputes."

Many states have recognized the Court's jurisdiction under the Optional Clause. A few have put *no* restrictions on the kinds of cases they will respond to. For example, Uganda's Optional Clause declaration states:

> I hereby declare on behalf of the government of Uganda, that Uganda recognizes as compulsory *ipso facto* and without special agreement, in relation to any other state accepting the same obligation, and on condition of reciprocity, the jurisdiction of the International Court of Justice in conformity with paragraph 2 of Article 36 of the Statute of the Court.
>
> New York, 3 October 1963
>
> (*Signed*) APPOLLO K. KIRONDE
> Ambassador and Permanent Representative
> of Uganda to the United Nations.[18]

Unrestricted Optional Clause declarations, however, are rare. Most states have added a wide variety of restrictions on the kinds of suits they are willing to let the Court hear without a special arrangement. An excellent example is the American Optional Clause declaration of 1946, even though it is no longer in force.[19] It states:

> I, Harry S. Truman, President of the United States of America, declare on behalf of the United States of America, under Article 36, paragraph 2, of the Statute of the International Court of Justice, and in accordance with the Resolution of 2 August 1946 of the Senate of the United States of America (two-thirds of the Senators present concurring therein), that the United States of America recognizes as compulsory *ipso facto* and without special agreement, in relation to any other state accepting the same obligation, the jurisdiction of the International Court of Justice in all legal disputes hereafter arising concerning—
>
> (a) the interpretation of a treaty;
> (b) any question of international law;
> (c) the existence of any fact which, if established, would constitute a breach of an international obligation;
> (d) the nature or extent of the reparation to be made for the breach of an international obligation;
>
> *Provided,* that this declaration shall not apply to—
>
> (a) disputes the solution of which the parties shall entrust to other tribunals by virtue of agreements already in existence or which may be concluded in the future; or

---

[15]Sometimes a special agreement is negotiated even though there is already another basis for jurisdiction. Thus, in the Arbitral Award (Honduras v. Nicaragua) Case, *International Court of Justice Reports,* vol. 1960, p. 160 (1960), the parties used a special agreement to refer a case involving the validity of an arbitral award made by the King of Spain even though the parties already were subject to the Court's jurisdiction under the Optional Clause.

[16]Statute of the International Court of Justice, Article 36(1).

[17]Latin: "by that very fact."

[18]*Multilateral Treaties Deposited with the Secretary-General, Status as at 31 August 2002,* posted on the UN's Web site at www.un.org/Depts/Treaty/final/ts2/newfiles/part_boo/ i_boo/i_4.html.

[19]On October 7, 1985, the United States informed the Secretary-General that it was terminating its Optional Clause declaration. *Id.,* p. 27.

The International Court of Justice, located at the Peace Palace in The Hague, Netherlands, is the main judicial organ of the United Nations. Established in 1946, it replaced the Permanent Court of International Justice, which had functioned as court for the League of Nations. The ICJ operates under a statute similar to that of its predecessor, which is an integral part of the Charter of the United Nations. (Photograph of the members of the court courtesy of ICJ. Photo: Van der Plas & Van den Eeden.)

(b) disputes with regard to matters which are essentially within the domestic jurisdiction of the United States of America as determined by the United States of America; or

(c) disputes arising under a multilateral treaty, unless (1) all parties to the treaty affected by the decision are also parties to the case before the Court, or (2) the United States of America specially agrees to jurisdiction; and

Provided further, that this declaration shall remain in force for a period of five years and thereafter until the expiration of six months after which notice may be given to terminate this declaration.

(Signed) HARRY S. TRUMAN.
Done at Washington this twenty-sixth day of August 1946.[20]

rule of reciprocity: A state has to respond to a suit brought against it before the International Court of Justice only to the extent that the state bringing the suit has also accepted the jurisdiction of the Court.

Article 36(2) requires that a state respond to a suit brought against it only if the state bringing the suit has also accepted the jurisdiction of the Court. This is known as the **rule of reciprocity**. When both states have limited the jurisdiction that they will recognize, the ICJ has power to decide a case only to the extent that both states have agreed to the same sort of matters. For example, in the *Norwegian Loans Case (France v. Norway)*, Norway objected to the Court taking jurisdiction on several grounds, including the lack of reciprocity in the declarations of the two parties. The Court said: ". . . since two unilateral declarations are involved, such jurisdiction is conferred upon the Court only to the extent to which the two declarations coincide in conferring it. A comparison between the two declarations shows that the French declaration accepts the Court's jurisdiction within narrower limits than the Norwegian declaration; consequently the common will of the parties, which is the basis of the Court's jurisdiction, exists within these narrower limits indicated by the French reservation."[21]

---

[20]*International Court of Justice Yearbook*, p. 77 (1976–1977).

[21]*International Court of Justice Reports*, vol. 1957, p. 9 (1957). Because the narrower of these two declarations "excludes from the jurisdiction of the Court the dispute which has been referred to it," the Court declined to hear the case. *Id.*

Term	Name	State	Term	Name	State
1946–1955	Alvarez, Alejandro	Chile	1970–1979	Ignacio-Pinto, Louis	Benin
1946–1965	Badawi Pashi, Ahdel Hamidb	Egypt	1970–1979	Jimenez de Aréchaga, Eduardo	Uruguay
1946–1964	Basdevant, Jules	France	1973–1985	Morozov, Planton D.[c]	Soviet Union
1946–1951	Barros e Azevedo, José P. de[b]	Brazil	1973–1981	Waldock, Humphrey[b]	United Kingdom
1946–1952	Fabela Alfaro, Isodor	Mexico	1973–1988	Singh, Nagendra[b]	India
1946–1959	Guerrero, José Gustavo[b]	El Salvador	1973–1991	Ruda, José Maria	Argentina
1946–1961	Hackworth, Green H.	United States	1976–1994	Elis, Taslim Olawale	Nigeria
1946–1957	Hsu Mo[b]	China	1976–1985	Mosler, Herman	West Germany
1946–1961	Klaestad, Helge	Norway	1976–2003	Oda, Shigeru	Japan
1946–1952	Krylov, Sergei Borisovich	Soviet Union	1976–1980	Tarazi, Salah El Dine[b]	Syria
1946–1955	McNair, Arnold Duncan	United Kingdom	1979–1995	Ago, Robert	Italy
1946–1958	Reed, John E.	Canada	1979–1980	Baxter, Richard R.[b]	United States
1946–1967	Winiarski, Bohdan	Poland	1979–1982	El-Erian, Abdullah Ali[b]	Egypt
1946–1958	Zoricic, Milovan	Yugoslavia	1979–1988	Camara, José Sette	Brazil
1951–1964	Fernandez Carneiro, Levi	Brazil	1981–1985	El-Khani, Abdallah Fikri	Syria
1952–1953	Golunski, Sergei Aleksandrovich[c]	Soviet Union	1981–2000	Schwebel, Stephen M.[c]	United States
1952–1953	Rau, Benegal	India	1982–1987	de Lacharrière, Guy Ladreit[b]	France
1952–1961	Armand Ugon, Enrique C.	Uruguay	1982–1995	Jennings, Robert Yewdall	United Kingdom
1953–1961	Kojeunikov, Feodor Ivanovick	Soviet Union	1982–1991	Mbaye, Kéba	Senegal
1954–1973	Khan, Mohammad Zafrulla	Pakistan	1982–2001	Bedjaoui, Mohammed[c]	Algeria
1955–1964	Cordova, Roberto	Mexico	1985–1994	Jens, Evensen	Norway
1955–1960	Lauterpacht, Hersch[b]	United Kingdom	1985–1994	Ni, Zhengyu	China
1955–1964	Moreno Quintana, Lucio M.	Argentina	1985–1995	Tarassov, Nikolai K.[b]	Russia
1957–1967	Koo, V. K. Wellington	China	1987–2009	Guillaume, Gilbert	France
1958–1967	Spender, Percy	Australia	1988–1997	Shahabuddeen, Mohamed	Guyana
1958–1967	Spiropoulos, Jean	Greece	1989–1991	Pathak, Raghunandan Swarup	India
1959–1963	Alfaro, Ricardo J.	Panama	1991–1995	Aguilar Mawdsley, Andrés[b]	Venezuela
1960–1973	Fitzmaurice, Gerald	United Kingdom	1991–2009	Ranjeva, Ranjeva	Madagascar
1961–1970	Bustamante y Rivero, José Luis	Peru	1991–2000	Weeramantry, Christopher G.	Sri Lanka
1961–1970	Jessup, Philip C.	United States	1993–2003	Herczegh, Geza	Hungary
1961–1970	Koretsky, Vladimir M.	Soviet Union	1994–2003	Shi, Jiuyong	China
1961–1970	Morelli, Gaetano	Italy	1994–2003	Fleischhauer, Carl-August	Germany
1961–1970	Tanaka, Kotaro	Japan	1994–2003	Koroma, Abdul G.	Sierra Leone
1964–1982	Forster, Isaac	Senegal	1995–2006	Vereshchetin, Vladlen S.	Russia
1964–1982	Gros, André	France	1995–1997	Bravo, Luigi Ferrari	Italy
1967–1976	Ammoun, Fouad	Lebanon	1995–2009	Higgins, Rosalyn	United Kingdom
1967–1976	Bengzon, Cesar	Philippines	1996–2009	Parra-Aranguren, Gonzalo	Venezuela
1967–1976	Onyeama, Charles D.	Nigeria	1997–2006	Kooijmans, Pieter H.	Netherlands
1967–1976	Petrén, Sture	Sweden	1997–2006	F. Rezek, Jose	Brazil
1967–1985	Lachs, Manfred	Poland	2000–2006	Buergenthal, Thomas	United States
1970–1979	de Castro, Federico	Spain	2000–2009	Al-Khasawneh, Awn Shawkat	Jordan
1970–1979	Dillard, Hardy C.	United States	2001–2006	Elaraby, Nabil	Egypt

EXHIBIT 3-1   Judges of the International Court of Justice[a]

[a]The International Court of Justice is made up of 15 permanent judges elected by the United Nations General Assembly and Security Council for terms of nine years. In addition, for contentious cases, if a party to a dispute is not represented by a judge on the Court, it may appoint an *ad hoc* judge. This list shows only permanent judges.

[b]Died while in office.

[c]Resigned.

Source: International Court of Justice: Composition and Organization of the Court, posted at www.icj-cij.org/icjwww/ igeneralinformation/igncompos.html.

Self-Judging Reservations   One questionable device that states have used to recognize the Court's jurisdiction under the Optional Clause but to still have a way out if they decide they do not want to respond to a particular suit is known as a **self-judging reservation** or Connally Reservation.[22] Such a clause allows a state to exclude from its acceptance of Optional Clause jurisdiction any matter that it later determines is within its own domestic jurisdiction. This can be a double-edged sword, however, because the principle of reciprocity allows would-be defendants to invoke the plaintiff's self-judging reservation. In fact, this happened in 1957 in a suit

self-judging reservation:
A reservation that allows a state to exclude from the jurisdiction of the International Court of Justice any dispute that it determines is a domestic matter.

---

[22]It is called the Connally Reservation after the U.S. senator who introduced an amendment to include a self-judging reservation in the American Optional Clause declaration when the declaration was being debated in the U.S. Senate. Actually, however, it was the brainchild of U.S. Secretary of State John Foster Dulles.

brought by the United States against Bulgaria after Bulgaria shot down an American aircraft that had strayed into Bulgaria's airspace. Bulgaria let it be known that it would invoke the self-judging reservation contained in the United States' Optional Clause declaration. To avoid embarrassment, the United States promptly withdrew its suit.[23]

The validity of self-judging reservations has been a matter of some speculation among legal writers. It seems to violate Article 36(6) of the Statute of the Court, which says that "in the event of a dispute as to whether the Court has jurisdiction, the matter shall be settled by the decision of the Court." The ICJ itself, however, has never definitively answered the question.[24]

Self-judging reservations were considered in Case 3–1, a case brought by Nicaragua against the United States. Although the majority of the Court again made no definitive statement about such reservations, they were considered in a dissenting opinion written by Judge Schwebel, the American judge on the Court.

---

[23]Aerial Incident of July 27, 1955 (United States v. Bulgaria), *International Court of Justice Reports,* vol. 1960, p. 146 (1959).

[24]It has had the opportunity on several occasions. In Interhandel (Switzerland v. United States), *International Court of Justice Reports,* vol. 1957, p. 77 (1957), the United States asserted its self-judging reservation in a suit brought by Switzerland, both at the hearing for interim measures and at the hearing on jurisdiction. The Court sidestepped the issue by holding that Switzerland had not exhausted all local remedies. In separate opinions, Judges Lauterpacht, Spender, and Klaestad commented on the reservation. All three agreed that the reservation violated Article 36(6). Judge Klaestad added: "These considerations have led me to the conclusion that the Court, both by its Statute and by the Charter, is prevented from acting upon that part of the Reservation which is in conflict with Article 36, paragraph 6 of the Statute, but that this circumstance does not necessarily imply that it is impossible for the Court to give effect to the other parts of the Declaration of Acceptance which are in conformity with the Statute."

In the Case Concerning Right of Passage over Indian Territory (Portugal v. India) (Preliminary Objections), *International Court of Justice Reports,* vol. 1957, p. 125 (1957), India sought to escape the ICJ's jurisdiction by arguing that the reservation in Portugal's Optional Clause declaration violated the basic principle of reciprocity. The Court stated: "[India has] contended that the condition [i.e., reservation] offends against the basic principle of reciprocity underlying the Optional Clause inasmuch as it claims for Portugal a right which in effect is denied to other signatories who have made a declaration without appending any such condition. The Court is unable to accept that contention. It is clear that any reservation notified by Portugal . . . becomes automatically operative against it in relation to other signatories of the Optional Clause."

Case 3–1   Case Concerning the Military and Paramilitary Activities in and Against Nicaragua (Jurisdiction and Admissibility) (Dissenting Opinion)

Nicaragua v. United States

International Court of Justice, 1984.
International Legal Materials, vol. 24, p. 38 at p. 142 (1985).

In the early 1980s, the United States supported the Nicaraguan contra rebels (Contras), whose aim, until the electoral defeat of the Sandinista government in 1990, was to overthrow the legitimate government of Nicaragua. In support of the Contras, the American Central Intelligence Agency (CIA)—among other things—covertly mined Nicaragua's harbors. Nicaragua brought suit in the International Court of Justice when one of its fishing

trawlers sank in the port of Corinto after striking a CIA mine. On April 6, 1984, shortly before the Nicaraguan government filed its complaint, the Reagan administration sent a new Optional Clause declaration to the United Nations Secretary-General modifying its August 26, 1946, declaration. This declaration stated that the United States would not subject itself to the jurisdiction of the Court concerning any matter relating to Central America for a period of two years.[25]

The United States then argued in a preliminary proceeding that the Court lacked jurisdiction to hear Nicaragua's

---

[25]The declaration read as follows: "I have the honor on behalf of the government of the United States of America to refer to the declaration of my government of August 26, 1946, concerning the acceptance by the United States of America of the compulsory jurisdiction of the International Court of Justice, and to state that the aforesaid Declaration shall not apply to disputes with any Central American state or arising out of or related to events in Central America, any of which disputes shall be settled in such manner as the parties to them may agree.

MAP 3-1 Nicaragua (1984)

complaint because of the new modified Optional Clause declaration. The majority of the Court rejected this argument, observing that the August 1946 declaration itself expressly provided that the United States had to give six months' notice before changing the provisions of its declaration, and the United States had not done so. The American Judge, Stephen M. Schwebel, dissented from this decision. One issue he addressed in his dissent was the effect of the United States' self-judging reservation on the jurisdiction of the Court.

DISSENTING OPINION OF JUDGE SCHWEBEL: . . .

* * *

Is the United States declaration of August 26, 1946, valid? . . .

It is well known that Judge Lauterpacht, in his dissenting opinion in the *Interhandel Case,*[26] concluded that the United States declaration of August 26, 1946, is invalid by reason of its incorporation of the automatic, self-judging proviso known as the "Connally Reservation." The United States thereby reserved from the Court's jurisdiction:

"(b) disputes with regard to matters which are essentially within the domestic jurisdiction of the United States of America as determined by the United States of America."

He reached a similar conclusion earlier in respect of a French self-judging reservation in the case of *Certain Norwegian Loans.*[27] Judge Lauterpacht in the *Interhandel Case* summarized his position in these terms:

"(a) the reservation in question, while constituting an essential part of the Declaration of Acceptance, is contrary to paragraph 6 of Article 36 of the Statute of the Court; it cannot, accordingly, be acted upon by the Court; which means that it is invalid;

"(b) that, irrespective of its inconsistency with the Statute, that reservation by effectively conferring upon the government of the United States the right to determine with finality whether in any particular case it is under an obligation to accept the jurisdiction of the Court, deprives the Declaration of Acceptance of the character of a legal instrument, cognizable before a judicial tribunal, expressing legal rights and obligations;

"(c) that reservation, being an essential part of the Declaration of Acceptance, cannot be separated from it so as to remove from the declaration the vitiating element of inconsistency with the Statute and of the absence of a legal obligation. The government of the United States, not having in law become a party, through the purported Declaration of Acceptance, to the system of the Optional Clause of Article 36(2) of the Statute, cannot invoke it as an applicant; neither can it be cited before the Court as defendant by reference to its Declaration of Acceptance."[28]

. . . I agreed with Judge Lauterpacht's position. . . . I continue to see great force in it, while appreciating the argument that, since declarations incorporating self-judging provisions apparently have been treated as valid, certainly by the declarants, for many years, the passage of time may have rendered Judge Lauterpacht's analysis less compelling today than it was when made. Were his position to be applied to the instant case, the result would be that there is no valid adherence by the United States to the Optional Clause in existence and that, accordingly, insofar as Nicaragua relies on that adherence, its Application must be dismissed.

"Notwithstanding the terms of the aforesaid declaration, this *proviso* shall take effect immediately and shall remain in force for two years, so as to foster the continuing regional dispute settlement process which seeks a negotiated solution to the interrelated political, economic, and security problems of Central America.

"(*Signed*) George Schultz, Secretary of State of the United States of America."

Multilateral Treaties Deposited with the Secretary-General, Status as at 31 December 1992, pp. 26–27 (1993).

[26]Judgment, *International Court of Justice Reports,* vol. 1959, pp. 6, 95 (1959).
[27]*Id.,* vol. 1957, p. 34 (1957).
[28]*International Court of Justice Reports,* vol. 1959, pp. 101–102 (1959).

On October 7, 1985, three days after the Court announced its opinion on the question of jurisdiction, George Schultz, the U.S. Secretary of State, sent the following notice to the Secretary-General of the United Nations: "I have the honor on behalf of the government of the United States of America to refer to the declaration of my government of August 26, 1946, as modified by my note of *April 6, 1984, concerning the acceptance of the United States of America of the compulsory jurisdiction of the International Court of Justice, and to state that the aforesaid declaration is hereby terminated, with effect six months from the date hereof." The United States then refused to participate in any further proceedings before the Court.* ■

Advisory Jurisdiction

advisory jurisdiction: The power of the International Court of Justice to give opinions about issues of international law at the request of the United Nations or one of its specialized agencies.

The ICJ's **advisory jurisdiction** exists so that the Court may give opinions about issues of international law at the request of the United Nations or one of its specialized agencies. The Court will reject a request for such an opinion, however, if it has the effect of making a state a party to a dispute without that state's consent. In the *Western Sahara Case*, the General Assembly had asked the ICJ to give an advisory opinion on the legal ties between the Spanish colony of Western Sahara and the neighboring states of Morocco and Mauritania. Spain objected to the request on the grounds that it was being made a party to a dispute without its consent. The Court said that it recognized "that lack of consent might constitute a ground for declining to give the opinion requested if, in the circumstances of a given case, considerations of judicial propriety should oblige the Court to refuse an opinion." It nevertheless denied that Spain was being made party to a dispute against its wishes. The General Assembly's request, the Court said, was made "to obtain from the Court an opinion which the General Assembly deems of assistance to it for the proper exercise of its functions concerning the decolonization of the territory [of Western Sahara]. . . . The settlement of this issue will not affect the rights of Spain today as the administering Power, but will assist the General Assembly in deciding the policy to be followed in order to accelerate the decolonization process in the territory."[29]

Judgments

A case can be concluded in one of three ways: (1) If the parties tell the Court that they have reached a settlement, the Court will issue an Order removing the case from its list,[30] (2) if the applicant state withdraws its suit, the Court will order the case to be removed from its list,[31] or (3) the Court will deliver a judgment.

Effect of Judgments "The decision of the Court has no binding force except between the parties and in respect of that particular case."[32] The Court's decisions, accordingly, have no precedential value (i.e., the doctrine of *stare decisis*[33] does not apply). It is free to depart from its earlier decisions, but it seldom does so, often citing earlier cases for authority in later opinions. The parties to a suit, however, are bound by the Court's decision. "The judgment is final and without appeal."[34]

The ICJ will, at the request of either party, interpret one of its judgments when there is uncertainty or disagreement about its meaning or scope.[35] The parties can also request that the Court revise its decision if some new fact comes to light that was not previously known to the Court or the party making the request. Requests must be made within six months after the new fact is discovered and within 10 years of the delivery of the original judgment.[36]

---

[29]Advisory Opinion, *International Court of Justice Reports,* vol. 1975, p. 12 (1975). *See* also the Interpretation of Peace Treaties with Bulgaria, Hungary, and Romania (Second Phase), Advisory Opinion, *International Court of Justice Reports,* vol. 1950, p. 65 (1950).

[30]The Court has yet to do this.

[31]If the Court is not in session, the President will issue the order.

[32]Statute of the International Court of Justice, Article 59.

[33]Latin: "let the decision stand." The Anglo-American common law doctrine that rules or principles laid down in earlier judicial decisions will be followed unless they contravene ordinary principles of justice.

[34]Statute of the International Court of Justice, Article 60.

[35]Requests for interpretation have been made only twice. In connection with the Asylum Case (Columbia v. Peru), *International Court of Justice Reports,* vol. 1950, p. 266 (1950); and the Continental Shelf Case (Tunisia v. Libya), *id.,* vol. 1982, p. 18 (1982).

[36]Statute of the International Court of Justice, Article 61. In Continental Shelf (Tunisia v. Libya), *id.,* the ICJ was asked to revise its 1982 judgment. The Court ruled in 1985 that the request was inadmissible and that its earlier judgment should be implemented. Application for Revision and Interpretation of the Judgment of 24 February 1982.

Compliance with ICJ Judgments   Most states have voluntarily complied with the judgments handed down by the Court. There have been exceptions, of course. Albania refused to pay the damages awarded the United Kingdom by the Court for the injuries suffered by the United Kingdom's ships in the Corfu Channel in 1946;[37] Iran refused to comply with the Court's judgment in the *United States Diplomatic and Consular Staff in Teheran Case;*[38] and the United States ignored the Court's decision in the *Nicaragua Case.*[39]

For all practical purposes, there is no way to force a state to comply with a judgment. The United Nations Charter says that if a party refuses to comply with a judgment, "the other party may have recourse to the Security Council, which may, if it deems necessary, make recommendations or decide upon measures to give effect to the judgment."[40] This has never been done.

World Trade Organization Dispute Settlement Procedures

World Trade Organization (WTO): International inter-governmental organization responsible for implementing and enforcing international rules regulating trade between nations.

The **World Trade Organization** (WTO) is responsible for implementing and enforcing international rules regulating trade between nations. The rules themselves are found in a wide-ranging collection of WTO agreements, including the General Agreement on Tariffs and Trade, the General Agreement on Trade in Services, and the Agreement on Trade-Related Aspects of Intellectual Property Rights. Each of these agreements has three main objectives: to help trade flow as freely as possible, to achieve further liberalization gradually through negotiation, and to set up an impartial means of settling disputes. The WTO's dispute settlement process itself is governed by an agreement known as the Understanding on Rules and Procedures Governing the Settlement of Disputes (the Dispute Settlement Understanding or DSU). This is a unified process that applies to all disputes arising under the WTO agreements.[41]

Consultation and Third-Party Participation

The *Dispute Settlement Understanding* encourages member states to resolve disputes through consultation with each other. Indeed, a member is obliged to enter into a consultation within 30 days of being asked to do so. If a member fails to respond within 10 days of a request or fails to consult within 30 days, or within a period agreed upon, the requesting member can seek the establishment of a WTO Dispute Settlement Panel.[42] Also, if no solution is reached within 60 days after a request for consultation is made, the complaining party can ask for the establishment of a panel.[43]

Besides consulting, the parties to a dispute may, if each of them agrees, seek the assistance of third parties in resolving their differences. Such assistance can take the form of good offices, conciliation, or mediation, and it may be sought at any time during the course of a dispute.[44] If the parties agree, good offices, conciliation, and mediation may continue while a Dispute Settlement Panel is considering a complaint.[45]

Dispute Settlement Organs

The organs charged with administering and carrying out the *Dispute Settlement Understanding* are (a) the Dispute Settlement Body, (b) the Dispute Settlement Panels, and (c) the Appellate Body.

Dispute Settlement Body   The Dispute Settlement Body (DSB) is actually the WTO General Council convened under its own Chairman and following its own rules of procedure.[46] It is

---

[37]Corfu Channel Case (United Kingdom v. Albania), *International Court of Justice Reports,* vol. 1949, p. 244 (1949).
[38]*Id.,* vol. 1980, p. 3 (1980).
[39]Case Concerning the Military and Paramilitary Activities in and against Nicaragua (Nicaragua v. United States), *International Legal Materials,* vol. 24, p. 38 (1985).
[40]United Nations Charter, Article 94(2).
[41]A separate WTO Trade Policy Review Mechanism exists to encourage WTO member states to liberalize their trade policies. The Mechanism is a political rather than a legal process, however, so the DSU does not apply to it.
    The WTO's Web site is at www.wto.org/.
[42]Understanding on Rules and Procedures Governing the Settlement of Disputes (1994), para. 4.3. The Understanding is posted on the WTO's Web site at www.wto.org/wto/dispute/dsu.htm.
    If a case is a matter of urgency, such as one involving perishable goods, consultations must be held within 10 days of a request; and, if they fail, a request for a panel may be made within 20 days. *Id.,* para. 4.8.
[43]*Id.,* para. 4.7.
[44]*Id.,* para. 5.3.
[45]*Id.,* para. 5.5.
[46]Agreement Establishing the World Trade Organization (1994), Article IV, para. 3.

responsible for establishing Panels, adopting their reports and those of the Appellate Body, monitoring implementation of rulings and recommendations, and authorizing the suspension of concessions and other obligations in appropriate cases.[47]

Dispute Settlement Panel Should a Dispute Settlement Panel[48] (that is, an *ad hoc* tribunal) be needed, it will be made up of three panelists unless the parties agree within 10 days of its establishment that it should consist of five panelists.[49] The WTO Secretariat will nominate individuals to be panelists and the parties must have "compelling reasons" to object to their appointment.[50] If no agreement is reached within 20 days as to the make-up of a Panel, the WTO Director-General in consultation with the Chairman of the DSB and the relevant Council or Committee will appoint the panelists, keeping in mind, after consulting with the parties, any special or additional considerations relevant to the particular case.[51]

Panelists serve in their individual capacities and not as representatives of any government or organization.[52] Individuals who are citizens of one of the state parties to a dispute are not to serve on a Panel concerned with that dispute unless the parties to the dispute agree otherwise.[53] If a dispute is between a developed member state and a developing member state, at least one of the panelists must be from a developing state if the developing member state party so requests.[54]

The function of a Dispute Settlement Panel is to assist the DSB by making an objective assessment of the matter referred to it, including the facts of the case and the applicability of and conformity with the pertinent WTO agreements, and by making findings that will help the DSB to make recommendations and rulings to resolve the dispute.[55]

So that a Panel may properly do its job, the party requesting its establishment must identify the specific matters that are in dispute. This requirement is discussed in Case 3–2.

---

[47]Understanding on Rules and Procedures Governing the Settlement of Disputes (1994), para. 2.1.

[48]For an excellent summary of the dispute settlement process, *see* the chart on the WTO's Internet Web site at www.wto.org/wto/about/dispute2.htm.

[49]*Id.,* para. 8.5.

[50]*Id.,* para. 8.6.

[51]*Id.,* para. 8.7. Whenever feasible, a single Panel will be established whenever there are multiple complaints dealing with the same issue. *Id.,* para 9.1. However, "[i]f more than one Panel is established to examine complaints related to the same matter, to the greatest extent possible the same persons shall serve as panelists on each of the separate Panels and the timetable for the panel process in such disputes shall be harmonized." *Id.,* para. 9.3.

[52]*Id.,* para. 8.9.

[53]*Id.,* para. 8.3.

[54]*Id.,* para. 8.10.

[55]*Id.,* para. 11.1.

Case 3–2 European Communities—Customs Classification of Certain Computer Equipment
United States v. European Communities

World Trade Organization, Appellate Body
Appellate Body Report AB–1998–2 (1998).[56]

INTRODUCTION

The European Communities appeals from certain issues of law covered in the Panel Report, *European Communities—Customs Classification of Certain Com-*

puter Equipment (the "Panel Report") and certain legal interpretations developed by the Panel in that Report. The Panel was established to consider complaints by the United States against the European Communities, Ireland, and the United Kingdom concerning the tariff treatment of Local Area Network (LAN) equipment and personal computers with multimedia capability (PCs with multimedia capability). The United States

---

[56]This Appellate Body Report is posted on the Internet at www.wto.org/wto/dispute/62abr.doc.

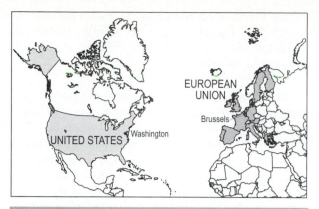

MAP 3-2 The United States and the European Communities (1998)

claimed that the European Communities, Ireland, and the United Kingdom accorded to LAN equipment and/or PCs with multimedia capability treatment less favorable than that provided for in Schedule LXXX of the European Communities (Schedule LXXX) and, therefore, acted inconsistently with their obligations under Article II:1 of the *General Agreement on Tariffs and Trade 1994* (the GATT 1994).

The Panel Report was circulated to the Members of the World Trade Organization (the WTO) on 5 February 1998. The Panel reached the conclusion that:

> . . . the European Communities, by failing to accord imports of LAN equipment from the United States treatment no less favorable than that provided for under heading 84.71 or heading 84.73, as the case may be, in Part I of Schedule LXXX, acted inconsistently with the requirements of Article II:1 of GATT 1994.

The Panel made the following recommendation:

The Panel recommends that the Dispute Settlement Body request the European Communities to bring its tariff treatment of LAN equipment into conformity with its obligations under GATT 1994.

* * *

ISSUES RAISED IN THIS APPEAL

The appellant, the European Communities, raises the following issues in this appeal:

> Whether the measures in dispute, and the products affected by such measures, were identified with sufficient specificity by the United States in its request for the establishment of a panel under Article 6.2 of the DSU. . . .

* * *

REQUEST FOR THE ESTABLISHMENT OF A PANEL

The first issue that we have to address is whether the measures in dispute, and the products affected by such measures, were identified with sufficient specificity by the United States in its request for the establishment of a panel under Article 6:2 of the DSU.

Article 6:2 of the DSU provides, in part, that the request for the establishment of a panel shall:

> . . . Identify the specific measures at issue and provide a brief summary of the legal basis of the complaint sufficient to present the problem clearly. . . .

The Panel considered that:

> . . . the substance of the present case is the actual tariff treatment by customs authorities in the European Communities and the evaluation of that treatment in the light of the tariff commitments in Schedule LXXX.

The Panel found that:

> Viewed from this perspective, . . . the United States has sufficiently identified the measures subject to the dispute, which concerns tariff treatment of LAN equipment and multimedia PCs by customs authorities in the European Communities.

The Panel found that the definitions given by the United States of the terms, LAN equipment and PCs with multimedia capability, are "sufficiently specific for the purposes of our consideration of this dispute."

The European Communities appeals these findings and submits that:

> The Panel erred where it found that the measures under dispute and the products affected by such measures were identified sufficiently specifically by the United States to include measures other than Commission Regulation (EC) No. 1165/95 as far as it concerns Local Area Network (LAN) adapter cards.

According to the European Communities, the request of the United States for the establishment of a panel:

> . . . Identifies one specific measure, namely Commission Regulation (EC) No. 1165/95 . . . [relating to] LAN adapter cards. The other alleged measures are only vaguely described, without clearly identifying the type of measure, the responsible authority, the date of issue and the reference.

We note that the request of the United States for the establishment of a panel reads in relevant part:

> Since June 1995, customs authorities in the European Communities, including but not limited to those in the United Kingdom and Ireland, have been applying tariffs to imports of all types of LAN equipment— including hubs, in-line repeaters, converters, concentrators, bridges and routers—in excess of those

provided for in the EC Schedules. Those products were previously dutiable as automatic data-processing equipment under category 8471, but, as a result of the customs authorities' action, are now subject to the higher tariff rates applicable to category 8517, "telecommunications apparatus." In addition, since 1995, customs authorities in the European Communities, particularly those in the United Kingdom, have increased tariffs on imports of certain personal computers (PCs) from 3.5 percent to 14 percent, which is above the rate provided for in the EC Schedules. These increases have resulted from the reclassification of PCs with multimedia capability from category 8471 to other categories with higher duty rates.

We consider that "measures" within the meaning of Article 6:2 of the DSU are not only measures of general application, i.e., normative rules, but also can be the application of tariffs by customs authorities. Since the request for the establishment of a panel explicitly refers to the application of tariffs on LAN equipment and PCs with multimedia capability by customs authorities in the European Communities, we agree with the Panel that the measures in dispute were properly identified in accordance with the requirements of Article 6:2 of the DSU.

With respect to the products affected by such measures, we note that the European Communities and the United States disagree on the scope of the terms, LAN equipment and PCs with multimedia capability. Regarding LAN equipment, the disagreement concerns, in particular, whether multiplexers and modems are covered by this term.

We note that Article 6:2 of the DSU does *not* explicitly require that the products to which the "specific measures at issue" apply be identified. However, with respect to certain WTO obligations, in order to identify "the specific measures at issue", it may also be necessary to identify the products subject to the measures in dispute.

LAN equipment and PCs with multimedia capacity are both generic terms. Whether these terms are sufficiently precise to "identify the specific measure at issue" under Article 6:2 of the DSU depends, in our view, upon whether they satisfy the purposes of the requirements of that provision.

In *European Communities — Bananas*, we stated that:

It is important that a panel request be sufficiently precise for two reasons: first, it often forms the basis for the terms of reference of the panel pursuant to Article 7 of the DSU; and, second, it informs the defending party and the third parties of the legal basis of the complaint.[57]

The European Communities argues that the lack of precision of the term, LAN equipment, resulted in a violation of its right to due process which is implicit in the DSU. We note, however, that the European Communities does not contest that the term, LAN equipment, is a commercial term which is readily understandable in the trade. The disagreement between the European Communities and the United States concerns its exact definition and its precise product coverage. We also note that the term, LAN equipment, was used in the consultations between the European Communities and the United States prior to the submission of the request for the establishment of a panel and, in particular, in an "Information Fiche" provided by the European Communities to the United States during informal consultations in Geneva in March 1997. We do not see how the alleged lack of precision of the terms, LAN equipment and PCs with multimedia capability, in the request for the establishment of a panel affected the rights of defense of the European Communities *in the course* of the panel proceedings. As the ability of the European Communities to defend itself was not prejudiced by a lack of knowing the measures at issue, we do not believe that the fundamental rule of due process was violated by the Panel.

The United States has stressed that "if the EC arguments on specificity of product definition are accepted, there will inevitably be long, drawn-out procedural battles at the early stage of the panel process in every proceeding. The parties will contest every product definition, and the defending party in each case will seek to exclude all products that the complaining parties may have identified by broader grouping, but not spelled out in 'sufficient' detail." We share this concern.

We agree with the Panel that the present case should be distinguished from *EEC — Quantitative Restrictions Against Hong Kong*. The request of the United States for the establishment of a panel refers to "all types of LAN equipment." Individual types of LAN equipment were only mentioned as examples. Therefore, unlike the panel in *EEC — Quantitative Restrictions Against Hong Kong*, we are not confronted with a situation in which an additional product item was added in the course of the panel proceedings.[58] This is not a case in which an attempt was

---

[57]*Appellate Body Report*, adopted 25 September 1997, WT/DS27/AB/R, para. 142.

[58]In paragraph 30 of the panel report in *EEC — Quantitative Restrictions against Hong Kong*, the panel stated:

The Panel considered that just as the terms of reference must be agreed between the parties prior to the commencement of the Panel's examination, similarly the product coverage must be clearly understood and agreed between the parties to the dispute.

We have already noted that Article 6.2 of the DSU does *not* require that the products at issue be specified in a request for the establishment of a panel. Also, Article 7 of the DSU provides that panels shall have standard terms of reference, unless the parties to the dispute agree otherwise within 20 days from the establishment of the panel.

made to "cure" a faulty panel request by a complaining party.[59]

In conclusion, we agree with the Panel that the request of the United States for the establishment of a

panel fulfilled the requirements of Article 6.2 of the DSU.... ■

---

[59]We recall that in our report in *European Communities — Bananas*, para. 143, we found that:

If a claim is not specified in the request for the establishment of a panel, then a faulty request cannot be subsequently "cured" by a complaining party's argumentation in its first written submission to the panel or in any other submission or statement made later in the panel proceeding.

A Panel report is adopted automatically by the DSB within 60 days after it has been circulated, even if a special meeting has to be convened for the purpose, unless (a) one of the parties to the dispute notifies the DSB that it is going to appeal or (b) the DSB decides by consensus not to adopt the report. If there is an appeal, the DSB will not consider the report until the appeal is completed.[60]

Appellate Body   The Appellate Body is an appeals board made up of seven persons, three of whom will serve on any one case.[61] The seven must be persons of recognized authority and with demonstrated expertise in law, international trade, and the subject matter of the WTO Agreement and its annexes.[62] The term of office is four years, renewable once.[63]

A Panel decision may be appealed to the Appellate Body only by parties directly involved in a dispute.[64] The appeal itself is limited to the legal issues contained in the Panel report and the legal interpretations developed by the Panel.[65]

The proceedings of the Appellate Body are confidential and the opinions expressed by its individual members in the report are anonymous.[66] The Appellate Body may uphold, modify, or reverse a Panel's findings and conclusions, and its report will automatically be adopted by the DSB unless the DSB decides by consensus not to do so.[67]

Enforcement

Panel and Appellate Body reports adopted by the Dispute Settlement Body are enforced by the DSB. The DSB is responsible for monitoring compliance and, should a state fail to comply with Panel or Appellate Body recommendations, the DSB may authorize either the noncomplying state to pay compensation or the injured state to retaliate.

Precedential Effect of Panel and Appellate Body Rulings   The Dispute Settlement Understanding provides:

The dispute settlement system of the WTO is a central element in providing security and predictability to the multilateral trading system. The members of the WTO recognize that it serves to preserve the rights and obligations of members under the covered [WTO] agreements, and to clarify the existing provisions of those agreements in accordance with customary rules of interpretation of public international law. Recommendations and rulings of the DSB cannot add to or diminish the rights and obligations provided in the covered agreements.[68]

In other words, the concept of legal precedent *does* apply to the new WTO dispute settlement system,[69] but it is the flexible system of precedent that is used in international tribunals

---

[60]Understanding on Rules and Procedures Governing the Settlement of Disputes, para. 16.4.
[61]*Id.,* para. 17.1.
[62]*Id.,* para. 17.3.
[63]*Id.,* para. 17.2.
[64]*Id.,* para. 17.4.
[65]*Id.,* para. 17.6.
[66]*Id.,* paras. 17.10 and 17.11.
[67]*Id.,* paras. 17.13 and 17.14.
[68]*Id.,* para. 3.2.
[69]Under GATT 1947, the question of whether or not the rulings of a Dispute Settlement Panel were to be treated as precedents for later Panels was a matter of some debate. On the one hand, Panels routinely referred to earlier Panel reports in support of their own rulings. Likewise, in GATT Council meetings, representatives of some contracting

and not the rigid system of British or even American common law. In other words, both the panels and the Appellate Body may rely on their own earlier legal rulings, but they are also free to deviate from those ruling as they think necessary. This is discussed in Case 3–3.

---

parties (notably the United States) argued that the Panel reports constituted GATT case law. On the other hand, other representatives argued that the reports had no precedential value, and a 1982 Ministerial Decision decided that dispute settlement decisions could "not add to or diminish the rights and obligations provided in the General Agreement," implying that there could be no such thing as case law or precedent. *See* GATT, *Analytical Index: Guide to GATT Law and Practice,* pp. 702–706 (6th ed., 1994).

Case 3–3   Japan — Taxes on Alcoholic Beverages

Canada v. Japan, European Communities v. Japan, United States v. Japan

World Trade Organization, Appellate Body, 1996
Appellate Body Report AB–1996–2[70]

INTRODUCTION

Japan and the United States appeal from certain issues of law and legal interpretations in the Panel Report, *Japan — Taxes on Alcoholic Beverages* (the Panel Report). That Panel (the Panel) was established to consider complaints by the European Communities, Canada and the United States against Japan relating to the Japanese Liquor Tax Law (*Shuzeiho*), Law No. 6 of 1953 as amended (the Liquor Tax Law).

* * *

ISSUES RAISED IN THE APPEAL

The . . . United States . . . raised the following issues in this appeal:

* * *

(h) whether the Panel erred in its characterization of panel reports adopted by the GATT CON-TRACTING PARTIES and the WTO Dispute Settlement Body as "subsequent practice in a specific case by virtue of the decision to adopt them."

* * *

STATUS OF ADOPTED PANEL REPORTS

In this case, the Panel concluded that,

. . . panel reports adopted by the GATT CONTRACT-ING PARTIES and the WTO Dispute Settlement Body constitute subsequent practice in a specific

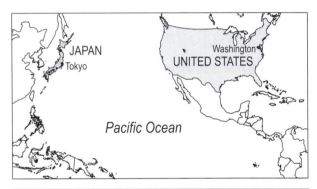

MAP 3-3   Japan and the United States (1996)

case by virtue of the decision to adopt them. Article 1(b)(iv) of GATT 1994 provides institutional recognition that adopted panel reports constitute subsequent practice. Such reports are an integral part of GATT 1994, since they constitute "other decisions of the CONTRACTING PARTIES to GATT 1947."

Article 31(3)(b) of the *Vienna Convention* [*on the Law of Treaties*] states that "any subsequent practice in the application of the treaty which establishes the agreement of the parties regarding its interpretation" is to be "taken into account together with the context" in interpreting the terms of the treaty. Generally, in international law, the essence of subsequent practice in interpreting a treaty has been recognized as a "concordant, common and consistent" sequence of acts or pronouncements which is sufficient to establish a discernible pattern implying the agreement of the parties regarding its interpretation. An isolated act is generally not sufficient to establish subsequent practice; it is a sequence

---

[70]This Appellate Body Report is posted on the Internet at www.wto.org/wto/dispute/alcohpr.wp5.

of acts establishing the agreement of the parties that is relevant.

Although GATT 1947[71] panel reports were adopted by decisions of the CONTRACTING PARTIES,[72] a decision to adopt a panel report did not under GATT 1947 constitute agreement by the CONTRACTING PARTIES on the legal reasoning in that panel report. The generally-accepted view under GATT 1947 was that the conclusions and recommendations in an adopted panel report bound the parties to the dispute in that particular case, but subsequent panels did not feel legally bound by the details and reasoning of a previous panel report.[73]

We do not believe that the CONTRACTING PARTIES, in deciding to adopt a panel report, intended that their decision would constitute a definitive interpretation of the relevant provisions of GATT 1947. Nor do we believe that this is contemplated under GATT 1994. There is specific cause for this conclusion in the *WTO Agreement*. Article IX:2 of the *WTO Agreement* provides: "The Ministerial Conference and the General Council shall have the exclusive authority to adopt interpretations of this Agreement and of the Multilateral Trade Agreements." Article IX:2 provides further that such decisions "shall be taken by a three-fourths majority of the Members." The fact that such an "exclusive authority" in interpreting the treaty has been established so specifically in the *WTO Agreement* is reason enough to conclude that such authority does not exist by implication or by inadvertence elsewhere.

Historically, the decisions to adopt panel reports under Article XXIII of the GATT 1947 were different from joint action by the CONTRACTING PARTIES under Article XXV of the GATT 1947. Today, their nature continues to differ from interpretations of the GATT 1994 and the other Multilateral Trade Agreements under the *WTO Agreement* by the WTO Ministerial Conference or the General Council. This is clear from a reading of Article 3:9 of the DSU, which states:

> The provisions of this Understanding are without prejudice to the rights of Members to seek authoritative interpretation of provisions of a covered agreement through decision-making under the WTO Agreement or a covered agreement which is a Plurilateral Trade Agreement.

Article XVI:1 of the *WTO Agreement* and paragraph 1(b)(iv) of the language of Annex 1A incorporating the GATT 1994 into the *WTO Agreement* bring the legal his-

tory and experience under the GATT 1947 into the new realm of the WTO in a way that ensures continuity and consistency in a smooth transition from the GATT 1947 system. This affirms the importance to the Members of the WTO of the experience acquired by the CONTRACTING PARTIES to the GATT 1947—and acknowledges the continuing relevance of that experience to the new trading system served by the WTO. Adopted panel reports are an important part of the GATT *acquis.*[74] They are often considered by subsequent panels. They create legitimate expectations among WTO Members, and, therefore, should be taken into account where they are relevant to any dispute. However, they are not binding, except with respect to resolving the particular dispute between the parties to that dispute.[75] In short, their character and their legal status have not been changed by the coming into force of the *WTO Agreement*.

For these reasons, we do not agree with the Panel's conclusion in paragraph 6.10 of the Panel Report that "panel reports adopted by the GATT CONTRACTING PARTIES and the WTO Dispute Settlement Body constitute subsequent practice in a specific case" as the phrase "subsequent practice" is used in Article 31 of the Vienna Convention. Further, we do not agree with the Panel's conclusion in the same paragraph of the Panel Report that adopted panel reports in themselves constitute "other decisions of the CONTRACTING PARTIES to GATT 1947" for the purposes of paragraph 1(b)(iv) of the language of Annex 1A incorporating the GATT 1994 into the *WTO Agreement*.

However, we agree with the Panel's conclusion in that same paragraph of the Panel Report that unadopted panel reports "have no legal status in the GATT or WTO system since they have not been endorsed through decisions by the CONTRACTING PARTIES to GATT or WTO Members." Likewise, we agree that "a panel could nevertheless find useful guidance in the reasoning of an unadopted panel report that it considered to be relevant."

* * *

CONCLUSIONS AND RECOMMENDATIONS

For the reasons set out in the preceding sections of this report, the Appellate Body has reached the following conclusions:

---

[71]By GATT 1947, we refer throughout to the General Agreement on Tariffs and Trade, dated October 30, 1947, annexed to the Final Act Adopted at the Conclusion of the Second Session of the Preparatory Committee of the United Nations Conference on Trade and Employment, as subsequently rectified, amended or modified.
[72]By CONTRACTING PARTIES, we refer throughout to the CONTRACTING PARTIES of GATT 1947.
[73]European Economic Community—Restrictions on Imports of Dessert Apples, BISD 36S/93, para. 12.1.
[74]French: "acquired." The acquired interpretation or gloss.]
[75]It is worth noting that the Statute of the International Court of Justice has an explicit provision, Article 59, to the same effect. This has not inhibited the development by that Court (and its predecessor) of a body of case law in which considerable reliance on the value of previous decisions is readily discernible.

the Panel erred in law in its conclusion that "panel reports adopted by the GATT CONTRACTING PARTIES and the WTO Dispute Settlement Body constitute subsequent practice in a specific case by virtue of the decision to adopt them." . . . ■

International Center for the Settlement of Investment Disputes

The International Center for the Settlement of Investment Disputes (ICSID) was created in 1965 at a conference in Washington, D.C., sponsored by the International Bank for Reconstruction and Development (popularly known as the World Bank). The underlying purpose of ICSID is to encourage private investment in underdeveloped countries. Many individuals and businesses had been reluctant to make investments, fearing they would be expropriated. To calm this fear, the World Bank drafted the Convention on the Settlement of Investment Disputes between States and Nationals of Other States (the Washington Convention),[76] creating ICSID, to provide a reliable mechanism for impartially resolving disputes between an investor and the country of investment. The Convention has now been ratified by 131 states.[77]

The ICSID Organization

The Center, headquartered at the World Bank's office in Washington, has an Administrative Council, a Secretariat, and two panels of experts. The Council is made up of representatives of the states parties to the Washington Convention and is chaired by the President of the World Bank.[78] It adopts the Center's rules regarding conciliation and arbitration and is responsible for its budget.[79] The Secretariat, made up of a Secretary-General (elected by the Council for a six-year term) and an administrative staff, serves as the Center's registrar.[80] The Council chooses the Panel of Arbitrators and the Panel of Conciliators from nominees submitted by states parties.[81]

ICSID Rules

The Administrative Council has enacted rules that regulate how conciliations and arbitrations are begun (called Institutional Rules) and rules for conducting conciliations (Conciliation Rules) as well as arbitral hearings (Arbitration Rules).[82] In the materials that follow, we will examine the rules relating to ICSID **arbitrations**.

The litigants (i.e., the investor or "private party," and the host state or "state party") may agree to the rules of law governing a particular arbitration. If they cannot agree, then both international law and the state party's law (including the state party's rules for deciding conflicts about the applicability of particular laws) are to apply.[83]

The most important basic rule established by the Washington Convention is that third-party states, including the state of the investor involved in the dispute, are not allowed to intervene. Article 27(1) of the Convention provides:

> No contracting state shall give diplomatic protection, or bring an international claim, in respect of a dispute which one of its nationals and another contracting state have consented to submit or shall have submitted to arbitration under this Convention, unless such other contracting party shall have failed to abide by and comply with the award rendered in such dispute.

This is a significant departure from traditional notions of international law, which required disputes between a state and the national of another state to be resolved only between the

arbitration: (From Latin *arbitrari:* "to give a decision.") The process by which parties to a dispute submit their differences to the binding judgment of an impartial third person or group selected by mutual consent.

---

[76]*United Nations Treaty Series,* vol. 5, p. 159.

[77]International Center for Settlement of Investment Disputes, List of Contracting States and Other Signatories of the Convention (as of October 27, 1998), posted on the ICSID Web site at www.worldbank.org/icsid/constate/constate.htm.

[78]Convention on the Settlement of Investment Disputes between States and Nationals of Other States, Article 5 (1965).

[79]*Id.,* Article 6.

[80]*Id.,* Articles 9 and 11.

[81]*Id.,* Article 13.

[82]The ICSID Rules were originally issued in 1968; they were last revised in 1984.

[83]Convention on the Settlement of Investment Disputes between States and Nationals of Other States, Article 42(1) (1965).

states alone.[84] States that are parties to the Washington Convention are not allowed to take up disputes on behalf of their nationals, unless the ICSID arbitration process fails.

Constituting an ICSID Arbitration Tribunal

Before ICSID can set up a tribunal to resolve a particular dispute, two preliminary steps must be taken. First, the state wherein the investment is being made (the host state) and the state of which the investor is a national (the home state) must both be parties to the Washington Convention. Second, the investor and the host state must both consent to ICSID jurisdiction.[85]

Both steps are vital to establishing the jurisdiction of ICSID to resolve a dispute. Neither can be **waived**. On the other hand, whereas the Convention must be properly signed and ratified, the acceptance of ICSID jurisdiction only needs to be in writing—no particular form is required.[86] As a practical matter, however, the ICSID arbitration agreement should be included in every contractual arrangement between the investor and the host state.

The *Holiday Inns v. Morocco Case*[87] involved an agreement between Morocco and two American companies—the Holiday Inns Group and Occidental Petroleum. At the request of Morocco, the companies agreed to build four hotels in that country. The "basic agreement" they signed contained an ICSID arbitration clause; however, this was not the only agreement governing the contract. To make it easier for the Moroccan government to make payments, the American companies established Moroccan subsidiaries. (This was done because Moroccan law made it difficult for the government to contract with foreign businesses.) The relationship between Morocco and the subsidiaries was described in separate agreements that did not have ICSID arbitration clauses. Thus, when Morocco failed to pay the Americans for building the hotels, both the parent American companies and their subsidiaries wanted to bring suit. However, because the agreements between Morocco and the subsidiaries had no ICSID arbitration clauses, the subsidiaries were not allowed to be parties to the arbitration proceedings. (Fortunately for the parent companies, the tribunal treated the agreements between the subsidiaries and Morocco as secondary documents that supplemented the basic agreement signed by the parents and Morocco. The parents were allowed, accordingly, to enforce those agreements.)

The Washington Convention, while speaking of "investors" and "investments," does not define either term. The drafters of the Convention attempted to do so, but they were unsuccessful. In Case 3–4, an ICSID Tribunal was faced with the issue of defining "investment."

waive: To voluntarily give up a legal right.

---

[84]*See* the Mavrommatis Palestine Concessions Case (Greece v. Great Britain) (Jurisdiction), *Permanent Court of International Justice Reports,* Series A, No. 2, p. 12 (1924); and Administrative Decision No. V. (United States v. Germany), Mixed Claims Commission, Opinion of Parker, Umpire, *United Nations Reports of International Arbitral Awards,* vol. 7, p. 119 (1924).

[85]Convention on the Settlement of Investment Disputes between States and Nationals of Other States, Article 25 (1965). Article 25 is the "cornerstone" of ICSID jurisdiction according to the directors of the World Bank.

[86]The host state must notify ICSID of the particular dispute or classes of disputes that it is willing to submit to ICSID arbitration. *Id.* It may do so in a contract with a foreign investor, in a bilateral treaty with another contracting state, or in a unilateral declaration made at the time of its ratification of the ICSID Convention or at any time thereafter. Since 1965, approximately 160 countries have entered into bilateral treaties with such provisions and some 30 countries have made unilateral declarations. Antonio R. Parra, "The Role of ICSID in the Settlement of Investment Disputes," *ICSID News,* vol. 16, No. 1, pp. 5–8 (Winter 1999), posted at www.worldbank.org/icsid/news/n-16–1–5.htm.

[87]Holiday Inns/Occidental Petroleum Corp. v. Government of Morocco, described in P. Lalive, "The First 'World Bank' Arbitration (Holiday Inn v. Morocco)—Some Legal Problems," *British Year Book of International Law,* vol. 51, p. 123 (1980).

Case 3–4   Fedax N.V. v. The Republic of Venezuela

International Centre for Settlement of Investment Disputes (1997)
International Legal Materials, vol. 37, p. 1378 (1998)

THE TRIBUNAL (Professor Francisco Orrego Vicuna, President; Professor Meir Heth; and Mr. Roberts B. Owen):

FACTS AND PROCEDURE

On June 17, 1996, a request for arbitration was submitted to the International Centre for Settlement of Investment Disputes (ICSID or the Centre) on behalf of Fedax N.V., a company established and domiciled in Curacao, Netherlands Antilles, against the Republic of Venezuela. The request concerns a dispute arising out of certain debt instruments, referred to below, issued by the Republic of Venezuela and assigned by way of endorsement to the Claimant Fedax N.V. The request invokes the provisions, discussed below, of an October 22, 1991, Agreement on Encouragement and Reciprocal Protection of Investments between the Kingdom of the Netherlands and the Republic of Venezuela (the Agreement).

* * *

On June 26, 1996, the Secretary-General of the Centre registered the request, pursuant to Article 36(3) of the Convention on the Settlement of Investment Disputes between States and Nationals of Other States (the Convention or the ICSID Convention). . . .

* * *

CONSIDERATIONS

* * *

The main jurisdictional question raised in this case concerns whether the dispute involves an "investment" within the meaning of Article 25 (1) of the Convention. In fact, the Republic of Venezuela has objected to the jurisdiction of the Centre in the matter of its dispute with Fedax N. V., on the ground that the latter company cannot be considered to have made an investment for the purposes of the Convention, because it acquired by way of endorsement the promissory notes issued by the Republic of Venezuela in connection with the contract made with the Venezuelan corporation Industrias Metalurgicas Van Dam C.A. The interpretation of the term "investment" is therefore crucial in determining the scope of the Centre's jurisdiction under the Convention.

The Republic of Venezuela has argued in this respect that Fedax N.V.'s holding of the above-mentioned promissory notes does not qualify as an "investment" because this transaction does not amount to a direct foreign investment involving "a long term transfer of financial resources—capital flow—from one country to another (the recipient of the investment) in order to acquire interests in a corporation, a transaction which normally entails certain risks to the potential investor." Neither would this transaction qualify, in Venezuela's view, as a portfolio investment to acquire titles to money since in that country this occurs "when the investor acquires shares of a corporation through the Stock Exchange—Caracas or Maracaibo—basically those known as 'Global Depository

EXHIBIT 3-4   Venezuela (1997)

Receipts' represented by GDS and ADR," a type of investment which is "only considered direct when the acquisition of the title is done in a primary way." Venezuela has further argued that in the light of the rule of interpretation laid down in Article 31.1 of the 1969 Vienna Convention on the Law of Treaties, the term "investment" should be interpreted "in good faith in accordance with the ordinary meaning to be given to the terms of the treaty in their context and in the light of its object and purpose." Under such an interpretation, in Venezuela's view, investment in an economic context means "the laying out of money or property in business ventures, so that it may produce a revenue or income." Venezuela contends that this particular interpretation is necessary to accommodate the definition of investments as comprising "every kind of asset" as that phrase appears in Article 1 (a) of the 1991 Agreement.

The Tribunal has examined with great attention the arguments put forward by the Republic of Venezuela since they express a legitimate concern about the interpretation of the Convention and the Agreement. The Tribunal has also carefully considered the jurisdictional arguments of the claimant contesting the views set out by the Republic of Venezuela. The Tribunal does of course concur with the Republic of Venezuela about the need to apply the rules of interpretation laid down in the Vienna Convention on the Law of Treaties. In order to satisfy these requirements the Tribunal shall examine the question in the light of Article 25 (1) of the Convention, Article 1 (a) and related provisions of the Agreement and other relevant considerations discussed below.

The Tribunal shall first examine the meaning of the term "investment" under Article 25 (1) of the Convention. It is well established that numerous attempts to define investments were made during the negotiations of the Convention,[88] but none were generally acceptable.[89] Because of this difficulty, it was finally decided to leave any definition of the "investment" to the consent of the parties.[90] As explained by the Report of the Executive Directors:

"No attempt was made to define the term 'investment' given the essential requirement of consent by the parties, and the mechanism through which Contracting States can make known in advance, if they so desire, the classes of disputes which they would or would not consider submitting to the Centre (Article 25 (4))."[91]

An account on these negotiations given by Mr. A. Broches is also most pertinent:

"During the negotiations several definitions of 'investment' were considered and rejected. It was felt in the end that a definition could be dispensed with 'given the essential requirement of consent by the parties.' This indicates that the requirement that the dispute must have arisen out of an 'investment' may be merged into the requirement of consent to jurisdiction. Presumably, the parties' agreement that a dispute is an 'investment dispute' will be given great weight in any determination of the Centre's jurisdiction, although it would not be controlling."[92]

In light of the above, distinguished commentators of the Convention have concluded that "a broad approach to the interpretation of this term in Article 25 is warranted,"[93] that it "is within the sole discretion of each Contracting State to determine the type of investment disputes that it considers arbitrable in the context of ICSID,"[94] or that the parties "thus have a large measure of discretion to determine for themselves whether their transaction constitutes an investment for the purposes of the Convention."[95] Within this broad framework for the definition of investment under the ICSID Convention, the Tribunal also notes that a number of transactions have been identified as qualifying as investments in given circumstances. It has also been noted by commentators of the Convention, and during the history of its negotiation, that jurisdiction over loans,[96] suppliers' credits,[97] outstanding payments,[98] ownership of shares[99] and construction contracts,[100] among other aspects, was left to the discretion of the parties.[101]

It is also most relevant to note the conclusions of a distinguished author in this respect:

"These new types of investment, and especially those relating to the supply of services are sometimes on the borderline between investment proper and commercial transactions, which would fall outside the scope of ICSID.

"However, the characterization of transnational loans as 'investments' has not raised difficulty. The reason is twofold. First, it has been assumed from the origin of the Convention that loans, or more precisely those of a certain duration as opposed to rapidly concluded commercial financial facilities, were included in the concept of 'investment.' This is evidenced by the first Draft of the Convention according to which:

For the purpose of this Chapter

(i) 'investment' means any contribution of money or other asset of economic value for an indefinite period or, if the period be defined, for not less than five years.

"Although attempts at defining the notion of investment were given up by the authors of the

---

[88]Christoph Schreuer: "Commentary on the ICSID Convention," *ICSID Review—Foreign Investment Law Journal,* vol. 11, 316, at pp. 355–358 (1996).

[89]Convention History, vol. 2 at pp. 835–837.

[90]*Ibid.,* at p. 1078; Carolyn B. Lamm and Abby Cohen Smutny: "The implementation of ICSID Arbitration Agreements," *ICSID Review—Foreign Investment Law Journal,* vol. 11, p. 64 at p. 80 (1996).

[91]"Report of the Executive Directors on the Convention on the Settlement of Investment Disputes between States and Nationals of Other States," Doc. ICSID/2, *ICSID Reports,* vol. 1, p. 23, para. 27 (1993).

[92]A. Broches: "The Convention on The Settlement of Investment Disputes: Some Observations on Jurisdiction," *Columbia Journal of Transnational Law,* vol. 5, pp. 261–280 at p. 268, footnote omitted (1966).

[93]C. F. Amerasinghe: "The Jurisdiction of the International Centre for the Settlement of Investment Disputes," *Indian Journal of International Law,* vol. 19, pp. 166–227 at p. 181 (1979).

[94]Georges R. Delaume: "ICSID and the Transnational Financial Community," *ICSID Review—Foreign Investment Law Journal,* vol. 1, pp. 237–256 at pp. 239–240 (1986); Ibrahim F. I. Shihata: "Towards a Greater Depoliticization of Investment Disputes: The Roles of ICSID and MIGA," *ICSID Review—Foreign Investment Law Journal,* vol. 1, p. 1 at p. 4 (1986).

[95]Carolyn B. Lamm and Abby Cohen Smutny: "The implementation of ICSID Arbitration Agreements," *ICSID Review—Foreign Investment Law Journal,* vol. 11, p. 64 at p. 80 (1996).

[96]Convention History, vol. II, at pp. 261, 474.

[97]*Ibid.,* at p. 451.

[98]*Ibid.,* at p. 542.

[99]*Ibid.,* at p. 661.

[100]*Ibid.,* at p. 500.

[101]Christoph Schreuer: "Commentary on the ICSID Convention," *ICSID Review—Foreign Investment Law Journal,* vol. 11, 316, at p. 357 (1996); C. F. Amerasinghe: "The Jurisdiction of the International Centre for the Settlement of Investment Disputes," *Indian Journal of International Law,* vol. 19, pp. 166–227 at p. 181 (1979).

Convention and this provision disappeared, there is no reason to doubt that loans can be considered as investments for the purposes of the Convention. Another reason why the issue of definition is not a serious one is that, in the case of loan contracts involving foreign public borrowers referring to ICSID as a means of settling loan disputes, the parties take the precaution of stipulating expressly that the loan is an investment for the purposes of the Convention."[102]

This matter will be discussed below in connection with the promissory notes as a form of loan or credit.

In addition to the background of Article 25 (1) of the Convention, there is also a problem of textual interpretation that the Tribunal must consider. The Republic of Venezuela has made the argument that the disputed transaction is not a "direct foreign investment" and therefore could not qualify as an investment under the Convention. However, the text of Article 25(1) establishes that the "jurisdiction of the Centre shall extend to any legal dispute arising directly out of an investment." It is apparent that the term "directly" relates in this Article to the "dispute" and not to the "investment." It follows that jurisdiction can exist even in respect of investments that are not direct, so long as the dispute arises directly from such transaction. This interpretation is also consistent with the broad reach that the term "investment" must be given in light of the negotiating history of the Convention.

Precisely because the term "investment" has been broadly understood in the ICSID practice and decisions, as well as in scholarly writings, it has never before been a major source of contention before ICSID Tribunals. This is the first ICSID case in which the jurisdiction of the Centre has been objected to on the ground that the underlying transaction does not meet the requirements of an investment under the Convention. On prior occasions ICSID Tribunals have examined on their own initiative the question whether an investment was involved, and in each such case have reached the conclusion that the "investment" requirement of the Convention has been met. In *Kaiser Bauxite v. Jamaica*,[103] as in *Alcoa Minerals of Jamaica Inc. v. Jamaica*,[104] the Tribunal established the Centre's jurisdiction both on the consent given by the parties and on the fact that the case "in which a mining company has invested substantial

amounts in a foreign State in reliance upon an agreement with that State, is among those contemplated by the Convention." Amounts paid out to develop a concession and other undertakings based on a concession agreement, were also considered to qualify as an investment under the Convention in LETCO v. Liberia.[105] Also in *SOABI v. Senegal* the Tribunal considered the issue of jurisdiction in respect of an operation encompassing separate agreements, but this dealt only indirectly with the existence of an investment.[106]

The issue of whether a given dispute arises directly out of an investment has been also raised in a number of cases, although such cases have not considered whether an investment was made in the first place. In *Holiday Inns v. Morocco*, for example, the Tribunal found that the Centre had jurisdiction over loan contracts that had their origin in agreements separate from the investment; although the respondent argued that these constituted different transactions, the Tribunal emphasized "the general unity of an investment operation."[107] In Amco Asia et al. v. Indonesia an *ad hoc* Committee also affirmed the Centre's jurisdiction in respect of an international tort arising from lack of protection to the claimant by the Indonesian Army and Police; the Tribunal stated that it "does not think of 'international tort' and 'investment dispute' as comprising mutually exclusive categories,' and that "[t]he jurisdiction of the Tribunal is not successfully avoided by applying a different formal characterization to the operative facts of the dispute."[108] In this same case an important distinction was made at a later stage in the following terms:

". . . the Tribunal believes that it is correct to distinguish between rights and obligations that are applicable to legal or natural persons who are within the reach of a host State's jurisdiction, as a matter of general law; and rights and obligations that are applicable to an investor as a consequence of an investment agreement entered into with that host State. Legal disputes relating to the latter will fall under Article 25 (1) of the Convention."[109]

* * *

The Tribunal considers that the broad scope of Article 25 (1) of the Convention and the ensuing ICSID practice and decisions are sufficient, without more, to

---

[102]Georges R. Delaume: "ICSID and the Transnational Financial Community," *ICSID Review—Foreign Investment Law Journal,* vol. 1, pp. 237–256 at p. 242, footnote omitted (1986).

[103]Kaiser Bauxite Company v. Government of Jamaica (1975), *ICSID Reports,* vol. 1, p. 296 (1993).

[104]Alcoa Minerals of Jamaica Inc. v. Government of Jamaica (1975), *Yearbook Commercial Arbitration,* vol. 4, p. 206 (1979).

[105]Liberian Eastern Timber Corporation v. Government of the Republic of Liberia (1984), *ICSID Reports,* vol. 2, p. 346 (1994).

[106]Societe Ouest Africaine des Betons Industriels v. State of Senegal, (1988), *id.,* vol. 2, p. 165 (1994).

[107]Holiday Inns S.A., Occidental Petroleum Corporation et al. v. Government of Morocco, Case No. ARB/72/1 . . . [in] P. Lalive: "The First 'World Bank' Arbitration (Holiday Inns v. Morocco)—Some Legal Problems, *British Year Book of International Law,* vol. 51, p. 123 (1980).

[108]Amco Asia Corporation, Pan American Development Limited and P.T. Amco Indonesia v. Republic of Indonesia (1986), *ICSID Reports,* vol. 1, p. 509 at p. 527 (1993).

[109]*Ibid.,* Resubmission (1988), *ICSID Reports,* vol. 1, p. 543 at p. 565 (1993).

require a finding that the Centre's jurisdiction and its own competence are wellfounded. In addition, as explained above, loans qualify as an investment within ICSID's jurisdiction, as does, in given circumstances, the purchase of bonds. Since promissory notes are evidence of a loan and a rather typical financial and credit instrument, there is nothing to prevent their purchase from qualifying as an investment under the Convention in the circumstances of a particular case such as this. This conclusion, however, has to be examined next in the context of the specific consent of the parties and other provisions which are controlling in the matter.

The Tribunal turns now to a consideration of the relevant terms and provisions of the Agreement between the Kingdom of the Netherlands and the Republic of Venezuela, which is the specific bilateral investment treaty governing the consent to arbitration by the latter Contracting Party. Under Article 9 (1) of this Agreement, disputes between one Contracting Party and a national of the other Contracting Party "concerning an obligation of the former under this Agreement in relation to an investment of the latter" shall be submitted to ICSID for settlement by arbitration or conciliation. In Article 9 (4) each Party "gives its unconditional consent" to such submission of disputes.

It follows that, as contemplated by the Convention, the definition of "investment" is controlled by consent of the Contracting Parties, and the particular definition set forth in Article 1 (a) of the Agreement is the one that governs the jurisdiction of ICSID:

"[T]he term Investments' shall comprise every kind of asset and more particularly though not exclusively: . . . .

(ii) rights derived from shares, bonds, and other kinds of interests in companies and joint ventures;

(iii) titles to money, to other assets or to any performance having an economic value . . ."

This definition evidences that the Contracting Parties to the Agreement intended a very broad meaning for the term "investment." The Tribunal notes in particular that titles to money in this definition are not in any way restricted to forms of direct foreign investment or portfolio investment, as argued by the Republic of Venezuela. Some such restrictions may perhaps apply to other types of investment listed in such definition, such as rights derived from shares or other similar types of investment, but they do not apply to the credit transactions of different categories that are embodied in the meaning of "titles to money" as referred to in subparagraph (iii) of the definition set out above. It should be noted, moreover, that titles to money are not necessarily excluded from the concept of direct foreign investment.

The Tribunal has also undertaken a close examination of other provisions of the Agreement which are related to the definition of an investment, including Article 5 of the Agreement, under which the Contracting Parties guarantee the transfer of payments related to an investment, including the transfer of interests (Article 5 (a)) and funds for the reimbursement of loans (Article 5(d)). The conclusion that the definition of "investment" and the meaning of "titles to money" under the Agreement include loans and related credit transactions is thus reinforced. It must also be noted that the Republic of Venezuela has not exercised its right under Article 25 (4) of the ICSID Convention to notify the Centre of any class or classes of disputes it would or would not consider submitting to the jurisdiction of the Centre. This provision allows Contracting States to put investors on notice as to what class of disputes they would or would not consider consenting to within the broad meaning of investment under the Convention.

A broad definition of investment such as that included in the Agreement is not at all an exceptional situation. On the contrary, most contemporary bilateral treaties of this kind refer to "every kind of asset" or to "all assets," including the listing of examples that can qualify for coverage; claims to money and to any performance having a financial value are prominent features of such listings. This broad approach has also become the standard policy of major economic groupings such as the European Communities. In providing for the protection of investments the EC have included "all types of assets, tangible and intangible, that have an economic value, including direct or indirect contributions in cash, kind or services invested or received." Among the transactions listed as investments are "stocks, bonds, debentures, guarantees or other financial instruments of a company, other firm, government or, other public authority or an international organization; claims to money, goods, services or other performance having economic value."[110] Since the Kingdom of the Netherlands is a prominent member of the European Communities, it is hardly surprising that a similar approach has been followed in its bilateral investment treaties.[111] . . .

* * *

The Tribunal . . . [is] satisfied that loans and other credit facilities are within the jurisdiction of the Centre under both the terms of the Convention and the scope of the bilateral Agreement governing consent in this case. . . .

* * *

---

[110]Council of the European Communities: "Community position on investment protection principles in the ACP States," ACP-CEE 2172/92, 3 November 1992, at p. 5.

[111]*See* for example the Agreement between the Kingdom of the Netherlands and the Republic of Paraguay on Encouragement and Reciprocal Protection of Investments, 29 October 1992, in Alejandro A. Escobar: "Introductory Note on Bilateral Investment Treaties Recently Concluded by Latin American States," ICSID Review—*Foreign Investment Law Journal*, Vol. 11, 1996, p. 86, at p. 197.

DECISION

For the foregoing reasons the Tribunal unanimously decides that the present dispute is within the jurisdiction of the Centre and the competence of the Tribunal. The Tribunal has, accordingly, made the necessary Order for the continuation of the procedure pursuant to Arbitration Rule 41(4). ■

Unilateral Withdrawal Is Ineffective   If the proper consent has been given to establish an ICSID tribunal, then the tribunal can be set up even when the host state or the investor refuses to participate.[112] Also, once consent has been given, it cannot be unilaterally withdrawn.[113] A state party cannot withdraw by filing a later reservation to the Convention[114] or even by denouncing the Convention.[115]

In *Alcoa Minerals of Jamaica, Inc. (United States) v. Jamaica*,[116] Alcoa, an American company, contracted with the Jamaican government to construct an aluminum factory in exchange for a 25-year bauxite mining concession, a promise of no increase in taxes for 25 years, and access to ICSID arbitration. Both the United States and Jamaica were parties to the Washington Convention, and Jamaica's ratification listed no reservations to the tribunal's jurisdiction. Alcoa built the plant and began mining bauxite. Then, in 1974, Jamaica decided to levy a tax on bauxite mining. Alcoa's tax bill that year was $20 million. To avoid a suit by Alcoa, Jamaica filed a reservation with ICSID excluding disputes relating to minerals or natural resources. Alcoa nevertheless went ahead and began an ICSID arbitration. Jamaica refused to participate, relying on its reservation. The tribunal decided that it had jurisdiction and that the proceedings would continue without Jamaica's participation.[117] It held that (a) consent to jurisdiction existed in writing, (b) consent existed at the time that the case was brought to ICSID, and (c) notification of the reservation did not affect any prior consent. The tribunal said that a reservation to the Convention would apply only to agreements made after the reservation was filed with the Center.

Selecting the Arbitrators   The Washington Convention offers a wide range of choices in the selection of arbitrators. The litigants may agree to any number, but if they want more than one, the number must be odd. The arbitrators may be any persons agreeable to the litigants; however, the majority must be nationals of states other than the state party to the dispute. Should one of the litigants refuse to cooperate in making the appointments, the Chairman of ICSID's Arbitration Council, at the request of either litigant and after consulting with both as far as possible, will provide the missing name or names from a list (called the Panel of Arbitrators) maintained by ICSID.[118]

Place of Arbitration   Arbitration proceedings are normally held at ICSID's headquarters in Washington, D.C. By agreement, the litigants can elect to have the arbitration held at the offices of any institution with which ICSID has made arrangements. At present ICSID has entered into arrangements with the Permanent Court of Arbitration at The Hague, the Asian-African Legal Consultative Committee's Regional Offices in Kuala Lumpur and in Cairo, the Australian Center for International Commercial Arbitration in Melbourne, the Australian Commercial Disputes Center in Sydney, the Singapore International Arbitration Center, and the Gulf Cooperation Council Commercial Arbitration Center in Bahrain.[119] Also, after consulting with ICSID's Secretary-General and with the permission of the arbitration tribunal, the litigants can agree to

---

[112]Convention on the Settlement of Investment Disputes between States and Nationals of Other States, Article 26 (1965).

[113]*Id.*, Article 25(1).

[114]*Id.*, Article 25(4).

[115]*Id.*, Article 72.

[116]*Yearbook of Commercial Arbitration*, vol. 4, p. 206 (1979).

[117]The tribunal cited Articles 38 and 42 of the Convention on the Settlement of Investment Disputes between States and Nationals of Other States (1965) as authority.

[118]*Id.*, Articles 38 and 40(1). These names may not be nationals of the state party.

[119]"About ICSID," International Center for the Settlement of Investment Disputes Web site, posted at www.worldbank.org/icsid/about/about.htm.

have the proceedings held at any other location.[120] So far, the arbitrations have been split fairly evenly between Washington and major European cities.[121]

Exclusive Remedy   Giving consent to ICSID arbitration is deemed to exclude all other remedies.[122] The case cannot be tried in a municipal or another international tribunal,[123] nor can the investor turn to the home state for diplomatic protection.[124]

Any dispute about the power of an ICSID tribunal to hear a matter is for the tribunal itself to decide.[125] The Convention requires the Secretary-General to register a request for arbitration unless the information contained in the request discloses that the dispute is "manifestly" outside the jurisdiction of the Center.[126] Thus, so long as there is some showing of a basis for arbitration, a tribunal will be convened.[127]

Jurisdiction   An ICSID tribunal must have jurisdiction both over the parties involved and over the subject matter of the dispute.

personal jurisdiction: The requirement that a tribunal must have power over the parties before it may hear a dispute.

Personal Jurisdiction.   In order for a tribunal to have **personal jurisdiction**, the parties appearing before it must be a "state party" and a "national of another contracting state." A state party includes the state itself, its agencies, and its subdivisions. Subdivisions include the "states" or provinces of a federal state, semiautonomous dependencies, and municipalities. When a dispute arises that involves an agency or a subdivision of a state, either the agency or subdivision *and* the state must have consented to ICSID jurisdiction before the Center will set up a tribunal to hear the matter.[128]

natural person: A human being.

A "national of another contracting state" can be either a natural or a juridical person. A **natural person** is a human being who has the nationality of a home state. That is, the home state must be a contracting party to the Convention and not itself a party to the dispute. In addition, the natural person must have home state nationality at two critical times: (1) on the date the parties consented to arbitration and (2) on the date that a request for the arbitration is registered with ICSID.[129]

juridical person: A legal entity created by national or international law.

A **juridical person** is a legal entity, other than a natural person, that has sufficient existence in the eyes of the law to function legally, sue and be sued, and make decisions through agents (e.g., a business firm). In order for a juridical person to be a party to an ICSID arbitration, it

---

[120]Convention on the Settlement of Investment Disputes Between States and Nationals of Other States, Articles 62 and 63 (1965).

[121]Georges R. DeLaume, "ICSID Arbitration," *Contemporary Problems in International Arbitration,* p. 33 (Julian Lew, ed., 1986).

[122]*See* Alcoa Minerals of Jamaica, Inc. (United States) v. Jamaica, *Yearbook of Commercial Arbitration,* vol. 4, p. 206 (1979); and Liberian Eastern Timber Corporation v. Liberia (1987), *International Legal Materials,* vol. 26, p. 647 (1988).

[123]The host state may, however, require that all local administrative and judicial remedies be exhausted before the dispute can be taken to ICSID. Convention on the Settlement of Investment Disputes between States and Nationals of Other States, Article 26 (1965).

[124]*Id.,* Article 27.

[125]*Id.,* Article 41.

[126]*Id.,* Article 36(3).

[127]There is no indication in the Convention about which party has the burden of proof to show that the Center has jurisdiction. However, in both Alcoa Minerals of Jamaica, Inc. (United States) v. Jamaica, *Yearbook of Commercial Arbitration,* vol. 4, p. 206 (1979), and the Klockner Industrie-Anlagen GmbH (Federal Republic of Germany) v. Cameroon (Award), *id.,* vol. 10, p. 71 (1985), the tribunals held that the burden was on the party seeking to show that the tribunal has jurisdiction.

[128]Convention on the Settlement of Investment Disputes between States and Nationals of Other States, Article 25(3) (1965). In Klockner Industrie-Anlagen GmbH (Federal Republic of Germany) v. Cameroon (Award), *Yearbook of Commercial Arbitration,* vol. 10, p. 71 (1985), a German company, Klockner, agreed to build and manage a fertilizer factory in the Cameroon for five years. The Cameroon government was to furnish the site and pay for construction by repaying the note taken out by Klockner. A joint venture, SOCAME, was set up in the Cameroon and in due course it became a party to an agreement with Klockner. The agreement between SOCAME and Klockner had an ICSID arbitration clause, as did the principal agreement between Klockner and the Cameroon government. After a year and a half, the factory was closed and SOCAME was declared bankrupt. Klockner thereupon filed with ICSID against both SOCAME and the Cameroon government, asking for the balance due on the loan. Because SOCAME had not been designated as an agent of the Cameroon government, it would not normally have qualified as a party to an ICSID arbitration. However, the Cameroon government wanted SOCAME to be party to its counterclaim against Klockner, so, before pleadings were submitted, the Cameroon government sent a letter to the tribunal stating that (a) SOCAME was an agency of that government and (b) the government approved of SOCAME's consent to ICSID arbitration. The tribunal tersely held that "the letter resolves the problem of jurisdiction affirmatively."

[129]Convention on the Settlement of Investment Disputes between States and Nationals of Other States, Article 25(2)(a) (1965).

must have had the nationality of a home state on the date the parties consented to arbitration.[130] However, companies under the control of foreign nationals will also be treated as nationals of another contracting state if the contracting parties agree that they should be treated as such.[131] This is an important point because host states often require that companies be incorporated locally before they can do business, acquire land, or obtain payment from the government.

The Convention does not define "foreign control," and the decisions in various cases have not been consistent. One case found foreign control where 51 percent of the shareholders were foreigners.[132] Another held that there was foreign control when foreigners dominated the management of the firm.[133]

Subject Matter Jurisdiction. ICSID arbitration tribunals can only decide matters that are (a) disputes that (b) arise out of an investment. The requirement that there be a dispute means that ICSID tribunals will not decide **collusive actions** (i.e., "test" cases) or give advisory opinions. In *AGIP Co. SpA (Italy) v. Congo*, an Italian investor, AGIP, breached its investment agreement with the Republic of the Congo. The Congo responded by nationalizing AGIP's subsidiary. AGIP then filed for arbitration, and the Congo answered by arguing that there was no dispute because it had compensated AGIP when it had nationalized the subsidiary. AGIP said that the dispute arose prior to the nationalization decree and that the compensation was inadequate. The tribunal could find no definition of a **legal dispute** in the Convention, so it turned to a statement made by the Executive Director of the World Bank at the time the Convention was opened for signature that defined a legal dispute as a conflict over rights rather than interests. Such a dispute, said the tribunal, has to relate to the existence of a legal right or a legal obligation, or to the nature and extent of compensation for the breach of such a right or obligation. Based on this definition, the tribunal concluded there had been no dispute prior to the nationalization decree. It therefore limited its inquiry to determining if the compensation made after nationalization was adequate.[134]

The Convention also does not define **investment**. The Executive Director of the World Bank once described this omission as purposeful, saying that drafters of the Convention thought the primary consideration should be the intent of the parties.[135] The intent of the parties was examined in the *Alcoa Minerals of Jamaica Case*, described earlier.[136] The tribunal said that the agreement of the parties as to what an investment is, while not the deciding factor, should be given great weight. And absent some agreement by them, the word should be given its ordinary meaning—that is, to put capital into a venture with the expectation of receiving a profit. In the *Alcoa Case*, the parties seemed to use the word *investment* in its ordinary way, so

collusive action: (From Latin *cullosio:* "a secret understanding.") A suit in which the parties are not at odds but in which they cooperate to obtain a judgment.

legal dispute: A disagreement as to the existence of a legal right or obligation, or as to the nature and extent of the compensation due for the breach of such a right or obligation.

investment: A commitment of money or capital in order to earn a financial return.

---

[130]The Convention does not expressly require a company to have home state nationality on the date that the filing is made with ICSID. This seems to indicate that a change in nationality of the company (from home to host state) would have no effect on the company's ability to began an arbitration. However, in Klockner Industrie-Anlagen GmbH (Federal Republic of Germany) v. Cameroon (Jurisdiction), *Yearbook of Commercial Arbitration,* vol. 10, p. 71 (1985), the tribunal implied that if foreign ownership ends before a case is filed with ICSID, personal jurisdiction would be lacking. (In Klockner, however, the jurisdiction was determined on different grounds.)

[131]Convention on the Settlement of Investment Disputes between States and Nationals of Other States, Article 25(2)(b) (1965). In Holiday Inns/Occidental Petroleum Corp. v. Government of Morocco, described in P. Lalive, "The First 'World Bank' Arbitration (Holiday Inns v. Morocco)—Some Legal Problems," *British Year Book of International Law,* vol. 51., p. 123 (1980), the tribunal narrowly interpreted the Convention and decided that foreign control would be implied only if no other implication would be made. However, in AMCO Asia Corp. et al. (United States) v. Indonesia (Jurisdiction), *International Legal Materials,* vol. 23, p. 351 (1985), a wider interpretation of the Convention was made. The tribunal looked at all the facts, assumed that the parties had acted in good faith, and concluded that foreign control would be implied because the host state knew that the company was dominated by foreigners, even though this was not expressly mentioned in the agreement containing the ICSID clause.

[132]In Holiday Inns/Occidental Petroleum Corp. v. Government of Morocco, described in P. Lalive, "The First 'World Bank' Arbitration (Holiday Inns v. Morocco)—Some Legal Problems," *British Year Book of International Law,* vol. 51, p. 123 (1980).

[133]Liberian Eastern Timber Corporation v. Liberia (1987), *International Legal Materials,* vol. 26, p. 647 (1988). The tribunal concluded that a local company was under French control for two independent reasons: (1) all of the shares were owned by French nationals and (2) French nationals dominated the management of the firm. A majority of directors and the manager were French.

[134]*International Legal Materials,* vol. 21, p. 740 (1983).

[135]Cited in Alcoa Minerals of Jamaica, Inc. (United States) v. Jamaica, *Yearbook of Commercial Arbitration,* vol. 4, p. 206 (1979).

[136]*Id.*

the tribunal decided that the nationalization of Alcoa's aluminum plant by Jamaica was a dispute arising directly out of an investment.

The parties can also limit the subject matter of a dispute by adding restrictions in their agreement to arbitrate. Additionally, the tribunal will only consider matters raised in the claim brought by the party initiating the arbitration proceeding[137] or raised in a counterclaim.[138]

Provisional Measures and Awards   An ICSID tribunal has the power to recommend provisional measures to preserve the respective rights of the parties[139] and to issue binding awards.[140]

Awards issued by an ICSID tribunal are binding but not final. The tribunal itself can review an award either to interpret it[141] or to revise it.[142] Appeal is also allowed to an *ad hoc* committee that has the power to annul an award.[143] An annulment proceeding was instituted in the *AMCO Asia Case* following a decision by the tribunal to award AMCO U.S. $2,472,490. The *ad hoc* committee determined that the evidence showed losses by AMCO of only $983,992, and it accordingly annulled the "award as a whole."[144]

Enforcement   ICSID awards are binding on the parties to an arbitration, and the states parties to the Washington Convention agree to comply with them. The courts of the states parties (including the courts of the state that was a party to the arbitration) are forbidden to review the award,[145] and the states themselves are obliged to enforce the pecuniary provisions of the award as if it were a final judgment of their own courts.[146] Should the courts of a state party to an ICSID arbitration seek to review an award, an investor can seek diplomatic remedies from its home state,[147] and other states parties to the Convention can protest as well.[148]

Other Arbitration Tribunals

Arbitration between private parties is not normally done on a purely *ad hoc* basis, with the parties appointing arbitrators and devising procedures and rules for the conduct of a proceeding on their own. More often the parties agree in advance to resolve their disputes using existing guidelines set up by one of several international arbitration organizations. The most prominent of these organizations are the American Arbitration Association, the London Court of International Arbitration, the International Chamber of Commerce, and the United Nations Commission on International Trade Law (UNCITRAL).[149] Each has an established set of arbitration rules and each maintains a panel (or list) of qualified arbitrators.[150] Despite some differences, the basic procedures used by all of them are similar and analogous to the procedures of the World Bank's International Center for the Settlement of Investment Disputes.

---

[137]Convention on the Settlement of Investment Disputes Between States and Nationals of Other States, Article 25 (1965).

[138]*Id.,* Article 46.

[139]*Id.,* Article 47.

[140]*Id.,* Article 53.

[141]Convention on the Settlement of Investment Disputes Between States and Nationals of Other States, Article 50 (1965).

[142]*Id.,* Article 51.

[143]*Id.,* Article 52. The *ad hoc* committee consists of three persons appointed from the Panel of Arbitrators by the Chairman of the Administrative Council (i.e., the President of the World Bank). Appeals to such a committee are allowed on the grounds "(a) that the Tribunal was not properly constituted; (b) that the Tribunal has manifestly exceeded its powers; (c) that there was corruption on the part of a member of the Tribunal; (d) that there has been a serious departure from a fundamental rule of procedure; or (e) that the award has failed to state the reasons on which it is based." *Id.*

[144]AMCO Asia Corp. et al. (United States) v. Indonesia (Annulment), *International Legal Materials,* vol. 26, p. 467 (1987).

[145]Convention on the Settlement of Investment Disputes Between States and Nationals of Other States, Article 53 (1965).

[146]*Id.,* Article 54.

[147]*Id.,* Article 27(1).

[148]*Id.,* Article 64.

[149]The American Arbitration Association can be found on the Internet at www.adr.org/; the International Chamber of Commerce at www.iccwbo.org/; and UNCITRAL at www.un.or.at/uncitral/.

[150]For a comparison of these organizations from an American perspective, *see* Steven J. Stein and Daniel R. Wotman, "International Commercial Arbitration in the 1980s: A Comparison of the Major Arbitral Systems and Rules," *Business Lawyer,* vol. 38, p. 1685 (1983).

C. SETTLEMENT OF DISPUTES IN MUNICIPAL COURTS

forum: (Latin: "an open square" or "market-place"; in Roman times, citizens met here to conduct business.) The court or locale wherein causes are judicially tried.

Municipal courts are often called upon to settle international disputes. These can include crimes and torts where the wrongful act did not occur within the **forum** state (i.e., the territory of the state wherein the court is located), or, if it did, where the defendant is not a national of the forum state. Similarly, in contract cases, the contract may not have been made in the forum state or may not have been carried out there, or both.

The competence or ability of a national court to exercise the power to try a case is known as jurisdiction. Under international law, the jurisdiction of municipal courts to try an international dispute is limited. Most governing rules are prohibitory—that is, they limit the court's powers. Indeed, there are few situations where international law requires a municipal court to take a case contrary to its wishes.

immunity: (From Latin immunitas: "freedom from public service.") Freedom or exemption from a burden or duty, such as from the obligation to appear before a court.

The ability of a party to escape the jurisdiction of a court is known as **immunity**. Natural and juridical persons have few (if any) immunities from the powers of a municipal court. Foreign states traditionally have had complete immunity, but this has changed substantially in the last four decades. State agencies that carry out commercial activities (such as national airlines or national shipping lines) are now commonly treated as having no immunity.

Jurisdiction in Criminal Cases

territoriality nexus: Criteria that allows a court to assume criminal jurisdiction over an the offense was committed within the forum state.

nationality nexus: Criteria that allows a court to assume criminal jurisdiction when the defendant is a national of the forum state.

protective nexus: Criteria that allows a court to assume criminal jurisdiction in cases in which a national interest of the forum state was injured.

universality nexus: Criteria that allows a court to assume criminal jurisdiction if the offenses is one recognized by the international community as being of universal concern.

In order for a municipal court to adjudicate in a criminal proceeding, there must be some connection, or nexus, between the regulating nation (the forum) and the crime or criminal. Four nexuses have been invoked by courts to justify their exercise of jurisdiction.[151] (1) The **territoriality nexus** holds that the place where an offense is committed—in whole or in part—determines jurisdiction.[152] (2) The **nationality nexus** looks to the nationality or national character of the person committing the offense to establish jurisdiction.[153] (3) The **protective nexus** provides for jurisdiction when a national or international interest of the forum is injured by the offender.[154] (4) The **universality nexus** holds that a court has jurisdiction over certain offenses that are recognized by the community of nations as being of universal concern, including piracy, the slave trade, attacks on or the hijacking of aircraft, genocide, war crimes, and crimes against humanity.[155]

It is not enough that these nexuses exist; the connection between the forum and the person or activity also must be "reasonable."[156] In determining reasonableness, courts consider one or more of the following factors, depending on the circumstances of the particular case:

---

[151]*Restatement (Third) of Foreign Relations Law of the United States,* §§ 402, 404 (1987); *Draft Convention on Jurisdiction with Respect to Crime,* arts. 3–10, reproduced in Harvard Research in International Law, "Jurisdiction with Respect to Crime," *American Journal of International Law,* vol. 35, p. 435 at pp. 439–442 (1935).

   For an analysis of these jurisdictional nexuses based primarily on longstanding American case law *see* American Bar Association Section Report, "Achieving Legal and Business Order in Cyberspace: A Report on Global Jurisdiction Issues Created by the Internet," *Business Lawyer,* vol. 55, p. 1801 (2000).

[152]An offense does not have to be consummated within the forum's territory for the forum to have jurisdiction. If an offense is commenced within the forum, even if it is completed or consummated abroad, the forum will have jurisdiction. Harvard Research in International Law, "Jurisdiction with Respect to Crime," *American Journal of International Law,* vol. 35, p. 435 at pp. 484–487 (1935). Logically, jurisdiction based on the place where an offense was commenced is the converse of jurisdiction based on the effects nexus, which focuses on the place where the offense is consummated. *See id.* at 487–94.

[153]*Restatement (Third) of Foreign Relations Law of the United States,* § 404 (1987).

[154]*Id.* § 404.

[155]*Id.* § 404 states that the universal nexus may "perhaps" include "certain acts of terrorism." *Id.* Comment b, asserts that "[u]niversal jurisdiction is increasingly accepted for certain acts of terrorism, such as assaults on the life or physical integrity of diplomatic personnel, kidnapping, and indiscriminate violent assaults on people at large," *id.* § 404, comment b, but it cites no cases or commentaries in support of its contention. It seems more likely, in light of the terrorist attacks on September 11, 2001, and the ensuing military action in Afghanistan, that the courts and commentators will treat terrorist acts as crimes against humanity. Crimes against humanity were originally defined in Article 6(c) of the Charter of the International Military Tribunal established after World War II (the Nuremberg Tribunal) as "murder, extermination, enslavement, deportation, and other inhumane acts committed against any civilian population." Charter of the International Military Tribunal, Nuremberg Trial Collection, The Avalon Project, Yale Law School *at* www.yale.edu/lawweb/avalon/imt/proc/ imtconst.htm (last visited Dec. 19, 2001). Because this broad definition includes the usual definition of terrorism (which is typically described as "the sustained clandestine use of violence, including murder, kidnapping, and bombings, for a political purpose) it seems unnecessary to separately define terrorism as one of the crimes covered by the universality nexus. *See* Ray August, *Public International Law,* pp. 345–346 (1995).

[156]*Restatement (Third) of Foreign Relations Law of the United States,* § 403 (1987).

- the extent to which the criminal or regulated activity takes place, or has a substantial, direct, and foreseeable effect, within the territory of the forum;[157]
- the extent to which the defendant or the injured party has a "genuine link" (i.e., an on-going and real relationship) with the forum;[158]
- the character of the activity (that is, its importance to the forum, whether other countries regulate it, and the extent to which countries generally regard it as appropriate for regulation);[159]
- the extent to which justified expectations will be protected or harmed by the regulation;[160]
- the extent to which another country has an interest in regulating the activity and the likelihood of a conflict with those regulations;[161]
- the importance of the regulation to the international community;[162] and
- the extent to which the regulation is consistent with the traditions of the international community.[163]

It is important to note that the four nexuses are not mutually exclusive. Courts routinely rely on more than one in assuming jurisdiction, as Case 3–5 demonstrates.

---

[157]*Id.* § 403(2)(b). The *Draft Convention on Jurisdiction with Respect to Crime, supra* note 151, art. 3, describes this same idea in terms of an "attempt" to commit a crime from outside the forum's territory. This attempt must be focused on conduct having its effect within the forum's territory.

[158]*Restatement (Third) of Foreign Relations Law of the United States,* § 403 comment e (1987). The classic discussion of the genuine link requirement appears in the Nottebohm (Liechtenstein v. Guatemala) Case, (Second Phase—Judgment of 6 April 1955), *International Court of Justice Reports,* vol. 1955, p. 4 (1955), in the context of a country's right to sponsor a national's suit before an international court.

[159]*Id.* § 403(2)(c).

[160]*Id.* § 403(2)(d).

[161]*Id.* § 403(2)(g) & (h).

[162]*Id.* § 403(2)(e).

[163]*Id.* § 403(2)(f).

Case 3–5   Attorney-General of the Government of Israel v. Eichmann

Israel, District Court of Jerusalem, 1961.
International Law Reports, vol. 36, p. 5 (1968).

In 1938, Adolf Eichmann was an official of the Austrian Nazi party who headed the Austrian office for Jewish emigration. His zeal for deporting Jews earned him a promotion to chief of the German Gestapo's Jewish Section in 1939. During World War II, he advocated the use of gas chambers for the mass extermination of Jews in concentration camps, and he oversaw the mistreatment and murder of millions of Jews. He was arrested in 1945 by the Allies but managed to escape to Argentina. In 1960, he was abducted by Israeli agents and taken to Israel for trial for crimes against humanity and the Jewish people.

JUDGMENT OF THE COURT: . . .

Learned defense counsel . . . submits: . . . that the Israel law, by imposing punishment for acts done outside the boundaries of the state and before its establishment, against persons who were not Israel citizens, and by a person who acted in the course of duty on behalf of a foreign country (Act of State) conflicts with international law and exceeds the powers of the Israel Legislature. . . .

[This Court does not agree.] . . . The law in force in Israel resembles that in force in England in [its application under international law]. . . .

Our jurisdiction to try this case is based on the Nazi and Nazi Collaborators (Punishment) Law, an enacted Law the provisions of which are unequivocal. The Court has to give effect to a law of the Knesset,[164] and we cannot entertain the contention that this Law conflicts with the principles of international law. . . .

We have, however, also considered the sources of international law . . . and have failed to find any foundation for the contention that Israel law is in conflict with the principles of international law. . . .

The abhorrent crimes defined in this Law are not crimes under Israel law alone. These crimes, which struck

---

[164][The Israeli legislature.]

MAP 3-5 Israel (1961)

at the whole of mankind and shocked the conscience of nations, are grave offenses against the law of nations itself (*delicta juris gentium*). Therefore, so far from international law negating or limiting the jurisdiction of countries with respect to such crimes, international law is, in the absence of an International Court, in need of the judicial and legislative organs of every country to give effect to its criminal interdictions and to bring the criminals to trial. The jurisdiction to try crimes under international law is universal.

The universal authority, namely the authority of the *forum deprehensionis* (the court of the country in which the accused is actually held in custody), was already mentioned in the *Corpus Juris Civilis*[165] and the towns of northern Italy had already in the Middle Ages followed the practice of trying specific cases of dangerous criminals (*banniti, vagabundi, assassini*) who happened to be within their area of jurisdiction, without regard to the place in which the crimes in question were committed. . . . Maritime nations have also since time immemorial acted on the principle of universal jurisdiction in

dealing with pirates, whose crime is known in English law, *piracy jure gentium.* . . .

The state of Israel's "right to punish" the accused derives, in our view, from two cumulative sources: a universal source (pertaining to the whole of mankind), which vests the right to prosecute and punish crimes of this order in every state within the family of nations; and a specific or national source, which gives the victim nation the right to try any who assault its existence.

This second foundation of criminal jurisdiction conforms, according to accepted terminology to the protective principle (*compétence réelle*). In England, which until very recently was considered a country that does not rely on such jurisdiction . . . it was said in *Joyce v. Director of Public Prosecutions*:[166]

The second point of appeal . . . was that in any case no English court has jurisdiction to try an alien for a crime committed abroad. . . . There is, I think, a short answer to this point. The statute in question deals with the crime of treason committed within or . . . without the realm: . . . No principle of comity demands that a state should ignore the crime of treason committed against it outside its territory. On the contrary a proper regard for its own security requires that all those who commit that crime, whether they commit it within or without the realm, should be amenable to its laws.

Oppenheim says[167] that the penal jurisdiction of the state includes "crimes injuring its subjects or serious crimes against its own safety." Most European countries go much further than this.[168]

Dahm says[169] . . . that the protective principle is not confined to those foreign offenses that threaten the "vital interests" of the state, and goes on to explain[170] in his reference to the "immanent limitations" of the jurisdiction of the state, a departure from which would constitute an "abuse" of its sovereignty, [that:] Penal jurisdiction is not a matter for everyone to exercise. It requires a "linking point" (*Anknuepfungpunkte*), a legal connection that links the punisher with the punished. The state may, insofar as international law does not contain rules to the contrary, punish only persons and acts *which concern it more than they concern other states.* . . . The "linking point" between Israel and the accused (and for that matter any person accused of a crime against the Jewish people under this Law) is striking in the case of "crime against the Jewish people," a crime that postulates an intention to exterminate the Jewish people in whole or in part. . . . The connection between the state of Israel and the Jewish people needs no explanation. . . .

---

[165]*See* Chapters 3 and 15, *ubi de criminibus agi oportet* ["it is proper to proceed in the place where the accused is held"].

[166]*Law Reports, Appeal Cases,* vol. 1946, p. 347 at p. 372 (1946).

[167]*International Law,* vol. I, § 147, p. 333 (7th ed., Lauterpacht, 1952).

[168]*See* Harvard Research in International Law, "Jurisdiction with Respect to Crime," *American Journal of International Law,* vol. 35, suppl., p. 546 *et seq.* (1935).

[169]Zur Problematik des Voelkerstrafrechts, p. 28 (1956).

[170]*Id.,* pp. 38–39.

. . . [T]his crime very deeply concerns the "vital interests" of the state of Israel, and under the "protective principle" this state has the right to punish the criminals. In terms of Dahm's thesis, the acts referred to in this law of the state of Israel "concern it more than they concern other states," and therefore according also to this author there exists a "linking point." The punishment of Nazi criminals does not derive from the arbitrariness of a country "abusing" its sovereignty but is a legitimate and reasonable exercise of a right of penal jurisdiction.

A people which can be murdered with impunity lives in danger, to say nothing of its "honor and authority."[171] This has been the curse of dispersion and the want of sovereignty of the people of Israel, upon whom any criminal could commit his outrages without fear of being punished by the people injured. Hitler and his associates exploited the defenseless position of the Jewish people in their dispersion, in order to perpetrate their total murder in cold blood. It was to provide some modicum of redress for the terrible injustice of the catastrophe that the sovereign state of the Jews, which enables the survivors to defend its existence by state means, was established on the recommendation of the United Nations. One of the means therefore is the punishment of the murderers who did Hitler's contemptible work. It is for this reasons that the Law in question was enacted.

Defense counsel contended that the protective principle cannot apply to this Law because that principle is designed to protect only an existing state, its security and its interests, whereas the state of Israel did not exist at the time of the commission of the said crimes. In his submission the same applies to the principle of "passive personality" which stems from the protective principle, and of which some states have made use through their penal legislation for the protection of their citizens abroad. Counsel pointed out that in the absence of a sovereign Jewish state at the time of the catastrophe, the victims of the Nazis were not citizens of the state of Israel when they were murdered.

In our view learned counsel errs when he examines the protective principle in this retroactive Law according to the time of the commission of the crimes, as is usual in the case of an ordinary law. This Law was enacted in 1950, to be applied to a specified period which had terminated five years before its enactment. The protected interest of the state recognized by the protective principle is in this case the interest existing at the time of the enactment of the Law, and we have already dwelt on the importance of the moral and defensive task which this Law is designed to fulfill in the state of Israel. . . .

We should add that the well-known judgment . . . in the *Lotus Case*[172] ruled that the principle of territoriality does not limit the power of a state to try crimes and, moreover, that any argument against such power must point to a specific rule in international law which negates that power. We have followed this principle which, so to speak, shifts the "onus of proof" upon him who pleads against jurisdiction, but have preferred to base ourselves on positive reasons for upholding the jurisdiction of the state of Israel.

The second contention of learned defense counsel was that the trial of the accused in Israel following upon his kidnapping in a foreign land, is in conflict with international law and takes away the jurisdiction of this Court. . . . [W]ith reference to the circumstances of the arrest of the accused and his transfer to Israel, the Republic of Argentina . . . lodged a complaint with the Security Council of the United Nations, which resolved on June 23, 1960, as follows:[173]

The Security Council, Having examined the complaint that the transfer of Adolf Eichmann to the territory of Israel constitutes a violation of the sovereignty of the Argentine Republic.

Considering that the violation of the sovereignty of a member state is incompatible with the Charter of the United Nations . . .

Mindful of the universal condemnation of the persecution of the Jews under the Nazis and of the concern of people in all countries that Eichmann should be brought to appropriate justice for the crimes of which he is accused . . .

1. Declares that acts such as that under consideration, which affect the sovereignty of a member state and therefore cause international friction, may, if repeated, endanger international peace and security;
2. Requests the government of Israel to make appropriate reparation in accordance with the Charter of the United Nations and the rules of international law;
3. Expresses the hope that the traditionally friendly relations between Argentina and Israel will be advanced.

Pursuant to this Resolution the two governments reached agreement on the settlement of the dispute between them, and on August 3, 1960, issued the following joint communiqué:

The governments of Argentina and Israel, animated by a desire to give effect to the Resolution of the Security Council of June 23, 1960, insofar as the hope was expressed that the traditionally friendly relations between the two countries will be advanced, resolve to regard as closed the incident which arose out of the action taken by citizens of Israel, which

---

[171]Grotius.
[[172]France v. Turkey, *Permanent Court of International Justice Reports,* vol. 1927, series A, no. 10, p. 23 (1927).]
[173]UN Doc. S/4349.

infringed the fundamental rights of the state of Argentina.

It is an established rule of law that a person being tried for an offense against the laws of a state may not oppose his trial by reason of the illegality of his arrest or of the means whereby he was brought within the jurisdiction of that state. The courts in England, the United States, and Israel have constantly held that the circumstances of the arrest and mode of bringing of the accused into the territory of the state have no relevance to his trial, and they have consistently refused in all instances to enter upon an examination of these circumstances. . . .

The Anglo-Saxon rule has been accepted by Continental jurists as well. . . . Criticism of English and American case law from the point of view of international law has been leveled by Dickinson[174] and Morgenstern.[175] It is not for us to enter into this controversy between international jurists, but we would draw attention to two important points for this case: (1) the critics admit that the established rule is as summarized above; (2) in the case before us the controversy is immaterial. . . .

By the joint decision of the governments of Argentina and Israel of August 3, 1960, . . . the country whose sovereignty was violated has waived its claims, including the claim for the return of the accused, and any violation of international law which might have been involved in the "incident" in question has been "cured." According to the principles of international law no doubt can therefore be cast on the jurisdiction of Israel to bring the accused to trail after August 3, 1960. After that date, no cause remained, in respect of a violation of international law, which could have served to support a plea against his trial in Israel.

Adolf Eichmann's conviction was affirmed. He was hanged in 1962. ■

---

[174]"Jurisdiction Following Seizure or Arrest in Violation of International Law," *American Journal of International Law,* vol. 28, p. 231 (1934).

[175]"Jurisdiction in Seizures Effected in Violation of International Law," *British Year Book of International Law,* vol. 29, p. 265 (1952). *See also* Lauterpacht, *Law Quarterly Review,* vol. 64, p. 100, note 14 (1948).

The *Eichmann Case* demonstrates that one state may try a criminal defendant even if he has been forcibly abducted from another state. In this case, the prosecution in Israel was allowed to go forward because Argentina, the country of the abduction, decided to drop its initial complaint that the abduction by Israeli agents had violated its sovereignty. The rule in the *Eichmann Case*, that a state may only try an abducted criminal defendant if the state from which he was abducted does not protest, is probably the most widely followed rule, but it is not the only one that states observe.

The spectrum of rules concerning the trial of a criminal defendant forcibly abducted from a foreign state runs from no prohibition to a complete bar. Thus, for example, the United States Supreme Court in 1992 in the case of *United States v. Alvarez-Machain* held that the American courts could try a Mexican national abducted from Mexico by agents of the U.S. Drug Enforcement Agency despite a United States-Mexican Extradition Treaty that seemed on its face to prohibit such activities and despite the protest of the Mexican government.[176] The U.S. Court stated simply that international law does not prohibit such abductions.[177] By comparison, in 1991 in the case of *State v. Ebrahim* the Appellate Division of the South African Supreme Court set aside the conviction of a South African national who had been abducted from Swaziland by South African government agents even though the government of

---

[176]*United States Reports,* vol. 504, p. 655 (1992).

[177]*Id.,* at p. 669.

    At the request of the Permanent Council of the Organization of American States, the Inter-American Judicial Committee was asked to consider whether the decision of the U.S. Supreme Court was in conformity with international law. The Committee concluded (nine votes in favor, with one abstention) that "the abduction in question was a serious violation of public international law since it was a transgression of the territorial sovereignty of Mexico," and it recommended that reparations be made by the United States to Mexico "[p]ursuant to the rules governing state responsibility in international law." In particular, it recommended that the United States repatriate Dr. Humberto Alvarez-Machain to his homeland. Inter-American Judicial Committee Legal Opinion in United States v. Alvarez-Machain, CJI/RES.II-15/92, *International Legal Materials,* vol. 32, p. 277 (1993).

    Following the U.S. Supreme Court's remand of the case to the trial court, Alvarez-Machain was acquitted. *See* Alvarez-Machain v. United States, *Federal Reporter, Third Series,* vol. 107, p. 696 at 699 (9th Circuit Ct. of Appeals 1996). Later, the Ninth Circuit Court of Appeals affirmed Alvarez-Machain's right to sue the United States for the tort of kidnapping. Alvarez-Machain v. United States, *Federal Reporter, Third Series,* vol. 266, p. 1045 (2001).

Swaziland did not protest.[178] The Appellate Division said that international law does not allow a state to come to court in a criminal proceeding unless it has "clean hands."[179]

Jurisdiction in Civil Cases

In civil suits, municipal courts can extend their jurisdiction over disputes between parties who appear within the territory of the forum state. Such jurisdiction is based on either *in personam*[180] or *in rem*.[181] principles.

Jurisdiction over Persons

in personam **jurisdiction:** The power of a court or tribunal to determine the rights of a party who appears before it.

In personam jurisdiction is the power of a court to decide matters relating to a natural or juridical person physically present within the forum state. Natural persons subject to *in personam* jurisdiction include nationals of the forum state, individuals physically present within the state, individuals domiciled in the state, and individuals who consent to such jurisdiction. Consent to personal jurisdiction can come about in any of the following ways: by the individual appearing in court after a suit has commenced, by a party agreeing to the personal jurisdiction of a particular court in a forum selection clause contained in a contract, or by a party appointing an agent within a state to receive service of process on his behalf.

As we mentioned earlier, juridical persons (or *persona ficta*[182]) are entities, other than natural persons, that have sufficient existence in the eyes of the law to function legally, sue and be sued, and make decisions through agents. Examples are business entities (including associations and corporations) and governmental and intergovernmental organizations. Juridical persons are subject to the *in personam* jurisdiction of a municipal court in much the same way that individuals are. Thus, legal entities created within a state are nationals of that state—they are called "domestic entities"—and they may sue or be sued there. Foreign entities, however, are amenable to the jurisdiction of another state's municipal courts only if (a) they are recognized in law as juridical persons and (b) they give their consent. Governments and intergovernmental organizations, accordingly, must be formally recognized (see Case 1–7, *Arab Monetary Fund v. Hashim and Others [No. 3]*), while other foreign entities (including business firms) must be created as juridical persons by recognized governments. Case 3–6 explores the requirement of recognition.

---

[178]*South Africa Law Reports*, vol. 1991, pt. 2, p. 553 (1991) (in Afrikäans); *International Legal Materials*, vol. 31, p. 888 (1992) (in English).
[179]*International Legal Materials*, vol. 31, p. 888 at p. 896 (1992).
[180]Latin: "against the person."
[181]Latin: "against the thing."
[182]Latin: "fictional person."

Case 3–6   Bumper Development Corp., Ltd. v. Commissioner of Police of the Metropolis and Others (Union of India and Others, Claimants)

England, Court of Appeal, Civil Division, 1991.
All England Law Reports, vol. 1991, p. 4, p. 638 (1991).

In 1976, an Indian laborer named Ramamoorthi, who lived near the site of a ruined Hindu temple at Pathur in the Indian state of Tamil Nadu, was excavating sand when his spade struck a metal object. The object was part of a series of bronze Hindu idols from the Chola period (ninth to thirteenth century A.D.); among these was a major idol known as the Siva Nataraja (or Pathur Nataraja because of its place of discovery).[183] Ramamoorthi realized that he had discovered something

---

[183]A Siva Nataraja is a representation of the Hindu god Siva (or Shiva), the destroyer, who is one of the three chief Hindu gods (Brahma, the creator, and Vishnu, the preserver, being the other two). As the Court of Appeal said: "The Siva Nataraja can be described in a thumb-nail sketch as

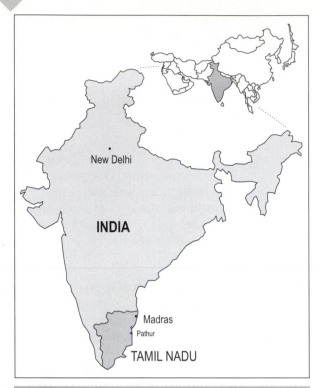

MAP 3-6 Tamil Nadu State, India (1991)

of value and he eventually sold the Pathur Nataraja to a dealer in religious objects. The Pathur Nataraja was in turn sold several times, with the last identified buyer being a man named Valar Prakash, who could not be traced but was last seen in Madras.

About the time that these sales were occurring, state officials in Tamil Nadu learned of them and began criminal investigations. Statements were taken from Ramamoorthi and others about the discovery of the Pathur Nataraja and its subsequent history. As of 1982, however, the whereabouts of the idol was unknown.

Although the Pathur Nataraja was lost, several other artifacts found at the temple site in Pathur remained at that place. Among them was a stone object of religious worship known as a Sivalingam.[184] In the typical Chola-period Hindu temple, this stone would have been positioned in the sanctum and would have been the focus of religious worship. Following its discovery, the Sivalingam was reinstated as an object of worship at the site of the ruined temple in Pathur.

In June 1982, Bumper Development Corp., Ltd., (Bumper) purchased in good faith in London a Siva Nataraja (the London Nataraja) from a dealer named Sherrier, who had produced a false provenance[185] of the idol for the purpose of making the sale. Bumper then sent the idol to the British Museum for appraisal and conservation. While the London Nataraja was at the British Museum, it was seized by the London Metropolitan police in compliance with the British government's policy of returning stolen religious artifacts to their owners. Bumper then brought this suit against the Commissioner of Police of the Metropolis of London and two of his officers seeking return of the London Nataraja.

At the trial, five claimants intervened in the case. They were the Union of India (the first claimant), the state of Tamil Nadu (the second claimant), and Thiru Sadagopan on his own behalf (as the third claimant) and on behalf of the temple itself (the fourth claimant). The Sivalingam, which had been reinstated as an object of worship at the temple site in Prathur after the trial had begun, was later added as an additional claimant (the fifth claimant). All of the claimants asserted that they were the rightful owners of the London Nataraja, which they claimed was one and the same as the Prathur Nataraja.

The trial court judge, Judge Ian Kennedy, held that the evidence of Ramamoorthi and others who had seen the Prathur Nataraja in 1976, as well as expert metallurgical, geological, and entomological evidence, proved that the Prathur Nataraja and the London Nataraja were one and the same. The judge also held that the temple at Prathur and the Sivalingam both had superior title to the Nataraja and that they were entitled to possession of the idol. Bumper appealed to the Court of Appeal.

The Court of Appeal first held that the evidence supported Judge Kennedy's conclusion that the London and Prathur Natarajas were the same. It then held that the law of the state of Tamil Nadu regarded the temple at Prathur as a juridical entity that possessed the right to sue and be sued and to own and possess property. The Court of Appeal then considered whether or not English law would look upon the temple as a legal entity.

LORD JUSTICE PURCHAS:

* * *

Having held that the temple is a legal person under the law of Tamil Nadu acceptable in the courts of that state

---

the god standing with his right foot upon a dwarf and surrounded by a 'halo' which represents the flames issuing from the mouths of two crocodiles situated to the left and right of the dwarf. At the top of the halo in some Natarajas there is to be found a design either in the form of a mask or a rosette or similar adornment known as a '*Kurti Muka.*' Round the halo there are a number of 'flames' issuing radially from the halo. Depending upon the period when and the area in which they were made the Siva Natarajas vary in many respects. The one with which this appeal is concerned is circular; but many others are oval in shape. The Nataraja with which this appeal is concerned had a lotus base mounted on a square-shaped peedam or pedestal.

"Returning to Siva, the design again varies according to date and place. The Chola Natarajas have a number of identifying features. . . . The god has two right and two left arms and hands but only two legs, right and left. He has on each side of his head horizontally flowing hair described as *jettas.* Various objects and representations are imposed upon or incorporated in the *jettas,* including a particular one called a '*ganga.*' In one of his right hands and around the wrist there is coiled a snake—a cobra. In one of his left hands he holds another flame. . . ."

[184]The Court of Appeal described it as "a carefully fashioned stone object representing a phallus."

[185]From French *provenir:* "to come forth with" or "to originate." A provenance is the history of ownership of a valued object, work of art, or literature.

as a party which, with the third claimant acting as representative, could have sued for the recovery of the Nataraja, we must now decide whether, as the judge held, it is likewise acceptable in the courts of this country.

The question whether a foreigner can be a party to proceedings in the English courts is one to be determined by English law (as the *lex fori*).[186] In the case of an individual no difficulty usually arises. And the same can be said of foreign legal persons which would be recognized as such by our own law, the most obvious example being a foreign trading company. It could not be seriously suggested that such a company could not sue in the English courts to recover property of which it was the owner by the law of the country of its incorporation.

The novel question which arises is whether a foreign legal person which would not be recognized as a legal person by our own law can sue in the English courts. The particular difficulty arises out of [the] English law's restriction of legal personality to corporations or the like, that is to say the personified groups or series of individuals. This insistence on an essentially animate content in a legal person leads to a formidable conceptual difficulty in recognizing as a party entitled to sue in our courts something which on one view is little more than a pile of stones.

There is an illuminating treatment of legal personality in *Salmond on Jurisprudence*,[187] from which we take two passages:

Legal persons, being the arbitrary creations of the law, may be of as many kinds as the law pleases. Those which are actually recognized by our own system, however, are of comparatively few types. Corporations are undoubtedly legal persons, and the better view is that registered trade unions and friendly societies are also legal persons though not verbally regarded as corporations. . . . No other legal persons are at present recognized by English law. If, however, we take account of other systems than our own, we find that the conception of legal personality is not so limited in its application, and that there are several distinct varieties, of which three may be selected for special mention. They are distinguished by reference to the different kinds of things which the law selects for personification. 1. The first class of legal persons consists of corporations, as already defined, namely, those which are constituted by the personification of groups or series of individuals. The individuals who thus form the *corpus*[188] of the legal person are termed its *members*. . . . 2. The second class is that in which the *corpus*, or object selected for personification, is not a group or series of persons, but an institution. The law may, if it pleases, regard a church or a

hospital, or a university, or a library, as a person. That is to say, it may attribute personality, not to any group of persons connected with the institution, but to the institution itself. Our own law does not, indeed, so deal with the matter. The person known to the law of England as the University of London is not the institution that goes by that name, but a personified and incorporated aggregate of human beings, namely, the chancellor, vice-chancellor, fellows, and graduates. It is well to remember, however, that notwithstanding this tradition and practice of English law, legal personality is not limited by any logical necessity, or, indeed, by any obvious requirement of expediency, to the incorporation of bodies of individual persons.

Thus *Salmond* recognizes the possibilities which may not be farfetched, of (say) a foreign Roman Catholic cathedral having legal personality under the law of the country where it is situated; and, in order to make the concept more comprehensible, let it be assumed that it is given that personality by legislation specifically empowering it to sue by its proper officer for the protection and recovery of its contents. It would, we think, be a strong thing for the English court to refuse the cathedral access simply on the ground that our own law would not recognize a similarly constituted entity as a legal person. The touchstone for determining whether access should be given or refused is the comity of nations, defined by the *Shorter Oxford English Dictionary*[189] as:

The courteous and friendly understanding by which each nation respects the laws and usages of every other, so far as may be without prejudice to its own rights and interests.

Arguing from the example of a Roman Catholic cathedral and in the belief that no distinction between institutions of the Christian church and those of other major religions would now be generally acceptable, we cannot see that in the circumstances of this case there is any offense to English public policy in allowing a Hindu religious institution to sue in our courts for the recovery of property to which it is entitled by the law of its own country. Indeed we think that public policy would be advantaged. . . .

* * *

We therefore hold that the temple is acceptable as a party to these proceedings and that it is as such entitled to sue for the recovery of the Nataraja.

* * *

---

[186]Latin: "law of the forum." The law of the state where the court hearing a case is located.]
[187]Pp. 306–308 (12th ed., 1966).
[188]Latin: "body."]
[189]3rd ed., 1944.

For the reasons set out in this judgment we dismiss the appeal on the ground that Judge Ian Kennedy correctly decided that the temple had a title to the Nataraja superior to that enjoyed by Bumper. ■

---

forum selection clause: A provision in a contract designating a particular court or tribunal to resolve any dispute that may arise concerning the contract.

As is the case for natural persons, a juridical person's consent to the jurisdiction of a foreign court may be given expressly or it may be implied. An example of express consent is a **forum selection clause**, that is, a clause in a contract that names the court or arbitration tribunal the parties want to have resolve any disputes relating to the contract. Consent will be implied if there are enough "contacts" between the juridical person and the foreign state. In the United States, for example, the Supreme Court has said that there must be at least certain minimum contacts that allow a court in fairness to extend its jurisdiction over a foreign corporation.[190] In determining if there are enough contacts, courts have to consider (a) whether the company has performed acts that relate to the forum state, (b) whether the suit is based on those acts, and (c) whether the company has indicated by its conduct that it intended to rely on the benefits (such as doing business) of the forum state.[191]

The enforceability of international forum selection clauses is examined in Case 3–7.

---

[190]International Shoe Co. v. State of Washington, *United States Reports*, vol. 326, p. 310 (Supreme Ct., 1945).
[191]*See* Case 4–5, Asahi Metal Industry Co., Ltd. v. Superior Court of California, for an example of a juridical person's implied consent to the jurisdiction of a foreign court.

Case 3–7   Shell v. R.W. Sturge, Ltd.   ⌒

United States Sixth Circuit Court of Appeals
Federal Reporter, Third Series, vol. 55, p. 1227 (1995).[192]

CIRCUIT JUDGE KENNEDY:

Plaintiffs, investors in the Society of Lloyd's, brought this diversity action against defendants R. W. Sturge, Ltd., the Society of Lloyd's, the Council of Lloyd's and the Corporation of Lloyd's seeking to rescind their investment contracts under Ohio securities law. Defendants filed a motion to dismiss for improper venue under Rule 12(b)(3) of the *Federal Rules of Civil Procedure* on the grounds that forum selection clauses in the investment contracts gave exclusive jurisdiction to the English courts. The District Court granted the motion to dismiss and plaintiffs now appeal, arguing that the forum selection clauses deprive them of their substantive rights under the Ohio securities laws and that Ohio public policy outweighs the policies served by enforcing the forum selection clauses. For the following reasons, we affirm.

I

The Society of Lloyd's, or Lloyd's of London, (Lloyd's) is not an insurance company, but rather is an insurance marketplace in which individual Underwriting Members, or Names, join together in syndicates to underwrite a par-

ticular type of business. The Corporation of Lloyd's (Corporation), which was created by an Act of Parliament, regulates the Lloyd's insurance market. The Corporation itself does not underwrite any insurance, but provides facilities and services to assist underwriters. The Corporation is managed by the Council of Lloyd's (Council) which controls the admission and discipline of Names, sets the Names' reserve requirements and establishes standards for Lloyd's policies.

To become a Name, one must apply and be sponsored by an existing member. Applicants must pass a means test to determine that they possess sufficient assets to satisfy claims. Those accepted as Names are required to obtain a letter of credit in favor of Lloyd's to serve as a security. The amount of the letter of credit, as well as a Name's means, determines the premium limit for each Name.

A Name cannot conduct insurance business directly, but instead enters into an Agency Agreement with a Members' Agent who acts on the Name's behalf. Names typically belong to several syndicates in order to spread their risks and the Members' Agents assist the Names in selecting the syndicates to join. Each Name is responsible for his or her proportionate share of a syndicate's losses up to his or her entire net worth.

Plaintiffs Andrew Hauck and West Shell are representatives of a putative class of Cincinnati-area individuals

---

[192]The text of this opinion is posted on the FindLaw Web site at caselaw.findlaw.com/uscircs/6th/ 950176p.html.

MAP 3-7   London, England (1995)

23. English Law:

This Agreement shall be read and construed and take effect in all respects in accordance with English Law.

24. English Jurisdiction:

Subject to Clause 22 hereof [permitting arbitration in London] the parties hereto irrevocably and unconditionally submit for all purposes of and in connection with this Agreement to the exclusive jurisdiction of the English Courts.

In most years, plaintiffs received profits, but in recent years they suffered losses. Although the outcome of their investments with Lloyd's is as yet undetermined, plaintiffs believe that their total losses will far exceed their profits.

On November 1, 1993, plaintiffs filed this action in the Court of Common Pleas in Hamilton County, Ohio, alleging that defendants Sturge, Lloyd's, the Corporation, and the Council violated Ohio securities law by selling unregistered and non-exempt securities in violation of chapter 1707 of the OHIO REVISED CODE. Under OHIO REVISED CODE § 1707.43, "[e]very sale or contract for sale made in violation of Chapter 1707 of the REVISED CODE, is voidable at the election of the purchaser." Plaintiffs sought to rescind the contracts and be returned to their original positions, offering to return any benefits which they had received from their investments with Lloyd's.

Defendants removed the action to the United States District Court for the Southern District of Ohio and filed a motion to dismiss for improper venue. Defendants have stipulated for purposes of their motion to dismiss that this action involves a security under Ohio securities law. A magistrate judge, following a hearing, recommended that the motion to dismiss for improper venue be granted. The District Court adopted this recommendation on December 22, 1993. Plaintiffs now appeal.

II

The enforceability of a forum selection clause is a question of law which we review de novo. The parties do not address the issue of whether federal or state law applies in determining the enforceability of forum selection clauses in a diversity action. However, we need not decide this issue because both Ohio and federal law treat these clauses in a similar manner.

A forum selection clause in an international agreement "should control absent a strong showing that it should be set aside."[194] "The correct approach [is] to

who invested in Lloyd's as Names. Each plaintiff executed a General Undertaking Agreement (General Agreement) with Lloyd's to become a Name. These General Agreements contain both a forum selection and a choice of law clause. The forum selection clause provides:

Each party hereto irrevocably agrees that the courts of England shall have exclusive jurisdiction to settle any dispute and/or controversy of whatsoever nature arising out of or relating to the Member's membership of, and/or underwriting of insurance business at, Lloyd's. . . .

The choice of law clause states:

The rights and obligations of the parties arising out of or relating to the Member's membership of, and/or underwriting of insurance business at, Lloyd's and any other matter referred to in this Undertaking shall be governed by and construed in accordance with the laws of England.

Each plaintiff also executed an Agency Agreement with R. W. Sturge, Ltd. ("Sturge") appointing Sturge as his Members' Agent. The Agency Agreements contain choice of law and forum selection clauses:[193]

---

[193]The Agency Agreements also contain a clause permitting arbitration in London at the request of either party. Defendants contend that the District Court's dismissal of this action can be upheld on the alternate ground that this arbitration clause is enforceable. Because we find the forum selection clause to be enforceable, we need not address this issue.

[194]Interamerican Trade Corp., *Federal Reporter, Second Series,* vol. 973, p. 487 at p. 489; The Bremen v. Zapata Off-Shore Co., *United States Reports,* vol. 407, p. 1 (Supreme Ct., 1972).

enforce the forum clause specifically unless" plaintiffs "[can] clearly show that enforcement would be unreasonable and unjust, or that the clause was invalid for such reasons as fraud or overreaching."[195] The presumptive validity of the forum selection clause may also be set aside if plaintiffs can show that "trial in the contractual forum will be so gravely difficult and inconvenient that [they] will for all practical purposes be deprived of [their] day in court"[196] or if "enforcement would contravene a strong public policy" of the forum state.[197]

In *The Bremen v. Zapata Off-Shore Co.* the Supreme Court emphasized the importance of upholding forum selection and choice of law clauses in international contracts. *Bremen* involved a contract for towing a drilling rig from Louisiana to Italy with a provision for judicial resolution of disputes in England. The Court observed:

> The expansion of American business and industry will hardly be encouraged if, notwithstanding solemn contracts, we insist on a parochial concept that all disputes must be resolved under our laws and in our courts.[198]

Subsequently, in *Scherk v. Alberto-Culver Co.*[199] the Court considered the validity of clauses providing for arbitration in France under Illinois law in a contract for the sale of several German businesses. In upholding the clauses, the Court stated:

> [U]ncertainty will almost inevitably exist with respect to any contract touching two or more countries, each with its own substantive laws and conflict-of-laws rules. A contractual provision specifying in advance the forum in which disputes shall be litigated and the law to be applied is, therefore, an almost indispensable precondition to achievement of the orderliness and predictability essential to any international business transaction.[200]

The *Scherk* Court also discussed the danger of ignoring contractual dispute resolution provisions:

> A parochial refusal by the courts of one country to enforce an international arbitration agreement would

not only frustrate these purposes, but would invite unseemly and mutually destructive jockeying by the parties to secure tactical litigation advantages.[201]

Given this background, we will now examine the enforceability of the forum selection provisions at issue in this appeal.

Plaintiffs contend that the clause is unenforceable because, together with the choice of law clause, it deprives investors of their substantive rights under Ohio securities law. Plaintiffs argue that they are entitled to a remedy based on what they classify as a "merit review" process under OHIO REVISED CODE § 1707.13. Section 1707.13 permits the Ohio Division of Securities to prohibit the sale of securities which are "being disposed of or purchased on grossly unfair terms, in such manner as to deceive or defraud . . . purchasers or sellers. . . ." Plaintiffs rely on *Mitsubishi Motors Corp. v. Soler Chrysler-Plymouth, Inc.*,[202] an antitrust action where the Court enforced a clause providing for arbitration in Japan. The Mitsubishi Court did not decide whether the choice of law clause providing for Swiss law should be upheld, but noted in dicta that if the forum selection and choice of law clauses "operate . . . in tandem as a prospective waiver of a party's right to pursue statutory remedies for antitrust violations," the Court would find the agreement to be against public policy.[203]

The Second Circuit addressed this issue in *Roby v. Corporation of Lloyd's*,[204] where the plaintiff Names, whose contracts contained substantially the same clauses as those in the present action, brought a federal securities and RICO[205] action against Lloyd's' syndicates and agents. The Names argued that the contract clauses effectively waived compliance with United States securities laws despite the anti-waiver provisions of these laws. The *Roby* court noted that forum selection and choice of law clauses could not be circumvented merely because foreign law or procedure might be different or less favorable than that of the United States.[206] "Instead, the question is whether the application of the foreign law presents a danger that the . . . Names 'will be deprived of any remedy or treated unfairly.' "[207] The court rejected the plaintiffs' arguments because it found that they had ample remedies under English law and

---

[195]Bremen, *United States Reports,* vol. 407 at p. 15.
[196]*Id.* at 18.
[197]*Id.* at 15.
[198]*Id.* at 9.
[199]*United States Reports,* vol. 417, p. 506 (Supreme Ct., 1974).
[200]*Id.* at 516.
[201]*Id.* at 516–517.
[202]*United States Reports,* vol. 473, p. 614 (Supreme Ct., 1985).
[203]*Id.* at p. 637 n.19.
[204]*Federal Reporter, Second Series,* vol. 996, p. 1353 (2d Circuit Ct. of Appeals), certiorari denied, *Supreme Court Reporter,* vol. 114, p. 385 (1993),
[205]Racketeer Influenced and Corrupt Organizations Act, *United States Code,* title 18, § 1961 et seq.
[206]*Federal Reporter, Second Series,* vol. 996 at p. 1363; Mitsubishi Motors, *United States Reports,* vol. 473 at p. 629.
[207]Roby, *Federal Reporter, Second Series,* vol. 996 at p. 1363 (quoting Piper Aircraft Co. v. Reyno, *United States Reports,* vol. 454, p. 235 at p. 255 (1981)).

nothing suggested that the English courts were biased or unfair. Both the Seventh and Tenth Circuits have also reached this result. In *Bonny v. Society of Lloyd's*[208] and *Riley v. Kingsley Underwriting Agencies, Ltd.*[209] some Names ignored the forum selection provisions in their contracts and brought suits in the United States alleging violations of state and federal securities law and common law fraud. The Seventh and Tenth Circuits examined English law and concluded that the Names would be able to adequately pursue their claims in England.

We agree that plaintiffs have remedies which they can pursue in England. Plaintiffs seek rescission of their contracts under Ohio Revised Code § 1707.43. The uncontroverted affidavit of Barrister John Lewis Powell shows that "[o]ne of the remedies under English law for misrepresentation (whether innocent, negligent or fraudulent) is rescission" and that a plaintiff "may also be entitled to an indemnity against liabilities incurred." Powell's affidavit also shows that plaintiffs can bring claims against defendants based on the tort of deceit, breach of contract, negligence, and breach of fiduciary duty.

Although the *Lloyd's Act* of 1982 provides Lloyd's some immunity from damages, it does not preclude Names from obtaining injunctive, declaratory, rescissionary or restitutionary relief or preclude Names from damages where Lloyd's has acted in bad faith.

Furthermore, Section 47 of *England's Financial Services Act* of 1986 provides a cause of action for any misleading statement or practice made for the purpose of inducing involvement in an investment agreement.

Finally, England's highest appellate court recently upheld a lower court's ruling that Member's Agents can be contractually liable for negligent underwriting by the Managing Agents who run the insurance syndicates at Lloyd's.[210]

According to plaintiffs, the remedies available in England are not the equivalent of the merit review because they are grounded in misrepresentation and fraud and do not address the underlying wrong of defendants' alleged failure to subject themselves to Ohio's registration requirements. The fact that parties will have to structure their case differently than if they were litigating in federal court is not a sufficient reason to defeat a forum selection clause. We adopt the Second Circuit's reasoning [in *Roby*] in rejecting this argument:

It defies reason to suggest that a plaintiff may circumvent forum selection and arbitration clauses merely by stating claims under laws not recognized by the forum selected in the agreement. A plaintiff simply would have to allege violations of his country's tort law or his country's statutory law or his country's property law in order to render nugatory any forum selection clause that implicitly or explicitly required the application of the law of another jurisdiction. We refuse to allow a party's solemn promise to be defeated by artful pleading.

Plaintiffs next argue that it would be unreasonable to enforce the forum selection clauses in light of the strong public policy behind Ohio's registration and merit review requirements. Citing *Bronaugh v. R. & E Dredging Co.*,[211] plaintiffs contend that Ohio's registration requirements are intended to "protect the public from its own stupidity, gullibility, and avariciousness."[212]

The District Court correctly held that under *Bremen*, plaintiffs must show that Ohio public policy outweighs the policies behind "supporting the integrity of international transactions."[213] In *Bonny*, the court upheld the forum selection clauses despite the federal and state policies underlying protection for investors against fraud and nondisclosure. These interests are at least equal to, if not greater than, the interest Ohio has in protecting the public from its own lack of knowledge. We agree with the court in *Bonny* that "[g]iven the international nature of the transactions involved here, and the availability of remedies under British law that do not offend the policies behind the securities laws, the parties' forum selection and choice of law provisions contained in the agreements should be given effect."[214]

Finally, plaintiffs contend that the District Court erred in enforcing the forum selection clauses in the contracts without first determining whether these contracts are void. Plaintiffs argue that the underlying contracts are voidable under Ohio Revised Code § 1707.43 and that if the District Court had found them to be void, the forum selection clauses would be void as well. This is essentially another way of restating plaintiffs' argument that enforcement of the forum selection clauses deprives plaintiffs of a hearing on the merits of their claim.

III

Accordingly, the District Court's order granting defendants' motion to dismiss is *AFFIRMED*. ∎

---

[208]*Federal Reporter, Third Series,* vol. 3, p. 156 (7th Circuit Ct. of Appeals, 1993).

[209]*Federal Reporter, Second Series,* vol. 969, p. 953 (10th Circuit Ct. of Appeals, 1992).

[210]Deeny v. Gooda Walker Ltd., slip op. (Queen's Bench Divisional Ct., Apr. 12, 1994), appeal dismissed, slip opinion (House of Lords, July 25, 1994).

[211]*North Eastern Reporter, Second Series,* vol. 242, p. 572 (Ohio, 1968).

[212]*Id.* at 576.

[213]*Federal Supplement,* vol. 850, p. 620 at p. 630 (S.D. Ohio, 1993); Bremen, *United States Reports,* vol. 407 at p. 15.

[214]*Federal Reporter, Third* Series, vol. 3 at p. 162.

Jurisdiction over Property

in rem jurisdiction: The power of a court to determine the ownership rights of persons as to property located within the forum state.

In rem[215] **jurisdiction** is the power of a court to determine the ownership rights of all persons with respect to particular property located within the territory of the forum state. For example, the ownership of real property would be determined by an *in rem* proceeding, as would the ownership of personal property physically within the state (such as a ship arrested in a port within the forum state).

D. IMMUNITIES OF STATES FROM THE JURISDICTION OF MUNICIPAL COURTS

Sovereign states are immune from the jurisdiction of foreign courts (1) when they engage in activities anywhere in the world that are unique to sovereigns and (2) when they act officially within their own territory. The first condition comes under the rubric of sovereign or state immunity; the second under the title of act of state.

Sovereign or State Immunity

sovereign or state immunity: Doctrine that municipal courts must decline to hear suits against foreign sovereigns.

The doctrine of **sovereign** or **state immunity** says that domestic courts must decline to hear cases against foreign sovereigns out of deference to their roles as sovereigns.[216] "Historically the rule may be traced to a time when most states were ruled by personal sovereigns who, in a very real sense, personified the state—'*L'Etat c'est moi.*'[217] In such a period, influenced by the survival of the principle of feudalism, the exercise of authority on the part of one sovereign over another inevitably indicated either the superiority of overlordship or the active hostility of an equal."[218] Today the sovereign is the state, its officers, its agencies, and its instrumentalities,[219] but the same notion of respect for a foreign state still holds true.

absolute sovereign immunity: Rule that a foreign state is immune from all types of suits.

Until the middle of the twentieth century, a rule of **absolute sovereign immunity** was generally accepted worldwide. That rule held that a state is absolutely immune and cannot be brought before a foreign court no matter what activities it is involved in or what injuries it may cause. This made sense in the days when states were involved in little more than tax collection, law enforcement, and national defense, but it does not make sense now that virtually every state is engaged in extensive social and commercial activities. Socialist countries especially are involved in operating all kinds of state-run businesses. The rule of absolute sovereign immunity would mean that individuals and businesses that contracted to buy from or sell goods or services to a foreign country would be unable to sue the country if the country breached its contract. Besides being unfair, this is bad business (even for a state-run business), and state governments and municipal courts eventually came to recognize that a change was needed. Lord Denning, then the Master of the Rolls of the English Court of Appeal, once observed:

> When the government of a country enter into an ordinary trading transaction, they cannot afterwards be permitted to repudiate it and get out of their liabilities by saying that they did it out of high governmental policy or foreign policy or any other policy.

---

[215]Latin: "against the thing."

[216]In The Schooner Exchange v. McFadden, *Cranch Reports,* vol. 7, p. 116 (1812), Chief Justice Marshall of the U.S. Supreme Court observed: "[A sovereign] being bound by obligations of the highest character not to degrade the dignity of his nation, by placing himself or its sovereign rights within the jurisdiction of another, can be supposed to enter a foreign territory only under an express license, or in the confidence that the [absolute] immunities belonging to his independent sovereign station, though not expressly stipulated, are reserved by implication, and will be extended to him."

[217]French: "the state is me."

[218]National American Corp. v. Federal Republic of Nigeria, *Federal Supplement,* vol. 448, p. 622 (Dist. Ct. for S. Dist. of N.Y., 1978).

[219]The 1976 U.S. Foreign Sovereign Immunities Act, § 1603(a), says: "A foreign State [includes] a political subdivision of a foreign State. . . ." And § 1603(b) says: "An 'agency or instrumentality of a foreign State' means any entity— (1) which is a separate legal person, corporate or otherwise, and (2) which is the organ of a foreign state or political subdivision thereof, or a majority of whose shares or other ownership interest is owned by a foreign state or political subdivision thereof, and (3) which is neither a citizen of a State of the United States . . . nor created under the laws of any third country."

The 1978 U.K. State Immunity Act, § 14(5), provides: "Her Majesty may by Order in Council provide for . . . this Act to apply to any [constituent territories of a federal state] specified in the Order as they apply to a state." And § 14(2) states: "A separate entity is immune from the jurisdiction of the courts of the United Kingdom if, and only if—(a) the proceedings relate to anything done by it in the exercise of sovereign authority; and (b) the circumstances are such that a state . . . would have been so immune."

They cannot come down like a god on to the stage, the *deus ex machina*,[220] as if they had nothing to do with it beforehand. They started as a trader and must end as a trader. They can be sued in the courts of law for their breaches of contract and for their wrongs just as any other trader can. They have no sovereign immunity.[221]

The preamble to the 1976 U.S. Foreign Sovereign Immunities Act[222] states: "The Congress finds that . . . [u]nder international law, states are not immune from the jurisdiction of foreign courts insofar as their commercial activities are concerned, and their commercial property may be levied upon for the satisfaction of judgments rendered against them in connection with their commercial activities."

restrictive sovereign immunity: Theory that a foreign state is not immune when the cause of action for a suit is based on conduct unrelated to the state's governmental activities.

The idea that a state should be responsible in a foreign municipal court for at least some of its conduct led to the adoption of the theory of **restrictive sovereign immunity**. This theory says that a state is immune from suit in cases involving injuries that are the result of its governmental actions (*jure imperii*[223]) but is not immune when the injuries result from a purely commercial or nongovernmental activity (*jure gestionis*[224]). This is now the prevalent rule in the world.[225]

Many states have enacted statutes adopting the restrictive sovereign immunity doctrine. Two widely emulated examples are the 1976 U.S. Foreign Sovereign Immunities Act and the 1978 U.K. State Immunity Act, which are remarkably similar in their approaches and reasonably representative of other acts that have been passed since. Both begin with a universal grant of immunity, then set out exceptions. The U.K. act provides: "A state is immune from the jurisdiction of the courts of the United Kingdom except as provided in the following provisions of . . . this Act."[226] The U.S. act states: "[A] . . . foreign state shall be immune from the jurisdiction of the courts of the United States and of the states [of the Union] except as provided in . . . this chapter."[227]

Both acts then describe exceptions. The principal exception is, of course, governmental participation in commercial activity, and both acts undertake to define such activity. The U.S. act defines it as "either a regular course of commercial conduct or a particular commercial transaction or act." The act then provides that "the commercial character of an activity shall be determined by reference to the *nature* of the course of conduct or particular transaction or act, *rather than* by reference to its *purpose*."[228] The U.K. act uses a similar approach, providing that

> "commercial transaction" means (a) any contract for the supply of goods or services; (b) any loan or other transaction for the provision of finance and any guarantee or indemnity in respect of any such transaction or of any other financial obligation; and (c) any other transaction or activity (whether of a commercial, industrial, financial, professional or other similar character) into which a state enters or in which it engages otherwise than in the exercise of sovereign authority; [but it does not include] a contract of employment between a state and an individual.[229]

The commercial activity exception is thus broadly defined. The U.K. act says that it includes any act or transaction that a state engages in "otherwise than in the exercise of sovereign

---

[220]Latin: "a god out of a machine." This expression alludes to a favorite stage trick used in classical tragedies of introducing a god, usually lowered mechanically from the rafters, to solve some otherwise insolvable entanglement in the plot.]

[221]I Congreso del Partido, *All England Law Reports*, vol. 1981, pt. 1, p. 1092 (Court of Appeal, 1979).

[222]*United States Code*, title 28, § 1602 *et seq.*

[223]Latin: "law of command."

[224]Latin: "law of management."

[225]"At this point there can be little doubt that international law follows the restrictive theory of sovereign immunity." Texas Trading and Milling Corp. v. Federal Republic of Nigeria, *Federal Reporter, Second Series*, vol. 647, p. 300 (Second Circuit Ct. of Appeals, 1981).

[226]U.K. State Immunity Act, § 1(1) (1978).

[227]U.S. Foreign Sovereign Immunities Act, § 1604 (1976).

[228]*Id.*, § 1603(d). Emphasis added. This "nature of the transaction" test had been criticized in the United States before it was adopted. "While this criterion is relatively easy to apply, it oftentimes produces rather astonishing results, such as the holdings of some European courts that purchases of bullets or shoes for the army, the erection of fortifications for defense, or the rental of a house for an embassy, are private acts. . . . Furthermore, this test merely postpones the difficulty, for particular contracts in some instances may be made only by states. (For example, any individual may be able to purchase a boat, but only a sovereign may be able to purchase a battleship. Should the purchase of a yacht be equated with the purchase of a battleship?)" Victory Transport Inc. v. Comisaria General de Abasteciminetos y Transportes, *Federal Reporter, Second Series*, vol. 336, p. 354 (Second Circuit Ct. of Appeals, 1964).

[229]U.K. State Immunity Act, § 3(3) (1978).

authority,"[230] and the U.S. act says that it includes conduct "not based upon the exercise of a discretionary function, or upon libel, slander, misrepresentation, or interference with contract rights."[231]

In addition to commercial activities, both acts deny states immunity from claims for death or personal injury,[232] for damage to or loss of tangible property,[233] for claims relating to real property,[234] and for actions based on intellectual property rights.[235] The U.K. act also denies immunity for suits that are based on claims for delinquent tariffs and taxes.[236]

However, the exceptions to immunity granted by both acts apply only if some connection exists between the activity and the forum state. In other words, the property must be located in the forum state[237] or the act or omission must take place or produce some direct effect there.[238] In the United States, this is constitutionally required by the due process clause;[239] in the United Kingdom, it is imposed by treaty obligations under the 1972 European Convention on State Immunity.[240]

Although both the U.S. and U.K. acts grant immunities to foreign states subject to exceptions, the burden of proof does not rest on the party suing the state to show that an exception exists, but rather on the state to show that it has immunity.[241] On the other hand, the remedies available to a plaintiff in a suit against a state are limited essentially to damages—injunctions[242] and orders of specific performance are not available.[243]

Both acts have substantially improved the ability of a party to enforce a judgment against a foreign state. Prior to their enactment, a state had to separately waive its immunity from the execution of a judgment. Now, a foreign state's assets located in the forum state may be seized for the satisfaction of a judgment unless they fit within certain categories. In the United Kingdom, the property of a foreign state's central bank is immune;[244] in the United States, the property of international institutions, central bank property, and property of a military character under the control of the foreign state's military are immune.[245]

In addition to the several exceptions already mentioned, immunity is also not available when it is waived by the state. It can be waived expressly at the time the suit is brought or in advance in a contract clause or implicitly by bringing or participating in a suit.[246]

---

[230]*Id.*

[231]U.S. Foreign Sovereign Immunities Act, § 1605(a)(5) (1976).

[232]U.K. State Immunity Act, § 5(a) (1978); U.S. Foreign Sovereign Immunities Act, § 1605(a)(5) (1976).
See Matter of SEDCO, Inc., *Federal Supplement,* vol. 543, p. 561 (Dist. Ct., S. Dist. of Texas, 1982) and Sugarman v. Aeromexico, *Federal Reporter, Second Series,* vol. 626, p. 270 (Dist. Ct. for S. Dist. of Texas, 1982).

[233]U.K. State Immunity Act, § 5(b) (1978); U.S. Foreign Sovereign Immunities Act, § 1605(a)(5) (1976).

[234]U.K. State Immunity Act, § 6 (1978); U.S. Foreign Sovereign Immunities Act, § 1605(a)(4) (1976).

[235]U.K. State Immunity Act, § 7 (1978); U.S. Foreign Sovereign Immunities Act, § 1605(a)(5) (1976).

[236]U.K. State Immunity Act, § 11(a) (1978).

[237]The 1978 U.K. State Immunity Act, § 5, requires that the act or omission relating to personal injury, death, or tangible property losses or damages occur in the United Kingdom; § 6 requires that in claims against real estate property the property be located in the United Kingdom; and § 7 requires that in actions based on intellectual property rights those rights apply in the United Kingdom. The 1976 U.S. Foreign Sovereign Immunities Act, § 1605(3), (4), and (5), imposes similar requirements.

[238]The 1976 U.S. Foreign Sovereign Immunities Act, § 1605, provides: "A foreign state shall not be immune . . . in any case . . . (2) in which the action is based upon a commercial activity carried on in the United States by the foreign state; or upon an act performed in the United States in connection with a commercial activity in the foreign state elsewhere; or upon an act outside the territory of the United States in connection with a commercial activity of the foreign state elsewhere and that act causes a direct effect in the United States."
The 1978 U.K. State Immunity Act, § 3(1), states: "A state is not immune as respects proceedings relating to— (a) a commercial transaction entered into by the state; or (b) an obligation of the state which by virtue of a contract (whether a commercial transaction or not) falls to be performed wholly or partly in the United Kingdom."

[239]See Timberlane Lumber Co. v. Bank of America, *Federal Reporter, Second Series,* vol. 549, p. 597 (Second Circuit Ct. of Appeals, 1976).

[240]*European Treaty Series,* No. 74; *International Legal Materials,* vol. 11, p. 470 (1972). In force since 1976.

[241]U.K. State Immunity Act, § 1(1) (1978); U.S. Foreign Sovereign Immunities Act, § 1604 (1976). "Once a basis for jurisdiction is alleged, the burden of proof rests on the foreign state to demonstrate that immunity should be granted." Matter of SEDCO, Inc., *Federal Supplement,* vol. 543, p. 561 (District Ct. for S. Dist. of Texas, 1982).

[242]Such as the so-called *Mareva* injunction granted in the Trendtex Case to keep a state from removing its assets from the forum jurisdiction.

[243]U.K. State Immunity Act, § 13(1) and (2) (1978); U.S. Foreign Sovereign Immunities Act, § 1605(a)(1) (1976).

[244]U.K. State Immunity Act, § 14(4) (1978).

[245]U.S. Foreign Sovereign Immunities Act, § 1611 (1976).

[246]U.K. State Immunity Act, § 13(3) (1978); U.S. Foreign Sovereign Immunities Act, § 1605(a)(1) (1976).

Case 3–8 examines whether or not the bank accounts of a foreign embassy are immune from judicial attachment.

The waiver must be knowingly made, however. "A foreign state does not waive its sovereign immunity merely by entering into a contract with another nation. There must be an intentional and knowing relinquishment of the legal right. . . . [While it may waive immunity by making a general appearance, it does] not waive the sovereign immunity defense by failing to timely answer." Castro v. Saudi Arabia, *Federal Supplement,* vol. 510, p. 309 (Dist. Ct. for W. Dist. of Texas, 1980).

Case 3–8   Abbott v. Republic of South Africa

Spain, Constitutional Court, 1992
Revista Electronica de Derecho Informatico, vol. 1992, p. 565 (1992).
International Law Reports, vol. 113, p. 412 (1999).

The plaintiff, a foreign national, was employed as a bilingual secretary by the Embassy of South Africa. It dismissed her in 1985 on the ground that she had performed her duties unsatisfactorily. She brought suit in the Labor Court of Madrid seeking reinstatement and arrears of salary. The Labor Court dismissed her suit for lacked jurisdiction and she appealed to the Supreme Court. The Supreme Court granted her appeal, holding that South Africa did not enjoy immunity from jurisdiction in the proceedings, and remanded the case to the Labor Court for a decision on the merits.

In 1990, the plaintiff obtained a judgment in her favor, but on appeal the High Court of Madrid held that South Africa was entitled to absolute immunity from execution. The plaintiff then brought this appeal in the Constitutional Court challenging that decision. She argued that the decision violated her right to effective judicial protection under Article 24(1) of the Spanish Constitution by not apply the doctrine of restrictive sovereign immunity.

JUDGMENT:

* * *

. . . [I]t remains to be decided to what extent, or alternatively, subject to what limits, a Spanish court can enforce a judgment against property of a foreign state held on Spanish territory.

In determining the question we must start from two general principles. First, international law bars execution on property of the foreign state used or intended to be used in activities of a sovereign or *de imperio* nature, per-

mitting it only in respect of property intended for the purposes of economic activities which do not involve the exercise of a state's sovereign power . . . Secondly, it must be particularly borne in mind that, of the various categories of property which may be held by foreign states on Spanish territory, the property of diplomatic and consular missions benefits from a special protective regime by virtue of Article 22(3) of the Vienna Convention on Diplomatic Relations, 1961,[247] and Article 31(4) of the Vienna Convention on Consular Relations, 1963.[248] In other words, the relative immunity of foreign states in respect of execution is founded on the distinction between property intended for activities carried on *jure imperii* and property intended for activities carried on *jure gestionis*. However, independently of this criterion, by virtue of the Vienna Conventions of 1961 and 1963, the property of diplomatic and consular missions enjoys absolute immunity from execution.

It follows from Article 22(3) of the Vienna Convention, 1961, that property of the Republic of South Africa situated within the confines of the Embassy, including the Embassy itself,, is absolutely immune from execution. However, doubt arises in the case of property of a foreign state which, while not physically present on Embassy premises nor expressly mentioned in Article 22(3) is intended by that state for the support of its diplomatic mission. In concrete terms, the problem consists in deciding whether bank accounts opened in the name of an embassy, or accounts whose assets are intended to fund embassy operations, are protected by the above rule, given that the order quashed by the decision now being challenged attached part of the funds held in a bank account opened in the name of the South African Embassy, an act which in South Africa's view involved a serious breach of relation between sovereign states.

[247 Article 22(3) provides: "3. The premises of the mission, their furnishings and other property thereon and the means of transport of the mission shall be immune from search, requisition, attachment or execution."]

[248 Article 31(4) provides: "4. The consular premises, their furnishings, the property of the consular post and its means of transport shall be immune from any form of requisition for purposes of national defense or public utility. If expropriation is necessary for such purposes, all possible steps shall be taken to avoid impeding the performance of consular functions, and prompt, adequate and effective compensation shall be paid to the sending State."]

Contemporary international practice clearly exempts bank accounts from any form of execution. . . . This is . . . the accepted approach in the most recent decisions of higher national courts.

In decision of April 12, 1984, in the case of *Alcom Ltd. v. Republic of Colombia*,[249] the English House of Lords held that under English law it was not possible to attach funds held in the embassy's bank account, even though such funds, as well as being applied to cover the embassy's day-to-day operating expenses, might also be used for commercial purposes. The account must be regarded as a single whole, held for the benefit of the diplomatic mission. Similarly, the German Federal Constitutional Court, in its decision of December 13, 1977 (*Philippines Embassy* case),[250] held that accounts of diplomatic missions could not be attached, being protected by virtue of the immunities accorded to diplomatic missions by international law. The maxim *ne impediatur legatio*[251] applied, since a bank account is a necessary tool for the proper functioning of the diplomatic mission. All that was required in this regard was a declaration by the competent agency of the state in question confirming that the account was intended to ensure the continuing operation of the embassy.

Such immunity from attachment of bank accounts held by a foreign state in banks situated on the territory [of the forum state] and used for purposes of the ordinary activity of diplomatic and consular missions represents the general international practice. It follows that the immunity in relation to execution enjoyed by states and by diplomatic and consular property prevents execution from being levied . . . , as regards property held in the forum state by diplomatic and consular missions, on such accounts. And this is the case even where the funds in the accounts may also be used for the purposes of activities not involving the foreign state's sovereignty, namely those carried on *jure gestionis*, to which the rationale justifying the immunity of diplomatic and consular property cannot apply. The fact that funds held in the account to cover the day-to-day functioning of diplomatic and consular missions may also be used for commercial purposes does not justify the exclusion of such funds from immunity against execution, and hence from attachment. This follows both from the single and indivisible nature of the funds and from the impossibility, in the case of an account operated by a diplomatic mission, of investigating the transactions, flow of funds, and purposes to which such funds are applied. Such an investigation would involve an interference with the mission's activity, in breach of the rules of public international law.

This Court is not unaware of the problems which the immunity from attachment of such accounts may sometimes poses in cases where it is sought to levy execution against a foreign state in circumstances where the state [is not exempt from jurisdictional] immunity. However, given the reasonableness of the immunity in such cases, having regard to the sovereignty and equality of states, we are led inevitably to the conclusion that the attachment of an embassy's bank account is an act forbidden by [the rules of public international law].

* * *

It may be that, in addition to those assets which cannot be attached because they are intended for performance of activities of diplomatic or consular missions, the foreign state against which execution is sought (in this case the Republic of South Africa) has other property on Spanish territory. As regards such property, in so far as it exists, immunity from execution pursuant to international law . . . extends only to property intended for of acts *jure imperii*, and not to property intended for activities *jure gestionis*. Thus, the ordinary courts, in order to give effect to the right of enforcement of judgments, have the power to order execution to be levied on property clearly intended for a foreign state's industrial or commercial activities, where there is no involvement of its sovereign power, inasmuch as its is conducting itself in accordance with the rules governing private-law transactions. In each case it is for the court ordering execution to determine, in accordance with the rules of Spanish law, which of the property specifically held by the foreign state on Spanish territory is clearly intended

MAP 3-8   South Africa (1992)

---

[249]*Appeal Cases,* vol. 1982, p. 888 (U.K. House of Lords 1982).
[250]*Entscheidungen des Bundesverfassungsgerichts,* vol. 46, p. 342 (German Federal Constitutional Court 1977).
[251]Latin: "Do not impede (the workings) of an embassy."]

MAP 3-9   Spain (1992)

In declaring a blanket immunity from execution in respect of all funds held in Spanish banking institutions by the State against which execution was being levied, irrespective of the purpose of such funds, and confirming closure of the [enforcement] proceedings, the judgment being challenged applied a rule of absolute immunity from execution in relation to the assets of the Republic of South Africa which is not required by [the rules of public international law], and hence amounts to a refusal to enforce a judgment without cause, contrary to the [Spanish constitutional] right to effective judicial protection. The order of the Labor Court and, to the extent it confirmed that order, the judgment being challenged, violated the respondent's right to effective judicial protection, in that it directed the proceedings to be closed without allowing any opportunity for possible enforcement of the judgment against other assets held by the Republic of South Africa on Spanish territory and intended not for the operation of its diplomatic or consular missions, but for the performance of activities in which the States was not exercising its sovereign power or authority.

* * *

The Constitutional Court, by the authority conferred upon it by the Constitution of the Spanish Nation, having regard to the foregoing considerations, has decided as follows:

* * *

3. To order that the proceedings be reopened before Madrid Labor Relations Court No. 11, in order that enforcement measures be pursued against any other assets of the defendant state not subject to immunity from execution in accordance with the terms . . . of this decision. ■

for purposes of economic activities in respect of which that state, rather than exercising its sovereign power, conducts itself as if it were a private individual. Moreover, where the condition is satisfied, it is not necessary that the property in respect of which execution is sought should be intended for the selfsame activity *jure gestionis* as that which provoked the dispute. To hold otherwise would be to render illusory the right to enforcement of judgments in cases like the present one, involving the dismissal of an embassy employee. Otherwise, notwithstanding that it has been accepted that such disputes fall outside the scope of states' jurisdictional immunity, no property would be excluded from protection against execution, since the only assets linked to the activity which provoked the dispute would be those of the embassy.

Act of State Doctrine

act of state doctrine:
Doctrine that the act of a government within the boundaries of its own territory is not subject to judicial scrutiny in a foreign municipal court. A municipal court will decline to hear a dispute based on such acts if to do so would interfere with the conduct of the forum state's foreign policy.

The **act of state doctrine** is a rule that restrains municipal courts in some countries from exercising jurisdiction over foreign states. This rule is most developed in the United States, where it is based on the U.S. constitutional requirement of separation of powers.[252] That is, because the U.S. Constitution assigns to the executive branch of the government responsibility for the conduct of foreign affairs, the courts (the judicial branch) must decline to hear cases that might adversely affect the executive's conduct of those affairs.[253] In particular, a U.S. court will decline to hear cases involving an official act of a foreign sovereign performed within its own territory when the relief sought or the defense raised in the case would require the court to declare invalid the foreign sovereign's official act.

Case 3–9 provides an example of how the act of state doctrine is applied.

---

[252]Countries with governmental structures similar to the United States, such as Mexico and Brazil, or countries whose courts are required to defer to the executive in the conduct of foreign affairs, such as the United Kingdom, also follow the act of state doctrine.

[253]W. S. Kirkpatrick & Co., Inc. v. Environmental Tectonics Corp., Int'l, *United States Reports,* vol. 493, p. 400 at p. 404 (Supreme Ct., 1990).

Case 3–9 *Regina v. Bartle and the Commissioner of Police for the Metropolis and Others (Ex Parte Pinochet)*

England, House of Lords, 1999.
All England Law Reports, vol. 1998, pt. 1, p. 97 (1999).

LORD BROWNE-WILKINSON:

My Lords,

As is well known, this case concerns an attempt by the Government of Spain to extradite Senator Pinochet from this country to stand trial in Spain for crimes committed (primarily in Chile) during the period when Senator Pinochet was head of state in Chile. . . .

* * *

THE FACTS

On September 11, 1973, a right-wing coup evicted the left-wing regime of President Allende. The coup was led by a military junta, of whom Senator (then General) Pinochet was the leader. At some stage he became head of state. The Pinochet regime remained in power until March 11, 1990, when Senator Pinochet resigned.

There is no real dispute that during the period of the Senator Pinochet regime appalling acts of barbarism were committed in Chile and elsewhere in the world: torture, murder and the unexplained disappearance of individuals, all on a large scale. Although it is not alleged that Senator Pinochet himself committed any of those acts, it is alleged that they were done in pursuance of a conspiracy to which he was a party, at his instigation and with his knowledge. He denies these allegations. None of the conduct alleged was committed by or against citizens of the United Kingdom or in the United Kingdom.

In 1998, Senator Pinochet came to the United Kingdom for medical treatment. The judicial authorities in Spain sought to extradite him in order to stand trial in Spain on a large number of charges. Some of those charges had links with Spain. But most of the charges had no connection with Spain. The background to the case is that to those of left-wing political convictions Senator Pinochet is seen as an arch-devil: to those of right-wing persuasions he is seen as the savior of Chile. It may well be thought that the trial of Senator Pinochet in Spain for offences all of which related to the state of Chile and most of which occurred in Chile is not calculated to achieve the best justice. But I cannot emphasize too strongly that that is no concern of your Lordships. Although others perceive our task as being to choose between the two sides on the grounds of personal preference or political inclination, that is an entire misconception. Our job is to decide two questions of law: are there any extradition crimes and, if so, is Senator Pinochet immune from trial for committing those crimes. If, as a matter of law, there are no extradition crimes or he is entitled to immunity in relation to whichever crimes there are, then there is no legal right to extradite Senator Pinochet to Spain or, indeed, to stand in the way of his return to Chile. If, on the other hand, there are extradition crimes in relation to which Senator Pinochet is not entitled to state immunity then it will be open to the Home Secretary to extradite him. The task of this House is only to decide those points of law.

On October 16, 1998, an international warrant for the arrest of Senator Pinochet was issued in Spain. On the same day, a magistrate in London issued a provisional warrant ("the first warrant") under section 8 of the *Extradition Act* 1989. He was arrested in a London hospital on October 17, 1998. On October 18 the Spanish authorities issued a second international warrant. A further provisional warrant ("the second warrant") was issued by the magistrate at Bow Street Magistrates Court on October 22, 1998, accusing Senator Pinochet of:

(1) Between January 1, 1988, and December 1992, being a public official intentionally inflicted severe pain or suffering on another in the performance or purported performance of his official duties;

(2) Between the first day of January 1988 and December 31, 1992, being a public official, conspired with persons unknown to intentionally inflict severe pain or suffering on another in the performance or purported performance of his official duties;

(3) Between the first day of January 1982 and January 31, 1992, he detained other persons (the hostages) and in order to compel such persons to do or to abstain from doing any act threatened to kill, injure or continue to detain the hostages;

he was charged. However, it had also been argued before the Divisional Court that certain of the crimes alleged in the second warrant were not "extradition crimes" within the meaning of the Act of 1989 because they were not crimes under U.K. law at the date they were committed. Whilst not determining this point directly, the Lord Chief Justice held that, in order to be an extradition crime, it was not necessary that the conduct should be criminal at the date of the conduct relied upon but only at the date of request for extradition.

The Crown Prosecution Service (acting on behalf of the Government of Spain) appealed to this House with the leave of the Divisional Court. The Divisional Court certified the point of law of general importance as being "the proper interpretation and scope of the immunity enjoyed by a former head of state from arrest and extradition proceedings in the United Kingdom in respect of acts committed while he was head of state." Before the appeal came on for hearing in this House for the first time, on 4 November 1998 the Government of Spain submitted a formal Request for Extradition which greatly expanded the list of crimes alleged in the second provisional warrant so as to allege a widespread conspiracy to take over the Government of Chile by a coup and thereafter to reduce the country to submission by committing genocide, murder, torture and the taking of hostages, such conduct taking place primarily in Chile but also elsewhere.

The appeal first came on for hearing before this House between 4 and 12 November 1998. The Committee heard submissions by counsel for the Crown Prosecution Service as appellants (on behalf of the Government of Spain), Senator Pinochet, Amnesty International as interveners and an independent *amicus*

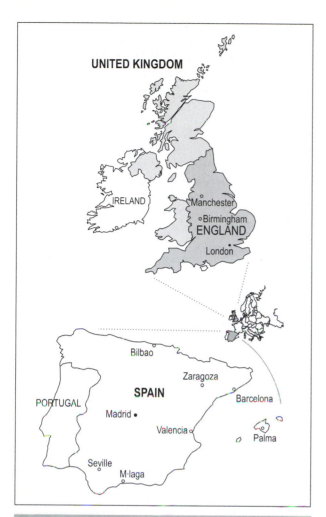

MAP 3-10 England and Spain (1999)

(4) Between the first day of January 1982 and January 31, 1992, conspired with persons unknown to detain other persons (the hostages) and in order to compel such persons to do or to abstain from doing any act, threatened to kill, injure or continue to detain the hostages;

(5) Between January 1976 and December 1992, conspired together with persons unknown to commit murder in a [*Vienna*] Convention [*on Diplomatic Relations*] country.

Senator Pinochet started proceedings for habeas corpus and for leave to move for judicial review of both the first and the second provisional warrants. Those proceedings came before the Divisional Court . . . which on October 28, 1998, quashed both warrants. Nothing turns on the first warrant which was quashed since no appeal was brought to this House. The grounds on which the Divisional Court quashed the second warrant were that Senator Pinochet (as former head of state) was entitled to state immunity in respect of the acts with which

MAP 3-11 Chile (1999)

curiae.[254] Written submissions were also entertained from Human Rights Watch. That Committee entertained argument based on the extended scope of the case as put forward in the Request for Extradition. It is not entirely clear to what extent the Committee heard submissions as to whether all or some of those charges constituted "extradition crimes." There is some suggestion in the judgments that the point was conceded. Certainly, if the matter was argued at all it played a very minor role in that first hearing. Judgment was given on November 25, 1998. The appeal was allowed by a majority (Lord Nicholls of Birkenhead, Lord Steyn and Lord Hoffmann, Lord Slynn of Hadley and Lord Lloyd of Berwick dissenting) on the grounds that Senator Pinochet was not entitled to immunity in relation to crimes under international law. On January 15, 1999, that judgment of the House was set aside on the grounds that the Committee was not properly constituted. The appeal came on again for rehearing on January 18, 1999, before your Lordships. In the meantime the position had changed yet again. First, the Home Secretary had issued to the magistrate authority to proceed under section 7 of the Act of 1989. In deciding to permit the extradition to Spain to go ahead he relied in part on the decision of this House at the first hearing that Senator Pinochet was not entitled to immunity. He did not authorize the extradition proceedings to go ahead on the charge of genocide: accordingly no further arguments were addressed to us on the charge of genocide which has dropped out of the case.

Secondly, the Republic of Chile applied to intervene as a party. Up to this point Chile had been urging that immunity should be afforded to Senator Pinochet, but it now wished to be joined as a party. Any immunity precluding criminal charges against Senator Pinochet is the immunity not of Senator Pinochet but of the Republic of Chile. Leave to intervene was therefore given to the Republic of Chile. The same *amicus*, Mr. Lloyd Jones, was heard as at the first hearing as were counsel for Amnesty International. Written representations were again put in on behalf of Human Rights Watch.

Thirdly, the ambit of the charges against Senator Pinochet had widened yet again. Chile had put in further particulars of the charges which they wished to advance. . . .

* * *

LORD MILLETT:

My Lords,

I have had the advantage of reading in draft the speech of my noble and learned friend, Lord Browne-Wilkinson. Save in one respect, I agree with his reasoning and conclusions. Since the one respect in which I differ is of profound importance to the outcome of this appeal, I propose to set out my own process of reasoning at rather more length than I might otherwise have done.

State immunity is not a personal right. It is an attribute of the sovereignty of the state. The immunity which is in question in the present case, therefore, belongs to the Republic of Chile, not to Senator Pinochet. It may be asserted or waived by the state, but where it is waived by treaty or convention the waiver must be express. So much is not in dispute.

The doctrine of state immunity is the product of the classical theory of international law. This taught that states were the only actors on the international plane; the rights of individuals were not the subject of international law. States were sovereign and equal: it followed that one state could not be impleaded in the national courts of another; *par in parem non habet imperium.*[255] States were obliged to abstain from interfering in the internal affairs of one another. International law was not concerned with the way in which a sovereign state treated its own nationals in its own territory. It is a cliche of modern international law that the classical theory no longer prevails in its unadulterated form. The idea that individuals who commit crimes recognized as such by international law may be held internationally accountable for their actions is now an accepted doctrine of international law. The adoption by most major jurisdictions of the restrictive theory of state immunity, enacted into English law by Part I of the *State Immunity Act* 1978, has made major inroads into the doctrine as a bar to the jurisdiction of national courts to entertain civil proceedings against foreign states. The question before your Lordships is whether a parallel, though in some respects opposite, development has taken place so as to restrict the availability of state immunity as a bar to the criminal jurisdiction of national courts.

Two overlapping immunities are recognized by international law; immunity *ratione personae*[256] and immunity *ratione materiae.*[257] They are quite different and have different rationales.

Immunity *ratione personae* is a status immunity. An individual who enjoys its protection does so because of his official status. It inures for his benefit only so long as he holds office. While he does so he enjoys absolute immunity from the civil and criminal jurisdiction of the national courts of foreign states. But it is only narrowly available. It is confined to serving heads of state and heads of diplomatic missions, their families and servants. It is not available to serving heads of government who are not also heads of state, military commanders and those in charge of the security forces, or their subordinates. It would have been available to Hitler but not to

---

[254]Latin: "friend of the court." A person not a party to a suit who participates in an appeal with the permission of the court.]
[255]Latin: "one equal to another does not have jurisdiction."]
[256]Latin: "based upon personality."]
[257]Latin: "based upon subject matter."]

Mussolini or Tojo. It is reflected in English law by section 20(1) of the *State Immunity Act* 1978, enacting customary international law and the *Vienna Convention on Diplomatic Relations* (1961).

The immunity of a serving head of state is enjoyed by reason of his special status as the holder of his state's highest office. He is regarded as the personal embodiment of the state itself. It would be an affront to the dignity and sovereignty of the state which he personifies and a denial of the equality of sovereign states to subject him to the jurisdiction of the municipal courts of another state, whether in respect of his public acts or private affairs. His person is inviolable; he is not liable to be arrested or detained on any ground whatever. The head of a diplomatic mission represents his head of state and thus embodies the sending state in the territory of the receiving state. While he remains in office he is entitled to the same absolute immunity as his head of state in relation both to his public and private acts.

This immunity is not in issue in the present case. Senator Pinochet is not a serving head of state. If he were, he could not be extradited. It would be an intolerable affront to the Republic of Chile to arrest him or detain him.

Immunity *ratione materiae* is very different. This is a subject-matter immunity. It operates to prevent the official and governmental acts of one state from being called into question in proceedings before the courts of another, and only incidentally confers immunity on the individual. It is therefore a narrower immunity but it is more widely available. It is available to former heads of state and heads of diplomatic missions, and any one whose conduct in the exercise of the authority of the state is afterwards called into question, whether he acted as head of government, government minister, military commander or chief of police, or subordinate public official. The immunity is the same whatever the rank of the office-holder. This too is common ground. It is an immunity from the civil and criminal jurisdiction of foreign national courts but only in respect of governmental or official acts. The exercise of authority by the military and security forces of the state is the paradigm example of such conduct. The immunity finds its rationale in the equality of sovereign states and the doctrine of non-interference in the internal affairs of other states. These hold that the courts of one state cannot sit in judgment on the sovereign acts of another. The immunity is sometimes also justified by the need to prevent the serving head of state or diplomat from being inhibited in the performance of his official duties by fear of the consequences after he has ceased to hold office. This last basis can hardly be prayed in aid to support the availability of the immunity in respect of criminal activities prohibited by international law.

Given its scope and rationale, it is closely similar to and may be indistinguishable from aspects of the Anglo-American Act of State doctrine. As I understand the difference between them, state immunity is a creature of international law and operates as a plea in bar to the jurisdiction of the national court, whereas the Act of State doctrine is a rule of domestic law which holds the national court incompetent to adjudicate upon the lawfulness of the sovereign acts of a foreign state.

Immunity *ratione materiae* is given statutory form in English law by the combined effect of section 20(1) of the *State Immunity Act* 1978, the *Diplomatic Privileges Act* 1964, and Article 39.2 of the *Vienna Convention*. The Act of 1978 is not without its difficulties. The former head of state is given the same immunity "subject to all necessary modifications" as a former diplomat, who continues to enjoy immunity in respect of acts committed by him "in the exercise of his functions." The functions of a diplomat are limited to diplomatic activities, i.e. acts performed in his representative role in the receiving state. He has no broader immunity in respect of official or governmental acts not performed in exercise of his diplomatic functions. There is therefore a powerful argument for holding that, by a parity of reasoning, the statutory immunity conferred on a former head of state by the Act of 1978 is confined to acts performed in his capacity as head of state, i.e. in his representative role. If so, the statutory immunity would not protect him in respect of official or governmental acts which are not distinctive of a head of state, but which he performed in some other official capacity, whether as head of government, commander-in-chief or party leader. It is, however, not necessary to decide whether this is the case, for any narrow statutory immunity is subsumed in the wider immunity in respect of other official or governmental acts under customary international law.

The charges brought against Senator Pinochet are concerned with his public and official acts, first as Commander-in-Chief of the Chilean army and later as head of state. He is accused of having embarked on a widespread and systematic reign of terror in order to obtain power and then to maintain it. If the allegations against him are true, he deliberately employed torture as an instrument of state policy. As international law stood on the eve of the Second World War, his conduct as head of state after he seized power would probably have attracted immunity *ratione materiae*. If so, I am of opinion that it would have been equally true of his conduct during the period before the coup was successful. He was not then, of course, head of state. But he took advantage of his position as Commander-in-Chief of the army and made use of the existing military chain of command to deploy the armed forces of the state against its constitutional government. These were not private acts. They were official and governmental or sovereign acts by any standard.

The immunity is available whether the acts in question are illegal or unconstitutional or otherwise unauthorized under the internal law of the state, since the whole purpose of state immunity is to prevent the legality of such acts from being adjudicated upon in the municipal courts of a foreign state. A sovereign state has the exclusive right to determine what is and is not illegal or unconstitutional under its own domestic law. Even before the end of the Second World War, however, it was questionable whether the doctrine of state immunity accorded protection in respect of conduct which was prohibited by international law. As early as 1841, according to Quincy Wright,[258] many commentators held the view that:

the Government's authority could not confer immunity upon its agents for acts beyond its powers under international law.

* * *

The landmark decision of the Supreme Court of Israel in *Attorney-General of Israel v. Eichmann*[259] is also of great significance. Eichmann had been a very senior official of the Third Reich. He was in charge of Department IV D-4 of the Reich Main Security Office, the Department charged with the implementation of the Final Solution, and subordinate only to Heydrich and Himmler. He was abducted from Argentina and brought to Israel, where he was tried in the District Court for Tel Aviv. His appeal against conviction was dismissed by the Supreme Court. The means by which he was brought to Israel to face trial has been criticized by academic writers, but Israel's right to assert jurisdiction over the offences has never been questioned.

The court dealt separately with the questions of jurisdiction and Act of State. Israel was not a belligerent in the Second World War, which ended three years before the state was founded. Nor were the offences committed within its territory. The District Court found support for its jurisdiction in the historic link between the State of Israel and the Jewish people. The Supreme Court preferred to concentrate on the international and universal character of the crimes of which the accused had been convicted, not least because some of them were directed against non-Jewish groups (Poles, Slovenes, Czechs, and gypsies).

As a matter of domestic Israeli law, the jurisdiction of the court was derived from an Act of 1950. Following the English doctrine of Parliamentary supremacy, the court held that it was bound to give effect to a law of the Knesset even if it conflicted with the principles of international law. But it went on to hold that the law did not conflict with any principle of international law. Following a detailed examination of the authorities, including the judgment of the Permanent Court of International Justice in the *Lotus* case, September 7, 1927, it concluded that there was no rule of international law which prohibited a state from trying a foreign national for an act committed outside its borders. There seems no reason to doubt this conclusion. The limiting factor that prevents the exercise of extra-territorial criminal jurisdiction from amounting to an unwarranted interference with the internal affairs of another state is that, for the trial to be fully effective, the accused must be present in the forum state.

Significantly, however, the court also held that the scale and international character of the atrocities of which the accused had been convicted fully justified the application of the doctrine of universal jurisdiction. It approved the general consensus of jurists that war crimes attracted universal jurisdiction. *See,* for example, [Morris] Greenspan's *The Modern Law of Land Warfare* (1959) where he writes at p. 420 that:

Since each sovereign power stands in the position of a guardian of international law, and is equally interested in upholding it, any state has the legal right to try war crimes, even though the crimes have been committed against the nationals of another power and in a conflict to which that state is not a party.

This seems to have been an independent source of jurisdiction derived from customary international law, which formed part of the unwritten law of Israel, and which did not depend on the statute. The court explained that the limitation often imposed on the exercise of universal jurisdiction, that the state which apprehended the offender must first offer to extradite him to the state in which the offence was committed, was not intended to prevent the violation of the latter's territorial sovereignty. Its basis was purely practical. The great majority of the witnesses and the greater part of the evidence would normally be concentrated in that state, and it was therefore the most convenient forum for the trial.

Having disposed of the objections to its jurisdiction, the court rejected the defense of Act of State. As formulated, this did not differ in any material respect from a plea of immunity *ratione materiae*. It was based on the fact that in committing the offences of which he had been convicted the accused had acted as an organ of the state, "whether as head of the state or a responsible official acting on the government's orders." The court applied Article 7 of the Nuremberg Charter (which it will be remembered expressly referred to the head of state) and which it regarded as having become part of the law of nations.

The case is authority for three propositions:

(1) There is no rule of international law which prohibits a state from exercising extraterritorial criminal jurisdiction in respect of crimes committed by foreign nationals abroad.

---

[258] *See American Journal of International Law,* vol. 41, at p. 71 (1947).

[259] *International Law Reports,* vol. 36, p. 5 (1962).

(2) War crimes and atrocities of the scale and international character of the Holocaust are crimes of universal jurisdiction under customary international law.

(3) The fact that the accused committed the crimes in question in the course of his official duties as a responsible officer of the state and in the exercise of his authority as an organ of the state is no bar to the exercise of the jurisdiction of a national court.

The case was followed in the United States in *Demjanjuk v. Petrovsky.*[260] In the context of an extradition request by the State of Israel the court accepted Israel's right to try a person charged with murder in the concentration camps of Eastern Europe. It held that the crimes were crimes of universal jurisdiction, observing:

International law provides that certain offences may be punished by any state because the offenders are enemies of all mankind and all nations have an equal interest in their apprehension and punishment.

The difficulty is to know precisely what is the ambit of the expression "certain offences."

Article 5 of the *Universal Declaration of Human Rights* of 1948 and Article 7 of the *International Covenant on Civil and Political Rights* of 1966 both provided that no one shall be subjected to torture or to cruel, inhuman or degrading treatment or punishment. A resolution of the General Assembly in 1973 proclaimed the need for international co-operation in the detection, arrest, extradition and punishment of persons guilty of war crimes and crimes against humanity. A further resolution of the General Assembly in 1975 proclaimed the desire to make the struggle against torture more effective throughout the world. The fundamental human rights of individuals, deriving from the inherent dignity of the human person, had become a commonplace of international law. Article 55 of the *Charter of the United Nations* was taken to impose an obligation on all states to promote universal respect for and observance of human rights and fundamental freedoms.

The trend was clear. War crimes had been replaced by crimes against humanity. The way in which a state treated its own citizens within its own borders had become a matter of legitimate concern to the international community. The most serious crimes against humanity were genocide and torture. Large scale and systematic use of torture and murder by state authorities for political ends had come to be regarded as an attack upon the international order. Genocide was made an international crime by the *Genocide Convention* in 1948. By the time Senator Pinochet seized power, the interna-

tional community had renounced the use of torture as an instrument of state policy. The Republic of Chile accepts that by 1973 the use of torture by state authorities was prohibited by international law, and that the prohibition had the character of *jus cogens*[261] or obligation *erga omnes.*[262] But it insists that this does not confer universal jurisdiction or affect the immunity of a former head of state *ratione materiae* from the jurisdiction of foreign national courts.

In my opinion, crimes prohibited by international law attract universal jurisdiction under customary international law if two criteria are satisfied. First, they must be contrary to a peremptory norm of international law so as to infringe a *jus cogens*. Secondly, they must be so serious and on such a scale that they can justly be regarded as an attack on the international legal order. Isolated offences, even if committed by public officials, would not satisfy these criteria. The first criterion is well attested in the authorities and text books: for a recent example, see the judgment of the international tribunal for the territory of the former Yugoslavia in *Prosecutor v. Anto Furundzija* (unreported) given on December 10, 1998, where the court stated:

At the individual level, that is, of criminal liability, it would seem that one of the consequences of the jus cogens character bestowed by the international community upon the prohibition of torture is that every state is entitled to investigate, prosecute, and punish or extradite individuals accused of torture who are present in a territory under its jurisdiction.

The second requirement is implicit in the original restriction to war crimes and crimes against peace, the reasoning of the court in *Eichmann*, and the definitions used in the more recent Conventions establishing ad hoc international tribunals for the former Yugoslavia and Rwanda.

Every state has jurisdiction under customary international law to exercise extra-territorial jurisdiction in respect of international crimes which satisfy the relevant criteria. Whether its courts have extra-territorial jurisdiction under its internal domestic law depends, of course, on its constitutional arrangements and the relationship between customary international law and the jurisdiction of its criminal courts. The jurisdiction of the English criminal courts is usually statutory, but it is supplemented by the common law. Customary international law is part of the common law, and accordingly I consider that the English courts have and always have had extra-territorial criminal jurisdiction in respect of crimes of universal jurisdiction under customary international law.

* * *

---

[260]*Federal Supplement,* vol. 603, p. 1468, affirmed *Federal Reporter, Second Series,* vol. 776, p. 571 (1985).
[261]Latin: "compulsory law." A peremptory norm of international law; one that all states must observe.]
[262]Latin: "applicable to everyone."]

In my opinion, the systematic use of torture on a large scale and as an instrument of state policy had joined piracy, war crimes and crimes against peace as an international crime of universal jurisdiction well before 1984. I consider that it had done so by 1973. For my own part, therefore, I would hold that the courts of this country already possessed extra-territorial jurisdiction in respect of torture and conspiracy to torture on the scale of the charges in the present case and did not require the authority of statute to exercise it. I understand, however, that your Lordships take a different view, and consider that statutory authority is required before our courts can exercise extra-territorial criminal jurisdiction even in respect of crimes of universal jurisdiction. Such authority was conferred for the first time by section 134 of the *Criminal Justice Act* 1988, but the section was not retrospective. I shall accordingly proceed to consider the case on the footing that Senator Pinochet cannot be extradited for any acts of torture committed prior to the coming into force of the section.

The *Convention Against Torture* (1984) did not create a new international crime. But it redefined it. Whereas the international community had condemned the widespread and systematic use of torture as an instrument of state policy, the Convention extended the offence to cover isolated and individual instances of torture provided that they were committed by a public official. I do not consider that offences of this kind were previously regarded as international crimes attracting universal jurisdiction. The charges against Senator Pinochet, however, are plainly of the requisite character. The Convention thus affirmed and extended an existing international crime and imposed obligations on the parties to the Convention to take measures to prevent it and to punish those guilty of it. . . . Whereas previously states were entitled to take jurisdiction in respect of the offence wherever it was committed, they were now placed under an obligation to do so. Any state party in whose territory a person alleged to have committed the offence was found was bound to offer to extradite him or to initiate proceedings to prosecute him. The obligation imposed by the Convention resulted in the passing of section 134 of the *Criminal Justice Act* 1988.

I agree, therefore, that our courts have statutory extra-territorial jurisdiction in respect of the charges of torture and conspiracy to torture committed after the section had come into force and (for the reasons explained by my noble and learned friend, Lord Hope of Craighead) the charges of conspiracy to murder where the conspiracy took place in Spain.

* * *

My Lords, we have come a long way from what I earlier described as the classical theory of international law—a long way in a relatively short time. But as the Privy Council pointed out in *In re Piracy Jure Gentium*,[263] international law has not become a crystallized code at any time, but is a living and expanding branch of the law. [Sheldon] Glueck observed[264] that:

unless we are prepared to abandon every principle of growth for international law, we cannot deny that our own day has its right to institute customs.

In a footnote to this passage he added:

Much of the law of nations has its roots in custom. Custom must have a beginning; and customary usages of states in the matter of national and personal liability for resort to prohibited methods of warfare and to wholesale criminalism have not been petrified for all time.

The law has developed still further since 1984, and continues to develop in the same direction. Further international crimes have been created. Ad hoc international criminal tribunals have been established. A permanent international criminal court is in the process of being set up. These developments could not have been foreseen by Glueck and the other jurists who proclaimed that individuals could be held individually liable for international crimes. They envisaged prosecution before national courts, and this will necessarily remain the norm even after a permanent international tribunal is established. In future those who commit atrocities against civilian populations must expect to be called to account if fundamental human rights are to be properly protected. In this context, the exalted rank of the accused can afford no defense.

* * *

The House of Lords granted the appeal to the "extent necessary to permit the extradition proceedings to continue in respect of the crimes of torture (and where it is alleged that torture resulted) of conspiracy to torture, allegedly committed by Senator Pinochet after December 8, 1988." ∎

---

[263]*Law Reports, Appellate Cases,* vol. 1934, p. 586 at p. 597 (1934).
[264]*Harvard Law Journal,* vol. 56, p. 396 at p. 398 (1946).

E. CHOOSING THE GOVERNING LAW

When faced with civil suits involving parties, acts, or transactions from different countries, municipal courts are confronted with the problem of deciding which law to apply. Should they apply the law of the forum state or the law of some other state? It would, of course, be simplest if courts applied the law of the forum state in all cases. Law writers and courts have long recognized, however, that this would be unfair. Individuals take actions in a particular place (such as signing contracts, buying property, operating equipment, making statements, hiring employees, etc.) based on the rules of law that apply in that place. To later have a court in another country apply different laws would discourage international exchanges of all kinds.

The idea that municipal courts should apply foreign laws in these kinds of cases was originally based on the idea of comity (i.e., respect for the interests of a foreign sovereign) because each state has an interest in protecting the rights of its subjects, and only by respecting the interests of foreign subjects can a state expect similar treatment for its subjects in other states.[265] This is no longer the rationale. As Chief Justice Fuller of the U.S. Supreme Court said in 1895:

> Now the rule is universal in this country that private rights acquired under the laws of foreign states will be respected and enforced in our courts unless contrary to the policy or prejudicial to the interests of the state where this is sought to be done; and although the source of this rule may have been the comity characterizing the intercourse between nations, it prevails today by its own strength and the right to the application of the law to which the particular transaction is subject is a juridical right.[266]

Although the obligation to apply foreign law exists today as a rule of law unto itself, its existence presents states with a difficult problem: how to decide which law to apply. Courts use what are called **choice of law** rules to determine if they should apply their own law or the law of another state in settling civil disputes.

Virtually all choice of law rules follow a two-step procedure.[267] First, if the parties to a dispute have agreed to the application of the law of a particular country, the court should apply that law. Second, if the parties have not agreed as to which law should apply (either expressly or impliedly), then the court should determine for itself which law it should apply by (a) following statutory dictates, (b) determining which state has the most significant relationship with the dispute, or (in a few states) (c) determining which state has the greatest interest in the outcome of the case.

choice of law: Rules used by municipal courts to determine which state's law they should apply in hearing a civil dispute.

Agreement of the Parties

The agreement of the parties as to which law should apply most commonly is a factor in contract cases. By the use of a **choice of law clause**, the parties agree in advance as to what law should apply. So long as the parties made the agreement freely, even if they have no factual connection with the country whose legal system they have adopted, their choice will be enforced.[268]

The agreement of the parties can also be made in statements to a court. For example, in *Multi Product International v. Toa Kogyo Co., Ltd.*, a Japanese court held:

> The plaintiff brought an action in this court and expressed, in preliminary proceedings as well as in the oral proceedings, the intention that the law of Japan should be the applicable law. . . . The defendant appeared in court and also expressed the same

choice of law clause: A provision in a contract designating the state whose law will govern disputes relating to the contract.

---

[265]Justice Joseph Story of the U.S. Supreme Court once wrote that American courts had an obligation to apply foreign laws out of "a sort of moral necessity to do justice, in order that justice may be done to us in return." *Commentaries on the Conflict of Laws* § 35 (1834). For a discussion of the relationship of comity to the choice of law problem, *see* Arthur K. Kuhn, *Comparative Commentaries on Private International Law of Conflict of Laws,* pp. 28–30 (1937).

[266]Hilton v. Guyot (dissenting opinion), *United States Reports,* vol. 159, p. 113 (Supreme Ct., 1895).

[267]One American commentator has observed: "Choice of law theory in most common law countries mirrors (with minor variations) U.S. approaches. Choice of law rules in non-common law countries are usually found in statutory codes or regional (or wider) international conventions. . . . Even in these codes and conventions, however, the more innovative U.S. approaches to choice of law [i.e., the most significant relationship and the governmental interests theories] find reflection, if not full acceptance." Joseph W. Dellapenna, *Suing Foreign Governments and Their Corporations,* pp. 233–234 (1988).

[268]Common law rulings to this effect include the following: Vita Food Products Inc. v. Unus Shipping Co., Ltd., *Law Reports, Appeal Cases,* vol. 1939, p. 277 at p. 290 (1939); Augustus v. Permanent Trustee Co. (Canberra), *Commonwealth Law Reports,* vol. 124, p. 245 at p. 252 (1971); John Kaldor v. Mitchell Cotts Freight, *Australian Law Reports,* vol. 90, p. 244 at pp. 256–257 (Supreme Ct. of New South Wales, 1989).

An example of a civil law code provision to this effect is Japan's *Law Concerning the Application of Laws in General* (Law No. 10 of 1898), Article 7: "(1) The intention of the parties shall determine what country's law will govern the creation and effect of a juristic act. (2) If the intention of the parties is uncertain, the law of the place of the act shall govern."

thing. . . . Therefore, both parties are held to have had the intent that the law of Japan shall apply to the matters at issue.[269]

In contract or other cases where the parties have not agreed to the applicable law, their intention that the law of a particular country should apply can sometimes be inferred. At least, this is the theory.[270] In practice, courts seldom (if ever) infer the parties' intention.[271] Instead, they go on to their second set of choice of law rules and apply the law specified in a statutory directive, the law with the most significant relationship, or the law of the state with most interest in the outcome.

Statutory Choice of Law Provisions

In civil law countries, the law that courts will apply in a dispute when the parties themselves have not made a choice is found in statutory codes or, sometimes, in international treaties. Traditionally, these provisions are based on a concept known as the "vesting of rights," and this approach to choosing the applicable law is, therefore, often called the **vested rights doctrine**. According to this doctrine, a court is to apply the law of the state where the rights of the parties to a suit vested (that is, where they legally became effective).[272]

vested rights doctrine:
Doctrine that courts should apply the law of the state where the rights of the parties legally became effective.

To determine where particular rights vest, the codes provide fairly simple and straightforward guidelines. Usually a provision can be found that covers the general case. A good example is the Japanese general choice of law provision, which provides:

> If the intention of the parties is uncertain, the law of the place of the act shall govern.[273]

delict: (From Latin *delictum:* "a fault.") In civil law countries, any private wrong or injury, or a minor public wrong or injury.

Beyond this, the courts look to the subject matter of the suit—such as delicts, contracts, or real property—and then choose the appropriate choice of law rule for that subject matter. Typical examples are these: If the suit involves a **delict** or tort, the governing law is the law of the place where the wrong was committed. If the suit is based on a contract, the law of the place where the contract was made governs questions of validity, and the law of the place where the contract was to be performed governs questions of performance. If the suit involves real property, the law of the place where the property is located governs.[274]

The codes also always contain a general limitation on the application of foreign law. That is, foreign law will not be followed if doing so would violate the public policy of the forum state. For example, the procedural rules of a foreign state will generally not be applied (because they would require courts to carry on their business in an unfamiliar manner);[275] a contract will not be enforced in a state that regards it as illegal (e.g., a gambling contract); foreign tax provisions

---

[269]*Hanreijiho,* No. 863, p. 100 (1977); *Japanese Annual of International Law,* no. 23, p. 187 (1980).

[270]*See Halsbury's Laws of England,* vol. 8, para. 585 (4th ed.).

[271]In John Kaldor v. Mitchell Cotts Freight, *Australian Law Reports,* vol. 90, p. 244 at p. 256 (Supreme Ct. of New South Wales, 1989), Judge Brownlie observed, "[It] has always been the case (at least so far as the submissions of counsel show, and my own research shows) that whenever a court has inferred an actual intention of the parties as what should be the proper law of the contract, that inferred intention has coincided with the view which the court would otherwise have imputed to the parties."

England's Lord Denning, in particular, was a strong adherent of skipping over any consideration of the parties' inferred intent. *See* Boissevain v. Weil, *Law Reports, King's Bench,* vol. 1949, pt. 1, p. 482 at pp. 490–491 (1949); and Armadora Occidental, S.A. v. Horace Mann Insurance Co., *Lloyd's Law Reports,* vol. 1977, pt. 2, p. 406 at p. 411 (1977). But see the doubt he expressed in Augustus v. Permanent Trustee Co. (Canberra), *Commonwealth Law Reports,* vol. 124, p. 245 at p. 260 (1971).

[272]The vested rights doctrine used to be applied by case law in many state courts in the United States.

[273]Law Concerning the Application of Laws in General, Article 7(2) (Law No. 10 of 1898).

[274]There are many other special rules for particular kinds of cases. The Boll Case (The Netherlands v. Switzerland), *International Court of Justice Reports,* vol. 1958, p. 55 (1958), involved the interpretation of a clause in a 1902 treaty governing the guardianship of minor children that provided that "the guardianship of an infant shall be governed by the national law of the infant." The case of Kiyomu Liu v. Public Prosecutor, *Kakyu Saibansho Minji Saibanreishu,* vol. 13, No. 10, p. 2146 (1962), *Japanese Annual of International Law,* No. 9, p. 229 (1965), involved the interpretation of the following rule for determining the applicable law for ascertaining a person's nationality: "(1) If a party has two or more nationalities and the law of the country of his nationality is to govern, the governing law shall be that of the country whose nationality he last acquired, provided Japanese law shall govern if one of the nationalities is Japanese. (2) As for a person who has no nationality, the law of the place of his domicile is deemed the law of his nationality. If his domicile is unknown, the law of the place of his residence governs. (3) Where a person's country has districts subject to different laws, the law of the district to which the person belongs shall govern."

[275]In cases dealing with title to real property, both the procedural and substantive law of the chosen state are applied.

will not be enforced (because they are a matter involving state sovereignty); nor will foreign penal provisions (because they are ordinarily territorial in scope).

The vested rights doctrine is the traditional device used by codes to determine the choice of law; however, it is not the only mechanism. In recent years, many civil law countries have modified their choice of law rules in response to objections that the vested rights doctrine is too rigid and fails to reflect the true interests of the states whose law may or may not be applied. The great majority of states have adopted the "most significant relationship" doctrine. Others have turned to the "governmental interests" doctrine.

Most Significant Relationship

most significant relationship doctrine:
Doctrine that courts should apply the law of the state that has the closest and most real connection with the dispute.

The **most significant relationship doctrine** has a court apply the law of the state that has the most "contacts" with the parties and their transaction. In essence, the courts will consider the following general factors in all cases: (a) Which state's law best promotes the needs of the international system? (b) Which state's law will be furthered the most by applying it to the case at hand? and (c) Which state's law will best promote the underlying policies of the legal subject-matter area involved?[276]

In addition, a court will consider "specific" factors depending on the kind of case that is before it. For tort cases, the specific factors are (a) the place of injury, (b) the place of the act, (c) the nationality, domicile, residence, or place of incorporation of the parties, and (d) the place where the relationship between the parties was centered. For personal property cases, they are (a) the location of the property and (b) the nationality, domicile, residence, or place of incorporation of the parties. For real property cases, the specific factor is the location of the property. And the specific factors in contract cases are (a) the place of contracting, (b) the place of negotiation, (c) the place of performance, (d) the location of the subject matter, and (e) the nationality, domicile, residence, or place of incorporation of the parties.

The most significant relationship doctrine is discussed in Case 3–10.

---

[276]This doctrine is adopted in *The Reinstatement (Second) of Laws: Conflicts, 1971,* according to which the following "general" factors are considered by a court applying this doctrine: (1) The application of which state's law will best promote the needs of the international legal system for harmony in the political and commercial relations of states? (2) Will the purpose of the forum state's own law be furthered by applying it to the particular case? (3) Will the purpose of the other states' law be furthered by applying it to the particular case? (4) If a contract is involved, which state's law will best advance the legitimate expectations of the parties? (5) The application of which state's law will best promote the underlying policies of the legal subject matter (e.g., torts, contracts, etc.) involved? (6) Which state's law will best promote certainty, predictability, and uniformity of result? (7) Which state's law is easiest to determine and apply?

Case 3–10   *Bank of India v. Gobindram Naraindas Sadhwani and Others*

Hong Kong, High Court, 1982.
Hong Kong Law Reports, vol. 2, p. 262 (1988).

The Bank of India (the Bank) initiated this suit against Gobindram Naraindas Sadhwani and his wife (the Gobindrams), who had acted as guarantors of a line of credit of 230,000,000 yen the Osaka branch of the Bank had provided Sadhwanis (Japan), Ltd. (SJL). The Gobindrams were residents of Hong Kong. The Bank was an Indian corporation and its head office was in Bombay. It had a regional office in Tokyo and a branch office in

Osaka, Japan. SJL, which carried on business in Osaka, was managed by Mr. Gobindram's brother, Kishinchand Naraindas Sadhwani (Mr. Kishinchand), who lived with his wife near Osaka. The Kishinchands owned 60 percent of SJL and the Gobindrams the remaining 40 percent. SJL had drawn bills of exchange that were supposed to have been paid by corporations in Sri Lanka and Nigeria that were run by other brothers of Mr. Gobindram and Mr. Kishinchand. When the bills were dishonored, the Bank sought payment from Mr. Kishinchand, only to be told by Mr. Kishinchand that it should pursue the

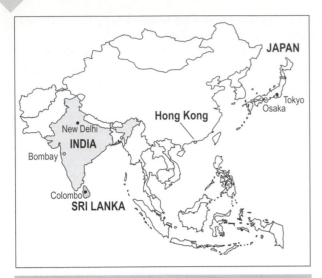

MAP 3-12 Hong Kong, Japan, and India (1982)

Hong Kong guarantors, the Gobindrams. The Bank did not care to sue the Gobindrams because, sometime before the bills of exchange had been drawn, the Bank had agreed to release the Gobindrams as guarantors. After the Bank obtained a provisional attachment of Mr. Kishinchand's property interests in Japan from the Japanese courts, Mr. Kishinchand went to the Bank's head office in Bombay and offered to bear all legal costs if the Bank would pursue its claims against the Gobindrams as guarantors and the Sri Lankan and Nigerian corporations as drawees of the bills of exchange. The Bank then sued the Gobindrams in Hong Kong, their place of residence. The Gobindrams in turn brought the Kishinchands into the proceeding as third parties.

At trial the Gobindrams argued that the proper law governing the guarantee contract was Japanese law and that Japanese law excused them from liability because the Bank had agreed to release them as guarantors. The Bank argued that either Indian or Hong Kong law should apply.

JUDGE NAZARETH: . . .

Determination of the Proper Law: The Test to Be Applied

The major issue between the parties is whether or not Japanese law is the proper law of the contract, i.e., the guarantee. The defendant contends for Japanese law in reliance upon the test of closest and most real connection. The plaintiff on the other hand contends otherwise in reliance upon the second of the three-stage or subrule test propounded thus in Dicey and Morris' *The Conflict of Laws*:

Rule 180: The term "proper law of a contract" means the system of law by which the parties intended the contract to be governed, or, where their intention is neither expressed nor to be inferred from the circumstances, the system of law with which the transaction has its closest and most real connection.

Subrule 1: When the intention of the parties to a contract, as to the law governing the contract, is expressed in words, this expressed intention, in general, determines the proper law of the contract.

Subrule 2: When the intention of the parties to a contract with regard to the law governing the contract is not expressed in words, their intention is to be inferred from the terms and nature of the contract, and from the general circumstances of the case, and such inferred intention determines the proper law of the contract.

Subrule 3: When the intention of the parties to a contract with regard to the law governing it is not expressed and cannot be inferred from the circumstances, the contract is governed by the system of law with which the transaction has its closest and most real connection.[277] . . .

I see no need to adumbrate the numerous authorities relied upon in the foregoing test, nor those through which counsel have conscientiously taken me and which I have carefully considered. The preponderance of authority clearly supports the three-stage criteria which in any event has been confirmed by the House of Lords in *Amin Rasheed v. Kuwait Insurance Co.*[278] Lord Diplock said:

As Lord Atkin put it in Rex v. International Trustee for the Protection of *Bondholders Aktiengesellschaft*:[279]

The legal principles which are to guide an English court on the question of the proper law of a contract are now well settled. It is the law which the parties intended to apply. Their intention will be ascertained by the intention expressed in the contract if any, which will be conclusive. If no intention be expressed the intention will be presumed by the court from the terms of the contract and the relevant surrounding circumstances. . . .

. . . If it is apparent from the terms of the contract itself that the parties intended it to be interpreted by reference to a particular system of law, their intention will prevail and the latter question as to the system of law with which, in the view of the court, the transaction to which the contract relates would, but for such intention of the parties, have had the closest and most real connection does not arise.[280]

---

[277]Vol. 2, p. 1161 (11th ed., 1985).
[278]*Law Reports, Appeal Cases,* vol. 1984, p. 50 at p. 61 (1984).
[279]*Id.,* vol. 1937, p. 500 at p. 529 (1937).
[280]Amin Rasheed v. Kuwait Insurance Co., *id.,* vol. 1984, p. 50 at p. 61 (1984).

It is true there are cases in which the courts have proceeded directly from the first to the third stage. In those drawn to my attention, which I see no need to list, there does not seem to me to have been any conscious or considered conclusion that the second stage does not exist. Moreover, none of those cases has the authority of the House of Lords' decision in *Amin Rasheed*. . . . I conclude, therefore, that in determining the proper law, the three-stage test must be applied, notwithstanding that it is clear from the authorities that the line between the second and third stages is fine, that both those stages often merge and that the same result generally emerges from the application of either of the two latter stages.[281]

Second Stage: Inferred or Implied Choice of Law

In the absence of express intention as to the proper law, I proceed to the second stage, i.e., the implied intention to be inferred "from the terms of the contract and the relevant surrounding circumstances" in the words of Lord Atkin adopted by Lord Diplock which I quoted earlier.

As may be expected, the courts have resorted to different factors from which to infer the intentions of the parties.[282] The same factors have not always prevailed, nor have they always been accorded the same weight. The classic process of weighing the factors must be followed. In that process the plaintiff sets much more store by the common law form in which the guarantee was framed. Many of its provisions are in common form and clearly must have been drafted by reference to particular rules of the common law and decisions of the English courts. Indeed, Mr. Anthony Dicks for the plaintiff submits that several of those provisions are only intelligible by reference to English law.

While the latter may explain their purpose and origins, I do not accept that the former are only intelligible by reference to common law. . . .

I have no doubt that the Bank's printed form of guarantee was used as a matter of routine convenience. Had the Bank wished Indian law (the only applicable common law system contemplated by the parties) to apply, I think it would most probably, if not certainly, have provided for that in the process of devising and printing the form. In that respect and having regard to Mr. Joshi's [the defendant's counsel's] evidence that it was good for Japanese law as well as other laws, the omission of a choice of law provision is of importance. The form in its original printed state referred to Indian currency, but this was replaced by typed references to Yen, which is indicative of Japanese law being the common choice.

The inability to enforce a contract according to one system of law has long been accepted as a relevant factor to be weighed in determining whether it is to be governed by some other law under which it is enforceable.[283] But in this case, as will be seen, the possibility of the guarantee not being enforceable wholly or partly is the result not so much of Japanese law, but of the conduct of the plaintiff in which it need not have indulged. Moreover that conduct was subsequent to the execution of the guarantee and could hardly have been foreseen. In the circumstances, I do not consider that the possibility (and it was not more than that) of the contract being unenforceable in Japanese law favors common law as the proper law intended by the parties.

Mr. Dicks also submits that notwithstanding its technical façade of a Japanese corporation, SJL was part of an Indian joint family business albeit in Japan, which resorted to the branch of an Indian bank also in Japan, to do business in an Indian way. That, again, may well be so but it does not in my view necessarily or even probably point to a choice of Indian law. Mr. Gobindram who acted both in his own behalf and on behalf of his wife, never gave the proper law a thought, and left it all to Mr. Kishinchand in Japan. There is no evidence that Mr. Kishinchand, who likewise acted on his wife's behalf, gave it any more thought.

Having regard to the foregoing considerations, the circumstances, counsels' comprehensive submissions, and taking account of the authorities pressed upon me, and the by no means unanimous views taken in them of similar circumstances, I am satisfied that no intention as to the proper law can be inferred from the guarantee and the surrounding circumstances. . . .

Third Stage: The System with Which the Guarantee Has the Closest and Most Real Connection

In determining the legal system with which a contract is most closely connected, the courts have given great weight to the law of the place of performance.[284] That is not to say that it is not to be weighed against the other factors. Notwithstanding the possibility of the Gobindrams paying in Hong Kong, on the evidence the place of performance must be regarded as Japan.

But that is far from being the only factor pointing to Japanese law as the system with which the guarantee has its closest and most real connection. Two of the four co-guarantors resided in Japan, and one of those two, Mr. Kishinchand, on the evidence was the only guarantor who played an active part and actually took decisions for the four. The negotiations between the parties took place in Japan. The guarantee formed part of the Sadhwani operations in Japan, and although the guarantee was legally an independent transaction and separate

---

[281]*See* Albert V. Dicey and J. H. C. Morris, *The Conflict of Laws,* vol. 2, pp. 1162–1163 (11th ed., 1985).
[282]*Halsbury's Laws of England,* vol. 8, para. 585 (4th ed.).
[283]*See* e.g., South African Breweries, Ltd. v. King, *Law Reports, Chancery,* vol. 1899, pt. 2, p. 173 at p. 181 (1899).
[284]Albert V. Dicey and J. H. C. Morris, *The Conflict of Laws,* vol. 2, p. 1193 (11th ed., 1985).

from the principal debtors' contract with the Bank, its connection with Japanese based operations is inescapable.

The principal sum guaranteed was expressed in Yen and the guarantee in addition bears a 100 Yen stamp.

All the guarantors had assets in Japan, although Mr. Joshi claimed there were other ways of reaching the Gobindrams.

Some of the factors considered in the context of the second stage are also of obvious relevance. I do not propose to repeat them. It seems to me perfectly plain that it is the system of Japanese law with which the guarantee has its closest and most real connection. The only alternative is Indian law and with that the connection is comparatively tenuous. I have at the second stage explained why I do not attach much weight to the common law form of the guarantee, the English language in which it is expressed and the role of the head office in Bombay.

In my judgment, therefore, the proper law of the contract of guarantee is Japanese law, being the system of law with which it has the closest and most real connection.

The proper law of the contract was Japanese law, and Japanese law excused the Gobindrams from liability. The plaintiff's case was dismissed. ∎

Governmental Interest

governmental interest doctrine: Doctrine that holds that courts should apply the law of the state that has the most interest in determining the outcome of the dispute.

Courts that apply the **governmental interest doctrine** will, first, make no choice of law unless asked to do so by the parties. If they are not asked, they will apply the law of their own state. If asked, they will then look to see which state has a legitimate interest in determining the outcome of the dispute. If only the forum state has an interest (a so-called "false conflicts" case), they will, of course, apply the forum state's law. If both the forum state and another state or states have some legitimate interest (a "true conflicts" case), then the forum state's laws should be applied, because the court obviously understands those interests better. If two states other than the forum state have legitimate interests (also a true conflicts case), then the court should dismiss the case if the state in which the court is located follows the doctrine of *forum non conveniens* (discussed later). Otherwise, the court has the choice of applying whichever law it feels is the sounder or the law that is most like that of the forum state.

The governmental interest doctrine was applied in Case 3–11.

Case 3–11   Reyno v. Piper Aircraft Company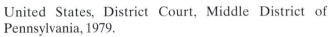

United States, District Court, Middle District of Pennsylvania, 1979.
Federal Supplement, vol. 479, p. 727 (1979).

In July 1976, a small commercial aircraft crashed in the Scottish highlands during the course of a charter flight from Blackpool to Perth. The pilot and five passengers were killed instantly. The decedents were all Scottish subjects and residents, as were their heirs and next of kin. There were no eyewitnesses to the accident. At the time of the crash, the plane was subject to Scottish air traffic control.

The aircraft, a twin-engine Piper Aztec, was manufactured in Pennsylvania by defendant Piper Aircraft Company (Piper). The propellers were manufactured in Ohio by defendant Hartzell Propeller, Inc. (Hartzell). At the time of the crash, the aircraft was registered in Great Britain and was owned and maintained by Air Navigation and Trading Co., Ltd. (Air Navigation). It was operated by McDonald Aviation, Ltd. (McDonald), a Scottish air taxi service. Both Air Navigation and

McDonald were organized in the United Kingdom. The wreckage of the plane was moved to a hangar in Farnborough, England.

The British Department of Trade investigated the accident several months after it occurred. A preliminary report found that the plane crashed after developing a spin and suggested that mechanical failure in the plane or propeller was responsible. At Hartzell's request, this report was reviewed by a three-member Review Board, which held a 9-day adversary hearing attended by all interested parties. The Review Board found no evidence of defective equipment and indicated that pilot error may have contributed to the accident. The pilot, who had obtained his commercial pilot's license only three months earlier, was flying over high ground at an altitude considerably lower than the minimum height required by his company's operations manual.

In July 1977, a California court appointed respondent Gaynell Reyno administratrix of the estates of the five passengers. Reyno was not related to and does not know any of the decedents or their survivors; she was a legal secretary to the attorney who filed this lawsuit. Several days after her appointment, Reyno commenced separate wrongful death actions against Piper and Hartzell in the Superior Court of California, claiming negligence and strict liability. Air Navigation, McDonald, and the estate of the pilot were not parties to this litigation. The survivors of the five passengers whose estates are represented by Reyno filed a separate action in the United Kingdom against Air Navigation, McDonald, and the pilot's estate. Reyno candidly admitted that the action against Piper and Hartzell was filed in the United States because its laws regarding liability, capacity to sue, and damages were more favorable to her position than were those of Scotland. Scottish law does not recognize strict liability in tort. Moreover, it permits wrongful death actions only when brought by a decedent's relatives. The relatives may sue only for "loss of support and society." On defendants' motion, this suit was moved to the United States District Court for the Central District of California. Piper then moved for transfer to the United States District Court for the Middle District of Pennsylvania, pursuant to United States Code, Title 28, § 1404(1).[285] The motion for transfer was granted.

Defendants Hartzell and Piper then moved to have the District Court in Pennsylvania dismiss the case. They argued, among other things, that the law of Scotland should control this case, and that according to Scottish law the plaintiff, Reyno, neither had standing to proceed in a wrongful death claim nor the right to bring a suit under a theory of strict liability. One question facing the court, then, was which law should be applied: California law, Pennsylvania law, or Scottish law.

DISTRICT JUDGE HERMAN:

* * *

The law is clear that we must apply the choice of law rule of the state in which we sit, Pennsylvania.[286] However, when a case is transferred pursuant to [*United States Code*, Title 28], § 1404(a), we then apply the choice of law rules of the state from which the case was transferred [pursuant to the procedure set out in *Van Dusen v. Barrack*].[287] Thus in this case we must apply the California choice of law rules to Defendant Piper. In applying the choice of law rules of California we have three choices of law, California, Pennsylvania, and Scottish. With respect to Defendant Hartzell, the applicable law is not as easily arrived at.

Defendant Hartzell, as previously noted, was found to have insufficient contact with the state of California and service was quashed. The District Court of

MAP 3-13 Scotland (1976)

California did not dismiss the action [against] Defendant Hartzell, but instead properly transferred the action to this forum. We use "properly" in the sense that the court had the power to transfer the action as to Defendant Hartzell even though service was quashed. Plaintiff argues that the *Van Dusen* rule applies to Hartzell as well as Defendant Piper, however, for the reasons that follow, we cannot accept this assertion.

The purpose of the *Van Dusen* rule was to prevent a party from obtaining a change in the law that would be applied to a case by seeking a transfer of the action. In essence, the *Van Dusen* Court ruled that a transfer under Section 1404 should result in a change of courtrooms only, not a change in the applicable law. In the instant case the district court of California held that the law of California could not apply to Defendant Hartzell because of insufficient contacts with the state. The question we are presented with is whether the Plaintiff in this action can capture the law of California under *Van Dusen* for transportation to this district and have it apply to Defendant Hartzell when service against Defendant Hartzell was improper in California. We hold that Plaintiff cannot accomplish this. Simply, the Plaintiff cannot take advantage of the law of California when she could not properly obtain jurisdiction over Defendant Hartzell there. Thus, to Hartzell we must apply Pennsylvania choice of law rules.

---

[285]The statement of facts up to this point is from the Supreme Court decision in this case.
[286]Klaxon Co. v. Stentor Electric Manufacturing Co., *United States Reports*, vol. 313, p. 587 (Supreme Ct., 1941).
[287]*Id.*, vol. 376, p. 612 (Supreme Ct., 1964).

First, we will briefly discuss whether California choice of law rules require that we apply California, Pennsylvania, or Scottish law to Defendant Piper. California courts follow the governmental interest approach in resolving conflict of law issues.[288] As Plaintiff states in her brief the "governmental interest approach differs greatly from the significant contacts approach utilized in Pennsylvania." The governmental interest approach, in determining the law applicable in a California forum, applies to situations involving a foreign country and the choice between the two.[289] The objective of the analysis is to determine the law that most appropriately applies to the issue involved.

The governmental interest approach involves three steps of analysis. First, the applicable legal issue and law must be identified. Second, the state interest underlying the law must be determined. Third, it must then be determined if that interest would be furthered through application of the states' law to resolve the specific issues involved in the case. . . .

Areas of conflict are present between these three jurisdictions, i.e., Pennsylvania, California, and Scotland. First, Scottish law does not allow a personal representative to bring an action of this kind in Scotland. Under Scottish law, a personal representative may only bring an action for funeral expenses. Otherwise, an action of this type may be brought only by the deceased's relatives or dependents. We have previously stated that Gaynell Reyno meets neither of these requirements. Both Pennsylvania and California appear to permit such suits. Second, the law of Scotland has not adopted and does not recognize the theory of strict products liability. The only basis for liability in Scotland for the manufacturer of a defective product is negligence. In contrast, both Pennsylvania and California recognize strict liability.

What interests of the state these laws promote must be identified by reference to the interpretations of the laws by the respective forum courts. California courts have held that the state's interest in creating a cause of action for wrongful death lies in governing the distribution of proceeds to beneficiaries and also the interest of deterring conduct within its borders that takes life.[290] For the purposes of this discussion we will assume that similar interests are promoted by the Pennsylvania laws. Since the accident did not occur in either Pennsylvania or California and because none of the decedents were residents of either of these states, it would appear that the application of either Pennsylvania or California law would not further the purpose of the wrongful death

laws. If the purpose of the Scottish law, permitting recovery for relatives of decedents, is similar, it would seem that its interests would be furthered by the application of the law of Scotland.

Particularly, this is true with respect to the rule of law in Scotland that only relatives or dependents of a deceased may bring an action of the type of the instant action and not a personal representative unrelated to the decedent. We, however, only have affidavits from lawyers from Scotland as to what the rules of law are in that country and thus we cannot make . . . any definitive ruling on the purpose of the Scottish law or thereby the choice of law. We do agree with the Plaintiff that in line with the California decisions, that the restrictions on recovery that exist in Scotland would generally not be applied in a choice of laws situation as the foreign country would likely have no interest in restricting any recovery its citizens might receive in foreign courts from foreign defendants.[291] We do not believe the provisions restricting suits of this nature to relatives of the decedents fall within this general principle however. Such a restriction would likely be for the purpose of ensuring that suits are brought by persons interested in the action so that competence of counsel and administration of a suit are in the hands of those parties with the ultimate interest.

We therefore [conclude] . . . that the law of California would not be applied under the choice of law rules of California as that state has no interest in having its laws apply. Plaintiff admits this fact. Furthermore, we believe that Pennsylvania also has no governmental interest in having its wrongful death laws apply. For the protection of the real parties in interest in this suit we believe that the application of Scottish law would further the purpose of the laws of Scotland with respect to the restrictions on proper plaintiffs. We believe that the California courts would therefore apply the law of Scotland to this suit.

There exists a conflict among the three forums in the law of products liability. Scotland only recognizes negligence as a basis for liability while the two states apply the rule of strict liability. California has no interest in having its product liability law apply and thus under California choice of law rules it would not apply its own law.[292] Our choice is thus between Scottish law and the law of Pennsylvania.

The law of Scotland in not recognizing strict liability is more limited in terms of liability than Pennsylvania. Generally, such a restriction provides an indication that the law seeks to limit the liability of its resident manufacturers to those cases where negligence can be shown;

---

[288]Reich v. Purcell, *California Reports, Second Series,* vol. 67, p. 551 (Supreme Ct., 1967); Hurtado v. Superior Court, *California Reports, Third Series,* vol. 11, p. 574 (Supreme Ct., 1974).

[289]Hurtado v. Superior Court, *id.,* vol. 11. p. 574 (Supreme Ct., 1974).

[290]*Id.*

[291]*Id.*

[292]*See* Bernhard v. Harrah's Club, *California Reports, Third Series,* vol. 16, p. 313 (Supreme Ct., 1976); Reich v. Purcell, *California Reports, Second Series,* vol. 67, p. 551 (Supreme Ct., 1967).

that only culpable conduct will result in liability. If the only purpose of the requirement of proof of negligence is to aid manufacturers in Scotland, then we may assume that the purpose of the law will not be furthered by applying it to American manufacturers.

Pennsylvania's interests in recognizing strict liability is foremost in ensuring that citizens will be compensated for injuries resulting from defective products. There does exist in the imposition of strict liability on manufacturers an element of deterrence. While the element of compensating injured residents outweighs the deterrence factor, at least some slight interest on the part of the state of Pennsylvania would be furthered if the law of Pennsylvania were applied to Defendant Piper. No Pennsylvania governmental interest, however, would be promoted by the application of Pennsylvania law to Defendant Hartzell. Since none of the decedents nor their relatives were Pennsylvania citizens, Pennsylvania's interest in compensating its injured citizens is of little weight. While the interest of Pennsylvania in applying its laws is indeed slight, neither of the other forums has any apparent interest in applying their laws and we therefore assume that California courts would apply Pennsylvania law under the choice of law rules of California.

In summary, under the California choice of law rules, it appears the law of Scotland would be applied to Defendant Piper with respect to the wrongful death laws. Under this interpretation, Plaintiff would not be a proper litigant. Second, the strict liability law of Pennsylvania would likely apply to Defendant Piper and not the negligence law of Scotland.

Next, we will briefly review the law that should apply to Defendant Hartzell under Pennsylvania choice of law rules. As Plaintiff accurately points out in her brief, the courts of Pennsylvania follow the significant contacts approach. In *Griffith v. United Airlines*,[293] the

Supreme Court of Pennsylvania adopted the rule of the *Restatement Second of Conflicts of Laws*, Section 145, which states that in a tort action, the rights and liabilities of the parties are determined by the local law which has the most significant relationship to the occurrence or to the parties. . . . Any analysis of the relevant contacts in the instant suit leads to the inevitable conclusion that the courts of Pennsylvania would apply the law of Scotland to this action.

To reiterate some of the crucial aspects of the contacts, we begin with the fact of the accident in Scotland. The conduct giving rise to the injury occurred in one of three places, Ohio, Pennsylvania, or Scotland. The real parties in interest are domiciled in Scotland, are residents of Scotland, while the Defendants are located in Ohio and Pennsylvania. We will not outline the contact in any more detail as we find the weight of the contacts with Scotland to be overwhelming. We hold that the law of Scotland would apply in the instant action to Defendant Hartzell.

We will now . . . turn our attention to the public interest factors. . . . If we attempted to try this action in this forum the administration and legal difficulties would be extreme. The legal problems include determining the serious and complex conflict of law questions, which this memorandum has only touched on. . . . All of these matters lead us to conclude that the public interest would be better served by a trial in Scotland.

Although the District Court concluded that an action based on strict liability could have gone forward against Piper, it nevertheless dismissed the suit on the grounds of forum non conveniens; *that is, that justice would be better served if the court declined to hear the case and the parties instead took their dispute to a Scottish court.* ∎

---

[293]*Pennsylvania State Reports,* vol. 416, p. 1 (Supreme Ct., 1964).

F. REFUSAL TO EXERCISE JURISDICTION

forum non conveniens:
(Latin: "inconvenient forum.") Doctrine that a municipal court will decline to hear a dispute when it can be better or more conveniently heard in a foreign court.

As indicated earlier, municipal courts are seldom required to exercise jurisdiction over cases involving international disputes. The doctrine used by common law courts to refuse jurisdiction is called ***forum non conveniens***. In essence, a court may refuse to exercise its power to hear a case when doing so is either inconvenient or unfair. To make such a determination the court will consider (1) the private interests of the parties (i.e., the ease and cost of access to documents and witnesses) and (2) the public interest factors (i.e., the interests of the forum state, the burden on the courts, and the notion of judicial comity).[294]

For example, in *Piper Aircraft Company v. Reyno* (see Case 3–11 above), the U.S. Supreme Court reversed the decision of the Court of Appeals and affirmed the decision of the trial court, which had dismissed the case on the basis of *forum non conveniens*.[295] The Supreme Court

---

[294]*See* Gulf Oil Corp. v. Gilbert, *United States Reports,* vol. 330, p. 501 at pp. 508–509 (Supreme Ct., 1947).
[295]*United States Reports,* vol. 454, p. 235 (1981).

agreed with the trial court that the private interest factors "pointed strongly to Scotland as the appropriate forum." It observed that "[a]lthough evidence concerning the design, manufacture, and testing of the plane and propeller is located in the United States, the connections with Scotland are otherwise 'overwhelming.' The real parties in interest are citizens of Scotland, as were all the decedents. Witnesses who could testify regarding the maintenance of the aircraft, the training of the pilot, and the investigation of the accident—all essential to the defense—are in Great Britain. Moreover, all witnesses to damages are located in Scotland. Trial would be aided by familiarity with Scottish topography, and by easy access to the wreckage." Similarly, the public factors pointed to a trial in Scotland. "Scotland has a very strong interest in this litigation. The accident occurred in its airspace. All of the decedents were Scottish. Apart from Piper and Hartzell, all potential plaintiffs and defendants are either Scottish or English." Finally, the Supreme Court said that the Court of Appeals "erred in holding that plaintiffs may defeat a motion to dismiss on the ground of *forum non conveniens* merely by showing that the substantive law that would be applied in the alternative forum is less favorable to the plaintiffs than that of the present forum." It added that it was not holding "that the possibility of an unfavorable change in law should *never* be a relevant consideration in a *forum non conveniens* inquiry." However, it said that courts should only do so "if the remedy provided by the alternative forum is so clearly inadequate or unsatisfactory that it is no remedy at all."

G. OPPOSITION TO THE EXERCISE OF JURISDICTION

anti-suit injunction:
Court order directing a person not to proceed with litigation in a foreign court.

When a litigant brings suit in a foreign court it sometimes happens that the litigant's home country is opposed to his doing so. The foreign court may dismiss the case using the doctrine of *forum non conveniens*; but if it does not, a court in the litigant's home country may intervene to prevent the litigant from proceeding with the case. The device the home country court uses is known as an **anti-suit injunction**. This injunction is directed at the litigant ordering him not to proceed with the case. Two different standards are used by courts to determine whether to issue an anti-suit injunction. The first requires a court to consider comity and to grant the injunction to protect its own jurisdiction or to prevent evasion of its public policies. The second allows a court to grant the injunction if the foreign proceedings are vexatious, oppressive or if they will otherwise cause inequitable hardship. These two standards are discussed in Case 3–12.

Case 3–12 Airbus Industrie G.I.E v. Patel ☞

House of Lords
Appeal Cases, vol. 1999, pt. 1, p. 119 (1998)

LORD GOFF OF CHIEVELEY:

My Lords,

This appeal is concerned with the circumstances in which an English court may grant what is usually called an "anti-suit injunction." The proceedings in question have arisen from a very serious air crash which occurred at Bangalore airport on 14 February 1990. An Airbus A-320 aircraft crashed when coming in to land. Many of the passengers died and the remainder were injured. Among the passengers on board were two families of Indian origin who were British citizens with homes in London. Four of them were killed, and the remaining four were injured. They are, or are represented by, the six

appellants in the appeal now before your Lordships' House. Following the publication in December 1990 of the Report of a Court of Inquiry in India, in which the cause of the crash was identified as error on the part of the pilots (both of whom were killed in the crash), claims were made by solicitors acting for the appellants, their primary claim being against Indian Airlines Corporation ("I.A.C."), the employers of the pilots. When it appeared that these claims would not be settled within the two-year time-limit for such proceedings in India, proceedings were commenced in India on 12 February 1992 against I.A.C., and also against Hindustan Aeronautics Ltd. ("H.A.L."), the airport authority at Bangalore airport. H.A.L. was criticized by the Court of Inquiry for failing to make adequate arrangements for dealing with accidents, and in particular for extinguishing fires such as that which broke out in the aircraft when it crashed; the

Court considered that, if such arrangements had been in place, the loss of life and the injuries suffered would not have been so severe. On 6 March 1992 the appellants settled their claim against I.A.C. for the full amount recoverable up to the limit of I.A.C.'s liability. This resulted in a total recovery of £120,000 by all the appellants which, taking into account irrecoverable expenses, left a net sum of no more than £75,000. Little progress has been made in the proceedings against H.A.L. This may be due to delay in the Indian proceedings; but there may also be difficulty in establishing that the death or injuries of the passengers in question were attributable to negligence on the part of H.A.L.

Meanwhile in February 1992, the appellants also commenced proceedings in Texas, where they sued a number of parties who might have had some connection with the aircraft or its operation. These included the respondent company, Airbus Industrie G.I.E. ("Airbus"), which designed and assembled the aircraft at Toulouse in France. Similar proceedings were brought in Texas in respect of three American passengers who died in the same crash. The two sets of proceedings were later consolidated. In response to these proceedings in Texas, on 21 November 1992 Airbus brought proceedings in the Bangalore City Civil Court against, inter alia, the appellants and the American claimants, and on 22 April 1995 the presiding judge made a number of declarations designed to deter the defendants in those proceedings (i.e. the appellants and the American claimants) from pursuing their claims in Texas. These included a declara-

tion that the appellants were not entitled to proceed against Airbus in any court in the world other than in India/Bangalore, and an injunction which purported to restrain the appellants from claiming damages from Airbus in any court in the world except the courts in India/Bangalore. However, since the appellants were not within the Indian jurisdiction, the injunction had little deterrent effect.

Airbus then issued an originating summons in this country with the purpose of (1) enforcing the Bangalore judgment against the appellants, and (2) obtaining an injunction from the English High Court restraining the appellants, who are resident in England, from continuing with their action against Airbus in Texas on the grounds that pursuit of that action by the appellants would be contrary to justice and/or vexatious or oppressive. The originating summons came before Judge Colman who, on 23 April 1996, refused to enforce or to recognise the Bangalore judgment and also refused to grant an injunction. Airbus then appealed to the Court of Appeal against the refusal of Judge Colman to grant an injunction, and on 31 July 1996 the Court of Appeal allowed the appeal and granted an injunction restraining the appellants from pursuing their action in Texas against Airbus. The appellants now appeal to your Lordships' House against that order, with the leave of this House.

* * *

The submissions of the appellants before the Appellate Committee

At the forefront of the appellants' case before the Appellate Committee was the submission that, where England is not the natural forum for the trial of the substantive dispute, the English court should not, as a matter of policy or law, restrain proceedings in one foreign jurisdiction where the purpose of the injunction is to favor proceedings in another jurisdiction. In other words, as Mr. Kentridge Q.C. summarized the point for the appellants, it is no part of the function of the English courts to act as an international policeman in matters of this kind. This submission raises an important question of principle.

* * *

The Underlying Principles

This part of the law is concerned with the resolution of clashes between jurisdictions. Two different approaches to the problem have emerged in the world today, one associated with the civil law jurisdictions of continental Europe, and the other with the common law world. Each is the fruit of a distinctive legal history, and also reflects to some extent cultural differences which are beyond the scope of an opinion such as this. On the continent of Europe, in the early days of the European Community, the essential need was seen to be to avoid any such clash between member States of the same community. A system, developed by distinguished scholars, was embodied

MAP 3-14 India (1998)

in the Brussels Convention, under which jurisdiction is allocated on the basis of well-defined rules. This system achieves its purpose, but at a price. The price is rigidity, and rigidity can be productive of injustice. The judges of this country, who loyally enforce this system, not only between United Kingdom jurisdictions and the jurisdictions of other member States, but also as between the three jurisdictions within the United Kingdom itself, have to accept the fact that the practical results are from time to time unwelcome. This is essentially because the primary purpose of the Convention is to ensure that there shall be no clash between the jurisdictions of member States of the Community.

In the common law world, the situation is precisely the opposite. There is, so to speak, a jungle of separate, broadly based, jurisdictions all over the world. In England, for example, jurisdiction is founded on the presence of the defendant within the jurisdiction, and in certain specified (but widely drawn) circumstances on a power to serve the defendant with process outside the jurisdiction. But the potential excesses of common law jurisdictions are generally curtailed by the adoption of the principle of forum non conveniens—a self-denying ordinance under which the court will stay (or dismiss) proceedings in favor of another clearly more appropriate forum. This principle, which has no application as between states which are parties to the Brussels Convention, appears to have originated in Scotland (partly, perhaps, because of the exorbitant Scottish jurisdiction founded upon arrestment of the defendant's goods in Scotland[296]), and to have been developed primarily in the United States; but, at least since the acceptance of the principle in England by your Lordships' House in *Spiliada Maritime Corporation v. Cansulex Ltd.*,[297] it has become widely accepted throughout the common law world—notably in New Zealand;[298] in Australia, though in a modified form;[299] in Canada;[300] and in India, as is exemplified by the litigation in the present case. It is of interest that it also appears to have been adopted in Japan, a country whose system has been much influenced by German law.[301] The principle is directed against cases being brought in inappropriate jurisdictions and so tends to ensure that, as between common law jurisdictions, cases will only be brought in a jurisdiction which is appropriate for their resolution. The purpose of the principle is therefore different from that which underlies the Brussels Convention. It cannot, and does not aim to, avoid all clashes between jurisdictions;

indeed parallel proceedings in different jurisdictions are not of themselves regarded as unacceptable. In that sense the principle may be regarded as an imperfect weapon; but it is both flexible and practical and, where it is effective, it produces a result which is conducive to practical justice. It is however dependent on the voluntary adoption of the principle by the state in question; and, as the present case shows, if one state does not adopt the principle, the delicate balance which the universal adoption of the principle could achieve will to that extent break down.

It is at this point that, in the present context, the jurisdiction to grant an anti-suit injunction becomes relevant. This jurisdiction has a long history, finding its origin in the grant of common injunctions by the English Court of Chancery to restrain the pursuit of proceedings in the English courts of common law, thereby establishing the superiority of equity over the common law. In the course of the 19th century we can see the remedy of injunction being employed to restrain the pursuit of proceedings in other jurisdictions within the United Kingdom, and even in other jurisdictions overseas. The principles upon which the jurisdiction may be exercised have recently been examined and restated by the Privy Council in *Aerospatiale*,[302] and it is therefore unnecessary for me to restate them in this judgment. . . . The broad principle underlying the jurisdiction is that it is to be exercised when the ends of justice require it. Generally speaking, this may occur when the foreign proceedings are vexatious or oppressive. . . . But, as was stressed in *Aerospatiale*, in exercising the jurisdiction regard must be had to comity, and so the jurisdiction is one which must be exercised with caution. This aspect of the jurisdiction . . . is, in my opinion, of particular relevance in the present case.

I must stress again that, as between common law jurisdictions, there is no system as such, comparable to that enshrined in the Brussels Convention. The basic principle is that each jurisdiction is independent. There is therefore, as I have said, no embargo on concurrent proceedings in the same matter in more than one jurisdiction. There are simply these two weapons, a stay (or dismissal) of proceedings and an anti-suit injunction. Moreover, each of these has its limitations. The former depends on its voluntary adoption by the state in question, and the latter is inhibited by respect for comity. It follows that, although the availability of these two weapons should ensure that practical justice is achieved in most cases, this may not always be possible.

---

[296]*See* The Atlantic Star, *Appeal Cases,* vol. 1974, p. 436, at p. 475 (House of Lords 1974), *per* Lord Kilbrandon.
[297]*Id.,* vol. 1987, p. 460 (1987).
[298]*See* Club Méditerranée N.Z. v. Wendell, *New Zealand Law Reports,* vol. 1989, pt. 1, p. 216 (Privy Council 1989).
[299]*See* Voth v. Manildra Flour Mills Pty. Ltd., *Australian Law Journal Reports,* vol. 65, p. 83 (High Ct. of Australia 1990).
[300]*See* Amchem Products Inc. *et al.* v. Workers' Compensation Board et al. *Dominion Law Reports, Fourth Series,* vol. 102, p. 96 (Supreme Ct. of Canada 1993).
[301]*See* the article by Ellen Hayes in *University of British Columbia Law Review,* vol. 26, p. 41 at p. 112 (1992).
[302]*Appeal Cases,* vol. 1987, p. 871 (1987).

The Problem in the Present Case

As I have already indicated, the first and crucial question which arises in the present case is whether the English court will grant an anti-suit injunction in circumstances where there is no relevant connection between the English jurisdiction and the proceedings in question other than that the appellants, who are resident in this country, are subject to the jurisdiction and so can effectively be restrained by an injunction granted by an English court.

I wish first to observe that this question may arise not only in cases such as the present, usually described as "alternative forum cases" (the two most relevant jurisdictions here being India and Texas), but also in what have been called "single forum cases," in which (for example) the English court is asked to grant an anti-suit injunction to restrain a party from proceeding in a foreign court which alone has jurisdiction over the relevant dispute. The distinction is of some importance in the present context, and I shall have to refer to it later. But for the moment it is enough for me to say that, in both categories of case, the basis of the jurisdiction has been traditionally stated in broad terms which are characteristic of the remedy of injunction as used in our domestic law. In alternative forum cases, it has been stated that the jurisdiction will be exercised as the ends of justice require, and in particular where the pursuit of the relevant proceedings is vexatious or oppressive; in single forum cases, it is said that an injunction may be granted to restrain the pursuit of proceedings overseas which is unconscionable. The focus is, therefore, on the character of the defendant's conduct, as befits an equitable remedy such as an injunction. In particular, although it has frequently been stated that comity requires that the jurisdiction to grant an anti-suit injunction should be exercised with caution, no requirement has been imposed specifically to prevent the grant of an anti-suit injunction in circumstances which amount to a breach of comity. The present case raises for the first time, and in a stark form, the question whether such a requirement should be recognized and, if so, what form it should take.

* * *

I turn to the United States of America, where the situation is more complicated. The principle of *forum non conveniens* has long been recognised in the United States.[303]

In the well-known anti-trust suit brought by Laker Airways Ltd. in the United States against (among others) the British Airways Board and British Caledonian Airways Ltd., in which the liquidator of Laker alleged a conspiracy among a number of major airlines to force Laker out of the market for transatlantic flights by predatory low pricing, there developed a battle of anti-suit injunctions between the courts of this country and those of the District of Columbia, where Laker's antitrust proceedings were brought. An injunction was granted in this country restraining Laker from so proceeding against certain European airlines; and Judge Greene, sitting in Washington, D.C., then granted an injunction restraining airlines which had not obtained such an injunction in England from seeking an anti-suit injunction here. His decision was affirmed by the Court of Appeals for the District of Columbia Circuit (see *Laker Airways Ltd. v. Sabena, Belgian World Airlines*[304]); but the matter was laid to rest by the decision of the House of Lords in *British Airways Board v. Laker Airways Ltd.*,[305] where it was made plain that no anti-suit injunction should have been granted in that case by the English courts. For present purposes, however, it is the judgment of Judge Wilkey in the District of Columbia Court of Appeals which is significant. In his judgment, for which I have expressed my respectful admiration on a previous occasion, Judge Wilkey stated that anti-suit injunctions are most often necessary (a) to protect the jurisdiction of the enjoining court, or (b) to prevent the litigant's evasion of the important public policies of the forum. Judge Wilkey's judgment has been most influential in the United States, but there has nevertheless developed a division of opinion among the Circuits as to the circumstances in which an anti-suit injunction may be granted. A valuable account of this is to be found in an article by Dr. Lawrence Collins.[306] One approach, embodying what Dr. Collins calls "the stricter standard," is applied by the Second Circuit, the Sixth Circuit and the District of Columbia Circuit. This is derived from Judge Wilkey's judgment in the *Laker* case. It requires that the court should have regard to comity, and should only grant an anti-suit injunction to protect its own jurisdiction or to prevent evasion of its public policies. The other approach, embodying what has been called a laxer standard, is applied in the Fifth, Seventh and Ninth Circuits. On this approach, an anti-suit injunction will be granted if the foreign proceedings are vexatious, oppressive or will otherwise cause inequitable hardship. In deciding whether to grant an injunction, the court will take into account the effect on a foreign sovereign's jurisdiction as one factor relevant to the grant of relief.

* * *

---

[303]*See* generally the *American Restatement of Conflict of Laws,* para. 84, and *Scole and Hay on Conflict of Laws, 2nd ed.,* pp. 373 et seq. (1992). . . .
[304]*Federal Reporter, Second Series,* vol. 731, p. 909 (District of Columbia Ct. of Appeals 1984).
[305]*Appeal Cases,* vol. 1985, p. 58 (1985).
[306]Contained in *Current Legal Issues in International Commercial Litigation* (published by the Faculty of Law of the National University of Singapore), p. 3 at pp. 6–8.

Comity

I approach the matter as follows. As a general rule, before an anti-suit injunction can properly be granted by an English court to restrain a person from pursuing proceedings in a foreign jurisdiction in cases of the kind under consideration in the present case, comity requires that the English forum should have a sufficient interest in, or connection with, the matter in question to justify the indirect interference with the foreign court which an anti-suit injunction entails.

* * *

The general principle which I have outlined above is, I understand, consistent with the approach adopted by the Supreme Court of Canada in the *Amchem Products* case. It is also close to the stricter approach adopted by the Second Circuit, the Sixth Circuit and the District of Columbia Circuit in the United States. It may be said that the traditional way in which the principles applicable in cases of anti-suit injunctions have been formulated in this country corresponds to the "laxer" approach applied in the Fifth, Seventh, and Ninth Circuits, in that the latter refers to vexation, oppression and inequitable hardship. But, as I see it, the problem which has arisen in such an acute form in the present case requires the English courts to identify, for the first time, the limits which comity imposes on the exercise of the jurisdiction to grant anti-suit injunctions. In truth, the solution which I prefer gives (as does the statement of the law by Judge Wilkey) due recognition to comity but, subject to that, maintains (as do the statements of the law by Judge Posner) the traditional basis of the jurisdiction as being to intervene as the ends of justice may require.

In any event, however, I am anxious that the principle which I have stated should not be interpreted too rigidly. I have therefore expressed it as a general rule. This is consistent with my statement of the law in *Aerospatiale*, an alternative forum case, to the effect that "as a general rule" the court granting the injunction must conclude that it is the natural forum for the trial of the action. It is also consistent with Judge Wilkey's statement that anti-suit injunctions are "most often" necessary for the two purposes which he specified. Indeed there may be extreme cases, for example where the conduct of the foreign state exercising jurisdiction is such as to deprive it of the respect normally required by comity, where no such limit is required to the exercise of the jurisdiction to grant an anti-suit injunction. In the present case Lord Justice Hobhouse attached particular importance to the fact that, at the material time, the State of Texas did not recognise the principle of *forum non conveniens*. For my part, however, I cannot accept that this was sufficient to entitle the English court to intervene in the present case, bearing in mind that the

principle is by no means universally accepted, and in particular is not accepted in most civil law countries.

The Present Case

I ask myself therefore whether there is any other aspect of the present case which would render the intervention of the English court consistent with comity. The facts upon which Airbus particularly relies are that there is a forum other than Texas, viz. India, which is indeed the natural forum for the dispute, but which is unable to grant effective injunctive relief restraining the appellants from proceeding in Texas because they are outside the jurisdiction of the Indian courts; however, since the appellants are amenable to the jurisdiction of the English courts, Airbus is in effect seeking the aid of the English courts to prevent the pursuit by the appellants of their proceedings in Texas, which may properly be regarded as oppressive but which the Indian courts are powerless to prevent.

I must first point out that, for the English court to come to the assistance of an Indian court, the normal process is for the English court to do so by enforcing a judgment of the Indian court. However, as the present proceedings have demonstrated, that is not possible here. An attempt was made by Airbus to persuade Judge Colman to enforce, or at least to recognize, the Indian judgment; but he declined to do so, and Airbus has not appealed from that part of Judge Colman's decision. So Airbus is relying simply on the English court's power of itself, without direct reliance on the Indian court's decision, to grant an injunction in this case where, unusually, the English jurisdiction has no interest in, or connection with, the matter in question. I am driven to say that such a course is not open to the English courts because, for the reasons I have given, it would be inconsistent with comity. In a world which consists of independent jurisdictions, interference, even indirect interference, by the courts of one jurisdiction with the exercise of the jurisdiction of a foreign court cannot in my opinion be justified by the fact that a third jurisdiction is affected but is powerless to intervene. The basic principle is that only the courts of an interested jurisdiction can act in the matter; and if they are powerless to do so, that will not of itself be enough to justify the courts of another jurisdiction to act in their place. Such are the limits of a system which is dependent on the remedy of an anti-suit injunction to curtail the excesses of a jurisdiction which does not adopt the principle, widely accepted throughout the common law world, of *forum non conveniens*.

CONCLUSION

For the reasons I have given, I would allow the appeal on the first issue, and set aside the injunction ordered by the Court of Appeal. It follows that the question of oppression does not arise. Had it done so the result would have been that the appeal would have been allowed on the terms of the undertakings offered by the appellants at the end of the hearing, with the effect that the respondent would have had the benefit of the undertakings, and there would have been an order for costs against the appellants. On the conclusion I have reached, however, that stage in the argument is not reached, and in my opinion the appeal should be allowed with costs, both before your Lordships' House and in the courts below. It should not however be inferred from the mere fact that your Lordships have not reviewed the decision of the Court of Appeal to interfere with Judge Colman's exercise of his discretion that, had the point arisen, your Lordships would necessarily have approved of the decision of the Court of Appeal in this respect.

POSTSCRIPT

I have no doubt that it will be of some comfort to your Lordships, though of none to Airbus, that the State of Texas has now, like other common law jurisdictions, adopted the principle of *forum non conveniens*, so that the situation which has arisen in the present case is unlikely to arise again. The principle is now so widespread that it may come to be accepted throughout the common law world; indeed, since it is founded upon the exercise of self restraint by independent jurisdictions, it can be regarded as one of the most civilized of legal principles. Whether it will become acceptable in civil law jurisdictions remains however to be seen. ■

In civil law countries, the problem of multiple courts assuming jurisdiction is dealt with in treaties and statutory rules. Typical of these rules are those in the European Union's Regulation on Jurisdiction and the Recognition and Enforcement of Judgments in Civil and Commercial Matters.[307] The regulation provides that a court has exclusive jurisdiction if the case involves (1) real property located within the forum, (2) the validity of a business organization formed or incorporated within the forum, (3) the validity of an entry in a public registry located in the forum, (4) the validity of intellectual property rights (such as trademarks, copyrights, and patents) that were granted by the forum government, and (5) the validity of judgments issued within the forum.[308] In cases were the type of proceeding does not dictate exclusive jurisdiction, then the court that first assumed jurisdiction over a matter has exclusive jurisdiction. All other courts are required to dismiss the case.[309]

H. PROVING FOREIGN LAW

Once a municipal court has decided that it is to apply the law of a foreign state, it must determine what that law is. Courts are held to know their own state's law; and the same assumption is made for international law—the court is assumed to know the rules of international law. Courts, however, are assumed *not* to know the law of foreign states. In most countries, as a consequence, a party must give advance notice if it intends to raise an issue that requires a court to determine the law of another state.[310] How the law is then ascertained varies from country to country.

---

[307]Council Regulation (EC) No 44/2001 of December 22, 2000. *Official Journal* L 012, 16/01/2001 p. 0001–0023. It is available on line from Eur-Lex at europa.eu.int/eur-lex/en/.

　　The EU Regulation is closely related to the rules in the draft Hague Convention on Jurisdiction and Foreign Judgments in Civil and Commercial Matters, a Convention being drafted by the Hague Conference on Private International Law. The work program for the Convention is available at www.hcch.net/e/workprog/jdgm.html. An October 1999 Draft, which is the latest complete draft, is posted at www.hcch.net/e/conventions/draft36e.html. A June 2001 Working Revision with proposed changes to October 1999 Draft is posted at ftp://hcch.net/doc/jdgm2001draft_e.doc. Both the EU Regulation and the draft Hague Convention are based on the 1968 Brussels Convention on Jurisdiction and Enforcement of Judgments in Civil and Commercial Matters, which was last amended in 1990. The consolidated text of the Brussels Convention in *EU Official Journal* C 027, 26/01/1998 p. 0001–0027.

[308]EU Regulation on Jurisdiction and the Recognition and Enforcement of Judgments in Civil and Commercial Matters, Art. 22.

[309]*Id.*, Art. 27.

[310]The point in time when a court requires a concerned party to give notice of the applicability of a foreign law varies widely from country to country and often from court to court. *See* "Report of the Committee on Comparative Procedure and Practice," in American Bar Association, Section of International and Comparative Law, *Proceedings*, 1960, pp. 148–176 (1961).

In France and countries deriving their law from the French Civil Code, and in the British Commonwealth countries, foreign law is regarded as a factual issue that the parties must prove in the same way they prove any fact.[311] In Germany and countries deriving their law from the German Civil Code, and in the Scandinavian states, foreign law is regarded as law that is to be ascertained by the judge[312] with the assistance, if necessary, of the parties or the Ministry of Justice.[313]

The federal courts and some of the state courts in the United States have recently given up the French and British practice of treating foreign law as a factual issue, and they now regard foreign law as judicially noticeable.[314] That is, judges are allowed to use any relevant source in determining the law of a foreign state whether or not a party introduces a particular source into evidence.[315] Unlike German judges, however, the American judges are not required to consult sources on their own if the parties fail to prove what the foreign law is.[316]

The sources that courts and parties may consult in determining the law of a foreign state include statutory materials, case decisions, commentaries, and (most commonly) expert opinion. This process is facilitated in Europe by the European Convention on Information on Foreign Law,[317] to which most member states of the Council of Europe are now signatories. The Convention requires signatory states to set up agencies to respond to requests from a court in another signatory state "with information on their law and procedure in civil and commercial fields as well as on their judicial organization."[318]

I. RECOGNITION OF FOREIGN JUDGMENTS

Judgments awarded by a municipal court are generally enforced with little difficulty in the forum state. When the court awards a judgment against a foreign defendant, however, the defendant may have few assets in the forum state; or, if the defendant is itself a foreign state, many of its assets may be immune from execution. As a consequence, a victorious plaintiff will often be forced to take the judgment abroad for enforcement.

When asked to convert a foreign judgment into an enforceable local judgment, a court will hold a hearing and, if it believes the request is justified, issue an appropriate order.[319] What it will consider in making this determination varies from state to state. The only universal consideration is that the foreign court must have had jurisdiction before handing down its judgment. Beyond this, the range of national rules runs the gamut from almost complete non-recognition to nearly obligatory recognition of any judgment granted by a court with jurisdic-

---

[311]For the rule in France, *see* Doris Jonas Freed, "Proof of Foreign Law in France," in *id.,* pp. 165–167. For the rule in Britain, *see* Bumper Development Corp., Ltd. v. Commissioner of Police, *All England Law Reports,* vol. 1991, pt. 4, p. 638 at p. 647 (1991).

[312]For the rule in Germany, *see* Martin Domke, "Proof of Foreign Law in (Western) Germany," in American Bar Association, Section of International and Comparative Law, *Proceedings, 1960,* pp. 163–165 (1961). *See also* Hans Koehler, "The Proof of Foreign Law in Poland," *id.,* pp. 148–150; Hans Koehler, "Pleading and Proof of Foreign Law—Rumania," *id.,* pp. 150–151; Allan Philip, "The Application of Foreign Law in Denmark," *id.,* pp. 151–157; Stojan Cizoj, "The Application of Foreign Law in Yugoslav Law of Procedure," *id.,* pp. 158–162; Paul L. Baeck, "Pleading and Proof of Foreign Law in Austria," *id.,* pp. 167–171; Paul L. Baek, "Pleading and Proof of Foreign Law in Czechoslovakia," *id.,* pp. 172–173; and Tauno Tirkkonen, "The Application of Foreign Law in Finland," *id,* pp. 174–176.

[313]For example, the Polish Law on Civil Procedure, § 331(1), provides: "If the necessity arises to apply foreign law, the court shall apply for an expert opinion of the Ministry of Justice, provided that the Court does not know this law or the same cannot be ascertained in the course of the proceedings." Quoted in Hans Koehler, "The Proof of Foreign Law in Poland," *id.,* p. 149.

[314]Some state courts continue to follow the French and British practice. *See,* for example, Doang Thi Hoang Anh v. Nelson, *North Western Reporter, Second Series,* vol. 245, p. 511 (Iowa Supreme Court, 1976).

[315]The rule for federal courts is set out in Federal Rules of Civil Procedure, Rule 44.1, and Federal Rules of Criminal Procedure, Rule 26.1. For examples of the rules in the states, *see* Volkswaggenwerk AG v. Superior Court of Alameda County, *California Reporter, Third Series,* vol. 176, p. 874 (1981); Vergnani v. Guidetti, *Massachusetts Reports,* vol. 308, p. 450 (Supreme Judicial Ct., 1941); and In re Duysburgh, *New York Supplement, Second Series,* vol. 584, p. 516 (1992).

[316]*See* Weiss v. Glemp, *Federal Supplement,* vol. 792, p. 215 (1992).

[317]United Nations Treaty Series, vol. 720, p. 147.

[318]European Convention on Information on Foreign Law, 1968, Article 1(1). In processing a request for information, "[t]he receiving agency may, in appropriate cases for reasons of administrative organization, transmit the request to a private body or to a qualified lawyer to draw up the reply." *Id.,* Article 6(2).

[319]In civil law countries, a court adds an endorsement—known as an *exequatur* (Latin: "he may perform")—to the transcript of a foreign judgment authorizing the judgment to be executed locally.

tion.[320] In the Netherlands, for example, a foreign judgment will not be recognized unless the state is a party to a treaty requiring the Dutch courts to do so. On the other hand, the U.S. state courts tend to go to the other extreme, especially in those states that have adopted the Uniform Foreign Money Judgment Recognition Act.[321]

Other criteria that courts consider are (1) Is recognition of a foreign judgment contrary to the public policy of the forum state? and (2) Is there reciprocity of recognition (i.e., will the court that handed down the foreign judgment recognize the judgments of the state holding the hearing)? Obviously, as to the first of these, the public policy of particular states varies greatly. Some courts will look at the choice of law determination made by the foreign court. Others may even consider whether the original decision was meritorious. Many courts will not enforce a default judgment or an interlocutory judgment.[322]

Arbitral awards (other than awards handed down by an International Center for the Settlement of Investment Disputes' tribunal) are treated quite differently. In states that are signatories to the United Nations Convention on the Recognition and Enforcement of Foreign Arbitral Awards,[323] a foreign arbitral award is recognized and enforced in the same way as a domestic award.[324] In other states, foreign arbitral awards can be enforced only if they are first converted into a judicial judgment in the state where the arbitration was heard.[325]

---

[320]Joseph Dellapenna, *Suing Foreign Governments and Their Corporations,* pp. 401–403 (1988). *See* also Peter E. Herzog, *Civil Procedure in France,* p. 586 (1967).

[321]*Uniform Law Acts,* vol. 13, p. 417 (1980).

[322]For the practice in Japan, *see* "Recognition and Enforcement of Foreign Judgments in Japan," *International Lawyer,* vol. 23, p. 29 (1989).

[323]*United Nations Treaty Series,* vol. 330, p. 3, and online on the UNCITRAL Web site at www.uncitral.org/english/texts/arbitration/NY-conv.htm. There are presently 125 states parties to the Convention. UNCITRAL, *Status of Conventions and Model Laws last updated on 17 January 2001* at www.uncitral.org/english/status/Status.pdf.

[324]In addition to the enforcement of arbitral awards, the Convention also provides (in Article II) for the enforcement of agreements to arbitrate.

[325]In civil law countries, an *exequatur* rather than a judgment is obtained in the state where the arbitration was held. This first *exequatur* is then taken abroad where another *exequator* is obtained. This procedure is known as "double exequatur." Andreas Lowenfeld, *International Litigation and Arbitration,* p. 344 n. 3 (1993).

Chapter Questions

1. State X has accepted the jurisdiction of the International Court of Justice (ICJ) in a unilateral declaration pursuant to Article 36(2) of the ICJ's Statute. The declaration, however, contains the following provision: "This declaration shall not apply to disputes with regard to matters which are essentially within the domestic jurisdiction of State X as determined by State X." (a) Is this provision valid? (b) In a suit between State X and State Y, may State Y invoke this provision as to matters it considers within its own domestic jurisdiction? Explain.

2. State A sues State B in the International Court of Justice. The ICJ hands down a judgment that is adverse to State B. State B refuses to comply with the judgment. What can State A do to get State B to comply?

3. State C and State D are both signatories of the Washington Convention that created the International Center for the Settlement of Investment Disputes (ICSID). Both have notified ICSID that they consider all types of investment disputes as arbitrable.

   Cee Co. is a multinational firm incorporated in State C. State D asked Cee Co. to set up a subsidiary in its territory and promised Cee Co. that it would give it a tax holiday (i.e., not charge it any local taxes) for a period of 20 years. Cee Co. agreed, but it required State D to sign an ICSID arbitration agreement.

   The government in State D has changed, and the new government has cancelled all tax holidays granted to foreign firms, including Cee Co. In anticipation of Cee Co. seeking ICSID arbitration, State D has informed ICSID that it no longer considers disputes relating to taxes as being arbitrable. Cee Co. does ask ICSID to convene an arbitration tribunal. Does the tribunal have jurisdiction to proceed? Explain.

4. In the preceding question, assume that Cee Co. obtains an award from the ICSID tribunal. Cee Co. now seeks to enforce the award in a State C court. State D pleads that it is immune from the jurisdiction of the court. What will the court decide? Discuss.

5. State U had a long-standing relationship with N, the President of State P. President N had regularly provided information to State U's national intelligence agency on activities of the political foes of State U both in State P and in the countries that neighbor State P. At the same time, State U had long ignored N's activities in helping drug runners transport illicit drugs into State U. Now, a change in the government in State U has caused State U not only to disassociate itself from the intelligence activities of President N but also to condemn his drug-related dealings. In need of a boost in the political polls, the President of State U orders his military to invade State P and apprehend President N. This is done. President N is then put on trial in a State U court for violation of State U's antidrug statutes. (a) Assuming that the court can be impartial, does it have jurisdiction to try President N? (b) Is President N immune from prosecution? Explain.

6. Eye Co., a shipping company headquartered and incorporated in State I, signed a contract with Kay Co., a company headquartered and incorporated in State K, to transport goods for Kay Co. from State K to State L. No provisions were made in the contract about where disputes would be settled or what law would be used to resolve them. As Eye Co.'s ship delivering the goods was entering the harbor of the capital city of State L, the ship blew up, destroying all of Kay Co.'s goods. Kay Co. brought suit in State L. Eye Co. now argues that the court does not have jurisdiction and that State L law should not be used to decide the dispute. (a) Does the court have jurisdiction? (b) What law should the court apply? Discuss.

7. The London Court of Arbitration has granted an arbitral award to Gee Co. The award requires H.R.R., the state-owned railway company in State H, to pay damages to Gee Co., a company headquartered and incorporated in State G, for breach of contract for the carriage of goods. Gee Co. seeks to enforce the award in a British court. H.R.R. pleads that it is immune. What will the court decide? Discuss.

8. State R decides to nationalize all property within its territory belonging to nationals of the United States. The United States objects that this violates international law, but State R goes ahead anyway. Afterward, R Bank, the national bank of State R, which has assumed ownership of all of the nationalized property, sells the expropriated goods of one Mr. Ess to Tee Co., a firm in the United States. Mr. Ess brings suit in a U.S. court demanding that Tee Co. pay him for goods it received from State R. R Bank intervenes and asks the court to dismiss the suit, claiming that a decision by the court in favor of Mr. Ess would violate the act of state doctrine. The U.S. State Department has declined an invitation to say what effect a decision would have on American foreign policy *vis-à-vis* State R. Should the court dismiss the case? Explain.

9. The A & B Tobacco Co., a U.S.-based multinational company with its headquarters in Dallas, Texas, has manufactured and sold cigarettes in the United States for more then a century. For the last 25 years or so, the U.S. Food and Drug Administration has required A & B to put warning labels on its cigarette packages that disclose the health risks involved in smoking. As a consequence of this and increasing concern for health in the United States, sales of A & B's cigarettes in the United States have declined sharply. To compensate for this, A & B began selling its cigarettes overseas, also about 25 years ago. Overseas sales have skyrocketed, especially in the developing state of Laissezfaireland. Laissezfaireland has no regulations concerning the sale of cigarettes, and A & B cigarettes sold in that country have never had health warning labels.

Twenty-eight thousand Laissezfaireans suffering from lung cancer caused by smoking A & B cigarettes have brought a class action suit in a United States court against A & B. They claim that by selling the cigarettes in Laissezfaireland without a health warning that A & B acted negligently. They also contend that the cigarettes are health hazards and that A & B is therefore strictly liable for the injuries they have suffered. Does the Texas court have jurisdiction to hear this case? Discuss.

Review Problem

You continue to be an assistant in the law department of MegaBranch Industries (MBI), a multinational enterprise that has branches in countries around the world. You are responsible for overseeing the legal affairs of several of its branches.

1. The MBI branch in Country A operates a fishing fleet in the waters of Country A. All the vessels in the fleet fly the flag of Country A. Recently, one of the fishing vessels was sunk by a torpedo shot from a submarine belonging to Country X. Country X claims that its submarine was carrying out normal military exercises in an area of the high seas that has been designated by international maritime authorities for such activity. You have asked the Foreign Ministry of Country A to make a claim against Country X for the loss of MBI's vessel. What nonjudicial procedures are open to the Foreign Ministry? What can MBI do to help?

2. The Foreign Ministry of Country A has been unsuccessful in getting Country X to pay compensation for the sunken fishing vessel. MBI wants to ask Country A to sue Country X in the International Court of Justice (ICJ). In making this request, it would like to inform Country A that the Court will have jurisdiction over this particular dispute. You have been given responsibility for providing this information. What must Country A show to establish that it can sue Country X in the ICJ?

3. MBI has been invited to set up a branch in Country B, a highly unstable Third World country. Country B has promised to give MBI several incentives for setting up the subsidiary, including tax breaks and nonexpropriation guarantees. MBI itself is incorporated and has its main office in a country that is a signatory of the Washington Convention that created the International Center for the Settlement of Investment Disputes (ICSID). Country B is also a signatory. MBI is willing to set up a branch in Country B but wants to make sure that it will have recourse to an impartial tribunal in the event anything goes wrong. What should MBI require of Country B before it begins setting up a branch there?

4. For several decades, MBI has manufactured military tanks at several of its branches around the world. One of those branches in Country C sells its tanks both to the army of Country C and to the army of Country D. MBI does not have a branch in Country D. After delivering several hundred tanks to Country D, that country has refused to pay for them, complaining that they were defective. (It has nonetheless deployed them as its frontline battle tanks.) The courts of Country D dismissed a breach of contract action brought by MBI several months ago, claiming that the army is immune from suit in its courts. Can MBI bring suit in a Country C court? Is Country D immune from the jurisdiction of this court?

5. Following a change in government, State E decided to nationalize MBI's branch in that country. Actually, the reason for nationalization was political. State E and MBI's home state (i.e., its state of incorporation) were at odds, and the only property that State E nationalized belonged to MBI.

   State E has now arranged to sell all of the assets in MBI's former branch to a competitor of MBI located in State F. Can MBI seek the assistance of a State F court to require the competitor to pay MBI the purchase price for the assets of MBI's former branch rather than State E? Will State E be successful if it asks the State F court to dismiss the suit by claiming that the nationalization was an act of state?

6. MBI's branch in Country G is TransShip, Ltd., a shipping company. Its manager signed a contract with the Erecto Co. in Country H to transport military weaponry manufactured by Erecto to the A.P.O. (Army Purchasing Organization) in Country I. TransShip is not to make delivery until the A.P.O. deposits the purchase price into an account in JumboBank in Country J and this fact is communicated to TransShip by Erecto.

   The goods were loaded aboard the TransShip vessel in Country H and the vessel has transported them to the point of destination in Country I. The A.P.O. did not, however, deposit the purchase price into JumboBank in Country J. Erecto refuses to pay TransShip for returning the goods to Country H or to agree not to hold it responsible if it delivers the goods to the A.P.O. TransShip has contacted MBI's legal office for assistance. Can TransShip sue Erecto or the A.P.O. or both? Where should the suit be brought? And, finally, what law governs the dispute?

C H A P T E R

The Multinational Enterprise

Chapter Outline

Introduction

The organization of a business is a matter of municipal law. Businesses are created by individual nations, even though they may operate internationally. As such, the organizational form that a business can assume depends on its place of creation. The variety of forms, however, is limited—essentially to partnerships and corporations—and the choices are remarkably similar from one state to another. Multinational enterprises (that is, businesses operating in more than one state) take on a variety of operational structures that reflect their international character. If the home or parent organization is located within a single state—a national multinational—the organization is usually fairly simple; however, enterprises with multiple parents located in multiple states—international multinationals—often have quite complex structures.

In states other than a firm's home state or states, the business operates through subordinate organizations. The choice of the particular form of these subordinates may be dictated by home and host state laws, but the range of choices is, again, remarkably limited—in this case to representative offices, agencies, branches, and subsidiaries.

Like the establishment of business forms, the regulation of multinationals is principally a matter of municipal law (although efforts to devise international standards have recently been made). As a general rule, home states regulate the parent firms and host states regulate the subordinates. Sometimes, however, home states are able to regulate foreign subordinates with extraterritorial laws, and host states may regulate the parents by piercing the fictional veil that separates the subordinates from their parents.

A. THE BUSINESS FORM

States authorize or forbid different business forms based on political ideology and economic and social needs. As a consequence, the company laws of every country in the world have many unique features. A prudent business investor planning to organize a firm abroad will, therefore, investigate in detail the company laws of the particular country involved. Nevertheless, for comparative and general planning purposes, it is useful to know the legal derivation of national company laws as they apply to categorizing business forms. Most national company laws are derived from (a) the civil law, especially French and German law, and (b) the common law, especially English law. We will examine the basic business forms in both of these legal systems. A summary of the different forms in both systems appears in Exhibit 4-1 on page 193.

Business Forms in Civil Law States

In the civil law states, including France and Germany, every form of business organization is a **company** (*société* in French, *Gesellschaft* in German) that must register with the state. In France, all companies are regarded as being **juridical entities** independent of their owners. In Germany, however, corporations are juridical entities, but partnerships are not.

Some civil law companies grant limited liability to their members, others do not. Thus, a **partnership** is a company of two or more persons who co-own and manage a business and who are each liable to the full extent of their personal assets for its debts. By comparison, a **corporation** is a company of capital whose owners have limited liability; that is, investors are responsible only to the extent of their financial investment.

Civil Law Partnerships

The **civil law partnership** (*société en nom collectif* [SNC] or *offene Handelsgesellschaft*) is a company of two or more persons organized to carry on a business.[1] Nevertheless, if the number of partners is reduced to one, the partnership, once established, can continue to function. In France, such a partnership may continue for some time (at least until dissolution is begun).[2] In Germany, a single person who purchases a partnership may continue to use the partnership's name to conduct business by himself indefinitely.[3]

In France, partnerships are considered as having separate legal or juridical personalities from the partners, and they thus may own property or sue or be sued in their own name. In Germany, however, they do not have a separate juridical personality. As a consequence, in Germany, partners are taxed individually for the income generated by their partnership, whereas in France they can elect to be taxed individually or to have the partnership treated as a separate entity and taxed as a corporation.[4]

Partnerships are supposed to involve partners in the sharing of profits and losses. In some countries, however, the partnership agreement may include a **Leonine Clause**. Such a clause excludes a particular partner from sharing in the losses of the company. In France, a Leonine Clause is void.[5] In Germany, however, a partnership agreement may exclude participation in profits or losses.[6]

A specialized form of partnership, the **limited partnership** (*société en commandite simple* [SCS] or *Kommanditgesellschaft* [KG]), is recognized in the civil law countries. At least one partner must be a general partner (with personal unlimited liability) and one must be a limited partner. Limited partners have limited liability of the kind that investors in stock companies have. They may only invest cash or property in France, but in Germany, services may be fixed and recognized as a contribution. In both countries, persons can be either a general or a limited partner, but they cannot be both.[7] In France limited partners may participate in the internal administration of the partnership but may not deal with third parties. In Germany, they can participate in internal administration and be given powers to deal with third parties on behalf of the partnership.[8]

Germany recognizes another type of partnership, known as the **silent partnership** (*stille Gesellschaft*). This is a secret relationship between the partners that is unknown to third parties.

---

company: An association of persons or of capital organized for the purpose of carrying on a commercial, industrial, or similar enterprise.

juridical entity: A legal person created by national or international law.

partnership: A company of two or more persons who co-own and manage a business and who are each liable to the full extent of their personal assets for its debts.

corporation: A company of capital whose owners have limited liability.

civil law partnership: A company of two or more persons who co-own and manage a business and who are each liable to the full extent of their personal assets for its debts.

Leonine Clause: A provision in a civil law partnership agreement that excludes a particular partner from sharing in the losses of the company.

civil law limited partnership: A company of two or more persons, at least one of whom has unlimited personal liability for the debts of the business and at least one other who is an investor having limited liability.

civil law silent partnership: A secret relationship between two or more persons, one of whom carries on a business in his name alone without revealing the participation of the other who has limited liability.

---

[1]Both Germany and France allow corporations to be partners, but other civil law countries, such as Switzerland, allow only natural persons to be partners. In Japan, a corporation may be a limited partner but not a general partner. Paul H. Vishny, *Guide to International Commerce Law,* § 6.53 (1981–2001).

[2]*Id.,* § 6.47.

[3]"Germany: Law Digest of the Federal Republic of Germany," *Martindale-Hubbell Law Digest,* p. GER-5 (1998).

[4]Paul H. Vishny, *Guide to International Commerce Law,* § 6.47 (1981–2001). In Colombia, general partnerships are taxed as separate entities at a rate lower than corporations. *Id.*

[5]Jacques Heenan, "Partnership and Other Personal Associations for Profit," *International Encyclopedia of Comparative Law,* vol. XIII, chap. 1, para. 22 (1975).

[6]*Id.,* para. 98.

[7]The ability of a person to be both a general and a limited partner appears to be a feature unique to U.S. law. Uniform Limited Partnership Act, § 12. Jacques Heenan, "Partnership and Other Personal Associations for Profit," *International Encyclopedia of Comparative Law,* vol. XIII, chap. 1, para. 160 (1975), calls this feature of the American law "remarkable."

[8]Paul H. Vishny, *Guide to International Commerce Law,* § 6.48 (1981–2001).

The active partner conducts the business in his name alone, never mentioning the silent partner. So long as the silent partner's participation is not disclosed, the silent partner's risk is limited to the amount he invested.[9] Silent partnerships are useful business forms for investment in Germany because the interest paid to the silent partner is treated as interest on a loan and is therefore tax deductible as a business expense from the earnings of the active partner.[10] In France, where partnerships are regarded as separate legal entities, a silent partnership (*société en participation*) is not recognized as a separate entity and, therefore, is not governed by partnership law; most commonly it is treated as a simple loan arrangement.[11]

A hybrid of the partnership and the stock corporation is the **partnership limited by shares** (*société en commandite par actions* [SCA] or *Kommanditgesellschaft auf Aktien* [KGaA]). This business form consists of one or more general partners with unlimited liability and limited participation by investors in the form of shares. In most countries where it exists, it is regarded as a capital company rather than an association of persons, and therefore governed by corporation law. Because it has the disadvantages of assigning unlimited liability to the general partners and is taxed as a corporation, it is seldom used.[12]

Civil Law Corporations

There are two basic kinds of civil law corporations: (1) stock corporations and (2) limited liability companies.[13]

The **stock corporation** (*société anonyme* [SA] or *Aktiengesellschat* [AG]) is the only civil law company that can raise money in the public marketplace.

One begins the organization of a stock corporation by drafting **Articles of Incorporation** and finding subscribers to purchase shares. The Articles contain such information as the company's name, the location of its registered office, the purpose of firm, and the capital invested.[14]

Subscriptions to corporate stock are raised in two ways. In the first, known as *incorporation by stages*, the promoters issue a prospectus and invite the public to subscribe. Subscribers are then called to a meeting to approve the draft Articles of Incorporation, to ratify the issuance of shares for other than cash, and to endorse other preliminary matters. The second and more common method is known as *simultaneous incorporation*. This procedure allows the promoters (or a group of bankers or venture capitalists) to form a syndicate that purchases the shares. Only after the business is incorporated are the shares sold to the general public.[15]

A minimum capitalization is required to establish a civil law corporation. In France, this is currently set at 1,500,000 francs and in Germany, at 100,000 deutsche marks.[16] Unlike common law countries, the civil law states generally do not recognize the concept of authorized but unissued shares. As a consequence, the entire capital must be subscribed before the corporation can be formally organized.[17]

---

civil law partnership limited by shares: A company of one or more general partners who have unlimited personal liability for the debts of the company and limited participation by investors in the form of shares. The company is taxed as a corporation.

civil law stock corporation: A corporation that can raise money in the public marketplace through the sale of freely transferable shares. Its financial statements have to be disclosed to the public.

Articles of Incorporation: The basic instrument creating and defining a particular corporation, which is filed with a state agency at the time of the firm's incorporation.

---

[9]Disclosure of the silent partner's participation without his consent will not destroy the silent partner's limited liability. Hans Würdinger, *German Company Law,* pp. 232–234 (1975).

[10]In Germany, if the active partner should become bankrupt, the silent partner will be treated, however, only as a general creditor. "Germany," *Company Law in Europe,* para. 40 (S. N. Frommel and J. H. Thompson, eds., 1975).

[11]French Law No. 66–537 of July 4, 1966, Article 419(1).

[12]Paul H. Vishny, *Guide to International Commerce Law,* § 6.50 (1981–2001).
In France, the law now provides for the conversion of partnerships limited by shares into corporations or limited liability companies upon the majority vote of both the shareholders and partners. "France Law Digest," *Martindale-Hubbell Law Digest,* p. FRA-7 (1998).

[13]In France, a special corporation called the simplified shares company (*société par actions simplifiée* [SAS]), was authorized by Law No. 94–1 of January 3, 1994. The SAS is meant to serve as a means for establishing joint ventures between companies. Only *sociétés anonymes* and *sociétés à responsabilité limitée,* as a consequence, may be shareholders. In practice, however, the SAS can be used to set up subsidiaries that are 99 percent foreign owned. "France Law Digest," *Martindale-Hubbell Law Digest,* p. FRA-6 (1998).

[14]The contents of the Articles of Incorporation are specified by statute, and this varies from state to state. Paul H. Vishny, *Guide to International Commerce Law,* § 6.04 (1981–2001). In France, for example, the Articles must state the corporate name, purpose and term of existence, the location of the corporate office, the amount of capital, the par value and type of shares to be issued, and the number of qualification shares for directors. "France Law Digest," *Martindale-Hubbell Law Digest,* p. FRA-3 (1998).

[15]Paul H. Vishny, *Guide to International Commerce Law,* § 6.09 (1981–2001).

[16]"France Law Digest," *Martindale-Hubbell Law Digest,* p. FRA-3 (1998); "Germany: Law Digest of the Federal Republic of Germany," *id.,* p. GER-6.

[17]Paul H. Vishny, *Guide to International Commerce Law,* § 6.06 (1981–2001).

Once subscriptions have been paid in, an initial organizational meeting is held, a board of directors is appointed or elected,[18] and the initial formalities are completed. The stock corporation must then register its Articles of Incorporation with the appropriate public offices, such as the Commercial Registrar. Additionally, some countries require that notice of registration be published in an official bulletin. Only after registration and publication (where required) occur does the stock corporation officially come into existence.[19]

Although the civil law generally requires that there be more than one subscriber to set up a stock corporation,[20] in Germany, after incorporation, the shares can be transferred to a single owner so that a wholly owned stock corporation can be set up.[21] In France, however, a stock corporation can have no fewer than seven shareholders; and if the number should fall below seven, the corporation can be forced to dissolve.[22]

Commonly, the only shares that subscribers may purchase are **par shares** (shares that have a specified face value).[23] Very few civil law countries recognize *no par shares* (i.e., shares that have no specified face value).[24] Payment can be made in either cash or property; however, when property is exchanged for shares, its value must be determined by independent auditors. Additionally, in France, shares received in exchange for property may not be negotiated for a 2-year period following the registration of the company.[25]

Traditionally, in civil law countries, the owners of corporate shares were entitled to vote on the operation of their stock corporation. *Nonvoting stock*, accordingly, was not allowed.[26] This is no longer the case. Both France and Germany now allow for the use of such stock.[27] Also, the use of *preferred stock* until recently was a rarity.[28] Both France and Germany now authorize corporations to issue preferred stock that gives special rights either to dividends or on dissolution.[29]

The right to transfer the stock of a stock corporation is presumed in the civil law countries. Indeed, to make the transfer easier, most corporations issue their share certificates in the form of bearer instruments.[30]

Shareholders in a stock corporation are responsible for electing the board of directors, reviewing the annual statements on earnings and operations, and declaring **dividends**.[31] Formal meetings are required. **Quorum** requirements (i.e., how many owners of a minimum number of

par share: A share that must be sold by a company for at least par value (the value printed on its face). This amount becomes part of the company's capital.

shareholder: The owner of a share interest in a company.

dividend: The distribution of current or accumulated earnings to the shareholders of a corporation in proportion to the number of shares each one owns.

quorum: The number of persons, or persons owning a number of shares, who must be present before a meeting of a deliberative body may be convened and business transacted.

---

[18]In Germany, the initial directors are named in the Articles of Incorporation. Richard M. Buxbaum, "The Formation of Marketable Share Companies," *International Encyclopedia of Comparative Law,* vol. XIII, chap. 3, para. 30 (1974).

[19]Paul H. Vishny, *Guide to International Commerce Law,* § 6.10 (1981–2001).
　　In some countries, such as Switzerland and the Scandinavian countries, two documents must be filed: a Deed of Incorporation and the Articles of Incorporation. In Germany and most other countries (but not France), these incorporation documents must be notarized. *Id.,* § 6.04.

[20]In some countries, including Denmark and Liechtenstein, a corporation may be organized initially with a single shareholder. "Introduction," *Company Law in Europe,* para. 88 (S. N. Frommel and J. H. Thompson, eds., 1975).

[21]"Germany: Law Digest of the Federal Republic of Germany," *Martindale-Hubbell Law Digest,* p. GER-2 (1998).

[22]"France Law Digest," *Martindale-Hubbell Law Digest,* p. FRA-3 (1998).

[23]France, Law No. 88–15 of January 5, 1988, provides that shares must have a minimum par value fixed in a corporation's bylaws. *Id.,* p. FRA-3. *See also* "Germany: Law Digest of the Federal Republic of Germany," *id.,* p. GER-2.

[24]Japan allows for the use of no par shares. Japanese Commercial Code, § 199, 213. Brazil does also. Pinheiro Neto & Cia., *Doing Business in Brazil,* app. A (1980–1981).

[25]Paul H. Vishny, *Guide to International Commerce Law,* § 6.07 (1981–2001).

[26]"Introduction," *Company Law in Europe,* para. 163 (S.N. Frommel and J.H. Thompson, eds., 1975).

[27]"France Law Digest," *Martindale-Hubbell Law Digest,* p. FRA-3 (1998); "Germany: Law Digest of the Federal Republic of Germany," *Martindale-Hubbell Law Digest,* p. GER-2 (1998). In Germany, however, the par value of nonvoting preferred stock cannot exceed that of the value of other stock. *Id.*

[28]Paul H. Vishny, *Guide to International Commerce Law,* § 6.15 (1981–2001).

[29]"France Law Digest," *Martindale-Hubbell Law Digest,* p. FRA-3 (1998); "Germany: Law Digest of the Federal Republic of Germany," *id.,* p. GER-2.

[30]In Germany, certificates must be in bearer form unless provided for otherwise in the Articles of Incorporation. "Germany: Law Digest of the Federal Republic of Germany," *Martindale-Hubbell Law Digest,* pp. GER-2, 3 (1998).
　　Since the adoption of Law 81–1160 of December 30, 1981 (effective November 3, 1984), French corporate shares have been "dematerialized." That is, shares are no longer represented by certificates; instead, ownership is shown by the entry of the shareholder's name in an account maintained by the issuing corporation or a financial institution approved by the French Ministry of Finance. "France Law Digest," *id.,* p. FRA-3.

[31]*Id.,* p. FRA-4; "Germany," *Company Law in Europe,* paras. 75, 112 (S.N. Frommel and J.H. Thompson, eds., 1975).
　　Dividends are declared by the shareholders after they examine the company's annual reports. Management, however, may establish reserves that are charged against the profits of the company, which effectively limits the amount of funds available for distribution. Additionally, company laws typically forbid the distribution of dividends that would impair the company's capital, and a certain percentage of annual earnings have to be set aside until the company's reserves meet a specified percentage of the company's capital. "Introduction," *Company Law in Europe,* paras. 242–245 (S.N. Frommel and J.H. Thompson, eds., 1975).

shares must be present before a meeting may be held) vary widely. In Germany, no quorum is required for ordinary resolutions. In France and many other countries, if a quorum cannot be met at a first meeting, then a second meeting may be held at which a lower percentage of shares will constitute a quorum and resolutions can then be adopted by a majority of those present.[32]

Corporate financial statements must be prepared annually in advance of the shareholders' meeting. Outside auditors or statutory auditors (i.e., government officials) must be employed by the stock corporation to examine its books. Such auditors frequently exercise supervisory authority over the company as well.[33] The financial statements, once prepared, must then be made available to the public. In addition, in many countries the statements must be published.[34]

The civil law **limited liability company** (*société à responsabilité limiteé* [SARL] or *Gesellschaft mit beschränkter Haftung* [GmbH]) is a popular corporate business entity both in France and Germany. In Germany, where the form originated, it is widely used for setting up subsidiaries.[35] In comparison to the stock corporation, the limited liability company is a simpler entity; it does not issue negotiable share certificates and it is subject to less stringent public disclosure laws.[36]

The process of forming a limited liability company is essentially the same as that for a stock corporation. Articles of Incorporation are drafted, capital is subscribed, an organizational meeting is held, an initial board of directors is appointed or elected, and the Articles of Incorporation are registered with the appropriate public offices.

The least amount of capitalization needed to set up a limited liability company varies greatly from country to country. As a general rule, the amount is less than that required for stock corporations. It is currently set at 50,000 francs in France and at 25,000 deutsche marks in Germany.[37]

Investors in a limited liability company are known as members—rather than shareholders—and are said to own a participation rather than shares. Formal meetings are normally required, but in Germany the members may approve any action of the company if all of them agree, and in France, the members may approve actions (other than the adoption of the annual statements) informally if such a procedure is authorized in the Articles of Incorporation.[38]

The transfer of a member's interest in a limited liability company is allowed, but the process is cumbersome in comparison to the stock corporation. Some countries do not provide for the issuance of participation certificates, and even where they are authorized and issued, they must be registered and be in the form of nonnegotiable instruments. The transfer is typically by a formal notarial act,[39] and restrictions on transfer (such as the right of approval or purchase by the other members) are both legal and commonplace.[40]

Business Forms in Common Law States

In the common law states (including England, the British Commonwealth countries, and the United States), not all businesses are companies that have to register with the state, nor are they all separate juridical entities, as is the case under the French civil law. Associations, such as

civil law limited liability company: A corporation owned by members that does not issue negotiable share certificates and is subject to minimal public disclosure laws.

---

[32]Paul H. Vishny, *Guide to International Commerce Law,* § 6.18 (1981–2001).
    In France, for example, a quorum for a regular shareholders' meeting is, upon first call, shareholders holding one-fourth of the registered shares. No minimum is specified for the second call. "France Law Digest," *Martindale-Hubbell Law Digest,* p. FRA-4 (1998).

[33]*Id.,* § 6.25. *See also* "France Law Digest," *Martindale-Hubbell Law Digest,* p. FRA-5 (1998).

[34]Paul H. Vishny, *Guide to International Commerce Law,* § 6.25 (1981–2001).

[35]Richard M. Buxbaum, "The Formation of Marketable Share Companies," in *International Encyclopedia of Comparative Law,* vol. XIII, chap. 3, paras. 9–10 (1974).

[36]Paul H. Vishny, *Guide to International Commerce Law,* § 6.02 (1981–2001).
    In many countries, the number of persons who may be members in a limited liability company is restricted. In Mexico and France, for example, the maximum number is 50. "Mexico Law Digest," *Martindale-Hubbell Law Digest,* p. MEX-3 (1998); "France Law Digest," *id.,* p. FRA-5.

[37]"France Law Digest," *Martindale-Hubbell Law Digest,* p. FRA-5 (1998); "Germany: Law Digest of the Federal Republic of Germany," *id.,* p. GER-3.

[38]Paul H. Vishny, *Guide to International Commerce Law,* § 6.16 (1981–2001).

[39]"Introduction," *Company Law in Europe,* paras. 110, 111 (S.N. Frommel and J.H. Thompson, eds., 1975).

[40]Paul H. Vishny, *Guide to International Commerce Law,* § 6.28 (1981–2001).

Civil Law Business Forms	**Common Law Business Forms**
company: An association of persons or of capital organized for the purpose of carrying on a commercial, industrial, or similar enterprise.	**company:** An association of persons organized for the purpose of carrying on a commercial, industrial, or similar enterprise.
partnership: A company of two or more persons who co-own and manage a business and who are each liable to the full extent of their personal assets for its debts.	**partnership:** An association of two or more persons who co-own and manage a business for profit and who are each liable to the full extent of their personal assets for its debts.
limited partnership: A company of two or more persons, at least one of whom has unlimited personal liability for the debts of the business and at least one other who is an investor having limited liability.	**limited partnership:** A partnership consisting of one or more general partners who manage the business and who are each liable to the full extent of their personal assets for its debts and one or more limited partners whose liability is limited to the funds they invest.
silent partnership: A secret relationship between two or more persons, one of whom carries on a business in his name alone without revealing the participation of the other who has limited personal liability.	**secret partnership:** A partnership in which the participation of one or more persons as partners is not disclosed to the public by any of the partners. All of the partners have unlimited personal liability.
partnership limited by shares: A company of one or more general partners who have unlimited personal liability for the debts of the company and with limited participation by investors in the form of shares. The company is taxed as a corporation.	**joint stock company:** An unincorporated association of persons whose ownership interests are represented by transferable shares. The shareholders have unlimited personal liability.
	common law limited liability company: An unincorporated association that is treated as a partnership for tax purposes and that provides limited liability for its owners.
	business trust: A business arrangement in which the owners of a property, known as beneficiaries, transfer legal title to that property to a trustee who then manages it for them. The beneficiaries hold transferable trust certificates entitling them to the income generated by the property and a residual equitable share at the time the trust is terminated. The trustee has unlimited personal liability whereas the beneficiaries have limited personal liability.
corporation: A company of capital whose owners have limited personal liability.	**corporation:** A separate juridical entity owned by shareholders who may have limited, unlimited, or no liability.
stock corporation: A corporation that can raise money in the public marketplace through the sale of freely transferable shares. Its financial statements have to be disclosed to the public.	**public corporation:** A corporation that can raise money in the public marketplace through the sale of freely transferable shares. Its financial statements have to be disclosed to the public.
limited liability company: A corporation owned by members that does not issue negotiable share certificates and is subject to minimal public disclosure laws.	**private corporation:** A corporation that may not ask the public to subscribe to its shares, bonds, or other securities and that is subject to less stringent public disclosure laws than a public corporation.
	unlimited liability corporation: A corporation whose members are liable in the event it is wound up and its assets are insufficient to cover its debts.
	no liability corporation: A corporation whose shareholders are not obligated to pay any call for contributions made by the firm or to pay any of the firm's debts, but who will not receive any dividends if a call is due and unpaid.

EXHIBIT 4-1   Comparison of Civil Law and Common Law Business Forms

partnerships, may be formed without registering with the state and are regarded as aggregates of persons rather than as separate juridical entities. Only corporations, which do register with the state, are separate juridical beings.

Common Law Partnerships

common law partnership: An association of two or more persons who co-own and manage a business for profit and who are each liable to the full extent of their personal assets for its debts.

A **common law partnership** is an association of two or more persons who co-own and manage a business for profit and who have full responsibility for its operation.[41] Although a partnership (at least in most common law countries) may sue or be sued and own and convey property in the partnership name, the partnership is nonetheless regarded as a mere aggregate of its partners, who are ultimately liable for its obligations.[42]

The fact that a partnership is an aggregate and not a separate juridical entity is significant in that partners are entitled to share in all of the profits (and losses) of the business. Also, a partnership is not a taxpaying entity. Income earned by the partnership is allocated to partners according to their partnership agreement (or equally, if they have not agreed otherwise) and then treated, for tax purposes, as the personal income of each partner.

common law limited partnership: A partnership consisting of one or more general partners who manage the business and who are each liable to the full extent of their personal assets for its debts and one or more limited partners whose liability is limited to the funds they invest.

A special form of partnership, based on the analogous civil law business form[43] and now found in all common law countries, is the **limited partnership**. This is a partnership consisting of one or more general partners who manage the business and who are jointly and severally responsible as ordinary partners for its obligations and one or more[44] limited partners who contribute a specific sum to the capital account and share in the profits. A limited partner does not participate in the management of the firm and does not have liability for the debts of the partnership beyond the funds he contributed.[45] Although a limited partnership can be formed only upon registration with the state, it is regarded, like an ordinary partnership, as an aggregate of its general partners and not a separate juridical entity.[46] As with an ordinary common law partnership, it is this characteristic that distinguishes the common law limited partnership from its civil law counterpart, as Case 4–1 points out.

---

[41]United States, Uniform Partnership Act, § 6(1) (1914). English Partnership Act, § 1(1) (1890).

In some jurisdictions, the number of persons who may be partners in a partnership is limited. In South Africa, for example, no more than 20 persons can be partners in a partnership, except that the limitation does not apply to persons carrying on the professions of public accountant, auditor, attorney, architect, quantity surveyor, professional engineer, or stockbroker. "South Africa Law Digest," *Martindale-Hubbell Law Digest,* p. SoA-2 (1998). Australia's states similarly limit partnerships (other than certain professional partnerships) to no more than 20 persons. "Australia Law Digest," *Martindale-Hubbell Law Digest,* p. AUS-19 (1998).

[42]Meyer & Co. v. Faber (No. 2), *Law Reports, Chancery,* vol. 1923, pt. 2, p. 421 (Court of Appeal, 1923).

[43]The limited partnership form was first introduced in the United States in 1822 when the state of New York adopted legislation based on the French Commercial Code. *See* Lanier v. Bowdoin, *New York Reports,* vol. 282, p. 32 (1940); and Moorhead v. Seymour, *New York Supplement,* vol. 77, p. 1050 (1901).

Although some have suggested that Bovill's Act, *Statutes of Victoria, Anni 26 & 27,* chap. 86 (1865), may have anticipated the possibility of the limited partnership form in England, it was not until the Limited Partnerships Act was adopted in 1907 that England clearly authorized this type of business. "Partnership," *Halsbury's Laws of England,* vol. 35, para. 206, n. 2 (4th ed., 1981).

[44]In England, a limited partnership may have no more than 10 limited partners if it is carrying on a banking business and no more than 20 if it is carrying on most other businesses. Limited partnerships of accountants, auctioneers, estate agents, estate managers, land agents, members of a recognized stock exchange, solicitors, and surveyors may have, however, any number of limited partners. English Limited Partnerships Act, § 4 (1907); Companies Act, §§ 120(3), 121(1) (1967).

[45]United States, Revised Uniform Limited Partnership Act, § 101(7) (1976). English Limited Partnerships Act, § 4(2) (1907).

In England, a limited partner who participates in management will lose his limited liability for the period in which he participates. English Limited Partnerships Act, § 6(1) (1907). In the United States, a limited partner will lose his limited liability if he participates in the "control" of the business, but only to persons who deal with the partnership believing, based on the limited partner's conduct, that he is a general partner. United States, Revised Uniform Limited Partnership Act, § 303(a) (1976).

[46]Although the common law limited partnership is modeled on the French limited partnership, the courts have interpreted the legislation creating the common law limited partnership according to the rules of the common law. *See* Moorhead v. Seymour, *New York Supplement,* vol. 77, p. 1050 (1901); and Re Barnard, Martins Bank v. Trustee, *Law Reports, Chancery,* vol. 1932, pt. 1, p. 269 at p. 272 (1932).

Case 4–1   Puerto Rico v. Russell & Co. et al.

United States, Supreme Court, 1933.
United States Reports, vol. 288, p. 476 (1933).

MR. JUSTICE STONE DELIVERED THE OPINION OF THE COURT:

The people of Puerto Rico,[47] the petitioner, brought this suit in the Insular District Court of San Juan, Puerto Rico, against the respondent, Russell & Co., a *sociedad en comandita*[48] organized under the laws of Puerto Rico, to recover certain assessments levied on lands of Russell & Co., under an act of the legislature of Puerto Rico. The individual respondents, members of the *sociedad*, none of whom are citizens of Puerto Rico or domiciled there, were not named as defendants. They appeared specially in the Insular Court and removed the cause to the United States District Court for Puerto Rico. That court denied a Motion to Remand[49] and gave its decree for respondents on the ground, first raised by the Answer,[50] that the assessments sued for were levied in violation of § 2 of the Organic Act of Puerto Rico, March 2, 1917, chapter 145, forbidding the enactment of any law impairing the obligation of contract. On appeal the Court of Appeals for the First Circuit affirmed; this Court granted *certiorari*.

Section 41 of the Organic Act confers on the United States District Court for Puerto Rico "jurisdiction of all cases cognizable in the district courts of the United States," and also "jurisdiction of all controversies where all of the parties on either side of the controversy are citizens of a foreign state or states, or citizens of a state, territory, or district of the United States and not domiciled in Puerto Rico, wherein the matter in dispute exceeds, exclusive of interest or cost, the sum or value of $3,000." . . .

Admittedly, if the individual members of the *sociedad* are "parties" within the meaning of the Organic Act, § 41, . . . the suit is one within the jurisdiction of the District Court because of their nonresidence, diversity of citizenship being unnecessary. And if the nonresidence of the individual members would confer jurisdiction upon the federal court in a suit against the *sociedad* originally instituted there, we will assume, for present purposes, that it would also suffice to justify removal by the individuals, even though the Insular Court refuses to recognize them as parties. The petitioner argues, nevertheless, that the suit was not removable because of citizenship for the reason that the *sociedad* is a juridical entity under Puerto Rican law and, as in the case of a corporation, its domicile rather than that of its members determines citizenship for purposes of federal jurisdiction. If the petitioner's contention is sound, the District Court was without jurisdiction. . . .

For almost a century, in ascertaining whether there is requisite diversity of citizenship[51] to confer jurisdiction on the federal courts, we have looked to the domicile of a corporation, not that of its individual stockholders, as controlling. In its final form this rule of jurisdiction was stated in terms of a "conclusive presumption" that shareholders are citizens of the corporate domicile, but even those who formulated the rule found its theoretical justification only in the complete legal personality with which corporations are endowed. Fictitious that personality may be, in the sense that the fact that the corporation is composed of a plurality of individuals, themselves legal persons, is disregarded, but "it is a fiction created by law with intent that it should be acted on as if true."[52] This treatment of the aggregate for other purposes as a person distinct from its members, with capacity to perform all legal acts, made it

---

[47]Puerto Rico was an overseas territory of Spain until 1898, when, by the Treaty of Paris ending the Spanish-American War, Spain ceded it to the United States. It remained under military control until 1900, when it became a territory of the United States with a governor and upper legislative chamber appointed by the President and an elected lower chamber. In 1917, the U.S. Congress granted its inhabitants U.S. citizenship. At the same time, Congress provided for the local election of both houses of Puerto Rico's legislature, but the governor and other key officials were appointed by the U.S. President. In 1946, Congress granted Puerto Rico increased autonomy, and in 1948, Puerto Rico was allowed to elect its first native governor. In 1952, Puerto Rico became a self-governing Commonwealth. This status was upheld in a referendum held in 1967, but debate still continues over whether Puerto Rico should be a Commonwealth, a U.S. state, or an independent nation.]

[48]Spanish: "limited partnership."]

[49]A Motion to Remand is a request to have one court send a case back to another court for further action.]

[50]The formal response of the defendant to the plaintiff's complaint.]

[51]Diversity of citizenship is a phrase used to refer to one basis of jurisdiction held by the federal courts. Under Article III, § 2 of the U.S. Constitution, the federal courts have jurisdiction over cases between citizens of different states—that is, when the party on one side of a lawsuit is a citizen of one state, and the party on the other side is a citizen of another state or an alien. A jurisdictional money amount must also be met.]

[52]Klein v. Board of Supervisors, *id.,* vol. 282, p. 19 at p. 24 (1930).

MAP 4-1 Puerto Rico (1933)

transact business, sue and be sued in its own name and right. Its members are not thought to have a sufficient personal interest in a suit brought against the entity to entitle them to intervene as parties defendant. It is created by articles of association filed as public records. Where the articles so provide, the *sociedad* endures for a period prescribed by them regardless of the death or withdrawal of individual members. Powers of management may be vested in managers designated by the articles from among the members whose participation is unlimited, and they alone may perform acts legally binding on the *sociedad*. Its members are not primarily liable for its acts and debts, and its creditors are preferred with respect to its assets and property over the creditors of individual members, although the latter may reach the interests of the individual members in the common capital. Although the members whose participation is unlimited are made contingently liable for the debts of the *sociedad* in the event that its assets are insufficient to satisfy them, this liability is of no more consequence for present purposes than that imposed on corporate stockholders by the statutes of some states. These characteristics under the Codes of Puerto Rico give content to their declaration that the *sociedad* is a juridical person. That personality is so complete in contemplation of the law of Puerto Rico that we see no adequate reason for holding that the *sociedad* has a different status for purposes of federal jurisdiction than a corporation organized under that law. In neither case may nonresidents of Puerto Rico, who have taken advantage of its laws to organize a juridical entity for the purpose of carrying on business there, remove from the Insular Courts controversies arising under local law.

* * *

The judgment below will be reversed and the cause remanded with instructions to remand it to the Insular Court from which it was removed.

Reversed. ■

possible and convenient to treat it so for purposes of federal jurisdiction as well. But status as a unit for purposes of suit alone, as in the case of a joint stock company, or a limited partnership, not shown to have other attributes of a corporation, has been deemed a legal personality too incomplete; what was but an association of individuals for so many ends and a juridical entity for only a few, was not easily to be treated as if it were a single citizen.

The tradition of the common law is to treat as legal persons only incorporated groups and to assimilate all others to partnerships. The tradition of the civil law, as expressed in the Code of Puerto Rico, is otherwise. Therefore, to call the *sociedad en comandita* a limited partnership in the common law sense, as the respondents and others have done, is to invoke a false analogy. In the law of its creation the *sociedad* is consistently regarded as a juridical person. It may contract, own property and

---

common law secret partnership: A partnership in which the participation of one or more persons as partners is not disclosed to the public by any of the partners. All of the partners have unlimited personal liability.

Like the civil law, the common law also recognizes **secret partnerships** in which the existence of one of the partners is not revealed to the public. Unlike in the civil law, however, the common law secret partner has the same liability as an ordinary partner.[53]

A common law **joint stock company** is analogous to the civil law's partnership limited by shares. It is an unincorporated association with ownership interests represented by transferable shares. As in the common law partnership, the owners of the shares have unlimited personal liability for the obligations of the company.[54]

---

[53]See In re Victor, *Federal Reports,* vol. 246, p. 727 at p. 731 (District Ct. N. District of Georgia, 1917).
[54]See Spotswood v. Morris, *Idaho Reports,* vol. 12, p. 360 (1906); and Weaver v. First Nat'l Bank, *Arkansas Reports,* vol. 216, p. 199 (1949). In England, a joint stock company may register and become a company limited by shares with limited liability. England, Companies Act, § 685(1) (1985).

common law joint stock company: An unincorporated association of persons whose ownership interests are represented by transferable shares. The shareholders have unlimited personal liability.

common law limited liability company: An unincorporated association that is treated as a partnership for tax purposes and that provides limited liability for its owners.

The common law **limited liability company** (LLC) is recognized only in the United States. The state of Wyoming authorized the first such company in 1977.[55] By 1997, all the other U.S. states had done so as well. The popularity of the LLC has to do with its tax status: It is treated as a partnership for tax purposes.[56] Prior to its creation, only sole proprietorships, general partnerships, limited partnerships, and very small corporations[57] were not subject to corporate taxation in the United States (the income of these businesses being attributed instead directly to their owners).

In addition to its tax status, the LLC is also popular because it gives its owners (called "members") limited liability. Members have no greater liability for their firm's obligations than do shareholders in a public or private corporation. Unlike limited partners or joint stock owners, the members of an LLC may participate in management without subjecting themselves to personal liability. Alternatively, they may delegate the management of their LLC to one or more managers who do not need to be members.[58]

An LLC is formed by filing Articles of Organization or a similar instrument with the state and paying a filing fee. The Articles of Organization is a public document that contains certain basic information including the company's purpose, place of business, the names and addresses of its initial manager or managers (or, if none, its initial members), and the latest date on which it must dissolve.[59] Yearly thereafter the LLC is required to file an annual report and to pay an annual fee, but it is generally not required to pay the franchise tax or state income tax normally due from corporations.

The operations and management of an LLC are described in an Operating Agreement. Unlike the Articles of Organization, the Operating Agreement is not a public document. The Agreement commonly contains provisions dealing with the voting rights of members, the members' rights to distributions and tax allocations, restrictions on the transfer of members' interests, and the rights of withdrawing members.[60]

common law business trust: A business arrangement in which the owners of a property, known as beneficiaries, transfer legal title to that property to a trustee who then manages it for them. The beneficiaries hold transferable trust certificates entitling them to the income generated by the property and a residual equitable share at the time the trust is terminated. The trustee has unlimited personal liability, whereas the beneficiaries have limited personal liability.

A **business trust** is an association that exists in the United States but not in the rest of the common law world. It is similar to a joint stock company, except that the owners of a property (the beneficiaries) transfer legal title to a trustee who then manages the property for them. The beneficiaries hold transferable trust certificates that entitle them to share in the income from the property and, on the termination of the trust, in the proceeds from its liquidation.[61] As is the case for limited partnerships, the trustees have unlimited personal liability, whereas the liability of the beneficiaries is limited to the amount of their contribution.[62]

Common Law Corporations

There are three main kinds of common law incorporated business entities: public corporations, private corporations, and limited liability companies. Additionally, some common law countries also recognize unlimited liability corporations and no liability corporations.[63]

---

[55]Thomas Earl Geu, "Understanding the Limited Liability Company: A Basic Comparative Primer," *South Dakota Law Review,* vol. 37, p. 44 at p. 45 (1992).

Wyoming acted at the request of a mineral company headquartered in Houston, Texas, that earlier had tried but failed to get limited liability companies authorized in Alaska. *Id.,* p. 48.

[56]In order to be taxed as a partnership rather than as a corporation, an LLC (1) has to be organized in accordance with a U.S. federal or state law that says it is not a corporation and (2) if owned by more than two members, must elect to be taxed as a partnership. *Internal Revenue Regulations,* Title 301, parts 7701-1, 7701-2, 7701-3 (effective January 1, 1997). Prior to 1997, in order for an LLC to be taxed as a partnership it had to lack at least two of the following four corporate characteristics: (1) continuity of life (i.e., the ability to exist in perpetuity), (2) free transferability of interests, (3) centralized management, and (4) limited liability for equity investors. *See* J. William Callison, *Overview of limited liability companies and limited liability partnerships, with particular emphasis on federal income tax aspects of LLCs (1998),* posted at http://www.faegre.com/docs/llc_llp.doc, and Revenue Ruling 93-49, *Internal Revenue Bulletin,* no. 1993-25, p. 11 (1993).

[57]These corporations are known as S Corporations in the U.S. tax code, and they may have no more than 35 shareholders. This numerical limitation does not apply to limited liability companies. Nevertheless, if an LLC has more than 500 members, the U.S. Internal Revenue Service may regard it as a "publicly traded partnership" and tax it as if it were a regular corporation. Robert R. Pluth Jr., "The Limited Liability Company: A New Alternative," *Trusts & Estates,* vol. 133, no. 9, p. 14 (September 1994).

[58]*Id.*

[59]*Id.,* p. 16. Some U.S. states require that an LLC dissolve after a specified number of years—commonly 30. *Id.*

[60]*Id.*

[61]Goldwater v. Oltman, *California Reports,* vol. 210, p. 408 (1930).

[62]Brown v. Bedell, *New York Reports,* vol. 263, p. 177 (1934).

[63]Because there is no standardized nomenclature, the names for the common law business forms used in this textbook are a synthesis of those used in the English-speaking world. Readers should be aware that the same names are sometimes used to describe different entities in different countries. For example, in England a limited liability company is any corporation with limited liability, whereas in the United States, it is the particular business form described in the materials that follow.

common law public corporation: A corporation that can raise money in the public marketplace through the sale of freely transferable shares. Its financial statements have to be disclosed to the public.

Memorandum of Association: An instrument creating and describing the basic details of a particular corporation, which is filed with a state agency at the time of the firm's incorporation.

Articles of Association: An instrument describing the internal regulations of a corporation.

no par share: A share that may be sold by a company for any value. The company may designate a "stated value," and the stated value amount becomes part of the company's capital.

classified stock: Stock that is categorized according to the persons who may own it or by the benefits it gives its owners.

preferred stock: Stock that gives its owners benefits that ordinary stockholders do not have.

cumulative voting: A system of voting by which a voter, having a number of votes equal to the offices to be filled, may concentrate the whole number upon one candidate or may distribute them as he sees fit.

Public corporations are recognized throughout the common law world.[64] In England, where they originated, a public corporation is organized by filing two documents with the Registrar of Companies: a Memorandum of Association and Articles of Association. The first, the **Memorandum of Association**, describes the basic details of the firm: its name, the location of its registered office, its purpose, a statement as to the limited liability of its members, and the capital shares subscribed.[65] The second, the **Articles of Association**, are provisions describing the internal regulations of the corporation, the duties of its directors, voting rights, and so on. A default set of Articles of Association is contained in the English Companies Act of 1985 as "Table A." If a corporation does not register its own Articles of Association, Table A applies. The Articles in Table A apply to the extent they are not excluded or modified by registered Articles.[66]

Prior to 1980, a minimum of seven subscribers were required to set up an English public corporation. The Companies Act of 1980 changed the minimum to two, but it mandated, for the first time, a minimum capitalization.[67] Now £50,000 has to be paid in or committed to the firm before a certificate of incorporation can be issued.[68] This is in keeping with the United Kingdom's role as a member of the European Union, whose other member states feel strongly that a commitment of capital is important for the protection of creditors. In the United States, by comparison, only a single subscriber is needed to incorporate and there is no minimum capital requirement.[69]

It is common for the Memorandum of Association to authorize the issuance of a larger number of shares than those needed to get a business started. Only the shares that are actually issued constitute the corporation's capital; the balance are "authorized but unissued shares." This is unlike the civil law system, where all of the shares authorized must be issued, and any additional issuance requires the filing of an amendment to a company's Articles of Incorporation.

Par shares are the only shares that public corporations may issue in England and most common law countries. **No par shares** (or shares without a specified face value) are the norm, however, in the United States, where their price—for the purpose of establishing the capitalization of a company—is set by the board of directors.[70] Shares may be issued in exchange for cash, property, or services, but when cash is not received a description or contract must be filed with the English Registrar. In the United States, the valuation of property or services exchanged for shares is left up to management, and in England, it is subject to good faith requirements.[71]

In the United States, a corporation may begin doing business as soon as it has filed its Articles of Incorporation with the appropriate governmental agency, usually the Secretary of State.[72] In England, no business can be done and no borrowing powers may be exercised until the Registrar of Companies issues a certificate substantiating that the firm has complied with the minimum share capital requirements set by the 1985 Companies Act.[73]

The stock issued by English and American corporations can be **classified**. **Preferred stock**—which entitles owners to a guaranteed dividend, a priority at the time of liquidation, or some other preference over ordinary shareholders—is permissible in both England and the United States, and widely used in the latter.[74] Also, in the United States, **cumulative voting** (an American innovation that allows minority shareholders to obtain proportionate representation on the board of directors) is either required or permitted by most states.[75]

---

[64]In England, they are known as Public Limited Corporations (PLC); in the United States, they are referred to simply as incorporated companies (Inc.) or corporations (Corp.).

[65]England, Companies Act, §§ 1, 2 (1985).
   In the United States, only Articles of Incorporation (which are similar to the English Memorandum of Association) are filed.

[66]*Id.,* § 8(2) (1985).

[67]The same provision was carried forward in the 1985 Companies Act, § 11.

[68]English corporations may be limited either by shares or by guarantees. Shares represent paid-in capital: guarantees represent commitments of the members to pay in specified amounts upon the winding up of the company. England, Companies Act, § 1(2)(b) (1985).

[69]Revised Model Business Corporation Act, § 2.01 (1984).

[70]The concept of par value was eliminated from the Revised Model Business Corporation Act (1984). This reflected the prevalent practice in the United States, which is for corporations to issue solely no par value shares.

[71]Paul H. Vishny, *Guide to International Commerce Law,* § 6.07 (1981–2001).

[72]Revised Model Business Corporation Act, § 2.03 (1984).

[73]England, Companies Act, §§ 117(1), 117(2) (1985).

[74]*Id.,* § 2(5)(a); U.S. Revised Model Business Corporation Act, § 6.01 (1984).

[75]U.S. Revised Model Business Corporation Act, § 7.28 (1984).
   Cumulative voting works in the following way: The number of votes a shareholder may cast is equal to the

Formal stockholder meetings are required in England to elect the board of directors and to carry out other duties specified in the Articles of Association.[76] In the United States, most of the states allow the shareholders to take all, or nearly all, actions by written consent rather than at a formal meeting.[77] When a meeting is held, a quorum in England is two shareholders present (unless the Articles specify otherwise).[78] In the United States, most states require a simple majority of the voting shares to be represented, and, while the Articles of Incorporation may change the quorum requirements, there is generally a prohibition against setting the quorum at less than a third or a fourth of the voting shares.[79]

In the United States, the corporate board of directors is authorized to declare dividends. The only limits are the requirements that (a) the corporation be solvent, (b) the issuance not violate the Articles of Incorporation, and (c) the source of the dividends be of a certain type (i.e., earnings, surplus, etc.).[80] The English Companies Act, on the other hand, does not specify who is to declare dividends. The model Articles contained in Table A, however, provide for the declaration to be made by the shareholders at their annual meeting, but the amount they can declare cannot exceed the amount recommended by the board of directors.[81]

common law private corporation: A corporation that may not ask the public to subscribe to its shares, bonds, or other securities and that is subject to less stringent public disclosure laws than a public corporation.

A **private corporation** in England is a juridical entity that may not ask the public to subscribe to its shares, bonds, or other securities.[82] Until 1980, private companies were also required to limit the number of their shareholders to 50 and to adopt restrictions on the transfer of shares.[83] Although both restrictions have been eliminated, most private corporations continue to be small in size, and their incorporating documents commonly contain provisions restricting the transfer of shares, including clauses that give the directors absolute direction to refuse a transfer.[84] In the United States, similar companies, known as close or closely held corporations, must meet similar definitional requirements.[85]

The principal advantage of organizing[86] a business as a private or close corporation is that it may dispense with many corporate formalities. In England, for example, a single director may be appointed rather than a board[87] and a shareholder may grant to a proxy all of his rights to attend and speak at meetings.[88] In the United States, the board of directors may be entirely dispensed with and the corporation may be run directly by the shareholders.[89]

---

number of shares he has, multiplied by the number of directors to be elected. All the nominees then stand for election at the same time.

[76]*Halsbury's Law of England,* vol. 7(1), para. 560 (1988).

[77]Paul H. Vishny, *Guide to International Commerce Law,* § 6.18 (1981–2001). And *see* Revised Model Business Corporation Act, § 7.04 (1984).

[78]England, Companies Act, § 370 (1985).

[79]Paul H. Vishny, *Guide to International Commerce Law,* § 6.18 (1981–2001). And *see* Revised Model Business Corporation Act, § 7.25 (1984).

[80]Revised Model Business Corporation Act, § 6.40 (1984).

[81]Paul H. Vishny, *Guide to International Commerce Law,* § 6.21 (1981–2001). *See* The Companies (Tables A to F) Regulations, Article 102 (1985).

[82]The name of a private company in England, with certain exceptions, must include the word *Limited* or its abbreviation, *Ltd.* In some British Commonwealth countries, the name must include the word *Proprietary* or its abbreviation, *Pty.* In the United States, no special name is given to the equivalent close corporations.

[83]England, Companies Act, §§ 28, 455(1) (1948).

[84]Paul H. Vishny, *Guide to International Commerce Law,* § 6.28 (1981–2001).

[85]Model Statutory Close Corporation Supplement to the Revised Model Business Corporations Act, § 3 (1984).

In addition to close corporations, a special corporate form—the professional corporation—is also recognized in virtually all U.S. states. The members of a professional corporation may only be certain designated professionals, including certified public accountants, doctors, and lawyers. The main reason professionals establish these corporations is that they give them better tax-planning, retirement, and disability options. *Corpus Juris Secundum,* vol. 18, § 5 (1995). In the majority of states that authorize the professional corporation, each professional member is liable for the professional malpractice of all the members, but is not individually liable for the nonprofessional obligations of the corporation. Professional corporations do not exist outside of the United States.

[86]The organizational procedures are essentially the same as those for public corporations. *See Halsbury's Laws of England,* vol. 7(1), para. 78 (1988); and Model Statutory Close Corporation Supplement to the Revised Model Business Corporations Act, § 3(a) (1984).

[87]England, Companies Act, § 282(3) (1985).

[88]*Id.,* § 372(1).

For other advantages of a private corporation *vis-à-vis* a public corporation, *see Halsbury's Laws of England,* vol. 7(1), para. 103 (1988). The main advantage of a private corporation as compared to a limited partnership is that the shareholding directors may assume the management of the private corporation without the risk of having unlimited liability for the debts it may incur. *Id.,* para. 104.

[89]Model Statutory Close Corporation Supplement to the Revised Model Business Corporations Act, §§ 20–21 (1984).

**common law unlimited
liability company:** A
corporation whose
members are liable in
the event it is wound
up and its assets are
insufficient to cover
its debts.

**common law no liability
corporation:** A corpora-
tion whose sharehold-
ers are not obligated to
pay any call for contri-
butions made by the
firm or to pay any of
the firm's debts, but
who will not receive
any dividends if a call is
due and unpaid.

An **unlimited liability corporation** is a company known in England[90] and in many of the Commonwealth countries[91] but not in the United States. The members of such a corporation are liable in the event that it is wound up and its assets are insufficient to cover its debts. These corporations are not subject to the same scrutiny as public and private corporations, and the annual information return they have to submit to the government is quite minimal.[92]

A **no liability corporation** is a company unique to Australia, where such companies are used for the operation of mines. A person who accepts a share in a no liability mining company is not obligated to pay any call for contributions made by the firm or to pay any of the firm's debts. The corporation, on the other hand, will not pay any dividends to a shareholder who has not paid on a call that is due and unpaid, and if the call remains unpaid for a prescribed period of time the share will be forfeited.[93]

The Importance of the Separate Legal Identity of Juridical Entities

Corporations and certain other companies[94] are juridical entities that have legal identities separate from that of their owners. This separate legal identity has several important consequences. First, it means that the liability of the owners is limited to their investment in their company. Thus, a company's owners are usually not required to pay the company's obligations from their personal estates. Second, it means that rights and benefits accruing to the company belong to the company and not its owners. In other words, only a company may lay claim to its own property. Additionally, for some companies (i.e., most kinds of corporations), the owners are neither managers nor agents nor representatives of the company; they may not on their own make decisions on behalf of the company, nor commit the company to perform contractually, nor commit crimes, torts, or delicts that would impose liability on the company.

In Case 4–2, the International Court of Justice was asked to ignore the separate legal identity of a Canadian corporation owned principally by Belgian nationals so that Belgium could bring a claim on the owners' behalf. The Court refused to do so.

---

[90]England, Companies Act, § 1(2)(c) (1985); *Halsbury's Laws of England,* vol. 7(1), para. 78 (1988).
[91]E.g., in Australia. "Australia Law Digest," *Martindale-Hubbell Law Digest,* p. AUS-19 (1998).
[92]*Halsbury's Laws of England,* vol. 7(1), para. 114 (1988).
[93]"Australia Law Digest," *Martindale-Hubbell Law Digest,* p. AUS-20 (1998).
[94]As discussed earlier, all companies in France are juridical entities. In Germany, however, partnerships are not juridi-
    cal entities, but other companies (including limited partnerships) are. In the common law countries, only corpora-
    tions (including limited liability companies) are juridical entities; partnerships and limited partnerships are not.

Case 4–2 Case Concerning Barcelona Traction, Light and Power Co. (Second Phase)

Belgium v. Spain

International Court of Justice, 1970.
International Court of Justice Reports, vol. 1970, p. 3 (1970); *International Law Reports,* vol. 46, p. 178 (1973).

The Barcelona Traction, Light, and Power Co. was incorporated in 1911 under Canadian law for the purpose of supplying electricity in Spain. In 1938, Spain declared the company bankrupt and took other actions detrimental to it and its shareholders. Canada would not bring a suit in the International Court of Justice, but, since an alleged 88 percent of the shareholders were Belgian, Belgium did. Spain objected

that Belgium could not sponsor a complaint on behalf of Barcelona Traction's owners because only the corporation had been injured and the corporation was not Belgian.

JUDGMENT OF THE COURT: . . .

Seen in historical perspective, the corporate personality represents a development brought about by new and expanding requirements in the economic field, an entity which in particular allows of operation in circumstances which exceed the normal capacity of individuals. As

MAP 4-2   Belgium and Spain (1970)

and shareholder is an important manifestation of this distinction. So long as the company is in existence, the shareholder has no right to the corporate assets.

It is a basic characteristic of the corporate structure that the company alone, through its directors or management acting in its name, can take action in respect of matters that are of a corporate character. The underlying justification for this is that, in seeking to serve its own best interests, the company will serve those of the shareholder too. Ordinarily, no individual shareholder can take legal steps, either in the name of the company or in his own name. If the shareholders disagree with the decisions taken on behalf of the company they may, in accordance with its articles or the relevant provisions of the law, change them or replace its officers, or take such action as is provided by law. Thus to protect the company against abuse by its management or the majority of shareholders, several municipal legal systems have vested in shareholders (sometimes a particular number is specified) the right to bring an action for the defense of the company, and conferred upon the minority of shareholders certain rights of the company *vis-à-vis*[95] its management or controlling shareholders. Nonetheless the shareholders' rights in relation to the company and its assets remain limited, this being, moreover, a corollary of the limited nature of their liability.

At this point the Court would recall that in forming a company, its promoters are guided by all the various factors involved, the advantages and disadvantages of which they take into account. So equally does a shareholder, whether he is an original subscriber of capital or a subsequent purchaser of the company's shares from another shareholder. He may be seeking safety of investment, high dividends or capital appreciation—or a combination of two or more of these. Whichever it is, it does not alter the legal status of the corporate entity or affect the rights of the shareholder. In any event he is bound to take account of the risk of reduced dividends, capital depreciation or even loss, resulting from ordinary commercial hazards or from prejudice caused to the company by illegal treatment of some kind.

Notwithstanding the separate corporate personality, a wrong done to the company frequently causes prejudice to its shareholders. But the mere fact that damage is sustained by both company and shareholder does not imply that both are entitled to claim compensation. Thus no legal conclusion can be drawn from the fact that the same event caused damage simultaneously affecting several natural or juristic persons. Creditors do not have any right to claim compensation from a person who, by wronging their debtor, causes them loss. In such cases, no doubt, the interests of the aggrieved are affected, but not their rights. Thus whenever a shareholder's interests are harmed by an act done to the company, it is to the latter that he must

such, it has become a powerful factor in the economic life of nations. Of this, municipal law has had to take due account, whence the increasing volume of rules governing the creation and operation of corporate entities, endowed with a specific status. These entities have rights and obligations peculiar to themselves.

There is, however, no need to investigate the many different forms of legal entity provided for by the municipal laws of states, because the Court is concerned only with that exemplified by the company involved in the present case: Barcelona Traction—a limited liability company whose capital is represented by shares. There are, indeed, other associations, whatever the name attached to them by municipal legal systems, that do not enjoy independent corporate personality. The legal difference between the two kinds of entity is that for the limited liability company it is the overriding tie of legal personality which is determinant; for the other associations, the continuing autonomy of the several members.

Municipal law determines the legal situation not only of such limited liability companies but also of those persons who hold shares in them. Separated from the company by numerous barriers, the shareholder cannot be identified with it. The concept and structure of the company are founded on and determined by a firm distinction between the separate entity of the company and that of the shareholder, each with a distinct set of rights. The separation of property rights as between company

---

[95French: "face to face"; in relation to each other.]

look to institute appropriate action; for although two separate entities may have suffered from the same wrong, it is only one entity whose rights have been infringed.

However, it has been argued in the present case that a company represents purely a means of achieving the economic purpose of its members, namely the shareholders, while they themselves constitute in fact the reality behind it. It has furthermore been repeatedly emphasized that there exists between a company and its shareholders a relationship describable as a community of destiny. The alleged acts may have been directed at the company and not the shareholders, but only in a formal sense: in reality, company and shareholders are so closely interconnected that prejudicial acts committed against the former necessarily wrong the latter; hence any acts directed against a company can be conceived as directed against its shareholders, because both can be considered in substance, i.e., from the economic viewpoint, identical. Yet even if a company is no more than a means for its shareholders to achieve their economic purpose, so long as it is *in esse*[96] it enjoys an independent existence. Therefore, the interests of the shareholders are both separable and indeed separated from those of the company, so that the possibility of their diverging cannot be denied.

It has also been contended that the measures complained of, although taken with respect to Barcelona Traction and causing it direct damage, constituted an unlawful act *vis-à-vis* Belgium, because they also, though indirectly, caused damage to the Belgian shareholders in Barcelona Traction. This again is merely a different way of presenting the distinction between injury in respect of a right and injury to a simple interest. But, as the Court

has indicated, evidence that damage was suffered does not *ipso facto*[97] justify a diplomatic claim. Persons suffer damage or harm in most varied circumstances. This in itself does not involve the obligation to make reparation. Not a mere interest affected, but solely a right infringed involves responsibility, so that an act directed against and infringing only the company's rights does not involve responsibility towards the shareholders, even if their interests are affected.

The situation is different if the act complained of is aimed at the direct rights of the shareholder as such. It is well known that there are rights which municipal law confers upon the latter distinct from those of the company, including the right to any declared dividend, the right to attend and vote at general meetings, the right to share in the residual assets of the company on liquidation. Whenever one of his direct rights is infringed, the shareholder has an independent right of action. On this there is no disagreement between the parties. But a distinction must be drawn between a direct infringement of the shareholder's rights, and difficulties or financial losses to which he may be exposed as the result of the situation of the company.

The Court found that the injured party was the company and not its owners. Therefore, Belgium could not bring suit against Spain on behalf of the company's Belgian owners.

The Court noted that Spain had made no objection to Canada bringing a complaint if it chose to do so. "The Canadian government's right of protection in respect of the Barcelona Traction Company," the Court concluded, "remains unaffected by the present proceedings." Canada, nevertheless, chose not to complain. ∎

[96Latin: "in being"; in actual existence.]
[97Latin: "by that very fact."]

B. THE MULTINATIONAL ORGANIZATION

The Parent Company

To carry out operations internationally, large business firms have adapted their organizational structures to share risks and to take advantage of economies of scale. The simplest international operating structure is the "nonmultinational enterprise," in which a firm organized in one country contracts with an independent foreign firm to carry out sales or purchasing abroad. Somewhat more complex is the "national multinational enterprise," in which a parent firm established in one country establishes wholly owned branches and subsidiaries in other countries. The most complex is the "international multinational enterprise" made up of two or more parents from different countries that co-own operating businesses in two or more countries.

The Nonmultinational Enterprise

nonmultinational enterprise: A domestic firm that operates internationally through independent foreign agents.

Many domestic firms function in the international marketplace through a foreign agent. The agent, who may be a private individual or an independent firm, acts on behalf of the domestic firm or "principal" to either sell the principal's goods or services abroad (in which case the agent is commonly called a "sales representative") or to buy goods or procure services for the principal (the agent sometimes being called a "factor"). Neither the principal nor the agent are truly multi-

Parent company	Company that acts as the head office for a multinational enterprise and that owns and controls the enterprise's subordinate entities.
Branch	Unit or part of a company. It is not separately incorporated.
Agent	An independent person or company with authority to act on behalf of the enterprise.
Representative office	A contact point where interested parties can obtain information about the company. It does not conduct business for the company.
Holding company	Company owned by parent or parents to supervise and coordinate the operations of subsidiary companies.
Subsidiary	Company owned by a parent or a parent's holding company. Unlike a branch, it is separately incorporated.
Joint venture	An association of persons or companies collaborating in a business venture for more than a transitory time period. May be set up as an association or a company.

EXHIBIT 4-2   The Parts of a Multinational Enterprise

national enterprises, however, because neither operates outside its home state. Their relationship is governed by an agency contract and by the agency laws of the home and host countries.

The National Multinational Enterprise

national multinational enterprise: An enterprise organized around a parent firm established in one state that operates through branches and subsidiaries in other states.

A **national multinational enterprise** consists of a firm in one country—the "parent"—operating in other countries through branches and subsidiaries. A branch is a unit or a part of the parent (such as an overseas purchasing office, assembly plant, manufacturing plant, or sales office), whereas a subsidiary is a company organized as a separate legal entity that is owned by the parent.

The parents of national multinationals are most likely to be found in the United States, Europe, or Japan. Examples are the Ford Motor Company, DaimlerChrysler, and the Mitsubishi Group (see Exhibit 4-3).[98] Incorporated in the United States in the state of Michigan in 1903, the Ford Motor Company in its early years employed sales representatives in many foreign countries. As sales increased, branch sales offices were opened, then branch assembly plants. Because of tax considerations and to insulate the parent company from local liability, the branches were converted into locally organized subsidiaries. For a brief period (from the late 1920s to the late 1940s), some of the foreign subsidiaries were jointly owned by local investors; but following World War II, Ford reacquired direct ownership of its entire overseas operation.

DaimlerChrysler, the world's third largest automobile manufacturer (after General Motors and Ford) was formed out of the merger of the German Daimler-Benz Company and the American Chrysler Corporation in 1998. Daimler-Benz itself was itself formed through the merger of two German companies, Daimler and Benz, in 1926. Chrysler began in 1920 when Walter Chrysler took over the Maxwell Motor Co., which was in receivership. He later named the company after himself, and then acquired the Dodge Motor Co. The merged DaimlerChrysler company is organized as a German *Aktiengesellschat* and headquartered in Stuttgart, Germany. Its North American operations are run as a division of the parent company. DaimlerChrysler also owns as subsidiaries Freightliner (a U.S. truck manufacturer), Western Star (a Canadian truck manufacturer), and Detroit Diesel (a heavy motor manufacturer).

The Mitsubishi Group is a Japanese multinational made up of about 40 individual companies. Unlike Ford, however, there is no parent company. Each of the Mitsubishi companies owns substantial portions of the shares of the others. Instead of a parent company exercising control over subsidiaries, the Group operates under the direction of a triumvirate of the three most important sister companies: the Mitsubishi Bank, the Mitsubishi Corporation, and Mitsubishi Heavy Industries. The senior managers of these three companies act as the cochairmen of a coordinating board called the Kinyo-Kai, or "Friday Conference." The Kinyo-Kai, which is made up of the top executives of 26 of the Mitsubishi companies, establishes common policies as a sort of "senior board of directors" for the entire Group.

---

[98]For a more detailed discussion of these companies, and the companies discussed in the following paragraphs, *see Hoover's Handbook of World Business 2002* (Hoover's Inc., 2002) at www.hoovers.com/.

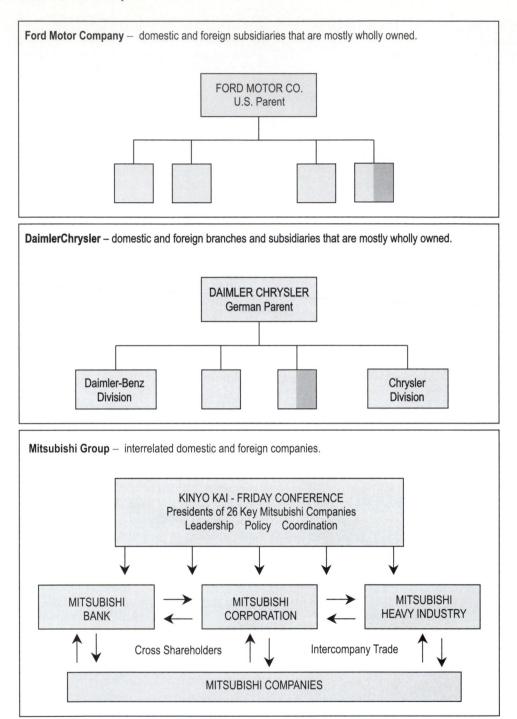

EXHIBIT 4-3   National Multinationals Enterprises

Sources: Hoover's Handbook of World Business 2002 (Hoover's Inc., 2002) and Robert E. Tindall, *Multi-national Enterprises: Legal & Management Structures & Interrelationship with Ownership, Control, Antitrust, Labor, Taxation, & Disclosure* (Dobbs Ferry, NY: Oceana Publications, 1975).

international multi-national enterprise: An enterprise made up of two or more parents from different states that co-own subordinate operating businesses in two or more states.

The International Multinational Enterprise

The **international multinational enterprise** is like a national multinational in that it operates through subsidiaries. The difference lies in its having two or more parent companies located in different states. Most international multinationals have come about from the merger of parent firms operating in different Western European countries.

Examples of international multinationals are Unilever, the Royal Dutch/Shell Group, and Reed Elsevier (see Exhibit 4-4).

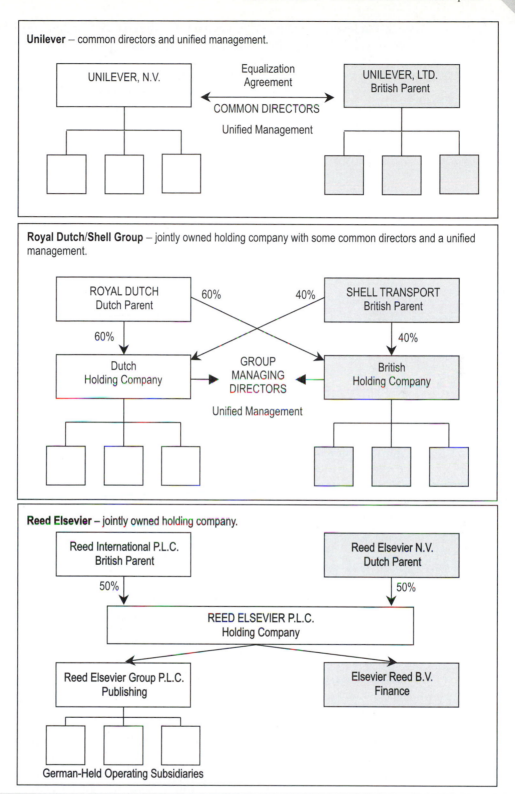

EXHIBIT 4-4   International Multinational Enterprises with Common Directorates

Sources: Hoover's Handbook of World Business 2002 (Hoover's Inc., 2002) and Robert E. Tindall, *Multinational Enterprises: Legal & Management Structures & Interrelationship with Ownership, Control, Antitrust, Labor, Taxation, & Disclosure* (Dobbs Ferry, NY: Oceana Publications, 1975).

Unilever, a consumer goods manufacturer, is a combination of Dutch and British parent companies that together own and operate subsidiaries around the world. The two parent companies are governed by an "equalization agreement" that has been incorporated into the Articles of Association of both. It arranges for the boards of both parents to be made up of the same individuals, and it guarantees equal treatment for both companies' shareholders.[99] To ensure that the directors are the same, both parents have set up wholly owned subsidiaries and transferred half of a special class of their own shares to each of these subsidiaries. This special class of shares has the exclusive right to nominate directors; the ordinary shareholders are only allowed to elect directors who are nominated by the wholly owned subsidiaries.

The Royal Dutch/Shell Group, an oil and gas company, is another combination of Dutch and British parents. Rather than having common directors sit on the boards of the two parents, the two parents jointly own two holding companies that in turn own the operating subsidiaries. The two holding companies share some directors in common, and these serve as the managing directors of the entire Group.

Reed Elsevier, a publishing and financing firm, is a third Dutch-British combination that came into being in 1993. Reed International P.L.C, incorporated in the United Kingdom, and Elsevier N.V., incorporated in the Netherlands, each own 50 percent of Reed Elsevier P.L.C., a holding company incorporated in the United Kingdom that owns the Reed Elsevier Group P.L.C., which operates publishing and information businesses, and Elsevier Reed Finance B.V., which is a financing firm.

Public Transnational Enterprises

A special variation of the international multinational enterprise is the **public transnational enterprise**. This is a government-controlled multinational enterprise created by a treaty between two or more states. An example is Air Afrique (see Exhibit 4-5).

The Subordinate Structure

To do business internationally, companies must establish a foreign presence. This requires the creation of subordinate entities, such as representative offices, agencies, branches, subsidiaries, joint ventures, and holding companies. See Exhibit 4-2 on page 203.

A **representative office** does not actually conduct business; rather, it functions as a foreign contact point where interested parties can obtain information about a particular firm.

An **agent** is an individual who is employed as an independent representative of a firm. Agents are subject to the supervision of the parent firm (or principal), and the authority that they can exercise is limited to what the parent delegates to them.

A **branch** is a unit of the parent company that involves not only the placement of individuals in a particular locale, but also the establishment of a facility, such as an assembly plant, mining operation, or service office. As with an agency, the authority of branch personnel, including the manager and employees, is limited to what the parent has delegated.

Establishing representative offices, agencies, and branches is advantageous because these entities allow the parent to maintain direct control of the foreign operation. The practice can be disadvantageous, however, because (1) the parent has to assume all of the risk of investing abroad, (2) a foreign firm (or its agent or its branch) is often taxed at higher rates than local firms, and (3) many developing states require local participation in order for a foreign firm to either invest or expand its local investment.

Because of these disadvantages, many multinational enterprises set up subsidiaries, joint ventures, and holding companies.

A **subsidiary** is an independently organized and incorporated company. Setting up a subsidiary can benefit a multinational firm because the subsidiary's company status insulates the parent from unlimited liability and because locally organized companies are commonly entitled to certain tax benefits that foreign branches are not.

A **joint venture** is an association of persons or companies that are involved in a "collaboration for more than a transitory period."[100] It can assume any type of business form, including

public transnational enterprises: A government-controlled multinational created by a treaty between two or more states.

representative office: A contact point where interested parties can obtain information about a company. It does not conduct business for the company.

agent: An independent person or company with authority to act on behalf of another.

branch: Unit or part of a company. It is not separately incorporated.

subsidiary: Company owned by a parent or a parent's holding company. Unlike a branch, it is separately incorporated.

joint venture: An association of persons or companies collaborating in a business venture for more than a transitory time period.

---

[99] The dividends paid to both companies' shareholders have to be the same; and both companies' shareholders are given the same rights should the enterprise ever be liquidated.

[100] Wolfgang G. Friedmann and George Kalmanoff, eds., *Joint International Business Venture*, p. 1 (1961).

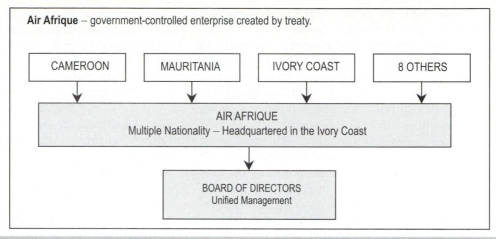

Air Afrique – government-controlled enterprise created by treaty.

```
CAMEROON          MAURITANIA          IVORY COAST          8 OTHERS
   │                  │                    │                   │
   ▼                  ▼                    ▼                   ▼
┌──────────────────────────────────────────────────────────────┐
│                        AIR AFRIQUE                             │
│        Multiple Nationality – Headquartered in the Ivory Coast │
└──────────────────────────────────────────────────────────────┘
                              │
                              ▼
                   ┌─────────────────────┐
                   │  BOARD OF DIRECTORS  │
                   │   Unified Management │
                   └─────────────────────┘
```

EXHIBIT 4-5   Public Transnational Enterprises

Sources: Hoover's Handbook of World Business 2002 (Hoover's Inc., 2002) and Robert E. Tindall, *Multinational Enterprises: Legal & Management Structures & Interrelationship with Ownership, Control, Antitrust, Labor, Taxation, & Disclosure* (Dobbs Ferry, NY: Oceana Publications, 1975).

that of an association, a partnership, a limited partnership, a secret partnership, or a limited liability company. Multinational enterprises use joint ventures as a way to share risk and to facilitate entry into foreign markets. Although the joint venturers may be from the same home state or two different home states, more commonly at least one is from the host state. Indeed, many developing states insist on local participation, and a joint venture may be the only practicable form for carrying on business in such a place.

holding company:
Company owned by a parent or parents to supervise and coordinate the operations of subsidiary companies.

A **holding company** is a subsidiary company that in turn owns other subsidiaries. Holding companies are created primarily (a) to establish a consolidated management team for a group of subsidiaries or subsidiaries owned by different parents or (b) for tax advantages (as we will discuss in chapter 13). Commonly, a holding company is a limited liability company whose shares are held by its parent or parents.

C. INTERNATIONAL REGULATION OF MULTINATIONAL ENTERPRISES

Rules of ethical behavior for multinational enterprises have been promulgated by several international organizations, including the Organization for Economic Cooperation and Development (OECD), the International Labor Organization (ILO), and the World Bank. Until recently, these were only suggested rules that multinationals were asked to voluntarily comply with, and most international rules continue to be voluntary.[101] One recent proposal for a voluntary compliance rule is described in Reading 4–1.

---

[101]The most recent guidelines are those of the World Bank Group, published in September 1992. They do not purport to establish a code of behavior for multinational enterprises; instead, they attempt to encourage foreign investment. Nevertheless, states are urged to take appropriate measures to prevent corrupt business practices and to cooperate in developing international procedures in this area. "World Bank Guidelines on the Treatment of Foreign Direct Investment," *ICSID Review—Foreign Investment Law Journal,* vol. 7, p. 297 (1992). The guidelines are also reproduced in *International Legal Materials,* vol. 31, p. 1363 (1992).

Reading 4–1   Proposed ISO Standard for Global Business Conduct

Alison Maitland, "An Acid Test for Better Conduct in Business," *Financial Times,* August 12 2001.

Unlike the Ten Commandments, there is little that is black and white about the many international agreements and principles drawn up in the past few years to promote ethical business conduct.

They abound with statements about contributing to economic progress, respecting human rights, promoting sustainable development and adhering to international and local rules. Most of these are open to interpretation, reflecting the difficulty of defining and agreeing what constitutes ethical and unethical behavior.

Now a completely different approach, creating an International Standards Organization standard for global business conduct, is being proposed by the U.S. Ethics Officer Association, a non-profit organization representing 400 mainly U.S.-based multinationals. Its members include General Motors, Microsoft, Pfizer, Philip Morris, and Royal Dutch/Shell.

"An ISO standard is all about process, not aspirations or objectives," says Edward Petry, executive director of the EOA. "It provides specific guidance as to what any new management system must include and it hopes to achieve consistency, clarity and measurability of internal processes."

Sergio Mazza, former president and chief executive of the American National Standards Institute (ANSI), says that the initiative is radical.

"Good business practice will be built into the culture and management systems of the company in the same way as quality or good financial controls," he says.

Modeled on the ISO 9000 standard for quality management and the ISO 14000 for environmental management, it would set out the internal structures, processes and resources that organizations need to ensure that they adhere to their stated principles. It would require them to draw up a policy for business conduct, implement it, assess how well it is working, make improvements and keep it under review.

On August 27, Mr. Petry and his team will put their case to the international committee of the ANSI. If approved, the proposal would go to the International Organization of Standardization in Geneva. Work on the standard would start once it had secured the support of national standards bodies in five countries.

The initiative is being driven by EOA members that are under pressure from stakeholders and the financial community to provide assurance of their own ethical commitments and are concerned about the potential risk to their reputation from relations with joint venture partners and suppliers, says Mr. Petry. An international standard may also help to fend off a series of requests to sign up to alternative codes and guidelines.

Significantly, the EOA is proposing that companies should be able to declare that they comply with the standard without having to seek certification by an external body.

"The standard we're proposing does not require third-party certification," he says. "We're hoping it will avoid some of the more costly regulations that might come—and some of the cost and burden of other standards being proposed. Many of our members feel they have years of experience in auditing and assessing their own programs and they can do that much better than most of the third-party certifiers."

Why should anybody take a company's word for it? "It comes down to who is making the declaration," says Mr. Mazza. "If the company has a sterling reputation and says: 'We comply', its customers will accept it. If it's a little company out of Taiwan that you've never heard of and it self-declares [compliance], people will say: 'I don't know about that.'"

Mr. Petry accepts that a lack of mandatory certification will not satisfy some stakeholder groups, "the ones that are very suspicious of business". Some companies may opt for external accreditation to comply with customers' or regulatory requirements or to enhance their reputation.

He says interested parties such as aid agencies will be able to take part in drawing up the standard. "It's not going to do away with the need for continued pressure and scrutiny from the NGO and stakeholder community but we think it will provide a useful tool to ensure that whatever progress is made is effective and measurable."

Might this not be rather self-serving for the EOA's members? Large companies that already have codes of practice and the resources and systems to communicate and implement them should not find it unduly burdensome to comply with the proposed standard. Smaller companies with less clout may be put off by the time and effort involved and by the cost of third-party verification. How will it allay concerns about the power of multinationals and the negative effects of globalization?

John Drummond, managing director of Integrity Works, an ethical business consultancy in the United Kingdom, says the search for universally accepted principles of good business conduct must continue. But some companies are using the lack of consensus as an excuse for failing to take the issue seriously.

"This [proposed standard] is saying: 'You don't have to wait. We can judge your processes against your own statement of values.' There's no ducking and diving if you come up short." ■

The main exception to the rule that international guidelines for ethical behavior should be voluntary is the OECD-sponsored *Convention on Combating Bribery of Foreign Public Officials in International Business Transactions*.[102] Adopted by 34 states in

---

[102]The Convention is posted at www.oecd.org//daf/nocorruption/20nov1e.htm.

1997[103] and ratified by all 34 states as of September 2001.[104] The Convention requires states parties to outlaw the "active bribery" of foreign officials. That is, states must make it a crime for individuals and juridical persons to bribe or attempt to bribe a foreign official. They are not required, however, to outlaw the acceptance of bribes.

The United States, which was the main advocate of the OECD Convention, has outlawed the bribing of foreign officials since 1977. Indeed, it pushed for adoption of the Convention in order to get its own multinational enterprises on a more level playing field with competitors from other countries, and it was one of the first countries to ratify the Convention.[105] The U.S. Foreign Corrupt Practices Act (discussed later in this chapter) is typical of the legislation currently being enacted in other countries to implement the Convention.[106]

Although the OECD Convention proves that international organizations can sponsor Conventions that regulate the ethical behavior of multinational establishes, most such regulation is a matter of municipal law. As a general rule, home states regulate the parent companies and host states regulate the subordinates. Sometimes, however, home states are able to regulate foreign subordinates with extraterritorial laws, and host states are able to regulate parent firms by piercing the fictional veil that separates the subordinates from their parents. We discuss both sorts of regulations in the materials that follow.

D. HOME STATE REGULATION OF MULTINATIONAL ENTERPRISES

To the extent that a multinational enterprise operates within the domestic marketplace of its home country, the home country regulates it in the same way that national enterprises are regulated. The most important forms of national regulation include (a) the regulation of competition, (b) the regulation of injuries caused by defective products, (c) the prohibition of sharp sales practices, (d) the regulation of securities, (e) the regulation of labor and employment, (f) the establishment of accounting standards, and (g) taxation. With the growth of international trade, many of these rules have been applied to activities that take place outside the territorial boundaries of a particular state, most notably, the first three: the regulation of competition, regulation of injuries caused by defective products, and the prohibition against fraudulent sales practices.[107] The country most willing to apply its laws extraterritorially has been the United States, an inclination the international community has not received kindly. Indeed, most countries regard such action as an intrusion into their domestic affairs. The United States has, nevertheless, persisted; and another major player in the international commercial community, the European Union, has begun to apply its internal regulations extraterritorially as well.

Unfair Competition Laws

Sherman Antitrust Act, Section 1: Forbids combinations and conspiracies in restraint of interstate and international trade.

rule of reason: Rule applied by courts on a case-by-case basis requiring them to consider all of the circumstances in deciding whether a restrictive practice should be prohibited as imposing an unreasonable restraint on competition in violation of Sherman Act § 1.

In the United States, the principal law regulating anticompetitive activity is the **Sherman Antitrust Act** of 1890. **Section 1** of the act prohibits contracts, agreements, and conspiracies that restrain interstate or international trade.[108] The American courts have interpreted this as applying only to conduct between two or more parties, and only to contracts that unreasonably restrain trade. In determining whether a particular activity violates §1, the courts ordinarily do so on a case-by-case basis using a so-called **rule of reason**. That is, "the factfinder weighs all of the circumstances of a case in deciding whether a restrictive practice should be prohibited as imposing an unreasonable restraint on competition."[109] Over the years, however, certain agreements or joint actions involving interstate

---

[103]The signatories were the 29 OECD member states plus Argentina, Brazil, Bulgaria, Chile, and the Slovak Republic.

[104]OECD, *Report of the Committee on International Investments and Multinational Enterprises, Convention on Combating Bribery of Foreign Public Officials in International Business Transactions and the 1997 Recommendation* posted at www.oecd.org/pdf/M00029000/M00029509.pdf.

[105]The U.S. Senate ratified the Convention on July 31, 1997.

[106]For a description of the actions being taken by states to implement the OECD Convention, *see* OECD, *Update On Steps Taken by Countries to Implement the Convention* (April 25, 2002), www.oecd.org/pdf/M00025000/M00025443.pdf.

[107]The other forms of regulation are discussed in later chapters.

[108]Sherman Antitrust Act of 1890, *United States Code,* Title 15, § 1: "Every contract, combination in the form of trust or otherwise, or conspiracy, in restraint of trade or commerce among the several states, or with foreign nations, is declared to be illegal. . . ."

[109]Business Elecs. Corp. v. Sharp Elecs. Corp., *United States Reports,* vol. 458, p. 717 at 723 (Supreme Ct. 1988).

(but not international) trade have come to be classified as automatically illegal, or *per se*[110] violations. These include (1) horizontal price fixing (where competitors at the same level expressly or impliedly agree to charge the same price for competing products), (2) vertical price fixing (where a seller at one level sells goods to a buyer at a different level on the condition that the latter will not resell below an agreed-upon price), (3) horizontal market division (where competitors agree not to sell in each other's territories), and (4) joint refusals to deal (i.e., group boycotts). Once a particular kind of activity is classified as a *per se* violation, the courts do not apply the case-by-case rule of reason analysis, but proceed directly to a consideration of the appropriate remedy in the particular case.

Sherman Antitrust Act, Section 2: Forbids monopolies and attempts to monopolize interstate and international trade.

Section 2 of the Sherman Antitrust Act forbids monopolies and attempts to monopolize commerce or trade either between the states of the United States or in international commerce affecting the United States.[111] Unlike Section 1, it applies to the conduct of a single enterprise, if the enterprise is a "dominant firm"; that is, a firm that "has the power to control the price" of the commodity it produces and has the ability to "exclude competitors from the market." To prove a violation, a plaintiff has to show that the defendant intended to monopolize the marketplace. This is normally done circumstantially, by showing a practice of discriminatory pricing, of dumping (i.e., selling goods below their cost of production), of using tying clauses (i.e., requiring purchasers of one product to buy other unrelated products), or similar conduct.

Clayton Act: Expands the enforcement provisions of the Sherman Antitrust Act. Defines exclusive dealing and tying clauses, mergers that result in monopolies, and interlocking directorates as being unfair business practices.

Robinson-Patman Act: Forbids price discrimination.

The **Clayton Act** of 1914 was enacted to give more teeth to the Sherman Antitrust Act, both by expanding its enforcement provisions and by defining certain specific acts that constitute unfair business competition. These include exclusive dealing and tying clauses, mergers that result in a monopoly, and interlocking directorates.[112] The **Robinson-Patman Act** of 1936 was added to the panoply of American antitrust law to make price discrimination illegal.[113]

Enforcement Provisions of U.S. Antitrust Laws

The enforcement provisions of the American antitrust acts are one of their two most controversial aspects. The U.S. Justice Department may bring criminal suits for egregious violations, and the U.S. Federal Trade Commission may bring civil actions (notably for injunctions) to ensure full compliance. More important, private persons are given the right to sue and recover treble damages for injuries they have suffered. This statutory treble damages provision has attracted foreign plaintiffs to American courts like flies to dead meat. One famous case was filed in the early 1980s by Laker Airways, a British air carrier, which brought a multimillion dollar action in the District Court for the District of Columbia against Pan American Airways, British Airways, British Caledonian, and other foreign airlines to take advantage of the treble damages provision that was unavailable in the home countries of the non-American defendants.[114]

---

[110]Latin: "by or in itself"; intrinsically.

[111]Sherman Antitrust Act of 1890, *United States Code,* Title 15, § 2: "Every person who shall monopolize, or attempt to monopolize, or combine or conspire with any other person or persons, to monopolize any part of the trade or commerce among the several states, or with foreign nations, shall be deemed guilty of a felony...."

[112]The Clayton Act of 1914, *United States Code,* Title 14, § 12: "(3) It shall be unlawful for any person engaged in commerce, in the course of such commerce, to lease or make a sale or contract for sale ... on the condition, agreement or understanding that the ... purchaser or lessee thereof shall not use or deal in the goods ... of a competitor of the seller." "(7) No corporation engaged in commerce shall acquire, directly or indirectly, the whole or any part of the stock ... or ... assets of another corporation, where in any line of commerce in any section of the country, the effect may be to substantially lessen the competition, or tend to create a monopoly." "(8) ... [N]o person at the same time shall be a director in any two or more competing corporations, any one of which has capital, surplus, and undivided profits aggregating more than $1 million, engaged in whole or in part in commerce, other than banks, banking associations, trust companies, and common carriers."

[113]Robinson-Patman Act of 1936, *id.,* Title 15, § 13: "It shall be unlawful for any person engaged in commerce, in the course of such commerce, either directly or indirectly, to discriminate in price between different purchasers of goods of like grade and quality [where the effect of such discrimination] may be to substantially lessen competition or tend to create a monopoly in any line of commerce, or injure, destroy, or prevent competition with any person who either grants or knowingly receives the benefit of such discrimination, or with customers of either of them...."

Other acts expand on these basic provisions, including the Federal Trade Commission Act, *id.,* Title 15, § 45; the Hart-Scott-Rodino Improvements Act of 1976, *id.,* Title 15, § 18a; the National Cooperative Research and Production Act, *id.,* Title 15, §§ 4301–4306; the Webb-Pomerene Act, *id.,* Title 15, §§ 61–65; and the Export Trading Company Act of 1982, *id.,* Title 12, § 372, 635 a-4, 1841, 1843, Title 15, §§ 6a, 45(a)(3), 4011–4021. *See* U.S. Department of Justice and Federal Trade Commission, "Antitrust Enforcement Guidelines for International Operations, April 1995," reproduced in *International Legal Materials,* vol. 34, p. 1080 (1995).

[114]Laker Airways, Ltd. v. Pan American World Airways, *Federal Supplement,* vol. 559, p. 1124 (District Ct. of the District of Columbia, 1983).

To make it easier to collect the evidence necessary to bring these cases, the U.S. Congress enacted the

Extraterritorial Application of U.S. Antitrust Laws

The other controversial feature of American antitrust law is the willingness of American courts to apply it extraterritorially. The statutory provision in the Sherman Antitrust Act declares that it applies to conduct affecting "trade or commerce among the several states, or with foreign nations," so the decisions of the courts can hardly be blamed solely on judicial largess. Indeed, the courts have imposed several jurisdictional tests that limit the legislative rule. They require a showing that, first, an alleged defendant is subject to the personal jurisdiction of the court, and, second, that the court has subject matter jurisdiction.

Personal Jurisdiction Requirements of U.S. Antitrust Laws   The American antitrust laws authorize a court to assume personal jurisdiction if a defendant has the contacts specified either by (a) Section 12 of the Clayton Act or (b) an applicable state "long arm statute." Section 12 of the Clayton Act allows a court to assume personal jurisdiction over an antitrust defendant who "transacts business" in the forum jurisdiction. Generally, this is given a broad interpretation, such that a foreign corporation lacking a full-time employee, an office, a bank account, or even related business property in the United States would still be subject to the personal jurisdiction of an American court.[115]

State **long arm statutes** are applicable to antitrust proceedings because of a provision in the U.S. Federal Rules of Civil Procedure that looks upon state law as an independent basis for exercising personal jurisdiction in federal cases.[116] For the most part, these state statutes give courts an even broader scope for assuming personal jurisdiction than does Section 12 of the Clayton Act.[117]

The principal limitation on the assumption of personal jurisdiction by U.S. courts is the federal constitutional requirement of due process. This forbids the court from assuming personal jurisdiction unless a defendant has **minimum contacts** with the forum.[118] In essence, a court has jurisdiction only if (a) the defendant purposefully did business in the forum and (b) the defendant reasonably could have anticipated that it would have to defend itself there.[119]

Subject Matter Jurisdiction Requirement of U.S. Antitrust Laws   Two tests are used to determine whether a court has subject matter jurisdiction in an American antitrust case: (1) the "effects test" and (2) the "jurisdiction rule of reason" test. Neither can be found in the statutory provisions of the antitrust laws; both are creatures of judicial legislation. Under the **effects test**, companies carrying on business outside the United States will come within the subject matter jurisdiction of an American court if their business activity is intended to affect U.S. commerce and it is not *de minimis*.[120]

long arm statute: A law defining the conduct of a foreign person within a state that will subject that person to the jurisdiction of the state.

United States minimum contacts test: A jurisdictional test required by due process that looks to see if a person had such contacts with a state that it could reasonably have anticipated that it would have to defend itself there.

United States effects test: A jurisdictional test which subjects foreign businesses to U.S. antitrust laws if their activities were intended to affect U.S. commerce and the effect was other than minimal.

International Antitrust Enforcement Assistance Act of 1994, U.S. Public Law No. 103–438 (November 2, 1994), authorizing U.S. government agencies to negotiate bilateral agreements with foreign governments to facilitate the exchange of documents and evidence in civil and criminal investigations. The act is reproduced in *International Legal Materials*, vol. 34, p. 494 (1995). Examples of existing cooperative accords include the 1984 Memorandum of Understanding as to Notification, Consultation, and Cooperation with Respect to Application of National Antitrust Laws between the United States and Canada, reproduced in *id.*, vol. 23, p. 275 (1984), and (subject to its formal reinstatement by the European Union) the 1991 Agreement between the Government of the United States of America and the Commission of European Communities Regarding the Application of Their Competition Laws, reproduced in *id.*, vol. 30, p. 1487 (1991).

[115]*See* Hunt v. Mobile Oil Corp., *Federal Supplement*, vol. 410, p. 4 (District Ct. for the S. Dist. of N.Y., 1975); Williams v. Canon, Inc., *Federal Supplement*, vol. 432, p. 376 (District Ct. for the Central Dist. of Calif., 1977), and Weinstein v. Norman M. Morris Corp., *Federal Supplement*, vol. 432, p. 337 (District Ct. for E. Dist. of Mich., 1977).

In Tiger Trash v. Browning-Ferris Industries, Inc., *Federal Reporter, Second Series*, vol. 560, p. 818 (7th Circuit Ct. of Appeals, 1977) and in O.S.C. Corp. v. Toshiba America Inc., *Federal Reporter, Second Series*, vol. 491, p. 1064 (9th Circuit Ct. of Appeals, 1974), personal jurisdiction was found to exist over a subsidiary incorporated in the United States that was owned and managed by a non-American parent corporation.

[116]*United States Code*, Title 28, Rule 4.

[117]Some examples of cases where courts have assumed personal jurisdiction on the basis of state long arm statutes include Hunt v. Mobile Oil Corp., *Federal Supplement*, vol. 410, p. 4 (District Ct. for the S. Dist. of N.Y., 1975), in which jurisdiction was based on the fact that the defendants held a small number of meetings related to an alleged conspiracy in the forum state; Wells Fargo & Co. v. Wells Fargo Exp. Co., vol. 556, p. 406 (9th Circuit Ct. of Appeals, 1977), where jurisdiction resulted from the negotiation and consummation of a single $10,000 loan; Cofinco Inc. v. Angola Coffee Co., A.C., *Trade Cases*, vol. 1975–2, para. 50,456 (District Ct. for the S. Dist. of N.Y., 1975), in which a court assumed jurisdiction on the basis of telex communications to and from New York; and King v. Hailey Chevrolet Co., *Federal Reporter, Second Series*, vol. 462, p. 63 (6th Circuit Ct. of Appeals, 1972), in which advertising within the forum state was sufficient to establish jurisdiction.

[118]*See* International Shoe Co. v. State of Washington, *United States Reports*, vol. 326, p. 310 (Supreme Ct., 1945).

[119]World-Wide Volkswagen Corp. v. Woodson, *United States Reports*, vol. 444, p. 286 (Supreme Ct., 1980).

[120]National Bank of Canada v. Interbank Card Association, *Federal Reporter, Second Series*, vol. 666, p. 6 (2nd Circuit Ct. of Appeals, 1981).

The effects test, which was originally set out in *United States v. Aluminum Co. of America*,[121] has been criticized on several grounds. Because international business practices may affect two or more nations, some critics contend that the effects test would (if it were adopted in other countries) allow courts in several states to simultaneously apply different and conflicting antitrust rules. Other critics contend that the test interferes with a state's sovereign right to control acts within its own territory. Still others note that the test seems to have the practical effect of shifting the burden of proof to a defendant to show that his activities do not affect the U.S. market.[122]

This criticism has led several other U.S. courts of appeals to adopt a different rule. In a widely cited pair of cases, *Timberlane Lumber Co. v. Bank of America* (*Timberland I*)[123] and *Timberlane Lumber Co. v. Bank of America* (*Timberlane II*),[124] the Ninth Circuit Court of Appeals adopted what it called a **jurisdictional rule of reason**. This set out a three-pronged test to determine jurisdiction in antitrust cases involving conduct outside the United States: (1) Was the alleged conduct intended to affect the foreign commerce of the United States? (2) Was it of such a type and magnitude to violate the Sherman Act? (3) As a matter of international comity and fairness, should a court assume extraterritorial jurisdiction over the matter? The last of these three prongs requires courts to balance the interests of the United States in assuming jurisdiction against various competing interests. The factors considered are:

- The degree of conflict with foreign law or policy
- The nationality or allegiance of the parties and the location or principal place of business of the companies
- The extent to which enforcement by the involved countries might be expected to achieve compliance
- The relative significance of the effects on the United States and other involved nations
- Whether the explicit purpose of the alleged conduct was to harm American commerce
- The foreseeability of the anticompetitive effects and the relative importance of the violations to commerce within the United States as compared with commerce abroad

This approach, although not uniformly followed in all of the U.S. courts of appeals, seems nevertheless to be the prevalent test in the United States.[125]

In Case 4–3, the Ninth Circuit described the jurisdictional rule of reason and applied it in a case involving a foreign company alleged to have monopolized trade in kitchen steamers.

> **United States jurisdictional rule of reason test:** A jurisdictional test that allows U.S. courts to assume jurisdiction over a foreign business for violation of U.S. antitrust laws if (1) the alleged conduct was intended to affect the foreign commerce of the United States, (2) it was of such a type and magnitude so as to violate the Sherman Act, and (3) as a matter of international comity and fairness, a U.S. court ought to assume extraterritorial jurisdiction over the matter.

De minimis is short for *de minimis non curat lex;* Latin: "the law does not concern itself with trifles." This phrase is used by courts to justify their refusal to hear suits that would take up their time on matters of little importance.

[121]*Federal Reporter, Second Series,* vol. 148, p. 416 (2nd Circuit Ct. of Appeals 1945). This case was originally appealed to the U.S. Supreme Court but, because six judges were not able to form a quorum to hear the case due to conflicts of interest, the case was assign to the Second Circuit.

[122]Robert Hammesfahr and Richard Blatt, "Extraterritorial Application of American Antitrust Laws: An Overview," *Chicago Bar Record,* vol. 65, p. 106 (1983).

[123]*Federal Reporter, Second Series,* vol. 549, p. 597 (9th Circuit Ct. of Appeals, 1976).

[124]*Id.,* vol. 749, p. 1378 (9th Circuit Ct. of Appeals 1984), certiorari denied, *United States Reports,* vol. 472, p. 1032 (Supreme Ct. 1985).

[125]It is consistent with the approaches set out in Restatement (Second) of Foreign Relations Law of the United States, §§ 23 and 42 (1965), and Restatement (Third) of Foreign Relations Law of the United States, § 402 and 403 (1984).

It is also consistent with the comity considerations set out in the U.S. Department of Justice and Federal Trade Commission, "Antitrust Enforcement Guidelines for International Operations, April 1995," at p. 20, reproduced in *International Legal Materials,* vol. 34, p. 1080 (1995).

Case 4–3   Metro Industries v. Sammi Corp.

United States Ninth Circuit Court of Appeals
Federal Reporter, Third Series, vol. 82, p. 839 (1996)

CIRCUIT JUDGE CHARLES WIGGINS:

Metro Industries, Inc., ("Metro"), an importer and wholesaler of kitchenware, sued Sammi Corp. ("Sammi"), a South Korean exporting company, and two of its American subsidiaries alleging, *inter alia*, that a Korean design registration system, which gives Korean holloware producers the exclusive right to export a particular holloware design for three years, constituted a market division that is a *per se* violation of section 1 of the Sherman Antitrust Act.

Metro alleges that Sammi used this registration system in 1983 to prevent Metro and other kitchenware importers from acquiring Korean-made stainless steel steamers from any of Sammi's competitors in Korea.

Metro appeals the district court's grant of Sammi's motion for summary judgment on Metro's Sherman Act § 1 claim. . . .

FACTS AND PROCEDURAL HISTORY

Metro is an importer and distributor of kitchenware products. Metro started a stainless steel kitchenware business in about 1977, importing mixing bowls from a Korean supplier called Haidong. In 1978 it began to purchase bowls from Sammi, and over the next few years, expanded its business to include other kitchenware. By 1981, importing and selling stainless steel kitchenware constituted Metro's principal business activity.

Sammi is a large Korean trading company that purchases a wide variety of finished products, including stainless steel steamers, for export to the United States and other countries. Sammi is a member of the Korea Holloware Association. This association, through a thirteen member design registration committee, grants pattern and design registration rights for particular products based on the shape, appearance, and color of the products. The registration committee consists of members from manufacturing companies, trading companies, the Korea Association of patent attorneys, and three members of Korean government organizations. A trading company, such as Sammi, can only hold a pattern design right jointly with a manufacturer. Registration gives the design holder the exclusive right to export a particular design for three years, and the rights can be extended for three additional years.

According to Metro, in late 1981, it raised the idea of a line of stainless steel steamers with Sammi, provided Sammi with models, and asked Sammi to develop samples and to prepare to supply the steamers. Sammi registered the steamer design and began to supply Metro with steamers. Metro experienced a disruption of steamer deliveries from Sammi at some time during 1983. Metro

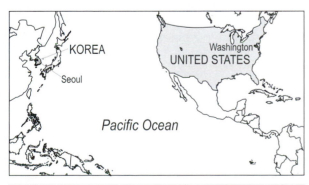

MAP 4-3 Korea and the United States (1996)

alleges that its attempts to order the steamers from another company were blocked by Sammi. Eventually, in late 1983, Metro was able to secure a source of steamers from a Korean company called Sambo and apparently had no further disruptions in its steamer shipments.

In December 1983, Metro filed a complaint in the United States District Court for the Central District of California against Sammi and two of its American subsidiaries alleging violations of §§ 1 and 2 of the Sherman Act. . . .

[In June 1984, Metro's case against Sammi was dismissed. In the meantime, the trial court began hearing another case, Vollrath Co. v. Sammi Corp., *based on similar facts and a similar claim, violation of §§ 1 and 2 of the Sherman Act. The jury found in favor of Vollrath but the trial judge overruled the finding and granted a judgment notwithstanding the verdict. While the* Vollrath *case was on appeal, Metro filed for leave to reinstitute its claim and it was allowed to do so. The trial judge ordered that Metro's case would remain off the calendar until the* Vollrath *appeal was decided. In December 1993, the Court of Appeals affirmed the trial judge's judgment.]*

. . . Subsequent to the district court's decision in the Vollrath case, Metro began arguing a new theory—that the Korean design registration system under which Sammi had the exclusive rights to manufacture a particular steamer design constituted a market division that was illegal per se under § 1 of the Sherman Act. In May 1994, Sammi filed a motion to dismiss all claims against Sammi and its subsidiaries. . . . The district court granted Sammi's motion . . . finding that Metro had failed to present sufficient evidence to carry its burden on any of its claims.

DISCUSSION

Metro appeals only the district court's grant of summary judgment in favor of Sammi on Metro's Sherman Act § 1 market division claim. . . .

Section 1 of the Sherman Antitrust Act, as amended in 1990, reads, in relevant part:

> Every contract, combination in the form of trust or otherwise, or conspiracy, in restraint of trade or commerce among the several States, or with foreign nations, is hereby declared to be illegal.[126]

Metro alleges that the Korean Holloware Association registration system constitutes a "naked" market division agreement, which is per se illegal under the Sherman Act. Thus, Metro argues, an examination of the impact of the registration system on competition in the United States is not necessary to find a violation of § 1.

Because conduct occurring outside the United States is only a violation of the Sherman Act if it has a sufficient negative impact on commerce in the United

---

[126]The 1990 amendments only increased the penalty provisions of § 1, and did not change the language quoted above.

States, *per se* analysis is not appropriate. Indeed, when the alleged illegal conduct occurred in a foreign country, we must examine the impact on commerce in the United States before we can determine that we have subject matter jurisdiction over a claim. . . .

I. *Per se* Treatment Is Inappropriate in This Case

"Ordinarily, whether particular concerted activity violates § 1 of the Sherman Act is determined through case-by-case application of the so-called rule of reason—that is, 'the factfinder weighs all of the circumstances of a case in deciding whether a restrictive practice should be prohibited as imposing an unreasonable restraint on competition.'"[127] "Certain categories of agreements, however, have been held to be *per se* illegal, dispensing with the need for case-by-case evaluation."[128] "Such agreements are those that always or almost always tend to restrict competition and decrease output."[129] In general, "[a] market allocation agreement between competitors at the same market level is a classic *per se* antitrust violation."[130]

A. The Korean Registration System Is Not Illegal *Per se*
Where the conduct at issue is not a garden-variety horizontal division of a market, we have eschewed a *per se* rule and instead have utilized rule of reason analysis. In deciding whether to extend the *per se* rule to a previously unexamined business practice, we are to examine whether "the practice facially appears to be one that would always or almost always tend to restrict competition and decrease output, . . . or instead one designed to 'increase economic efficiency and render markets more, rather than less, competitive.'"[131]

The Korean registration system is not a classic horizontal market division agreement in which competitors at the same level agree to divide up the market for a given product. Metro does not point to, and we have not found, a single instance in which an arrangement similar to the Korean manufacturer-exporter design registration system has undergone judicial scrutiny in the Sherman Act context. The novelty of this arrangement, "strongly supports application of rule-of-reason analysis."[132]

Further, as discussed below, there is no evidence of a negative effect on competition, which also militates against extension of the *per se* rule.[133] The record reveals

that the registration protection was limited to particular designs of a product "based on shape, appearance, and color of the products." The protection extends for only three years, renewable for three additional years. Contrary to Metro's assertions, the record does reveal the output increasing potential of the registration system. Sammi's general manager of housewares indicated that tooling and production of a new product takes several years. Thus, the limited protection could encourage manufacturers to develop and produce new products, knowing that they would have the exclusive right to export a particular design for a limited period of time.

Finally, there is no evidence that the purpose of the design registration system was to restrain trade, which also counsels in favor of rule of reason analysis.[134] The Korean association was apparently a quasigovernmental group (in that it was sanctioned by the Korean government and three of its thirteen members were representatives of the Korean government) that was formed to ensure product and design quality and to protect from copying. Sammi's general manager of housewares indicated that the system was designed "to promote the manufacturer to develop better quality product, a better quality design, and protect them from copy[ing] by other manufacturers."

Accordingly, rule of reason analysis is appropriate in this case.

B. Foreign Conduct Cannot Be Examined Under the *Per se* Rule
Even if Metro could prove that the registration system constituted a "market division" that would require application of the *per se* rule if the division occurred in a domestic context, application of the *per se* rule is not appropriate where the conduct in question occurred in another country. Determining whether the registration system was a violation of the antitrust laws would still require an examination of the impact of the system on commerce in the United States. "The Sherman Act does reach conduct outside our borders, but only when the conduct has an effect on American commerce."[135] According to a leading treatise:

[T]he conventional assumptions that courts make in appraising restraints in domestic markets are not necessarily applicable in foreign markets. A foreign joint venture among competitors, for example, might be

---

[127]Business Elecs. Corp. v. Sharp Elecs. Corp., *United States Reports,* vol. 458, p. 717 at 723 (Supreme Ct. 1988). . . .
[128]*Id.*
[129]United States v. Brown, *Federal Reporter, Second Series,* vol. 936, p. 1042 at p. 1045 (9th Circuit Ct. of Appeals 1991).
[130]*Id.*
[131]Broadcast Music, Inc. v. Columbia Broadcasting Sys., *United States Reports,* vol. 441, p. 1 at pp. 19–20 (Supreme Ct. 1979).
[132]Northrop v. McDonnell Douglas Corp., *Federal Reporter, Second Series,* vol. 705, p. 1030 at p. 1051 (9th Circuit Ct. of Appeals 1983); *see also* United States v. Topco Assoc., Inc., *United States Reports,* vol. 405, p. 596 at pp. 607–08 (Supreme Ct. 1972): "It is only after considerable experience with certain business relationships that courts classify them as *per se* violations of the Sherman Act."
[133]Northrop, *Federal Reporter, Second Series,* vol. 705 at p. 1052.
[134]*Id.* at p. 1053.
[135]Matsushita Elec. Indus. Co. v. Zenith Radio Corp., *United States Reports,* vol. 475, p. 574 at p. 582 n.6, (Supreme Ct. 1986). *See also* Hartford Fire Ins. Co. v. California, *id.,* vol. 509, p. 764 (Supreme Ct. 1993): "[I]t is well established by now that the Sherman Act applies to foreign conduct that was meant to produce and did in fact produce some substantial effect in the United States."

more "reasonable" than a comparable domestic transaction in several respects: the actual or potential harms touching American commerce may be more remote; the parties' necessities may be greater in view of foreign market circumstances; and the alternatives may be fewer, more burdensome, or less helpful.

The fact that foreign conduct would be a *per se* offense—one that is condemned without proof of particular effects and with little regard for possible justifications in the particular case—when entirely domestic does not call for a fundamentally different analysis. Domestic antitrust policy uses *per se* rules for conduct that, in most of its manifestations, is potentially very dangerous with little or no redeeming virtue. That rationale would be inapplicable to foreign restraints that, in many instances, either pose very little danger to American commerce or have more persuasive justifications than are likely in similar restraints at home. For example, price fixing in a foreign country might have some but very little impact on United States commerce.[136]

Thus, the potential illegality of actions occurring outside the United States requires an inquiry into the impact on commerce in the United States, regardless of the inherently suspect appearance of the foreign activities. Consequently, where a Sherman Act claim is based on conduct outside the United States, we apply rule of reason analysis to determine whether there is a Sherman Act violation.

II. Jurisdictional Inquiries Are Required When a Sherman Act Claim Is Based On Foreign Conduct

When we examine foreign conduct to determine if there is an antitrust violation, our jurisdiction is not a foregone conclusion. "When foreign conduct is involved, the courts customarily appraise its substantive antitrust significance only after deciding whether the Sherman Act asserts jurisdiction over it. . . ." [J]urisdictional" and "substantive" inquiries are not wholly independent."[137] We examined the jurisdictional considerations in applying the Sherman Act to foreign conduct in *Timberlane Lumber Co. v. Bank of America*[138] (*Timberlane I*), and *Timberlane Lumber Co. v. Bank of America*[139] (*Timberlane II*). Both cases concerned an American lumber producer's Sherman Act claims based on its allegations that Bank of America and several co-conspirators had conspired and acted to preclude a subsidiary of Timberlane from competing in the Honduran lumber market and exporting lumber into the United States.

In *Timberlane I*, we articulated a "jurisdictional rule of reason," to be applied to Sherman Act claims arising

out of foreign conduct. The inquiry requires the weighing of the answers to three questions:

Does the alleged restraint affect, or was it intended to affect, the foreign commerce of the United States? Is it of such a type and magnitude so as to be cognizable as a violation of the Sherman Act? As a matter of international comity and fairness, should the extraterritorial jurisdiction of the United States be asserted to cover it?

The comity question alone requires the consideration of several elements, including:

the degree of conflict with foreign law or policy, the nationality or allegiance of the parties and the locations or principal places of business of corporations, the extent to which enforcement by either state can be expected to achieve compliance, the relative significance of effects on the United States as compared with those elsewhere, the extent to which there is explicit purpose to harm or affect American commerce, the foreseeability of such effect, and the relative importance to the violations charged of conduct within the United States as compared with conduct abroad.

* * *

[In *Timberlane II*] . . . we found that Timberlane adequately pleaded that there was an actual or intended effect on American foreign commerce and that Timberlane had made the minimal injury allegations necessary to support an a Sherman Act claim, thus satisfying the first two prongs of the *Timberlane I* test. As for the comity prong, we found that the conduct in Honduras at issue was allowed or even encouraged by Honduran law; thus the factor considering "the degree of conflict with foreign law or policy," weighed strongly against Sherman Act jurisdiction.

Other factors, including the relative insignificance of the actions to the U.S. lumber market compared with the significant impact on the Honduran lumber market, the lack of evidence of intent to affect the U.S. market, and the lack of foreseeability of an effect on the U.S. market, also counseled against jurisdiction. We concluded that the exercise of federal jurisdiction would not be proper.

Metro has made sufficient allegations to state a claim under the Sherman Act. Comity considerations are less compelling here than they were in Timberlane. . . . [T]here is no conflict with foreign law or policy because the Korean holloware registration system was not compelled by the Korean government, even though three government representatives serve on the design and pattern registration committee. Though Sammi is a foreign corporation, it apparently does a great deal of business

---

[136]Phillip Areeda and Donald F. Turner, *Antitrust Law,* vol. 1, p 237 (1978).
[137]*Id.*
[138]*Federal Reporter, Second Series,* vol. 549, p. 597 (9th Circuit Ct. of Appeals 1976).
[139]*Id.,* vol. 749, p. 1378 (9th Circuit Ct. of Appeals 1984), certiorari denied, *United States Reports,* vol. 472, p. 1032 (Supreme Ct. 1985).

in the United States, so it has assets which could be used to secure any judgment against it. The impact of the registration is felt more in the United States than in Korea because the registration system only limits the export of particular designs, and it was certainly foreseeable that these export restrictions could affect the United States. Considering all the factors, principles of comity and fairness do not deprive this court of jurisdiction.

As *Timberlane II* makes clear, the other two prongs of the "jurisdictional rule of reason" test are substantially intertwined with the merits of Metro's Sherman Act claim. Thus, while we could ultimately determine that we lack subject matter jurisdiction over Metro's Sherman Act claim because of a lack of impact in the United States, such a conclusion would only come after the factual inquiry into markets, market power, and other factors necessary to find a substantive violation of the Sherman Act. By alleging in its complaint that because of Sammi's manipulation of the registration system "existing and potential competition in the relevant markets has been unreasonably restrained and substantially lessened, independent United States importer-distributors have been severely damaged or eliminated from the markets, concentration has been increased in those markets, and a tendency towards monopoly has been created," Metro has made the minimal allegations about the impact on competition in the United States necessary to state a claim for a Sherman Act violation. We have jurisdiction to review Metro's claims, and examine Sammi's alleged conduct under the rule of reason.

III. Metro Cannot Show a Substantial Anticompetitive Effect in the United States or Antitrust Injury

Under the rule of reason, a plaintiff must establish "antitrust injury," that is, that the conduct at issue actu-

ally caused "injury to competition, beyond the impact on the claimant, within a field of commerce in which the claimant is engaged."[140] Because Metro relies almost entirely on a *per se* argument, it points to little evidence of the impact of the Korean registration system on competition in the United States. It merely suggests that it could present evidence of "the harm and consequent damage to Metro and its customers". . . . We conclude that . . . a rational trier of fact could not find in favor of Metro on its Sherman Act claim.

To show an injury to competition, the plaintiff ordinarily "must delineate a relevant market and show that the defendant plays enough of a role in that market to impair competition significantly."[141] . . .

Metro has produced no evidence of actual injury to competition in the United States. Rather, based on its own conclusion that the relevant market consists only of stainless steel steamers, it asserts that Sammi has a monopoly in that market and that output would only be reduced in the United States if Sammi chose to do so. . . . [But] Metro has produced no evidence of reduced output or increased prices. These assertions are insufficient to satisfy [the] requirement that Metro come forward with specific facts supporting its claims of injury to competition when responding to a motion for summary judgment.

* * *

CONCLUSION

For the reasons stated above, we AFFIRM the district court's grant of summary judgment in favor of Sammi. . . . ∎

---

[140]Austin v. McNamara, *Federal Reporter, Second Series,* vol. 979, p. 728 (9th Circuit Ct. of Appeals 1992).
[141]Bhan v. NME Hosp., Inc., *Federal Reporter, Second Series,* vol. 929, p. 1404 at p. 1413 (9th Circuit Ct. of Appeals 1991).

Regulation of Anticompetitive Behavior in the European Union

European Community Treaty, Article 81: Forbids competitors from entering into agreements to prevent, restrain, or distort trade.

The European Community Treaty contains two articles—Articles 81 and 82—that regulate business competition.[142] **Article 81** (which is analogous to Section 1 of the U.S. Sherman Antitrust Act) prohibits normal arm's length competitors from entering into agreements or carrying on concerted practices that either prevent, restrain, or distort trade. The following activities are expressly prohibited: (a) fixing any trading condition, including price fixing; (b) limiting or controlling production, markets, technical development, or investment; (c) allocating markets or sources of supply; (d) applying unequal terms to parties furnishing equivalent consideration; and (e) using unrelated tying clauses.[143] Paragraph 3 of Article 81 also sets out an

---

[142]The Treaty of Amsterdam, adopted in 1997 and effective May 1, 1999, renumbered the articles of the principle European Union treaties, including the Treaty Establishing the European Community. Articles 81 and 82 were previously numbered as Articles 85 and 86.
[143]Treaty Establishing the European Community, Article 81(1): "The following shall be prohibited as incompatible with the common market: all agreements between undertakings, decisions by associations of undertakings and concerted practices which may affect trade between member states and which have as their object or effect the prevention, restriction

exception, providing that agreements or practices that both (1) contribute to improved production, improved distribution of goods, or improved technical processes and (2) do not prevent competition in a substantial part of the market in question are exempted from the application of the basic rule.[144]

Because of the exception in Article 81 paragraph 3, the EC Courts have held that the rule of reason that applies to Section 1 of the Sherman Act cannot similarly apply to the European provision, as Case 4–4 explains.

---

or distortion of competition within the common market, and in particular those which: (a) directly or indirectly fix purchase or selling prices or any other trading condition; (b) limit or control production, markets, technical development, or investment; (c) share markets or sources or supply; (d) apply dissimilar conditions to equivalent transactions with other trading parties, thereby placing them at a competitive disadvantage; (e) make the conclusion of contracts subject to acceptance by the other parties of supplementary obligations which, by their nature or according to commercial usage, have no connection with the subject of such contracts."

[144]*Id.,* Article 81(3): "The provisions of paragraph 1 may, however, be declared inapplicable in the case of: any agreement or category of agreements between undertakings; any decision or category of decisions by associations of undertakings; any concerted practice or category of concerted practices; which contributes to improving the production or distribution of goods or to promoting technical or economic progress, while allowing consumers a fair share of the resulting benefit, and which does not: (a) impose on the undertakings concerned restrictions which are not indispensable to the attainment of these objectives; (b) afford such undertakings the possibility of eliminating competition in respect of a substantial part of the products in question."

Case 4–4   *Métropole Télévision (M6) v. Commission of the European Communities*

European Union, Court of First Instance (Third Chamber). Case T-112/99 (2001).

JUDGMENT

General Background to the Case

Description of the Operation   This case relates to Commission Decision 1999/242/EC of 3 March 1999 relating to a proceeding pursuant to Article 85 [now Article 81] of the EC Treaty concerning the creation of Télévision par Satellite (hereinafter "TPS"), whose object is to devise, develop and broadcast, in digital mode by satellite, a range of television programs and services, against payment, to French-speaking television viewers in Europe.

TPS, which was set up in the form of a partnership (*société en nom collectif*) under French law by six major companies active in the television sectors (Metropole television [M6], Télévision Française 1 SA [TF1], France 2, and France 3) or in the telecommunication and cable distribution sectors (France Telecom and Suez-Lyonnaise des Eaux) is a new entrant on markets that are very much dominated by a long-standing operator, namely Canal+ and its subsidiary CanalSatellite.

* * *

The Notification and the Notified Agreements   The parties first contacted the Commission . . . in the summer of 1996, with a view to [giving] notification under Council Regulation (EEC) No 4064/89 of 21 December 1989 on the control of concentrations between undertakings. . . . [O]n 18 October 1996 they [filed notice with] the Commission and requested negative clearance and/or exemption pursuant to [Council] Regulation No 17 of . . . 1962 . . . implementing Articles 85 and 86 of the Treaty.

Four agreements were notified. The basic principles governing the operation of TPS are set out in the Agreement of 11 and 18 April 1996 (hereinafter 'the Agreement); they were expressed in more concrete and structured terms in the subsequent Associates' Pact signed on 19 June 1996 and in the TPS and TPS [Management Annexes] of the same date. The agreements were [to last] for a period of 10 years.

Three clauses contained in those agreements were the subject of the Commission's attention in the contested decision. They are . . . second, the clause relating to special-interest channels and, third, the exclusivity clause.

* * *

The Clause Relating to Special-Interest Channels   Article 6 of the Agreement (under the heading 'Digital programs and services) and Article 5.4 of the Associates' Pact cited above, provide that TPS has a right of priority and a right of final refusal with regard to the production of special-interest channels and television services by its shareholders. The clause is worded as follows:

"In order to supply TPS with the programs it requires, the parties have agreed to give TPS first

MAP 4-4 France (2001)

refusal in respect of the programs or services which they themselves operate or over which they have effective control within the producing company, and in respect of the programs and services which they produce. TPS is also entitled to final refusal or acceptance on the best terms proposed by competitors with regard to any programs or services which its shareholders offer to third parties. If it accepts them, whether on exclusive terms or not, TPS will apply financial and contractual terms which are at least equivalent to those which the programs and services could receive elsewhere.

"As regards the acquisition of these channels and services, TPS will freely decide, on the basis of its own assessment, whether or not to agree to integrate them into its digital bouquet, either exclusively or non-exclusively; however, the parties underline their objective of having programs and services in TPS's digital bouquet on an exclusive basis."

The Exclusivity Clause   Lastly, Article 6 of the Agreement provides that the general-interest channels (M6, TF1, France 2, and France 3, are to be broadcast exclusively by TPS. TPS is to meet the technical costs of transporting and broadcasting the programs but will not pay any remuneration for them.

The Contested Decision   On 3 March 1999, the Commission adopted the contested decision.

* * *

. . . [T]he Commission concluded that:

* * *

- with regard to the exclusivity clause and the clause relating to special-interest channels [that those clauses infringed Article 85(1), but that] those provisions could benefit from an exemption under Article 85(3) of the Treaty for a period of three years, namely until 15 December 1999.

[The applicants challenge this decision, arguing, in part, that the Commission failed to apply a rule of reason in analyzing the applicability of Article 85(1) to the circumstances of their request for an exemption; and that the Commission erroneously calculated the period for the exemption.]

* * *

Misapplication of Article 85(1) of the Treaty (failure to apply a rule of reason)

Arguments of the Parties   The applicants submit that the Commission should have applied Article 85(1) of the Treaty in the light of a rule of reason rather than as an abstract rule. Under a rule of reason, an anti-competitive practice falls outside the scope of the prohibition in Article 85(1) of the Treaty if it has more positive than negative effects on competition on a given market. They submit that the existence of a rule of reason in Community competition law has already been confirmed by the Court of Justice.[145] They also assert that, contrary to the Commission's submission, those two judgments are relevant in the present case because the creation of TPS also took place in conditions and on a market that are wholly [unique].

The applicants submit that the application of a rule of reason would have shown that Article 85(1) of the Treaty did not apply to the exclusivity clause and to the clause relating to the special-interest channels. They observe that, as follows implicitly from the reasoning adopted by the Commission in regard to Article 85(3) of the Treaty, those clauses, rather than restricting competition on the pay-TV market in France, in fact favor such competition as they allow a new operator to gain access to a market which was dominated until then by a single operator, CanalSatellite and its parent company Canal+, (the service offered by AB Sat not really being a competitor, but rather complementary to that of Canal+).

According to the applicants, the line of reasoning that Article 85(1) of the Treaty does not apply to the exclusivity clause and the clause relating to the special-interest channels is all the more compelling in the light of the case-law of the Court of Justice. It is apparent from that case-law that, first, a clause granting exclusive sales rights must be the subject of an economic assess-

---

[145]Case 258/78, Nungesser and Eisele v. Commission, *European Court Reports,* vol. 1982, p. 2015 (1982) and Case 262/81, Coditel v. Ciné-Vog Films, *id.,* vol. 1982, p. 3381, paragraph 20 (1982).

ment and is not necessarily caught by Article 85(1) of the Treaty[146] and that, second, an exclusive right granted with a view to penetrating a new market is not caught by the prohibition laid down in that article.[147]

The Commission disputes that it infringed Article 85(1) of the Treaty by not applying a rule of reason, as suggested by the applicants, when [the Commission determined] the compatibility with [Article 85(1)] of the exclusivity clause and of the clause relating to the special-interest channels.

Findings of the Court   According to the applicants, as a consequence of the existence of a rule of reason in Community competition law, when Article 85(1) of the Treaty is applied it is necessary to weigh the pro and anti-competitive effects of an agreement in order to determine whether it is caught by the prohibition laid down in that article. It should, however, be observed, first of all, that, contrary to the applicants' assertions, the existence of such a rule has not, as such, been confirmed by the Community courts. Quite to the contrary, in various judgments the Court of Justice and the Court of First Instance have been at pains to indicate that the existence of a rule of reason in Community competition law is doubtful.[148]

Next, it must be observed that an interpretation of Article 85(1) of the Treaty, in the form suggested by the applicants, is difficult to reconcile with the rules prescribed by that provision.

Article 85 of the Treaty expressly provides, in its third paragraph, for the possibility of exempting agreements that restrict competition where they satisfy a number of conditions, in particular where they are indispensable to the attainment of certain objectives and do not afford undertakings the possibility of eliminating competition in respect of a substantial part of the products in question. It is only in the precise framework of that provision that the pro and anti-competitive aspects of a restriction may be weighed.[149] Article 85(3) of the Treaty would lose much of its effectiveness if [a rule of reason] examination [first] had to be carried out . . . under Article 85(1) of the Treaty.

It is true that in a number of judgments the Court of Justice and the Court of First Instance have favored a more flexible interpretation of the prohibition laid down in Article 85(1) of the Treaty.[150]

Those judgments cannot, however, be interpreted as establishing the existence of a rule of reason in Commu-

nity competition law. They are, rather, part of a broader trend in the case-law according to which it is not necessary to hold, wholly abstractly and without drawing any distinction, that any agreement restricting the freedom of action of one or more of the parties is necessarily caught by the prohibition laid down in Article 85(1) of the Treaty. In assessing the applicability of Article 85(1) to an agreement, account should be taken of the actual conditions in which it functions, in particular the economic context in which the undertakings operate, the products or services covered by the agreement and the actual structure of the market concerned.[151]

That interpretation, while observing the substantive scheme of Article 85 of the Treaty and, in particular, preserving the effectiveness of Article 85(3), makes it possible to prevent the prohibition in Article 85(1) from extending wholly abstractly and without distinction to all agreements whose effect is to restrict the freedom of action of one or more of the parties. It must, however, be emphasized that such an approach does not mean that it is necessary to weigh the pro and anti-competitive effects of an agreement when determining whether the prohibition laid down in Article 85(1) of the Treaty applies.

In the light of the foregoing, it must be held that, contrary to the applicants' submission, in [making its] decision the Commission correctly applied Article 85(1) of the Treaty to the exclusivity clause and the clause relating to the special-interest channels inasmuch as it was not obliged to weigh the pro and anti-competitive aspects of those agreements outside the specific framework of Article 85(3) of the Treaty.

It did, [in this Court's view,] assess the restrictive nature of those clauses in their economic and legal context in accordance with the case-law. Thus, it rightly found that the general-interest channels presented programs that were attractive for subscribers to a pay-TV company and that the effect of the exclusivity clause was to deny TPS' competitors access to such programs. As regards the clause relating to the special-interest channels, the Commission found that it resulted in a limitation of the supply of such channels on that market for a period of 10 years.

This objection must therefore be rejected.

* * *

[I]nfringement of Article 85(3) of the Treaty

* * *

---

[146]Case 56/65 *Société Technique Minière, id.,* vol. 1966, p. 337 (1966).
[147] *Nungesser and Eisele* v *Commission,* cited . . . above, and *Société Technique Minière,* cited above. . . .
[148]*See* Case C-235/92, P. Montecatini v Commission, *id.,* vol.1999, pt. 1, p. 4539, paragraph 133 (". . . even if the rule of reason did have a place in the context of Article 85(1) of the Treaty"). . . .
[149]*See,* to that effect, Case 161/84, *Pronuptia, id.,* vol. 1986, p. 353, paragraph 24. . . .
[150]*See,* in particular, *Société Technique Minière* . . . cited . . . above. . . .
[151]*See,* in particular, joined cases T-374/94, T-375/94, T-384/94 and T-388/94, European Night Services and Others v. Commission, *id.,* vol. 1998, pt. 2, p. 3141 (1988). . . .

The Argument Alleging Erroneous Assessment of the Duration of the Individual Exemption

Arguments of the Parties   The applicants submit that the Commission committed an error of assessment in taking the view in the contested decision that the duration of the exemption in respect of the exclusivity clause had to be fixed at three years. [The Commission's reasons for doing so were] that the restriction is indispensable for TPS only during the launch period and its indispensability will lessen over time inasmuch as TPS will be able to sign up subscribers, gain experience in the pay-TV sector and so improve its offer . . .

[The applicants] state that the indispensability of the exclusivity will not diminish but, quite to the contrary, will increase, having regard to the unassailable positions which the Canal+ group holds on the market. They observe that without exclusive rights to transmit the general-interest channels the viability of TPS is in danger.

The applicants consider that it is necessary to refer to the *Cégétel* decision,[152] in which an exclusive distribution clause for certain telephony services was exempted for a period of 10 years, in particular on the ground that Cégétel would not be able to make the investments in those telecommunication services pay until an extremely long period had expired.

* * *

Findings of the Court   It must be observed, first, that it is settled law that the exercise of the Commission's powers under Article 85(3) of the Treaty necessarily involves complex evaluations on economic matters, which means that judicial review of those evaluations must confine itself to an examination of the relevance of the facts and of the legal consequences which the Commission deduces from them.[153]

That principle applies especially with regard to the Commission's determination of the period during which a restriction is considered indispensable.

Second, . . . the applicants do not dispute any of the facts on the basis of which the Commission took the view that the indispensability of those clauses would necessarily diminish over time and held that three years was the minimum period during which they were indispensable for TPS.

Third, it must be observed that the applicants are wrong in referring to the *Cégétel* decision. As the Commission correctly states, only the exclusive distribution of certain products was the subject of an exemption in that decision and the distribution of those products was merely a small part of Cégétel's activities, whereas the exclusive right to transmit the general-interest channels is an essential element of the services offered by TPS.

It must therefore be found that the Commission did not commit a manifest error of assessment in limiting the period of exemption to three years.

This part of the applicants' argument must therefore be rejected.

* * *

On those grounds, THE COURT OF FIRST INSTANCE (Third Chamber), hereby:

1. Dismisses the application;
2. Orders the applicants to bear their own costs and to pay those incurred by the Commission and by the intervener. ■

---

[152]Commission Decision 1999/573/EC of 20 May 1999.
[153]*See,* in particular, the judgment in Case 56/64 and 58/64 Consten and Grundig v. Commission, *id.,* vol. 1966, p. 382. . . .

European Community Treaty, Article 82: Forbids dominant businesses from taking advantage of their position to the detriment of consumers.

Article 82 (which is analogous to Section 2 of the Sherman Antitrust Act) forbids businesses with a dominant position[154] in their marketplace[155] from taking improper advantage[156] of their position to the detriment of consumers. As with Article 81, specific prohibitions are listed. They are (a) directly or indirectly imposing unfair prices or trading conditions; (b) limiting production, markets, or technical developments to the prejudice of consumers; (c) applying unequal conditions to equivalent transactions with different trading partners; and (d) imposing unrelated tying clauses.[157] Unlike Article 81, there is no exception clause.

---

[154]A firm in a dominant position is one having the power to behave independently without taking into account, to any substantial extent, competitors, purchasers, or suppliers.
[155]A market is the merchandising of products regarded as similar by customers. It is a "substantial" market, and thus one covered by Article 82, if it is appreciably large, even if it is entirely within the territory of a single member state.
[156]An improper advantage is any action reducing supplies to purchasers. Note that there need not be a causal connection between dominance and improper advantage for Article 82 to apply.
[157]*Id.,* Article 82: "Any abuse by one or more undertakings of a dominant position within the Common Market or a substantial part of it shall be prohibited as incompatible with the Common Market insofar as it may affect trade between member states. Such abuse may, in particular, consist in: (a) directly or indirectly imposing unfair purchase

Determining compliance with Articles 81 and 82 is left solely to the European Commission, which can impose substantial fines in its own right.[158] For non-EU firms, the most significant aspect of the Union's business competition rules is their extraterritorial impact. The European Commission and the European Court of Justice have applied the rules to foreign firms to the extent that the firm's activities have an effect on trade or commerce within the EU. (In essence, the Commission and the Court are using the American effects test.) Thus, a foreign firm that conspires with EU firms to monopolize trade within the Union would be in breach of the EC Treaty. Similarly, a parent firm would be responsible for the acts of its subsidiaries to the extent that it controls those acts. Also, a foreign firm seeking to acquire a competitor within the EU must convince the Union that the resulting merger will not improperly monopolize the marketplace.

Opposition to the Extraterritorial Application of Unfair Competition Laws

At the beginning of the nineteenth century, an English judge once asked:

> Can the island of Tobago pass a law to bind the rights of the whole world? Would the world submit to such an assumed jurisdiction?[159]

The willingness of American and European Union courts to apply antitrust laws extraterritorially has been roundly criticized by many countries, most especially Third World states. The most prominent developed state to object to this practice has been the United Kingdom, especially before it joined the EU.[160] Even afterward, however, it has taken a dim view of the practice, especially in regard to U.S. decisions. In 1978, in the case of *Rio Tinto Zinc Corporation v. Westinghouse Electric Corporation*, the English House of Lords observed that it may be the policy of one country to defend what is the policy of another to attack.[161] In that case, Viscount Dilhorne said the following about American policy:

> For many years now the United States has sought to exercise jurisdiction over foreigners in respect of acts done outside the jurisdiction of that country. This is not in accordance with international law and has led to legislation on the part of other states, including the United Kingdom, designed to protect their nationals from criminal proceedings in foreign courts where the claims to jurisdiction by those courts are excessive and constitute an invasion of sovereignty.[162]

The British objections to the American antitrust laws are twofold. One, they dislike the fact that suits for punitive treble damages can be brought by private plaintiffs. The British public, business community, and government often characterize these plaintiffs as menaces. Two, they dislike the discriminatory application of U.S. antitrust laws. Although the United States' Sherman Antitrust Act requires foreign exporters to act competitively in the international marketplace, its Webb Pomerene Act exempts U.S. export associations from having to comply with the Sherman Act.[163] Thus, there is a curious double standard.

These two "negative" features of the U.S. antitrust laws have led to diplomatic protests and to the enactment of "blocking statutes," not only by Britain, but by many states. Indeed, one

---

or selling prices or unfair trading conditions; (b) limiting production, market or technical development to the prejudice of consumers; (c) applying dissimilar conditions to equivalent transactions with other trading parties, thereby placing them at a competitive disadvantage; (d) making the conclusion of contracts subject to acceptance by the other parties of supplementary obligations which, by their nature or according to commercial usage, have no connection with the subject of such contracts."

[158]The fines for noncompliance are up to 5,000 euros for each day of noncompliance. For supplying false or misleading information for an Articles 81/82 investigation, the fines are 5,000 euros. For violating Articles 81/82, the fines can be up to 1 million euros.

[159]Buchanan v. Rucker, *English Reports,* vol. 108, p. 546 (1808).

[160]In 1953, the English Court of Appeal enjoined one of the parties involved in litigation based on the Sherman Antitrust Act from obeying an order of a U.S. court. United States v. Imperial Chemical Industries, Ltd., *Federal Supplement,* vol. 100, p. 504 (District Ct. for the S. Dist. of N.Y., 1951), *Federal Supplement,* vol. 105, p. 215 (District Ct. for the S. Dist. of N.Y., 1952); British Nylon Spinners, Ltd. v. Imperial Chemical Industries, Ltd., *Law Reports, Chancery,* vol. 1953, p. 19 (1953), *Law Reports, Chancery,* vol. 1955, p. 37 (1955).

[161]*Law Reports, Appeal Cases,* vol. 1978, p. 547 at p. 617 (1978).

[162]*Id.,* p. 631.

[163]The Webb Pomerene Act is not unique in exempting export associations from the application of anticompetition laws. Statutes in the United Kingdom, Canada, Germany, Japan, and Australia grant similar exemptions.

commentator has noted that "there have been five diplomatic protests of U.S. antitrust cases for every instance of express diplomatic support, and three blocking statutes for every cooperation agreement."[164]

blocking statute: Law enacted in some states to obstruct the extra-territorial application of U.S. antitrust laws by limiting a plaintiff's rights to obtain evidence or to enforce a judgment, and that allows a defendant to bring suit locally to recover punitive damages paid in the United States.

Blocking Statutes   **Blocking statutes** are possibly the most forceful of the responses that states have made to the extraterritorial application of American antitrust laws.[165] These statutes typically have three features: (1) they limit the extent to which a U.S. plaintiff can obtain evidence or seek production of commercial documents outside of the United States for use in investigations or proceedings in the United States; (2) they make it difficult for a successful plaintiff to enforce a U.S. judgment outside the United States; and (3) by virtue of a "clawback" provision, they allow defendants to bring suit in their home country to recover the punitive damages they paid in the United States.

Anti-Suit Injunctions   In addition to foreign legislators' attempts to curtail the extraterritorial application of American antitrust legislation, foreign courts have sometimes been willing to hand down injunctions forbidding one of their nationals from initiating an antitrust suit in the United States against another of their nationals. The use of anti-suit injunction is discussed in the case of *Airbus Industrie G.I.E v. Patel* (Case 3–12).

Products Liability Laws

products liability: Liability of a manufacturer for the injuries caused by its defective products.

Products liability laws attempt to discourage manufacturers from putting defective products into the marketplace by requiring them to assume liability for the injuries their products cause.

Products Liability Theories

Three theories are commonly relied upon to do this: (1) breach of contract, (2) negligence, and (3) strict liability. Most states (including Japan and most of the states of the developing world) use only the first two of these. The common law countries (i.e., the United States and the British Commonwealth countries) use all three. The European Union now relies principally on the last.

Japanese Products Liability Laws   The Japanese Civil Code provides two ways to impose liability for defective products: breach of contract and negligence. See Exhibit 4-6.

The remedies provided by contract law are quite restricted. In essence, they are based on (a) a seller's failure to perform and (b) a seller's breach of an implied warranty not to deliver a defective product.

A seller's obligation with respect to every sales contract is to deliver a product that is fit for the purpose for which it was sold.[166] Failure to perform by delivering a defective product is both a breach of the seller's obligation and the contract. The seller is then responsible for damages for personal and property losses, and (unlike the common law and European Union states) for economic losses as well.

privity: A legal relationship sufficiently close and direct to support a legal claim on behalf of or against another with whom the relationship exists.

burden of proof: The responsibility of proving a disputed charge or allegation.

This remedy is limited, however, by two familiar rules: privity and burden of proof. **Privity** only allows the immediate purchaser to sue (although a few Japanese courts have recently extended liability to foreseeable users as well as purchasers). Because contracts are part of the Japanese law of obligations, the **burden of proof** is on the plaintiff to show that the seller was at fault. Moreover, even when this can be done, the seller can avoid liability by showing that the defect was due to some factor beyond the seller's control, or that the seller took reasonable steps to prevent the defect.

Liability for breach of the implied warranty not to deliver a latent defect is also a very limited remedy.[167] First, privity restricts recovery to the immediate purchaser. Second, the buyer cannot be aware of the defect at the time the product was purchased. Third, the seller's liability is limited to repairing or replacing the product.

With respect to both breach of contract and breach of warranty actions, the seller is allowed to limit liability by issuing disclaimers. Although the disclaimers cannot violate public policy and must meet certain content requirements, they do effectively allow sellers to avoid all

---

[164]P. C. F. Pettit and C. J. D. Styles, "The International Response to the Extraterritorial Application of United States Antitrust Laws," *The Business Lawyer,* vol. 37, p. 697 (1982).

[165]*See id.* for a discussion of the United Kingdom's Protection of Trading Interest Act 1980 and related acts in Western Europe.

[166]Japanese Civil Code, Article 415.

[167]*Id.,* Article 570.

	Breach of Contract	**Negligence**
Products covered	All products	All products
Basic test	Was the product unfit for the purpose for which it was sold?	Considering all of the circumstances, was reasonable care exercised?
Elements	1. Contractual duty not to deliver defective product 2. Breach of express or implied contractual duty 3. Breach caused injury or damage	1. Duty of care 2. Breach of duty 3. Breach caused injury or damage
Defenses	1. Claimant was not in privity with defendant 2. Defendant had disclaimed liability 3. Intervening or superceding event caused defect 4. Defendant exercised reasonable care in attempting to prevent defect 5. If claim is for breach of implied duty, claimant cannot have been aware of the defect at the time of the purchase	1. Exercise of reasonable care 2. Intervening or superceding event caused injury or damage 3. Claimant unreasonably assumed risk 4. Claimant was negligent 5. Defect could not have been discovered using the scientific or technical means available at the time the product was put in circulation
Damages available	1. Personal injury 2. Property loss 3. Economic loss	1. Personal injury 2. Property loss 3. Economic loss

EXHIBIT 4-6   Bases for Imposing Products Liability in Japan

liability. For all of these reasons, the usefulness of contract law to impose liability on a seller for a defective product is minimal.

negligence: The neglect or omission of reasonable precaution or care.

Negligence is a more likely basis for imposing liability. Even so, the proof requirements are relatively demanding. A claimant must prove (a) the existence of a defect, (b) that the defect was the result of the defendant's conduct, (c) that the plaintiff suffered an injury, (d) that the injury was caused by the defect, and (e) that the defendant breached a duty of care to the plaintiff.[168]

Some Japanese trial courts have recently begun to relax some of these proof requirements. In particular, these courts will not require the plaintiff to show that certain products—especially foodstuffs and pharmaceuticals—are defective. Also, causation may be shown inferentially through the use of statistical data.

The remedies available upon proof of the defendant's negligence are the same as those for breach of a seller's contractual duty to perform. That is, damages for personal, property, and economic losses.

Common Law Products Liability Rules   Liability for defective products may be shown in the common law countries through breach of contract, negligence, or strict liability. See Exhibit 4-7. Because of the limitations of privity, breach of contract is seldom used.[169] Instead,

---

[168]*Id.*, Article 709.
[169]The proof requirements to show a common law breach of contract are the same as those set out in the Japanese Civil Code.

	Negligence	**Strict Liability**
Products covered	All products	Product dangerously defective in design or manufacture
Basic test	Considering all of the circumstances, was reasonable care exercised?	Was there a defect making the product unreasonably dangerous?
Elements	1. Duty of care 2. Breach of duty 3. Breach caused injury or damage	1. Unreasonably dangerous defect 2. Defect caused injury or damage
Defenses	1. Exercise of reasonable care 2. Intervening or superceding event caused injury or damage 3. Claimant unreasonably assumed risk 4. Claimant was negligent 5. Defect could not have been discovered using the scientific or technical means available at the time the product was put in circulation	1. Defect did not exist when product left defendant's control 2. Claimant misused the product in an unforeseeable manner 3. Claimant unreasonably assumed risk 4. Claimant was negligent 5. Defect could not have been discovered using the scientific or technical means available at the time the product was put in circulation
Damages available	1. Personal injury 2. Property loss	1. Personal injury 2. Property loss

EXHIBIT 4-7   Bases for Imposing Products Liability in Common Law States

claimants in these countries most often rely on the theories of negligence and (if a product is unreasonably dangerous) strict liability.

The common law negligence theory (as it relates to products liability) is essentially the same as the theory used in Japan; however, two doctrines make it somewhat easier for a common law claimant to meet the proof requirements. One is the doctrine of **res ipsa loquitur** (a Latin phrase meaning "the thing speaks for itself"). This excuses an injured claimant who can show that a product was defective when it left the hands of the defendant from having to prove that the defendant caused the defect. The other doctrine is **negligence *per se*.**[170] This excuses a claimant from showing that the defendant breached a duty of care in those cases where the defendant violated a statutory manufacturing or disclosure requirement. For example, a manufacturer who sells a stove that does not meet statutory safety requirements could be sued on the grounds that failure to observe the requirements is in and of itself an automatic breach of the manufacturer's duty of reasonable care.

Under the common law theory of **strict liability**, defendants can be held liable for acts that are unreasonably dangerous no matter what their intentions may have been or whether or not they exercised reasonable care. The theory is succinctly set out in the *Restatement of Torts* as follows:

(1) One who sells any product in a defective condition unreasonably dangerous to the user or consumer or to his property is subject to liability for physical harm thereby caused to the ultimate user or consumer or to his property, if

    (a) the seller is engaged in the business of selling such a product, and

    (b) it is expected to and does reach the user or consumer without substantial change in condition in which it is sold.

(2) The rule stated in Subsection (1) applies although

    (a) the seller has exercised all possible care in the preparation and sale of his product, and

    (b) the user or consumer has not bought the product from or entered into any contractual relation with the seller.[171]

res ipsa loquitur: (Latin: "the thing speaks for itself.") A rule of evidence that excuses an injured claimant who can show that a product was defective when it left the hands of the defendant from having to prove that the defendant caused the defect.

negligence per se: Conduct defined by statute as automatically constituting negligence.

strict liability: Imposing liability on an actor regardless of fault.

---

[170]*Per se* is Latin for "by or in itself"; intrinsically.
[171]American Law Institute, *Restatement, Second, Torts,* § 402A (1965).

The major advantage of strict liability from the claimant's perspective is that it does not require the showing of negligence. There is, however, a significant limitation: the defective product must be "unreasonably dangerous." This means that the claimant has to show either (1) that the product was dangerous beyond the expectations of the ordinary consumer or (2) that a less dangerous alternative was economically feasible for the manufacturer to produce and the manufacturer failed to produce it.

European Union Products Liability Rules

A European Union Directive establishes a common minimum products liabilities standard for all EU member states.[172] See Exhibit 4-8. This standard is similar to the strict liability theory used in the common law countries. However, it does not require the claimant to show that a defect is unreasonably dangerous. The Directive provides:

(1) A product is defective when it does not provide the safety which a person is entitled to expect, taking all circumstances into account, including:

    (a) the presentation of the product;
    (b) the use to which it could reasonably be expected that the product would be put;
    (c) the time when it was put into circulation.

(2) A product does not have a defect for the sole reason that a better product is subsequently put into circulation.[173]

The EU Directive is similar to the common law strict liability rule as it is applied in the British Commonwealth countries (but not in the United States) in that it allows EU member states to set a total maximum liability limit that a product producer may have to pay. It states that "any member state may provide that a producer's total liability for damage resulting from a death or personal injury and caused by identical items with the same defect shall be limited to an amount which may not be less than 70 million euros."[174]

Extraterritorial Application of Products Liability Laws

As is the case with unfair competition laws, the U.S. courts have been the most willing to apply their domestic products liability laws extraterritorially. The American courts consider two

	Strict Liability
Products Covered	Products other than primary agricultural products and game
Basic test	Considering all of the circumstances, was the product unsafe?
Elements	1. Unsafe defect
	2. Defect caused injury or damage
Defenses	1. Defendant did not put product into circulation
	2. Defect did not exist when product left defendant's control
	3. Defendant did not make the product for sale or distribution and did not himself sell or distribute it
	4. Defect results from compliance with a mandatory regulation issued by a public authority
	5. Defect could not have been discovered using the scientific or technical means available at the time the product was put in circulation
	6. If defendant is the manufacturer of a component, the defect relates to the design of the product to which the component is a part or the instructions provided by the manufacturer of the product
Damages available	1. Personal injury
	2. Property loss

EXHIBIT 4-8   Basis for Imposing Products Liability in the European Union

[172]European Community (now European Union) Directive No. 85/374 on the Approximation of the Laws, Regulations, and Administrative Provisions of the Member States Concerning Liability for Defective Products, *Official Journal,* No. L 210/29 (August 7, 1985).
[173]*Id.,* Article 6.
[174]*Id.,* Article 16(1). As of July 2002, 70 million euros was approximately U.S. $69 million.

issues when deciding whether they can exercise jurisdiction in a product liability case: personal jurisdiction and *forum non conveniens*.

The Personal Jurisdiction Requirements of U.S. Products Liability Laws   Products liability is a creature of the laws of the individual states of the United States rather than federal law. As a consequence, personal jurisdiction must be found in the individual states' long arm statutes. These are the same statutes that apply in antitrust cases. Most are quite broad and virtually any business activity in the local forum will be enough to establish long arm jurisdiction.

As with the antitrust cases, however, establishing long arm jurisdiction is not enough by itself. A claimant must also satisfy the federal constitutional requirement of due process by showing that the defendant had "minimum contacts" with the forum. In short, the minimum contacts test allows a court to assume jurisdiction only if (a) the defendant purposefully availed itself of doing business in the forum and (b) the defendant reasonably could have anticipated that it would have to defend itself there. The minimum contacts test is discussed in Case 4–5.

Case 4–5   Asahi Metal Industry Co., Ltd. v. Superior Court of California, Solano County   ◁~

United States Supreme Court.
United States Supreme Court Reports, vol. 480, p. 102 (1987).

JUSTICE O'CONNOR ANNOUNCED THE JUDGMENT OF THE COURT. . . .

This case presents the question whether the mere awareness on the part of a foreign defendant that the components it manufactured, sold, and delivered outside the United States would reach the forum State in the stream of commerce constitutes "minimum contacts" between the defendant and the forum state such that the exercise of jurisdiction "does not offend 'traditional notions of fair play and substantial justice.'"[175]

On September 23, 1978, on Interstate Highway 80 in Solano County, California, Gary Zurcher lost control of his Honda motorcycle and collided with a tractor. Zurcher was severely injured, and his passenger and wife, Ruth Ann Moreno, was killed. In September 1979, Zurcher filed a product liability action in the Superior Court of the state of California in and for the County of Solano. Zurcher alleged that the 1978 accident was caused by a sudden loss of air and an explosion in the rear tire of the motorcycle, and alleged that the motorcycle tire, tube, and sealant were defective.

Zurcher's complaint named, *inter alia*,[176] Cheng Shin Rubber Industrial Co., Ltd. (Cheng Shin), the Taiwanese manufacturer of the tube. Cheng Shin in turn filed a cross-complaint seeking indemnification from its codefendants and from petitioner, Asahi Metal Industry Co., Ltd. (Asahi), the manufacturer of the tube's valve assembly. Zurcher's claims against Cheng Shin and the other defendants were eventually settled and dismissed, leaving only Cheng Shin's indemnity action against Asahi.

California's long-arm statute authorizes the exercise of jurisdiction "on any basis not inconsistent with the Constitution of this state or of the United States."[177] Asahi moved to quash Cheng Shin's service of summons, arguing the state could not exert jurisdiction over it consistent with the Due Process Clause of the Fourteenth Amendment.

In relation to the motion, the following information was submitted by Asahi and Cheng Shin. Asahi is a Japanese corporation. It manufactures tire valve assemblies in Japan and sells the assemblies to Cheng Shin, and to several other tire manufacturers, for use as components in finished tire tubes. Asahi's sales to Cheng Shin took place in Taiwan. The shipments from Asahi to Cheng Shin were sent from Japan to Taiwan. Cheng Shin bought and incorporated into its tire tubes 150,000 Asahi valve assemblies in 1978; 500,000 in 1979; 500,000 in 1980; 100,000 in 1981; and 100,000 in 1982. Sales to Cheng Shin accounted for 1.24 percent of Asahi's

---

[175]International Shoe Co. v. Washington, *United States Reports,* vol. 326, p. 310 at p. 316 (Supreme Ct., 1945), quoting Milliken v. Meyer, *id.,* vol. 311, p. 457 at p. 463 (Supreme Ct., 1940).
[176]Latin: "among other things."]
[177]California Civil Procedure Code Annotated, § 410.10 (West Pub. Co., 1973).

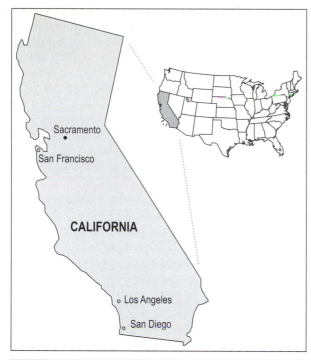

income in 1981 and 0.44 percent in 1982. Cheng Shin alleged that approximately 20 percent of its sales in the United States are in California. Cheng Shin purchases valve assemblies from other suppliers as well, and sells finished tubes throughout the world.

In 1983, an attorney for Cheng Shin conducted an informal examination of the valve stems of the tire tubes sold in one cycle store in Solano County. The attorney declared that of the approximately 115 tire tubes in the store, 97 were purportedly manufactured in Japan or Taiwan, and of those 97, 21 valve stems were marked with the circled letter "A", apparently Asahi's trademark. Of the 21 Asahi valve stems, 12 were incorporated into Cheng Shin tire tubes. The store contained 41 other Cheng Shin tubes that incorporated the valve assemblies of other manufacturers. An affidavit of a manager of Cheng Shin whose duties included the purchasing of component parts stated: "In discussions with Asahi regarding the purchase of valve stem assemblies, the fact that my Company sells tubes throughout the world and specifically the United States has been discussed. I am informed and believe that Asahi was fully aware that valve stem assemblies sold to my Company and to others would end up throughout the United States and in California." An affidavit of the president of Asahi, on the other hand, declared that Asahi "has never contemplated that its limited sales of tire valves to Cheng Shin in Taiwan would

subject it to lawsuits in California." The record does not include any contract between Cheng Shin and Asahi.

Primarily on the basis of the above information, the Superior Court denied the motion to quash summons, stating: "Asahi obviously does business on an international scale. It is not unreasonable that they defend claims of defect in their product on an international scale."[178]

The Court of Appeal of the state of California issued a peremptory writ of mandate commanding the Superior Court to quash service of summons. The court concluded that "it would be unreasonable to require Asahi to respond in California solely on the basis of ultimately realized foreseeability that the product into which its component was embodied would be sold all over the world including California."

The Supreme Court of the state of California reversed and discharged the writ issued by the Court of Appeal. The court observed: "Asahi has no offices, property or agents in California. It solicits no business in California and has made no direct sales [in California]." Moreover, "Asahi did not design or control the system of distribution that carried its valve assemblies into California." Nevertheless, the court found the exercise of jurisdiction over Asahi to be consistent with the Due Process Clause. It concluded that Asahi knew that some of the valve assemblies sold to Cheng Shin would be incorporated into tire tubes sold in California, and that Asahi benefited indirectly from the sale in California of products incorporating its components.

The court considered Asahi's intentional act of placing its components into the stream of commerce—that is, by delivering the components to Cheng Shin in Taiwan—coupled with Asahi's awareness that some of the components would eventually find their way into California, sufficient to form the basis for state court jurisdiction under the Due Process Clause.

We granted certiorari and now reverse.

II
A

The Due Process Clause of the Fourteenth Amendment limits the power of a state court to exert personal jurisdiction over a nonresident defendant. "[T]he constitutional touchstone" of the determination whether an exercise of personal jurisdiction comports with due process "remains whether the defendant purposefully established 'minimum contacts' in the forum state."[179] Most recently we have reaffirmed the oft-quoted reasoning of [our decision in] *Hanson v. Denckla*[180] that minimum contacts must have a basis in "some act by which the defendant purposefully avails itself of the

[178]Order Denying Motion to Quash Summons, Zurcher v. Dunlop Tire & Rubber Co., No. 76180 (Super. Ct., Solano County, California, April 20, 1983).
[179]Burger King Corp. v. Rudzewicz, *United States Reports,* vol. 471, p. 462 at p. 474 (Supreme Ct., 1985), quoting International Shoe Co. v. Washington, *id.,* vol. 326 at p. 316.
[180]*Id.,* vol. 357, p. 235 at p. 253 (1958).

privilege of conducting activities within the forum state, thus invoking the benefits and protections of its laws." [In] *Burger King*[181] [we said:] "Jurisdiction is proper . . . where the contacts proximately result from actions by the defendant himself that create a 'substantial connection' with the forum state."

Applying the principle that minimum contacts must be based on an act of the defendant, the Court in *World-Wide Volkswagen Corp. v. Woodson*[182] rejected the assertion that a consumer's unilateral act of bringing the defendant's product into the forum state was a sufficient constitutional basis for personal jurisdiction over the defendant. It had been argued in *World-Wide Volkswagen* that because an automobile retailer and its wholesale distributor sold a product mobile by design and purpose, they could foresee being haled into court in the distant states into which their customers might drive. The Court rejected this concept of foreseeability as an insufficient basis for jurisdiction under the Due Process Clause. The Court disclaimed, however, the idea that "foreseeability is wholly irrelevant" to personal jurisdiction, concluding that "[t]he forum state does not exceed its powers under the Due Process Clause if it asserts personal jurisdiction over a corporation that delivers its products into the stream of commerce with the expectation that they will be purchased by consumers in the forum state."[183] The Court reasoned:

> "When a corporation 'purposefully avails itself of the privilege of conducting activities within the forum state,'[184] it has clear notice that it is subject to suit there, and can act to alleviate the risk of burdensome litigation by procuring insurance, passing the expected costs on to customers, or, if the risks are too great, severing its connection with the state. Hence if the sale of a product of a manufacturer or distributor . . . is not simply an isolated occurrence, but arises from the efforts of the manufacturer or distributor to serve, directly or indirectly, the market for its product in other states, it is not unreasonable to subject it to suit in one of those states if its allegedly defective merchandise has there been the source of injury to its owners or to others."[185]

In *World-Wide Volkswagen* itself, the state court sought to base jurisdiction not on any act of the defendant, but on the foreseeable unilateral actions of the consumer. Since *World-Wide Volkswagen*, lower courts have been confronted with cases in which the defendant acted by placing a product in the stream of commerce, and the stream eventually swept defendant's product into the forum state, but the defendant did nothing else to purposefully avail itself of the market in the forum state. Some courts have understood the Due Process Clause, as interpreted in *World-Wide Volkswagen,* to allow an exercise of personal jurisdiction to be based on no more than the defendant's act of placing the product in the stream of commerce. Other courts have understood the Due Process Clause and the above-quoted language in *World-Wide Volkswagen* to require the action of the defendant to be more purposefully directed at the forum state than the mere act of placing a product in the stream of commerce.

The reasoning of the Supreme Court of California in the present case illustrates the former interpretation of *World-Wide Volkswagen*. The Supreme Court of California held that, because the stream of commerce eventually brought some valves Asahi sold Cheng Shin into California, Asahi's awareness that its valves would be sold in California was sufficient to permit California to exercise jurisdiction over Asahi consistent with the requirements of the Due Process Clause. The Supreme Court of California's position was consistent with those courts that have held that mere foreseeability or awareness was a constitutionally sufficient basis for personal jurisdiction if the defendant's product made its way into the forum state while still in the stream of commerce.[186]

Other courts, however, have understood the Due Process Clause to require something more than that the defendant was aware of its product's entry into the forum state through the stream of commerce in order for the state to exert jurisdiction over the defendant. In the present case, for example, the state Court of Appeal did not read the Due Process Clause, as interpreted by *World-Wide Volkswagen*, to allow "mere foreseeability that the product will enter the forum state [to] be enough by itself to establish jurisdiction over the distributor and retailer." In *Humble v. Toyota Motor Co.*[187] an injured car passenger brought suit against Arakawa Auto Body Company, a Japanese corporation that manufactured car seats for Toyota. Arakawa did no business in the United States; it had no office, affiliate, subsidiary, or agent in the United States; it manufactured its component parts outside the United States and delivered them to Toyota Motor Company in Japan. The Court of Appeals, adopting the reasoning of the District Court in that case, noted that although it "does not doubt that Arakawa could have foreseen that its product would find its way into the United States," it would be "manifestly unjust" to require Arakawa to defend itself in the United States.

---

[181]*Id.*, vol. 471 at p. 475.
[182]*Id.*, vol. 444, p. 286 (1980).
[183]*Id.*, at pp. 297–298.
[184]Hanson v. Denckla, *id.*, vol. 357 at p. 253.
[185]*Id.*, at 297.
[186]*See* Bean Dredging Corp. v. Dredge Technology Corp., *Federal Reports, Second Series,* vol. 744, p. 1081 (5th Circuit Ct. of Appeals, 1984);
    Hedrick v. Daiko Shoji Co., *id.*, vol. 715, p. 1355 (9th Circuit Ct. of Appeals, 1983).
[187]*Id.*, vol. 727. p. 709 (8th Circuit Ct. of Appeals, 1984).

We now find this latter position to be consonant with the requirements of due process. The "substantial connection," between the defendant and the forum state necessary for a finding of minimum contacts must come about by an action of the defendant purposefully directed toward the forum state. The placement of a product into the stream of commerce, without more, is not an act of the defendant purposefully directed toward the forum state.

Additional conduct of the defendant may indicate an intent or purpose to serve the market in the forum state, for example, designing the product for the market in the forum state, advertising in the forum state, establishing channels for providing regular advice to customers in the forum state, or marketing the product through a distributor who has agreed to serve as the sales agent in the forum state. But a defendant's awareness that the stream of commerce may or will sweep the product into the forum state does not convert the mere act of placing the product into the stream into an act purposefully directed toward the forum state.

Assuming, *arguendo*,[188] that respondents have established Asahi's awareness that some of the valves sold to Cheng Shin would be incorporated into tire tubes sold in California, respondents have not demonstrated any action by Asahi to purposefully avail itself of the California market. Asahi does not do business in California. It has no office, agents, employees, or property in California. It does not advertise or otherwise solicit business in California. It did not create, control, or employ the distribution system that brought its valves to California. There is no evidence that Asahi designed its product in anticipation of sales in California. On the basis of these facts, the exertion of personal jurisdiction over Asahi by the Superior Court of California exceeds the limits of due process.

B

The strictures of the Due Process Clause forbid a state court to exercise personal jurisdiction over Asahi under circumstances that would offend "traditional notions of fair play and substantial justice."[189]

We have previously explained that the determination of the reasonableness of the exercise of jurisdiction in each case will depend on an evaluation of several factors. A court must consider the burden on the defendant, the interests of the forum state, and the plaintiff's interest in obtaining relief. It must also weigh in its determination "the interstate judicial system's interest in obtaining the most efficient resolution of controversies; and the shared interest of the several states in furthering fundamental substantive social policies."[190]

A consideration of these factors in the present case clearly reveals the unreasonableness of the assertion of jurisdiction over Asahi, even apart from the question of the placement of goods in the stream of commerce.

Certainly the burden on the defendant in this case is severe. Asahi has been commanded by the Supreme Court of California not only to traverse the distance between Asahi's headquarters in Japan and the Superior Court of California in and for the County of Solano, but also to submit its dispute with Cheng Shin to a foreign nation's judicial system. The unique burdens placed upon one who must defend oneself in a foreign legal system should have significant weight in assessing the reasonableness of stretching the long arm of personal jurisdiction over national borders.

When minimum contacts have been established, often the interests of the plaintiff and the forum in the exercise of jurisdiction will justify even the serious burdens placed on the alien defendant. In the present case, however, the interests of the plaintiff and the forum in California's assertion of jurisdiction over Asahi are slight. All that remains is a claim for indemnification asserted by Cheng Shin, a Taiwanese corporation, against Asahi. The transaction on which the indemnification claim is based took place in Taiwan; Asahi's components were shipped from Japan to Taiwan. Cheng Shin has not demonstrated that it is more convenient for it to litigate its indemnification claim against Asahi in California rather than in Taiwan or Japan.

Because the plaintiff is not a California resident, California's legitimate interests in the dispute have considerably diminished. The Supreme Court of California argued that the state had an interest in "protecting its consumers by ensuring that foreign manufacturers comply with the state's safety standards." The state Supreme Court's definition of California's interest, however, was overly broad. The dispute between Cheng Shin and Asahi is primarily about indemnification rather than safety standards. Moreover, it is not at all clear at this point that California law should govern the question whether a Japanese corporation should indemnify a Taiwanese corporation on the basis of a sale made in Taiwan and a shipment of goods from Japan to Taiwan. The possibility of being haled into a California court as a result of an accident involving Asahi's components undoubtedly creates an additional deterrent to the manufacture of unsafe components; however, similar pressures will be placed on Asahi by the purchasers of its components as long as those who use Asahi components in their final products, and sell those products in California, are subject to the application of California tort law.

[188Latin: "for the sake of the argument."]
189International Shoe Co. v. Washington, *United States Reports,* vol. 326, p. 310 at p. 316 (Supreme Ct., 1945), quoting Milliken v. Meyer, *id.,*
  vol. 311, p. 457 at p. 463 (Supreme Ct., 1940).
190World-Wide Volkswagen, *id.,* vol. 444 at p. 292.

World-Wide Volkswagen also admonished courts to take into consideration the interests of the "several states," in addition to the forum state, in the efficient judicial resolution of the dispute and the advancement of substantive policies. In the present case, this advice calls for a court to consider the procedural and substantive policies of other nations whose interests are affected by the assertion of jurisdiction by the California court. The procedural and substantive interests of other nations in a state court's assertion of jurisdiction over an alien defendant will differ from case to case. In every case, however, those interests, as well as the Federal Government's interest in its foreign relations policies, will be best served by a careful inquiry into the reasonableness of the assertion of jurisdiction in the particular case, and an unwillingness to find the serious burdens on an alien defendant outweighed by minimal interests on the part of the plaintiff or the forum state. "Great care and reserve should be exercised when extending our notions of personal jurisdiction into the international field."[191]

Considering the international context, the heavy burden on the alien defendant, and the slight interests of the plaintiff and the forum state, the exercise of personal jurisdiction by a California court over Asahi in this instance would be unreasonable and unfair.

III

Because the facts of this case do not establish minimum contacts such that the exercise of personal jurisdiction is consistent with fair play and substantial justice, the judgment of the Supreme Court of California is reversed, and the case is remanded for further proceedings not inconsistent with this opinion.

It is so ordered. ■

---

[191]United States v. First National City Bank, *id.,* vol. 379, p. 378 at p. 404 (1965) (Justice Harlan dissenting).

---

forum non conveniens: (Latin: "inconvenient forum.") Doctrine that a municipal court will decline to hear a dispute when it can be better or more conveniently settled in a foreign forum.

sharp practices: Business dealings meant to obtain a benefit for a person or firm regardless of the means used.

Forum Non Conveniens   Unlike their approach to antitrust cases, American courts do not apply a separate test for subject matter jurisdiction in products liability cases. Nevertheless, the considerations the courts look at in antitrust cases are sometimes explored in products liability cases through the device of *forum non conveniens*. This allows courts applying this device to determine if the forum state has enough interest in the outcome of the dispute to take jurisdiction. The factors considered are (a) the private interests of the parties (i.e., the ease and cost of access to documents and witnesses) and (b) the public interest factors (i.e., the interest of the forum state, the burden on the courts, and notions of judicial comity).[192]

Sharp Practices

Sharp practices are dishonest business dealings meant to obtain a benefit for an individual or firm regardless of the means used. They include such conduct as misrepresentation and bribery. Generally, in the past, only host states regulated the sharp practices of investors and multinational enterprises. However, with the adoption of the OECD Convention on Combating Bribery of Foreign Public Officials in International Business Transactions—discussed earlier—sharp practices are now to be regulated by home states as well. Because the OECD's member states are the wealthiest countries—including Japan, Germany, France, Italy, the United Kingdom, and the United States—nearly all of the world's major multinational enterprises will soon be subject to these regulations.

The one exception to the old rule that sharp practices were regulated only by host states was the United States. In 1977, in response to several scandals involving American companies bribing foreign government officials to obtain lucrative contracts (especially Lockheed Aircraft's bribing of the Prime Minister of Japan to secure sales of jet fighter planes), the United States enacted the Foreign Corrupt Practices Act (FCPA).[193]

The FCPA, as currently written,[194] attacks sharp practices in two ways. First, it imposes accounting obligations on companies as a means of indirectly deterring bribery. These require

---

[192]*See* Gulf Oil Corp. v. Gilbert, *id.,* vol. 330, p. 501 at pp. 508–509 (Supreme Ct., 1947).
[193]Public Law 95–213, *Statutes at Large,* vol. 91, p. 1494 (December 19, 1977), amending *United States Code,* Title 15, §§ 78q(b), 78dd, 78ff(a) (1976).
[194]As it was originally enacted, the FCPA proved difficult to interpret and apply. Its attempts to distinguish between prohibited "bribery" payments and permissible "facilitating" payments were confusing. Terms and phrases such as "essentially ministerial or clerical," "obtaining or retaining business," "reason to know," "such thing of value," and

MNEs (a) to account with "reasonable detail" for all company transactions (especially the transfer of assets) and (b) to maintain a system of internal accounting controls that provide "reasonable assurances" that all transactions are properly authorized by the company.[195]

Second, the FCPA makes it illegal for American companies, foreign companies registered with the U.S. Securities and Exchange Commission, or their officers, agents, or employees to knowingly bribe a foreign government official, a foreign political party official, or a candidate for foreign political office.[196] That is, firms and individuals will be criminally liable if they make a payment "knowing" or in "conscious disregard" that it will be used as a bribe—a bribe being the giving of, or the promise to give, anything of value to influence a foreign official to let the firm or individual making the payment to engage in a new business or to allow that firm or individual to continue its existing business.

The FCPA's antibribery provisions do not apply to so-called "routine governmental actions." That is, a person is not engaging in bribery by paying a foreign official to obtain permits, licenses, or documents that allow the person to do business in the official's country. Nor is it a bribe to pay an official to process papers, such as visas; to obtain work orders, police protection, or mail, phone, power, or water services; to schedule inspections; or to do any other acts of a "similar nature." In addition, a person charged with violating the FCPA may defend himself by showing that the payment was lawful under the written laws of the foreign country or by showing that the payment was a "reasonable and bona fide expenditure" related to carrying out or executing a contract.

Not all of the participants in a bribery scheme are subject to prosecution under the Foreign Corrupt Practices Act. Case 4–6 points out that one group was not the intended target of this legislation.

"corruptly" were not defined. As a consequence, many American exporters, uncertain about the applicability of the act and their potential liability, retreated from the global marketplace.

In response to the "chilling effect" that some of the provisions in the act were having on American competitiveness abroad, Congress amended the FCPA as part of the Omnibus Trade and Competitiveness Act of 1988.

[195]"Reasonable detail" and "reasonable assurances" are defined as "such level of detail and degree of assurance as would satisfy prudent officials in the conduct of their own affairs." Criminal liability will attach, but only if persons "knowingly circumvent or knowingly fail" to maintain the system of accounting controls required by the act. The accounting provisions, however, are not meant to impose liability on a company for inadvertent or technical errors in maintaining books and records.

[196]*United States Code,* Title 15, §§ 78dd-2(b)(1)(B)(3), 78ff(c)(3) (1976). In United States v. McLean, *Federal Reporter, Second Series,* vol. 738, p. 644 (1984), the court held that a company's officers, agents, and employees could only be prosecuted after their company was first convicted. This requirement, it said, was necessary to keep the company from using its officers, agents, and employees as scapegoats.

Case 4–6 United States v. Blondek, Tull, Castle, and Lowry

United States District Court for the Northern District of Texas, 1990.
Federal Supplement, vol. 741, p. 116 (1990).

CHIEF JUDGE BAREFOOT SANDERS

All four defendants in this case are charged in a one-count indictment with conspiring to violate the *Foreign Corrupt Practices Act* of 1977 (FCPA).[197] Defendants Castle and Lowry have moved to dismiss the indictment against them on the grounds that as Canadian officials, they cannot be convicted of the offense charged against them. The two other defendants, Blondek and Tull, are U.S. private citizens, and they do not challenge their indictment on this ground. The Court has considered supplemental briefing and oral argument on the motions.

The indictment charges all four defendants with conspiring to bribe foreign officials in violation of FCPA. Blondek and Tull were employees of Eagle Bus Company, a U.S. concern as defined in the FCPA.

---

[197]*United States Code,* Title 15, §§ 78dd-1, 78dd-2.

According to the indictment, they paid a $50,000 bribe to defendants Castle and Lowry to ensure that their bid to provide buses to the Saskatchewan provincial government would be accepted.

There is no question that the payment of the bribe by defendants Blondek and Tull is illegal under the FCPA, and that they may be prosecuted for conspiring to violate the Act. Nor is it disputed that defendants Castle and Lowry could not be charged with violating the FCPA itself, since the Act does not criminalize the receipt of a bribe by a foreign official. The issue here is whether the government may prosecute Castle and Lowry under the general conspiracy statute[198] for conspiring to violate the FCPA. Put more simply, the question is whether foreign officials, whom the government concedes it cannot prosecute under the FCPA itself, may be prosecuted under the general conspiracy statute for conspiring to violate the Act.

In *Gebardi v. United States*,[199] the Supreme Court confronted a similar issue: whether a woman who agreed to be transported by her lover across state lines to engage in sexual intercourse could be convicted of a conspiracy to violate the Mann Act. The Mann Act prohibited the transportation of women across state boundaries for immoral purposes, but did not criminalize the conduct of the women being transported. Acknowledging that it could not prosecute the woman for violating the Mann Act itself, the government prosecuted her instead for conspiring to violate the Mann Act. The woman objected to her conviction on the grounds that the Mann Act exempted her from prosecution for her participation.

The Court noted first that the incapacity of a person to commit the substantive offense does not necessarily imply that he may conspire with others to commit the offense with impunity, since the state may criminalize the collective planning of the criminal conduct.[200] For example, it is a crime for a bankrupt to conceal property from his trustee, and thus only bankrupts may be convicted of the substantive offense of concealing property. But convictions of others for conspiring with the bankrupt to conceal property have been upheld.[201]

The Court distinguished the case before it on the grounds that a violation of the Mann Act necessarily required the agreement of the woman to the criminal act—her transportation across a state line. Yet the Act did not make the woman's consent a crime. The Court concluded that by excluding the transported woman from prosecution under the Mann Act, Congress evinced an affirmative legislative policy "to leave her acquiescence unpunished."[202] A necessary implication of that policy was that the woman's agreement to participate was immune from any kind of prosecution, including prosecution for conspiring to violate the Mann Act. To do otherwise, the Court reasoned, would allow the executive branch to extend the reach of the Act beyond the scope of Congress' intention. . . .[203] On this basis, the Court reversed the conviction of the woman for conspiring to violate the Mann Act.

The principle enunciated by the Supreme Court in *Gebardi* squarely applies to the case before this Court. Congress intended in both the FCPA and the Mann Act to deter and punish certain activities which necessarily involved the agreement of at least two people,[204] but Congress chose in both statutes to punish only one party to the agreement.

In *Gebardi*, the Supreme Court refused to disregard Congress' intention to exempt one party by allowing the executive to prosecute that party under the general conspiracy statute for precisely the same conduct. Congress made the same choice in drafting the FCPA, and by the same analysis, this Court may not allow the executive to override the congressional intent not to prosecute foreign officials for their participation in the prohibited acts.

In drafting the Mann Act, Congress was probably motivated by a protective instinct toward women based on a belief that most women would not participate in the activity without coercion or duress by the man involved. The government tries to distinguish *Gebardi* on this ground, asserting that "the exception" provided in *Gebardi* to prosecution for conspiracy only applies to individuals belonging to the class of persons the criminal statute was designed to protect.

Nothing in *Gebardi* indicates that only "protected" persons are exempted from conspiracy charges; rather, the Court explicitly built its analysis on Congress' clear intention, evinced by the plain language of the statute, to exempt the transported women from *all* prosecutions for their involvement in the prohibited activities. A similar intent is apparent from the language of the FCPA, especially when compared to other bribery statutes which criminalize both the payment and receipt of bribes. . . .

Even accepting the general idea that Congress must have some reason for exempting from prosecution a class of persons necessarily involved in the prohibited conduct, Congress was quite explicit about its reasons, but none of these reasons have anything to do with foreign

---

[198]*Id.*, Title 18, § 371.

[199]*United States Reports*, vol. 287, p. 112 (Supreme Ct., 1932).

[200]*Id.*, at pp. 120–121.

[201]*See id.* at p. 120 n. 5 and the cases cited therein.

[202]*Id.*, at p. 123.

[203]*Id.*

[204]In the Mann Act, the two necessary parties were the transporter and the transported woman, and in the FCPA the necessary parties were the U.S. company paying the bribe and the foreign official accepting it.

officials. Instead, the exclusive focus was on the U.S. companies and the effects of their conduct within and on the United States.

First, Congress was concerned about the domestic effects of such payments. In the early 1970s, the Watergate affair and resulting investigations revealed that the payment of bribes to foreign officials was a widespread practice among U.S. companies. In the House Report accompanying an earlier version of the Act, it was noted that more than 400 companies had admitted making such payments, distributing well over 300 million dollars in corporate funds to foreign officials.[205] Such massive payments had many negative domestic effects, not the least of which was the distortion of, and resulting lack of confidence in, the free market system within the United States.

The payment of bribes to influence the acts or decision[s] of foreign officials . . . is unethical. It is counter to the moral expectations and values of the American public. But not only is it unethical, it is bad business as well. It erodes public confidence in the integrity of the free market system. . . . In short, it rewards corruption instead of efficiency and puts pressure on ethical enterprises to lower their standards or risk losing business.[206]

The House Committee further noted that many of the payments were made not to compete with foreign companies, but rather to gain an edge over a competitor in the United States.[207]

Congress' second motivation was the effect of such payments by U.S. companies on the United States' foreign relations. The legislative history repeatedly cited the negative effects the revelations of such bribes had wrought upon friendly foreign governments and officials.[208] Yet the drafters acknowledged, and the final law reflects this, that some payments that would be unethical or even illegal within the United States might not be perceived similarly in foreign countries, and those payment should not be criminalized. For example, grease payments, those payments made "to assure or to speed the proper performance of a foreign official's duties," are not illegal under the Act since they were often a part of the custom of doing

business in foreign countries.[209] Additionally, the Act was later amended to permit an affirmative defense on the grounds that the payment was legal in the country in which it was made.[210] These exclusions reinforce the proposition that Congress had absolutely no intention of prosecuting the foreign officials involved, but was concerned solely with regulating the conduct of U.S. entities and citizens.[211]

The government argues that the following statement in the House Report evinces a clear intent by Congress to allow conspiracy prosecutions of foreign officials: "The concepts of aiding and abetting and joint participation would apply to a violation under this bill in the same manner in which those concepts have always applied in both SEC][212] civil actions and implied private actions brought under the securities laws generally."[213] The government's reliance is misplaced. Congress included this statement to clarify the rights of *civil* litigants in pursuing a private right of action under the Act, an area entirely different from criminal prosecutions.

This language does not refute the overwhelming evidence of a congressional intent to exempt foreign officials from prosecution for receiving bribes, especially since Congress knew it had the power to reach foreign officials in many cases, and yet declined to exercise that power.[214] Congress' awareness of the extent of its own power reveals the fallacy in the government's position that only those classes of persons deemed by Congress to need protection are exempted from prosecution under the conspiracy statute. The question is not whether Congress *could have* included foreign officials within the Act's proscriptions, but rather whether Congress *intended to do so*, or more specifically, whether Congress intended the general conspiracy statute, passed many years before the FCPA, to reach foreign officials.

The drafters of the statute knew that they could, consistently with international law, reach foreign officials in certain circumstances. But they were equally well aware of, and actively considered the "inherent jurisdictional, enforcement, and diplomatic difficulties" raised by the application of the bill to noncitizens of the United

[205]House of Representatives Report No. 640, p. 4 (95th Congress, 1st Session, 1977).
[206]*Id.*, at pp. 4–5. *See also* Senate Report No. 114, p. 4 (95th Congress, 1st Session, 1977).
[207]House of Representatives Report No. 640, at p. 5 (95th Congress, 1st Session, 1977).
[208]*Id. See also* Senate Report No. 114, p. 4 (95th Congress, 1st Session, 1977).
[209]House of Representatives Report No. 640, at p. 8 (95th Congress, 1st Session, 1977); *see also United States Code,* Title 15, § 78dd-2(b).
[210]*United States Code,* Title 15, § 78dd-2(c)(1).
[211]Congress considered, and rejected, the idea that a demand for a payment by a foreign official would be a valid defense to a criminal prosecution under the Act, because "at some point the U.S. company would make a conscious decision whether or not to pay a bribe. That the payment may have been first proposed by the recipient rather than the U.S. company does not alter the corrupt purpose on the part of the person paying the bribe."
   Senate Report No. 114 at pp. 10–11, *United States Code, Congressional & Administrative News,* at p. 4108 (1977). The very fact that Congress considered this issue underscores Congress' exclusive focus on the U.S. companies in *making* the payment. If the drafters were concerned that a demand by a foreign official might be considered a defense to a prosecution, they clearly were expecting that only the payors of the bribes, and not the foreign officials demanding and/or receiving the bribes, would be prosecuted.
[212Securities and Exchange Commission. A U.S. government agency created by the Securities Exchange Act of 1934 that is responsible for protecting the interests of investors and the public in connection with the public issuance and sale of corporate securities.]
[213]House of Representatives Report No. 640, at p. 8 (95th Congress, 1st Session, 1977).
[214]*See* House of Representatives Report No. 640, at p. 12, n. 3 (95th Congress, 1st Session, 1977) (United States has power to reach conduct of noncitizens under international law).

States.[215] In the conference report, the conferees indicated that the bill would reach as far as possible, and listed all the persons or entities who could be prosecuted. The list includes virtually every person or entity involved, including foreign nationals who participated in the payment of the bribe when the U.S. courts had jurisdiction over them.[216] But foreign officials were not included.

It is important to remember that Congress intended that these persons would be covered by the Act itself, without resort to the conspiracy statute. Yet, the very individuals whose participation was required in every case—the foreign officials accepting the bribe—were excluded from prosecution for the substantive offense. Given that Congress included virtually every possible person connected to the payments except foreign officials, it is only logical to conclude that Congress affirmatively chose to exempt this small class of persons from prosecution.

Most likely, Congress made this choice because U.S. businesses were perceived to be the aggressors, and the efforts expended in resolving the diplomatic, jurisdictional, and enforcement difficulties that would arise upon the prosecution of foreign officials was not worth the minimal deterrent value of such prosecutions. Further minimizing the deterrent value of a U.S. prosecution was the fact that many foreign nations already prohibited the receipt of a bribe by an official.[217] In fact, whenever a nation permitted such payments, Congress allowed them as well.[218]

Based upon the language of the statute and the legislative history, this Court finds in the FCPA what the Supreme Court in *Gebardi* found in the Mann Act: an affirmative legislative policy to leave unpunished a well-defined group of persons who were necessary parties to the acts constituting a violation of the substantive law. The government has presented no reason why the prosecution of defendants Castle and Lowry should go forward in the face of the congressional intent not to prosecute foreign officials. If anything, the facts of this case support Congress' decision to forego such prosecutions since foreign nations could and should prosecute their own officials for accepting bribes. Under the revised statutes of Canada the receipt of bribes by officials is a crime, with a prison term not to exceed five years,[219] and the Royal Canadian Mounted Police have been actively investigating the case, apparently even before any arrests by U.S. officials.[220] In fact, the Canadian police have informed defendant Castle's counsel that charges will likely be brought against defendants Castle and Lowry in Canada.[221] Thus, prosecution and punishment will be accomplished by the government which most directly suffered the abuses allegedly perpetrated by its own officials, and there is no need to contravene Congress' desire to avoid such prosecutions by the United States.

As in *Gebardi*, it would be absurd to take away with the earlier and more general conspiracy statute the exemption from prosecution granted to foreign officials by the later and more specific FCPA. Following the Supreme Court's admonition in an analogous criminal case that "[a]ll laws are to be given a sensible construction; and a literal application of a statute, which would lead to absurd consequences, should be avoided whenever a reasonable application can be given to it, consistent with the legislative purpose,"[222] the Court declines to extend the reach of the FCPA through the application of the conspiracy statute.

Accordingly, defendants Castle and Lowry may not be prosecuted for conspiring to violate the *Foreign Corrupt Practices Act*, and the indictment against them is dismissed. ■

---

[215]*See* House of Representatives Conference Report No. 831, p. 14 (95th Congress, 1st Session, 1977).
[216]*Id.*
[217]*See* Senate Report No. 114, at p. 4 (95th Congress, 1st Session, 1977) (testimony of Secretary Blumenthal that in many nations such payments are illegal).
[218]*See United States Code,* Title 15, § 78dd-2(c)(1).
[219]*See* Criminal Code, *Revised Statutes of Canada,* chap. C-46, § 121 (pp. 81–84) (1985).
[220]Defendant Castle's and Lowry's Supplemental Memorandum in Support of Motion to Dismiss, filed May 14, 1990, at p. 10.
[221]*Id.* at p. 10 and nn. 3, 4.
[222]United States v. Katz, *United States Reports,* vol. 271, pp. 354, 357 (Supreme Ct., 1926).

E. HOST STATE REGULATION OF MULTINATIONAL ENTERPRISES

Host states regulate multinational enterprises in much the same way that home states do. Thus, host states will apply their own unfair competition, products liability, and sharp practices rules to foreign multinationals operating within their territory. The focus of host state regulation, however, is not on making the local parent company responsible for the conduct of a foreign subsidiary, but on making the foreign parent responsible for the conduct of the local subsidiary. This generally leads host state courts to make three types of investigations: (1) whether a foreign company has consented to the jurisdiction of the host state; (2) whether a local firm is part of a common enterprise with a foreign firm, making both liable for activities of the local firm;

and (3) whether the independent corporate status of a subsidiary can be ignored so that liability can be imposed on its parent.

Consent to the Jurisdiction of the Host State

As we have seen earlier, a person or company must give its consent (either expressly or impliedly) before either will be subject to the jurisdiction of a local state. A company that incorporates or has its main office in a state is said to have expressly consented to the jurisdiction of that state. Similarly, a foreign company that applies to obtain a certificate to do business in a host state must expressly consent to the state's jurisdiction as a condition of obtaining the certificate. One must distinguish between applying for a certificate to do business and setting up a subsidiary. Whereas the subsidiary is a local firm and therefore subject to the jurisdiction of the local state, the parent is merely a foreign shareholder that has not consented to the state's jurisdiction.

Implied consent to the jurisdiction of a state can be found from a foreign firm doing business within the state. As we have already discussed, courts will look to local long arm statutes that define "doing business" and to basic concepts of fairness before they will exercise jurisdiction over a foreign company. Commonly, jurisdiction will be found if a company is—either directly or through an agent—carrying on a business, soliciting business, or engaging in any other "persistent" conduct related to the making of a profit.

Common Enterprise Liability

When individuals or companies (including related subsidiary companies of a multinational firm) function as part of a common enterprise, courts will treat them as if they were members of a joint venture or partnership, with each of them having joint[223] or joint and several[224] liability for the obligations of the entire enterprise. In determining whether persons or firms are members of a common enterprise, courts look at the intent of the parties. If the parties have not entered into a formal agreement creating a partnership or joint venture, the courts will consider several factors in determining intent, including (a) sharing of profits or losses, (b) sharing in the management, and (c) joint ownership of the business.

The significance of **common enterprise liability** is illustrated by Case 4–7.

common enterprise liability: Each member of a common enterprise will have liability for the conduct of the entire enterprise.

---

[223]"Joint liability" means that all of the members in a venture must be sued together.

[224]"Joint and several liability" means that any one of the members in a venture may be sued separately whether or not the other members are sued.

Case 4–7 Touche Ross & Co. v. Bank Intercontinental, Limited

The Cayman Islands, Grand Court, 1986.
The Cayman Islands Law Reports, vol. 1986–87, p. 156 (1988).

Touche Ross & Co., a firm of accountants practicing in the Cayman Islands, carried out audit work in the Cayman Islands for the Bank Intercontinental, Limited., a company incorporated under Cayman law. The Bank brought suit in Florida alleging professional negligence against a firm named as Touche Ross & Co., maintaining that it was a multinational partnership of accountants with offices in Florida, New York, the Cayman Islands, and worldwide. Individuals alleged to be partners in this multinational

firm, who were resident in Florida and various other parts of the world, were joined as defendants in the suit.

Touche Ross & Co., a firm of accountants constituted under the laws of New York, then initiated suit in the Cayman Islands seeking to restrain the Bank from continuing to prosecute the Florida suit. The New York firm (the plaintiff in this case and the defendant in Florida) argued that the audit work had been carried out exclusively by the Cayman firm of the same name according to the terms of a contract between that firm and the defendant that was governed by Cayman law. It urged the court to hold that the proper forum for the trial of the Bank's suit was the Cayman Islands, because the suit had no real connection

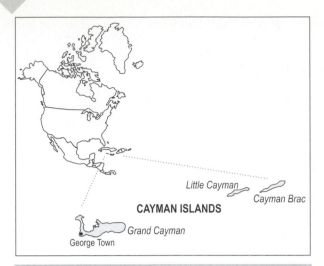

MAP 4-6 Cayman Islands (1988)

with Florida and the Bank only alleged that Touche Ross & Co. was a single worldwide partnership (with partners resident in Florida) so that it could bring the suit there.

This Court initially granted an ex parte[225] injunction based on the plaintiff's allegations that the Florida proceedings appeared to be an attempt to cloak Touche Ross & Co. in a multinational mantle with connections to Florida as a pretext for suing there. This Court gave the Bank (the defendant in this case and the plaintiff in Florida) leave to apply to discharge the injunction and the Bank did so. Its decision on the Bank's application follows.

JUDGE HULL: . . .

In the *ex parte* application, Mr. Foster [counsel] for the plaintiff in Cayman relied on affidavits sworn by Mark Edward Davidson, a New York attorney-at-law, Richard Surgeson, a chartered accountant in the Cayman Islands, and Mr. Foster himself.

Mr. Foster submitted that the evidence supporting his application showed that the Bank was a Cayman company and that the Florida action related to audit work performed by chartered accountants in the Cayman Islands and in substance alleged professional negligence. He said that the work had been performed by "Touche Ross & Co.," a Cayman firm of chartered accountants, pursuant to a contract between that firm and the Bank. The evidence showed that the contract was to be interpreted in accordance with the law of the Cayman Islands, and that the plaintiff in Cayman (i.e. "Touche Ross & Co. of New York") was a separate entity from the Cayman firm and had in no way been

connected with the contract or with any audit work undertaken by the Cayman firm for the Bank. The Cayman Islands were the proper forum for the action. The matter had no real connection with Florida. The Bank had alleged that the defendant in the Florida action was one worldwide firm in order to bring the action there. Mr. Foster said that he had to satisfy me that it was acting in bad faith; he submitted that the evidence showed that the allegation was specious.[226]

. . . In his affidavit, Mr. Surgeson stated that Touche Ross & Co. in the Cayman Islands was an entirely separate and different legal entity from the partnership known as "Touche Ross & Co. of New York." He deposed that the firms had separate partners, that neither had any proprietary or other interest in the other, that they determined independently the conduct of their respective businesses, and that the Cayman firm had no offices or records in the United States. He also deposed that to the best of his knowledge and belief the New York firm did not have offices or operate here, nor were any of its partners or employees authorized to practice as accountants here, and that none of the partners or employees in the Cayman firm were authorized to practice public accounting within the United States.

Mr. Surgeson said that the only relationship between the two firms was that they were both affiliated to a Swiss *verein*[227] known as "Touche Ross International," which was an association made up of various firms throughout the world to enhance professional co-operation and cooperation between its affiliates. These firms however remained separate entities and none was subject to control by any of the others. They determined separately which clients they would serve and were individually responsible for their own obligations to their clients' affiliates. The *verein* did however undertake so far as possible to assist other affiliates by providing services on request within its own jurisdiction. The bank, Mr. Surgeson said, had been a client of the Cayman firm which had audited its accounts for the years 1980, 1981, and 1982. This work was done at the request of the bank. The New York firm had not been involved in any way in that work, nor to the best of his knowledge or belief had the bank ever been its client or had professional services provided by it.

Mr. Davidson deposed that he was the New York attorney for the New York firm. . . .

Mr. Davidson's evidence was . . . that the New York firm was legally a separate entity from the Cayman firm. They were not authorized in law to practice in each other's jurisdiction. The Cayman firm had no officers in the United States, the bank was a Cayman company, the firm which had done the work in issue was Caymanian, and the papers

---

[225]Latin: "from one party or side." An *ex parte* injunction is one that is granted upon the request and for the benefit of one party only, and without notice to the party or parties adversely interested and without the latter being present or having the opportunity to contest the granting of the injunction.]

[226]Specious: "having a false look of truth or genuineness."]

[227]German: "association, alliance, or syndicate."]

and the witnesses were located here. The alleged injury occurred here and involved issues of Cayman law. . . .

. . . In support of its application to discharge the injunction, the Bank filed two affidavits.

One was by Mr. George Cassidy, stating that he was the Chairman of the Board of the Bank and that he was authorized to make the affidavit. The other was sworn by Mr. Stephen Martin Zukoff, who deposed that he was an attorney-at-law licensed to practice in the States of New York and Florida and the District of Columbia, and that he was one of the attorneys representing the Bank in the action in Florida. Each affidavit contains argument and even invective. Leaving that aside, they assert the following matters of fact.

Mr. Zukoff said that there had been over 120 pleadings and extensive hearings in the Florida action. All the matters which Mr. Davidson raised in this court had been heard and determined in Florida. . . .

Mr. Cassidy's affidavit contains various statements relating to the state of the action in Florida. . . .

. . . Mr. Cassidy also exhibited various documents which, the Bank contends, indicate that the defendant in Florida held itself out as a worldwide multinational firm, ready to perform international services and to handle work anywhere in the world, and that it allowed all of its offices to be listed as one firm. He also deposed that the Bank was ready, on advice, to have the Florida action tried without "the work papers," and that all current officers and directors of the Bank resided in the United States.

. . . As I now see the matter, it is essential for the determination of this case to have a clear understanding of the Bank's allegations as to the nature and extent of the entity that is suing in Florida and to distinguish those allegations from the one's put forward by the present plaintiff here as to the nature and extent of its own identity. Although it may seem a little pedantic at times, it is for those reasons that I have used the expressions "the plaintiff in Cayman" and "the defendant in Florida" in contra-distinction.

The Bank in the Florida action is averring that the defendant there, which is admittedly a firm practicing accountancy in the United States, is in fact a multinational firm that also practices in these Islands and elsewhere. A central issue in the present application is whether or not this is a specious assertion, made in bad faith. . . .

. . . Having seen the Bank's affidavits and those for the plaintiff in Cayman in reply, it was clear to me that in the unsuccessful motion for dismissal by the defendant in Florida, the question whether or not it was one worldwide partnership was in issue. . . . [A]fter considering all the affidavits in the *inter partes*[228] hearing, I attached weight (which I had not previously done) to the fact that the defendant in Florida had failed to persuade the court

there, summarily as it were, that the allegation of a worldwide partnership was specious. . . .

Mr. Davidson in his . . . affidavit . . . disclosed that the Bank was relying on certain public relations materials. He said that none of these described Touche Ross & Co. as a "worldwide partnership" as alleged in the complaint and went on to say:

> Indeed, as stated in a publication frequently cited by [Bank Intercontinental, Limited]—*A World of Professional Services*" . . . Touche Ross International today has unified 54 national firms into one worldwide organization. Led by respected national businessmen and professionals, the practice in each country is locally owned and managed.

Mr. Cassidy's affidavit exhibited material of this nature. One exhibit is headed, prominently, "LOCAL ATTENTION FROM A WORLD CLASS ORGANIZATION." It then continues—

> Touche Ross is one of the largest multinational accounting, tax and management consulting firms operating in 87 countries with a staff of 20,000 including 8,000 in the United States. Our professionals include CPAs, lawyers, MBAs . . . and other highly skilled individuals. There are seven offices located in Florida. . . .

Then follows profiles of the Florida partners. Another exhibit is a brochure. It refers to "Touche Ross International." It is headed "A FIRM WITH A DIFFERENCE" and it begins:

> Having pioneered in structuring the first truly multinational professional services firm, Touche Ross International today has unified 54 national firms into one worldwide organization. Led by respected national businessmen and professionals, the practice in each country is locally owned and managed. The parties in each country are joined together through membership in Touche Ross International, a legal entity formed under Swiss law. Our national firms, the experience of our professionals, and our common standards of professional performance are assets to international clients. Universal quality control and financial responsibility apply to all work done in the Touche Ross name.

That paragraph includes the sentence referred to by Mr. Davidson: "Led by . . . locally owned and managed." Moreover, I have not quoted the whole of the exhibit. And it is talking about "Touche Ross International." Later it refers to "the member firms of Touche Ross International" (under a subheading "Our Firm Worldwide," however). Also, of course, this public relations material has to be considered in conjunction with the

---

[228]Latin: "between parties." An *inter partes* hearing is one held when all of the parties are present and participating.]

affidavits on the *ex parte* application describing the organization of individuals using the style "Touche Ross."

Nevertheless, I think it has to be said (whatever the "Touche Ross" label may eventually be held to mean in law in any given situation) that these materials undoubtedly convey and must be intended to convey, at first sight, the impression not only that there is a multinational entity called "Touche Ross" but also that it is one which at least has a professional relationship with its constituent elements, and more than that (because one exhibit says so in its terms) one which controls in terms of *quality* and *financial responsibility* the work done in the Touche Ross name.

The legal nature of the Swiss entity is not explained in the public relations material so exhibited. The plaintiff in Cayman has not sought to dissociate itself from this public relations material. It is very difficult to avoid the inference that those who are associated with it are holding themselves out as members of a single worldwide entity with collective professional responsibility, or at the least that anyone who alleges this cannot be dismissed as raising a patently specious argument. The impression given by the publicity material certainly stands in marked contrast to the subsequent, detailed explanations of the precise relationship of "Touche Ross" associates given in the affidavits of . . . Surgeson. . . .

* * *

Although, as I see it, the present application does not turn solely on those exhibits, they are in my view very material. They go directly to the question whether the bank, by alleging one worldwide firm, was contriving a pretext for the Florida action. I granted the injunction *ex parte* on the strength of the affidavits of the plaintiff in Cayman as they then stood. If I had been aware of these exhibits and had had (at least as I now see it) a sharper appreciation of the failure of the defendant in Florida to have the action there dismissed on an interlocutory application, I would at least have been very much more circumspect about doing so. In any case, I have changed my initial view. . . .

The view I therefore came to, after hearing both sides, was that the submission that the allegation in Florida of a worldwide firm was patently a pretext could not be sustained.

* * *

. . . The action has already continued for some time in the United States. The court in Florida has not thrown it out. It has ordered pretrial discovery, on the evidence for the plaintiff in Cayman, to enable the Bank to explore the evidence supporting its allegation of one worldwide firm. I am not familiar enough with American pretrial discovery to comment on that adversely; in any case I suspect that it may be parochial to do so. The weight of the evidence and submissions in the case in my view point clearly to the fact that a court of superior jurisdiction in the United States is seized of the matters in issue. It has not seen fit to dismiss the action. . . . The reality, I think, is that by suing here, the present plaintiff is in effect trying to prevent the determination in Florida of an issue which can and ought properly to be left to be decided there. I am not satisfied that the injunction should be continued.

For these reasons, I discharged it.

On appeal, the Cayman Islands Court of Appeal reversed the decision of Judge Hill and reinstated the injunction. It did so because it believed that the issue of whether or not Touche Ross & Co. was a multinational enterprise with responsibility for the Cayman Island firm was an issue that could be tried in either Florida or the Cayman Islands and that the genuiness or otherwise of the assertion of the firm's multinational character was not sufficient by itself to determine the question of whether the Florida proceedings should be stayed. Rather than focusing on this issue, Judge Hill should have been looking at whether or not the granting of the injunction preventing the Bank from bringing the case in Florida would have had the effect of depriving the Bank of a legitimate personal or judicial advantage. Because the Bank had been unable to show that it had been deprived of an advantage, and because the cause of action itself arose in the Cayman Islands, Judge Hill should not have discharged the injunction. The Court of Appeal, accordingly, reinstated it.[229] ■

---

[229]*The Cayman Islands Law Reports,* vol. 1986–1987, p. 268 (1988).

---

pierce the company veil: An expression indicating that the legal fiction that a company is a separate legal entity will be set aside and the shareholders of the company will be held liable for its conduct as if they were partners in a partnership.

Piercing the Company Veil

In some unusual situations, a company is used by its owners to perpetrate a fraud, to circumvent the law, or in some other way to carry out illegal activities. In such cases, a court will ignore the corporate structure of a company and **pierce the company veil**, exposing the shareholders to personal liability.

There are four circumstances under which courts will pierce the corporate veil: (1) the controlled company, (2) the alter ego company, (3) undercapitalization, and (4) personal assumption of liability.

The Controlled Company

The corporate status of a controlled company will be ignored if (1) its financing and management are so closely connected to its parent that it does not have any independent decision-making authority and (2) it is induced to enter into a transaction beneficial to the parent but detrimental to it and to third parties.

The Alter Ego Company

alter ego: (Latin: "another self.") An *alter ego* company is one that is not treated by its owners as a separate entity.

The company veil will be pierced if the company is not treated by its shareholders as a separate juridical entity—that is, it is treated as the **alter ego** of the shareholders. Examples of such conduct include the commingling of corporate and personal assets, the use of company assets by shareholders for their own personal benefit, and the failure to hold and record minutes of board of directors' meetings.

Undercapitalization

When a company has insufficient capital at the time it is formed to meet its prospective debts or potential liabilities, the courts will sometimes set aside the corporate veil. This is especially so if the corporation later fails to obtain the amount of insurance that any reasonable business would be expected to have as a matter of public responsibility.

Personal Assumption of Liability

Shareholders can, of course, personally assume liability for the obligations of a company. This is especially common if a company is new or small or marginally successful. Creditors will seldom lend money to such a company without the shareholders personally guaranteeing the performance of the company.

The Case 4–8 illustrates how difficult it is to pierce the veil of a company.

Case 4–8   Garden Contamination Case (No. 2)

Federal Republic of Germany, District Court (*Amtsgericht*) of Bonn, 1987.

Praxis des Internationalen Privat- und Verfahrensrechts, vol. 1988, p. 354 (1988); *International Law Reports*, vol. 80, p. 378 (1990).

JUDGMENT OF THE COURT

On April 26, 1986, an explosion occurred at the nuclear power station [operated by AES Chernobyl, a Soviet state enterprise], located at Chernobyl in the Ukraine. As a result, a radioactive cloud was emitted that, because of prevailing wind conditions, drifted westward. Two days later, this poisonous cloud reached northwestern Germany, contaminating the house and garden of the plaintiff in Dörverden-Barme. At that time, the plaintiff was growing various fruit and vegetables in an area of 780 square meters.

On April 30, 1986, the radiation damage seemed to the plaintiff to be especially bad and he destroyed—without having been paid to do so—fruit and vegetables worth 45 deutsche marks. The plaintiff also discontinued his gardening because of the radiation pollution.

The plaintiff has now sued the Soviet Union for his losses, which he claims are at least 750 deutsche marks. This claim is based on the loss of the 45 deutsche marks worth of fruit and vegetables which the plaintiff destroyed and a sum of not less than 705 deutsche marks for lost enjoyment. . . .

There is no legal basis for the plaintiff's claim. First, the plaintiff can point to no international agreements between West Germany and the Soviet Union on which such a claim can be founded. This is because, quite simply, there have never been any treaties between the Federal Republic of Germany and the Soviet Union.

Second, there is no remedy available to the plaintiff under the general principles of international law. He argues that the Soviet Union failed to meet its international obligations to provide information about the events of April 26, 1986. The plaintiff, however, cannot use this alleged breach as a basis for obtaining compensation. It is true that under international law a state has obligations to provide certain kinds of information and that a failure to do so can lead to a duty to compensate the injured party. Such obligations, however, only exist between subjects of international law. In this case, it would be the Federal

MAP 4-7 West Germany and the Soviet Union (1988)

both of these agencies for commissioning the installation [at Chernobyl] and for carrying on its operation is AES Chernobyl. AES Chernobyl is, under Soviet law, an independent legal person, with the right to possess property of its own and the responsibility for any damages that it may cause. AES Chernobyl is, therefore, the operator of the Chernobyl nuclear installation within the meaning of the Atomic Energy Act.... Under Section 25(1) of that Act, only the operator—AES Chernobyl—may be sued to obtain compensation [for damage caused by the Chernobyl nuclear plant] and not the Soviet Union....

Fourth, [the plaintiff may not impute liability to the defendant] based on a claim made in delict[230] under Article 823(1) of the German Civil Code.... This is because the actions taken by AES Chernobyl which caused the damage cannot be imputed to the defendant, the Soviet Union, because of the extensive devolution of authority and responsibility within the Soviet energy system. In particular, the AES is an independent legal person with direct responsibility for the operation of the installation....

[The plaintiff has argued against this conclusion] by suggesting that the state is always responsible for the delicts of a state enterprise.... While it is true that such liability is said to exist in theory, it does not exist in practice.[231] ...

[The plaintiff also suggests that liability can be imputed to the Soviet Union in its role as the parent of its subsidiary, AES Chernobyl.] In German law, the imputing of liability [to a parent for the conduct of a subsidiary] is usually discussed in the context of company law. In the field of company law, we find four main ways in which such liability can be imputed: (1) the controlled company, (2) undercapitalization, (3) the commingling of assets, and (4) the assumption of personal liability. None of these apply, however, to the circumstances of this case.

As to the first of these, we need to see if the overall control of the particular state enterprise—the AES Chernobyl—rests with the Soviet Union. For this to be so, the finances and administration of the enterprise must be so closely intertwined with that of the state that it can only be concluded that the enterprise retains no independent decision-making authority of its own.... Then we must also find that the enterprise was induced into entering into some disadvantageous transactions. In this case, the extensive devolution of control [from the state to state enterprises] within the Soviet administrative system argues against a finding of close control. Additionally, the plaintiff has made no suggestion as to how this control might have been used. We note that the socialist legal system does not automatically assume that the state has complete control over a state enterprise. And we observe that where (as here) the provisions of that system give an

Republic of Germany which is entitled to assert a claim that it suffered damage to its national integrity as a consequence of another state's failure to give warning, provide information, and clarify any misunderstandings. To reiterate, only a state—not an individual—could assert this particular claim for compensation....

Third, the plaintiff's reliance on Section 25(1) of the Federal Republic of Germany's Atomic Energy Act [of 1985] is misplaced....

... Section 25(1) of the Atomic Energy Act only imposes liability on the operator of a nuclear installation. As ... defined in that Act, an operator is a person designated as such by the appropriate public authority. With respect to the installation at Chernobyl ... the operator can be identified by examining the multilayered Soviet administrative structure. The Ministry of Energy and Electrification of the USSR is responsible for the establishment of nuclear installations. The All-Union Atomic Energy Association is responsible for overall supervisory functions. The entity designated by

---

[230From Latin *delictum:* "a fault." In civil law countries, a delict is a private wrong or injury (similar to a tort in common law countries) or a minor public wrong or injury (a misdemeanor in common law countries).]

231*See* Böckstiegel, Der Durchgriff auf den Staat, p. 13 (1972); von Hoffmann in Fischer and von Hoffmann, Staatsunternehmen im Völkerrecht und im Internationalen Privatrecht, p. 66, (1984).

enterprise an adequate measure of organizational independence, financial autonomy, and freedom to enter into commercial transactions, then no liability can be imputed to the state on the basis of control. If the plaintiff had been able to show that AES Chernobyl had been dominated by the government's organs and by government officials acting under the instructions of those organs, a different conclusion might have been reached. But he did not do so, even in general terms.

The result is the same when we consider the issue of liability based on undercapitalization. Here, as well, the plaintiff needs to show in detail such things as the source of AES Chernobyl's finances, why they were inadequate, and whether or not any insurance or other financial guarantees had been arranged for [in the event that the finances were inadequate to cover any liability that might reasonably be anticipated]. This requirement to provide proof to substantiate a claim is both a matter of general legal principles and a requirement of Articles 117 and 118 of the Code of Civil Procedure. It is for the plaintiff to provide this proof; it is not for the Court to obtain it by ordering the defendant to provide it. As mentioned earlier, AES Chernobyl is an independent legal person with its own assets and responsibility for its own liabilities. It is not clear to the Court what financial resources belong to AES Chernobyl. The possibility that it is underfunded to the extent that this would cause unreasonable injury to its creditors cannot be automatically excluded. But the plaintiff, in order to succeed, would have to present detailed proof establishing that AES Chernobyl is underfunded to the injury of its creditors, and he has not done so.

The same proof requirement applies to the issues of liability based on commingling of assets and on the assumption of personal liability by the defendant. Again, no exceptions to the proof requirement are allowed, so, here too, the plaintiff is required to produce detailed evidence of the facts. He has not done this and, therefore, he is unable to impute liability to the defendant.

. . . In view of all of the above, the plaintiff's cause of action is untenable.

The plaintiff's case was dismissed. On appeal to the Provincial Court (Landgericht) of Bonn, the trial court's decision was affirmed, with the appeal court stating that the trial court correctly rejected the plaintiff's petition because it had "no real prospect of success." ■

Chapter Questions

1. Regal Shipping, Ltd., is a publicly traded company incorporated in the United Kingdom. It carries freight between Europe and the United States. Two years ago it lowered its fares to half that of its competitors. The competitors (i.e., Plebeian Shipping Lines, Ltd., a U.K. company, and seven other shipping companies incorporated in the United States, Canada, France, Germany, Italy, and Japan) were enraged by Regal's action, and they secretly agreed to lower their own prices until they could run Regal out of business. Regal suffered huge losses and is on the brink of bankruptcy. It hopes to recoup its losses and stay in business by bringing an antitrust suit in the United States against its competitors.
   a. In connection with its suit in the United States, Regal asks an English court to compel Plebeian to turn over corporate documents showing the extent of the conspiracy between Plebeian and the other seven of Regal's competitors. Will Regal succeed? Discuss.
   b. Plebeian brings an appropriate action in an English court asking the court to issue an injunction to bar Regal from suing Plebeian in the United States. Will Plebeian succeed? Discuss.
   c. The other competitors bring a separate action in England asking the English court to enjoin Regal from continuing with its suit in the United States. Will they succeed? Discuss.
   d. Assume that Regal was successful in its suit in the United States and that the U.S. court awarded it treble damages. Is there anything Plebeian can do to minimize the amount of the judgment it is supposed to pay Regal? Discuss.

2. The Buena Banana Co., a U.S. corporation, has several subsidiaries in Central America that purchase bananas from local producers. Buena then sells the bananas under its trademark to wholesalers in the United States. The Compañia del Plátano Puro, SA (Puro), an Argentine corporation that markets bananas throughout South America, recently set up several subsidiaries in Central America in direct competition with those of Buena. Puro's subsidiaries have offered the Central American producers an arrangement that is remarkably generous by international standards. It will give them a guaranteed 10-year contract to purchase their entire production at 10 percent above world market prices. (Buena, by comparison, has never agreed to a long-term contract and only pays the going world prices.) Puro's sales are

presently limited to South America, but it hopes to begin selling throughout the United States soon. In preparation for this, it has set up a small branch in Miami, Florida, and it is testing the local market with sales to several upscale market chains.

In the meantime, Buena has brought suit against Puro in a U.S. federal court in Miami. It claims that Puro is attempting to monopolize the banana trade in Central America (there is only one other large banana exporting company in competition with Buena and Puro). Buena claims that Puro's activities in Central America will force Buena to raise its prices and that this will affect American consumers. Does the U.S. court have jurisdiction to hear the case? Discuss.

3. I Company is a large American manufacturer of computers. It controls approximately 65 percent of the market in the European Community. It refuses to share the patents and copyrights it owns for the operating system software that controls its computers, thus not allowing other manufacturers to make computers that are compatible with I's computers (i.e., other manufacturers cannot make and sell computers that will run the same programs as I Company's computers). Is this a violation of Article 81 or 82 of the European Community Treaty? Discuss.

4. Could I Company, in the previous question, be charged with violating American antitrust laws? Discuss.

5. The Mighty Motor Car Co. and the Novel Automobile Corp. manufacture cars and trucks in Country J. They recently entered into a non-competition agreement with the approval of the Country J Ministry of Trade. The agreement provides (1) that Mighty will sell its vehicles in the United States and that Novel will not; and (2) that Novel will sell its vehicle in the European Union and that Mighty will not.

Since the signing of this agreement, the Foreign Car and Truck Import Co., a U.S. importer of Novel cars and light trucks, is unable to obtain vehicles to import to the United States. As a consequence, it has brought suit against Novel in a U.S. court alleging that the agreement between Mighty and Novel violated the U.S. Sherman Antitrust Act. Novel has asked the court to dismiss the case for lack of subject matter jurisdiction. Should it do so? Discuss.

6. Assume the same facts as in the preceding question. Does the arrangement between Mighty and Novel violate either Article 81 or 82 of the European Community Treaty? Can the EU Commission take action against either Mighty or Novel? If it can, what action can it take? Discuss.

7. The dictator of State X lets it be known that a certain lucrative contract will be granted only to the foreign company that gives the most expensive "birthday present" to the dictator's 7-year-old son. An American, a Japanese, and a European company are all vying for the contract. With what legal and ethical limitations must they comply? Discuss.

8. Good, Better & Best (GBB) is the name used by several firms of business consultants located in many different countries, including countries in Western Europe, North America, South America, and the Orient. Depending on local laws, the firms are organized either as partnerships or limited liability stock companies. The senior partners or presidents of the several firms meet on a regular basis to coordinate worldwide advertising and standardize the policies and practices of the several firms. The firms exchange information and they share employees as the need may arise. Multinational clients are assured that they will be served by the local GBB firm in any country where the client does business.

One of the GBB firms in Country X (GBB-X) provided marketing information to Local Company. The information had been negligently prepared by GBB-X and it contained gross errors. Relying on that information, Local made several disastrous investments, and it lost most of its net worth. Local wants to sue GBB-X, but it knows that GBB-X has few assets. Will Local be successful if it asks the court in which it is suing the GBB-X firm to join others of the GBB firms as codefendants? Would the choice of the court in which GBB brings its suit be important in deciding this? Discuss.

9. Big Shipping Lines is a transoceanic freight company incorporated in Country Z. To avoid potential liability from shipping crude oil from the Persian Gulf to Europe in the antiquated single-hull ships that it owns, it set up 14 different companies (including the Small Shipping Co.) and transferred ownership of one ship to each of them. Each company then purchased insurance to cover the losses of the ship and the ship's cargo, but nothing else.

The SS *Small,* which belonged to the Small Shipping Co., negligently ran aground on a shoal in the Eastern Mediterranean Sea spilling its entire load of some five million barrels of crude oil. The oil has washed ashore in Greece, Turkey, Cyprus, Syria, Lebanon, Israel, Egypt, and Libya. Each of these countries has brought suit in Country Z against the Small Shipping Co., its sister companies, and against Big Shipping Lines. The sister companies and Big Shipping Lines have asked the court to dismiss the complaints against them. They contend that the Small Shipping Co. is a separate company and solely liable for its own torts. How should the court rule? Discuss.

Review Problem

You are a now a Senior Assistant in the law department of MegaBranch Industries (MBI), a multinational enterprise that has branches in countries around the world. You are responsible for providing MBI's board of directors with legal advice on its worldwide operations.

1. MBI is setting up subsidiaries in France, Germany, and England. In determining the appropriate company form to use, what factors should be considered?
2. MBI would like to set up a holding company in France to operate its French subsidiaries. What company form would be best suited for this?
3. MBI plans to start up a large subsidiary in Germany. It will employ some 5,000 blue-collar workers and 50 managers. What procedures must it follow to organize a German company that can issue stock and that will have limited liability? What kind of internal corporate structure must the company have? What are the rights of the employees? Of shareholders? Of management?
4. MBI has representative offices and branches in 27 countries in Africa. Should these be converted to subsidiaries? If they are, how should they be incorporated into the multinational structure of MBI?
5. How should MBI regard the international rules for multinational enterprises that have been drafted or are being drafted by the International Chamber of Commerce, the International Labor Organization, and the International Standards Organization?
6. What general policies should MBI adopt to avoid U.S. and European Community unfair competition regulations?
7. How can MBI structure itself to minimize its losses from possible products liability suits?
8. What possible impact does the U.S. Foreign Corrupt Practices Act have on MBI's operations outside of the United States?
9. What can MBI do to ensure that it and its subsidiaries will not be linked together as a common enterprise should any one of the subsidiaries ever be sued?
10. In structuring its multinational operations, what can MBI do to avoid the possibility that the corporate veil of one of its subsidiaries might be pierced, thereby exposing MBI to direct liability?

CHAPTER 5

Foreign Investment

Chapter Outline

A. FOREIGN INVESTMENT LAWS AND CODES

The regulations governing foreign investments are commonly set out in "investment laws" and "investment codes." In socialist countries (such as the People's Republic of China and Vietnam) that allow investments only in the form of joint ventures, the regulations are usually called "joint venture laws." The purpose of these laws is the creation of a legal framework that will attract and put to work foreign capital.

A few states do not have general laws but rather special investment acts that apply to particular sectors of the economy, such as agriculture, technology, tourism, and so on. And some, such as Brazil, have a complex network of laws that control investment incentives, subsidized financing, tariffs, taxes, foreign exchange, prices, technology transfers, and other matters, such that the combination functions as an investment code.

The provisions commonly found in these investment codes and general laws are sometimes incorporated in bilateral investment treaties (BITs).[1] These treaties are most often arrangements between a developed state and that state's favored developing states, but a few are between developing states themselves.[2] For the most part, the provisions in BITs are the same

---

[1] The use of these treaties has grown popular in recent years. A study conducted in 1996 by the International Center for the Settlement of Investment Disputes identified more than 1,100 BITs. Of these, more than 800 were entered into after 1987. ICSID, *Bilateral Investment Treaties: 1959–1996* (1999), posted at www.worldbank.org/icsid/treaties/treaties.htm.

[2] The ICSID study, mentioned in the previous footnote, lists 155 countries who were parties to BITs as of 1996. *Id.*
   Albania, Argentina, Armenia, Azerbaijan, Bangladesh, Belarus, Bolivia, Bulgaria, Cameroon, Congo, Democratic Republic of the, Congo, Republic of, Croatia, Czech Republic, Ecuador, Egypt, El Salvador, Estonia, Georgia, Grenada, Haiti, Honduras, Jamaica, Jordan, Kazakhstan, Kyrgyzstan, Latvia, Lithuania, Moldova, Mongolia, Morocco, Mozambique, Nicaragua, Panama, Poland, Romania, Russia, Senegal, Slovakia, Sri Lanka, Trinidad and

as those in the more progressive municipal codes and laws.[3] In addition, however, many BITs contain international dispute settlement provisions, such as a commitment to refer disputes to the International Center for the Settlement of Investment Disputes.[4]

National Foreign Investment Policies

Although the form that foreign investment regulations take varies from country to country, the underlying purposes of the regulations are generally the same worldwide. These include (a) promoting local productivity and technological development, (b) encouraging local participation, and (c) minimizing foreign competition in economic areas already well served by local businesses.[5]

To carry out these purposes, investment laws establish basic policies for screening and regulating foreign investment applications. These generally fall into three categories. The first is to encourage investments through incentives and minimal regulations. Most states with this policy are in sub-Saharan Africa and the Far East. The second is to use investment incentives but also to require "local participation quotas." Countries with this policy are generally found in the Middle East and North Africa. The third is a policy of allowing foreign investment subject to local screening and supervision.[6] States of this kind are generally found in Latin America.[7]

Tobago, Tunisia, Turkey, Ukraine, and Uzbekistan. U.S. Trade Representative, "U.S. Bilateral Investment Treaty Program" (March 18, 1999) at www.ustr.gov/agreements/bit.pdf.

[3] A copy of "The 1994 U.S. Prototype Bilateral Investment Treaty" is posted on the Internet at www.ita.doc.gov/legal/modelbit.html.

[4] *See International Legal Materials,* vol. 21, p. 1208 (1982). A dispute involving a BIT between Sri Lanka and the United Kingdom was heard by ICSID in Asian Agricultural Products, Ltd. (United Kingdom) v. Republic of Sri Lanka (ICSID, 1990), *id.,* vol. 30, p. 577 (1991).

In May 1995, the member states of the Organization for Economic Cooperation and Development (OECD) began negotiations to draft a Multilateral Agreement on Investments (MAI). *See* www.preamble.org/ mai/interweb.html. The aim of the negotiations was to establish a system of uniform rules on both market access and legal security that would provide a worldwide "level playing field" for foreign investors.

A nearly final draft MAI text was agreed to in May 1998. The scope of the draft text was broad, applying to a wide range of investments (including foreign direct investments, portfolio investments, rights under contract, public debt, and real estate) in all market sectors and at all levels of government. It guaranteed foreign investors and foreign investments nondiscriminatory treatment (including both national treatment and most-favored-nation treatment), the right to compensation in the event of expropriation, and the right to the free cross-border transfer of funds. Finally, it established a system of binding disputes settlement procedures.

This draft text was the result of three years of essentially closed-door negotiations. The OECD's MAI Negotiating Team relied solely on member state delegations and internal OECD committees for comments and suggestions. Not until October 1997 did the Negotiating Team hold a 1-day consultation with non-OECD business and labor organizations, and this was done only after leaked copies of the developing MAI text had come under harsh criticism from organized labor and international environmental groups. They argued that the MAI would force governments to lower their domestic health, safety, environmental, and labor standards to attract and retain foreign investment.

Beginning in mid-1997, opponents of the MAI mounted a campaign to halt the negotiations. They posted critical comments on Internet Web pages and sent voluminous admonitory electronic mail to OECD member state governments. *See,* for example, the U.S. Western Governors Association analysis and critique of the MAI posted at www.westgov.org/wga/publicat/maiweb.htm. In October 1998, the OECD—citing "significant concerns" relating to "sovereignty, protection of labor rights and environment, culture and other important matters"—announced that the negotiations had been indefinitely suspended.

The OECD did not completely throw in the towel. At its October 1998 session its members agreed that studies would be undertaken to determine if the goals of the MAI negotiations could be reached by a new series of negotiations. The new negotiations, they noted, needed to involve non-OECD countries as participants and "discussions with representatives of civil society (business, labor, non-governmental organizations, consumer and other groups)." *See* www.oecd.org/news_and_events/release/nw98–100a.htm.

[5] These can be seen in the criteria set out in Canada's Foreign Investment Review Act (1973–1974) for the screening of foreign investment applications: "(a) the effect of the acquisition or establishment on the level and nature of economic activity in Canada, including, without limiting the generality of the foregoing, the effect on employment, on resource processing, on the utilization of parts, components and services produced in Canada, and on exports from Canada; (b) the degree and significance of participation by Canadians in the business enterprise or new business and in any industry or industries in Canada of which the business enterprise or new business forms or would form a part; (c) the effect of the acquisition or establishment on productivity, industrial efficiency, technological development, product innovation and product variety in Canada; (d) the effect of the acquisition or establishment on competition within any industry or industries in Canada; and (e) the compatibility of the acquisition or establishment with national industrial and economic policies, taking into consideration industrial and economic policy objectives enunciated by the government or legislature of any province likely to be significantly affected by the acquisition or establishment." Statutes of Canada, vol. 1973–1974, chap. 46, § 2(2), p. 620.

[6] The main features of this third category are "(a) case-by-case screening of all foreign investment; (b) fewer tax incentives for foreign investment; (c) separate screening of technology transfers, (d) limitations on foreign managerial control; (e) repatriation ceilings on fees and royalties as well as on profits; (f) regulation of debt financing; [and] (g) local adjudication of investment disputes." Center on Transnational Corporations, *National Legislation and Regulations Relating to Transnational Corporations,* p. 11 (UN Doc. ST/CTC/6, UN Sales No. E.78.II.A.3, 1978).

[7] *Id.*

Screening Foreign Investment Applications

Most (but not all) countries require foreign investors to (a) register with the government and (b) obtain governmental approval of their proposed venture.

The Screening Agencies

Commonly, foreign investors register and file proposals with a single central agency set up specifically to facilitate foreign investments. The central agency may itself conduct the screening process or it may simply coordinate the process. In both the Philippines and South Korea, for example, the central agency has a multidisciplinary staff that is organized to independently evaluate most proposals.[8] In Chile, India, Kenya, and Mexico, on the other hand, the role of the central agency is primarily a coordinating one with most of the evaluation being done by other specialized departments and agencies.[9]

Not all countries have a central agency. In Brazil and Nigeria, for instance, the evaluation of proposals is handled directly by the departments and agencies concerned. If coordination is needed, they will directly contact other governmental units as necessary for advice and assistance.[10]

Proposals Requiring Screening

The criteria for determining which proposals need screening vary greatly. A few states may subject all foreign investment to some form of screening. Other states limit their reviews to proposals seeking investment incentives, to those which involve a certain percentage of foreign investment, or to those whose projected investment exceeds a certain amount of capital.[11]

In Brazil, for example, no governmental authorization is needed unless a foreign investor wants to take advantage of certain industrial incentives.[12]

The Board of Investments of the Philippines screens all new investments in which foreigners have a 40 percent or greater share, and all expansions or additional investments in existing firms that have foreign ownership of 40 percent or more.[13]

In Argentina, investments of less than U.S. $5 million do not require approval unless a majority of the shares in a locally owned company is to be bought by foreigners.

Several countries follow different procedures depending on the magnitude of the investment. In Argentina, new foreign investments of more than U.S. $20 million or the foreign acquisition of a majority interest in a locally owned company worth more than U.S. $10 million require prior approval of the President. Investments of lesser amounts—but greater than the minimum amount of U.S. $5 million for new investments—require approval of the Under-Secretariat of External Investments.

In Algeria, the prefect of the département concerned screens investments that do not exceed 500,000 Algerian dinars and that do not contain a request for financial incentives. Otherwise, the Secretariat of the National Investment Board must review the application. France has a similar arrangement. Investments of more than 10 million francs are screened in Paris; others are reviewed locally.

Proposals Requiring Special Screening

In many countries, certain kinds of foreign investment proposals require the approval of specialized agencies. Commonly, investments in natural resource–based industries (e.g., hydrocarbons, minerals, and forestry) need the approval of agencies that formulate special criteria tailored to the

[8]Philippines Omnibus Investments Code of 1987 (Executive Order No. 226), arts. 3 to 9; available on the Chan Robles Virtual Law Library at www.chanrobles.com/default8eono226.htm. South Korea, Foreign Investment Promotion Act (Revised Act No.5982, 24, 1999), art. 27; available on the South Korean Ministry of Finance and Economy's Web site at www.mofe.go.kr/mofe/kor/fdi/html/act.htm.

[9]Center on Transnational Corporations, National Legislation and Regulations Relating to *Transnational Corporations,* p. 10 (UN Doc. ST/CTC/26, UN Sales No. E.83.II.A.7, 1983).

[10]*Id.*

[11]*Id.*

[12]*Id.*

[13]Philippines Omnibus Investments Code of 1987 (Executive Order No. 226), art. 32. The Code is available on Chan Robles Virtual Law Library at www.chanrobles.com/default8eono226.htm.

specific requirements of the industries involved. In South Korea, investments in certain strategic industries need special government authorization.[14]

Information That Must Be Disclosed

Foreign investors are required to supply screening agencies with quite detailed information about their proposals. This typically includes the following:[15]

a. The industry to be established and the nature of the product to be produced
b. A financial plan, showing the amount of investment in external and local capital
c. A production scheme showing the annual volume and value of the production
d. A services scheme showing what services will be created and their volume and value
e. The owners, the management structure, and the relative share of local and foreign control
f. Machinery and equipment needed, and their sources and cost
g. An import and export scheme showing the expected volume of imports and exports
h. The extent that local inputs (including raw materials) will be used and an estimate of the local value added
i. An employment scheme, including a program for training nationals to operate and manage the enterprise
j. A marketing study of the domestic and export market
k. Product pricing and projected profits and rate of return
l. The proposed location of the industry

Evaluation Criteria

A foreign investment proposal is judged, in general, on the extent to which it conforms with a country's national development objectives. Some investment laws establish standards for screening projects in general or for the granting of incentives in particular. The criteria, of course, vary greatly, depending on a country's goals. Nevertheless, certain broad criteria are considered by the screening agencies of most countries, as follows:[16]

a. The impact on the balance of payment
b. The number of jobs created
c. The impact of technical know-how and the training program for indigenous employees
d. The impact on the local market (including any possible negative consequences for already-established national enterprises)
e. The contribution to the development of less economically developed zones or regions
f. The ratio between foreign and national capital contribution
g. The export diversification and stimulation, and import substitution
h. The use of national inputs and components in the manufacture of the product
i. The effect on price levels and the quality of the product

Formal and Informal Application Process

The investment application submitted by a foreign investor must demonstrate two things to the local regulatory authority: first, that the proposed investment fits the guidelines of the investment law; second, and most important, that the investment agrees with the investment philosophy of the host country.

Although compliance with the statutory provisions is reasonably straightforward, conforming to the regulatory philosophy can prove difficult. It may be difficult because the regulatory authority is secretive and unsympathetic to foreign investors. It may difficult because the investor is insensitive to the investment environment in the host country, as Reading 5–1 points out.

---

[14]South Korea, Foreign Investment Promotion Act (Revised Act No.5982, 24, 1999), art. 6(3); available on the South Korean Ministry of Finance and Economy's Web site at www.mofe.go.kr/mofe/kor/fdi/html/act.htm.
[15]Center on Transnational Corporations, National Legislation and Regulations Relating to *Transnational Corporations,* p. 11 (UN Doc. ST/CTC/26, UN Sales No. E.83.II.A.7, 1983).
[16]*Id.,* p. 12.

Reading 5–1   The Informal Application Process

Michael Skapinker, "How Monsanto Got Bruised in a Food Fight," *Financial Times*, March 7, 2002.

When Monsanto brought its genetically modified food to Europe, Greenpeace was waiting. How did the U.S. company respond? "We sent over our American scientists and lawyers," Kate Fish, Monsanto's vice-president for public policy, says witheringly.

In a speech to a conference on corporate citizenship in New York [in April 2002], Ms. Fish mercilessly dissected her company's failure in the 1990s to deal with European fears about genetically modified foods. Monsanto's executives had become so caught up in the work done in their laboratories that they barely knew how to talk to non-scientists.

"For a company that believes in science, it's very difficult. When the Prince of Wales started talking about interfering with the realms of God, we weren't equipped to deal with that," she told the conference.

Ms. Fish was no stranger to environmentalism. In 1989, she founded EarthWays, an environmental group. Her first contact with Monsanto came soon afterwards, when it approached her about supporting Earth Day, which she was organizing in St. Louis, Missouri, the company's home town.

Monsanto's work on genetically modified foods—which, the company said, would lower pesticide use, increase crop yields and promote more efficient land use—appeared perfectly aligned with her belief in sustainable development.

She joined Monsanto's external advisory council in 1990 and when the company offered her a job in 1996, it seemed the perfect way to pursue her ideals. "I had a sense of being employed doing something I wanted to do that could have some effect in the world," she says.

Monsanto's promotion of genetically modified food enjoyed great success in the U.S. The products won regulatory approval and the amount of land under cultivation for such crops expanded rapidly. Taking the products to Europe seemed the natural next step. It did not occur to Ms. Fish and her colleagues that European environmentalists would be anything other than enthusiastic. "When I was an environmentalist and first started looking at these products, I thought this was exciting stuff. When you spend time in the labs, you get comfortable with it. It doesn't seem so scary," she says.

Some Monsanto staff in Europe warned that genetically modified foods might not enjoy the easy ride they had had in the U.S. They were ignored. "We heard the signals coming from Europe. Our people in Europe were saying: 'There are some issues here.' But they weren't

Parody advertisement for Monsanto's Bovine Steroid Treated milk that appeared in 1999 in *Splice Magazine*, a publication of the Genetics Forum, a British environmental advocacy group. It depicts a carton of milk with the following text: "Take the plunge into steroid abuse on a global scale. Forced into your food-stores by the WTO. Our cows are specially injected with Monsanto's B.S.T growth hormone to increase productivity. Sadly the cows get crippled, and were not sure whether the B.S.T gets through to YOU the consumer. Oh Well."

loud enough. They were perceived as fringe signals. Until it starts to hurt, they're very hard to hear."

The introduction of genetically modified foods into Europe was a fiasco. The environmental movement's campaign against them won huge public support. Supermarkets promised to banish such foods from their shelves. Crop trials were sabotaged. European governments imposed a moratorium on approval of genetically modified crops, which has been in force for more than three years.

This has given Ms. Fish and Monsanto—which is now a subsidiary of Pharmacia, the pharmaceuticals group—plenty of time to consider the lessons. The first lesson is that what works in the U.S. does not necessarily work anywhere else.

Americans, Ms. Fish says, trust their regulators. Europeans do not—for good reason. Monsanto was attempting to introduce its products following the BSE (mad cow disease) crisis, where government assurances that beef was safe had turned out to be false.

Monsanto also appeared to be imposing genetically modified foods on Europe without consultation. "You don't alter people's food without asking them first. It was as if their babies were being attacked," Ms. Fish says. "There was a sense of outrage because it didn't appear that people had a choice. I think the whole industry didn't spend the time dealing with the consumer issues, talking about the technology. When consumers first heard about it, it was from Greenpeace, it wasn't from the industry."

Is there any chance that, if Monsanto had spent more time listening and consulting, European consumers would have been willing to give genetically modified foods a try? "It's so hard to say," Ms. Fish says. "Certainly, we could have done it differently."

Monsanto realizes that winning Europe round will take years. In 2000, Hendrik Verfaillie, Monsanto's chief executive, announced a "pledge" not to use genes from humans or animals in products intended for food or animal feed. Monsanto said it would never sell a product into which a known allergen had been introduced. Addressing an issue that has caused particular concern, it also promised "not to pursue technologies that result in sterile seeds".

Ms. Fish now spends much of her time in Brussels. Mr. Verfaillie believes the way forward is for Monsanto to attempt to find common ground with its critics rather than confront them. It has been holding meetings with European environmental groups. "I can't give you names but we went to our most outspoken critics," he says.

Did he find these campaigners reasonable? "It was absolutely amazing. We obviously had significant disagreements on certain points but they were very willing to engage. We may not agree with everything they say but they have a point of view that reflects at least a part of society. It's very difficult to get the most extreme critics to agree to anything but the middle-of-the-road organizations have as their objective improving the environment."

Mr. Verfaillie and Ms. Fish are trying to convince those organizations that they and Monsanto have a common interest. Using genetically modified crops to reduce pesticide use is a line Monsanto continues to pursue. In Brazil, Mr. Verfaillie says, planting of such crops has reduced leakage of pesticides into rivers. Increasing crop yields around the world would mean fewer forests and wetlands being taken over by agricultural production.

Monsanto is also talking to European farmers. "How do we build and align what we're offering with the needs of European agriculture?" Ms. Fish asks. "Agriculture in the U.K. is very efficient but farmers' income is low. The U.K.'s got one of the highest uses of pesticide in Europe, much higher than the U.S. Only the Netherlands' is higher."

Mr. Verfaillie sees signs that European public opinion is starting to turn. "We do market research. We're still not where we need to be. But we see consumers in the U.K. and [the Netherlands] have gone from 20 percent saying they would consume [GM] products to over 50 percent," he says.

The European Commission last year warned that the moratorium on approving new varieties of genetically modified crops were damaging the European Union's attempt to become the world's most dynamic economy. "Europe cannot afford to miss the opportunity that these new sciences and technologies offer," the Commission said. "Biotechnology research efforts could and should be used to develop new GM varieties to improve yields and enable cultivation by small-scale and poor farmers." It added that Europe risked losing more scientists to the U.S.

European ministers were unmoved, insisting last year that the moratorium could not be lifted until new rules on labeling and tracing genetically modified ingredients were in place. This could take another three years. Greenpeace's Web site continues to insist: "Genetic scientists are altering life itself—artificially modifying genes to produce plants and animals which could never have evolved naturally." It warns that such ingredients are still "sneaking into the food chain through animal feed". ■

Approval of Foreign Investment Applications

Upon completion of the screening process, the host state will approve or disapprove a foreign investor's proposal. If the proposal did not ask for the host to grant any incentives, and if the host state does not insist upon any concessions from the investor, the approval will often be in the form of a letter from the appropriate agency. If the host state grants an incentive or the investor agrees to some concession, the arrangement will be set out in a formal investment agreement. Such an agreement will be governed by the host state's contract laws and any disputes will be resolved in that state's courts, unless the parties agree otherwise.

As Case 5–1 makes clear, the burden for ensuring that the proper approval has been granted rests with the investor.

Case 5–1 Arab Republic of Egypt v. Southern Pacific Properties, Ltd. et al.

France, Court of Appeals of Paris, 1984.
International Legal Materials, vol. 23, p. 1048 (1984).

On September 23, 1974, Southern Pacific Properties, Ltd. (SPP), a company organized and headquartered in Hong Kong, entered into an investment agreement with the Egyptian Minister of Tourism, who was representing the Arab Republic of Egypt (ARE), and the Egyptian General Organization for Tourism and Hotels (EGOTH), an Egyptian state-owned corporation. This three-party agreement provided for the establishment of two tourist complexes, one of which was to be located near the site of the pyramids at Giza, and which later became the center of controversy in this case. Under the agreement, the Egyptian government undertook to secure title and possession to land where the complexes were to be built and EGOTH and SPP agreed to incorporate an Egyptian company to be known as the Egyptian Tourist Development Company (ETDC). EGOTH would subscribe to 40 percent of the shares and SPP to 60 percent. Title to the land was then to be transferred by EGOTH and the Egyptian government to ETDC.[17]

The three-party agreement further required SPP to provide the expertise and the financing to construct, market, and manage the complexes. Finally, the Minister of Tourism was to supply the roads and other infrastructural elements necessary to make the sites accessible.

On December 12, 1974, EGOTH and SPP entered into a Supplemental Agreement reaffirming and explaining the obligations and rights of these two parties. Most important, this Supplemental Agreement reaffirmed the applicability of Egyptian law, including a statutory provision that put the tourist complexes and their development under the supervision of the Minister of Tourism. The Agreement also provided that SPP could assign its rights to a locally incorporated subsidiary (known as Southern Pacific Properties [Middle East] Ltd. [SPP-ME]). In addition, a "statement" signed by the two parties (EGOTH and SPP) was attached. This said that EGOTH's obligations under the agreements were contingent on receipt of all necessary governmental approval and of satisfactory results from a feasibility study.

The Supplemental Agreement contained one final important provision (one that was not in the original three-party agreement): an arbitration clause. This clause

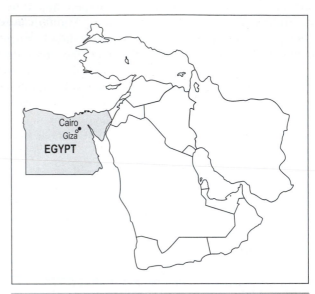

MAP 5-1 Egypt (1984)

provided for disputes to be settled by the Court of Arbitration of the International Chamber of Commerce (ICC) in Paris, France.

The Supplemental Agreement was signed and dated by both EGOTH and SPP. The Minister of Tourism added the words "approved, agreed and ratified" and then his signature. On that same day, December 12, 1974, the Egyptian Minister of Housing and Reconstruction told SPP that the government would indeed provide the roads and other infrastructural elements up to the boundaries of the sites.

Subsequently, ETDC was incorporated, title to the land was transferred to it, the Minister of Tourism approved the master plan, the feasibility study was completed, financing was obtained, and construction was begun. All did not go smoothly, however. The parties had various differences and a certain degree of misunderstanding arose between them.

In the meantime, environmentalists began a worldwide campaign opposing development of the tourist complex at Giza, and they called upon the Egyptian government to protect this ancient place. Following various investigations, the government declared the plain surrounding the Giza pyramids to be part of the public domain. It ordered work on the complex stopped, invali-

---

[17]Title was actually transferred in *usufruct. Usufruct* (from Latin *usus,* "use" and *fructus,* "fruit") is the right to enjoy a thing that belongs to another and to derive from it all the profits or benefit it may produce, provided that such right be exercised without altering or damaging the substance of the thing.

dated the transfer of the land, and appointed a legal administrator to take over management of ETDC. Finally, the government cancelled the entire "Pyramids" project.

Following the cancellation of the project, SPP and its subsidiary, SPP-ME, initiated an arbitration proceeding before the ICC in accordance with the arbitration clause in the Supplemental Agreement. They argued that the Minister of Tourism's signature at the end of the Supplemental Agreement bound Egypt to the arbitration clause in that contract. The ICC Court held that the ARE had been a party to both agreements and therefore that it had agreed to participate in the arbitration. It also found that the ARE had breached its obligations under the agreements and that it had to pay SPP and SPP-ME damages of U.S. $12,500,000.

The ARE then brought this suit in the French Court of Appeals of Paris, asking the Court to set aside the decision of the ICC's Court of Arbitration on the ground that it had not been a party to the Supplemental Agreement—which contained the arbitration clause—and therefore it had never agreed to the jurisdiction of the ICC Court.

THE COURT: . . .

WHEREAS the ARE maintains that it did not wish to sign any document containing an arbitration clause;

* * *

WHEREAS the approval of the Minister of Tourism as described above does not imply the will of the state to become a party to the contract by waiving its immunity from jurisdiction;

WHEREAS the notation "approved, agreed and ratified" must be understood in accordance with Egyptian law, which confers supervision of tourist sites upon the Minister of Tourism (Statute No. 2-73) and grants him the power to approve the creation of economic complexes (Statute No. 60-71) as well as the creation, operation and management of tourist and hotel establishments (Statute No. 1-73);

WHEREAS these statutes, the latter two of which are cited in Article 21 of the [Supplemental] Agreement, convincingly account for the intervention by this Minister, . . . [and clearly demonstrate that he did not intend for the ARE] to become a party to this contract. . . .

WHEREAS, furthermore, the three aforementioned words must also be construed in the context of the statement signed by the "contracting parties—EGOTH and SPP," which . . . [provided] that the obligations placed the same day upon EGOTH would be "subject to the approval of the competent governmental authorities";

WHEREAS, in this regard, SPP and SPP-ME cannot claim, without contradicting themselves, that on the one hand, the signature affixed by the Ministry of Tourism manifests "the permanency of the state's commitment," and, on the other, that the joint statement only concerns "various and routine administrative authorizations," which could have constituted an obstacle to the performance of the contract if not obtained;

WHEREAS, in reality, given the words employed, their location at the end of the document and the connection which must be made with the attached statement, it appears that the ratification which follows the signatures of SPP and EGOTH constitutes, not a solemn commitment by the state to enter into the contract, but specifically the material manifestation of approval by the supervising authority mentioned in the statement;

WHEREAS the existence of said statement provides clear confirmation that, even though the Minister of Tourism did indeed grant his approval, the Egyptian state was not itself a party to the contract; . . .

WHEREAS, therefore, the result of the foregoing reasons is that the ARE did not agree to be bound by an arbitration clause, and that the award of February 16, 1983, was rendered with no arbitration agreement as far as the Egyptian state is concerned.

* * *

FOR THESE REASONS

SETS ASIDE Award No. 3493, given on February 16, 1983, by the Arbitration Court set up under the auspices of the International Chamber of Commerce; Orders Southern Pacific Properties, Ltd. (SPP) and Southern Pacific Properties (Middle East), Ltd. (SPP-ME) to pay costs. . . .

In 1987, the French Court of Cassation affirmed the decision of the Court of Appeals of Paris. ■

Business Forms

International investors seeking to set up a foreign operation may be limited in the kinds of business forms they are allowed to use. Most states generally prefer that foreigners limit themselves to businesses that (a) have local participation and (b) fully disclose their activities to the public. In terms of local participation, this means some form of joint venture, which can be organized either as a partnership, a limited liability company, or a publicly traded stock corporation. Saudi Arabia, for example, allows a foreign company to set up a local branch without any Saudi participation, but the company is not eligible for any of the incentives, such as tax holidays, to which a company that has at least 25 percent Saudi ownership is entitled.[18] Tax holidays and other incentives are available only to investors who form a local company and register with the Saudi Ministry of Commerce. Additionally, Saudi government contracts are granted to companies in the following order of preference: (1) 100 percent Saudi owned, (2) more than 50 percent Saudi owned, (3) 50 percent Saudi owned, (4) less than 50 percent Saudi owned, and (5) 100 percent foreign owned.[19] (In Saudi Arabia, this is an important consideration because the government is by far the biggest purchaser in the country.) As a consequence, the most common company form used by foreign investors in Saudi Arabia is the limited liability company.[20]

Host state laws requiring public disclosure of the activities of large firms or firms with foreign ownership is a second factor affecting the choice of business form. In Pakistan, for example, companies that have more than 20 million rupees in assets cannot be organized as limited liability companies (which do not have to prepare financial prospectuses or make their prospectuses available to the public); they must be set up as stock companies that offer their shares on the local stock exchange. Also, as a matter of preference, Pakistan encourages all firms that have more than a token amount of foreign participation to organize themselves as stock companies.[21]

It is important to note that not all countries try to encourage their companies to disclose their financial and other activities. So-called "tax haven" countries, which try to attract foreign multinational investment, commonly impose no disclosure requirements. Indeed, some (including the Bahamas, Bermuda, the Cayman Islands, the Turks and Caicos Islands, and Vanuatu) tacitly encourage the organization of partnerships and limited liability companies (which are not required to disclose their financial activities).[22]

Limitations on Foreign Equity

Foreign investment laws frequently forbid or limit the percentage of equity that foreigners may own in local businesses. For example, in India, foreign ownership is generally limited to 40 percent[23] and in Mexico to 49 percent.[24]

Notwithstanding these general restrictions, exceptions are occasionally made for the purpose of attracting capital to selected industries and sometimes as a matter of administrative discretion.

Sectoral Limitations

Foreign investment is commonly restricted by economic sector. Regulations typically (a) reserve certain sectors of the economy exclusively to the state or its nationals, (b) permit a limited percentage of foreign capital participation in certain sectors, or (c) define certain sectors in which full or majority foreign ownership is allowed or encouraged.

Closed Sectors

closed sectors: Sectors of a state's economy which are not open to foreign investors.

Most states close certain economic sectors to foreign ownership. Among those most often closed are

- Public utilities
- Vital or strategic industries[25]

---

[18]*See* the Saudi Arabian Regulations for Companies, § 228, Royal Decree No. M/6 of 22.3.1385 A.H. (1968); and the Saudi Arabian Foreign Capital Investment Code, Royal Decree No. M/4 of 2.2.1399 A.H. (1979).

[19]Saudi Arabian Tender Regulations, Article 1(d)(3), Royal Decree No. M/14 of 7.4.1397 A.H. (1977).

[20]*See* Frederick W. Taylor Jr., "Alternative Structures for Doing Business in Saudi Arabia: Distributorship, Agency, Branch, Joint Venture, and Professional Office," *Case Western Reserve Journal of International Law,* vol. 12, p. 77 at p. 90 (1980).

[21]*Center on Transnational Corporations, National Legislation and Regulations Relating to Transnational Corporations,* pp. 44–45 (UN Doc. ST/CTC/26, UN Sales No. E.83.II.A.7, 1983).

[22]The encouragement results in part from the reluctance of these countries to cooperate with foreign tax authorities in providing those authorities with income statements of local companies.

[23]Center on Transnational Corporations, *National Legislation and Regulations Relating to Transnational Corporations,* p. 58 (UN Doc. ST/CTC/26, UN Sales No. E.83.II.A.7, 1983).

[24]*Id.,* p. 323. The Mexican Foreign Investment Act of 1993 requires approval of the country's National Commission of Foreign Investments before foreigners may invest in excess of 49 percent in the limited fields in which such an investment is allowed (e.g., port and shipping services, legal services, the administration of air traffic terminals, cellular telephones, etc.). Foreign Investment Act, 1993, Article 8, in *Diario Oficial de la Federación,* pt. 1, p. 92 (December 27, 1993), English translation in *International Legal Materials,* vol. 33, p. 207 (1994) and online at the Signet Ramos Abogados Web site at www.signetramos.com/laws/foreign investment.htm.

[25]France reserves broadcasting, postal and telecommunications, railroads, gas, and electricity exclusively to state agencies or state-owned companies. Center on Transnational Corporations, *National Legislation and Regulations Relating to Transnational Corporations,* p. 16 (UN Doc. ST/CTC/26, UN Sales No. E.83.II.A.7, 1983).

- Industries that are sufficiently developed[26]
- Medium- or small-scale industries that can be developed by domestic entrepreneurs[27]

To illustrate, Cuba forbids foreign investment in educational and the health care industries.[28] Mexico reserves the following industries to the state: petroleum and other hydrocarbons, basic petrochemicals, nuclear energy, electric power, and telegraphic and postal services. In addition, the following industries are reserved for Mexicans or Mexican companies: radio and television, railroads, urban and interurban land transportation, and retail gasoline sales.[29] Russia forbids foreign investment in the insurance industry, in securities exchanges, and in brokerages.[30]

Restricted Sectors

restricted sectors: Sectors of a state's economy that are not fully open to foreign investors.

Many states limit the percentage of foreign investment allowed in certain economic sectors. Commonly, this is done to limit the influence that foreigners have in domestic political, social, and economic affairs. Australia, for instance, limits foreign investment in its radio and television companies to 20 percent.[31] Canada restricts the amount of equity ownership that foreigners may have in television broadcasting; insurance; local and trust companies; fishing; newspapers; banks; and federal oil, gas, and mining leases.[32]

Foreign Priority Sectors

foreign priority sectors: Sectors of a state's economy in which foreigners are encouraged to invest.

Foreigners are often encouraged to invest in sectors where local development resources are limited, where foreign investment will increase the number of local jobs, and where the foreign export trade will grow. Developing countries, especially, allow foreign capital participation in "pioneer" industries and in industries that are capital intensive, use advanced technology, increase employment, are export oriented, and whose products have a high degree of local value added. Tanzania, for instance, encourages foreign participation in agriculture and livestock development, natural resources, tourism, manufacturing, petroleum and mining, construction, transport, transit trade with neighboring countries, and computers and high technology.[33]

Geographic Limitations

A few countries limit the geographic areas in which foreign investors may conduct business or own land. Argentina, for example, restricts foreign ownership of land and businesses adjacent to its land and ocean frontiers.[34] Chile does not allow foreigners to participate in coastal trade, except for very small vessels.[35] And Indonesia forbids foreigners from owning

---

[26]Foreign investment in flour milling, for example, is forbidden in Ireland. Organization for Economic Cooperation and Development, *Controls and Impediments Affecting Inward Direct Investment*, pp. 13, 45 (1987); and foreigners may not participate in leather and leather products manufacturing in Japan, *id.*, pp. 13, 48 (1987).

[27]Tanzania reserves the following areas for local investors: the retail and wholesale trade; product brokerage; business representation of foreign companies; public relations firms; taxis; barber shops, hairdressing, and beauty salons; butcheries; and ice cream making and ice cream parlors. Tanzania, National Investment (Promotion and Protection) Act of 1990, *International Legal Materials*, vol. 30, p. 890 at p. 912 (1991).

[28]Cuba, Foreign Investment Act, 1995, art. 10, English translation is online at the unofficial Republic of Cuba Web site at www.geo.unipr.it/~davide/cuba/economy/law95/.

[29]Foreign Investment Act, 1993, as amended, Articles 5, 6, in *Diario Oficial de la Federación*, (December 27, 1993, May 12, 1995, June 6, 1995, December 24, 1996, January 23, 1998 and January 19, 1999), English translation in *International Legal Materials*, vol. 33, p. 207 (1994) and online at the Signet Ramos Abogados Web site at www.signetramos.com/laws/foreign investment.htm.

[30]*Guide to International Business Practices*, p. 300 (William S. Hein & Co., 1997).

[31]Organization for Economic Cooperation and Development, *Controls and Impediments Affecting Inward Direct Investment in OECD Member Countries*, p. 31 (1987).

[32]Center on Transnational Corporations, *National Legislation and Regulations Relating to Transnational Corporations*, p. 16 (UN Doc. ST/CTC/26, UN Sales No. E.83.II.A.7, 1983). Most of these restrictions were removed for United States and Mexican investors with the adoption of the North American Free Trade Agreement. *Guide to International Business Practices*, p. 59 (William S. Hein & Co., 1997).

[33]Tanzania, National Investment (Promotion and Protection) Act of 1990, *International Legal Materials*, vol. 30, p. 890 at pp. 910–911 (1991).

[34]*Guide to International Business Practices*, p. 29 (William S. Hein & Co., 1997).

[35]*Id.*, p. 67. Belize forbids foreign commercial fishing inside its barrier reef. *Id.*, p. 40.

land.[36] Moreover, some countries sometimes forbid foreign investment in their entire territories. This was true of the Soviet Union and its allies prior to the mid-1980s.

The right of a state to restrict foreign investment in particular geographic areas is respected by other states as an expression of the state's sovereign authority, as Case 5–2 points out.

---

[36]*Id.,* p. 398. Thailand restricts the purchase of land by foreigners. *Id.* at p. 469. Tunisia does not allow foreigners to own agricultural land. *Id.* at p. 544.

Case 5–2   Brady v. Brown

United States, Ninth Circuit Court of Appeals.
Federal Reporter, Third Series, vol. 51, p. 810 (1995).

CIRCUIT JUDGE BOOCHEVER: . . .

Facts and Procedure

In 1969, California businessmen William T. Brady ("Brady") and James Cardwell ("Cardwell") decided to acquire coastal land in Mexico. Through Guido Natali ("Natali"), a Mexican attorney, Brady and Cardwell learned that a parcel of more than 3300 hectares[37] with seventeen kilometers of beachfront on the Gulf of California (the "Boca property") was available. Brady and Cardwell retained Fred A. Orleans ("Orleans"), a lawyer licensed to practice in Texas and in Mexico, to help them obtain an interest in the Boca property. Orleans hired Chester Brown ("Brown"), the appellant in this action, to perform services in Mexico in connection with the purchase and development of the land. Brown is a United States citizen, a resident of Mexico, and a United States-trained lawyer licensed to practice in Mexico.

In early September 1969, Brown advised Orleans that foreigners could not hold an ownership interest in the Boca property. The Boca property was in Mexico's "Forbidden Zone," an area within fifty kilometers of the shore in which the Mexican Constitution prohibited foreigners from acquiring ownership interests. Based on advice from Brown, Orleans wrote Brady and Cardwell proposing the formation of a corporation wholly owned by Mexican citizens to acquire the land:

It should be kept in mind that legally you can never own shares in the land owning corporation and while there are instances where Mexican citizens have permitted foreigners to use their names to acquire land in the forbidden zone, thus violating the Mexican Constitution, this should not be done. Instead you can obtain better results by associating with bona fide Mexican investors to develop the land and taking their just share in the profits.

Orleans wrote Brown, identifying Brady, Cardwell, and the Mexican participants in the proposed transaction. Brown drew up three agreements, each called "Contract of Association in Participation," sending a draft to Brady on October 24, 1969. In an accompanying letter, Brown advised Brady:

[I]t would be a serious mistake to attempt to purchase land in the forbidden zone in open defiance of the Mexican Constitution. To use Mexicans who are willing to lend you the use of their names as a subterfuge would merely lay you open to the eventual confiscation of the land if the authorities became aware of the subterfuge. . . .

* * *

I believe you can accomplish what you want without violating any law whatsoever by resorting to the use of legitimate contractual relations. Your purpose in any case is to promote the use and sale of the land, and possibly its prior development. It is quite common for promoting and developing groups to associate with property owners to develop land and after recovering their costs, to share the profits with the owners.

Brady, Cardwell, and the four Mexican citizens selected by Orleans (three lawyers associated with Orleans, and Natali's wife) signed the agreements on November 3, 1969 (the "November 1969 agreements"). The November 1969 agreements provided that the Mexican citizens would purchase the Boca property with money contributed by Brady and Cardwell, and would eventually sell or lease the land to Mexican corporations that would be formed to hold and develop the property. The agreements also gave Brown irrevocable powers of attorney from the Mexican citizens over future transactions. The four Mexican citizens purchased the entire Boca property shortly thereafter. Later in November, Brown ended his relationship with Orleans and became Brady and Cardwell's lawyer.

---

[37]A hectare is a unit of land measure equal to 10,000 square meters, or 2.471 acres. The land eventually transferred amounted to 3570 hectares.

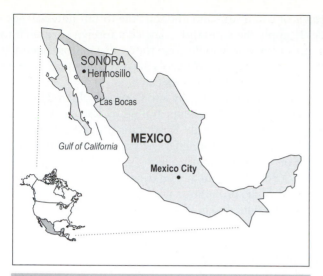

MAP 5-2 Mexico (1995)

In 1972, the Mexican government published new controls forbidding the use of "straw men," Mexican citizens who would hold title to Forbidden Zone property for foreigners. The regulations, which became law in 1973, authorized the Ministry of Foreign Affairs to grant permits to Mexican credit institutions to buy in trust coastal land intended for tourist activities, to be held for the benefit of foreign nationals such as Brady and Cardwell (an arrangement called a "*fideicomiso*").[38] The new law also "required the Ministry's authorization before a foreigner could acquire or lease more than 25 percent of the capital, or 49 percent of the assets of a business enterprise.

Brown sent a copy of the regulations to Brady and Cardwell, but did not advise them to create a trust. Although the law as eventually enacted provided that those required to register their investments had 180 days in which to do so, Brown told Brady and Cardwell they could not benefit from such an arrangement. Instead, he counseled Brady and Cardwell that the new regulations prevented them from owning more than 49 percent of any Mexican business or enterprise, and advised them to sign a new Contract of Association in Participation.

Subsequently, through a complex series of transactions, Brown used his power of attorney to orchestrate the transfer of the property to his family and to business entities controlled by his family, all of whom were Mexican citizens. First, on December 15, 1972, Brady and Cardwell signed the new participation contract, which transferred partial ownership of the Boca property to Brown's son, Eric Brown, and Brown's wife, Maria Brown.

In early 1973, Maria Brown entered into an agreement with Robert Gooden ("Gooden"), a U.S. citizen, for hotel development on 32 hectares of her Boca property. Gooden formed a California limited partnership, Bahia

Ventana Company ("Bahia"), which then formed with Maria Brown a Mexican limited partnership, Cueva del Leon, in which Maria Brown was the general partner with a 51 percent interest, and Bahia was the limited partner with a 49 percent interest. Maria Brown invested no money, and made no decisions regarding the partnership.

In 1975, Brown exercised his power of attorney to transfer to his daughter, Lorna Brown, the remaining interest in the Boca property. The district court found that the Brown defendants paid a total of only $19,200 for the entire Boca property, while Brady and Cardwell eventually invested over $1 million in the purchase and development of the Boca land.

Gooden withdrew from the hotel development project in 1977, and Brady and Cardwell acquired his interest in the project and in Bahia. Later in the year, Dar-Kel Corporation ("Dar-Kel"), a California corporation formed by Brady and Cardwell, signed a contract styled as a non-recourse loan to Maria Brown, transferring funds to Mexico to build the Hotel Las Arenas ("Hotel"). Construction continued from 1977 to 1980.

In 1980, Cueva del Leon became a Mexican corporation, Hotel Las Arenas, S.A. de C.V. (the "Hotel corporation"), with Maria Brown as its majority shareholder. That same year, Maria Brown, as administrator of the Hotel corporation, signed a "Commission Agency Contract" with Dar-Kel, to provide a method for Dar-Kel to receive funds from the Hotel's operation. She also executed a contract related to the loans from Dar-Kel and leased the Hotel to the Hotel corporation. All this was done under Brown's direction, with the ostensible purpose of giving Brady and Cardwell the benefits of ownership without any conflict with Mexican law.

The Hotel opened in 1980. After several years of operation, Brady and Cardwell argued with Brown and Maria Brown regarding ownership and management issues. In 1985, Maria Brown called a shareholders meeting of the Hotel corporation, and claimed control of and title to the Hotel as majority shareholder.

In September 1985, Brady, Cardwell, and Dar-Kel filed suit against Brown, Maria Brown, Eric Brown, Lorna Brown, and Nelly Brown (Eric Brown's wife) alleging . . . state law claims of fraud, conversion, constructive trust, and breach of fiduciary duty. Brown filed a cross-claim against the Hotel Las Arenas corporation, and Maria Brown filed a counterclaim against Brady, Cardwell, and Dar-Kel, alleging . . . fraud.

After an early settlement fell through, the case was eventually tried before the district court from October 5, 1988, to January 17, 1990. The court issued findings of fact and conclusions of law in final form on February 3, 1992. The district court granted summary judgment to Brady and Cardwell on Maria Brown's counterclaim on September 10, 1992. Brown's cross-claim was dismissed

---

[38 A *fideicomiso* is a statutory 50-year renewable trust in which a bank serves as trustee.]

on January 31, 1993.[39] Final judgment was entered March 26, 1993. The court found Brown liable for fraud, and found the other Brown defendants were not bona fide purchasers of the Hotel and the Boca property. As a remedy, the district court imposed a constructive trust to avoid unjust enrichment, ordering all the defendants to execute irrevocable powers of attorney to an agent to transfer the Hotel and the Boca property into a Mexican government-approved trust, or *"fideicomiso,"* for the benefit of Brady and Cardwell.

Chester Brown appeals from the final judgment as do the other Browns (hereinafter collectively referred to as Brown's family), who also appeal from the district court's grant of summary judgment on their counterclaim.

DISCUSSION

* * *

II. Comity

Brown argues that Brady and Cardwell's actions, and the court's eventual remedy, violated the Mexican prohibition of the ownership of coastal land by foreigners. Brown's family joins in his argument. Brown asserts that the California law[40] of comity requires the district court to apply Mexican law, and therefore to refuse to grant Brady and Cardwell any interest in the property. This court reviews the district court's interpretation of foreign law *de novo.*[41] . . .

The doctrine of comity [according to *Wong v. Tenneco, Inc.*] is based on "respect for the sovereignty of other states or countries," and under it "the forum state will generally apply the substantive law of a foreign sovereign to causes of action which arise there."[42] California courts therefore defer to Mexico's laws prohibiting foreign ownership or control of Mexican land.

At the time that Brady and Cardwell entered into the November 1969 agreements drafted by Brown, Article 27, Section I of the Mexican Constitution provided: "Under no circumstances may foreigners acquire direct ownership of lands or waters within a zone of . . . fifty kilometers along the shores of the country." Acts done and contracts made in violation of the prohibition were absolutely void. Later legislation continued to limit foreign investment. . . . [43]

California courts have deferred to Mexican law and declined to enforce California citizens' claims of ownership of Mexican property and businesses in violation of Mexican law. In *Stockton v. Ortiz*,[44] a California businessman created two Mexican corporations to take title to coastal property in Mexico, and operated a motel business on the property. When the business suffered adversity, Stockton sued to recover his investment. Because he was not listed anywhere as having a legal interest in the corporations that owned the property, the California Court of Appeal held that he had no derivative cause of action. It also held that the attempt to acquire the land through the corporations was illegal and void under the Mexican Constitution and laws in effect before 1973. While citing the principle of comity as justification for denying any relief and for "leav[ing] the parties where we found them," the court noted: "This

---

[39]Brown does not appeal the dismissal of his cross-claim.

[40]Brown does not dispute the district court's conclusion that California law applies to the comity issue. We thus apply California law to determine whether comity considerations bar Brady and Cardwell's state law claims.

[[41]Latin: "from new" or "from the beginning." A *de novo* review is a completely new review conducted by the appellate court as if it were the trial court.]

[42]*California Reporter,* vol. 216, p. 412 at p. 417 (California Supreme Ct., 1985).

[43]The 1973 "Law to Promote Mexican Investment and to Regulate Foreign Investment" provides:

ARTICLE 5. . . . In cases where legal provisions or regulations do not specify a given percentage, foreign investment may hold up to 49 percent of the capital of business enterprises provided it is not empowered, by any title, to control the management of the business enterprise. . . .

ARTICLE 7. Foreigners, foreign companies, and Mexican companies without an exclusion of foreigners clause may not acquire direct dominion (title) over land and water in a 100-kilometer strip along the country's borders or in a 50-kilometer strip inland from its coast.

Foreign companies may not acquire dominion over land and water or obtain concessions for water exploitation.

Foreign individuals may acquire dominion over the properties to which the preceding paragraph refers by permission from the Ministry of Foreign Affairs and after signing the agreement to which Section 1, Paragraph 4, of Article 27 of the Political Constitution of the United Mexican States refers.

ARTICLE 8. Authorization by the corresponding Ministry, according to the economic activity involved, shall be required where one or more of the individuals or companies to which Article 2 refers, in one or several actions, or a succession of actions, acquires or acquire more than 25 percent of the capital, or over 49 percent of the fixed assets of a business enterprise. The leasing of a business enterprise or of essential assets required for its functioning, shall be considered equivalent to the acquisition of assets.

Also requiring authorization are actions by which the administration of a business enterprise is acquired by foreign investors, or by which foreign investment is empowered, by any title, to control the management of the business enterprise.

The authorization to which this Article refers shall be granted when it is considered in the interest of the country, pursuant to ruling by the National Commission of Foreign Investment.

Actions undertaken without such authorization shall be null and void. . . .

ARTICLE 18. In accordance with Section 1, Article 27, of the Political Constitution of the United Mexican States and its Organic Law, the Ministry of Foreign Affairs is hereby empowered to decide, in each case, the advisability of granting credit institutions the authorization to acquire in trust the title to real estate intended for industrial and tourist activities, within a strip of 100 kilometers wide along Mexico's borders and 50 kilometers wide inland from its coasts, provided that the purpose of the acquisition is to permit the use of such real estate by the trust beneficiaries without thereby creating ownership rights over it. For this purpose the trustee may issue nominal, nonamortizable participation certificates.

National Commission for Foreign Investment, *Foreign Investment: Legal Framework and Its Application* (1986).

[44]*California Appellate Reports, Third Series,* vol. 47, p. 183 (California Ct. of Appeal, 1975).

does not mean that a person innocently defrauded into believing he can own or lease certain Mexican land cannot seek redress in California courts. Each case must be decided on its own facts."

Also citing comity considerations, the California Supreme Court in *Wong* denied recovery to a California grower who lost his illegal farming operation in Mexico. Wong used Mexican citizens as front men to lease farmlands and hold title in and run his produce farming operation in Mexico, an arrangement Wong knew violated Mexican law. Wong's marketing agreement with a produce broker soured when the broker bypassed Wong to remit the sales proceeds directly to the Mexican growers, treating them as the true owners of the farming operation. After a jury verdict for Wong in his action for breach of contract against the produce broker, the trial judge barred Wong from recovery because the entire arrangement was illegal under Mexican law.

The California Supreme Court affirmed, holding that "[t]he trial court properly declined to involve our courts in this flagrant effort to circumvent Mexican law."[45] "Comity teaches that a contract . . . made with a view of violating the law of another country, though not otherwise obnoxious to the law . . . of the forum . . . will not be enforced"[46] and Wong's violation of Mexican law rendered all his transactions related to the Mexican operation illegal. As in *Stockton*, the court left the parties where it found them.

Brown argues that because Brady and Cardwell attempted to acquire ownership interests in violation of Mexican law, all of their actions were null and void, and the district court should have followed Wong and Stockton to leave the parties where they were (in this case, apparently with Brown's family holding title to the Boca land, and the controlling interests in the Hotel and the Hotel corporation). Brady and Cardwell seek to avoid the application of Wong and Stockton on several grounds. First, they sued for fraud, not for breach of contract. Second, they argue that the relief ordered does not offend comity, as Mexican law authorizes such trust arrangements.

A. Fraud   Brady and Cardwell distinguish their fraud action from Wong and Stockton, in which the plaintiffs attempted to enforce contracts that were illegal under Mexican law. They point out that the California courts did not bar recovery for fraud in either case: in Wong the plaintiff made no fraud claim similar to Brady and Cardwell's,[47] and the *Stockton* court considered the plaintiff's fraud allegation and found it without merit,

because Stockton knew of the legal problems with holding title to Mexican lands. They point out that Stockton suggested the possibility that an innocent party could maintain a fraud action.

We find that this argument has merit. *Stockton* expressly reserves judgment on whether an innocent party could maintain a suit for fraud, stating that "[e]ach case must be decided on its own facts."[48] *Wong* leaves open the question whether comity would bar an action for fraud, emphasizing that in Wong's case his "purposeful violation of Mexican law is clear" because Wong, far from attempting to comply with the law, "concocted an elaborate scheme" to deceive the Mexican authorities.[49] The court found that Wong entered into the marketing contract "with full knowledge that the farming operations upon which the agreement depended were being carried out in violation of Mexican law."[50]

In this case, Brady and Cardwell do not allege that Brown breached any of the contracts related to the Boca property, and the district court did not find that those contracts were illegal under Mexican law. Instead, the fraud claimed by Brady and Cardwell and found by the district court is that Brown advised Brady and Cardwell to sign the 1969 agreement, assuring them that it was entirely legal; three years later, when the new Mexican foreign investment law was published, he misrepresented to them that they could not profit from a trust arrangement under the new Mexican law; and instead of suggesting such a trust, Brown manipulated the subsequent agreements to transfer all the rights in the property to him and his family and to the detriment of Brady and Cardwell, claiming throughout that he was doing so to comply with Mexican law.

On the facts as found by the district court, the doctrine of comity does not require us to apply Mexican law to bar Brady and Cardwell from recovering on their fraud claim.

B. The Nature of the Relief   Brown and the other defendants argue that the relief ordered by the district court violates Mexican law, because the district court attempted to give Brady and Cardwell "all of the attributes of ownership of the Boca land." The court did not do so. Instead, it ordered Brown to execute a power of attorney so that the defendants' interest in the land and the Hotel could be transferred into a trust with a bank approved by the Mexican government for the benefit of Brady and Cardwell.

---

[45]*California Reporter,* vol. 216, p. 412 at p. 417. The court also noted that although the 1973 Law to Promote Mexican Investment and to Regulate Foreign Investment was not in effect when Wong began operation, he could have complied with the law by registering during the 180-day grace period provided for in the transitional rules. *California Reporter,* vol. 216, p. at p. 415 n. 2.
[46]*Id.* at p. 418
[47]Wong's contract suit was against the produce broker who had bypassed him to deal directly with the Mexican citizens holding title to the farmland; he did not name the Mexican citizens themselves.
[48]*California Reporter,* vol. 120 at p. 465 n. 5.
[49]*Id.,* vol. 216 at p. 418.
[50]*Id.* at p. 417.

The remedy devised by the district court is essentially a "*fideicomiso*," authorized by Article 18 of the 1973 foreign investment law. Brown's statement to Brady and Cardwell that they could not benefit from such a trust is a basis of the district court's finding of fraud. Such an arrangement, if it can be accomplished, does not violate Mexican law.

Moreover, the district court retained jurisdiction to consider alternative remedies if the trust could not be established under Mexican law. We find that the district court's judgment did not violate Mexican law.

C. The Brown Defendants Other than Chester Brown

Brown's family claims that because the district court found that only Chester Brown was liable on the fraud claim, Wong and Stockton bar the action against his family, because the contracts were illegal under Mexican law. The district court, however, did not find that the various contracts were illegal. Rather, the court granted Brady and Cardwell relief against Brown's family on the basis of unjust enrichment. The court's finding of unjust enrichment is affirmed in the memorandum disposition filed concurrently with this opinion.

Wong and Stockton do not bar the action against Brown's family.

CONCLUSION

The district court properly exercised pendent jurisdiction over Brady and Cardwell's state law claims. Wong and Stockton do not bar Brady and Cardwell from recovering against Brown and his family. We AFFIRM the district court's judgment after trial in favor of Brady and Cardwell and its grant of summary judgment against Maria Brown on her counterclaim. ◼

Free Zones

free zones:
Geographical areas wherein goods may be imported and exported free from customs tariffs and in which a variety of trade-related activities may be carried on.

Virtually all states encourage multinational enterprises to invest in their economies by setting up **free zones**[51]—that is, geographical areas wherein goods may be imported and exported free from customs tariffs and in which a variety of trade-related activities may be carried on (from simple storage to manufacturing and retailing). One writer has described the free zone as

> a neutral, stockaded area which offers trade-related services and exemptions from laws for the specific purposes of attracting direct foreign investment, encouraging exports, or promoting trade in general. The zone is authorized by the law of the country where the zone is to be located and can [be] either privately or publicly owned. The users of the zone generally pay rent for their usage of space and services.[52]

These zones can be categorized by their geographical size and by the kinds of activities that may be carried on within them.[53]

Free Zones Categorized by Size

free trade areas:
Geographical areas made up of two or more states that have agreed to let some or all of each other's enterprises carry on their trades across and within each state's borders free from customs tariffs and other restrictions.

Free zones vary greatly in size, from large multistate regions to small subzones located in a single building. The largest are called **free trade areas** (FTAs) and are made up of two or more states that have agreed to let some or all of each other's enterprises carry on their trades across and within each state's borders free from customs tariffs and other restrictions. For example, both the North American Free Trade Agreement and the European Community Treaty establish FTAs.[54]

---

[51]In 1967, the United Nations Economic and Social Council (ECOSOC) adopted a resolution encouraging the use of free zones in developing countries as a tool for promoting exports. Resolution of August 4, 1967, United Nations Economic and Social Council Plenary Session No. 1056. In 1970, the United Nations Industrial Development Organization also made the same recommendation. UNIDO, *Free Trade Zones Around the World and Their Use for Export-Oriented Industrial Operations,* UN Document 1D/WG.112/26 (1972).

More recently, the use of free zones has been criticized. Alex Rubner, *The Export Cult: A Global Display of Economic Distortions,* p. 165 (1987), writes: "Free Trade Zones . . . are very much in vogue because they enable governments to flout the spirit of GATT by bestowing distinctive favors on exporters. . . . [T]he FTZ is also a useful device to assuage the nationalist and/or socialist susceptibilities of politicians. By creating a ghetto, in which manufacturers produce either exclusively or predominantly for export, a country puts up with 'obnoxious' corporate practices that would sully the politicians' social conscience if carried on outside the ghetto."

[52]Bettwy, "Mexico's Development: Foreign Trade Zones and Direct Foreign Investment, *Comparative Juridical Review,* vol. 22, p. 49 at pp. 54–55 (1985).

[53]The terms used to describe the various types of free zones are not consistently applied in the literature or from country to country. The terms used here were chosen because they seem to be most commonly used and/or to best describe the particular zone.

[54]The European Union, a common market, is both a free-trade area (in which goods, services, and labor move freely among its 15 member states) and a customs union (in that the Union applies a common external tariff for all member states). *See* Chapter 7.

A state may provide for its entire territory to open up some or all of its economic sectors to international trade. An example is Singapore.[55] Similarly, they may open certain regions. Examples are China's Special Economic Zones[56] and the free perimeters (*perímetros libres*) found along the international borders of some Latin American countries.[57]

The oldest type of free zone is the **free city** (or free port), in which a port city is opened to international trade. Historical examples include Hamburg, which was granted a city charter in 1189 by Frederick I, emperor of the Holy Roman Empire, exempting it from collecting customs duties from merchant ships operating on the lower Elbe River, and the free cities of Bremen, Copenhagen, Genoa, Leghorn, and Trieste.[58] A modern example is Hong Kong.[59]

The **free trade zone** (or Foreign Trade Zone [FTZ] as it is known in the United States) is the modern variant of the free city. Rather than granting free trade status to an entire city, states instead designate smaller areas, usually within or near port cities,[60] as free trade zones. In the United States, for example, there are now more than 180 FTZs.[61] In addition to free trade zones, some states also create special purpose **subzones** associated with, but physically apart from, those zones to accommodate limited-purpose trading activities (such as a single manufacturing plant). The United States, to illustrate, has more than 210 such subzones.[62]

In Case 5–3, the question arose as to whether goods imported into a U.S. subzone would be subject to customs duties.

free city: An entire port city which has been opened to international trade.

free trade zone: A free zone located within or near a port city.

subzone: A special purpose free zone associated with, but physically apart from, a free trade zone, in which limited purpose trading activities are carried on.

---

[55] Walter H. Diamond and Dorothy B. Diamond, *Tax-Free Trade Zones of the World*, p. xi (1987).
[56] *See* Sonoko Nishitateno, "China's Special Economic Zones: Experimental Units for Economic Reform," *International and Comparative Law Quarterly*, vol. 32, p. 175 (1983).
[57] Mexico, for example, has a free perimeter some 20 kilometers wide that parallels its international borders with the United States, Guatemala, and Belize. Michael J. Tucker, "Foreign Trade Zones in Latin America: A Spectrum of Possible Uses," *Texas International Law Journal*, vol. 23, p. 117 at p. 118 (1988). The southern extremity of Argentina is also a free perimeter. *Id.*
[58] Most of the free cities of Europe lost their free trading privileges before 1900 and all lost them prior to World War II. Alfred L. Lomax, *The Foreign-Trade Zone*, pp. 8–9 (1947).
[59] Walter H. Diamond and Dorothy B. Walter H. Diamond and Dorothy B. Diamond, *Tax-Free Trade Zones of the World*, p. xi (1987).
[60] In the United States, free trade zones must be within 60 miles or 90 minutes driving time from a port of entry. Regulations of the Foreign-Trade Zones Board, *Code of Federal Regulation*, Title 15, § 400.21(b)(2)(i).
[61] A list of U.S. FTZs can be found in Helen K. Bonk, *Foreign Trade Zones and Subzones: Their Uses and Effects for U.S. Manufacturers*, app. A, pp. 203–225 (1992).
[62] *Id.*, app. C, pp. 235–249.

Case 5–3   *Nissan Motor Mfg. Corp., U.S.A. v. United States*

United States Court of Appeals, Federal Circuit, 1989. *Federal Reporter, Second Series*, vol. 884, p. 1375 (Federal Circuit Ct. of Appeals, 1989).

CIRCUIT JUDGE ARCHER:

Nissan Motor Mfg. Corp., U.S.A. (Nissan) appeals from the summary judgment of the United States Court of International Trade holding that machinery imported by Nissan from Japan into a foreign trade zone subzone for use in the production of motor vehicles is subject to duty as prescribed by the United States Customs laws.[63] We affirm.

Background

The Foreign Trade Zones Act[64] authorizes the establishment of foreign trade zones within the United States. The Act is administered by a Board which has authority "to grant to corporations[65] the privilege of establishing, operating, and maintaining foreign trade zones in or adjacent to ports of entry under the jurisdiction of the United

---

[63] Nissan Motor Mgf. Corp., U.S.A. v. United States, *Federal Supplement*, vol. 693, p. 1183 (Ct. of Int'l Trade, 1988).
[64] *United States Code*, Title 19, §§ 81a–81u (1982).
[65] "Public" and "private" as defined in the Act, *id.*, § 81a.

States."[66] "Merchandise" may be brought into a foreign trade zone for the purposes set forth in the statue "without being subject to the customs laws of the United States."[67]

According to the trial court:

> In 1952, the Board promulgated regulations pursuant to *United States Code*, title 19, § 81h to authorize "zones for specialized purposes" or "subzones" in areas separate from existing free trade zones "for one or more of the specialized purposes of storing, manipulating, manufacturing, or exhibiting goods" when the Board finds that existing or authorized zones will not serve adequately the convenience of commerce with respect to the proposed purposes.[68] In contrast to general purpose zones where a municipal corporation leases a portion of the zone to firms that subsequently locate within that zone, subzones are generally used by a single firm.[69]

A foreign trade zone subzone was established at Nissan's motor vehicle manufacturing and assembly plant in Smyrna, Tennessee.

Nissan imported production machinery for use in the subzone which consisted of a highly automated, integrated system of industrial robots, automated conveyor and stamping systems, and a complex computerized interface. Nissan requested a ruling from the United States Customs Service[70] regarding its obligation for duties. Nissan noted that it was uncertain whether the proposed final configuration of the machinery would be capable of full-scale production of motor vehicles and that the machinery needed to be assembled, installed and tested. Nissan stated that based on these tests some or all of the machinery might be returned to the foreign manufacturers, replaced, redesigned, or scrapped.

Customs decided, based on these facts, that production equipment imported into Nissan's subzone was not "merchandise" for purposes of the Foreign Trade Zones Act and was therefore dutiable. Customs deferred assessment of duties, however, until the machinery was completely installed and tested in full-scale production of motor vehicles in the subzone.[71]

After installation and testing, Customs required that formal duty-paid entries be made even though the equipment was to remain in the subzone. The production equipment was valued at approximately $116,314,883 with over $3,000,000 in assessed duties. Nissan entered the merchandise as required by Customs and, upon liq-

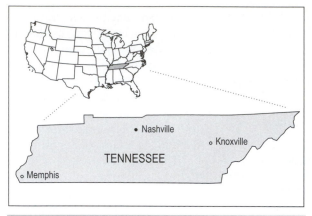

MAP 5-3 Tennessee (1989)

uidation, filed a protest. The protest was denied and Nissan commenced this proceeding. The Court of International Trade held that "[b]ased on the language of the Foreign Trade Zones Act, as amended, and the relevant legislative history . . . [Nissan's] production machinery and related capital equipment are dutiable."[72] Congress authorized the creation of foreign trade zones in the Foreign Trade Zones Act of 1934.[73] In 1950, section 3 of the Act was amended to provide:

> Foreign and domestic *merchandise of every description*, except such as is prohibited by law, may, without being subject to the customs laws of the United States, except as otherwise provided in this chapter, be brought into a zone and *may be stored, sold, exhibited, broken up, repacked, assembled, distributed, sorted, graded, cleaned, mixed with foreign or domestic merchandise, or otherwise manipulated, or be manufactured* except as otherwise provided in this chapter, and be exported, destroyed, or sent into customs territory of the United States therefrom, in the original package or otherwise; but when foreign merchandise is so sent from a zone into customs territory of the United States it shall be subject to the laws and regulations of the United States affecting imported merchandise.[74] . . .

Nissan contends that the trial court erred in concluding that Customs could properly impose a duty on the equipment, because a foreign trade zone is considered to be outside the Customs territory of the United States. It

---

[66]*Id.*, § 81b(a).
[67]*Id.*, § 81c (1982).
[68]*Federal Register*, vol. 17, § 5316 (June 11, 1952), now codified without amendment at *Code of Federal Regulations*, vol. 15, § 400.304 (1988).
[69]*Federal Supplement*, vol. 693 at p. 1185.
[70]Under *Code of Federal Regulations*, vol. 19, § 177.1(a)(1) (1988).
[71]Customs Service Decision 82–103, *Customs Bulletin & Decisions*, vol. 16, p. 869 at p. 870 (March 4, 1982).
[72]*Federal Supplement*, vol. 693 at p. 1189.
[73]Public Law No. 566, *Statutes at Large*, vol. 64, p. 249 (1950) (codified as amended at *United States Code*, Title 19, § 81c (1982)).
[74]*Id.* (Emphasis added.)

argues that merchandise entered into a zone becomes subject to duty only if the merchandise is thereafter sent "into the customs territory of the United States."

The government urges that the Foreign Trade Zone Act does not authorize the use of a foreign trade zone to avoid or defer payment of duties on production equipment installed, used and consumed in the foreign trade zone. Such equipment, according to the government, is not "merchandise" within the meaning of the Act and the installation and use of the equipment are not covered by the activities enumerated in the Act.

The Court of International Trade rejected Nissan's position and held that "imports . . . used or intended to be used to produce motor vehicles" are not within the activities enumerated in *United States Code,* title 19, § 81c (1982).[75] Applying a general rule of statutory construction that the expression of one thing is the exclusion of the alternative, *expressio unius est exclusio alterius*, the court stated that "[n]one of the activities that Congress identified in its comprehensive list permit [*sic*] installation or operation of production equipment without payment of duties."[76] The court also pointed to the legislative history of the 1950 amendment,[77] which stated that "[t]he amended proviso would not authorize consumption of merchandise in a zone. . . ."

Nissan's reading of the Act to mean that duties cannot be imposed on any article brought into a foreign trade zone unless or until it is sent into the Customs territory of the United States is overbroad. The Court of International Trade was correct in our view in determining that Congress signaled its intention to make the imposition of immediate duties dependent on the operations that occur in a foreign trade zone when it listed the activities that could be performed on merchandise brought into a zone. The fact that a comprehensive listing is set forth in the statute indicates that Congress did not intend a blanket exclusion from Customs duties irrespective of what is done with the imported merchandise.

The activities performed by Nissan in the foreign trade zone subzone with the imported equipment are not among those permitted by a plain reading of the statute. Section 81c provides that merchandise brought into a foreign trade zone may be "stored, sold, exhibited, broken up, repacked, assembled, distributed, sorted, graded, cleaned,

mixed with foreign or domestic merchandise, or otherwise manipulated, or be manufactured. . . ."[78] The Act does not say that imported equipment may be "installed," "used," "operated" or "consumed" in the zone, which are the kinds of operations Nissan performs in the zone with the subject equipment. Alternative operations of a different character should not be implied when Congress has made so exhaustive a list.[79]

. . . The Customs Service, in a decision relating to other production machinery from Japan, has similarly ruled that "the list [of activities] does not permit an article to be brought into a zone, free of duty, to be used as production equipment to make other articles."[80]

Nissan relies upon the case of *Hawaiian Independent Refinery v. United States*[81] in support of its position. The merchandise there involved was crude oil which was entered into a foreign trade zone for manufacture into fuel oil products. This, of course, is an activity delineated by the Act and entry into the zone was exempted from Customs duties. Thereafter, a portion of the crude oil was consumed in the manufacturing process and Customs assessed duty on the theory that there had been a "constructive" entry into the Customs territory of the United States. In holding that the assessment was improper, the Court of International Trade did not have to deal with the question at issue here of whether the initial entry into the zone was exempt. Clearly, in that case the crude oil was exempt at the time of entry. Thus, the Court of International Trade properly concluded that the *Hawaiian Independent Refinery Case* was not dispositive of this case.

We are convinced that the Court of International Trade correctly determined that the importation by Nissan of the machinery and capital equipment at issue into the foreign trade zone subzone was not for the purpose of being manipulated in one of the ways prescribed by the statute. Instead it was to be used (consumed) in the subzone for the production of motor vehicles. Under the plain language of the 1950 amendment to the Act and the legislative history of that amendment, and Customs' published decision interpreting the Act as amended, such a use does not entitle the equipment to exemption from Customs duties. Accordingly, the judgment of the Court of International Trade is affirmed. ∎

---

[75] *Federal Supplement,* vol. 693 at p. 1186.

[76] *Id.*

[77] Senate Report No. 1107, 81st Congress, 2d Session, reprinted in *United States Code, Congressional and Administrative News,* vol. 1950, p. 2533 at pp. 2535–2536 (1950).

[78] *United States Code,* Title 19, § 81c.

[79] *See* United States v. Douglas Aircraft Co., *Federal Reporter, Second Series,* vol. 510, p. 1387 at p. 1392 (Ct. of Customs and Patent Appeals, 1975).

[80] *See* Customs Service Decision 79–418, *Customs Bulletin & Decisions,* vol. 13, p. 1627 at pp. 1629–1630 (May 24, 1979). *See also* Senate Report No. 308, 98th Congress, 2d Session, pp. 35–36, reprinted in *United States Code, Congressional and Administrative News,* vol. 1984, p. 4910 at pp. 4944–4945, which, in discussing the 1984 amendments to the Foreign Trade Act, described the "current law" as providing that the "exemption does not apply to machinery and equipment that is imported for use (for manufacturing or the like) within a foreign trade zone."

[81] *Federal Supplement,* vol. 460, p. 1249 (Customs Ct., 1978).

Free Zones Categorized by Activities

The range of activities that can take place within a free zone includes storage, distribution, manufacturing, and retailing; however, not all zones permit all of these activities. What is allowed varies both according to the state in which the zones are located and according to the type of zones. Typically, the full range of these activities is allowed in a free trade zone, as, for example, in U.S. Foreign Trade Zones.[82] Examples of zones with a more limited range of activities are export processing zones and free retail zones.

export processing zones: Free zones in which manufacturing facilities are allowed to process foreign goods and materials for export without paying tariffs or duties either when the goods or materials are imported or when they are exported.

Export processing zones (EPZs) are free zones in which manufacturing facilities process raw materials or assemble parts imported from abroad and then export the finished product. For customs purposes, the materials and parts are treated as if they never enter the host country at all. Accordingly, no tariffs or other duties are paid either when they are imported or when they are exported.[83]

EPZs have proven to be popular in developing states because they are specifically designed to encourage foreign multinational enterprises to employ local workers and, at least in some states, to take on local joint venturers.[84] Popular as they are, however, they have not always been successful and there have been "many notable failures."[85] Some international agencies, including the United Nations Conference on Trade and Development (UNCTAD) and the United Nations Industrial Development Organization (UNIDO), which initially encouraged developing countries to establish EPZs, have recently become more cautious in that respect. The main problem with EPZs seems to have been their popularity. Their increasing numbers having generated "excessive inter-zone competition."[86]

An important example of the successful use of export processing zones is Mexico's *maquiladora* program. A *maquiladora*[87] is a Mexican business entity—usually organized as a wholly owned subsidiary of a foreign multinational enterprise—that assembles, refines, or finishes goods imported from abroad and then exports all of its production. The major advantage for the parent multinational is that it can use inexpensive Mexican labor to assemble its products without having to pay Mexican tariffs. For Mexico, the *maquiladora* program has led to the creation of many new jobs.[88] (In the industrialized states where the work used to be performed, however, the *maquiladora* program is not always viewed with sympathy.)[89]

free retail zones: Areas in international airports and harbors where travelers can buy goods free of local sales and excise taxes.

Free retail zones (or duty-free zones) are found in international airports and harbors and near some border crossings. They cater to tourists and other travelers who are leaving a country by offering them goods free of local sales and excise taxes. These zones are usually of little economic significance in industrial countries, but they are often an important source of income in countries that depend on tourism, especially in the Caribbean.

bonded warehouse: A facility at a port of entry where shippers can store goods until they clear customs.

Analogous to, but somewhat different from, free zones are **bonded warehouses**. These facilities are found at the ports of entry of most countries. Privately owned and operated by transportation firms, they provide a place where shippers can store goods from the time of their

---

[82]United States Foreign Trade Zones Act of June 18, 1934, *Statutes at Large,* vol. 48, pp. 998–1003, *United States Code,* Title 19, §§ 81a–81u.
   Retail trade is allowed only by special permit and it may involve only domestic or duty-paid or duty-free merchandise that entered the zone from a U.S. Customs territory. *Id.,* at § 81*o*(d).

[83]Antoine Basile and Dimitri Germidis, *Investing in Free Export Processing Zones,* p. 20 (1984).

[84]*Id.* at p. 22.
   Recently, some states that had required joint venture participation have modified their rules and now allow for wholly owned foreign subsidiaries to operate within their zones. For example, the Emirate of Dubai, part of the United Arab Emirates, which created the Jebel Ali Free Zone in 1985 to encourage international trade and the use of the Jebel Ali Port, authorized the establishment of wholly owned foreign subsidiaries within the Zone as of 1992. Dubai was the first Persian Gulf nation to do so. Hassen A. Ferris and Joe M. Hawbaker, "100% Foreign Ownership Allowed in Jebel Ali," *Middle East Executive Reports,* vol. 15, No. 11, p. 9 (November 1992).

[85]*Id.,* at p. 22.

[86]*Id.,* at p. 23.

[87]From Spanish *maquila:* the charge collected by millers in Colonial Mexico for processing grain. *Maquiladora* is used today as a generic term for those firms that "process" (assemble and/or transform in some way) components imported into Mexico and then reexported.

[88]As of 2001, on average, some 2,834 *maquiladora* plants employed more than 992,877 workers. Instituto Nacional de Estadística, Geografía e Informática, Indicadores de la industria maquiladora: Establecimientos y empleo para estados y municipios fronterizos (2002), posted on the Network of Border Economics/Red de la Economía Fronteriza Web site at www.nobe-ref.org/Databases/Empl_Plants.xls.

[89]*See A Fair Deal* (1999) posted at www.afsc.org/border/maquila.htm, and Norris C. Clement, "An Overview of the Maquiladora Industry," *California Western International Law Journal,* vol. 18, p. 55 (1987).

arrival from overseas to the time they clear customs and are taken away by importers. They are not intended to be places for trade or business but are rather an efficient solution to the problem that customs authorities would otherwise have if they had to provide storage and access to foreign goods while they were being processed for entry into the country. An importer who uses a bonded warehouse cannot avoid tariffs, quotas, or any other form of regulation. Customs forms have to be filled out when goods enter the warehouse and when they leave, and the goods are maintained under guard while they are there. Goods can be stored only for a limited time, and permission from the customs authorities has to be obtained before they can be cleaned, packaged, sorted, labeled, repaired, or destroyed. No manufacturing activities are allowed inside bonded warehouses.[90]

Foreign Investment Guarantees

Host countries provide a variety of guarantees to foreign investors to make investment in their territories more attractive. The most important guarantees relate to the following:[91]

- Compensation in the event of nationalization of a foreign-owned enterprise and repatriation of the payments made
- Repatriation of the proceeds upon the sale of the enterprise
- Repatriation of profits and dividends
- Repatriation of other forms of current income (such as royalties, licensing fees, and fees for managerial and other services)
- Repatriation of the principal and interest from loans
- Nondiscriminatory treatment
- Stabilization of taxes and other regulations
- Convertibility of local currency

Guarantees are granted either (a) automatically when an investment application is "approved" or "certified" by the appropriate host state agency or (b) on an *ad hoc* basis.

Particular guarantees are found in the constitutions, legislation, policy statements, and legal and administrative practices of countries.[92]

Constitutional provisions most commonly deal with the compensation due foreign investors in the event of **nationalization** or **expropriation**. These describe how property is to be taken and, sometimes, how it is to be paid for. India's constitution provides only that no person shall be deprived of his property except by the authority of law. The German constitution requires that a taking be in the public interest and pursuant to the law. Mexico's constitution says that private property cannot be expropriated except for a public use and upon payment of compensation. The constitutions of Argentina, Iraq, Malaysia, the Philippines, the Sudan, and Yugoslavia all say that a taking must be in the public interest, by means of a law or procedures established by law, and that "fair," "just," or "adequate" compensation must be provided. Kenya's constitution states that a taking has to be in the public interest and be such as to afford "reasonable justification for the hardship caused to the owner," and, also, that compensation must be "prompt" and "full" and able to be remitted freely within a reasonable period. Both Ghana and Kenya add specific guarantees assuring access to their countries' highest courts for anyone whose interests are affected.[93]

The guarantees found in legislation—especially in foreign investment laws—tend to be both more detailed and more extensive than those found in constitutions. The procedures to be followed in the event of nationalization, for instance, are more detailed. Russia's Federal Law on

nationalization:
Acquisition by a state of property previously held by private persons or companies usually in exchange for some consideration.

expropriation:
Depriving a person or company of private property without compensation.

---

[90]Helen K. Bonk, *Foreign Trade Zones and Subzones: Their Uses and Effects for U.S. Manufacturers,* p. 14 (1992).

[91]Center on Transnational Corporations, *National Legislation and Regulations Relating to Transnational Corporations,* pp. 48, 50 (UN Doc. ST/CTC/26, UN Sales No. E.83.II.A.7, 1983).

[92]Foreign investment guarantees are also granted through bilateral investment-protection agreements. Generally, these give foreign investors protection or guarantees with respect to (a) nationalization and compensation, (b) repatriation and transfer of funds, (c) national treatment, (d) most-favored-nation treatment, (e) subrogation, and (f) dispute settlement. Center on Transnational Corporations, *National Legislation and Regulations Relating to Transnational Corporations,* p. 51 (UN Doc. ST/CTC/26, UN Sales No. E.83.II.A.7, 1983). Also, with the adoption of the General Agreement on Trade in Services (GATS), many of these agreements are incorporated in the Schedules of Commitments that World Trade Organization member states have annexed to GATS. *See* Chapter 8.

[93]*Id.,* p. 48.

Foreign Investment provides that foreign investors will be fairly compensated for property that is nationalized and that disputes with investors will be resolved as provided for by international treaties or Russian law.[94] Indonesia's Foreign Capital Investment Law provides that compensation should be mutually agreed upon in accordance with international law and that any disagreements shall be resolved by binding arbitration. Ghana's Capital Investment Decree directs that disputes about compensation are to be referred to an arbitrator appointed by the parties or, should they be unable to agree upon an arbitrator, then to arbitration held under the auspices of the International Center for Settlement of Investment Disputes. The Encouragement of Investment Act of the Sudan provides that compensation will be paid in yearly installments over a period not exceeding five years and that it will be paid in the same currency that the investor used in starting up the business or in any other currency the parties mutually specify.[95]

Foreign investment laws also deal with guarantees that are not always found in constitutions, especially repatriation guarantees, assurances of nondiscrimination, and stability clauses.

repatriation guarantee: The assurance of a host state government that foreign investors will be able to take out of the state both the investment capital they brought in and the profits they earned.

The most common **repatriation guarantees** relate to the right of foreign investors to remit profits and investment capital to their home country in the event of the partial or complete termination of their enterprise.[96] Less common are guarantees relating to the repatriation of other kinds of current income (such as royalties, licensing fees, and fees for managerial and other services) and to the remittance of the principal and interest from loans.[97]

In many countries, monetary remittances abroad are subject to a variety of qualifications. Some of the more common are listed here:

a. Transfers may be limited or forbidden in case of very tight foreign exchange situations.

b. The transfer of capital may be restricted for a certain period after an investment is made.[98]

c. Transfers of profits and dividends or other forms of income will be subjected to the requirement of paying taxes and complying with auditing requirements.[99]

d. The transfer of proceeds from the sale or liquidation of an investment may require governmental approval.

nondiscrimination guarantee: The assurance of a host government that foreign investors will be treated in the same way as local investors.

Nondiscrimination guarantees are found in many investment laws, as well as in the constitutions of several countries, especially in Latin America. The constitutional provisions generally are guarantees that foreign investors will be treated in the same manner as national investors. The statutory provisions often specify that equality of treatment relates to ownership rights, taxation, and, sometimes, social matters.[100]

---

[94]Federal Law on Foreign Investment in the Russian Federation of July 2, 1999, arts. 8 and 10; English translation in *International Legal Materials,* vol. 39, p. 894 (2000) and online at the Russian federal government's Web site at www.economy.gov.ru/MinEc/english/legislation/law.html.

[95]Center on Transnational Corporations, *National Legislation and Regulations Relating to Transnational Corporations,* p. 49 (UN Doc. ST/CTC/26, UN Sales No. E.83.II.A.7, 1983). For another example, *see* Bretton G. Sciaroni, "New Investment Law Creates Favorable Framework," *East Asian Executive Reports,* vol. 16, no. 7, p. 7 (July 15, 1994), describing the Cambodian foreign investment law that became effective on August 5, 1994.

[96]*See* Federal Law on Foreign Investment in the Russian Federation of July 2, 1999, art. 11; English translation in *International Legal Materials,* vol. 39, p. 894 (2000) and online at the Russian federal government's Web site at www.economy.gov.ru/MinEc/english/legislation/law.html.

[97]Center on Transnational Corporations, *National Legislation and Regulations Relating to Transnational Corporations,* pp. 49, 50 (UN Doc. ST/CTC/26, UN Sales No. E.83.II.A.7, 1983). Sometimes host countries will underwrite foreign loans; that is, they will guarantee the repayment of foreign loans and interest. Algeria, Brazil, Ghana, Kenya, Saudi Arabia, and the Sudan have such a guarantee in their investment promotion laws. *Id.,* p. 50.

[98]The Chilean Foreign Investment Statute of 1977 does not allow capital to be transferred abroad until three years after it is first brought into the country. Net income, however, can be remitted at any time. *Id.,* p. 49.

[99]*Id.,* p. 49. Algeria's investment laws state that the investors' share in distributed profits that can be transferred abroad may not exceed the ratio of the investors' contribution in imported capital to the total investment capital of an enterprise; and, in any event, the maximum amount that can be repatriated in any year is 15 percent of the investors' equity participation. *Id.*

[100]Algeria's investment laws guarantee equality before the law for investors, especially in relation to taxation. *Id.,* p. 50.
The Argentine Foreign Investment Law of 1977 promises that foreign investors have the same rights and obligations that the constitution and national laws grant to national investors, subject to any qualifications in that law and to rules provided by special and promotional statutes. *Id.*
Brazil's Foreign Capital Investment Law states that foreign capital is to receive the same treatment before the law as that accorded Brazilian capital under similar situations, and that any discrimination not specifically provided for in the law is prohibited. *Id.*
Chile's Foreign Investment Statute guarantees that foreign investments will be subject to the same general regulations that apply to national investments and that there is to be no discrimination, direct or indirect, except that access by foreign investors to internal credit may be limited. *Id.*

stabilization clause: The promise of a host government that any future changes it makes in its tax, foreign exchange, or other legal régimes will not apply to a particular foreign investor.

Stabilization clauses are a special kind of investment guarantee provided by a few countries. Such a clause promises foreign investors that the host government will not change its tax, foreign exchange, or other legal régime for a certain period of time, or that changes subsequent to the establishment of an enterprise will not affect that enterprise. For example, Algeria's investment code contains a clause that promises that any future changes in the code will not affect an enterprise that has already been approved under the existing code, unless the conditions benefit the enterprise.[101]

A stabilization clause, like any contractual provision, can be changed by the mutual agreement of the parties. Changes in the surrounding circumstances and changes in the way the parties perform may also modify such a clause.

A stabilization clause cannot prevent a state from nationalizing or expropriating a foreign investment. Under international law, every state ultimately has the power to nationalize property. The violation of a stabilization clause, however, may change the character of a nationalization decree, from lawful to a breach of contract. Nevertheless, while a state may surrender its "right" to nationalize, it cannot surrender its "power."

B. SUPERVISION OF FOREIGN INVESTMENT

Start-Up Standards

The foreign investor whose application has been approved by the host state is usually subject to some time limit in which to start construction and/or begin operation. Saudi Arabia, for example, gives licensed investors six months in which to implement an approved project; otherwise their license may be revoked. In Tunisia, the period is one year; while Chile requires foreign investors to fully capitalize their investments within six years (or eight years in the case of mining ventures).[102]

Additionally, most countries require investors to submit periodic reports during the start-up period that describe their progress in importing capital (including capital goods), constructing facilities, hiring and training personnel, and beginning production. For example, in Indonesia, during the construction and trial production period, investors have to submit monthly reports to the Bank of Indonesia so that the bank can track the amount of foreign currency brought into the country, and semiannual reports to the Investment Coordinating Board so that the Board can follow the operational progress of the project.[103]

Operational Reviews

Once a foreign-owned enterprise is in full operation, it is usually subject to periodic monitoring. This may involve the submission of information (commonly on a yearly basis) on various aspects of the enterprise's business activities, plus regular inspections of its plant, facilities, and records to ensure that it is in compliance with the local investment regulations and, if appropriate, a specific investment agreement. If a single central agency is responsible for approving and supervising foreign investments, it will commonly collect the reports and conduct the inspections. Otherwise, a variety of specialized agencies may be involved. In Tanzania, for example, the Investment Promotion Center monitors and enforces compliance with the country's investment regulations.[104]

Tunisia's Investment Code of January 1, 1994, recognizes the principle of nondiscrimination and equality before the law for foreign investors, especially in tax and social matters. *Id.*

Russia's Federal Law on Foreign Investment in the Russian Federation of July 2, 1999, art. 5 provides that foreign investors will be treated the same as Russian investors. *See* English translation in *International Legal Materials,* vol. 39, p. 894 (2000) and online at the Russian federal government's Web site at www.economy.gov.ru/MinEc/english/legislation/law.html.

[101]*Id.,* p. 50; and *see* Federal Law on Foreign Investment in the Russian Federation of July 2, 1999, art. 9.

[102]Center on Transnational Corporations, *National Legislation and Regulations Relating to Transnational Corporations,* p. 12 (UN Doc. ST/CTC/26, UN Sales No. E.83.II.A.7, 1983).

[103]*Id.,* p. 13.

[104]Tanzania, National Investment (Promotion and Protection) Act of 1990, § 4(2)(m), *International Legal Materials,* vol. 30, p. 890 at p. 898 (1991).

In Indonesia the Investment Coordinating Board performs these duties and in Ghana they are performed by the Capital Investment Board. Center on Transnational Corporations, *National Legislation and Regulations Relating to Transnational Corporations,* p. 13 (UN Doc. ST/CTC/26, UN Sales No. E.83.II.A.7, 1983).

In Saudi Arabia, both the Investment Bureau and the Ministry of Industry and Electricity share such responsibility.[105]

Modification of Foreign Investment Agreements

Investment laws usually provide that any modification to an investment agreement, including an increase or decrease in the size or scope of a project, has to be approved by the host state. Sudan's Encouragement of Investment Act of 1980, for example, provides that any change in the size or purpose of a project has to be approved by the Minister of Finance and National Economy. Similarly, any transfer of ownership of all or any part of a project needs the Minister's approval.[106]

Protection of Subsidiaries

Foreign investors, whether natural persons or companies, are generally recognized as having the same rights to manage a company in a host state as do local persons and companies. At the same time, foreigners are not allowed to take advantage of the fact that they are not physically present in the host state as a way of escaping full responsibility for their investments. They and the subsidiary firms they establish are subject to the same obligations as local firms. In addition, they are also subject to a variety of special regulations designed to prevent them from abusing either their local subsidiaries, their subsidiaries' employees, or their subsidiaries' creditors.

Disclosure of Information

All firms, whether foreign subsidiaries or domestic enterprises, are subject to basic disclosure obligations. The reason companies are required to disclose information about their organizational structure and their activities is to serve one basic purpose: protection of the public (i.e., shareholders and creditors) from fraud and misrepresentation.

There are two basic sets of disclosure rules: (1) initial or organizational disclosure reports that must be made when a company is first organized and (2) periodic reports that require companies to update changes in their organization and activities. In federal states, such as Argentina, Brazil, and the United States, the constituent federal states enact the initial or organizational disclosure rules, and the central (or federal) government enacts the periodic disclosure laws. Of course, in unitary states, both sets of rules are enacted by the national government.

In common law countries, a company's Memorandum of Association and/or Articles of Incorporation are filed with a registrar who maintains a copy that can be examined by the public. In civil law countries, the organizational documents are notarized and entered in the Commercial Register, which is also open to the public. Additionally, most countries, in both systems, now require that a company's organizational documents be published in a state or national gazette or in a newspaper of general circulation.[107]

Along with the organizational documents, the information that a company has to submit as part of its initial disclosure—whether registration takes place through the Registrar of Companies or the notarization process—generally includes the following:[108]

a. Names, nationality, and domicile of the shareholders of the company
b. Purpose or objectives of the company
c. Company name or designation
d. Amount of capital and classes of shares and any division therein
e. Amount of contribution of each shareholder in cash and the method of calling for unpaid subscriptions
f. Manner in which the company will be managed and powers of the board of directors or its equivalent

---

[105]*Id.*

[106]*Id.*

[107]In Ghana, for example, all company documents filed with the registrar have to be published. In Indonesia, the Memorandum of Incorporation of a limited liability company (*perseroan terbatas: PT*), which is the form of business organization commonly used by foreign investors, has to be approved by the Minister of Justice, recorded in court, and published in the official gazette. In the Philippines, incorporation documents are filed with the Securities and Exchange Commission, notarized, and published in a newspaper of general circulation. In Saudi Arabia, a company's Memorandum, Articles of Association, and basic details have to notarized and published in the official gazette. *Id.,* pp. 44, 45.

[108]*Id.,* pp. 45–46.

g. Rights and liabilities of shareholders and creditors

h. Appointment of executives and staff

i. Method of distributing profits and losses

j. Circumstances under which a company may be dissolved and liquidators appointed

The information that companies have to provide annually usually includes the following:[109]

a. Balance sheet

b. Profit and loss account

c. Directors' report

d. Auditors' report

The detail of information in these reports varies from country to country, as do the accounting methods that are used.

The annual reporting procedures also vary. In Ghana, for example, an annual report has to be published in the national gazette and in one national newspaper. In Brazil, company reports are published in the national gazette and a local newspaper and are made available to shareholders. In India, corporate reports are filed with the Registrar of Companies and sent to holders of shares and debentures.[110]

Publicly traded companies, as mentioned earlier, generally have to provide more extensive information in their annual reports. Privately held companies are usually required to file only limited information. In India, for example, a private company files only a balance sheet and an auditor's report.

Foreign-owned corporations in some countries (such as Argentina, Ghana, and Malaysia) are subject to the same disclosure requirements as domestic companies. In a few countries, they are also subject to special additional reporting requirements. For example, in India, a foreign branch has to submit both its own annual financial statements and that of its head office to the Registrar of Joint Stock Companies.

Some attempts have been made to harmonize the information collected by different countries. The International Accounting Standards Committee (IASC), which has 42 member countries, has established standards for the preparation of audited financial statements. The International Federation of Accountants (IFAC), with 53 member countries, has established international auditing guidelines. Recently, the United Nations established an *Ad Hoc* Intergovernmental Working Group of Experts on International Standards of Accounting and Reporting. This group is reviewing existing arrangements, and it plans to issue a code that will provide for greater harmonization of international standards.[111]

Compliance with a country's disclosure requirements is generally enforced both by the agencies that collect the disclosure reports and by the country's Department or Ministry of Justice. In Argentina, for example, corporate activities are regulated through the office of the syndic (*sindicatura*) and a vigilance council (*consejo de vigilancia*). Both agencies have extensive investigatory powers. They may inspect records and solicit information necessary to conduct their investigations satisfactorily. The General Inspection Service (*Inspection General de Personas Jurídicas*), a division of the Ministry of Justice, has supervisory, investigatory, and enforcement powers. It must approve all of a company's organizational documents before the company can commence business, as well as any amendments that affect the company's powers. It has extensive subpoena powers that enable it to examine a company's books and investigate a company's affairs. It also may initiate suits to ensure that a company observes the law.[112]

In addition to these basic disclosure requirements, many European countries also require affiliated companies to file consolidated financial statements or, as a minimum, to submit

---

[109]*Id.,* p. 46.

[110]In addition to annual reports, several countries also require special reports on various aspects of a company's activities. *Id.*

[111]United Nations Center on Transnational Corporations, *National Legislation and Regulations Relating to Transnational Corporations,* p. 47 (UN Doc. ST/CTC/26, UN Sales No. E.83.II.A.7, 1983).

[112]*Id.,* p. 45.

information on the financial status of the entire group. In the Netherlands, for example, a Dutch parent may choose between publishing consolidated annual accounts or publishing the accounts of all of its subsidiaries.[113]

Protection of the Subsidiary

The laws of several countries, including Belgium, France, Germany, Norway, and Switzerland, provide some protection for subsidiaries from the disadvantageous decisions by their parent company. In general, these provisions try to preserve the capital basis and the financial viability of the subsidiary.

German law, for example, treats parent and subsidiary companies as *de facto*[114] combines and requires the parent to compensate its subsidiaries for any disadvantageous effects that result from its instructions. If a parent and its subsidiaries enter into a formal "contract of domination," this formal combine is subject to special rules. The subsidiary is required to set up a special reserve; the amount of profits that can be transferred to the parent is limited; and the parent company must assume the annual losses of the subsidiary.[115]

Protection of a Subsidiary's Minority Shareholders

appraisal rights: The right of a dissenting shareholder to require the company to purchase his shares at their fair market value.

Corporate law, securities regulations, or stock exchange rules often grant minority shareholders appraisal rights or rights to minimum guaranteed dividends. **Appraisal rights** are the rights of a dissenting shareholder to require the company to purchase his shares at their fair market value. Under German law, for instance, minority shareholders can exercise their appraisal rights whenever a subsidiary enters into a special "contract of domination" with its parent involving, for example, a transfer of profits. In the alternative, they can demand adequate compensation for their investment in the form of guaranteed minimum dividends.[116]

In addition, in Belgium, France, and other countries, a minority shareholder is entitled to initiate a legal action against decisions imposed on a subsidiary by a controlling parent company if the decisions are manifestly contrary to the subsidiary's interests.[117]

Protection of a Subsidiary's Creditors

Parent companies are sometimes held to be responsible for the debts of their subsidiaries, or, in the event of liquidation of the subsidiary, the parent's claims will be subordinated to those of other creditors. In Portugal, for example, affiliates of "a complementary group of enterprises" are mutually liable for each other's debts in the case of the insolvency of any member of the group.[118]

Like minority shareholders, creditors are often entitled to bring actions to enjoin a subsidiary from complying with the instructions of a parent. In addition, the host state may intervene, through the appointment of a temporary or permanent administrator to operate the subsidiary, to protect the interests of the minority shareholders and local creditors.[119] Case 5–4 describes the actions taken by government agencies in Italy to protect the interests of the employees and creditors of an American-owned subsidiary.

---

[113]Organization for Economic Cooperation and Development, *International Investment and Multinational Enterprises: Responsibility of Parent Companies for their Subsidiaries,* p. 10 (1980).

[114]Latin: "from the fact" or "in fact"; in effect although not formally recognized.

[115]Organization for Economic Cooperation and Development, *International Investment and Multinational Enterprises: Responsibility of Parent Companies for Their Subsidiaries,* p. 10 (1980).

[116]*Id.,* p. 11.

[117]For example, in Fruehauf v. Massardy, in Dalloz-Sirey, *Jurisprudence,* vol. 1968, p. 147 (1965), the Paris Court of Appeals accepted a complaint brought by minority shareholders who contested the instructions of an American parent that had ordered its French subsidiary to breach a contract with a company in a third country in order to comply with trade restrictions based on U.S. law. The Court held that the parent, as the majority shareholder, had abused its position because the breach would have resulted in the subsidiary being liable for damages that would have threatened its very existence. The Court, accordingly, appointed a judicial administrator to carry out the contract. *Id.,* p. 12.

[118]*Id.,* p. 13.

[119]An example is the Badger Case. *See* Stephen Lee Smith, "Badger Revisited," *International Tax and Business Law,* vol. 11, pp. 125–130 (1983).

Case 5–4 *Case Concerning Elettronica Sicula, SpA*

United States v. Italy

International Court of Justice, 1989.
International Court of Justice Reports, vol. 1989, p. 15
(1989); *International Legal Materials*, vol. 28, p. 1109 (1989).

The United States initiated this proceeding against Italy before a Chamber of the International Court of Justice. The United States claimed that Italy violated its international obligations under the Treaty of Friendship, Commerce, and Navigation concluded by Italy and the United States in 1948 (the FCN Treaty) and its Supplementary Agreement of 1951 in connection with Italy's treatment of two American companies, the Raytheon Company (Raytheon) and one of Raytheon's wholly owned subsidiaries, Machlett Laboratories Incorporated (Machlett). Raytheon and Machlett were the owners of an Italian subsidiary, Raytheon-Elsi, SpA (previously known as Elettronica Sicula, SpA [ELSI]), that operated a plant in Palermo, Sicily. ELSI employed some 900 workers, who manufactured microwave tubes, cathode-ray tubes, semiconductor rectifiers, X-ray tubes, and surge arresters. For a variety of reasons, the venture was not successful. ELSI's management blamed a major part of its lack of success on its having trained and employed an excessively large workforce and on the opposition of a local employees union to its attempts to reduce that workforce. In an attempt to modernize and expand its plant, ELSI had also incurred large debts to one U.S. and several Italian banks, some of which were guaranteed by Raytheon. In addition, it had had little success in penetrating the Italian electronics market. As a consequence, between February 1967 and March 1968, it solicited the help of the Italian government, the Sicilian government, and the private sector to find an Italian joint venturer with economic power and influence that would make it both more competitive and more likely to obtain development assistance from the Italian government.

When efforts to work out a mutually satisfactory arrangement between the Italian officials and the companies proved impossible, Raytheon and Machlett immediately began planning to liquidate ELSI. On March 7, 1968, Raytheon notified ELSI that it would not subscribe to any further shares of ELSI's stock or guarantee any additional loans. On March 16, ELSI's Board of Directors shut down the operation of the plant and, effective March 29, terminated all commercial activities and employment contracts. On April 1, representatives of ELSI met with representatives of its bank creditors in an attempt to work out an orderly

liquidation. The banks were unwilling to cooperate. That same day the Mayor of Palermo issued an order requisitioning ELSI's plant for a period of six months, citing a "grave public necessity" and the possibility of rioting by ELSI's employees. An administrator took over the operation of the plant on April 6. ELSI protested the requisition order and sought relief in a local court, to no avail. On April 26, 1968, ELSI filed for bankruptcy. In the bankruptcy proceeding, creditors filed claims against ELSI totaling some 13 billion lira and the Court ordered that ELSI be liquidated. The liquidation realized only some 6.4 billion lira.

Raytheon had guaranteed ELSI's indebtedness to several banks; and on ELSI's bankruptcy, it was accordingly liable for, and paid, 5.8 billion lira to the banks in accordance with the terms of the guarantees. Raytheon and Machlett then sought the assistance of the United States to press a claim against Italy for the loss of their subsidiary. The United States did so initially through diplomatic channels, but when diplomacy failed, the United States brought suit in the International Court of Justice. The United States claimed that Italy had deprived Raytheon and Machlett of their ownership and control of ELSI in violation of the U.S.-Italian FCN Treaty.

JUDGMENT: . . .

The Chamber is faced with a situation of mixed fact and law of considerable complexity, wherein several different strands of fact and law have to be examined both separately and for their effect on each other: the meaning and effect of the relevant articles of the FCN Treaty and Supplementary Agreement; the legal status of the Mayor's requisition of ELSI's plant and assets; and the legal and practical significance of the financial position of ELSI at material times, and its effect, if any, upon ELSI's plan for orderly liquidation of the company. It will be convenient to begin by examining these considerations in relation to the applicant's claim that the requisition order was a violation of Article III of the FCN Treaty.

Article III of the FCN Treaty is in two paragraphs. Paragraph 1 provides for rights of participation of nationals of one High Contracting Party, in corporations and associations of the other High Contracting Party, and for the exercise by such corporations and associations of their functions. Since there is no allegation of treatment less favorable than is required according to the standards set by this paragraph, it need not detain

MAP 5-4 Italy (1989)

the Chamber. Paragraph 2 of Article III is, however, important for the applicant's claim; it provides:

> The nationals, corporations and associations of either High Contracting Party shall be permitted, in conformity with the applicable laws and regulations within the territories of the other High Contracting Party, to organize, control and manage corporations and associations of such other High Contracting Party for engaging in commercial, manufacturing, processing, mining, educational, philanthropic, religious and scientific activities. Corporations and associations, controlled by nationals, corporations and associations of either High Contracting Party and created or organized under the applicable laws and regulations within the territories of the other High Contracting Party, shall be permitted to engage in the aforementioned activities therein, in conformity with the applicable laws and regulations, upon terms no less favorable than those now or hereafter accorded to corporations and associations of such other High Contracting Party controlled by its own nationals, corporations and associations.

... [T]here is no allegation of treatment of ELSI according to standards less favorable than those laid down in the second sentence of the paragraph. The allegation by the United States of a violation of this paragraph by Italy relates to the first sentence.

In terms of the present case, the effect of the first sentence of this paragraph is that Raytheon and Machlett are to be permitted, in conformity with the applicable laws and regulations within the territory of Italy, to organize, control and manage ELSI. The claim of the United States focuses on the right to "control and manage"; the right to "organize," apparently in the sense of the creation of a corporation, is not in question in this case. Is there, then, a violation of this Article if, as the United States alleges, the requisition had the effect of depriving ELSI of both the right and practical possibility of selling off its plant and assets for satisfaction of its liabilities to its creditors and satisfaction of its shareholders?

... The essence of the applicant's claim has been throughout that Raytheon and Machlett, which controlled ELSI, were by the requisition deprived of the right, and of the practical possibility, of conducting an orderly liquidation of ELSI's assets. ...

The crucial question is whether Raytheon, on the eve of the requisition, and after the closure of the plant and the dismissal, on 29 March 1968, of the majority of the employees, was in a position to carry out its orderly liquidation plan, even apart from its alleged frustration by the requisition. That plan, as originally conceived, contemplated that the disposal of plant and assets might produce enough to pay all creditors 100 percent of their dues, with a modest residue for the shareholders. In one of the affidavits ... [submitted on behalf of the applicant] it is stated: "If the assets had been disposed of at book value all liabilities, including those payable to Raytheon Company, would have been paid in full. ...

* * *

Nevertheless ... the possibility of paying creditors in full depended upon putting the orderly liquidation plan into operation in good time. Time was running out because money was running out. As the position worsened daily, the moment might at any time arrive when liabilities exceeded assets, or default resulted from lack of liquidity. ELSI's management had prepared the assessment of ... [a] "quick-sale value," ... which was markedly less than book value, being aware that the sale of the company's assets might fail to provide sums approximating to book value. There were plans also to approach the large bank creditors in the hope of securing their agreement to settlements of 50 percent.

Did ELSI, in this precarious position at the end of March 1968, still have the practical possibility to proceed with an orderly liquidation plan? The successful implementation of a plan of an orderly liquidation would have depended upon a number of factors not under the control of ELSI's management. Since the company's coffers were dangerously low, funds had to be forthcoming to maintain the cash flow necessary while the plan was being carried out. Evidence has been produced by the applicant that Raytheon was prepared to supply cash flow and other assistance necessary to effect the orderly liquidation, and the Chamber sees no reason to question that Raytheon had entered or was ready to enter into such a commitment. Other factors governing the matter, however, give rise to some doubt.

First, for the success of the plan it was necessary that the major creditors (i.e., the banks) would be willing to wait for payment of their claims until the sale of the assets released to settle them; and this applied not only to the capital sums outstanding, which may not at the time have yet been legally due for repayment, but also the agreed payments of interest or installments of capital. Though the Chamber has been given no specific information on this point, this is of the essence of such a liquidation plan: the creditors had to be asked to give the company time. If ELSI had been confident of continuing to meet all its obligations promptly and regularly while seeking a buyer for its assets, no negotiations with creditors, and no elaborate calculations of division of the proceeds, on different hypotheses, such as have been produced to the Chamber, would have been needed.

Secondly, the management were by no means certain that the sale of the assets would realize enough to pay all creditors in full; in fact, the existence of the calculation of a "quick-sale value" suggests perhaps more than uncertainty. . . .

Nor should it be overlooked that the dismissed employees of ELSI ranked as preferential creditors for such sums as might be due to them for severance pay or arrears. In this respect Italy has drawn attention to the Sicilian regional law of 13 May 1968, providing for the payment

> for the months of March, April, and May 1968, to the dismissed employees of Raytheon-Elsi of Palermo of a special monthly indemnity equal to the actual monthly pay received until the month of February 1968.

From this it could be inferred, said Italy, that ELSI did not pay its employees for the month of March 1968. Further it was conceded by the former Chairman of ELSI, when he appeared as a witness and was cross-examined, that the cash available at 31 March 1968 ("22 million in the kitty") would have been insufficient to meet the payroll of the full staff even for the first week of April ("at least 25 million"). . . .

Thirdly, the plan as formulated by ELSI's management involved a potential inequality among creditors: unless enough was realized to cover the liabilities fully, the major creditors were to be content with some 50 percent of their claims; but the smaller creditors were still to be paid in full. . . . According to the evidence, when in late March 1968 ELSI started using funds made available by Raytheon to pay off small creditors in full, "the banks intervened and said that they did not want this to happen as that was showing preference." Once the banks adopted this attitude, the whole orderly liquidation plan was jeopardized. . . .

Fourthly, the assets of the company had to be sold with the minimum delay and at the best price obtainable — desiderata which are often in practice irreconcilable. . . .

Fifthly, there was the attitude of the Sicilian administration. The company was well aware that the administration was strongly opposed to a closure of the plant, or more specifically, to a dismissal of the workers. . . . The company's management had been told before the staff dismissal letters were sent out that such dismissals would lead to a requisition of the plant.

All these factors point towards a conclusion that the feasibility at 31 March 1968 of a plan of orderly liquidation, an essential link in the chain of reasoning upon which the United States claim rests, has not been sufficiently established.

. . . It is important, in the consideration of so much detail, not to get the matter out of perspective. Given an undercapitalized, consistently loss-making company, crippled by the need to service large loans, which company its stockholders had themselves decided not to finance further but to close and sell off because, as they were anxious to make clear to everybody concerned, the money was running out fast, it cannot be a matter of surprise if, several days after the date at which the management itself had predicted that the money would run out, the company should be considered to have been actually or virtually in a state of insolvency for the purposes of Italian bankruptcy law.

If, therefore, the management of ELSI, at the material time, had no practical possibility of carrying out successfully a scheme of orderly liquidation under its own management, and may indeed already have forfeited any right to do so under Italian law, it cannot be said that it was the requisition that deprived it of this faculty of control and management. Furthermore, one feature of ELSI's position stands out: the uncertain and speculative character of the causal connection on which the applicant's case relies, between the requisition and the results attributed to it by the applicant. There were several causes acting together that led to the disaster to ELSI. No doubt the effects of the requisition might have been one of the factors involved. But the underlying cause was ELSI's headlong course towards insolvency; which state of affairs it seems to have attained even prior to the requisition. There was the warning loudly proclaimed about its precarious position; there was the socially damaging decision to terminate the business, close the plant, and dismiss the workforce; there was the position of the banks as major creditors. In short, the possibility of the solution of orderly liquidation, which Raytheon and Machlett claim to have been deprived of as a result of the requisition, is purely a matter of speculation. The Chamber is therefore unable to see here anything which can be said to amount to a violation by Italy of Article III, paragraph 2, of the FCN Treaty.

* * *

THE CHAMBER, . . .

By four votes to one, *finds* that the Italian Republic has not committed any . . . breaches . . . of the Treaty of Friendship, Commerce, and Navigation between the parties signed at Rome on 2 February 1948, or of the Agreement Supplementing that Treaty signed by the parties at Washington on 26 September 1951. ■

Protection of a Subsidiary's Tort Victims

If a subsidiary injures persons within the host state in tort or in delict, the host state may assume responsibility for acting on their behalf and pursing remedies both in the local courts and in foreign courts as well. The landmark decision upholding the right of a national government to take over the suit of victims injured by the subsidiary of a multinational enterprise is the *Bhopal* case. The Supreme Court of India's rationale for its decision is set out in the following excerpt (see Case 5–5).

Case 5–5   The Bhopal Case
Charan Lal Sahu v. Union of India

India, Supreme Court, 1989.
All India Reporter, Supreme Court, vol. 1990, p. 1480 (1989); *International Law Reports*, vol. 118, p. 451 (2000).

On December 2, 1984, enormous amounts of lethal gas leaked from the storage tanks of Union Carbide (I) Ltd. in Bhopal, India causing death and injury to a large number of people living nearby. Union Carbide (I) was incorporated in India as a subsidiary of the Union Carbide Corporation of New York.

After cases were brought on behalf of the victims in the United States by American lawyers, the Indian Parliament adopted the Bhopal Gas Disaster Leak (Processing of Claims) Act 1985 ("Bhopal Act"). This act authorized the Indian central government, the Union of India, to take over the claims of the victims of the gas leak, and it promptly brought suit for damages in the District Court of Bhopal. Soon thereafter, the plaintiffs in the cases that had been taken over filed petitions with the Supreme Court of India challenging the constitutionality of the Bhopal Act.

MAP 5-5   India (1984)

CHIEF JUSTICE SABYASACHI MUKHARJI:

* * *

Before we deal with the question of constitutionality, it has to be emphasized that the Act in question deals with the Bhopal gas leak disaster and it deals with the claims . . . arising out or connect with the disaster for compensation of damages for loss of life or any personal injury. . . . The Act in question does not purport to deal with . . . criminal liability. . . . The Act does not, either, expressly or impliedly deal with the extent of the damages or liability. . . . The expression:

"the Central Government shall, and shall have the exclusive right to represent, and act in place of (whether within or outside India) every person who has made, or is entitled to make, a claim for all purposes connected with such claim in the same manner and to the same effect as such person" . . .

means that the Central Government is substituted and vested with the exclusive right to act in place of the victims. This happens by operation of Section [of] the legislation in question. . . . However, in cases where . . . suits or proccedings have been instituted before the [enactment] of the Act in any court or before any authority outside India, . . . the Central Government . . . has the right to act in place of, or along with, such claimant, provided such court or authority so permits. . . . Therefore, the Central Government is authorized to act with the claimants in respect of proceedings instituted outside India subject to the orders of such courts or authorities. Is such a right valid and proper?

The Union Carbide Plant at Bhopal (Photo: © Alain Nogues/CORBIS SYGMA.)

There is the concept known both in this country and abroad, called *parens patriae*.[120] Dr. B. K. Mukherjuea,[121] referring to the concept of *parens patriae*, has noted that in English law, the Crown as *parens patriae* is the constitutional protector of all property subject to charitable trusts, such trusts being essentially matters of public concern. . . . In the *Words and Phrases* permanent edition[122] it is stated that *parens patriae* is the inherent power and authority of a legislature to provide protection to the person and property of persons *non sui juris*,[123] such as minor, insane, and incompetent persons. . . . *Parens patriae* jurisdiction, it has been explained, is a right of the sovereign and imposes a duty on the sovereign, in the public interest, to protect persons under a disability who have no rightful protector. . . . [Thus,] the Government is within its duty to protect and to control persons under a disability. . . .

Our Constitution makes it imperative for the state to secure to all its citizens the rights guaranteed by the Constitution and, where the citizens are not in a position

to assert and secure their rights, the state must come into the picture and protect and fight for the rights of the citizens. The preamble to the Constitution, read with the Directive Principles, Articles 38, 39, and 39A, enjoins the state to take up these responsibilities. It is necessary for the state to ensure the fundamental rights in conjunction with the Directive Principles of State Policy to effectively discharge its obligations and for this purpose, if necessary, to deprive some rights and privileges of the individual victims or their heirs to protect their rights better and secure these further.

Reference may be had to *Alfred L. Snapp & Sons, Inc. v. Puerto Rico*[124] in this connection. There it was held by the Supreme Court of the United States of America that the Commonwealth of Puerto had standing to sue as *parens patriae* to enjoin apple growers [from discriminating] against Puerto Rico migrant farmworkers. . . . Justice White [in a separate opinion] emphasized that the *parens patriae* action had its roots in the common-law concept of the "royal prerogative." The royal prerogative included the right or responsibility to take care of persons who were legally unable, on account of mental incapacity, whether it proceeds from nonage, idiocy, or lunacy, to take proper care of them and their property. This prerogative of *parens patriae* is inherent in the supreme power of every state, whether that power is lodged in a royal person or in the legislature, and is a most beneficent function. . . . Justice White [further] observed . . . that in order to maintain an action in *parens patriae* the state must articulate an interest apart from the interests of particular parties, i.e. the state must be more than a nominal party. The state must express a quasi-sovereign interest. . . .

Therefore, conceptually and from the jurisprudential point of view, especially [in light of] . . . the preamble to the Constitution of India and mandate of the Directive Principles, it is possible [for Parliament] to authorize the Central Government to take over the claims of the victims. . . .

Ms. Indira Jaising, . . . on behalf of some [of the] victims, . . . drew our attention to the fact that the Act was [adopted] to meet a specific situation that had arisen after the tragic disaster and the [appearance] of American lawyers seeking to represent the victims in American courts. The Government's view, according to her, as was manifest from the . . . debates of the Parliament, etc., was that the interests of the victims would be best served if the Central Government was given the right to represent the victims in the courts of the United States as they would otherwise be exploited by "ambulance chasers" working on contingency fees. The Government also proceeded initially

[120Latin: "parent of the country." The expression refers to the role of the state as sovereign and guardian of persons under disabilities.]
121"Hindu Law of Religious and Charitable Trusts," *Tagore Law Lectures,* p. 454 (5th ed.).
122Vol. 33 at p. 99.
[123Latin: "not his own master." Term describing someone who lacks the capacity to act for himself.]
124*United States Reports,* vol. 458, p. 592 (U.S. Supreme Ct. 1982).

on the hypothesis that the U.S. was the most convenient forum in which to sue the Union Carbide Company. The Government, however, feared that it might not have *locus standi*[125] to represent the victims in the courts of the United States of America unless a law was passed to enable it to sue on behalf of the victims. The dominant object of the Act, therefore, according to her, was to give the Government of India *locus standi* to sue on behalf of the victims in a foreign jurisdiction, a standing which it otherwise would not have had. According to her, the Act was never intended to give exclusive rights to the Central Government to sue on behalf of the victims in India or abroad. . . . We are unable to agree. As we have indicated before, conceptually and jurisprudentially . . . the Government [may] represent the victims in a domestic forum if the situation so warrants. . . .

* * *

It was contended that the procedure evolved under the Act for the victims is peculiar and has a good deal of disadvantages for the victims. Such special disadvantageous procedure and treatment is unequal treatment, it was suggested. It was therefore violative of Article 14 of the Constitution, that is the argument advanced.

The Act does provide for a special procedure in respect of the rights of the victims and to that extent the Central Government takes upon itself the rights of the victims. It is a special Act providing a special procedure for a kind of special class of victims. In view of the enormity of the disaster, the victims of the Bhopal gas leak disaster, as they were placed against a multinational and a big Indian corporation, and in view of the presence of foreign contingency lawyers to whom the victims were exposed, the claimants and victims can legitimately described as a class by themselves different and distinct, and sufficiently identifiable to be entitled to special treatment for the [most] effective, speedy, equitable, and . . . advantageous settlement of their claims. There indubitably is differentiation. The disaster being unique in its character and in the recorded history of industrial disasters, situated as the victims were against a mighty multinational with the presence of foreign contingency lawyers looming on the scene, in our opinion, there were sufficient grounds for such differentiation and different treatment. In treating the victims of the gas leak disaster differently and providing them with a procedure which was just, fair, [and] reasonable . . . was not unwarranted or unauthorized by the Constitution. . . .

* * *

In this connection, the concept of *parens patriae* in [procedural] jurisprudence may be examined. . . . It was asserted on behalf of the victims by learned counsel that the concept of *parens patriae* . . . can only be applied in cases of persons who under a disability and would not be applicable in respect of those who are able to assert their own rights. It is true that the victims or their representatives are . . . not legally incapable of suing or pursuing the remedies for their rights; yet they are at a tremendous disadvantage in the broader . . . sense of the term. The victims cannot be considered to be any match to the multinational companies or the government with whom—in the conditions that the victims or their representatives were after the disaster, physically, mentally, financially, economically and also because of the [location] of the litigation—would have to contend. In such a predicament, the victims can legitimately be considered to be disabled. They were in no position by themselves to look after their own interests effectively or purposefully. . . . In the situation in which the victims were, the state had to assume the role of a parent protecting the rights of the victims who must come within the protective umbrella of the state of the common sovereignty of the Indian people. As we have noted, the Act is an exercise of the sovereign power of the state. It is an appropriate . . . expression of sovereignty in the situation that had arisen. We must recognize and accept it as such.

* * *

[*The applicants' petition is dismissed.*]

JUSTICE SINGH:

* * *

The Bhopal gas tragedy has raised several important questions regarding the function of multinationals in third world countries. After the Second World War, colonial rule came to an end in several parts of the globe as a number of nations secured independence from foreign rule. The political domination was over, but the newly born nations were beset with various problems on account of lack of finance and development. A number of multinationals and transnational corporations offered their services to the underdeveloped and developing countries to provide finances and technical know-how by setting up their own industries in those countries on their own terms that brought problems with regard to control over the functioning of the transnational corporations. Multinational companies in many cases exploited the underdeveloped nations and in some case they influenced political and economic policies of host countries which subverted the sovereignty of those countries. There have been complaints against the multinationals for adopting unfair and corrupt means to advance their interests in the host countries.

[125Latin: "a place for standing." Term refers to the right of a person to appear in court, or before a legislative body, in a given case or dispute.]

Since this was a worldwide phenomenon, the United Nations took up that matter for consideration. The Economic and Social Council of the United Nations established a Commission on Transnational Corporations to conduct research on various political economic, and social aspect relating to transnational corporations. On a careful and detailed study the Commission submitted its Report in 1985 for evolving a Code of Conduct for Transnational Corporations. The Code was adopted in 1986 to which a large number of countries of the world are signatories. Although it has not been fully finalized as yet, the Code presents a comprehensive instrument formulating the principles of a Code of Conduct for transnational corporations carrying on their enterprises in underdeveloped and developing countries. . . . The Code also laid down guidelines for the determination of settlement of disputes arising out of accident and disaster and also for liability of transnational corporations and the jurisdiction of courts. The Code is binding on the countries which formally accept it. It was stated before us that India has accepted the Code. If that be so, it is necessary that the Government should take effective measures to translate the provisions of the Code into specific actions and policies backed by appropriate legislation and enforc-

ing machinery to prevent any accident or disaster and to secure the welfare of the victims of any industrial disaster.

In the context of our national dimensions of human rights—right to life, liberty, pollution-free air and water guaranteed by the Constitution under Articles 21, 48A, and 51(g)—it is the duty of the state to take effective steps to protect the guaranteed constitutional rights. The rights must be integrated and illumined by the evolving international dimensions and standards, having regard to our sovereignty, as highlighted by . . . the UN Code of Conduct of Transnational Corporations. . . . A transnational corporation should be made liable and subservient to the laws of out country and its liability should not be restricted to an affiliate company only, but the parent corporation should also be made liable for any damage caused. . . .

. . . The Government and the Parliament should therefore take immediate steps for enacting laws, having regard to these suggestions, consistent with the international norms and guidelines contained in the United Nations Code of Conduct for Transnational Corporations.

With these observations, I agree with the order proposed by my learned brother, Chief Justice Sabyasachu Mukharji. ■

Penalties for Noncompliance

Investment laws usually establish a variety of penalties for foreign investors who violate the law or fail to comply with an investment agreement. Violators may be subject to penalties ranging from fines to the suspension of their right to engage in business or to the revocation of the facilities they were granted.[126]

C. SECURITIES REGULATIONS

security: a share, participation, or other interest in an enterprise or other property, or a debt obligation.

stock: Share in the ownership of a company that entitles its owner to rights in the company, including a proportionate part of the dividends and, upon liquidation, of the capital assets.

bond: Contractual obligation of a company (or government) to repay the holder the amount of his original investment plus interest at a specified future date.

National governments regulate securities transactions. This includes defining the form that securities take, overseeing the markets in which securities are traded, establishing disclosure requirements to protect buyers and sellers, adopting clearance and settlement procedures, limiting insider trading, and regulating takeovers.

Securities

Businesses raise much of their operating capital by issuing securities. A **security** is (a) a share, participation, or other interest in an enterprise or other property or (b) a debt obligation.[127] **Stock** (or an equity security) represents an ownership interest in a business and a **bond** (or debt security) represents an obligation to pay money.

---

[126]Center on Transnational Corporations, *National Legislation and Regulations Relating to Transnational Corporations,* p. 13 (UN Doc. ST/CTC/26, UN Sales No. E.83.II.A.7, 1983).

[127]United States Uniform Commercial Code, § 8.102(1). An investment contract is "a contract, transaction, or scheme whereby a person invests his money in a common enterprise and is led to expect profits solely from the efforts of the promoter or a third party. . . ." Securities and Exchange Commission v. W. J. Howey Co., *United States Reports,* vol. 328, p. 293 (U.S. Supreme Ct., 1946).

certificated security: A security that is in the form of a negotiable instrument of the type commonly dealt in on securities exchanges.

registered security: A certificated security made out to a named owner and registered on the books of the issuer.

bearer security: A certificated security made out to "bearer." It is not registered on the books of the issuer.

bona fide purchaser: Someone who buys a security or other negotiable instrument in good faith, pays value, and is unaware that the transferor is not the rightful owner.

uncertificated security: A security whose ownership is recorded only on the books of the issuer.

par value: The minimum price, stated on the face of a stock certificate, for which the certificate may be sold by the issuer.

A security can take several forms. If it is in the form of an instrument of the "type commonly dealt in on securities exchanges"[128] it is called a **certificated security**. Such a security is a negotiable instrument that can be transferred by negotiation.[129] If it is made out to a named owner it is called a **registered security** because the issuer must maintain a register with the names of owners of such certificates. If it is made out to "bearer" (that is, to whomever is properly in possession of the certificate) it is a **bearer security** and no register of owners is maintained.

Most countries authorize the use of both registered and bearer securities. Some, however, insist that stock certificates be registered securities. India, for example, requires that stock certificates be registered within three months after they are paid for.[130] Bearer securities commonly have coupons attached to them that can be detached so that the bearer can send them to the issuer to collect dividends or interest as they come due. In a few countries, such as Mexico, registered stock certificates must also have coupons.[131]

Registered securities are transferred by (1) endorsement directly on the certificate and (2) delivery of the certificate. The new owner then sends the endorsed certificate to the issuer for registration and to obtain a new certificate made out to himself. Bearer securities are transferred simply by delivery of the certificate. In most countries, a bona fide purchaser of a bearer security acquires ownership even if the transferor was not the owner.[132] A **bona fide purchaser** is someone who buys in good faith, pays value, and is unaware that the transferor is not the rightful owner.

Securities do not have to be put into tangible form. An **uncertificated security** is one whose ownership is recorded only on the books of the issuer. Most developed countries authorize companies to use uncertificated certificates.[133] Moreover, some countries forbid companies whose shares are not traded publicly (such as a civil law limited liability company) to issue certificated securities.[134]

Whether certificated or uncertificated, stock certificates in most countries must state a minimum **par value** on their face.[135] If the certificate is in bearer form, the issuer may not sell it for less than its par value. Registered stock may be sold for less than par value; however, the stockholder will be liable to the corporation for the difference.[136] Only in Brazil, Japan, and the United States, can stock be issued without a par value.[137]

Trading in Securities

Most nations limit the persons who may trade in securities. Typically, these are brokers and dealers who have registered with a commission that oversees traders and exchanges.[138] Additionally, banks, lawyers, accountants, and other experts are commonly allowed to provide advice about securities transactions, but only if this is incidental to their principal business.[139]

Securities Exchanges

securities exchange: Marketplace where member brokers and dealers buy and sell securities on behalf of investors.

Securities brokers and dealers have grouped together in many countries to form **securities exchanges** that is, marketplaces where member brokers and dealers buy and sell securities on behalf of investors. These marketplaces exist because they make it easier for securities'

---

[128]United States Uniform Commercial Code, § 8.102(1).

[129]*See* the discussion on the negotiation and transfer of bills and notes in Chapter 12.

[130]"India Law Digest," *Martindale-Hubbell International Law Digest,* p. IND-5 (2001).

[131]"Mexico Law Digest," *id.*, p. MEX-2.

[132]*See* "Netherlands Law Digest," *id.*, p. NTH-2.

[133]*See* United States Uniform Commercial Code § 8.102(1); Japanese Commercial Code § 226(2).

[134]*Id.*

[135]In Switzerland, for example, the minimum allowable par value is 10 Swiss francs. "Switzerland Law Digest," *Id.*, p. SWZ-2. In Germany, the minimum par value must be no less than 5 marks. "Germany Law Digest," *id.*, p. GER-2. In France the par value of shares must be stated in a corporation's bylaws. France, Law No. 88–15 of January 5, 1998, cited in "French Law Digest," *id.*, p. FRA-3.

[136]"Switzerland Law Digest," *Id.*, p. SWZ-2; "Germany Law Digest," *id.*, p. GER-2.

[137]No par shares were recently introduced in Brazil. Pinheiro Neto & Cia., Doing Business in Brazil, app. A (1980–1981); Japanese Commercial Code §§ 199, 213, cited in "Japan Law Digest," Martindale-Hubbell International Law Directory, p. JPN-2; U.S. Revised Model Business Corporation Act § 6.21 (which states that the board of directors is to determine the amount to be received for shares and does not require them to specify a par value).

[138]*See,* for example, Canadian Securities Act, § 25, *Revised Statutes of Canada,* chap. C-44.

[139]*Id.*, § 34. In Germany, trading in securities is done by banks that buy and sell securities on exchanges for their customers through registered brokers. "Germany Law Digest," *Martindale-Hubbell International Law Digest,* GER-8 (2001).

issuers to find investors and for investors to exchange their securities.[140] The six largest (in annual trading volume), respectively, are the New York Stock Exchange, the NASDAQ Stock Market, the Tokyo Stock Exchange, the London Stock Exchange, the Frankfurt Stock Exchange, and the Paris Stock Exchange. Together, they account for close to 90 percent of all securities transactions in the world. Exhibit 5-1 lists the world's securities exchanges.

Issuance of Securities

prospectus: Printed statement given to prospective securities investors setting out a full, true, and plain disclosure of all material facts relating to the securities and the issuer.

In order for a corporation or other person to offer securities to the general public it must prepare and register a prospectus to accompany the offer. A **prospectus** is a printed statement setting out a "full, true, and plain disclosure of all material facts" relating to the securities and the issuer.[141] The required contents of prospectuses are generally quite similar from country to country.[142] Germany, for example, requires prospectuses to set out:

1. A history of the issuer and a description of its purpose and goals
2. A description of the issuer's business and its present and anticipated course
3. A current financial statement with an explanation of all significant transactions
4. Profits earned and dividends paid for the previous three years[143]

Prospectuses must be signed by the officers and directors of the issuer,[144] and by any promoters[145] and underwriters[146] who may be involved. By signing, they certify that a prospectus constitutes, to the best of their knowledge, a full, true, and plain disclosure of all material facts relating to the securities being offered.[147]

Finally, to be effective, a prospectus must be registered. In some countries a prospectus is submitted to the listing committee of the securities exchange on which it will be offered;[148] in others it is filed with a national supervisory agency, such as the Securities and Exchange Commission in the United States. The "waiting period" during which the listing committee or supervisory agency reviews the filing varies in length from 10[149] to 20[150] days. During the waiting period an issuer may *offer* its securities orally, by distributing a preliminary prospectus (called a "red herring prospectus" in the United States because it must bear a legend in red ink that it is not final), and by means of a limited advertisement (colloquially known as a "tombstone advertisement") that identifies the security, its price, and who will execute orders. Only after the listing committee or supervisory agency approves the prospectus may sales of the securities take place.

Exemptions from Registration

Certain kinds of securities and certain transactions are exempt from registration. Exempt securities typically include those issued by governmental bodies, by banks, and by not-for-profit

---

[140]Businesses, of course, do not have to sell their securities on an exchange. They can sell them privately or arrange for an equity stock trade. Private sales (in most countries) are subject to few governmental regulations, so that method is often preferred. It is often difficult, however, to raise large sums of money privately. For example, equity stock trades are a convenient device for setting up a joint venture with a host country firm but of little value in acquiring cash for the actual operation of a business.

[141]Canadian Securities Act, § 56, *Revised Statutes of Canada,* chap. C-44.

[142]The contents of prospectuses may vary depending on the kind of issuer involved. Senior issuers (those who have issued securities in the past and who have a substantial market valuation) in some countries are allowed to use "short form" prospectuses. E.g., *id.,* § 74. Also, senior issuers may be excused from issuing a new prospectus for every issuance of shares. In such instances, they may sell securities "off the shelf" on a delayed or continuous basis so long as an original prospectus is kept current and accurate. The registration of such a prospectus is known as "shelf registration." E.g., United States Securities and Exchange Commission Rule 415.

[143]Germany, Securities Prospectus Act of December 13, 1990, *Bundesgesetzblatt,* vol. I, p. 2749 (1990), cited in "Germany Law Digest," *Martindale-Hubbell International Law Directory,* p. GER-8. The required contents of a U.S. prospectus are described in the U.S. Securities Act of 1933, app. A.

[144]The particular officers and the minimum number of directors varies from country to country.

[145]A promoter is any person who associates himself with a firm for the purpose of organizing a company, securing a charter, issuing a prospectus, raising subscriptions, and so forth.

[146]An underwriter is any person, bank, or syndicate that guarantees to furnish an agreed amount of money by an agreed date to an issuer of securities in exchange for the securities.

[147]E.g., Canadian Securities Act, § 59, *Revised Statutes of Canada,* chap. C-44.

[148]*See* "Germany Law Digest," *Martindale-Hubbell International Law Digest,* GER-8 (2001).

[149]E.g., Canadian Securities Act, § 65, *Revised Statutes of Canada,* chap. C-44.

[150]E.g., United States Securities Act of 1933, § 8.

Alberta (Canada) Stock Exchange
American (United States) Stock Exchange
Amman (Jordan) Financial Market
Amsterdam (Netherlands) Stock Exchange
Arizona (United States) Stock Exchange
Athens (Greece) Stock Exchange
Australian Stock Exchange
Australian Stock Exchanges, Australia
Bahrain Stock Exchange
Bangalore (India) Stock Exchange
Barcelona (Spain) Stock Exchange
Bavarian (Germany) Stock Exchange
Beirut (Lebanon) Stock Exchange
Berlin (Germany) Stock Exchange
Bermuda Stock Exchange
Bilbao (Spain) Stock Exchange
Bogotá (Colombia) Stock
Bolivian Stock Exchange
Bombay (India) Stock Exchange
Boston (Massachusetts, United States) Stock Exchange
Bratislava (Slovakia) Stock Exchange
Bremen (Germany) Stock Exchange
Bucharest (Romania) Stock Exchange
Budapest (Hungary) Stock Exchange
Buenos Aires (Argentina) Stock Exchange
Bulgarian Stock Exchange
Caracas (Venezuela) Stock Exchange
Casablanca (Morocco) Stock Exchange
Cayman Islands Stock Exchange
Channel Islands Stock Exchange
Chicago (United States) Board Options Exchange
Chicago (United States) Stock Exchange
Chilean Commercial Stock Exchange
Chilean Electronic Stock Exchange
Chittagong (Bangladesh) Stock Exchange
Colombo (Sri Lanka) Stock Exchange
Copenhagen (Denmark) Stock Exchange
Costa Rica Electronic Stock Exchange
Costa Rica National Stock Exchange
Cyprus Stock Exchange
Delhi (India) Stock Exchange Association
Dhaka (Bangladesh) Stock Exchange
Düsseldorf (Germany) Stock Exchange
European Association of Securities Dealers Automated Quotation
  (EASDAQ—Belgium) Stock Exchange
Frankfurt (Germany) Stock Exchange
Geneva (Switzerland) Stock Exchange
Ghana Stock Exchange
Guayaquil (Ecuador) Stock Exchange
Hamburg (Germany) Stock Exchange
Hanover (Germany) Stock Exchange
Helsinki (Finland) Stock Exchange
Hong Kong Stock Exchange
Iceland Stock Exchange
Istanbul (Turkey) Stock Exchange
Italian Stock Exchange
Jakarta (Indonesia) Stock Exchange
Jamaica Stock Exchange
Johannesburg (South Africa) Stock Exchange
Karachi (Pakistan) Stock Exchange
Kazakhstan Stock Exchange
Korea Stock Exchange
Kuala Lumpur (Malaysia) Stock Exchange
Kuwait Stock Exchange
Lahore (Pakistan) Stock Exchange,
Le Nouveau Marché (France) Stock Exchange
Lima (Peru) Stock Exchange

Lisbon (Portugal) Stock Exchange
Ljubljana (Slovenia) Stock Exchange
London (United Kingdom) Stock Exchange
Lusaka (Zambia) Stock Exchange
Luxembourg Stock Exchange
Macedonian Stock Exchange
Madrid (Spain) Stock Exchange
Mexican Stock Exchange
Moldova Stock Exchange
Mongolian Stock Exchange
Montreal (Canada) Stock Exchange
Munich (Germany) Stock Exchange
Nagoya (Japan) Stock Exchange
Nairobi (Kenya) Stock Exchange
Namibian Stock Exchange
National Association of Securities Dealers Automated
  Quotation (NASDAQ—United States) Stock Market
National Stock Exchange of India
National Stock Exchange of Lithuania
New York (United States) Stock Exchange
New Zealand Stock Exchange
Nicaragua Stock Exchange
NouveauMarche, France
Occidente Stock Exchange (Colombia)
Osaka (Japan) Securities Exchange
Oslo (Norway) Stock Exchange
Pacific (San Francisco, California, United States) Exchange
Palestine Securities Exchange
Panama Stock Exchange
Paris (France) Stock Exchange
Philadelphia (United States) Stock Exchange
Philippines Stock Exchange
Port Moresby (Papua New Guinea) Stock Exchange
Prague (Czech Republic) Stock Exchange
Quito (Ecuador) Stock Exchange
Rhine-Westphalian (Germany) Stock Exchange
Riga (Latvia) Stock Exchange
Rio de Janeiro (Brazil) Stock Exchange
Russian Exchange
San Diego (United States) Stock Exchange
Santiago (Chile) Stock Exchange
São Paulo (Brazil) Stock Exchange
Shenzhen (China) Stock Exchange
Stock Exchange of Mauritius
Stock Exchange of Singapore
Stock Exchange of Thailand
Stockholm (Sweden) Stock Exchange
Stuttgart (Germany) Stock Exchange
Surabaya (Indonesia) Stock Exchange
Swaziland Stock Exchange
Swiss Stock Exchange
Taiwan Stock Exchange
Tallinn (Estonia) Stock Exchange
Tehran (Iran) Stock Exchange
Tel Aviv (Israel) Stock Exchange
Tokyo (Japan) Stock Exchange
Toronto (Canada) Stock Exchange
Tradepoint (United Kingdom) Stock Exchange
Trinidad and Tobago Stock Exchange
Vancouver (Canada) Stock Exchange
Venezuela Electronic Stock Exchange
Vienna (Austria) Stock Exchange
Virt-X Stock Exchange (Switzerland)
Warsaw (Poland) Stock Exchange
Winnipeg (Canada) Stock Exchange
Zagreb (Croatia) Stock Exchange

EXHIBIT 5-1   Securities Exchanges of the World

Sources: Nasdaq at www.nasdaq.com/help/helpfaq.stm and World Federation of Exchange at www.world-exchanges.org.

corporations.[151] Exempt transactions commonly include nonpublic offerings and limited offerings. In Poland, for example, offerings circulated to fewer than 300 persons are not public offerings and are exempt from registration.[152] Limited offerings are those for small monetary amounts. Thus, in the United States, offerings of less than $1 million in a 12-month period are exempt from registration.[153]

Foreign Registration

Securities may be offered on a foreign exchange so long as they are registered locally. To simplify this process, many countries allow an issuer to use the same prospectus they registered in their home country. For example, the United States allows a foreign issuer to register a copy of its home-country prospectus plus a report (Form 20-F) that essentially explains the differences between its home-country prospectus and an American prospectus.[154]

Clearance and Settlement Procedures

clearance and settlement: Procedure by which a buyer turns over the purchase price and the seller turns over the securities in a securities transaction.

Clearance and settlement is the procedure by which a buyer turns over the purchase price and the seller turns over the securities in a securities transaction. This procedure differs from country to country. A securities "transaction" is actually a contract to be performed in the future—at the time the buyer delivers the purchase price and the seller delivers the debt or equity certificate. In the United States, the National Securities Clearing Corporation (NSCC), a nationwide clearinghouse, handles the clearance and settlement of all securities traded on American exchanges. Since the 1970s, settlement has occurred in the United States by entries made on the books of the Depository Trust Company (DTC).[155] The DTC holds global certificates for publicly traded firms, and settlement is done simply by debiting the account of a seller and crediting the account of a buyer on the DTC's books.[156] Similar procedures are followed in other developed countries.[157] In most developing countries, however, the buyer's and seller's brokers must get together and make an actual trade. Although sales are settled within five business days in developed countries, the settlement process can take several weeks in developing countries.[158]

---

[151]E.g., United States Securities Act of 1993, § 3.

[152]Poland, Law of March 22, 1991, on Public Trading in Securities and on Trust Funds, cited in "Poland Law Digest," *Martindale-Hubbell International Law Directory*, p. POL-10.

[153]United States Securities and Exchange Commission Rule 504. Other limited offerings are allowed if some or all of the purchasers are "accredited investors," such as banks, registered brokers and dealers, and persons with a net worth of more than $1 million and an annual income in excess of $200. If no more than 35 purchasers are unaccredited, the offering may be up to $5 million in a 12-month period. *Id.,* Rule 505. If all the purchasers are accredited investors, there is no monetary limit. Securities Act of 1933, § 4(6).

[154]Robert G. Pozen, "Disclosure and Trading in the International Security Market," *International Lawyer,* vol. 15, p. 84 (1981).

[155]The Depository Trust Company's home page on the Internet is at www.dtc.org/.

[156]Uniform Commercial Code § 8–320(1) provides: "In addition to other methods, a transfer, pledge, or release of a security or any interest therein may be effected by the making of appropriate entries on the books of a clearing corporation reducing the account of the transferor, pledgor, or pledgee and increasing the account of the transferee, pledgee, or pledgor by the amount of the obligation or the number of shares or rights transferred, pledged, or released, if the security is shown on the account of a transferor, pledgor, or pledgee on the books of the clearing corporation; is subject to the control of the clearing corporation; and (a) if certificated [i.e., it is in the form of a negotiable instrument], (i) is in the custody of the clearing corporation, another clearing corporation, a custodian bank, or a nominee of any of them; and (ii) is in bearer form or endorsed in blank by an appropriate person or registered in the name of the clearing corporation, a custodian bank, or a nominee of any of them; or (b) if uncertificated, is registered in the name of the clearing corporation, another clearing corporation, a custodian bank, or a nominee of any of them."

[157]Companies performing the same function as the Depository Trust Company include:
- CIK, Caisse Interprofessionnelle de Dépots de Virements de Titres S.A., Brussels, Belgium
- DBC, Deutsche Börse Clearing, Frankfurt, Germany
- JSCC, Japan Securities Clearing Corporation, Tokyo, Japan
- Monte Titoli S.p.A., Milan, Italy
- NECIGEF, Nederlands Centraal Instituut voor Giraal Effectenverkeer B.V., Amsterdam, Netherlands
- OEKB, Oesterreichische Kontrollbank AG, Vienna, Austria
- SEGA, Schweizerische Effekten-Giro AG, Zurich, Switzerland
- SICOVAM, Société Interprofessionnelle pour la Compensation des Valeurs Mobilières, Paris, France

[158]*See* Brandon Becker and Thomas C. Etter Jr., "International Clearance and Settlement," *Brooklyn Journal of International Law,* vol. 14, p. 283 (1988), and Robert P. Austin, "Regulatory Principles and the Internationalization of Securities Markets," *Law and Contemporary Problems,* vol. 50, p. 221 at pp. 234–237 (1987).

International Clearance and Settlement

Two international clearinghouses handle the clearance and settlement of securities sold internationally: Euroclear and Cedel Bank. Euroclear, which has its operating offices in Brussels, deals in more than 100,000 securities from 80 different countries. Daily transactions exceed U.S. $125 million. Most transactions are domestic securities traded in some 30 different markets.[159] Cedel Bank, headquartered in Luxembourg, also deals in more than 100,000 securities. Its daily transactions are worth U.S. $60 billion.[160]

In addition to Euroclear and Cedel Bank, the Emerging Market Clearing Corporation (EMCC) guarantees the clearance of debt securities from developing countries.[161] Either Euroclear or Cedel Bank actually carries out the clearance and settlement process on the instructions of EMCC.

Depository Receipts

depository receipt: A negotiable instrument issued by a bank that represents a foreign company's public traded securities and that in turn is traded on a local securities exchange.

To facilitate foreign trading in shares, brokerage firms use depository receipts. A **depository receipt** is a negotiable instrument issued by a bank that represents a foreign company's public traded securities and that in turn is traded on a local securities exchange. A depository receipt is created by a broker purchasing a company's shares in its home country, depositing them in a custodian bank in that country in the name of a depository bank in another country, and then instructing the depository bank to issue the receipt.[162] When the depository bank is a U.S. bank, the instruments are known as American Depository Receipts. European Depository Receipts are issued by European banks, Global Depository Receipts by other banks. Currently, there are over 1,600 companies whose securities stand behind depository receipts.[163]

Depository receipts are convenient because the shares of the company do not have to leave the home state—it is the receipt that is sent abroad. Additionally, the physical delivery requirements of many countries can be avoided by trading the receipt on an American securities exchange. Also, the stock transfer taxes imposed by some home states can be avoided in part because the stock itself remains registered in the name of the depository bank.

Depository receipts are not identical, of course, with the securities themselves. The law of the state where an issuer is incorporated sometimes specifically defines the rights of depository receipt holders. In the Netherlands, for example, only shareholders may vote in corporate elections; depository receipt holders may not.[164] In addition, the deposit agreement between the broker, custodian bank, and depository bank may also define the rights of the holders of such receipts, as Case 5–6 points out.

---

[159]See the Euoclear Web site at www.euroclear.com/.

[160]Cedel Bank, Product Brochure: Clearing and Settlement Procedures, posted at www.cedelgroup.com/ publi/ brochure/clear.htm.

[161]The EMCC's home page is at www.e-m-c-c.com/.

[162]In the past, depository receipts were sometimes created without the participation of the issuer. Known as unsponsored depository receipts, they are now seldom used. Virtually all depository receipts are created on behalf of the issuer and they are known as sponsored depository receipts. Bank of New York, "An Overview of Depository Receipts," at www.bankofny.com/adr/aovrview.htm.

[163]See id.

[164]"Netherlands Law Digest," *Martindale-Hubbell International Law Digest,* p. NTH-3 (2001).

Case 5–6   Batchelder v. Kawamoto   ⌖

United States, Ninth Circuit Court of Appeals.
Federal Reporter, Third Series, vol. 147, p. 915 (1998).

CIRCUIT JUDGE DIARMUID F. O'SCANNLAIN:

We must decide whether the holder of an American Depository Receipt has standing to bring a shareholder derivative action against a Japanese corporation.

I

This is a derivative action brought by Harry C. Batchelder, Jr. on behalf of Honda Motor Company, Ltd. ("Honda Japan") and American Honda Motor Company, Inc. ("American Honda") for wrongs allegedly committed by directors, officers, and employees of Honda Japan and American Honda (the "Director Defendants"), and by certain third parties, including Lyon & Lyon and Roland

Smoot (collectively, "Lyon & Lyon"). Honda Japan was incorporated under the laws of Japan. It is the sole shareholder of American Honda, a California corporation.

Harry C. Batchelder, Jr., alleges that at all times relevant to this case he owned 1,246 American Depository Receipts ("ADRs"), each of which reflects ownership of ten shares of stock in Honda Japan. The ADRs are issued by the depository, Morgan Guaranty Trust Company of New York. Batchelder purchased his ADRs under the terms and conditions of a deposit agreement ("Deposit Agreement") with Honda Japan and Morgan Guaranty. Batchelder alleges that the directors of both Honda Japan and American Honda breached their fiduciary duties by failing adequately to protect the companies from harm caused by the actions of certain American Honda employees who were involved in a bribery and kickback scheme. Batchelder also purports to bring suit against the law firm of Lyon & Lyon, American Honda's former general counsel, and two of its partners, Roland Smoot and James Short, who, Batchelder claims, assisted in "covering up" the fraudulent scheme. Batchelder has asserted "shareholder" derivative claims for breach of duty, waste of corporate assets, abuse of control, constructive fraud, mismanagement, and dissemination of false and misleading proxy statements in violation of *United States Code*, title 15, § 78n(a).

MAP 5-6   *California and Japan (1998)*

Following the Director Defendants' motion to dismiss, the district court entered a scheduling order staying all discovery in the case pending its resolution. Thereafter, American Honda and Lyon & Lyon also filed motions to dismiss on numerous grounds. Following a hearing, the district court dismissed Batchelder's complaint with prejudice. The district court ruled that Batchelder's complaint failed as a matter of law because, *inter alia*: (1) based on the Deposit Agreement, Batchelder's standing to bring a derivative action must be determined under Japanese law; [and] (2) under Japanese law, Batchelder is not a shareholder and therefore lacks standing to bring a derivative action on behalf of Honda Japan. . . .

Batchelder timely appealed.

II

Batchelder maintains that the district court erred in holding that he lacks standing to bring a shareholder derivative action on behalf of Honda Japan and American Honda. According to Batchelder, the district court erroneously held that his "standing and his right to bring a derivative action . . . must be determined under Japanese law," and wrongly concluded that, as an owner of Honda Japan ADRs, he "is not a shareholder and lacks standing to bring a derivative action on behalf of Honda . . . under governing Japanese law." Batchelder contends that whereas Japanese law provides the substantive law to adjudicate his claims against the Director Defendants, it does not control his standing to bring California and federal claims on behalf of Honda Japan and American Honda. According to Batchelder, the district court must perform "the requisite conflicts of law analysis" to determine what law governs his right to bring a derivative suit. Batchelder contends that either the *Federal Rules of Civil Procedure*, Rule 23.1 ("Derivative Actions by Shareholders") or the California *Corporation Code* § 800 ("Shareholder Derivative Actions") provides the standing requirements for his claim, not Japanese law.

A

Batchelder's right to bring derivative claims on behalf of Honda Japan and American Honda is indeed governed by Japanese law. Batchelder purchased his ADRs pursuant to the Deposit Agreement, which expressly provides that the law of Japan governs shareholder rights. Section 7.07 of the Deposit Agreement, entitled "Governing Law," states:

> This Deposit Agreement and the [American Depository] Receipts and all rights hereunder and thereunder and provisions hereof and thereof shall be governed by and construed in accordance with the laws of the state of New York, United States of America. It is understood that notwithstanding any present or future provision of the laws of the state of New York, *the rights of holders of Stock and other Deposited Securities, and the duties and obligations of the Company in respect of such holders, as such, shall be governed by the laws of Japan.* (Emphasis added).

The first sentence of § 7.07 provides that contract rights contained in the Deposit Agreement itself or in the ADR certificates, as well as the construction of the Deposit Agreement, are to be governed by the laws of New York. The second sentence of § 7.07, however, explicitly provides that Japanese law governs shareholder rights and the rights of holders of other Deposited Securities, including ADRs. Thus, if an ADR holder seeks to assert a right belonging to shareholders or a right not specifically granted to ADR holders in the Deposit Agreement, the laws of Japan apply. Section 7.07 is simply a choice-of-law clause.

1. We analyze the validity of choice-of-law clauses under *The Bremen v. Zapata Off-Shore Co.*,[165] in which the Supreme Court stated that courts should enforce choice-of-law and choice-of-forum clauses in cases of "freely negotiated private international agreements." There is every reason to believe that the Depository Agreement was such an agreement. . . .

Batchelder has never contended that the Deposit Agreement itself grants ADR holders the right to bring shareholder derivative claims. He argues instead that he is entitled to bring derivative claims because he "is a Honda shareholder" through his ownership of ADRs. Because Batchelder is attempting to assert a right not expressly granted to him by the Deposit Agreement—the right to bring a derivative suit—the plain language of the second sentence of § 7.07 directs this court to apply Japanese law to determine the existence and scope of Batchelder's right. No conflicts-of-law analysis is required.

* * *

III

Batchelder next argues that, even under Japanese law, he *is* a Honda Japan shareholder who is entitled to bring suit on behalf of the parent company *and* assert a double derivative claim on behalf of its subsidiary, American Honda. According to Batchelder, the district court "ignored the fact that ADRs are the equivalent of shares of a foreign corporation and ADR holders are equivalent to a shareholder [sic] of that corporation, whether under Japanese law or U.S. law." Batchelder further maintains that the district court erred in finding that he failed properly to assert "double derivative" claims on behalf of Honda Japan and American Honda. He contends that the district court also "ignored the fact that California substantive law applies to derivative claims asserted by Batchelder on behalf of American Honda" as well as "numerous precedents recognizing the validity of 'double derivative' claims under these circumstances."

Article 267 of the Japanese *Commercial Code*, which establishes the derivative remedy, states:

1. Any shareholder who has held a share continuously for the last six months may demand, in writing, that the stock company institute an action to enforce the liability of directors.

2. If the stock company has failed to institute such action within thirty days from the date on which the demand referred to in the preceding paragraph was made, the shareholder referred to in the preceding paragraph may institute such action on behalf of the company.

Notwithstanding his concessions that he holds ADRs, not shares, in Honda Japan, and that Article 267 confers derivative standing only on "any shareholder," Batchelder claims, that as an ADR holder, he is "equivalent to a shareholder" and should have been permitted to proceed with his derivative suit. The weight of authority, however, is against him.

Honda's Japanese law experts testified that only shareholders appearing on Honda Japan's shareholders' register may institute a derivative action under Article 267(1). "ADR holders are not shareholders of record" under Japanese law and therefore "are not allowed to make the demand and then institute a derivative action." According to one of Honda's experts, Professor Kitazawa, "the law on this point is undisputed; I know of no case or scholarly opinion that argues otherwise." Another of Honda's experts stated unequivocally that "Under Japanese law, a holder of [ADRs] would not be considered under Japanese law to be a registered shareholder and, therefore, would have no right or power to make the requisite pre-suit demand or to initiate the instant derivative litigation."

Batchelder has submitted no authority to compel a different conclusion.

* * *

In light of the foregoing, the district court correctly found that Batchelder lacked standing as an ADR holder under Japanese law to bring his shareholder derivative action on behalf of Honda Japan.

* * *

For the foregoing reasons, we conclude that the district court did not err in holding that Batchelder, as an ADR holder, lacks standing to bring a shareholder derivative suit on behalf of Honda Japan. . . . The district court's dismissal of Batchelder's action is therefore AFFIRMED. ∎

---

[165]*United States Reports*, vol. 407, p. 1 (Supreme Ct., 1972).

---

insider trading: The use of material nonpublic information about a company or the securities market to buy or sell securities for personal gain.

Insider Trading Regulations

Insider trading occurs when someone takes advantage of material nonpublic information about a corporation or the securities market to buy or sell securities for his personal benefit. Some countries (notably the United States, Canada, the United Kingdom, and

Germany)[166] regard insider trading as unjust and dishonest. For example, during the U.S. Congressional hearings leading up to the adoption of the 1934 Securities Exchange Act that criminalized insider trading, a Senate committee observed:

> Among the most vicious practices unearthed at the hearings before the subcommittee was the flagrant betrayal of their fiduciary duties by directors and officers of corporations who used their positions of trust and the confidential information which came to them in such positions, to aid them in their market activities.[167]

This is not the uniform view, however. Many other countries look upon insider trading as a normal business practice.[168]

The United States' prohibitions against insider trading are found in Section 10(b) of the Securities Exchange Act of 1934 and in the Securities and Exchange Commission's Rule 10b-5, which implements Section 10(b) of the 1934 act. These forbid an **insider** (e.g., a corporate officer, director, or majority shareholder) who has access to material nonpublic information from buying or selling shares for his own account when he knows that the information is unavailable to the person or persons with whom he is dealing. In addition, a **tipper** who has inside information that he discloses to a **tippee** and a tippee who acts on that information knowing it is not available to the public are both liable for the profits made by the tippee.[169]

Courts interpreting these provisions have held that information is **material** when it is such that a reasonable investor would act upon it, and information becomes "public" once it becomes available to the general public (although an insider must refrain from trading for a "reasonable waiting period" to allow news to be translated into investment action).

Case 5–7 is a recent U.S. Supreme Court decision expanding the scope of Section 10(b) and Rule 10b-5.

insider: A person, such as a corporate officer, director, or majority shareholder, who has access to material nonpublic information about a company or the securities market.

tipper: A person who has access to material nonpublic information about a company or the securities market who discloses it to a tippee.

tippee: A person who acts for his own personal account on information received from a tipper knowing that the information is not available to the public.

material: According to United States law, when something is of significance to a reasonable person (i.e., an investor).

---

[166]The German Securities Trading Act defining and criminalizing insider trading came into effect on August 1, 1994. *Bundesgesetzblatt,* vol. I, p. 1749. India adopted similar legislation that came into effect in February 1992. *See* "India Law Digest," *Martindale-Hubbell International Law Digest,* p. IND-7 (2001).

[167]Report of the Committee on Banking and Currency, "Stock Exchange Practices," Senate Report No. 1455, 73rd Congress, Second Session, p. 55 (1934).

[168]Countries with small exchanges generally pay little attention to insider trading because few companies are publicly owned and those that are publicly traded are generally owned by only a limited number of individuals. For an excellent, although somewhat dated, comparative study of insider trading, *see* Barry A. Rider and H. Leigh French, *The Regulation of Insider Trading* (1979).

[169]Usually insider traders are persons with an employment or other relationship of trust with the corporation, but they do not have to be. Thus, in United States v. Carpenter, *United States Reports,* vol. 484, p. 19 (1987), the U.S. Supreme Court held that a columnist for the *Wall Street Journal* who tipped information about what would be in his investment advice column to tippees before the column appeared in print was liable, as an insider and a tipper, for the profits made by the tippees.

Case 5–7   United States v. O'Hagan

United States Supreme Court.
United States Reports, vol. 521, p. 642 (1997).
Justice Ginsburg DELIVERED THE OPINION OF THE COURT.

* * *

I

Respondent James Herman O'Hagan was a partner in the law firm of Dorsey & Whitney in Minneapolis, Minnesota. In July 1988, Grand Metropolitan PLC (Grand Met), a company based in London, England, retained Dorsey & Whitney as local counsel to represent Grand Met regarding a potential tender offer for the common stock of the Pillsbury Company, headquartered in Minneapolis. Both Grand Met and Dorsey & Whitney took precautions to protect the confidentiality of Grand Met's tender offer plans. O'Hagan did no work on the Grand Met representation. Dorsey & Whitney withdrew from representing Grand Met on September 9, 1988. Less than a month later, on October 4, 1988, Grand Met publicly announced its tender offer for Pillsbury stock.

On August 18, 1988, while Dorsey & Whitney was still representing Grand Met, O'Hagan began purchasing

MAP 5-7 Minnesota (1997)

charged with [among other things] . . . 17 counts of securities fraud, in violation of § 10(b) of the Securities Exchange Act of 1934 . . . and SEC Rule 10b-5. . . . A jury convicted O'Hagan on all . . . counts, and he was sentenced to a 41-month term of imprisonment.

A divided panel of the Court of Appeals for the Eighth Circuit reversed all of O'Hagan's convictions. Liability under § 10(b) and Rule 10b-5, the Eighth Circuit held, may not be grounded on the "misappropriation theory" of securities fraud on which the prosecution relied. . . . Judge Fagg, dissenting, stated that he would recognize and enforce the misappropriation theory. . . .

Decisions of the Courts of Appeals are in conflict on the propriety of the misappropriation theory under § 10(b) and Rule 10b-5. . . . We granted certiorari and now reverse the Eighth Circuit's judgment.

* * *

A

In pertinent part, § 10(b) of the Exchange Act provides:

> It shall be unlawful for any person, directly or indirectly, by the use of any means or instrumentality of interstate commerce or of the mails, or of any facility of any national securities exchange—

* * *

> (b) To use or employ, in connection with the purchase or sale of any security registered on a national securities exchange or any security not so registered, any manipulative or deceptive device or contrivance in contravention of such rules and regulations as the [Securities and Exchange] Commission may prescribe as necessary or appropriate in the public interest or for the protection of investors.

The statute thus proscribes (1) using any deceptive device (2) in connection with the purchase or sale of securities, in contravention of rules prescribed by the Commission. The provision, as written, does not confine its coverage to deception of a purchaser or seller of securities; rather, the statute reaches any deceptive device used "in connection with the purchase or sale of any security."

Pursuant to its § 10(b) rulemaking authority, the Commission has adopted Rule 10b-5, which, as relevant here, provides:

> It shall be unlawful for any person, directly or indirectly, by the use of any means or instrumentality of interstate commerce, or of the mails or of any facility of any national securities exchange,
>
> (a) To employ any device, scheme, or artifice to defraud, [or]

* * *

call options for Pillsbury stock. Each option gave him the right to purchase 100 shares of Pillsbury stock by a specified date in September 1988. Later in August and in September, O'Hagan made additional purchases of Pillsbury call options. By the end of September, he owned 2,500 unexpired Pillsbury options, apparently more than any other individual investor. O'Hagan also purchased, in September 1988, some 5,000 shares of Pillsbury common stock, at a price just under $39 per share. When Grand Met announced its tender offer in October, the price of Pillsbury stock rose to nearly $60 per share. O'Hagan then sold his Pillsbury call options and common stock, making a profit of more than $4.3 million.

The Securities and Exchange Commission (SEC or Commission) initiated an investigation into O'Hagan's transactions, culminating in a 57-count indictment. The indictment alleged that O'Hagan defrauded his law firm and its client, Grand Met, by using for his own trading purposes material, nonpublic information regarding Grand Met's planned tender offer. According to the indictment, O'Hagan used the profits he gained through this trading to conceal his previous embezzlement and conversion of unrelated client trust funds. O'Hagan was

(c) To engage in any act, practice, or course of business which operates or would operate as a fraud or deceit upon any person, in connection with the purchase or sale of any security.

Liability under Rule 10b-5, our precedent indicates, does not extend beyond conduct encompassed by § 10(b)'s prohibition.[170] Under the "traditional" or "classical theory" of insider trading liability, § 10(b) and Rule 10b-5 are violated when a corporate insider trades in the securities of his corporation on the basis of material, nonpublic information. Trading on such information qualifies as a "deceptive device" under § 10(b), we have affirmed, because "a relationship of trust and confidence [exists] between the shareholders of a corporation and those insiders who have obtained confidential information by reason of their position with that corporation."[171] That relationship, we recognized, "gives rise to a duty to disclose [or to abstain from trading] because of the 'necessity of preventing a corporate insider from . . . taking unfair advantage of . . . uninformed . . . stockholders.' "[172] The classical theory applies not only to officers, directors, and other permanent insiders of a corporation, but also to attorneys, accountants, consultants, and others who temporarily become fiduciaries of a corporation.[173]

The "misappropriation theory" holds that a person commits fraud "in connection with" a securities transaction, and thereby violates § 10(b) and Rule 10b-5, when he misappropriates confidential information for securities trading purposes, in breach of a duty owed to the source of the information. Under this theory, a fiduciary's undisclosed, self-serving use of a principal's information to purchase or sell securities, in breach of a duty of loyalty and confidentiality, defrauds the principal of the exclusive use of that information. In lieu of premising liability on a fiduciary relationship between company insider and purchaser or seller of the company's stock, the misappropriation theory premises liability on a fiduciary-turned-trader's deception of those who entrusted him with access to confidential information.

The two theories are complementary, each addressing efforts to capitalize on nonpublic information through the purchase or sale of securities. The classical theory targets a corporate insider's breach of duty to shareholders with whom the insider transacts; the misappropriation theory outlaws trading on the basis of nonpublic information by

a corporate "outsider" in breach of a duty owed not to a trading party, but to the source of the information. The misappropriation theory is thus designed to "protect the integrity of the securities markets against abuses by 'outsiders' to a corporation who have access to confidential information that will affect the corporation's security price when revealed, but who owe no fiduciary or other duty to that corporation's shareholders."[174]

In this case, the indictment alleged that O'Hagan, in breach of a duty of trust and confidence he owed to his law firm, Dorsey & Whitney, and to its client, Grand Met, traded on the basis of nonpublic information regarding Grand Met's planned tender offer for Pillsbury common stock. This conduct, the Govern-ment charged, constituted a fraudulent device in connection with the purchase and sale of securities.[175]

B

We agree with the Government that misappropriation, as just defined, satisfies § 10(b)'s requirement that chargeable conduct involve a "deceptive device or contrivance" used "in connection with" the purchase or sale of securities. We observe, first, that misappropriators, as the Government describes them, deal in deception. A fiduciary who "[pretends] loyalty to the principal while secretly converting the principal's information for personal gain" . . . "dupes" or defrauds the principal.

We addressed fraud of the same species in *Carpenter v. United States*,[176] which involved the mail fraud statute's proscription of "any scheme or artifice to defraud."[177] Affirming convictions under that statute, we said in *Carpenter* that an employee's undertaking not to reveal his employer's confidential information "became a sham" when the employee provided the information to his coconspirators in a scheme to obtain trading profits. A company's confidential information, we recognized in *Carpenter*, qualifies as property to which the company has a right of exclusive use. The undisclosed misappropriation of such information, in violation of a fiduciary duty, the Court said in *Carpenter*, constitutes fraud akin to embezzlement—" 'the fraudulent appropriation to one's own use of the money or goods entrusted to one's care by another.' " *Carpenter*'s discussion of the fraudulent misuse of confidential information, the Government

[170]*See* Ernst & Ernst v. Hochfelder, *United States Reports,* vol. 425, p. 185 at p. 214 (Supreme Ct., 1976). . . .

[171]Chiarella v. United States, *id.,* vol. 445, p. 222 at p. 228 (1980).

[172]*Id.,* at 228–229. . . .

[173]*See* Dirks v. Securities and Exchange Commission, *id.* vol. 463, p. 646 at p. 655, n.14 (1983).

[174]Ibid.

[175]The Government could not have prosecuted O'Hagan under the classical theory, for O'Hagan was not an "insider" of Pillsbury, the corporation in whose stock he traded. Although an "outsider" with respect to Pillsbury, O'Hagan had an intimate association with, and was found to have traded on confidential information from, Dorsey & Whitney, counsel to tender offeror Grand Met. Under the misappropriation theory, O'Hagan's securities trading does not escape Exchange Act sanction, as it would under the dissent's reasoning, simply because he was associated with, and gained nonpublic information from, the bidder, rather than the target.

[176]*United States Reports,* vol. 484, p. 19 (1987).

[177]*United States Code,* title 18, § 1341.

notes, "is a particularly apt source of guidance here, because [the mail fraud statute] (like Section 10(b)) has long been held to require deception, not merely the breach of a fiduciary duty."

Deception through nondisclosure is central to the theory of liability for which the Government seeks recognition. As counsel for the Government stated in explanation of the theory at oral argument: "To satisfy the common law rule that a trustee may not use the property that [has] been entrusted [to] him, there would have to be consent. To satisfy the requirement of the Securities Act that there be no deception, there would only have to be disclosure."[178]

The misappropriation theory advanced by the Government is consistent with *Santa Fe Industries, Inc. v. Green*,[179] a decision underscoring that § 10(b) is not an all-purpose breach of fiduciary duty ban; rather, it trains on conduct involving manipulation or deception. In contrast to the Government's allegations in this case, in *Santa Fe Industries*, all pertinent facts were disclosed by the persons charged with violating § 10(b) and Rule 10b-5; therefore, there was no deception through nondisclosure to which liability under those provisions could attach. Similarly, full disclosure forecloses liability under the misappropriation theory: Because the deception essential to the misappropriation theory involves feigning fidelity to the source of information, if the fiduciary discloses to the source that he plans to trade on the nonpublic information, there is no "deceptive device" and thus no § 10(b) violation—although the fiduciary-turned-trader may remain liable under state law for breach of a duty of loyalty.[180]

We turn next to the § 10(b) requirement that the misappropriator's deceptive use of information be "in connection with the purchase or sale of [a] security." This element is satisfied because the fiduciary's fraud is consummated, not when the fiduciary gains the confidential information, but when, without disclosure to his principal, he uses the information to purchase or sell securities. The securities transaction and the breach of duty thus coincide. This is so even though the person or entity defrauded is not the other party to the trade, but is, instead, the source of the nonpublic information. A misappropriator who trades on the basis of material, nonpublic information, in short, gains his advantageous market position through deception; he deceives the source of the information and simultaneously harms members of the investing public.

The misappropriation theory targets information of a sort that misappropriators ordinarily capitalize upon to gain no-risk profits through the purchase or sale of securities. Should a misappropriator put such information to other use, the statute's prohibition would not be implicated. The theory does not catch all conceivable forms of fraud involving confidential information; rather, it catches fraudulent means of capitalizing on such information through securities transactions.

* * *

The misappropriation theory comports with § 10(b)'s language, which requires deception "in connection with the purchase or sale of any security," not deception of an identifiable purchaser or seller. The theory is also well-tuned to an animating purpose of the Exchange Act: to insure honest securities markets and thereby promote investor confidence. Although informational disparity is inevitable in the securities markets, investors likely would hesitate to venture their capital in a market where trading based on misappropriated nonpublic information is unchecked by law. An investor's informational disadvantage vis-à-vis a misappropriator with material, nonpublic information stems from contrivance, not luck; it is a disadvantage that cannot be overcome with research or skill.

In sum, considering the inhibiting impact on market participation of trading on misappropriated information, and the congressional purposes underlying § 10(b), it makes scant sense to hold a lawyer like O'Hagan a § 10(b) violator if he works for a law firm representing the target of a tender offer, but not if he works for a law firm representing the bidder. The text of the statute requires no such result. The misappropriation at issue here was properly made the subject of a § 10(b) charge because it meets the statutory requirement that there be "deceptive" conduct "in connection with" securities transactions.

C

The Court of Appeals rejected the misappropriation theory primarily on two grounds. First, as the Eighth Circuit comprehended the theory, it requires neither misrepresentation nor nondisclosure. As we just explained, however, deceptive nondisclosure is essential to the § 10(b) liability at issue. Concretely, in this case, "it [was O'Hagan's] failure to disclose his personal trading to Grand Met and Dorsey, in breach of his duty to do so, that made his conduct 'deceptive' within the meaning of [§]10(b)."

---

[178]Under the misappropriation theory urged in this case, the disclosure obligation runs to the source of the information, here, Dorsey & Whitney and Grand Met. Chief Justice Burger, dissenting in *Chiarella*, advanced a broader reading of § 10(b) and Rule 10b-5; the disclosure obligation, as he envisioned it, ran to those with whom the misappropriator trades. *United States Reports*, vol. 445 at p. 240 ("a person who has misappropriated nonpublic information has an absolute duty to disclose that information or to refrain from trading"); *see also id.*, at p. 243, n.4. The Government does not propose that we adopt a misappropriation theory of that breadth.

[179]*Id.*, vol. 430, p. 462 (Supreme Ct., 1977).

[180]Where, however, a person trading on the basis of material, nonpublic information owes a duty of loyalty and confidentiality to two entities or persons—for example, a law firm and its client—but makes disclosure to only one, the trader may still be liable under the misappropriation theory.

Second and "more obvious," the Court of Appeals said, the misappropriation theory is not moored to § 10(b)'s requirement that "the fraud be 'in connection with the purchase or sale of any security.' " According to the Eighth Circuit, three of our decisions reveal that § 10(b) liability cannot be predicated on a duty owed to the source of nonpublic information: *Chiarella* v. *United States*;[181] *Dirks* v. *SEC*;[182] and *Central Bank of Denver, N. A.* v. *First Interstate Bank of Denver, N. A.*[183] "Only a breach of a duty to parties to the securities transaction," the Court of Appeals concluded, "or, at the most, to other market participants such as investors, will be sufficient to give rise to § 10(b) liability." We read the statute and our precedent differently, and note again that § 10(b) refers to "the purchase or sale of any security," not to identifiable purchasers or sellers of securities.

Chiarella involved securities trades by a printer employed at a shop that printed documents announcing corporate takeover bids. Deducing the names of target companies from documents he handled, the printer bought shares of the targets before takeover bids were announced, expecting (correctly) that the share prices would rise upon announcement. In these transactions, the printer did not disclose to the sellers of the securities (the target companies' shareholders) the nonpublic information on which he traded. For that trading, the printer was convicted of violating § 10(b) and Rule 10b-5. We reversed the Court of Appeals judgment that had affirmed the conviction.

The jury in *Chiarella* had been instructed that it could convict the defendant if he willfully failed to inform sellers of target company securities that he knew of a takeover bid that would increase the value of their shares. Emphasizing that the printer had no agency or other fiduciary relationship with the sellers, we held that liability could not be imposed on so broad a theory. There is under § 10(b), we explained, no "general duty between all participants in market transactions to forgo actions based on material, nonpublic information." Under established doctrine, we said, a duty to disclose or abstain from trading "arises from a specific relationship between two parties."

The Court did not hold in *Chiarella* that the *only* relationship prompting liability for trading on undisclosed information is the relationship between a corporation's insiders and shareholders. That is evident from our response to the Government's argument before this Court that the printer's misappropriation of information from his employer for purposes of securities trading—in violation of a duty of confidentiality owed to the acquiring companies—constituted fraud in connection with the purchase or sale of a security, and thereby satisfied the terms of § 10(b). The Court declined to reach that poten-

tial basis for the printer's liability, because the theory had not been submitted to the jury. . . .

Chiarella thus expressly left open the misappropriation theory before us today. Certain statements in *Chiarella*, however, led the Eighth Circuit in the instant case to conclude that § 10(b) liability hinges exclusively on a breach of duty owed to a purchaser or seller of securities. The Court said in *Chiarella* that § 10(b) liability "is premised upon a duty to disclose arising from a relationship of trust and confidence *between parties to a transaction*," and observed that the printshop employee defendant in that case "was not a person in whom the sellers had placed their trust and confidence." These statements rejected the notion that § 10(b) stretches so far as to impose "a general duty between all participants in market transactions to forgo actions based on material, nonpublic information," and we confine them to that context. The statements highlighted by the Eighth Circuit, in short, appear in an opinion carefully leaving for future resolution the validity of the misappropriation theory, and therefore cannot be read to foreclose that theory.

Dirks, too, left room for application of the misappropriation theory in cases like the one we confront. . . .

* * *

Last of the three cases the Eighth Circuit regarded as warranting disapproval of the misappropriation theory, *Central Bank* held that "a private plaintiff may not maintain an aiding and abetting suit under § 10(b)." We immediately cautioned in *Central Bank* that secondary actors in the securities markets may sometimes be chargeable under the securities Acts: "Any person or entity, including a lawyer, accountant, or bank, who employs a manipulative device or makes a material misstatement (or omission) *on which a purchaser or seller of securities relies* may be liable as a primary violator under 10b-5, assuming . . . the requirements for primary liability under Rule 10b-5 are met." (Emphasis added). The Eighth Circuit isolated the statement just quoted and drew from it the conclusion that § 10(b) covers only deceptive statements or omissions on which purchasers and sellers, and perhaps other market participants, rely. It is evident from the question presented in *Central Bank*, however, that this Court, in the quoted passage, sought only to clarify that secondary actors, although not subject to aiding and abetting liability, remain subject to primary liability under § 10(b) and Rule 10b-5 for certain conduct.

* * *

In sum, the misappropriation theory, as we have examined and explained it in this opinion, is both consistent with the statute and with our precedent.

---

[181]*United States Reports,* vol. 445, p. 222 (1980).
[182]*Id.,* vol. 463, p. 646 (1983).
[183]*Id.* vol. 511, p. 164 (1994).

* * *

The judgment of the Court of Appeals for the Eighth Circuit is reversed, and the case is remanded for further proceedings consistent with this opinion.

It is so ordered. ■

The United Kingdom's prohibitions on insider trading are found in the 1985 Company Securities (Insider Dealing) Act, in particular Chapter 8, Section 1. Insiders are defined as persons who are knowingly connected with a company (or were knowingly connected with a company in the last 6 months). They are forbidden from trading in the shares of the company if they have information they know to be generally unavailable and that is likely to materially affect the price of the company's shares.[184] Insiders are also forbidden from trading in the shares of another company when they acquired information about that company as a result of its negotiations with their own firm.[185] Additionally, tippees are forbidden from using the information they obtain from these insiders.[186]

material: According to British law, when the price of something (i.e., a security) would be significantly affected.

Whereas the British law has some similarities to the American law, it is also very different. Individual victims have no civil remedy in Britain (as they do in the United States). Also, the **materiality** of inside information is ascertained by a different standard. Rather than looking to whether "a reasonable man would attach importance [to the particular information] in determining his choice of action in the transaction in question,"[187] as is done in the United States, the British law asks whether the information would affect the price of a security.[188] Finally, violation of the law does not, of itself, make a transaction void.

Japan's insider trading provisions are found in Article 58 of its Securities and Exchange Law. This article parallels Section 10(b) of the United States Securities Exchange Act, making insider transactions voidable if they are based on deceit, and making directors liable for damages if their conduct amounts to bad faith or gross negligence. However, like the British act, Article 58 does not provide for civil remedies.

Despite the existence of this legislation, traditionally the Japanese did not view insider trading as being improper, and its insider trading provisions were seldom enforced. In the late 1980s, however, several scandals—including one that involved the passing of insider information to politicians—brought about calls for reform; and in 1988 the Securities Exchange Law was amended to give it more teeth.[189] The Ministry of Finance, the agency responsible for enforcing the law, can now require "the issuer of a security listed on the stock exchange, as well as the stock exchange itself, to submit reports concerning the operation of the exchange. . . ."[190] Additionally, the punishment for insider trading is now set at "not more than six months or a fine of not more than 500,000 yen."[191]

France, like Japan, also had a tradition of ignoring insider trading violations that was brought to an end by scandals implicating some of its senior politicians.[192] In 1989, it amended its insider trading laws to give the *Commission des Opérations de Bourse* (the Stock Exchange Oversight Commission) authority "to require the production of documents and testimony from any person" and to impose civil sanctions, in addition to its existing authority to bring criminal charges.[193]

---

[184]Company Securities Act (Insider Dealing), 1985, chap. 8, § 1(1).
[185]*Id.,* § 1(2).
[186]*Id.,* § 1(3).
[187]List v. Fashion Park, Inc., *Federal Reporter, Second Series,* vol. 340, p. 457 at p. 462 (2nd Circuit Ct. of Appeals, 1965), *certiorari* denied, *United States Reports,* vol. 382, p. 811 (Supreme Court, 1965).
[188]Company Securities Act, 1985, chap. 8, § 1(1)(c).
[189]James A. Kehoe, "Exporting Insider Trading Laws: The Enforcement of U.S. Insider Trading Laws Internationally," *Emory International Law Review,* vol. 9, p. 345 at pp. 356–357 (1995).
[190]Tomoko Akashi, "Regulation of Insider Trading in Japan," *Columbia Law Review,* vol. 89, p. 1296 at p. 1304 (1989).
[191]*Id.,* p. 1306.
[192]James A. Kehoe, "Exporting Insider Trading Laws: The Enforcement of U.S. Insider Trading Laws Internationally," *Emory International Law Review,* vol. 9, p. 345 at pp. 356–357 (1995).
[193]Michael D. Mann and Lise A. Lustgarten, "Internationalization of Insider Trading Enforcement—A Guide to Regulation and Cooperation," in American Bar Association National Institute on White Collar Crime, *White Collar Crime,* p. 511 at p. 555 (1990).

Takeover Regulations

Financiers became actively involved in foreign acquisitions, mergers, and takeovers in the 1980s. British, Canadian, and Japanese corporate raiders made headlines for bidding on or taking over American entertainment, liquor, and publishing businesses. At the same time, efforts by American raiders to reciprocate were usually rebuffed. T. Boone Pickens' failure to gain a seat on the board of directors of the Japanese firm of Koito Manufacturing in 1988 is just one such example.

The reason foreign raiders were generally successful in the United States but unsuccessful elsewhere is that securities regulations outside the United States are biased against takeovers. Common barriers to takeover attempts are (1) restrictions on share transferability, (2) cross-ownership of shares, and (3) restrictions on the voting rights of publicly held shares.

In the United States and the United Kingdom, stock exchange listing requirements prohibit restrictions on the transferability of shares of publicly held companies.[194] This is not the case in other countries. In Canada, for example, publicly offered shares may contain restrictions prohibiting their sale to non-Canadians.[195] French law allows a *socièté anonyme* (SA) to forbid the transfer of its shares without the company's consent.[196] And in Switzerland, a corporation can go so far as to prohibit any transfer of registered shares.[197]

Cross-ownership of shares is the placing of large blocks of stock in friendly hands to protect against a hostile takeover. In Japan, cross-ownership of shares is a prevalent practice, although its use now is much less common than it was before World War II.[198]

Voting restrictions on publicly held shares also inhibit takeovers. Continental European corporation statutes impose caps on the total percentage of shares any one owner may vote. For example, in Belgium, no single shareholder may cast more than one fifth of the total votes.[199] A similar restriction applies in Germany.[200]

In contrast to the countries with takeover barriers, the countries with an active acquisition marketplace—notably the United Kingdom and the United States—have legislation or exchange rules that directly regulate the takeover process.[201] The goal of such regulations is neutrality: to put the raider and the management of the target company on roughly equal footing.

Without takeover barriers or takeover regulations, the takeover process is weighted heavily in favor of the raider. For example, in the United States, prior to the enactment of the Williams Act of 1968, a tender offer (i.e., a raider's offer to buy publicly held shares) was governed by the principle of *caveat venditor*.[202] The offeror was free to define the terms and conditions of his offer and to hold offerees (shareholders) to a binding contract from the moment they accepted. Commonly, the offer was held open for only a short period of time to exclude the possibility that a competing offer might appear or that the target firm's management could take some defensive action. It was also subject to a variety of conditions that allowed the offeror to back out if he was unable to complete the takeover to his satisfaction. In essence, the offerees were faced with a take-it-or-leave-it proposition, and the target firm's management had little ability to protect itself, while the raider's risks were minimal.

Williams Act: Law enacted by the United States in 1968 that authorizes the Securities and Exchange Commission to issue rules regulating takeover bids.

In the United States, the **Williams Act** attempts to put the contestants on a level playing field by authorizing the Securities and Exchange Commission to issue rules governing tender offers for securities of companies registered under the Securities Exchange Act of 1934. The Williams Act and the SEC's rules require an offeror to disclose information about his finances

---

[194]Deborah A. Demott, "Comparative Dimensions of Takeover Regulation," *Washington University Law Quarterly,* vol. 65, p. 69 at p. 76 (1987). In the United States, the New York Stock Exchange and the Pacific Exchange prohibit the listing of stock with limitations on transferability. Other exchanges permit such restrictions. *Id.,* p. 74.

[195]*See,* e.g., Ontario Business Corporations Act, § 42(2), Ontario Statutes, chap. 4 (1982).

[196]French *Code des Sociètés,* Article 274.

[197]*See* "Doing Business in Europe," *Common Market Reporter,* para. 29,215 (summarizing the Swiss Code of Obligations).

[198]*See* Thomas F.M. Adams and N. Kobayashi, *The World of Japanese Business,* p. 53 (1969), Bradley M. Richardson and Taizo Ueda, *Business and Society in Japan,* p. 23 (1981), and Deborah A. Demott, "Comparative Dimensions of Takeover Regulation," *Washington University Law Quarterly,* vol. 65, p. 78 (1987).

[199]*See* "Doing Business in Europe," *Common Market Reporter,* para. 21,256 (summarizing the Belgian *Commercial Companies Code*).

[200]*Id.,* at para. 23,213.

[201]An excellent summary and comparison of the takeover regulations of Australia, Canada, the United Kingdom, and the United States can be found in Deborah A. Demott, "Comparative Dimensions of Takeover Regulation," *Washington University Law Quarterly,* vol. 65, p. 69 (1987).

[202]Latin: "let the seller beware."

and his reasons for attempting a takeover either before or at the time he announces his offer, and the target's management must be given time to circulate its views on the proposal. The offer must be kept open for a minimum period, and if the offer is for less than all of a target's shares, it may not be accepted on a "first-come, first-served" basis. An oversubscribed offer must be allocated among tendering subscribers on a pro rata basis. Also, subscribers may withdraw the shares they have tendered within specified time limits. Finally, anyone who acquires more than 5 percent or more of a publicly traded company's equity securities must disclose their holdings within ten days after the acquisition.[203]

One important aspect of the Williams Act is that it does not restrict the ability of offerors to set conditions that allow them to withdraw their offer. As a consequence, American offerors commonly include in their offers terms that permit them to revoke their offers if financing is unavailable, or too expensive, or their offers are challenged in court.

On the other hand, the Williams Act does not restrict the defensive actions that a target's management may take.[204] The restrictions that do exist are imposed by the states, and principally by the state courts. In Delaware and New York, the two states whose courts have addressed the issue most extensively, management is allowed to take any defensive measure that complies with the business judgment rule. That rule allows management to exercise reasonable business discretion, so long as it does so in the best interest of the corporation as a whole.[205]

The City Code on Takeovers and Mergers: Rules of the London Stock Exchange issued by the Exchange's Panel on Takeovers and Mergers that regulate takeover bids.

Takeovers in the United Kingdom are regulated by the London Stock Exchange's **City Code on Takeovers and Mergers** that is issued by the Exchange's Panel on Takeovers and Mergers.[206] The City Code is similar to the Williams Act in that it (a) requires extensive disclosure by offerors, (b) sets a minimum duration for offers, (c) requires prorated acceptance for oversubscribed partial offers, and (d) grants tendering shareholders limited withdrawal rights.[207] Unlike the Williams Act, it regulates conditions set by the offeror, and it forbids conditions "depending solely on subjective judgments by the directors of the offeror."[208] Also, partial offers may be made only with the consent of the Panel, and an offeror who acquires more than 30 percent of the shares of a target must offer to buy out the remaining shareholders at the highest price paid during the previous year for comparable shares.[209] Finally, the responses that a target's Board of Directors may take are more structured. The Board, to which the offeror must initially make his offer, has to obtain "competent independent advice" on the offer and share that advice both with its own shareholders and, if requested, any other legitimate offeror.[210] The target Board must also obtain shareholder approval of any defensive action it takes that is intended to frustrate a takeover bid.[211]

D. ENFORCEMENT OF SECURITIES REGULATIONS INTERNATIONALLY

International cooperation in the enforcement of securities regulations is a relatively recent development. In 1961, the Organization for Economic Cooperation and Development (OECD) adopted a Code of Liberalization of Capital Movements, which it hoped would abolish stock

---

[203]*United States Code,* Title 15, § 78m(d).

[204]Examples of immediate defenses to a takeover bid are (a) the "self tender" (an offer by a target to buy its own stock from its shareholders to maintain control); (b) the "white knight" defense (the target arranges a favorable merger with another corporation); (c) the "Pac Man" defense (the target offers to purchase the raiding corporation); (d) greenmail (the target offers to buy the stock bought by the raider at a premium); and (e) a suit for an injunction (the target claims that the resulting merger or consolidation would violate some state or federal statute, such as the federal antitrust laws).

Long-term tactics that make a corporation more generally unattractive to takeover bids are (a) the "scorched earth" ploy (the target arranges to sell off its principal assets or it has loans which become due immediately after a takeover occurs); (b) the "shark repellent" scheme (the target changes its charter or bylaws to require a higher than normal shareholder vote to approve a merger or consolidation); (c) the "poison pill" (the target's shares are redeemable for cash in the event of a takeover); and (d) "golden parachutes" (which provide for high payments to officers and directors in the event that they are discharged or demoted).

[205]*See* Unocal Corp. v. Mesa Petroleum Co., *Atlantic Reporter, Second Series,* vol. 493, p. 946 (Delaware Supreme Ct., 1985); and Norlin Corp. v. Rooney, Pace, Inc., *Federal Reporter, Second Series,* vol. 744, p. 255 (2nd Circuit Ct. of Appeals, 1984) (applying New York law).

[206]"England Law Digest," *Martindale-Hubbell International Law Digest,* p. ENG-4 (2001).

[207]Panel on Takeovers and Mergers, *The City Code on Takeovers and Mergers,* Rules 10, 24, 31.1, 34, and 36.7 (1985).

[208]*Id.,* Rule 13.

[209]*Id.,* Rules 36 and 9.

[210]*Id.,* Rules 3.1 and 19.4.

[211]*Id.,* Rule 21.

exchange restrictions among its member states. Many members, however, filed reservations to the Code, demonstrating that attitudes about securities regulations were then too diverse for the international community to agree upon a single regulatory mechanism. Also, the Code had no effective enforcement provisions, and the OECD member states, in practice, ignored it.[212]

Until the 1980s, no other attempts were made to establish any formal mechanism of international cooperation. Then the United States began pushing its major trading partners to enter into cooperative agreements, and the Council of Europe began work on an insider trading convention.

Memorandums of Understanding

The U.S. efforts have centered on securing "memorandums of understanding" (MOUs), which it regards as the most feasible tool for preventing international securities fraud and enforcing compliance with its own domestic disclosure rules.[213] During the 1980s, it entered into MOUs with Switzerland, the United Kingdom, and Japan.

The U.S.-Swiss MOU is a unilateral agreement designed to overcome Switzerland's banking secrecy laws. Under the MOU, the American Securities and Exchange Commission can ask the Swiss Bankers Association to provide information and to freeze insider trading profits deposited in a Swiss bank account. In making its request, the SEC must (a) show that it has reasonable grounds for suspecting insider trading that would violate both American and Swiss law, (b) place all of its evidence before the Association, and (c) promise not to disclose any information provided by the Association except in connection with the enforcement of its insider trading laws. It is up to the Swiss Bankers Association, however, to decide if the SEC has an adequate case; and, if it decides that the SEC does not, it can refuse to honor the request.[214]

Unlike the Swiss agreement, the U.S.-U.K. Memorandum of Understanding is a bilateral agreement designed to help both countries enforce their securities (and futures) laws through information sharing. The U.S.-U.K. MOU defines securities transactions broadly: (a) it does not require a violation of both U.S. and U.K. laws; (b) local authorities are to honor a request for information unless they can show "substantial grounds" in writing why it should be denied; and (c) both countries have an affirmative duty to turn over any information they discover that points to a violation of the other country's laws even without a request.[215]

The U.S.-Japanese MOU is both brief and informal. Both sides promise to "facilitate . . . requests for surveillance and investigatory information on a case-by-case basis," but no mechanism for making or honoring requests is established. The memorandum only requires that the parties use "good faith" in working out their procedural differences, as that becomes "necessary or appropriate."[216]

The Convention on Insider Trading

In 1983, the Council of Europe sponsored a colloquy in Milan, Italy, to review national regulations and to examine the deficiencies in international law with respect to insider trading. The colloquy led to the appointment of a Committee of Experts (drawn from the Council's member states, Finland, the United States, and the Commission of the European Community) to draft a convention on insider trading. On April 20, 1989, the Council formally adopted the Convention on Insider Trading and opened it for signature.

---

[212]*International Capital Markets and Securities Regulation,* vol. 10, § 2.02 (Harold S. Blumenthal and Samuel Wolff, eds., 1982).

[213]*See* Ken S. Nakata, "The SEC and Foreign Blocking Statutes: Need for a Balanced Approach," *University of Pennsylvania Journal of International Business Law,* vol. 9, p. 549 (1987); and Elizabeth E. Barlow, "Enforcing Securities Regulations through Bilateral Agreements with the United Kingdom and Japan: An Interim Measure or a Solution?" *Texas International Law Journal,* vol. 23, p. 251 (1988).

[214]Memorandum of Understanding to Establish Mutually Acceptable Means for Improving International Law Enforcement Cooperation in the Field of Insider Trading, August 31, 1982, United States-Switzerland, reprinted in *International Legal Materials,* vol. 22, p. 1 (1983).

[215]Memorandum of Understanding on Exchange of Information between the United States Securities and Exchange Commission and the United Kingdom Department of Trade and Industry in Matters Relating to Securities and between the United States Commodity Futures Trading Commission and the United Kingdom Department of Trade and Industry in Matters Relating to Futures, September 23, 1986, reprinted in *id.,* vol. 25, p. 1431 (1986).

[216]Memorandum of the United States Securities and Exchange Commission and the Securities Bureau of the Japanese Ministry of Finance on the Sharing of Information, May 23, 1986, reprinted in *id.,* vol. 25, p. 1429 (1986).

The Convention's purpose is to assist the regulatory agencies of its signatory states by establishing a mechanism for the exchange of information so that those agencies can better supervise their securities markets. In particular, "because of the internationalization of markets and the ease of present-day communications," it focuses on uncovering the insider trading activities "on the market of a state by persons not resident in that state or acting through persons not resident there."[217] The Convention does not attempt to establish uniform enforcement provisions or sanctions.

In essence, the Convention allows one state to request the assistance of another in uncovering conduct by an individual or individuals in the latter's territory that constitutes insider trading in the requesting state. The requesting state must make a full disclosure of the facts that lead it to believe that insider trading has taken place, and it must state what it will do with the information it receives.[218] The state receiving the request then follows the procedures set up by its own laws in responding to the request, subject to an overall obligation to keep both the request and the assistance it provides secret.[219] The requested state can refuse to honor a request if it is too broad or if the conduct described does not constitute a violation of both states' insider trading rules.[220]

Extraterritorial Application of U.S. Securities Laws

One important example of the many attempts to apply securities regulations internationally has been the enforcement of United States securities laws extraterritorially. Consideration of this is especially important because American laws apply to a much wider range of activities than those of any other country. The U.S. Securities Act of 1933 requires companies to disclose their financial standing before issuing new shares. The Securities and Exchange Act of 1934 requires managers and owners of large percentages of stock to disclose their ownership interests, and it forbids insider trading and other fraudulent securities transactions. The Williams Act requires corporate raiders to disclose their finances and their reasons for making a takeover bid.

To ensure that persons operating outside the United States do not avoid these laws, the SEC and the U.S. Department of Justice (which are responsible for their enforcement) have regularly instituted suits involving nonresident aliens. This has forced courts to determine if the U.S. securities laws give them the necessary jurisdiction to hear these cases. Case 5–8 examines this question.

---

[217]Council of Europe, Convention on Insider Trading, Preamble, reprinted in *id.,* vol. 29, p. 309 (1990).
[218]*Id.,* Article 5.
[219]*Id.,* Article 6.
[220]*Id.,* Article 7. By a special declaration, a signatory state can—subject to reciprocity—agree to provide information on all types of securities regulations, not just insider trading. *Id.,* Article 3.

Case 5–8   Securities and Exchange Commission v. Knowles

United States, Tenth Circuit Court of Appeals.
Federal Reporter, Third Series, vol. 87, p. 413 (1996).

CIRCUIT JUDGE MURPHY:

This case arises out of the enforcement by the district court against the appellant, a foreign national, of two administrative subpoenas *duces tecum*[221] issued by the Securities and Exchange Commission. The appellant argues that the district court lacked personal jurisdiction to enforce the subpoenas. The district court held that it did not need personal jurisdiction over the appellant to do so.

The question presented is whether the appellant has the requisite minimum contacts to justify the district court's exercise of personal jurisdiction over him. This court holds that he does and that the district court properly enforced the subpoenas.

---

[221]Latin: "under penalty . . . bring with you." An order requiring a person to bring stated items to a court proceeding.]

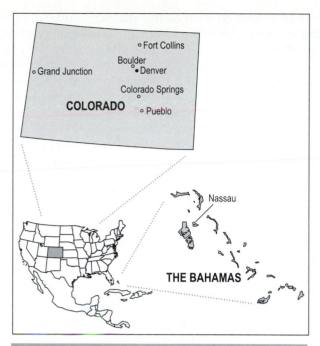

MAP 5-8   Colorado and the Bahamas (1996)

I. BACKGROUND AND PROCEDURAL SETTING

On June 14, 1995, and again on June 30, 1995, the Securities and Exchange Commission (the "SEC") issued administrative subpoenas *duces tecum* in the name of the appellant, Gaye B. Knowles. The SEC served Knowles with the first subpoena by hand at LaGuardia Airport in New York City. It later served the second on Knowles's counsel in Miami, Florida. These subpoenas were issued in connection with the Formal Order of Investigation in the nonpublic investigation conducted by the SEC out of its Denver, Colorado, office, *In the Matter of the Rockies Fund, Inc., Redwood Microcap Fund, Inc., and Combined Penny Stock Fund, Inc., et al.*[222] The SEC issued these subpoenas pursuant to its authority under *United States Code*, title 15, §§ 77s(b), 78u(b), and 80a-41(b).

Knowles is presently a Bahamian citizen and resident and has been so since 1951. He is an independent investment consultant and, at the times the subpoenas were served on him, was also the president of two Bahamian companies, Global Petrol Trading and Swiss EuroFund, Inc. In the investigation, the SEC sought to determine whether bank accounts in the names of these two companies were used to bribe brokers in the United States to sell certain stock of American companies in violation of federal securities laws. The first subpoena directed Knowles to appear at a deposition and to pro-

duce certain personal documents and documents relating to the bank accounts of Global Petrol Trading. The second subpoena directed the same and called for Knowles to produce documents relating to the bank accounts of Swiss EuroFund, Inc.

In response to the subpoenas, Knowles appeared for deposition in Miami, Florida, on July 12, 1995. Knowles produced certain corporate documents pursuant to the subpoenas but objected to producing monthly banking statements and other banking documents of the two companies. In order to enforce the subpoenas, the SEC applied to the district court in the judicial district where it is conducting the investigation, as authorized in *United States Code*, title 15, §§ 77v(b), 78u(c), and 80a-41(c).

The SEC filed an Ex Parte Application for an Order to Show Cause and Application for an Order Compelling Compliance with Administrative Subpoenas *Duces Tecum*. The United States District Court for the District of Colorado subsequently issued an Order to Show Cause. Thereafter, the SEC served Knowles with the Order to Show Cause outside his home in Nassau, Bahamas. Knowles responded to the Order to Show Cause and moved the district court to dismiss the SEC's application for lack of personal jurisdiction over him.

In an Amended Memorandum Order and Opinion, the district court held that it did not need personal jurisdiction over Knowles in order to enforce the subpoenas against him. It held, instead, that judicial enforcement of an administrative subpoena may be had where the agency can show that: (1) the inquiry is conducted pursuant to a lawfully authorized, legitimate purpose; (2) it is reasonably relevant to an investigation which the agency has authority to conduct; and (3) all administrative prerequisites have been met. The district court determined that the SEC met this three-pronged burden and that Knowles had adduced no evidence to the contrary. It therefore ordered Knowles to comply with the subpoenas within ten days. This court subsequently granted Knowles's Motion to Stay the Amended Memorandum Order and Opinion pending appeal. This appeal followed.

On appeal, Knowles argues that the district court erred when it determined it did not need personal jurisdiction over him in order to enforce the subpoenas. He also argues that the district court could not properly exercise jurisdiction over him because of his lack of personal contacts with the United States. In response, the SEC maintains that the district court had personal jurisdiction over Knowles based upon sufficient minimum contacts with the United States in relation to: (1) the subpoenas; (2) the matters under investigation by the SEC; and (3) his general business. In the alternative, the SEC argues that the minimum contacts analysis is not

---

[222]The Formal Order of Investigation is not a part of the record in this case; the SEC claims that it is a nonpublic document. The Formal Order was available to the district court for *in camera* [in the judge's chambers] inspection, but its scope and contents are in no way related to the issues here on appeal.

required because the district court had personal jurisdiction over Knowles based upon the SEC's service of the subpoenas on Knowles within the territorial limits of the United States. The SEC does not argue that personal jurisdiction is not required in order to enforce the subpoenas, as the district court held.

II. JURISDICTION

* * *

The issue here is a narrow one: whether the district court had personal jurisdiction over Knowles to enforce the administrative subpoenas *duces tecum*. . . .

A. Minimum Contacts

Under the due process clause of the Fifth Amendment, personal jurisdiction over a party does not exist unless that party has sufficient "minimum contacts" with the jurisdiction.[223] The exercise of jurisdiction must not "offend 'traditional notions of fair play and substantial justice.'"[224] Furthermore, the party's activities within the jurisdiction must render it foreseeable that the party should reasonably anticipate being haled into the forum court.[225]

Under Federal Rule of Civil Procedure 4(k)(2), the service of a summons with respect to a claim under federal law in which Congress has authorized worldwide service establishes personal jurisdiction over the defendant, subject to constitutional limits. The Securities Exchange Act permits the exercise of personal jurisdiction to the limits of the Due Process Clause of the Fifth Amendment. Congress has provided [in *United States Code*, title 15, § 77v(a)] for worldwide service of process in cases of the enforcement of subpoenas issued by the SEC. The language of § 77v(a) authorizes the service of process on a defendant in any district "of which the defendant is an inhabitant or wherever the defendant may be found." Under § 80a-41(c), the SEC is entitled to invoke the aid of the district court in which it is conducting its investigation.

Knowles was served by the SEC with the Order to Show Cause outside his home in Nassau, Bahamas. When the personal jurisdiction of a federal court is invoked based upon a federal statute providing for extraterritorial service, the relevant inquiry is whether the respondent has had sufficient minimum contacts with the United States. Specific contacts with the district in which enforcement is sought, in this case Colorado, are unnecessary.

The question then before this court is whether Knowles has sufficient minimum contacts with the United States to enable the district court to exercise personal jurisdiction over him consistent with the Due Process Clause of the Fifth Amendment. We thus look to the constitutional sufficiency of the contacts with the United States which Knowles concedes. Knowles acknowledges the following contacts: (1) that he visited the United States "on a number of occasions" for purposes of meeting with investment clients; (2) that during his visits to Florida to meet with the sole shareholder n6 of Global Petrol Trading and Swiss EuroFund, Inc., "he signed a handful of letters and checks"; and (3) he opened a brokerage trading account for Global Petrol Trading during one of his trips to Florida.

Here the SEC has produced affidavits outlining more extensive contacts between Knowles and the United States, mainly in the forms of active trading through additional American brokerage accounts and the wiring of proceeds from stock sales to Bahamian banks. Knowles, however, generally contests these alleged contacts. He argues that they are based on hearsay and expert opinions concerning securities industry practices and handwriting identification which are without foundation. He contends that his actions on behalf of Global Petrol Trading and Swiss EuroFund, Inc., are limited to those he has admitted.

The district court did not resolve these disputed jurisdictional facts. As a result, this court is hesitant to consider the evidence of contacts presented by the SEC. Based only on the contacts Knowles admits, however, we hold that the district court does have personal jurisdiction over him.

B. Analysis

The source of a federal district court's jurisdiction may be twofold: specific and general jurisdiction. Specific jurisdiction may be exercised where the defendant has "purposefully directed" its activities toward the forum jurisdiction and where the underlying action is based upon activities that arise out of or relate to the defendant's contacts with the forum.[226] A nonresident defendant may be subjected to the forum's general jurisdiction even where the alleged activities of the defendant upon which the claims are based are unrelated to his contacts with the forum. The forum court's general jurisdiction may be invoked over the defendant on any matter if the defendant's unrelated contacts are sufficiently "'continuous and systematic'" that the exercise of jurisdiction is "'reasonable and just.'"[227] Our focus here is on specific jurisdiction.

In this case, all of Knowles's admitted contacts with the United States concern his activities as the former

---

[223]International Shoe Co. v. Washington, *United States Reports,* vol. 326, p. 310 at p. 316 (Supreme Ct., 1945).
[224]*Id.*
[225]World-Wide Volkswagen Corp. v. Woodson, *id.,* vol. 444, p. 286 at p. 297 (Supreme Ct., 1980).
[226]Burger King Corp. v Rudzewicz, *id.,* vol. 471, p. 462 at p. 472 (1985). . . .
[227]Helicopteros Nacionales de Colombia v. Hall, *id.,* vol. 466, p. 408 at p. 415 (1984) (quoting Perkins v. Benguet Consol. Mining Co., *id.,* vol. 342, p. 437 at p. 438 (1952)).

president of Global Petrol Trading and Swiss EuroFund, Inc. Those contacts involve activities that are the very source of the SEC's interest in the two corporations. The underlying investigation and this subpoena enforcement action arise out of Knowles's contacts with the United States and thus support the exercise of specific jurisdiction in order to secure enforcement.

Knowles, however, contends that the contacts of the two corporations cannot be factored into the analysis of whether he has minimum contacts with the United States. His argument is that the jurisdiction of the district court based upon these corporate contacts does not extend to him. Knowles is mistaken. As the Supreme Court held in *Calder v. Jones,* employees of a corporation that is subject to the personal jurisdiction of the courts of the forum may themselves be subject to jurisdiction if those employees were primary participants in the activities forming the basis of jurisdiction over the corporation.[228] That the subpoenas were served on Knowles without explicit reference to his former capacity as president of the two corporations has no bearing on whether the district court has jurisdiction over him with regard to the corporate activities in which Knowles was a primary participant. Personal jurisdiction over him would extend at least as far as matters relating to the activities of the two corporations in the forum in which he was a primary participant.

Knowles has purposefully directed his activities on behalf of Global Petrol Trading and Swiss EuroFund, Inc., toward the United States. Moreover, those activities are directly related to matters in the underlying SEC investigation. As Knowles concedes, he was the individual who took the actions on behalf of the two corporations that are the basis of jurisdiction. Knowles was then a primary participant in these activities. Based upon his admitted contacts, the exercise of specific jurisdiction over him is reasonable and just and satisfies traditional notions of fair play.

Even a single purposeful contact may be sufficient to meet the minimum contacts standard when the underlying proceeding is directly related to that contact.[229] Those contacts admitted by Knowles involve an ongoing business relationship and a brokerage account. They are sufficient to support the exercise of specific personal jurisdiction because the underlying SEC investigation concerns these admitted contacts.

Knowles's contacts involve trading activities on behalf of an American shareholder of the corporations that employed him as president, through an American brokerage firm, that were "purposefully directed" toward the United States. Moreover, they represent a deliberate affiliation with the forum that renders foreseeable the possibility of being haled into court in the United States at least as to those specific contacts. The actions Knowles took on behalf of Global Petrol Trading and Swiss EuroFund, Inc., indicate that Knowles, through the corporations, purposefully availed himself of the benefits and protections of the laws of the United States.

From these contacts, Knowles and the two corporations enjoyed the privileges of conducting activities within the United States and he could reasonably anticipate being subject to the jurisdiction of the United States. Knowles's continuing investment contacts with United States citizens, companies, and brokerage accounts were not random, fortuitous, or attenuated. Rather, they were purposeful, continuous, and systematic. The district court's exercise of specific personal jurisdiction over him thus comported with "'traditional notions of fair play and substantial justice.'"[230]

For the foregoing reasons, the district court's order to Knowles to comply with the SEC's administrative subpoenas duces tecum is AFFIRMED. ◼

---

[228]Calder v. Jones, *id.,* vol. 465, p. 783 at p. 790 (1984).
[229]*See* McGee v. International Life Ins. Co., *id.,* vol. 355, p. 220 at p. 223 (Supreme Ct., 1957).
[230]*See* International Shoe, *id.,* vol. 326 at p. 316 (quoting Milliken, *id.,* vol. 311 at p. 463).

Chapter Questions

1. Overseas Investment Co. (OIC), a multinational enterprise with its headquarters in State W, entered into a joint venture with Investment Promotions Facility, Ltd. (IPF), a state-owned company whose board of directors and principal officers had been appointed by the Minister of Finance of State X. The joint venture agreement provided that, in the event of any dispute, the dispute would be resolved by arbitration. Additionally, because the law of State X says that all foreign investment agreements must be approved by the Minister of Finance, the Minister was present at the signing of the agreement; and after representatives of the two parties put their signatures on the document, the Foreign Minister added the words "approved and ratified" and his own signature.

   Unfortunately, a dispute did arise, and OIC initiated an arbitration proceeding according to the procedures set out in the joint venture agreement, naming both IPF and State X as parties. State X responded to this by arguing that the arbitration tribunal has no jurisdiction over it. Should State X be excused from participating in the suit? Discuss.

2. The Video Assembly Co. (VAC), a company organized in State Z, entered into an agreement with the U.S. government to assemble video cassette recorders from foreign manufactured parts inside a U.S. foreign trade zone. Before this could be done, however, VAC had to set up an assembly plant. Rather than using an American facility, it imported a completely prefabricated plant. The plant consisted of the building, all of the assembly and packaging equipment, and all of the ancillary tools. The U.S. Customs Service claims that the plant itself did not qualify for exemption from customs duties at the time it came into the foreign trade zone because it was not "merchandise" for assembly, as required by U.S. law; and the Customs Service levied duties on the plant. VAC has appealed to the U.S. Court of International Trade, asking for an order compelling the Customs Service to return the duties it collected. How should the Court rule? Discuss.

3. In 1980, the Lumber Harvesting Co. (LHC) entered into a long-term development contract with State A, a small developing country, to harvest lumber from 20 million acres of forestland within State A. At that time this forest constituted about 80 percent of the land of State A, and only a few primitive peoples inhabited it. The contract also contained a stabilization clause promising that no subsequent laws enacted by State A would affect the relationship between LHC and State A. Over the years, however, LHC has bowed to demands from State A to pay it an ever-increasing percentage of royalties and taxes. Also, under pressure from State A, LHC has always assumed responsibility for relocating and retraining the individuals displaced by its harvesting activities.

    Today, nearly 15 million acres of the forest have been clear-cut. The damage to State A's ecosystem has been devastating. May State A modify the contract with LHC to put a stop to its destructive harvesting practices? May State A require LHC to repair the damage it has caused? May State A, if necessary, expropriate LHC's investment within its territory? Discuss.

4. The Modern Exploration Co. (MEC), a firm organized in State P, entered into an investment contract with State Q to explore for and harvest magnesium nodules from the seabed of State Q's continental shelf. MEC agreed to pay State Q U.S. $100 million in advance for this privilege. State Q, however, did not inform MEC that it would be promulgating certain environmental protection laws within days after signing this contract that would make the endeavor so expensive that it would be effectively impossible for MEC to perform. When MEC discovered this, it asked State Q to either modify the environmental laws or give MEC back its money. State Q refused. MEC then initiated an arbitration proceeding under the auspices of the International Center for the Settlement of Investment Disputes, in accordance with the terms of the investment agreement and State Q law. How should the tribunal rule? Discuss.

5. Turnip Company, a multinational enterprise headquartered in State T, ordered its subsidiary in State R, the Radish Company, to close and to declare itself bankrupt. The Radish Company did so. In doing so, however, it did not give its employees adequate notice of its closing, and its assets were inadequate for funding the termination payments due the employees under State R law. In the bankruptcy proceeding, the employees asked the bankruptcy tribunal to order Turnip to fund the termination payments that Radish owed the employees. In support of this, the employees introduced evidence establishing that Turnip had known for some time that Radish was an unprofitable subsidiary and would have to be closed; and that, in anticipation of this, it had taken assets belonging to Radish out of the state so that they would be unavailable at the time of the bankruptcy liquidation. How should the tribunal rule? Discuss.

6. Two securities brokerage firms, Western Brokerage and Eastern Brokerage, entered into a contract for Western to physically deliver 5,000 shares of stock in a certain company to Eastern within 10 to 15 days. Western failed to do so, and neither Western nor Eastern noticed the error for several months. When it was discovered, Western insisted that Eastern must take delivery of the stock, but Eastern refused. Western then brought suit to compel Eastern to accept and pay for the stock. Eastern defends itself by saying that Western

breached its duty to make a timely delivery and therefore had no right to complain. What should the decision be? Discuss.

7. Little, Ltd., is a small publicly traded stock company that owns a valuable patent. Little has approximately 1,000 shareholders and about 100,000 shares authorized and outstanding. Big Company would like to have use of the patent, but Little has refused to grant it a license. Big offered to buy out all of Little's assets, but Little's board of directors refused the offer. Big has now tendered an offer to all of Little's shareholders offering to pay them U.S. $10 a share for their shareholdings, a price that is slightly above their current fair-market price. What can Little do to prevent Big from succeeding? Discuss.

8. Miscellaneous, Ltd. was a company set up as a joint venture in Country M. Its foreign investor was Mammoth Enterprises, Ltd., a company organized in Country N. Mammoth owned 51 percent of Miscellaneous's shares and it therefore was able to elect all of the directors of Miscellaneous. The other 49 percent of Miscellaneous's shares had been sold through a stock exchange in Country M to the local public. For several years, Miscellaneous had been unprofitable; then, when it was just about to become profitable, its board of directors bought up all of the company's public shares without revealing its current economic status. The Country M agency that supervises securities transactions has learned of this, and it seeks to force Miscellaneous to rescind these purchases. Will it be successful? Discuss.

Review Problem

You continue to be a Senior Assistant in the law department of MegaBranch Industries (MBI), a multinational enterprise that has branches in countries around the world. You are responsible for providing MBI's board of directors with legal advice on its worldwide operations.

1. MBI is considering setting up a new subsidiary in State A to manufacture refrigerators for both domestic consumption and export. State A presently has no refrigeration manufacturing firm.
   a. List the kinds of state agencies that MBI will need to contact to obtain approval for this venture, and list the kinds of information that MBI will need to provide them.
   b. What business form would be best suited for this subsidiary?
   c. What can MBI do to avoid having to enter into a joint venture with local investors?
   d. Are there any kinds of activities that will be closed to the subsidiary? or that State A might discourage the subsidiary from entering into?
   e. Would it be advantageous to set up this subsidiary in a foreign trade zone?
   f. What investment guarantees should MBI seek from State A?
   g. What kind of supervision of its investment can MBI expect from State A prior to the time when the subsidiary is fully operational?
   h. What kind of supervision can MBI expect after the subsidiary begins operating normally?
   i. Should it be necessary for MBI or State A to modify its investment arrangement, how can this be done? Will there be any constraints?
   j. What say will the local employees, creditors, and (assuming there are any) shareholders have in the operation of the subsidiary?
2. MBI is considering selling its shares on a foreign stock exchange, in particular an exchange in State B.
   a. What information must MBI disclose to State B about itself and its worldwide operations?
   b. Describe the clearance and settlement procedures that MBI, or its underwriters, will have to comply with in selling its shares.
   c. Assuming that MBI does not want to physically deliver any of its share certificates outside of its home state, can it do anything to avoid that?
3. MBI wants to take over a competing company, the Competitor Company (CC), the stock of which is traded on an exchange in State C.
   a. How should MBI go about doing this?
   b. What kind of responses can it expect from CC?

4. One of MBI's subsidiaries in State D has just discovered a new drug that it believes will actually prevent baldness, and, if it proves successful, make MBI lots of money. This information must be kept secret, however, until further tests can be made. Are there any precautions that MBI, its subsidiaries, or their officers, directors, or employees should take during this time period in connection with the sale or purchase of the stock of MBI or any of its subsidiaries?

5. If MBI wishes to avoid the securities regulations of State E, may it do so by conducting all of its securities transactions in State E through a subsidiary set up in State F?

CHAPTER 6

Money and Banking

Chapter Outline

The world's money and banking system is neither coherent nor well organized. In the absence of a convenient set of laws or regulations, custom and practice regulate much of it. The system is highly informal. On the international plane, its players include national institutions governed by national laws, as well as international agencies, such as the International Monetary Fund and the Bank for International Settlements, whose operations are governed as often by informal agreements, plans, and accords as they are by treaties or conventions. On the domestic level, each country (or small group of countries) has its own national monetary system and its own specialized and often unique institutions.

A. MONEY

money: Anything customarily used as a medium of exchange and measure of value.

According to one dictionary, **money** is "anything customarily used as a medium of exchange and measure of value." Economists generally attribute three characteristics to money: it acts (a) as a means of exchange, (b) as a unit of measure or value, and (c) as a medium for storing value over time.[1]

Money can be both private and official. Private money commonly consists of a basket of official currencies, but it can also be a stock of rare metal or any other commodity that is easily transferable and reasonably nonspoilable. Official money is a unit of exchange issued by a

---

[1] J. Carter Murphy, "International Moneys: Official and Private," *International Lawyer,* vol. 23, p. 921 at p. 923 (1989).

government agency (such as a treasury department) or government-controlled financial institution (such as a central bank).[2]

Private money can be used only for making payments between private parties who agree in advance to its use. Most official money (i.e., coins and currency) can be used to pay debt of any kind, whether private or public. However, some types of official money, known as reserve currencies, (such as the International Monetary Fund's Special Drawing Right—the SDR may be used only by governments to pay other governments.

The Value of Money

While the value of property and services is measured by money, the value of money (i.e., official money) is "nominally" constant. That is, if one agrees to purchase something for 100 units of a specified currency (such as dollars, marks, pounds, or yen), the obligation can be discharged only by paying those particular 100 units. The obligation does not change because the purchasing power or conversion value of the currency has fluctuated. This principle is known as **nominalism**.[3]

If the parties to a contract have not taken care to anticipate changes in the value of the currency they use, the principle of nominalism "puts the risk of depreciation on the creditor and the risk of appreciation (or revaluation) on the debtor and neither part[y] can be heard to complain about unexpected losses."[4] National law in a few countries has mediated the harshness of this rule in extreme circumstances. In Germany, for example, the courts are allowed to revalue money if a currency has totally or almost totally collapsed.[5] In Argentina, Belgium, Germany, and Uruguay, claims are allowed where one party suffers because another fails to pay in a timely fashion and the value of the currency depreciates in the meantime. In England, Italy, and the United States, on the other hand, revaluation is not allowed.[6]

Application of the principle of nominalism can be avoided in the special case where currency is to be delivered not as money, but as a commodity. For example, the seller of a rare coin might be able to set aside the sale if he learns the coin is much more valuable than the agreed-upon price. In the case of *Richard v. American Union Bank*,[7] a dealer in foreign currency successfully argued that the currency he had agreed to buy was a commodity that had become worthless and therefore he was not obliged to accept delivery.

The Choice of Money

In domestic transactions, obligations are paid in local currency. In international transactions, the parties must designate the money that the buyer has to deliver. Actually, two monies have to be selected. First is the **money of account**. This is the money that expresses the amount of obligation owed. Second is the **money of payment**. This is the money that the buyer must use to pay for the items purchased. In most situations, the money chosen for both will be the same, but it does not have to be. For example, a seller may agree to deliver a product worth one million Australian dollars, and a buyer may agree to pay for it in Swiss francs.

In addition to selecting the money of account and the money of payment, contracting parties also need to select the place of payment. This is important because virtually all countries allow a foreign money obligation to be satisfied by payment in the local currency at the exchange rate effective on the date payment is due.[8] Absent a selection by the parties, the courts will determine

nominalism: The principle that an obligation to pay a particular sum of money is fixed and does not change even if the purchasing power or foreign exchange rate of the money does change.

money of account: The money used to define the amount of an obligation.

money of payment: The money used to pay off an obligation.

---

[2]The U.S. Uniform Commercial Code definition is typical of most countries. Section 1–201(24) states: "'Money' means a medium of exchange authorized or adopted by a domestic or foreign government and includes a monetary unit of account established by an intergovernmental organization or by agreement between two or more nations."

[3]F. A. Mann, *The Legal Aspect of Money,* pp. 80–114 (4th ed., 1982).

[4]*Id.,* p. 272.

[5]*Id.,* p. 285.

[6]*Id.,* p. 286–287. Keith S. Rosenn, "The Effects of Inflation on the Law of Obligations in Argentina, Brazil, Chile and Uruguay," *British Columbia International and Comparative Law Review,* vol. 2, p. 274 (1979).

In France the case law is inconsistent and no settled rule has evolved. F. A. Mann, *The Legal Aspect of Money,* p. 287 (4th ed., 1982).

[7]*New York Reports,* vol. 253, p. 166 (1930).

[8]F. A. Mann, *The Legal Aspect of Money,* p. 308 (4th ed., 1982). The conversion rate for foreign currency is specified in the U.S. Uniform Commercial Code as "the current bank-offered spot rate at the place of payment for the purchase of dollars on the day on which the instrument is paid." § 3-107. A similar formula is applied in most other countries.

the place of payment, and that determination can vary from country to country.[9] For example, if the United Nations Convention on Contracts for the International Sale of Goods applies, the place of payment will be the place of delivery (if such a place was designated), otherwise it will be the seller's place of business.[10]

By choosing a money of account, a money of payment, and a place for payment, the parties to a contract are also authorizing the courts in the states that issue those monies or the court in the state wherein payment is to take place to resolve disputes related to the interpretation or performance of the contract. This point is considered in Case 6–1.

---

[9]In some countries, payment is due at the seller's place of business; in others, at the buyer's place of business. F. A. Mann, *The Legal Aspect of Money,* pp. 214–219 (4th ed., 1982).
[10]Article 57(1).

Case 6–1   Republic of Argentina et al. v. Weltover, Inc. et al.

United States, Supreme Court, 1992.
United States Reports, vol. 504, p. 607 (1992).[11]

JUSTICE SCALIA DELIVERED THE OPINION OF THE COURT.

This case requires us to decide whether the Republic of Argentina's default on certain bonds issued as part of a plan to stabilize its currency . . . had a "direct effect in the United States" so as to subject Argentina to suit in an American court under the Foreign Sovereign Immunities Act of 1976.[12] . . .

Since Argentina's currency is not one of the mediums of exchange accepted on the international market, Argentine businesses engaging in foreign transactions must pay in U.S. dollars or some other internationally accepted currency. In the recent past, it was difficult for Argentine borrowers to obtain such funds, principally because of the instability of the Argentine currency. To address these problems, petitioners, the Republic of Argentina, and its central bank, Banco Central (collectively Argentina), in 1981 instituted a foreign exchange insurance contract program (FEIC), under which Argentina effectively agreed to assume the risk of currency depreciation in cross-border transactions involving Argentine borrowers. This was accomplished by Argentina's agreeing to sell to domestic borrowers, in exchange for a contractually predetermined amount of local currency, the necessary U.S. dollars to repay their foreign debts when they matured, irrespective of intervening devaluations.

MAP 6-1   Argentina (1992)

Unfortunately, Argentina did not possess sufficient reserves of U.S. dollars to cover the FEIC contracts as they became due in 1982. The Argentine government

---

[11]The text of this opinion is posted on the FindLaw Internet Web site at laws.findlaw.com/U.S./504/607.html.
[12]*United States Code,* Title 28, § 1602 et seq.

thereupon adopted certain emergency measures, including refinancing of the FEIC-backed debts by issuing to the creditors government bonds. These bonds, called "Bonods," provide for payment of interest and principal in U.S. dollars; payment may be made through transfer on the London, Frankfurt, Zurich, or New York market, at the election of the creditor. Under this refinancing program, the foreign creditor had the option of either accepting the Bonods in satisfaction of the initial debt, thereby substituting the Argentine government for the private debtor, or maintaining the debtor/creditor relationship with the private borrower and accepting the Argentine government as guarantor.

When the Bonods began to mature in May 1986, Argentina concluded that it lacked sufficient foreign exchange to retire them. Pursuant to a Presidential Decree, Argentina unilaterally extended the time for payment, and offered bondholders substitute instruments as a means of rescheduling the debts. Respondents, two Panamanian corporations and a Swiss bank who hold, collectively, $1.3 million of Bonods, refused to accept the rescheduling, and insisted on full payment, specifying New York as the place where payment should be made. Argentina did not pay, and respondents then brought this breach of contract action in the United States District Court for the Southern District of New York, relying on the Foreign Sovereign Immunities Act of 1976 as the basis for jurisdiction. Petitioners moved to dismiss for lack of subject matter jurisdiction, lack of personal jurisdiction, and *forum non conveniens*.[13] The District Court denied these motions, and the Court of Appeals affirmed. We granted Argentina's petition for *certiorari*,[14] which challenged the Court of Appeals' determination that, under the Act, Argentina was not immune from the jurisdiction of the federal courts in this case.

. . . The . . . question is whether Argentina's unilateral rescheduling of the Bonods had a "direct effect" in the United States.[15] . . . As the Court of Appeals recognized, an effect is "direct" if it follows "as an immediate consequence of the defendant's . . . activity."[16]

The Court of Appeals concluded that the rescheduling of the maturity dates obviously had a "direct effect" on respondents. It further concluded that the effect was sufficiently "in the United States" for purposes of the FSIA, in part because "Congress would have wanted an American court to entertain this action" in order to preserve New York City's status as "a preeminent commercial center."[17] The question, however, is not what Congress "would have wanted" but what Congress enacted in the FSIA. Although we are happy to endorse the Second Circuit's recognition of "New York's status as a world financial leader," the effect of Argentina's rescheduling in diminishing that status (assuming it is not too speculative to be considered an effect at all) is too remote and attenuated to satisfy the "direct effect" requirement of the FSIA.[18]

We nonetheless have little difficulty concluding that Argentina's unilateral rescheduling of the maturity dates on the Bonods had a "direct effect" in the United States. Respondents had designated their accounts in New York as the place of payment, and Argentina made some interest payments into those accounts before announcing that it was rescheduling the payments. Because New York was thus the place of performance for Argentina's ultimate contractual obligations, the rescheduling of those obligations necessarily had a "direct effect" in the United States: Money that was supposed to have been delivered to a New York bank for deposit was not forthcoming. We reject Argentina's suggestion that the "direct effect" requirement cannot be satisfied where the plaintiffs are all foreign corporations with no other connections to the United States. We expressly stated in *Verlinden* [*B.V. v. Central Bank of Nigeria*] that the FSIA permits "a foreign plaintiff to sue a foreign sovereign in the courts of the United States, provided the substantive requirements of the Act are satisfied."[19]

Finally, Argentina argues that a finding of jurisdiction in this case would violate the Due Process Clause of the Fifth Amendment [of the United States Constitution], and that, in order to avoid this difficulty, we must construe the "direct effect" requirement as embodying the "minimum contacts" test of *International Shoe Co. v. [State of] Washington*.[20] Assuming, without deciding, that a foreign state is a "person" for purposes of the Due Process Clause,[21] we find that Argentina possessed "minimum contacts" that would satisfy the constitutional test. By issuing negotiable debt instruments denominated in U.S. dollars and payable in New York

---

[13Latin: "inconvenient forum." Doctrine that a municipal court will decline to hear a dispute when it can be better or more conveniently heard in a foreign court.]

[14Latin: "to be made certain" or "to be certified." It is an order from a superior to an inferior court requiring the latter to produce a certified record of a particular case tried therein.]

15*United States Code,* Title 28, § 1602(a)(2).

16*Federal Reporter, Second Series,* vol. 941, p. 145 at p. 152 (Second Circuit Court of Appeals, 1991).

17*Id.,* at p. 153.

18*Id.*

19*United States Reports,* vol. 461, p. 480 at 489 (Supreme Court, 1983).

20*Id.,* vol. 326, p. 310 at p. 316 (Supreme Court, 1945). Argentina concedes that this issue "is before the Court only as an aid in interpreting the direct effect requirement of the Act" and that "[w]hether there is a constitutional basis for personal jurisdiction over [Argentina] is not before the Court as an independent question." Brief for Petitioners, p. 36, n. 33.

21*Confirm* South Carolina v. Katzenbach, *id.,* vol. 383, p. 301 at pp. 323–324 (Supreme Court, 1966) (states of the Union are not "persons" for purposes of the Due Process Clause).

and by appointing a financial agent in that city, Argentina "purposefully avail[ed] itself of the privilege of conducting activities within the [United States]."[22]

We conclude that Argentina's issuance of the Bonods . . . [and] its rescheduling of the maturity dates on those instruments . . . had a "direct effect: in the United States; and that the District Court therefore properly asserted jurisdiction, under the FSIA, over the breach of contract claim based on that rescheduling. Accordingly, the judgment of the Court of Appeals is *affirmed*. ■

[22]Burger King Corp. v. Rudzewicz, *id.,* vol. 471, p. 462 at p. 475 (Supreme Court, 1985), quoting Hanson v. Denckla, *id.,* vol. 357, p. 235 at p. 253 (Supreme Court, 1958).

Maintaining Monetary Value

maintenance of value clause: A contractual provision that says that the price will be adjusted according to the inflation rate.

A seller agrees to deliver 10,000 barrels of crude oil within three months to a buyer in Country X, with payment to be made in Country X's currency at the time of delivery. Country X's currency is inflating at 1,000 percent a year. How does the seller ensure that he will receive a fair price for the oil? Commonly, this is done by including a **maintenance of value clause** in the sales contract. Such a clause stipulates that the price is to be adjusted according to the inflation rate.[23]

A seller of commodities can also avoid the problem of inflation (and the buyer the problem of deflation) by designating a money of account which traditionally maintains its value. The currency most commonly used for this purpose is the American dollar, but the European Union euro, the Japanese yen, and the British pound are also widely used.

currency basket: A selected group of currencies whose weighted average is used to define the amount of an obligation.

A third mechanism for avoiding currency fluctuations is the use of a **currency basket**. That is, the money of account in a contract is defined by a weighted average of a selected group of currencies. The basket (or group of currencies) may be created *ad hoc* for a particular agreement. For example, the parties may agree that the money of account for their contract will be a "basket currency" made of American dollars, British pounds, and Japanese yen, with the dollar making up 50 percent of the value, the pound 30 percent, and the yen 20 percent. More commonly, however, parties will use an official basket currency established by intergovernmental organizations, such as the International Monetary Fund's Special Drawing Right (SDR).

Originally, the SDR was created to permit governments to discharge their international obligations. However, because the IMF publishes daily quotations on the exchange value of the SDR, the SDR has become widely accepted as a private currency basket. Today, private banks commonly accept deposits denominated in SDRs; and loans, especially those made by governments dealing with the IMF, are denominated in SDRs. (The current SDR basket, past changes in the makeup of the basket, a current valuation of the SDR in U.S. dollars, and change in the valuation of the SDR over the past 30 years are shown in Exhibit 6-1.)

B. THE INTERNATIONAL MONETARY FUND

Origin of the IMF

international monetary system: The world's informal money and banking system.

Because there is no single international currency that can be spent around the world, foreign currencies have to be converted into local currencies. The set of rules and procedures by which different national currencies are exchanged for each other in world trade is known as the **international monetary system**.

gold standard: A monetary system that provided for the free circulation between states of gold coins of standard specification.

The first modern international monetary system was the **gold standard**. In operation during the late nineteenth and early twentieth centuries, it provided for the free circulation between nations of gold coins of standard specification. The advantage of the gold standard was its stabilizing influence. If a state exported more than it imported, it would receive gold in payment for the difference. This influx of gold would raise domestic prices. These higher prices would then decrease demand for the state's exports and increase the state's internal demand for relatively cheap foreign imports. The result was an eventual return to the original price level. The principal

[23]The inflation rate is typically ascertained by reference to a published index. Until the value of gold began to fluctuate dramatically in the 1970s, gold was commonly used as a standard for ascertaining inflation. F. A. Mann, *The Legal Aspect of Money*, pp. 138–156, 161–172 (4th ed., 1982).

SDR Basket (For the 5-year period from January 1, 2002, to December 31, 2005)

Currency	Weight (%)
British pound	11
European Union euro	29
Japanese yen	15
U.S. dollar	45

Changes in SDR Basket

Date	Basket
January 1,1970	0.088867088 grams (1/35 of an ounce) of gold.
July 1, 1974	Australian dollar, Austrian schilling, Belgian franc, British pound, Canadian dollar, Danish krone, Dutch guilder, French franc, German mark, Italian lira, Japanese yen, Norwegian krone, South African rand, Spanish peseta, Swedish krona, U.S. dollar.
July 1, 1978	Australian dollar, Austrian schilling, Belgian franc, British pound, Canadian dollar, Dutch guilder, French franc, German mark, Iranian rial, Italian lira, Japanese yen, Norwegian krone, Saudi Arabian riyal, Spanish peseta, Swedish krona, U.S. dollar.
January 1, 1981	British pound, French franc, German mark, Japanese yen, U.S. dollar.
January 1, 2001	British pound, European Euro, Japanese yen, U.S. dollar.

SDR Valuation on July 10, 2002

Currency	Currency Amount[a]	Exchange Rate on July10[b]	U.S. Dollar Equivalent[c]
European Union euro	0.4260	0.99450	0.423657
Japanese yen	21.0000	117.72000	0.178389
British pound	0.0984	1.55210	0.152727
U.S. dollar	0.5770	1.00000	0.577000
		Total	1.331773

[a]The currency components of the SDR basket.

[b]Exchange rates in terms of currency units per U.S. dollar, except for the pound sterling, which is expressed in U.S. dollars per pound.

[c]The U.S. dollar equivalents of the currency amounts divided by the exchange rates.

Changes in SDR Valuation

Date	Valuation Basis	U.S. Dollar Equivalent
January 1, 1970	Gold	SDR 1.00 = U.S. $1.0000
July 1, 1974	Currency basket	SDR 1.00 = U.S. $1.2063
July 1, 1978	Currency basket	SDR 1.00 = U.S. $1.2395
January 1, 1981	Currency basket	SDR 1.00 = U.S. $1.2717
February 4, 1987	Currency basket	SDR 1.00 = U.S. $1.2677
August 26, 1991	Currency basket	SDR 1.00 = U.S. $1.3346
August 15, 1994	Currency basket	SDR 1.00 = U.S. $1.4561
August 28, 1998	Currency basket	SDR 1.00 = U.S. $1.3422
July 10, 2002	Currency basket	SDR 1.00 = U.S. $1.3318

EXHIBIT 6-1 The International Monetary Fund's Special Drawing Right (SDR)

Sources: IMF Survey (January 1981), *IMF Survey* (September 1991), *IMF Survey* (Supplement, August 1994), Special Drawing Rights: A Factsheet (April 15, 2002) posted on the Internet at www.imf.org/external/np/exr/facts/sdr.htm, and SDR Valuation (July 10, 2002) posted at www.imf.org/external/np/tre/sdr/basket.htm.

EXHIBIT 6-2

Harry Dexter White (1892–1948) **and John Maynard Keynes** (pronounced "canes," 1883–1946) were the two great intellectual founders of the IMF. Keynes, who served at the British Treasury before and during World War II, had revolutionized 20th Century economics with his classic book, *The General Theory of Employment, Interest and Money* (1936), in which he advocated government deficit-spending during depressions. White was the chief international economist for the United States Treasury from 1942 to 1944 and Assistant Secretary of the Treasury from 1944 to 1946. Both worked on developing a post-World War II economic system and both agreed on the need for international cooperation and for a mechanism for controlling currency exchanges. Keynes advocated the creation of a world central bank that could regulate the flow and distribution of credit. White proposed the creation of an international equalization "fund" that would promote the growth of international trade and preserve the role of the U.S. dollar in international trade. White's proposal prevailed at the 1944 Bretton Woods Conference, where the IMF Charter was drafted, because the United States was the dominant economic power at that time. Ultimately, the link to the dollar proved untenably and the Charter was amended in 1968 to provide for IMF's own reserve currency: the Special Drawing Right.

The Intellectual Founders of the International Monetary Fund Harry Dexter White and John Maynard Keynes (Photo: IMF.)

---

gold bullion standard:
A monetary system that required states to buy and sell gold bullion with paper currency at a fixed price.

Bretton Woods Conference: UN-sponsored monetary and financial conference held in Bretton Woods, New Hampshire, in July 1944. It led to the creation of the International Monetary Fund and the World Bank.

disadvantage of the gold standard was its inherent lack of liquidity: the world's supply of money was necessarily limited by the world's supply of gold. Additionally, any sizeable increase in the supply of gold, such as the discovery of a rich new mine, would cause prices to rise abruptly.

Because of its disadvantages, the gold standard broke down in 1914. It was replaced in the 1920s by the **gold bullion standard**. Under this system, states no longer minted gold coins; instead they backed their paper currencies with gold bullion and agreed to buy and sell the bullion at a fixed price.[24]

With the onset of the worldwide economic depression of the 1930s, the exchange of currencies became both unreliable and expensive. Deteriorating domestic economies[25] led to a widespread lack of confidence in paper money and a demand for gold that national treasuries could not meet. Nations with limited gold reserves, including the United Kingdom, were forced to abandon the gold standard, and because their money no longer bore a fixed relation to gold, its exchange became difficult.

Coupled with the difficulties of currency exchange were other detrimental depression-era economic policies, including protectionist tariffs and truculent international trade policies. In July 1944, the United Nations convened a meeting in the small town of Bretton Woods, New Hampshire, for the purpose of creating a new international monetary system and an international organization to oversee that system. Representatives of 44 nations attended the UN Monetary and Financial Conference (known as the **Bretton Woods Conference**)[26] to draft the

---

[24]*The Columbia Encyclopedia,* p. 1349 (5th ed., 1993).

[25]Between 1929 and 1932, prices of goods fell 48 percent worldwide and the value of international trade fell 63 percent. David D. Driscoll, *What Is the International Monetary Fund?* p. 3 (1989).

[26]This conference also created the International Bank for Reconstruction and Development (popularly known as the World Bank). The World Bank is discussed in Chapter 12.

International Monetary Fund (IMF): Intergovernmental organization headquartered in Washington. Using funds contributed by its members, it will purchase a currency on the application of a member to help the member discharge its international indebtedness and stabilize its currency exchange rates.

charter for the **International Monetary Fund (IMF)**. The IMF came into being on December 29, 1945, when its charter, formally known as the Articles of Agreement of the IMF, was signed by 29 states. The organization itself began operations in May 1946 at headquarters in the city of Washington.[27] Today, virtually every country in the world is a member of the IMF.[28]

The IMF was created to combat the international monetary and trade conditions that had helped to produce and prolong the Great Depression of the 1930s. The intellectual fathers of the IMF, British economist John Maynard Keynes and U.S. Treasury official Harry Dexter White, identified two such conditions: (1) currency inconvertibility and (2) the lack of a standard for determining the value of national currencies (because of the collapse of the gold bullion standard). To correct these conditions, the IMF was made the overseer of its member states' monetary and exchange rate policies and the guardian of a code of conduct. In particular, the Articles of Agreement establish a system of currency exchange (originally related to the value of gold but later, following an amendment to the Articles, based on exchange agreements) and a system for currency support (that allows the IMF to provide short-term financial resources to member states to help them correct payment imbalances).[29]

The Articles (as they are now amended) also establish a system of surveillance to ensure that member states abide by a code of conduct in their external monetary relations—specifically, that they do not borrow or lend at unsustainable levels, engage in protracted one-way interventions in the exchange market, or follow unwarranted monetary or fiscal policies for balance-of-payments purposes. The surveillance mechanism involves both the carrying on of regular bilateral consultations between the IMF and each member state and the preparation of semi-annual reviews (undertaken as part of a so-called World Economic Outlook exercise) that report on the economic and financial conditions of all of the IMF member states.[30]

In addition to currency exchange, currency support, and surveillance, the IMF maintains an extensive program of technical assistance through staff missions to member states. These staff missions help member states to reform their fiscal systems and budgetary controls and to establish or adapt institutional machinery, such as central banking and exchange systems.[31]

IMF Quotas

IMF quota: The amount of funds that a member of the International Monetary Fund is required to contribute. It determines the voting rights of a member and the sum of IMF funds that a member may draw upon to stabilize its currency and to meet balance-of-payments obligations.

To become a member of the IMF, a state must contribute a certain sum of money (expressed in SDRs) called a **quota** subscription.[32] (See Exhibit 6-3.) The quota is based on the relative size of a member state's economy, and it serves various purposes. First, members' quotas make up a pool of funds on which the IMF can draw to lend to a particular member having financial difficulties. Second, quotas determine how much a contributing member can borrow from the Fund and how much it will receive in periodic allocations of SDRs. Third, quotas determine the members' voting power in the IMF.[33] Those who contribute the most to the Fund are given the greatest say in setting its policies. For example, the United States currently has about 370,000 votes, or about 17 percent of the total, while Palau has only about 280 votes.[34] Currently, the IMF has a membership of 183 nations, the total amount of quotas is SDR 212.4 billion, and the total number of votes is 2,166,749.[35]

Quotas for a state seeking to join the IMF are determined initially by the IMF staff based on formulas that take into consideration the state's gross domestic product, its current account transactions, the variability of its current receipts, and its official reserves. The results of the

[27]David D. Driscoll, *What Is the International Monetary Fund?* p. 5 (1989); Margaret Garritsen de Vries, "Bretton Woods and the IMF's First 35 Years," *IMF Survey,* vol. 23, p. 217 (July 11, 1994).

[28]For a current list of members, *see* Exhibit 6–3.

[29]Union of International Associations, *Yearbook of International Organizations 1994/1995,* pp. 968–969 (1994).

[30]James M. Boughton, "IMF since 1979: Revolutions in the World Economy," *IMF Survey,* vol. 23, p. 220 (July 11, 1994).

[31]Union of International Associations, *Yearbook of International Organizations, 1994/1995,* p. 969 (1994).

[32]Seventy-five percent of a member's quota may be paid in its own currency; the other 25 percent has to be in a major convertible currency (such as British pounds, French francs, German marks, Japanese yen, or U.S. dollars). Articles of Agreement of the International Monetary Fund, Article III, § 3(a).

[33]Every member is given 250 basic votes plus 1 vote for each SDR 100,000 of its quota. *Id.,* Article XII, § 5(a).

[34]"IMF Members' Quotas and Voting Power, and IMF Governors" (June 28, 2002), posted at www.imf.org/external/np/sec/memdir/members.htm.

[35]*Id.*

Afghanistan	120.4	France[1]	10,738.5
Albania	48.7	Gabon[1]	154.3
Algeria[1]	1,254.7	Gambia[1]	31.1
Angola	286.3	Georgia[1]	150.3
Antigua and Barbuda[1]	13.5	Germany[1]	13,008.2
Argentina[1]	2,117.1	Ghana[1]	369.0
Armenia[1]	92.0	Greece[1]	823.0
Australia[1]	3,236.4	Grenada[1]	11.7
Austria[1]	1,872.3	Guatemala[1]	210.2
Azerbaijan	160.9	Guinea[1]	107.1
Bahamas[1]	130.3	Guinea-Bissau[1]	14.2
Bahrainf[1]	135.0	Guyana[1]	90.9
Bangladesh[1]	533.3	Haiti[1]	60.7
Barbados[1]	67.5	Honduras[1]	129.5
Belarus[1]	386.4	Hungary[1]	1,038.4
Belgium[1]	4,605.2	Iceland[1]	117.6
Belize[1]	18.8	India[1]	4,158.2
Benin[1]	61.9	Indonesia[1]	2,079.3
Bhutan	6.3	Iran	1,497.2
Bolivia[1]	171.5	Iraq	504.0
Bosnia and Herzegovina	169.1	Ireland[1]	838.4
Botswana[1]	63.0	Israel[1]	928.2
Brazil[1]	3,036.1	Italy[1]	7,055.5
Brunei Darussalam[1]	150.0	Jamaica[1]	273.5
Bulgaria[1]	640.2	Japan[1]	13,312.8
Burkina Faso[1]	60.2	Jordan[1]	170.5
Burundi	77.0	Kazakhstan[1]	365.7
Cambodia[1]	87.5	Kenya[1]	271.4
Cameroon[1]	185.7	Kiribati[1]	5.6
Canada[1]	6,369.2	Korea[1]	1,633.6
Cape Verde	9.6	Kuwait[1]	1,381.1
Central African Republic[1]	55.7	Kyrgyz Republic[1]	88.8
Chad[1]	56.0	Laos	52.9
Chile[1]	856.1	Latvia[1]	126.8
China[1]	6,369.2	Lebanon[1]	203.0
Colombia	774.0	Lesotho[1]	34.9
Comoros[1]	8.9	Liberia	71.3
Congo, Democratic Republic of[2]	291.0	Libya	1,123.7
Congo, Republic of[1]	84.6	Lithuania[1]	144.2
Costa Rica[1]	164.1	Luxembourg[1]	279.1
Côte d'Ivoire[1]	325.2	Macedonia[1]	68.9
Croatia[1]	365.1	Madagascar[1]	122.2
Cyprus[1]	139.6	Malawi[1]	69.4
Czech Republic[1]	819.3	Malaysia[1]	1,486.6
Denmark[1]	1,642.8	Maldives	8.2
Djibouti[1]	15.9	Mali[1]	93.3
Dominica[1]	8.2	Malta[1]	102.0
Dominican Republic[1]	218.9	Marshall Islands[1]	3.5
Ecuador[1]	302.3	Mauritania[1]	64.4
Egypt	943.7	Mauritius[1]	101.6
El Salvador[1]	171.3	Mexico[1]	2,585.8
Equatorial Guinea[1]	32.6	Micronesia[1]	5.1
Eritrea	15.9	Moldova[1]	123.2
Estonia[1]	65.2	Mongolia[1]	51.1
Ethiopia	133.7	Morocco[1]	588.2
Fiji[1]	70.3	Mozambique	113.6
Finland[1]	1,263.8	Myanmar	258.4

(continued)

EXHIBIT 6-3   International Monetary Fund Quotas (in Million SDRs), as of June 28, 2002

Namibia[1]	136.5	Slovakia[1]	357.5
Nepal[1]	71.3	Slovenia[1]	231.7
Netherlands[1]	5,162.4	Solomon Islands[1]	10.4
New Zealand[1]	894.6	Somalia	44.2
Nicaragua[1]	130.0	South Africa[1]	1,868.5
Niger[1]	65.8	Spain[1]	3,048.9
Nigeria	1,753.2	Sri Lanka[1]	413.4
Norway[1]	1,671.7	Sudan	169.7
Oman[1]	194.0	Suriname[1]	92.1
Pakistan[1]	1,033.7	Swaziland[1]	50.7
Palau[1]	3.1	Sweden[1]	2,395.5
Panama[1]	206.6	Switzerland[1]	3,458.5
Papua New Guinea[1]	131.6	Syria	293.6
Paraguay[1]	99.9	Tajikistan	87.0
Peru[1]	638.4	Tanzania[1]	198.9
Philippines[1]	879.9	Thailand[1]	1,081.9
Poland[1]	1,369.0	Togo[1]	73.4
Portugal[1]	867.4	Tonga[1]	6.9
Qatar[1]	263.8	Trinidad and Tobago[1]	335.6
Romania[1]	1,030.2	Tunisia[1]	286.5
Russia[1]	5,945.4	Turkey[1]	964.0
Rwanda[1]	80.1	Turkmenistan	75.2
St. Kitts and Nevis[1]	8.9	Uganda[1]	180.5
St. Lucia[1]	15.3	Ukraine[1]	1,372.0
St. Vincent and the Grenadines[1]	8.3	United Arab Emirates[1]	611.7
Samoa[1]	11.6	United Kingdom[1]	10,738.5
San Marino[1]	17.0	United States[1]	37,149.3
São Tomé and Príncipe	7.4	Uruguay[1]	306.5
Saudi Arabia[1]	6,985.5	Uzbekistan	275.6
Senegal[1]	161.8	Yemen[1]	243.5
Seychelles[1]	8.8	Yugoslavia	467.7
Sierra Leone[1]	103.7	Zambia[1]	489.1
Singapore[1]	862.5	Zimbabwe[1]	353.4

EXHIBIT 6-3 Continued

[1]These countries have accepted the obligations of Article VIII, Sections 2, 3, and 4 of the Articles of Agreement.

[2]The Democratic Republic of the Congo's voting rights were suspended effective June 2, 1994, pursuant to Article XXVI, Section 2(b) of the Articles of Agreement.

Source: IMF Members' Quotas and Voting Power, and IMF Governors, posted at www.imf.org/external/np/sec/memdir/members.htm.

staff's initial calculations are adjusted both in light of data from existing members of comparable economic size and characteristics and through negotiations with the applicant state. Then the IMF Executive Board and finally the IMF Board of Governors must approve the quota.[36]

The Board of Governors is required to make a general review of quotas at intervals of not more than five years and propose any adjustments that it considers appropriate, taking into consideration the growth of the world economy and changes in the relative economic positions of the members. Any quota changes must then be approved by member states having at least 70 percent of the Fund's total votes. In addition, the change is not effective for a particular state until the state itself both approves of the change and pays for it.[37]

The weighted majority vote and the requirement that each member state must approve its own quota change are considered in Case 6–2.

---

[36]"Where Does the IMF Get its Money? A Factsheet" (April 2002) posted at www.imf.org/external/np/exr/facts/finfac.htm.

[37]Articles of Agreement of the International Monetary Fund, Article III, §§ 2(a), 2(c), and 2(d); "Member Countries' Quotas Guide Their Access to IMF Resources," *IMF Survey,* pp. 6–7 (Supplement, August 1994).

Case 6–2   Re Law Authorizing an Increase in the French Quota to the International Monetary Fund

France, Constitutional Council, 1978.
Revue générale de droit international public, vol. 1979, p. 217 (1979); *International Law Reports*, vol. 74, p. 685 (1987).

On March 22, 1976, the International Monetary Fund's Board of Governors passed a resolution to increase the quotas of the IMF member states. At that time the IMF Articles of Agreement required changes in quotas to be approved by member countries having 85 percent of the IMF votes.[38] In addition, each member state had to consent to its own particular quota change.[39]

On April 30, 1976, the Board of Governors approved another resolution. Known as the Second Amendment Resolution, this measure was to amend the Articles of Agreement to abolish the requirement of defining currencies in terms of their value in gold and to allow member states to establish the exchange rate (or parity) of their currency by the standard of their choice. Because this was an amendment to the Articles of Agreement themselves, it had to be approved by a different criterion. In certain special circumstances, including proposals to change the par value of a member state's currency, an amendment had to be unanimously approved. Otherwise, an amendment came into force when it was approved by 60 percent of the members having at their disposal 80 percent of the total votes.[40] This latter majority was applied to the Second Amendment Resolution.

Both the quota change resolution and the Second Amendment Resolution were approved by their required majorities and came into force on April 1, 1978.

France, having been one of the states that had not acted to ratify the Second Amendment Resolution, then moved to approve the change in its quotas. The French government had not done this earlier because it did not believe that the Second Amendment Resolution itself would be adopted by the IMF member states.

Because the Second Amendment was already in effect, the government did not ask the French National Assembly for its approval. Instead, it asked only for the adoption of a law accepting the new quota established by the March 22, 1976, resolution (and which referred only indirectly to the fact that the Second Amendment had come into force). To have ratified the Second Amendment, the National Assembly would have had to follow the special procedures set out in Article 53 of the French Constitution. The approval of the change in the quota required no such special procedure.

On April 27, 1978, some 60 members of the National Assembly petitioned the French Constitutional Council asking it to find unconstitutional the law authorizing an increase in France's International Monetary Fund quota. They argued that the increase in France's quota could not be disassociated from the amendment to the Articles of Agreement of the Fund, and that the National Assembly could not consider the increase unless the amendment was considered too.

The basis for the petitioner's argument was the principle of national sovereignty. This, according to the petitioners, holds that no state can be a party to an international agreement unless it specifically agrees to do so. Thus, they contended, because France had not ratified the Second Amendment, it could not be a party to the IMF Articles of Agreement. And since France was not a party, the National Assembly should not have been asked to vote on the change in the French quota. Only, they claimed, if the National Assembly had first considered and then ratified the Second Amendment would it have been able to approve the change in the quota. Because the National Assembly had not considered the Second Amendment, its vote to adopt the quota change was, the petitioners said, unconstitutional.

DECISION OF THE CONSTITUTIONAL COUNCIL: . . .

In an attempt to show that the law providing for an increase in France's International Monetary Fund (IMF) quota is unconstitutional, the petitioners have argued that it cannot be disassociated from the proposal to amend the IMF Articles of Agreement. If this were so, then the two measures ought to have been presented to Parliament together for a vote in accordance with

---

[38]Article III, Section 2(c). As of December 30, 1991, quota changes can be approved by 70 percent.
[39]Article III, Section 2(d).
[40]Article XVII.

MAP 6-2   France (1978)

Article 53 of the Constitution and the principle of national sovereignty.

[The Adjustment of Quotas]

The adjustment of IMF quotas (which are now being changed for the sixth time since the IMF was established) is to be done in accordance with Article III, Section 2, of the original Articles of Agreement. That provision states:

> The Fund shall at intervals of five years review, and if it deems it appropriate propose an adjustment of, the quotas of the members.

By comparison, any proposal to amend the Articles of Agreement has to be done according to the special procedures laid down in Article XVII.

These two kinds of measures, which involve two different kinds of considerations, are legally independent of each other. This is underscored by the fact that the particular measures under consideration here were decided upon in two separate resolutions of the IMF Board of Governors and adopted on two different dates: March 22, 1976, for the Resolution relating to quotas and April 30, 1976, for the Resolution concerning the Second Amendment.

It is true that the March 22, 1976, resolution provided that no increase in quotas would take effect until after the Second Amendment Resolution was approved and the Second Amendment came into force. This provision, however, had no effect on the Second Amendment and it does not imply any interdependence between itself and the Second Amend-ment. . . . Accordingly, France's participation in the decision to increase quotas is a matter distinct and separate from its consideration of the Second Amendment and it can be decided independently of any consideration of that Amendment.

[The Principle of National Sovereignty]

As for the adoption of an amendment to the original Articles of Agreement of the Fund, Article XVII provides that such an amendment will come into force only after it is ratified by three-fifths of the members having at their disposal four-fifths of the total IMF votes. Only in three cases is unanimous approval required. Those cases are set out in Article XVII, paragraph b, and they include amendments that would alter the so-called parity provision; that is "that no change may be made in the par value of a member's currency except on the proposal of that member." The Second Amendment does not alter this provision.[41]

. . . The purpose of the parity rule is to safeguard the sovereignty of the member states of the IMF. . . . Indeed, the sovereignty of the member states is enhanced by the Second Amendment because it recognizes that each state is free to choose whatever system of exchange it wishes.

It cannot be denied that the vote on the Second Amendment attained the majority specified by Article XVII and that it subsequently came into force in all IMF member states on April 1, 1978. The Second Amendment is binding upon France by virtue of France having ratified the original International Monetary Fund Agreement according to the proper procedure on December 26, 1945. This is so, even though the procedure for obtaining the approval of the National Assembly that is set out in Article 53 of the Constitution was not followed in respect to the adoption of the Second Amendment.

In conclusion, the law submitted for the review of the Council is contrary neither to the provisions of Article 53 of the Constitution nor to the principle of national sovereignty.

The Constitutional Council therefore declares: *First*—The law authorizing an increase in France's quota to the International Monetary Fund is in conformity with the Constitution.

Second—This decision shall be published in the *Journal Officiel* of the French Republic. . . . ∎

---

[41]It was part of Article IV, Section 5(b) of the original text of the Articles of Agreement and it is repeated in the amended text in paragraph 6 of Annex C.

Organization of the IMF

The Board of Governors is the highest authority of the International Monetary Fund. It comprises a Governor and an Alternate Governor representing each IMF member state. The individuals who serve as Governors and Alternate Governors are usually the ministers of finance or the heads of the central banks of their states.[42] They convene at an annual meeting and may participate in votes by mail or by other means during the remainder of the year. Many of the powers of the Board of Governors have been delegated to an Executive Board made up of 24 directors, although the election of Directors, the conditions for the admission of new members, the adjustment of quotas, and certain other important matters remain the responsibility of the Board of Governors.[43]

The Executive Directors meet at least three times a week in formal sessions to oversee the implementation of the policies set by the Board of Governors. Seven of the 24 Directors represent individual member states: China, France, Germany, Japan, Saudi Arabia, the United Kingdom, and the United States. The other Directors represent groupings of the remaining states. The Executive Board seldom makes decisions on the basis of a formal vote; instead, it acts only when its members reach a consensus, a practice that minimizes confrontations on sensitive issues and that ensures full cooperation on the decisions that are taken.[44]

The Executive Board appoints a Managing Director to both chair the Executive Board and act as the IMF's head of staff. By tradition, the Managing Director is European. The international staff of some 2,650 is made up mainly of economists but also includes statisticians, researchers, experts in public finance and taxation, linguists, writers, and support personnel. Most of the staff are employed at the Fund's headquarters in Washington, but a few are assigned to small offices in Paris, Geneva, and New York. Unlike the Executive Directors, who represent particular states or groups of states, the Managing Director and the staff are responsible to the member states as a whole in carrying out the policies of the IMF.[45]

IMF Operations

A member state obligates itself upon joining the IMF to observe a code of conduct. This code requires the state to (1) keep other members informed of its arrangements for determining the value of its money relative to the money of other states, (2) refrain from placing restrictions on the exchange of its money, and (3) pursue economic policies that will increase in a constructive and orderly way both its own national wealth and that of all the IMF member states.[46] It is important to note that observation of this code is essentially voluntary. The IMF has no mechanism for compelling member states to conform, although it can and does exert moral pressure to encourage its members to comply. Should a state persistently ignore the code of conduct, the Board of Governors may declare that it is ineligible to borrow money from the IMF, or, as a last resort, an offending member can be expelled from the IMF by a vote of "a majority of the Governors having 85 percent of the total voting power."[47]

Since the Fund's creation in 1945, its member states have given it a variety of responsibilities that have changed with the times. Today, the Fund is responsible for (a) supervising a cooperative system of currency exchange, (b) lending money to members in order to support their currencies and their economies, and (c) providing auxiliary services to assist members in establishing and carrying out their external debt and other financial policies.[48]

C. CURRENCY EXCHANGE

Currency Exchange Obligations of IMF Member States

IMF par value system:
The currency exchange mechanism specified by the International Monetary Fund prior to 1971, which required all members to declare a value (the par value) at which their currencies could be converted into gold.

The currency exchange mechanism established in 1945 by the Articles of Agreement of the International Monetary Fund was called the **par value system**. That is, every member of the IMF, on joining the Fund, had to declare a value at which its currency could be converted into gold.

---

[42]"The IMF at a Glance: A Factsheet" (April 15, 2002) posted at www.imf.org/external/np/exr/facts/glance.htm.
[43]*Id.*
[44]*Id.*
[45]*Id.*
[46]*Id.*
[47]Articles of Agreement of the International Monetary Fund, Article XXVI, § 2(b).
[48]The IMF at a Glance: A Factsheet (April 15, 2002) posted at www.imf.org/external/np/exr/facts/glance.htm.

The U.S. dollar, for example, was pegged at 1/35 of an ounce of gold. Members were obliged to keep the value of their currency within 1 percent of this par value, and only upon consultation with the IMF and the other members of the Fund could a member make a change.[49]

The par value system worked well so long as inflation rates remained stable and unemployment was low in the major developed countries. It fell apart in the early 1970s, however, when inflation rates and unemployment grew sharply in the United States while remaining low in Europe and Japan. Foreign claims on American gold reserves increased[50] as the U.S. balance-of-payments deficit soared. The system effectively came to an end on August 15, 1971, when President Nixon terminated the convertibility of the dollar into gold. Its final breakdown occurred in 1973, when the United States announced a 10 percent devaluation of the dollar.

Three years lapsed before the IMF system could be reformed. The member states adopted the **Second Amendment** to the Articles of Agreement in 1976, effective in 1978. This new accord, which remains in effect today, allows members to define the value of their currency by any criteria except gold. Many member countries peg their currencies to the currencies of other countries, or to the IMF's Special Drawing Right, or to a currency basket. Others simply allow the value of their currencies to "float," that is, to be determined by international supply and demand.[51]

Although a member is free to adopt its own exchange arrangements, it is forbidden from "manipulating exchange rates or the international monetary system in order to prevent effective balance-of-payments adjustment or to gain an unfair competitive advantage over other members."[52] A member is also required "to collaborate with the Fund to promote exchange stability, to maintain orderly exchange arrangements with other members, and to avoid competitive exchange alterations."[53] In addition, members with floating exchange rates are required to "intervene on the foreign exchange market as necessary to prevent or moderate sharp and disruptive fluctuations from day to day and from week to week in the exchange value of its currency."[54]

Enforcement of Exchange Control Regulations of IMF Member States

Article VIII, Section 2(b), of the Articles of Agreement of the International Monetary Fund provides: "Exchange contracts which involve the currency of any member and which are contrary to the exchange control regulations of that member maintained or imposed consistently with this Agreement shall be unenforceable in the territories of any member. . . ."

The purpose of this provision is twofold: (1) to prevent one IMF member from frustrating the legitimate exchange controls of another member and (2) to deter private persons from violating exchange control regulations.[55] It can be invoked in three situations: (1) as a defense to a suit for the breach of an executory contract,[56] (2) as a cause of action for a foreign government to compel rescission or to obtain damages after the execution of a contract that violated its

---

IMF Second Amendment system: The currency exchange mechanism established by the International Monetary Fund in 1978 that allows members to define the value of their currency by any means other than by reference to the value of gold.

---

[49]For the history of the IMF and the par value system, *see* Robert Solomon, *The International Monetary System, 1945–1976* (1977); David D. Driscoll, *What Is the International Monetary System?* (1989), and "What Is the International Monetary Fund?" (August 2001) posted at www.imf.org/external/pubs/ft/exrp/what.htm.

[50]The exchange rate of $35 for an ounce made gold an irresistible bargain—so much so that U.S. gold reserves were inadequate to meet the demand. David D. Driscoll, *What Is the International Monetary System?* p. 9 (1989).

[51]Articles of Agreement of the International Monetary Fund, Article IV, § 2(b): " . . . [E]xchange arrangements may include (i) the maintenance by a member of a value for its currency in terms of the Special Drawing Right or another denominator, other than gold, selected by the member, or (ii) cooperative arrangements by which members maintain the value of their currencies in relation to the value of the currency or currencies of other members, or (iii) other exchange arrangements of a member's choice."

[52]*Id.,* Article IV, § 1(iii).

[53]*1974 International Monetary Fund Annual Report,* p. 112 (1974).

[54]*Id.,* p. 113.

[55]Keith L. Baker, "Enforcement of Contracts Violating Exchange Control Laws," *International Trade Law Journal,* vol. 3, p. 247 (1977); George B. Schwab, "The Unenforceability of International Contracts Violating Foreign Exchange Regulations: Article VIII, Section 2(b) of the International Monetary Fund Agreement," *Virginia Journal of International Law,* vol. 25, p. 967 (1985).

[56]*See* Perutz v. Bohemian Discount Bank in Liquidation, *New York Reports,* vol. 304, p. 533 (New York Ct. of Appeals, 1953); Southwestern Shipping Corp. v. National City Bank of New York, *New York Reports, Second Series,* vol. 6, p. 454 (New York Ct. of Appeals, 1959); J. Zeevi & Sons, Ltd. v. Grindlays Bank, Ltd. (Uganda), *New York Reports, Second Series,* vol. 37, p. 220 (New York Ct. of Appeals, 1975); Libra Bank, Ltd. v. Banco Nacional de Costa Rica, SA, *Federal Supplement,* vol. 570, p. 870 (District Ct. for the Southern District of New York, 1983).

exchange provisions,[57] and (3) as a cause of action for a private person to compel rescission or to obtain damages after the execution of a contract that violates a foreign exchange provision.[58]

The IMF Agreement grants to the Executive Board of the Fund the authority to interpret the provisions of the Agreement.[59] Pursuant to this authority, the Directors have interpreted Article VIII, Section 2(b), to mean that the principle of unenforceability is "effectively part [of every member country's] national law."[60] Courts in France, Luxembourg, and the United States have held that they are bound by the Directors' interpretation, and most commentators agree that the Directors' interpretation is binding on all member states' courts and agencies.[61]

The IMF Directors have not interpreted the meaning of the term "exchange contracts," although these words have been the focus of most of the litigation over Article VIII, Section 2(b). Courts on the European continent have generally given the term a broad meaning. In essence, they define **exchange contracts** as contracts that "in any way affect a country's exchange resources."[62]

An example of how the broad interpretation of "exchange contract" has been applied is provided in Case 6–3.

> **Continental European definition of "exchange contract":** Any contract that in any way affects the currency exchange resources of a country.

-----

[57]*See* Banco do Brasil, SA v. A. C. Israel Commodity Co., *New York Reports, Second Series,* vol. 12, p. 371 (New York Ct. of Appeals, 1963).

[58]*See* Banco Frances e Brasileiro, SA v. Doe, *New York Reports, Second Series,* vol. 36, p. 592 (New York Ct. of Appeals, 1975).

[59]Article XXIX(a).

[60]International Monetary Fund Annual Report, app. XIV, p. 82 (1949).

[61]The three court cases are: De Boer, Widow Moojen v. Ducro et al., Judgment of June 20, 1961, Court of Appeal of Paris, *Journal du droit International,* vol. 89, p. 719 (1962), *International Law Reports,* vol. 41, p. 46 (1963); Banco do Brasil, SA v. A. C. Israel Commodity Co., *New York Reports, Second Series,* vol. 12, p. 371 at pp. 376–377 (New York Ct. of Appeals, 1963); Société Filature et Tissage X. Jourdain v. Époux Heynen-Binter, Judgment of Feb. 1, 1956, Tribunal d'Arrondissement de Luxembourg, *Pasicrisie Luxembourgeoise,* p. 35 (1957), *International Law Reports,* vol. 22, p. 727 (1958). The commentators include John S. Williams, "Extrater-ritorial Enforcement of Exchange Control Regulations under the International Monetary Fund Agreement," *Virginia Journal of International Law,* vol. 15, p. 319 (1975); and George B. Schwab, "The Unenforce-ability of International Contracts Violating Foreign Exchange Regulations: Article VIII, Section 2(b) of the Inter-national Monetary Fund Agreement," *Virginia Journal of International Law,* vol. 25, p. 967 at p. 974 (1985).

[62]F. A. Mann, "The Private International Law of Exchange Contracts under the International Monetary Fund Agreement," *International & Comparative Law Quarterly,* vol. 2, p. 102 (1953).

Case 6–3 De Boer, Widow Moojen v. Ducro et al.

France, Court of Appeal of Paris, 1961.
Journal du droit international, vol. 89, p. 719 (1962);
International Law Reports, vol. 41, p. 46 (1963).

Pieter Moojen, a Dutch architect, owned 290 of the 300 shares issued by a French company, Gutenberg Immobilier, SARL, which operated an apartment building in Boulougne-sur-Seine, France. In 1950, while residing in a nursing home in the Netherlands, Moojen, a Dutch citizen, assigned 230 of his shares to his goddaughter, Eleonore Guese, a German citizen and the wife of Mr. von Reichert, for the sum of 1,380,000 French francs payable over two years. Pieter Ducro, who owned the other 10 shares in the company, was secretly a party to the assignment.

In 1953, Moojen sought to have the assignment set aside, and he brought suit in the Tribunal of Haarlem against Mrs. von Reichert and Pieter Ducro. He argued that the assignment was void because both he and his assignee had violated Dutch exchange laws in making the transaction; that the transaction was actually a disguised gift; and that due to his poor health at the time, he was unaware of the contents of the agreement. Some two and one-half weeks after Pieter Moojen died on April 1, 1955, the Tribunal found in his favor, holding that Dutch exchange control regulations require Dutch residents to obtain a license from the Netherlands National Bank before they dispose of foreign assets. The Court of Appeal of Amsterdam affirmed the Tribunal's decision the following year.

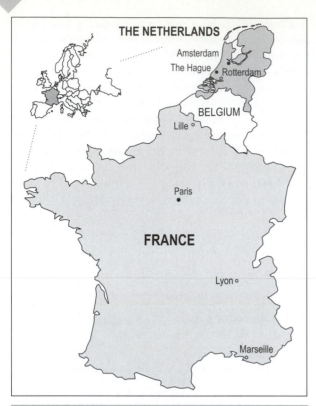

MAP 6-3 France and the Netherlands (1961)

In 1957, Anna de Boer, widow of Pieter Moojen, sought to obtain an exequatur[63] *from a Tribunal in Paris so that the Dutch judgment could be enforced in France. The Tribunal refused, stating that Pieter Moojen had been a resident of France at the time the assignment had been made and that French law therefore controlled. Anna de Boer appealed.*

THE COURT:

. . . France and the Netherlands both participated in the United Nations Monetary Conference held at Bretton Woods from July 1 to July 22, 1944, and they both subsequently became members of the International Monetary Fund (IMF) set up at that conference. Article VIII, Section 2, of the IMF's Articles of Agreement provides that "exchange contracts which involve the currency of any member and which are contrary to the exchange control regulations of that member maintained or imposed consistently with this Agreement shall be unenforceable in the territories of any member." The Articles of Agreement of the IMF confer on the [Executive Board of the] Fund the power to interpret its provisions.[64] By virtue of this power, the [Executive Board of the] Fund has interpreted Article VIII, Section 2, as follows:

1. Parties entering into exchange contracts involving the currency of any member of the Fund and contrary to the exchange control regulations of that member which are maintained or imposed consistently with the Fund Agreement will not receive the assistance of the judicial or administrative authorities of other members in obtaining the performance of such contracts. That is to say, the obligations of such contracts will not be implemented by the judicial or administrative authorities of member countries, for example, by decreeing performance of the contracts or by awarding damages for their nonperformance.
2. By accepting the Fund Agreement, members have undertaken to make the principle mentioned above effectively part of their national law. . . .

As a consequence of this interpretation, this Court is precluded from holding that the Dutch court orders giving effect to the Dutch currency control legislation of October 10, 1945, are contrary to French international public policy or that they violate French rules on the conflicts of laws.

Nevertheless, this Court may consider whether the facts support the conclusion reached by the Dutch courts that the transaction in question violated Dutch currency exchange regulations.

The facts show that Moojen, who had an apoplectic fit in Paris on December 2, 1949, was taken to The Hague on December 30 of that same year. The facts further show that on April 12, 1950, while in a nursing home in The Hague, he executed the contract of assignment of shares. Thus, the facts establish that Moojen had his actual residence in the Netherlands at the time of the execution of that contract. . . .

Despite the fact that Moojen had his residence in the Netherlands at the time, the respondents (Mr. and Mrs. von Reichert, Gutenberg Immobilier, SARL, and Mr. Ducro) argue that the April 12th contract was not an "exchange contract" within the meaning of Article VIII, Section 2, of the Articles of Agreement of the International Monetary Fund because (a) it involved the sale of shares in a French real estate company, and (b) the price of the sale was expressed in French francs (i.e., the legal currency of the country where the Company has its registered office and carries on its business).

The respondents assert that the true function of the International Monetary Fund (as it was agreed to at the Bretton Woods Conference) is to establish and maintain stable currency exchange rates. Accordingly, the Articles of Agreement of the IMF seek to limit the currency exchange

---

[63]Latin: "he may perform." An endorsement added by a court in a civil law country to the transcript of a foreign judgment that authorizes the judgment to be executed locally.

[64]Article XVIII [now Article XXIX following the adoption of the Second Amendment to the IMF Articles of Agreement].

controls of member states to those which are necessary to maintain stable rates (and, in particular, to prevent what is commonly called "capital flight"). In other words, any such controls have to be restrictively construed.

The respondents further argue that a law regulating the exchange of an asset located abroad for a currency also located abroad cannot in itself have any effect on the stability of a country's currency exchange rate. This is because currency exchange rates are effected only by the exchange of currency located within the regulating country for foreign currency or assets located outside that country. In this case, the respondents assert, no flight of Dutch capital was to be feared. The transaction in question did not affect the stability of the guilder or the foreign currency reserves of the National Bank of the Netherlands either directly or indirectly.

This Court disagrees that currency exchange controls are to be interpreted restrictively. It must be recalled that the primary purpose of the Agreements signed at Bretton Woods [creating the International Monetary Fund and the World Bank] was "to promote international monetary cooperation." Thus, in order to implement this goal of efficient cooperation as fully as possible, this Court will consider whether the contract in question might have any detrimental effect on the financial situation of the concerned member state. In other words, we will consider whether this particular transaction was apt, in any way, to affect the currency resources of that country.

We believe that the April 12, 1950, contract, even though it was expressed in French francs, can affect the Dutch economy. This is because the Dutch Treasury can expect that its resident nationals, having obtained a fair price for shares sold abroad, will repatriate the currency they have obtained.

The respondents next contend that the wording of Article VIII . . . requires, as does the general focus of the Agreements signed at Bretton Woods, that the scope of the term "exchange contract" used in paragraph (b) of Article VIII be limited by the restrictions set out in paragraph (a). In other words, they say, the exchange contract described in paragraph (b) is only concerned with transfers and payments involving current international transactions. Thus, because Moojen's assignment of shares was neither a capital transfer within the meaning of Article VI, Section 3, nor a transfer or payment involving a current transaction, as defined by Article XIX, paragraph 1, the respondents conclude that the Dutch attempt to restrict that assignment violates the IMF Articles of Agreement.

We do not agree. Looking at the whole of the text of the articles just referred to, especially at the titles, it is clear that while the signatories of the IMF Agreement meant, on the one hand, to prohibit member states from imposing restrictions on the payment of current international transactions without the approval of the Fund, they did not mean, on the other hand, to impose the same prohibitions on other kinds of transactions such as the sale or transfer by a national of assets located abroad.

* * *

Finally, the respondents argue that the words "*non exécutoire*" in Article VIII (which are translated as "unenforceable" in the corresponding English text) indicate that the only consequence of a breach of Article VIII is that the affected contract is unenforceable in a court; it is not, however, void. Thus, outside of a court, the contract would continue to be valid as a sort of natural obligation.

We have to rule against such an interpretation. . . . To allow either party, at his or her discretion, to chose, or to refuse, to carry out a contract would produce anarchy. . . .

The appeal was allowed. Anna de Boer's request to have the Dutch court order enforced in France was granted. ◼

Anglo-American definition of "exchange contract": A contract having as its immediate object the international exchange of mediums of payment.

American and British courts restrictively define the term **exchange contract**.[65] They hold that an exchange contract is one having as its immediate object the exchange of international mediums of payment, which is usually the exchange of one currency for another.[66] This interpretation excludes (1) securities contracts, (2) sales contracts (including sales of precious metals),

---

[65] In Mansouri v. Singh, *All England Law Reports,* vol. 2, p. 619 (1986), Lord Justice Neill stated for the English Court of Appeal: "The term 'exchange contract' in § 2(b) of article VIII is to be interpreted narrowly. The term is confined to contracts to exchange the currency of one country for the currency of another; it does not include contracts entered into in connection with sales of goods which require the conversion by the buyer of one currency into another in order to enable him to pay the purchase price. . . ."

[66] This definition originated with Arthur Nussbaum in his article "Exchange Control and the International Monetary Fund," *Yale Law Journal,* vol. 59, p. 426 (1949). *See* John S. Williams, "Extraterritorial Enforcement of Exchange Controls under the International Monetary Fund Agreement," *Virginia Journal of International* Law, vol. 15, p. 333 (1975); and George B. Schwab, "The Unenforceability of International Contracts Violating Foreign Exchange Regulations: Article VIII, Section 2(b) of the International Monetary Fund Agreement," *Virginia Journal of International Law,* vol. 25, p. 982 (1985).

and (3) loans (including letters of credits).[67] Case 6–4 illustrates the reasoning used by courts for adopting the narrow interpretation of Article VIII, Section 2(b).

[67]*See* Arthur Nussbaum, "Exchange Control and the International Monetary Fund," *Yale Law Journal,* vol. 59, p. 426 (1949) (securities contracts); Wilson, Smithett & Cope, Ltd. v. Terruzzi, *All England Law Reports,* vol. 1976, pt. 1, p. 817 (1976) (sales of metals); Libra Bank Ltd. v. Banco Nacional de Costa Rica, *Federal Supplement,* vol. 570, p. 899–900 (U.S. District Court for the Southern District of New York, 1983) (loans). But compare United City Merchants (Investment) Ltd. v. Royal Bank of Canada, *All England Law Reports,* vol. 1982, pt. 2, p. 720 at p. 729 (1982), which held that a letter-of-credit transaction was a "monetary contract in disguise."

Case 6–4   Wilson, Smithett & Cope, Ltd. v. Terruzzi

England, Court of Appeal, 1976.
All England Law Reports, vol. 1976, pt. 1, p. 817 (1976).

LORD DENNING, MASTER OF THE ROLLS:

Signor Terruzzi lives in Milan. He is a dealer in metals, trading under the name Terruzzi Metalli. But he is also, it seems, a gambler in differences. He speculates on the rise or fall in the price of zinc, copper and so forth. He speculated in 1973 on the London Metal Exchange. He did so in plain breach of the Italian laws of exchange control. These provide that residents in Italy are not to come under obligations to non-residents save with ministerial authority. Signor Terruzzi never obtained permission.

In making his speculations, Signor Terruzzi established an account with London dealers, Wilson, Smithett & Cope, Ltd. He was introduced to them by their Milan agent, Signor Giuliani, and made his deals through him. All the transactions were in sterling and reduced into writing on the standard contract forms of the London Metal Exchange. Sometimes Signor Terruzzi was a "bull." That is, he thought that the price was likely to rise in the near future. So he bought metal from the London dealers at a low price for delivery three months ahead, not meaning ever to take delivery of it, but intending to sell it back to the London dealers at a higher price before the delivery date, thus showing him a profit in his account with the London dealers. At other times he was a "bear." That is, he thought that the price was likely to fall in the near future. So he sold metal "short" (which he had not got) to the London dealers at a high price for delivery three months ahead, not meaning ever to deliver it, but intending to buy back from the London dealers a like quantity at a lower price before the delivery date, thus showing him a profit in his account with the London dealers. Such transactions would have been gaming contracts if *both* parties had never intended to make or accept delivery, and they would not have been enforced by the English courts. But the London dealers were not parties to any such intention. They always intended to make or accept delivery according to the contracts they made. So far as the London dealers were concerned, they were genuine commercial transactions. They were enforceable accordingly by the English courts.[68] But they were not enforceable in the Italian courts because they infringed the exchange control.

The critical months here were October and November 1973. The price of zinc was very high. The price for "forward" delivery (that is for delivery three months ahead) had been steadily rising from £465 on 18th October 1973 to £520 on 7th November. Signor Terruzzi thought that the price was much too high and that it was likely to fall soon. So he made a series of contracts with the London dealers whereby he sold to them 1,200 tons of zinc for delivery in the next three months. He sold "short," that is he had then no zinc to meet his obligations. Unfortunately for Signor Terruzzi, his forecast was wrong. Even after 7th November the price did not fall. It rose steeply. So much so that within a week it had risen to £650 a ton. By 12th November 1973 the London dealers were anxious as to the ability of Signor Terruzzi to meet his commitments. They asked him to provide a deposit or "margin" of £50,000, as they were entitled to do under the contracts. On the evening of Tuesday, 13th November, Signor Giuliani, on behalf of the London dealers, met Signor Terruzzi at the Café Ricci in Milan. He told him the state of the account. Signor

[68]*See* Bassett v. Sanker, *Times Law Reports,* vol. 41, p. 660 (1925) (London Metal Exchange); Weddle, Beck & Co. v. Hackett, *All England Law Reports,* vol. 1928, p. 539 (1928) (London Stock Exchange); Woodward v. Wolfe, *All England Law Reports,* vol. 1936, pt. 3, p. 529 (1936) (Liverpool Cotton Exchange); Garnac Grain Co., Inc. v. HMF Faure & Fairclough, Ltd., and Bunge Corp. *All England Law Reports,* vol. 1965, pt. 3, p. 273 (1965) (contracts for lard).

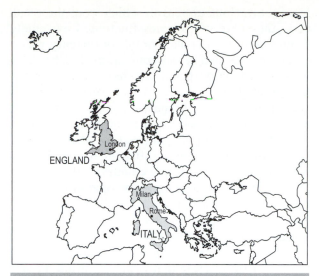

MAP 6-4   Italy and England (1976)

Nations. The object was to organize their monetary systems so as to meet the post-war problems. At this conference the United Kingdom was represented by the distinguished economist, Lord Keynes, and by the legal adviser to the Foreign Office, Sir Eric Beckett. In July 1944, Articles of Agreement were drawn up and signed. By the Agreement the International Monetary Fund was established and provisions were made (amongst other things) "to promote international monetary cooperation" and "to promote exchange stability." In 1945, Parliament passed an Act to give effect to the Agreement. In January 1946, an order in council, the Bretton Woods Agreements Order in Council 1946, was made giving the force of law to this provision, among others:

> *Article VIII, Section 2(b).* Exchange contracts which involve the currency of any member and which are contrary to the exchange control regulations of that member maintained or imposed consistently with this Agreement shall be unenforceable in the territories of any member. . . .

That provision is part of the law of England, but it has given rise to much controversy, particularly as to the meaning of the words "exchange contracts." There are two rival views. First, the view of Professor Nussbaum set out in 1949 in the *Yale Law Journal*.[69] He said that "an exchange contract" is exclusively concerned with the handling of international media of payment as such. Therefore, contracts involving securities or merchandise cannot be considered as exchange contracts except when they are monetary transactions in disguise. This view is in accord with the meaning given by Lord Radcliffe in *Re United Railways of the Havana and Regla Warehouses, Ltd.*:[70]

> . . . a true exchange contract . . . is a contract to exchange the currency of one country for the currency of another. . . .

Second, the view of Dr. F. A. Mann set out in 1949 in the *British Year Book of International Law* and in his book, *The Legal Aspect of Money*. He said that "exchange contracts" are contracts which in any way affect a country's exchange resources—a phrase which I accepted without question in *Sharif v. Azad*,[71] in the belief that, coming from such a source, it must be right. Dr. Mann recognizes that his view makes the word "exchange" redundant and thus seems counter to established methods of interpretation. But he contends that it is in better harmony with the purpose of the Agreements.

Dr. Mann suggests that the lawyers did not take much part in drafting the Bretton Woods Agreements. In this he is mistaken. I trust that I may be forgiven a

Terruzzi flamed with anger. He said that he was not going to pay anything to the London dealers by way of margin, or otherwise, and they could take him to court. Signor Giuliani telephoned the London dealers. They were fearful that the price might go still higher. There were frantic telexes. In the result the London dealers "closed" the contracts with him, as they were entitled to do under the written terms thereof. They sold back to him 1,200 tons of zinc at the ruling price. They telexed him with details. The result showed a balance due to the London dealers amounting to £220,440.38; and credit was due to him on previous profits of £25,418.37. So on balance the sum of £195,022.01 was due from him to them. On 10th January 1974 they issued a writ against him for that amount in the High Court in England. He got leave to defend by swearing, quite untruly, that the transactions had been carried out without his knowledge or authority. Afterwards he took a different line. He said that the London dealers had failed to advise him properly about the transactions. The trial opened on 9th October 1974. He came to London for the first day. He went back to Italy for the weekend. He had a heart attack there. He never returned to the trial. All his defenses crumbled. So did his counterclaim. The only point which remained was that the contracts were "exchange contracts" and were unenforceable against him by reason of the Bretton Woods Agreements. Judge Kerr decided against him. Signor Terruzzi appeals to this court.

Now for the Bretton Woods Agreements. Bretton Woods is a small town in New Hampshire, U.S.A, but it has a place in history. During the Second World War, even in the midst of raging hostilities, there was a conference there attended by the members of the United

---

[69]*Yale Law Journal,* vol. 59, p. 421 at pp. 426, 427 (1949).
[70]*All England Law Reports,* vol. 1960, pt. 2, p. 332 at p. 350 (1960).
[71]*Id.,* vol. 1966, pt. 3, p. 785 at p. 787 (1966).

digression if I borrow from the argument of counsel for the plaintiffs and recite part of the speech which Lord Keynes made at the Final Act of the Conference (as recorded by Sir Roy Harrod in his biography of Keynes):

> And, for my own part, I should like to pay a particular tribute to our lawyers. All the more so because I have to confess that, generally speaking, I do not like lawyers. I have been known to complain that, to judge from results in this lawyer-ridden land, the *Mayflower*, when she sailed from Plymouth, must have been entirely filled with lawyers. When I first visited Mr. Morgenthau in Washington some three years ago accompanied only by my secretary, the boys in your Treasury curiously enquired of him—where is your lawyer? When it was explained that I had none— "Who then does your thinking for you?" was the rejoinder. . . . [O]nly too often [our lawyers] have had to do our thinking for us. We owe a great deal of gratitude to Dean Acheson, Oscar Cox, Luxford, Brenner, Collado, Arnold, Chang, Broches and our own Beckett of the British Delegation.[72]

So the lawyers did play a large part. I have no doubt that they had in mind an evil which was very much in evidence in the years after the First World War. It is strikingly illustrated by the notorious case of *Ironmonger & Co. v. Dyne*[73] in which a lady, Mrs. Bradley Dyne, speculated in foreign currency. She did it at the instance of prominent officials in the Foreign Office. She dealt with bankers in Throgmorton Street. She used to buy from the bankers French francs and Italian lire for delivery three months in the future; but, before the time for delivery arrived, she sold them again. If the price went up, she took the difference as a "profit." If the price went down, she was liable to pay the difference as a "loss." In no single case was any currency delivered. She operated on an enormous scale. In three years the turnover amounted to 421 million francs and 17 million lira, and large sums in other currencies as well. At the end she was much in debt to the bankers for her "losses." They sued her for it. She pleaded the Gaming Act. Her plea failed because, so far as the bankers were concerned, they were genuine transactions which created obligations to fulfill the contracts according to their tenor if circumstances required it. She was held liable. The British government declared that the transactions were a disgrace to the Civil Service and punished the Foreign Office officials who had engaged in them. But the case is important for present purposes because it shows the great mischief which can be done by such speculations. Lord Justice Scrutton described it in these words:

> The transactions in question were not of a pleasant nature. After the War, while Europe was recovering from the various upheavals which were the result of it, the value of currency fluctuated extremely. Contracts for the purchase or sale of currency, which, before the War had been a comparatively sober business, became very speculative in their making and their result. It was possible to make very large profits and equally possible to make very great losses, and, as was to be expected when great profits might be made, the birds of prey gathered together. Reckless speculators, absolutely indifferent to the damage that they were doing to the country in the currency of which they were dealing, began operations. People bought and sold currency to a very large extent, with the most disastrous results to the countries concerned. That was particularly the case with regard to the sales and purchases of French currency, which went near to bringing that country to ruin. People who indulged in those speculations were beneath contempt and ought to be condemned. They were utterly selfish, and had no regard at all to the enormous injury which they were inflicting on the legitimate trade of the country in whose exchange they were speculating.[74]

The mischief being thus exposed, it seems to me that the participants at Bretton Woods inserted Article VIII, § 2(b), in the Agreement so as to stop it. They determined to make exchange contracts of that kind—for the exchange of currencies—unenforceable in the territories of any member. I do not know of any similar mischief in regard to other contracts, that is contracts for the sale or purchase of merchandise or commodities. Businessmen have to encounter fluctuations in the price of goods, but this is altogether different from the fluctuations in exchange rates. So far from there being any mischief, it seems to me that it is in the interest of international trade that there should be no restriction on contracts for the sale and purchase of merchandise and commodities; and that they should be enforceable in the territories of the members.

The Bretton Woods Agreements made provision to that end. Thus Article 1(ii) says that one of the purposes of the International Monetary Fund is to "facilitate the expansion and balanced growth of international trade. . . ." Article VI, § 3, and Article VIII, § 2(a), coupled with Article XIX(i), say that no member is to impose restrictions on payments due "in connection with foreign trade, other current business, including services, and normal short-term banking and credit facilities."

In conformity with those provisions, I would hold that the Bretton Woods Agreements should not do anything to hinder legitimate contracts for the sale or purchase of merchandise or commodities. The words

---

[72]R. F. Harrod, *Life of John Maynard Keynes,* p. 583 (1951).
[73]*Times Law Reports,* vol. 44, p. 497 (1928).
[74]*Id.,* at p. 498.

"exchange contracts" in Article VIII, § 2(b), refer only to contracts to exchange the currency of one country for the currency of another. The words "which involve the currency of any member" fit in well with this meaning, but it is difficult to give them any sensible meaning in regard to other contracts. They show that the section is only dealing with the currencies of members of the fund, and not with the currencies of nonmembers. The reference to regulations "maintained or enforced consistently with this Agreement" covers such regulations as those of Italy here.

It is no doubt possible for men of business to seek to avoid Article VIII, § 2(b), by various artifices. But I hope that the courts will be able to look at the substance of the contracts and not at the form. If the contracts are not legitimate contracts for the sale or purchase of merchandise or commodities, but are instead what Professor Nussbaum calls "monetary transactions in disguise,"[75] as a means of manipulating currencies, they would be caught by § 2(b).

I will not say more save to express my appreciation of the judgment of Justice Kerr. He has covered the whole subject most satisfactorily. In my opinion the contracts here were legitimate contracts for the sale and purchase of metals. They were not "exchange contracts." The London dealers are entitled to enforce them in this country. I would dismiss the appeal accordingly.

The appeal was dismissed and leave to appeal to the House of Lords was refused. ■

---

[75]*Yale Law Journal,* vol. 59, p. 421 at p. 427 (1949).

Finally, the International Monetary Fund's Articles of Agreement do not describe what constitutes currency exchange regulations, other than to note that they must be "maintained or imposed consistently" with the Articles of Agreement.[76] As with other regulations, however, it seems evident that they need to be adopted in accordance with a member state's constitution and laws and properly promulgated.

Enforcement of Exchange Control Laws in the Absence of IMF Membership

The provision in Article VIII, Section 2(b), of the IMF's Articles of Agreement requiring member states to give effect to the currency exchange regulations of other members is at odds with a longstanding choice of law rule that holds that states do not enforce the revenue laws of other states. The civil code in civil law countries often expressly prohibits the enforcement of foreign revenue laws, including currency exchange regulations.[77] The common law countries apply a court-made rule to the same effect, which they trace to a now famous dictum by Lord Mansfield in an international smuggling case that "no country ever takes notice of the revenue laws of another."[78]

The rationale for this rule (both in civil law and common law countries) is that the enforcement of foreign revenue laws infringes on the sovereign rights of the forum state. The rule and the rationalization have been criticized, however, as legally and economically unsound in light of the contemporary interdependence of nations.[79] Nevertheless, the rule continues to be universally observed.

However, because most nations of the world are members of the International Monetary Fund, the provision in Article VIII, Section 2(b), of the IMF Articles of Agreement effectively overrides the traditional nonenforcement rule in most cases. Of course, not all countries are members of the IMF. When their currency exchange regulations are at issue, those regulations will not, as Case 6–5 illustrates, be enforced abroad.

---

[76]Article VIII, § 2(b).
[77]*See* Basso v. Janda, *Bulletin des ârrets de la Cour de cassation, première section civile,* no. 2967, p. 222 (1967); *International Law Reports,* vol. 48, p. 229 (1975).
[78]Holman v. Johnson, *English Reports,* vol. 98, p. 1120 at p. 1121 (1775).
[79]Banco Frances e Brasiliero, SA v. Doe, *North Eastern Reporter, Second Series,* vol. 331, p. 502 at pp. 505–506 (1975).

Case 6–5   Menendez v. Saks and Company

United States, Court of Appeals, Second Circuit, 1973.
Federal Reporter, Second Series, vol. 485, p. 1355 (1973).

On September 15, 1960, the Cuban government "inter-
vened"[80] in the operation of (i.e., it nationalized) the five
leading manufacturers of Cuban cigars (F. Palacio y
Compañia, SA; Tabacaler José L. Piedra, SA; Por
Larranga, SA; Cifuentes y Compañia; and Menendez,
Garcia y Compañia, Limitada). These manufacturers for
many years had produced cigars of the highest quality
and reputation and had sold them to importers in the
United States, principally the parties being sued in this
case, Faber, Coe & Gregg (Faber), Alfred Dunhill of
London (Dunhill), and Saks & Company (Saks). The
importers paid for the cigars in U.S. dollars by checks
drawn on New York banks and made payable either (1) to
the Cuban exporter, (2) to a New York bank acting as the
exporter's collecting agent, or (3) to the order of the
Cuban exporter and/or the New York collecting bank.
Payments made to the New York collecting banks were
transmitted by those banks to the Banco Nacional de
Cuba, which in turn credited the exporters with pesos in
their own Cuban banks.[81]

Upon the Cuban government's intervention, the
owners were immediately ousted and the government
designated persons called "interventors" as its agents
to manage the businesses. The interventors continued
to operate the businesses and to export cigars under
the same company names to the same importers in the
United States. The importers continued to make some
payments through their usual channels, but most of these
payments were intended to cover only the amounts still
owing for the preintervention shipments. Although the
importers accepted the cigars shipped after the interven-
tion, they did not pay for most of them. Shipments from
Cuba to the U.S. importers continued until February
1961, when relations between the interventors and the
importers deteriorated for various reasons. In February
1962, the U.S. government declared an embargo on future
trade with Cuba.

Immediately after the Cuban government seized the
cigar manufacturing companies, the owners of those busi-
nesses fled to the United States and brought actions in
New York against the importers to collect the sums due
for cigars shipped from their factories in Cuba. Shortly
thereafter, the interventors sought to intervene in these
actions to replace the owners in prosecuting claims

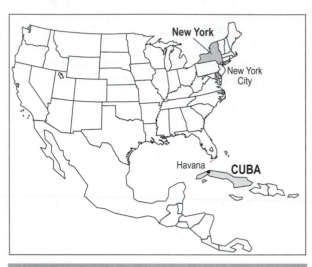

MAP 6-5   Cuba and the United States (1973)

against the importers. The government of Cuba also inter-
vened to support the claims of the interventors.

The trial court held that the importers had to pay the
original owners for the cigars exported to the United States
before their companies were nationalized and the inter-
ventors for the cigars sold after that time. The importers
were also allowed to offset monies they had previously
paid the interventors. All of the parties appealed.

CIRCUIT JUDGE MANSFIELD:

* * *

. . . The interventors insist that they, rather than the
owners, are entitled to the proceeds paid or payable by
the importers for the preintervention shipments. They
claim that the owners' accounts receivable were
included in the property effectively seized by the intervention. They further argue that even if the owners'
accounts receivable were not effectively seized, the
owners are entitled at most to Cuban pesos, which is all
that they would have been permitted to retain had they
collected on these accounts while still in Cuba, since
Cuban currency regulations require a Cuban exporter
who receives payment in a foreign currency to deliver
the foreign currency to the "Cuban Stabilization Fund"
for exchange into pesos.

* * *

---

[80]"Intervention" was the euphemistic term used for seizure of a business by the Cuban government in 1960.
[81]This method of making payment through a New York collecting bank was imposed on the exporters by the Castro government soon after it
  came to power to ensure that the dollars would be available to the Cuban government rather than be kept or used abroad by the exporters.

[As for interventors' claim that they are entitled to the proceeds from the preintervention shipments of cigars, we are compelled to deny their request because of] our decision in *Republic of Iraq v. First National City Bank.*[82] Application of the principles of that case here satisfies us that since the owners' accounts receivable had their *situs*[83] in the United States rather than in Cuba at the time of intervention and since the Cuban government's purported seizure of them without compensation is contrary to our own domestic policy, the act of state doctrine does not apply, the confiscation was ineffective, and the interventors' claim must be rejected. The owners rather than the interventors remain entitled to collect these accounts.

* * *

... Cuba and the interventors argue that even if the intervention did not deprive the owners of their right to collect on their accounts receivable from the importers, the district court erred in failing to apply Cuban currency regulations, which would limit the owners to ultimate receipt of pesos rather than dollars for these accounts. ... Relying on *Auten v. Auten*,[84] Cuba and the interventors insist that Cuban law was applicable because the contracts were made and were to be performed in Cuba. A Cuban currency regulation in effect since 1959 required all exporters who received payment in a foreign currency to deliver the currency within three days to the Cuban Currency Stabilization Fund for exchange into pesos. The interventors argue that by ignoring these and other regulations[85] the district court has given the owners an unwarranted windfall at the ultimate expense of the interventors and the Republic of Cuba.[86]

Neither the invoices nor other documents evidencing the agreement between the parties specify that payment was to be made in Cuba or in pesos. On the contrary, the business practice of the parties was that the importers for the most part would pay in dollars by checks drawn and delivered to collecting banks located in New York, which acted as the sellers' agents. In those instances where checks were sent directly to the exporters in Cuba, the checks were drawn on New York banks so that final payment was made in New York. Ordinarily, where a contract or agreement authorizes performance in any of several places, the law governing the agreement is that of the place of performance actually chosen.[87]

... Nor are we persuaded that Cuba's currency control regulations should here be given effect on the ground that not to do so would give the owners the benefit of a dollar windfall in lieu of the pesos which the Cuban government would have required them to accept in exchange for their dollars if they had remained in Cuba. The broad question of whether extraterritorial effect should be given to a foreign government's currency controls is not to be resolved on the basis of what the effect will be in a particular case but upon basic policy grounds. Currency controls are but a species of revenue law.[88] As a general rule one nation will not enforce the revenue laws of another,[89] at least in the absence of an agreement between the nations involved to do so.[90] While Article VIII of the Bretton Woods [*International Monetary Fund*] *Agreement* evidenced a commitment on the part of signatory nations to enforce each other's exchange controls as a matter of international cooperation,[91] Cuba has long since withdrawn from the Fund Agreement. Cuba cannot, therefore, predicate its attempted enforcement of its currency regulations upon any treaty or international agreement with the United States.

... Here the agreement bound the importers to pay dollars, not pesos. ... Although the effect of our judgment is to award to the owners dollars, which are worth more on the market than the pesos which the owners would be required by Cuban law to accept if they were in Cuba, this does not constitute a valid ground for enforcement here of Cuba's revenue laws. ...

The judgment of the trial court was affirmed. ■

---

[82]*Federal Reporter, Second Series,* vol. 353, p. 47 (Second Circuit Ct. of Appeals, 1965), *certirorari* denied, *United States Reports,* vol. 382, p. 1027 (Supreme Ct., 1966).

[[83]Latin: "situation" or "location." The location of a place of business.]

[84]*New York Reports,* vol. 308, p. 155 (New York Ct. of Appeals, 1954), [which holds that the] law of [the] state with [the] most significant contacts governs contractual obligations.

[85]Other regulations or "instructions" established the method of payment through New York collecting banks whereby the exporters would receive only pesos. ...

[86]The theory of the interventors and Cuba is that if the owners had been awarded pesos rather than dollars, in effect they would have recovered nothing since presently there is no exchange between pesos and dollars. A nominal recovery by the owners, according to the theory, would have reduced the importers' setoff against the interventors.

[87]*See,* e.g., Anglo-Continentale Treuhand, AG v. St. Louis Southwest Railway, *Federal Reporter, Second Series,* vol. 81, p. 11 (Second Circuit Ct. of Appeals, 1936), *certirorari* denied, *United States Reports,* vol. 298, p. 655 (Supreme Ct., 1936).

[88]*Confirm* Banco do Brasil, SA v. A. C. Israel Commodity Co., *New York Reports, Second Series,* vol. 12, p. 371 (New York Ct. of Appeals, 1963), *certirorari* denied, *United States Reports,* vol. 376, p. 906 (Supreme Ct., 1963).

[89]*See* Colorado v. Harbeck, *New York Reports,* vol. 232, p. 71 (New York Ct. of Appeals, 1921).

[90]*See,* e.g., Bretton Woods *International Monetary Fund Agreement.*

[91]*See,* e.g., Meyer, "Recognition of Exchange Controls After the International Monetary Fund Agreement," *Yale Law Journal,* vol. 62, p. 867 (1953).

Enforcement of Other IMF Member State Currency Exchange Obligations

The "General Obligations of Members" of the Fund are contained in Article VIII of the IMF Articles of Agreement. Section 2(b), as we have seen, makes exchange contracts that violate a member's currency regulations unenforceable in other member states. Section 2(a) forbids member states from imposing restrictions on the payments or transfers involving "current international transactions."[92] A **current international transaction** is any transaction other than the transfer of capital.[93] Restrictions on the transfer of currency between member countries are therefore forbidden on transactions that involve any of the following:[94]

a. All payments due in connection with foreign trade, other current business, including services, and normal short-term banking and credit facilities

b. Payments due as interest on loans and as net income from other investments

c. Payments of moderate amount for amortization of loans or for depreciation of direct investments

d. Moderate remittances for family living expenses

Section 3 of Article VIII forbids a member from engaging in any "discriminatory currency arrangements" or "multiple currency practices,"[95] and Section 4 requires a member to buy its own currency from other members who have acquired it as the result of "current transactions." Sections 5, 6, and 7 require members to furnish information to the IMF, to consult with other members when adopting special or temporary currency exchange restrictions, to collaborate in promoting international liquidity, and to work with other members to make the "special drawing right the principal reserve asset in the international monetary system."

Except for Section 2(b) of Article VIII, the member states' obligations do not give rise to any private rights. As a consequence, the other provisions of the IMF Articles of Agreement are seldom the subject of court disputes.[96]

Exemptions for New Members from IMF Member State Currency Exchange Obligations

Upon joining the IMF, a state does not have to accede to all of the currency exchange obligations set out in Article VIII (Sections 2, 3, and 4) of the IMF's Articles. Article XIV sets out transitional provisions that give a new member the option of maintaining the restrictions on payments and transfers for current international transactions in effect on the date it becomes a member. Only those restrictions may be maintained, however. Any later restrictions will automatically fall under Article VIII and will require IMF approval.

At the time the IMF Agreement was first signed in 1945, only the United States and nine other countries (all from Latin America) did not claim this exemption. Today, more than 150 states (more than three-quarters of all IMF members) have agreed to comply with the obligations imposed by Article VIII, including many of the more advanced developing states.[97] This is a significant development, as it indicates that most IMF members are committed to pursuing sound economic policies and will forgo any future reimposition of exchange restrictions.

D. CURRENCY SUPPORT

In addition to its principal function as the regulatory body for the international currency exchange system, the IMF serves as a short-term source of funds for member states having difficulty meeting their balance-of-payments obligations. These funds are drawn principally from the quota subscriptions paid by members, although the IMF also borrows from commercial

---

current international transaction: Any currency transaction other than the transfer of capital.

[92] Article VIII, § 2(a).

[93] Article XXX(d).

[94] *Id.*

[95] "Multiple currency practices" is the maintenance of several different rates of exchange for a currency, such as one rate for nationals, another for foreign individuals, and a third for government agencies.

[96] Article IX, which establishes the Fund's status, immunities, and privileges, was the focus of a dispute before the U.S. Federal Communications Commission in International Bank for Reconstruction and Development & International Monetary Fund v. All America Cables and Radio, Inc., *Federal Communications Commission Reports,* vol. 17, p. 450 (1966). In that decision, the FCC held that the IMF was entitled to the same privileges for transmitting its international cables as those given to foreign governments.

[97] *See* Exhibit 6-3.

banks. As of June 2002, the total quota subscriptions amounted to 212.4 billion SDRs or U.S. $265 billion.[98]

IMF Facilities

IMF facilities: The financial assistance programs available to International Monetary Fund members.

The IMF's financial resources are made available to its members through a variety of **facilities**. These facilities are funded from (1) the General Resources Account (consisting of funds from the members' subscriptions and funds borrowed from banks by the IMF), (2) the Special Disbursement Account (made up of funds derived originally from the sale of the IMF's gold holdings between 1976 and 1980, and later from interest paid by borrowers), and (3) the Enhanced Structural Adjustment Facility Trust Fund (which has resources from loans and donations from members). As of February 28, 2002, the IMF had credits and loans outstanding to 88 countries for an amount of SDR 61.7 billion (U.S.$ 77 billion).[99]

The IMF provides regular, concessional, and special facilities for its member states.

Regular IMF Facilities

Facilities available to *all* IMF member states include the following:

tranche: (French: "installment" or "block of shares.") A percentage of an IMF member's quota that it may withdraw to stabilize its currency or to meet balance-of-payments obligations.

Reserve *Tranche*   Each member has an IMF ***tranche*** that it may withdraw at any time, and that technically does not constitute the use of an IMF credit. This *tranche* consists of that share of a member state's quota that it did not contribute in its own currency (i.e., 25 percent of quota).[100]

Credit *Tranche*   A member is entitled to four credit *tranches*, each equivalent to 25 percent of its quota. The first one is generally made available when a member faces relatively minor balance-of-payments difficulties and is subject to few conditions. Subsequent *tranches* (collectively known as "upper credit *tranches*") are subject to progressively more stringent conditions.[101]

Extended Fund Facility   These facilities help member states overcome balance-of-payments problems for longer periods (i.e., financing is available for up to three years) and for amounts larger (i.e., up to 140 percent of the member's quota) than those available under the credit *tranche*.[102]

Standby Arrangements   These facilities are in essence "bridging loans" provided to member states while the IMF deliberates about whether to provide other funds to the particular member state.[103] Typically they are granted for 12 to 18 months.[104]

Concessional IMF Facility

The IMF has one facility, established in 1987, enlarged and extended in 1994, and renamed and revised in 1999, that is designed for low-income member countries with protracted balance-of-payment problems. The *Poverty Reduction and Growth Facility* provides loans at concessional interest rates of 0.5 percent per annum to such countries. Seventy-nine low-income countries are currently eligible to use this facility.[105]

Special IMF Facilities

Compensatory Financing Facility   Created in 1963, this facility helps a country deal with a temporary depletion of its foreign exchange reserves when this comes about as the consequence of economic developments beyond its control (such as a crop failure or natural disaster).[106]

---

[98]IMF Members' Quotas and Voting Power, and IMF Governors, posted at www.imf.org/external/np/sec/memdir/members.htm.

[99]The IMF at a Glance: A Factsheet (April 15, 2002) posted at www.imf.org/external/np/exr/facts/glance.htm.

[100]Financial Organization and Operations of the IMF, p. 22 (IMF Pamphlet Series No. 45, 6th ed. 2001) posted at www.imf.org/external/pubs/ft/pam/pam45/contents.htm.

[101]*Id.*, p. 20.

[102]*Id.*, p. 42.

[103]"Highlights of the IMF's 50-Year History," IMF Survey, p. 229 (July 11, 1994).

[104]"How Does the IMF Lend? A Factsheet" (April 15, 2002) posted at www.imf.org/external/np/exr/facts/howlend.htm.

[105]"The IMF's Poverty Reduction and Growth Facility (PRGF): A Factsheet (March 2001) posted at www.imf.org/external/np/exr/facts/prgf.htm.

[106]Organization and Operations of the IMF, pp. 44–45 (IMF Pamphlet Series No. 45, 6th ed. 2001) posted at www.imf.org/external/pubs/ft/pam/pam45/contents.htm.

Supplemental Reserve Facility   This facility provides short-term financial assistance for exceptional balance-of-payments difficulties due to a large short-term financing need that is the result of a sudden and disruptive loss of market confidence.[107]

Contingent Credit Lines   Established in 1999 as a response to the spread of turmoil through global financial markets during the Asian Crisis, this is a precautionary facility designed to help members with strong economic policies and sound financial systems that find themselves threatened by a crisis elsewhere in the world economy—a phenomenon known as "financial contagion."[108]

IMF "Conditionality"

Use of the IMF's resources is limited by the policies set out in the Articles of Agreement and the policies adopted under them. This requirement is known as **conditionality**.

> **IMF conditionality:** Principle that a member's right to the use of credit *tranches* and credit facilities will be conditioned on its progress in regularizing its balance-of-payments obligations and in developing sustained economic growth.

The essence of conditionality is that access to the IMF's credit *tranches* and other credit facilities is linked to a member's progress in implementing policies to restore balance-of-payments viability and sustainable economic growth. It is based not on a rigid set of operational rules but on a general set of guidelines. The current guidelines, which the Executive Board adopted in 1979, encourage members to adopt corrective measures at an early stage, stress the importance of respecting the member state's domestic social and political objectives, limit the number and content of performance criteria, and emphasize that IMF arrangements are not contractual agreements but rather decisions of the IMF that set out the conditions for continued financial assistance.[109]

E. DEVELOPMENT BANKS

There exist on the international, regional, and national levels specialized financial organizations that promote economic development. The International Bank for Reconstruction and Development (IBRD)—known informally as the **World Bank**—was established, along with the International Monetary Fund, at the United Nations meeting at Bretton Woods in 1944. Membership in the Bank is restricted to the members of the IMF, and, in essence, the Bank operates as the development arm of the IMF.

> **World Bank:** Informal name for the International Bank for Reconstruction and Development. An intergovernmental organization, headquartered in Washington, that provides development financing for its members.
>
> **International Development Agency (IDA):** A subsidiary of the World Bank that provides concessional development financing to less developed countries.
>
> **International Finance Corporation (IFC):** A subsidiary of the World Bank that provides development financing to private enterprises.
>
> **Global Environment Facility (GEF):** A World Bank source of grant and concessional funding for protecting and improving the global environment.

Complementing the World Bank are two subsidiaries: the **International Development Agency** (IDA), and the **International Finance Corporation** (IFC). The World Bank provides development financing to the national governments and political subdivisions of its member states. The IDA provides less restrictive financing for less developed countries, and the IFC provides loans to private enterprises.[110] Together, the World Bank, the IDA, and the IFC are the world's largest providers of development assistance to developing countries and countries in transition, providing some $20 billion in new loans each year.[111]

The World Bank is also responsible for managing the Trust Fund of the **Global Environment Facility** (GEF). The GEF, which became a permanent international facility in 1994, provides grant and concessional monies to developing countries to fund projects dealing with four global environmental problems: climate change, biological diversity, international waters, and ozone layer depletion.[112] Only countries that are parties to the Climate Change Convention[113] or the Convention on Biological Diversity[114] are eligible to receive funds from the GEF. Unlike

---

[107]Id., p. 42.

[108]"The IMF's Contingent Credit Lines: A Factsheet (June 2001) posted at www.imf.org/external/np/exr/facts/ccl.htm.

[109]IMF Policy Development and Review Department, "Conditionality in Fund-Supported Programs—Overview," (February 20, 2001) posted at www.imf.org/external/np/pdr/cond/2001/eng/overview/index.htm.

[110]As of August 24, 1998, the World Bank had 181 members; the IDA had 160; and the IFC had 174. The World Bank's Web site is at www.worldbank.org/.

[111]*See* www.worldbank.org/html/extdr/faq/faq.htm.

[112]Instrument for the Establishment of the Restructured Global Environment Facility, Article I, § 2.

[113]The Climate Change Secretariat's home page at www.unfccc.de/ contains the full text of the United Nations Framework Convention on Climate Change. As of August 1998, there were 176 states parties.

[114]The Biological Diversity Secretariat's home page at www.biodiv.org/ has the full text of the convention. As of May 1998, there were 174 states parties.

Name	Objectives
African Development Bank	Complementary regional economic development
Asian Development Bank	Complementary regional economic development
Arab Bank for Economic Development in Africa	African economic independence through Arab-African cooperation
Arab Fund for Economic and Social Development	Joint Arab development projects
Caribbean Development Bank	Economic cooperation and integration
Central African States Development Bank	Multinational development projects leading to economic integration
Central American Bank for Economic Integration	Economic integration and balanced economic development
East African Development Bank	Regional economic development
Inter-American Development Bank	Economic growth and development
Islamic Development Bank	Economic development in accordance with Islamic law
Nordic Investment Bank	Nordic economic development and Nordic exports
OPEC Fund for International Development	Economic cooperation and development
Southern African Development Coordination Conference	Regional economic integration
West African Development Bank	Economic integration and development

EXHIBIT 6-4   Regional Development Organizations

Source: Based on Robert Fraser, *The World Financial System,* pp. 398–454 (Phoenix: Oryx Press, 1987).

International Fund for Agricultural Development (IFAD): An intergovernmental organization, headquartered in Rome, that provides financing to its developing member states to promote food production.

in other World Bank facilities, an independent Council made up of 32 states participating in the GEF determines which projects will be funded.[115]

Another international development organization, the **International Fund for Agricultural Development** (IFAD), was created by a special UN conference held in Rome in 1976. Membership is open to any UN member.[116] The IFAD's primary objective is to provide financing for projects that introduce, expand, and improve food production systems in its developing member states.

Regional development organizations exist to promote the economic and social development of regional groups. The names and purposes of the major regional organizations are listed in Exhibit 6-4.

National development agencies exist in virtually every developed country. The most important are discussed in Chapter 12, "Financing."

F. THE BANK FOR INTERNATIONAL SETTLEMENTS

Bank for International Settlements (BIS): Intergovernmental organization, headquartered in Basel, that functions as a bank for the world's central banks.

The oldest international organization involved in monetary cooperation is the **Bank for International Settlements** (BIS), headquartered in Basel, Switzerland.[117] Founded in 1930, it has three main purposes: (1) to act as a bank for the world's central banks, (2) to promote international monetary cooperation, and (3) to act as an agent for international settlements. It currently holds and invests between 10 and 15 percent of all of the world's monetary reserves.

The legal structure of the BIS is somewhat unique. While it is clearly endowed with international personality and the privileges and immunities of an international organization, it is also a limited company incorporated under Swiss law.[118] This structure is partly the result of historical accident and partly intentional. In 1930, most of the central banks that helped found the BIS

[115]Instrument for the Establishment of the Restructured Global Environment Facility, Article I, § 16. Any UN member may become a participant in the GEF by depositing an instrument of participation with the GEF Secretariat or by making a deposit in the Trust Fund. *Id.,* Article I, § 7. As of fall 1998, there were 164 member countries. *See* www.worldbank.org/ html/extdr/faq/faq.htm.

[116]The International Fund for Agricultural Development has 161 member countries. *See* the IFAD home page at www.unicc.org/ifad/home.html.

[117]The BIS's home page is at www.bis.org/.

[118]The current international status of the BIS is defined in the Swiss Headquarters Agreement of 1987: Accord entre le Conseil fédéral suisse et la Banque des Règlements Internationaux en vue de déterminer le statut juridique de la Banque en Suisse, du 10 février 1987, *Recueil officiel des lois fédérales,* p. 8 (March 3, 1987). Reprinted (in English) in *Bank for International Settlements: Basic Texts,* pp. 29–39 (1987). An edited version of the Agreement is posted on the Internet at www.bis.org/about/hq-ex.htm. For a discussion of the debate on the legal character of the BIS, *see* Mario Giovanoli, "The Role of the Bank for International Settlements in International Monetary Cooperation and Its Tasks Relating to the European Currency Unit," *International Lawyer,* vol. 23, p. 841 at pp. 847–848 (1989).

were private corporations rather than public institutions.[119] More important, however, the Bank's founders were concerned that the BIS should be insulated, as much as possible, from direct governmental influence. The BIS is structured, therefore, as a banking company limited by shares. Originally, when the BIS's initial capital was issued, part of the Belgian and French issues and all of the American issue were sold to the public. After an Extraordinary General Meeting held January 2001, the BIS Statutes were amended to restrict ownership of shares exclusively to central banks, and the 14 percent of the shares that then remained in private hands shares were bought back. Now, all of the shares are owned solely by central banks.[120]

Today, the central banks of 50 countries are represented at the BIS.[121] General meetings of shareholders are held at least once a year, and voting rights are exercised in proportion to the number of shares subscribed (including those held privately) in the state that a central bank represents. A Board of Directors is dominated by the largest European central banks. Its membership is made up of (a) the Governors of the central banks of Belgium, France, Germany, Italy, and the United Kingdom and the Chairman of the Board of Governors of the United States Federal Reserve; (b) for each of these Governors, a second director of the same nationality appointed by that Governor; and (c) up to nine additional directors elected by the Board from among the Governors of the central banks of other members states.[122] The Board meets at least 10 times a year and makes decisions by majority vote from among those present or represented by proxy. The Board selects the President of the Bank from among its own members. The President serves both as the titular head of the Bank and the Chairman of the Board. In turn, the President nominates a General Manager, who is appointed by the Board. The General Manager is responsible for appointing the staff and carrying out the day-to-day operations of the Bank.[123]

The Central Banks' Bank

One of the BIS's main functions is to serve as a bank for the world's central banks. It does so by helping some 120 central banks manage and invest their monetary reserves (now amounting to some U.S. $130 billion).[124] Most of these funds are placed in the world's money market in the form of commercial bank deposits and short-term negotiable instruments (such as certificates of deposit).

BIS facilities: The financial assistance programs available to central banks from the Bank for International Settlements.

bridging loan: Short-term loan that allows a debtor to meet its current obligations until a permanent loan can be obtained.

Beyond placing surplus funds in the international marketplace, the BIS occasionally makes liquid resources available to central banks. Such transactions (called **facilities**) include swaps of currency for gold, credits advanced against a pledge of gold or marketable short-term securities, and, less frequently, unsecured credits and standby credits. The Bank also carries on exchange transactions in foreign currency and gold both with the central banks and with the markets.

Recently, the Bank has undertaken a new role as a source of large-scale, short-term **bridging loans** to help the central banks of developing countries with their balance-of-payments difficulties. These loans have helped the central banks of Latin American and Eastern European countries cope with cash flow problems pending the receipt of credits from the International Monetary Fund.

[119]The National Bank of Belgium and the Bank of Switzerland remain limited companies. The central banks of most countries have now been nationalized, or, upon the establishment of their governments, were created as public institutions. Mario Giovanoli, "The Role of the Bank for International Settlements in International Monetary Cooperation and Its Tasks Relating to the European Currency Unit," *International Lawyer,* vol. 23, p. 841 at p. 845 (1989).

[120]BIS, *Profile 2001,* p. 2 (June 2001) at www.bis.org/about/profil2001.pdf.

[121]Argentina, Australia, Austria, Belgium, Bosnia and Herzegovina, Brazil, Bulgaria, Canada, China, Croatia, the Czech Republic, Denmark, Estonia, Finland, France, Germany, Greece, Hong Kong SAR, Hungary, Iceland, India, Ireland, Italy, Japan, Korea, Latvia, Lithuania, the Republic of Macedonia, Malaysia, Mexico, the Netherlands, Norway, Poland, Portugal, Romania, Russia, Saudi Arabia, Singapore, Slovakia, Slovenia, South Africa, Spain, Sweden, Switzerland, Thailand, Turkey, the United Kingdom, the United States, and Yugoslavia, as well as the European Central Bank. *Id.,* p. 1.

[122]Traditionally, the Presidents of the Netherlands Bank and the Swiss National Bank along with the Governor of the Bank of Sweden have been among these nine..

[123]*See* BIS, *Profile 2001,* p. 1 (June 2001) at www.bis.org/about/profil2001.pdf.

[124]Id., p. 5.

Promoter of International Monetary Cooperation

The BIS undertakes a variety of functions to encourage cooperation among the world's bankers. The Bank's offices in Basel regularly host meetings of the world's finance ministers, central bank Governors, and banking experts. The BIS also staffs the permanent secretariats of the Committee of Governors of the European Union's central banks, the Board of Governors of the European Monetary Cooperation Fund, and the Committee on Banking Regulations and Supervisory Practices of the so-called Group of Ten (G-10) countries.[125] These secretariats collect data on national banking regulations and national surveillance systems, identify problem areas, and suggest measures for safeguarding bank solvency and liquidity. In addition, the Bank itself collects and publishes banking statistics on a quarterly basis.

Agent for International Settlements

Much of the impetus for the creation of the BIS came from the need to settle the problem of German reparations to the victorious allies in the aftermath of World War I. The solution the founders agreed to was the reduction and commercialization of the German payments under the supervision of the Bank. The BIS was put in charge of the loans floated by Germany and Austria, and it managed them until the onset of World War II.[126]

From time to time since then, the Bank has entered into settlement arrangements with various countries and international organizations. It managed the currency exchange settlements system set up by the European Payments Union and its successor, the European Monetary Agreement, during the 1950s and 1960s. During the 1970s, the Bank managed the Organization for Economic Cooperation and Development's Exchange Guarantee Agreement, which again involved a multilateral system for settling currency exchanges. From 1973 to 1993, the BIS managed the European Monetary Cooperation Fund for the European Community.[127] And in 1994, the BIS assumed responsibility for rescheduling Brazil's external debt. It assumed similar responsibilities for Peru beginning in 1997 and for the Ivory Coast in 1998.[128]

G. REGIONAL MONETARY SYSTEMS

Several groups of countries have set up regional monetary organizations. These vary in their structure and evolution, from those that emulate the IMF in promoting currency exchange and financial support for balance-of-payments obligations to those that have established a complete monetary union.

Regional organizations that carry on many of the same functions as the IMF include the Central American Monetary Union (*Unión monetaria centroamericana*, or *UMCA*)[129] and the Arab Monetary Fund (AMF).[130] Both work to maintain the values of their members' currencies, stabilize their exchange ratios, jointly manage foreign exchange reserves, and promote eventual monetary union.[131]

The most developed monetary unions are the West African Economic and Monetary Union (*Union economique et monétaire ouest-africaine*, or *UEMOA*), the Eastern Caribbean

---

[125]The Group of Ten is an informal organization of the finance ministers of the 10 major free-market countries. They have met regularly since 1961 to discuss the world's banking problems. Members are Belgium, Canada, France, Germany, Italy, Japan, the Netherlands, Sweden, the United Kingdom, and the United States. *Id.,* p. 3.

[126]The old obligations were revived under new terms in 1953, and they were again managed by the BIS.

[127]Beginning January 1, 1994, the functions of the European Monetary Cooperation Fund were taken over by the European Monetary Institute. *See* "The Bank for International Settlements: Profile of an International Organization" at www.bis.org/about/prof-gh.htm.

[128]*Id.*

[129]Established in 1964 by Costa Rica, El Salvador, Guatemala, Honduras, and Nicaragua.

[130]Established in 1976, its current members are Algeria, Bahrain, Iraq, Jordan, Kuwait, Lebanon, Libya, Mauritania, Morocco, Oman, Palestine, Qatar, Saudi Arabia, Somalia, Sudan, Syria, Tunisia, United Arab Emirates, and Yemen. Goals of the AMF include "correcting disequilibria in the balances of payments of the member states," stabilizing currency exchange ratios, promoting economic integration, and "paving the way for the creation of a unified Arab currency." *Agreement on the Arab Monetary Fund,* quoted in Robert Fraser, *The World Financial System,* at p. 346 (1987).

[131]*Id.,* pp. 357–360 (1987).

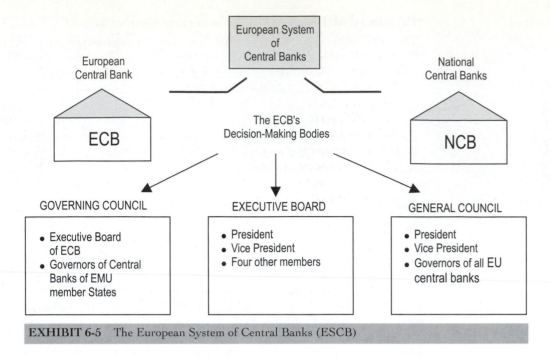

EXHIBIT 6-5   The European System of Central Banks (ESCB)

Currency Authority (ECCA), and the Customs and Economic Union of Central Africa (*Union douanière et économique de l'Afrique centrale*, or *UDEAC*). Each has established a central bank, a common currency, and a single pool of exchange reserves.[132]

The European Union (EU) is currently in the process of establishing a fully integrated economic and monetary union (known as the European Monetary Union or EMU). The criteria for setting up the EMU were agreed to in 1992 with the adoption of the Maastricht Treaty.[133] In May 1998, 11[134] of the 15[135] EU member states met the qualifications and agreed to participate in the EMU. At that time they elected the President, Vice President, and four other Executive Board members of a new European Central Bank (ECB).[136] The ECB came into being on June 1, 1998.[137]

Because the Maastricht Treaty envisioned that some EU member states would not be participating in the EMU, it established a rather complex structure to oversee the EU's monetary policies. This is known as the European System of Central Banks (ESCB) and is made up of the European Central Bank and the 15 EU national central banks (NCBs). However, the NCBs of the four member states of the EU that are not participating in the EMU have a special status. Most importantly, they do not participate in setting the monetary policies of the EMU. See Exhibit 6-5.

---

[132]Current members of *UEMOA* are Benin, Burkina Faso, Ivory Coast, Mali, Niger, Senegal, and Togo. Its bank is the Central Bank of West African States and its currency is the franc. *See* the UEMOA Web site at www.uemoa.int/. Current members of the ECCA are Antigua, Dominica, Grenada, Montserrat, Saint Kitts and Nevis, Saint Lucia, and Saint Vincent and the Grenadines. Its bank is the Eastern Caribbean Central Bank and its currency is the dollar. *See* Frits van Beek et al., "The Eastern Caribbean Currency Union: Institutions, Performance, and Policy Issues," International Monetary Fund Occasional Papers No. 195 (August 11, 2000) at www.imf.org/external/pubs/nft/op/195/. Current members of *UDEAC* are Cameroon, Central African Republic, Chad, Congo, Equatorial Guinea, and Gabon. Its bank is the Bank of Central African States and its currency is the franc. Robert Fraser, *The World Financial System,* at pp. 353–354. (1987).

[133]The Treaty on European Union sets out the monetary policy of the EU in Articles 105–109. *See* hyperion.advanced.org/19110/english/treaty/treaty.html.

[134]The 11 EMU participants are Austria, Belgium, Finland, France, Germany, Ireland, Italy, Luxembourg, the Netherlands, Portugal, and Spain.

[135]The non-EMU states are Britain, Denmark, Greece, and Sweden. Britain and Denmark chose not to participate in the EMU at its outset, but they may join later. Greece failed all the criteria for entry into the EMU and Sweden failed because of its volatile currency. Both are committed to joining as soon as they can.

[136]The European Central Bank's Web site is at www.ecb.int/.

[137]Between June 1, 1998, and January 1, 1999, the ECB took over the functions of the European Monetary Institute (established in 1993), which it replaced. These were (1) to strengthen central bank cooperation and monetary policy coordination and (2) to make the preparations required for the establishment of the European System of Central Banks (ESCB). *See* "Constitution of the ESCB: History — Three Stages towards EMU" at www.ecb.int/about/ab2con.htm.

The main responsibilities of the ESCB are (1) defining and implementing the monetary policy of the EU, (2) conducting foreign exchange operations, (3) holding and managing the official foreign reserves of the EU member states, and (4) promoting the smooth operation of payment systems. In addition, the ESCB advises the EU organs—the Commission, Council, Parliament, and so on—about the banking matters it is responsible for.

The ESCB is governed by the decision-making bodies of the European Central Bank: the Governing Council, the Executive Board, and the General Council. The Governing Council is made up of the six members of the Executive Board and the Governors of the national banks of the 11 EMU states. It sets the monetary policy—including interest rates—for the EMU independent of the EU Commission, Council, and Parliament, much like the German central bank (the *Bundesbank*) on which it was modeled.[138] The Executive Board is then responsible for carrying out this policy.

The General Council of the ECB is made up of the President and Vice President of the Executive Board and the Governors of the 15 EU national central banks. It is responsible for establishing common accounting and reporting provisions for the EU, collecting and disseminating statistical information, and setting the capital contribution requirements for the ECB.

On January 1, 1999, the ESCB began functioning as the central banking authority for the EU. On that same date, the "euro" became the new currency for the EMU. Euro coins and notes, however, did not begin circulating until January 1, 2002. During the intervening three years, national currencies continued to be legal tender at permanent exchange rates that were based on the exchange rates that existed on December 31, 1998. As of June 30, 2002, only euro coins and notes were legal tender in the EMU.

H. NATIONAL MONETARY SYSTEMS

National Monetary Organizations

There are three types of organizations that operate on the national plane to implement national monetary policies. At the highest level is a political agency of the national government that sets national fiscal policy and carries on the financial functions of the government. In most countries, this is a cabinet-level agency, such as a Ministry of Finance or a Treasury Department.

central bank: A state's bank that is responsible for issuing the state's currency, regulating the quantity of its money in circulation, maintaining currency reserves, and acting as a lender of last resort.

At the next level is a **central bank**, such as the Bank of England, the Bank of Japan, or the U.S. Federal Reserve System.[139] In most countries, it is owned by the national government, but through a variety of mechanisms (such as lengthy fixed terms for directors), the bank is given some degree of independence from the government and from the day-to-day pressures of politics. Its most important functions are (a) to issue bank notes and coins, (b) to regulate the quantity of money in circulation, (c) to maintain and invest currency reserves, and (d) to act as a lender of last resort.

commercial bank: A business firm that maintains custody of money deposited by its customers and pays on drafts written by its customers. It earns its profits by investing the money it has on deposit.

At the third level are the **commercial banks** that accept and manage deposits, make loans, and offer trust services.[140] In the domestic arena one finds a variety of financial institutions (such as savings banks, savings and loan associations, and credit unions), but, internationally, the commercial bank is the institution most likely to be involved. Commercial banks may be owned privately or by the government.[141]

---

[138]The Governing Council, which uses English as its common language, meets every other Thursday, just as the German *Bundesbank* used to do. "The Euro: What It All Means," CNN Financial Network (December 8, 1998), posted at cnnfn.com/worldbiz/europe/9812/08/definitions/.

[139]*See* Yahoo!'s listing of national central banks at dir.yahoo.com/Business_and_Economy/Finance_and_Investment/Banking/Central_Banks/.

[140]*See* Yahoo!'s listing of commercial banks at dir.yahoo.com/Business_and_Economy/Companies/Financial_Services/Banking/Banks/.

[141]A commercial bank's particular structural organization and its authority to participate in international banking depends upon the laws of its home country. In the United States, a commercial bank's ability to operate abroad through branches is regulated by the Federal Reserve Act and Federal Reserve Board Regulations. *United States Code,* Title 12, §§ 601 and 604(a) and *Code of Federal Regulations,* Title 12, § 211 *et seq.* The Edge Act of 1919 authorizes federally chartered corporations to engage in international banking and permits U.S. national banks to invest in them. *United States Code,* Title 12, § 611. The International Banking Act of 1978 eliminates those provisions of the Edge Act (such as restrictions on liabilities and reserve requirements) that put American banks at a competitive disadvantage with foreign banks. *United States Code,* Title 12, § 611a. Finally, since 1981, American

Bank Deposits

bank deposit: Money held by a bank. The bank may freely use this money as it best sees fit. A depositor only has a claim against the bank as a general creditor and not as a bailor of specific property deposited with the bank.

Bank deposits are monies placed with a bank for its use. The term "deposit" suggests the notion of a bailment,[142] which implies that a bank has an obligation to keep the funds it receives in a vault for safekeeping. This is not the case. Except for monies delivered for a designated purpose, deposits become a bank's funds. A bank can commingle them and use them as it sees fit. Most commonly, banks use these funds to make short- and medium-term loans. The depositor, in return for his deposit, receives a claim against the bank as a general, unsecured creditor. Additionally, for some accounts, a depositor acquires the authority to write checks, payment orders, or drafts for the benefit of third parties, with the value of the checks, orders, or drafts being deducted from his claim.[143]

In Case 6–6 the nature of the relationship of banker and depositor is examined. In this landmark case, the banker contended that he had no special obligation to the depositor, whereas the depositor argued that the banker was his fiduciary[144] and therefore had a duty to manage his money with utmost care.

---

banks are authorized to establish International Banking Facilities; that is, they can set up segregated asset and liability accounts for foreign customers that otherwise would be subject to the liability and reserve restrictions of domestic accounts. *Code of Federal Regulations,* Title 12, §§ 204 and 217.

[142] A bailment is an arrangement by which property is delivered in trust to another for a special purpose and for a limited time.

[143] The statutory provisions governing bank deposits in countries with major financial centers are reasonably consistent around the world. Most provide for charter supervision, liquidation, the regulation of business practices, and the status of depositors. However, with few exceptions, these statutes do not contemplate deposits made by foreign persons, deposits made at foreign branch banks, or the problem of conflicts with regulations issued by a foreign sovereign. Peter S. Smedresman and Andreas F. Lowenfeld, "Eurodollars, Multinational Banks, and National Laws," *New York University Law Review,* vol. 64, p. 733 at pp. 737–738 (1989).

[144] A fiduciary is a person having a duty, created by his undertaking, to act primarily for another's benefit in matters connected with the undertaking. In particular, a fiduciary is to act in good faith, and with trust, special confidence, and candor towards another.

Case 6–6   The Banker's Case
Foley v. Hill et al.

England, House of Lords, 1848.
English Reports, vol. 9, p. 1002 (1901).

Thomas Hill was a banker in Stourbridge, Worcestershire, England. Edward Foley opened an account with Thomas Hill in 1829, depositing the sum of £6,117 10s. Thomas Hill agreed to pay 3 percent annual interest on the funds in the account. Interest was posted in the banker's account books through December 25, 1831, but not thereafter. Only two checks were ever drawn on the account by Foley, and the account effectively remained dormant for some seven years.

In January 1838, Foley filed a bill (i.e., brought suit) in a court of equity seeking an accounting of all of the funds and of the interest earned in his account and to obtain the monies due him. Thomas Hill asked the court to dismiss the case because, the banker contended, it involved a legal dispute (i.e., one to be resolved in a law court) and not an equi-

table dispute (i.e., one heard by a court of equity). The trial judge (the Vice-Chancellor of England) ruled in favor of Foley, but this was overruled on appeal (by Lord Chancellor Lyndhurst). Foley then appealed to the House of Lords.

THE LORD CHANCELLOR

. . . [I]t is said a Court of Equity . . . has . . . jurisdiction [in this case because of] the supposed fiduciary character existing between the banker and his customer.

No case has been produced in which that character has been given to the relation of banker and customer; but it has been attempted to be supported by reference to other cases supposed to be analogous. These are cases where bills have been filed as between principal and agent, or between principal and factor. Now, as between principal and factor, there is no question whatever that . . . [disputes relating to

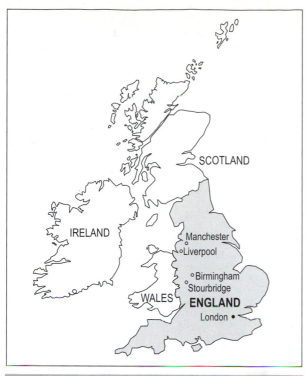

MAP 6-6   England (1848)

But the analogy entirely fails, as it appears to me, when you come to consider the relative situation of a banker and his customer; and for that purpose it is quite sufficient to refer to the authorities . . . and to the nature of the connection between the parties. Money, when paid into a bank, ceases altogether to be the money of the principal; it is then the money of the banker, who is bound to return an equivalent by paying a similar sum to that deposited with him when he is asked for it. The money paid into the banker's [possession] is money known by the principal to be placed there for the purpose of being under the control of the banker; it is then the banker's money; he is known to deal with it as his own; he makes what profit he can, which profit he retains to himself, paying back only the principal, according to the custom of bankers in some places, or the principal and a small rate of interest, according to the custom of bankers in other places. The money placed in the custody of a banker is, to all intents and purposes, the money of the banker, to do with it as he pleases; he is guilty of no breach of trust in employing it; he is not answerable to the principal if he puts it into jeopardy, if he engages in hazardous speculation; he is not bound to keep it or to deal with it as the property of the principal; but he is, of course, answerable for the amount, because he has contracted, having received that money, to repay to the principal, when demanded, a sum equivalent to that paid into his hands.

That has been the subject of discussion in various cases, and that has been established to be the relative situation of banker and customer. That being established to be the relative situation of banker and customer, the banker is not an agent or factor, but he is a debtor. Then the analogy between that case and those that have been referred to [by the appellant's counsel in his argument to the House of Lords] entirely fails; and the ground upon which those cases have, by analogy to the doctrine of trusteeship, been held to be the subject of the jurisdiction of a Court of Equity, has no application here, as it appears to me.

The appeal was dismissed. The case should have been brought in a law court and not a court of equity as a banker is not a fiduciary with respect to a customer. ■

the character of their relationship are] within the jurisdiction of a Court of Equity, because . . . [the factor is employed in the manner] of a trustee. Partaking of the character of a trustee, the factor—as the trustee for the particular matter in which he is employed as factor—sells the principal's goods, and accounts to him for the money. The goods, however, remain the goods of the owner or principal until the sale takes place, and the moment the money is received the money remains the property of the principal. So it is with regard to an agent dealing with any property; he obtains no interest himself in the subject matter beyond his remuneration; he is dealing throughout for another, and though he is not a trustee according to the strict technical meaning of the word, he is a *quasi* trustee for that particular transaction for which he is engaged; and therefore in these cases the Court of Equity has assumed jurisdiction.

Commonly, banks pay interest on the monies they hold on deposit. When large sums are deposited for short-term investment, banks typically issue certificates of deposit (CDs), which generally provide a higher rate of interest than funds left in a general deposit account. Not all banks, however, pay interest. As Reading 6–1 points out, interest payments are forbidden in countries following Islamic law. Instead of earning interest, depositors in Islamic banks become the equivalent of joint venturers in the investments that their banks underwrite.

Reading 6–1 Islamic Banking
Traute Wohlers-Scharf

Arab and Islamic Banks: New Business Partners for Developing Countries, p. 74 (1983).

UNDERLYING CONCEPTS OF ISLAMIC ECONOMICS AND BANKING

Across the Muslim world there is a move to create Islamic financial institutions. This is but one manifestation of a much broader phenomenon, the revival of Islam and its values. The contribution of the Muslim world to a new international economic order could be based upon the application of the Shari'a to modern economic and financial transactions.

An Islamic economic order represents for the world's Muslims an alternative to capitalistic and socialist systems. Islamic concepts are different from capitalism by their opposition to excessive accumulation of wealth and, in contradiction to socialism, by their protection of the rights to property, including ownership of the means of production.

As defined by the "Egyptian Study", the Islamic economic system is based upon a number of principles that regulate human life. They constitute a sum of wisdom accumulated over the centuries by Islamic thinkers, who addressed themselves to broad political and economic issues and the history of human societies. For them, a true Islamic society must not be an arena where opposing interests clash, but rather a place where harmonious relations can be achieved through a sense of shared responsibilities. The individual's rights must be equitably balanced against those of society at large.

Islamic economics are regulated by [the] Shari'a, the laws derived from the Koran and Sunna. Unlike the Christian world, Islam makes no distinction between secular and religious law. It follows that the economic and financial practices of Islamic banks must abide by these guiding principles, although they do have a certain flexibility to adapt to new economic situations.

The traits that distinguish Islamic economy and finance from their Western counterparts reflect a different understanding of the value of capital and labor. In lieu of a lender-borrower relationship, Islamic finance relies on equitable risk-sharing between the person who provides the capital and the entrepreneur. This practice derives from the central tenet of Islamic banking based on the Koran, which forbids *riba*, that is, interest charges or payments.

Contrary to what Westerners often think, interest-free banking should not be considered as merely a con-

MAP 6-7 The Islamic World (2002)

cessionary or subsidized financial practice. Viewed in its historic context, Islamic law on interest was above all practical. The economy of the Arabian peninsula in the seventh century was that of trading city-states living in a hostile environment. In economic terms, the constraints were illiquidity and scarcity and the results were usury and hoarding. Islamic precepts aimed to control such undesirable social phenomena. If interest rates imposed on long-distance traders were too high, this either discouraged trade or substantially increased the cost of commodities for investors as well as consumers, resulting in a net loss to the community.

The original ban on interest charges stemmed from the fact that moneylenders were exploiting the poor by charging usurious rates. Even if this may no longer apply to modern, monetized economies, a different rationale has evolved to justify the principle of banning interest. There is no need for loan financing, it is claimed, because an active involvement in a company through profit sharing is a superior way to direct capital into productive outlets without putting an additional financial burden on the community.

For Islamic economists, the economic rationale for profit sharing is not only distributive justice but efficiency, economic stability and growth. M. N. Siddiqui, for example, argues that interest financing can be very unfair, when entrepreneurs alone incur the losses or, on the contrary, reap disproportionately high benefits. As far as public debts are concerned, interest financing is felt to be inequitable in the case of national emergencies, such as crop failures or floods, and inefficient for development aid purposes. The role of interest in international debt comes in for heavy criticism, as the following statement aptly sums up: "Three decades of debt financing did not help the debtor countries to become self-sufficient, or less dependent, or capable of generating a surplus to pay back".

As far as allocative efficiency is concerned, it is contended that debt financing usually goes to the most creditworthy borrower and not necessarily to the most productive and potentially profitable projects. As for stability, the argument is advanced that an interest-based economy has a built-in tendency towards inflation because the creation of money is not linked to productive investment at the level either of central banks or of commercial banks. Lastly, interest charges decrease the supply of risk capital and therefore hamper economic growth.

Some Islamic economists hold different views on the interdiction of interest in today's economies. Islamic "modernists" find a literal reading of the Koran too restrictive and favor an interpretation of the spirit of the law. They thus contend that the Koran has prohibited usury but not legitimate interest. Nevertheless, the vast majority of Islamic economists maintain—and Islamic banks concur—that interest should be prohibited.

Today no Islamic bank charges or pays interest, although certain fiduciary business operations allow partners to circumvent this difficulty. Charging interest is permissible for financial transactions with "Dar Al Harb", that is, non-Muslim countries, or for Muslims living beyond the rule of Islam, known as "Dar Al Islam".

A second tenet governing money matters is that it is forbidden to hoard. Men have a moral obligation to put money to productive use, for themselves and for the good of the community, by investing in profitable opportunities. Though Islamic banks are trying to promote such schemes, this is still an ideal. Until a complete Islamic system is instituted, hoarding continues to be widespread. It has been estimated that some $80 billion are sitting idle in Muslim countries. If Islamic banks could attract broader segments of the population, which have till now considered Western-style banking with distrust, it could mobilize this capital into productive outlets.

Another important aspect of Islamic finance is a tax called *Zakat,* in some ways similar to the Christian tithe. Paying *Zakat* is one of the five imperative religious obligations for a Muslim. It is levied on traded goods and revenues from business and real estate, but not on personal property like houses, furniture or jewelry. Computation is complex: as a rule, peasants pay anywhere from 5 to 10 percent on their produce, while the rest of the population contributes 2.5 percent of their revenues. . . .

Individuals may give their *Zakat* contribution directly to a beneficiary or else to a special institution set up to distribute funds. Most Islamic banks administer *Zakat* funds in a separate account and can use them, if

necessary, to help out depositors in temporary difficulty. Contributions are over and above secular taxes.

RECENT DEVELOPMENTS IN DOCTRINE AT INTERGOVERNMENTAL LEVEL

During the Seventies, several Muslim countries undertook various efforts at the international level to define basic concepts and applications of Islamic banking in today's world. These endeavors included conceptual studies, the establishment of an inter-governmental Islamic development bank, the creation of international training and research institutions as well as control by monetary authorities over Islamic institutions.

A study presented by the Arab Republic of Egypt on the "Institution of an Islamic Bank, Economics and Islamic Doctrine" was discussed and adopted on the occasion of the Third Islamic Conference of Foreign Ministers in Jeddah [in] 1972. Experts from 18 Muslim countries prepared this document under the leadership of the Egyptian Ministry of Economics. The basic issues addressed were the functioning and operations of Islamic banks. It was clearly postulated that loan finance based on interest should be replaced by profit-and-loss sharing participation schemes. Three phases were suggested to implement this novel financial concept.

As a first step, it was proposed that an Islamic advisory agency be established to deal with problems of Islamic economics and banking. Its mandate would be to help establish new Islamic financial institutions and advise them how to operate.

The second proposed step was to set up an international Islamic bank which would manage the income from interest received from non-Muslim countries, as well as from *Zakat* funds. Furthermore, it would serve as a clearinghouse for international payments between Muslim countries and finance reciprocal trade. At the national level, central agencies would be created to prepare for the subsequent establishment of local Islamic banks.

In a third step, Islamic savings, investment and development banks would be created to complement the umbrella institutions at the national and international levels.

What actually developed was somewhat different. The advisory agency, the International Association of Islamic Banks (IAIB), was established only in 1977, after the Islamic Development Bank (IsDB) in 1975 and then commercial Islamic banks had been set up in several countries. A central agency to help establish Islamic banks at the local level has yet to be founded in the various Muslim countries. Nevertheless, the "Egyptian Study" was instrumental in furthering the development and implementation of Islamic banks, and many of its conceptual proposals have been adopted along the lines laid down.

* * *

TRADITIONAL AND NEW ISLAMIC FINANCIAL INSTRUMENTS

Since Islamic law does not recognize corporations in the Western sense, companies are based on partnerships, originally only between two individuals but later extended to more. Two legal forms are basically utilized to provide funds on the basis of profit-and-loss sharing: *Musharaka* and *Modaraba*. Both are old Arab/pre-Islamic constructions which were originally developed for the requirements of trading city-states in a hostile environment to cope with socially undesirable phenomena, like scarcity of goods and usury for credit.

The *Musharaka* contract is formally a limited partnership, whereby both the bank and the customer provide capital for a specific project. Another possibility is the participation of the bank in an existing enterprise by means of a capital contribution. The pro-rata distribution of profits between bank and customer is subject to a contract between the parties. Losses are shared according to capital contribution. The bank may participate in the management, but it may also waive this right.

There exist *Musharaka* contracts with either constant or decreasing participation. The latter form is offered by the Jordan Islamic Bank, for example where the participation of the bank decreases over time. The bank keeps the profit share of the customer to pay back the capital contribution.

The *Modaraba* contract is formally a silent partnership with a clear distinction between the capital provider and the entrepreneur who controls the management of the project. Remuneration is again based upon a predetermined percentage of profits; losses have to be borne by capital providers alone. The entrepreneur then foregoes remuneration for his work.

Literature on Islamic banking has extensively commented on *Modaraba* contracts. Originally, the bank was the capital provider (*Raab Al-Mal*); it financed a project proposed by an entrepreneur (*Modareb*). Today, *Modarabas* can be applied to various economic activities, the most important of which are described below.

In banking, the institution offers its services as a manager of capital (*Mudareb*) and invites deposits from the public (*Raab Al-Mal*). The customer is offered a variety of fixed term instruments (e.g. security accounts, investment accounts, etc.) and shares with the bank the risk of the operations. He is guaranteed neither a profit nor the full return of his principal. In the case of current accounts, the bank assumes all risks alone, but does not share profits with the depositor (often Islamic banks specify a minimum balance above which no handling charges on current accounts are levied).

In investment, the bank issues nominal or bearer certificates (often negotiable) which entitle the holder to share in the profits of the activities being undertaken by the investment company. This can be specific to a single project, or a general share in all activities. The duration can be for a fixed date, at fixed intervals, on call, etc.

For the supply of goods and equipment, Islamic banks use the *Murabaha* contract. The financial institution purchases raw materials, goods or equipment at cost and sells them to the client on a cost-plus-negotiated-margin basis. Other transactions are rental financing (*Ijara*), whereby the bank acquires equipment or buildings and makes them available to the client on a straightforward rental basis. In the case of hire-purchase financing (*Ijara Wa Iktina*), a similar construction is applied. The client, however, has the possibility of acquiring ownership of the rental equipment or buildings by paying installments into a savings account. The reinvestment of this accumulated capital works in favor of the client, allowing him to offset rental cost. ■

Eurocurrency Deposits

Eurocurrency deposits: Foreign currency on deposit in a bank, on which the bank pays interest in the same foreign currency.

Accounts in domestic banks that are maintained and paid in a foreign currency are generally known as **Eurocurrency deposits**.[145] Such deposits are commonly free of the monetary control restrictions imposed by their issuing country. American dollars (or "Eurodollars"[146]) are the most common Eurocurrency; however, British pounds, Canadian dollars, European Union euros, Japanese yen, and Swiss francs are also used.

The Interbank Deposit Market

The worldwide economic expansion that began in the 1950s put such enormous financial demands on commercial banks that they were unable to service their "core" or customer-placed deposits. Because banks operating in the United States were (and are) generally forbidden to open

---

[145]The "Euro" prefix stems from its origins in London's currency market and is, of course, no longer accurate. For a short history of the Eurocurrency market *see* F. A. Mann, *The Legal Aspect of Money*, pp. 61–62 (4th ed., 1982).

[146]Eurodollars are financial assets denominated as U.S. dollars and having at any given time the same value as a U.S. dollar in the United States, but which are not subject to the control exercised by the U.S. central bank (the Federal

branches and solicit deposits from outside the geographical area of their parent bank, they had to turn to other sources for raising funds.[147] Thus they began to borrow from banks and corporations with short-term surpluses. By the 1970s, this interbank market had become international, with banks in New York, London, Tokyo, and the world's other financial centers operating as active international traders.[148] Trades are made throughout the day and night, every day of every year, by telephone and over the Internet in a global marketplace that is virtually unregulated.

certificate of deposit: A promissory note issued by a bank in which the bank promises to repay money it has received, plus interest, at a time certain.

A variety of short-term liquid instruments are traded in this interbank market, but the most common is the **certificate of deposit** (CD), issued in multiples of U.S. $1 million for maturity periods of 1, 3, and 6 months. A CD is a form of commercial paper, defined as "an instrument containing an acknowledgment by a bank that a sum of money has been received by the bank and a promise by the bank to repay the sum of money."[149] As such, it is a negotiable instrument. However, because interbank CDs have relatively short maturities, they are seldom transferred from one holder to another.

Banks are no longer the principal purchasers of CDs. Money market funds and corporations with excess cash have supplanted them, in part, because CDs held by American banks are not regarded (under the U.S. Federal Reserve System's regulations) as the equivalent of cash and, therefore, cannot be used to reduce a bank's obligation to maintain reserves.[150] Even so, banks do deposit huge sums of money in other banks as a means of rate positioning based on their differing perceptions about the market's direction. Often these trades are made in rapid-fire order and commonly without the use of certificates. In the fastest-moving sector of the interbank market, both the issuance and the safekeeping of certificates would be burdensome. Trades are made over the telephone, confirmed in brief messages sent by telex or fax, and then followed up with a written "ticket" that is mailed by the depositary to the depositor.

The Foreign Exchange Market

A buyer in Lusaka, Zambia, wants to buy 100,000 gallons of maple syrup from a seller in Toronto, Canada. The buyer is able to pay with Zambian kwachas, but the seller requires Canadian dollars. To carry out the purchase (which is called a **foreign exchange**), the buyer will contact his bank in Lusaka to buy the needed dollars. If the Lusaka bank does not have Canadian dollars on hand (which is likely the case), it will undertake to buy them on the world's **foreign exchange market**. Despite its name, the foreign exchange market does not exist in any place. It is, rather, an informal network of banks, foreign exchange brokers, and foreign exchange dealers. The Lusaka bank's foreign currency trader will contact them in the hopes of making an exchange. This may be difficult, however, because the international market for kwachas is limited, and the bank may only have a limited supply of other currencies (called hard currencies) that it can readily convert into Canadian dollars. Hard currencies (i.e., the currencies of the major free-market nations) are freely exchangeable. The currencies of developing countries, like Zambia's kwacha, are commonly called soft currencies because they are not freely exchangeable.

foreign exchange: The conversion of the money of one state into that of another state.

foreign exchange market: An informal network of banks, foreign exchange brokers, and foreign exchange dealers who facilitate the exchange of currencies.

If the Lusaka bank is unable to purchase sufficient Canadian dollars to carry out the transaction for the buyer, it will have to turn to Zambia's central bank for assistance. The Bank of Zambia may or may not have enough Canadian dollars or other hard currencies to sell to the Lusaka bank. If it does not, it may contact the Bank for International Settlements to exchange gold or whatever currencies it does have for dollars. Should this be impossible, the central bank will ask the Zambian government to exchange the Special Drawing Rights that it holds in the International Monetary Fund for Canadian dollars. If the central government does not have

---

Reserve System) over either interest rates or money supply. Peter S. Smedresman and Andreas F. Lowenfeld, "Euro-dollars, Multinational Banks, and National Laws," *New York University Law Review,* vol. 64, p. 733 at p. 744 (1989).

[147]*United States Code,* Title 12, § 36(c) (1998), requires national banks to comply with the branch banking rules of the state in which they operate. Section 1831(u) allows banks to maintain branches in different states following a merger (occurring after June 1, 1997), but not if this would violate an express state prohibition.

[148]The top 10 banks in the interbank foreign exchange market as of May 1997 were (1) Citibank, (2) NatWest, (3) Merrill Lynch, (4) Deutsche Morgan Greenfell, (5) Chase Manhattan, (6) SEC Warburg, (7) JP Morgan, (8) Goldman Sachs, (9) HSBC Markets/Midland, and (10) BZW. From "Foreign Exchange," *Euromoney* (May 1997) as noted in *Foreign Currency Trading, From the Fundamentals to the Fine Points,* posted at www.pforex.com/book/book.htm.

[149]United States, *Uniform Commercial Code,* § 3–104.

[150]United States, *Code of Federal Regulations,* Title 12, § 204.3(f)(1) (1998).

SDRs, it may arrange for a short-term loan from the IMF, or the World Bank, to acquire the needed dollars.

Once the dollars have been acquired, they will be deposited in a major bank in one of the major financial centers, such as New York, London, or Tokyo, for the account of the Lusaka bank. The major bank in this instance is known as a **correspondent bank**. When the buyer confirms that the seller has delivered the maple syrup, the Lusaka bank will instruct its correspondent bank to transfer the dollars to the seller's bank or to that bank's correspondent bank.

This somewhat simplified example of a foreign currency exchange highlights the principal participants involved in the transaction. Normally, the two major actors are commercial and central banks. In addition, arbitrageurs, importers, exporters, multinational firms, tourists, governments, and intergovernmental organizations may become involved. The transaction itself is generally unregulated, although governments in developing countries sometimes impose licensing requirements on banks and traders and often require that all exchanges be made through their central banks.

Commercial banks participate in the foreign exchange market both as intermediaries for importers, exporters, multinational corporations, and the like, and as correspondent banks in the interbank marketplace. In combination, they play three important roles: (1) they operate the payment mechanism, (2) they extend credit, and (3) they help to reduce the risk of international transactions.

Central banks participate as lenders of last resort and as regulators of currency exchange rates. In addition to providing funds for local transactions when no other funds are readily available, central banks may independently intervene in the foreign currency market to maintain orderly trading conditions. This sometimes involves the purchase of weaker currencies. For example, in the 1980s, Germany and Japan helped support the U.S. dollar by purchasing the American currency at a time when its value was falling.

In making currency exchanges, traders typically use a widely traded intermediary currency. For instance, in the previous example, the buyer's bank in Lusaka might purchase U.S. dollars, which in turn would be converted by the seller's bank in Toronto to Canadian dollars. The most commonly used intermediary, or international exchange currency, is the American dollar. Exchange rates for converting the dollar into the world's other hard currencies are published on a daily basis in major newspapers around the world. Exchange rates for other currencies are published on a weekly basis in major financial newspapers (such as the *Financial Times* and the *Wall Street Journal*) and can be obtained from major banks on a more frequent basis.

Foreign Exchange Contracts

Foreign exchange contracts may be made as spot, future, forward, or option contracts. A **spot contract** is simply a transaction involving the immediate sale and delivery of a commodity, such as a currency.[151] A **future contract** (or "future") is simply a promise to buy or sell a commodity (e.g., a currency) for a specified price with both delivery and payment to be made at a specified future date. Because there is a market in futures (they are sold on commodity exchanges), such contracts are both standardized and transferable.[152] Trading in futures, however, seldom results in the physical delivery of the commodity. More often, the obligations of the parties are extinguished by offsetting transactions that produce a net profit or loss. Futures are used primarily as a way to transfer price risks from suppliers, processors, and distributors (called "hedgers" when they become parties to these "hedging" contracts) to those who are more willing to take the risk (called "speculators").[153]

The uses of hedging as well as the risks involved in such contracts are explored in Case 6–7.

correspondent bank: A bank that acts as an agent of another bank, especially in carrying a deposit balance for the latter.

spot contract: A contract for the immediate sale and delivery of a commodity, such as a currency.

future contract: A promise to buy or sell a commodity (e.g., a currency) for a specified price with both delivery and payment to be made at a specified future date.

---

[151]The Federal Reserve Bank of New York posts spot foreign exchange rates for the New York interbank market at www.ny.frb.org/pihome/mktrates/forex10.shtml.

[152]Futures contracts are characterized as being fungible, that is, being readily transferable or exchangeable. Salomon Forex, Inc. v. Tauber, *Federal Reporter, Third Series,* vol. 8, p. 966 at p. 967 (Fourth Circuit Ct. of Appeals, 1993).

[153]*Id.*

Case 6–7   Hunt et al. v. Alliance North American Government Income Trust, Inc. et al.   ⌐~

United States, Second Circuit Court of Appeals.
Federal Reporter, Third Series, vol. 159, p. 723, 1998.[154]

CIRCUIT JUDGE LEVAL:

Plaintiffs are shareholders in Alliance North American Government Income Trust, Inc. (the Fund), an open-ended mutual fund formed to make investments in government-guaranteed securities of Mexico, Canada, the United States, and countries in Central and South America. Plaintiffs brought this action against the Fund (and related persons and entities[155]) alleging various violations of the federal securities laws and common law claims after the value of their shares declined dramatically due to the collapse of the Mexican peso in December 1994. The United States District Court for the Southern District of New York (Judge Lawrence M. McKenna) dismissed the original complaint. The court also denied plaintiffs' motion for leave to replead on the ground that the Proposed Amended Complaint failed to state an actionable claim. . . .

Background

Plaintiffs purchased their shares in the Fund from March 27, 1992, to December 23, 1994 (the Relevant Period). During the Relevant Period the Fund was an open-ended mutual fund that sold shares on a continuing basis pursuant to registration statements and prospectuses. Between February 1992 and December 1994, the Fund issued seven prospectuses, each containing representations that were substantially identical for the purposes of this case.[156] The prospectuses represented that the Fund's investment objective was to "seek . . . the highest level of current income, consistent with what the Fund's Adviser considered to be a prudent investment risk, that is available from a portfolio of debt securities issued or guaranteed by the governments of the United States, Canada, and Mexico, their political

subdivisions, . . . agencies, instrumentalities, or authorities. . . ." The prospectuses also stated, "There can be, of course, no assurance that the Fund will achieve its investment objective." The Fund would invest at least 65 percent of its total assets in debt securities issued or guaranteed by the governments of the United States, Canada, and Mexico. The balance of the Fund's assets would be invested in debt securities issued by the governments of countries located in Central and South America.

The prospectuses explained that investing in securities issued by foreign governments involved "possible risks not typically associated with investing in U.S. Government Securities." The value of the Fund's assets could be diminished by, *inter alia*, changes in currency exchange rates. The prospectuses stated,

> If not hedged . . . currency fluctuations could affect the unrealized appreciation and depreciation of non-U.S. Government Securities as expressed in U.S. dollars.
>
> . . . Because Fund assets will be invested in fixed income securities denominated in . . . foreign currencies and because a substantial portion of the Fund's revenues will be received in currencies other than the U.S. Dollar, the U.S. Dollar equivalent of the Fund's net assets and distributions will be adversely affected by reductions in the value of certain foreign currencies relative to the U.S. Dollar.

The prospectuses discussed several techniques available to the Fund Adviser to hedge against currency risk, including futures contracts and options on futures contracts, options on foreign currencies, forward foreign currency exchange contracts, and options on U.S. and Foreign Government securities. For example, the prospectuses stated the Fund "may" enter into futures contracts and options on futures contracts, which "will be used only to hedge against anticipated future changes in interest or exchange rates which otherwise might

---

[154]The text of this case is posted on the FindLaw Internet Web site at caselaw.findlaw.com/uscircs/2nd/979477v2.html.

[155]In addition to the Fund, the defendants are: Alliance Capital Management, L.P., the Fund's investment adviser; Alliance Capital Management Corporation, general partner of the investment adviser; Alliance Fund Distributors, Inc., a subsidiary of the investment adviser and the principal underwriter for the Fund; and Equitable Companies Inc., the corporate parent of the investment adviser. The individual defendants are current or former officers, directors, or employees of these entities.

[156]Unless otherwise indicated all references will be to the initial prospectus and Statement of Additional Information ("SAI") dated February 21, 1992.

adversely affect the value of the Fund's portfolio securities . . . ," and that

the Fund intends to write covered put and call options and purchase put and call options on U.S. Government Securities and foreign government securities that are traded on United States and foreign securities exchanges. . . . The Fund intends to write call options for cross-hedging purposes.

Regarding these hedging techniques, the prospectuses stated,

The successful use of the foregoing investment practices draws upon the Adviser's special skills and experience with respect to such instruments and usually depends on the Adviser's ability to forecast interest rate and currency exchange rate movements correctly. Should interest or exchange rates move in an unexpected manner, the Fund may not achieve the anticipated benefits of futures contracts, options or forward contracts or may realize losses and thus be in a worse position than if such strategies had not been used. Unlike many exchange-traded futures contracts and options on futures contracts, there are not daily price fluctuation limits with respect to options on currencies and forward contracts, and adverse market movements could therefore continue to an unlimited extent over a period of time. In addition, the correlation between movements in the prices of such instruments and movements in the price of the securities and currencies hedged or used for cover will not be perfect and could produce unanticipated losses.

The Fund's ability to dispose of its position in futures contracts, options and forward contracts will depend on the availability of liquid markets in such instruments. Markets in options and futures with respect to a number of fixed-income securities and currencies are relatively new and still developing. It is impossible to predict the amount of trading interest that may exist in various types of futures contracts, options, and forward contracts. If a secondary market does not exist with respect to an option purchased or written by the Fund over-the-counter, it might not be possible to effect a closing transaction in the option (i.e., dispose of the option) with the result that (i) an option purchased by the Fund would have to be exercised in order for the fund to realize any profit and (ii) the Fund may not be able to sell currencies or portfolio securities covering an option written by the Fund until the option expires or it delivers the underlying security, futures contract or currency upon exercise. Therefore, no assurance can be given that the Fund will be able to utilize these instruments effectively for the purposes set forth above. Furthermore, the Fund's ability to engage in options and futures transactions may be limited by tax considerations.

The Fund held significant investments in Mexican and Argentine government securities in the months leading up to December 1994. These positions were disclosed to shareholders in annual and semi-annual reports dated November 30, 1993, and May 31, 1994, respectively. The reports did not state whether the Fund had employed hedging techniques to reduce currency risk.

In December 1994, the Mexican government devalued the peso over 15 percent against the U.S. dollar and, in a change of policy, allowed the peso to float freely against the dollar. As a consequence, the value of the peso fell rapidly against the dollar, investors sold large quantities of Mexican and other Central and South American securities, and the Fund's net asset value declined dramatically.

Procedural History

In early 1995, plaintiffs filed several class action complaints against the Fund and related entities . . . alleging [among other things] . . . that the Fund had falsely represented it would use hedging techniques to reduce currency risk.

The district court granted defendants' motion to dismiss. . . . Regarding the hedging techniques claim, the court found that

in combination with the other warnings contained in the prospectus, a reasonable investor should have been fully apprised of the risks that the Fund would be unable to effectively hedge its foreign investments.

* * *

In light of these disclosures, this Court finds that even assuming that no devices were practically available to hedge against the losses the Fund suffered due to its investments in Mexican and Argentine securities, due to the explicit warnings of such devices' possible unavailability and ineffectiveness, any misstatements or omissions were immaterial as a matter of law.

Accordingly, the court dismissed the Consolidated Complaint, stating it would entertain a motion for leave to replead.

Plaintiffs then moved for leave to replead. . . . The Proposed Amended Complaint alleges . . . that the prospectuses falsely stated that the Fund would use hedging devices when it knew or recklessly disregarded the fact that such devices were too expensive to be used. . . .

* * *

The district court denied plaintiff's motion for leave to replead. . . . [T]he court found again that the claim was legally insufficient. The court reasoned that no reasonable investor could have been "misled after examination of the Fund's offering materials as to the risk that hedging the Fund's investments might be impossible" because the prospectuses specifically stated that "no assurance can be given that the Fund will be able to utilize these instruments effectively for the purposes set forth [in the prospectus]."

* * *

Plaintiffs appealed. . . .

* * *

Discussion

* * *

In our view, the amended claim that the Fund's representations concerning the availability of hedging devices, "taken together and in context, would have misled a reasonable investor,"[157] adequately pleads an actionable claim. The prospectuses stated that the Fund would be exposed to risk resulting from currency fluctuations, that hedging devices could reduce this risk, and that the Fund intended to use hedging devices. The prospectuses set forth in a ten-paragraph discussion that several hedging devices were available to the Fund Adviser—futures contracts and options on futures contracts, options on foreign currencies, forward foreign currency exchange contracts, and options on U.S. and Foreign Government securities.

They stated the Fund "may" enter into futures contracts and options on futures contracts, which "*will be used* only to hedge against anticipated future changes in interest or exchange rates which otherwise might adversely affect the value of the Fund's portfolio securities . . ." (Emphasis added). They also stated that

> the Fund intends to write covered put and call options and purchase put and call options on U.S. Government Securities and foreign government securities that are traded on United States and foreign securities exchanges. . . . The Fund intends to write call options for cross-hedging purposes.

A reader of these passages and others reasonably could have understood them to mean that these hedging techniques were available (even if they were not foolproof) and that the Fund would attempt to hedge against currency risk by using these techniques. By alleging that the Fund managers knew (or recklessly disregarded) that these hedging techniques were not available (because they were too costly), plaintiffs stated an actionable claim for misrepresentation.

Defendants contend they cannot be liable because the prospectuses contain cautionary language warning that the Fund might be ineffective in reducing currency risk through hedging. They note the prospectuses warn that the "successful use of [hedging] practices . . . usually depends on the Adviser's ability to forecast interest rate and currency exchange rate movements correctly." . . .

* * *

The cautionary language contained in the prospectus does not necessarily foreclose liability because it warned investors of a different contingency than that which plaintiffs allege was misrepresented. . . .

* * *

In the instant case . . . the prospectuses did not warn of the risk plaintiffs claim was not disclosed. Plaintiffs claim the prospectuses promised the Fund would attempt to use hedging devices when in fact it could not. Because we agree a reasonable investor could have been misled by the prospectuses, and would have considered the availability of hedging devices important in deciding whether to purchase Fund shares, we find the Proposed Amended Complaint states a claim for which relief can be granted. We therefore reverse the district court's order denying leave to replead this claim. ∎

---

[157]McMahan & Co. v. Wherehouse Entertainment, Inc., *Federal Reporter, Second Series,* vol. 900, p. 576 at p. 579 (Second Circuit Ct. of Appeals, 1990).

---

forward contract: A contract in which a commodity is presently sold and the price presently paid, but delivery is, by agreement, delayed to a later date.

option contract: A contract that creates the right—but not the obligation—to buy or sell a specific amount of a commodity (e.g., currency) at a fixed price within an agreed-upon period of time.

A **forward contract** (or, in the case of currency, a "cash forward contract") is simply a transaction in which a commodity is presently sold and the price presently paid, but the delivery is, by agreement, delayed to a later date. In comparison with a future contract, which is readily transferable, a forward contract is generally negotiated individually by the parties who will actually make and receive physical delivery of the goods involved.[158]

An **option contract** (or "option") creates the right—but not the obligation—to buy or sell a specific amount of a commodity (e.g., currency) at a fixed price within an agreed-upon period of time. If the right is to buy a commodity, the option is known as a "call"; if the right is to make a sale, the option is known as a "put." If the right involves a combination of these—to either buy or sell—the option is known as a "straddle" or "spread eagle."[159] Unlike spot, futures, or forwards contracts, the holder of an option is not required to go through with the transaction. The holder must pay a fee

---

[158]*Id.*

[159]*Black's Law Dictionary,* p. 1094 (6th ed., 1990).

or some other consideration to acquire the option, but the total risk assumed in purchasing it is the loss of that fee.[160]

Arbitrage

arbitrage: (From French *arbitrer:* "to arbitrate" or "to regulate.") The nearly simultaneous purchase of currencies (or other commodities) in one market and their resale in another in order to profit from the price differential.

Arbitrage is the nearly simultaneous purchase of a commodity (such as a currency) in one market and its sale in another to profit from the price differential. Because there are differences in the prices of the world's currencies, both over time and between locations, arbitrageurs are active participants in the international foreign exchange market.[161] For example, suppose that the European Union euro is trading among traders in London at U.S. $0.9725 and among traders in Tokyo for U.S. $0.9735. An arbitrageur would buy euros in London and sell them in Japan. For example, assuming that the arbitrageur purchases 1,028,278 euros (i.e., U.S. $1 million) in London and sells them in Tokyo, he will receive $1,010,286, for a net profit of $10,286 or 1.3 percent. Of course, the purchase of euros in London will drive up their price there, and their sale in Tokyo will drive down their price in Japan. The process will continue until the exchange rate becomes the same in both places.[162]

Today, arbitrageurs and other currency traders carry on their transactions at lightning speed using telephones and the Internet. The minimum contract is normally U.S. $25,000, but contracts of $1 million are more common. Offers have to be accepted immediately, and then performed regardless of a later dispute. If there is a dispute, traders commonly split the difference.

The Transfer of Money

instruction: Order to a bank to disburse funds to a particular person.

bill of exchange (also known as a draft): A three-party instrument on which the drawer makes an unconditional order to a drawee to pay a named payee.

A bank transfers money internationally by setting up a correspondent bank relationship with a foreign bank and depositing funds to its own account in that bank. When a customer goes to his own bank and asks to transfer money overseas, the bank accepts the customer's money at its domestic office, then arranges for the correspondent bank to disburse funds in the foreign country to whomever the customer has designated. This may be done by **instruction**, in which case the domestic bank directs its correspondent to pay funds directly to a particular payee, or by the use of a **bill of exchange** that is drawn on the domestic bank's account at the foreign correspondent bank. In the latter case, the bill of exchange is given to the customer, who in turn sends it to the payee. The payee then cashes it at the correspondent bank.[163]

The actual physical delivery of currency internationally is seldom done. When required, it is arranged for by central banks, and commonly managed by the Bank for International Settlements.

Some of the problems of transferring money, especially by instruction, are described in Reading 6–2.

---

[160]Salomon Forex, Inc. v. Tauber, *Federal Reporter, Third Series,* vol. 8, p. 966 at p. 967 (Fourth Circuit Ct. of Appeals, 1993).
[161]Suk H. Kim, *International Business Finance,* pp. 111–116 (1983).
[162]Arbitrageurs, by taking advantage of momentary discrepancies in prices between markets, perform the economic function of making these markets more efficient.
[163]Ralph H. Folsom, Michael W. Gordon, John A. Spanogle Jr., *International Business Transactions in a Nutshell,* pp. 313–314 (3rd ed., 1988).

Reading 6–2   The Illicit Transfer of Money

Jonathan M. Winer, "How to Clean up Dirty Money," *Financial Times* (March 22, 2002).

It was only a generation ago that a sitting U.S. President was forced to resign after two investigative reporters were given whispered advice by a deep throat in a garage: "Follow the money."

One could track money then, prior to the transformation of currencies into electronic digits, and the blowing away of local controls and the overseeing of who managed the cash.

Poor Richard Nixon, having to rely on hush-money payments in local currency, and denied the money-laundering choices available to even small-timers today, not to mention the world's more significant criminals, terrorists, and kleptocrats.

Where once the ability to stash your cash was limited to those sufficiently affluent to stop over in Zurich between schussing in Gstaad, globalization has rapidly democratized money laundering.

The results, in much of the world have been horrific, as the U.S. learned on September 11 [2001]. How simple it was for al-Qaeda's terrorists to have $500,000 wired from a bank in Dubai for anonymous use in automatic teller machines in Florida and Maine. How difficult, even with the backing of United Nations resolutions and 150 nations, it has proved to find out who raised and sent those dollars.

Long before September 11, many other victims of wrongdoing have found that global evil-doers are better at taking advantage of the financial infrastructure of globalization than the world's police and regulators are at catching them.

Indeed, with remarkable frequency, governments themselves have been infected by the money-laundering disease, with senior officials hiding wrongdoing in the same nooks and crannies of the global financial system used by the denizens of the lower depths.

Over the past decade, this pattern has been played out repeatedly, as political conflict, narcotics trafficking, arms smuggling, civil war, grand corruption, and terrorism have been facilitated and sustained by illicit finance networks embedded in the world's legal financial services infrastructure.

Massive (and largely untraceable) electronic money outflows paved the way in 1994 for the collapse of the Mexican peso, costing Mexico a quarter-century of economic growth amid evidence of drug-money laundering and huge high-level corruption involving the president's family. Billions vanished as governments collapsed in Ecuador, Peru, and, most recently, Argentina. Fraudulent pyramid schemes decapitalized nations in transition in Albania, Bulgaria, and Latvia.

Meanwhile, taking advantage of the archipelago of global finance, kleptocrats were able to steal and sequester the national wealth of the Congo/Zaire, Indonesia, Nigeria, and Russia. The use of offshore financial centers to mask large financial losses facilitated the industrial, corporate and governmental corruption that has burdened the economies of Japan, South Korea, and Taiwan.

The tiny principality of Liechtenstein was able simultaneously to handle political slush funds for former German Chancellor Helmut Kohl, the corrupt proceeds of illicit arms trafficking by the son of the late French President Francois Mitterrand, the proceeds of various West African dictators, and funds set aside by some of Latin America's most successful drug lords.

Illicit finance has also made possible the trade in diamonds that fuelled civil conflict in Liberia, Angola, and Sierra Leone, and their accompanying arms deals and payoffs. It has sustained the narcotics trade and accompanying insurrections in Afghanistan, Burma, and Colombia.

Spreading financial scandals have given birth to mushrooming government initiatives. The UN, the European Union, the Council of Europe, the Organization of American States, and other international bodies have concocted new global standards to promote financial transparency and achieve the required level of international co-operation.

Leading self-regulatory organizations, such as the Basle Committee for Banking Supervision and the International Organization of Securities Commissions, have focused on extending standards for international financial regulation to cover transparency issues. In Paris, the OECD and the Financial Action Task Force, created by the G7 in 1989 to clean up drug money, conduct assessments of who has been naughty and who has been nice.

The two organizations take turns to name jurisdictions that will face sanctions if they do not behave. Those threatened with financial isolation, including such international thoroughfares as Dominica and Nauru and the U.K.'s Crown or Caribbean dependencies, protest at the unfairness of it all—but have marched lock-step in compliance with regulatory demands—unable to risk loss of access to the world's most substantial financial markets.

And yet, amid all this regulatory and enforcement activity, dodgy money continues to remain an artful dodger indeed.

Is something wrong, then, with the way regulators are trying to implement financial transparency? Or is it simply over-ambition for domestic, national, and public entities to join together to try to regulate the dark side of an infrastructure that is inherently cross-border, international and private?

Each existing government initiative is based on the premise that national financial service regulators have the capacity to determine whether their own "local" institutions meet the standards. Under the principle of consolidated supervision, each home country regulator of an international financial institution is solely responsible for exercising oversight over the global operations of that institution.

However, evidence is mounting to justify questioning whether global financial institutions, operating transnationally to move money instantaneously across national borders, can be readily regulated or supervised by any one country. With local branches and subsidiaries in dozens of nations, it may be beyond the capacity of any single state to police such institutions.

In practice, even the most sophisticated and best-regulated financial centers have proved incapable of adequately overseeing the global enterprises they license. Suppose the nation state of Nauru, population 18,000, wished to impose rigorous anti-money-laundering standards on banks it licenses. How, precisely, is it supposed to assess what the branch offices of those banks are doing in say, Lebanon, Liberia, Gibraltar, or Macao?

In contrast to such governments, international financial institutions would seem better situated to regulate money-laundering and financial crime, and to enforce self-regulation on a global basis. Whatever the largest global financial institutions may lack, it is not human resources, or organizational capacity. Rather, what would appear to be lacking to date is an appropriate system of incentives.

Today, at any international bank, a compliance office is a cost of doing business, while a trader is a profit generator. Under the circumstances, it is easy to understand why, at any given bank on any given day, those creating a profit-making scheme involving an off-shore trust in Belize, that in turn owns a Turks and Caicos company, tend to win battles with those asking questions about the venture. In the long run, an institution faces a reputational risk in taking advantage of financial secrecy in remote parts of the world, but, in the short term, profits are to be made so that bonuses may be paid.

Thus, while governments scurry about ranking one another's efforts against financial crime, international financial institutions face no comparable review, at least at a global level. No organization, public or private, has ranked leading international institutions for the greatest or least laundering of dirty money, although such a ranking might be compiled from court documents, public investigations and press reports.

Nor has there been a seal or certificate system to endorse institutions that have put into place a series of best practices to promote transparency. The most relevant initiative has been the adoption over the past two years of the Wolfsberg Principles by 11 of the world's largest banks.

These banks, the Wolfsberg Group, have agreed to adopt "know your customer" principles to discourage abuses of private banking by those engaged in grand corruption, and, most recently, to prevent themselves from being used to facilitate terrorist finance.

The Wolfsberg Principles have been a unique development in the world of international banking. All participating institutions have agreed to impose the principles on a global basis—from Liechtenstein to London, Nauru to New York.

However, unlike government name-and-shame exercises, the Wolfsberg Principles lack an assessment mechanism and any practical carrots or sticks for the group's members. While a reputation is a terrible thing to waste, many large international financial institutions have weathered scandals that would have felled heads of government.

The question, therefore, is whether a new initiative could bring together the principles of universal private-sector self-regulation, and the concept of lists and mutual assessment used to some effect among nation states through the OECD and the Financial Action Task Force exercises. Such an initiative could not be used to create a blacklist for private-sector institutions. Neither markets nor politics would tolerate such an intrusion into global finance. But imagine instead a white list, to make compliance a profit centre, rather than a burden on a bank. A white list—and a reward for being on it.

The World Bank and its regional cousins control billions of dollars for lending around the world. While holding these funds, these organizations deposit them not only in central banks, but also in commercial ones. The UN and other international organizations also control substantial sums in development assistance, also necessarily deposited in and handled by banks, as do government-sponsored entities such as export-import banks, the world's many national and international development programs, private foundations, and non-governmental organizations.

Today, financial transparency is not a criterion for the selection of one financial institution over another. An international bank involved in money-laundering scandals or terrorist finance has about the same chance of obtaining a lucrative source of government resources as does an international bank that has imposed the highest standards of transparency and anti-money laundering policies. No wonder the compliance officer is seen as a profit drain.

An additional incentive for financial institutions to adhere to a comprehensive, global code of conduct would seem a logical goal for an international community increasingly focused on risks created by financial secrecy. It would supplement the work of nations by asking institutions that operate in many jurisdictions to adhere to the same standards in all of them, even where the governments themselves have little ability directly to regulate or enforce these standards.

To make a white-list system work, the UN could, for example, ask the world's financial institutions to adopt existing international anti-money laundering guidelines on a global basis throughout their institutions.

The institutions would be required to agree to maintain know-your-customer and other anti-money laundering policies and procedures in every office, regardless of location. They would accept the principle of having others conduct regular external assessments of its compliance with the standards, and the publication of comprehensive reports, describing how they had met the standards.

An institution that has agreed to an assessment, and passed it, would be named on a white list and, after a transition period, be rewarded with a preference for selection in processing funds controlled by the UN and other international organizations.

The opponents of globalization have sometimes characterized the process as a race to the bottom when it comes to the enforcement of laws and regulations.

Its supporters have promised globalization as a deliverer of opportunity and prosperity. At this juncture, we may find ourselves like Alice. Having eaten the comfit, with hand on head, we ask ourselves: "Which way? Which way?"

The establishment of a global white list could help us insure a regulatory race to the top, so that the benefits of globalization are not eclipsed by its dark side. ∎

Branch Banking

International banks, unlike most other multinational companies, prefer to operate in host countries through branches rather than subsidiaries. And in most major host countries, including France, Germany, Japan, Switzerland, the United Kingdom, and the United States, branch operations (without separate incorporation) are not only allowed, they are encouraged.[164] On the one hand, host countries impose few regulations limiting the operations of foreign banks. On the other hand, they assume few supervisory responsibilities. Thus, unlike domestic banks, foreign banks do not have to maintain reserves to cover potential losses. Foreign banks, however, cannot turn to the host country's central bank as a lender of last resort. From the perspective of the host country, a foreign bank is required to stand behind the local obligations of its branches with its entire worldwide assets.

Although host states generally impose minimal regulations on foreign branches, the presence of a foreign branch has sometimes been used as a means to obtain information from a foreign parent bank. In particular, the U.S. government, in an effort to curtail the use of foreign banks as conduits for laundering illegal profits from narcotics smuggling, income tax evasion, securities fraud, and other business crimes, has attempted to extend its regulatory jurisdiction over foreign banks by asking courts to issue subpoenas exercisable against their U.S. branches.[165] Such subpoenas require the U.S. branch to obtain information from the parent and then turn it over to the American government. Needless to say, many countries regard the American actions as an invasion of their sovereign rights, and legislation to counter the U.S. efforts is not uncommon.[166]

Not only foreign countries but the U.S. courts as well have taken a dim view of this attempt by the political arms of the U.S. government to exercise extraterritorial jurisdiction over foreign banks. Case 6–8 illustrates the reaction of one appellate court to the U.S. government's use of a grand jury subpoena to compel one branch of a foreign bank to produce records held by its parent.[167]

---

[164]*See*, for example, U.S. Treasury Department, *Report to Congress on Foreign Government Treatment of U.S. Commercial Banking Organizations,* p. 19 (1979).

Prior to becoming a party to the North American Free Trade Agreement, Canada required local incorporation of banks. Canada Bank Act, *Revised Statutes of Canada,* vol. 1, chap. B-1, § 302(1)(b) (1985). Now, foreign banks may establish branches so long as the bank's home state provides like treatment for foreign banks. *Id.,* vol. 1, chap. B-1.01, § 24 (1991). Canada's statutes are posted on the Internet at canada.justice.gc.ca/Loireg/index_en.html.

[165]A report issued by the U.S. House of Representatives Committee on Banking and Currency in 1970 stated that secret foreign bank accounts encourage "white collar" crimes. *House of Representatives Report No. 975,* 91st Congress, 2nd Session, p. 12 (1970).

[166]*See,* e.g., Foreign Proceedings (Prohibition of Certain Evidence) Act, 1976, *Acts of the Parliament of the Commonwealth of Australia,* No. 121; amended by Foreign Proceedings (Prohibition of Certain Evidence) Amendment Act, 1976, *id.,* No. 202; repealed and replaced by Foreign Proceedings (Excess of Jurisdiction) Act, 1984, *id.,* No. 3. Foreign Extraterritorial Measures Act, *Statutes of Canada,* chap. 49 (1984). Confidential Relationships (Preservation) Law, Cayman Islands Law 16 of 1976 and the Confidential Relationships (Preservation) (Amendment) Law, Cayman Islands Law 26 of 1979.

Sometimes, however, states other than the United States seek to obtain information from banks located abroad. *See* In re Request for Assistance from Ministry of Legal Affairs of Trinidad and Tobago, *Federal Reporter, Second Series,* vol. 848, p. 1151 (Eleventh Circuit Court of Appeals, 1988).

[167]An excellent discussion of the conflict-of-laws implications that arise from the use of subpoenas to compel foreign banks to produce evidence can be found in Silvia B. Piñera-Vàzquez, "Extraterritorial Jurisdiction and International Banking: A Conflict of Interest," *University of Miami Law Review,* vol. 43, p. 449 (1988).

Case 6–8   In re Sealed Case   ⌒

United States, Court of Appeals, District of Columbia Circuit, 1987.
Federal Reporter, Second Series, vol. 825, p. 494 (1987).

PER CURIAM:[168]

These consolidated appeals are taken from orders in a miscellaneous proceeding below collateral to a grand jury investigation. The government sought and obtained orders in the district court compelling appellants, a bank and an individual, to respond to a grand jury subpoena by producing documents and giving testimony. When appellants continued to refuse to respond to the grand jury's demands, the court found appellants in contempt. The grand jury investigation has not been completed, and the records in the district court and this court have been sealed. In order to maintain this secrecy, we do not identify the parties in this opinion.

I.

* * *

From the beginning, the manager and the bank have cooperated to a certain extent with the investigation. The manager has come to Washington several times to meet with the prosecutors and testify before the grand jury about his knowledge of the targets and their activities that he learned in his personal capacity (not through bank operations). Except for information concerning three customers from whom they obtained releases, however, the manager and the bank refused to testify before the grand jury about the targets' banking activities or produce documents on the ground that to do so would violate Country Y's banking secrecy laws and subject the manager and the bank to criminal prosecution in Country Y.

The bank has taken the position that the government should use other means to attempt to obtain the documents from Country Y, a course that the government believes is inappropriate and would be ineffective. The manager based his refusal to testify on Fifth Amendment grounds, claiming that the act of testifying would subject him to criminal sanctions in Country Y. The government secured use immunity for the manager but he continues to decline to answer on the ground that a United States court could not immunize him from

criminal prosecution in Country Y. Since the act of testifying would violate the laws of Country Y, he contends that to require him to testify would violate his Fifth Amendment protection against self-incrimination.

* * *

II.

The manager's Fifth Amendment claim is based on his assertion that Country Y could convict him of a crime solely for revealing information protected by Country Y's banking secrecy law. He does not claim that the substance of his testimony would incriminate him for any crime that he has committed, under either the laws of the United States, of Country X, or of Country Y. The manager argues that, despite the district court's grant of immunity, his real and substantial fear of prosecution in Country Y cloaks his refusal to testify with Fifth Amendment protection. We disagree.

* * *

The district court concluded that even if the Fifth Amendment does apply to a situation in which the witness asserts the threat of foreign prosecution, it "[was] not convinced that the fear of prosecution in this case is 'real' as required by *Zicarelli v. New Jersey Comm'n of Investigation*."[169] . . . It based this finding on the strict secrecy provisions of Rule 6(e) of the Federal Rules of Criminal Procedure.

We agree that the manager's fear of prosecution is not real, but for a different reason. The manager could only be prosecuted by Country Y as a result of his own voluntary act—returning to Country Y. We recognize his substantial connections to Country Y, but he no longer lives or works there. He is not himself a citizen of that country and his immediate family is with him in this country. As the manager concedes, the offense with which he could be charged by Country Y for his testimony here is not an offense for which he could be extradited. He could only be punished for this offense if he were to return voluntarily. "It is well established that the [Fifth Amendment] privilege protects against real dangers, not remote and speculative possibilities."[170] We only add that it does not protect against dangers voluntarily assumed. We, therefore, affirm the order of the district court holding the manager in contempt for refusing to testify before the grand jury.

---

[168]Latin: "by the court." A phrase used to indicate that the whole court rather than any one judge wrote the opinion.]
[169]*United States Reports,* vol. 406, p. 472 at pp. 478–81 (Supreme Ct., 1972).
[170]*Id.,* at p. 478.

III.

The bank argues that the district court erred in entering a civil contempt order that compels it to act in violation of the laws of Country Y. The federal courts have disagreed about whether a court may order a person to take specific actions on the soil of a foreign sovereign in violation of its laws and about what sanctions the court may levy against a person who refuses to comply with such an order. . . .

. . . Be that as it may, here we simply conclude that even if a court has the power to issue such contempt orders under certain circumstances, on the peculiar facts of this case the order should not have issued. Most important to our decision is the fact that these sanctions represent an attempt by an American court to compel a foreign person to violate the laws of a different foreign sovereign on that sovereign's own territory. In addition, the bank, against whom the order is directed, is not itself the focus of the criminal investigation in this case but is a third party that has not been accused of any wrongdoing. Moreover, the bank is not merely a private foreign entity, but is an entity owned by the government of Country Y. We recognize that one who relies on foreign law assumes the burden of showing that such law prevents compliance with the court's order, . . . but here the government concedes that it would be impossible for the bank to comply with the contempt order without violating the laws of Country Y on Country Y's soil. The district court specifically found that the bank had acted in good faith throughout these proceedings. The executive branch may be able to devise alternative means of addressing this problem, but the bank cannot.

* * *

A decision whether to enter a contempt order in cases like this one raises grave difficulties for courts. We have little doubt, for example, that our government and our people would be affronted if a foreign court tried to compel someone to violate our laws within our borders. The legal expression of this widespread sentiment is found in basic principles of international comity. But unless we are willing simply to enter contempt orders in all such cases, no matter how extreme, in utter disregard of comity principles, we are obliged to undertake the unseemly task of picking and choosing when to order parties to violate foreign laws. It is conceivable that we might even be forced to base our determination in part on a subjective evaluation of the content of those laws; an American court might well find it wholly inappropriate to defer to a foreign sovereign where the laws in question promote, for example, torture or slavery or terrorism.

. . . We have no doubt that Congress could empower courts to issue contempt orders in any of these cases, or that the executive branch could negotiate positive agreements with other nations to the same end. If we were asked to act in accord with such a distinct and express grant of power, it would be our duty to do so. Indeed, any such measures would be a welcome improvement over the difficulties and uncertainties that now pervade this area of law.

In sum, we emphasize again the limited nature of our holding on this issue. If any of the facts we rest on here were different, our holding could well be different. And though we reserve the district court's order holding the bank in civil contempt on the facts of this case, we of course intend no challenge to proposition that the vital role of grand jury investigations on our criminal system endows the grand jury with wide discretion in seeking evidence. It is therefore also relevant to our conclusion that the grand jury is not left empty-handed by today's decision. The manager will be available and able to testify as to many of the facts that the grand jury may wish to ascertain. The government may find alternative means to obtain additional information from or through the bank. Though we recognize that the grand jury's investigation may nonetheless be hampered, perhaps significantly, we are unable to uphold the contempt order against the bank.

Affirmed in part and reversed in part. ■

From the perspective of the parent bank, the foreign branch is often treated as a separate business unit, with its own profit-and-loss statement, its own foreign tax liabilities, and its own separate account with the parent bank.[171] In terms of home state law, however, the treatment of foreign branches is not so easily described. Inconsistency is the common rule, both between and within states. Sometimes foreign branches are treated as peculiar separate entities. For example, statutes commonly require a parent bank to get permission from its home state banking authority before it may establish a foreign branch.[172] Similarly, some courts have refused to

[171] Peter S. Smedresman and Andreas F. Lowenfeld, "Eurodollars, Multinational Banks, and National Laws," *New York University Law Review,* vol. 64, p. 733 at p. 742 (1989).

[172] *United States Code,* Title 12, § 601 (1998), requires a federally chartered bank to obtain authorization from the Board of Governors of the Federal Reserve System before opening a foreign branch.

issue subpoenas directed against foreign branches,[173] and others have treated letter-of-credit transactions between a parent and branch bank as if the two were unrelated entities.[174]

Sometimes, however, home country statutes and courts treat foreign branches as mere extensions of their parents. For example, in 1979, in response to the Iranian hostage crisis, the United States froze Iranian government assets held in U.S. banks *and* their foreign branches.[175] Courts, similarly, have held that a parent bank can be ordered to freeze the account of a foreign corporation held in the bank's foreign branches.[176] And courts commonly hold that a parent bank is liable for the debts incurred by its foreign branches, because the branch is subject to the supervision and control of the parent.[177]

In Case 6–9, the U.S. Second Circuit Court of Appeals considered the responsibilities of a parent bank for funds deposited in a foreign branch when the foreign branch and its assets are seized by the host country.

---

[173]In McCloskey v. Chase Manhattan Bank, *New York Reports, Second Series,* vol. 11, p. 936 (1962), the New York Court of Appeals held that an attachment served on a New York bank does not reach deposits made at its foreign branch.

[174]Pan-American Bank & Trust Co. v. National City Bank of New York, *Federal Reporter, Second Series,* vol. 6, p. 762 (Second Circuit Ct. of Appeals, 1925).

[175]*See Weekly Compilation of Presidential Documents,* vol. 15, p. 2117 (November 14, 1979), and *United States Code,* Title 50, §§ 1701–1706 (1982 and Supp. V, 1987).

[176]In United States v. First National City Bank, *United States Reports,* vol. 379, p. 378 (Supreme Ct., 1964), the U.S. Supreme Court reasoned that a foreign bank branch is not a separate entity and, therefore, its parent has both actual and practical control of its operations.

[177]Sokoloff v. National City Bank of New York, *New York Miscellaneous Reports,* vol. 130, p. 66 (New York Supreme Court, 1927). A different rationale was used in Wells Fargo Asia, Ltd., v. Citibank, N.A., *Federal Supplement,* vol. 695, p. 1450 at p. 1456 (1988). There, the U.S. District Court for the Southern District of New York concluded that "under New York law, which governs this question, Citibank is liable for the debt of its Manila branch and plaintiff is entitled to look to Citibank's worldwide assets for satisfaction of its deposits." For additional similar cases, *see* Patrick Heininger, "Liability of U.S. Banks for Deposits Placed in Their Foreign Branches," *Law and Policy in International Business,* vol. 11, p. 903 (1979).

Case 6–9   *Vishipco Line et al. v. Chase Manhattan Bank, N.A.*

United States, Court of Appeals, Second Circuit, 1981. *Federal Reporter, Second Series*, vol. 660, p. 854 (1981).

CIRCUIT JUDGE MANSFIELD:

* * *

From 1966 until April 24, 1975, Chase operated a branch office in Saigon. Among its depositors were the ten corporate plaintiffs, which were principally engaged at that time in providing shipping services to the U.S. Government in Southeast Asia, and the individual plaintiff, who owned a 200 million piastre CD issued by Chase's Saigon branch. Chase's operations in Saigon came to an end at noon on April 24, 1975, after Chase officials in New York determined that Saigon would soon fall to the Communists. After closing the branch without prior notice to depositors, local Chase officials balanced the day's books, shut the vaults and the building itself, and delivered keys and financial records needed to operate the branch to personnel at

the French Embassy in Saigon. Saigon fell on April 30th, and on May 1st the new government issued a communiqué which read as follows:

All public offices, public organs, barracks, industrial, agriculture and commercial establishments, banks, communication and transport, cultural, educational and health establishments, warehouses, and so forth — together with documents, files, property and technical means of U.S. imperialism and the Saigon administration — will be confiscated and, from now on, managed by the revolutionary administration.

Shortly thereafter, the French embassy turned over records from the Chase branch to the new government.

Tran Dinh Truong, who is a major shareholder of most, if not all, of the ten corporate plaintiffs and who represents them here, fled South Vietnam just prior to the Communist takeover, as did Nguyen Thi Cham, the individual plaintiff. After arriving in the United States,

Truong and Cham demanded that Chase repay the piastre deposits made in Saigon, but Chase refused to do so. . . . Truong, acting under his powers of attorney, subsequently caused the plaintiffs to bring this action against Chase for breach of contract, seeking recovery of the dollar value of the piastre deposits held by its Saigon branch for them at the time it was closed, as well as the value of the certificate of deposit owned by Cham.

The evidence was undisputed that on April 24, 1975, the ten corporate plaintiffs held demand piastre deposits (or overdrafts) with Chase in the following sums:

Name of Account	Balance
Vishipco Line VN	$22,995,328
Ha Nam Cong Ty	9,053,016
Dai Nam Hang Hai C.T.	9,397,598
Rang Dong Hang Hai C.T.	8,974,556
Mekong Ship Co. SARL	7,239,661
Vishipco SARL	(12,498,573)
Thai Binh C.T.	68,218
VN Tau Bien C.T.	5,925,249
Van An Hang Hai C.T.	87,439,199
Cong Ty U Tau Sao Mai	380,419

Chase also concedes that on November 27, 1974, it issued to Ms. Cham a CD in the sum of 200,000,000 Vietnamese piastres, payable on May 27, 1975, and that the CD bore interest at the rate of 23.5 percent per annum, payable at maturity.

* * *

DISCUSSION

* * *

Chase . . . argues that the Vietnamese decree confiscating the assets which maritime corporations such as the corporate plaintiffs had left behind had the effect of seizing the piastre deposits at issue in this case. As a result, according to Chase, the corporate plaintiffs may not sue to recover the deposits because they no longer own them, and the act of state doctrine bars any challenge to the validity of the governmental seizure. We disagree. There is no evidence that plaintiffs' existence as corporate entities was terminated. Moreover, it is only by way of a strained reading of the Vietnamese confiscation announcement that one can even argue that choses[178] in action were meant to be included. The plain meaning of the statement that

the Saigon-Gia Dinh Management Committee quickly took over the management of all mari-

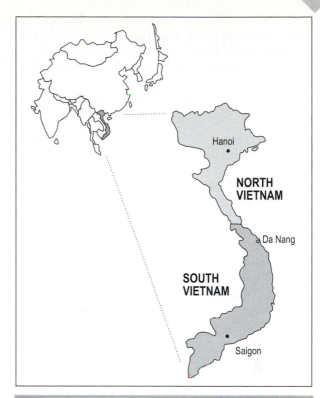

MAP 6-8   Vietnam (1975)

time transportation *facilities* abandoned by their owners (emphasis supplied)

is that the seizures involved physical assets only and did not reach whatever claim the corporate plaintiffs might have on their departure for payment of the amounts owed to them by Chase.

More importantly, however, upon Chase's departure from Vietnam the deposits no longer had their *situs*[179] in Vietnam at the time of the confiscation decree. As we have said in the past, "[f]or purposes of the act of state doctrine, a debt is not 'located' within a foreign state unless that state has the power to enforce or collect it."[180] The rule announced in *Harris v. Balk*[181] continues to be valid on this point: the power to enforce payment of a debt depends on jurisdiction over the debtor. Since Chase had abandoned its Saigon branch at the time of the Vietnamese decree, and since it had no separate corporate identity in Vietnam which would remain in existence after its departure, the Vietnamese decree could not have had any effect on its debt to the corporate plaintiffs. As one qualified commentator has observed:

The *situs* of a bank's debt on a deposit is considered to be at the branch where the deposit is carried, but if

---

[178French: "a thing." A "chose in action" is a right to bring a suit or to recover a debt or money.]
[179Latin: "location."]
180Menendez v. Saks and Co., *Federal Reporter, Second Series,* vol. 485, p. 1355 at p. 1364 (Second Circuit Ct. of Appeals, 1973), reversed on other grounds in the case of Alfred Dunhill of London, Inc. v. Republic of Cuba, *United States Reports,* vol. 425, p. 682 (Supreme Ct., 1976).
181*United States Reports,* vol. 198, p. 215 (Supreme Ct., 1905).

the branch is closed, . . . the depositor has a claim against the home office; thus, the *situs* of the debt represented by the deposit would spring back and cling to the home office. . . . [U]nder the act of state doctrine, the courts of the United States are not bound to give effect to foreign acts of state as to property outside the acting state's territorial jurisdiction.[182]

. . . Since in our case Chase's branch in Saigon was neither open nor operating at the time of the confiscation and had in fact been abandoned prior to that time, the Vietnamese decree was ineffective as against Chase's debt to the plaintiffs.

* * *

Chase next argues that under Vietnamese law its failure to repay plaintiffs' deposits in the period prior to May 1, 1975, was not a breach of its deposit contract, because the conditions prevailing in Saigon at the time rendered payment impossible. In support of this argument, Chase cites various sections of the South Viet-namese Civil Code which excuse performance under various extenuating circumstances, as well as the provisions included in the deposit contracts used by the Saigon branch which purported to discharge the bank's responsibility for losses to depositors resulting from a variety of unexpected and uncontrollable sources.

This argument must be rejected for the reasons that impossibility of performance in Vietnam did not relieve Chase of its obligation to perform elsewhere. By operating in Saigon through a branch rather than through a separate corporate entity, Chase accepted the risk that it would be liable elsewhere for obligations incurred by its branch. As the official referee in the *Sokoloff* [*v. National City Bank of New York*] case . . . summarized the law:

> [W]hen considered with relation to the parent bank, [foreign branches] are not independent agencies; they are, what their name imports, merely branches, and are subject to the supervision and control of the parent

bank, and are instrumentalities whereby the parent bank carried on its business. . . . *Ultimate liability for a debt of a branch would rest upon the parent bank.*[183]

U.S. banks, by operating abroad through branches rather than through subsidiaries, reassure foreign depositors that their deposits will be safer with them than they would be in a locally incorporated bank. . . . Indeed, the national policy in South Vietnam, where foreign banks were permitted to operate only through branches, was to enable those depositing in foreign branches to gain more protection than they would have received had their money been deposited in locally incorporated subsidiaries of foreign banks. Chase's defenses of impossibility and *force majeure*[184] might have succeeded if the Saigon branch had been locally incorporated or (more problematically) if the deposit contract had included an explicit waiver on the part of the depositor of any right to proceed against the home office. But absent such circumstances the Saigon branch's admitted inability to perform did not relieve Chase of liability on its debts in Saigon, since the conditions in Saigon were no bar to performance in New York or at other points outside of Vietnam. . . .

A bank which accepts deposits at a foreign branch becomes a debtor, not a bailee,[185] with respect to its depositors. In the event that unsettled local conditions require it to cease operations, it should inform its depositors of the date when its branch will close and give them the opportunity to withdraw their deposits or, if conditions prevent such steps, enable them to obtain payment at an alternative location. . . . In the rare event that such measures are either impossible or only partially successful, fairness dictates that the parent bank be liable for those deposits which it was unable to return abroad. To hold otherwise would be to undermine the seriousness of its obligations to its depositors and under some circumstances (not necessarily present here) to gain a windfall.

Reversed and remanded for further proceedings consistent with the foregoing. ■

---

[182]Patrick Heininger, "Liability of U.S. Banks for Deposits Placed in Their Foreign Branches," *Law and Policy in International Business,* vol. 11, p. 903 at p. 975 (1979).
[183]Sokoloff v. National City Bank of New York, *New York Miscellaneous Reports,* vol. 130, p. 66 at p. 73 (New York Supreme Court, 1927).
[184French: "superior force." An event or effect that cannot be anticipated or controlled.]
[185A bailee is a person to whom personal property is delivered that is to be returned to the person who delivered it, the bailor, after it has been held for some purpose.]

Conflicts between Host and Home State Regulations

State X enacts legislation requiring foreign branches of its domestic banks to comply with its rules regulating deposits. State Y enacts legislation requiring the local branches of foreign parent banks to comply with State Y rules regulating deposits. Bank P, with its headquarters in State X, has a foreign branch in State Y. Which law does the branch obey?

Two commentators have suggested that a branch bank should be subject only to the rules and regulations of the host country, regardless of the directives given by the home country to the parent bank. They argue that such a rule "would most accurately reflect the expectations" of banks and depositors, and would be perceived by governments as the "most reasonable allocation" of their powers to regulate banks and bank deposits.[186] Their rule, however, is only a proposal. No case law has clearly emerged to cover this circumstance, although cases involving conflicting regulations have become more and more common in recent years.[187] Case 6–10 describes one British judge's solution to this enigma.

---

[186]Peter S. Smedresman and Andreas F. Lowenfeld, "Eurodollars, Multinational Banks, and National Laws," *New York University Law Review,* vol. 64, p. 733 at p. 800 (1989).

[187]In the United States, the court in Wells Fargo Asia, Ltd. v. Citibank, N.A., *Federal Supplement,* vol. 695, p. 1450 (District Ct. for S. District of New York, 1988), reached a conclusion at odds with Smedresman and Lowenfeld's proposed rule. However, in the companion cases of Braka v. Bancomer, SA, *Federal Supplement,* vol. 589, p. 1465 (District Ct. for S. District of New York, 1984), affirmed in *Federal Reporter, Second Series,* vol. 762, p. 222 (Second Circuit Court of Appeals, 1985), and Callejo v. Bancomer, SA, *id.,* vol. 764, p. 1101 (Fifth Circuit Court of Appeals, 1985), the decisions support the rule.

Some developments in reaching international accords for the joint supervision of branch banks, especially in the area of capital adequacy, have begun to take shape. The Committee of Banking Regulations and Supervisory Practices, established by the central banks of the member countries of the Group of Ten, has recently issued several reports suggesting how supervisory responsibility should be allocated. Several of the member countries, including the United States and the United Kingdom, have started the process of enacting the recommendations into law. *See* Joseph J. Norton and Sherry C. Whitley, *Banking Law Manual,* § 15.09 (1990).

Case 6–10   *Libyan Arab Foreign Bank v. Bankers Trust Company*

England, High Court of Justice, Queen's Bench Division, Commercial Court, 1987.
Lloyd's Reports, vol. 1988, pt. 1, p. 259 (1988); *International Legal Materials,* vol. 26, p. 1600 (1987).

On January 8, 1986, the Libyan Arab Foreign Bank (Libyan Bank)[188] *had over $131.5 million deposited in a "call" account with the London branch of Bankers Trust Company (Bankers Trust), a New York corporation (and $161.4 million in a "demand" account in New York). On that day, effective 4:10 P.M., the President of the United States "froze" all Libyan assets "in the United States." According to New York law, but not according to English law, that included the Libyan Bank's London deposit. The Libyan Bank sued Bankers Trust in the United Kingdom for, among other claims, recovery of its deposit. Bankers Trust argued that it was not liable because (a) New York law governed the deposit arrangement and (b) New York law prohibited it from making transfers out of the London account. In particular, Bankers Trust points to an agreement between the parties made in December 1980 (the managed account arrangement) that provided for the New York office of Bankers Trust to oversee the Libyan Bank's accounts in* both New York and London as support for its argument that New York law applied.

MR. JUSTICE STAUGHTON:

* * *

As a general rule the contract between a bank and its customer is governed by the law of the place where the account is kept, in the absence of agreement to the contrary. . . . [T]here was no challenge to that as a general rule. . . .

That rule accords with the principle, to be found in the judgment of Lord Justice Atkin in *N. Joachimson v. Swiss Bank Corporation,*[189] and other authorities, that a bank's promise to repay is to repay at the branch of the bank where the account is kept.

In the age of the computer it may not be strictly accurate to speak of the branch where the account is kept. Banks no longer have books in which they write entries; they have terminals by which they give instructions; and the computer itself with its magnetic tape, floppy disc or some other device may be physically located elsewhere. Nevertheless it should not be difficult to decide where an

---

[188]The Libyan Arab Foreign Bank was a Libyan corporation wholly owned by the Central Bank of Libya. It carried on an offshore banking business and did not engage in domestic banking in Libya.

[189]*Law Reports, King's Bench,* vol. 1921, pt. 3, p. 110 at p. 127 (1921).

account is kept for this purpose; and is not in the present case. The actual entries on the London account were, as I understand it, made in London, albeit on instructions from New York after December 1980. At all events I have no doubt that the London account was at all material times "kept" in London.

Mr. Sumption [the attorney representing Bankers Trust] was prepared to accept that the proper law governing the London account was English law from 1973 to December 1980. But he submitted that a fundamental change then took place, when the managed account arrangement was made. I agree that this was an important change, and demands reconsideration of the proper law from that date. That the proper law of a contract may be altered appears from *James Mill & Partners, Ltd. v. Whitworth Street Estates, Ltd.*[190]

Mr. Cresswell, for the Libyan Bank, submits that there then arose two separate contracts, of which one related to the London account and remained governed by English law; alternatively he says that there was one contract, again governed by English law; or that it had two proper laws, one English law and the other the law of New York. Mr. Sumption submits that there was from December 1980 one contract only, governed by New York law.

Each side has relied on a number of points in support of its contentions. I do not set them out, for they are fairly evenly balanced, and in my view do little or nothing to diminish the importance of the general rule, that the proper law of a bank's contract is the law of the place where the account is kept. Political risk must commonly be an important factor to those who deposit large sums of money with banks; the popularity of Swiss bank accounts with some people is due to the banking laws of the Cantons of Switzerland. And I have already found on the evidence of Bankers Trust, that the Iranian crisis was at the back of everyone's mind in 1980. Whatever considerations did or did not influence the parties to this case, I believe that banks generally and their customers normally intend the local law to apply. So I would require solid grounds for holding that the general rule does not apply, and there do not appear to me to be such grounds in this case.

I have, then, to choose between the first and third of Mr. Cresswell's arguments—two separate contracts or one contract with two proper laws. It would be unfortunate if the result of this case depended on the seemingly unimportant point whether there was one contract or two. But if it matters, I find the notion of two separate contracts artificial and unattractive. . . .

Mr. Sumption argues that difficulty and uncertainty would arise if one part of the contract was governed by English law and another by New York law. I do not see that this would be so, or that any difficulty which arose would be insuperable.

There is high authority that branches of banks should be treated as separate from the head office. See for example *R. v. Grossman*,[191] where Lord Denning, Master of the Rolls, said:

> The branch of Barclays Bank in Douglas, Isle of Man, should be considered as a different entity separate from the head office in London.

That notion, of course, has its limits. A judgment lawfully obtained in respect of the obligation of a branch would be enforceable in England against the assets of the head office. (That may not always be the case in America). As with the theory that the premises of a diplomatic mission do not form part of the territory of the receiving state, I would say that it is *true for some purposes* that a branch office of a bank is treated as a separate entity from the head office.

This reasoning would support Mr. Cresswell's argument that there were two separate contracts, in respect of the London account and the New York account. It also lends some support to the conclusion that if, as is my preferred solution, there was only one contract, it was governed in part by English law and in part by New York law. I hold that the rights and obligations of the parties in respect of the London account were governed by English law.

The High Court allowed the Libyan Bank to recover the $131.5 million on deposit in the London branch of Bankers Trust as well as $161.4 million of the funds in the New York office because, according to the managed account arrangement, Bankers Trust was supposed to have transferred that sum from its New York office to its London branch on the morning prior to the Presidential freeze and it had no excuse for not having done so. ■

---

[190]*Law Reports, Appeal Cases,* vol. 1970, p. 583 (1970), per Lord Reid at p. 603, Lord Wilberforce at p. 615.
[191]{195} *Law Reports, Criminal Appeal Reports,* vol. 73, p. 302 at p. 307 (1981).

Chapter Questions

1. X and Y are foreign exchange traders in Germany. X agreed to sell 100 million Mexican pesos to Y for delivery within 1 week at an agreed price in German marks. X was 3 days late in making delivery. During those 3 days, the Mexican government acted to devalue the Mexican peso by 20 percent. Y now sues in a German court to have the contract set aside. Will Y be successful? Explain.

2. X in State A and Y in State B plan to enter into a contract. What can they do to avoid the impact of a fluctuation in the value of their money of account?

3. The State of Q forbids its citizens from taking more than 1,000 units of its currency out of the country in any 1-month period. To avoid this limitation, Ms. Ecks, a State Q citizen who lives abroad in State X, engages in the following scheme with a friend, Mr. Zed, a travel agent in Tokyo, Japan. Ms. Ecks buys yen from Mr. Zed at a sizable premium. She pays for the yen with checks, made out to Mr. Zed, that she draws on her account with QueBank, a bank located in the capital city of State Q. Mr. Zed regularly accompanies tour groups to State Q and when he is there he cashes Ms. Ecks's check at QueBank. Mr. Zed, accordingly, makes a nice profit from selling yen to Ms. Ecks, and Ms. Ecks is able to get as much money as she wants out of State Q. Somehow the government of Q State learned of this transaction, and it ordered QueBank to freeze Ms. Ecks's account so long as she is abroad. Mr. Zed, unable to cash Ms. Ecks's latest checks, sues Ms. Ecks in State X to get back the money he had already advanced her. Both State Q and State X, as well as Japan, are members of the International Monetary Fund. Will Mr. Zed succeed? Explain.

4. MultiBank is a large London, England, bank with a branch office in Boston, Massachusetts. The American government believes that a prominent American underworld figure, Mr. Z, has been depositing stolen money in MultiBank's Boston branch as well as with the bank's home office in London. The government's prosecutor has asked an American court to issue a subpoena ordering the manager of the Boston branch to turn over all records relating to Mr. Z from both the Boston branch and the London home office. Should the court issue the subpoena? Explain.

5. You are an arbitrageur in London. Swiss francs are presently selling in London for U.S. $0.67. You anticipate that they will increase in value and be selling for U.S. $0.70 in 30 days. You purchase $1 million worth of francs on the spot market. Is there anything that you can do to hedge your bet? That is, is there some way to ensure that you won't lose all of your money in case the value of the franc plummets?

6. Q Bank, located in State A, has a branch in State B. X has State A currency on deposit in that branch. X directs the branch to transfer the funds to a branch of P Bank that is located in State B. P Bank itself is, like Q Bank, located in country A. The customary method for making such a transfer is for Q Bank's branch to request its parent to make a transfer through State A's central bank, debiting its own account with its parent and crediting P Bank's account at the central bank. In turn, P Bank will credit its branch's account with the transfer. State A, however, has imposed an embargo on all transfers relating to monies belonging to X, and neither Q Bank nor P Bank will make the transfer. X files suit in State B and seeks an order for the two branches to make the transfer locally without going through their parent banks or State A's central bank. Will X be successful?

Review Problem

As the Senior Chief Assistant in the law department of MegaBranch Industries (MBI), you are responsible for overseeing the legal aspects of all the financial transactions of MBI and its subsidiaries. (Unless stated otherwise, MBI and its subsidiaries are all located in states that belong to the International Monetary Fund.)

1. MBI wants to sell electrical parts to a buyer in State A. MBI's financial officer is worried, however, about the value of State A's money. What can be done in connection with this sale to avoid (or minimize) the possibility that the money will decrease in value?

2. A candidate for the legislature in the state where MBI has its headquarters is campaigning to have the state promote a return by the International Monetary Fund to the pre-1971 par value system. MBI's Board of Directors has asked you to advise it as to whether it should support this candidate on this issue.

3. An MBI subsidiary in State B has entered into a sales contract with a buyer in State C. The contract requires the buyer to transfer abroad State C currency and securities. In addition, the transaction will be financed by the subsidiary, and the State C buyer will be required to pay off the loan to the subsidiary in State B using State C currency. Assuming that State C has monetary regulations that affect all of these transfers, will the authorities in State B

respect and enforce those regulations in the event of a dispute between the subsidiary and the buyer? What if State C is not a member of the IMF?

4. In the previous situation, how can the subsidiary in State C know what is a State B currency regulation?

5. MBI wants to close down its subsidiary in State E and repatriate all of the capital that it had invested in State E back to MBI's home state. Can State E put any limits on the repatriation of these assets?

6. MBI's subsidiary in State F wants to send to MBI the dividends that MBI has earned on its stock in that subsidiary. Can State F put any limits on the transfer abroad of these assets?

7. State G is a very poor developing country. It is having trouble both in meeting its balance-of-payments obligations and in raising new capital to undertake local development projects. It has asked MBI (which has more lawyers on its staff than State G has in the entire country) to advise it—as a matter of courtesy—on what assistance it can get from the IMF. State G also wants to know what conditions the IMF may put on the assistance it provides.

8. MBI has several subsidiaries in the European Union. What effect will the adoption of a common EU currency have on their operations?

9. MBI owns one of the largest commercial banks in the United States. That bank, in turn, owns a large number of shares in the Bank for International Settlements. The other American banks with shares in BIS have recently elected the MBI bank to send the American delegate to the General Meeting of the BIS. The MBI bank has asked you to help screen the bank's employees to select someone appropriate to be the delegate. What does that person need to know about the BIS and its operations?

10. MBI's subsidiary in State H would like to see that state build a new hydroelectric power plant that would supply the subsidiary with cheap electricity. The subsidiary has encouraged State H to seek funding from the World Bank. What kind of funding is available? If State H is unsuccessful, could the subsidiary itself apply directly to the World Bank, or one of its agencies, for funding to build the plant?

11. MBI has decided to set up a moneylending subsidiary in State I. It can escape many of the legal regulations imposed on moneylenders if it can qualify to be a bank. What must it do to become a bank?

12. If MBI sets up a bank in an Islamic country, what kind of restrictions on its operations is this bank likely to face?

13. The MBI subsidiary in State J needs to buy foreign currency to pay a supplier in State K in State K funds. Where can it get the funds? Would it have been a good idea to have contracted to buy the goods for future delivery at the time it originally agreed to buy the goods from the supplier?

14. Should MBI's overseas banks be organized as independent subsidiaries or as branches of a single bank? What are the advantages and disadvantages of each arrangement?

If MBI's overseas banks are set up as branches, must they abide by the regulations of the home or the host state?

CHAPTER

Trade in Goods

Chapter Outline

A. HISTORY OF CONTEMPORARY INTERNATIONAL TRADE LAW

International trade has grown dramatically in the last 50 years. In great measure, this is because the world's nations have cooperated in eliminating protectionist domestic legislation and in promoting the free exchange of goods.[1]

The Great Depression of the 1930s in many ways was a direct consequence of protectionism. When the United States raised tariffs on more than 900 items with the Hawley-Smoot Tariff Act of 1930, the major trading nations of the world reciprocated with similar increases. The United Kingdom, for one, enacted its first major protective trade legislation of the twentieth century in 1931. That same year, the League of Nations tried to cool what had become a tariff war by convening a Tariff Truce Conference, but the effort failed. By 1932, world trade had fallen 25 percent from its 1929 level, and the world's industrial production had fallen 30 percent. In 1933, the last major prewar multilateral conference on trade, the World Monetary and Economic Conference, adjourned without results because the participants refused to relax their trade restrictions. Not until 1936 did industrial production return to its 1929 level, and not until 1940 did international trade return to its pre-Depression levels.

Recovery from the Great Depression was U.S. President Franklin Roosevelt's main goal upon his election in 1932, and liberalization of international trade was at the heart of his program for achieving that end. Beginning in 1934, the United States entered into bilateral trade negotiations with its major trading partners to reduce tariffs on a reciprocal (instead of a unilateral) basis. The United States kept up this program until, during, and after World War II.

The idea that tariffs should be reduced through bilateral and multilateral negotiations became part of the Atlantic Charter, the declaration issued by President Roosevelt and British Prime

---

[1]For a brief history of developments leading up to the establishment of the World Trade Organization, *see* "About the WTO. Roots: from Havana to Marrakesh," at www.wto.org/wto/about/facts4.htm.

U.S. President Frankling Roosevelt (center) and British Prime Minister Winston Churchill (left) aboard a ship off Newfoundland from which they issued the Atlantic Charter on August 14, 1941. (Photo: 24469 UN/DPI.)

Minister Winston Churchill in 1941 as a rallying cry for nations opposing the military and economic aggression of fascist Germany, Italy, and Japan. In addition to calling for the permanent renunciation of territorial aggrandizement and the disarmament of all aggressor states, the Charter set out goals for the postwar era, many of which were based on international economic cooperation. Among these was the assertion that every nation has the right to expect that its legitimate trade will not be diverted or diminished by excessive tariffs, quotas, or restrictive unilateral or bilateral practices.

During World War II, the protectionist sentiments of the 1930s were rejected as destructive, and they were swept aside in a rush to arrange a comprehensive network of multilateral agreements to settle the world's political and economic problems. The nations fighting Germany, Italy, and Japan allied themselves as the United Nations; and in 1943, they called for the creation of a permanent international organization to replace the League of Nations and an integrated international system to encourage trade liberalization and multilateral economic cooperation. Both efforts began the following year. A first draft of a United Nations Charter was agreed to at a conference at Dumbarton Oaks (a mansion in Georgetown, Washington, D.C.) and an international conference on economic relations convened at Bretton Woods, New Hampshire. A final draft of the UN Charter was approved and adopted at San Francisco in 1945.

The Bretton Woods System

The negotiators who met for the United Nations Monetary and Financial Conference in Bretton Woods in July 1944 were determined to create a system that would promote trade liberalization and multilateral economic cooperation. The Bretton Woods System was meant to be an integrated undertaking by the international community to establish a multilateral institutional framework of rules and obligations.

As originally planned, the Bretton Woods System was to have had at its core three major international organizations: the International Monetary Fund (IMF), the International Bank for Reconstruction and Development (IBRD or World Bank), and the ill-fated International Trade Organization (ITO). Together they were to collectively administer and harmonize world trade. The IMF was to ensure monetary stability and facilitate currency exchange. The World Bank was to assist war-ravaged and developing countries reconstruct or upgrade their economies. The ITO was to administer a comprehensive code governing the conduct of world trade. This code was to be broad and encompassing, dealing with a wide range of issues, including trade and trade barriers, labor and employment, economic development, restrictive business practices, and intergovernmental commodity agreements.

The Articles of Agreement of the IMF were adopted at Bretton Woods and ratified in 1945. See Exhibit 7-1. The World Bank was organized and its Agreement ratified in 1945 as well. Not until 1946 did the United Nations Economic and Social Council (ECOSOC) appoint a Preparatory Committee to draft an agenda and set up a conference to create the ITO.

The strongest advocate of an International Trade Organization was the U.S. government, which produced a "Suggested Charter" for consideration by the Committee that met in London in October 1946. After a second session in Geneva in 1947, the ITO Charter was adopted in a "Final Act" and its contents were agreed to by the 53 countries participating in a UN-sponsored Conference on Trade and Employment in Havana in 1948. But the American government, which had worked hard to create the ITO in 1946, withheld support in 1948. President Truman, fearing that the ITO Charter (or Havana Charter) would be rejected by an opposition Congress that had become conservative and protectionist and that American foreign policy would be adversely affected, did not submit the ITO Charter to the Senate for ratification. All but two of the other participants at the Havana conference had waited to see if the United States would ratify the Charter, and when it did not, no further effort was made to establish the organization.

The 1947 General Agreement on Tariffs and Trade

General Agreement on Tariffs and Trade 1947: Multilateral agreement that set out the rules under which the contracting states parties were committed to negotiate reductions in customs tariffs and other impediments to international trade in goods.

Instead of creating an International Trade Organization, the developed market-economy countries entered into an accord in 1947 called the **General Agreement on Tariffs and Trade** (GATT 1947).[2] The original contracting states parties were the same states that had formed the

---

[2]The Final Act Embodying the Results of the Uruguay Round of Multilateral Trade Negotiations (1994) refers to the original GATT as "GATT 1947" to distinguish it from the GATT annexed to the Agreement Establishing the World Trade Organization, which it calls "GATT 1994." The same nomenclature will be used here.

EXHIBIT 7-1   The Bretton Woods Conference

Representatives from 44 countries participated in the United Nations Monetary and Financial Conference in Bretton Woods, New Hampshire, July 1–22, 1944. The Conference drafted the Articles of Agreement of the International Monetary Fund and proposed the creation of the International Bank for Reconstruction and Development (IBRD) and an International Trade Organization (ITO). The International Monetary Fund came into being in 1945, the IBRD in 1946, but the ITO did not come into being (as the World Trade Organization) until 1994. (Photo: Gamma Liaison.)

Preparatory Committee that had drafted the ITO Charter, and they borrowed liberally from that document in drafting GATT 1947.[3]

GATT 1947 was a multilateral treaty that set out the principles under which its contracting states,[4] on the basis of "reciprocity and mutual advantage," were to negotiate "a substantial reduction in customs tariffs and other impediments to trade." With the addition of other states in subsequent years, GATT 1947 came to govern almost all of the world's trade.

The main principles of GATT 1947 were as follows: (1) Trade discrimination was forbidden. Each contracting state had to accord the same trading privileges and benefits (or most-favored-nation status) to all other contracting states equally; and, once foreign trade goods were imported into one contracting state from another, the foreign goods had to be treated (according to the national treatment principle) the same as domestic goods. (2) With some exceptions, the only barriers that one contracting state could use to limit the importation of goods from another contracting state were customs tariffs. (3) The trade regulations of contracting states had to be "transparent," that is, published and available to other contracting states and their nationals. (4) Customs unions and free trade agreements between contracting states were regarded as legitimate means for liberalizing trade so long as they did not, on the whole, discriminate against third-party states that were also parties to GATT. (5) GATT-contracting states were allowed to levy only certain charges on imported goods: (a) an import tax equal in amount to internal taxes, (b) "antidumping" duties to offset advantages obtained by imported goods that were sold below the price charged in their home market or below their actual cost, (c) "countervailing" duties to counteract foreign export subsidies, and (d) fees and other proper charges for services rendered.[5]

---

[3]For a history of GATT through the completion of the Tokyo Round (1973–1979), *see* Frank Stone, *Canada, the GATT and the International Trade System* (1984), and "About the WTO. Roots: from Havana to Marrakesh," at www.wto.org/wto/about/facts4.htm. For its subsequent history, *see* Jeffrey J. Schott and Johanna W. Buurman, *The Uruguay Round: An Assessment* (1994), and "About the WTO. The Uruguay Round," at www.wto.org/wto/about/facts5.htm.

[4]There were 23 original contracting states parties to GATT 1947. At that time they accounted for 80 percent of the world's trade.

[5]GATT 1947, in addition to these basic principles, contained various exceptions that could be invoked in special situations. These included balance-of-payments disequilibriums, serious and unexpected damage to domestic production,

The legal framework established at Geneva in 1947 remained essentially unchanged until the creation of the World Trade Organization (WTO) in 1994. Even under that agreement, the substantive provisions of GATT 1947 live on, becoming one of the annexes to the Agreement Establishing the WTO (under the name of GATT 1994).[6]

Multilateral Trade Negotiations

round: A meeting of the contracting parties of the General Agreement on Tariffs and Trade to participate in multilateral trade negotiations.

To keep GATT 1947 up to date, the contracting parties regularly participated in multilateral trade negotiations (MTNs), informally called **rounds**. Including the Geneva Round in 1947, when the General Agreement was originally adopted, eight rounds of MTNs were held. Most were held at Geneva, the location of the GATT headquarters.[7]

The first five rounds were devoted almost exclusively to tariff reductions, while the last three rounds (the Kennedy, Tokyo, and Uruguay Rounds) expanded their agendas to nontariff matters. Negotiations in the early rounds were generally carried on bilaterally, on a product-by-product basis. That is, the two states most interested in a particular product would negotiate a bargain through the time-honored process of offer, counteroffer, and agreement. Agreed-upon concessions in the form of bound tariff rates were then extended to all other GATT contracting parties as a consequence of the most-favored-nation principle.

Kennedy Round: GATT multilateral trade negotiations held from 1964 to 1967 that established the practice of setting an agenda for and defining the techniques to be used during GATT negotiations.

More comprehensive negotiating techniques were proposed and used for the first time in the **Kennedy Round** (1964–1967). At a plenary session of the contracting parties held immediately prior to this MTN, the contracting states (represented by ministerial-level officials) issued a declaration defining the agenda and the negotiation techniques to be used. The declaration also called for two kinds of across-the-board tariff reductions. One was a uniform percentage reduction in tariffs among all contracting parties. The other was the use of various mathematical formulas to make the various tariff schedules more consistent; that is, higher tariffs were reduced more and lower tariffs less. Fifty-four states participated in the negotiations and 400,000 tariff headings were covered. The result was an average 35 percent reduction in duties levied on industrial products that was phased in over a five-year period. In addition to the negotiations on tariffs, the Round also dealt with the problems of non-reciprocity for developing states and with nontariff obstacles. The developing states parties successfully added a new part to the General Agreement entitled "Trade and Development," which called for stabilization, as far as possible, of raw material prices; reduction or elimination of customs duties and other restrictions that unreasonably differentiate between products in the primary (or raw) state and the same products in their finished form; and renunciation by the developed states of the principle of reciprocity in their relations with developing states. In the area of nontariff barriers to trade, the Kennedy Round produced an agreement on antidumping (popularly called the Antidumping Code).

Tokyo Round: GATT multilateral trade negotiations held from 1973 to 1979 that produced six nontariff codes.

The next multilateral trade negotiations, known as the **Tokyo Round** (1973–1979), were characterized by an ambitious agenda and the participation of non-GATT states. In all, 102 states participated. As with the Kennedy Round, formulas for negotiating tariffs were again applied, but with less success. For a variety of political reasons, tariff rates for some items (e.g., agricultural products and exempt industrial products) were not cut at all, and the cuts on other items were larger or smaller than they would have been if the formulas had been applied. Nevertheless, the tariffs on industrial products were cut, again, an average of 35 percent, to an overall range of 5 to 8 percent among the developed states parties.

Also, following the example of the Kennedy Round, the Tokyo Round produced several special agreements (popularly known as "codes") to regulate nontariff matters as well as several sectoral agreements to promote trade in particular commodities. These codes, which were sponsored but not administered by GATT, were multilateral treaties open to ratification by any state. Six codes were completed: (1) customs valuation, (2) subsidies and countervailing measures, (3) antidumping, (4) standards, (5) import licensing, and (6) government procurement. In addition, three sectoral agreements were concluded on trade in civil aircraft, dairy products, and bovine meat.

---

the need to promote economic development, the need to protect the production of domestic raw materials, and the need to protect domestic national security interests.

[6]The provisions of GATT 1947 are carried forward to GATT 1994 with few changes. Essentially, only the Protocol of Provisional Application was not readopted.

[7]The eight rounds were Geneva (parallel with the negotiation of GATT 1947); Annecy, France (1949); Torquay, England (1950–1951); Geneva (1955–1956); the "Dillon Round" in Geneva (1961–1962); the "Kennedy Round" in Geneva (1964–1967); the "Tokyo Round" in Geneva (1973–1979); and the "Uruguay Round" in Montevideo, Geneva, Montreal, and Marrakesh (1986–1994).

The Uruguay Round

Uruguay Round:
GATT multilateral trade negotiations held from 1986 to 1994 that resulted in the establishment of the World Trade Organization.

The **Uruguay Round** (1986–1994)[8] brought about a major change in the institutional structure of the GATT, replacing the informal GATT institution with a new institution: the World Trade Organization.[9] The Round concluded on April 15, 1994, when representatives of 108 states signed its Final Act[10] at a ceremony in Marrakesh, Morocco, and committed their governments to ratify the results of the Round.[11] Again, as it had with the International Trade Organization Charter, the world waited to see if the U.S. Congress would approve of the new institution. This time, after much delay, including time out for an election, Congress convened in an extraordinary session and ratified the Final Act on December 8, 1994. Moments after the vote was announced in Washington, the representatives of the old GATT convened an Implementation Conference in Geneva and agreed that its successor institution, the World Trade Organization, would officially come into existence on January 1, 1995.[12]

The Uruguay Round Final Act is made up of three parts that together form a single whole. The first part, the formal Final Act itself, is a one-page "umbrella" that introduces the other two parts. Most importantly, this first part provides that its signatories agree to (1) submit the Agreement Establishing the World Trade Organization (WTO Agreement) and its annexes (with the exception of four Plurilateral Trade Agreements) to their appropriate authorities for ratification and (2) adopt the Ministerial Declarations, Decisions, and Understandings agreed to during the course of the negotiations.

The second part of the Final Act is made up of the WTO Agreement and its annexes, of which there are two kinds: Multilateral Trade Agreements and Plurilateral Trade Agreements. The first are "integral parts" of the WTO Agreement and are "binding on all members" of the WTO.[13] They consist of (a) 14 Agreements on Trade in Goods (including GATT 1994), (b) the General Agreement on Trade in Services (GATS), (c) the Agreement on Trade-Related Aspects of Intellectual Property Rights (TRIPS), (d) the Understanding on Rules and Procedures Governing the Settlement of Disputes (DSU), and (e) the Trade Policy Review Mechanism (TPRM). The four Plurilateral Trade Agreements are also "part" of the WTO Agreement, but they are only binding on those member states that have accepted them. They "do not create either obligations or rights for members that have not accepted them."[14]

The third and final part comprises the Ministerial Declarations, Decisions, and Understandings just mentioned.[15] See Exhibit 7-2.

B. THE WORLD TRADE ORGANIZATION

World Trade Organization: Intergovernmental organization responsible for (1) implementing, administering, and carrying out the WTO Agreement and its annexes, (2) acting as a forum for ongoing multilateral trade negotiations, (3) serving as a tribunal for resolving disputes, and (4) reviewing the trade policies and practices of WTO member states.

The **World Trade Organization** is best described as an umbrella organization under which the agreements that came out of the Uruguay Round of multilateral trade negotiations are

---

[8]Calls for a new round of multilateral trade negotiations were made soon after the Tokyo Round was completed. GATT set up a preparatory committee in 1982 to create an agenda for a new round, but it was not until 1986, after much debate, that the GATT members formally began negotiations.

[9]For a historical overview of the Uruguay Round, *see* "About the WTO. The Uruguay Round," at www.wto.org/wto/about/facts5.htm.

[10]Its full title is the Final Act Embodying the Results of the Uruguay Round of Multilateral Trade Negotiations.

[11]The European Community (now the European Union) and 108 states signed the Final Act at Marrakesh. Bureau of National Affairs, *International Trade Reporter,* vol. 11, p. 610 (April 20, 1994). At the conclusion of the Uruguay Round, 125 states were participating in the negotiations. John Kraus, *The GATT Negotiations: A Business Guide to the Results of the Uruguay Round,* p. 6 (1994).

[12]GATT 1947 was itself to continue to function "in tandem" with the WTO until the end of 1995 so that the business then being carried on by GATT could gradually be turned over to the WTO. GATT states parties became free to withdraw from GATT 1947 at the end of 1995. Bureau of National Affairs, *International Trade Reporter,* vol. 11, p. 1925 (December 14, 1994).

[13]Agreement Establishing the World Trade Organization, Article II, para. 2 (1994).

The requirement that the member states of the WTO have to participate in the Multilateral Trade Agreements (which include updated versions of many of the Tokyo Round codes) "ends the free ride of many GATT members that benefited from, but refused to join, new agreements negotiated in the GATT since the 1970s." Many states, especially developing states, must now adopt trade rules to bring themselves into compliance. In this respect, the WTO Agreement requires a higher degree of commitment from its members than the old GATT, which had allowed its contracting states to decline participation in its ancillary agreements. Jeffrey J. Schott and Johanna W. Buurman, *The Uruguay Round: An Assessment,* p. 133 (1994), quoting John H. Jackson.

[14]Agreement Establishing the World Trade Organization, Article II, para. 3 (1994).

[15]The Final Act, the WTO Agreement, and a selection of the annexes and ministerial decisions and declarations are reproduced in *International Legal Materials,* vol. 33, pp. 1–152 (1994). They are also available on the Internet at www.wto.org/wto/legal/legal.htm.

I. FINAL ACT

II. AGREEMENT ESTABLISHING THE WORLD TRADE ORGANIZATION (WTO AGREEMENT)

Annex 1A: Agreements on Trade in Goods

1. General Agreement on Tariffs and Trade 1994
2. Uruguay Round Protocol to the General Agreement on Tariffs and Trade 1994
3. Agreement on Agriculture
4. Agreement on Sanitary and Phytosanitary Measures
5. Agreement on Textiles and Clothing
6. Agreement on Technical Barriers to Trade
7. Agreement on Trade-Related Investment Measures
8. Agreement on Implementation of Article VI [concerning antidumping]
9. Agreement on Implementation of Article VII [concerning customs valuation]
10. Agreement on Preshipment Inspection
11. Agreement on Rules of Origin
12. Agreement on Import Licensing Procedures
13. Agreement on Subsidies and Countervailing Measures
14. Agreement on Safeguards.

Annex 1B: General Agreement on Trade in Services
Annex 1C: Agreement on Trade-Related Aspects of Intellectual Property Rights
Annex 2: Understanding on Rules and Procedures Governing the Settlement of Disputes
Annex 3: Trade Policy Review Mechanism
Annex 4: Plurilateral Trade Agreements
Annex 4(a): Agreement on Trade in Civil Aviation
Annex 4(b): Agreement on Government Procurement
Annex 4(c): International Dairy Agreement[a]
Annex 4(d): International Bovine Meat Agreement[b]

III. MINISTERIAL DECISIONS AND DECLARATIONS

EXHIBIT 7-2   Outline of the Final Act Embodying the Results of the Uruguay Round of Multilateral Trade Negotiations

[a]The International Dairy Agreement was terminated at the end of 1997. *See* "About the WTO. The Agreements," posted at www.wto.org/wto/about/agmnts0.htm.
[b]The International Bovine Meat Agreement was also terminated at the end of 1997. *See id.*

gathered.[16] As the WTO Agreement states, the WTO is meant to provide the "common institutional framework" for the implementation of those agreements.[17] The WTO thus serves four basic functions: (1) to implement, administer, and carry out the WTO Agreement and its annexes,[18] (2) to act as a forum for ongoing multilateral trade negotiations,[19] (3) to serve as a tribunal for resolving disputes,[20] and (4) to review the trade policies and practices of member states.[21] Additionally, the WTO is to cooperate with the International Monetary Fund and the World Bank in order to achieve greater coherence in global economic policy making.[22]

The WTO Agreement

The Agreement Establishing the World Trade Organization (WTO Agreement) has been described as a "mini-charter"[23] because it is much less complex than the International Trade Organization's Havana Charter. The Havana Charter, of course, was never ratified—GATT

---

[16]The WTO home page is at www.wto.org. For the WTO's own description of what it does, *see* "What Is the World Trade Organization?" at www.wto.org/wto/about/facts1.htm.
[17]Agreement Establishing the World Trade Organization, Article II, para. 1 (1994).
[18]*Id.*, Article III, para. 1.
[19]*Id.*, para. 2.
[20]*Id.*, para. 3.
[21]*Id.*, para. 4.
[22]*Id.*, para. 5.
[23]Jeffrey J. Schott and Johanna W. Buurman, *The Uruguay Round: An Assessment,* p. 133 (1994), quoting John H. Jackson.

1947 was adopted instead. What the WTO Agreement does is to transform GATT 1947, which was a trade accord serviced by a professional secretariat, into a membership organization.[24]

The WTO Agreement, to reiterate, is not a reenactment of the stillborn Havana Charter. Its provisions are exclusively institutional and procedural, unlike those of the Havana Charter, which contained substantive provisions of its own.[25] The WTO Agreement in essence establishes a legal framework to bring together the various trade pacts that were negotiated under GATT 1947. Thus, the WTO was created as a unified administrative organ to oversee all of the Uruguay Round Agreements. This unification solves two problems that hampered the old GATT. First, because GATT 1947 dealt with trade in goods, there was no obvious mechanism for handling agreements relating to trade in services and the protection of intellectual property rights. The WTO Agreement, which "separates the institutional concepts from the substantive rules,"[26] takes care of this difficulty. Second, because the ITO never came into existence, the old GATT had no formal institutional structure. The establishment of the WTO rectifies this.

The WTO Agreement, however, is not substantially different either in scope or function from the old GATT. It does not create a new supranational organization with the power to usurp sovereignty from its members.[27] In fact, the WTO is to be guided by the procedures, customary practices, and decisions of the old GATT.[28] As Professor John Jackson, the author of an early draft of what was to become the WTO Agreement, told the U.S. Senate Finance Committee about the WTO, it "has no more real power than that which existed for the GATT under the previous agreements."[29]

Later in this chapter, GATT 1994 and the other multilateral agreements relating to trade in goods are examined in some detail. The General Agreement on Trade in Services (GATS) is discussed in Chapter 8 and the Agreement on Trade-Related Aspects of Intellectual Property Rights (TRIPS) is explored in Chapter 9.

The Membership of the WTO

The 133 members of the World Trade Organization[30] comprise both states and customs territories that conduct their own trade policies.[31] States that were members of GATT 1947 on January 1, 1995,[32] along with the European Union, were eligible to become "original members" of the WTO.[33] These members agreed to adhere to all of the Uruguay Round multilateral

---

[24]*Id.*

[25]Thomas J. Dillon Jr., "The World Trade Organization: A New Legal Order for World Trade," *Michigan Journal of International Law,* vol. 16, p. 349 at p. 355 (1995).

[26]Uruguay Round Legislation, March 23, 1994, Hearings before the Senate Finance Committee, 103rd Congress, Second Session, p. 195 at p. 197 (testimony of John H. Jackson).

[27]Thomas J. Dillon Jr., "The World Trade Organization: A New Legal Order for World Trade," *Michigan Journal of International Law,* vol. 16, p. 349 at pp. 355–356 (1995).

[28]Agreement Establishing the World Trade Organization, Article XVI, para. 1 (1994).

[29]Uruguay Round Legislation, March 23, 1994, Hearings Before the Senate Finance Committee, 103rd Congress, Second Session, p. 195 at p. 197 (testimony of John H. Jackson).

[30]For a current list of WTO members, *see* www.wto.org/english/thewto_e/whatis_e/tif_e/org6_e.htm. As of January 1, 2002, there were 144 members, plus 31 countries or territories that had applied for admission and that had observer status, and 1 other country (the Vatican) with observer status. The members were Albania, Angola, Antigua and Barbuda, Argentina, Australia, Austria, Bahrain, Bangladesh, Barbados, Belgium, Belize, Benin, Bolivia, Botswana, Brazil, Brunei Darussalam, Bulgaria, Burkina Faso, Burundi, Cameroon, Canada, Central African Republic, Chad, Chile, China, Colombia, Congo, Costa Rica, Côte d'Ivoire, Croatia, Cuba, Cyprus, Czech Republic, Democratic Republic of the Congo, Denmark, Djibouti, Dominica, Dominican Republic, Ecuador, Egypt, El Salvador, Estonia, European Community, Fiji, Finland, France, Gabon, Gambia, Georgia, Germany, Ghana, Greece, Grenada, Guatemala, Guinea Bissau, Guinea, Guyana, Haiti, Honduras, Hong Kong, Hungary, Iceland, India, Indonesia, Ireland, Israel, Italy, Jamaica, Japan, Jordan, Kenya, Kuwait, Kyrgyz Republic, Latvia, Lesotho, Liechtenstein, Lithuania, Luxembourg, Macao, Madagascar, Malawi, Malaysia, Maldives, Mali, Malta, Mauritania, Mauritius, Mexico, Moldova, Mongolia, Morocco, Mozambique, Myanmar, Namibia, Netherlands, New Zealand, Nicaragua, Niger, Nigeria, Norway, Oman, Pakistan, Panama, Papua New Guinea, Paraguay, Peru, Philippines, Poland, Portugal, Qatar, Romania, Rwanda, Saint Kitts and Nevis, Saint Lucia, Saint Vincent and the Grenadines, Senegal, Taiwan, Sierra Leone, Singapore, Slovakia, Slovenia, Solomon Islands, South Africa, South Korea, Spain, Sri Lanka, Suriname, Swaziland, Sweden, Switzerland, Tanzania, Thailand, Togo, Trinidad and Tobago, Tunisia, Turkey, Uganda, United Arab Emirates, United Kingdom, United States of America, Uruguay, Venezuela, Zambia, and Zimbabwe.

[31]Agreement Establishing the World Trade Organization, Article XII, para. 1 (1994).

[32]On December 8, 1994, Guinea became the 125th member of GATT 1947, and the last state to qualify for becoming an original member of the WTO. Bureau of National Affairs, *International Trade Reporter,* vol. 12, p. 36 (January 4, 1995).

[33]Agreement Establishing the World Trade Organization, Article XI, para. 1 (1994).

agreements and to submit their Schedules of Concessions and Commitments concerning industrial and agricultural goods and their Schedules of Specific Commitments concerning services within a year after joining.[34] Original members, however, that are recognized by the United Nations as being among the least developed states were required to undertake only commitments and concessions consistent with their individual development, financial, and trade needs, and within their administrative and institutional capabilities.[35] They also were given an additional year in which to submit their schedules.[36]

A state that did not qualify for admission as an original member must negotiate entry into the WTO on terms to be agreed between it and the WTO, and approved by the WTO Ministerial Conference by a two-thirds majority of the member states of the WTO.[37]

At the time a state becomes a member of the WTO, but only then, it may take advantage of Article XIII of the WTO Agreement entitled "Nonapplication of Multilateral Trade Agreements between Particular Members." This provision (which is analogous to GATT Article XXXV) allows one member state to ignore another member state's participation in the WTO Agreement or in the Multilateral Trade Agreements.

Finally, a member may withdraw from the WTO 6 months after notifying the Director-General of its intention to do so.[38]

Structure of the WTO

The WTO has five main organs: (1) a Ministerial Conference, (2) a General Council that also functions as the WTO's Dispute Settlement Body and Trade Policy Review Body, (3) a Council for Trade in Goods, (4) a Council for Trade in Services, and (5) a Council for Trade-Related Aspects of Intellectual Property Rights. In the tradition of GATT, the Ministerial Conference and the General Council are made up of representatives from all the member states.[39] In essence, they are each "committees of the whole." The General Council names the members of the other main organs.[40] See Exhibit 7-3.

The composition of the Ministerial Conference and especially the General Council has been criticized on the grounds that "[m]ass management does not lend itself to operational efficiency or serious policy discussion."[41] However, attempts at the Uruguay Round to establish a small executive body, similar to the executive boards of the International Monetary Fund and the World Bank, were not successful. The smaller states oppose this type of structure as it would undoubtedly be dominated by the larger trading states, as is the case for the IMF and the World Bank. In the absence of some such arrangement, however, it is likely that the major trading states will continue to resort, as they did under GATT 1947, to extralegal mechanisms like the Quad (an informal group made up of the United States, the European Union, Canada, and Japan). Or, as was the case for the Uruguay Round negotiations on agriculture, the United States and the EU may simply "cut their own deal" and then insist that the other states accept it.[42]

In addition to the main organs of the WTO, there is also a Secretariat headed by a Director-General,[43] who is appointed by the Ministerial Conference.[44] The staff of the GATT 1947 Secretariat became the staff of the WTO Secretariat on the latter's inauguration. Traditionally, the

---

[34]*Id.,* Article XIV, para. 1.
  A state eligible for original membership that became or becomes a member after January 1, 1995 (when the WTO Agreement came into force), must "implement those concessions and obligations in the Multilateral Trade Agreements that are to be implemented over a period of time starting with the entry into force of this Agreement as if it had accepted this Agreement on the date of its entry into force." *Id.,* Article XIV, para. 2.
[35]*Id.,* Article XI, para. 2.
[36]Ministerial Decision on Measures in Favor of Least-Developed Countries, para. 1 (1994).
[37]Agreement Establishing the World Trade Organization, Article XII, paras. 1–2 (1994).
[38]*Id.,* Article XV, para. 1.
[39]*Id.,* Article IV, paras. 1–4.
[40]*Id.,* Article IV, para. 5.
[41]Jeffrey J. Schott and Johanna W. Buurman, *The Uruguay Round: An Assessment,* p. 139 (1994).
[42]*Id.*
[43]Renato Ruggiero of Italy became the first WTO Director-General on May 1, 1995, succeeding Peter Sutherland, the GATT 1947 Director-General who had served as Acting Director-General since the WTO's inauguration on January 1, 1995. "WTO Formally Accepts Ruggiero as Its First Director-General," Bureau of National Affairs, *International Trade Reporter,* vol. 12, p. 567 (March 29, 1995).
[44]Agreement Establishing the World Trade Organization, Article VI, para 2 (1994).

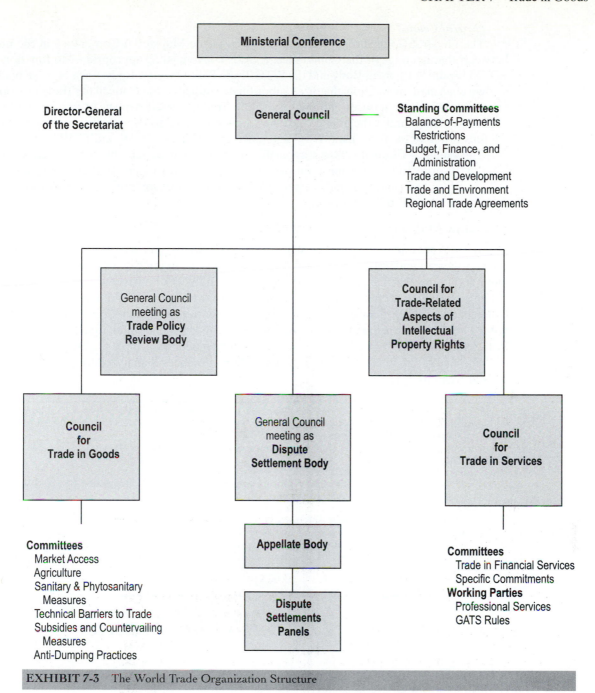

EXHIBIT 7-3 The World Trade Organization Structure

role of the GATT Secretariat was limited, and its small budget put tight restraints on the staff's ability to initiate studies or carry on programs on its own. The responsibility of the Secretariat has grown because of its new role in assessing member state trade policies in support of the Trade Policy Review Body; nevertheless, it is likely that the staff will remain relatively small.

Ministerial Conference

The Ministerial Conference meets at least every other year to oversee the operation of the WTO. Five standing committees deal with (1) trade and development; (2) balance-of-payments restrictions; (3) budget, finance, and administration; (4) trade and the environment; and (5) regional agreements.[45]

---

[45]The first three committees are specified in *id.,* Article IV, para. 7. The committee on trade and environment was added by the Ministerial Conference meeting at Marrakesh in April 1994, and the committee on regional

General Council

The General Council carries on the functions of the Ministerial Conference in the intervals between the meetings of the Conference. It also "convene[s] as appropriate" to function as the WTO Dispute Settlement Body and the WTO Trade Policy Review Body. Each of these bodies has its own chairman. In addition, the three subordinate councils—the Council for Trade in Goods, the Council for Trade in Services, and the Council for Trade-Related Aspects of Intellectual Property Rights—function under the guidance of the General Council to oversee the implementation and administration of the three main WTO agreements (GATT 94, GATS, and TRIPS).[46]

The General Council is also responsible for making arrangements for "effective cooperation" with other intergovernmental organizations whose responsibilities are related to the WTO and for "consultation and cooperation" with nongovernmental organizations involved in matters of interest to the WTO.[47]

Decision Making Within the WTO

consensus: The making of a decision by general agreement and in the absence of any voiced objection.

The WTO Agreement says that the WTO will "continue the practice of decision making by consensus followed under the GATT 1947."[48] **Consensus** is the making of a decision by general agreement and in the absence of any voiced objection.[49] The WTO, however, can make a decision by a vote if a consensus cannot be reached. At meetings of the Ministerial Conference and the General Council, each WTO member state has one vote, with the European Union having a number of votes equal to (but not more than) the number of its member states that are members of the WTO. Should a vote be required, the decision will be made by a simple majority in most cases.[50]

The role of the WTO and of its decision-making practices is analyzed from differing perspectives in Reading 7–1.

---

agreements by the Ministerial Conference meeting at Singapore in December 1996. *See* Jeffrey J. Schott and Johanna W. Buurman, *The Uruguay Round: An Assessment,* p. 137 (1994); and Ministerial Declaration of December 18, 1996, at www.wto.org/wto/archives/ wtodec.htm.
[46]Agreement Establishing the World Trade Organization, Article IV, paras. 2–5 (1994).
[47]*Id.,* Article V.
[48]*Id.,* Article IX, para. 1.
[49]*See* Understanding on Rules and Procedures Governing the Settlement of Disputes, para. 2.4, n. 1 (1994).
[50]Agreement Establishing the World Trade Organization, Article IX, para. 1 (1994).
Decisions that require a larger than simple majority vote include decisions to adopt interpretations of the WTO Agreement and the Multilateral Trade Agreements (*id.,* Article IX, para. 2); waivers of obligations imposed on members by the WTO Agreement and the Multilateral Trade Agreements (*id.,* Article IX, para. 3); amendments to the WTO Agreement or the Multilateral Trade Agreements (*id.,* Article X); and decisions of the General Council when convened as the Dispute Settlement Body (Understanding on Rules and Procedures Governing the Settlement of Disputes, para. 2.4 [1994]).

Reading 7–1   The Battle for Seattle

The Ministerial Conference, the WTO's main decision making body, meets at least every two years. At the Conference held in Seattle in December 1999, protesters campaigning for causes ranging from the environment to animal rights took to the streets and, despite the tear gas and rubber bullets of the police, eventually brought the Conference to a standstill. The following two stories describe the opposing views of the protesters and supporters of the WTO.

THE PROTESTORS' VIEW

"Behind the Screen at the WTO" by Judith Ann Maltz[51]

As the tumultuous scene of the World Trade Organization events unfolded in Seattle this week, the world was awakening to the realization that the scope of the WTO reached far beyond the closeted world of Geneva and into the very roots of democratic values and the lives of individuals.

Over 70,00 people and 500 global civil society organizations brought the attention of the world to the streets of Seattle where people of all ages, from many countries and all walks of life demonstrated their concerns about the ambitions of the World Trade Organization (WTO) to corporatize all areas of the global commons including food security, health care, public education, cultural

---

[51]*The Watertalk Forum* (December 5, 1999) at www.watertalk.org/forum/WTO-Seattle.html.

integrity, water, air, forest conservation, labor standards, human rights, local development, intellectual property rights and patents on plant, animal, and even human genetic material.

Two years later, in November 2001, protestors again march in Seattle in opposition to the WTO. (Photo © Terry Divyak 2001.)

From the roar of 35,000 trade union representatives chanting "Fix it or nix it", raising placards and banners reading "If it doesn't work for working families, it doesn't work", to the voices of thousands of others sounding "This is what democracy looks like"—the emerging international global citizens movement sprung to challenge the WTO's credo that: globalization is natural and irreversible, that it benefits the developing countries and that free trade is really free, despite the volumes of rules governing its form of highly regulated, corporate managed trade.

At the point (Tuesday morning) at which mass education about the WTO and its agenda was about to become the focus of global media, unknown provocateurs began smashing windows downtown. The first rumor reached the union marchers as they headed to the downtown core. Word was passed that a group of extremely violent individuals was roaming the streets. As the marchers—including those dressed as sea turtles—and other environmental representatives neared downtown, they were split and diverted away from the main demonstration already jamming the streets and were sidelined to a sit-down protest some blocks away. The disgust of many participants—who envisioned labor as providing need leadership and muscle to remind the WTO and everyone else that it was they who had the power to shut down the West Coast ports for the day—was palpable.

By nightfall the curfew had been announced and first scenes of excessive and indiscriminate use of force were starting to be reported and broadcast on television. Stunned viewers saw protestors, largely engaged in peaceful acts of civil disobedience, being brutalized by forces in fully equipped riot gear; true life gratuitous violence, capturing the attention of the world. While media coverage riveted viewers on the street action, the "Battle of Seattle" was also taking place within the Trade and Convention Center itself, and in a myriad of venues throughout the downtown core where discussions and debates flourished.

Rumors were rife, action lines and curfew boundaries kept moving, buses to events were cancelled in largely unsuccessful attempts to thwart public mobility and access; ministers and delegates from developing nations within the WTO scrambled to find meetings scheduled in unknown locations (infamous "green rooms" only announced to select participants) and called the WTO's own internal process "the ultimate in non-transparency".

Various delegates and non-governmental organization (NGO) representatives left the Ministerial to give briefings and exchange information on strategies and breaking developments at other independent Media Centers. Often just a handful of journalists were present to hear how intensely and by what means the African bloc and developing nations were being pressured for agreements; or how the United States and European Union were proposing the establishment of on-going working forums to side-step the fundamental consensus process in areas of genetic manipulation and bio-genetic organisms. Streamlined recommendations could potentially be passed to committees to draft policies, and then presented to signatories in coming rounds.

Often the chaos being reported from the streets was mirrored in much more subtle forms within the Convention Center itself. The much-touted scheduled NGO Symposium (a WTO first) became farcical after being postponed by three hours to become an hour and a half lecture to the NGO's by the presiding table chaired by Charlene Barshevsky and Michael Moore on the benefits of trade. Finally, only a small number of NGO representatives were allowed to address the table and "in the interest of time for all," not permitted to ask questions. NGO's were firmly told that their only participation would and could be through governmental representation.

Trade ministers from member countries in Plenary Sessions (designed to hear participants positions on the scope of the proposed agenda and their country's experiences under the first five years of WTO measures) were repeatedly displaced—often when the weight of evidence tended towards opposing views—by United States requests for its own speakers. Countries such as Jamaica, India, Pakistan, and the African bloc felt they had not only not benefited being signatories at the first WTO Uruguay Round, but had in actuality been penalized. Their call went out to sign nothing without carefully reading and reviewing of texts.

France, Mexico, Brazil, and the United Kingdom supported addressing the concerns of civil society, creating balanced policies on environment, services and social justice issues ("We can not forget about people"). Trade ministers from Canada, Australia, Hong Kong China, New Zealand, the European Union, and the United States vigorously pressed for immediate and comprehensive expansion of the free trade/investment agenda and the establishment of a biotechnical working group. Agricultural subsidies and fears of U.S. imposed protectionist union labor standards became the major stumbling blocks.

The words shared by Hamidon Ali, Ambassador of Malaysia upon arrival for registration Monday morning, proved to be prophetic "I think in the final hours we will stand with the representatives of civil society." Developing nations stood united in resisting last-minute attempts to force compliance despite threats of severe financial penalties.

Canadians who are wondering what all the fuss is really about and why they need to know about the WTO, need only to reflect on the current lawsuit currently underway. U.S. based Sunbelt Corp which is suing the B.C. government (i.e. B.C. taxpayers) for $15.75 billion dollars under NAFTA Section 11 regulations for denial of what it considers to be its right to license for bulk export of B.C. water. Under proposed WTO regulations all multinational corporations who desire access to resources or markets—even those contrary to existing labor, environmental, health or other sovereign nation's legislation anywhere in the world—must be compensated if attempts are made to deny such access. And that is only the beginning.

By turning a blind eye on excessive police responses at the start, those in Seattle with decision-making power tacitly sanctioned such actions, thus guaranteeing there would little, if any room, left on the television screens for any substantive coverage and questions about WTO's policies, processes and proposals themselves.

If this was not deliberate strategy, it was one which successfully obscured most telling commentary through malevolent neglect and abuse of the public interest, including that of those unfortunates often herded with teargas and rubber bullets through Seattle streets to locations guaranteeing maximum media exposure. How many people, who knew little about the WTO before the Seattle Round began, know much more about it now, other than to remember the unforgettable images played out endlessly and repeatedly before their eyes?

The challenge to create dialogue between the global corporate agenda, the exclusionary structure and arbitrary decision-making power of the WTO and the voices of people and organizations demanding true participation in the decision-making processes that fundamentally affect their futures, will be actively carried forward globally. The cry "*Bastante* (enough)" has been heard around the world and by the WTO itself. Could it be there will begin to evolve just and equitable means to address the pressing question: Who will make the rules that govern us all and how?

... Already there is talk of changing the decision-making process from consensus to something else (top-down as opposed to bottom up). There is little doubt that the major players will attempt to "adjust" the whole

process to insure the desired outcomes regardless of whatever opposition there might be either from the inside of the WTO itself or from civil society interests outside, and to do so without even having to talk about it. Speculation about bi-lateral agreements or the United States "going it alone" began the day after the collapse of the WTO. Pressures on individual developing nations are sure to escalate in a "divide and conquer" strategy and information on the progress of the WTO will likely become more impenetrable and obscure. It will probably be a very long time before the WTO risks bringing its agenda out into the open again after Seattle.

The process, however, will continue to unfold at an alarming rate under various guises through which well established and entrenched institutions that will be attempting to appropriate the language of protest into written policies and public relation campaigns.

The public still needs to be convinced of the benefits of unfettered global corporatism, where citizens and governments of all nations are left no choice but to become serfs and servants to corporate profits and consumate control. Anyone with investment portfolios, holding pension funds, or other financial instruments, may need to inspect their consciences clearly, hold them up to the ensuing darkness of the WTO agenda, and ask themselves how willing they are to be investors in the possible demise of the future.

THE SUPPORTERS' VIEW

"The WTO is Not a World Government and No One has any Intention of Making it One," by Mike Moore.[52]

A decade and a half ago the Uruguay Round was launched in the face of public apathy. No one can say that about Seattle, that's a deliverable. We have gone from apathy to anxiety and even anger, not just from the demonstrators in the streets, but from people around the world who feel that for too long they have been locked out of the benefits of growth, and from those who fear for their security in a time of uncertainty and change.

Mike Moore, WTO Director General
(Photo: Reuters.)

[52] WTO Press Release 155, November 29, 1999.

If people—especially young people—say unemployment is too high, they are right. If unions want better wages and conditions for working people, they are right. If environmentalists say that growth must be sustainable—and not destroy the planet's ecological balance—they are right. When developing countries say they are not getting fair access and economic justice, they are absolutely right.

First let's be clear about what the WTO does not do. The WTO is not a world government, a global policeman, or an agent for corporate interests. It has no authority to tell countries what trade policies—or any other policies—they should adopt. It does not overrule national laws. It does not force countries to kill turtles or lower wages or employ children in factories. Put simply, the WTO is not a supranational government—and no one has any intention of making it one.

Our decisions must be made by our Member States, agreements ratified by Parliaments and every two years Ministers meet to supervise our work. There's a bit of a contradiction with people outside saying we are not democratic, when inside over 120 Ministers all elected by the people or appointed by elected presidents, decide what we will do.

The WTO is an international organization that mediates trade disputes, seeks to reduce barriers between countries, and embodies the agreements. As President Clinton said, globalization is not a policy choice, it's a fact. Globalization is being driven above all by the power of technology—by faster and cheaper transportation, by new communications, by the increasing weightlessness of our economies—the financial services, telecommunications, entertainment, and e-commerce that make up a growing share of global trade. It's also driven by common values of freedom, democracy and the desire to share what the world has to offer.

The real question we should ask ourselves is whether globalization is best left unfettered—dominated by the strongest and most powerful, the rule of the jungle—or managed by an agreed system of international rules, ratified by sovereign governments.

How will the global economy be made more stable by undermining its foundation of rules and cooperation? By returning to the same system of regional blocs and trade anarchy that helped plunge us into world war in the 1930's?

How are developing countries helped by shutting our markets, restricting their exports, and worsening their marginalization?

How is the global environment improved by retarding growth, distorting prices, or subsidizing the consumption of scarce resources?

Command economies have the worst consequences for the environment, for human rights, and for jobs, education, and health. And, incidentally, totalitarian countries always pose a greater threat to peace.

How will we find jobs for the unemployed—or homes for the dispossessed—by making our economies and societies poorer? Consider this: exports have accounted for more than a quarter of U.S. economic growth in the United States in the past six years. And almost 20 million new jobs.

The United States uses less steel now than 30 years ago. Trade between countries can do no more violence to the environment than trade within countries. Of course, we can do better, that's why you and I are here.

The OECD has concluded that a new round of tariff liberalization would boost world economic output by 3 percent—or over 1.2 trillion dollars—and that developing countries would benefit most. India's GDP would grow by 9.6 percent, China's by 5.5 percent, sub-Saharan Africa's by 3.7 percent.

I'm not suggesting that the pain and the problems associated with technological and economic change are not real. They are. And we must address them with the appropriate domestic policies: that's the function of governments.

Remember when the Berlin wall came down, when Nelson Mandela walked to freedom, when the last imperial European Empire collapsed, when the Colonels returned to their barracks in South America? From the Congo to Cambodia, Poland to Chile, we all celebrated these universal values of freedom. No one condemned globalization or the ideals of freedom. Why is it when the smoke clears, people chose freedom? And now these same freedom fighters are in Seattle, demanding an opportunity to trade freely. Are you going to tell them the old days and ways were better? I won't. I'm here to open the door for working men and women.

Those who oppose and protest are not all bad or mad. Many want to improve the WTO. Others want to capture it to reflect their interests—which is a form of flattery I suppose. Most seek honest engagement. The World Wide Fund for Nature—to take just one example—has made several constructive suggestions about improving the interface between trade and the environment. We should listen, reflect, then act. Earlier I spoke to the International Confederation of Free Trade Unions. Here too there is a surprising degree of shared understanding about how trade can help improve labor standards—and vice versa.

If we lift living standards we will improve and lift labor standards, human rights, and get better results for those who are sick and those who yearn to learn.

Trade is not the answer to all our problems, but it provides part of the solution. 50,000 people may be demonstrating against us at Seattle. But remember too, that over 30 countries—some 1.5 billion people—want to join the WTO. They know what it offers and they want to be part of it. Ask them what they want.

And what's wrong in wanting China and Russia to be part of a rules-based world? It is one of those great contradictions, that while the world celebrates political freedom as it has spread throughout Europe, Africa,

Asia, and South America, the open minds that celebrate these freedoms frequently close their minds to the economic freedoms that trade offers. There's a contradiction among those who give generously at Church on Sunday when there is a flood or earthquake in the third world, then on Monday sign a petition to lock out the products their workers create.

What are we fighting for in Seattle? We are fighting for a multilateral trading system that is an essential component of the architecture for international cooperation—a firm foothold in an uncertain world. The world would not be a safer place without the UN, IMF, World Bank, or WTO despite their imperfections. The GATT/WTO system is a force for international peace and order. A fortification against disorder. This is reason enough to insist on the rightness of what we are doing.

We are also fighting to reduce poverty and to create a more inclusive world. We all want a fairer world, a world of opportunity accessible to all. Just ask the mother with a sick child who wants the best medical advice the world has to offer—whether its from Boston or Oxford or Johannesburg.

When I was a boy it would have taken a year's wages of a worker to buy the Encyclopedia Britannica for their children. Today, it's free on the Internet. Who wants to visit a dentist based on technology 20 years old? Think of what technology and science are doing for education and health.

The old divides of North-South, of left and right, no longer apply. What divides us today is the difference between those that welcome the future and those that fear it. Today the WTO comprises 135 countries—compared to just 23 who negotiated the GATT in 1948. None of these countries wants less trade, less investment, fewer jobs, technology or research. No, they want the same things for their families as we want.

Lastly we are fighting to create a world that is more open and interdependent, a world of lower barriers and greater freedom. "Freedom is indivisible"—President Kennedy reminded us over 35 years ago. This should be remembered by all those who would resurrect the walls between us. Of course economic freedom is not the only freedom. But it is an indispensable part of all the other freedoms we hold important—freedom of speech, freedom of conscience, the freedom of choice and opportunity.

There is a strong argument that economic, social and political freedom is a basic pre-requisite for development.

I began by asking what the world would be like without the multilateral trading system? Let me answer my own question. It would be a poorer world of competing blocs and power politics—a world of more conflict, uncertainty, and marginalization. Too much of this century was marked by force and coercion. Our dream must be a world managed by persuasion, the rule of law, the settlement of differences peacefully by the law and in co-operation. Seattle ought to be remembered then with confidence, in our case that economic and political freedom means higher living standards and a better lifestyle. Let's hope our vision of the new century matches that of our parents who lived through depression and war, then created us and our institutions. Let's honor them. Thank you. ∎

Waivers

waiver: The relinquishment of an obligation owed by another.

GATT 1947 was sometimes characterized as a system of loopholes held together by **waivers**.[53] The WTO agreements dramatically changed this. First, with one exception,[54] the waivers of obligations in existence under GATT 1947 terminated expiry or, in any event, no later than two years after the inauguration of the WTO.[55] Second, the procedures for obtaining new or continuing waivers are more rigorous. Thus, an applying member state must (a) describe the measures that it proposes to take, (b) specify the policy objectives it seeks to obtain, and (c) explain why it cannot achieve those objectives without violating its obligations under GATT 1994.[56] Third, waivers must be approved by the Ministerial Conference, which has up to 90 days to do so by consensus. If a consensus cannot be reached in that period, waivers must then be approved by a three-quarters majority of the members.[57] Waivers are reviewed annu-

---

[53]John Kraus, *The GATT Negotiations: A Business Guide to the Results of the Uruguay Round*, p. 78 (1994).
[54]The exception allows the waiver that applies to the U.S. Jones Act (which restricts the use, sale, or lease of non-U.S. ships in the movement of goods between points in national waters or the waters of an exclusive economic zone) to continue in force, subject to a first review after five years, and then subsequent reviews every two years by the WTO Ministerial Conference. General Interpretive Note to Annex IA (GATT 1994), para. 1:e.
[55]Understanding in Respect of Waivers of Obligations under GATT 1994, para. 2.
    A list of these waivers can be found in footnote 7 to the General Interpretive Note to Annex 1A (GATT 1994). Among these are waivers relating to German unification, the United Kingdom's dependent overseas territories, the U.S.–Canada Auto Pact, the U.S. Caribbean Basin Economic Recovery Act, and the U.S. Andean Trade Preference Act.
[56]Understanding in Respect of Waivers of Obligations under GATT 1994, para. 1.
[57]Agreement Establishing the World Trade Organization, Article IX, para. 3 (1994).

ally thereafter.[58] Fourth, any dispute that arises in connection with a waiver, whether or not the waiver is being carried out in conformity with its terms and conditions, can be referred for settlement under the Dispute Settlement Understanding.[59]

Dispute Settlement

The *Understanding on Rules and Procedures Governing the Settlement of Disputes* (the Dispute Settlement Understanding or DSU) carries forward and improves on the dispute settlement procedures of GATT 1947.[60] Most importantly, the DSU establishes a unified system for settling disputes that arise under the WTO Agreement and its annexes (other than the annex establishing the Trade Policy Review Mechanism).[61] See Chapter 3 for a discussion of the WTO's dispute settlement procedures.

Trade Policy Review

Annex 3 of the WTO Agreement establishes a Trade Policy Review Mechanism. This "mechanism" is built around a Trade Policy Review Board (TPRB) that is meant to be the WTO's auditor or watchdog. It is responsible for promoting "improved adherence" by all WTO member states to the WTO Multilateral Trade Agreements and, for the member states that are signatories, the Plurilateral Trade Agreements. The TPRB, however, is meant neither to enforce the agreements nor to settle disputes between members.[62] To accomplish its goal, the TPRB (a) carries out periodic reviews of the trade policies and practices of all member states and (b) prepares an annual overview of the international trading environment.

C. THE 1994 GENERAL AGREEMENT ON TARIFFS AND TRADE

General Agreement on Tariffs and Trade 1994: Annex to the Agreement Establishing the World Trade Organization that sets out the rules under which the member states of that organization are committed to negotiate reductions in customs tariffs and other impediments to international trade in goods.

The current **General Agreement on Tariffs and Trade** (GATT 1994, see Exhibit 7-4) is made up essentially of the same set of rules as GATT 1947. The changes in the text of GATT 1994 amount mainly to changes in terminology (e.g., "member" replaces "contracting party" and references to the "contracting parties acting jointly" are taken to mean to the World Trade Organization or its Ministerial Conference).[63] Even so, despite the similarity between GATT 1994 and GATT 1947, they are described by the WTO Agreement as "legally distinct" instruments.[64]

The significance of the two instruments being legally distinct is that (1) the WTO is not the "legal successor"[65] to the old GATT organization and (2) the members states of GATT 1994 owe no legal obligations to the contracting parties of GATT 1947. Thus, the WTO is not bound to service GATT 1947 nor is it bound by any obligations made by the previous GATT organization except to the extent it expressly assumes those responsibilities.

In addition, states that become member states of GATT 1994 without withdrawing from GATT 1947 will be bound by two different sets of commitments involving two different lists of states. Similarly, states that withdraw from GATT 1947 after becoming members of GATT 1994 (which they may do any time after December 31, 1995) will only continue to have GATT obligations under GATT 1994.[66]

Although GATT 1994 is not the legal successor of GATT 1947, most of the past decisions of the GATT Council, the GATT contracting parties acting jointly, and the GATT Dispute

---

[58]*Id.*, para. 4.

[59]Understanding in Respect of Waivers of Obligations under GATT 1994, para. 3.

[60]At the Uruguay Round, negotiators identified and worked to remedy three basic flaws in the old dispute settlement procedures: (1) the long times taken by panels in concluding their proceedings, (2) the ability of participating states to deny the consensus needed to approve the panel findings and to authorize retaliation, and (3) the difficulty of obtaining compliance with panel decisions.

[61]The Trade Policy Review Mechanism (1994) is meant to be a political rather than a legal process, and its exclusion from the DSU is therefore quite logical.

[62]Trade Policy Review Mechanism, para. A(i) (1994).

[63]*See* General Interpretive Note to Annex 1A, paragraph 1(d) (1994).

[64]Agreement Establishing the World Trade Organization, Article II, para. 4 (1994).

[65]Statement of GATT Director-General Peter Sutherland quoted in Amelia Porges, "Introductory Note, General Agreement on Tariffs and Trade—Multilateral Trade Negotiations (the Uruguay Round): Final Act Embodying the Results of the Uruguay Round if Trade Negotiations," *International Legal Materials*, vol. 33, p. 1 at p. 4 (1994).

[66]*Id.*

Article I: General Most-Favored-Nation Treatment
- To be applied by each member to the imports and exports of all other members.

Article II: Schedules of Concessions
- Individual country tariff concessions, as annexed to the Agreement, to be applied to all other members.

Article III: National Treatment on Internal Taxation and Regulation
- Products of one member imported into the territory of another must be accorded treatment no less favorable than that given like products of national origin in respect to their internal sale or distribution.

Article VI: Antidumping and Countervailing Duties
- Antidumping duties to be imposed only if goods are sold for export at a price below that which they are sold for domestic consumption.
- Antidumping duties may not be greater than the amount by which the domestic price exceeds the export.
- Countervailing duties may not be greater than the amount of the estimated "bounty" or subsidy.
- Antidumping and countervailing duties may be imposed only if there is a threat of material injury to an established industry in the importing country or if it materially retards the establishment of such an industry.

Article XI: General Elimination of Quantitative Restrictions
- Import and export quotas and licenses are prohibited, with certain exceptions for critical shortages, grading or marketing standards, and domestic marketing or production programs.

Article XII: Restrictions to Safeguard the Balance of Payments
- Permits nondiscriminatory quotas as necessary to forestall a serious decline in monetary reserves to increase such reserves from too low a level.
- Requires annual consultation procedures and progressive relaxation of the restrictions.
- Developing countries operate under the separate but similar provisions of Article XVIII, which requires consultations at 2-year intervals.

Article XIII: Nondiscriminatory Administration of Quantitative Restrictions
- Requires that export and import quotas be administered on a nondiscriminatory basis.
- Requires that import quotas be fairly allocated among suppliers.

Article XVI: Subsidies
- Seeks to avoid use of subsidies generally and prohibits use of export subsidies (other than on primary products).
- Requires reporting of subsidies, consultations with parties affected, and equitable sharing of markets for primary products.

Article XVIII: Government Assistance to Economic Development
- Permits developing countries to modify or withdraw tariff concessions by agreement with parties affected and after efforts to provide compensatory concessions.
- Recognizes persistent balance-of-payment pressures on developing countries and permits quantitative restrictions to deal with them.
- Specifies procedures whereby developing countries may use protective import quotas to promote infant industries.

Article XIX: Emergency Action on Imports of Particular Products
- The "escape clause" of the General Agreement.
- Authorizes importing country to suspend, withdraw, or modify tariff concessions if increased imports threaten serious injury to domestic producers.
- Requires notice and consultation with parties affected and permits exporting country to restore previous balance of concessions.

Article XXII: Consultation
- Provides for bilateral consultation and settlement of disputes.

Article XXIII: Nullification or Impairment
- Establishes procedures for bilateral consultation and for referral of disputes to a plenary session of the members for a recommendation and a ruling, whether or not the issue in dispute constitutes a violation of the Agreement.

Article XXIV Territorial Application; Frontier Traffic; Customs Unions and Free Trade Areas
- Deals with the application of the General Agreement to colonial territories.
- States exceptions to the rule of nondiscrimination for customs unions and free trade areas.

EXHIBIT 7-4   Selected Descriptive Contents of the General Agreement on Tariffs and Trade 1994

Article XXVIII: Modification of Schedules
- Permits a member, at the beginning of each three-year period, or under "special circumstances," to modify or withdraw a concession after renegotiation with the members affected.

Article XXXV: Nonapplication of the Agreement between Particular Members
- Permits a member to withhold the application of its tariff concessions from another member with which it has not entered into tariff negotiations.

Article XXXVI: Trade and Development: Principles and Objectives
- Expresses the need and desire of the members to give special preferences to developing countries.

EXHIBIT 7-4   Continued

Settlement Panels relating to the text of the General Agreement continue to have force.[67] Some decisions, however, were modified at the time GATT 1994 came into force by a series of "Understandings" annexed to the new General Agreement.

Direct Effect

direct effect: The principle whereby a treaty may be invoked by a private person to challenge the actions of a state that is a party to the treaty.

Some of the provisions of GATT 1994 are **directly effective**. That is, they may be relied upon by private persons (including both natural and juridical persons) to challenge the actions of a member state. In particular, those provisions that prohibit a state from taking action contrary to the General Agreement are directly effective. Those that require a contracting state to take some positive action may only be challenged by individuals if the state adopts implementing legislation authorizing such a challenge. This rule is set out in Case 7–1.

---

[67]Agreement Establishing the World Trade Organization, Article XVI, para. 1 (1994), provides: "Except as otherwise provided for under this Agreement or the Multilateral Trade Agreements, the WTO shall be guided by the decisions, procedures, and customary practices followed by the CONTRACTING PARTIES of the GATT 1947 and the bodies established in the framework of the GATT 1947."

Case 7–1   Finance Ministry v. Manifattura Lane Marzotto, SpA

Italy, Court of Cassation (Joint Session), 1973.
Foro Italiano, vol. 1, p. 2443 (1973); *Italian Yearbook of International Law*, vol. 1976, p. 383 (1976); *International Law Reports*, vol. 77, p. 551 (1988).

Manifattura Lane Marzotto, SpA, an Italian manufacturer of woolen goods, sued the Italian Finance Ministry after being charged an "administrative services duty" (dirrito per servizi amministrativi) on wool it imported from Australia, claiming that this duty violated the General Agreement on Tariffs and Trade. GATT 1947, Article III(1)(b), prohibits member states from charging duties in excess of those set out in the Agreement's annexes and schedules, or from increasing its duties after the time the member state accedes to the General Agreement. Because the law that first imposed the administrative services duty was enacted after Italy acceded to the General Agreement, Marzotto claimed that it was ille-

gal. The Finance Ministry asked the court to dismiss the case, contending that Article III(1)(b) was not directly effective because parliament had not adopted implementing legislation. The trial court in Milan dismissed the suit, but the Court of Appeal reversed, ruling that the duty was illegal. The Finance Ministry appealed to the Court of Cassation.

JUDGMENT OF THE COURT:

* * *

Article III . . . of the General Agreement deals first with ordinary customs duties and provides that they are applicable to the products included in the schedules at a rate not higher than that indicated in those same lists. It then establishes that duties other than ordinary customs duties may not be higher than those in force on the date of the General Agreement. . . .

Law No. 295 of 5 April 1950, which implemented the GATT Agreement, provides in Article 2:

> The aforementioned Agreements, Annexes and Protocols are fully and entirely implemented as from the time limits established by the Protocol of Annecy. . . . .

As Italy has fully integrated into its legal system the first part of the General Agreement—including the provision concerning customs duties—it remains to be seen whether this provision is merely a simple declaration of principle, deprived of any direct legal effect within the country. If that is so, the member states would only be obliged to each other to harmonize their laws, and there would be no immediate right for individuals to bring actionable claims. According to the Finance Ministry, parliament is the only entity that can properly determine when and to what extent the existing customs laws should be modified, and no other person or entity should be allowed to do so.

This Court cannot agree. It seems clear to us that the provision of the General Agreement that we are examining is directly effective, giving rights both to the member states of the GATT and to individuals within those states, without any need for additional legislative implementation. The provision—which is essentially a prohibition against increasing duties above those in effect on the date a member state accedes to the General Agreement—is clearly one which imposes on the acceding state an obligation *not* to act. There is, therefore, no need for the state *to* act. Accordingly, this prohibition is complete and directly effective not only between the member states but also between the member states and their nationals. . . .

MAP 7-1 Italy (1973)

Thus, in compliance with the law implementing the General Agreement, we hold that goods imported from one GATT member state to another are not subject to internal duties and charges of any kind which are higher than those that were in force on the date the General Agreement became effective. . . .

The judgment of the Court of Appeal was affirmed. ■

Nondiscrimination

The most fundamental principle of GATT is that international trade should be conducted without discrimination. This principle is given concrete form in the "most-favored-nation" (MFN) and "national treatment" rules.

The Most-Favored-Nation Rule

Article I of GATT requires each member to apply its tariff rules equally to all other members. Paragraph 1 of that Article provides:

> . . . [A]ny advantage, favor, privilege, or immunity granted by any member to any product originating in or destined for any other country shall be accorded immediately and unconditionally to the like product originating in or destined for the territories of all other members.

The MFN rule is not without exceptions, however. The rule does not apply to

1. The use of measures to counter dumping and subsidization[68]
2. The creation of customs unions and free trade areas[69]
3. Restrictions that protect public health, safety, welfare, and national security[70]

---

[68]General Agreement on Tariffs and Trade 1994, Article VI.
[69]*Id.,* Article XXIV, para. 8.
[70]*Id.,* Articles XX and XXI.

In addition to these three exceptions[71] to the most-favored-nation rule and the principle of nondiscrimination, GATT provides for a special exception in the case of developing states. In order both to promote and protect the economies of developing states, GATT encourages the developed states not to demand reciprocity from them in trade negotiation and it authorizes developed member states to adopt measures that give preferences to developing member states.[72]

The contracting parties to GATT 1947 approved two preferential treatment schemes that are carried forward into GATT 1994. One, the **Generalized System of Preferences** (GSP), allows developing countries to export all (or nearly all) of their products to a participating developed country on a nonreciprocal basis. The hope is that the GSP will make developing countries more competitive in world markets and less dependent on the production of raw or primary goods.[73] The other, the **South-South Preferences** (so called because most developing nations are in the Southern Hemisphere), lets developing countries exchange tariff preferences among themselves without extending the same preferences to developed states.[74]

The National Treatment Rule

The **national treatment rule** is the second manifestation of the principle of nondiscrimination that appears in the General Agreement on Tariffs and Trade. In contrast to the MFN rule, which requires nondiscrimination at a country's border, the national treatment rule requires a country to treat products equally with its own domestic products once they are inside its borders.[75] Article III, paragraph 4, of GATT provides:

> The products of the territory of any member state imported into the territory of any other member state shall be accorded treatment no less favorable than that accorded to like products of national origin in respect of all laws, regulations and requirements affecting their internal sale, offering for sale, purchase, transportation, distribution, or use. . . .

Article III, paragraph 2, sets out the same nondiscriminatory requirement with respect to internal taxes. In Case 7–2, a WTO Panel was asked to determine if Japan was taxing imported alcoholic beverages differently than a domestically produced beverage known as *shochu*.

Generalized System of Preferences: A GATT scheme that allows a developing state to obtain tariff concessions from a developed state on a nonreciprocal basis.

South-South Preferences: A GATT scheme that allows developing states to grant tariff preferences to each other without having to grant them to developed states.

national treatment rule: Once imported goods are within the territory of a state, that state must treat those goods no less favorably than it treats its own domestic goods.

---

[71]These three exceptions are discussed later in this chapter.
[72]*Id.*, Article XXXVI, para. 8, provides: "The developed members do not expect reciprocity for commitments made by them in trade negotiations to reduce or remove tariffs and other barriers to the trade of less-developed members."
[73]GATT, *Analytical Index: Guide to GATT Law and Practice*, pp. 49–50, 53–54 (6th ed., 1994).
 Eleven developed states, plus the European Union, presently participate in the GSP. The states are Australia, Austria, Canada, the Czech Republic, Finland, Hungary, Japan, New Zealand, Norway, Switzerland, and the United States. *Id.*, p. 50.
[74]*Id.*, pp. 50–51, 53–54.
[75]Section 801(a)(2) of the *Restatement of Foreign Relations Law of the United States, Tentative Draft No. 4* (1983) states that " 'national treatment' by a state means according to the nationals of another state treatment equivalent to that which the state accords to its own nationals."
 To ensure that member states comply with the national treatment standards, GATT requires them to promptly notify other members of any new trade regulations they may enact. *See* General Agreement on Tariffs and Trade 1994, Article X, para. 1.

Case 7–2   Japan — Taxes on Alcoholic Beverages

World Trade Organization, Dispute Settlement Panel, 1998.
Panel Reports WT/DS8/R, WT/DS10/R, WT/DS11/R.[76]

Canada, the European Union, and the United States complained that Japan imposed lower taxes on shochu, a locally produced alcoholic beverage, than it did on

---

[76]This Dispute Settlement Panel Report is posted on the WTO's Internet Web site at www.wto.org/wto/dispute/alcoh.wp5.

imported alcoholic beverages, including vodka, in violation of Article III, paragraph 2, of the 1994 General Agreement on Tariffs and Trade.

REPORT OF THE PANEL

* * *

The Panel noted that the complainants are essentially claiming that the Japanese *Liquor Tax Law* is inconsistent with GATT Article III:2 (hereinafter "Article III:2"). Article III:2 reads:

> The products of the territory of any contracting party imported into the territory of any other contracting party shall not be subject, directly or indirectly, to internal taxes or other internal charges of any kind in excess of those applied, directly or indirectly, to like domestic products. Moreover, no contracting party shall otherwise apply internal taxes or other internal charges to imported or domestic products in a manner contrary to the principles set forth in paragraph 1.

GATT Article III:1 (hereinafter "Article III:1"), which is referred to in Article III:2, reads:

> The contracting parties recognize that internal taxes and other internal charges, and laws, regulations, and requirements affecting the internal sale, offering for sale, purchase, transportation, distribution, or use of products, and internal quantitative regulations requiring the mixture, processing, or use of products in specified amounts or proportions, should not be applied to imported or domestic products so as to afford protection to domestic production.

* * *

ARTICLE III:2, FIRST SENTENCE

a) Overview

* * *

The Panel first turned to the test proposed by Japan and the United States. The Panel noted, in this respect, that the proposed aim-and-effect test is not consistent with the wording of Article III:2, first sentence. The Panel recalled that the basis of the aim-and-effect test is found in the words "so as to afford protection" contained in Article III:1. The Panel further recalled that Article III:2, first sentence, contains no reference to those words. Moreover, the adoption of the aim-and-effect test would have important repercussions on the burden of proof imposed on the complainant. The Panel noted in this respect that the complainants, according to the aim-and-effect test, have the burden of showing not only the effect of a particular measure, which is in principle discernible, but also its aim, which sometimes can be indiscernible. The Panel also noted that

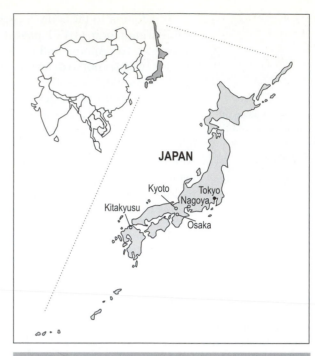

MAP 7-2 Japan (1998)

very often there is a multiplicity of aims that are sought through enactment of legislation and it would be a difficult exercise to determine which aim or aims should be determinative for applying the aim-and-effect test. Moreover, access to the complete legislative history, which according to the arguments of the parties defending the aim-and-effect test, is relevant to detect protective aims, could be difficult or even impossible for a complaining party to obtain. Even if the complete legislative history is available, it would be difficult to assess which kinds of legislative history (statements in legislation, in official legislative reports, by individual legislators, or in hearings by interested parties) should be primarily determinative of the aims of the legislation. The Panel recalled in this respect the argument by the United States that the aim-and-effect test should be applicable only with respect to origin-neutral measures. The Panel noted that neither the wording of Article III:2, nor that of Article III:1 support a distinction between origin-neutral and origin-specific measures.

The Panel further noted that the list of exceptions contained in Article XX of GATT 1994 could become redundant or useless because the aim-and-effect test does not contain a definitive list of grounds justifying departure from the obligations that are otherwise incorporated in Article III. The purpose of Article XX is to provide a list of exceptions, subject to the conditions that they "are not applied in a manner which would constitute a means of arbitrary or unjustifiable discrimination between countries where the same conditions prevail, or a disguised restriction of international trade", that could justify deviations from the obligations imposed under GATT. Consequently, in principle, a WTO Member could, for example, invoke protection of health in the context of invoking the aim-and-effect test. The Panel noted that if this were the case, then the standard of proof established in Article XX would effectively be circumvented. WTO Members would not have to prove that a health measure is "necessary" to achieve its health objective. Moreover, proponents of the aim-and-effect test even shift the burden of proof, arguing that it would be up to the complainant to produce a *prima facie*[77] case that a measure has both the aim and effect of affording protection to domestic production and, once the complainant has demonstrated that this is the case, only then would the defending party have to present evidence to rebut the claim. In sum, the Panel concluded that for reasons relating to the wording of Article III as well as its context, the aim-and-effect test proposed by Japan and the United States should be rejected.

b) Like Products

The Panel noted that the term "like product" appears in various GATT provisions. The Panel further noted that it did not necessarily follow that the term had to be interpreted in a uniform way. In this respect, the Panel noted the discrepancy between Article III:2, on the one hand, and Article III:4 on the other: while the former referred to Article III:1 and to like, as well as to directly competitive or substitutable products (see also Article XIX of GATT), the latter referred only to like products. If the coverage of Article III:2 is identical to that of Article III:4, a different interpretation of the term "like product" would be called for in the two paragraphs. Otherwise, if the term "like product" were to be interpreted in an identical way in both instances, the scope of the two paragraphs would be different. This is precisely why, in the Panel's view, its conclusions reached in this dispute are relevant only for the interpretation of the term "like product" as it appears in Article III:2.

The Panel noted that previous panel and working party reports had unanimously agreed that the term "like product" should be interpreted on a case-by-case basis. The Panel further noted that previous panels had not established a particular test that had to be strictly followed in order to define likeness. Previous panels had used different criteria in order to establish likeness, such as the product's properties, nature and quality, and its end-uses; consumers' tastes and habits, which change from country to country; and the product's classification in tariff nomenclatures. In the Panel's view, "like products" need not be identical in all respects. However, in the Panel's view, the term "like product" should be construed narrowly in the case of Article III:2, first sentence. This approach is dictated, in the Panel's view, by two independent reasons: (i) because Article III:2 distinguishes

between like and directly competitive or substitutable products, the latter obviously being a much larger category of products than the former; and (ii) because of the Panel's conclusions reached with respect to the relationship between Articles III and II. As to the first point, the distinction between "like" and "directly competitive or substitutable products" is discussed in paragraph 6.22. As to the second point, as previous panels had noted, one of the main objectives of Article III:2 is to ensure that WTO Members do not frustrate the effect of tariff concessions granted under Article II through internal taxes and other internal charges, it follows that a parallelism should be drawn in this case between the definition of products for purposes of Article II tariff concessions and the term "like product" as it appears in Article III:2. This is so in the Panel's view, because with respect to two products subject to the same tariff binding and therefore to the same maximum border tax, there is no justification, outside of those mentioned in GATT rules, to tax them in a differentiated way through internal taxation. . . .

* * *

. . . In the view of the Panel, the term "like products" suggests that for two products to fall under this category they must share, apart from commonality of end-uses, essentially the same physical characteristics. In the Panel's view its suggested approach has the merit of being functional, although the definition of likeness might appear somewhat "inflexible." Flexibility is required in order to conclude whether two products are directly competitive or substitutable. In the Panel's view, the suggested approach can guarantee the flexibility required, since it permits one to take into account specific characteristics in any single market; consequently, two products could be considered to be directly competitive or substitutable in market A, but the same two products would not necessarily be considered to be directly competitive or substitutable in market B. The Panel proceeded to apply this approach to the products in dispute in the present case.

The Panel next turned to an examination of whether the products at issue in this case were like products, starting first with vodka and shochu. The Panel noted that vodka and shochu shared most physical characteristics. In the Panel's view, except for filtration, there is virtual identity in the definition of the two products. The Panel noted that a difference in the physical characteristic of alcoholic strength of two products did not preclude a finding of likeness especially since alcoholic beverages are often drunk in diluted form. The Panel then noted that essentially the same conclusion had been reached in the 1987 Panel Report, which

. . . agreed with the arguments submitted to it by the European Communities, Finland, and the United

---

[77Latin: "on first appearance." A case that is legally sufficient unless later disproved.]

States that Japanese shochu (Group A) and vodka could be considered as 'like' products in terms of Article III:2 because they were both white/clean spirits, made of similar raw materials, and the end-uses were virtually identical".

Following its independent consideration of the factors mentioned in the 1987 Panel Report, the Panel agreed with this statement. The Panel then recalled its conclusions concerning the relationship between Articles II and III. In this context, it noted that (i) vodka and shochu were currently classified in the same heading in the Japanese tariffs . . . and (ii) vodka and shochu were covered by the same Japanese tariff binding at the time of its negotiation. Of the products at issue in this case, only shochu and vodka have the same tariff applied to them in the Japanese tariff schedule. The Panel noted that, with respect to vodka, Japan offered no further convincing evidence that the conclusion reached by the 1987 Panel Report was wrong, not even that there had been a change in consumers' preferences in this respect. The Panel further noted that Japan's basic argument is not that the two products are unlike, in terms of the criteria applied in the 1987 Panel Report, but rather that they are unlike because the Japanese tax legislation does not have the aim and effect to protect shochu. The Panel noted, however, that it had already rejected the aim-and-effect test. Consequently, in light of the conclusion of the 1987 Panel Report and of its independent consideration of the issue, the Panel concluded that vodka and shochu are like products. In the Panel's view, only vodka could be considered as like product to shochu since, apart from commonality of end-uses, it shared with shochu most physical characteristics. Definitionally, the only difference is in the media used for filtration. Substantial noticeable differences in physical characteristics exist between the rest of the alcoholic beverages at dispute and shochu that would disqualify them from being regarded as like products. More specifically, the use of additives would disqualify liqueurs, gin and genever; the use of ingredients would disqualify rum; lastly, appearance (arising from manufacturing processes) would disqualify whisky and brandy. . . .

c) Taxation in Excess of That Imposed on Like Domestic Products

The Panel then proceeded to examine whether vodka is taxed in excess of the tax imposed on shochu under the Japanese *Liquor Tax Law*. The Panel noted that what was contested in the Japanese legislation was a system of specific taxes imposed on various alcoholic drinks. In this respect, it noted that vodka was taxed at 377,230 Yen per kiloliter—for an alcoholic strength below 38°—that is 9,927 Yen per degree of alcohol, whereas shochu A was taxed at 155,700 Yen per kiloliter—for an alco-

holic strength between 25° and 26°—that is 6,228 Yen per degree of alcohol. The Panel further noted that Article III:2 does not contain any presumption in favor of a specific mode of taxation. Under Article III:2, first sentence, WTO Members are free to choose any system of taxation they deem appropriate provided that they do not impose on foreign products taxes in excess of those imposed on like domestic products. The phrase "not in excess of those applied . . . to like domestic products" should be interpreted to mean at least identical or better tax treatment. The Japanese taxes on vodka and shochu are calculated on the basis of and vary according to the alcoholic content of the products and, on this basis, it is obvious that the taxes imposed on vodka are higher than those imposed on shochu. Accordingly, the Panel concluded that the tax imposed on vodka is in excess of the tax imposed on shochu.

The Panel then addressed the argument put forward by Japan that its legislation, by keeping the tax/price ratio "roughly constant", is trade neutral and consequently no protective aim and effect of the legislation can be detected. In this connection, the Panel recalled Japan's argument that its aim was to achieve neutrality and horizontal tax equity. The Panel noted that it had already decided that the existence or non-existence of a protective aim and effect is not relevant in an analysis under Article III:2, first sentence. To the extent that Japan's argument is that its *Liquor Tax Law* does not impose on foreign products (i.e., vodka) a tax in excess of the tax imposed on domestic like products (i.e., shochu), the Panel rejected the argument for the following reasons:

(i) The benchmark in Article III:2, first sentence, is that internal taxes on foreign products shall not be imposed in excess of those imposed on like domestic products. Consequently, in the context of Article III:2, first sentence, it is irrelevant whether "roughly" the same treatment through, for example, a "roughly constant" tax/price ratio is afforded to domestic and foreign like products or whether neutrality and horizontal tax equity is achieved.

(ii) Even if it were to be accepted that a comparison of tax/price ratios of products could offset the fact that vodka was taxed significantly more heavily than shochu on a volume and alcoholic content basis, there were significant problems with the methodology for calculating tax/price ratios submitted by Japan, such that arguments based on that methodology could only be viewed as inconclusive. More particularly, although Japan had argued that the comparison of tax/price ratios should be done on a category-by-category basis, its statistics on which the tax/price ratios were based excluded domestically produced spirits from the calculation of tax/price ratios for spirits and whisky/brandy. Since the prices of the domestic spirits and whisky/brandy are much lower than the prices of the imported goods, this exclusion has the impact of reducing considerably the tax/price ratios cited by Japan for those products. In this connection, the Panel noted that one consequence of the Japanese tax system was to make it more difficult for cheaper imported brands of spirits and whisky/brandy to enter the Japanese market. Moreover, the Panel further noted that the Japanese statistics were based on suggested retail prices and there was evidence in the record that these products were often sold at a discount, at least in Tokyo. To the extent that the prices were unreliable, the resultant tax/price ratios would be unreliable as well.

(iii) Nowhere in the contested legislation was it mentioned that its purpose was to maintain a "roughly constant" tax/price ratio. This was rather an *ex post facto*[78] rationalization by Japan and at any rate, there are no guarantees in the legislation that the tax/price ratio will always be maintained "roughly constant". Prices change over time and unless an adjustment process is incorporated in the legislation, the tax/price

ratio will be affected. Japan admitted that no adjustment process exists in the legislation and that only *ex post facto* adjustments can occur. The Panel lastly noted that since the modification in 1989 of Japan's Liquor Tax Law there has been only one instance of adjustment.

* * *

Consequently, the Panel concluded that, by taxing vodka in excess of shochu, Japan is in violation of its obligation under Article III:2, first sentence.

* * *

[The Panel also found that "shochu, whisky, brandy, rum, gin, genever, and liqueurs are 'directly competitive or substitutable products' and Japan, by not taxing them similarly, is in violation of its obligation under Article III:2, second sentence, of the General Agreement on Tariffs and Trade 1994."]

* * *

The Panel *recommends* that the Dispute Settlement Body request Japan to bring the *Liquor Tax Law* into conformity with its obligations under the General Agreement on Tariffs and Trade 1994. ■

[78Latin: "After the fact."]

As with the most-favored-nation rule, exceptions apply to the application of the national treatment rule. These include:

1. The maintenance of preferences existing at the time GATT 1947 came into effect[79]
2. Discrimination in the procurement of goods by government agencies for governmental purposes only[80]
3. Discrimination in the payment of subsidies to domestic producers[81]
4. Discrimination in the screening of domestically produced cinematographic films[82]

Protection Through Tariffs

tariffs: Governmental charges imposed on goods at the time they are imported into a state.

The second major principle of the General Agreement on Tariffs and Trade is that each member state may protect its domestic industries only through the use of **tariffs**. Quotas and other quantitative restrictions that block the function of the price mechanism are forbidden by Article XI of GATT.[83] Additionally, to ensure that internal taxes are not disguised as tariffs, Article II requires that tariffs be collected "at the time or point of importation."

79General Agreement on Tariffs and Trade, 1994, Article III, para. 6.
80*Id.*, para. 8(a).
81*Id.*, para. 8(b).
82*Id.*, para. 10, and Article IV.
83*Id.*, Article XI, para. 1, states: "No prohibitions or restrictions other than duties, taxes or other charges, whether made effective through quotas, import or export licenses, or other measures, shall be instituted or maintained by any member on the importation of any product of the territory of any other member or on the exportation or sale for export of any product destined for the territory of any other member."

As with the other GATT principles, exceptions apply to the principle of protection through tariffs. The main exceptions include:

1. The imposition of temporary export prohibitions or restrictions to prevent or relieve critical shortages of foodstuffs or other essential products[84]
2. The use of import and export restrictions related to the application of standards or regulations for classifying, grading, or marking commodities[85]
3. The use of quantitative restrictions on imports of agricultural and fisheries products to stabilize national agricultural markets[86]
4. The use of quantitative restrictions to safeguard a state's balance of payments[87]
5. The use of quantitative restrictions by a developing state to further its economic development[88]

GATT requires member states not only to use customs tariffs as the primary device for protecting their domestic trade, but also to work toward their "substantial reduction." Tariff reductions are negotiated among the member states and then recorded as Schedules of Concessions annexed to the General Agreement on Tariffs and Trade. A **bound tariff rate** represents the highest rate that a member state may set on an item under the terms of GATT (tariffs are "bound" to this rate). Once such a rate is negotiated, the member state is required to extend it to all other GATT members by the most-favored-nation rule.[89]

> **bound tariff rates:** The highest tariff rates a WTO member state may set on imports from another member state.

Transparency

> **transparency:** Principle that governments must make their rules, regulations, and practices open and accessible to the public and other governments.

Essential to the operation of GATT is the principle of transparency. **Transparency**, as defined in Article X, is the requirement that governments *disclose* to the public and other governments the rules, regulations, and practices they follow in their domestic trade systems. Complementing this principle is the requirement, found in Article VIII, that member states must strive to *simplify* their import and export formalities. The operation of both of these principles can be seen in the way countries *classify imports* for the purpose of imposing duties.

While negotiations were underway in Geneva in 1947 to set up the original GATT, discussions were also being held in Western Europe to establish a customs union. For political reasons, this early attempt to put together a customs union failed, but the participants agreed to take advantage of the accords that had been reached to establish a standardized system (or "nomenclature") for classifying goods for the purpose of imposing customs duties. In 1950, the Convention on Nomenclature for the Classification of Goods in Customs Tariffs was signed, and the Customs Cooperation Council (CCC), an international organization based in Brussels, was established to administer it.

> **Harmonized System:** A system of classifying goods for customs purposes established by the Convention on Nomenclature for the Classification of Goods in Customs Tariffs.

Most countries have ratified this Convention. On January 1, 1989, the United States—the last major holdout—brought its tariff schedules into line with the CCC or "Harmonized" system. The **Harmonized System** (HS) is made up of a schedule of about 900 tariff headings, which are interpreted through explanatory notes and classification opinions published and regularly updated by the CCC. Both the notes and opinions are commonly incorporated into the tariff interpretation rules used by states that have adopted the HS.

The rationale underlying Article XI was provided in a statement by the U.S. delegate at the First Preparatory Session of GATT: "In the case of a tariff the total volume of imports can expand with the expansion of trade. There is flexibility in the volume of trade. Under a quota system the volume of trade is rigidly restricted, and no matter how much more people may wish to buy or consume, not one single more unit will be admitted than the controlling authority thinks fit.

"In the case of tariffs, the direction of trade and the source of import can shift with changes in quality and cost and price. Under a quota system the direction of trade and the sources of imports are rigidly fixed by public authority without regard to quality, cost or price. Under a tariff, equality of treatment of all other states can be assured. Under a quota system, no matter how detailed our rules, no matter how carefully we police them, there must almost inevitably be discrimination as amongst other states." UN Document EPCT/A/PV. 221 at pp. 16–17 (1947).

[84]General Agreement on Tariffs and Trade 1994, Article XI, para. 2(a).

[85]*Id.*, para. 2(b).

[86]*Id.*, para. 2(c).

[87]*Id.*, Article XII, para. 1, provides: ". . . [A]ny member, in order to safeguard its external financial position and its balance of payments, may restrict the quantity or value of merchandise permitted to be imported. . . ."

[88]*Id.*, Article XVIII, para. 4(a).

[89]*Id.*, Article XXVIII(*bis*).

Regional Integration

GATT seeks to promote international trade through regional economic integration. It accordingly encourages WTO member states to participate in free trade areas and customs unions. A **free trade area** consists of a group of states that have reduced or eliminated tariffs between themselves, but who maintain their own individual tariffs as to other states.[90] A **customs union** involves a group of states that have reduced or eliminated tariffs between themselves and have also established a common tariff for all other states.[91]

WTO member states may participate in these regional groups, however, *only* if the groups do not establish higher duties or more restrictive commercial regulations with respect to other WTO countries. The same prohibition also applies to interim agreements leading to the establishment of these groups.[92]

Any member state seeking to participate in a free trade area or customs union is required to "promptly notify" the WTO of its intentions. The proposed agreement and a transition schedule are then reviewed by WTO working parties to ensure that they comply with GATT Article XXIV. The results of this review are reported to the WTO Ministerial Conference, which in turn approves the proposal or makes "recommendations" for modification. Recommendations are actually demands to make changes. GATT Article XXIV, paragraph 7(b), says that "members shall not maintain or put into force . . . such [an] agreement if they are not prepared to modify it in accordance with these recommendations."

Once a free trade area or customs union is established, GATT rules apply to the area or union as a whole and not to its constituent states.

In many respects, a customs union or free trade area operates as a regional GATT, with its own tariff and nontariff codes. The North American Free Trade Agreement (see Exhibit 7-5) illustrates this.

Commodity Arrangements

Commodity arrangements are trade regulations meant to stabilize the production and supply of basic or "primary" commodities through the intergovernmental regulation of supply and demand. **Primary commodities** are, generally speaking, those derived by extraction (fuels and ores) or harvest (foodstuffs and fish) and that require minimal industrial processing before being used or consumed. The list commonly includes bananas, bauxite, cocoa, coffee, copper, cotton and cotton yarns, hard fibers and their products, iron ore, jute and its products, manganese, meat, phosphates, rubber, sugar, tea, tropical timber, tin, and vegetable oils including olive oil and oil seeds.

The General Agreement on Tariffs and Trade allows member states to participate in commodity agreements provided that they involve both exporting and importing countries and are submitted to the WTO for approval.[93] In developing and overseeing commodity agreements in the past, the GATT 1947 organization cooperated with both the UN Economic and Social Council (ECOSOC) and the UN Conference on Trade and Development (UNCTAD). The most active of the three in promoting commodity agreements was UNCTAD. At a meeting in Nairobi in 1976, UNCTAD adopted (under pressure from its developing member states) an **Integrated Program for Commodities** (IPC). The IPC called for the early conclusion of commodity agreements covering 10 "core" commodities: cocoa, coffee, copper, cotton, hard fibers, jute, rubber, sugar, tea, and tin; and for the establishment of a $6 billion internationally financed Common Fund to underwrite the costs of maintaining the buffer stocks commonly used in stabilizing the supply of the core commodities. To date, commodity arrangements have been set up

---

free trade area: A group of states that have reduced or eliminated tariffs between themselves but that maintain their own individual tariffs as to other states.

customs union: A group of states that have reduced or eliminated tariffs between themselves and have also established a common external tariff.

commodity arrangements: Intergovernmental agreements regulating the production and supply of primary commodities.

primary commodities: Products obtained by extraction or harvest that require minimal processing before being used.

Integrated Program for Commodities: Proposal of developing countries that would establish a Common Fund to underwrite the costs of maintaining a buffer stock of primary commodities as a way to stabilize supplies.

---

[90]General Agreement on Tariffs and Trade 1994, Article XXIV, para. 8(b).

[91]*Id.,* Article XXIV, para. 8(a).
   Free trade areas and customs unions can exist between "customs territories" (areas within states that are treated as separate territories for customs purposes) as well as between states. *Id.,* para. 8.

[92]*Id.,* Article XXIV, paras. 5(a) and 5(b).

[93]*Id.,* Article XX(h), authorizes members to enforce measures "undertaken in pursuance of obligations under any intergovernmental commodity agreement which conforms to criteria submitted to the World Trade Organization and not disapproved by the WTO or which is itself so submitted and not so disapproved."

Tariffs. The North American Free Trade Agreement (NAFTA) will eliminate all tariffs on products traded between Canada, Mexico, and the United States by 2007. Tariffs between Canada and the United States were eliminated at the end of 1998 under a free trade agreement between those two states that was agreed to prior to the establishment of NAFTA.

Rules of Origin. Only those Canadian, Mexican, and U.S. products that meet NAFTA's rules of origin will qualify for preferential tariff treatment. In other words, only products that are principally produced or manufactured in Canada, Mexico, or the United States will qualify for the special tariff rates.

Safeguards. Should imports from a NAFTA member state seriously injure or threaten to seriously injure another member state's businesses or workers, the affected state may temporarily impose quotas or tariffs on the goods causing the injury.

Investment. NAFTA removes investment barriers (in particular, government approval is no longer required for member state nationals to invest in a wide range of business activities); it removes investment distortions (by eliminating requirements as to domestic content, the transfer of technology to local competitors, and minimum levels of exports and maximum levels of imports); and it protects investors (by guaranteeing the right to repatriate capital and profits, the right to obtain fair compensation in the event of expropriation, and the right to use international arbitration in the event of a dispute between an investor and a government).

Services. Virtually all service areas (except for air and maritime transport and basic telecommunications) are opened to service providers from the three member states. That is, firms in one member state do not have to relocate to another member state in order to provide services. The licensing of professionals, including accountants, doctors, and lawyers, will be based on competency rather than nationality or residency.

Border-Crossing Procedures. NAFTA streamlines border-crossing procedures for business visitors, professionals, traders and investors, and intracompany transferees and assures that qualified persons will be permitted entry. The right of blue-collar workers to move across borders to take jobs, however, is not provided for.

Government Procurement. NAFTA authorizes firms in its member states to compete on an equal basis for a wide range of government contracts as well as contracts with government-controlled enterprises. Government procurement procedures are to be transparent and subject to independent review.

Standards. Standards (including both voluntary and mandatory technical specifications that specify the characteristics of a product, such as quality, performance, or labeling) have to be applied on a nondiscriminatory basis. The process of developing new standards has to be open and transparent, and nationals of the other member states are allowed to participate in this process.

Dispute Resolution. NAFTA creates a Trilateral Trade Commission to oversee trade relations and to appoint bilateral or trilateral panels to resolve disputes. Disputes must be resolved in no more than 8 months. Member states must comply with panel recommendations or offer acceptable compensation. If they do not, then the affected state can retaliate by withdrawing "equivalent trade concessions." Special provisions apply in certain areas, including investment and commercial disputes. These allow investors and merchants to go directly to international arbitration.

EXHIBIT 7-5   Principal Features of the North American Free Trade Agreement

for cocoa, coffee, rubber, sugar, and tin, but the money needed to establish the Common Fund has yet to be found.[94]

Once established, the organizations created by commodity agreements operate independently of the WTO, ECOSOC, or UNCTAD. They typically come under the supervision of a council made up of representatives of all participating states and a permanent secretariat appointed by the council. To support both supplies and prices, the agreements set up one or

---

[94]Frank Stone, *Canada, the GATT, and the International Trade System,* pp. 120–124, 139–154 (1984).
   Note that no commodity agreements were ever submitted to the GATT 1947 organization for its approval under Article XX(b). GATT, *Analytical Index: Guide to GATT Law and Practice,* p. 547 (6th ed., 1994).

more stabilization programs. Typically, these include contractual arrangements to buy and sell the goods at agreed-upon prices; export quotas to limit the quantities available to the world market during stressful times; and internationally financed buffer stocks, operated by a central body, which buys and sells from those stocks to stabilize market prices.[95]

Escape Clause

escape clause: Allows a WTO member state to temporarily escape from its GATT obligations when there is a surge in the number of imports coming from other member states.

Article XIX of GATT 1994—entitled "Emergency Action on Imports of Particular Products"—is an **escape clause** or safety valve that allows a member state to avoid, temporarily, its GATT obligations when there is a surge in the number of imports coming from other member states. The injured state can impose emergency restrictive trade measures—known as safeguards—if it can demonstrate that there is an actual or seriously threatened injury to one of its domestic industries.[96]

A state making use of the escape clause must notify the WTO and consult with the affected exporting state to arrange for compensation.[97] If a notifying country fails to negotiate, the injured exporting countries are authorized to "retaliate"—that is, withhold "substantially equivalent concessions" in order to restore the previous balance of trade between the two states.[98] The procedures for engaging in consultations and for withholding concessions are incorporated in a new Safeguards Agreement, discussed later in this chapter.

Exceptions

The drafters of the General Agreement on Tariffs and Trade realized that states sometimes need to take certain measures as a matter of public policy that conflict with GATT's general goal of liberalizing trade. Article XX sets out "General Exceptions" and Article XXI, "Security Exceptions."

general exceptions: Excuses that allow a WTO member state from complying with its GATT obligations in order for the state to protect certain essential public policy objectives.

The **general exceptions** excuse a member state from complying with its GATT obligations so long as this is not done as "a means of arbitrary or unjustifiable discrimination" or as "a disguised restriction on international trade." They allow a state to take measures contrary to the General Agreement on Tariffs and Trade that

a. are necessary to protect public morals;

b. are necessary to protect human, animal, or plant life or health;

c. relate to the importation or exportation of gold or silver;

d. are necessary to secure compliance with laws or regulations that are not inconsistent with GATT;

e. relate to the products of prison labor;

f. protect national treasures of artistic, historic, or archaeological value;

g. relate to the conservation of exhaustible natural resources;

h. are undertaken in accordance with an intergovernmental commodity agreement;

i. involve restrictions on exports of domestic materials needed by a domestic processing industry during periods when the domestic price of those materials is held below world prices as part of a governmental stabilization plan; or

j. are essential to acquiring products in short supply.

In Case 7–3, the Appellate Body explains how these general exceptions are interpreted and applied.

---

[95]Frank Stone, *Canada, the GATT, and the International Trade System*, pp. 144–145 (1984).
[96]General Agreement on Tariffs and Trade 1994, Article XIX, para. 1(a).
[97]*Id.*, Article XIX, para. 2.
[98]*Id.*, Article XIX, para. 3. *See* GATT, *Analytical Index: Guide to GATT Law and Practice*, pp. 488–489 (6th ed., 1994).

Case 7–3 United States—Import Prohibition of Certain Shrimp and Shrimp Products

World Trade Organization, Appellate Body, 1998.
Appellate Body Report WT/DS58/AB/R.[99]

I. INTRODUCTION: STATEMENT OF THE APPEAL

This is an appeal by the United States from certain issues of law and legal interpretations in the Panel Report, *United States—Import Prohibition of Certain Shrimp and Shrimp Products.* . . .

* * *

The United States issued regulations in 1987 pursuant to the *Endangered Species Act* of 1973[100] requiring all United States shrimp trawl vessels to use approved Turtle Excluder Devices ("TEDs") or tow-time restrictions in specified areas where there was a significant mortality of sea turtles in shrimp harvesting.[101] These regulations, which became fully effective in 1990, were modified so as to require the use of approved TEDs at all times and in all areas where there is a likelihood that shrimp trawling will interact with sea turtles, with certain limited exceptions.

. . . Section 609(b)(1) imposed . . . an import ban on shrimp harvested with commercial fishing technology which may adversely affect sea turtles. Section 609(b)(2) provides that the import ban on shrimp will not apply to harvesting nations that are certified. . . . According to the 1996 [*Administrative*] *Guidelines [for Implementing the Endangered Species Act]*, the Department of State "shall certify any harvesting nation meeting the following criteria without the need for action on the part of the government of the harvesting nation: (a) any harvesting nation without any of the relevant species of sea turtles occurring in waters subject to its jurisdiction; (b) any harvesting nation that harvests shrimp exclusively by means that do not pose a threat to sea turtles, e.g., any nation that harvests shrimp exclusively by artisanal means; or (c) any nation whose commercial shrimp trawling operations take place exclusively in waters subject to its jurisdiction in which sea turtles do not occur."

Second, certification shall be granted to harvesting nations that provide documentary evidence of the adoption of a regulatory program governing the incidental tak-

MAP 7-3   United States (1998)

ing of sea turtles in the course of shrimp trawling that is comparable to the United States program *and* where the average rate of incidental taking of sea turtles by their vessels is comparable to that of United States vessels.[102] According to the 1996 *Guidelines*, the Department of State assesses the regulatory program of the harvesting nation and certification shall be made if the program includes: (i) the required use of TEDs that are "comparable in effectiveness to those used in the United States. Any exceptions to this requirement must be comparable to those of the United States program . . . "; and (ii) "a credible enforcement effort that includes monitoring for compliance and appropriate sanctions." . . .

* * *

In the Panel Report, the Panel reached the following conclusions:

. . . [W]e conclude that the import ban on shrimp and shrimp products as applied by the United States on

---

[99]This report is posted at the WTO's Web site at www.wto.org/wto/dispute/58abr.doc.

[100]Public Law 93-205, *United States Code*, title 16, § 1531 et. seq.

[101]United States Federal Regulation, title 52, para. 24244, June 29, 1987 (the "1987 Regulations"). Five species of sea turtles fell under the regulations: loggerhead (*Caretta caretta*), Kemp's ridley (*Lepidochelys kempi*), green (*Chelonia mydas*), leatherback (*Dermochelys coriacea*) and hawksbill (*Eretmochelys imbricata*).

[102]Section 609(b)(2)(A) and (B).

the basis of Section 609 of Public Law 101-162 is not consistent with article XI: 1 of GATT 1994, and cannot be justified under article XX of GATT 1994.

* * *

IV. ISSUES RAISED IN THIS APPEAL

The issues raised in this appeal by the appellant, the United States, are the following:

* * *

(b) whether the Panel erred in finding that the measure at issue constitutes unjustifiable discrimination between countries where the same conditions prevail and thus is not within the scope of measures permitted under article XX of the GATT 1994.

VI. APPRAISING SECTION 609 UNDER ARTICLE XX OF THE GATT 1994

* * *

A. [Introduction]

* * *

Article XX of the GATT 1994 reads, in its relevant parts:

ARTICLE XX
GENERAL EXCEPTIONS
Subject to the requirement that such measures are not applied in a manner which would constitute a means of arbitrary or unjustifiable discrimination between countries where the same conditions prevail, or a disguised restriction on international trade, nothing in this agreement shall be construed to prevent the adoption or enforcement by any Member of measures:

* * *

(g) relating to the conservation of exhaustible natural resources if such measures are made effective in conjunction with restrictions on domestic production or consumption;

* * *

In *United States—[Standards for Reformulated and Conventional] Gasoline*,[103] we enunciated the appropriate method for applying article XX of the GATT 1994:

In order that the justifying protection of article XX may be extended to it, the measure at issue must not only come under one or another of the particular exceptions—paragraphs (a) to (j)—listed under article XX; it must also satisfy the requirements imposed by the opening clauses of article XX. *The analysis is, in other words, two-tiered: first, provisional justification by reason of characterization of the measure under XX(g); second, further appraisal of the same measure under the introductory clauses of article XX.* (emphasis added)

The sequence of steps indicated above in the analysis of a claim of justification under article XX reflects, not inadvertence or random choice, but rather the fundamental structure and logic of article XX. The Panel [in its Report] appears to suggest, albeit indirectly, that following the indicated sequence of steps, or the inverse thereof, does not make any difference. To the Panel, reversing the sequence set out in *United States—Gasoline* "seems equally appropriate." We do not agree.

* * *

We hold that the findings of the Panel . . . and the interpretative analysis embodied therein, constitute error in legal interpretation and accordingly reverse them.

* * *

B. Article XX(g): Provisional Justification of Section 609

In claiming justification for its measure, the United States primarily invokes article XX(g). . . .

1. "Exhaustible Natural Resources"   We begin with the threshold question of whether Section 609 is a measure concerned with the conservation of "exhaustible natural resources" within the meaning of article XX(g). . . . India, Pakistan, and Thailand contended that a "reasonable interpretation" of the term "exhaustible" is that the term refers to "finite resources such as minerals, rather than biological or renewable resources." In their view, such finite resources were exhaustible "because there was a limited supply which could and would be depleted unit for unit as the resources were consumed." Moreover, they argued, if "all" natural resources were considered to be exhaustible, the term "exhaustible" would become superfluous. . . .

We are not convinced by these arguments. Textually, article XX(g) is *not* limited to the conservation of "mineral" or "non-living" natural resources. The complainants' principal argument is rooted in the notion that "living" natural resources are "renewable" and therefore cannot be "exhaustible" natural resources. We do not believe that "exhaustible" natural resources and "renewable" natural resources are mutually exclusive. One lesson that modern biological sciences teach us is that living species, though in principle, capable of reproduction and, in that sense, "renewable", are in certain circumstances indeed susceptible of depletion, exhaustion and extinction, frequently

---

[103Appellate Body Report WT/DS2/AB/R, posted on the WTO's Web site at www.wto.org/wto/dispute/gas1.htm.]

because of human activities. Living resources are just as "finite" as petroleum, iron ore and other non-living resources.

* * *

Given the recent acknowledgement by the international community of the importance of concerted bilateral or multilateral action to protect living natural resources, and recalling the explicit recognition by WTO Members of the objective of sustainable development in the preamble of the WTO Agreement, we believe it is too late in the day to suppose that article XX(g) of the GATT 1994 may be read as referring only to the conservation of exhaustible mineral or other non-living natural resources. Moreover, two adopted GATT 1947 panel reports previously found fish to be an "exhaustible natural resource" within the meaning of article XX(g).[104] We hold that, in line with the principle of effectiveness in treaty interpretation, measures to conserve exhaustible natural resources, whether *living* or *non-living*, may fall within article XX(g).

We turn next to the issue of whether the living natural resources sought to be conserved by the measure are "exhaustible" under article XX(g). That this element is present in respect of the five species of sea turtles here involved appears to be conceded by all the participants . . . in this case. The exhaustibility of sea turtles would in fact have been very difficult to controvert since all of the seven recognized species of sea turtles are today listed in Appendix 1 of the Convention on International Trade in endangered Species of Wild Fauna and Flora ("CITES"). The list in Appendix 1 includes "all species *threatened with extinction* which are or may be affected by trade." (emphasis added)

* * *

For all the foregoing reasons, we find that the sea turtles here involved constitute "exhaustible natural resources" for purposes of article XX(g) of the GATT 1994.

[The Appellate Body also held that Section 609 was "related to the conservation of exhaustible natural resources" and that it was "made effective in conjunction with restrictions on domestic production or consumption" as required by paragraph (g) of Article XX of the GATT 1994.]

* * *

C. The Introductory Clauses of Article XX: Characterizing Section 609 Under the Chapeau's Standards

* * *

Although provisionally justified under article XX(g), Section 609, if it is ultimately to be justified as an excep-

tion under article XX, must also satisfy the requirements of the introductory clauses—the "chapeau"[105]—of article XX, that is,

ARTICLE XX
GENERAL EXCEPTIONS
Subject to the requirement that such measures are *not applied in a manner which would constitute a means of arbitrary or unjustifiable discrimination between countries where the same conditions prevail*, or a *disguised restriction on international trade*, nothing in this agreement shall be construed to prevent the adoption or enforcement by any Member of measures: (emphasis added)

We turn, hence, to the task of appraising Section 609, and specifically the manner in which it is applied under the chapeau of article XX; that is, to the second part of the two-tier analysis required under article XX.

* * *

In *United States—Gasoline*, we stated that "the purpose and object of the introductory clauses of article XX is generally the prevention of 'abuse of the exceptions of [article XX].'" We went on to say that:

. . . The chapeau is animated by the principle that while the exceptions of article XX may be invoked as a matter of legal right, they should not be so applied as to frustrate or defeat the legal obligations of the holder of the right under the substantive rules of the General Agreement. If those exceptions are not to be abused or misused, in other words, the measures falling within the particular exceptions must be applied reasonably, with due regard both to the legal duties of the party claiming the exception and the legal rights of the other parties concerned.

At the end of the Uruguay Round, negotiators fashioned an appropriate preamble for the new WTO Agreement, which strengthened the multilateral trading system by establishing an international organization, *inter alia*,[106] to facilitate the implementation, administration and operation, and to further the objectives, of that agreement and the other agreements resulting from that Round. In recognition of the importance of continuity with the previous GATT system, negotiators used the preamble of the GATT 1947 as the template for the preamble of the new WTO Agreement. Those negotiators evidently believed, however, that the objective of "full use of the resources of the world" set forth in the preamble of the GATT 1947 was no longer appropriate to the world trading system of the 1990's. As a result, they decided to qualify the original objectives of the GATT 1947 with the following words:

---

[104]United States—Prohibition of Imports of Tuna and Tuna Products from Canada, adopted 22 February 1982, BISD 29S/91, para. 4.9; Canada—Measures Affecting Exports of Unprocessed Herring and Salmon, adopted 22 March 1988, BISD 35S/98, para. 4.4.
[105]French: "hat."]
[106]Latin: "among other things."]

... while allowing for the optimal use of the world's resources in accordance with the objective of sustainable development, seeking both to protect and preserve the environment and to enhance the means for doing so in a manner consistent with their respective needs and concerns at different levels of economic development, ...

[T]his language demonstrates a recognition by WTO negotiators that optimal use of the world's resources should be made in accordance with the objective of sustainable development. As this preambular language reflects the intentions of negotiators of the WTO Agreement, we believe it must add color, texture and shading to our interpretation of the agreements annexed to the WTO Agreement, in this case, the GATT 1994. ...

* * *

Turning then to the chapeau of article XX, we consider that it embodies the recognition on the part of WTO Members of the need to maintain a balance of rights and obligations between the right of a Member to invoke one or another of the exceptions of article XX, specified in paragraphs (a) to (j), on the one hand, and the substantive rights of the other Members under the GATT 1994, on the other hand. Exercise by one Member of its right to invoke an exception, such as article XX(g), if abused or misused, will, to that extent, erode or render naught the substantive treaty rights ... of other Members. ... The chapeau was installed at the head of the list of "General exceptions" in article XX to prevent such far-reaching consequences.

In our view, the language of the chapeau makes clear that each of the exceptions in paragraphs (a) to (j) of article XX is a *limited and conditional* exception from the substantive obligations contained in the other provisions of the GATT 1994, that is to say, the ultimate availability of the exception is subject to the compliance by the invoking Member with the requirements of the chapeau. ...

* * *

2. "Unjustifiable Discrimination" We scrutinize first whether Section 609 has been applied in a manner constituting "unjustifiable discrimination between countries where the same conditions prevail". Perhaps the most conspicuous flaw in this measure's application relates to its intended and actual coercive effect on the specific policy decisions made by foreign governments, Members of the WTO. Section 609, in its application, is, in effect, an economic embargo which requires *all other exporting Members*, if they wish to exercise their GATT rights, to adopt *essentially the same* policy (together with an approved enforcement program) as that applied to, and enforced on, United States domestic shrimp trawlers. As enacted by the Congress of the United States, the *statutory* provisions of Section 609(b)(2)(A) and (B) do not,

in themselves, *require* that other WTO Members adopt *essentially the same* policies and enforcement practices as the United States. Viewed alone, the statute appears to permit a degree of discretion or flexibility in how the standards for determining comparability might be applied, in practice, to other countries. However, any flexibility that may have been intended by Congress when it enacted the statutory provision has been effectively eliminated in the implementation of that policy through the 1996 *Guidelines* promulgated by the Department of State and through the practice of the administrators in making certification determinations.

According to the 1996 *Guidelines*, ... any exceptions to the requirement of the use of TEDs must be comparable to those of the United States program. ... [And] in practice, the competent government officials only look to see whether there is a regulatory program requiring the use of TEDs or one that comes within one of the extremely limited exceptions available to United States shrimp trawl vessels.

The actual *application* of the measure, through the implementation of the 1996 *Guidelines* and the regulatory practice of administrators, *requires* other WTO Members to adopt a regulatory program that is not merely *comparable*, but rather *essentially the same*, as that applied to the United States shrimp trawl vessels. Thus, the effect of the application of Section 609 is to establish a rigid and unbending standard by which United States officials determine whether or not countries will be certified, thus granting or refusing other countries the right to export shrimp to the United States. Other specific policies and measures that an exporting country may have adopted for the protection and conservation of sea turtles are not taken into account, in practice, by the administrators making the comparability determination.

... It may be quite acceptable for a government, in adopting and implementing a domestic policy, to adopt a single standard applicable to all its citizens throughout that country. However, it is not acceptable, in international trade relations, for one WTO Member to use an economic embargo to *require* other Members to adopt essentially the same comprehensive regulatory program, to achieve a certain policy goal, as that in force within that Member's territory, *without* taking into consideration diffcrent conditions which may occur in the territories of those other Members.

Furthermore, when this dispute was before the Panel and before us, the United States did not permit imports of shrimp harvested by commercial shrimp trawl vessels using TEDs comparable in effectiveness to those required in the United States if those shrimp originated in waters of countries not certified under Section 609. In other words, *shrimp caught using methods identical to those employed in the United States* have been excluded from the United States market solely because they have been caught in waters of *countries that have not been certified by the United States.* The resulting situation is difficult to reconcile with the declared policy objective of protecting and conserving sea turtles. This suggests to us that this measure, in its application, is more concerned with effectively influencing WTO Members to adopt essentially the same comprehensive regulatory regime as that applied by the United States to its domestic shrimp trawlers, even though many of those Members may be differently situated. We believe that discrimination results not only when countries in which the same conditions prevail are differently treated, but also when the application of the measure at issue does not allow for any inquiry into the appropriateness of the regulatory program for the conditions prevailing in those exporting countries.

* * *

3. "Arbitrary Discrimination" We next consider whether Section 609 has been applied in a manner constituting "arbitrary discrimination between countries where the same conditions prevail." We have already observed that Section 609, in its application, imposes a single, rigid and unbending requirement that countries applying for certification under Section 609(b)(2)(A) and (B) adopt a comprehensive regulatory program that is essentially the same as the U.S. program, without inquiring into the appropriateness of that program for the conditions prevailing in the exporting countries. Furthermore, there is little or no flexibility in how officials make the determination for certification pursuant to these provisions.[107] In our view, this rigidity and inflexibility also constitute "arbitrary discrimination" within the meaning of the chapeau.

* * *

. . . The certification processes under Section 609 consist principally of administrative *ex parte*[108] inquiry or verification by staff of the Office of Marine Conservation in the Department of State with staff of the United States National Marine Fisheries Service. With respect to both types of certification, there is no formal opportunity for an applicant country to be heard, or to respond to any arguments that may be made against it, in the course of the certification process before a decision to grant or to deny certification is made. Moreover, no formal written, reasoned decision, whether of acceptance or rejection, is rendered on applications for either type of certification, whether under Section 609(b)(2)(A) and (B) or under Section 609(b)(2)(C). Countries which are granted certi-

fication are included in a list of approved applications published in the Federal Register; however, they are not notified specifically. Countries whose applications are denied also do not receive notice of such denial (other than by omission from the list of approved applications) or of the reasons for the denial. No procedure for review of, or appeal from, a denial of an application is provided.

* * *

We find, accordingly, that the United States measure is applied in a manner which amounts to a means not just of "unjustifiable discrimination", but also of "arbitrary discrimination" between countries where the same conditions prevail, contrary to the requirements of the chapeau of article XX. The measure, therefore, is not entitled to the justifying protection of article XX of the GATT 1994. . . .

In reaching these conclusions, we wish to underscore what we have *not* decided in this appeal. We have *not* decided that the protection and preservation of the environment is of no significance to the Members of the WTO. Clearly, it is. We have *not* decided that the sovereign nations that are Members of the WTO cannot adopt effective measures to protect endangered species, such as sea turtles. Clearly, they can and should. And we have *not* decided that sovereign states should not act together bilaterally, plurilaterally or multilaterally, either within the WTO or in other international fora,[109] to protect endangered species or to otherwise protect the environment. Clearly, they should and do.

What we *have* decided in this appeal is simply this: although the measure of the United States in dispute in this appeal serves an environmental objective that is recognized as legitimate under paragraph (g) of article XX of the GATT 1994, this measure has been applied by the United States in a manner which constitutes arbitrary and unjustifiable discrimination between Members of the WTO, contrary to the requirements of the chapeau of article XX. . . .

* * *

The Appellate Body *recommends* that the DSB request the United States to bring its measure found in the Panel Report to be inconsistent with article XI of the GATT 1994, and found in this Report to be not justified under article XX of the GATT 1994, into conformity with the obligations of the United States under that agreement. ∎

---

[107]In the oral hearing, the United States stated that "as a policy matter, the United States government believes that all governments should require the use of turtle excluder devices on all shrimp trawler boats that operate in areas where there is a likelihood of intercepting sea turtles" and that "when it comes to shrimp trawling, we know of only one way of effectively protecting sea turtles, and that is through TEDs."

[108]Latin: "from one party or side." An *ex parte* inquiry is one conducted without notice to the other party or parties adversely interested and without the latter being present or having the opportunity to contest the decision made there.]

[109]Plural of "forum." A meeting place, such as a court or tribunal.]

The **security exceptions** set out in Article XXI allow member states to avoid any obligations they may have under GATT that are contrary to their "essential security interests" or that
conflict with their duties "under the United Nations Charter for the maintenance of international peace and security."

Export Controls

Member states commonly employ GATT exceptions to limit certain kinds of exports.
Noteworthy examples of export controls that fit under the general exceptions found in Article XX are several multilateral treaties that limit the removal of cultural artifacts from their
countries of origin. Examples of export controls that relate to the security exceptions set out in
Article XXI include export restrictions for national security reasons or in support of actions
taken by the United Nations in maintaining the peace.

The Protection of Cultural Property

The United Nations Education, Scientific, and Cultural Organization (UNESCO), the
Organization of American States (OAS), and the International Institute for the Unification of
Private Law (Unidroit) have each sponsored conventions to control the international transfer
of cultural artifacts.[110] The UNESCO-sponsored Convention for the Protection of Cultural
Property in the Event of Armed Conflict, signed at The Hague in 1954, is the oldest of these
agreements.[111] It is important in defining cultural property (i.e., "movable or immovable property of great importance to the cultural heritage of every people"); in prohibiting the theft, pil-
lage, misappropriation, or exportation of cultural property during an armed conflict; and in
establishing the principle that obligations under cultural property conventions are not retroactive.[112] The UNESCO-sponsored Convention on the Means of Prohibiting and Preventing the
Illicit Import, Export, and Transfer of Ownership of Cultural Property, signed at Paris in 1970,
establishes that the import, export, and transfer of ownership of cultural property is illegal if it
is done contrary to laws adopted by states to protect their national heritage. The Convention
also requires member states to take all steps necessary to return stolen cultural properties to
their state of origin.[113]

The OAS's 1976 Convention on the Protection of the Archaeological, Historical, and
Artistic Heritage of the American Nations copies most of the provisions of the 1970 UNESCO
Convention, adding articles that make enforcement easier.[114]

The 1995 Unidroit Convention on Stolen or Illegally Exported Cultural Objects requires
member states to return stolen cultural objects. Claims must be made within three years
after the owner learns of the location of such property and within 50 years of the time of
the theft.[115]

---

[110]UNESCO's Convention Concerning the Protection of the World Cultural and Natural Heritage (1972) is concerned principally with the identification and protection of cultural sites within the borders of member states. The
Council of Europe's European Convention on the Protection of the Archaeological Heritage (Revised 1992) primarily regulates the exploration of archaeological sites; it only peripherally restricts the exportation of cultural
property. The text of the Convention is posted on the Council of Europe's Web site at
www.coe.fr/eng/legaltxt/143e.htm.

[111]The text is in *The Protection of Cultural Property I: Compendium of Legislative Texts*, pp. 335–356 (UNESCO,
1984). It is also posted on UNESCO's Web site at www.unesco.org/ general/eng/legal/cltheritage/hague/index.html.
Currently, 88 states are parties to this Convention. *See* www.unesco.org/general/eng/legal/cltheritage/hague/
rat.html.

[112]*See* Autocephalous Greek-Orthodox Church of Cyprus v. Goldberg & Feldman Fine Arts, Inc., *Federal Supplement*,
vol. 717, p. 1374 (1989), for an example of a case where the recipient of artifacts expropriated by an occupying military force was required to return them to their country of origin.

[113]The text is in *The Protection of Cultural Property I: Compendium of Legislative Texts*, pp. 357–364 (UNESCO,
1984). It is also posted on UNESCO's Web site at www.unesco.org/general/ eng/legal/
cltheritage/bh572.html. Currently, 85 states are parties to this Convention. *See* www.unesco.org/general/eng/legal/
cltheritage/bh572-rat.html.

[114]The text is in *id.*, at pp. 370–374. It is also posted on the OAS's Web site at www.oas.org/En/prog/juridico/english/
Treaties/c-16.html. The current member states are Costa Rica, Ecuador, El Salvador, Guatemala, Nicaragua,
Panama, and Peru. *See* www.oas.org/En/prog/ juridico/english/Sigs/c-165.html.

[115]The Convention is posted on the Unidroit Web site at www.unidroit.org/english/ conventions/c-cult.htm. The
Convention entered into force on July 1, 1998. Currently, there are seven states parties. *See* www.unidroit.org/
english/implement/i-95.htm.

The Maintenance of National Security

States have long imposed restrictions on strategically important exports as a matter of national security. Following World War II, export restrictions became a prominent feature of the West's Cold War with the East, and by 1949, the United States and its West European allies had enacted legislation limiting exports to the Soviet Union and its Eastern European allies. The U.S. Export Control Act of 1949, for example, restricted American exports of strategic commodities to Communist countries for three reasons: (1) national security, (2) foreign policy, and (3) to preserve materials in short supply. In 1949, the United States and its allies formed the Coordinating Committee on Multilateral Export Controls (COCOM). COCOM maintained a list of commodities and technological information that each country agreed not to export to Communist and certain other states. In 1993, with the Cold War at an end, the COCOM member states agreed that its East-West focus was no longer an appropriate basis for establishing export controls, and they agreed to bring the committee to an end. The following year, at a meeting in Wassenaar, Netherlands, the member states formally terminated COCOM and agreed to establish a new multilateral arrangement.

Wassenaar Arrangement:
Intergovernmental arrangement and organization to coordinate national policies so that transfers of conventional arms and dual use goods and technologies do not contribute to the development or enhancement of military capabilities that undermine international and regional security and are not diverted to support such capabilities.

The Wassenaar Arrangement In July 1996, 33 countries[116]—including Canada, France, Great Britain, Japan, Russia, and the United States—approved the **Wassenaar Arrangement** on Export Controls for Conventional Arms and Dual-Use Goods and Technologies.[117] Its goals are to promote transparency, the exchange of views and information, and greater responsibility in transfers of conventional arms and dual-use goods and technologies. Member countries, through their own national policies, seek to ensure that such transfers do not contribute to the development or enhancement of military capabilities that undermine international and regional security and are not diverted to support such capabilities. The Arrangement, however, is not meant to impede bona fide transactions and, unlike COCOM, is not directed against any state or group of states.[118]

Member countries are required to maintain export controls on a list of agreed-upon items.[119] They meet regularly in Vienna, where a small Secretariat is located,[120] to update the list and to exchange information. Additionally, they make semiannual reports on the transfer of arms and controlled dual use items.

Membership is open to all countries on a nondiscriminatory basis. A member must be a producer of arms or an exporter of industrial equipment; maintain nonproliferation policies and appropriate national policies, including adherence to relevant nonproliferation regimes and treaties; and maintain fully effective export controls.[121]

Other Multilateral Export-Control Programs

In addition to the Wassenaar Arrangement, there are four other multilateral export-control programs. The **Australia Group** is an informal multilateral group of states established in 1984 to address concerns about the proliferation of chemical and biological warfare capabilities.[122] Members[123] meet annually to share information about proliferation dangers and to harmonize their national export controls in an effort to curb the transfer of materials or equipment that could be used in the creation of chemical or biological weapons. The Group maintains lists of

Australia Group:
Multilateral group of states concerned with curbing the proliferation of chemical and biological weapons.

---

[116]The 33 countries are Argentina, Australia, Austria, Belgium, Bulgaria, Canada, the Czech Republic, Denmark, Finland, France, Germany, Greece, Hungary, Ireland, Italy, Japan, Luxembourg, the Netherlands, New Zealand, Norway, Poland, Portugal, Romania, Russia, Slovakia, South Korea, Spain, Sweden, Switzerland, Turkey, Ukraine, the United Kingdom, and the United States. Wassenaar Secretariat at www.wassenaar.org/.

[117]The "Initial Elements" of the Wassenaar Arrangement are posted at www.wassenaar.org/docs/IE96.html.

[118]*See* "What Is the Wassenaar Arrangement?" at www.wassenaar.org/docs/talkpts.html.

[119]The lists are posted at www.wassenaar.org/List/Table%20of%20Contents%20-%2098web.html.

[120]The Secretariat maintains a Web site at www.wassenaar.org/.

[121]Links to Web sites describing the export-control programs of all the Wassenaar Agreement member states are located on the Secretariat's home page at www.wassenaar.org/.

[122]The Australia Group Secretariat maintains a Web site at www.australiagroup.net.

[123]Currently there are 34 members: Argentina, Australia, Austria, Belgium, Bulgaria, Canada, Cyprus, Czech Republic, Denmark, European Commission, Finland, France, Germany, Greece, Hungary, Iceland, Ireland, Italy, Japan, Luxembourg, Netherlands, New Zealand, Norway, Poland, Portugal, Romania, Slovakia, South Korea, Spain, Sweden, Switzerland, Turkey, United Kingdom, and United States. Australia Group Secretariat at www.australiagroup.net/agpart.htm.

items that should be controlled, as well as "warning" lists of items whose purchase may indicate proliferation activities.[124]

Zangger Committee: Exporting states parties to the Treaty on Non-Proliferation of Nuclear Weapons that seek to harmonize their interpretations of the Treaty's export-control provision.

The **Zangger Committee** was set up the year after the Treaty on Non-Proliferation of Nuclear Weapons[125] came into force in 1970.[126] Also known as the Non-Proliferation Treaty Exporters' Committee,[127] it works to harmonize the member states' interpretations of the export-control provision contained in the Treaty.[128] This provision calls for exporters to require International Atomic Energy Agency safeguards as a condition for the supply of nuclear material or items "especially designed or prepared for the processing, use, or production of special fissionable material." The safeguards include peaceful end-use assurances and assurances that an item will not be re-exported to a non-Treaty non–nuclear weapon state unless the receiving state accepts safeguards on the item.[129]

Nuclear Suppliers Group: Group of nuclear supplier states concerned with limiting the proliferation of nuclear weapons.

The **Nuclear Suppliers Group** (NSG) is a group of nuclear supplier countries—including members and nonmembers of the Treaty on Non-Proliferation of Nuclear Weapons—that seeks to contribute to the nonproliferation of nuclear weapons by maintaining control lists for nuclear exports and nuclear-related exports.[130] The NSG's lists aim to ensure that nuclear trade for peaceful purposes does not contribute to the proliferation of nuclear weapons or other nuclear explosive devices without hindering international trade and cooperation in the nuclear field.[131]

Missile Technology Control Regime: Group of states concerned with limiting the proliferation of missiles capable of delivering nuclear warheads.

The **Missile Technology Control Regime** was established in 1987 to limit the proliferation of missiles "capable of delivering nuclear weapons." This is an informal group with no permanent organization; each member administers its missile-related export controls independently. The members convene at regular meetings to exchange information and to agree on the goods and technologies that need to be controlled.[132]

United Nations Action to Maintain International Peace

The United Nations Charter authorizes the UN Security Council to impose sanctions, including the adoption of bans on trade, upon states whose actions threaten international peace,[133] and on several occasions it has imposed such sanctions. For example, in 1966, when Rhodesia's minority white government unilaterally declared independence from the United Kingdom in the hopes of preserving white domination of the country, the UN Security Council ordered

---

[124]The lists are posted at www.australiagroup.net/agcomcon.htm.

[125]The text of the treaty is posted on the U.S. Arms Control and Disarmament Agency Web site at www.acda.gov/treaties/npt1.htm.

[126]*See* U.S. Department of Statement, Bureau of Nonproliferation, "Factsheet" (January 20, 2001) at www.state.gov/t/np/rls/fs/2001/3054.htm.

[127]The Zangger Committee was named in honor of Professor Claude Zangger of Switzerland, who chaired the Committee from its inception in 1971 until 1989. U.S. Arms Control and Disarmament Agency, Annual Report, chap. 6 (1997), posted at www.acda.gov/reports/annual/chpt6.htm.

[128]There are 35 member states of the Zangger Committee: Argentina, Australia, Austria, Belgium, Bulgaria, Canada, China, Czech Republic, Denmark, Finland, France, Germany, Greece, Hungary, Ireland, Italy, Japan, Luxembourg, Netherlands, Norway, Poland, Portugal, Republic of Korea, Romania, Russia, Slovakia, Slovenia, South Africa, Spain, Sweden, Switzerland, Turkey, Ukraine, United Kingdom, and United States. U.S. Department of Statement, Bureau of Nonproliferation, "Factsheet" (January 20, 2001) at www.state.gov/t/np/rls/fs/2001/3054.htm.

[129]U.S. Arms Control and Disarmament Agency, Annual Report, chap. 6 (1997), posted at www.acda.gov/reports/annual/chpt6.htm.

[130]The 39 current members are Argentina, Australia, Austria, Belarus, Belgium, Brazil, Bulgaria, Canada, Cyprus, Czech Republic, Denmark, Finland, France, Germany, Greece, Hungary, Ireland, Italy, Japan, South Korea, Latvia, Luxembourg, Netherlands, New Zealand, Norway, Poland, Portugal, Romania, Russia, Slovakia, Slovenia, South Africa, Spain, Sweden, Switzerland, Turkey, Ukraine, United Kingdom, and United States. Nuclear Suppliers Group Secretariat at www.nuclearsuppliersgroup.org/member.htm.

[131]*See* Nuclear Suppliers Group Secretariat Web site at www.nuclearsuppliersgroup.org.

[132]Arms Control Association, "Fact Sheet: Missile Technology Control Regime," at www.armscontrol.org/factsheets/mtcr.asp.

   The 33 current members are Argentina, Australia, Austria, Belgium, Brazil, Canada, Czech Republic, Denmark, Finland, France, Germany, Greece, Hungary, Iceland, Ireland, Italy, Japan, Luxembourg, Netherlands, New Zealand, Norway, Poland, Portugal, Russia, South Africa, South Korea, Spain, Sweden, Switzerland, Turkey, Ukraine, United Kingdom, and United States.

[133]Article 41 of the United Nations Charter provides: "The Security Council may decide what measures not involving the use of armed force are to be employed to give effect to its decisions, and it may call upon members of the United Nations to apply such measures. These may include complete or partial interruption of economic relations and of rail, sea, air, postal, telegraphic, radio, and other means of communication, and the severance of diplomatic relations." The Charter is posted on the UN's Web site at www.un.org/aboutun/charter/.

members of the United Nations to suspend trade in certain commodities with Rhodesia.[134] In 1977, in reaction to the use of apartheid laws, the Security Council imposed a mandatory ban on the sale of arms to South Africa.[135] And most recently, following Iraq's invasion of Kuwait, the Security Council imposed an economic embargo on Iraq that is still in place.[136]

D. MULTILATERAL TRADE AGREEMENTS

In addition to GATT 1994, there are 13 other Agreements on Trade in Goods annexed to the WTO Agreement: nine of these deal with regulatory matters; two are "sectoral agreements" that extend the General Agreement on Tariffs and Trade to goods not covered under GATT 1947; one is a program to devise a new agreement; and one is a protocol. The regulatory agreements deal with (1) customs valuation, (2) preshipment inspection, (3) technical barriers to trade, (4) sanitary and phytosanitary measures, (5) trade-related investment measures, (6) import-licensing procedures, (7) subsidies and countervailing measures, (8) antidumping, and (9) safeguards.[137] The sectoral agreements cover (1) agriculture and (2) textiles and clothing. The program to devise a new agreement relates to rules of origin. The protocol describes how the Schedules of Commitments and Concessions of the member states were phased in following the adoption of the WTO Agreement.

The most significant aspect of these agreements is that they have to be acceded to by all WTO member states. Under GATT 1947, member states were not required to participate in its nontariff codes and many did not.[138] This change is certain to produce much greater international harmony in the way trade is conducted.

Another important harmonizing factor found in all of the new nontariff agreements is that disputes between member states over their application are now uniformly governed by the WTO Dispute Settlement Understanding. Previously, each agreement had its own dispute settlement provisions. Procedures to settle disputes between individuals and governments over the latter's compliance with the provisions of a particular agreement continue, however, to be specified in each agreement.

Customs Valuation

Agreement on Implementation of Article VII of GATT 1994 (Customs Valuation Code): Harmonizes the methods used by WTO member states for determining the value of goods for customs purposes.

transaction value: Customs value of imported goods that is based on the price actually paid or payable for goods at the time they were sold for export.

When goods cross an international frontier, they are charged a tariff that is based on a percentage of their value. The Customs Valuation Code, or **Agreement on Implementation of Article VII of GATT 1994**, is designed to harmonize the methods used by WTO member states to determine the value of those goods.[139] Its detailed rules are meant to provide for a fair, neutral, and uniform system of customs valuation. A primary method and fallback methods are established.

The primary method of customs valuation is to figure the **transaction value** of the imported item. This is based on "the price actually paid or payable for the goods when sold for export to the country of importation"[140] plus certain amounts reflecting packing costs, commissions paid by the buyer, any royalties or license fees paid by the buyer, and any resale, disposal, or use proceeds that accrue to the seller.[141]

If the transaction value of imported items cannot be fairly determined (which is the case, for example, when the seller and buyer are related), then fallback methods are used. The first

---

[134]The text of the UN Declaration is in *International Legal Materials*, vol. 5, p. 141 (1967).

[135]Security Council Resolution 418 (November 4, 1977), in *UN Monthly Chronicle*, p. 10 (December 1977), and posted on the UN Web site at gopher://gopher.undp.org:70/00/undocs/scd/scouncil/s77/16.

[136]Security Council Resolution 661 (August 6, 1990), posted on the UN Web site at gopher:// gopher.undp.org:70/00/ undocs/scd/scouncil/s90/15.

[137]The Agreement on Government Procurement, adopted at the Tokyo Round, was carried forward as a Plurilateral Trade Agreement under the WTO rather than a Multilateral Trade Agreement.

[138]*See* the table setting out acceptances of the Tokyo Round agreements in GATT, *Analytical Index: Guide to GATT Law and Practice*, pp. 1056–1059 (6th ed., 1994).

[139]The Agreement on Implementation of Article VII of GATT 1994 reproduces the text of the 1979 Tokyo Round agreement. This is supplemented in Part III of the Final Act by a "Decision Regarding Cases Where Customs Administrations Have Reasons to Doubt the Truth or Accuracy of the Declared Value" and by "Texts Relating to Minimum Values and Imports by Sole Agents, Sole Distributors, and Sole Concessionaires." These supplements address concerns of developing countries relating to difficulties they commonly encounter in determining the value of goods for customs purposes.

[140]Agreement on Implementation of Article VII of GATT 1994, Article 1, para. 1.

[141]*Id.*, Article 8, para. 1.

such method involves determining the "transaction value of identical goods" sold for export to the same importing country at about the same time.[142] If this value cannot be established, then the second method is to determine the "transaction value of similar items" sold for export to the importing country at about the same time.[143] Third, if neither of these values can be ascertained, the **deductive value** method is used. In this case, the customs value is based on the price actually paid for the greatest number of units sold to unrelated persons in the importing country at about the same time.[144] Under the fourth method, the **computed value** is derived from the sum of (a) the cost or value of the materials, including the cost of fabrication or processing, (b) the profit and overhead that customarily apply to the particular goods in the exporting country, and (c) charges for handling, transportation, and insurance.[145] Finally, if none of these methods can be applied, a **derived value** is used. This is determined by applying whichever of the other methods best fits and adjusting it to the particular circumstances.[146]

Case 7–4 examines the circumstances when it is appropriate to use the deductive value instead of the transaction value for imported goods.

deductive value: Customs value of imported goods that is based on the price actually paid for similar goods by unrelated persons in the importing country at about the same time.

computed value: Customs value of goods that is based on their price calculated from the cost of manufacture, overhead, and handling.

derived value: Customs value of goods that is determined by using whichever of the other methods best fit and adjusting it to the particular circumstances.

---

[142]*Id.,* Article 2, para. 1(a).
[143]*Id.,* Article 3, para. 1(a).
[144]*Id.,* Article 5, para. 1(a).
[145]*Id.,* Article 6, para. 1(a).
    At the request of the importer, the order of application of the deductive value and the computed value methods will be reversed. *Id.,* Article 4.
[146]*Id.,* Article 7, para. 1

Case 7–4   Orbisphere Corp. v. United States

United States, Court of International Trade.
Federal Supplement, vol. 726, p. 1344 (1989).

JUDGE MUSGRAVE:

The primary issue in this case is whether, in valuing plaintiff's products for purposes of customs duties, the Customs Service properly used as its measure of value the "transaction value" of the imported merchandise, or should instead have used the "deductive value" of the merchandise as requested by the plaintiff here. . . .

BACKGROUND

Plaintiff Orbisphere Corp. (Orbisphere) sells scientific devices that detect, measure, and analyze oxygen and other gases. These devices are manufactured in Switzerland by Orbisphere Laboratories (Orbisphere Labs), a subsidiary of Orbisphere. Both Orbisphere and Orbisphere Labs are incorporated in Delaware. The operation's administrative offices are in Geneva and most of its executive personnel are based there. Orbisphere maintains four sales offices in the United States in Emerson, New Jersey; Houston, Texas; Mount Prospect, Illinois; and Huntington Beach, California.

At the time of the transactions at issue, sales orders for the analyzers were solicited from U.S. customers by Orbisphere sales staff working at the four U.S. sales

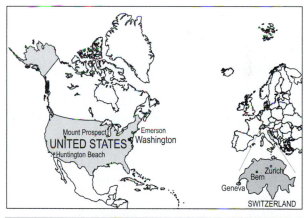

MAP 7-4   United States and Switzerland (1989)

offices. Once received, the orders are forwarded to the New Jersey office, which then forwarded the order to the Orbisphere Labs Geneva office where the ordered item was manufactured. The completed item was then shipped from Geneva to the New Jersey office where the merchandise was unpacked, inspected, adjusted if necessary, repacked in a different container, and then shipped to the U.S. purchaser. Invoices were sent to the purchaser from the New Jersey office which office also received payment from the customer and deposited the payment in the company's U.S. bank account. All revenues from these sales in excess of the salaries and other costs attributable to the U.S. sales offices were ultimately remitted to the Geneva office; the U.S. offices, therefore, were "cost centers," not "profit centers."

CONTENTIONS OF THE PARTIES AND APPLICABLE STATUTES

In support of the Customs Service's use of transaction value for appraising the merchandise in this case, the defendant argues that the sales of the products were consummated not by the U.S. sales offices, but, rather, by the Geneva office directly with the U.S. purchasers. Consequently, argues the defendant, the merchandise was sold by and from the Geneva office for export to the United States, and was therefore correctly appraised on the basis of transaction value under 19 U.S.C. § 140la(b).

Section 1401a(a) provides that

(1) . . . imported merchandise shall be appraised, for purposes of this chapter, on the basis of the following:

   (A) The transaction value provided for under subsection (b) of this section.

   (B) The transaction value of identical merchandise . . .

   (C) The transaction value of similar merchandise . . . if the value referred to in subparagraph (B) cannot be determined.

   (D) The deductive value provided for under subsection (d) of this section, if the value referred to in subparagraph (C) cannot be determined . . .

The parties have framed their dispute in this case as a contest over whether the applicable standard for appraisal is the transaction value of the merchandise under subparagraph (A), or the deductive value under subparagraph (D).

Subsection (b) of this section defines "transaction value" as the price actually paid or payable for the merchandise when sold for exportation to the United States, plus amounts equal to—

(A) the packing costs incurred by the buyer with respect to the imported merchandise;

(B) any selling commission incurred by the buyer with respect to the imported merchandise;

(C) the value, apportioned as appropriate, of any assist;

(D) any royalty or license fee related to the merchandise that the buyer is required to pay, directly or indirectly, as a condition of the sale of the imported merchandise for exportation to the United States; and

(E) the proceeds of any subsequent resale, disposal, or use of the imported merchandise that accrue, directly or indirectly, to the seller.

This subsection provides further that the transaction value shall be augmented by the items in paragraphs (A) through (E) above only to the extent that the amount in such a paragraph:

   (i) is not otherwise included within the price paid or actually payable; and

   (ii) is based on sufficient information.

If sufficient information is not available with respect to one of these amounts then the transaction value of the product shall be treated as undeterminable, and the product must be valued under one of the alternative bases provided in section 1401a.

In the context of the present controversy, the most critical language in subsection (b) is that defining "transaction value" as the price paid or payable for the merchandise "when sold for export to the United States." The defendant argues that the sales in this case were concluded by Orbisphere's Geneva office directly with the purchasers in the United States. This is so, the defendant claims, because all of Orbisphere's major business decisions were made from the Geneva office by the company's executive personnel, all of whom were based at that office. The Geneva office set the prices at which Orbisphere's products were offered for sale and the terms and conditions governing the sale contracts. The U.S. sales offices, after receiving an order, transmitted to the Geneva office a telex describing the items ordered and stating, "Please accept the following order(s)". After manufacturing the items, the Geneva office shipped the items to the New Jersey office for delivery to the U.S. customer, and paid whatever costs were incurred by the company in transporting the items from Switzerland to New Jersey. When final payment for the items was received by the New Jersey office, these sums were remitted from Orbisphere's U.S. bank account to the Geneva office, less amounts necessary to meet the operating expenses and overhead costs of the U.S. offices.

Additionally, the defendant argues that the commercial practice of Orbisphere in these transactions was accurately stated in the terms printed on the pre-1984 invoices, namely, that all shipments were F.O.B.[147] Geneva, that the risk of loss of the goods shifted to the buyer at that location and, most importantly, that all orders received by the U.S. sales offices were acceptable only by, and at the sole discretion of, the Geneva office. The defendant contends that the charges made in these terms on Orbisphere's invoices after 1983 were merely changes in form, and that the actual practice of the company in later

---

[[147]F.O.B., as used here, is a U.S. trade term that stands for "free on board" and means that goods have been delivered to a carrier at a named place; in this case, Geneva.]

transactions remained the same as that described in the earlier invoices. The U.S. sales, argues the defendant, were always accepted by, indeed could only be accepted by, the Geneva office, and were thus sales "for export to the United States" within the meaning of section 1401a(b).

The plaintiff flatly contradicts the defendant's primary argument and insists that it was the New Jersey office that accepted the orders placed with Orbisphere by customers in the United States. Plaintiff argues further that the ordered goods were shipped from Switzerland F.O.B. New Jersey, and that Orbisphere bore the cost of insuring, and the risk of loss of, the goods during their trans-Atlantic shipment. On the basis of this argument, the plaintiff contends that the sales of the items at issue here were concluded in the United States, and that they were therefore not sales "for export to the United States" as required to make possible transaction value appraisal under section 1401a(b). The plaintiff argues that instead of transaction value, the "deductive value" of the goods is the proper basis for their valuation under section 140la(d).

"Deductive value" is defined in this section as:

... (d) (2) (A) ... whichever of the following prices (as adjusted under paragraph (3)) is appropriate depending upon when and in what condition the merchandise concerned is sold in the United States:

(i) If the merchandise concerned is sold in the condition as imported at or about the date of importation of the merchandise being appraised, the price is the unit price at which the merchandise concerned is sold in the greatest aggregate quantity at or about such date.

(ii) If the merchandise concerned is sold in the condition as imported but not sold at or about the date of importation of the merchandise being appraised, the price is the unit price at which the merchandise concerned is sold in the greatest aggregate quantity after the date of importation of the merchandise being appraised but before the close of the 90th day after the date of such importation.

(iii) If the merchandise concerned was not sold in the condition as imported and not sold before the close of the 90th day after the date of importation of the merchandise being appraised, the price is the unit price at which the merchandise being appraised, after further processing, is sold in the greatest aggregate quantity before the 190th day after the date of such importation ...

* * *

Plaintiff's first witness at trial, Mr. William J. Miller, joined Orbisphere in 1979, and was the manager of its New Jersey Branch at the time of importation of the merchandise at issue here. When presented at trial with copies of several pre-1984 invoices containing the earlier terms, Mr. Miller testified that these earlier terms did not reflect the way Orbisphere operated in the United States from the time he joined the company. He professed not to know why these terms remained on the backs of the company's invoices when the U.S. operations did not conform to those terms. Mr. Miller also stated that in 1984 when it became necessary to reprint more invoices, he realized that the earlier terms printed on the invoices were inconsistent with Orbisphere's U.S. business practices, and that he consequently then modified the invoices to their present form. According to his testimony, these modified terms on the post-1983 invoices accurately describe Orbisphere's practices with regard to U.S. sales from the time he began working for the firm in 1979. In a colloquy with the Court, Mr. Miller stated that notwithstanding the terms printed on the earlier invoices, the practice of the company during his employment there was that goods were sold to U.S. customers F.O.B. New Jersey, that risk of loss of the goods passed to the customers at New Jersey, and that freight was charged to the customers only from that point to the point of ultimate delivery at the customer's places of business.

Mr. Miller's testimony was supported at trial by Mr. John Franklin who has been employed by Orbisphere in its Geneva office since 1983 as the company's financial comptroller. Mr. Franklin testified that Orbisphere maintained an open freight insurance policy covering all shipments of manufactured products from the company's factory in Geneva to the point of delivery at the U.S. sales offices. Like Mr. Miller, Mr. Franklin stated that in the event of a loss of these products during shipment to the U.S. offices the U.S. purchaser would not be liable for payment, and Orbisphere would suffer the loss.

Plaintiff's argument is in essence that given this scenario the shipments of the products from the Geneva factory to the New Jersey office were merely movements of the goods "from one warehouse to another" in Mr. Franklin's words; that the actual sales were concluded wholly within the United States.

DISCUSSION

The resolution of this controversy depends substantially upon where the sales of the merchandise are deemed to have occurred.

* * *

All of the sales orders from U.S. customers were solicited and/or received by the U.S. sales offices of Orbisphere, a U.S. corporation. None was ever solicited or received directly by the Geneva office; indeed the Geneva office never had direct communications of any kind with U.S. customers. The terms and conditions printed on the sales invoices for all of the products involved here clearly stated that orders were acceptable only by the New Jersey office, that title and risk of loss on all sales passed to the buyer on delivery of the products to the ultimate carrier at the FOB point stated in the invoice, and that this FOB point was Orbisphere's . . . New Jersey office. These invoices, moreover, were produced by the New Jersey office when the particular orders were received, and copies were sent to the customers by this same office along with the products. All payments for U.S. sales were sent to the New Jersey office which deposited the amounts in Orbisphere's New York bank account. This scenario constitutes the archetypal United States sales contract.

Defendant contests this conclusion primarily with circumstantial evidence. Whatever were the terms and conditions printed on the back of Orbisphere's invoices at times past, all of its invoices during the time of the present transactions contained the terms and conditions described in the preceding paragraph. The company therefore was legally bound by these terms and conditions in these transactions, and consequently, for purposes of this case the provisions should prevail over any inconsistent provisions contained in other invoices from earlier times not relevant here. . . .

* * *

Finally, and underlying its entire argument, the defendant asserts that it was the Geneva office that in reality retained control over all of Orbisphere's important obligations, including the acceptance of orders from U.S. customers. The Court has stated its objections to specific portions of this argument, such as those concerning the invoices and telexes. In conclusion, the Court notes that both Orbisphere and Orbisphere Labs were at all times involved here American corporations. Orbisphere Labs, the manufacturing arm of the company was an American subsidiary of Orbisphere, also an American company. The Geneva office was simply a foreign office of this company. Mr. John Franklin testified that literally there was no entity known as "Orbisphere Switzerland", nor as "Orbisphere Geneva", nor as "Orbisphere New Jersey". Rather there was Orbisphere, Inc., a United States corporation which sold products to U.S. customers through its New Jersey office. The defendant does not directly contradict this.

Based on these circumstances, the plaintiff has proved to the satisfaction of the Court that the sales at issue in this case were consummated within the United States, thus rebutting the presumption of the correctness of Customs' valuation, and establishing "deductive value" as the correct basis for valuation of the entries.

Both parties agree that in the event of such a finding, the Court should remand the case to the Customs Service under 28 U.S.C. § 2643(b) (1982) for calculation of duties based on the deductive value of the merchandise. The Court hereby finds for the plaintiff, dismisses plaintiff's counterclaims, and remands this case to the Customs Service for re-calculation of duties on the basis of deductive value, taking into account all relevant data, and in accordance with this opinion. ■

Preshipment Inspection

Developing states frequently engage private companies to verify price, quantity, quality, customs classifications, and other characteristics of goods before the goods are shipped from other states. This "preshipment inspection" (or PSI) is meant to prevent over- and under-invoicing and fraud, and thus prevent the flight of capital and the evasion of customs duties.

Agreement on Preshipment Inspection: Allows WTO developing member states to use preshipment inspections, subject to certain criteria, to prevent over- and under-invoicing and fraud.

The **Agreement on Preshipment Inspection** authorizes developing states (other states are not mentioned) to make use of PSI, but it also tries to limit its harmful trade effects. Accordingly, WTO member states that use PSI must ensure that

a. PSI activities are carried out in a nondiscriminatory manner;[148]

b. products subject to PSI activities and imported from other member states are accorded no less favorable treatment than national products;[149]

c. inspections are carried out either in the state of export or the state of manufacture;[150]

d. quantity and quality inspections are performed in accordance with the standards defined by the buyer and seller in their purchase agreement or, in the absence of those standards, according to relevant international standards;[151]

---

[148] Agreement on Preshipment Inspection, Article 2, para. 1 (1994).
[149] *Id.,* para. 2.
[150] *Id.,* para. 3.
[151] *Id.,* para. 4.

e. PSI activities are conducted in a transparent manner;[152]

f. information, guidelines, and regulations relating to PSI must be readily available to exporters;[153]

g. information received as part of the PSI be treated as business confidential;[154]

h. conflicts of interest between entities engaged to carry out PSI activities and entities subject to those activities be avoided;[155] and

i. unreasonable delays are avoided in carrying out PSI activities.[156]

Central to the PSI process is the verification of prices. The PSI Agreement allows an entity engaged to carry out PSI activities to reject a contract price it believes wrong only if the entity follows certain guidelines.[157] Most importantly, it may only compare the contract price of the goods being exported to "the price(s) of identical or similar goods offered for export from the same country of exportation at or about the same time, under competitive and comparable conditions of sale, in conformity with customary commercial practices and net of any applicable standards discounts."[158]

In addition to the states making use of PSI, the states in which PSI activities are carried out also have certain obligations. These states must ensure that their laws and regulations relating to PSI activities are applied nondiscriminatorily and transparently. If requested, they also must offer to provide technical assistance to the states engaging in PSI activities within their territories.[159]

Disputes between an exporter and an entity engaged to carry out PSI activities are to be resolved by mutual accord.[160] If not, either party may refer the matter for review to an independent review body[161] that will appoint a panel of three trade experts to decide the matter within eight working days.[162] The decision of the panel will be binding on both the PSI entity and the exporter.[163]

Technical Barriers to Trade

The **Agreement on Technical Barriers to Trade**, or TBT Agreement, establishes rules governing the way WTO member states draft, adopt, and apply technical regulations and standards to ensure that they (a) provide an appropriate level of protection for the life and health of humans, animals, and plants, as well as for the environment; (b) prevent deceptive practices; and (c) do not create unnecessary obstacles to trade.[164] **Technical regulations** are *mandatory* laws and provisions specifying (a) the characteristics of products; (b) the processes and production methods for creating products; and (c) the terminology, symbols, packaging, marking, or labeling requirements for products, processes, or production methods.[165]

Standards are *voluntary* guidelines that specify the same kind of requirements.[166] **Conformity assessment procedures** include the sampling, testing, and inspecting of products; their evaluation, verification, and assurance of conformity; and their registration, accreditation, and approval.[167]

Agreement on Technical Barriers to Trade: Establishes rules governing the way WTO member states draft, adopt, and apply technical regulations and standards.

technical regulations: Mandatory laws and provisions that specify the characteristics of products; the processes and production methods for creating products; and the terminology, symbols, packaging, marking; or labeling requirements for products, processes, or production methods.

standards: Voluntary guidelines that specify the same things that technical regulations mandatorily specify.

conformity assessment procedures: Any procedure used, directly or indirectly, to determine that relevant requirements in technical regulations or standards are fulfilled.

---

[152]*Id.,* para. 5.

[153]*Id.,* paras. 6–8.

[154]*Id.,* para. 9.

[155]*Id.,* para. 14.

[156]*Id.,* para. 15.

[157]*Id.,* para. 20(a).

[158]*Id.,* para. 20(b).

[159]*Id.,* Article 3.

[160]The entity carrying out the PSI activities must designate officials to receive, consider, and promptly render decisions on grievances. *Id.,* Article 2, para. 21(a).

[161]This body will be constituted jointly by an organization representing PSI entities and an organization representing exporters. *Id.,* Article 4, para. (a).

[162]*Id.,* para. (g).

[163]*Id.,* para. (h).

[164]The 1994 TBT Agreement replaces the 1979 Tokyo Round Agreement on Technical Barriers to Trade (popularly known as the Standards Code).

[165]Agreement on Technical Barriers to Trade, Annex I, para. 1 (1994).

[166]*Id.,* para. 2.

[167]*Id.,* para. 3.

All products, including agricultural and industrial products, are covered by the TBT Agreement, but purchasing specifications related to the production or consumption requirements of governmental bodies (which are covered by the Agreement on Government Procurement) and sanitary and phytosanitary measures (which are covered by the Agreement on Sanitary and Phytosanitary Measures) are not.[168] The TBT Agreement applies to local governments and nongovernmental organizations, and central governments are required to take "reasonable measures" (in other words, to try their best) to see that these bodies do so.[169] Ultimately, however, only the central governments are responsible for the observance of this Agreement.

The main provisions of the TBT Agreement are as follows:

1. WTO member states must establish one or more offices where information and assistance about technical regulations, standards, and conformity assessment procedures can be obtained by other member states and any interested parties.[170]

2. Accepted international systems should be used in devising technical regulations, standards, and conformity assessment procedures wherever possible.[171]

3. With respect to the application of technical regulations, standards, and conformity assessment procedures, WTO member states shall ensure that products imported from other member states shall be accorded no less favorable treatment than like national products or like products originating in any other state.[172]

4. Technical regulations, standards, and conformity assessment procedures are not to be prepared, adopted, or applied so as to create unnecessary obstacles to international trade.[173]

5. Technical regulations, standards, and conformity assessment procedures are to be adopted or amended openly, unless international standards are used.[174]

6. If requested, WTO member states are to provide technical assistance to other member states and especially to developing member states.[175]

Sanitary and Phytosanitary Measures

Agreement on the Application of Sanitary and Phytosanitary Measures: Defines the measures that WTO member states may take to protect the life and health of humans, animals, and plants.

The Agreement on the Application of Sanitary and Phytosanitary[176] Measures, or SPS Agreement, is meant to complement the Agreement on Technical Barriers to Trade by defining the measures that may be taken by WTO member states to protect human, animal, and plant life and health. Member states may protect the life and health of living things, but they may not do so as a disguised means for restricting international trade,[177] nor may they act arbitrarily to unjustifiably discriminate between states where identical or similar conditions exist.[178] In addition, the measures taken must be justified by scientific evidence (although in cases where the evidence is limited, measures may be adopted provisionally).[179]

Case 7–5 illustrates how the SPS Agreement is applied.

---

[168]*Id.,* Article 1, paras. 3–5.

[169]*Id.,* Article 3, para. 1.

[170]In the United States, the National Institute of Standards and Technology, part of the Department of Commerce, maintains a National Center for Standards and Certification Information. A description of the Center can be found on the Institute's Web site at ts.nist.gov/ts/htdocs/210/217/ bro.htm.

The United States also monitors and provides information about the standards programs of other countries. *See* the Global Standards Program page on the National Institute of Standards and Technology's Web site at ts.nist.gov/ts/htdocs/210/216/216.htm.

[171]Agreement on Technical Barriers to Trade, Article 9 (1994). The International Organization for Standardization (ISO) is the principal intergovernmental organization responsible for establishing international standards. It is a worldwide federation of national standards bodies from 130 countries. Its Web site is at www.iso.ch/.

[172]*Id.,* Article 2, para. 1; Article 4, para. 1; Article 5, para. 1.1.

[173]*Id.,* Article 2, para. 2; Article 4, para. 1; Article 5, para. 1.2.

[174]*Id.,* Article 2, para. 9; Article 4, para. 1; Article 5, para. 6.

[175]*Id.,* Article 11.

[176]From Greek *phyto*, meaning "plant," and from sanitary, meaning "of or pertaining to health or the conditions affecting health." Phytosanitary measures are measures taken to ensure the health of plants.

[177]Agreement on the Application of Sanitary and Phytosanitary Measures, Preamble and para. 20 (1994).

[178]*Id.,* para. 7.

[179]*Id.,* paras. 6 and 22.

Case 7–5   Australia—Measures Affecting Importation of Salmon ⌂~
Canada v. Australia

World Trade Organization, Appellate Body.
Case AB-1998-5 (1998).

REPORT OF THE APPELLATE BODY

I. INTRODUCTION

Australia and Canada appeal from certain issues of law and legal interpretations in the Panel Report, *Australia—Measures Affecting Importation of Salmon.*[180] The Panel was established to consider a complaint by Canada regarding Australia's prohibition on the importation of fresh, chilled, or frozen salmon from Canada under Quarantine Proclamation 86A ("QP86A"), dated 19 February 1975 and any amendments or modifications thereto.

Before the promulgation of QP86A on 30 June 1975, Australia imposed no restrictions on the importation of salmonid products. QP86A "prohibit[s] the importation into Australia of dead fish of the sub-order Salmonidae, or any parts (other than semen or ova) of fish of that sub-order, in any form unless: . . . prior to importation into Australia the fish or parts of fish have been subject to such treatment as in the opinion of the Director of Quarantine is likely to prevent the introduction of any infectious or contagious disease, or disease or pest affecting persons, animals, or plants." Pursuant to QP86A and in accordance with the authority delegated therein, the Director of Quarantine has permitted the entry of commercial imports of heat-treated salmon products for human consumption as well as non-commercial quantities of other salmon (primarily for scientific purposes) subject to prescribed conditions. Canada requested access to the Australian market for fresh, chilled or frozen, i.e., uncooked, salmon. Australia conducted an import risk analysis for uncooked, wild, adult, ocean-caught Pacific salmonid product ("ocean-caught Pacific salmon"). This category of salmon is to be distinguished from the other categories of salmon for which Canada seeks access to the Australian market ("other Canadian salmon"). The risk analysis on ocean-caught Pacific salmon was first set forth in the 1995 Draft Report, revised in May 1996 and final-ized in December of 1996 (the "1996 Final Report").[181] The 1996 Final Report concluded that:

> . . . it is recommended that the present quarantine policies for uncooked salmon products remain in place.

The Director of Quarantine, on the basis of the 1996 Final Report, decided on 13 December 1996 that:

> . . . having regard to Australian Government policy on quarantine and after taking account of Australia's international obligations, importation of uncooked, wild, adult, ocean-caught Pacific salmonid product from the Pacific rim of North America should not be permitted on quarantine grounds.

> * * *

> . . . The Panel found that Australia has acted inconsistently with Articles 5.1, 5.5 and 5.6 and, by implication, Articles 2.2 and 2.3 of the *Agreement on the Application of Sanitary and Phytosanitary Measures* (the "*SPS Agreement*"). In paragraph 9.1 of its Report, the Panel reached the following [conclusion, among others]:

> * * *

> (ii)   Australia, by adopting arbitrary or unjustifiable distinctions in the levels of sanitary protection it considers to be appropriate in different situations (on the one hand, the salmon products at issue from adult, wild, ocean-caught Pacific salmon and, on the other hand, whole, frozen herring for use as bait and live ornamental finfish), which result in discrimination or a disguised restriction on international trade, has acted inconsistently with the requirements contained in Article 5.5 of the Agreement on the Application of Sanitary and Phytosanitary Measures and, on that ground, has also acted inconsistently with the requirements contained in Article 2.3 of that Agreement . . .

> * * *

---

[180]WT/DS18/R, 12 June 1998.
[181]Department of Primary Industries and Energy, Salmon Import Risk Analysis: An assessment by the Australian Government of quarantine controls on uncooked, wild, adult, ocean-caught Pacific salmonid product sourced from the United States of America and Canada, Final Report, December 1996.

MAP 7-5 Australia and Canada (1998)

ARTICLE 5.5 OF THE SPS AGREEMENT

The next issue we address is whether the Panel erred in law in finding that Australia has acted inconsistently with Article 5.5 of the *SPS Agreement*.

Following our Report in *European Communities—Hormones*,[182] the Panel considered:

> . . . that three elements are required in order for a Member to act inconsistently with Article 5.5:
>
> • the Member concerned adopts different appropriate levels of sanitary protection in several "different situations";
>
> • those levels of protection exhibit differences which are "arbitrary or unjustifiable"; and
>
> • the measure embodying those differences results in "discrimination or a disguised restriction on international trade."

The Panel found that all three conditions are fulfilled. . . .

* * *

Australia appeals from this finding of inconsistency with Article 5.5 and, by implication, Article 2.3 of the *SPS Agreement*. Without challenging the Panel's three-step legal test for inconsistency with Article 5.5 as such, Australia contends that the Panel has made a series of errors of law in the interpretation and application of the test. . . .

FIRST ELEMENT OF ARTICLE 5.5

With regard to the first element of Article 5.5, namely, the existence of distinctions in appropriate levels of protection in different situations, the Panel cited our Report in

European Communities—Hormones, where we stated that "situations . . . cannot, of course, be compared, unless they are comparable, that is, unless they present some common element or elements sufficient to render them comparable."[183] The Panel found that:

> . . . in the circumstances of this dispute, we can compare situations under Article 5.5 if these situations involve either a risk of "entry, establishment or spread" of the same or a similar disease *or* of the same or similar "associated biological and economic consequences" and this irrespective of whether they arise from the same product or other products. (emphasis added)

On this basis, the Panel determined that the import prohibition on fresh, chilled or frozen salmon for human consumption *and* the admission of imports of (i) uncooked Pacific herring, cod, haddock, Japanese eel and plaice for human consumption; (ii) uncooked Pacific herring, Atlantic and Pacific cod, haddock, European and Japanese eel and Dover sole for human consumption; (iii) herring in whole, frozen form used as bait ("herring used as bait"); and (iv) live ornamental finfish, are "different" situations which can be compared under Article 5.5 of the *SPS Agreement*.

* * *

Australia . . . contends that the Panel erred in determining that its examination on the comparability of different situations must be limited solely to those disease agents positively detected. According to Australia, the Panel diminished Australia's right to a cautious approach to determine its own appropriate level of protection. Australia argues that the Panel failed to interpret the provisions of Article 5.5 in their context and in the light of the object and purpose of the *SPS Agreement*. According to Australia, the terms "likelihood" and "potential" in regard to the definition of "risk assessment" contained in paragraph 4 of Annex A, and the terms "scientific principles" and "sufficient scientific evidence" contained in Article 2.2, make it clear that the basic SPS right set out in Article 2.1 to take SPS measures necessary for the protection of animal life or health, is not contingent on positive scientific evidence of disease detection.

We note that, contrary to what Australia argues, the Panel did not limit its examination under Article 5.5 to diseases positively detected in fresh, chilled or frozen ocean-caught Pacific salmon. On the contrary, it appears clearly from Annex 1 to the Panel Report, entitled "The Four Comparisons under Article 5.5", that the Panel examined diseases of concern which, according to Australia, may be carried by fresh, chilled or frozen ocean-caught Pacific salmon but which have not yet been positively detected in

---

[182]Adopted 13 February 1998, WT/DS26/AB/R, WT/DS48/AB/R para. 214.
[183]Adopted 13 February 1998, WT/DS26/AB/R, WT/DS48/AB/R para. 217.

this type of salmon. We also note that the Panel stated explicitly that:

> . . . To the extent that both the other products and the salmon products further examined are known to be hosts to one of these disease agents or—for the salmon products—give rise to an alleged concern for that disease agent, they can be associated with the same kind of risk, namely a risk of entry, establishment or spread of that disease. (emphasis added)

In addition, we believe that for situations to be comparable under Article 5.5, it is sufficient for these situations to have in common a risk of entry, establishment or spread of *one* disease of concern. There is no need for these situations to have in common a risk of entry, establishment or spread of *all* diseases of concern. Therefore, even if the Panel had excluded from its examination *some* diseases of concern not positively detected in fresh, chilled or frozen ocean-caught Pacific salmon, this would not invalidate its finding . . . on comparable situations under Article 5.5.

We, therefore, uphold the Panel's finding . . . that the import prohibition on fresh, chilled or frozen salmon for human consumption *and* the admission of imports of other fish and fish products are "different" situations which can be compared under Article 5.5 of the *SPS Agreement*.

SECOND ELEMENT OF ARTICLE 5.5

With regard to the second element of Article 5.5, namely, the existence of arbitrary or unjustifiable distinctions in appropriate levels of protection in different situations, the Panel began its analysis by noting that in view of the difference in SPS measures and corresponding levels of protection for salmon products, on the one hand, and the four categories of other fish and fish products, on the other, one might expect some justification for this difference, such as a higher risk from imported salmon. However, as the Panel noted:

> . . . the arguments, reports, studies and expert opinions submitted to us in this respect—rather than pointing in the direction of a higher risk related to . . . [ocean-caught Pacific salmon], in order to justify the stricter sanitary measures imposed for these products—all provide evidence that the two categories of non-salmonids [herring used as bait and live ornamental finfish], for which more lenient sanitary measures apply, can be presumed to represent at least as high a risk—if not a higher risk—than the risk associated with . . . [ocean-caught Pacific salmon].

The Panel, therefore, found that, on the basis of the evidence before it, the distinctions in levels of sanitary protection reflected in Australia's treatment of, on the one hand, ocean-caught Pacific salmon and, on the other, herring used as bait and live ornamental finfish, are "arbitrary or unjustifiable" in the sense of the second element of Article 5.5.

Australia argues that the Panel erred in determining that its examination under Article 5.5, second element, must be limited solely to those disease agents positively detected in ocean-caught Pacific salmon. Australia raises the same objections to this limitation as it did in the context of the first element discussed above.

We do not agree with Australia that the Panel excluded diseases of concern which have not been positively detected in ocean-caught Pacific salmon from its examination under Article 5.5. The Panel explicitly took into account diseases which have not been positively detected in ocean-caught Pacific salmon but had been detected in herring used as bait and live ornamental finfish. . . .

THIRD ELEMENT OF ARTICLE 5.5

With regard to the third element of Article 5.5, i.e., that the arbitrary or unjustifiable distinctions in levels of protection result in "discrimination or a disguised restriction on international trade", we note that the Panel identified three "warning signals" as well as three "other factors more substantial in nature" ("additional factors"). The Panel considered that each of these "warning signals" and "additional factors" can be taken into account in its decision on the third element of Article 5.5. In . . . its Report, it concluded:

> On the basis of all "warning signals" and factors outlined above, considered cumulatively, . . . the distinctions in levels of protection imposed by Australia for, on the one hand, . . . [ocean-caught Pacific salmon] and, on the other hand, herring . . . use[d] as bait and live ornamental finfish, . . . result . . . in "a disguised restriction on international trade", in the sense of the third element of Article 5.5. (emphasis added)

Australia contends that the Panel made a number of substantive errors of law in using these "warning signals" and "additional factors" to come to its conclusion on the third element of Article 5.5.

The first "warning signal" the Panel considered was the arbitrary or unjustifiable character of the differences in levels of protection. It noted what we stated in *European Communities—Hormones*:

> . . . the arbitrary or unjustifiable character of differences in levels of protection . . . may in practical effect operate as a "warning" signal that the implementing measure in its application might be a discriminatory measure or might be a restriction on international trade disguised as an SPS measure for the protection of human life or health.[184]

---

[184]Adopted 13 February 1998, WT/DS26/AB/R, WT/DS48/AB/R, para. 215.

The Panel, therefore, considered that:

> . . . In this dispute, . . . the arbitrary character of the differences in levels of protection is a "warning signal" that the measure at issue results in "a disguised restriction on international trade."

According to Australia, the Panel erred in according the first "warning signal", the status of evidence which demonstrates that the measure results in a disguised restriction on international trade. We note however, that it appears clearly from the Panel Report, and in particular, from the reference therein to our Report in *European Communities—Hormones*, that the Panel considered the arbitrary or unjustifiable character of differences in levels of protection as a "warning signal" for, and not as "evidence" of, a disguised restriction on international trade.

The second "warning signal" considered by the Panel was the *rather substantial difference* in levels of protection between an import prohibition on ocean-caught Pacific salmon, as opposed to tolerance for imports of herring used as bait and of live ornamental finfish. The Panel noted our statement in *European Communities—Hormones* that:

> . . . the degree of difference, or the extent of the discrepancy, in the levels of protection, is only one kind of factor which, along with others, may cumulatively lead to the conclusion that discrimination or a disguised restriction on international trade in fact results from the application of a measure.[185] (emphasis added)

On that basis, the Panel stated:

> . . . we do consider that the rather substantial difference in levels of protection is one of the factors we should take into account in deciding whether the measure at issue results in "a disguised restriction on international trade", as argued by Canada.

Australia contends that this second "warning signal" is effectively no different in character from the first "warning signal" and should therefore be discounted. We note, however, that in this case the degree of difference in the levels of protection (prohibition *versus* tolerance) is indeed, as the Panel stated, "rather substantial." We, therefore, consider it legitimate to treat this difference as a separate warning signal.

The third "warning signal" the Panel considered was the inconsistency of the SPS measure at issue with Articles 5.1 and 2.2 of the *SPS Agreement*. The Panel considered that its earlier finding of inconsistency with Articles 5.1 and 2.2:

> . . . may, together with other factors, lead to the conclusion that the measure at issue results in a "disguised

restriction on international trade." Indeed, considering these violations of Articles 5.1 and 2.2 it would seem that the measure at issue constitutes an import prohibition, i.e., a restriction on international trade, "disguised" as a sanitary measure. We do stress, however, that this additional "warning signal" as such cannot be sufficient to conclude that the measure results in a "disguised restriction on international trade."

Australia objects to the use of this inconsistency as a warning signal in the context of the third element of Article 5.5. It argues that inconsistency with Article 5.1 cannot "presume" or pre-empt a finding under Article 5.5. We note that a finding that an SPS measure is not based on an assessment of the risks to human, animal or plant life or health—either because there was no risk assessment at all or because there is an insufficient risk assessment—is a strong indication that this measure is not really concerned with the protection of human, animal, or plant life or health but is instead a trade-restrictive measure taken in the guise of an SPS measure, i.e., a "disguised restriction on international trade." We, therefore, consider that the finding of inconsistency with Article 5.1 is an appropriate warning signal for a "disguised restriction on international trade."

The first "additional factor" considered by the Panel is the fact that the two substantially different SPS measures that Australia applies (import prohibition versus import tolerance) lead to discrimination between salmon, on the one hand, and herring used as bait and live ornamental finfish on the other. In the Panel's view, the concept of "disguised restriction on international trade" in Article 5.5 includes, among other things, restrictions constituting arbitrary or unjustifiable discrimination between certain products.

Australia contends that this first "additional factor" is merely a combination of the first two "warning signals" and does not, therefore, constitute additional "evidence". . . .

We believe that the first "additional factor" should indeed be excluded from the examination of the third element of Article 5.5. All "arbitrary or unjustifiable distinctions" in levels of protection will lead logically to discrimination between products, whether the products are the same (e.g., discrimination between imports of salmon from different countries or between imported salmon and domestic salmon) or different (e.g., salmon versus herring used as bait and live ornamental finfish). The first "additional factor" is therefore not different from the first warning signal, and should not be taken into account as a *separate factor* in the determination of whether an SPS measure results in a "disguised restriction on international trade."

The second "additional factor" considered by the Panel was the substantial, but unexplained change in con-

---

[185]Adopted 13 February 1998, WT/DS26/AB/R, WT/DS48/AB/R, para. 240.

clusion between the 1995 Draft Report (which recommended allowing the importation of ocean-caught Pacific salmon under certain conditions) and the 1996 Final Report (which recommended continuing the import prohibition). The Panel suggested that the decisive reason for the reversal of the 1995 draft recommendation "might well have been inspired by domestic pressures to protect the Australian salmon industry against import competition."

Australia argues that the Panel erred in considering this difference as a factor to be taken into account in the examination of the third element of Article 5.5. Australia contends that the Panel has incorrectly accorded a draft recommendation the status of an SPS measure and that no provision of the *SPS Agreement* requires WTO Members to implement draft recommendations absent new scientific evidence. Moreover, Australia argues that the Panel refused to consider its arguments and evidence on the role of draft reports and recommendation in the decision-making process of governments. Australia contends that the Panel mischaracterized the reasons for the introduction of QP86A. In Australia's view, the Panel also erred in speculating about the presence and role of lobbying in Australia's decision to adopt the 1996 Final Report.

We consider Australia's arguments to be without merit. First, we note that paragraph 1 of Annex A of the *SPS Agreement* defines a sanitary measure of the type relevant in this dispute as a measure applied to protect animal life or health within the territory of a Member from risks arising from the entry, establishment or spread of diseases. In the light of this definition, the Panel was correct to consider the recommendation of the 1995 Draft Report to allow *under certain conditions* the importation of ocean-caught Pacific salmon to be a recommendation of an SPS measure.

Second, we note that the Panel did not at any point state that WTO Members are obliged to implement draft recommendations absent new scientific evidence. It did not introduce such obligation. We note that the Panel explicitly acknowledged that the substantial but unexplained reversal of the 1995 draft recommendation does not constitute, in itself, sufficient proof that the measure results in a disguised restriction on trade. The Panel merely considered that this factor "can be taken into account cumulatively with other factors" in the examina-

tion under the third element of Article 5.5. We agree with the Panel. . . .

The third "additional factor" considered by the Panel was the absence of controls on the internal movement of salmon products within Australia compared to the prohibition of the importation of ocean-caught Pacific salmon. The Panel did not come to a conclusion on the existence or nature of this alleged difference, but considered that its doubts whether Australia applies similarly strict sanitary standards, "though probably not conclusive as such, can also be taken into account, cumulatively with other factors, in [its] decision on whether the measure at issue results in a 'disguised restriction on international trade.'"

Australia contends that the Panel erred in implying that consistency with Article 5.5, requires either restrictions on the internal movement of salmon products within Australia or, alternatively, that Australia apply import zoning to grant access to Australia for ocean-caught Pacific salmon.

We note that, as acknowledged by Australia, the Panel did not conclude that the alleged absence of internal controls constituted a violation of Article 5.5 or any other provision of the *SPS Agreement*. The Panel merely stated its doubts on whether Australia applies similarly strict sanitary standards on the internal movement of salmon products within Australia as it does on the importation of salmon products and considered that as *a* factor which can be taken into account in the examination under the third element of Article 5.5. We consider that these doubts do not carry much weight, but we agree with the Panel that they can nevertheless be taken into consideration.

In the above analysis, we have upheld the Panel's findings on the first, second and third "warning signals" as well as its findings on the second and third "additional factors." We have only reversed the Panel's finding on the first "additional factor." We consider, however, that this reversal does not affect the validity of the Panel's conclusion . . . that the "warning signals" and "other factors", *considered cumulatively*, lead to the conclusion that the distinctions in the levels of protection imposed by Australia result in a disguised restriction on international trade.

We, therefore, uphold the Panel's finding that, by maintaining the measure at issue, Australia has acted inconsistently with its obligations under Article 5.5, and, by implication, Article 2.3 of the *SPS Agreement*. ■

Trade-Related Investment Measures

The **Agreement on Trade-Related Investment Measures**, or TRIMs Agreement, is aimed at facilitating foreign investment and eliminating some of the provisions commonly found in foreign investment laws that distort or reduce international trade. In particular, the Agreement forbids provisions in investment laws that discriminate unfavorably against foreigners (i.e., that do not accord them "national treatment")[186] and that impose quantitative restrictions on the

[186]Agreement on Trade-Related Investment Measures, Article 2, para. 1 (1994).

Agreement on Trade-Related Investment Measures: Forbids provisions commonly found in foreign investment laws that distort or reduce international trade, including provisions that discriminate unfavorably against foreigners and that impose quantitative restrictions on the use of foreign products by foreign-owned local enterprises.

Agreement on Import-Licensing Procedures: Requires that the import-licensing procedures of WTO member states be neutral in their application and that they be administered in a fair and equitable manner.

Agreement on Implementation of Article VI of GATT 1994 (Antidumping Code): Allows WTO member states to counter dumping through the application of antidumping duties.

dumping: Selling exported goods at prices below their normal value.

use of foreign products by foreign-owned local enterprises.[187] Examples include requirements that a foreign-owned enterprise must purchase or use a certain amount or proportion of domestic products ("local contents requirements") and requirements that restrict the volume or value of an enterprise's imports by linking them to the volume or value of its exports ("trade-balancing requirements") or by correlating an enterprise's access to foreign exchange to its foreign exchange earnings ("foreign exchange balancing restrictions").[188]

Import-Licensing Procedures

Because licensing requirements may restrict or distort trade, the **Agreement on Import-Licensing Procedures** seeks to ensure that import-licensing procedures are neutral in their application and administered in a fair and equitable manner.[189] Forms and procedures are to be as simple as possible and applicants should have to deal only with a single administrative body.[190] Import licenses are not to be denied because of minor errors in completing the application;[191] nor are imports to be barred because of minor deviations in the value, quantity, or weight designated on the license.[192]

Antidumping

The **Agreement on Implementation of Article VI of GATT 1994**, or the Antidumping Code, replaces codes negotiated during the Tokyo and Kennedy Rounds. The current Code defines **dumping** in the following way:

> . . . [A] product is to be considered as being dumped, i.e., introduced into the commerce of another country at less than its normal value, if the export price of the product exported from one country to another is less than the comparable price, in the ordinary course of trade, for the like product when destined for consumption in the exporting country.[193]

Significantly, the Antidumping Code does not prohibit dumping. It recognizes instead that the dumping of imports may be countered through the application of antidumping duties, but only if an investigation determines that the dumped imports cause or threaten to cause material injury to, or materially retard the establishment of, a domestic industry within the importing country.[194] A "domestic industry" is defined by the Code as the domestic producers as a whole of like products or those domestic producers whose collective output of products makes up a major share of the total output of such products within their state.[195]

An investigation to determine the existence, degree, and effect of an alleged dumping may be initiated (1) "upon a written application by or on behalf of the [effected] domestic industry";[196] (2) "in special circumstances" by governmental authorities of the affected state;[197] or (3) by an application made by authorities of an effected third country.[198] In any of these cases, the application must disclose evidence showing (a) dumping, (b) material injury or threat of injury to, or material retardation to the establishment of, a domestic industry, and (c) a causal link between the dumped imports and the alleged injury.[199]

---

[187]*Id.,* para. 2.

Developed member states were given until December 31, 1996, to eliminate any provisions inconsistent with the TRIMs Agreement. Developing states have until December 31, 1999, and the least-developed member states have until December 31, 2001. *Id.,* Article 5, para. 2.

[188]*Id.,* Annex, paras. 1–2.

[189]Agreement on Import Licensing Procedures, Article 1, para. 3 (1994).

[190]*Id.,* paras. 5–6.

[191]*Id.,* para. 7.

[192]*Id.,* para. 8.

[193]Agreement on Implementation of Article VI of GATT 1994, Article 2, para. 1.

[194]*Id.,* Article 3, n. 9.

[195]*Id.,* Article 4, para. 1.

[196]*Id.,* Article 5, para. 1.

[197]*Id.,* Article 5, para. 6.

[198]*Id.,* Article 14, para. 1.

[199]*Id.,* Article 5, paras. 2 and 6; and Article 14, para. 2.

The investigation will be terminated and no antidumping duties will be imposed if "the margin of dumping is *de minimis,* or [if] the volume of dumped imports, actual or potential, or the injury, is negligible. The margin of

The authorities carrying out an investigation must give all interested parties notice of the investigation, an opportunity to present written evidence, and the opportunity to examine and rebut adverse evidence.[200] Even so, the investigation is to be carried out expeditiously, and the procedures that allow interested parties to participate may not be used by the parties as a means of delaying the investigation, from reaching a preliminary or final decision, or from applying provisional or final antidumping measures.[201]

Provisional measures (that is, the imposition of a provisional antidumping duty or the deposit of a security equal to a provisionally estimated antidumping duty) may be imposed after an investigation has been initiated, a preliminary determination has been made of dumping and consequential injury to a domestic industry, and the authorities concerned believe that such measures are necessary to prevent injury being caused during the course of the investigation.[202] Final antidumping duties may be imposed at the discretion of the authorities concerned upon the completion of an investigation and a final determination that dumping, injury, and a causal link between them exist.[203]

The monetary amount of an antidumping duty may not exceed the difference between a product's normal value (i.e., the price charged for the same or similar products exported to third countries, or their cost of production plus a reasonable amount for administrative and other costs and for profits) and the price at which it was actually exported.[204] Such a duty may remain in force as long as necessary to counteract dumping that is causing injury.[205]

Subsidies and Countervailing Measures

A **subsidy** is a financial contribution made by a government (or other public body) that confers a benefit on an enterprise, group of enterprises, or an industry. Examples of subsidies are (a) direct transfers of funds (e.g., grants, loans, and equity infusions), (b) potential direct transfers of funds (e.g., loan guarantees), (c) the foregoing of revenues (e.g., tax credits), (d) the providing of goods or services (other than general infrastructure), and (e) the conferring of any form of income or price support.[206] Subsidies, moreover, may be made directly by a government or indirectly through funding mechanisms or private bodies.[207]

When improperly used by a government to promote its export trade to the detriment of another state, subsidies are forbidden by GATT 1994. If subsidies have an unreasonable impact on another country's internal market, that country can impose countervailing duties to offset their impact, but only if it follows certain conditions to ensure that its reaction is justified, appropriate, and not excessive.

The **Agreement on Subsidies and Countervailing Measures** or SCM Agreement, replaces the 1979 Subsidies Code concluded at the Tokyo Round. The 1979 Code was criticized because it failed to define a subsidy, to establish criteria for determining if harm had been or was about to be caused by a subsidy, and to calculate a subsidy's impact.[208] These deficiencies are all remedied in the new Agreement.

subsidy: A financial contribution made by a government or other public body that confers a benefit on an enterprise, a group of enterprises, or an industry.

Agreement on Subsidies and Countervailing Duties: Classifies subsidies as prohibited, actionable, and nonactionable; forbids the first class and allows affected WTO member states to request consultation, to obtain a remedy from the WTO, or to independently impose countervailing duties.

---

dumping shall be considered to be *de minimis* if this margin is less than 2 percent, expressed as a percentage of the export price. The volume of dumped imports shall normally be regarded as negligible if the volume of dumped imports from a particular country is found to account for less than 3 percent of imports of the like product in the importing country unless countries which individually account for less than 3 percent of the imports of the like product in the importing country collectively account for more than 7 percent of imports of the like product in the importing country." *Id.*, Article 5, para. 8.

[200]*Id.*, Article 6, paras. 1–2.

Interested parties include: "(i) an exporter or foreign producer or the importer of a product subject to investigation, or a trade or business association a majority of the members of which are producers, exporters, or importers of such product; (ii) the government of the exporting country; and (iii) a producer of the like product in the importing country or a trade and business association a majority of the members of which produce the like product in the importing country." *Id.*, para 11.

[201]*Id*, para. 14.

[202]*Id.*, Article 7, paras. 1–3.

[203]*Id.*, Article 9, para. 1.

[204]*Id.*, Article 9, para. 3; and Article 2.

[205]*Id.*, Article 11, para. 1.

Reviews must be held periodically and, if no review is conducted for a five-year period, the duty will automatically terminate. *Id.*, Article 11, paras. 2 and 3.

[206]Agreement on Subsidies and Countervailing Measures, Article 1 (1994).

[207]*Id.*

[208]John Kraus, *The GATT Negotiations: A Business Guide to the Results of the Uruguay Round*, p. 33 (1994).

The SCM Agreement clearly states that its "disciplines" (i.e., member state obligations) apply only to "specific" subsidies—that is, subsidies that target (a) a specific enterprise or industry, (b) specific groups of enterprises or industries, or (c) enterprises in a particular region.[209] The disciplines do not apply to (a) nonspecific subsidies, (b) certain specific subsidies defined in the Agreement, and (c) agricultural subsidies (which are governed by the Agreement on Agriculture).

Categories of Specific Subsidies

Specific subsidies (that is, those regulated by the SCM Agreement) are divided into three categories: (1) prohibited subsidies (informally referred to as "red" subsidies), (2) actionable subsidies ("yellow"), and (3) nonactionable subsidies ("green").

prohibited subsidy: A subsidy that is presumed to be trade distorting because it requires export performance or is contingent upon the use of domestic instead of imported goods.

Prohibited subsidies (red subsidies) are subsidies that either (a) depend upon export performance (in other words, on a firm's or industry's success in exporting its products)[210] or (b) are contingent upon the use of domestic instead of imported goods (e.g., subsidies based on so-called domestic content rules.)[211] Red subsidies are presumed to be trade distorting and WTO member states are forbidden from granting or maintaining them.[212]

actionable subsidy: A subsidy that may be challenged as trade distorting if it injures the domestic industry of another WTO member state, nullifies or impairs the benefits due another member state, or causes or threatens to cause serious prejudice to the interests of another member state.

Actionable subsidies (yellow subsidies) are subsidies that may or may not be trade distorting depending upon how they are applied (thus the reason for their designation as yellow). They are defined[213] as specific subsidies that, in the way they are used, (1) injure a domestic industry of another member state, (2) nullify or impair benefits due another member state under GATT 1994, or (3) cause or threaten to cause "serious prejudice"[214] to the interests of another member state. WTO member states are discouraged, but not forbidden, from using actionable subsidies.[215]

nonactionable subsidy: A subsidy that is permissible and nonchallengeable, such as government funding to underwrite research activities, to aid disadvantaged regions, or to help existing facilities adapt to new environmental requirements.

Nonactionable subsidies (green subsidies) consist of nonspecific subsidies and certain specific infrastructural subsidies. These infrastructural subsidies involve government funding to (1) assist (but not fully cover) the costs of research activities carried on by or on behalf of business firms, (2) aid disadvantaged regions (i.e., regions with low per capita income or high unemployment), or (3) help existing facilities adapt to new environmental requirements.[216] They are known as green subsidies because, as a general rule, they are permissible and nonchallengeable.[217]

---

[209]Agreement on Subsidies and Countervailing Measures, Article 2 (1994).

[210]*Id.,* Article 3, para. 1(a).

    An illustrative list of 12 examples is provided in Annex I of the SCM Agreement.

[211]*Id.,* para. 1(b).

[212]*Id.,* para. 2.

[213]*Id.,* Article 5.

[214]Serious prejudice "may arise in any case where one or several of the following apply: (a) the effect of the subsidy is to displace or impede the imports of like product into the market of the subsidizing member; (b) the effect of the subsidy is to displace or impede the exports of like product of another member from a third country market; (c) the effect of the subsidy is a significant price undercutting by the subsidized products as compared with the price of a like product of another member in the same market or significant price suppression, price depression, or lost sales in the same market; (d) the effect of the subsidy is an increase in the world market share of the subsidizing member in a particular subsidized primary product or commodity as compared to the average share it had during the previous period of three years and this increase must follow a consistent trend over a period when subsidies have been granted." *Id.,* Article 6, para. 3.

    Serious prejudice is presumed to exist "in the case of: (a) the total *ad valorem* subsidization of a product exceeding 5 percent; (b) subsidies to cover operating losses sustained by an industry; (c) subsidies to cover operating losses sustained by an enterprise, other than one-time measures which are nonrecurrent and cannot be repeated for that enterprise and which are given merely to provide time for the development of long-term solutions and to avoid acute social problems; (d) direct forgiveness of debt, i.e., forgiveness of government-held debt, and grants to cover debt repayment." *Id.,* para. 1.

    A subsidizing member state can nevertheless overcome these presumptions by showing that none of the effects first mentioned above (Article 6, para. 3) apply. *Id.,* para. 2.

[215]The SCM Agreement, Article 5, uses the permissive phrase "no member *should*" in describing the obligations of member states in connection with actionable subsidies.

[216]*Id.,* Article 8, para. 2.

[217]Nonactionable subsidies may be challenged, nonetheless, if a member state believes that they have caused serious adverse effects to one of its domestic industries. Such a challenge begins with consultations between the concerned

Remedies and Countervailing Measures

A WTO member state that believes that its domestic industries have been injured by either prohibited subsidies or actionable subsidies is given four options: (1) do nothing, (2) request consultations, (3) seek a remedy from the WTO, or (4) independently impose countervailing duties. If an injured member state chooses to do nothing, neither the WTO nor any other member state is entitled to intervene.[218]

To obtain a remedy from the WTO, a member state claiming an injury must first consult with the subsidizing member state.[219] If the two states are unable to find a mutually acceptable solution, either one may refer the matter to the WTO's Dispute Settlement Body (DSB) for the latter to set up a Panel.[220] If the Panel—which may seek the assistance of a Permanent Group of Experts (a body established by the SCM Agreement)—concludes that there is a prohibited subsidy, it will recommend the subsidy's withdrawal; if it concludes that there is an actionable subsidy, it will recommend that the subsidizing member state either remove the subsidy's adverse effects or withdraw the subsidy.[221] If neither party appeals to the DSB's Appellate Body, the DSB must promptly adopt the report (unless it rejects it by consensus).[222] If there is an appeal, the Appellate Body's decision must be unconditionally observed.[223]

If a member state does not comply with a DSB-adopted report or Appellate Body decision, the DSB will authorize (unless it agrees by consensus not to do so) a complaining member state to adopt countervailing measures.[224] A **countervailing measure** is defined in the SCM Agreement simply as a duty specially levied to offset a subsidy.[225]

countervailing measures: A duty specifically levied to offset a subsidy.

As an alternative to seeking a WTO-authorized remedy, a state may independently impose countervailing duties so long as it follows the procedures specified in the SCM Agreement[226] (which are the same as those used in the Antidumping Code for the adoption of antidumping measures). The reason why a state may prefer to independently adopt countervailing duties instead of seeking a WTO-authorized remedy is that its administrative agencies will have greater control over the process. On the other hand, a state with limited resources will find the WTO-funded process more economical.

Case 7–6 illustrates the procedures that must be followed for a state to impose countervailing duties.

---

state members. If they are unable to agree to a solution, either one may refer the matter to the Committee on Subsidies and Countervailing Measures, a body created by the SCM Agreement, which will review the matter. If the Committee determines that the adverse effects exist, it may recommend to the subsidizing member state to modify its program. If that member state does not comply, the Committee may then authorize the complaining state to take appropriate countermeasures. *Id.,* Article 9.

[218] Articles 4 and 7 of the SCM Agreement, which provide for the consultations and WTO remedies, and Articles 10 through 23, which authorize the imposition of countervailing duties, only allow a member state claiming an injury to one of its domestic industries to initiate these proceedings.

[219] Agreement on Subsidies and Countervailing Measures, Article 4, para 1, and Article 7, para. 1 (1994).

[220] The referral may be made after 30 days in the case of prohibited subsidies, *id.,* Article 4, para. 4; and after 60 days in the case of actionable subsidies, *id.,* Article 7, para. 4.

[221] The report must be submitted within 90 days for prohibited subsidies, *Id.,* Article 4, para. 4; and 120 days for actionable subsidies, Article 7, para. 4.

[222] This must be done within 30 days. *Id.,* Article 4, para. 8; Article 7, para. 6.

[223] The Appellate Body must hand down its decision within 30 (in exceptional circumstances 60) days for prohibited subsidies, *Id.,* Article 4, para. 9; and within 60 (in exceptional circumstances 90) days for actionable subsidies, Article 7, para. 7.

   A prohibited subsidy must be withdrawn within a time period specified by the panel, *id.,* Article 4, para. 7; and an actionable subsidy must be withdrawn within 6 months of the DSB or Appellate Body's decision, *id.,* Article 7, para. 9.

[224] *Id.,* Article 4, para. 10; Article 7, para. 9.

[225] *Id.,* Article 10, provides: "The term 'countervailing duty' shall be understood to mean a special duty levied for the purpose of offsetting any subsidy bestowed directly or indirectly upon the manufacture, production, or export of any merchandise, as provided for in Article VI:3 of the GATT 1994."

[226] *Id.,* Articles 10–23.

Case 7–6 Mukand Ltd. v. Council
of the European Union

European Union, Court of First Instance.
Case T-58/99 (2001).

JUDGMENT

Facts

The applicants produce and export to the Community stainless steel bright bars (hereinafter "SSBBs").

On 26 September 1997, the Commission received a complaint from Eurofer, the European confederation of iron and steel industries, alleging that imports of SSBBs originating in India were benefiting from subsidies and were thus causing material injury to the Community industry. A notice of initiation of anti-subsidy proceedings concerning the imports was published in the Official Journal of the European Communities of 30 October 1997.

* * *

On 17 July 1998, the Commission adopted Regulation (EC) No 1556/98 imposing a provisional countervailing duty on imports of stainless steel bars originating in India (hereinafter "the Provisional Regulation").

* * *

On 13 November 1998, the Council adopted Regulation (EC) No 2450/98 imposing a definitive countervailing duty on imports of stainless steel bars originating in India and collecting definitively the provisional duty imposed (hereinafter "the Contested Regulation").

* * *

Substance

The applicants . . . in support of their action . . . allege infringement [by the Council] of Article 1(1), Article 8(1), (6) and (7) and Article 15(1) of [Council Regulation (EC) No 2026/97 of 6 October 1997 on Protection Against Subsidized Imports from Countries Not Members of the European Community (hereinafter "the Basic Regulation")] and Articles 15 and 19 of the Agreement on Subsidies and Countervailing Measures concluded within the World Trade Organization in the context of the Uruguay Round of Negotiations (hereinafter "the ASCM"), and a manifest error of assessment, in that the Contested Regulation imposes a countervailing duty without there being any proper and substantiated finding

that imports of the product in question have caused significant damage to Community undertakings producing similar products. . . .

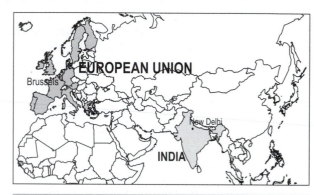

MAP 7-6   European Union and India (2001)

Arguments of the Parties

The applicants argue that, in accordance with Article 1(1), Article 8(1), (6) and (7) and Article 15(1) of the Basic Regulation and Articles 15 and 19 of the ASCM, countervailing duties may be imposed only if it has been concluded, through proper investigation, that the subsidized imports cause material injury to a Community industry. Any harm caused by other factors, in particular by anti-competitive conduct on the part of Community industry itself, must not be attributed to the imports in question.

The applicants refer to paragraph 16 of the judgment of the Court of Justice in *Extramet Industrie v. Council*[227] (hereinafter "Extramet II") and submit that, in the present case, the Community institutions similarly failed in their duty properly to assess what injury might have been caused. As a result, the institutions made a manifest error of assessment of both the injury caused and the question of causation.

In their pleadings, the applicants argue that Community producers of SSBBs engaged in the same anti-competitive practices as those imputed [by the Commission] in Decision 98/247 to Community producers of flat products. They also argue, in the alternative, that, whether or not Community producers of SSBBs did engage in such practices, the practices of Community producers of flat products necessarily influenced the price of SSBBs. Whichever is the case, the Community institutions

---

[227]Case C-358/89, European Court Reports, vol. 199, pt. 1, p. 3813.

neglected to take these factors into account in their assessment of the injury.

The applicants explain, . . . that, throughout the period under consideration in the anti-subsidy investigation, Community producers of SSBBs systematically applied, in respect of their European sales, a surcharge system that was identical, *mutatis mutandis*,[228] to the alloy surcharge system censured in Decision 98/247, the surcharge applied to SSBBs simply being the product of multiplying the surcharge applicable to flat products by a "yield factor" of 1.35. The fact that all Community producers of SSBBs uniformly applied that factor was confirmed by the Commission in . . . [a decision it made on] 21 April 1999.

The applicants conclude that, from February 1994 onwards, SSBBs produced within the Community were also being sold at inflated prices. They emphasize that, according to . . . Decision 98/247, following the imposition of the alloy surcharge, the price of stainless steel increased almost two-fold between January 1994 and March 1995. They also point out that the price of SSBBs changed in much the same way as did the price of flat products over the course of the years in question and maintain that such significant price distortion could not have been overlooked in the anti-subsidy proceedings, particularly in establishing price undercutting, the appropriate level of profitability in the Community industry and loss of market share.

. . . Thus, other than the worsening results of the Community industry, the Commission had no adequate, reliable information from which it could reach a firm view of any injury caused.

As regards causation, the applicants argue, similarly, that the adverse effects allegedly sustained by the Community industry are attributable not to imports of SSBBs from India but to "other factors," namely the conduct of producers of flat products and its effect on the price of SSBBs.

* * *

In response to the argument advanced by the applicants, the Council contends that the prices charged on the SSBB market could not be regarded as artificially high given that Community SSBB producers had not acted in concert to fix those prices. The application of the yield factor and the fixing of its level, as well as the fixing of the final price of SSBBs, was a matter of free choice for each SSBB producer and was not the inevitable result of decisions taken in concert by producers of flat products. The Council submits that these are distinct products which are not substitutable for SSBBs and that there are therefore no grounds for concluding that anti-competitive conduct of the part of producers of flat products had any effect on the prices charged on the market for SSBBs.

Findings of the Court

According to Article 1(1) of the Basic Regulation, a countervailing duty may be imposed for the purpose of offsetting any subsidy granted, directly or indirectly, for the manufacture, production, export, or transport of any product whose release for free circulation in the Community causes injury.

Article 8 of the Basic Regulation provides:

1. For the purposes of this regulation, the term "injury" shall, unless otherwise specified, be taken to mean material injury to the Community industry. . . .

* * *

6. It must be demonstrated, from all the relevant evidence . . . , that the subsidised imports are causing injury within the meaning of this regulation. . . .
7. Known factors other than the subsidised imports which are injuring the Community industry at the same time shall also be examined to ensure that injury caused by these other factors is not attributed to the subsidised imports pursuant to paragraph 6. Factors which may be considered in this respect include . . . restrictive trade practices of . . . third country and Community producers. . . .

Under Article 15(1) of the Basic Regulation,

"[w]here the facts as finally established show the existence of countervailable subsidies and injury caused thereby, and the Community interest calls for intervention . . . , a definitive countervailing duty shall be imposed by the Council. . . .

Articles 15 and 19 of the ASCM, headed "Determination of Injury" and "Imposition and Collection of Countervailing Duties" respectively, contain substantially the same provisions as those cited in . . . present judgment.

As regards the implementation of those provisions by the Community institutions, it must be remembered that the question whether a Community industry has suffered injury and, if so, whether that injury is attributable to dumped or subsidized imports involves the assessment of complex economic matters in respect of which, according to settled case-law, the institutions enjoy a wide discretion. Consequently, judicial review of any such assessment must be confined to ascertaining whether the procedural rules have been complied with, whether the facts on which the contested decision is based have been accurately stated

---

[228Latin: "with the necessary changes having been made."]

and whether there has been any manifest error of assessment of the facts or any misuse of powers.[229]

As regards, more specifically, review of compliance with the procedural rules, the Court of Justice held, in paragraph 16 of its judgment in Extramet II, a case involving dumping, that, in determining the injury, the Council and the Commission are under an obligation to consider whether the injury on which they intend to base their conclusions actually derives from dumped imports and must disregard any injury deriving from other factors, particularly from the conduct of Community producers themselves. In that case, having found nothing in the preamble to the regulation at issue to show that the institutions had actually considered whether the Community industry might itself have contributed, by its refusal to sell, to the damage sustained or that the institutions had established that the injury found did not derive from the factors mentioned by Extramet, the Court held that the Community institutions had not followed the proper procedure in establishing the injury.

In the present case, however, it is clear from both . . . recital[s] in . . . the Provisional Regulation and . . . the Contested Regulation that the institutions did consider whether the Community industry might not itself have contributed, by its anti-competitive conduct, to the injury suffered, as the applicants alleged during the administrative procedure. So, as regards the procedural requirement laid down by the Court of Justice in Extramet II, the institutions did, formally at least, set about determining the injury in the proper way.

It nevertheless remains to be established whether the institutions made a manifest error of assessment in as much as, when deciding whether or not injury had been caused and whether or not there was any causal link between any such injury and the subsidised imports, they overlooked all factors other than the imports in question, including the matters which the applicants alleged were damaging the Community industry at the same time. It is for the applicants to adduce evidence to enable the Court of First Instance to find that such an error was made.[230]

In this connection, the applicants have argued that SSBB prices had been artificially inflated either by concerted application of the alloy surcharge by SSBB producers themselves, this being the applicants' principal argument, abandoned at the hearing, or by concerted application by producers of flat products of the alloy surcharge in conjunction with uniform application by SSBB producers of the yield factor, this being the applicants' alternative argument, maintained at the hearing. SSBB prices could not, therefore, provide a reliable basis on which to establish price undercutting in respect of Indian products.

In the present proceedings the Council does not dispute the fact that, as a matter of practice in the Community iron and steel industry, SSBB prices are calculated by adding together a base price and an alloy surcharge calculated by multiplying the alloy surcharge applied by producers of flat products by a yield factor of 1.35. Moreover, in its decision of 21 April 1999, the Commission acknowledged that Community producers of SSBBs had been applying this factor of 1.35 for at least 10 years. It also emerged from information provided by the institutions at the hearing that the Commission discovered in the course of its investigations that producers of hot-rolled bars (a product falling . . . constituting the main input in the manufacture of SSBBs to the extent of making up approximately 85 percent of their final sale price) also calculated the alloy surcharge applicable to their own products by multiplying the alloy surcharge for flat products by a factor of 1.2. The Council does not take issue with the transparency for buyers of this mechanism, especially in view of the mandatory publication of the price lists of ECSC producers and dealers.

Nevertheless, the institutions emphasise that they have no evidence that the implementation and application of this formula for calculating the alloy surcharge for SSBBs amounts to a concerted practice by SSBB producers. In its pleadings, the Council argues, more specifically, that each SSBB producer freely exercised its own discretion in fixing the level of, and applying, the yield factor and in fixing the final price of SSBBs, and was not constrained by decisions taken in concert by producers of flat products. Given that these are distinct, non-substitutable products, there are no grounds for concluding that anti-competitive conduct on the part of producers of flat products had any effect on the market prices of SSBBs.

This argument of the institutions cannot be accepted and it must be held that their assessment of the injury and of the causal link between the injury and the subsidised imports set out in the Contested Regulation is vitiated by a manifest error.

Indeed, in circumstances such as those of the present case, the simple fact that it could not be proved that the final sale prices of SSBBs were fixed by Community producers acting in concert does not mean that those prices were to be regarded as reliable and consistent with normal market conditions in the determination of the injury sustained by those producers as a result of subsidised Indian imports. On the contrary, given that changes in the price of flat products were closely mirrored by changes in the price of hot-rolled bars and SSBBs, because producers of hot-rolled bars and SSBBs uniformly and consistently applied to the alloy surcharge for flat products a yield factor of 1.2 and 1.35 respectively, the institutions ought to have accepted that the anti-competitive conduct of producers of flat products could have had significant repercussions on SSBB prices, most likely increasing

---

[229]*See, inter alia* . . . Case T-51/96 Miwon v Council, *European Court Reports*, vol. 2000, pt. 1, p. 1841, para. 94.
[230]*See* Case T-121/95 EFMA v Council, *id.*, vol. 1997, pt. 2, p. 2391, para. 106. . . .

them artificially, even though SSBB prices themselves were not directly the subject of any unlawful concerted practice on the part of producers.

That is all the more true in a context in which the Commission found, in its decision of 21 April 1999, that "flat products represent about 85 pecent of the ECSC finished products, delivered by EU producers" and that, "due to the importance of flat products, price developments in the stainless steel markets are very often driven by pricing decisions of flat products producers."

Thus, by failing to take account of the uniform, consistent industrial practice of Community producers of SSBBs and hot-rolled bars, the objective effect of which was automatically to mirror, in the markets for those products, the artificial price increases achieved through concertation by producers of flat products, the institutions disregarded a known factor, other than the subsidised imports, which might have been a concurrent cause of the injury sustained by the Community industry.

* * *

Moreover, contrary to the Council's submission, the incontrovertible fact that one component of the final sale price of SSBBs (namely the amount of alloy surcharge applied to flat products, before application of the yield factor of 1.35) was artificially increased as a result of unlawful concerted practices on the part of producers of flat products was bound to affect the final sale prices of SSBBs, rendering them unreliable.

First of all, in a market where it is industry practice to calculate the final sale price of a product by adding together a number of distinct items, it is clear that external factors affecting the amount of one or other of those

items will, in the absence of exceptional circumstances, necessarily have an effect on the final sales price. That effect is likely to be even more marked in a market such as the market in SSBBs, where the prices of the principal manufacturing input, which represented approximately 85 percent of their final sale price . . . , will also have been affected by the same external factors and where the mechanism determining the prices of that input is transparent and understood by purchasers and vendors alike, in particular, by virtue of ECSC price lists.

Secondly, the Council's reasoning stands in contradiction to the Commission's own finding in Decision 98/247. There, the Commission found that the concerted amendment of the reference values for the formula for calculating the alloy surcharge applicable to flat products, whilst not being the sole cause of the near doubling of prices of stainless steel flat products between January 1994 and March 1995, had nevertheless "greatly contributed to it through the mechanical price increase that it caused."

* * *

In view of the foregoing, the Court finds that the argument which the applicants put forward in the alternative is well founded.

* * *

On those grounds, THE COURT OF FIRST INSTANCE (First Chamber, Extended Composition), hereby . . . Annuls Council Regulation (EC) No 2450/98 of 13 November 1998 imposing a definitive countervailing duty on imports of stainless steel bars originating in India. . . . ∎

Developing States and States Transitioning to Market Economies

Developing states are given special treatment in the SCM Agreement. The least-developed states and developing states with a per capita income of less than U.S. $1,000 are allowed to use subsidies based on export performance and are given until the year 2003 to phase out subsidies based on domestic content.[231] Other developing states were required to phase out both kinds of subsidies by the end of 1999.[232] Less rigorous procedures were also applied to developing countries with respect to remedies and countervailing duties.[233]

States in the process of transforming themselves from centrally planned to market economies were allowed to adopt programs necessary to facilitate the transformation, and they were given until 2002 to phase out any existing prohibited and actionable subsidies.[234]

Safeguards

Safeguards are emergency actions that a WTO member state may take to protect its domestic industries from serious injury from a sudden increase in the quantity of an imported product. Until the **Agreement on Safeguards** was adopted with the inauguration of WTO, the provisions

safeguard: An emergency action that a WTO member state may take in order to protect its domestic industry from serious injury from a sudden increase in the quantity of an imported product.

Agreement on Safeguards: Establishes multilateral controls over the use of safeguards by WTO member states.

---

[231]Agreement on Subsidies and Countervailing Measures, Article 27, paras. 2 and 2 bis (1994).
[232]*Id.*
[233]*Id.,* Article 27, paras. 6–14.
[234]*Id.,* Article 29, paras. 1–2.

of Article XIX (entitled "Emergency Actions on Imports of Particular Products") of GATT 1947 governed safeguards. The problem with this was that Article XIX was simply ignored by the GATT 1947 contracting parties.[235] Instead of withdrawing concessions in the manner provided for by Article XIX, states found it easier to resort to alternative protectionist devices that limited exports instead of imports. Examples were "orderly marketing arrangements" (OMAs)[236] and "voluntary export restraints" (VERs).[237]

Even though OMAs, VERs, and other similar arrangements are restraints on exports, they nevertheless violate GATT,[238] and it is the purpose of the new Agreement on Safeguards to establish multilateral control over them and over safeguards in general. Thus, safeguard measures in existence at the time the WTO was inaugurated[239] had to be phased out by the end of 1999,[240] and new safeguards can be instituted only in specific limited cases and only for limited time periods.

A WTO member state may apply safeguard measures against a product only after conducting an official investigation to determine that the product is being imported into its territory in such increased quantities and under such conditions as to cause or threaten to cause serious injury to the domestic industry that produces like or directly competitive products.[241] The measures must then be applied to a product (a) regardless of its origin (i.e., the GATT principle of nondiscrimination applies)[242] and (b) only for the time and to the extent necessary to prevent or remedy serious injury and to facilitate adjustment.[243]

To encourage domestic industries to make adjustments, any safeguard measure that is to last longer than one year must be progressively liberalized at regular intervals over its lifetime. If it is to last for more than three years, a review must be made by its midterm to determine if the measure should be withdrawn or liberalized more quickly.[244]

Agriculture

Agreement on Agriculture: Establishes guidelines for initiating a process of reform to progressively integrate international trade in agricultural products into the GATT system.

The **Agreement on Agriculture** establishes guidelines for "initiating a process of reform of trade in agriculture."[245] Its ultimate goal is the establishment of a market-oriented system for trade in agricultural products that is free of restrictions and distortions.

To begin the process of reform, the Agreement (1) specifies the agricultural products it governs; (2) requires that nontariff barriers to agricultural imports be converted into customs tariffs; (3) defines permissible forms of domestic supports; (4) defines export subsidies; (5) phases in initial reductions in tariffs, impermissible domestic support measures, and export subsidies during a six-year implementation period (developing countries are given a 10-year period); and (6) progressively integrates international trade in agricultural products into the GATT system.

---

[235]John Kraus, *The GATT Negotiations: A Business Guide to the Results of the Uruguay Round*, p. 37 (1994).

[236]Orderly marketing arrangements (OMAs) are formal agreements between importing and exporting states as to the quantity of a particular product that the exporting state will export to the importing state. OMAs that include industry participation are known as voluntary restraint agreements (VRAs). Organization for Economic Cooperation and Development, *Obstacles to Trade and Competition*, p. 17 (1993).

[237]Voluntary export restraints (VERs) are government-sponsored arrangements among exporting firms that limit exports to a predetermined ceiling. *Id.*

[238]Although sometimes classed as being within a "gray area" under GATT because they involved exports (*id.,* p. 21), both VERs and OMAs, as well as other forms of export restraint agreements, clearly violate GATT. Article XI, para. 1, of GATT provides: "No prohibitions or restrictions other than duties, taxes, or other charges, whether made effective through quotas, import or *export* licenses, or other measures, shall be instituted or maintained by any member on the importation of any product of the territory of any other member or on the *exportation or sale for export* of any product destined for the territory of any other member." (Emphasis added.)

[239]*See* Kent A. Jones, *Export Restraint and the New Protectionism: The Political Economy of Discriminatory Trade Restrictions*, pp. 12–17 (1994), for a list of voluntary restraints and similar measures that were in existence as of mid-1990.

[240]Agreement on Safeguards, paras. 21 and 22(b) (1994).

An exception allowed each importing member state to maintain one existing OMA or VER until the end of 1999. *Id.,* para. 23. One example is mentioned in the Annex to the Agreement on Safeguards. It involves an agreement between the European Union and Japan on certain types of motor vehicles. According to the WTO, no other member took advantage of this exception. *See* "About the WTO—Agreements: Anti-dumping, subsidies, safeguards, contingencies, etc." posted on the Internet at www.wto.org/about/agmnts7.htm.

[241]*Id.,* para. 2.

[242]*Id.,* para. 5.

[243]*Id.,* para. 10.

[244]*Id.,* para. 13.

[245]Agreement on Agriculture, Preamble (1994).

The agricultural products governed by the Agreement include foodstuffs (except for fish and fish products), hides, skins, animal hairs, raw cotton, raw flax, raw hemp, raw silk, and certain related products.[246]

Upon becoming members of the WTO and parties to the Agreement on Agriculture, states agreed to convert their existing nontariff barriers to agricultural imports (including quotas, levies, and licenses)[247] into equivalent customs tariffs. The process for doing this involved taking the difference in internal and external prices and making appropriate adjustments (for differences in quality or variety, for freight and other charges, and for other elements that provided protection to domestic producers).[248] These tariff rates were then incorporated into a Schedule of Concessions that each member state deposited with the GATT Secretariat to be appended to GATT 1994 along with its commitment to reduce its tariff rates during the implementation period.[249] On average, agricultural tariffs will be reduced 36 percent for developed countries and 24 percent for developing countries.[250] With a few exceptions, all of these tariffs will be "bound" (that is, guaranteed against increase).[251]

Domestic agricultural support measures can sometimes restrict or distort trade. Developed states have agreed to reduce the monetary impact of measures that have this effect by 20 percent and developing countries by 13.3 percent (two-thirds of 20 percent) during the implementation period.[252] Not all support measures restrict or distort trade, however, and the Agreement on Agriculture defines those that are exempt. Exempt measures must satisfy two basic requirements: (1) they must be publicly funded government programs and (2) they must not have the effect of providing price supports to producers. Examples include support for research, pest and disease control, training services, extension and advisory services, inspection services, marketing and promotion services, and infrastructure services; food security and domestic food aid; direct payments to producers (including income support that is not linked to production); participation in social or crop disaster insurance; structural adjustment assistance; environmental protection; and regional assistance programs.[253]

Export subsidies for agricultural products can similarly restrict or distort trade. As with domestic support measures, the developed states have agreed to reduce export subsidies by 36 percent and developing states by 24 percent during the implementation period.[254] These measures are defined in the Agreement on Agriculture as subsidies that are contingent upon export performance.[255] Examples include direct government payments that are contingent upon export performance; the sale for export of governmental noncommercial stocks of agricultural products at less than their fair market value; government payments to exporters even when financed from levies on the exports; subsidies for marketing or transporting exports; and subsidies on farm products contingent on their incorporation in exported products.[256]

The Agreement on Agriculture provides for the gradual phasing in of member state obligations. In addition to the six-year implementation period (10 years for developing states) for reducing tariffs, impermissible domestic support measures, and export subsidies, there is a nine-year transition period during which measures and supports maintained in conformity with the Agreement will not be subject to actions otherwise available under the GATT and the SCM Agreement unless they cause or threaten to cause injury.[257] Even then, member states agree to exercise "due restraint" before initiating any countervailing duty investigations.[258]

---

[246]*Id.,* Article 2.
[247]*Id.,* Article 4, para. 2, n. 1.
[248]*Id.,* Attachment to Annex 5.
[249]Uruguay Round Protocol to the General Agreement on Tariffs and Trade 1994, para. 1.
[250]*See* "About the WTO—Agreements: Agriculture," posted on the Internet at www.wto.org/wto/ about/agmnts3.htm.
[251]Agreement on Agriculture, Article 4, para. 1 (1994).
[252]*See* "About the WTO—Agreements: Agriculture," posted on the Internet at www.wto.org/wto/ about/agmnts3.htm. The means for determining the value of these support measures is described in Agreement on Agriculture, Article 1(a), (d), and (h) (1994).
[253]*Id.,* Annex 2.
[254]*See* "About the WTO—Agreements: Agriculture," posted on the Internet at www.wto.org/wto/ about/agmnts3.htm.
[255]Agreement on Agriculture, Article 1(e) (1994).
[256]*Id.,* Article 9, para. 1.
[257]*Id.,* Article 13, paras. 1 and 3.
[258]*Id.,* paras. 2(a) and 3(a).

Textiles and Clothing

Agreement on Textiles and Clothing: Establishes a process for the phasing out of existing special arrangements governing international trade in textiles and clothing and the integration of those products into the GATT system.

The **Agreement on Textiles and Clothing** is designed to eliminate the current system of special arrangements governing international trade in these products. Prior to its adoption, a series of collateral arrangements had been entered into by the states principally involved in the clothing and textiles trade that created an exception to the GATT principle of protection through tariffs.

These arrangements came about because of the rapid growth in the 1950s of cotton textile imports into the United States from low-cost suppliers, most notably Japan. Under pressure from its own textile industry, the U.S. government negotiated concessions from Japan and other low-cost exporters to voluntarily limit their textile exports. Then, in 1961, the United States proposed that GATT agree to administer an "arrangement for the orderly development of the trade in such products . . . while at the same time avoiding disruptive conditions in import markets."[259] The European Community (which had a longstanding policy of restricting the importation of nearly all textiles) and other importing states supported the American initiative. The low-cost exporting states reluctantly agreed to the proposal, both in the hopes that it might improve access to the European market and that it might avoid the unilateral imposition of restrictions by the other importing states, especially the United States. A one-year Short-Term Arrangement Regarding Trade in Cotton Textiles, adopted in 1961, evolved into a Long-Term Arrangement Regarding Trade in Cotton Textiles, that was replaced in 1973 by the Arrangement Regarding International Trade in Textiles, commonly known as the Multi-Fiber Arrangement (MFA).[260]

The Multi-Fiber Arrangement was important because it applied to about half of the developed world's $100 billion worth of imports from developing countries. It allowed participating states to establish quantitative limits on imports of textiles through bilateral restraint agreements. Unlike the Generalized System of Preferences and the South-South Preferences (discussed earlier), the MFA was not designed to give preferences to developing states. Quite to the contrary, it overtly allowed developed states to discriminate *against* developing states. Although the MFA itself came to an end with the adoption of the Agreement on Textiles and Clothing, the quotas it established and that were in existence on December 31, 1994, were carried forward under the new agreement.

The Agreement on Textiles and Clothing provides for the complete elimination of the MFA at the end of a 10-year transition period. Upon the Agreement's adoption, WTO member states had to remove at least 16 percent of their textile and clothing imports from quota controls. An additional 17 percent was removed as of 1998, another 18 percent as of 2001, and the remaining quotas are to be removed by 2005. At that time, all the WTO member states' international trade in clothing and textiles is to be fully "integrated" into GATT 1994, and all quantitative restrictions inconsistent with GATT are to be abolished.[261]

Once textiles and clothing are fully integrated into the GATT system, the Agreement on Textiles and Clothing itself will come to an end. It is the only WTO multilateral agreement that provides for its own termination.[262]

Rules of Origin

Agreement on Rules of Origin: Establishes a three-year program aimed at bringing about an international system of harmonized rules of origin.

rules of origin: Laws, regulations, and administrative procedures used by states for determining the country of origin of goods.

The **Agreement on Rules of Origin** is essentially a program outlining procedures for bringing about an international system of harmonized rules of origin. **Rules of origin** are the laws, regulations, and administrative procedures used by states to determine the country of origin of goods.[263] The program for harmonization was instituted with the inauguration of the WTO and is being carried out in conjunction with the Customs Cooperation Council (CCC).[264] The Agreement called for the program to be completed by mid-1998; however, "due to the complexity of issues" involved, the WTO postponed the completion date to November 1999.[265]

---

[259]Gardner Paterson, *Discrimination in International Trade: The Policy Issues, 1945–1965*, p. 309 (1966).
[260]*See GATT Secretariat Study, Textiles and Clothing in the World Economy* (1984).
[261]Agreement on Textiles and Clothing, Article 2, paras. 6, 8 (1994).
[262]*See* "About the WTO—Agreements: Textiles," posted on the Internet at www.wto.org/wto/ about/agmnts4.htm.
[263]Agreement on Rules of Origin, Article 1, para. 1 (1994).
[264]*Id.,* Article 9, para. 1.
[265]*See* "What's New [at the WTO]—WTO to Continue Work on Harmonizing Rules of Origin," posted at www.wto.org/wto/new/press106.htm.

According to the guidelines set out in the Agreement, the resulting rules of origin are to be (1) coherent;[266] (2) objective, understandable, and predictable;[267] (3) administered in a consistent, uniform, impartial, and reasonable manner;[268] (4) applied equally to each member state's nonpreferential commercial policy instruments (e.g., most-favored-nation treatment, antidumping and countervailing duties, safeguard measures, origin marking requirements, quantitative restrictions, and tariff quotas);[269] and (5) based on a positive standard (i.e., one that states what confers, rather than what does not confer, origin).[270] Furthermore, the rules are not to be used as instruments of trade policy nor should they restrict, distort, or disrupt trade.[271] Finally, the "country of origin" is to be the one where a particular good was obtained, or, when more than one country is involved in its production, the one in which the last substantial transformation is carried out.[272]

During the transition period, these same principles are to govern the member states' existing rules.[273] In addition, both during and after the transition, member states are required to observe the basic GATT principles of nondiscrimination[274] and transparency.[275] Finally, the usual GATT 1994 procedures for review, consultation, and dispute settlement apply.[276]

---

[266] Agreement on Rules of Origin, para. 1(f) (1994).

[267] *Id.,* para. 1(c).

[268] *Id.,* para. 1(e).

[269] *Id.,* para. 1(a).

[270] *Id.,* para. 1(g).

[271] *Id.,* para. 1(d).

[272] *Id.,* para. 1(b).

[273] *Id.,* Article 2.

[274] *Id.,* Article 3(d).

[275] *Id.,* Article 3(e).

  A member state's laws, regulations, administrative actions, and court decisions establishing, implementing, or interpreting rules of origin must be promptly published. *Id.* Also, copies must be filed with the WTO Secretariat. *Id.,* Article 5.

[276] *Id.,* Articles 6, 7, and 8.

Chapter Questions

1. The Widget Company has just imported 10,000 widgets into State A. Describe how the Customs Service of State A, a signatory of the Customs Valuation Code, will go about determining the value of these goods in the process of collecting an import tariff.

2. Several automobile manufacturers from State J are importing large numbers of cars to State K, taking over a large share of K's automobile market and putting K's own automobile manufacturers and workers out of business. State J's manufacturers are not subsidized by State J nor are they dumping their cars at below cost. Under GATT 1994, what can State K do? Discuss.

3. State D and State V are both members of the WTO. At the time of joining the WTO, State D prohibited the importation of foreign-grown rice. The prohibition has never been lifted. Presently, rice in State D sells for about four times the world price. State V, a large grower of rice, wants access to State D's market. Under GATT 1994, what can State V do? Discuss.

4. State R, a country with a centrally planned economy, uses prison labor to manufacture export goods at very low cost. When State S finds out about this, it imposes an import embargo on these goods. Both countries are members of the WTO, and State R complains to the WTO's Dispute Settlement Body. Assuming that a Dispute Settlement Panel is appointed to resolve this matter, how will the Panel rule? Explain.

5. Recently, State E, concerned that its nationals are being poisoned by chemical growth stimulants that are fed to livestock to make them grow faster and heavier, enacted legislation that forbids its livestock producers from using these stimulants and also forbids the sale of any meat from such animals within its territory. The law also forbids the importation of any animal fed a growth stimulant or any animal product from such an animal. Because it is impossible to detect the growth stimulant in either live animals or in their meat, the legislation requires importers to certify that the animals (or the animals from which an animal product is derived) have never been fed a growth stimulant.

The livestock producers in State F have been using growth stimulants for many years to grow larger animals at lower cost, and they believe any possible health risk to consumers is insignificant. State F's Ministry of Health also agrees that growth stimulants pose little risk to consumers and it encourages its livestock producers to use them. Because State F's livestock producers are no longer able to export their animals or the animal products from those animals to State E, they have asked their government to take action through the WTO on their behalf. Both State E and State F are members of the WTO. Consultation with State E proved unsuccessful, so State F asked the WTO's Dispute Settlement Body to appoint a Dispute Settlement Panel. This has been done. How should the Panel rule on State F's request for a finding that State E's legislation violates the latter's obligations under GATT 1994? Discuss.

6. State H provides general subsidies to all of its export manufacturers by means of low-cost loans, foreign currency exchange guarantees, and discounted prices for fuel and electricity purchased from the state's energy monopoly. HowdyDoo Company, a State H manufacturer of shampoos that has taken advantage of all of these subsidies, exports its goods to State I, where its products are in direct competition with several local manufacturers. State I's manufacturers have complained to their government, asking it to impose a countervailing duty on HowdyDoo. Both State H and State I are members of the WTO. Should the countervailing duty be imposed? Explain.

7. The Snicker Company, the largest manufacturer of Snickerdoodles in State F, decided about two years ago to enter the cookie market in State G. Several small companies in State G manufacture Snickerdoodles, but the market has traditionally been very small. When Snicker entered State G's market, it undertook a widespread advertising campaign to promote Snickerdoodle consumption and to encourage consumers to try its product by publishing coupons in newspapers that allowed purchasers to buy Snicker's Snickerdoodles below their actual cost. As a consequence of this campaign, the sales of Snickerdoodles in State G have skyrocketed. In addition, the sales of Snickerdoodles manufactured by the State G firms have more than tripled. State G's Snickerdoodle manufacturers are, nonetheless, displeased, because their market share has gone from 100 percent to 30 percent in two years. Concerned with this loss, they have asked State G to impose antidumping duties on Sincker, since its snickerdoodles are being sold below cost. Both State F and State G are members of the WTO. Should State G impose antidumping duties on Snicker? Explain.

8. Many years ago, State X enacted a law forbidding its government agencies and subdivisions from purchasing materials produced in any other country. Recently, one of State X's municipalities, Gotham City, solicited bids for artworks to be incorporated into the new city hall. Gotham's specifications for bidders state that bids will be accepted only from citizens of State X. Now, Ms. Yokum, a world-renowned artist and a citizen of State Z, brings suit in a State X court asking that the court rule that the bid specifications violate State X's obligations to the WTO (of which it is a member) and to the Government Procurement Code of 1994 (of which it is a signatory). Will Ms. Yokum win? Explain.

9. State C is a major exporter of lumber products (especially plywood) to State U. State C's lumber companies are able to manufacture and sell their products in State U inexpensively because (unlike State U) State C's government charges only a nominal fee for cutting lumber in its national forests. In State U, on the other hand, the cutting fee is substantial, adding 15 to 20 percent to the cost of the finished lumber product. One of State U's plywood lumber companies, Multi-Ply, Inc., has lost much of its market share in State U due to imports from State C. Multi-Ply has complained to State U's government, arguing that State C is unfairly subsidizing its lumber companies by charging such a low forest-cutting fee. Multi-Ply would like State U's government to impose a countervailing duty on imports of plywood from State C. May State U do so? Note that both State C and State U are members of the WTO. Discuss.

10. State Z's automobile manufacturing industry is one of the largest and most highly regarded in the world. The industry is concerned that it may lose some of its domestic market share to inexpensive, low-quality cars manufactured in newly industrialized countries. To avoid this, the industry lobbies the State Z government until it enacts new standards for the sale

of cars in the country. The standards are set in such a way that only cars manufactured in State Z can meet them. Assuming that State Z is a member of the WTO, can the governments of those newly industrialized countries (also members of the WTO) do anything to get State Z to rescind its new standards? Explain.

11. Eve, a national of State A, owns the technology for manufacturing a video game called "Porn-Man" that involves the use of the latest and most advanced computer technology to show lifelike images of Porn-Man doing truly obscene things. State A is a member of the WTO and of the Coordinating Committee on Multilateral Export Controls (COCOM). State A's government has issued an administrative order prohibiting Eve from (1) exporting the computer chips to State O (a country that is listed in State A's export-control legislation as being "off limits" for all high-technology exports), where the video games are supposed to be assembled, and (2) re-importing assembled and operational video games back into State A. Eve has brought suit in a State A court to obtain the appropriate order to lift the government's prohibition. What are the chances of her success? Discuss.

Review Problem

You have been promoted to the job of Chief Assistant in the law department of MegaBranch Industries (MBI) and put in charge of overseeing all the import and export transactions of MBI and its subsidiaries.

1. In honor of your promotion, the local bar association has invited you to give a short talk. They would like you to describe the World Trade Organization (WTO), its history, its successes, and its present usefulness. Prepare an outline of your talk.

2. An MBI subsidiary in State A exported goods to State B and was charged a tariff by State B that the subsidiary believes violates GATT 1994. Both State A and State B are members of the WTO. Will the subsidiary be successful if it brings a suit in a State B court asking the court to order the government to return the tariff to the subsidiary, assuming that the only law the subsidiary can cite in support of its position is GATT 1994?

3. MBI wants to set up a new overseas subsidiary, and it has narrowed the choices of location down to State C and State D. State C is a developed country. State D is a developing country. State D has been the beneficiary of preferences extended by the United States and the European Union under the Generalized System of Preferences. State D has also entered into several South-South Preferences. Assuming all else is equal, which country should MBI chose?

4. Does a labeling law that requires all products to have a label or tag identifying the place where they were made violate GATT 1994's national treatment rule?

5. State E imposes tariffs on component parts when they enter the country. It also imposes a tariff on those parts after they are assembled by local subsidiaries of foreign multinationals. One such company is an MBI subsidiary. Does this practice violate State E's obligations under GATT 1994?

6. MBI's subsidiaries in Africa want to know if they should support or oppose the creation of an African Economic Union (that would be similar to the European Union). How would you advise them?

7. MBI's subsidiary in State F grows coffee, the single most important crop in State F. Should it encourage State F to participate in the creation of a coffee commodity arrangement? If so, how should the arrangement be organized?

8. For what reasons may a country enact laws or regulations that are otherwise contrary to its GATT 1994 obligations?

9. An MBI subsidiary in State G deals in rare art and religious relics. Will it have any difficulty exporting these items?

10. An MBI subsidiary in State H deals in arms sales. Will it have any difficulty exporting them?

11. Your talk about the WTO's history, and so forth, was so successful that the bar association has asked you back for an encore. This time it would like you to describe how the WTO organization works, how disputes between member states are resolved, and what goes on at the multilateral trade negotiations. Prepare a summary of this talk.

12. An MBI subsidiary in County I exports goods to another MBI subsidiary in State J. The price that the purchaser pays is dictated (somewhat arbitrarily) by the MBI parent firm. How will the State J Customs Service go about determining the value of these goods for the purpose of collecting its import tariffs?

13. One of MBI's product lines is widgets. It wants to export these to State K. State K, however, requires that the packaging have no writing on it in any language other than the language spoken in State K (a language that is spoken nowhere else). Does this requirement violate State K's obligations as a member of the WTO?

14. The Chief Executive Officer of MBI wants to take his dog with him to State L for a short visit. State L, however, requires that all dogs entering the country be put in quarantine for six months to ensure that they are free from rabies and other similar diseases, which do not exist in State L. Is State L acting contrary to its GATT 1994 obligations?

15. State M, following a recent dramatic downturn in its economy, adopted a new foreign exchange rule. The rule forbids foreign investors from transferring any earnings out of the country during the first year after making an investment in the country, and limits transfers to 50 percent for the next three years. MBI, which is planning to invest in a joint venture in State M, wants to know if State M is in violation of its GATT 1994 obligations.

16. How does one find out about the import-licensing requirements of a foreign country?

17. What can MBI do to ensure that it and its subsidiaries will not have to pay antidumping duties?

18. An MBI subsidiary in State N would like to take advantage of the export subsidies offered by that country. Does this mean it will have to pay a countervailing duty to State O, the destination for its goods?

19. What effect might the Agreement on Textiles and Clothing have on the MBI subsidiary in State O that manufactures clothing for export?

20. How does a Customs Service agent decide where goods come from?

CHAPTER

8

Services and Labor

Chapter Outline

Introduction

This chapter examines the international rules that govern services and labor. The rules on services are now found principally in the General Agreement on Trade in Services and in the agreements creating certain regional economic organizations such as the European Union and the North American Free Trade Area. The rules governing labor—especially the movement of laborers—are to be found in the international labor standards promulgated by the International Labor Organization, in the agreements creating some regional organizations, and in national legislation.

A. GENERAL AGREEMENT ON TRADE IN SERVICES

General Agreement on Trade in Services: Multilateral agreement in force from January 1, 1995, that contains rules and principles governing international trade in services and establishes guidelines for negotiating the future liberalization of such trade.

The **General Agreement on Trade in Services** (GATS) came into effect on January 1, 1995, as one of the three main multilateral annexes to the Agreement Establishing the World Trade Organization (the other two being the General Agreement on Tariffs and Trade [GATT] and the Agreement on Trade-Related Aspects of Intellectual Property Rights [TRIPS]). The purpose of GATS is to give to international trade in services a set of rules and principles and a basis for liberalization similar to those that GATT has applied to goods for the last five decades.

GATS is made up of three interrelated components: (1) the Agreement itself (often called the Framework Agreement),[1] which contains the rules applicable to all member states of the World Trade Organization (who are automatically parties to the GATS); (2) the sectoral annexes that deal with issues unique to particular economic sectors (i.e., movement of natural

---

[1]John Kraus, *The GATT Negotiations: A Business Guide to the Results of the Uruguay Round,* p. 40 (1994). The texts of GATS and other WTO agreements are available on the Internet at www.wto.org/ wto/legal/legal.htm.

persons, air transport services, financial services, maritime transport services, and telecommunications), and (3) the national Schedules of Specific Commitments each member state has agreed to undertake, which were agreed to mainly through negotiations undertaken as part of the Uruguay Round of Multilateral Trade Negotiations that produced the WTO Agreement (see Chapter 7).

The Framework Agreement

The Framework Agreement lays out the basic parameters of GATS in six parts. These parts deal with (1) the scope and definition of GATS, (2) general obligations and disciplines of member states, (3) obligations and disciplines concerning specific commitments of member states, (4) a schedule for progressively liberalizing the world's trade in services, (5) the institutional structure for implementing GATS, and (6) miscellaneous provisions (including definitions of key terms).

Although much of GATS is based on the provisions in the General Agreement on Tariffs and Trade and uses much of the same terminology, the "architecture" of GATS is significantly different. Unlike GATT, which provides for a single set of obligations that apply to all measures affecting trade in goods, GATS contains two sets of obligations: (1) a set of general principles and rules that apply to *all* measures affecting trade in services and (2) a set of principles and rules that apply *only* to the specific sectors and subsectors that are listed in a member state's Schedule. The consequence of this division of obligations is that the principles and rules in GATS, as we shall see, are less "binding" than those in GATT.[2]

Scope and Definition

The Framework Agreement covers all trade in services in any sector except those supplied in the exercise of governmental functions; however, the Agreement does not define either service or service sector. In common usage, a **service** is an act or an action, such as work rendered or performed for another,[3] and this definition seems to fit with the use of the term in the Agreement. The dictionary definition of a sector is a division or a part,[4] and the Agreement and the GATS annexes provide several examples of service sectors, including banking, finance, insurance, telecommunications, and transportation. Thus, while not defined, the services referred to in the Framework Agreement seem to mean the work performed by one person for another, while **service sectors** are any parts of the economy related to the performance of such work. The Annex on Movement of Natural Persons makes clear, however, that the GATS rules apply neither to laborers, except those temporarily involved in delivering a service, nor to member states' laws governing the permanent employment of natural persons.[5] Also, because GATS is but one of the three main annexes to the Agreement creating the WTO, it is clear that GATS governs neither trade in goods (which is covered by GATT) nor the trade-related aspects of intellectual property rights (which are covered by TRIPS).

The Framework Agreement does define trade in services. It does so in terms of "modes of supply." Four modes are described: (1) the cross-border supply of services that do not require the physical movement of either the supplier or the consumer (such as telecommunications), (2) the supply of services that require the consumer to go to the supplier (such as tourism), (3) services

service: An act or action, such as work rendered or performed for another.

service sectors: Any parts of the economy involving the performance of a service.

---

[2]Bernard Hoekman, "The General Agreement on Trade in Services," a paper presented to an OECD Workshop on The New World Trading System, Paris, April 25–26, 1994, reprinted in John H. Jackson, William J. Davey, and Alan O Sykes Jr. *Legal Problems of International Economic Relations,* pp. 921–930 (3rd ed., 1995).

   The reason for the difference in the architecture of GATS and GATT relates to the interests of the states involved in its negotiation. The United States, which saw trade liberalization as a means for enhancing its competitiveness, proposed that rules on most-favored-nation (MFN) treatment and national treatment be applied, as they are in GATT, equally to all member states as a general obligation. The European Union and several of the major developing countries, which were reluctant to open their markets to foreign (especially U.S.) service suppliers, opposed this concept of "hard" obligations and offered a proposal of "soft" obligations meant to achieve comparable access to markets on a sector-by-sector basis for all participating states. Ultimately, this second proposal prevailed. Thus, MFN treatment was adopted subject to exemptions and national treatment (discussed below) and was made to apply only to the sectors the member states included in their Schedules of Commitments. *Id.*

[3]*See* Indiana Department of State Revenue, Sales Tax Division v. Cable Brazil, Inc., *North Eastern Reporter, Second Series,* vol. 380, p. 555 at p. 561 (Indiana Ct. of Appeals, 1978).

[4]*The American Heritage Dictionary,* p. 1109 (2nd ed., 1985).

[5]Annex on Movement of Natural Persons Supplying Services under the Agreement, paras. 1–2.

supplied by a service supplier[6] from one member state by means of a commercial presence[7] in another member's territory (such as banking), and (4) services supplied in the territory of a member state by a service supplier from another member state by means of the temporary presence of natural persons of another member state (such as construction or consulting work).[8] This four-sided definition is significant both because it broadly covers all forms of trade in services and because member states are allowed to exclude, as to particular service sectors or subsectors, one or more of these modes of supply in their Schedules of Specific Commitments.[9]

Case 8–1, the issue arose as to whether GATT and GATS could apply to the same factual situation or whether they are mutually exclusive.

---

[6]The Framework Agreement defines the term "service supplier" as "any person that supplies a service" (General Agreement on Trade in Services, Article XXVIII, para. g [1994]). It further defines a "person" as "either a natural person or a juridical person" (*id.*, para. [j]).

[7]A commercial presence means any type of business or professional establishment, which may be in the form of a subsidiary, a branch, or a representative office. General Agreement on Trade in Services, Article XXVIII, para. (d).

[8]*Id.*, Article I, § 2.

[9]Although the right of member states to make exclusions as to modes of supply is not specifically stated in GATS, this may be inferred from Article XVI, § 1, n. 9, and Article XVII, § 1.

Case 8–1   *European Communities—Regime for the Importation, Sale, and Distribution of Bananas*

Ecuador, Guatemala, Honduras, Mexico, United States v. European Communities

Case WT/DS27/AB/R, AB-1997-3.
World Trade Organization, Appellate Body (1997).

The European Communities [the name used by the WTO to refer to the European Union] and Ecuador, Guatemala, Honduras, Mexico, and the United States (the "Complaining Parties") appeal from certain issues of law and legal interpretations in the Panel Reports, *European Communities—Regime for the Importation, Sale and Distribution of Bananas* (the "Panel Reports"). The Panel was established on 8 May 1996 to consider a complaint by the Complaining Parties against the European Communities concerning the regime for the importation, sale and distribution of bananas established by Council Regulation (EEC) No. 404/93 of 13 February 1993 on the common organization of the market in bananas ("Regulation 404/93"), and subsequent EC legislation, regulations and administrative measures, including those reflecting the provisions of the Framework Agreement on Bananas (the "BFA"), which implement, supplement, and amend that regime. [The EC legislation, regulations, and measures provided for preferential tariff treatment for former colonies of EC member states that were importing bananas to the EC. The WTO Panel held that the EC was in violation of the General Agreement on Tariffs and Trade of 1994 (GATT 1994) and the General Agreement on Trade in Services (GATS). The Panel recommended that the EC amend its banana tariff regulations to bring them into compliance

with both GATT 1994 and GATS. In most respects, the Appellate Body affirmed the Panel's holding on the applicability of GATT 1994. The Appellate Body then considered the applicability of GATS.]

* * *

C. GENERAL AGREEMENT ON TRADE IN SERVICES

1. Application of the GATS

There are two issues to consider in this context. The first is whether the GATS applies to the EC import licensing procedures. The second is whether the GATS overlaps with the GATT 1994, or whether the two agreements are mutually exclusive. With respect to the first issue, the Panel found that:

> . . . no measures are excluded *a priori* from the scope of the GATS as defined by its provisions. The scope of the GATS encompasses any measure of a Member to the extent it affects the supply of a service regardless of whether such measure directly governs the supply of a service or whether it regulates other matters but nevertheless affects trade in services.

For these reasons, the Panel concluded:

> We therefore find that there is no legal basis for an *a priori* exclusion of measures within the EC banana import licensing regime from the scope of the GATS.

MAP 8-1 European Union (1997)

The European Communities argues that the GATS does not apply to the EC import licensing procedures because they are not measures "affecting trade in services" within the meaning of Article I:1 of the GATS. In the view of the European Communities, Regulation 404/93 and the other related regulations deal with the importation, sale, and distribution of bananas. As such, the European Communities asserts, these measures are subject to the GATT 1994, and not to the GATS.

In contrast, the Complaining Parties argue that the scope of the GATS, by its terms, is sufficiently broad to encompass Regulation 404/93 and the other related regulations as measures affecting the competitive relations between domestic and foreign services and service suppliers. This conclusion, they argue, is not affected by the fact that the same measures are also subject to scrutiny under the GATT 1994, as the two agreements are not mutually exclusive.

In addressing this issue, we note that Article I:1 of the GATS provides that "[t]his Agreement applies to measures by Members affecting trade in services". In our view, the use of the term "affecting" reflects the intent of the drafters to give a broad reach to the GATS. The ordinary meaning of the word "affecting" implies a measure that has "an effect on", which indicates a broad scope of application. This interpretation is further reinforced by the conclusions of previous panels that the term "affecting" in the context of Article III of the GATT is wider in scope than such terms as "regulating" or "governing".[10] We also note that Article I:3(b) of the

GATS provides that "'services' includes *any service* in *any sector* except services supplied in the exercise of governmental authority" (emphasis added), and that Article XXVIII(b) of the GATS provides that the "'supply of a service' includes the production, distribution, marketing, sale, and delivery of a service". There is nothing at all in these provisions to suggest a limited scope of application for the GATS. We also agree [with the Panel] that Article XXVIII(c) of the GATS does not narrow "the meaning of the term 'affecting' to 'in respect of.'" For these reasons, we uphold the Panel's finding that there is no legal basis for an *a priori* exclusion of measures within the EC banana import licensing regime from the scope of the GATS.

The second issue is whether the GATS and the GATT 1994 are mutually exclusive agreements. The GATS was not intended to deal with the same subject matter as the GATT 1994. The GATS was intended to deal with a subject matter not covered by the GATT 1994, that is, with trade in services. Thus, the GATS applies to the supply of services. It provides, *inter alia,*[11] for both MFN treatment and national treatment for services and service suppliers. Given the respective scope of application of the two agreements, they may or may not overlap, depending on the nature of the measures at issue. Certain measures could be found to fall exclusively within the scope of the GATT 1994, when they affect trade in goods as goods. Certain measures could be found to fall exclusively within the scope of the GATS, when they affect the supply of services as services. There is yet a third category of measures that could be found to fall within the scope of both the GATT 1994 and the GATS. These are measures that involve a service relating to a particular good or a service supplied in conjunction with a particular good. In all such cases in this third category, the measure in question could be scrutinized under both the GATT 1994 and the GATS. However, while the same measure could be scrutinized under both agreements, the specific aspects of that measure examined under each agreement could be different. Under the GATT 1994, the focus is on how the measure affects the goods involved. Under the GATS, the focus is on how the measure affects the supply of the service or the service suppliers involved. Whether a certain measure affecting the supply of a service related to a particular good is scrutinized under the GATT 1994 or the GATS, or both, is a matter that can only be determined on a case-by-case basis. This was also our conclusion in the Appellate Body Report in *Canada—Periodicals.*[12]

---

[10]*See,* for example, the panel report in *Italian Agricultural Machinery,* adopted 23 October 1958, BISD 7S/60, para. 12.
[11]Latin: "among other things."]
[12]Appellate Body Report, WT/DS31/AB/R, adopted 30 July 1997, p. 19.

For these reasons, we agree with the Panel that the EC banana import licensing procedures are subject to both the GATT 1994 and the GATS, and that the GATT 1994 and the GATS may overlap in application to a particular measure.

2. Whether Operators Are Service Suppliers Engaged in Wholesale Trade Services

The European Communities raises two issues concerning the definition of wholesale trade services and the application of that definition. Both these issues relate to the Panel's finding that:

> . . . operators in the meaning of Article 19 of Regulation 404/93 and operators performing the activities defined in Article 5 of Regulation 1442/93 are service suppliers in the meaning of Article I:2(c) of GATS provided that they are owned or controlled by natural persons or juridical persons of other Members and supply wholesale services. When operators provide wholesale services with respect to bananas which they have imported or acquired for marketing, cleared in customs or ripened, they are actual wholesale service suppliers. Where operators form part of vertically integrated companies, they have the capability and opportunity to enter the wholesale service market. They could at any time decide to re-sell bananas which they have imported or acquired from EC producers, or cleared in customs, or ripened instead of further transferring or processing bananas within an integrated company. Since Article XVII of GATS is concerned with conditions of competition, it is appropriate for us to consider these vertically integrated companies as service suppliers for the purposes of analyzing the claims made in this case.

First, the European Communities questions whether the operators within the meaning of the relevant EC regulations are, in fact, service suppliers in the sense of the GATS, in that what they actually do is buy and import bananas. The European Communities argues that "when buying or importing, a wholesale trade services supplier is a buyer or importer and not covered by the GATS at all, because he is not providing any reselling services". The European Communities also challenges the Panel's conclusion that "integrated companies", which may pro-

vide some of their services in-house in the production or distribution chain, are service suppliers within the meaning of the GATS.

On the first of these two issues, we agree with the Panel that the operators as defined under the relevant regulations of the European Communities are, indeed, suppliers of "wholesale trade services" within the definition set out in the Headnote to Section 6 of the [Central Product Classification, an international agreement classifying services activities, which is abbreviated as] CPC.[13] We note further that the European Communities has made a full commitment for wholesale trade services (CPC 622), with no conditions or qualifications, in its Schedule of Specific Commitments under the GATS.[14] Although these operators, as defined in the relevant EC regulations, are engaged in some activities that are not strictly within the definition of "distributive trade services" in the Headnote to Section 6 of the CPC, there is no question that they are also engaged in other activities involving the wholesale distribution of bananas that are within that definition.

The Headnote to Section 6 of the CPC defines "distributive trade services" in relevant part as follows:

> . . . the principal services rendered by wholesalers and retailers may be characterized as reselling merchandise, accompanied by a variety of related, subordinated services. . . . (emphasis added)

We note that the CPC Headnote characterizes the "*principal* services" rendered by wholesalers as "reselling merchandise". This means that "reselling merchandise" is not necessarily the *only* service provided by wholesalers. The CPC Headnote also refers to "a variety of related, subordinated services" that may accompany the "principal service" of "reselling merchandise". It is difficult to conceive how a wholesaler could engage in the "principal service" of "reselling" a product if it could not also purchase or, in some cases, import the product. Obviously, a wholesaler must obtain the goods by some means in order to resell them.[15] In this case, for example, it would be difficult to resell bananas in the European Communities if one could not buy them or import them in the first place.

The second issue relates to "integrated companies". In our view, even if a company is vertically-integrated, and even if it performs other functions related to the production, importation, distribution, and processing of a product, to the extent that it is also engaged in providing

---

[13]Provisional Central Product Classification, United Nations Statistical Papers, Series M, No. 77, 1991, p. 189.
[14]European Communities and their Member States' Schedule of Specific Commitments, GATS/SC/31, 15 April 1994, p. 52.
[15]After all, as the European Communities has pointed out, "goods cannot walk" or be resold by themselves (EC's appellant's submission, para. 236).

"wholesale trade services" and is therefore affected in that capacity by a particular measure of a Member in its supply of those "wholesale trade services," that company is a service supplier within the scope of the GATS.

For these reasons, we uphold the Panel's findings on both these issues.

* * *

The Appellate Body *recommends* that the Dispute Settlement Body request the European Communities to bring the measures found in this Report and in the Panel Reports, as modified by this Report, to be inconsistent with the GATT 1994 and the GATS into conformity with the obligations of the European Communities under those agreements. ■

General Obligations and Disciplines

most-favored-nation treatment: GATS requirement that its member states accord immediately and unconditionally to services and service suppliers of other members treatment that is no less favorable than that it accords to like services and service suppliers of any other state.

Two general obligations in the Framework Agreement apply to all WTO member states: (1) most-favored-nation (MFN) treatment and (2) transparency. The **most-favored-nation treatment** provision provides that "each member shall accord immediately and unconditionally to services and service suppliers of any other member treatment no less favorable than that it accords to like services and service suppliers of any other country."[16] This means that a privilege a state grants to any country (including non-WTO members), such as allowing a foreign bank to operate within its territory, must be granted immediately and unconditionally to other WTO members.

The MFN treatment rule in the Framework Agreement (unlike the rule in GATT) is not, it is important to note, a binding requirement that must be uniformly observed. During the Uruguay Round negotiations, the representatives of service industries in a number of industrialized nations opposed binding and unconditional MFN treatment on the ground that the level of market openness at that time varied too greatly among countries. They argued that unconditional MFN treatment would allow states with restrictive laws governing services to keep those laws in place while their own service suppliers would get a "free ride" into the markets of states with more open laws. To force states with closed markets to open them, the service industry representatives successfully advocated the use of MFN exemptions.[17] An annex was added to GATS that (a) allowed the original WTO member states to submit a list of MFN exemptions that became effective when GATS came into force and (b) provided that any later applications for exemptions will be considered using the ordinary WTO waiver procedures.[18] The MFN exemptions, furthermore, are to be limited in time (lasting no longer than 10 years) and subject to periodic review and to negotiation in future trade liberalization rounds.[19] Nevertheless, while this provision for exemptions does put pressure on states with restrictive laws to open up their markets, it clearly diminishes the effectiveness of GATS, making it (like the old GATT 1947) little more than a collection of loopholes held together by waivers.[20]

transparency: GATS requirement that its member states publish their regulations affecting trade in services, that they notify the Council for Trade in Services of any relevant changes, and that they respond promptly to requests for information from other members.

The **transparency** provision in GATS requires member states to publish prior to their entry into force all of their national measures and international agreements that affect their obligations under GATS.[21] Additionally, they have to notify the Council for Trade in Services of any relevant changes to those measures and agreements at least annually,[22] and they are obliged to promptly respond to another member state's requests for information and to establish points of inquiry to facilitate this.[23]

In addition to its core obligations of MFN treatment and transparency, the Framework Agreement establishes other general criteria governing trade in services (most of which are

---

[16]General Agreement on Trade Services, Article II, § 1 (1994).

[17]Bernard Hoekman, "The General Agreement on Trade in Services," paper presented to an OECD Workshop on the New World Trading System, Paris, April 25–26, 1994, reprinted in John H. Jackson, William J. Davey, and Alan O Sykes Jr., *Legal Problems of International Economic Relations,* pp. 921–930 (3rd ed., 1995).

[18]Annex on Article II Exemptions (1994).

[19]*Id.,* para. 6.

[20]*See* John Kraus, *The GATT Negotiations: A Business Guide to the Results of the Uruguay Round,* p. 78 (1994).

[21]General Agreement on Trade in Services (1994), Article III, § 1.

[22]*Id.,* § 3.

[23]*Id.,* § 4.

analogous to similar provisions in GATT). To encourage the participation of developing countries, the Agreement authorizes developed and developing member states to enter into negotiations (similar to those that produced GATT's General System of Preferences and South-South Preferences) targeted at improving the capacity, efficiency, and competitiveness of the developing members.[24]

GATS seeks to encourage regional economic integration both in trade in services and in the movement of labor with provisions comparable to those in GATT that deal with the establishment of common markets and free trade areas for goods. A service integration agreement among member states is required to have substantial sectoral coverage[25] and must provide for the elimination of all or substantially all discrimination among the parties in the sectors it covers.[26] A labor-market integration agreement has to exempt nationals of states parties from residency and work permit requirements.[27] In either case, the participating states parties have to "notify" the Council for Trade in Services of their proposed agreement for the Council's review and approval.[28]

GATS requires its member states to ensure that their domestic regulations affecting trade in services are administered in a reasonable, objective, and impartial manner. It forbids them from applying their existing licensing, qualification requirements,[29] and technical standards in a burdensome, restrictive, or nontransparent manner; and, as soon as the Council on Trade in Services adopts harmonizing guidelines in these areas, it will require them to bring their practices into compliance with those guidelines.[30]

A member state may grant monopoly rights to a service supplier (such as the granting of an assigned frequency to a radio or television broadcaster), but in doing so, it must not allow the supplier to act inconsistently with the member's MFN treatment obligation or its specific commitments.[31] As for other business practices which restrain competition and therefore restrict international trade in services, GATS requires each member state, at the request of any other, to participate in consultations aimed at the eventual elimination of those practices.[32]

No restrictions may be applied by member states to international transfers and payments for current transactions[33] relating to a member state's specific commitments. Nevertheless, restrictions, including those just mentioned, may be adopted or maintained if a member state suffers serious balance-of-payments difficulties, especially if the member is developing or is in transition to a market economy.[34] When restrictions are imposed, they must not discriminate among member states nor unnecessarily damage another member's economic interests; they must conform to the Articles of Agreement of the International Monetary Fund; they may not be excessive; and they must be temporary and progressively phased out as their purpose is achieved.[35]

---

[24]*Id.*, Article IV, § 1(a).

[25]"This condition is [to be] understood in terms of number of sectors, volume of trade affected, and modes of supply." *Id.*, Article V, § 1(a), n. 1.

[26]*Id.*, Article V, § 1(b).

[27]*Id.*, Article V *bis.*
A footnote to Article V *bis* notes that "[t]ypically, such integration provides citizens of the parties concerned with a right to free entry to the employment markets of the parties and includes measures concerning conditions of pay, other conditions of employment, and social benefits."

[28]While the Framework Agreement requires only that the Council be notified, one can anticipate that the Council will treat this notification process in the same way that the CONTRACTING PARTIES under the old GATT 1947 treated a similar notification requirement—that is, that notification means submission, review, and approval. *See* Chapter 7.

[29]"Qualification requirements" are the training or experience requirements that a service provider must have before offering a service.

[30]General Agreement on Trade in Services (1994), Article VI, §§ 1, 4, and 5.
So that service suppliers are able to meet local criteria for operating, GATS encourages mutual recognition of education, experience, licenses, and certifications. Similarly, member states that are parties to existing bilateral or multilateral recognition agreements are encouraged to let other member states join or negotiate comparable new agreements. *Id.*, Article VII, §§ 1 and 2.

[31]*Id.*, Article VIII, § 1.

[32]*Id.*, Article IX, § 2.

[33]*Id.*, Article XI, § 1. For the definition of a current transaction, *see* Chapter 4.

[34]*Id.*, Article XII, § 1.

[35]*Id.*, Article XII, § 2.

In addition to the core requirements on MFN treatment and transparency, as well as the other obligations just discussed, still other obligations and disciplines were being considered for inclusion in the Framework Agreement during the Uruguay Round but did not get put in before the Round came to an end. The negotiating parties, nevertheless, agreed to continue multilateral negotiations on these items.[36] Negotiations to devise rules on emergency safeguard measures, government procurement of services, and trade-distorting subsidies began in January 1997, and are still on going.[37] Negotiations to agree on rules concerning the links between the services trade and the environment began in January 1995, and they are also still ongoing.[38] The Framework Agreement provides for general exceptions[39] and security exceptions[40] that are analogous to those found in GATT. The GATS general exceptions include, additionally, a provision that provides for a departure from the principle of national treatment (discussed later) to ensure that direct taxes may be effectively collected on services or from foreign service suppliers,[41] as well as a provision that authorizes an exception to the MFN treatment rule when the difference in treatment is the result of an agreement for the avoidance of double taxation.[42]

Specific Commitments

GATS is designed to open up specific service sectors of the WTO member states' markets to international access on a sector-by-sector and a state-by-state basis. Following negotiations, or on its own initiative, a member is to submit a Schedule of Specific Commitments for annexation to GATS that lists the sectors (or subsectors) it is opening to market access.[43] The member may also list limitations that apply to these sectors and it *must* do so as to six categories of limitations if it wants those six to apply. The categories of limitations that the member must either list or not apply are limitations on (1) the number of service suppliers allowed, (2) the total value of transactions or assets, (3) the total quantity of service output or the number of service operations, (4) the number of natural persons that may be employed in a particular service sector, (5) the type of legal entity or joint venture arrangement that a service supplier may use in supplying a service, and (6) the participation of foreign capital in terms of a maximum percentage limit on foreign shareholding or the total value of individual or aggregate foreign investment.[44]

For the sectors listed in a member state's Schedule of Specific Commitments, and subject to the limitations listed there, the member must observe two specific obligations: market access and national treatment. **Market access** is defined as giving services and service suppliers of other members "treatment no less favorable" than that listed in the member's Schedule.[45] **National treatment** is giving services and service suppliers of other members "treatment no less favorable" than what the member grants its own like services and service suppliers.[46]

As mentioned earlier, the arrangement in GATS that separates obligations into two sets, general and specific, and that only requires a member state to observe its specific obligations to the extent that it opens its markets to international access, means that GATS is a much weaker agreement than the General Agreement on Tariffs and Trade (since GATT does not correlate the observance of any of its obligations to commitments on market access). Considering, however, that GATT was, at its outset, observed more often in the breach than in its performance, the decision to limit the extent to which members are required to subject themselves to the obligations and disciplines of GATS, at least in its initial version, was undoubtedly prudent.

market access: GATS requirement that a WTO member state accord to services and service suppliers of other member states treatment no less favorable than that listed in its GATS Schedule.

national treatment: GATS requirement that a WTO member state accord to services and service suppliers of other member states treatment no less favorable than what the member grants its own like services and service suppliers.

---

[36]*See id.,* Articles X, XIII, and XV, and the Ministerial Decision on Trade in Services and the Environment (1994).

[37]General Agreement on Trade in Services, Article X (1994), required the WTO to issue rules for emergency safeguard measures no later than January 1, 1998. The member states were unable to do so, and they extended the deadline to June 1999. *See* "GATS Rules," posted at www.wto.org/eol/e/wto06/wto6_40.htm. As of August 1999, however, the rules had not been issued and no notice of a new deadline had been agreed upon.

[38]*See* "About Trade and the Environment in the WTO," posted at www.wto.org/wto/environ/environm.htm.

[39]General Agreement on Trade in Services, Article XIV (1994).

[40]*Id.,* Article XIV bis.

[41]*Id.,* para. (d).

[42]*Id.,* para. (e).

[43]*Id.,* Article XX, § 1.

[44]*Id.,* Article XVI, § 2.

[45]*Id.,* § 1.

[46]*Id.,* Article XVII, § 1.

Progressive Liberalization

The long-term objective of GATS is to encourage its member states to open as many of their service sectors to market access as possible. Article XIX, Section 1, describes how this is to be done:

> In pursuance of the objectives of this Agreement, members shall enter into successive rounds of negotiations, beginning not later than five years from the date of entry into force of the WTO Agreement and periodically thereafter, with a view to achieving a progressively higher level of liberalization. Such negotiations shall be directed to the reduction or elimination of the adverse effects on trade in services of measures as a means of providing effective market access. This process shall take place with a view to promoting the interests of all participants on a mutually advantageous basis and to securing an overall balance of rights and obligations.

Although progressive liberalization is the goal of GATS, member states are not permanently bound to the commitments they make in their Schedules. After a period of three years from the entry into force of a commitment, a member may modify or withdraw it. Before doing so, however, the member must give the Council for Trade in Services at least three months notice; and, if a member state affected by the change asks, the notifying member must participate in negotiations to agree on appropriate compensatory adjustments.[47]

Institutional Structure

Council for Trade in Services: A committee of representatives of all WTO member states that oversees the General Agreement on Trade in Services.

The operation of GATS is overseen by a **Council for Trade in Services** made up of representatives of all WTO member states.[48] Subordinate to the Council are several bodies, including sectoral committees responsible for the operation of the different sectoral annexes (e.g., the Committee on Trade in Financial Services).[49]

The Council for Trade in Services is meant to function within the WTO structure. Thus, the Council is, in essence, the WTO Secretariat that provides technical assistance to developing countries on matters related to trade in services.[50] And both consultations and dispute settlements related to GATS are governed by the WTO's Understanding on Rules and Procedures Governing the Settlement of Disputes.[51]

GATS Annexes

As stated earlier, the annexes are the second component part of GATS. Together with several supplementary instruments (Ministerial Decisions and Ministerial Understandings), they deal with special aspects of particular service sectors or issues. The provisions of these annexes are summarized in Exhibit 8-1.

GATS Schedules of Specific Commitments

Each WTO member state is required to submit for annexation to GATS a Schedule of Specific Commitments regarding the service sectors that it has opened to international market access. For each such sector, its Schedule must specify (as discussed earlier) (a) terms, limitations, and conditions on market access, (b) conditions and qualifications on national treatment, (c) undertakings relating to additional commitments, (d) the time frame for implementing its commitments (if that applies), and (e) the date of entry into force of its commitments.[52]

Of course, members are not required to open all of their service sectors and one preliminary study indicates that developing countries have only opened about one-fifth of their service

---

[47]*Id.,* Article XXI, § 1(b), § 2(a).

[48]*Id.,* Article XXIV.

[49]Decision on Institutional Arrangements for the General Agreement on Trade in Services (1994).

[50]General Agreement on Trade in Services, Article XXV, § 2 (1994).

[51]Panelists for the dispute settlement panels in service matters, however, are taken from a special list of persons with special knowledge of GATS and/or trade in services, and panels for disputes regarding sectoral matters must be made up of persons with the necessary expertise relative to the sector concerned. Decision on Certain Dispute Settlement Procedures for the General Agreement on Trade in Services (1994).

[52]General Agreement on Trade in Services, Article XX, § 1 (1994).

EXHIBIT 8-1 Annexes to the General Agreement on Trade in Services

Annex on Movement of Natural Persons Supplying Services under the Agreement

Provides that the entry into and temporary residence of natural persons within a WTO member state's territory may be regulated by that member state unless it makes a commitment to the contrary. More particularly, this Annex makes clear that GATS does not apply either to measures of WTO member states affecting natural persons seeking employment or to measures regarding citizenship, residence, or employment on a permanent basis.[a]

Annex on Air Transport Services

Makes clear that GATS does not replace the various bilateral and multilateral agreements on air traffic rights (i.e., rights to carry passengers, cargo, or mail for remuneration to, within, or across a country) and related services. In particular, GATS is to apply only to

(a) aircraft repair and maintenance services, (b) the selling and marketing of air transport services, and (c) computer reservation system (CRS) services.

Annex on Financial Services

States that a WTO member state may adopt, in regulating financial services (i.e., insurance, banking, and their related services), prudential measures to protect investors, depositors, policyholders, and others, and it may take such other actions as are necessary to protect its financial system as a whole. Additionally, member states are free to maintain or adopt measures that protect the confidentiality of financial service customers.[b]

Annex on Negotiations on Maritime Transport Services

Provides that member states are not obliged to list in their Schedules of Commitments measures applicable to maritime transport services that are inconsistent with most-favored-nation treatment until the negotiations on such services (that began in 1994) are concluded.[c]

Annex on Telecommunications

Requires WTO member states that have granted market access to service suppliers of other members to ensure that those suppliers have access to the use of public telecommunications transport networks and services (other than cable and broadcast radio and television) on reasonable and nondiscriminatory terms within their territories and across their borders. Permits member states to place conditions on access to and use of these networks and services, but only to (a) ensure that they are available to the public generally, (b) protect their technical integrity, or (c) prevent suppliers from providing services that are not listed on the concerned member's Schedule of Specific Commitments.[d]

---

[a]This Annex is supplemented by the Decision on Negotiations on Movement of Natural Persons (1994). The Decision called for negotiations on liberalization of the movement of natural persons to begin in May 1994 and to conclude in June 1995.

[b]A Second Annex on Financial Services (1994) gave member states an extension of up to six months after the entry into force of the WTO Agreement in which to list, modify, or withdraw their specific commitments regarding financial services.

[c]Member states must submit their list of commitments related to maritime transport services not later than (a) the date the Negotiating Group on Maritime Transport Services specifies for implementing the results of its negotiations or (b) if the negotiations fail, the date when the Group issues its final report. A Decision on Negotiations on Maritime Transport Services (1994) called for the negotiations to be completed by June 1996. At the end of June 1996, however, the member states were unable to reach an agreement and they suspended the negotiations indefinitely. *See* "GATS: Maritime Transport," posted on the WTO Web site at www.wto.org/eol/e/wto06/wto6_41.htm

[d]In 1997, the WTO concluded negotiations on market access for basic telecommunications services. Sixty-nine governments agreed to offers that were annexed to the Fourth Protocol of the GATS. The one-page Protocol and its annexed schedules and MFN exemption lists entered into force on February 5, 1998. *See* "GATS: Basic Telecommunications," posted at www.wto.org/eol/e/wto06/wto6_34.htm.

sectors and developed countries about two-thirds of theirs.[53] Nevertheless, GATS is new and it is but a first step. The Framework Agreement requires, and the member states have agreed, that negotiations continue to liberalize the international trade in services. If GATS is as successful in the future as GATT has been in the past, it seems likely that international trade in services will grow dramatically in the decades to come.

---

[53]Bernard Hoekman, "The General Agreement on Trade in Services," paper presented to an OECD Workshop on the New World Trading System, Paris, April 25–26, 1994, reprinted in John H. Jackson, William J. Davey, and Alan O Sykes Jr., *Legal Problems of International Economic Relations*, pp. 921–930 (3rd ed., 1995).

B. REGIONAL INTERGOVERNMENTAL REGULATIONS ON TRADE IN SERVICES

European Union Law on Trade in Services

The European Union is a common market not only for goods but also for services and (as discussed later in the chapter) labor. In comparison with the General Agreement on Trade in Services, the Treaty Establishing the European Community (EC Treaty), the principal source of law in the European Union (EU), creates a much more open and liberal market for services (and business in general) between and among its member states. The EC Treaty provides that, within the EU, "restrictions on the freedom to provide services"[54] and "restrictions on the freedom of establishment"[55] are to be progressively abolished. In essence, service suppliers and entrepreneurs are acquiring (as the EU integrates and EU law evolves) the right to do business in all European Union member states.

The **freedom to provide services** relates to economic activities carried out on a temporary or nonpermanent basis. It applies, for example, when a Danish firm of consultants advises businesses in Greece, or an Italian construction company erects a building in Spain.

The **right of establishment** authorizes a natural person or a company to settle permanently in a member state and carry on a business.[56] It includes the right to set up and carry on a business both as an individual and as an employer.[57]

Concern has been expressed that some cases fall between the scope of both these guarantees.[58] An example would be a British camera crew filming scenes in France and Germany. Because the crew is neither establishing itself nor providing or receiving services, neither of the two guarantees fit exactly. However, in several cases, the European Court of Justice has read the two provisions together and hinted that it regards them as part of a general right of a self-employed person to pursue activities throughout the Union regardless of the location of his principal office or the kind of economic endeavor he is involved in.[59]

To ensure that the right of establishment and the freedom to provide services are meaningful guarantees, the EC Treaty declares that the self-employed and the employees of service suppliers are entitled to travel freely within the member states of the Union and to carry on their activities free from discrimination.[60] These are not absolute rights, however. Entry can be limited on the grounds of public policy, public security, and public health,[61] and contracts with the public service can be limited to nationals of the member state.[62] These limitations are narrowly construed, however, as Case 8–2 points out.

> **EU freedom to provide services:** Right of member state nationals and firms to market their services on a temporary or nonpermanent basis throughout the European Union.
>
> **EU right of establishment:** Right of member state nationals and firms to settle permanently and carry on a business throughout the European Union.

---

[54]Treaty Establishing the European Community, Article 59.
[55]*Id.,* Article 52.
[56]Derrick Wyatt and Alan Dashwood, *The Substantive Law of the EEC,* p. 198 (2nd ed., 1987).
[57]Fearon, Case 182/83, *European Court Reports,* vol. 1984, p. 3677 (1984).
[58]Derrick Wyatt and Alan Dashwood, *The Substantive Law of the EEC,* p. 199 (2nd ed., 1987).
[59]*See* Coenen v. Sociaal-Economische Raad, Case 39/75, *European Court Reports,* vol. 1975, p. 1547 (1975); and Koestler, Case 15/78, *European Court Reports,* vol. 1978, p. 1971 (1978).
[60]Treaty Establishing the European Community, Articles 52 and 59.
[61]*Id.,* Articles 56 and 66.
[62]*Id.,* Articles 55 and 66.

Case 8–2   *Jany v. Staatssecretaris van Justitie*   ⌒

European Union, European Court of Justice Case C-268/99.
European Court Reports, vol. 2001, part 1, p. 8615 (2001).

JUDGMENT

[*The District Court for The Hague referred this case to the Court of Justice for a preliminary ruling on questions* concerning *the interpretation of Association Agreements between the European Communities and Poland and the Czech Republic.*]

The questions have arisen in proceedings brought by Ms. Jany and Ms. Szepietowska, who are Polish nationals, and Ms. Padevetova, Ms. Zacalova, Ms. Hrubcinova and Ms. Überlackerova, who are Czech nationals, against the

Staatssecretaris van Justitie (the Netherlands Secretary of State for Justice) ("the Secretary of State") contesting his . . . decisions refusing them residence permits to enable them to work as self-employed prostitutes.

The Association Agreement Between the Communities and Poland

* * *

Article 44(3) and (4) of the Association Agreement between the Communities and Poland . . . provides:

3. Each Member State shall grant, from entry into force of this Agreement, a treatment no less favorable than that accorded to its own companies and nationals for the establishment of Polish companies and nationals as defined in Article 48 and shall grant in the operation of Polish companies and nationals established in its territory a treatment no less favorable than that accorded to its own companies and nationals.
4. For the purposes of this Agreement:
   (a) "establishment" shall mean
      (i) as regards nationals, the right to take up and pursue economic activities as self-employed persons and to set up and manage undertakings, in particular companies, which they effectively control. Self-employment and business undertakings by nationals shall not extend to seeking or taking employment in the labor market or confer a right of access to the labor market of another Party. The provisions of this chapter do not apply to those who are not exclusively self-employed;

* * *

   (c) "economic activities" shall in particular include activities of an industrial character, activities of a commercial character, activities of craftsmen and activities of the professions.

Article 53(1) of the Association Agreement between the Communities and Poland provides:

The provisions of this chapter shall be applied subject to limitations justified on grounds of public policy, public security, or public health.

* * *

The Association Agreement Between the Communities and the Czech Republic

* * *

. . . [T]he Association Agreement between the Communities and the Czech Republic contain provi-

MAP 8-2   Netherlands and the European Union (2001)

sions that are similar to those set out in . . . the Association Agreement between the Communities and Poland. . . .

The National Legislation   Under Article 11(5) of the [Dutch the Law on Aliens,] residence permits for the Netherlands may be refused to any foreigner on grounds of public interest.

Under the policy followed by the Secretary of State in applying that provision . . . ("the Circular on Aliens") . . . nationals of a non-member country with which the European Communities or their Member States have concluded an association agreement, such as the Republic of Poland or the Czech Republic, must, in order to be allowed to become established in terms of those agreements as self-employed persons in the Netherlands:

(a) satisfy the conditions generally governing access to an activity as a self-employed person and any special conditions applicable to the exercise of the planned activity;

(b) have sufficient financial resources;

(c) not represent a danger to public peace, public order, or national security.

* * *

The Dispute . . .   Ms. Jany, Ms. Szepietowska, Ms. Padevetova, Ms. Zacalova, Ms. Hrubcinova and Ms. Überlackerova declare that they established their residence in the Netherlands at various dates between May 1993 and October 1996 on the basis of the Law on Aliens. All of them work in Amsterdam as "window prostitutes."

* * *

The six applicants . . . applied . . . for residence permits to enable them to work as self-employed prostitutes for "compelling humanitarian reasons." Those applications were rejected by the Secretary of State . . . on the ground that prostitution is a prohibited activity or at least not a socially acceptable form of work and cannot be regarded as being either a regular job or a profession.

[*The applicants then filed suit in the District Court for The Hague, which referred several preliminary questions to the Court of Justice.*]

The Questions Submitted for Preliminary Ruling
[*Among the questions referred for a preliminary ruling was the following:*]

3. Do Article 44 of the Agreement with Poland and Article 45 of the Agreement with the Czech Republic allow prostitution to be excluded from the notion of "economic activities as self-employed persons" . . . on the ground that prostitution is prohibited in (a majority of) the associate countries, and on the ground that it gives rise to problems concerning the freedom of action of prostitutes and their independence which are difficult to monitor?

* * *

The Third Question   By its third question, the national court is asking in substance whether Article 44 of the Association Agreement between the Communities and Poland and Article 45 of the Association Agreement between the Communities and the Czech Republic must be construed as meaning that prostitution does not come under those provisions on the ground that it cannot be regarded as an economic activity pursued in a self-employed capacity, as defined in those provisions:

- in view of its illegal nature;
- for reasons of public morality;
- on the ground that it would be difficult to control whether persons pursuing that activity are able to act freely and are therefore not, in reality, parties to disguised employment relationships.

According to the Commission, [which supports the petition of the applicant,] the third question is in part based on a false premise. In most Member States, prostitution is not prohibited as such, and prohibitions relate more to certain wider phenomena such as soliciting, white-slaving, prostitution of minors, procuring, and the clandestine residence of workers.

As regards the question of disguised employment relationships, the Commission observes that [the Association Agreements between the Communities and Poland and the Czech Republic] authorize the host Member State to impose substantive requirements allowing rigorous

checks to determine whether prostitutes wishing to become established within its territory are genuinely self-employed workers and whether they remain so after being admitted there.

In contrast, the Netherlands and Belgian Governments argue that prostitution cannot be treated as an activity performed in a self-employed capacity within the meaning of the Association Agreements between the Communities and Poland and the Czech Republic because it is not possible to determine whether a prostitute has voluntarily moved to the host Member State or pursues her activities there freely. Although prostitution lends itself to an "appearance of independence" since the criminal prohibition of procuring means that any employment relationships must be organized illegally, prostitutes are normally in a subordinate position in relation to a pimp.

* * *

So far as concerns the question of the immorality of that activity, raised by the referring court, it must also be borne in mind that, as the Court has already held, it is not for the Court to substitute its own assessment for that of the legislatures of the Member States where an allegedly immoral activity is practiced legally.[63]

Far from being prohibited in all Member States, prostitution is tolerated, even regulated, by most of those States, notably the Member State concerned in the present case.

Admittedly, as follows from [the provisions of the Association Agreements between the Communities and Poland and the Czech Republic] . . . the host Member State may derogate from application of the provisions of those Agreements governing establishment on grounds of, *inter alia*, public policy.

However, as the United Kingdom Government and the Commission have correctly pointed out, under the Court's case-law a national authority's use of a public-policy derogation presupposes that there is a genuine and sufficiently serious threat affecting one of the fundamental interests of society.[64]

Although Community law does not impose on Member States a uniform scale of values as regards the assessment of conduct which may be considered to be contrary to public policy, conduct may not be considered to be of a sufficiently serious nature to justify restrictions on entry to, or residence within, the territory of a Member State of a national of another Member State where the former Member State does not adopt, with respect to the same conduct on the part of its own nationals, repressive measures or other genuine and effective measures intended to combat such conduct.

---

[63]*See,* with regard to abortion, Case C-159/90 Society for the Protection of Unborn Children Ireland, *European Court Reports,* vol. 1991, pt. 1, p. 4685, para. 20, and, with regard to lotteries, Case C-275/92 Schindler, *id.,* vol. 1994, pt. 1, p. 1039, para. 32.
[64]*See* Joined Cases 115/81 and 116/81 Adoui and Cornuaille, *id.,* vol. 1982, p. 1665, para. 8. . . .

Consequently, conduct which a Member State accepts on the part of its own nationals cannot be regarded as constituting a genuine threat to public order within the context of the Association Agreement between the Communities and Poland and that between the Communities and the Czech Republic. Applicability of the public-policy derogation set out in Articles 53 and 54 of those Agreements respectively is thus subject, in the case of Polish and Czech nationals wishing to pursue the activity of prostitution within the territory of the host Member State, to the condition that that State has adopted effective measures to monitor and repress activities of that kind when they are also pursued by its own nationals.

That condition is not met in the present case. . . . [W]indow prostitution and street prostitution are permitted in the Netherlands and are regulated there at communal level.

In its third question, the referring court also alludes to the difficulties in monitoring the conditions under which prostitution is practiced and the consequent risk that the establishment provisions of the Association Agreements between the Communities and Poland and the Czech Republic may be abused in their application to Polish or Czech nationals who might in fact wish to use them as a way to gain access to the labor market of the host Member State.

* * *

It is clear, in this regard [that the Association Agreements between the Communities and Poland and the Czech Republic] . . . do not in principle preclude a system of prior control which makes the issue by the competent immigration authorities of leave to enter and remain subject to the condition that the applicant must show that he genuinely intends to take up an activity as a self-employed person. . . .

* * *

It is [permissible, therefore] for the national court to determine in each case, in the light of the evidence adduced before it, whether the conditions allowing it to be concluded that prostitution is being carried on by the person concerned in a self-employed capacity are satisfied, that is to say:

- outside any relationship of subordination concerning the choice of that activity, working conditions and conditions of remuneration;
- under that person's own responsibility; and
- in return for remuneration paid to that person directly and in full.

* * *

On those grounds, THE COURT, in answer to the questions referred to it by the [District Court of The Hague] . . . hereby rules:

* * *

[The Association Agreements between the Communities and Poland and the Czech Republic] must be construed to the effect that prostitution is an economic activity pursued by a self-employed person as referred to in those provisions, where it is established that it is being carried on by the person providing the service:

- outside any relationship of subordination concerning the choice of that activity, working conditions and conditions of remuneration;
- under that person's own responsibility; and
- in return for remuneration paid to that person directly and in full.

It is for the national court to determine in each case, in the light of the evidence adduced before it, whether those conditions are satisfied. ∎

Provisions Governing Trade in Services in the North American Free Trade Agreement

The trade-in-services provisions in the North American Free Trade Agreement (NAFTA) are very similar to those found in GATS. There are, nonetheless, some differences.

As is the case with GATS, each of the NAFTA countries (Canada, Mexico, and the United States) has to observe the basic rules of transparency,[65] most-favored-nation treatment,[66] and national treatment.[67] In addition, each NAFTA country is required to accord the better of national or most-favored-nation treatment to services and service suppliers of the other two countries.[68]

---

[65]North American Free Trade Agreement, Articles 1306, 1411, and 1802 (1993).
[66]*Id.*, Articles 1103, 1203, and 1406.
[67]*Id.*, Articles 1102, 1202, and 1405.
[68]*Id.*, Articles 1104, and 1204.

Also, like GATS, service providers establishing a commercial presence in NAFTA countries, including providers from non-NAFTA states, are granted several important rights, including the right to be free from performance requirements,[69] the right to make inward and outward transfers,[70] the right to have the international standard of care doctrine applied to expropriations,[71] and the right to have investor-state disputes resolved by binding international arbitration.[72]

One important difference between GATS and NAFTA is that NAFTA does not deal with services generally, but rather by sectors. Its main service provisions, accordingly, are in three core service chapters (cross-border trade in services, telecommunications, and financial services), two associated chapters (investment and temporary entry of businesspeople), and three annexes (land transportation, professional services, and specific reservations and exceptions).[73] Because of this arrangement, rules such as transparency, most-favored-nation treatment, and national treatment are repeated (with minor variations) in different chapters.

Another difference is that NAFTA does not specifically define the four basic "modes of supply" as GATS does, and instead deals with them piecemeal. NAFTA's chapter on cross-border trade in services covers that mode.[74] The chapter on investments generally covers the commercial presence mode of supply. Other chapters cover the movement of consumers and the temporary movement of natural persons.

A third difference between NAFTA and GATS is the manner in which NAFTA deals with sectoral coverage. Unlike GATS, which requires states to list the sectors covered (a so-called "positive list") and then list the limitations that apply to them (a "negative list"), NAFTA requires its countries to set out the sectors that are not covered by the Agreement (a negative list) and the limitations that apply to them (a negative list). Thus, if a NAFTA country does not list a sector or a limitation, NAFTA's rules automatically apply.[75]

Finally, the NAFTA countries may modify their lists of sectors and limitations. However, they may not, unlike GATS member states, make the lists more restrictive.[76]

C. INTERNATIONAL LABOR LAW

International law has been concerned with the rights of laborers from the beginning of the twentieth century. Following World War I, as part of the Treaty of Versailles, the international community agreed to establish the International Labor Organization (ILO) and the ILO has subsequently become the principal international advocate of workers. With the creation of the United Nations after World War II, the right of laborers to have reasonable working conditions became part of the basic human rights that were incorporated in the UN's Universal Declaration of Human Rights. In the materials that follow, we discuss both the International Labor Organization and those human rights rules that apply to workers.

---

[69]*Id.,* Article 1106.

[70]*Id.,* Article 1109.

[71]*Id.,* Article 1110.

[72]*Id.,* Article 1120.

[73]Harry G. Broadman, "International Trade and Investment in Services: A Comparative Analysis of the NAFTA," *International Lawyer,* vol. 27, p. 623 at pp. 637–644 (1993).

[74]Significantly, the Agreement provides that NAFTA countries may not compel a cross-border service provider to establish an office or maintain a local presence. North American Free Trade Agreement, Article 1205 (1993).

[75]*Id.,* Articles 1108, 1206, 1409.

  NAFTA itself lists one service sector that is not covered by the Agreement: the general civil aviation sector. *Id.,* Article 1201, para. 2(b).

  The principal exempted service sectors that the NAFTA countries have listed are: (a) government provided social services (exempted by all three countries), (2) basic telecommunications services (all three countries), (3) cultural industries (Canada), (4) sectors that are constitutionally reserved to nationals (Mexico), (5) legal services (Mexico and the United States), and (6) maritime transport services (all three countries). Harry G. Broadman, "International Trade and Investment in Services: A Comparative Analysis of the NAFTA," *International Lawyer,* vol. 27, p. 623 at p. 919 (1993).

[76]North American Free Trade Agreement, Article 1108, para. 1(c); Article 1206, para. 1(c); Article 1409, para. 1(c) (1993).

The International Labor Organization

The **International Labor Organization** (ILO) has as its primary goal the improvement of working conditions, living standards, and the fair and equitable treatment of workers in all countries. Created in 1919 by the Treaty of Versailles, it became a specialized agency of the United Nations in 1946. Headquartered in Geneva, the ILO carries out its objectives by issuing recommended labor standards, organizing conferences to draft international labor conventions,[77] monitoring compliance with its recommendations and its conventions, and providing technical assistance to member states.

The ILO's institutional structure is made up of a **General Conference** that acts as a legislative body, approving conventions and adopting recommendations; a **Governing Body** that serves as the executive; and an **International Labor Office** headed by a Director-General that functions as the organization's secretariat. The membership of the General Conference comprises representatives from government, labor, and management. Each national delegation includes four representatives: two from government, one representing labor, and one representing employers. The same tripartite representation also exists in the Governing Body, which is composed of 56 members, half of whom are appointed by governments, a quarter by workers' groups, and a quarter by employers' organizations. Of the 28 seats reserved for government representatives, 10 are further reserved for delegates from the world's principal industrial powers.

The authors of the ILO's Constitution probably meant for the organization to involve itself primarily with manual, or blue-collar, labor, and not with other forms of employment. This reflected the interests of the labor movement at the end of World War I, but it did not represent its concerns only a few years later. In the *Employment of Women at Night Case*, the Permanent Court of International Justice considered whether the ILO could sponsor conventions that did not involve manual labor, in particular, a 1919 Convention Concerning Employment of Women at Night. The PCIJ stated:

> It is certainly true that the amelioration of the lot of the manual laborer was the main preoccupation of the authors of Part XIII of the Treaty of Versailles of 1919; but the Court is not disposed to regard the sphere of activity of the International Labor Organization as circumscribed so closely, in respect of the persons with which it was to concern itself, as to raise any presumption that "Labor convention" must be interpreted as being restricted in its operation to manual workers, unless a contrary intention appears. . . .
>
> To justify the adoption of a rule for the interpretation of "Labor conventions" to the effect that words describing general categories of human beings such as "persons" or "women" must *prima facie*[78] be regarded as referring only to manual workers, it would be necessary to show that it was only with manual workers that the International Labor Organization was intended to concern itself . . .
>
> The text . . . of Part XIII does not support the view that it is workers doing manual work—to the exclusion of other categories of workers—with whom the International Labor Organization was to concern itself. . . .[79]

The PCIJ's decision makes clear that the scope of the ILO's concerns includes all forms of labor, whether it be blue-collar or white-collar, for hire or done gratuitously, and whether employed by the state or the private sector.

International Labor Standards

To carry out its goal of improving the lot of all working people, the ILO attempts to establish rules or "standards" that have international effect. Three reasons are sometimes given for why these standards need to have international effect. The first, and most practical, is that individual states are not inclined to enact domestic labor laws because this would put them at a

---

[77]The ILO has sponsored more than 180 conventions.
[[78]Latin: "at first sight." A fact presumed to be true until disproved by some contrary evidence.]
[79]Advisory Opinion, *Permanent Court of International Justice Reports,* Series A/B, No. 50 (1932).

competitive disadvantage in the world market by increasing local labor costs. The adoption of an internationally effective agreement would, accordingly, keep multinational companies from practicing what is sometimes called "social dumping."[80] Second, the establishment of fair and equitable labor standards helps promote world peace. Third, the establishment of uniform labor standards is a matter of both justice and humanity.[81]

ILO conventions: Labor conventions sponsored by the ILO.

ILO recommendations: International Labor Office opinions as to proper labor practices and as to how ILO conventions should be interpreted.

Two instruments are used to create international standards: **ILO conventions** and **ILO recommendations**. Conventions are sponsored by the ILO when there is substantial agreement in the international community about a particular labor practice. Recommendations are issued by the International Labor Office staff when the situation is more amorphous—for example, when the subject at hand is complex, or when there is no consensus on how a problem should be solved, or sometimes as a supplement to a convention that covers a matter in more general terms.

Over the years, ILO conventions and ILO recommendations have dealt principally with three concerns. First, they focused on the basic issues of labor protection, such as employment conditions (e.g., hours of work, weekly rest, holidays with pay, etc.) and the protection of women and children. (In general, these were also the issues the ILO addressed during its own earliest years.) Second, they concentrated on setting up the basic machinery and institutions that are needed to make labor protection effective (e.g., labor inspection, employment service, labor statistics, and minimum wage-fixing machinery). Third (and this has been the focus of much of the ILO's work since the end of World War II), they have taken aim at promoting and protecting the human rights and fundamental freedoms of workers (e.g., freedom of association, freedom from forced labor, and freedom from discrimination in employment and occupation).

International Labor Organization Reports

The member states of the ILO are obliged to provide annual reports to verify compliance with the conventions they have ratified,[82] and irregular reports (when solicited by the Director-General) to provide information on both recommendations and unratified conventions.[83] The report format required for both recommendations and conventions is essentially the same. In general, it consists of four main parts, which require the submitting country to provide the following:

Part I	Copies of the state's statutory legislation and administrative regulations dealing with the particular convention or recommendation and any documentary material (such as forms, booklets, handbooks, and reports) interpreting these.
Part II	An interpretation of the materials provided in Part I, showing how they have given effect to the provisions of the particular convention or recommendation.
Part III	(a) A description of the actions that need to be taken to modify existing legislation or practice to give effect to all or part of the provisions of the particular convention or recommendation; (b) reasons why those actions have not been taken; and (c) a statement as to whether or when those actions will be taken.
Part IV	The names of employers and workers' organizations to which copies of the report were given, and the comments that those organizations made.

ILO Committee of Experts on the Application of Conventions and Recommendations: A committee of the ILO's Governing Body that analyzes annual reports to determine the extent of member state compliance with ILO recommendations and conventions.

A summary of the information contained in the member states' reports is prepared annually by the International Labor Office for use by the General Conference. Since 1927, this has been the job of the **Committee of Experts on the Application of Conventions and Recommendations**.

---

[80]Social dumping is the practice of directing services to the wealthy (e.g., developed countries) and letting the poor (e.g., underdeveloped countries) fend for themselves because of the high cost of providing services to the poor.

[81]*See* Nicholas Valticos, "The International Labor Organization," in *The Effectiveness of International Decisions: Papers of a Conference of the American Society of International Law and the Proceedings of the Conference*, p. 134 (Stephen M. Schwebel, ed., 1971).

[82]International Labor Organization Constitution, Article 22, states: "Each of the members agrees to make an annual report to the International Labor Office on the measures which it has taken to give effect to the provisions of conventions to which it is a party. These reports shall be made in such form and shall contain such particulars as the Governing Body may request."

[83]*Id.*, Article 19.

The Committee's members are appointed by the Governing Body as individuals and not as representatives of particular governments or groups. They must have a reputation for being impartial, independent, and knowledgeable of international labor law. Commonly they are drawn from the judiciary and academia.

The Committee of Experts does more than merely prepare a summary of the aforementioned reports. It analyzes and evaluates the submissions, indicating, in the case of unratified treaties and ILO recommendations, how close international practice is with the standards set by the Organization; and, in the case of ILO conventions, the extent to which the parties have complied with their obligations.

ILO Conference Committee on the Application of Conventions and Recommendations: Committee of the ILO General Conference responsible for making a list of member states that have defaulted on their obligations to the ILO.

special list: List of member states that have defaulted on their obligations to the ILO.

A special **Conference Committee on the Application of Conventions and Recommendations** reviews the summary at the General Conference. This Conference Committee, after hearing comments from governments, employers, and workers, compiles a **special list** of the governments that have defaulted on their obligations to the ILO. The list contains seven categories of deficiencies. Six deal with the failure of particular governments to submit reports, to respond to requests for information, or to participate in discussions concerning an alleged failure to comply with an ILO convention obligation. The seventh and most serious alleges that certain governments have failed to fully implement one or more of the ILO conventions they have ratified.

Each year the Conference Committee's special list is presented to the General Conference for review and adoption. This is often an awkward time for those states named on the list, especially those in Category 7. One especially memorable debate occurred in 1974, when the Soviet Union was named in Category 7. The U.S.S.R. was included for an alleged breach of the 1930 Convention Concerning Forced or Compulsory Labor because, among other things, its laws did not allow a collective farm laborer to quit work without the permission of the farm's management. After a lengthy and heated discussion, the General Conference was unable to obtain a quorum when a vote was called, so the special list was not adopted.[84]

The failure of the General Conference to take action against the U.S.S.R., together with Soviet bloc and Third World nation interference with the independence of employee and employer groups, and an increase in political debates at the General Conference, led the United States to withdraw from the ILO in 1977. The withdrawal had a dramatic impact on the ILO, in part because the United States was the major financial supporter of the Organization. By 1980, when the United States rejoined, the ILO had adopted resolutions to strengthen the tripartite system of decision making; it also had censured the Soviet Union, adopted the use of secret ballots, defeated an anti-Israeli resolution, begun screening out resolutions that violated ILO procedures, and reduced the number of meetings dealing with political affairs.[85]

Settlement of Disputes between ILO Member States

If an ILO member state violates the ILO Constitution, an ILO convention that it has ratified, or the ILO Convention on the Freedom of Association (whether it is a party to it or not), there are several dispute-resolution procedures that can be invoked to reach a settlement. These include (a) the investigation of complaints of noncompliance with ratified conventions by commissions of inquiry, (b) the investigation of abuses by the Fact-Finding and Conciliation Commission on Freedom of Association, and (c) interpretations of the ILO Constitution and ILO conventions by the International Labor Office.

inquiry: (From Latin *inquirere:* "to seek.") The process by which an impartial third party makes an investigation to determine the facts underlying a dispute without resolving the dispute itself.

Commission of Inquiry   Article 26(1) of the ILO Constitution authorizes any member state to file a complaint with the ILO "if it is not satisfied that any other member is securing the effective observance of any convention which both have ratified." Upon receiving such a complaint, the "Governing Body may appoint a Commission of Inquiry to consider the complaint and to report thereon."[86]

---

[84]*See* "Proceedings Regarding Soviet Inclusion in the Special List," International Labor Conference, 59th Session, *Record of Proceedings,* pp. 733–760 (1974).

[85]Linda L. Moy, "The U.S. Legal Role in International Labor Organization Conventions and Recommendations," *International Lawyer,* vol. 22, pp. 768–769 (1988).

[86]International Labor Organization Constitution, Article 26(2).

Although this procedure has been available since the ILO was founded, the first Commission of Inquiry was appointed only in 1961, and only a few other Commissions have been appointed since.[87]

The Fact-Finding and Conciliation Commission on Freedom of Association　The Preamble of the ILO Constitution establishes the "recognition of the principle of freedom of association" as one of the Organization's primary purposes. To implement this principle, the General Conference adopted two labor conventions: the Convention Concerning Freedom of Association (ILO Convention No. 87) and the Convention Concerning the Application of the Principles of the Right to Organize and to Bargain Collectively (ILO Convention No. 98). The first grants workers the right to form and join trade unions free from governmental interference; the second protects workers from antiunion discrimination and protects unions from employer domination.

Although both conventions have been widely ratified,[88] it was feared at first that they would not be. Because the Commission of Inquiry procedure allowed by Article 26 of the ILO Constitution can be invoked only if both the complaining and the offending state have ratified the convention involved, the expected delay in ratification of the two freedom of association conventions meant that Commissions of Inquiry could not be used. This was unacceptable to the Governing Body, which regarded the two conventions as especially important, so it established a special commission, modeled on the Article 26 Commission of Inquiry, but not depending on the ratification of a convention to carry out its tasks.[89]

Together with the UN Economic and Social Council (ECOSOC), the Governing Body established in 1950 a nine-member **Fact-Finding and Conciliation Commission** to consider complaints involving violations of the two freedom of association conventions. Under the guidelines established for the Commission, it can hear complaints against a state that has ratified either of the conventions; and, if the state against whom a complaint has been made gives its consent, the Commission can consider a complaint even though the state has not ratified either.[90]

Few states have consented to investigations by the Fact-Finding and Conciliation Commission; however, as the two conventions have become widely ratified in recent years, the requirement of consent has become of less concern. Most recent investigations have involved states that are parties to one or both of the freedom of association conventions. In these cases the Fact-Finding and Conciliation Commission is, except for its name and the focus of its investigation, nothing more than an Article 26 Commission of Inquiry.

The International Labor Office　The ILO Constitution provides that "[a]ny questions or dispute relating to the interpretation . . . of any convention . . . shall be referred for decision to the International Court of Justice." Only one case, however, has ever been considered by the ICJ. As a practical matter, reference to the ICJ is cumbersome and expensive, so governments in doubt about the meaning of an ILO convention have taken to the practice of asking for the International Labor Office to express an opinion. As the Office has stated:

> The Office has always considered it to be a duty to assist governments in this manner, though it has invariably pointed out that it has no special authority to interpret texts of Conventions; the opinions given by the Office have, when of sufficient general interest, been submitted to the Governing Body and published. Though not authoritative in the same final sense as an interpretation by the Court, these interpretations therefore enjoy such authority as derives from their having been formulated by the International

ILO Fact-Finding and Conciliation Commission on Freedom of Association: Special ILO committee of inquiry that considers complaints that a state has violated the ILO's freedom of association conventions. If the state consents, the inquiry can proceed even though the state is not a member of the ILO.

---

[87] *See* Clarence Wilfred Jenks, *Social Justice in the Law of Nations: The ILO Impact after Fifty Years,* p. 48 (1970).

[88] They have not been ratified by the United States.

[89] *See* James A. Nafziger, "The International Labor Organization and Social Change: The Fact-Finding and Conciliation Commission on Freedom of Association," *New York University Journal of International Law & Politics,* vol. 2, p. 1 at p. 11 (1969).

[90] The requirement that a state that has not ratified a convention must consent to an investigation by the Fact-Finding and Conciliation Commission was thought necessary because there is no provision in the ILO Constitution for setting up commissions other than the one in Article 26. Even with the addition of this requirement, the establishment of this commission was thought to be unconstitutional by Australia and South Africa. For a discussion of the debate on the establishment of the Commission, *see* Clarence Wilfred Jenks, *The International Protection of Trade Union Freedom,* pp. 190–193 (1957).

Labor Office in its official capacity at the request of governments of members of the Organization.[91]

Settlement of Disputes between Intergovernmental Organizations and Their Employees

The **Administrative Tribunal** of the International Labor Organization[92] is a special court that hears complaints from employees in the secretariats of the ILO and 39 other intergovernmental organizations (IGOs) that have recognized the competence of the Tribunal.[93] The Tribunal's jurisdiction extends to disputes involving the "nonobservance, in substance or in form, of the terms of appointment of officials," and to violations of the Staff Regulations of the ILO or other IGO.[94]

Currently, more than 2,000 cases have been heard by the three-judge Tribunal,[95] and almost all of the decisions have been accepted and implemented by the officials and organizations involved.[96] The power of the Administrative Tribunal to issue judgments, however, is limited. It has the power to "order the rescinding of the decision impugned or the performance of the obligation relied upon." It does not have the power to order an IGO to undertake an action it has not begun on its own, as Case 8–3 demonstrates.

---

[91]International Labor Office, *The International Labor Code, 1951*, vol. 1, Preface, p. cix (1952).

[92]The Tribunal maintains a home page at www.ilo.org/public/english/tribunal/.

[93]The IGOs that have recognized the competence of the ILO's Administrative Tribunal are: World Health Organization (WHO), Pan American Health Organization (PAHO), United Nations Educational, Scientific and Cultural Organization (UNESCO), International Telecommunication Union (ITU), World Meteorological Organization (WMO), Food and Agriculture Organization of the United Nations (FAO), European Organization for Nuclear Research (CERN), World Trade Organization (WTO), International Atomic Energy Agency (IAEA), World Intellectual Property Organization (WIPO), European Organization for the Safety of Air Navigation (Eurocontrol), Universal Postal Union (UPU), European Southern Observatory (ESO), Intergovernmental Council of Copper Exporting Countries (CIPEC), European Free Trade Association (EFTA), Inter-Parliamentary Union (IPU), European Molecular Biology Laboratory (EMBL), World Tourism Organization (WTO), European Patent Organization (EPO), African Training and Research Centre in Administration for Development (CAFRAD), Intergovernmental Organization for International Carriage by Rail (OTIF), International Center for the Registration of Serials (CIEPS), International Office of Epizootics (OIE), United Nations Industrial Development Organization (UNIDO), International Criminal Police Organization (Interpol), International Fund for Agricultural Development (IFAD), International Union for the Protection of New Varieties of Plants (UPOV), Customs Co-operation Council (CCC), Court of Justice of the European Free Trade Association (EFTA Court), Surveillance Authority of the European Free Trade Association (ESA), International Service for National Agricultural Research (ISNAR), International Organization for Migration (IOM), International Centre for Genetic Engineering and Biotechnology (ICGEB), Organization for the Prohibition of Chemical Weapons (OPCW), International Hydrographic Organization (IHO), Energy Charter Conference (ECC), International Federation of Red Cross and Red Crescent Societies, Preparatory Commission for the Comprehensive Nuclear-Test-Ban Treaty Organization (CTBTO PrepCom), European and Mediterranean Plant Protection Organization (EPPO), and International Plant Genetic Resources Institute (IPGRI). *See id.*

A UN Administrative Tribunal has a similar responsibility for the United Nations, the International Civil Aviation Organization (ICAO), and the International Maritime Organization.

[94]Statute of the International Labor Organization Administrative Tribunal, Article 2.

[95]All of the Tribunal's judgments are available online at www.ilo.org/public/english/tribunal/.

[96]The judgments of the Administrative Tribunal are "final and without appeal," except that challenges to the court's jurisdiction and claims of a "fundamental fault in the procedure followed" can be appealed to the International Court of Justice. *Id.,* Articles 7 and 12.

Case 8–3   Duberg v. UNESCO

International Labor Organization Administrative Tribunal, 1955.
Judgment No. 17, *International Labor Organization Official Bulletin*, vol. 38, no. 7, p. 251 (1955).

In 1949, Peter Duberg, an American citizen, began working for the United Nations Educational, Scientific and

Cultural Organization (UNESCO) in Paris, France. In 1953, the U.S. government sent him a loyalty questionnaire that required him to swear that he was loyal to the United States and not sympathetic with any subversive organizations or ideas, including communism. When he did not return the questionnaire, the U.S. government asked him to appear before an International Employees Loyalty

MAP 8-3 France (1955)

Board at its Embassy in Paris. He refused as a matter of conscience. In 1954, the Director-General of UNESCO refused to renew his employment contract, citing Duberg's failure to appear before the Loyalty Board as the reason for doing so. The Director-General's letter of dismissal stated, "In the light of what I believe to be your duty to the Organization, I have considered very carefully your reasons for not appearing before the International Employees Loyalty Board where you would have had an opportunity of dispelling suspicions and disproving allegations which may exist regarding you." Duberg requested the Director-General to reconsider, and, while his request was being reviewed, the Chairman of the Loyalty Board wrote the Director-General that "[it] has been determined on all of the evidence that there is a reasonable doubt as to the loyalty of Norwood Peter Duberg to the government of the United States" and that "this determination, together with the reasons therefore, in as much detail as security considerations permit, are submitted for your use in exercising your rights and duties with respect to the integrity of the personnel employed by the United Nations Educational, Scientific and Cultural Organization." The Director-General refused to reconsider Duberg's employment. Duberg appealed to UNESCO's Appeals Board. The Board issued an opinion that Duberg should be rehired, but the Director-General informed the Board that he would not comply with its recommendation. Duberg appealed to the International Labor Organization's Administrative Tribunal.

THE ADMINISTRATIVE TRIBUNAL OF THE INTERNATIONAL LABOR ORGANIZATION: . . .

A.

Considering that the defendant Organization holds that the renewal or nonrenewal of a fixed-term appointment depends entirely on the personal and sovereign discretion of the Director-General, who is not even required to give his reasons therefore; . . .

B.

Considering that if the Director-General is granted authority not to renew a fixed-term appointment and so to do without notice or indemnity, this is clearly subject to the implied condition that this authority must be exercised only for the good of the service and in the interest of the Organization; . . .

* * *

E.

Considering that . . . the ground for complaint of the Director-General is based solely on the refusal of the official to participate in measures of verbal or written inquiry to which his national government considers it necessary to subject him; That the Director-General of an international organization cannot associate himself with the execution of the policy of the government authorities of any state member without disregarding the obligations imposed on all international officials without distinction and, in consequence, without misusing the authority which has been conferred on him solely for the purpose of directing that organization towards the achievement of its own, exclusively international, objectives; That this duty of the Director-General is governed by Article VI, paragraph 5, of the Constitution of the defendant Organization, in the following terms:

The responsibilities of the Director-General and of the staff shall be exclusively international in character. In the discharge of their duties they shall not seek or receive instructions from any government or from any authority external to the Organization. They shall refrain from any action which might prejudice their position as international officials. Each state member of the Organization undertakes to respect the international character of the responsibilities of the Director-General and the staff, and not to seek to influence them in the discharge of their duties;

Considering that the fact that in this case the matter involved is an accusation of disloyalty brought by a government which enjoys in all respects the highest prestige must be without any influence upon the consideration of the facts in the case and the determination of the principles whose respect the Tribunal must ensure;

That it will suffice to realize that if any of the 72 states and governments involved in the defendant Organization brought against an official, one of its citizens, an accusation of disloyalty and claimed to subject him to an inquiry in similar or analogous conditions, the attitude adopted by the Director-General would constitute a precedent obliging him to lend his assistance to such inquiry and, moreover, to invoke the same disciplinary or statutory consequences, the same withdrawal of confidence, on the basis of any opposal by the person concerned to the action of his national government; That if this were to be the case there would result for all international officials, in matters touching on conscience, a state of uncertainty and insecurity prejudicial to the performance of their duties and liable to provoke disturbances in the international administration such as cannot be imagined to have been in the intention of those who drew up the Constitution of the defendant Organization; Considering, therefore, that the only ground for complaint adduced by the Director-General to justify the application to the complainant of an exception to the general rule of renewal of appointments, that is to say his opposal to the investigations of his own government, is entirely unjustified;

* * *

Considering that it results therefrom that the decision taken must be rescinded; but that nevertheless the Tribunal does not have the power to order the renewal of a fixed-term appointment, which requires a positive act of the Director-General over whom the Tribunal has no hierarchical authority;

That in the absence of such a power, and unless the Director-General should consider himself in a position to reconsider his decision in this manner, the Tribunal

is nonetheless competent to order equitable reparation of the damage suffered by the complainant by reason of the discriminatory treatment of which he was the object; . . .

That the decision not to renew the appointment is one which should not only be rescinded in the present case, but also constitutes a wrongful exercise of powers and an abuse of rights which consequently involves the obligation to make good the prejudice resulting therefrom; that this prejudice was aggravated by the publicity given to the withdrawal of confidence as being due to lack of integrity, this ground having been given in a press communiqué issued by the defendant Organization, without it being possible seriously to maintain the view that there could have existed the slightest doubt as to the identity of the persons to which the said communiqué referred; . . .

That redress will be ensured *ex aequo et bono*[97] by the granting to the complainant of the sum set forth below;

ON THE GROUNDS AS AFORESAID— THE TRIBUNAL,

* * *

Orders the decision taken to be rescinded and declares in law that it constitutes an abuse of rights causing prejudice to the complainant;

In consequence, should the defendant not reconsider the decision taken and renew the complainant's appointment, orders the said defendant to pay the complainant the sum of 15,500 dollars, plus children's allowance for two years, the whole together with interest at 4 per centum from 1 January 1955;

Orders the defendant Organization to pay to the complainant the sum of 300 dollars by way of participation in the costs of his defense. ■

[[97]Latin: "according to what is just and good." Maxim that disputes shall be resolved amicably and by compromise and conciliation.]

The Human Rights of Workers

The basic principles underlying contemporary international labor law are found in the Universal Declaration of Human Rights and in the International Covenant on Economic, Social and Cultural Rights. Both the Declaration, which was adopted by the United Nations General Assembly in 1948, and the Covenant, adopted by the General Assembly in 1966 and in force from 1976, reflect the international community's aspiration and sensibilities following World War II.

The civilized world was shocked by the Nazi's attempt during the course of the war to annihilate all the Jews of Europe and to enslave and destroy millions of others, including Poles, gypsies, Soviet prisoners of war, homosexuals, and the mentally and physically handicapped. For many, the efforts of the Allied forces to defeat the Nazi's and their allies became synonymous with a struggle for human rights.

EXHIBIT 8-2

Eleanor Roosevelt

Eleanor Roosevelt (1884–1962), the wife of President Franklin Roosevelt (1882–1945), was one of the world's great humanitarians. Born in New York City to a socially prominent family, she married Franklin Roosevelt in 1905 and over the next 11 years gave birth to six children. During World War I she was actively involved with the Red Cross and after the war she was active in the League of Women Voters, the Women's Trade Union League, and the women's division of the Democratic Party. In 1921, her husband was stricken with polio and she became his close adviser and political stand-in in his campaigns for governor of New York in 1928 and the presidency in 1932, 1936, 1940, and 1944. As First Lady she held weekly conferences with women reporters, had her own radio program, wrote her own newspaper column, and lectured widely. Traveling around the country, she was her husband's eyes and ears and a strong advocate for the underprivileged and racial minorities. Following the death of her husband and the end of World War II, President Harry Truman made her a member of the U.S. delegation to the United Nations. As chairman of the Commission on Human Rights she was instrumental in the drafting and adoption of the

Eleanor Roosevelt with a copy of the Universal Declaration of Human Rights (Photo: UN/DPI)

Universal Declaration of Human Rights. She resigned from the UN in 1952 only to be appointed again in 1961 by President John Kennedy.

Impetus for establishing the universal recognition of basic human rights came from U.S. President Franklin D. Roosevelt's Four Freedoms speech before the United States Congress in 1941. Roosevelt's speech asserted that there were four basic freedoms that could never be legitimately abridged; freedom of speech and expression, freedom of worship, freedom from want, and freedom from fear.[98] U.K. Prime Minister Churchill likewise asserted that an Allied victory would bring about the "enthronement of human rights." In August 1941, Roosevelt and Churchill jointly issued the Atlantic Charter, announcing their goals in the war. The Charter reiterated Roosevelt's four freedoms and proclaimed that allies sought "the object of securing for all improved labor standards, economic advancement, and social security."[99]

With Germany's defeat, there was more news of Nazi atrocities and this brought about a determination to secure enduring respect for human rights. The cause was taken up at the "Conference on International Organization," held in San Francisco in April 1946, to draft a charter for the United Nations. While many human rights advocates had hoped that the Charter would contain a Bill of Rights, they were nevertheless pleased that the Charter committed the international community to protect and preserve human rights.

The Preamble to the United Nations Charter declares that human rights are one of the four founding purposes of the United Nations. Article 1 declares that member states agree to work together "in promoting and encouraging respect for human rights." Article 55 states that the UN will promote "universal respect for, and observance of, human rights and fundamental freedoms" and Article 56 says that the members "pledge themselves to take joint and separate action" to achieve that respect.

---

[98]The Four Freedom Speech is available at www.libertynet.org/~edcivic/fdr.html.
[99]The Atlantic Charter is posted on the U.S. State Department's Web site at usinfo.state.gov/usa/infousa/facts/democrac/53.htm.

Soon after the United Nations came into existence, the UN's Economic and Social Council accepted the recommendation of a "nuclear commission," chaired by Eleanor Roosevelt (see Exhibit 8-2 on page 437), and established a Commission on Human Rights. Among the Commission's first acts was the creation of a subcommittee to draft an International Bill of Rights. At the suggestion of Eleanor Roosevelt, who was aware of the political difficulties of getting a human rights treaty adopted, the subcommittee began working on a declaration—the Universal Declaration of Human Rights—to be issued by the UN General Assembly, as well as two treaties, one dealing with civil and political rights, the other the International Covenant on Economic, Social, and Cultural Rights.

The Universal Declaration of Human Rights

The Universal Declaration of Human Rights was promulgated by the General Assembly on December 10, 1946. It proclaims civil and political rights as well as economic, social, and cultural rights. The first of these—the civil and political rights—are based on the traditional Western civil liberties and political rights derived from the English Bill of Rights of 1689, the French Declaration of the Rights of Man and Citizen of 1789, the United States Bill of Rights of 1790, and similar instruments. The economic, social, and cultural rights were included at the insistence of the Soviet Union, its allies, and of other non-Western countries.

The economic, social, and cultural rights listed in the Universal Declaration of Human Rights include provisions dealing with the rights of laborers. These are expressed as follows:

Everyone has the right to:

• "freedom of peaceful assembly and association" (Article 20)

No one shall be

• "held in slavery" (Article 4)
• "subject to torture" (Article 5)
• "compelled to belong to an association" (Article 20)

Everyone has the right to:

• "social security" (Article 22)
• "work" (Article 23)
• "equal pay for equal work" (Article 23)
• "just and favorable remuneration" (Article 23)
• "form and . . . join trade unions" (Article 23)
• "rest and leisure" (Article 24)
• "a standard of living adequate for the health and well-being of himself and of his family" (Article 25)
• "education" (Article 26)

Legal Effect of the Universal Declaration of Human Rights   The Universal Declaration is not a treaty. From its beginnings, however, commentators have argued at length about whether or not it constitutes customary international law.[100] Eleanor Roosevelt campaigned in the United States for the Declaration's adoption by arguing that it was not legally binding. Some of the members in the General Assembly, however, were not so sure. South Africa and the Soviet Union, among others, expressed fears that the Declaration would impose new legal obligations, and six states joined them in abstaining from the final vote of adoption.[101]

In the years since its adoption, more and more writers have made the case that the Declaration is a statement of customary international law. Several developments can be cited in support of this argument: (1) The United Nations consistently relies on the Universal Declaration

---

[100]*See* Josef L. Kunz, "The United Nations Declaration of Human Rights," *American Journal of International Law,* vol. 43, p. 316 (1949); Egon Schwelb, "The Influence of the Universal Declaration of Human Rights on International and National Law," *American Society of International Law Proceedings,* vol. 1959, p. 217 (1959); and Richard Lillach and Frank Newman, *International Human Rights,* pp. 53–121 (1979).

[101]Howard Tolley, Jr., *The UN Commission on Human Rights,* pp. 23–24 (1987).

when it applies the human rights provisions of the UN Charter.[102] (2) The General Assembly has said that the rights delineated in the Universal Declaration "constitute basic principles of international law."[103] (3) International conferences attended by large numbers of states have adopted resolutions stating that the Universal Declaration "constitutes an obligation for the members of the international community."[104] (4) More than seventy states have incorporated the Universal Declaration in their constitutions or main laws.[105] (5) Court decisions have held that the Universal Declaration is customary international law.[106]

Among the most influential of the case decisions supporting the idea that the Universal Declaration is a statement of customary international law is the U.S. Second Circuit Court of Appeals case of *Filartiga v. Pena-Irala*.[107] That case, which dealt with issue of whether torture is a violation of international law, held that the prohibition against a state torturing its citizens "has become part of customary international law, as evidenced by the Universal Declaration of Human . . . which states in the plainest terms, "no one shall be subject to torture."

Case 8–4, which relies on the *Filartiga* decision, deals with the question of whether or not forced labor is prohibited by international law.

---

[102]Humphrey Waldock, "Human Rights in Contemporary International Law and the Significance of the European Convention," *The European Convention of Human Rights*, p. 1 at p. 14 (*International & Comparative Law, Supplementary Publication* No. 11, 1965).

[103]General Assembly Resolution 2625 (XXV) (October 24, 1970).

[104]United Nations International Conference on Human Rights at Teheran, 1968, *American Journal of International Law*, vol. 62, p. 674 (1969).

[105]The adoption of the Universal Declaration in a state's constitution has sometimes been advised by the UN Commission on Human Rights in the reports it has made following its investigation of human rights violations. Such was the case for Equatorial Guinea. Commission on Human Rights Resolution 32 (XXXVII), 1981; United Nations Doc. E/CN.4/1494 (1981).

[106]*See* Case 1–9, De Sanchez v. Banco Central de Nicaragua, *Federal Reporter, Second Series*, vol. 770, p. 1385 (5th Circuit Ct. of Appeals 1985) for a listing of cases looking to the Universal Declaration as a source of human rights law.

[107]*Federal Reporter, Second Series*, vol. 630, p. 876 (1980).

Case 8–4   Doe v. Unocal Corp.

United States District Court for the Central District of California.
Federal Supplement, Second Series, vol. 110, p. 1294 (2000).

DISTRICT JUDGE RONALD S.W. LEW:

* * *

I. Introduction

* * *

Plaintiffs allege that Unocal entered into a joint venture with Total S.A. ("Total"), a French oil company, and the Myanmar government, to extract natural gas from oil fields off the coast of Burma and to transport the gas to the Thai border via a gas pipeline. Plaintiffs further allege that Unocal is liable for international human rights violations perpetrated by the Burmese military in furtherance and for the benefit of the pipeline portion of the joint venture project.

* * *

II. Background

The Court considered all admissible evidence submitted by both parties. However, because it is neither practical nor necessary to summarize all of the evidence, the Court presents only those facts necessary to support its conclusions.

Burma's elected government was overthrown by a military government in 1958. In 1988, Burma's military government suppressed massive pro-democracy demonstrations by jailing and killing thousands of protesters and imposing martial law. At that time, a new military government took control naming itself the State Law and Order Restoration Council ("SLORC") and renaming the country Myanmar. In May 1990, SLORC held multiparty elections in which the National League for Democracy, the leading opposition party, won 80 percent of the parliamentary seats. After the elections, SLORC refused to relinquish power and jailed many political leaders.

The international community has closely scrutinized the SLORC's human rights record since it seized power in 1988. Foreign governments, international organizations, and human rights groups have criticized SLORC for committing such human rights abuses as torture, abuse of women, summary and arbitrary executions, forced labor, forced relocation, and arbitrary arrests and detentions.

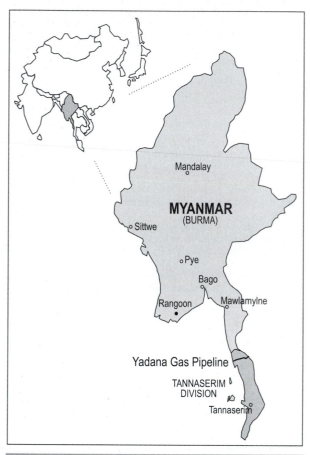

MAP 8-4 Myanmar (2000)

In 1982, large natural gas deposits that were to become known as the Yadana field were discovered in the Andaman Sea off the coast of Burma. Sometime in the late 1980s and early 1990s, Unocal conducted an oil and gas exploration in central Burma, and in or about 1991, several international oil companies, including Unocal, began negotiating with SLORC regarding oil and gas exploration in Burma. . . .

* * *

In 1992, the Myanmar government established a state-owned company, the Myanma Oil and Gas Enterprise ("MOGE"), to hold the government's inter-

est in its energy products and to produce and sell the nation's oil and gas resources. MOGE then auctioned off a license to produce, transport, and sell the natural gas discovered in the Andaman Sea. Despite Control Risk Group's report, Unocal bid on the contract but lost to the French oil company, Total. Total set up a subsidiary, Total Myanmar Exploration and Production ("TMEP"), to receive Total's interest in the contract, and on July 9, 1992, TMEP and MOGE formed the Moattama Gas Project (the "Project") by entering into two agreements: the Production Sharing Contract (the "PSC") and the Memorandum of Understanding (the "MOU," collectively the "Agreements").

The Agreements set forth the rights and obligations of the parties and established TMEP as the Operator and Contractor of the Project. The Agreements further provided that "MOGE shall assist and expedite Contractor's execution of the Work Program by providing . . . security protection and rights of way and easements as may be requested by Contractor." . . .

. . . The Agreements also provided that the Project would consist of two entities. The first entity, referred to as the Joint Venture, was responsible for the production of gas. The second entity, referred to as the Gas Transportation Company, was charged with constructing and operating the gas pipeline.

The pipeline was to run eastbound through Burma's Tenasserim region, a rural area in the southern portion of Burma that is home to "rebels" who disfavor the SLORC. Accordingly, the Myanmar military increased its presence in the pipeline region to provide security for the Project. In addition, the military prepared for a Commercial Discovery by building army barracks and helipads and clearing roads along the proposed pipeline route. Plaintiffs are Tenasserim villagers who allege that the Burmese military committed human rights violations against them in connection with the Project. According to the deposition testimony of Plaintiffs and witnesses, the military forced Plaintiffs and others, under threat of violence, to work on these projects and to serve as porters for the military for days at a time. Plaintiffs further contend that the military forced entire villages to relocate for the benefit of the pipeline project. The deposition testimony recounted numerous acts of violence perpetrated by Burmese soldiers in connection with the forced labor and forced relocations. Plaintiffs allege international law violations including torture, rape, murder, forced labor, and forced relocation . . .[108]

In 1992, Unocal and Total negotiated an assignment of a portion of Total's interest in the Project to Unocal. On November 25, 1992, Unocal made an $8.6 million offer for a 47.5 percent participating interest in Total's

---

[108]The violence perpetrated against Plaintiffs is well documented in the deposition testimony filed under seal with the Court and need not be recited in detail in this Order.

rights and interests under the Agreements, which Total accepted in December 1992. Unocal then incorporated Unocal Myanmar Offshore Company ("UMOC") to hold Unocal's interest in the Project and on January 22, 1993, UMOC acquired an undivided 47.5 percent interest in TMEP's rights under the Agreements.

During the negotiations, Unocal and Total discussed the potential problems of having the Myanmar military provide security for the Project. Stephen Lipman, Unocal's Vice President of International Affairs, testified that

> in our discussions between Unocal and Total, we said that the option of having the military provide protection for the pipeline construction and operation of it would be they might proceed in the manner that would be out of our control and not be in a manner that we would like to see them proceed, I mean, going to the excess. So we didn't know. It's an unknown, and it's something that we couldn't control. So that was the hazard we were talking about. It was out of our control if that kind of full relinquishment of security was given to the government.

* * *

In early 1995, representatives from Unocal met with Human Rights Watch ("HRW"). In this meeting, the HRW representatives told Unocal that HRW was not against investment in foreign countries, even those nations without spotless human rights records. Myanmar, though, was an exception. HRW's director informed Unocal that forced labor was "so pervasive" in the country that HRW cannot condone any investment that would enrich the current regime.

Before the trial in *Doe v. Unocal*, human's rights activists failed in their attempt to get Unocal's shareholders to adopt resolutions to withdraw from its operations in Myanmar. While the shareholder's meeting was in progress one Burmese demonstrated outside the company's headquarters. (Photo: Dang Ngo.)

A 1995 letter written by a consultant to Unocal states:

> My conclusion is that egregious human rights violations have occurred, and are occurring now, in southern Burma. The most common are forced relocation without compensation of families from land near/along the pipeline route; forced labor to work on infrastructure projects supporting the pipeline (the SLORC calls this government service in lieu of payment of taxes); and imprisonment and/or execution by the army of those opposing such actions. Unocal, by seeming to have accepted SLORC's version of events, appears at best naive and at worst a willing partner in the situation.

* * *

In April 1996, Unocal CEO Roger Beach and Unocal President John Imle visited the Project. A report was prepared, apparently for their review, which provides charts representing the amount of money paid by the Project to local "project helpers" by month. One chart documents the numbers of "villagers" hired by Army Battalions. Another chart documents money spent on food rations for the army and villagers.

A U.S. State Department cable summarizes a conversation the U.S. government official had with Unocal's Joel Robinson regarding the Project's relationship to the Myanmar military. The State Department official noted:

> Robinson acknowledged that army units providing security for the pipeline construction do use civilian porters, and Total/Unocal cannot control their recruitment process. Robinson said Total meets the porters at the marshaling camp, where a Total doctor gives them a physical exam. Some are sent home due to their poor physical condition (the companies accept only males between 18–45 years of age). Robinson said Total keeps careful records of the porters to ensure they are paid. He said these records of workers and porters showed that they had not been overly drawn from just one village, in fact, the most that had been drawn from a particular village was three.

Another State Department cable dated May 20, 1996 stated:

> Forced labor is currently being channeled, according to NGO reports, to service roads for the pipeline to Thailand. The mode of operation apparently is to build the service road first, then lay pipe alongside. There are plans for a helicopter pad and airstrip in the area . . . in part for use by oil company executives. When foreigners come on daily helicopter trips to inspect work sites, involuntary laborers are forced into the bush outside camera range.

* * *

III. Discussion

. . . Plaintiffs allege that Unocal is liable for torts committed against them by the Myanmar military for the benefit of the Project. According to Plaintiffs, Unocal, Total, and the Myanmar government formed a joint venture to produce natural gas and transport it via pipeline from the Andaman Sea to the Thai border. The Agreements executed by and between the parties placed responsibility for the security of the pipeline with the Myanmar government. The Myanmar military did provide security as well as other services for the benefit of the Project such as road clearing and the construction of helipads and army barracks.

Plaintiffs filed these related claims in the United States District Court pursuant to the Alien Tort Claims Act ("ATCA"). . . . Unocal now moves for summary judgment on all of Plaintiffs' claims.

* * *

B. The Alien Tort Claims Act

1. The Act The Alien Tort Claims Act ("ATCA"), [which is codified in *United States Code*, title 28, § 1350,] states:

> The district courts shall have original jurisdiction of any civil action by an alien for a tort only, committed in violation of the law of nations or a treaty of the United States.

The ATCA provides both subject matter jurisdiction and a cause of action.[109] To state a claim under the ATCA, a plaintiff must allege (1) a claim by an alien, (2) alleging a tort, and (3) a violation of the law of nations (international law). The parties do not dispute that the first two elements are satisfied. The issue is whether the conduct of the Myanmar military violated international law, and if so, whether Unocal is liable for these violations.

Actionable violations of international law must be of a norm that is specific, universal, and obligatory.[110] When ascertaining the content of the law of nations, the Court must interpret international law not as it was in 1789 (the year the ATCA was enacted), but as it has evolved and exists among the nations of the world today.[111] The norms of the law of nations are found by consulting juridical writings on public law, considering the general practice of nations, and referring to judicial decisions recognizing and enforcing international law.[112]

* * *

2. State Action Requirement and Individual Liability The Second Circuit's decision in *Filartiga* [*v. Pena-Irala*] marked the beginning of a new era of reliance on section 1350 in international human rights cases and was the first Circuit decision interpreting the ATCA. "Construing this rarely-invoked provision, [the Court held] that deliberate torture perpetrated under color of official authority violates universally accepted norms of international law of human rights."[113]

. . . [T]he Second Circuit's decision in *Kadic* [*v. Karadzic*] provides a reasoned analysis of the scope of the private individual's liability for violations of international law. There, the court disagreed with the proposition "that the law of nations, as understood in the modern era, confines its reach to state action. Instead, [the court held] that certain forms of conduct violate the law of nations whether undertaken by those acting under the auspices of a state or only as private individuals."[114] While crimes such as torture and summary execution are proscribed by international law only when committed by state officials or under color of law, the law of nations has historically been applied to private actors for the crimes of piracy and slave trading, and for certain war crimes.[115]

3. Liability as a State Actor "The 'color of law' jurisprudence of *United States Code*, title 42, § 1983 is a relevant guide to whether a defendant has engaged in official action for purposes of jurisdiction under the Alien Tort Claims Act."[116] A private individual acts under "color of law" within the meaning of section 1983 when he acts together with state officials or with significant state aid.

* * *

Plaintiffs argue that Unocal's participation in the Joint Venture constitutes state action under the joint action test. Under the joint action test, state action is present if a private party is a "willful participant in joint

---

[109]In re Estate of Ferdinand Marcos, Human Rights Litigation, *Federal Reporter, Third Series,* vol. 25, p. 1467 at pp. 1474–75 (9th Circuit Ct. of Appeals 1994).

[110]*Id.* at p 1475 citing Filartiga v. Pena-Irala, *Federal Reporter, Second Series,* vol. 630, p. 876 at p. 881 (2nd Circuit Ct. of Appeals 1980)); Tel-Oren v. Libyan Arab Republic, *id.,* vol. 726, p. 774 at p. 781 (District of Columbia Circuit Ct. of Appeals 1984).

[111]Kadic v. Karadzic, *Federal Reporter, Third Series,* vol. 70, p. 232 at p. 238 (2nd Circuit Ct. of Appeals 1995). . . .

[112]*Id.* at p. 241.

[113]*Federal Reporter, Second Series,* vol. 630, at p. 878.

[114]*Federal Reporter, Third Series,* vol. 70, at p. 239.

[115]*Id.* at p. 239.

[116]*Id.* at p. 245.

action with the State or its agents."[117] "Courts examine whether state officials and private parties have acted in concert in effecting a particular deprivation of constitutional rights."[118]

* * *

In *Gallagher* [*v. Neil Young Freedom Concert*, a case before the Tenth Circuit Court of Appeals] a group of concert goers sued the concert's promoter and the security guard provider under section 1983 after being subjected to a pat-down search before entering a Neil Young concert at the University of Utah. Two weeks before the concert, University officials met with the promoter and the security team to discuss security for the event. At this meeting, the promoter directed the security company to perform the type of pat-down searches generally performed by the security company at rock concerts. The Tenth Circuit concluded that the joint action test did not apply in this situation because the evidence did not show that University officials jointly participated in the pat-down searches. The Tenth Circuit commented that in applying the joint action test,

> some courts have adopted the requirements for establishing a conspiracy under Section 1983. These courts [require] that both public and private actors share a common, unconstitutional goal. Under this conspiracy approach, state action may be found if a state actor has participated in or influenced the challenged decision or action.[119]

The Tenth Circuit then stated that other courts require a "'substantial degree of cooperative action' between state and private officials." "However, some state involvement is too minimal to establish that a private actor and a state official have jointly participated in a deprivation of constitutional rights." In applying the test to the facts, the Court held that the University's silence as to the kind of security provided or its acquiescence in the practices of the parties does not establish state action under the joint action test. Moreover, the fact that the defendants and the University shared the common goal of producing a profitable music concert does not establish the necessary degree of concerted action. "Under [the joint action] approach, state and private entities must share a specific goal to violate the plaintiff's constitutional rights by engaging in a particular course of action."

Here, Plaintiffs present evidence demonstrating that before joining the Project, Unocal knew that the military had a record of committing human rights abuses; that the Project hired the military to provide security for the Project, a military that forced villagers to work and entire villages to relocate for the benefit of the Project; that the military, while forcing villagers to work and relocate, committed numerous acts of violence; and that Unocal knew or should have known that the military did commit, was committing, and would continue to commit these tortious acts. As in *Gallagher*, Unocal and SLORC shared the goal of a profitable project. However, as the *Gallagher* Court stated, this shared goal does not establish joint action. Plaintiffs present no evidence that Unocal "participated in or influenced" the military's unlawful conduct; nor do Plaintiffs present evidence that Unocal "conspired" with the military to commit the challenged conduct.

* * *

5. Forced Labor   As discussed above, individual liability under the ATCA may be established for acts rising to the level of slavery or slave trading. Plaintiffs contend that forced labor is "modern slavery" and is therefore one of the "handful of crimes" to which individual liability under section 1350 attaches. . . .

The International Labor Organization ("ILO") is the agency within the United Nations that has primary responsibility for all matters related to the rights of workers. The ILO sets international labor standards in binding treaties called Conventions. Burma joined the ILO in 1948 and has ratified 21 ILO Conventions, including Forced Labor Convention No. 29. Convention 29 prohibits the use of forced labor and defines forced labor as "all work or service which is exacted from any person under the menace of any penalty and for which the said person has not offered himself voluntarily." Over the past 40 years, the ILO has repeatedly condemned Burma's record of imposing forced labor on its people contrary to Convention 29. In 1996, for only the tenth time in its almost 80 year history, the ILO established a Commission of Inquiry to investigate allegations concerning Burma's non-compliance with Convention 29. On July 2, 1998, the Commission issued its report. This report acknowledges that the definition of slavery has historically been a narrow one, but then states that the term "slavery" now encompasses forced labor.

> In international law, the prohibition of recourse to forced labor has its origin in the efforts made by the international community to eradicate slavery, its institutions and similar practices, since forced labor is considered to be one of these slavery-like practices. . . . Although certain instruments, and particularly those adopted at the beginning of the nineteenth century,

---

[117]Dennis v. Sparks, *United States Reports*, vol. 449, p. 24 at pp. 27–28 (Supreme Ct. 1980).
[118]Gallagher v. Neil Young Freedom Concert, *Federal Reporter, Third Series*, vol. 49, p. 1442 at p. 1453 (10th Cir. 1995). . . .
[119]*Id.* at p. 1454.

define slavery in a restrictive manner, the prohibition of slavery must now be understood as covering all contemporary manifestations of this practice.[120]

[In this case there] is ample evidence in the record linking the Myanmar government's use of forced labor to human rights abuses. . . . Moreover, there is an issue of fact as to whether the forced labor was used to benefit the Project as opposed to the public's welfare.

6. Unocal's Role in the Forced Labor   To prevail on their ATCA claim against Unocal, Plaintiffs must establish that Unocal is legally responsible for the Myanmar military's forced labor practices. Plaintiffs contend that under international law principles of direct and vicarious liability, Unocal is legally responsible for the Myanmar military's forced labor practices. . . .

Plaintiffs . . . argue that *Iwanowa v. Ford Motor Co.*[121] supports their argument that Unocal is liable for the Myanmar military's forced labor practices. In *Iwanowa*, the plaintiff alleged that after being abducted by Nazi troops and transported from Rostov, Russia to Germany, Ford Werke, a German subsidiary of Ford Motor Co., purchased her and forced her to perform heavy labor from 1942 until Germany surrendered in 1945. The district court denied Ford's motion to dismiss

for lack of jurisdiction, finding there to be jurisdiction for the plaintiff's claims of slave labor under the ATCA. The court held that Ford Werke's "use of unpaid, forced labor during World War II violated clearly established norms of customary international law."

In this case, there are no facts suggesting that Unocal sought to employ forced or slave labor. In fact, the Joint Venturers expressed concern that the Myanmar government was utilizing forced labor in connection with the Project. In turn, the military made efforts to conceal its use of forced labor. The evidence does suggest that Unocal knew that forced labor was being utilized and that the Joint Venturers benefited from the practice. However, because such a showing is insufficient to establish liability under international law, Plaintiffs' claim against Unocal for forced labor under the Alien Tort Claims Act fails as a matter of law.

* * *

IV. Conclusion

For the reasons set forth above, Unocal's motion for summary judgment as to Plaintiffs' federal claims is GRANTED. . . . ■

---

[120]"Forced Labor in Myanmar (Burma): Report of the Commission of Inquiry Appointed Under Article 26 of the Constitution of the International Labor Organization to Examine the Observance by Myanmar of the Forced Labor Convention, 1930 (No. 29)," ILO, Part IV.9.A. p. 198 (1998).

[121]*Federal Supplement, Second Series*, vol. 67. p. 424 (District Court for the District of New Jersey 1999).

International Covenant on Economic, Social, and Cultural Rights

The International Covenant on Economic, Social, and Cultural Rights was adopted by the UN General Assembly on December 18, 1966. It entered into force on January 3, 1976. Currently, 145 states are parties to the Covenant,[122] including the member countries of European Union, Brazil, China, India, Japan, and Russia; but not the United States.[123]

---

[122]As of July 10, 2002, the states parties were: Afghanistan, Albania, Algeria, Angola, Argentina, Armenia, Australia, Austria, Azerbaijan, Bangladesh, Barbados, Belarus, Belgium, Benin, Bolivia, Bosnia and Herzegovina, Brazil, Bulgaria, Burkina Faso, Burundi, Cambodia, Cameroon, Canada, Cape Verde, Central African Republic, Chad, Chile, China, Colombia, Congo, Costa Rica, Côte d'Ivoire, Croatia, Cyprus, Czech Republic, Democratic Republic of the Congo, Denmark, Dominica, Dominican Republic, Ecuador, Egypt, El Salvador, Equatorial Guinea, Eritrea, Estonia, Ethiopia, Finland, France, Gabon, Gambia, Georgia, Germany, Ghana, Greece, Grenada, Guatemala, Guinea, Guinea-Bissau, Guyana, Honduras, Hungary, Iceland, India, Iran, Iraq, Ireland, Israel, Italy, Jamaica, Japan, Jordan, Kenya, Kuwait, Kyrgyzstan, Latvia, Lebanon, Lesotho, Libya, Liechtenstein, Lithuania, Luxembourg, Macedonia, Madagascar, Malawi, Mali, Malta, Mauritius, Mexico, Moldova, Monaco, Mongolia, Morocco, Namibia, Nepal, Netherlands, New Zealand, Nicaragua, Niger, Nigeria, North Korea, Norway, Panama, Paraguay, Peru, Philippines, Poland, Portugal, Romania, Russia, Rwanda, Saint Vincent and the Grenadines, San Marino, Senegal, Seychelles, Sierra Leone, Slovakia, Slovenia, Solomon Islands, Somalia, South Korea, Spain, Sri Lanka, Sudan, Suriname, Sweden, Switzerland, Syria, Tajikistan, Tanzania, Thailand, Togo, Trinidad and Tobago, Tunisia, Turkmenistan, Uganda, Ukraine, United Kingdom, Uruguay, Uzbekistan, Venezuela, Vietnam, Yemen, Yugoslavia, Zambia, and Zimbabwe. UN High Commissioner for Human Rights, "Status of Ratifications of the Principal International Human Rights Treaties (July 10, 2002) posted at www.unhchr.ch/pdf/report.pdf.

[123]Conservatives in the United States government have opposed the Covenant for a variety of reasons. Originally, segregationists saw it as a device for ending segregation. Later, economic conservatives looked upon the Covenant as an assault on capitalism. During the administration of Ronald Reagan (1981–1989), Secretary of State Alexander Haig approved a memorandum that denied that economic, social, and cultural rights were "rights." The memorandum stated that U.S. foreign policy regarded human rights as "meaning political rights and civil liberties" only and

The Covenant implements the rights set out in the Universal Declaration of Human Rights and gives them the binding force of treaty law. The extent to which the provisions apply, however, varies from country-to-county. Article 2(1) provides:

> Each State Party to the present Covenant undertakes to take steps, individually and through international assistance and cooperation, especially economic and technical, to the maximum of its available resources, with a view to achieving progressively the full realization of the rights recognized in the present Covenant by all appropriate means, including in particular the adoption of legislative measures.

In other words, countries that ratify the Covenant do not undertake to give immediate effect to its provisions. Rather, a country only commits itself to taking steps "to the maximum of its available resources" to achieve "progressively the full realization" of those provisions.

D. REGIONAL INTERGOVERNMENTAL REGULATIONS ON LABOR

Workers' rights are protected by a variety of regional intergovernmental organizations. Among those that are the most active in advancing the interests of labor are the European Union, the Organization for Economic Cooperation and Development, and the Council of Europe.

Employment Laws in the European Union

EU freedom of movement for workers: Right of member state nationals to seek and accept employment throughout the European Union.

The **freedom of movement of workers** between the member states of the European Union is a basic tenet in the treaties that constitute the fundamental instruments creating the Union.[124] The European Atomic Energy Community forbids any restrictions based on nationality in the employment of qualified workers in the atomic energy industry.[125] Treaty Establishing the European Community (EC Treaty), which is meant to promote the comprehensive economic integration of EU member states, provides that "freedom of movement for workers shall be secured" within the European Union.[126]

Article 39 of the EC Treaty allows workers, no matter what their occupations, to accept offers of employment and to remain in any member state to carry out that employment.[127] Article 40 authorizes the EU Council to remove and harmonize administrative procedures that obstruct the free movement of workers and to set up the machinery necessary to match job hunters in one state with job offers in another. Article 42 grants the Council the power to "adopt such measures in the field of social security as are necessary to provide freedom of movement for workers."[128]

---

it directed members of the administration to "move away from 'human rights' as a term, and [to] begin to speak of 'individual rights,' 'political rights,' and 'civil liberties.'" Memorandum quoted in Hurst Hannum and Dana D. Fischer, eds., *U.S. Ratification of the International Covenants on Human Rights*, p. 15 (1993).

[124]For current information on the status of the movement of workers in the European Union *see* the European Parliament's Fact Sheet on the Freedom of Movement of Workers on the Parliament's Web site at www.europarl.eu.int/factsheets/3_2_2_en.htm.

[125]European Atomic Energy Community Treaty, Article 48.

[126]Treaty Establishing the European Community, Article 39 (formerly Article 48).

[127]*Id.,* Article 39, provides:

"1. Freedom of movement for workers shall be secured within the [Union]. . . .

"2. Such freedom of movement shall entail the abolition of any discrimination based on nationality between workers of the member states as regards employment, remuneration and other conditions of work and employment.

"3. It shall entail the right, subject to limitations justified on grounds of public policy, public security, or public health: (a) to accept offers of employment actually made; (b) to move freely within the territory of member states for this purpose; (c) to stay in a member state for the purposes of employment in accordance with the provisions governing the employment of nationals of that state laid down by law, regulation or administrative action; (d) to remain in the territory of a member state after having been employed in that state, subject to conditions which shall be embodied in implementing regulations to be drawn up by the Commission.

"4. The provisions of this Article shall not apply to employment in the public service."

[128]Articles 40 and 42 were previously numbered 49 and 51 prior to renumbering of the Treaty Establishing the European Community agreed to by the Treaty of Amsterdam. For a table of equivalencies *see* Annex IV of the Treaty of Amsterdam at europa.eu.int/eur-lex/en/treaties/selected/livre550.html.

In 1968, the Council of Ministers enacted Directive 68/360 to implement the EC Treaty provisions on the free movement of workers. The directive guarantees workers (and their families)[129] the right to leave their own country and to enter any other member state both to take up and to search for a job.[130] Workers must produce an identity card or passport, but no exit or entry visa can be required. And workers who secure employment are entitled to an automatically renewable residence permit allowing them to remain within a member state for at least 5 years, subject only to the requirement that they do not voluntarily quit their job or absent themselves from the country for a prolonged period.[131]

Article 39(2) of the EC Treaty states that workers who are citizens of a member state cannot be treated differently because of their nationality.[132] This guarantee is implemented by Regulation 1612/68, which declares that national laws and administrative rules are void to the extent they explicitly or implicitly limit the right of a worker to take up and pursue employment. Examples of improper requirements that relate to the finding of a job include those which

1. prescribe a special recruitment procedure for foreign nationals;
2. limit or restrict the advertising of vacancies in the press or through any other medium or subject it to conditions other than those applicable in respect of employers pursuing their activities in the territory of that member state; and
3. subject eligibility for employment to conditions of registration with employment offices or impede recruitment of individual workers where persons who do not reside in the territory of that state are concerned.[133]

Once a worker has found employment, discrimination in the amount of "remuneration" is improper. Thus, a foreign worker is entitled to "enjoy the same social and tax advantages as national workers"[134] and to "enjoy all the rights and benefits accorded to national workers in matters of housing, including the ownership of the housing he needs."[135] Finally, foreign workers may not be treated differently in the manner in which they are dismissed or in their "reinstatement or reemployment" if they have become unemployed.[136]

The right of workers to move freely across the borders of EU member states is subject to three broad limitations: Travel can be denied on the grounds of public policy, public security, and public health.[137] However, these limitations apply only to the right to enter or leave a member state and not to the right of equal treatment once a worker has been admitted to a state.[138]

The scope of these limitations was narrowed gradually in the 1970s and 1980s in a series of cases decided by the European Court of Justice. In 1974 in the case of *Van Duyn v. Home Office*, the Court recognized that a member state had the right to restrict the entry of a foreign national for public policy reasons.[139] The next year in *Rutili v. French Minister of the Interior*,

---

[129]A worker's family is defined by Regulation 1612/68 as "(a) his spouse and their descendants who are under the age of 21 years or are dependents; (b) dependent relatives in the ascending line of the worker and his spouse."

[130]The right to search for a job is not expressly contained in either article 39 of the EC Treaty or in Directive 68/360. However, in construing both the Treaty and the Directive, the European Court of Justice, in Procurer du Roi v. Royer, Case 48/75, *European Court Reports*, vol. 1976, p. 496 (1976), stated that a worker had the right to enter the territory of any member state to "look for" employment.

[131]Workers looking for employment are allowed three months to find a job.

[132]Treaty Establishing the European Community, Article 39(2).

[133]European Union, Regulation 1612/68, Article 3.

[134]*Id.*, Article 9. Some of the social advantages that foreign workers are entitled to include guaranteed minimum subsistence allowance (Hoeckx, Case 249/83, *European Court Reports*, vol. 1985, p. 973 [1985]); old-age benefits for individuals without a pension entitlement under the national social security system (Frascogna, Case 157/84, judgment of June 6, 1985); and a guaranteed minimum income for the elderly (Castelli, Case 261/83, *European Court Reports*, vol. 1984, p. 3199 [1984]).

[135]European Union, Regulation 1612/68, Article 9(1).

[136]*Id.*, Article 7.

[137]Treaty Establishing the European Community, Article 39(3).

[138]"On the grounds of public policy or public security a foreigner may not be permitted to enter a country and take up employment there, but those considerations have no bearing on conditions of work once employment has been taken up in an authorized manner." Advocate General Gand in Ugioli, Case 15/69, *European Court Reports*, vol. 1969, p. 369 (1969).

[139]Case 41/74, *European Court Reports*, vol. 1974, p. 1337 (1974).

the Court stated that "restrictions cannot be imposed on the right of a national of any member state to enter the territory of another member state, to stay there [or] to move within it unless his presence or conduct constitutes a *genuine and sufficiently serious threat* to public policy."[140] Then in 1977, the Court added that the genuine and serious threat had to affect "one of the fundamental interests of society."[141] Finally, in 1981 in *Adoni*, the Court defined the fundamental interests of society as those listed in the European Convention on Human Rights, which, it pointed out, has been ratified by all the member states.[142]

A final limitation to the free movement of workers is found in a clause in Article 39 of the EC Treaty that states that the "provisions of this Article shall not apply to employment in the public service." This does not mean that foreign nationals are forbidden from working in any job in the public service, nor does it allow discrimination in the terms and conditions of employment once a worker has been hired. The public service limitation applies only to jobs that are related to the activity of governing. In *Commission v. Belgium (No. 1)*, the Court of Justice said: "Such posts in fact presume on the part of those occupying them the existence of a special relationship of allegiance to the state and reciprocity of rights and duties which form the foundation of the bond of nationality."[143] In *Commission v. Belgium (No. 2)*, the Court gave examples of public service and nonpublic service jobs. Head technical office supervisor, principal supervisor, works supervisor, and stock controller for the municipalities of Brussels and Auderghem fell within the first group, while railway shunters, drivers, platelayers, signalmen and nightwatchmen, nurses, electricians, joiners, and plumbers employed by the same municipalities fell in the second group.[144]

Employment Standards of the Organization for Economic Cooperation and Development

The Organization for Economic Cooperation and Development (OECD)[145] has worked to better the working standards of laborers. In order "to encourage the positive contributions" of multinational enterprises (MNEs), "to minimize and resolve the difficulties" that can arise out of their operations, and "to contribute to improving the foreign investment climate," the **OECD's Guidelines for Multinational Enterprises** establishes norms for the employment of workers in both home and host countries. These norms are as follows:

> **OECD Guidelines for Multinational Enterprises:** Norms suggested by the OECD for the operation of multinational firms both in home and host states.

EMPLOYMENT AND INDUSTRIAL RELATIONS

Enterprises should, within the framework of law, regulations, and prevailing labor relations and employment practices, in each of the countries in which they operate:

1. respect the right of their employees to be represented by trade unions and other bona fide organizations of employees, and engage in constructive negotiations, either individually or through employers' associations, with such employee organizations with a view to reaching agreements on employment conditions, which should include provisions for dealing with disputes and for ensuring mutually respected rights and responsibilities;

2. (a) provide such facilities to representatives of the employees as may be necessary to assist in the development of effective collective agreements; (b) provide to representatives of employees information which is needed for meaningful negotiations on conditions of employment;

3. provide to representatives of employees where this accords with local law and practice, information which enables them to obtain a true and fair view of the performance of the entity or, where appropriate, the enterprise as a whole;

4. observe standards of employment and industrial relations not less favorable than those observed by comparable employers in the host country;

---

[140]Case 36/75, *id.,* vol. 1975, p. 1219 (1975). (Emphasis added.)
[141]Regina v. Bouchereau, Case 30/77, *id.,* vol. 1977, p. 1999 (1977).
[142]Cases 115 and 116/81, *id.,* vol. 1982, p. 1665 (1982).
[143]Case 149/79, No. 1, *id.,* vol. 1980, p. 3881 (1980).
[144]Case 149/79, No. 2, *id.,* vol. 1982, p. 1845 (1982).
[145]The OECD's Web site is at www.oecd.org.

5. in their operations, to the greatest extent practicable, utilize, train and prepare for upgrading members of the local labor force in cooperation with representatives of their employees and, where appropriate, the relevant governmental authorities;

6. in considering changes in their operations which would have major effects upon the livelihood of their employees, in particular in the case of the closure of an entity involving collective layoffs or dismissals, provide reasonable notice of such changes to representatives of their employees, and where appropriate to the relevant governmental authorities, and cooperate with the employee representative and appropriate governmental authorities so as to mitigate to the maximum extent practicable adverse effects;

7. implement their employment policies including hiring, discharge, pay, promotion, and training without discrimination unless selectivity in respect of employee characteristics is in furtherance of established governmental policies which specifically promote greater equality of employment opportunity;

8. in the context of bona fide negotiations with representatives of employees on conditions of employment or while employees are exercising a right to organize, not threaten to utilize a capacity to transfer the whole or part of an operating unit from the country concerned in order to influence unfairly those negotiations or to hinder the exercise of a right to organize;

9. enable authorized representatives of their employees to conduct negotiations on collective bargaining or labor management relations issues with representatives of management who are authorized to make decisions on the matters under negotiation.[146]

Although the Guidelines are only voluntary, they have had some influence because they establish, in essence, minimum international standards. Companies that fall below these standards are put in an awkward position when dealing with local governments, local unions, and the local and international media.

Protection of Workers' Rights by the Council of Europe

European Convention on Human Rights of 1950: Establishes and guarantees civil and political rights for the nationals of the member states of the Council of Europe.

The Council of Europe is responsible for enforcing the **European Convention on Human Rights of 1950**[147] and the European Social Charter of 1961.[148] The Human Rights Convention is concerned mainly with civil and political rights, whereas the Social Charter deals primarily with economic, social, and cultural rights. Despite the division in emphasis, there is some overlap between the two treaties.

In particular, the Human Rights Convention includes, as part of its guarantee of freedom of assembly, the right to join a trade union. Article 11 of the Convention provides as follows:

1. Everyone has the right to freedom of peaceful assembly and to freedom of association with others, including the right to join trade unions for the protection of his interests.

2. No restrictions shall be placed on the exercise of these rights other than such as are prescribed by law and are necessary in a democratic society in the interests of national security or public safety, for the prevention of disorder or crime, for the protection of health or morals, or for the protection of the rights and freedoms of others. This Article shall not prevent the imposition of lawful restrictions on the exercise of these rights by members of the armed forces, of the police or of the administration of the State.

---

[146]"Guidelines for Multinational Enterprises," Declaration on International Investment and Multinational Enterprises by the Governments of the OECD Member Countries (June 21, 1976). The Guidelines and information about their application are available on the OECD's Web site at www.oecd.org/EN/home/0,,EN-home-93-3-no-no-no,00.html.

[147]*European Treaty Series*, No. 5 (1950). Forty-one states were parties as of 1999. *See* Council of Europe, Chart of Signatures and Ratifications, Convention for the Protection of Human Rights and Fundamental Freedoms, posted on the Council of Europe Web site at www.coe.fr/tablconv/5t.htm.

[148]*United Nations Treaty Series*, vol. 529, p. 90. There were 22 parties as of 1999. *See* Council of Europe, Chart of Signatures and Ratifications, European Social Charter, posted at www.coe.fr/tablconv/35t.htm.

European Social Charter of 1961: Establishes and guarantees economic, social, and cultural rights for the nationals of the member states of the Council of Europe.

Much broader provisions protecting the rights of workers are found in the **European Social Charter.**[149] Part I lays out, in general terms, the "rights and principles" that the Charter aims to protect:

1. Everyone shall have the opportunity to earn his living in an occupation freely entered upon.
2. All workers have the right to just conditions of work.
3. All workers have the right to safe and healthy working conditions.
4. All workers have the right to a fair remuneration sufficient for a decent standard of living for themselves and their families.
5. All workers and employees have the right to freedom of association in national or international organizations for the protection of their economic and social interests.
6. All workers and employers have the right to bargain collectively.
7. Children and young persons have the right to a special protection against the physical and moral hazards to which they are exposed.
8. Employed women, in case of maternity, and other employed women as appropriate, have the right to a special protection in their work.
9. Everyone has the right to appropriate facilities for vocational guidance with a view to helping him choose an occupation suited to his personal aptitude and interests.
10. Everyone has the right to appropriate facilities for vocational training.
11. Everyone has the right to benefit from any measures enabling him to enjoy the highest possible standard of health attainable.
12. All workers and their dependents have the right to social security.
13. Anyone without adequate resources has the right to social and medical assistance.
14. Everyone has the right to benefit from social welfare services.
15. Disabled persons have the right to vocational training, rehabilitation, and resettlement, whatever the origin and nature of their disability.
16. The family as a fundamental unit of society has the right to appropriate social, legal, and economic protection to ensure its full development.
17. Mothers and children, irrespective of marital status and family relations, have the right to appropriate social and economic protection.
18. The nationals of any one of the contracting parties have the right to engage in any gainful occupation in the territory of any one of the others on a footing of equality with the nationals of the latter, subject to restrictions based on cogent economic or social reasons.
19. Migrant workers who are nationals of a contracting party and their families have the right to protection and assistance in the territory of any other contracting party.

Part II contains articles describing in detail these rights and principles. For example, Article 4 describes the "Right to a Fair Remuneration" as follows:

With a view to ensuring the effective exercise of the right to a fair remuneration the contracting parties undertake:

1. to recognize the right of workers to a remuneration such as will give them and their families a decent standard of living;
2. to recognize the right of workers to an increased rate of remuneration for overtime work, subject to exceptions in particular cases;
3. to recognize the right of men and women workers to equal pay for work of equal value;

---

[149]It is reproduced in *United Nations Treaty Series*, vol. 529, p. 90 (1965). The Charter, signed on October 18, 1961, came into force on February 26, 1965.

4. to recognize the right of all workers to a reasonable period of notice for termination of employment;

5. to permit deductions from wages only under conditions and to the extent prescribed by national laws or regulations or fixed by collective agreements or arbitration awards.

The exercise of these rights shall be achieved by freely concluded collective agreements, by statutory wage-fixing machinery, or by other means appropriate to national conditions.

Part III of the European Social Charter sets out the specific obligations that the contracting parties must undertake after ratifying the Charter. They are not required to adhere to all 19 "rights and principles" described in Parts I and II. Rather, they must adhere to "at least" 10 articles or 45 numbered paragraphs.[150] This formulation has created a bizarre maze of adoptions.

For example, paragraph 3 of Article 4 (which establishes the right to equal pay for equal work) has been adopted in about half the contracting states and ignored in the other half. Articles 1, 3, 5, 6, 13, 14, 15, 16, and 17, on the other hand, have been adopted in their entirety by nearly all the parties.

Transnational Organized Labor

Transnational labor unions, with the ability to represent employees across international boundaries, can exist only where intergovernmental organizations have the power to sanction them. Both the European Union and the Council of Europe have such power. Although the EU has yet to authorize the establishment of any transnational labor unions, the Council of Europe's European Social Charter specifically provides for them. Article 5 declares that the "Right to Organize" includes "the freedom of workers and employers to form local, national or international organizations for the protection of their economic and social conditions and to join such organizations." As noted earlier, Article 5 has been adopted by nearly all of the states that have ratified the Social Charter.

Several transnational labor organizations have been set up as coordinating bodies by municipal labor unions. They are designed to encourage cooperative action, to support national organizations, and to advocate the rights of workers before regional IGOs. Two reasonably successful examples are the International Secretariat of the World Auto Council and the European Confederation of Trade Unions. In addition to exchanging information about labor conditions and advocating labor issues, transnational labor organizations have been actively involved in collecting and disbursing "solidarity funds" to support national labor actions.

E. MOVEMENT OF WORKERS

The Universal Declaration of Human Rights, promulgated by the United Nations in 1948, states that "everyone has the right to leave any country, including his own, and to return to his country."[151] This is not, however, the generally accepted rule in international law today. Many

---

[150]European Social Charter, Article 20(1), states: "Each of the contracting parties undertakes: (a) to consider Part I of this Charter as a declaration of aims to which it will pursue by all appropriate means, as stated in the introductory paragraph of that Part; (b) to consider itself bound by at least five of the following Articles of Part II of the Charter: Articles 1, 5, 6, 12, 13, 16, and 19; (c) in addition to the Articles selected by it in accordance with the preceding subparagraph, to consider itself bound by such a number of Articles or numbered paragraphs of Part II of the Charter as it may select, provided that the total number of Articles or numbered paragraphs by which it is bound is not less than 10 Articles or 45 numbered paragraphs."

[151]Universal Declaration of Human Rights, Article 13(2) (1948). A more detailed provision is contained in the International Covenant on Civil and Political Rights (1966). Article 12 provides:

"1. Everyone lawfully within the territory of a State shall, within that territory, have the right to liberty of movement and freedom to choose his residence.

"2. Everyone shall be free to leave any country, including his own.

"3. The above-mentioned rights shall not be subject to any restrictions except those which are provided by law, are necessary to protect national security, public order, public health or morals, or the rights and freedoms of others, and are consistent with the other rights recognized in the present Covenant.

"No one shall be arbitrarily deprived of the right to enter his own country."

passport: A warrant of protection and authority to travel between nations.

countries require that their citizens have a **passport** and permission from the government before traveling abroad. The U.S. government, for example, has repeatedly held that American citizens do not have a right to have a passport or a right to leave the country.[152] In the case of *Haig v. Agee*,[153] the U.S. Supreme Court observed:

> A passport is, in a sense, a letter of introduction in which the issuing sovereign vouches for the bearer and requests other sovereigns to aid the bearer. . . .
>
> With the enactment of travel control legislation making a passport generally a requirement for travel abroad, a passport took on certain added characteristics. Most important for present purposes, the only means by which an American can lawfully leave the country or return to it—absent a Presidentially granted exception—is with a passport. . . . As a travel control document, a passport is both proof of identity and proof of allegiance to the United States. Even under a travel control statute, however, a passport remains in a sense a document by which the government vouches for the bearer and for his conduct. . . .
>
> Revocation of a passport undeniably curtails travel, but the freedom to travel abroad with a "letter of introduction" in the form of a passport issued by the sovereign is subordinate to national security and foreign policy considerations; as such, it is subject to reasonable governmental regulations. The Court has made it plain that the *freedom* to travel outside the United States must be distinguished from the *right* to travel within the United States.[154]

A similar rule was applied in the United Kingdom before it joined the European Community (now the European Union) on January 1, 1973. Until that time, passports could not be obtained as a matter of right, and a passport, once granted, could be impounded or canceled at any time. The European Union requires its member states to issue and renew passports valid for travel throughout the EU, and it forbids member states from requiring exit visas or equivalent documents for travel to other EU member states.[155] To the extent that the EU rules do not apply (i.e., to travel outside the Union), U.K. law still regards the issuance of a passport as a matter of "royal prerogative."[156]

Case 8–5 illustrates how one country justifies its restrictions on issuing passports.

---

[152]American citizens, however, may hold passports from other countries, as can the nationals of most states.
[153]*United States Reports*, vol. 453, p. 280 (Supreme Ct., 1981).
[154]*Id.,* at pp. 293–306.
[155]EC Directive 68/360 (October 15, 1968), *Official Journal*, p. L257/13 (1968).
[156]*See* David E. Williams, "British Passports and the Right to Travel," *International Comparative Law Quarterly*, vol. 23, p. 642, at pp. 647–648, 652–653 (1974).

Case 8–5　State v. Nagami

Japan, Nagasaki District Court, 1968.
Criminal Case 267, *Hanreijiho*, No. 599, p. 8 (1968); *Japanese Annual of International Law*, No. 16, p. 103 (1972).

Akie Nagami, a Japanese national, sought to obtain a Japanese passport that would allow her to visit China with her husband, Earle L. Reynolds, a United States national. Nagami and Reynolds were activists in the world peace movement and they hoped to visit the People's Republic of China to promote understanding between China, Japan, and the United States. Japan did not recognize China at this

time, and its Passport Law required nationals who wanted to visit an unrecognized country to obtain and attach to their passport applications an entrance permit from the particular country. Nagami was unable to obtain an entrance permit from China; and Japan, accordingly, refused to grant her a passport endorsed for entrance into China. Undaunted, Nagami and Reynolds sailed for China on Reynolds' yacht anyway. The Nagasaki harbor police, having had notice that this might happen, arrested both Nagami and Reynolds, charging her with leaving the country without a valid passport, and him with being an accessory to her crime. At their trial, the accused argued that denying a

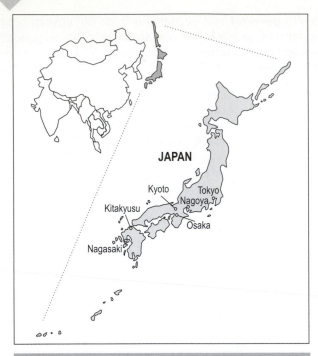

MAP 8-5 Japan (1968)

person a passport is a breach of a fundamental human right as well as a breach of the Japanese constitutional provision establishing the right to travel.

JUDGMENT OF THE COURT:

* * *

Article 3 of the Passport Law specifies the papers that an applicant must submit to the Foreign Minister in order to obtain a passport. . . .

The Court will now consider whether this provision [i.e., Article 3] gives too much discretion to the Foreign Minister to restrict the freedom of travel to foreign countries. . . .

Because this provision imposes a substantial restriction on a fundamental human right—the right of an individual to travel freely to foreign countries—it has to be narrowly interpreted. Because a passport serves not only to identify an individual and establish his nationality, but also as a letter from a government asking another government to ensure the care and safety of a traveler, it is appropriate to conclude that procedures established by the Passport Law are meant to ensure that the bearer will be safe and secure in the country being visited. In this respect, Article 19(1)(4) of the Passport Law specifically provides that the Foreign Minister or a consular official may demand that an individual return a passport in circumstances where the Minister or official believes that the individual's life, person, or property are at risk. It seems appropriate, accordingly, that if an individual is subject to these same risks at

the time that he applies for a passport, that the passport need not be given him.

The government's evidence establishes that it has long followed the practice of requiring nationals who want to visit a country with which Japan has no diplomatic relations to obtain and attach to their passport applications an entrance permit from that country. Several reasons are given for this practice. First, entrance into a country with which Japan does not have diplomatic relations may prove difficult for an individual who has not made advance arrangement. Second, after a person enters an unrecognized foreign state, it is not possible for the government to protect them or provide them with any assistance.

Considering that the practice of requiring applicants seeking to enter an unrecognized country to obtain an entrance permit is long standing, that the procedure is consistent with the general purpose of the Passport Law, and that there are good reasons for imposing this requirement, one cannot conclude that the discretionary authority given to the Foreign Minister in Article 3(1)(7) is overly broad or that it has been misused.

The Court will now consider whether the regulations of the Foreign Minister implementing Article 3(1)(7) of the Passport Law violate the guarantee set out in Article 22(2) of the Constitution, which establishes that freedom of travel is a fundamental right, or whether those regulations are an exception to that guarantee permitted by the Constitution's public welfare clause. We must begin by observing that the freedom of movement is not an unlimited or unrestricted right. We also observe that a restriction on a fundamental right in the interest of public welfare is allowed if it is based on substantial and rational reasons, and is not unduly burdensome.

The Foreign Minister's regulations, we note, are clear cut and succinct: they forbid travel to the People's Republic of China by anyone who cannot obtain an entrance permit from that country's government. While it may be difficult to obtain this authorization, it is not impossible. The government's evidence established that more than 3,000 Japanese visited China in 1968, having first received entrance permits. Consequently, it cannot be said that the procedure established by the Foreign Minister's regulations is unduly burdensome. Also, because the purpose of the regulations is to insure that travelers are safe in their person and property, it is obvious that they are based on substantial reasons and reasons rationally related to objectives of the Passport Law.

. . . The accused contend that it is irrational to punish individuals who do not wish to have the protection of their government, especially when that protection is realistically unavailable. In this regard, it has to be noted that Japan, which is a signatory of a Security Treaty with United States, follows the U.S. lead in international relations, and, as a consequence, is opposed internationally to China. . . . It is also a fact, as established by the government's evidence, that the People's Republic of China has not given adequate protection to the Japanese who reside there. As a consequence, the probability that Japanese visitors will be in danger in China is very high.

The contention that protection should not be forced on persons who do not want it is untenable for the following reasons. First, the government has the responsibility—which it cannot relinquish—of ensuring the safety and security of Japanese who are abroad, and it was quite proper in this case that it took an interest in the accused and attempted to protect them from the dangers which they were very likely to face in the People's Republic of China. . . . Second, an important reason why the govern-

ment is concerned with the safety of persons traveling overseas . . . is that foreign travel has, by its nature, a close connection with international relations and national security. In this regard, we cannot ignore the historical fact that the persecution or injury of nationals in foreign countries has often produced international tension. In sum, the government, in restricting the foreign travel of nationals, is acting both out of concern for the safety of the individual and also for the country's national security.

For these reasons, we hold that the Foreign Minister, acting out of concern for the public welfare, acted properly in restricting the travel of [Akie Nagami]. . . .

Akie Nagami was fined 50,000 yen. Her husband, Earle L. Reynolds, having been an accessory, was fined 30,000 yen. ■

Visas

visa: Formal authorization to enter a country.

Visas are a host state's counterpart of the passport. They grant permission for an alien to enter a country. As with passports, issuance is discretionary with the host state, and both the length of time that an alien may stay in a country and the activities the alien may carry on while there can be limited. With respect to their duration, visas are classified as either temporary or permanent. An alien who receives a temporary visa is expected to leave the country after a stated time period. An alien who receives a permanent visa is allowed to stay indefinitely, and often an alien who seeks a permanent visa is expecting to apply for nationalization.

Commonly, an alien who wishes to obtain a visa must go to a state's overseas embassies or consulates and make an application before traveling to the state. An alien who is already inside a host state and has questions about his visa or wants to change from one kind of visa to another needs to contact the state's immigration service. For example, in the United States this is known as the Immigration and Naturalization Service, in Canada it is called Citizenship and Immigration Canada, and in the United Kingdom it is called the Immigration and Nationality Directorate.[157]

Some countries, especially developing countries, allow aliens to obtain a visa upon their arrival in the country. When this is the case, aliens have a duty to contact the immigration service within a reasonable period of time to obtain a visa, as Case 8–6 points out.

---

[157]For information about U.S. immigration laws and policies, visit the U.S. Immigration and Naturalization Service's home page at www.ins.usdoj.gov/. The United Kingdom's Immigration and Nationality Directorate home page is at www.homeoffice.gov.uk/ind/hpg.htm. Canada's Citizenship and Immigration Canada bureau's home page is at cic-net.ci.gc.ca/. Information on other countries' immigration laws and policies can be obtained from their embassies. For a list of embassy home pages, *see* the Yahoo! listing at dir.yahoo.com/Government/ Embassies_and_ Consulates/.

Case 8–6   *Republic v. Mussa and Five Others*

Malawi, High Court, 1974.
Malawi Law Reports, vol. 7, p. 320 (1974).

Mr. Mussa drove his vehicle across the border between the Portuguese colony of East Africa (which became

Mozambique in 1975) and the Republic of Malawi, at a place near Sopi, on his way from one part of Portuguese East Africa to another. The vehicle, which was full of merchandise, also carried three of Mr. Mussa's servants (Karim, Sedqve, and Mambal) and two casual passengers

MAP 8-6 Malawi and Portuguese East Africa (1974)

(Bernet and Bakali). The six occupants of the vehicle were all subjects of Portuguese East Africa.

A police officer stopped the vehicle in the Phalombe area and asked Mr. Mussa where he was going. Mr. Mussa said that he was just passing through Malawi. The officer asked him if he had reported to the nearest customs officer when he had entered the country. Mr. Mussa said he had not, and his passengers confirmed this. The police officer then charged the six men with having illegally entered Malawi in violation of Section 14(1) of Malawi's Immigration Act, which requires persons entering the country to report to an immigration officer within 24 hours of their entry.

At trial at the Magistrate's Court in Mulange, the six accused all pleaded guilty and were convicted and fined amounts varying from 10 to 30 Malawian kwacha (or, if any of them could not pay, they were to serve a jail term instead).

The convictions and sentences were forwarded to the High Court for confirmation.

JUDGE MEAD: . . .

None of the accused persons has been served with notice of the hearing of this case; all are believed by the police authorities concerned to have returned to Portuguese East Africa. The orders made on the hearing of this case are not to the prejudice of any of the accused persons.

The . . . accused entered Malawi at Sopi from Portuguese East Africa. . . . [Mr. Mussa] said they were all on their way from Milange in Portuguese East Africa to Mazimbi in Portuguese East Africa, passing through Malawi as being a short route between the two places. It was stated by the prosecutor at the trial that the customs officers do not recognize Sopi as a place for entering into Malawi. The accused persons were asked by the police officer who questioned them whether they had reported to the nearest customs officer and each accused stated he had not reported. The police officer did not say where the nearest customs or immigration officer was to be found.

The onus was on the prosecution . . . to prove where the immigration officer nearest to Sopi was to be found and that the six accused persons (all or any one or more of them) had failed to present themselves or himself to that officer within 24 hours of arrival at Sopi. I would add that in the particulars of the offense there is no reference to the accused or any of them having failed to report within that time limit.

It is conceded by learned State Advocate there is no evidence that on the six accused persons' arrival at Sopi there was either an immigration or a customs officer, and that there is no evidence that the accused persons or any of them had been in Malawi for a period of 24 hours. Until the accused persons or any one or more of them had been in Malawi for a period of 24 hours and had failed within that period of time to present themselves to the immigration officer nearest to Sopi, wherever that may be, an offense under the Immigration Act, § 14(1) had not been committed. Each of the accused persons' plea of guilty . . . was misconceived. No offense had been committed by any of the six accused persons under the Immigration Act, § 14(1). Learned State Advocate does not seek to support the convictions.

I quash the conviction of each of the six accused persons, Mussa, Karim, Sedqve, Mambal, Bernet and Bakali under the Immigration Act, § 14(1). I set aside the fines imposed on each of the accused, the fines having been paid to be refunded to each of the accused persons. ■

Temporary Visas

Most countries' immigration laws establish a great many categories of temporary visas, reflecting the many different activities that aliens may carry on while temporarily residing in a host country. The U.S. Immigration and Nationality Act, for instance, establishes the following categories of nonimmigrant aliens who are allowed to enter the United States for limited periods of time:

a. Foreign government officials
b. Visitors
c. Transits
d. Crewmen
e. Traders and investors
f. Students in colleges, universities, seminaries, conservatories, academic high schools, other academic institutions, and in language training programs
g. Representatives of international organizations
h. Temporary employees
i. Representatives of information media
j. Exchange aliens
k. Fiancées and fiancés of U.S. citizens
l. Intracompany transferees
m. Students in established vocational or other recognized nonacademic institutions, other than language training programs
n. Parents and children of certain special immigrants
o. Aliens of extraordinary ability
p. Artists, athletes, and entertainers
q. International cultural exchange visitors
r. Religious workers
s. NATO nonimmigrant aliens
t. Alien witnesses and informants[158]

The most common temporary visas are visitor visas for tourists.[159] Tourists ordinarily have to apply for a visa at an overseas embassy or consulate of the country they intend to visit. Many countries, however, have a "Visa Waiver Program" that allows tourists from designated countries (usually countries with a reciprocal arrangement) to enter without a visa. The United States, for example, does not require visas for tourists from Andorra, Argentina, Australia, Austria, Belgium, Brunei, Denmark, Finland, France, Germany, Iceland, Ireland, Italy, Japan, Liechtenstein, Luxembourg, Monaco, the Netherlands, New Zealand, Norway, Portugal, San Marino, Singapore, Slovenia, Spain, Sweden, Switzerland, the United Kingdom, and Uruguay.[160]

Another common temporary visa is given to business visitors.[161] Most countries allow business visitors to enter for short-term visits (typically for no more than six months) to contact customers, attend trade shows and conventions, show samples, take orders, and engage in other business activities. They must be acting on behalf of a foreign firm, however, and not working for a local employer.[162]

Most developed countries have a special category of visa for students.[163] To qualify, students typically must obtain a statement in advance from the educational institution showing that they have been admitted to a course of study.[164] They also need to prove that they have sufficient

---

[158]*United States Code*, Title 8, §§ 1101, 1103, 1182, 1184, 1186a, 1187, 1221, 1281, and 1282.
[159]In the United States, these are known as B-1 visas.
[160]*United States Code of Federal Regulations*, Title 8, part 217.2 (January 1, 2002). U.S. immigration laws and regulations are available on the U.S. Immigration and Nationalization Service's Web site at www.ins.usdoj.gov/law/inserts.html.
[161]In the United States, these are called B-2 visas.
[162]The United States allows business visitors to "be admitted for not more than one year" and they "may be granted extensions of temporary stay in increments of not more than six months." *United States Code of Federal Regulations*, Title 8, § 214.2(b).
[163]In the United States, these are F-1 visas for students in academic institutions and M-1 visas for students in vocational programs.
[164]A student seeking to study in the United States must have the U.S. institution complete a form I-20 A-B/I-20 ID, "Certificate of Eligibility for Nonimmigrant (F-1) Student Status," or form I-20M-N, "Certificate of Eligibility for Nonimmigrant (M-1) Student Status." *Id.,* §§ 214.2(f)(1)(I)(A) and 214.2(m)(1)(i)(A).

resources to cover their course of study and to return home upon its completion.[165] Some countries allow students to work on campus,[166] but many do not.[167]

Other important temporary visas are those given to temporary employees[168] and the intra-company transferees of multinational enterprises.[169] Typically, these visas are granted only on the petition of an employer,[170] and an alien who has such a visa who changes jobs must get the new employer to apply for a new visa.[171]

Permanent Visas

All states limit the number of permanent visas that they grant to immigrants. This is because they want to ensure that the persons who are granted permanent visas will contribute to the state's society and will not be a burden on it. States typically establish a scheme that gives certain classes of persons a priority claim to visas with permanent immigrant status and that limits the total number of aliens that may enter from particular foreign countries.

For example, the U.S. Immigration and Nationality Act[172] establishes two categories of aliens with priority claims to permanent visas: (1) aliens who are family members of American citizens or of aliens who are already permanent residents of the United States[173] and (2) aliens with special skills.[174] Among this second category are aliens with extraordinary ability (such as well-known writers and philosophers), outstanding professors and researchers, and highly qualified multinational executives and managers.[175]

Once all of the aliens with priority claims to permanent visas have been granted them, then persons who do not have such a claim are given visas, usually on a first-to-apply basis. There is ordinarily a limit on the number of visas that will be granted to aliens from any particular country and on the number of visas that will be granted in any one year. For example, the total number of visas that the United States grants annually is 675,000.[176]

Most immigration schemes also provide for special cases, especially refugees and aliens seeking political asylum. Ordinarily, these applicants are not considered in determining the total number of visas that are granted on an annual basis.[177]

Compliance with Visa Obligations

Aliens are obliged to comply with the terms of their visas and to leave a country when their visa expires or when it is withdrawn. Moreover, the issuance or denial of a visa, the extension or

---

[165]*Id.,* §§ 214.2(f)(1)(i)(B) and 214.2(m)(1)(i)(A). Students enrolled at academic institutions are allowed to leave and return on the same visa for annual vacations. § 214.2(f)(5)(iii).

[166]*Id.,* § 214.2(f)(9). Students in U.S. vocational programs may only work in practical training programs after completing their course of study. *Id.,* § 214.2(m)(i)(13) and (14).

[167]United Kingdom, *Immigration Rules* (HC 395), para. 57(vii).

[168]In the United States, these are known as H-1 visas.

[169]These are called L-1 visas in the United States.

[170]For example, *United States Code,* Title 8, § 1101(a)(15)(H), provides that an alien may be authorized to come to the United States temporarily to perform services or labor for, or to receive training from, an employer, if petitioned for by that employer. The alien must be a registered nurse, a fashion model, a temporary or seasonal agricultural worker, a trainee, a participant in a special education exchange visitor program, or an individual who will perform services in a specialty occupation, or services relating to a Department of Defense cooperative research and development project or coproduction project, or who is of distinguished merit and ability. *See United States Code of Federal Regulations,* Title 8, § Sec. 214.2(h)(1)(i).

    United States Code, Title 8, § 1101(a)(15)(L), provides that an alien who within the preceding three years has been employed abroad for one continuous year by a qualifying organization may be admitted temporarily to the United States to be employed by a parent, branch, affiliate, or subsidiary of that employer in a managerial or executive capacity, or in a position requiring specialized knowledge.

[171]*See United States Code of Federal Regulations,* Title 8, § 214.2(h)(2)(i)(c).

[172]*United States Code,* Title 8, § 1101 et seq.

[173]These are known as "family-sponsored immigrants" and they have priority in the following order: first, unmarried sons and daughters of citizens; second, spouses and unmarried sons and unmarried daughters of permanent resident aliens; third, married sons and married daughters of citizens; and, fourth, brothers and sisters of citizens. *Id.,* § 1153.

[174]*Id.*

[175]Other aliens with priority claims to permanent residency visas based on special skills are (in order of preference) aliens who are members of the professions and who hold advanced degrees or who have exceptional ability; skilled workers whose skill requires two or more years of training or experience; professionals; other workers who have qualifications that are not available in the United States; and persons who have or will establish a business in the United States. *Id.*

[176]*Id.,* § 1151.

[177]For example, *see id.,* § 1157 (for refugees).

the refusal to extend an existing visa, as well as the revocation of a visa are all matters of executive discretion. As a consequence, such decisions are noncontestable in the courts of most countries, as Case 8–7 illustrates.

Case 8–7   England and Another v. Attorney-General of St. Lucia

Court of Appeal of the Eastern Caribbean States, Civil Division, 1985.
West Indian Reports, vol. 35, p. 171 (1987).

The appellants, David and Jean England, who were British subjects, moved to St. Lucia with their family in 1968 and became residents (but not citizens). On August 9, 1983, David England was informed by the Prime Minister of St. Lucia that the government had information indicating that he was helping political extremists in their efforts to recruit St. Lucians for terrorist training in Libya. The Prime Minister did not indicate the source of this information. He did, however, tell David England that the government regarded him as a threat to the security of the state and that he was no longer welcome.

David England, through his solicitor, denied these allegations, and he asked to present his side of the matter before the government took any action. The government did not give him the opportunity. On September 2, two Orders concerning David and Jean England were made by the Governor-General in Council under Section 4(3)(b) of St. Lucia's Immigration Ordinance. The Orders declared the Englands to be prohibited immigrants and authorized the Chief Immigration Officer to remove them from the country on or before September 4. On September 5, the solicitor for the Englands filed motions challenging the procedure taken by the government and the validity of its two Orders.

ASSOCIATE JUSTICE BISHOP DELIVERED THE JUDGMENT OF THE COURT: . . .

On 1st September 1983 the Immigration Ordinance (Amendment) Act became law in St. Lucia. As a result, the Immigration Ordinance and Deportation (British Subjects) Ordinance were significantly affected. For the purposes of the instant case, in the former Ordinance there was no longer the section that created a class of persons who were "deemed to belong" to St. Lucia and the immigration of persons or of any person specified in an Order made by the Governor-General in Council was

prohibited, unless there was some statutory barrier to such prohibition. Put another way, Section 2(2) and that part of Section 5 to which I alluded earlier were both deleted. The whole of the Deportation (British Subjects) Ordinance was repealed. The result was that the England family were without the description or classification of persons who were deemed to belong to St. Lucia for immigration and for deportation purposes. Further, they could be deemed prohibited immigrants under the Immigration Ordinance, as amended.

In my view, from the date when St. Lucia became an independent sovereign country, there were those persons who became citizens without more, there were persons who became citizens upon registration, and there were those persons who were not citizens, some of whom could apply for citizenship. It is clear and undisputed that, on 22nd February 1979 and after, the Englands were not registered as citizens and were not citizens. It does not arise for determination in this appeal whether the Englands could or should be registered as citizens on making application in the proper form. If and when

MAP 8-7   Saint Lucia (1987)

application is made, that decision or a declaration from this court may become necessary. For the moment it is sufficient, in my opinion, to say that there was no application made for registration as citizens. The Englands did not have a right, in law, to reside in St. Lucia. They did not have a right, in law, not to be deported from St. Lucia. They did not have a right in law, not to be declared prohibited immigrants.

On 2nd September 1983, around 3.30 p.m, two Orders (the David England (Prohibited Immigrant) Order and the Jean England (Prohibited Immigrant) Order) were served on the parties therein named. They were similar in substance and in their terms, the sole difference being the names, and so I shall quote only one of them.

WHEREAS by Paragraph (b) of Subsection (3) of Section 4 of the Immigration Ordinance, Chapter 76, it is provided that where the Governor-General in Council is satisfied on information or advice that any person is undesirable as an inhabitant of, or a visitor to St. Lucia, he may by Order declare such a person to be a prohibited immigrant and direct that such person be removed from St. Lucia forthwith or by such time as shall be stipulated,

AND WHEREAS the Governor-General in Council is satisfied on information received that David England is undesirable as an inhabitant of, or a visitor to St. Lucia,

NOW THEREFORE the Governor-General in Council in pursuance to the power conferred upon him as aforesaid orders and declares and it is hereby ordered and declared as follows:

1. *Short Title.* This Order may be cited as the David England (Prohibited Immigrant) Order 1983.
2. *Declaration of Prohibited Immigrant.* David England is declared to be a prohibited immigrant as an inhabitant of, or a visitor to St. Lucia.
3. *Removal of Prohibited Immigrant.* The Chief Immigration Officer is hereby authorized to remove David England from St. Lucia by Sunday 4th September 1983.

Made by the Cabinet under the authority of Subsection (3) of Section 4 of the Immigration Ordinance, Chapter 76, 2nd September 1983.

On 3rd September 1983, David and Jean England through their solicitor, prepared and signed notices of motions and supporting affidavits, as a direct consequence of the service of the above Orders. These notices were filed on 5th September 1983 after the Englands had been removed from St. Lucia. Upon completion of the hearing of the motion the trial judge reserved his decision for delivery on 23rd November 1983 and, as I have already indicated, he refused all the relief and prayers sought by the Englands in their motions.

. . . It was submitted by counsel for the Englands that the Governor-General in Council acting under Section 4(3) of the Immigration Ordinance, as amended, was an authority prescribed by law for the determination of the existence or extent of the civil right of persons falling in the category created by Section 102(1)(b) of the Constitution of St. Lucia and that, if that were so, the rules of natural justice ought to have been observed in arriving at the decision to remove the Englands from St. Lucia as the Governor-General in Council was made a *quasi*-judicial body.

Counsel for the Attorney-General submitted that the Governor-General in Council was not a tribunal nor was any exercise of a judicial or *quasi*-judicial function required under Section 4(3) of the Immigration Ordinance. He submitted, further, that it could not be reasonable, when the Governor-General in Council was satisfied that a person should be removed, to expect that that person should then be called and told of the information or advice given, as well as its source, so that that person could be afforded an opportunity to be heard. According to counsel, there were certain areas in government which were reserved for the state (for example, security and deportation) and "the courts could not substitute themselves for the state." . . .

In my opinion the Governor-General in Council was not acting as judicial tribunal nor was the function required by the Section one of a *quasi*-judicial nature. When it is borne in mind that the Governor-General is Her Majesty the Queen's representative in St. Lucia (Section 19 of the St. Lucia Constitution) and when the Immigration Ordinance (as amended in 1983) is considered, it becomes clear that under Section 4(3)(b) the Governor-General in Council, in September 1983, acted solely under executive powers and in no sense as a court.[178] As I perceive it, the Governor-General in Council was not called upon or empowered by the Section to adjudicate in any matter of contention between parties, nor was any procedure laid down or any provision made for anyone to be heard or for the person who would be affected by an Order to make any representation, oral or written. The Section did not state, either expressly or by implication, that the Governor-General in Council should conduct an inquiry. If Parliament had so intended or wished it would have been simple to state in the Section that the Governor-General in Council should be satisfied "after holding due inquiry," and not "on information or advice." So that there was no statutory requirement that there be evidence or that the source of information or advice on which the Governor-General in Council acted be disclosed or be controlled in accordance with any law.

---

[178]Eshugbayi Eleko v. Officer Administering the Government of Nigeria, *Law Reports, Appeal Cases*, vol. 1931, p. 662 (1931).

Indeed, it must be obvious that disclosure of the source, or of the information or advice, to the person who may be affected by the Order of the Governor-General in Council, would not only be highly understandable but could involve disclosure of confidential national matters, including defense policy, security and the internal safety of the public. Again, as was indicated by the Chief Justice, the Earl of Reading, in *R. v Leman Street Police Station Inspector, ex parte Venicoff*:[179]

It might well be that a person against whom it was proposed to make such an order would take care, if he had notice of such an inquiry, not to present himself, and, as soon as he knew that an inquiry would be held, would take steps to prevent his apprehension.

There was no claim that the Governor-General in Council acted other than in good faith. Of course, had there been any assertion of bad faith, it would have had to be specifically alleged, with particulars, and the burden of proof would have been on the Englands. Nor could it have been asserted that the Governor-General in Council was not satisfied on information received that David England and Jean England were undesirable as inhabitants of, or visitors to St. Lucia.

* * *

. . . I have found no cause to disturb the decision of the trial judge and would therefore dismiss the appeal.

* * *

The appeal was dismissed. ∎

---

[179]*All England Law Reports*, vol. 1920, p. 157 (1920).

Regulation of Foreign Workers

Aliens who enter a country to work must obtain an appropriate entry visa (i.e., one that allows them to be gainfully employed), and they must comply with the host state's employment laws. Commonly, the same labor laws that apply to nationals govern foreign workers once they are allowed to enter a country. This is often so even when a foreign worker and a foreign employer agree to abide by the labor laws of their home state, as Case 8–8 points out.

Case 8–8   George v. International Air Service Co., Ltd.

Japan, Tokyo District Court, 1965.
Case 2237/1964, *Hanreijiho*, No. 408, p. 14 (1965); *Japanese Annual of International Law*, No. 10, p. 189 (1966).

The respondent, International Air Service Co., Ltd. (IASC), was an American company incorporated in the state of California with an office at Tokyo International Airport. Its main business was to supply crewmen to airline companies in Japan and other countries, including Japan Air Lines, Ltd. (JAL) and Japan Domestic Air Lines, Ltd. (JDAL). Frank George (the petitioner), an American citizen, was employed for a period of one year by IASC as a planemaster on April 1, 1960. George's employment agreement provided, among other things, that he would be assigned to work with JAL and that any claims relating to death, dis-ease, or injury would be resolved according to the Workmen's Compensation Law of California.

George's employment was renewed each year for the next four years. In September 1964, however, George filed a complaint with the manager of IASC's Tokyo office, complaining that it had recommended to JAL that JAL promote two other employees who were junior in seniority to him. IASC rejected George's complaint. George responded by forming a "Temporary Employees Committee" along with two other IASC employees assigned to JAL to talk with IASC about its promotion policies. At the same time, the Committee sent a letter to JAL's foreign operations supervisor suggesting to him that JAL should postpone all of its forthcoming promotions until George's complaint could be reconsidered by IASC. The Committee also distributed circulars to the IASC crewmen assigned to JAL informing them of the actions it had taken.

IASC's Tokyo Office Manager met with the Committee in October 1964 and he agreed that the company would be willing to discuss employment conditions with three representatives elected by the employees and that any understandings reached would be forwarded to the IASC's Board of Directors for its approval. That same month, the Committee distributed to the IASC crewmen assigned to JAL a letter describing the agreement it had made and a ballot that asked the recipient to (a) vote for three individuals to serve on the Committee and (b) state whether or not a labor union should be formed to represent the employees in the event that the main office of IASC refused to deal with the Committee.

Meanwhile, on September 28, 1964, IASC's acting chief pilot asked George to submit an explanation for why he had contacted the JAL foreign operations supervisor concerning his grievance. On October 3, George delivered a written explanation. On October 7, IASC's Tokyo Office Manager sent George notice in the mail (which he received on the 10th) telling George that he was fired effective October 30. The notice said that George was being dismissed because he had contacted the JAL foreign operations supervisor to the detriment of IASC and its employees assigned to JAL and also because he had done so using IASC stationery without the company's permission.

George brought suit in the Tokyo District Court asking to be reinstated in his job. IASC responded that the court lacked jurisdiction because it was not a Japanese company, and that even if it had jurisdiction, the dispute was governed by California law because the dismissal related to the employment contract between IASC and George.

JUDGMENT OF THE COURT:

* * *

1. Jurisdiction

A corporation organized under the laws of a foreign country is subject to the jurisdiction of the Japanese courts if it has offices in Japan and is engaged in business in Japan.[180] Accordingly, the respondent company's assertion that this court does not have jurisdiction over it is incorrect, since the evidence shows that it is doing business at offices at the Tokyo International Airport. . . .

2. Applicable Law

With respect to the employment agreement involved in this case, the Court notes that the parties have chosen . . . California law . . . as the applicable governing law. This is

because: (1) the petitioner is an American citizen and the respondent is an American company incorporated in California, and (2) the agreement requires the petitioner to maintain his residence in the United States so as "to avoid any state other than the United States from having jurisdiction in disputes as to labor conditions."

Nevertheless, the petitioner lives in Minato-ku, Tokyo; he was assigned to JAL pursuant to his employment agreement with the respondent; and he was working under JAL's supervision on JAL's domestic aircraft as a planemaster. The respondent's representative who delivered the notification of dismissal to the petitioner was James C. Jack, the respondent's Tokyo Office Manager and its agent in charge of the company's foreign operations.

Under these circumstances, even though the dismissal is related to the employment agreement, the laws of Japan govern this case since the labor was actually supplied in Japan. The general rule in Article 7 of the Law Concerning the Application of Laws in General [—that the courts should apply the law designated by the parties—] does not apply in this case. This is because labor laws, unlike contract laws, are not of a consistent nature or character in the different countries of the world. Nations differ in the ways that they regulate employment contracts and in the way that they restrict or limit collective bargaining agreements. The Court believes that when labor is actually supplied in Japan on a continuous basis, as in this case, then both public policy and the nature of labor law (which has a limited territorial scope) compel the Court to ignore the general principle expressed in Article 7—that the parties are free to chose the appropriate governing law—and hold to the contrary.

The Court will now consider the action taken by IASC in light of the general objectives and purposes set out in Article 7(1) of the Labor Union Law [which states that all employees have the right to organize freely to establish a labor union]. IASC contends that it dismissed the petitioner because . . . he used the company's letterhead without its permission . . . and because he contacted JAL directly. Although it may be a little imprudent of the petitioner to have used the respondent's stationery without the company's consent, there was no danger that the letter might give the impression that it was an official request made by the company since (a) the letter was written in the name of the petitioner to inform JAL that the petitioner "had lodged a complaint with the respondent company," and (b) it only asked that JAL delay its promotion decisions until the dispute between the petitioner and the respondent company could be resolved according to their employment agreement. Additionally, there is no evidence that the peti-

---

[180]Code of Civil Procedure, Article 4(3).

tioner's request to JAL in anyway affected the interests of the respondent or any of the respondent's employees.

On the other hand, the Court has found the following: (1) While IASC pretended that the dismissal notice received by the petitioner on October 10th was made in response to the statement submitted by the petitioner on October 3rd (which had been solicited by the respondent's acting chief pilot on September 28th), the dismissal was actually ordered by William R. Rivers, a Director of IASC on September 19th (that is, before the petitioner submitted his explanatory letter). (2) That James C. Jack, the respondent's Tokyo Office Manager, who had promised to the petitioner on September 21st

that he would meet with the Temporary Employment Committee on September 23rd, went instead to San Francisco to meet with William Rivers. (3) That at the time Jack was in San Francisco, he believed that the petitioner was going to start a labor union.

Considering all of the above, the Court believes that it may reasonably conclude that the decision to dismiss the petitioner was done for the purpose of interfering with the establishment of a labor union. Since this is clearly in conflict with the stated objective of Article 7(1) of the Labor Union Law, the petitioner's dismissal is null and void. ■

---

percentile legislation: A law requiring a certain percentage of employees to be local nationals.

Many states impose special rules on foreign workers. Some use **percentile legislation** to ensure that a certain percentage of the local work force is made up of nationals.[181] Others limit the benefits that foreign employees can be given. Singapore, for example, requires that alien employees be paid at the same rate as nationals. Singapore employers, furthermore, are responsible for ensuring that their alien employees get adequate housing and that a physician examines them before entering the country; the employers additionally must make social security contributions and assume the cost of the employees' repatriation.[182]

Sometimes the rules governing foreign workers seem to grant them special privileges. This seems especially to be the case when the rules are set out in a treaty. For example, treaties of Friendship, Commerce, and Navigation commonly establish a reciprocal right for the national businesses of either signatory state to employ certain categories of their national workers within the territory of the other state. An example is the 1953 Japanese–United States Friendship, Commerce, and Navigation Treaty:[183]

> Nationals and companies of either party shall be permitted to engage, within the territories of the other party, accountants and other technical experts, executive personnel, attorneys, agents, and other specialists of their choice. Moreover, such nationals and companies shall be permitted to engage accountants and other technical experts regardless of the extent to which they may have qualified for the practice of a profession within the territories of such other party, for the particular purpose of making examinations, audits and technical investigations exclusively for, and rendering reports to, such nationals and companies in connection with the planning and operation of their enterprises, and enterprises in which they have a financial interest, within such territories.
>
> Nationals of either party shall not be barred from practicing the professions within the territories of the other party merely by reason of their alienage. . . .

On its face, this provision allows a foreign business to discriminate in favor of its national employees by assigning its nationals to senior executive positions and by denying promotions to employees in the host state. This was not, however, the intent of the treaty's drafters. As Case 8–9

---

[181]Oman's Ministry of Social Affairs and Labor has issued regulations that are a variant of percentile legislation. Ministerial Decision No. 51, effective from August 17, 1993, provides that foreign workers may be employed only when Omani labor is inadequate. In addition, no more than 15 non-Omanis may be employed in Oman Chamber of Commerce and Industry category four companies, 30 in category three companies, and 60 in category two companies. Also, some industries, such as fishing, are forbidden from employing non-Omani workers; whereas others, such as tailoring, are not. Adrian Creed, "Oman Issues New Rules for Non-Omani Workers," *Middle East Executive Reports*, vol. 16, no. 12, p. 17 (December 1993).

[182]International Labor Organization, "Protecting the Most Vulnerable of Today's Workers," Chap. 4 (1997) posted at www.ilo.org/public/english/protection/migrant/papers/protvul/index.htm.

[183]Article VIII, paras. 1–2, *United States Treaties and Other International Agreements*, vol. 4, pt. 2, p. 2063 at p. 2070 (1953).

points outs, foreign employers and foreign workers are both subject to the employment laws of the host state, unless a treaty or domestic law clearly and specifically provides otherwise.

Case 8–9   *Spiess et al. v. C. Itoh & Co. (America), Inc.*

United States, District Court, Southern District of Texas, 1979.
Federal Supplement, vol. 469, p. 1 (1979).

DISTRICT JUDGE CARL O. BUE, JR.:

Plaintiffs, non-Japanese employees of the defendant, have filed suit against defendant pursuant to Title VII of the Civil Rights Act of 1964, . . . alleging racially discriminatory employment practices. C. Itoh & Co. (America), hereinafter "Itoh-America," is a domestic corporation incorporated under the laws of New York and a wholly-owned subsidiary of C. Itoh & Co., Ltd., of Japan, hereinafter "Itoh-Japan," a Japanese corporation which is not a party to the instant suit. Presently before the Court for consideration is Itoh-America's . . . motion to dismiss for failure to state a claim upon which relief may be granted. The issue presented is a novel question of first impression: Does the 1953 Treaty of Friendship, Commerce and Navigation between the United States and Japan provide American subsidiaries of Japanese corporations with the absolute right to hire managerial, professional and other specialized personnel of their choice, irrespective of American law proscribing racial discrimination in employment? . . .

. . . Itoh-America asserts that the Treaty gives it three absolute rights, the combined effect of which "is to create an absolute right on the part of United States and Japanese nationals and companies to send their own nationals to the other country to hold managerial and specialized positions within their respective affiliates and subsidiaries." The rights claimed are:

1. The absolute right to establish, maintain, control, and manage a wide variety of commercial enterprises by nationals and companies of one country in the other country (Article VII, paragraph 1).
2. The absolute right of nationals of the two countries to enter the other country for the purpose of carrying on trade and engaging in related commercial activities between the two countries (Article I, paragraph 1).
3. The absolute right of nationals and companies of either country to engage, within the other country, managerial, professional, and other specialized personnel "of their choice," including their own nationals (Article VIII, paragraph 1).

. . . The crucial section of the Treaty relied upon by Itoh-America is Article VIII(1) which by its terms provides that "nationals and companies of either party shall be permitted to engage within the territories of the other party [personnel] of their choice." Stated otherwise in terms of the instant inquiry, a company of Japan is entitled to engage within the territory of the United States personnel of its choice. Thus, the pivotal issue becomes the nationality of Itoh-America. Plaintiffs urge that the Treaty's own definitional section provides the unequivocal answer to this question: Article XXII(3) provides that "[c]ompanies constituted under the applicable laws and regulations within the territories of either party shall be deemed companies thereof. . . ." Under this definition Itoh-America is a company of the United States because it is incorporated under the laws of the State of New York. Its business operations in the United States are, therefore, those of a United States company in the United States, not the activities of a company of one party within the territory of the other party. Accordingly, plaintiffs argue any immunity from United States discrimination laws conveyed by Article VIII(1) does not apply to Itoh-America.

. . . This analysis is supported by the case of *United States v. R. P. Oldham*,[184] wherein the court used a similar standard for determining corporate nationality for purposes of the 1953 Japanese-American Treaty. Kinoshita & Co., Ltd., U.S.A. ("Kinoshita-America"), an American subsidiary of Kinoshita & Co., Ltd., Tokyo, was indicted along with others for conspiracy in restraint

---

[184]*Federal Supplement*, vol. 152, p. 818 (District Ct., N. Dist. of Calif., 1957).

of commerce in Japanese wire nails. Kinoshita-America argued that Article XVIII of the Treaty dealing with antitrust violations provided the exclusive remedy available to the government in dealing with antitrust violations by American corporations which are wholly owned by Japanese corporations. The District Court held that Article XVIII was not intended as an exclusive remedy; rather than replace American antitrust laws Article XVIII was intended to supplement them. This conclusion was based on the fact that "[t]he tenor of the entire Treaty is *equal* treatment to nationals of the other party, not better treatment."[185] . . . The Court further held that even if Article XVIII were held to provide an exclusive remedy for antitrust violations, Kinoshita-America lacked standing to invoke its protection.

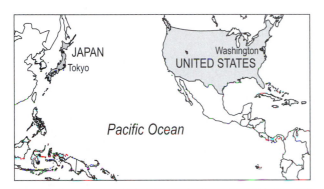

MAP 8-8 Japan and United States (1979)

The Court engaged in a two-step process to arrive at the conclusion that Kinoshita-America was not shielded from United States antitrust laws by Article XVIII. The first step was the determination of the nationality of Kinoshita-America. In order to resolve this question the Court looked to Article XXII, the only definitional section of the Treaty, and pursuant to paragraph three of that Article determined that:

[B]y the terms of the Treaty itself, as well as by established principles of law, a corporation organized under the laws of a given jurisdiction is a creature of that jurisdiction, with no greater rights, privileges or immunities than any other corporation of that jurisdiction.[186]

Once the question of the nationality of Kinoshita-America was determined, the Court completed the two-step inquiry by concluding that an American corporation has no standing to invoke Article XVIII as a defense to the

United States antitrust laws. Any protection against application of United States law would extend only to Japanese corporations, concluded the Court:

If . . . conspirator Kinoshita & Co., Ltd., Tokyo had wished to retain its status as a Japanese corporation while doing business in this country, it could easily have operated through a branch. Having chosen instead to gain privileges accorded American corporations by operating through an American subsidiary, it has for the most purposes surrendered its Japanese identity with respect to the activities of this subsidiary.[187]

* * *

Despite the fact that the Treaty's own definitional section provides that the place of incorporation determines the nationality of a company for purposes of the Treaty and the fact that the Court in *Oldham* determined that an entity identically situated to Itoh-America was an American corporation for purposes of the Treaty, Itoh-America urges this Court to reach a different result.

As support for its argument that it should be considered a Japanese corporation, Itoh-America refers to guidelines promulgated by the Department of State for use by consular officials in determining whether a foreigner seeking admission to the United States qualifies as a "treaty-trader". Article I, paragraph 1 of the Japanese-American Treaty authorizes Japanese nationals to enter the United States as so-called treaty-traders "for the purpose of carrying on trade between the territories of the two parties and engaging in related commercial activities. . . ." In order to qualify as a treaty-trader an alien must satisfy Department of State regulations which require, among other things, that the alien "be employed by an individual employer having the nationality of the treaty company, or by an organization which is principally owned by a person or persons having the nationality of the treaty country."[188] Department of State guidelines provide further that:

[t]he nationality of the employing firm is determined by those persons who own more than 50 percent of the stock of the employing corporation "regardless of the place of incorporation."

. . . Since it is wholly owned by Japanese interests, and thus is a Japanese corporation for treaty-trader purposes, Itoh-America urges that it should be considered a

[185]*Id.*
[186]*Id.,* at p. 823.
[187]*Id.*
[188]*Code of Federal Regulations,* Title 22, § 41.40 (1977).

Japanese corporation for purposes of Article VIII(3). Any other conclusion, it argues, requires the absurd result that once a Japanese corporation exercises the right given to it by Article VII(1) to incorporate an American subsidiary, that subsidiary loses all other rights under the Treaty.

The Court finds that resort to the treaty-trader guidelines to determine corporate nationality for purposes of interpretation of the Treaty provisions is unwarranted in the face of the clear definitional provisions included in Article XXII(3) of the Treaty itself. Article XXII(3) unequivocally states that for the purpose of the Treaty the nationality of a corporation is determined by the place of incorporation. The fact that nationality is determined by a different standard for other purposes cannot alter the clearly stated test of the Treaty itself.

. . . Given the Treaty's own definitional terms, Itoh-America is a company of the United States for purposes of the interpretation of Articles VIII(1). Thus, it can claim no direct protection under Article VIII(1), which applies only to companies of one party within the territories of the other party. Furthermore, even assuming that Article VIII(1) provides absolute immunity from Title VII to Itoh-Japan and that Itoh-America has standing to assert Itoh-America's Treaty rights in this action, questions the Court need not resolve, the motion to dismiss must be denied. Any absolute rights granted to Itoh-Japan apply only to its own hiring decisions; the practices challenged in the present litigation are those of Itoh-America. Itoh-America is a United States company for purposes of Title VII and, like other United States companies, is subject to suit on the grounds that its employment practices are racially discriminatory. Accordingly, Itoh-America's motion to dismiss for failure to state a claim upon which relief may be granted is hereby denied. ∎

Application of Home State Labor Laws Extraterritorially

Traditionally, countries have refused to apply their labor laws extraterritorially. For example, as long ago as 1804, the U.S. Supreme Court ruled that the laws of the United States will not be interpreted to violate the laws of other nations unless no other interpretation is possible.[189] In keeping with this, the Supreme Court has denied a Danish seaman's petition to have American tort law apply to an injury he suffered on a Danish ship in Havana harbor;[190] it has refused to give the National Labor Relations Board the authority to regulate collective bargaining among crewmen serving on foreign ships;[191] and it has held that the Equal Pay Act does not apply outside the territorial jurisdiction of the United States.[192]

However, even though the U.S. Supreme Court ordinarily assumes that the U.S. Congress does not intend for its legislation to apply extraterritorially, it does recognize that Congress "has the authority to enforce its laws beyond the territorial boundaries of the United States."[193] And Congress—contrary to the practice in most other countries—has enacted labor-related laws that expressly apply extraterritorially, including the antidiscrimination provisions of Title VII of the Civil Rights Act of 1964[194] and the Americans with Disabilities Act of 1990, which apply to American citizens working for American employers overseas.[195]

In Case 8–10, a U.S. federal court was asked to determine if Congress intended for the Age Discrimination Employment Act of 1967 to apply extraterritorially.

---

[189]The Charming Betsy, *United States Reports*, vol. 6, p. 64 (Supreme Ct., 1804).

[190]Lauritzen v. Larsen, *id.,* vol. 345, p. 571 (Supreme Ct., 1953).

[191]Benz v. Compañia Naviera Hidalgo, SA, *id.,* vol. 353, p. 138 (1957).

[192]Windward Shipping (London), Ltd. v. American Radio Assn., AFL-CIO, *id.,* vol. 415, p. 104 (Supreme Ct., 1974).

[193]Equal Employment Opportunity Commission v. Arabian American Oil Co., *United States Reports*, vol. 499, p. 244 at p. 248 (1991).

[194]*United States Code*, Title 42, § 2000e(f), as amended by Public Law 102-166 of 1991. This amendment was adopted after the Supreme Court held in Equal Employment Opportunity Commission v. Arabian American Oil Co., *United States Reports*, vol. 499, p. 244 (1991), that the Civil Right Act did not apply to American employees working for American employers overseas.

[195]*Id.,* Title 42, § 12111(4), Public Law 101–336, § 2 of 1990.

While Congress may adopt regulations that apply extraterritorially, the states of the United States may not do so, as these regulations can conflict with the power of the federal government to regulate international commerce. Crosby, Secretary of Administration and Finance of Massachusetts v. National Foreign Trade Council, *United States Reports*, vol. 530, p. 363 (U.S. Supreme Ct. 2000).

Case 8–10   Morelli v. Cedel

United States, Second Circuit Court of Appeals.
Federal Reporter, Third Series, vol. 141, p. 39 (1998).

RICHARD D. CUDAHY, CIRCUIT JUDGE:

This appeal requires us to decide whether the domestic employees of certain foreign corporations are protected under the Age Discrimination and Employment Act of 1967 (the ADEA), and, if so, whether a foreign corporation's foreign employees are counted for the purpose of determining whether the corporation has enough employees to be subject to the ADEA. We answer both questions in the affirmative.

BACKGROUND

After the defendant fired the plaintiff, the plaintiff sued the defendant. The plaintiff's amended complaint asserted that the defendant violated the ADEA. . . . The district court dismissed the complaint on the grounds that the defendant was not subject to the ADEA. . . . The plaintiff appeals. . . .

As alleged in the complaint, the facts relevant to this appeal are as follows. The plaintiff, Ida Morelli, was born on April 11, 1939. The defendant is a Luxembourg bank. On or about June 29, 1984, the defendant hired the plaintiff to work in its New York office. On or about February 26, 1993, the plaintiff became an assistant to Dennis Sabourin, a manager in the defendant's New York office. Mr. Sabourin summoned the then 54-year-old plaintiff to his office on January 18, 1994, handed her a separation agreement, and insisted that she sign it.

Under the terms of the separation agreement, a copy of which was attached to the complaint, the plaintiff would resign, effective April 30, 1994. She would continue to receive her salary and benefits until the effective date of her resignation, but she would be relieved of her duties as an employee, effective immediately. Both the defendant and the employee would renounce all claims arising out of "their past working relationship." Mr. Sabourin told the plaintiff that she would receive the three months' severance pay, medical coverage for three months, and her pension only on the condition that she sign the agreement on the spot. The plaintiff had never seen the separation agreement before and had no warning that she was going to be asked to resign. But in the face of Mr. Sabourin's ultimatum, she did sign the agreement immediately and returned it to him. The defendant, however, never provided her with a pension distribution.

MAP 8-9   Luxembourg (1998)

DISCUSSION

1. Age Discrimination

(a) Does the ADEA Cover a U.S.-Based Branch of a Foreign Employer?   The ADEA was enacted in 1967 to prevent arbitrary discrimination by employers on the basis of age. In order to determine whether the defendant is subject to the ADEA, we must first determine whether the ADEA generally protects the employees of a branch of a foreign employer located in the United States.

It is undisputed that Cedel is a foreign employer with fewer than 20 employees in its sole U.S. branch. . . .

Section 4(h)(2) of the ADEA provides that "the prohibitions of [the ADEA] shall not apply where the employer is a foreign person not controlled by an American employer." At a minimum, this provision means that the ADEA does not apply to the foreign operations of foreign employers — unless there is an American employer behind the scenes. An absolutely literal reading of § 4(h)(2) might suggest that the ADEA also does not apply to the domestic operations of foreign employers. But the plain language of § 4(h)(2) is not necessarily decisive if it is inconsistent with Congress' clearly expressed legislative purpose.

Section 4(h)(2) was not part of the original ADEA. It was added in 1984. The context in which it was added reveals that Congress' purpose was not to exempt the domestic workplaces of foreign employers from the ADEA's prohibition of age discrimination. Instead, the purpose of adding this exclusion was to limit the reach of an extraterritorial amendment adopted as part of the same legislation.

In 1984, before § 4(h)(2) was added, several courts of appeals had concluded that the ADEA did not apply to "Americans employed outside the United States by American employers."[196] . . . Within a few months of the 1984 court decisions, Congress amended the ADEA in a way that superseded the holding of these cases by "providing for limited extraterritorial application" of the ADEA.

The 1984 amendments amplified the definition of "employee" in § 11(f) of the ADEA, which had previously embraced any "individual employed by any employer," except for certain elected public officials and political appointees. One of the 1984 amendments specified that "the term 'employee' includes any individual who is a citizen of the United States employed by an employer in a workplace in a foreign country."

Companion amendments dealt with the cases of foreign persons not controlled by an American employer— now § 4(h)(2) of the ADEA—and foreign corporations controlled by American employers—now § 4(h)(1). . . .

The 1984 revision to the definition of "employee" in § 11(f) was intended "to assure that the provisions of the ADEA would be applicable to any citizen of the United States who is employed by an American employer in a workplace outside the United States."[197] The other 1984 amendments, to § 4 of ADEA, conform the ADEA's reach to "the well-established principle of sovereignty, that no nation has the right to impose its labor standards on another country."[198] Thus § 4(h)(2) of the ADEA merely limits the scope of the amended definition of employee, so that an employee at a workplace in a foreign country is not protected under the ADEA if the employer is a foreign person not controlled by an American employer.[199] There is no evidence in the legislative history that these amendments were intended to restrict the application of the ADEA with respect to the domestic operations of foreign employers.

* * *

If § 4(h)(2) does not exempt the domestic operations of foreign companies from the ADEA, there is no other basis for such an exemption. . . . International comity does not require such an exemption; the 1984 amendments anticipate that American corporations operating abroad will be subject to foreign labor laws, and Congress presumably contemplated that the operations of foreign corporations here will be subject to U.S. labor laws.

We have previously concluded that even when a foreign employer operating in the United States can invoke a Friendship, Commerce and Navigation treaty to justify employing its own nationals, this "does not give [the employer] license to violate American laws prohibiting discrimination in employment."[200] . . .

We therefore agree with the E.E.O.C., the agency charged with the enforcement of the ADEA, that the law generally applies "to foreign firms operating on U.S. soil."[201] For the reasons we have discussed, we are confident that Congress has never clearly expressed a contrary intent.

(b) Are Employees Based Abroad Counted in Determining Whether a U.S.-Based Branch of a Foreign Employer Is Subject to the ADEA? Cedel will still not be subject to the ADEA by virtue of its U.S. operations unless Cedel is an "employer" under the ADEA. A business must have at least twenty "employees" to be an "employer."[202] Cedel maintains that, in the case of foreign employers, only domestic employees should be counted. The district court agreed, and, since Cedel had fewer than 20 employees in its U.S. branch, the court granted Cedel's motion to dismiss for lack of subject matter jurisdiction without considering the number of Cedel's overseas employees.

* * *

The district court reasoned that the overseas employees of foreign employers should not be counted because they are not protected by the ADEA. But there is no requirement that an employee be protected by the ADEA to be counted; an enumeration, for the purpose of ADEA coverage of an employer, includes employees under age 40, who are also unprotected, see 29 U.S.C. § 631(a). The nose count of employees relates to the scale of the employer rather than to the extent of protection.

* * *

---

[196]Cleary v. United States Lines, Inc., *Federal Reporter, Second Series*, vol. 728, p. 610 (3d Circuit Ct. of Appeals, 1984). . . .

[197]Senate Report 98-467, at p. 27 (1984) . . . ; *see* EEOC v. Arabian American Oil Co., *United States Reports*, vol. 499, p. 244 at pp. 258–59 (Supreme Ct., 1991).

[198]Senate Report at p. 27.

[199]*See id.* at pp. 27–28 ("The amendment . . . *does not* apply to foreign companies which are not controlled by U.S. firms.") (emphasis added).

[200]Avigliano v. Sumitomo Shoji America, Inc., *Federal Reporter, Second Series.*, vol. 638, p. 552 at p. 558 (2d Circuit Ct. of Appeals, 1981), vacated on other grounds, *United States Reports*, vol. 457, p. 176 (Supreme Ct., 1982);

[201]E.E.O.C. Policy Guidance, N-915.039, Empl. Prac. Guide (CCH) paras. 5183, 6531 (March 3, 1989).

[202]*United States Code*, title 29, § 630(b).

... Cedel contends that because it has fewer than 20 employees in the United States, it is the equivalent of a small U.S. employer. This is implausible with respect to compliance and litigation costs; their impact on Cedel is better gauged by its worldwide employment. Cedel would not appear to be any more a boutique operation in the United States than would a business with ten employees each in offices in, say, Alaska and Florida, which would be subject to the ADEA. Further, a U.S. corporation with many foreign employees but fewer than 20 domestic ones would certainly be subject to the ADEA.

Accordingly, in determining whether Cedel satisfies the ADEA's 20-employee threshold, employees cannot be ignored merely because they work overseas. We therefore vacate the judgment on the plaintiff's ADEA count.

* * *

CONCLUSION

The judgment is vacated ... and the case is remanded for further proceedings not inconsistent with this opinion. ■

Chapter Questions

1. State A, an Eastern European country, is in the process of transforming its command economy to a market economy. It is also a WTO member state that has granted market access to its financial services sector to foreign banks. Unfortunately, it recently began to have difficulty with its balance-of-payments obligations. After notifying the GATS Council on Trade in Services and the International Monetary Fund, it issued a decree restricting the right of foreign banks to transfer funds abroad. It put no similar limitations, however, on its own banks or on the banks of other Eastern European countries making the transition to market economies. Big Bank, a bank with its place of establishment in State B and a branch in State A, objected to the State A decree and sought the help of State B to get State A to modify or rescind its decree. State A has contacted State B for consultations and both parties have notified the WTO Dispute Settlement Body of their intent to engage in consultations. How should this dispute be resolved? Explain.

2. State C is a WTO member state and a party to NAFTA. It has made no specific agreements under either GATS or NAFTA as to its road transport sector. Now, two freight companies, one from State D (a WTO member state) and one from State E (a party to both the WTO and NAFTA), wish to provide overland freight transportation services in State C using trucks operating out of terminals in their states of establishment. May they do so? If so, to what extent? Explain.

3. State A has not ratified either the ILO Convention Concerning Freedom of Association or the ILO Convention Concerning the Application of the Principles of the Right to Organize and Bargain Collectively. Several workers within State A have lodged complaints with the ILO about their right to associate and bargain collectively. Can the ILO's Fact-Finding and Conciliation Commission consider their complaints?

4. Armstrong worked for a United Nations specialized agency in Geneva for seven years. As part of his job, he tracked the civil rights activities of the agency's member states. One state did not appreciate his listing of certain civil rights abuses that he alleged that country was perpetrating against its nationals. The country refused to pay its dues to the agency unless he was fired. The Secretary-General of the agency then fired him. Armstrong appealed this decision to the ILO's Administrative Tribunal, which has jurisdiction over these kinds of disputes. Armstrong asked the Tribunal to order the agency to rehire him; or, if it could not, then to order the agency to pay him compensation for the loss of his job. How should the Tribunal rule? Discuss.

5. Barton works as a freelance reporter covering stories in State F, a member state of the European Union (EU). Her revealing stories, which she sells to a variety of progressive independent newspapers throughout the EU, have caused a great deal of embarrassment to a certain Minister in the State F government; and the Minister has asked the State F Parliament to pass a law forbidding foreign news reporters from working in State F without the permission of that Minister's office. Parliament has asked the State F Attorney General for an opinion on the legality of the Minister's request in light of State F's membership in the EU. What advice should the Attorney General give Parliament? Discuss.

6. Caruso, a national of State G, is licensed to be a lawyer in that state. Caruso, however, wants to work as a courtroom advocate in State H. May Caruso do so, despite the fact that State H has a law that says only citizens may be courtroom advocates in State H? (Both State G and State H are members of the European Union.) Discuss.

7. Dickens is a dual national of the United States and Ireland. The United States has a prohibition on travel and employment of U.S. nationals in Cuba. If Dickens goes to work in Cuba using his Irish passport to enter and leave Cuba, may the United States take any action against Dickens? Discuss.

8. The faculty of Public University (PU), located in State I, has invited Karl Engels, a "revolutionary Marxist" from State J, and Bishop Biggott, an advocate of apartheid from State K, to participate in a symposium at PU. Both individuals have agreed to attend, but both have been denied visas to enter State I by that state's Foreign Ministry. The Ministry acted according to State I law, which grants the Ministry authority to deny visas for reasons of public policy, public safety, or public health. The PU faculty petitioned the Ministry for a waiver, but the Foreign Minister refused to grant it. The faculty members have now brought a suit claiming that (1) *their* rights under State I's Constitution (that guarantees both freedom of speech and freedom of assembly) to hear the viewpoints of Mr. Engels and Bishop Biggott have been denied and (2) that the government has no basis on which to deny either applicant admission to State I. Will the faculty succeed on either of these grounds? Discuss.

9. Americana, Inc., a large multinational corporation with its headquarters in the United States, has a subsidiary in Tokyo. It refuses to appoint any Japanese nationals to the senior executive posts of the subsidiary, claiming that it is specifically allowed to do so by the 1953 Japanese-United States Friendship, Commerce, and Navigation Treaty. Is this true? Explain.

10. Edison, an employee of Big Corporation, works for Big at its subsidiary in State Y. Edison is an American citizen and Big is an American corporation. Big fires Edison because he is a member of a racial group that is generally despised in State Y. Edison now brings a suit in the United States claiming that his American civil rights have been violated. Have they? Explain.

Review Problem

In your position as Chief Assistant in the law department of MegaBranch Industries (MBI), you are responsible for overseeing the service operations and employment practices of MBI and its subsidiaries.

1. MBI owns a small private university in State A that has a worldwide reputation for excellence in teaching. The university has decided to teach many of its courses via the Internet, and it now seeks to promote and sell those courses internationally. How should it go about determining the countries in which it may offer its courses? How can it be sure that it will receive full payment from the overseas students who register for its courses?

2. MBI has a subsidiary in Luxembourg that sells insurance and insurance services. To what extent may the subsidiary sell its insurance and offer its other insurance services in the other member states of the European Union?

3. MBI's legal division in the United States wants to provide legal services to MBI's subsidiaries in Canada and Mexico. May it do so? To what extent?

4. MBI has been asked to review the annual report being submitted by MBI's home country to the International Labor Organization (ILO). What does this entail? What will happen to the report and MBI's comments?

5. What legal and practical effects do the ILO's international labor standards have on the operation of MBI's businesses?

6. One of MBI's senior Directors took a leave of absence last year to serve in the International Labor Office in Geneva, Switzerland, for 12 months. Her employment contract with the ILO called for the ILO to pay for her medical insurance; the ILO failed to do so, and her health insurance policy lapsed as a consequence. While the policy was not in

effect, she suffered a short but expensive illness. She has received U.S. $75,000 in doctors' and hospital bills. She has asked the ILO to pay these bills, but it has refused. Can she appeal this to the ILO's Administrative Tribunal? If so, what kind of relief can she obtain from the Tribunal?

7. MBI is planning on setting up a new subsidiary in the European Union and knows it will have to hire new employees. MBI prefers to employ English speakers as this makes it easier for MBI to train them. May MBI refuse to hire non-English speakers? May it avoid the problem by setting up the subsidiary in the United Kingdom and advertising that it wishes to employ U.K. nationals only?

8. An MBI subsidiary that is organized as a French company maintains several employees in London who observe the operation of the London Stock Exchange and report on its operation to the subsidiary's headquarters in Paris. One of the employees is a French national, another is Dutch, a third is German, and a fourth is Canadian. Will the employees have any difficulty in continuing to live and work in London?

9. If MBI seeks to send employees from one subsidiary to work for another subsidiary in a different country, what labor regulations must it comply with in both states?

10. Should MBI concern itself with the extraterritorial application of its home country labor laws in any of the countries where it has subsidiaries?

CHAPTER 9

Intellectual Property

Chapter Outline

Introduction

intellectual property:
Useful artistic and industrial information and knowledge.

artistic property:
Artistic, literary, and musical works.

industrial property:
Inventions and trademarks.

Intellectual property is, in essence, useful information or knowledge. It is divided, for the purposes of study (and for establishing legal rights), into two principal branches: artistic property and industrial property. **Artistic property** encompasses artistic, literary, and musical works. These are protected, in most countries, by copyrights and neighboring rights.

Industrial property is itself divided into two categories: inventions and trademarks. Inventions include both useful products and useful manufacturing processes. They are protected in a variety of ways, the most common protection being in the form of patents, petty patents, and inventors' certificates. Trademarks include "true" trademarks, trade names, service marks, collective marks, and certification marks. All of these are markings that identify the ownership rights of manufacturers, merchants, and service establishments. They are protected by trademark laws.

Regardless of its form, intellectual property is a creature of municipal law. International law does not create it. International law does, however, set down guidelines for its uniform definition and protection, and it sets up ways that make it easier for owners to acquire rights in different countries.

National law—and sometimes regional law—is also important in establishing the rules for assigning and licensing intellectual property. Recently, the international community has given some effort to establishing international norms for the transfer of intellectual property, but so far the effort has not been successful.

These aspects of intellectual property law—its creation, protection, and transfer—form the subject matter of this chapter. Each will be discussed in its turn.

A. THE CREATION OF INTELLECTUAL PROPERTY RIGHTS

The realm of information that can be owned, assigned, and licensed is as broad as human inventiveness and imagination. Such information can involve either statutory or nonstatutory rights. The former include copyrights, patents, and trademarks. The latter include "know-how." (Know-how is a word of American origin that has now been adopted as a term of art in many languages.[1]) However categorized, they are all products of municipal law.

Copyrights

copyright: An incorporeal statutory right that gives the author of an artistic work, for a limited period, the exclusive privilege of making copies of the work and publishing and selling the copies.

A **copyright** is title to certain "pecuniary rights" and, in most countries, certain "moral rights" for a specified period of time. These rights belong to the authors of any work that can be fixed in a tangible medium for the purpose of communication, such as literary, dramatic, musical, or artistic works; sound recordings; films; radio and television broadcasts; and (at least in some countries) computer programs. Unlike a patent, a copyright does not give its owner the rights to prevent others from using the idea or the knowledge contained in the copyrighted work; it only restricts the use of the work itself. That is, anyone can use the information in the work to make, use, or sell a product; but they will be limited in the way they may use a particular copy.

The Duke of Milan issued the first known copyright—a grant of the exclusive right to print a work—in 1481 to the printer of a local history. Similar grants were given to other printers in Germany, France, Italy, and Spain at about the same time. The first true Copyright Act, which protected authors without their having to obtain an individual grant from their sovereign, was enacted in England in 1709. Similar statutes appeared in Spain in 1764, in the United States in 1790, in revolutionary France in 1791, and in the German Confederation in 1837. Comprehensive acts, granting both pecuniary and moral rights to authors with minimal formality, appeared on the European Continent in the 1880s—the Belgian Copyright Law of 1886 being the first of several. Also, in 1886, 10 countries, including Belgium, Britain, France, Germany, Italy, Spain, and Switzerland, signed the Berne Convention[2]—by far the most influential international copyright convention—at Berne, Switzerland. This convention followed the Continental European model, requiring signatory states to impose minimal formalities and to protect both pecuniary and moral rights. Today, most of the nations of the world have ratified the Berne Convention, including—as of March 1989—the United States, thereby giving substantial (but certainly not complete) uniformity to the world's copyright laws.

Pecuniary Rights

pecuniary right: Right of an author to exploit a copyrighted work for economic gain.

Economic or **pecuniary rights** are legislative or judicial grants of authority that entitle an author to exploit a work for economic gain. Historically, there were only two channels for doing so. One was through the printed medium (i.e., a work was printed and then distributed through book shops, music stores, poster shops, etc.), and the other was through an entertainment establishment (i.e., a work was performed or shown at theaters, music halls, galleries, etc.). Today, as a consequence, most of the nearly 100 countries that grant copyrights protect two kinds of pecuniary rights: the "right of reproduction" (which, in many jurisdictions, also includes the rights to exhibit and disseminate a work) and the "right of public performance." An example of the pecuniary protection granted in a typical statute is found in Section 15 of the German Copyright Law:

I.   The author shall have the exclusive right to exploit his work in material form; the right shall comprise in particular:

1. the right of reproduction;
2. the right of distribution;
3. the right of exhibition.

---

[1]Paul H. Vishny, *Guide to International Commerce Law,* vol. 1, § 3.09 (1994).
[2]Berne Convention for the Protection of Literary and Artistic Works (Paris 1886, revised in Paris 1896, Berlin 1908, Berne 1914, Rome 1928, Brussels 1948, Stockholm 1967, and Paris 1971).

> II. The author shall further have the exclusive right to publicly communicate his work in nonmaterial form (right of publicly communicating); the right shall comprise in particular:
>
>   1. the right of recitation, representation and performance;
>   2. the right of broadcasting;
>   3. the right of communicating the work by means of sound or visual records;
>   4. the right of connecting broadcast transmissions.

right of reproduction:
Exclusive right of an author to make multiple copies of a copyrighted work.

Reproduction, the oldest and most common of the "copy-right" rights, is consistently defined in the market countries of the West. For example, the German statute defines it as the "right to make copies of a work, irrespective of the method or number";[3] the British Copyright Act refers to "reproducing the work in any material form";[4] the French Copyright Law defines a work reproduction as "the material fixation of a work by any method that permits indirect communication to the public";[5] and the United States Copyright Act refers merely to the making of "copies."[6]

In socialist countries, although a copyright *does* include the right of reproduction, the right can only effectively be exercised by state agencies. As a consequence, copyright holders have to assign their rights to an agency—commonly their employer—and hope that the agency will promote their copyrighted work.[7]

right of distribution:
The right of an author to place a copy of a copyrighted work into circulation for the first time.

Distribution rights, unlike reproduction rights, are neither consistently defined nor consistently granted from one country to another. To understand distribution rights, one has to consider two questions: (a) What is meant by distribution? and (b) When are distribution rights "exhausted"?

The German Copyright Law defines *distribution* as "the right to offer to the public,[8] or to place in circulation, the original work or copies of the work."[9] Similar provisions are found in the American, Austrian, British, Scandinavian, and Swiss statutes.[10] Most countries do not directly grant such a right. For example, while the French Copyright Law does not directly grant a right of distribution, it does provide for essentially the same thing in the form of a limitation on a transferee's rights. Thus, a transferee only acquires those rights "specifically mentioned in the transfer agreement,"[11] and any attempt to assume greater rights is considered a crime. A French transferee who attempts "the sale, exportation or importation of unlawful copies of [copyrighted] works" is subject to penal sanctions.[12]

doctrine of exhaustion:
Once a copy of a copyrighted work is in circulation, the author has no further right to control its distribution.

In most countries, once a particular copy of a work has been sold to a public transferee, the author's right to control any subsequent transfers ends. This is known as the **doctrine of exhaustion**.[13]

---

[3]Germany, Copyright Law, § 16 (September 9, 1965, as amended).

[4]United Kingdom, Copyright Act, § 2(5) (1956 as amended).

[5]France, Law No. 57-298, Article 28 (March 11, 1957, as amended). Similar language appears in the Russian Civil Code, Article 479.

[6]United States, Copyright Act, § 106(1) (1976).

[7]For an illustration of one individual's trials and tribulations in the old Soviet Union, *see* Peter Gumbel, "Tetris Game Wins Big for Nintendo but Not for Soviet Inventors: They're Left Out as Software Falls into Western Hands and Then into Litigation," *Wall Street Journal,* June 8, 1990.

[8]While the statutory provisions do not define "public," the commentators generally agree that the circulation of one or two copies to members of one's family or to close friends is not a public distribution. *See* Stig Strömholm, "Copyright—Comparison of Laws," *International Encyclopedia of Comparative Law,* vol. 14, chap. 3, p. 52.

[9]Germany, Copyright Law, § 17(1) (September 9, 1965, as amended).

[10]United States, Copyright Act, § 106(1) (1976); Austria, Copyright Law, § 16; United Kingdom, Copyright Act, § 2(5) (1956 as amended); Switzerland, Federal Copyright Law, Article 12(1) (December 7, 1922, as amended). An example of the Scandinavian provisions is Sweden's Law No. 729 on Copyrights, § 2(3) (1960 as amended).

[11]France, Law No. 57–298, Article 31(3) (March 11, 1957, as amended).

[12]France, Penal Code, Article 425(3).

[13]The doctrine of exhaustion was first introduced in the nineteenth century by Josef Kohler, a German law professor, and his ideas are now incorporated in the German Copyright Law, § 17(2), and in the other copyright laws that provide for an express grant of the right of distribution.

   The United States' exhaustion-of-rights rule is set out in § 27 of the U.S. Copyright Act, which states that "nothing in this title shall be deemed to forbid, prevent, or restrict the transfer of any copy of a copyrighted work the possession of which has been lawfully obtained.

Practically, this doctrine is a necessary corollary to the right of distribution; otherwise, the copyright owner would be able to control every transfer of every copyrighted work.

There are three important limitations to the doctrine of exhaustion. The first is that the right only applies to sales. An author who transfers an original or a copy by lending, leasing, or as part of an exhibition retains his distribution right as to any subsequent transfer. The second limitation is that the doctrine only applies to the right of distribution. The right to reproduce the original work, as well as other rights (such as performance rights and moral rights), is not affected. For example, making photocopies of a book purchased by a transferee is still an infringement of the copyright holder's right of reproduction. The third limitation has to do with the author's right to limit rentals of distributed original works and copies. By a widely subscribed international agreement, authors are entitled (at least with regard to computer programs and motion pictures) to prohibit commercial rentals of their copyrighted works.[14]

right of performance:
The right of an author to communicate a copyrighted work to the public.

In addition to reproduction and distribution rights, copyright owners also have a pecuniary **right of performance**. There are basically two approaches to the granting of this right. One, set out in the British, French, and U.S. laws, among others, is to grant a *general* right of performance (*droit de représentation*). The French law, which was extensively amended in 1985, provides a good example of this method. The right of performance is the right "to communicate the work to the public by any means whatsoever, including public recitation, lyrical performance, public presentation, public projection, and telecommunication."[15]

The second approach, followed in various countries, but most fully utilized in Germany, is to create several *subsidiary* rights[16]—in particular, the right to recite a literary work, the right to perform a musical work, the right to make a remote presentation over loudspeakers or similar devices, the right to make a projected image, the right to communicate by visual or sound records, and the right to make radio and television broadcasts.[17]

Regardless of the approach, the right of performance applies only to public performances. Private performances—that is, performances limited to a small group of people "interconnected personally by mutual relations or by a relationship to the organizer"[18]—do not infringe the copyright. Examples of public performances from U.K. case law (all of which will infringe the copyright holder's performance right) include the performance of a play by members of a ladies' club to other members of the same club, and playing music in the lobby of a hotel, in a television showroom, in a record shop, over loudspeakers to workers in a factory, and to members of a dance club.[19] A private performance would be a reading of a book to one's family or to a small group of close friends. The difference between public and private performances is examined in Case 9–1.

The European Union's exhaustion-of-rights rule is a court-made rule. It was first applied by the European Court of Justice in a copyright dispute in the case of Deutsche Gramophone v. Metro, Case 78/70, *European Community Reports*, vol. 1971, p. 487 (1971); and then fully set out in Musik-Vetrieb Membran v. GEMA, joined Cases 55/80 and 57/80, *European Community Reports*, vol. 1981, p. 147 (1981).

[14]The Agreement on Trade-Related Aspects of Intellectual Property Rights, Article 11 (1994), provides: "In respect of at least computer programs and cinematographic works, a [World Trade Organization] member shall provide authors and their successors in title the right to authorize or to prohibit the commercial rental to the public of originals or copies of their copyright works. A member shall be excepted from this obligation in respect of cinematographic works unless such rental has led to widespread copying of such works which is materially impairing the exclusive right of reproduction conferred in that member or authors and their successors in title. In respect of computer programs, this obligation does not apply to rentals where the program itself is not the essential object of the rental."

[15]France, Law No. 57-298, Article 27 (March 11, 1957, as amended). Similar provisions are in the United Kingdom Copyright Act, §§ 2(5) and 3 (1956 as amended), and the United States Copyright Act, §§ 101 and 106(4) (1976).
   This same general prohibition was incorporated into the Agreement on Trade-Related Aspects of Intellectual Property Rights Article 14 (1994). This Agreement is discussed later in this chapter.

[16]*See,* as well, Italy's Law No. 633 for the Protection of Copyrights, Article 16 (April 22, 1941, as amended).

[17]Germany, Copyright Law, §§ 15(2), 19 (September 9, 1965, as amended).

[18]*Id.,* § 15(3).

[19]*See* Stig Strömholm, "Copyright—Comparison of Laws," *International Encyclopedia of Comparative Law,* vol. 14, chap. 3, p. 57.

Case 9–1   Performing Right Society, Limited v. Hickey

Zambia, High Court at Lusaka, 1978.
The Zambia Law Reports, vol. 1979, p. 66 (1979).

JUDGE SAKALA:

The plaintiff's claim is for an injunction to restrain the defendant—whether by himself or by his servants or agents—from authorizing or procuring communication to the public of the musical works "Kung Fu Fighting," "House of Exile," and "Money Won't Save You," or any other musical works the copyright of which vests in the plaintiff. The plaintiff also claims for damages.

In support of the claim, Ronald Clarence Chipumza, an accountant with Lightfoot Advertising, told the Court that he is also the Zambian Agent for the Performing Right Society, Limited, the plaintiff in this case. He testified that the objective of the plaintiff is to protect the copyright of musical writers, artists, and composers. The Society represents them and collects fees on behalf of its members, which in the end is distributed to the members. In Zambia, the position of the plaintiff is to represent the copyright of the affiliated societies throughout the world. He testified that in early 1975 a search was conducted at the defendant's premises to determine the extent to which the copyright of the society members was being violated. He told the Court that in September a letter was sent to the defendant advising him that the plaintiff's copyright was being infringed. Another letter was sent in October 1975 reminding the defendant of the consequence of performing copyrighted music without the consent of the copyright owner. The witness further testified that he also wrote the defendant suggesting to him to take out the society's license. But there was no reply to any of these letters. Further, the defendant made no attempt to arrange for a meeting. In the end the matter was referred to the plaintiff's solicitors. The witness further testified that he physically, on several occasions, made searches at the defendant's premises. First of these occasions was on the 4th of April 1975. He discovered that the Society's copyright was being infringed. The inspections were carried out after the defendant failed to reply to the correspondence. At the time of the inspections, the songs that were being performed were "Kung Fu Fighting," "House of Exile," and "Money Won't Save You." These last two songs were composed by Jimmy Cliff, while "Kung Fu Fighting" was by Carl Douglas. He testified that copyright in these works subsists in the plaintiff. The witness also told the Court that

after the institution of the present proceedings, he carried out another search at the defendant's premises on the 11th of July 1978. It was again established that the copyright of the Society was still being violated. He said about five searches in all were carried out by him personally. He said that other works of the plaintiff are still being infringed, in addition to those specifically mentioned in the pleadings. . . .

In defense, Francis Anthony Hickey testified that he is one of the proprietors of Bar-B-Que Drive-in Restaurant. He agreed that on the 26th of April, 1976, he caused to be heard in public three records, namely, "Kung Fu Fighting," "House of Exile," and "Money Won't Save You." He said that it is not his intention to carry on breaking the copyright. He said, before then, he received several letters from the plaintiff's solicitors asking him to stop playing copyrighted music, but he did not know what they were asking him. He has never in his life heard that there is a copyright in music. He testified that he has bought records and played them. The letters he received did not mention any specific records and the pamphlet he received did not specify the music. He said he only realized that the letters referred to "Kung Fu Fighting," "House of Exile," and "Money Won't Save You" when he approached his lawyer who explained [the letters] to him. Otherwise, before then, he had no idea. He said he does not intend to play these records until he obtains a license from the rightful owner. He told the Court that nobody approached him at his restaurant asking him to stop playing the records. He said he holds about one dance a week depending on the license allocated to him by the police.

In cross-examination, he said on receipt of the various letters from the plaintiff, he asked his various friends who run discos and in their case, they did not know anything of copyright and as he was a beginner himself, he thought that these letters were some sort of a money making racket. He said he does not remember whether he read the pamphlet sent to him. He said he understood the word copyright to mean that you cannot manufacture the item in question.

. . . The contention by the plaintiff is that, they have lost royalty fees by reason of the defendant's refusal and/or negligence to take out the plaintiff's license. As a result, they are claiming for an injunction to restrain the defendant by himself, or by his servants or agents, from causing to be heard in public at the defendant's premises, the said musical works or any other such work

MAP 9-1 Zambia (1978)

the copyright of which vests in the plaintiff or from authorizing performance without a license from the plaintiff. They also ask for damages for infringement of the copyright.

... The defense is, that, the performance was done innocently and under mistake. The submission on behalf of the defendant was that, in matters of copyright infringement it is a good defense that at the time of the infringement that the defendant was not aware and had no reasonable grounds for suspecting that copyright subsisted. A further submission on behalf of the defendant is that if the plaintiff suffered any damages, the damages should only relate to the one day as pleaded. In the circumstances, counsel for the defendant urged that the damages should either by nominal or nil. It is conceded on behalf of the defendant in the submissions that the granting of an injunction cannot be opposed and was never at any stage objected to. The plaintiff's contention is that regard being had to all the correspondence sent to the defendant, the defense of innocence must be rejected. The law governing copyright of musical works and other works in Zambia is contained in the *Copyright Act,* Chapter 701. I must confess that, in my research, I have not come across any Zambian authority based on the *Copyright Act.* Even in the submissions, I was not referred to any local decided cases. Musical works under the Act are eligible for copyright. Infringement of copyright is specifically provided for in § 13 of the Act. Section 13 reads as follows:

Copyright shall be infringed by any person who does, or causes any other person to do, an act falling within the copyright without the license of the person in whom is vested either the whole of the copyright or, where there has been a partial assignment or partial testamentary disposition, the relevant portion of the copyright.

In the instant case, the defendant admits that on the 26th of April, 1976, he did perform or cause the performance of the three musical works without a license.

* * *

... Section 13(3) provides a defense to infringements of copyright. The subsection reads as follows:

Where in an action for infringement of copyright it is proved or admitted—(a) that an infringement was committed; but (b) that at the time of the infringement the defendant was not aware, and had no reasonable grounds for suspecting, that copyright subsisted in the work or other subject matter to which the Section relates;

the plaintiff shall not be entitled under this Section to any damages against the defendant in respect of the infringement, but shall be entitled to an account of profits in respect of the infringement whether any other relief is granted under this Section or not.

As already mentioned, the defense raised is one of innocence. Quite clearly, § 13(3) of Chapter 701 provides a good defense of innocence of infringements of copyright. Although there is no decided authority in Zambia, ... English decisions based on the English *Copyright Act* of 1956 ... have very strong persuasive value ... bearing in mind that the wording of § 13(3) of Chapter 701 is the same as § 17(2) of the English Copyright Act of 1956. ... Innocence as a defense under this Section has been considered in a number of English cases, reference to which will be found in *Halsbury's Laws of England.*[20] Part of that paragraph reads as follows:

In general, any invasion of a right of property gives a cause of action to the owner against the person responsible for the invasion, whether it is intentional or not. Consequently, innocence is no defense to an action for infringement of copyright or for the conversion or detention of any infringing copy or a plate.

Where, however, it is proved or admitted in an action for infringement that an infringement was committed, but that at the time of the infringement the defendant was not aware and had no reasonable

---

[20] 4th ed., vol. 9 at paragraph 938, p. 602.

grounds for suspecting that copyright subsisted in the work or other subject matter to which the action relates, the plaintiff is not entitled to damages, but is entitled to an account of profits whether any other relief is granted to not.

On the evidence before me, I am satisfied and find as a fact that at the time of the defendant's admitted infringement, he was not aware and had no reasonable grounds for suspecting that copyright subsisted in the plaintiff's three musical works. This being the case, I hold that the plaintiff is not entitled to any damages against the defendant in respect of the infringement. The Sec-

tion, on the other hand, provides an alternative to damages in that the plaintiff is entitled to an amount of profits in respect of the infringement whether any other relief is granted or not. On the defendant's admission of the infringement of the plaintiff's copyright of the three musical works on April 26th, 1976, I hold that the plaintiff is entitled to the profits made on that day. As to quantum, I grant the parties liberty to apply in chambers. The defendant, at least from the evidence, does not appear to object to the injunction being granted. In the circumstances, I grant the injunction in respect of the three works pleaded. ■

Moral Rights

moral rights: The right of an author to prohibit others from tampering with a copyrighted work.

The personal rights of authors to prohibit others from tampering with their works are called **moral rights**. These rights are independent of the author's pecuniary rights, and in most states that grant moral rights, they continue to exist in the author even after the pecuniary rights have been transferred. In France, for example, they are inalienable.

The concept of moral rights is a product of nineteenth-century German legal philosophy. Starting in the period of the natural law thinkers (such as Locke, Montesquieu, and Pufendorf) a belief gained currency that there existed in nature certain legal rights (called *Persönlichkeitsrecht* or personal rights) that were inherent in the persons of individuals. Later, the positivists, including Hegel, Jellinek, and Triepel, accepted that such rights ought to exist, even if they did not exist in nature. For example, Immanuel Kant, the eminent eighteenth-century German philosopher, looked upon the *Persönlichkeitsrecht* as a grant of freedom essential to the existence of an ethical society.[21]

The principal nineteenth-century German legal commentators—the Pandectists—were generally opposed to the notion of *Persönlichkeitsrecht*; it did not fit into the patterns of Roman law, which they regarded as conclusive and unimprovable. Nonetheless, a small group of writers, who studied German rather than Roman laws, were adamant defenders of the idea. These "personalists," led by Otto von Gierke, took the view that a copyright was a single *unified* privilege that included both economic rights (i.e., reproduction and distribution) and moral rights. For these writers, a copyright was essentially personal; it could not be transferred, seized, or banned.[22]

Although the unitary view of von Gierke and the other personalists may have been philosophically and logically sound, it did not reflect actual practice. Copyright laws in every country allowed authors to transfer, at a minimum, their pecuniary rights. Josef Kohler proposed, about 1880, a *dualist* theory of copyright law. This divided copyrights into economic and moral rights—the latter being those rights that reflected the creative interests and concerns of the author. Kohler's theory was based on extensive studies of British and French case law (German case materials were generally unavailable at that time), and his ideas were especially influential in France.

Judicial decisions in France in the 1870s—under the influence of German scholarship—came to recognize moral rights as separate and distinct from economic rights. The French decisions, and Kohler's dualist theory, were incorporated in statutory form for the first time in the Belgian Copyright Law of 1886.

The 1886 Belgian Copyright Law recognized what today are considered the three basic moral rights: (1) the right to object to distortion, mutilation, or modification (*droit de respect*),

---

[21]In "Von der Unrechtmässihkeit des Büchernachdruckes," *Berlinische Monatsschrift,* at p. 416 (1785), Kant described a copyright as "not a right in the thing . . . but an innate right, inherent in the author's person, which implies the faculty to protest against another making him speak unwillingly to the public."

[22]*Deutsches Privatrecht,* vol. 1, pp. 756–766 (1895).

(2) the right to be recognized as the author (*droit à la paternité*), and (3) the right to control public access to the work (*droit de divulgation*). These same rights were recognized in French and German copyright laws at the beginning of the twentieth century; and, in 1928, the Berne Convention (which provides for the international recognition of national copyright laws) was amended to specifically recognize these three moral rights. France and Germany have subsequently added a fourth moral right—the right to correct or retract a work (*droit de repentir, Rückrufsrecht*); but it is not as universally recognized as the other three.

Moral rights are not recognized in the copyright laws of the United Kingdom, the United States, and countries that have inherited their law from England. The United Kingdom, which is a signatory of the Berne Convention and therefore obliged to protect the moral rights of authors, complies with its international obligations, at least arguably, by claiming that an author can bring an action for libel to complain of distortion, mutilation, or modification, and an action for passing off to protect the author's rights of paternity. It also has argued that the right to control public access is inseparable from the economic right of reproduction, and therefore similarly protected.

American courts and legal writers have often denied the existence of moral rights in the United States. It was long suggested that the principal reason that the United States refused to become a signatory of the Berne Convention was the treaty's requirement that member states recognize moral rights. With U.S. ratification of the Berne Convention in 1989, however, such explanations are no longer viable. A few American writers have suggested—in the fashion of British commentators—that moral rights are protected by tort and contract law.[23] These suggestions, however, have been halfhearted at best and, with the recent adoption of the Agreement on Trade-Related Aspects of Intellectual Property Rights, probably no longer necessary.

The Agreement on Trade-Related Aspects of Intellectual Property Rights (TRIPS Agreement), which is an annex to the Agreement Establishing the World Trade Organization, requires WTO member states to comply with provisions of the Berne Convention (whether or not they are parties to that Convention) with one significant exception: Member states are not required to grant moral rights to authors.[24] It seems likely as a consequence, at least for now, that authors in the United Kingdom, the United States, and other countries that follow the English tradition will continue to do without moral rights, despite the provisions in the Berne Convention and the practice in most of the rest of the world.

Works Covered

work: An artistic, literary, musical, or scientific creation.

The object of copyright protection is a **work**, that is, an intellectual creation in the fields of art, literature, music, or science. Particular examples of works covered are provided in many copyright laws.[25] For example, the 1976 U.S. Copyright Act lists seven categories of works that are eligible for copyright protection:

1. Literary works
2. Musical works, including any accompanying words
3. Dramatic works, including any accompanying music
4. Pantomimes and choreographic works
5. Pictorial, graphic, and sculptural works
6. Motion pictures and other audiovisual works
7. Sound recordings

originality: Creative effort invested by an author into raw materials that gives them a new quality or character.

Not every work that falls within these categories qualifies for copyright protection, however. A work must also be **original**; that is, an author must infuse creativity into it. As Lord Atkinson once stated in a famous Privy Council case: "To secure [a] copyright . . . it is necessary that labor, skill and capital should be expended sufficiently to impart to the product some quality or

---

[23]*See* Earl Kinter and Jack Lahr, *An Intellectual Property Law Primer,* p. 335 (1975).
[24]Agreement on Trade-Related Aspects of Intellectual Property Rights, Article 9, para. 1 (1994).
　　The Agreement specifies that WTO member states are to comply with the Berne Convention as revised in Paris in 1971.
[25]A similar list of examples can be found in the United Kingdom Copyright Act, § 3 (1956 as amended); the German Copyright Law, § 2 (September 9, 1965 as amended); and French Law No. 57-298, Article 3 (March 11, 1957 as amended).

character which the raw material did not possess, and which differentiates the product from the raw material."[26] Originality, however, should not be confused with the patent law requirements of novelty or merit. Two painters, for example, may paint the same still life. Each painting is an original, since it reflects the creativity of the maker. Accordingly, even though neither is novel, and even if they both lack any artistic merit whatsoever, both painters are entitled to a copyright for their works.

What is protected is not the idea or knowledge contained in the work, but the expression of the work. That is, copyrights do not apply to "ideas, procedures, methods of operations, or mathematical concepts as such."[27] Anyone may use the information or knowledge in the work; they are limited only in the way they may use the original or a particular copy.[28]

Of course, before there can be a copy, there must be an original. The original must be such that it is capable of being "fixed in any tangible medium of expression, now known or later developed."[29] A story written down on paper with pen and ink is the classic example of an original work that has been fixed in a tangible medium. So, too, is a picture painted with oils onto a canvas, an image sculpted into marble, and music recorded on a record, tape, or compact disc.

Most copies (other than performances) must also be fixed in a tangible medium. That being so, is a copy made when the data that are stored on a computer disk are placed into the computer's central memory? The court in *MAI Systems v. Peak Computer*[30] was faced with this question. In that case, MAI Systems, a computer programming company, wrote unique operating system programs for its customers' computers, which were stored on the computers' hard disks. MAI also serviced those computers whenever they needed it. Peak Computer, a rival programming company, contracted to service many of MAI's customers' computers for substantially less than MAI Systems. MAI was not happy about this, and it sought to stop Peak by suing for copyright infringement. MAI, which had licensed only its customers to use the operating system programs installed on their computers, claimed that Peak had made unauthorized copies whenever it turned on the computers. The court agreed. Peak was able to view the error log generated by MAI's operating system program when a computer with the program was turned on. This meant that a perceivable copy of the program was taken from the hard disk and placed in the computer's operating memory. Although the copy was removed when the computer was shut down, it still existed for "more than a transitory period." That is all that is required. The court, therefore, enjoined Peak from infringing MAI's copyrights. (Because this meant that Peak could not turn on the computers with MAI's programs, Peak was effectively stopped from competing against MAI.)

Neighboring Rights

Copyright laws generally apply to most works of an artistic, literary, musical, or scientific nature. Technology, however, has a habit of producing new kinds of works that fall outside of existing definitions. Two recent examples are computer programs and semiconductor chips. Legislatures respond to such changes in different ways. Sometimes they make amendments to existing copyright laws to incorporate these new works. Copyright laws in most developed countries were amended in the mid-1980s to include protection for computer programs.[31] Sometimes, however, new laws, parallel but separate from the existing copyright statutes, are enacted. The rights created by such laws are often called **neighboring rights** (from the French *droits voison*) because they are neighbors to, but not part of, an author's copyright. For ex-

neighboring rights:
Rights similar to copyrights that are protected by different statutes.

---

[26] MacMillan & Co., Ltd. v. Cooper, *Times Law Reports,* vol. 40, p. 188 (Privy Council, 1923).

[27] Agreement on Trade-Related Aspects of Intellectual Property Rights, Article 9, para. 2 (1994).

[28] This principle is formally stated in many copyright laws. E.g., Colombia, Law No. 23 on Copyright, Article 6(2) (January 28, 1982), provides: "The ideas or conceptual content of literary, artistic and scientific works may not be the subject of appropriation."

[29] United States, Copyright Act, § 102 (1976). Similar provisions are found in Argentina, Law No. 11,723 on Copyright, Article 1 (September 28, 1933, as amended); Colombia, Law No. 23 on Copyright, Article 2 (January 28, 1982); Ghana, Copyright Law, § 2(2) (March 21, 1985); Kenya, Copyright Law, § 3(2) (Act No. 3 of February 24, 1966, as amended); Malaysia, Copyright Act, § 7(3)(b) (April 30, 1987); Nigeria, Law No. 61 on Copyright, § 1(2)(b) (December 30, 1970); and Uganda, Copyright Act, § 2 (1966).

[30] *Federal Reporter, Second Series,* vol. 991, p. 511 (9th Circuit Ct. of Appeals, 1993).

[31] E.g., the German Copyright Law, § 2(1) (September 9, 1965, as amended in 1985), now includes computer programs among the examples it provides of "literary writings"; the U.K. Copyright (Computer Software) Amendments Act (1985), amends the U.K. Copyright Act (1956) to grant protection to computer programs; and the U.S. Computer Software Protection Act (1980) amends § 117 of the U.S. Copyright Act (1976) to make computer programs copyrightable.

This change was also incorporated in the Agreement on Trade-Related Aspects of Intellectual Property Rights,

ample, in 1989, two new international treaties governing rights similar to, but different from, the traditional copyright were adopted: the Treaty on the International Registration of Audiovisual Works and the Treaty on Intellectual Property in Respect of Integrated Circuits.[32]

Formalities

The Berne Convention, as amended in Berlin in 1908, established that the title granted by copyright laws is subject to no formalities. When the United States became a member of the Berne Convention in March of 1989, this became the rule throughout the world.[33]

Prior to March 1989, the United States was the only country that required authors to observe certain formalities to obtain a copyright. In particular, all publicly distributed copies of a work had to include a copyright notice consisting of the symbol (c) or the word "Copyright" or the abbreviation "Copr."; the year the work was first published; and the name of the copyright owner. In addition, two copies of certain kinds of works (e.g., books and phonographs) had to be deposited with the Copyright Office of the U.S. Library of Congress.[34] This is no longer the case.

Scope

A copyright applies only within the territory of the state granting it. A state will not prevent the making of copies of copyrighted material outside its territory. However, most states will keep unauthorized copies of copyrighted works from being imported into their territory.[35]

In Case 9–2, the United States Supreme Court was asked to determine whether authorized copies of a copyrighted work sold outside the United States could be imported back into the country.

Article 10, para. 1 (1994) (which applies to all World Trade Organization member states). It provides: "Computer programs, whether in source or object code, shall be protected as literary works under the Berne Convention ([as amended in Paris in] 1971)."

[32]The substantive provisions of the Treaty on Intellectual Property in Respect of Integrated Circuits have been made applicable to WTO member states by the Agreement on Trade-Related Aspects of Intellectual Property Rights, Article 35 (1994).

[33]Argentina requires copyright holders to deposit copies of certain works (e.g., books and phonographs) with the government, subject to a "suspension of the rights of the author" for failing to comply. Argentina, Law No. 11,723 on Copyright, Articles 47–63 (September 28, 1933 as amended). France also requires registration of films, videograms, and contracts relating to such works, but failure to comply does not affect the author's copyright in the works. *See* Roland Dumas, *La Propriété littéraire et artistique*, pp. 325–327 (1987).

[34]United States, Copyright Act, §§ 401–407 (1976 as amended). A copyright holder also has a right (but no duty) to register a copyright with the Copyright Office. *Id.*, §§ 408–412.

[35]For example, *United States Code*, Title 17, § 602(a), provides that the unauthorized importation of copyrighted works constitutes infringement even when the copies were lawfully made abroad.

Case 9–2   *Quality King Distributors, Inc. v. L'anza Research International, Inc.*

Supreme Court of the United States
United States Reports, vol. 523, p. 135 (1998).

JUSTICE STEVENS DELIVERED THE OPINION OF THE COURT:

Section 106(3) of the Copyright Act of 1976 (Act)[36] gives the owner of a copyright the exclusive right to distribute copies of a copyrighted work. That exclusive right is expressly limited, however, by the provisions of §§ 107 through 120. Section 602(a) gives the copyright owner the right to prohibit the unauthorized importation of copies. The question presented by this case is whether the right granted by § 602(a) is also limited by §§ 107 through 120. More narrowly, the question is whether the "first sale" doctrine endorsed in § 109(a) is applicable to imported copies.

---

[36]*United States Code*, title 17, § 106(3).

I

Respondent, L'anza Research International, Inc. (L'anza), is a California corporation engaged in the business of manufacturing and selling shampoos, conditioners, and other hair care products. L'anza has copyrighted the labels that are affixed to those products. In the United States, L'anza sells exclusively to domestic distributors who have agreed to resell within limited geographic areas and then only to authorized retailers such as barber shops, beauty salons, and professional hair care colleges. L'anza has found that the American "public is generally unwilling to pay the price charged for high quality products, such as L'anza's products, when they are sold along with the less expensive lower quality products that are generally carried by supermarkets and drug stores." L'anza promotes the domestic sales of its products with extensive advertising in various trade magazines and at point of sale, and by providing special training to authorized retailers.

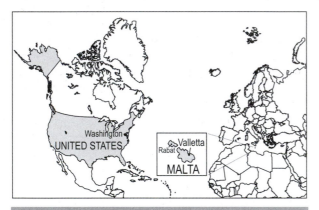

MAP 9-2　United States and Malta (1998)

L'anza also sells its products in foreign markets. In those markets, however, it does not engage in comparable advertising or promotion; its prices to foreign distributors are 35 percent to 40 percent lower than the prices charged to domestic distributors. In 1992 and 1993, L'anza's distributor in the United Kingdom arranged the sale of three shipments to a distributor in Malta; each shipment contained several tons of L'anza products with copyrighted labels affixed. The record does not establish whether the initial purchaser was the distributor in the United Kingdom or the distributor in Malta, or whether title passed when the goods were delivered to the carrier or when they arrived at their destination, but it is undisputed that the goods were manufactured by L'anza and first sold by L'anza to a foreign purchaser.

It is also undisputed that the goods found their way back to the United States without the permission of L'anza and were sold in California by unauthorized retailers who had purchased them at discounted prices from Quality King Distributors, Inc. (petitioner). There is some uncertainty about the identity of the actual importer, but for the purpose of our decision we assume that petitioner bought all three shipments from the Malta distributor, imported them, and then resold them to retailers who were not in L'anza's authorized chain of distribution.

After determining the source of the unauthorized sales, L'anza brought suit against petitioner and several other defendants. The complaint alleged that the importation and subsequent distribution of those products bearing copyrighted labels violated L'anza's "exclusive rights under *United States Code*, title 17, §§ 106, 501 and 602 to reproduce and distribute the copyrighted material in the United States." The District Court rejected petitioner's defense based on the "first sale" doctrine recognized by § 109 and entered summary judgment in favor of L'anza. Based largely on its conclusion that § 602 would be "meaningless" if § 109 provided a defense in a case of this kind, the Court of Appeals affirmed. Because its decision created a conflict with [a decision from] the Third Circuit,[37] we granted the petition for certiorari.

II

This is an unusual copyright case because L'anza does not claim that anyone has made unauthorized copies of its copyrighted labels. Instead, L'anza is primarily interested in protecting the integrity of its method of marketing the products to which the labels are affixed. Although the labels themselves have only a limited creative component, our interpretation of the relevant statutory provisions would apply equally to a case involving more familiar copyrighted materials such as sound recordings or books. Indeed, we first endorsed the first sale doctrine [in 1908] in a case [*Bobbs-Merrill Co.* v. *Straus*] involving a claim by a publisher that the resale of its books at discounted prices infringed its copyright on the books.[38]

In that case, the publisher, Bobbs-Merrill, had inserted a notice in its books that any retail sale at a price under $1.00 would constitute an infringement of its copyright. The defendants, who owned Macy's department store, disregarded the notice and sold the books at a lower price without Bobbs-Merrill's consent. We held that the exclusive statutory right to "vend" applied only to the first sale of the copyrighted work:

"What does the statute mean in granting 'the sole right of vending the same? Was it intended to create a right which would permit the holder of the copy-

[37]*See* Sebastian Int'l, Inc. *v.* Consumer Contacts (PTY) Ltd., *Federal Reporter, Second Series,* vol. 847, p. 1093 (1988).
[38]*United States Report,* vol. 210, p. 339 (1908).

right to fasten, by notice in a book or upon one of the articles mentioned within the statute, a restriction upon the subsequent alienation of the subject-matter of copyright after the owner had parted with the title to one who had acquired full dominion over it and had given a satisfactory price for it? It is not denied that one who has sold a copyrighted article, without restriction, has parted with all right to control the sale of it. The purchaser of a book, once sold by authority of the owner of the copyright, may sell it again, although he could not publish a new edition of it.

"In this case the stipulated facts show that the books sold by the appellant were sold at wholesale, and purchased by those who made no agreement as to the control of future sales of the book, and took upon themselves no obligation to enforce the notice printed in the book, undertaking to restrict retail sales to a price of one dollar per copy."

The statute in force when *Bobbs-Merrill* was decided provided that the copyright owner had the exclusive right to "vend" the copyrighted work. Congress subsequently codified our holding in *Bobbs-Merrill* that the exclusive right to "vend" was limited to first sales of the work. Under the 1976 Act, the comparable exclusive right granted in *United States Code*, title 17. § 106(3) is the right "to distribute copies . . . by sale or other transfer of ownership." The comparable limitation on that right is provided not by judicial interpretation, but by an express statutory provision. Section 109(a) provides:

"Notwithstanding the provisions of section 106(3), the owner of a particular copy or phonorecord lawfully made under this title, or any person authorized by such owner, is entitled, without the authority of the copyright owner, to sell or otherwise dispose of the possession of that copy or phonorecord. . . ."

The *Bobbs-Merrill* opinion emphasized the critical distinction between statutory rights and contract rights. In this case, L'anza relies on the terms of its contracts with its domestic distributors to limit their sales to authorized retail outlets. Because the basic holding in *Bobbs-Merrill* is now codified in § 109(a) of the Act, and because those domestic distributors are owners of the products that they purchased from L'anza (the labels of which were "lawfully made under this title"), L'anza does not, and could not, claim that the statute would enable L'anza to treat unauthorized resales by its domestic distributors as an infringement of its exclusive right to distribute copies of its labels. L'anza does claim, however, that contractual provisions are inadequate to protect it from the actions of foreign distributors who

may resell L'anza's products to American vendors unable to buy from L'anza's domestic distributors, and that § 602(a) of the Act, properly construed, prohibits such unauthorized competition. To evaluate that submission, we must, of course, consider the text of § 602(a).

III

The most relevant portion of § 602(a) provides:

"Importation into the United States, without the authority of the owner of copyright under this title, of copies or phonorecords of a work that have been acquired outside the United States is an infringement of the exclusive right to distribute copies or phonorecords under section 106, actionable under section 501. . . ."

It is significant that this provision does not categorically prohibit the unauthorized importation of copyrighted materials. Instead, it provides that such importation is an infringement of the exclusive right to distribute copies "under section 106." Like the exclusive right to "vend" that was construed in *Bobbs-Merrill*, the exclusive right to distribute is a limited right. The introductory language in § 106 expressly states that all of the exclusive rights granted by that section—including, of course, the distribution right granted by subsection (3)—are limited by the provisions of §§ 107 through 120. One of those limitations, as we have noted, is provided by the terms of § 109(a), which expressly permit the owner of a lawfully made copy to sell that copy "notwithstanding the provisions of section 106(3)."

After the first sale of a copyrighted item "lawfully made under this title," any subsequent purchaser, whether from a domestic or from a foreign reseller, is obviously an "owner" of that item. Read literally, § 109(a) unambiguously states that such an owner "is entitled, without the authority of the copyright owner, to sell" that item. Moreover, since § 602(a) merely provides that unauthorized importation is an infringement of an exclusive right "under section 106," and since that limited right does not encompass resales by lawful owners, the literal text of § 602(a) is simply inapplicable to both domestic and foreign owners of L'anza's products who decide to import them and resell them in the United States.

Notwithstanding the clarity of the text of §§ 106(3), 109(a), and 602(a), L'anza argues that the language of the Act supports a construction of the right granted by § 602(a) as "distinct from the right under Section 106(3) standing alone," and thus not subject to § 109(a). Otherwise, L'anza argues, both the § 602(a) right itself and its exceptions would be superfluous. Moreover, supported by various *amici curiae*,[39] including the Solicitor General

---

[[39]Latin: "friends of the court." Refers to legal briefs submitted by a person interested in the proceeding but not a party to the suit.]

of the United States, L'anza contends that its construction is supported by important policy considerations. We consider these arguments separately.

IV

L'anza advances two primary arguments based on the text of the Act: (1) that § 602(a), and particularly its three exceptions, are superfluous if limited by the first sale doctrine; and (2) that the text of § 501 defining an "infringer" refers separately to violations of § 106, on the one hand, and to imports in violation of § 602. The . . . answer to both of these arguments is that neither adequately explains why the words "under section 106" appear in § 602(a). . . .

* * *

V

The parties and their *amici* have debated at length the wisdom or unwisdom of governmental restraints on what is sometimes described as either the "gray market" or the

practice of "parallel importation." In *K mart Corp.* v. *Cartier, Inc.*[40] we used those terms to refer to the importation of foreign-manufactured goods bearing a valid United States trademark without the consent of the trademark holder. We are not at all sure that those terms appropriately describe the consequences of an American manufacturer's decision to limit its promotional efforts to the domestic market and to sell its products abroad at discounted prices that are so low that its foreign distributors can compete in the domestic market. But even if they do, whether or not we think it would be wise policy to provide statutory protection for such price discrimination is not a matter that is relevant to our duty to interpret the text of the Copyright Act.

* * *

The judgment of the Court of Appeals is reversed. ■

---

[40]*United States Reports,* vol. 486, p. 281 (1988).

Duration

The common rule for the duration of a copyright was established in 1948 in a revision to the Berne Convention. That is, a copyright lasts for 50 years *post mortem auctoris* (i.e., for 50 years following the author's death).[41] The WTO's newly adopted Agreement on Trade-Related Aspects of Intellectual Property Rights follows this precedent, requiring WTO member states to provide copyright protection of *at least* 50 years.[42]

Exceptions to Copyright Protection

Virtually every copyright law describes certain uses of works that do not constitute an infringement of the author's copyright. These exceptions, however, vary widely, and only a few main examples will be listed here.

Copyrighted material can be used lawfully in at least some countries (a) in a court or administrative proceeding or by the police should the material (such as a portrait) be needed to maintain public safety;[43] (b) for instructional purposes in schools;[44] (c) for a purely private use (except that computer programs may not be copied, regardless of the use involved);[45] (d) in

---

[41]Berne Convention for the Protection of Literary and Artistic Works, Article 7, para. (1) (1886 as revised in Brussels in 1948).

[42]Agreement on Trade-Related Aspects of Intellectual Property Rights, Article 12 (1994).

Some WTO member states provide for longer terms of coverage. Germany, Austria, and Switzerland grant protection for 70 years. France grants protection for 70 years for musical compositions. Spain grants protection for 60 years. Brazil follows a 60 years *post mortem auctoris* rule, the United States 70 years *post mortem,* Colombia and Guinea 80 years *post mortem,* and the Ivory Coast 99 years *post mortem.*

All states provide for similar terms when a work is created by a business firm or other juridical entity. Currently, the United States establishes a term of 95 years from the date of first publication or 120 years from the date of creation, whichever expires first, for such works. Sonny Bono Copyright Term Extension Act, Public Law 105–298 (1998) amending United States, *Copyright Act,* § 102(b) (1976).

[43]E.g., Germany, Copyright Law, § 47 (September 9, 1965, as amended).

[44]E.g., United States, Copyright Act, § 110(01) (1976).

[45]E.g., Germany, Copyright Law, § 53 (September 9, 1965, as amended).

brief quotations in scholarly or literary works, or in reviews;[46] and (e) in extended quotations of newsworthy speeches or political commentaries.[47]

Patents

A **patent** is "a statutory privilege granted by the government to inventors, and to others deriving their rights from the inventor, for a fixed period of years, to exclude other persons from manufacturing, using, or selling a patented product or from utilizing a patented method or process."[48] Although a patent is commonly referred to as a monopoly, it is not truly so. The owner of a patent may be prevented from exploiting the grant by other laws (such as national security laws or unfair competition laws) or by contractual agreement. What a patent grants, rather, is the *protection* of a monopoly. As the U.S. Supreme Court of the United States put it in *Zenith Radio Corp. v. Hazeltine Research, Inc.*:

> The heart of [a patentee's] legal monopoly is the right to invoke the state's powers to prevent others from utilizing his discovery without his consent.[49]

Historically, two reasons have been given to justify the granting of patents. One is that patents are a confirmation of the private property rights of the inventor. The other is that a patent is a grant of a special monopoly to encourage invention and industrial development.

The first of these two justifications—that patents are private property rights—can be found in the wording of the eighteenth- and nineteenth-century patent legislation of several continental European countries. For example, the French Patent Law of 1791 states:

> Every novel idea whose realization or development can become useful to society belongs primarily to the person who conceived it, and it would be a violation to the very essence of the rights of man if an industrial invention were not regarded as the property of its creator.

This private property justification for patents was also incorporated into the Paris Convention for the Protection of Industrial Property in 1878. The Paris Convention—now the principal international patent and trademark convention—includes the following statement:

> The right of inventors and of industrial creators in their own work, or the right of manufacturers and businessmen over their trademarks, is a property right. The law enacted by each nation does not create these rights, but only regulates them.

The private-property-right approach to patents has, however, some theoretical shortcomings. In particular, it does not take into account the restrictions that governments commonly impose on patents. Among these are a patent's fixed duration, its inapplicability to certain kinds of inventions, and its forfeiture or compulsory licensing when it is not worked. As a consequence, the second explanation for granting patents—to encourage inventors and public development—seems the better explanation.

This second public-interest justification for granting a patent monopoly appears in some of the very earliest of patent laws. For example, the Preamble to the Patent Law of 1474 of the Republic of Venice states that it was meant to serve as an incentive to inventors. It also is the underlying rationale of the English Patent Law of 1623, the first modern patent law.

In England, in the fourteenth and fifteenth centuries, the grant of a patent monopoly was a matter of sovereign prerogative. That power, however, was used almost exclusively as a way of raising revenue. As a consequence, many of the early English patents involved day-to-day necessities completely lacking in novelty or invention. To combat what was clearly an abuse of the royal prerogative, the English Parliament enacted the Statute of Monopolies in 1623. This made

---

[46]E.g., United Kingdom, Copyright Act, § 6(2) (1956 as amended).
[47]E.g., France, Law No. 57-298, Article 41(3) (March 11, 1957, as amended).
[48]*The Role of Patents in the Transfer of Technology to Developing Countries,* p. 9 (UN Doc. Sales No. 65.II.B.1, 1964).
[49]*United States Reports,* vol. 395, p. 100 (Supreme Ct., 1917).

illegal all monopolies, grants, and patents that had given individuals the right to buy, sell, or use particular things within the country. Only one category was excepted: patents for inventions.

The English Statute of Monopolies also set down, for the first time, the principle that patents were to be made available on a uniform basis "to the true and first inventor" for the purpose of encouraging inventions and manufacturing. Later, a court decision construed the words "true and first inventor" to include the first person to introduce a new process or procedure from abroad, thereby extending patent protection to imported technologies, as well as to completely new inventions.

The idea that patents should be granted to reward inventors for advancing the public interest was incorporated in the U.S. Constitution of 1789. The Constitution gives the U.S. Congress the power "to promote the progress of science and useful arts by securing for a limited time to authors and inventors the exclusive right to their respective writings and discoveries."

In 1809, the Emperor of Brazil promulgated the fourth modern patent law (following the British, U.S., and French statutes), which set out the following policy:

> It being highly convenient that inventors of any new machinery should have an exclusive privilege for a certain time, I hereby order that no matter who should be in such a position to submit the plans of his invention to the Royal Board of Trade which, verifying that such invention is really worthy, should be given the exclusive right for the period of fourteen years after which the invention should be published so that all the nation might have the right to share the benefits of such invention.

Today, both the private rights of inventors and the public's interests in promoting development continue to be the primary justifications given both in patent acts and by legal writers for the granting of inventors' privileges. In some respects, however, a patent is now viewed as a device for reconciling these two competing interests. For example, a 1964 United Nations study that compared the patent laws of the world concluded that a patent is "essentially a process in which account is taken of, and an attempt is made to reconcile and satisfy, the whole scheme of public and private interests pressing for recognition."[50] On the private side are the inventor's claims for recognition and economic advantage. On the public side, there is not only the interest of the government in promoting economic development but also the social benefit in encouraging invention, as well as the desire of consumers to purchase goods for fair value.

Patents and Other Inventor's Grants

The primary method of protecting and rewarding inventors is the patent. As defined earlier, a patent is an exclusive privilege granted to an inventor, for a fixed term, to manufacture, use, and sell a product or to employ a method or a process. Most countries, accordingly, grant three basic kinds of patents:

design patent: Patent granted to protect new and original designs of an article of manufacture.

plant patent: Patent granted for the creation or discovery of a new and distinct variety of a plant.

utility patent: Patent granted for the invention of a new and useful process, machine, article of manufacture, or composition of matter.

- **Design patents** are granted to protect new and original designs of an article of manufacture.
- **Plant patents** are granted for the creation or discovery of a new and distinct variety of a plant.
- **Utility patents** are granted for the invention of a new and useful process, machine, article of manufacture, or composition of matter.

There are also several variations on these basic patents, including *confirmation patents* (which are issued for inventions already patented in another country),[51] *patents of addition* (which cover improvements on already patented inventions), and *precautionary patents* (which are issued for short periods of time to an inventor who has not completely perfected an invention, so that he will be notified when any other inventors apply for a patent on the same invention, and so that he will have the opportunity to object to their applications).

In addition, a few countries provide protection for lesser inventions (i.e., technical improvements of a minor nature). Developed in Germany and Japan and adopted in a few

---

[50]*The Role of Patents in the Transfer of Technology to Developing Countries,* p. 10 (UN Doc. E/3861, 1964).

[51]Confirmation patents are most commonly recognized in Latin America, where they are seen as a device for promoting the introduction and domestic exploitation of foreign inventions. A similar device called a *patent of importation* is available in Belgium and Spain.

petty patent: A statutory right given to the authors of minor inventions.

new: An invention is new if no other inventor has obtained a patent for the same invention.

inventive step: That the subject matter of an invention was not obvious at the time of the invention's making to a person having ordinary skill in the art of the subject matter.

capable of industrial application: That the product or process of an invention can be used in industry or commerce.

other countries (most notably Spain), this form of protection is known as a **petty patent** or an inventor's right in a *utility model.*

The German system of *Gebrauchmuster* (utility or working models) was established in 1891; the Japanese Utility Model Law was enacted in 1905. In Germany, a petty patent will be granted for a period of three years following a determination by the German Patent Office that the invention is novel (i.e., that no other inventor has obtained a patent or petty patent for the same invention). In Japan, a petty patent, which lasts for 15 years, will only be issued after the Patent Office determines both novelty and inventiveness (i.e., that the invention is not something that was obvious to the scientific community at the time of its invention).

Inventions That Qualify for Patent Protection

Patents may be obtained for inventions in every field of technology, whether products or processes, as long as they are "new, involve an inventive step, and are capable of industrial application."[52] An invention is **new** if no other inventor has obtained a patent for the same invention; it involves an **inventive step** if the "subject matter" of the invention was not "obvious at the time the invention was made to a person having ordinary skill in the art to which said subject matter pertains";[53] and it is **capable of industrial application** if the product or process is one that can be used in industry or commerce.

Case 9–3 examines more fully what is meant by the term "inventive step."

---

[52]Agreement on Trade-Related Aspects of Intellectual Property Rights, Article 27, para. 1 (1994).

"For the purposes of this Article, the terms 'inventive step' and 'capable of industrial application' may be deemed by a member to be synonymous with the terms 'nonobvious' and 'useful' respectively." *Id.,* n. 5.

[53]United States, Patent Act, § 103 (1952).

Case 9–3   *Monsanto Co. v. Coramandal Indag Products, (P) Ltd.*

India, Supreme Court, 1986.
Supreme Court Journal, vol. 1, p. 234 (1986).

JUDGE CHINNAPPA REDDY:

The long and grasping hand of a multinational company, the Monsanto Company of St. Louis, Missouri, United States of America, has reached out to prevent the alleged infringement of two of their patents (Numbers 104120 and 125381) by the defendant, an Indian Private Limited Company. Though the suit, as initially laid, was with reference to two patents, the suit was ultimately confined to one patent only (Number 125381), the period for which the other patent (104120) was valid having expired during the pendency of the suit. . . .

We may first refer to a few preliminary facts. Weeds, as is well known, are a menace to food crops, particularly crops like rice which belong to the grass variety. Research has been going on for years to discover a weed killer which has no toxic effect on rice, that is to say, a herbicide which will destroy the weeds but allow rice to survive without any deleterious effect. For long the

research was futile. But in 1966–67 came a breakthrough. A scientist, Dr. John Olin, discovered CP 53619 with the formula 2-Chloro-2, 6-Diethyl-N-(Butoxy-Methyl)-Acetanilide, which satisfied the requirement of a weed killer which had no toxic effect on rice. The annual report of the International Rice Research Institute for 1968 stated: "Weed control in rice was an important part of the agronomy program. The first agronomic evidence of the efficacy of granular-trichloroethyl styrene for the selective control of annual grasses in transplanted rice was obtained at the Institute. *Another accession, CP 53619, gave excellent weed control in transplanted flooded and nonflooded, upland rice.*" It was further stated: "CP 53619 at 2 and 4 kg/ha appeared at least twice among the 20 best treatments," and "the most outstanding new pre-emergence herbicide was 2-Chloro-2, 6-Diethyl-N-(Butoxy-Methyl)-Acetanilide (CP 53619)." The annual report of the International Rice Institute for 1969 shows that the herbicide CP 53619 came to acquire the name of Butachlor.

. . . The first plaintiff is the Monsanto Company and the second plaintiff is a subsidiary of the first plaintiff

MAP 9-3 India (1986)

registered as a company in India. It was stated in the plaint that the first plaintiff was the patentee of inventions entitled "Phytotoxic Compositions" and "Grass Selective Herbicide Compositions," duly patented under patent numbers 104120 dated March 1, 1966, and 125381 dated February 20, 1970. The claims and the particulars relating to the inventions . . . stated . . . and this is very important, "the active ingredient mentioned in the claim is called 'Butachlor.'" It suggested, without expressly saying it, that the plaintiffs' patents covered Butachlor also, which in fact it did not, as we shall presently see. It was next stated that the first plaintiff had permitted the second plaintiff to work the patents from 1971 onwards under an agreement dated September 3, 1980. . . . It came to the notice of the plaintiffs, it was averred, that the defendant was attempting to market a formulation of Butachlor covered by the said patents. They, therefore, wrote to the defendants drawing their attention to the existence of the patents in their favor. Some correspondence ensued. In the second week of May, 1981, the second plaintiff found that the defendant was marketing a formulation of Butachlor covered by the patents of the first plaintiff. Sample tins of "Butachlor 50" manufactured by the defendant were purchased by the plaintiffs. . . .

According to the plaintiffs, the legends on the tins containing substance manufactured by the defendant showed that what was sold by the defendant was nothing but a reproduction of the first plaintiff's patented formulation. The formulations of the defendant were sent to the Shri Ram Institute for analysis and they were said to contain the chemical "Butachlor, the chemical formula for which is 2 Chloro, 6-Diethyl-N-(Butoxymethyl) Acetanilide." On these averments the plaintiffs alleged that the defendant had infringed their patents, numbers 104120 and 125381, by selling formulations covered by them. The plaintiffs sued for an injunction. . . .

. . . [T]he defendant claimed, as he was entitled to do under Section 107 of the Patents Act 1970, that the patents were liable to be revoked. . . . The defendant also made a counterclaim seeking revocation of the patents.

A close scrutiny of the plaint and a reference to the evidence of the witnesses for the plaintiff at once exposes the hollowness of the suit. We must begin with the statement in the plaint that "the active ingredient mentioned in the claim is called 'Butachlor,'" which suggests that Butachlor was covered by the plaintiffs' patents and the circumstance now admitted that no one, neither the plaintiff nor any one else, has a patent for Butachlor. The admission was expressly made by PW-2, the power of attorney holder of the first plaintiff and Director of the second plaintiff company. The learned counsel for the plaintiffs also admitted the same before us. PW-1, Dr. Dixon, a chemist of the first plaintiff company, after explaining the use of an emulsifying agent, in answer to a direct question, whether his company claimed any patent or special knowledge for the use of any particular solvent or particular emulsifying agent, in the formulation in their patent, had to admit that they had no such patent or special knowledge. He further admitted that the use of solvent and emulsifying agent on the active ingredient was one of the well-known methods used in the pesticide industry to prepare a marketable product. He also expressed his inability to say what dilutents or other emulsifying agents the defendant used in their process. PW-2 admitted that Butachlor was a common name and that the Weed Science Society of America had allotted the common name. He stated that "Machete" was the brand name under which their company manufactured Butachlor. He also stated that there could be a number of concerns all over the world manufacturing Butachlor, but he was not aware of them. He admitted that they did not claim a patent for Butachlor. He stated that though his company did not claim a patent for Butachlor, they claimed a patent for the process of making a Butachlor emulsifiable concentrate to be used as a herbicide composition for rice. Pursued further in cross-examination, he was forced to admit that they used kerosene as a solvent for Butachlor and an emulsifier manufactured by a local Indian company was an emulsifying agent. He then proceeded to state that he claimed secrecy with regard to the manufacture of their formulation. When he was asked further whether the secrecy claimed was with regard to the solvent or with regard to the stabilizer, he answered in the negative. He finally admitted that his secret was confined to the active ingredient Butachlor about which, as we know, there is no secret. . . .

We, therefore, see that Butachlor (which was the common name for CP 53619) was discovered prior to 1968 as a herbicide possessing the property of nontoxic effect on rice. The formula for the herbicide was published in the report of the International Rice Research Institute for the year 1968 and its common name Butachlor was also mentioned in the report of the International Rice Research Institute for the year 1969. No one patented the invention Butachlor and it was the property of the population of the world. Before Butachlor, or for that matter any herbicide could be used for killing weeds, it had to be converted into an emulsion by dissolving it in a suitable solvent and by mixing the solution with an emulsifying agent. Emulsification is a well-known process and is no one's discovery. In the face of the now indisputable fact that there is no patent for or any secrecy attached to Butachlor, the solvent, or the emulsifying agent, and the further fact that the process of emulsification is no new discovery, the present suit based on the secrecy claimed in respect of the active ingredient Butachlor and the claim for the process of emulsification must necessarily fail. Under Section 61(1)(d) [of the Patents Act, 1970], a patent may be revoked on the ground that the subject of any claim of the complete specification is not an invention within the meaning of the Act. Under Section 64(e), a patent may be revoked if invention so far as claimed in any claim of the complete specifications is not new, having regard to what was publicly known or publicly used in India before the date of the claim, etc. Under Section 64(1)(f), a patent may be revoked if the invention so far as claimed in any claim of the complete specification is obvious or does not involve any inventive step having regard to what was publicly known or publicly used in India or was published in India before the priority date of the claim (the words "or elsewhere" are omitted by us as the patents in the present case were granted under the Indian Patents and Designs Act, 1911, i.e., before the Patents Act, 1970). "Inventions" has been defined by Section 2(j) as follows:

Invention means any new and useful—(i) art, process, method, or manner of manufacture; (ii) machine, apparatus, or other article; (iii) substance produced by manufacture, and includes any new and useful improvement of any of them, and an alleged invention.

It is clear from the facts narrated by us that the herbicide CP 53619 (Butachlor) was publicly known before patent number 125381 was granted. Its formula and use had already been made known to the public by the report of the International Rice Institute for the year 1968. No one claimed any patent or any other exclusive right to Butachlor. To satisfy the requirement of being publicly known as used in clauses (e) and (f) of the Section 64(1), it is not necessary that it should be widely used to the knowledge of the consumer public. It is sufficient if it is known to the persons who are engaged in the pursuit of any knowledge of the patented product or process, either as men of science or men of commerce or consumers. The section of the public who, as men of science or men of commerce, were interested in knowing about herbicides which would destroy weeds but rice, must have been aware of the discovery of Butachlor. There was no secret about the active ingredient Butachlor, as claimed by the plaintiffs, since there was no patent for Butachlor, as admitted by the plaintiffs. Emulsification was a well-known and common process by which any herbicide could be used. Neither Butachlor nor the process of emulsification was capable of being claimed by the plaintiffs as their exclusive property. The solvent and the emulsifier were not secrets and they were admittedly ordinary market products. From the beginning to the end, there was no secret and there was no invention by the plaintiffs. The ingredients, the active ingredient, the solvent, and the emulsifier, were known; the process was known; the product was known; and the use was known. The plaintiffs were merely camouflaging a substance whose discovery was known throughout the world and trying to enfold it in their specification relating to patent number 125381. The patent is, therefore, liable to be revoked. . . . The appeal is dismissed with costs. ■

Determining Qualifications

Questions about the existence or nonexistence of newness, inventive steps, and industrial application can arise at various stages in the life of a patent. They may arise during the initial review of an application, during the appeal of a denial, during a revocation or cancellation hearing, or in suits for infringement where the person charged with infringement disputes the validity of the patent.

With regard to the first of these—the review of an application by a patent office—procedures vary from country to country. They range from a simple review of the application form to an extensive search of domestic and foreign materials to determine if the product or process is both novel and inventive. The different procedures (for a select group of countries) are summarized in Exhibit 9-1.

In completing an application form, an inventor is uniformly required to disclose sufficient information about the product or process "in such full, clear, concise, and exact terms as to enable any person skilled in the art to which it pertains, or with which it is most clearly connected, to make and use the same."[54] In addition, in the United States the application must disclose the "best mode" known to the inventor for carrying out the invention.[55] Most other countries, however, allow an applicant to elect to disclose only one mode, and that does not necessarily have to be the best mode.

In Europe and Japan, and in most of the developing world, the information contained in a patent application has to be published before a patent will be granted. In the developing world, this publication requirement acts as a substitute for an examination of novelty and inventiveness by a patent office. In Colombia, for example, a patent will issue 30 days after publication in the *Diario Official* (official journal) unless some private party raises an objection.[56] In the developed world, the publication date is the date on which the patent vests, although it will not be enforceable until it is formally granted by a patent office.

Publication during the application process is not required in the United States. Nevertheless, most litigation in the United States concerning the validity of a patent application arises during the application process. In part, this is because of the size and nature of the U.S. Patent Office. In most other countries (despite the requirements for disclosure during the application process), most challenges to the validity of a patent arise after a patent is granted.[57]

EXHIBIT 9-1   Procedures Used in Reviewing Patent Applications

Procedure	Countries Using Procedure
1. Examination of the application form only.	Egypt, Iran, Italy, Lebanon, Liberia, Morocco, Spain, Switzerland,[a] Tunisia, Turkey
2. Examination as to form, then publication followed by a period in which the public may object to the grant of a patent.	Colombia, Peru, Venezuela
3. Examination as to form and novelty. Only domestic patents are searched in ascertaining novelty.	Argentina
4. Examination as to form and novelty. Domestic and foreign patents are searched in ascertaining novelty.	India, Israel
5. Examination as to form and inventiveness. Domestic and foreign developments are searched in ascertaining inventiveness.	France
6. Examination as to form, novelty, and inventiveness. Only domestic patents and developments are searched in ascertaining novelty and inventiveness.	Mexico
7. Examination as to form, novelty, and inventiveness. Domestic and foreign patents and developments are searched in ascertaining novelty and inventiveness.	Brazil, Canada, Czechoslovakia, Germany, Japan, the Netherlands, Pakistan, Russia, Sweden, United Kingdom, United States

[a]Switzerland requires an examination as to form, novelty, and inventiveness for patents involving textiles and textile dyes.

---

[54]United States, Patent Act, § 112 (1952).
[55]*Id.*
[56]Colombia, Patent Law (1925 as amended).
[57]Alan Gutterman, "A Legal Due Diligence Framework for Inbound Transfers of Foreign Technology Rights," *The International Lawyer,* vol. 24, p. 982 (1990).

Inventions Excluded from Patent Protection

Patents may be denied to inventions that do not meet the basic definition of patentability (i.e., being new, involving an inventive step, and being capable of industrial application). They may also be denied to inventions that violate basic social policies. The Agreement on Trade-Related Aspects of Intellectual Property Rights, for example, allows a WTO member state to deny a patent to an inventor in order "to protect *ordre public* or morality" so long as the state also forbids the commercial exploitation of the invention.[58] (That is, a state cannot deny an inventor a patent on this basis and still let the invention be exploited freely by others.) In particular, patents may be denied for this reason in order to protect the lives or health of humans, animals, or plants, or to protect the environment from serious injury.

The TRIPS Agreement also allows WTO member states to deny patents for certain inventions without also prohibiting their commercial exploitation. (In other words, the invention may be freely exploited within the territory of the state.) These inventions may include (a) diagnostic, therapeutic, and surgical methods for the treatment of humans and animals; (b) plants and animals other than microorganisms (except that member states must provide patent protection or its equivalent for plant varieties); and (c) essentially biological processes for the production of plants or animals.[59]

Duration of Patents

With the coming into force of the TRIPS Agreement on January 1, 1995, the minimum term of protection for patents has now been set at 20 years for WTO member states.[60] Previously, the terms that countries had established varied widely, ranging from three to 26 years (including extensions).[61] The uniformity provided by the new 20-year standard should greatly encourage inventors, who will now be able to exploit their inventions much more widely and for an overall longer period than they were able to do in the past.

The Scope of Patents

A patent is valid only within the territory of the state granting it; hence, states cannot prevent the use of patented technology outside their territory. States will, however, stop the importation of goods from third countries that infringe a patent. On the other hand, many states will not stop someone inside their territory from using patented technology to produce a product for export and sale abroad.[62]

Trademarks

Merchants and others use five marks to identify themselves and their products. These are (1) trademarks (or sometimes "true trademarks" to distinguish them from other marks), (2) trade names, (3) service marks, (4) collective marks, and (5) certification marks. In practice, all five are commonly called trademarks.

true trademark: A mark or symbol used to identify goods of a particular manufacturer or merchant.

trade name: A mark or symbol used to identify a manufacturer or merchant.

A **true trademark** is "any word, name, symbol, or device or any combination thereof adopted and used by a manufacturer or merchant to identify his goods and distinguish them from those manufactured or sold by others."[63] It is different from a **trade name**, which is the name of the manufacturer rather than the manufacturer's products. *PepsiCo*, for example, is the well-known trade name of *PepsiCo, Inc.*, a company that manufactures and sells products under trademarks such as *Pepsi-Cola, Fritos,* and *Gatorade*.

---

[58]Agreement on Trade-Related Aspects of Intellectual Property Rights, Article 27, para. 2 (1994).
[59]*Id.*, para. 3.
[60]*Id.*, Article 33.
[61]*See* Ray August, *International Business Law: Text, Cases, and Readings,* pp. 610–611 (1st ed., 1993).
[62]For example, in Deepsouth Packing Co. v. Laitram Corp., *United States Reports,* vol. 406, p. 518 at pp. 526–529 (1972), the U.S. Supreme Court held that the shipment overseas of materials that, when assembled in combination, violated a U.S. patent did not result in liability for contributory infringement. The U.S. Congress subsequently reversed this decision by statute. *See* Patent Law Amendments of 1984, codified as amended at *United States Code,* Title 35, § 271(f) (1992). In the United States, accordingly, the manufacture of a product in the United States using a U.S. patented process will infringe the patent, even if the product is intended for shipment abroad and requires final assembly overseas.
[63]Lanham Trademark Act (1946), in *United States Code,* Title 15, § 1127.

service mark: A mark or symbol used to identify a person who provides services.

A **service mark** is a "mark used in the sale or advertising of services to identify the services of one person and distinguish them from the services of another."[64] *Yum! Brands, Inc.,* for example, uses the service marks of *KFC, Pizza Hut,* and *Taco Bell* to identify its service establishments.

As the examples indicate, a mark can be used for more than one purpose. Thus, *KFC* is both a trademark and a service mark. Similarly, *Coca-Cola* is used both as a trade name and a trademark.

collective mark: A mark or symbol used by a group to identify itself to its members.

When trademarks or service marks are used by members of an association, collective, or cooperative organization to identify their products or services to members, they are called **collective marks.** Examples include the identifying names and insignias of the American Greek letter fraternities and sororities or the uniforms or cookies of Boy Scouts and Girl Scouts.

certification mark: A mark or symbol used by a licensee or franchisee to indicate that a particular product meets certain standards.

A **certification mark** is a mark used exclusively by a licensee or franchisee to indicate that a product meets certain standards. Examples include "*Champagne,*" "*Roquefort,*" and "*Grown in Idaho,*" which indicate places of origin;[65] and the "*Underwriters' Seal of Approval,*" which attests to certain standards of quality. Unlike true trademarks, trade names, and service marks, a licensor or franchisor may not use a certification mark.

Trademarks (using the term broadly) have several functions. From the perspective of an owner, a trademark is the right to put a product protected by the mark into circulation for the first time.[66] From the viewpoint of a consumer, a trademark serves to (a) designate the origin or source of a product or service, (b) indicate a particular standard of quality, (c) represent the goodwill of the manufacturer, and (d) protect the consumer from confusion.[67]

Acquiring Trademarks

Trademarks are acquired in two ways: by use and by registration. In a few countries, registration is not available. In two countries—Canada and the Philippines—a trademark can be registered only if it has already been put into use. In the rest of the world, a mark can be registered even if it has never been used in commerce.[68]

The fact that a trademark cannot be registered does not mean that its owner is without rights. In *McDonald's Corp. v. Hassan Arzouni,* the Civil Court of Sharjah, one of the United Arab Emirates, held that McDonald's could enjoin a local entrepreneur from using its name and golden arches logo on a restaurant, even though Sharjah has no trademark registration law. The court said:

> The fact that such trademark has not been registered in the U.A.E. is irrelevant, because of the fame of this trademark worldwide and the possibility of the simultaneous presence of the two products in the U.A.E. market, considering the ease of transportation, the wide range of commerce, and the fact that the U.A.E. imports most of its consumer products, including foodstuffs.[69]

As the *Hassan Arzouni* case points out, "famous" trademarks (i.e., ones well known throughout the world) may not have to be registered to be protected. In another case involving McDonald's, *Colourprint Ltd. v. McDonald's Corp.,* the American fast-food retailer opposed an

[64]*Id.*
[65]The Agreement on Trade-Related Aspects of Intellectual Property Rights, Article 22 (1994), requires WTO Member States to provide the legal means for interested parties to prevent the use of geographical indications of origin that mislead the public. Geographical indications of origin relating to wine are protected even if they are not misleading (for instance, even if the true geographical origin is accompanied by words such as "kind," "type," imitation," etc., it may not be used). *Id.,* Article 23. Also, the TRIPS Council (established by the Agreement) is to undertake negotiations to establish a multilateral system for notifying and registering geographical indications of the origins of wines. *Id.,* para. 4.
[66]Centrafarm v. Winthrop, Case 16/74, *European Court Reports,* vol. 1974, p. 1183 (1974).
[67]J. Gilson, *Trademark Protection and Practice,* § 1.03 (1975). *See,* as well, Hanover Star Milling Co. v. Metcalf in *United States Reports,* vol. 240, at p. 412 (Supreme Ct., 1916).
[68]Prior to 1988, the United States also required that a trademark could not be registered until it had been put in use. Now, a trademark will be granted based on the applicant's intent to use the mark. The mark must then be used within six months (although extensions can be obtained so that the period can be three years) or the registration will be revoked. The Trademark Law Revision Act, Public Law 100-667, § 134 (1988).
[69]Case No. 823/85, decided January 13, 1986 (unpublished); quoted in *Trademark Reporter,* vol. 76, p. 354 (1986).

application in Kenya by a local company to register the McDonald's name and double arches logo as a trademark. McDonald's had not registered its trademark and did not have it in any restaurants in Kenya. Nevertheless, the Kenyan Deputy Registrar of Trademarks would not allow the local company to register the mark as its own. The Deputy stated:

> I have no doubt in my mind that local reputation of the mark is very important, but I am also of the view that reputation outside Kenya cannot be ignored altogether. It is also important to consider whether any section of the Kenyan public were aware of the existence of the opponents' mark at the time when the applicants' mark was filed for registration. This is relevant because the likelihood of confusion or deception must be considered at the time of the application.
>
> A section of the Kenya public has not only seen the opponent's mark in the magazines referred to, but I accept that they have traveled to some countries outside Africa where the opponents' mark is well known. The opponents run the business of hotels [*sic*] and no doubt some Kenyans are familiar with the products of the opponent.[70]

The same result has been reached in Australia, Canada, Colombia, India, New Zealand, the United Kingdom, and the United States. In other countries (e.g., Panama and Taiwan), a foreign owner of a famous unregistered trademark can oppose registration but cannot sue a local company for infringement. In still other countries (e.g., most of South America), only a locally registered owner can protest either registration or infringing use.[71]

Of course, in any of the countries that allow an unregistered foreign trademark holder to either challenge a competing registration or an infringing use, the trademark in question must be well-known. For example, in *Wienerwald Holding, A.G. v. Kawn, Wong, Tan, and Fong*, the High Court of Hong Kong concluded that the name "Wienerwald Restaurant," which was the service mark of a Swiss restaurant company, was so little known in Hong Kong that the Swiss owner could not object to a competing registration in Hong Kong by a local firm of chartered accountants.[72]

In addition to the objections that can be raised by famous trademark holders, most countries allow a local user of a mark to object to its registration by another individual—even if the mark is not famous—so long as the opponent's local use began before that of the applicant. However, a few states will register a trademark to the first person to apply for it, regardless. Thus prior users are denied the right to challenge the application or to later seek cancellation of the registration.[73]

Registration

One registers a trademark to publicly notify other potential users of one's claim in a mark. The registration process commonly begins with an examination done by an official in the Trademark Office to determine a mark's suitability for registration. In most countries this consists simply of an examination of the application form for compliance with statutory definitions and an examination of the Office's own records to ensure that the mark has not been previously registered. In wealthier countries with the resources to maintain a large library and a large staff, the examination can include the examination of records from other countries, records of the states of a federal or economic union, or private materials, such as newspapers, magazines, or trademark association reports.

Registration Criteria

distinctive: Possessing a unique design that distinguishes a product from other similar products.

The common statutory definitional criterion that appears in all trademark laws is **distinctiveness**. This means that a mark must possess a unique design that functions to distinguish the

---

[70]Decision by Deputy Registrar of Trademarks in Kenya, TM No. B23964, May 21, 1980, at p. 9 (unreported); quoted in Thomas Hoffmann and Susan Brownstone, "Protection of Trademark Rights Acquired by International Reputation without Use of Registration," *Trademark Reporter,* vol. 71, pp. 21–22 (1981).

[71]*Id.,* pp. 1–37.

[72]*Fleet Street Patent Law Reports,* vol. 1979, p. 381 (January 20, 1979).

[73]American Bar Association, Section of Patent, Trademark and Copyright Law, *1990 Committee Reports,* p. 96 (1990).

product on which it is used from other similar products. In sum, to be registered, a trademark must (a) not infringe on another mark and (b) be distinctive.

In Case 9–4, an international arbitration panel had to determine whether an Internet domain name—which is treated very much like a trademark—was confusingly similar to a registered mark.

Case 9–4   Experience Hendrix, L.L.C. v. Hammerton

World Intellectual Property Organization Arbitration and Mediation Center.
Administrative Panel Decision, Case No. D2000-0364, August 2, 2000.

PANELIST MARYLEE JENKINS:

1. The Parties

Experience Hendrix, L.L.C. ("Complainant"), is a Washington limited liability company with a principal place of business at 14501 Interurban Avenue South, Tukwila, Washington, 98168, U.S.A. The company was formed in 1995 by the family of the late Jimi Hendrix, an internationally known guitarist and musician. Experience Hendrix, L.L.C., is the owner and administrator of substantially all rights relating to Jimi Hendrix, including rights in his music, name, image, and recordings.

The Respondent, Denny Hammerton ("Mr. Hammerton"), an individual, is listed as the administrative contact for the registration of the domain name in issue and lists a mailing address of P.O. Box 1103, Minneola, Florida, 34744, U.S.A. The Respondent, The Jimi Hendrix Fan Club ("Fan Club"), added by amendment to the Complaint, is the registrant of the domain name registration and has the same mailing address as Mr. Hammerton.

* * *

5. Factual Background

The Complainant is the owner of all rights in the name "JIMI HENDRIX", including all common law rights therein, and is the owner of several trademarks and service marks registered or pending with the U.S. Patent and Trademark Office. . . .

* * *

The Complainant is also the registrant of the domain names "jimi-hendrix.com," "jimi-hendrix.org," and "jimihendrix.org" and is the owner and operator of the "Experience Hendrix Interactive—The Official Jimi Hendrix Web site" located at "www.jimi-hendrix.com."

MAP 9-4   Washington and Florida (2000)

A search result from a query of the Registrar's Whois database shows that the domain name in issue was registered on April 5, 1996, to "The Jimi Hendrix Fan Club" with Mr. Hammerton listed as the administrative contact.

Some time between the domain name registration and April 30, 1997, the Respondent created a Web site at "www.jimihendrix.com" that offered for sale vanity e-mail addresses incorporating the "jimihendrix.com" domain name ("Site").

The Complainant's representatives communicated with the Registrar and asked the Registrar to initiate the Registrar's Domain Name Dispute Policy then in effect with respect to the domain name "jimihendrix.com." On April 30, 1997, the domain name was placed on "Hold" status by the Registrar.

In a letter dated March 21, 2000, the Registrar notified the Complainant's representatives that on May 2, 2000, the Registrar would terminate the dispute, remove the domain name registration from "Hold" status and reactivate the domain name unless the Registrar received either a complaint filed pursuant to the Policy or a file-stamped complaint filed in a court of competent jurisdiction which involved the subject domain name registration and named the domain name registrant as a party. The Complainant commenced this proceeding in response to the Registrar's March 21st letter.

6. Parties' Contentions

Complainant The Complainant contends that the domain name "jimihendrix.com" is identical or confusingly similar to the name and marks owned by the Complainant.

The Complainant contends that the Respondent has no rights or legitimate interests in the domain name based upon:

(i) the Respondent choosing the domain name in issue not arbitrarily but intending to misappropriate and use the goodwill in the Complainant's marks for his own commercial benefit by advertising vanity e-mail addresses for sale on a Web page located at "www.jimihendrix.com."

(ii) the Complainant having not at any time, assigned, granted, licensed, sold, or otherwise transferred any of its rights in the name and mark JIMI HENDRIX to the Respondent.

(iii) the Respondent's use of the domain name being purely commercial in nature with the effect of diluting and harming the Complainant's legitimate rights in the name and mark.

(iv) the Respondent, Mr. Hammerton, being a domain name speculator and registering and selling domain names for no legitimate purpose other than to profit from the name relying on a front page article in the *San Francisco Chronicle* quoting Mr. Hammerton as saying "[s]ome people like it, some people don't—that's tough. . . . It's real estate is what it is. If I buy land that somebody wants, then lucky me." The Complainant further quotes the article as stating that Mr. Hammerton claimed to own rights to "some 2,000 Web site names, including, www.jimihendrix.com, www.jethrotull.com, and www.fleetwoodmac.com."

The Complainant contends that the Respondent has registered and used the domain name in bad faith based upon:

(i) the Respondent knowing at all times prior to, during, and following registration of the domain name that he did not own or have

any legal rights to the name or mark JIMI HENDRIX.

(ii) the Respondent trying to benefit commercially by offering to sell the domain name to the Complainant for "an exorbitant amount of money.

(iii) a recent search of a domain name reseller site showing Mr. Hammerton advertising to sell the "jimihendrix.com" domain name for $1 million dollars as "the most unique domain/jimi was a 'hit' maker."

(iv) the Respondent having made it clear to the Complainant and the world that the Respondent intends to prevent the Complainant from reflecting the Complainant's mark in a corresponding domain name based on comments posted on the Web site located at "www.johnlennon.com" and an e-mail message from Mr. Hammerton.

(v) Mr. Hammerton being a domain name speculator that registers and sells domain names for no legitimate purpose other than to profit from the name.

(vi) Mr. Hammerton advertising to sell the domain names "elvispresley.net" for $39,000, "jethrotull.com" for $8,000, "lindamccartney.com" for $15,000–$25,000, "mickjagger.com" for $25,000, "paulmccartney.com" for $25,000–$51,000, "ringo.com" for $15,000–$21,000, "rodstewart.com" for $15,000–$21,000, and "twiggy.com" for $10,000 on different domain name reseller sites.

(vii) the Respondent also having registered and having since transferred or sold the domain names "johnlennon.com," "eltonjohn.com," "otisredding.com," "whitneyhouston.com," and "barrymanilow.com" based on archived news, a domain resale bulletin board and Whois records.

(viii) the Respondent, by using the domain name, having intentionally attempted to attract, for commercial gain, Internet users to his Web site by creating a likelihood of confusion with the Complainant's mark as to source, sponsorship, affiliation, and endorsement of his Web site or the services he offers on the site;

(ix) a search by the Complainant of a database of fictitious names in Florida, where Mr. Hammerton resides, showing that the name "The Jimi Hendrix Fan Club" is not registered as a "dba" in that state and that no such entity has ever been created in Florida;

(x) the Respondent, although having registered the domain name "jimihendrix.com" in the name of a fan club, not being a true "fan club" existing at the address "www. jimihendrix.com" or providing any traditional fan club services, but being nothing more than a sales promotion site—selling vanity e-mail addresses.

(xi) Mr. Hammerton operating or having operated under a number of aliases including "Benny Hammerton," "D, Ralph," "Denny Rhammerton," "Denny Thedom Hammerton," "Denny Trad Hammerton," "King, Richard," "Denny Nexus Hammerton," "Denny McBeatle Hammerton," and "Count Cybergod";

(xii) Mr. Hammerton understanding that using a trademarked name has legal consequences, as can be seen from his Trademark Services Web site at "www.dalemabry.com/mark. htm" which states, "[r]eserving your Domain Name does not guarantee that the name will be free of trademark conflicts. If your Domain Name matches a registered trademark, the owner of that trademark has the power to take the Domain Name away from you. Don't let this happen to your business."

Based upon the above, the Complainant requests that the Panelist transfer the domain name "jimihendrix.com" to it.

Respondent The Respondent, Mr. Hammerton, contends that he registered the domain "jimihendrix.com" on April 5, 1996. Before registering the domain name, he contends that he conducted a search of the USPTO database for any trademarks on "Jimi Hendrix" and found none.

The Respondent contends that from April of 1996, he ran a Web site for "The Jimi Hendrix Internet Fan Club" on the Internet until a complaint by the Complainant was sent to the Registrar in 1997 resulting in the domain name "jimihendrix.com" being placed on Hold.

The Respondent contends that his registration of the domain name precedes the Complainant's trademark.

The Respondent contends that a word with a .com on the end is not identical to a word without a .com on the end and inferentially asserts that the domain name is not identical or confusingly similar to the Complainant's mark.

The Respondent contends that he has never offered "jimihendrix.com" as a domain name for sale.

The Respondent contends that he has never used the domain name "jimihendrix.com" in bad faith.

The Respondent contends that "it becomes a violation of human rights and free speech that an arbitrary board such as WIPO which contradicts itself case after case should have any rights over any domain which is owned by the original paying domain name owner."

The Respondent contends that "once WIPO takes [*sic*] that domain name away from the original owner it constitutes theft under the American Constitution in that the Jurisdiction under Human Rights should not allowed."

7. Discussion and Findings

* * *

The Proceeding—Three Elements Paragraph 4(a) of the Policy [of the domain name registrar, Network Solutions, Inc., governing dispute settlements, which the respondent agreed to be bound by,] states that the domain name holder is to submit to a mandatory administrative proceeding in the event that a third party complainant asserts to an ICANN approved dispute provider that:

(i) the domain name holder's domain name is identical or confusingly similar to a trademark or service mark in which the complainant has rights ("Element (i)"); and

(ii) the domain name holder has no rights or legitimate interests in respect of the domain name ("Element (ii)"); and

(iii) the domain name of the domain name holder has been registered and is being used in bad faith ("Element (iii)").

Element (i) - Domain Name Identical or Confusingly Similar to Mark The Complainant is the owner of both the common law trademark rights in the name JIMI HENDRIX as well as the registered trademarks identified above. Although the Respondent contends that a word with a ".com" on the end is not identical to a word without a ".com" on the end, the COM suffix is not relevant in determining whether a domain name is identical or confusingly similar to a mark. Rather, one looks to the second-level domain "jimihendrix" of the domain name for such a determination since the suffix COM is merely descriptive of the registry services and is not an identifier of a source of goods or services. Accordingly, the Panelist concludes that the domain name is identical to the mark JIMI HENDRIX and that Element (i) has been satisfied.

Element (ii) - Rights or Legitimate Interests in the Domain Name Paragraph 4(c) of the Policy sets out circumstances, in particular but without limitation, which, if found by the Panelist to be proved based on its evaluation of all evidence presented, can demonstrate the holder's rights to or legitimate interests in the domain name. These circumstances include:

(i) before any notice to the holder of the dispute, the holder's use of, or demonstrable preparations to use, the domain name or a name corresponding to the domain name in connection with a bona fide offering of goods or services; or

(ii) the holder (as an individual, business, or other organization) has been commonly known by the domain name, even if the holder has acquired no trademark or service mark rights; or

(iii) the domain name holder is making a legitimate noncommercial or fair use of the domain name, without intent for commercial gain to misleadingly divert consumers or to tarnish the trademark or service mark at issue.

The Respondent contends that he registered the domain name prior to the Complainant's registration of the Complainant's marks and was unaware of the Complainant's trademark registrations at the time of registration. However based upon the evidence presented, the registration and use of the domain name by the Respondent do not predate the Complainant's use and rights in the name but rather appears to be an attempt to usurp the Complainant's rights therein. Indeed, the registration of the domain name by "The Jimi Hendrix Fan Club" is a clear indication of the Respondent's awareness of the wide recognition and fame associated with the name JIMI HENDRIX. The Respondent's alleged lack of knowledge concerning the trademark registrations involved in this proceeding is insufficient.

The Respondent further contends that the domain name was registered to "The Jimi Hendrix Fan Club" and that he was operating a Web site for the Fan Club. A review of the submitted evidence, however, shows that the Respondent was not operating as a fan club site but rather had created a site at "www.jimihendrix.com" advertising vanity e-mail addresses incorporating the domain name "jimihendrix.com" for sale on the Site. No evidence was presented that at any time had the Complainant ever assigned, granted, licensed, sold, transferred, or in any way authorized the Respondent to register or use the name and mark JIMI HENDRIX in any manner. Accordingly, the Panelist finds that the Respondent, prior to any notice of this dispute, had not used the domain name in connection with any type of bona fide offering of goods or services.

Additionally, no evidence has been presented that the Respondent is commonly known by the domain name or has been making any legitimate noncommercial or fair use of the domain name without the intent for commercial gain to misleadingly divert consumers or to tarnish the mark at issue. Indeed, the Respondent's use of the domain name cannot be characterized as noncommercial or fair use based on: (i) the creation and use of the Site located at "www.jimihendrix.com" for selling vanity e-mail addresses incorporating the "jimihendrix.com" domain name; (ii) the offering for sale of the domain name itself for $1,000,000 on a domain name reseller site; and (iii) a news article identifying Mr. Hammerton as a domain name speculator and quoting him as the owner of the rights to some 2,000 domain names for sale including "jimihendrix.com".

The Respondent also contends that this proceeding is a "violation of human rights", "free speech," and "theft under the American Constitution." The Panelist finds that these contentions lack foundation and that no evidence has been submitted by the Respondent to support these contentions.

Based upon the above, the Panelist concludes that the Respondent has no rights or legitimate interests in the domain name and that Element (ii) has been satisfied.

Element (iii) - Domain Name Registered and Used in Bad Faith   Paragraph 4(b) of the Policy states that evidence of registration and use in bad faith by the holder includes, but is not limited to:

(i) circumstances indicating that the holder has registered or has acquired the domain name primarily for the purpose of selling, renting, or otherwise transferring the domain name registration to the complainant who is the owner of the trademark or service mark or to a competitor of that complainant, for valuable consideration in excess of the holder's documented out-of-pocket costs directly related to the domain name; or

(ii) the holder has registered the domain name in order to prevent the owner of the trademark or service mark from reflecting the mark in a corresponding domain name, provided that the holder has engaged in a pattern of such conduct; or

(iii) the holder has registered the domain name primarily for the purpose of disrupting the business of a competitor; or

(iv) by using the domain name, the holder has intentionally attempted to attract, for commercial gain, Internet users to the holder's Web site or other online location, by creating a likelihood of confusion with the complainant's mark as to the source, sponsorship, affiliation, or endorsement of your Web site or location or of a product or service on the holder's Web site or location.

Based upon the Respondent's contention that he registered the domain name prior to the Complainant's registrations of the above-identified marks, the Panelist finds that the Respondent had actual knowledge at the time he registered the domain name of the use and rights of the Complainant in the name JIMI HENDRIX. Indeed, the record demonstrates that at the time of registering the domain name "jimihendrix.com" the Respondent was well aware of the name JIMI HENDRIX and the Respondent has not submitted evidence or argued to the contrary.

The Complainant also contended that the Respondent offered to sell the domain name to the Complainant for "an exorbitant amount of money". However, the Complainant provided no evidence in support of this contention. The Respondent has contended that he never offered the domain name "jimihendrix.com" for sale and has never used the domain name in bad faith. The Complainant did submit copies of Web pages from a domain name reseller site located at "www.domainsmart.com" where the domain name "jimihendrix.com" is being offered for sale for $1,000,000. The Respondent has provided no evidence in rebuttal.

To further support its contention of bad faith by the Respondent, the Complainant submitted evidence of other domain names incorporating the names of well-known celebrities that the Respondent registered and which are being advertised for sale on different domain name reseller sites. Additionally, the Complainant submitted news articles that identified Mr. Hammerton as a domain name speculator who had registered and sold several domain names incorporating names of other celebrities.

Based upon these facts, the Panelist finds that the Respondent registered the domain name "jimihendrix.com" in order to prevent the Complainant from reflecting the name and mark in a corresponding domain name and that the Respondent has engaged in "a pattern of such conduct" of registering and offering for sale domain names incorporating well-known names in which the Respondent has no rights or legitimate interests.

The Panelist therefore concludes that the Respondent has registered and used the domain name "jimihendrix.com" in bad faith and that Element (iii) has been satisfied.

8. Decision

The Panelist concludes: (i) that the domain name in issue is identical to the Complainant's mark; (ii) that the Respondent has no rights or legitimate interests in the domain name; and (iii) that the Respondent registered and used the domain name in bad faith. Accordingly, the Panelist requires that the registration of the domain name "jimihendrix.com" be transferred to the Complainant. ■

Refusing Registration

The statutory grounds for refusing a trademark vary from country to country. Nevertheless, most criteria are reasonably similar. For example, a mark or name will be denied in the United States if it

1. does not function as a trademark to identify the goods or services as coming from a particular source (for example, the matter applied for is merely ornamentation);

2. is immoral, deceptive, or scandalous;

3. may disparage or falsely suggest a connection with persons, institutions, beliefs, or national symbols, or bring them into contempt or disrepute;

4. consists of or simulates the flag or coat of arms or other insignia of the United States, or a state or municipality, or any foreign nation;

5. is the name, portrait, or signature of a particular living individual, unless he has given written consent; or is the name, signature, or portrait of a deceased President of the United States during the lifetime of his widow, unless she has given her consent;

6. so resembles a mark already registered in the Patent and Trademark Office as to be likely, when applied to the goods of the applicant, to cause confusion, or to cause mistake, or to deceive;

7. is merely deceptive or deceptively misdescriptive of the goods or services;

8. is primarily geographically descriptive or deceptively misdescriptive of the goods or services of the applicant; or

9. is primarily merely a surname.[74]

---

[74]U.S. Patent and Trademark Office, *Trademark Manual of Examining Procedure,* chap. 1200 (2002) at www.uspto.gov/web/offices/tac/tmep/.

Registration Review

Once a Trademark Office official determines that a mark is suitable for registration, the mark will be published in the office's official gazette. Opponents to the registration then have a period of time—typically 30 to 90 days—in which to oppose the registration or to ask for an extension to do so. An "opposition" hearing is then held before a review board of the Trademark Office. If no opposition is filed or if the review board rules in favor of the applicant, a registration will issue.[75]

The Term of Registered Trademarks

The newly adopted Agreement on Trade-Related Aspects of Intellectual Property Rights requires WTO member states to protect trademarks for terms of at least seven years. Additionally, it provides that trademarks are to be indefinitely renewable.[76]

Usage Requirements

After a trademark is registered, many countries require the holder to present proof, upon the renewal of registration, that the mark was actually used within the country during the prior term.[77]

A few countries require the trademark owner to make an interim proof of use before the term expires. Mexico, for example, requires the holder to present evidence of usage at the end of the third year. The United States requires the same thing at the end of the sixth year.

What constitutes proof varies, of course, and many countries do not specify what may be used. Colombia does, and its listing is representative of actual practice in other countries. Colombia permits the trademark holder to use any of the following to establish usage: newspaper and magazine advertisements, catalogs, samples, sales invoices, sales licenses, import licenses, Chamber of Commerce certificates, Health Department registrations, advertising agency billings, depositions, and inspections by the reviewing officer.[78]

In addition to requiring the user to prove use at the time of renewal, many countries allow third parties to bring actions to cancel the trademark if it has not been used for some specified period of time. The TRIPS Agreement now sets this period of time at no less than three years.[79]

It must be pointed out that not all countries have a user requirement[80] and that a few, such as Canada and the United States, make it difficult for challengers to establish nonuse by additionally requiring them to prove that the owner intentionally abandoned use of a trademark.[81] Also, it must be noted, that challenges for nonuse are uncommon. Many trademark owners have a policy of never initiating a nonuse action against others for fear of retaliatory actions against their own unused marks. Similarly, challenges against new registrants attempting to file marks that are alike or identical to marks already in use are equally

---

[75]In the United States, the average length of time in which a mark will be registered or an application abandoned is 13 months from the date the application was filed. *Id.*

[76]Agreement on Trade-Related Aspects of Intellectual Property Rights, Article 18 (1994).

[77]The requirement is contained in the Trademark Law Treaty adopted in Geneva in 1994 to which the following states were parties as of April 15, 2002: Australia, Burkina Faso, Cyprus, Czech Republic, Denmark, Egypt, Guinea, Hungary, Indonesia, Ireland, Japan, Kyrgyzstan, Latvia, Liechtenstein, Lithuania, Moldova, Monaco, Netherlands, Romania, Russia, Slovakia, Slovenia, Spain, Sri Lanka, Switzerland, Trinidad and Tobago, Ukraine, United Kingdom, United States, Uzbekistan, and Yugoslavia. *See* www.wipo.int/treaties/ip/tlt/. The text of the treaty is posted at www.wipo.int/treaties/ip/.

The 1977 Bangui Agreement creating African and Malagasy Intellectual Property Organization contains the same requirement. States parties to the agreement as of November 23, 2000, were Benin, Burkina Faso, Cameroon, Central African Republic, Chad, Congo, Côte-d'Ivoire, Equatorial Guinea, Gabon, Guinea, Guinea Bissau, Mali, Niger, Senegal, and Togo. *See* www.oapi.wipo.net/. The text of the agreement, in French, is posted at www.eldis.org/ipr/.

[78]American Bar Association, Section of Patent, Trademark and Copyright Law, *1987 Committee Reports,* p. 98 (1987).

[79]Agreement on Trade-Related Aspects of Intellectual Property Rights, Article 19 (1994).

Prior to the adoption of this Agreement, there was an extensive debate over what the proper time period of nonuse should be. *See* Richard Taylor, "Loss of Trademark Rights through Nonuse: A Comparative Worldwide Analysis," *Trademark Reporter,* vol. 80, p. 207–208 (1990).

[80]E.g., Bolivia, Chile, Costa Rica, Denmark, El Salvador, Norway, and Uruguay.

[81]In the United States, nonuse during the initial two-year period following registration gives rise to a presumption of abandonment, thereby shifting the burden of proof to the trademark owner.

uncommon. What is more likely, in such a case, is a settlement and the establishment of a co-existence agreement.

Know-How

Know-how is practical expertise acquired from study, training, and experience. It has been defined as

> factual knowledge, not capable of separate description but which, when used in an accumulated form, after being acquired as a result of trial and error, gives to the one acquiring it an ability to produce something which he otherwise would not have known to produce with the same accuracy of precision found necessary for commercial success.[82]

Unlike other forms of intellectual property, know-how is generally not protected by specific statutory enactments. It is protected, rather, by contract, tort, and other basic legal principles. When know-how is kept secret, it is protected in some countries by trade secrecy laws.

The Agreement on Trade-Related Aspects of Intellectual Property Rights requires WTO member states to protect what the Agreement calls "undisclosed information."[83] That is, natural and legal persons must be given the legal means to prevent information from being disclosed to, acquired by, or used by others without their consent in a manner contrary to honest commercial practice. The information, however, must (a) be secret, (b) have commercial value because it is a secret, and (c) have been reasonably protected from disclosure by its owner.[84]

Most commonly the legal protection given know-how comes about in connection with its use by an assignee, licensee, or employee. That is, the owner of know-how may prevent an assignee, licensee, or employee from disclosing secret know-how to third parties and may require these same people to pay for the training or assistance or use of the know-how they acquire from the owner. Because owners' rights in know-how are determined by the contractual relationship they have with assignees, licensees, and employees, the discussion of these rights is included with the materials on transfer and licensing considered later in this chapter.

B. INTERNATIONAL INTELLECTUAL PROPERTY ORGANIZATION

Two main international organizations take an active role in defining and protecting international intellectual property rights: the World Intellectual Property Organization (WIPO) and the Council for Trade-Related Aspects of Intellectual Property Rights (TRIPS Council) of the World Trade Organization.[85]

World Intellectual Property Organization

The **World Intellectual Property Organization** (WIPO) was created in 1967 with the adoption of the Stockholm Convention.[86] WIPO succeeded the International Bureau of Paris and the International Bureau of Berne, which had administered the International Convention for the

---

[82]Mycalex Corp. of America v. Pemco Corp., *Federal Supplement,* vol. 64, p. 425 (Dist. Ct. for Maryland, 1946).
[83]Agreement on Trade-Related Aspects of Intellectual Property Rights, Article 39 (1994).
[84]*Id.,* para. 2.
[85]With the advent of the WTO and the WTO's TRIPS Council, the international influence of other organizations has diminished. The Intergovernmental Copyright Committee of the United Nations Educational, Scientific and Cultural Organization (UNESCO) no longer plays much of a role in this area following the decision by the United States and several other states to become parties to the Berne Convention and to, in effect, abandon their commitments under the Universal Copyright Convention that UNESCO had sponsored and overseen. The United Nations Conference on Trade and Development (UNCTAD), which was primarily interested in devising a Code of Conduct on Technology Transfer, has seen many of its proposals incorporated into the Agreement Establishing the World Trade Organization and that Agreement's annexes. Moreover, the institutional role that UNESCO had played has now been taken over by the WTO.
[86]The Convention is formally known as the Convention Establishing the World Intellectual Property Organization. It is posted on the Internet at www.wipo.int/treaties/convention/index.html.

Protection of Industrial Property (Paris Convention) and the Berne Convention for the Protection of Literary and Artistic Works (Berne Convention). These two bureaus had been supervised by the Swiss Federal Council and, functionally, were joined together as the United International Bureaus for the Protection of Intellectual Property (*Bureaux Internationaux Réunis pour la Protection de la Propriéte Intellectuelle*—BIRPI).

In contrast to its predecessors, WIPO has much broader authority. It is responsible for administering the Paris and Berne Conventions (as well as several new conventions established since its creation) and, generally, promoting intellectual property rights. WIPO's governing body, the General Assembly, is made up of representatives of states parties to the Stockholm Convention who are also parties to either the Paris or Berne Conventions. WIPO is also a specialized agency of the United Nations.[87] There are now 179 states that are parties to the Stockholm Convention.[88]

WIPO's promotional activities include the sponsoring and hosting of conferences for the development of new intellectual property rights agreements. The Patent Cooperation Treaty, for example, was the result of a WIPO initiative. WIPO also studies, through the appointment of expert committees, new legal and technological developments, and it regularly reports the results through both monthly journals and occasional reports.[89]

One of WIPO's more important tasks is to facilitate the transfer of technology, especially to and among developing countries. Two permanent committees—one for Development Cooperation Related to Industrial Property and one for Development Cooperation Related to Copyrights and Neighboring Rights—are responsible for helping countries modernize their national intellectual property laws, for helping them develop administrative agencies for supervising those laws, and for helping them increase, both in quantity and quality, the creation of new intellectual property by their own nationals.

A new responsibility recently taken on by WIPO is that of resolving Internet domain disputes. In 1999, WIPO's Arbitration and Mediation Center was selected by the Internet Corporation for Assigned Names and Numbers (ICANN), which oversees the Internet, was given responsibility for implementing ICANN's Uniform Domain Name Dispute Resolution Policy. The Policy gives holders of trademarks a procedure for efficiently resolving disputes involving bad faith cybersquatting of trademarks. The Center is authorized to resolve disputes if: (1) the domain name registered by the domain name registrant is identical or confusingly similar to the complainant's trademark or service mark; and (2) the domain name registrant has no rights or legitimate interests in the disputed domain name; and (3) the domain name was registered and is being used in bad faith.[90] (See Case 9–4 for an example of a trade name dispute.)

---

[87]For more information about the history and operation of WIPO, *see* its home page on the Internet at www.wipo.int/.

[88]The states parties as of July 2002 were Albania, Algeria, Andorra, Angola, Antigua and Barbuda, Argentina, Armenia, Australia, Austria, Azerbaijan, Bahamas, Bahrain, Bangladesh, Barbados, Belarus, Belgium, Belize, Benin, Bhutan, Bolivia, Bosnia and Herzegovina, Botswana, Brazil, Brunei Darussalam, Bulgaria, Burkina Faso, Burundi, Cambodia, Cameroon, Canada, Cape Verde, Central African Republic, Chad, Chile, China, Colombia, Congo, Costa Rica, Côte d'Ivoire, Croatia, Cuba, Cyprus, Czech Republic, Democratic Republic of the Congo, Denmark, Djibouti, Dominica, Dominican Republic, Ecuador, Egypt, El Salvador, Equatorial Guinea, Eritrea, Estonia, Ethiopia, Fiji, Finland, France, Gabon, Gambia, Georgia, Germany, Ghana, Greece, Grenada, Guatemala, Guinea, Guinea-Bissau, Guyana, Haiti, Holy See, Honduras, Hungary, Iceland, India, Indonesia, Iran, Iraq, Ireland, Israel, Italy, Jamaica, Japan, Jordan, Kazakhstan, Kenya, Kuwait, Kyrgyzstan, Laos, Latvia, Lebanon, Lesotho, Liberia, Libya, Liechtenstein, Lithuania, Luxembourg, Macedonia, Madagascar, Malawi, Malaysia, Mali, Malta, Mauritania, Mauritius, Mexico, Moldova, Monaco, Mongolia, Morocco, Mozambique, Myanmar, Namibia, Nepal, Netherlands, New Zealand, Nicaragua, Niger, Nigeria, North Korea, Norway, Oman, Pakistan, Panama, Papua New Guinea, Paraguay, Peru, Philippines, Poland, Portugal, Qatar, Romania, Russia, Rwanda, Saint Kitts and Nevis, Saint Lucia, Saint Vincent and the Grenadines, Samoa, San Marino, Sao Tome and Principe, Saudi Arabia, Senegal, Seychelles, Sierra Leone, Singapore, Slovakia, Slovenia, Somalia, South Africa, South Korea, Spain, Sri Lanka, Sudan, Suriname, Swaziland, Sweden, Switzerland, Tajikistan, Thailand, Togo, Tonga, Trinidad and Tobago, Tunisia, Turkey, Turkmenistan, Uganda, Ukraine, United Arab Emirates, United Kingdom, United Republic of Tanzania, United States, Uruguay, Uzbekistan, Venezuela, Vietnam, Yemen, Yugoslavia, Zambia, and Zimbabwe. *See* WIPO, "Member States" at www.wipo.int/members/members/.

[89]The *WIPO Magazine* and other WIPO publications are posted on the Internet at www.wipo.int/publications/general/.

[90]*See* WIPO's Domain Name Dispute Resolution Service at arbiter.wipo.int/domains/.

Council for Trade-Related Aspects of Intellectual Property Rights

Council for Trade-Related Aspects of Intellectual Property: Organ of the World Trade Organization responsible for administering the Agreement on Trade-Related Aspects of Intellectual Property Rights.

The **Council for Trade-Related Aspects of Intellectual Property Rights** (Council for TRIPS) was created in 1995 with the adoption of the Agreement Establishing the World Trade Organization (WTO Agreement). The Council is charged with overseeing the operation of the Agreement on Trade-Related Aspects of Intellectual Property Rights, which is an annex to the WTO Agreement. In particular, the Council is responsible for monitoring WTO member state compliance with the Agreement on TRIPS, for helping members consult with each other on trade-related aspects of intellectual property rights, and for assisting members in settling disputes. The Council consults with WIPO and cooperates with WIPO's constituent bodies.[91]

C. INTELLECTUAL PROPERTY TREATIES

Intellectual property rights are protected and regulated internationally both by bilateral treaties and multilateral conventions. Bilateral treaties were the original means of preventing illegal copying, and they were once quite commonplace. With the growing popularity of multilateral conventions in the mid-nineteenth century, their use has diminished. Today, most bilateral intellectual property treaties are used by states that are not parties to the multilateral conventions. This does not mean that parties to multilateral agreements are prevented from entering into bilateral arrangements. For example, the Berne Convention for the Protection of Literary and Artistic Works specifically provides:

> The governments of the countries of the Union reserve their rights to enter into special agreements among themselves, in so far as such agreements grant to authors more extensive rights than those granted by the Convention, or contain other provisions not contrary to the Convention.[92]

Similar provisions can be found in the International Convention for the Protection of Industrial Property.[93]

Nevertheless, multilateral treaties nowadays regulate most matters relating to intellectual property rights. These treaties generally cover industrial property or artistic property, but not both together. Moreover, patents, petty patents, and trademarks are commonly dealt with in a single treaty, while copyrights are dealt with separately. As already mentioned, most of these conventions are administered by the World Intellectual Property Organization and the Council for Trade-Related Aspects on Intellectual Property Rights.

Comprehensive Agreements

The principal comprehensive agreement establishing general intellectual property obligations for most of the world's states is the Agreement on Trade-Related Aspects of Intellectual Property Rights.

Agreement on Trade-Related Aspects of Intellectual Property Rights

Agreement on Trade-Related Aspects of Intellectual Property Rights: Annex to the Agreement Establishing the World Trade Organization; it creates a multilateral and comprehensive set of rights and obligations governing the international trade in intellectual property.

The **Agreement on Trade-Related Aspects of Intellectual Property Rights** (TRIPS Agreement), which is an annex to the Agreement Establishing the World Trade Organization, came into effect with the WTO in 1995.[94] As is the case for the WTO Agreement's other multilateral annexes, all of the WTO member states are automatically members of the TRIPS Agreement.

The purpose of the TRIPS Agreement is to create a multilateral and comprehensive set of rights and obligations governing the international trade in intellectual property. As a consequence, the Agreement establishes a common minimum of protection for intellectual property

---

[91]Agreement on Trade-Related Aspects of Intellectual Property Rights, Article 68 (1994).
[92]Berne Convention for the Protection of Literary and Artistic Works, Article 20(1) (1886, as revised in 1971).
[93]International Convention for the Protection of Industrial Property, Article 19 (1883 as revised in 1967).
[94]The Agreement is posted on the Internet at www.wto.org/english/docs_e/legal_e/27-trips.pdf.

rights applicable within all the WTO member states. It does this in five ways.[95] First, it requires WTO members to observe the substantive provisions of the most important existing multilateral intellectual property treaties: the 1883 International Convention for the Protection of Industrial Property (Paris Convention) as revised in 1967; the 1886 Berne Convention for the Protection of Literary and Artistic Works (Berne Convention) as revised in 1971; the 1961 International Convention for the Protection of Performers, Producers of Phonograms, and Broadcasting Organizations (Rome Convention); and the 1989 Treaty on Intellectual Property in Respect of Integrated Circuits (IPIC Treaty). Moreover, the TRIPS Agreement provides that its substantive provisions do not in any way reduce the obligations of WTO member states under the Paris, Berne, and Rome Conventions or the IPIC Treaty.[96]

Second, the substantive provisions of the TRIPS Agreement create obligations that are meant to "fill in the gaps" in the other international intellectual property conventions. Some important provisions are otherwise missing, such as the length of life for a patent.[97]

Third, the TRIPS Agreement establishes criteria for the effective and appropriate enforcement of intellectual property rights[98] and for the prevention and settlement of disputes between the governments of the WTO member states.[99]

Fourth, to encourage the widest possible adoption and application of the common rules and obligations set out in the TRIPS Agreement, the Agreement establishes transitional arrangements that give more time to developing member states and to member states in transition from a centrally planned economy to a free market economy to comply, and even more time to those that are the least developed. Developed member states were required to be in full compliance by January 1, 1996; developing member states and states transitioning to a market economy were required to comply by January 1, 2000; and the least-developed states have until January 1, 2016.[100]

Finally, and most importantly, the TRIPS Agreement extends the basic principles of the General Agreement on Tariffs and Trade (GATT) to the field of international intellectual property rights. The national treatment principle requires each member state to extend to nationals of other members treatment no less favorable than that which it gives its own nationals regarding protection of intellectual property.[101] The transparency principle requires member states to publish and notify the Council for TRIPS of all relevant laws, regulations, and the like and to respond to requests from other members for information.[102]

National treatment and transparency provisions are found, of course, in other intellectual property agreements. The TRIPS Agreement is unique, however, in including a provision requiring most-favored-nation treatment for such property. Under this provision, "any advantage, favor, privilege, or immunity granted by a member to the nationals of any other country [whether or not it is a WTO member] shall be accorded immediately and unconditionally to the nationals of all other members."[103] Read together with the national treatment provision and the transparency provision, this requires each member state to treat the nationals of other member states as least as well (and possibly better) than it treats its own nationals.[104]

Artistic Property Agreements

The main international agreements dealing with artistic property are the Berne Convention for the Protection of Literary and Artistic Works; the International Convention for the Protection of Performers, Producers of Phonograms, and Broadcasting Organizations; the Patent Cooperation Treaty; the Satellite Transmission Convention; and the WIPO Copyright Treaty.

---

[95]Agreement on Trade-Related Aspects of Intellectual Property Rights, Preamble (1994).

[96]*Id.,* Articles 1–2.

[97]*Id.,* Articles 9–40.

[98]*Id.,* Articles 41–62.

[99]*Id.,* Articles 63–64.

[100]*Id.,* Articles 65–66. The date for compliance for least developed states was extended to 2016 at the WTO Doha Ministerial Conference. WTO, "Declaration on the TRIPS Agreement and Public Health," WT/MIN(01)/DEC/220 (November 14, 2001) at www.wto.org/english/thewto_e/minist_e/min01_e/mindecl_trips_e.htm.

[101]Agreement on Trade-Related Aspects of Intellectual Property Rights, Article 3 (1994).

[102]*Id.,* Article 63.

[103]*Id.,* Article 4.

[104]John Kraus, *The GATT Negotiations: A Business Guide to the Results of the Uruguay Round,* p. 52 (1994).

Berne Convention for the Protection of Literary and Artistic Works: Requires member states to establish common minimum rules to protect the pecuniary and moral rights of authors without requiring them to comply with particular formalities.

nonconditional protection principle: Protection is not to be conditioned on the use of formalities.

protection independent of protection in the country of origin principle: Protection is granted to any person publishing a work in a member state, even if he is not a national of a member state.

common rules principle: Common minimum standards for granting copyrights must be observed by all member states.

International Convention for the Protection of Performers, Producers of Phonograms, and Broadcasting Organizations: Prohibits the unauthorized recording of live performances, the unauthorized reproduction of recordings, and the unauthorized recording or rebroadcasting of broadcasts.

Berne Convention

Adopted in Paris in 1886, the **Berne Convention for the Protection of Literary and Artistic Works** (Berne Convention) came into force in 1887.[105] Its nine original member countries[106] have now grown to 149.[107]

The original text of the Convention established procedures for its revision, and revisions have been regularly made: in Paris in 1896, Berlin in 1908, Berne in 1914, Rome in 1928, Brussels in 1948, Stockholm in 1967, and Paris in 1971.

The Convention establishes a "union" of states that is responsible for protecting artistic rights. Four basic principles underlie the members' obligations: (1) The principle of *national treatment* requires each member state to extend to nationals of other member states treatment no less favorable than that which it gives its own nationals. (2) **Nonconditional protection** is the requirement that member states must provide protection without any formalities. A country of origin may, however, condition protection on the author's first making an application for registration, or registering the work, or reserving rights in a contract of sale, or a similar condition. (3) The principle of **protection independent of protection in the country of origin** allows authors who are nationals of nonmember states to obtain protection within the Berne Union by publishing their works in a member state. (4) The principle of **common rules** establishes minimum standards for granting copyrights common to all member states. These, and the other requirements of the Berne Convention, are summarized in Exhibit 9-2.

Rome Convention

The **International Convention for the Protection of Performers, Producers of Phonograms, and Broadcasting Organizations** (Rome Convention) was agreed to in 1961.[108] The draft for the Convention was prepared by a joint committee of experts appointed by the Berne Union, UNESCO, and the International Labor Organization. The Convention, accordingly, attempts to balance the interests of performers, producers of phonograms, and broadcasting organizations. Currently, there are 69 states parties.[109]

The Rome Convention protects artists from the unauthorized recording of their original performances and from the use of authorized recordings for a purpose other than what the artist consented to. Producers of phonograms are protected from the direct or indirect reproduction of their works. Broadcasters are protected from the unauthorized recording, rebroadcasting, and use of their broadcasts.

In addition to these rights, the Rome Convention provides that a broadcaster making a public communication or broadcast of an authorized phonogram is required to pay the pro-

---

[105]The text of the Convention is posted on the Internet at www.wipo.int/treaties/ip/.

[106]Belgium, Britain, France, Germany, Haiti, Italy, Spain, Switzerland, and Tunisia. Haiti, however, withdrew in 1941, and it did not rejoin until 1996.

[107]As of July 2002 the member states were Albania, Algeria, Antigua and Barbuda, Argentina, Armenia, Australia, Austria, Azerbaijan, Bahamas, Bahrain, Bangladesh, Barbados, Belarus, Belgium, Belize, Benin, Bolivia, Bosnia and Herzegovina, Botswana, Brazil, Bulgaria, Burkina Faso, Cameroon, Canada, Cape Verde, Central African Republic, Chad, Chile, China, Colombia, Congo, Costa Rica, Côte d'Ivoire, Croatia, Cuba, Cyprus, Czech Republic, Democratic Republic of the Congo, Denmark, Djibouti, Dominica, Dominican Republic, Ecuador, Egypt, El Salvador, Equatorial Guinea, Estonia, Fiji, Finland, France, Gabon, Gambia, Georgia, Germany, Ghana, Greece, Grenada, Guatemala, Guinea, Guinea-Bissau, Guyana, Haiti, Holy See, Honduras, Hungary, Iceland, India, Indonesia, Ireland, Israel, Italy, Jamaica, Japan, Jordan, Kazakhstan, Kenya, Kyrgyzstan, Latvia, Lebanon, Lesotho, Liberia, Libya, Liechtenstein, Lithuania, Luxembourg, Macedonia, Madagascar, Malawi, Malaysia, Mali, Malta, Mauritania, Mauritius, Mexico, Moldova, Monaco, Mongolia, Morocco, Namibia, Netherlands, New Zealand, Nicaragua, Niger, Nigeria, North Korea, Norway, Oman, Pakistan, Panama, Paraguay, Peru, Philippines, Poland, Portugal, Qatar, Romania, Russia, Rwanda, Saint Kitts and Nevis, Saint Lucia, Saint Vincent and the Grenadines, Senegal, Singapore, Slovakia, Slovenia, South Africa, Spain, Sri Lanka, Sudan, Suriname, Swaziland, Sweden, Switzerland, Tajikistan, Tanzania, Thailand, Togo, Tonga, Trinidad and Tobago, Tunisia, Turkey, Ukraine, United Kingdom, United States, Uruguay, Venezuela, Yugoslavia, Zambia, and Zimbabwe. *See* www.wipo.int/treaties/ip/berne/.

[108]The text of the Convention is posted on the Internet at www.wipo.int/treaties/ip/.

[109]The states parties as of April 15, 2002 were Albania, Argentina, Australia, Austria, Barbados, Belgium, Bolivia, Brazil, Bulgaria, Burkina Faso, Canada, Cape Verde, Chile, Colombia, Congo, Costa Rica, Croatia, Czech Republic, Denmark, Dominica, Dominican Republic, Ecuador, El Salvador, Estonia, Fiji, Finland, France, Germany, Greece, Guatemala, Honduras, Hungary, Iceland, Ireland, Italy, Jamaica, Japan, Latvia, Lebanon, Lesotho, Liechtenstein, Lithuania, Luxembourg, Macedonia, Mexico, Moldova, Monaco, Netherlands, Nicaragua, Niger, Nigeria, Norway, Panama, Paraguay, Peru, Philippines, Poland, Portugal, Romania, Saint Lucia, Slovakia, Slovenia, Spain, Sweden, Switzerland, Ukraine, United Kingdom, Uruguay, and Venezuela. *See* www.wipo.int/treaties/ip/rome/.

EXHIBIT 9-2   Principal Provisions of the Berne Convention

Provision	Description
Persons entitled to protection	Nationals and habitual residents of any member state and persons of any state who publish first or simultaneously in a member state
Definition of "publication"	Manifestation in a tangible form (may not include intangible reproduction by performance or telecommunication)
Definition of "simultaneous publication"	Publication within a 30-day period
Protected works	Literary, artistic, scientific, and architectural
Author's rights	Pecuniary and moral rights
Formalities	Member states may not require formalities (except that protection in the country of origin may be conditioned on application, registration, reservation of rights, etc.)
Translations	Author loses right to make a translation if it is not published within 10 years of original publication
Exemptions for developing countries	Developing country may grant a nonexclusive nonassignable compulsory license to make copies for use in teaching, scholarship, and research if the author fails to grant such a license
Term	Author's life plus 50 years

ducer or the artist, or both, a single equitable payment. This caused some consternation among several countries, which feared that such a system of compensation would diminish the proceeds that their artists were entitled to under their own laws. As a consequence, the Convention allows member states to make reservations to this provision.

Phonogram Piracy Convention

The **Convention for the Protection of Producers of Phonograms Against Unauthorized Duplication of Their Phonograms** was signed in 1971 at Geneva.[110] It provides that member states must protect producers of phonograms from the unauthorized reproduction and importation of their works for a period of not less than 20 years. The means for doing this, however, is left to each individual state. In the common law countries, including the United Kingdom and the United States, protection is provided through copyright legislation. Most of the countries of continental Europe use neighboring rights laws. Japan provides protection with penal sanctions. At present, there are 57 states parties to the Phonogram Piracy Convention.[111]

Satellite Transmission Convention

The **Convention Relating to the Distribution of Program-Carrying Signals Transmitted by Satellite** sponsored jointly by WIPO and UNESCO, was concluded in Brussels in 1974.[112] It requires member states to take "adequate measures" to prevent the unauthorized distribution in or from their territory of any program-carrying signal transmitted by satellite. As with the

Convention for the Protection of Producers of Phonograms Against Unauthorized Duplication of Their Phonograms: Requires member states to protect producers of phonograms from the unauthorized reproduction of their works.

Convention Relating to the Distribution of Program-Carrying Signals by Satellite: Requires member states to prevent the unauthorized transmission of electronic communications by satellite from their territory.

---

[110]The text of the Convention is posted on the Internet at www.wipo.int/treaties/ip/.

[111]The states parties as of April 15, 2002, were Argentina, Australia, Austria, Azerbaijan, Barbados, Brazil, Bulgaria, Burkina Faso, Chile, China, Colombia, Costa Rica, Croatia, Cyprus, Czech Republic, Democratic Republic of the Congo, Denmark, Ecuador, Egypt, El Salvador, Estonia, Fiji, Finland, France, Germany, Greece, Guatemala, Holy See, Honduras, Hungary, India, Israel, Italy, Jamaica, Japan, Kazakhstan, Kenya, Latvia, Liechtenstein, Lithuania, Luxembourg, Mexico, Monaco, Netherlands, New Zealand, Nicaragua, Norway, Panama, Paraguay, Peru, South Korea, Moldova, Romania, Russia, Saint Lucia, Slovakia, Slovenia, Spain, Sweden, Switzerland, Macedonia, Trinidad and Tobago, United Kingdom, United States, Ukraine, Uruguay, and Venezuela. *See* www.wipo.int/treaties/ip/geneva/.

    A related convention is the 1996 WIPO Performances and Phonograms Treaty, which establishes both moral and pecuniary rights for performers and creators of phonograms. The text of that Treaty is posted on the Internet at www.wipo.int/treaties/ip/.

[112]The text of the Convention is posted on the Internet at www.wipo.int/treaties/ip/.

Agreement on Phonogram Piracy, the means of implementing this convention is left up to each member state. The number of states parties at present is 23.[113]

WIPO Copyright Treaty

The **World Intellectual Property Organization Copyright Treaty** was adopted in 1996 by a conference of member states of the Berne Union for the purpose of extending the provisions of the Berne Convention to computer programs and databases and protecting copyright ownership information embedded in programs and databases.[114] There are currently 35 states parties.[115]

Industrial Property Agreements

The principal international conventions concerned with industrial property are the International Convention for the Protection of Industrial Property, the Treaty on Intellectual Property in Respect of Integrated Circuits, the Madrid Agreement for the Repression of False or Deceptive Indications of Sources of Goods, the Patent Cooperation Treaty, and the Trademark Law Treaty.

Paris Convention

Drafted in 1880, the **International Convention for the Protection of Industrial Property** (Paris Convention) was ratified by 11 states[116] in 1883 and came into effect in 1884.[117] Since then the number of participants has grown to 163.[118]

The Convention establishes a "union" of states responsible for protecting industrial property rights. Among the members' duties is the obligation to participate in regular revisions. Revision conferences to expand the coverage of the Convention have been held regularly: in Rome in 1886, Madrid in 1890 and 1891, Brussels in 1897 and 1900, Washington in 1911, The Hague in 1925, London in 1934, Lisbon 1958, and Stockholm in 1967.

Three basic principles are incorporated in the Paris Convention: (1) national treatment, (2) right of priority, and (3) common rules. *National treatment* is the requirement that each member state must grant the same protection to the nationals of other states that it grants to its own nationals. The **right of priority** gives an applicant who has filed for protection in one member country a grace period of 12 months in which to file in another member state, which then

World Intellectual Property Organization Copyright Treaty: Requires member states to extend the provisions of the Berne Convention to computer programs and databases.

International Convention for the Protection of Industrial Property: Requires member states to provide national treatment, right of priority, and common minimum rules to protect owners of industrial property rights.

right of priority: For a period of one year, an application for a patent in a second member country will be treated as though it had been filed on the same date as the application made in the first member country.

---

[113]The states parties as of April 15, 2002, were Austria, Bulgaria, Cuba, France, Guinea, Kyrgyzstan, Luxembourg, Mexico, Netherlands, Poland, Republic of Moldova, Romania, Saint Lucia, Slovenia, Sweden, Trinidad and Tobago, Tunisia, Turkey, and Uruguay. *See* www.wipo.int/treaties/ip/brussels/.

[114]The text of the Convention is posted on the Internet at www.wipo.int/treaties/ip/.

[115]The states parties as of April 15, 2002 were Argentina, Belarus, Bulgaria, Burkina Faso, Chile, Colombia, Costa Rica, Croatia, Czech Republic, Ecuador, El Salvador, Gabon, Georgia, Guinea, Honduras, Hungary, Indonesia, Jamaica, Japan, Kyrgyzstan, Latvia, Lithuania, Mali, Mexico, Moldova, Panama, Paraguay, Peru, Romania, Saint Lucia, Senegal, Slovakia, Slovenia, Ukraine, and United States. *See* www.wipo.int/treaties/ip/wct/.

[116]The original parties were Belgium, Brazil, El Salvador, France, Guatemala, Italy, the Netherlands, Portugal, Serbia, Spain, and Switzerland.

[117]The text of the Convention is posted on the Internet at www.wipo.int/treaties/ip/.

[118]As of April 15, 2002, the states parties to the Paris Convention as revised in 1967 were Albania, Algeria, Antigua and Barbuda, Armenia, Australia, Austria, Azerbaijan, Bahrain, Bangladesh, Barbados, Belarus, Belgium, Belize, Benin, Bhutan, Bolivia, Bosnia and Herzegovina, Botswana, Brazil, Bulgaria, Burkina Faso, Burundi, Cambodia, Cameroon, Canada, Central African Republic, Chad, Chile, China, Colombia, Congo, Costa Rica, Côte d'Ivoire, Croatia, Cuba, Cyprus, Czech Republic, Democratic Republic of the Congo, Denmark, Djibouti, Dominica, Ecuador, Egypt, El Salvador, Equatorial Guinea, Estonia, Finland, France, Gabon, Gambia, Georgia, Germany, Ghana, Greece, Grenada, Guatemala, Guinea, Guinea-Bissau, Guyana, Haiti, Holy See, Honduras, Hungary, Iceland, India, Indonesia, Iran, Iraq, Ireland, Israel, Italy, Jamaica, Japan, Jordan, Kazakhstan, Kenya, Kyrgyzstan, Laos, Latvia, Lesotho, Liberia, Libya, Liechtenstein, Lithuania, Luxembourg, Macedonia, Madagascar, Malawi, Malaysia, Mali, Mauritania, Mauritius, Mexico, Moldova, Monaco, Mongolia, Morocco, Mozambique, Nepal, Netherlands, Nicaragua, Niger, North Korea, Norway, Oman, Panama, Papua New Guinea, Paraguay, Peru, Poland, Portugal, Qatar, Romania, Russia, Rwanda, Saint Kitts and Nevis, Saint Lucia, Saint Vincent and the Grenadines, San Marino, Sao Tome and Principe, Senegal, Sierra Leone, Singapore, Slovakia, Slovenia, South Africa, South Korea, Spain, Sri Lanka, Sudan, Suriname, Swaziland, Sweden, Switzerland, Tajikistan, Togo, Tonga, Trinidad and Tobago, Tunisia, Turkey, Turkmenistan, Uganda, Ukraine, United Arab Emirates, United Kingdom, United States, Uruguay, Uzbekistan, Venezuela, Vietnam, Yugoslavia, and Zimbabwe.

In addition, Argentina, Bahamas, Malta, Nigeria, Philippines, Tanzania, and Zambia were parties to the Convention as revised in 1958; Lebanon, New Zealand, Sri Lanka, and Syria were parties to the Convention as revised in 1934; and the Dominican Republic was a party to the Convention as revised in 1925. *See* www.wipo.int/treaties/ip/paris/.

must treat the application as if it were filed on the same day as the original application. The principle of *common rules* sets minimum standards for the creation of intellectual property rights. These are as follows: (a) a member state may not deny protection to industrial property because the work incorporating an invention was not manufactured in that state; (b) member states must protect trade names without requiring registration; (c) member states must outlaw false labeling (i.e., any indication that falsely identifies the source of goods, or the trader or manufacturer); and (d) each member state is required to take "effective" measures to prevent unfair competition. Beyond these common rules, the convention leaves to each member the right to make rules governing the application, registration, scope, and duration of patents, trademarks, and other forms of industrial property.

Treaty on Intellectual Property in Respect of Integrated Circuits

Treaty on Intellectual Property in Respect of Integrated Circuits: Requires member states to provide national treatment and common minimum rules to protect owners of integrated circuits.

The **Treaty on Intellectual Property in Respect of Integrated Circuits** (the Washington Treaty), adopted in 1989, obligates member states to protect the designs used in integrated circuits (such as the designs of computer memory chips).[119] Like the Berne Convention, this treaty incorporates the principles of national treatment and common rules. The common rules include the obligation of member states to protect against the making of unauthorized copies and the importing of contraband copies.[120]

Although the member states of the World Trade Organization are obliged to comply with the provisions of the Washington Treaty,[121] the treaty itself is not currently in force.[122]

Patent Cooperation Treaty

Patent Cooperation Treaty: Establishes an international mechanism that allows inventors to make a single application for patent protection that is equivalent to making a filing in all of the member states.

The **Patent Cooperation Treaty**, agreed to in 1970, establishes a mechanism for making an international application whose effect in each member state is the same as if a national patent had been filed for.[123] Applications are submitted to a member state's patent office, which forwards them to one of several international searching authorities, where an international search is made to determine novelty. The goal of the treaty is the elimination of unnecessary repetition by both patent offices and applicants. Eventually, the member states plan to establish a single international search authority. Currently there are 116 states parties to the Patent Cooperation Treaty.[124]

---

[119]The text of the Washington Treaty is posted on the Internet at www.jus.uio.no/lm/ip.integrated.circuits.treaty. washington.1989/toc.html.

[120]Article 6.

[121]Agreement on Trade-Related Aspects of Intellectual Property Rights, Articles 1 and 2 (1994).

[122]*See* World Trade Organization, "Intellectual Property: Protection and Enforcement," posted at www.wto.org/ english/thewto_e/whatis_e/tif_e/agrm6_e.htm.

[123]The text of the Patent Cooperation Treaty is posted on the Internet at www.wipo.int/treaties/registration/.

[124]The state parties as of April 15, 2002, were Albania, Algeria, Antigua and Barbuda, Armenia, Australia, Austria, Azerbaijan, Barbados, Belarus, Belgium, Belize, Benin, Bosnia and Herzegovina, Brazil, Bulgaria, Burkina Faso, Cameroon, Canada, Central African Republic, Chad, China, Colombia, Congo, Costa Rica, Côte d'Ivoire, Croatia, Cuba, Cyprus, Czech Republic, Denmark, Dominica, Ecuador, Equatorial Guinea, Estonia, Finland, France, Gabon, Gambia, Georgia, Germany, Ghana, Greece, Grenada, Guinea, Guinea Bissau, Hungary, Iceland, India, Indonesia, Ireland, Israel, Italy, Japan, Kazakhstan, Kenya, Kyrgyzstan, Latvia, Lesotho, Liberia, Liechtenstein, Lithuania, Luxembourg, Macedonia, Madagascar, Malawi, Mali, Mauritania, Mexico, Moldova, Monaco, Mongolia, Morocco, Mozambique, Netherlands, New Zealand, Niger, North Korea, Norway, Oman, Philippines, Poland, Portugal, Romania, Russia , Saint Lucia, Saint Vincent and the Grenadines, Senegal, Sierra Leone, Singapore, Slovakia, Slovenia, South Africa, South Korea, Spain, Sri Lanka, Sudan, Swaziland, Sweden, Switzerland, Tajikistan, Tanzania, Togo, Trinidad and Tobago, Tunisia, Turkey, Turkmenistan, Uganda, Ukraine, United Arab Emirates, United Kingdom, United States, Uzbekistan, Vietnam, Yugoslavia, Zambia, and Zimbabwe. *See* www.wipo.int/treaties/ registration/pct/.

Related treaties are the 1925 Hague Agreement Concerning the International Deposit of Industrial Designs (posted on the Internet at www.wipo.int/treaties/registration/, which sets up a mechanism for registering industrial designs with WIPO, which then handles individual filings in member states; the 1968 Locarno Agreement Establishing an International Classification for Industrial Designs (posted on the Internet at www.wipo.int/treaties/ classification/); and the 1971 Strasbourg Agreement Concerning the International Patent Classification (posted at www.wipo.int/treaties/classification/), which classifies technologies in eight main categories and approximately 52,000 subcategories, each of which is assigned a symbol.

Additionally, Articles 25 and 26 of the Agreement on Trade-Related Aspects of Intellectual Property Rights (1994) address industrial designs. This Agreement establishes, among other things, that the term of protection is a minimum of 10 years. *Id.,* Article 26, para. 3.

Madrid Agreement for the Repression of False or Deceptive Indications of Sources of Goods: Requires member states to deny importation to goods bearing false or misleading indications as to their source.

Agreement on Sources of Goods

The **Madrid Agreement for the Repression of False or Deceptive Indications of Sources of Goods**, drafted in 1891, requires its members to either deny importation to or confiscate at the time of importation any goods bearing false or deceptive indications about their source.[125] There are 33 states parties to the Agreement at present.[126]

Trademark Law Treaty: Requires member states to establish common minimum rules to protect trademarks

Trademark Law Treaty

The **Trademark Law Treaty**, adopted in 1994, is meant to simplify both national and regional trademark registration systems by establishing common minimum rules.[127] In addition, the term for renewal of a trademark is set at 10 years. Currently 28 states are parties to the treaty.[128]

D. THE INTERNATIONAL TRANSFER OF INTELLECTUAL PROPERTY

There are five ways in which intellectual property rights are transferred from one country to another: (1) the owner may work the property rights abroad, (2) the owner may transfer or assign the rights to another, (3) the owner may license another to work them, (4) the owner may establish a franchise, or (5) a government may grant a compulsory license so that a third party may exploit them.

The procedures and international regulations for setting up a business, a subsidiary, or a joint venture were discussed in chapters 4 and 5. Those same procedures and regulations apply to firms established to work intellectual property rights.

The rules and procedures for transferring or making a full assignment of an owner's rights in intellectual property are the same as those for any other sale. Those rules and procedures are discussed in Chapter 10.

license: Authority granted by the owner of an intellectual property to another allowing the latter the right to use it in some limited way.

A **license** is a nonexclusive revocable privilege that allows a licensee to use a licensor's property. A license is created by contract, and standard contractual rules are used to interpret it. It is to be distinguished from a **franchise**, which is a specialized license that requires a franchisee to work the property under the supervision and control of a franchisor.

franchise: Special license that requires the franchisee to work the licensed property under the supervision and control of the franchisor.

A license allows a licensee to use a property for the licensee's own purposes. Depending on the licensing agreement, the licensee may use the property as a component in its own products, it may sell the property or the products derived from it under the licensor's name, or it may do the same thing under its own name. Sometimes the licensee may even sell the property, or the products derived from it, in direct competition to the licensor.

---

[125]The text of the Madrid treaty is posted at www.wipo.int/treaties/ip/.

[126]As of April 15, 2002, the states parties to the Madrid Agreement as revised in 1958 were Algeria, Bulgaria, Cuba, Czech Republic, Dominican Republic, France, Germany, Hungary, Ireland, Israel, Italy, Japan, Liechtenstein, Monaco, Morocco, Poland, San Marino, Slovakia, Spain, Sweden, Switzerland, United Kingdom, and Yugoslavia; the parties to the agreement as revised in 1934 were Lebanon, Moldova, New Zealand, Sri Lanka, Syria, Tunisia, and Turkey and the parties to the agreement as revised in 1925 were Brazil, Egypt, and Portugal. *See* www.wipo.int/treaties/ip/madrid/.

    Another agreement dealing with the origins of goods is the 1958 Lisbon Agreement for the Protection of Appellations of Origin and Their International Registration (posted on the Internet at www.wipo.int/treaties/registration/), which provides protection for geographic names used to designate agricultural products (e.g., wines, spirits, cheeses, etc.).

[127]The text of the treaty is posted at www.wipo.int/treaties/ip/.

[128]The signatories as of April 15, 2002, were Australia, Burkina Faso, Cyprus, Czech Republic, Denmark, Egypt, Guinea, Hungary, Indonesia, Ireland, Japan, Kyrgyzstan, Latvia, Liechtenstein, Lithuania, Moldova, Monaco, Netherlands, Romania, Russia, Slovakia, Slovenia, Spain, Sri Lanka, Switzerland, Trinidad and Tobago, Ukraine, United Kingdom, United States, Uzbekistan, and Yugoslavia. *See* www.wipo.int/treaties/ip/tlt/.

    Other agreements dealing with trademarks are the 1881 Madrid Agreement Concerning the International Registration of Marks (posted on the Internet at www.wipo.int/treaties/registration/), which establishes a mechanism for registering marks with WIPO, which then handles the filing in the individual member states where registration is sought; the 1957 Nice Agreement Concerning the International Classification of Goods and Services for the Purposes of the Registration of Marks (posted at www.wipo.int/treaties/classification/), which sets up a uniform classification system involving 34 classes of goods and eight classes of services; the 1973 Vienna Agreement Establishing an International Classification for the Figurative Elements of Marks (posted at www.wipo.int/treaties/classification/); and the 1981 Nairobi Treaty for the Protection of the Olympic Symbol (posted at www.wipo.int/treaties/ip/).

By contrast, a franchisee has more limited rights. The key difference is that a franchisee is regarded as a unit or element of the franchisor's business. Three types of franchises have evolved since their initial establishment at the beginning of the twentieth century: (1) distributorships, (2) chain-style businesses, and (3) manufacturing or processing plants.

distributorship: A franchise in which a manufacturer licenses a dealer to sell its products.

A **distributorship** franchise exists when a manufacturer licenses a dealer to sell its products. A common example is the automobile dealership.

chain-style business: A franchise in which a franchisee operates under the franchisor's trade name and is identified as part of the franchisor's business.

A **chain-style business** franchise is an arrangement in which a franchisee operates under a franchisor's trade name and is identified as part of the franchisor's business chain. Examples include McDonald's, KFC, Pizza Haven, and other fast-food restaurants.

manufacturing or processing plant franchise: A franchise in which the franchisee sells products it manufactures from a formula or from ingredients provided by the franchisor.

A **manufacturing** or **processing plant** franchise comes about when a franchisor provides the franchisee with the formula or the essential ingredients to make a particular product. The franchisee then wholesales or retails the product according to the standards established by the franchisor. Examples of this kind of franchise are Coca-Cola, Pepsi-Cola, and the other soft-drink firms.

Although a franchisee has more limited rights than a licensee, the rules and regulations that govern franchise agreements are the same as those governing licenses.

Compulsory licenses are common in most countries of the world, especially in developing countries. In these countries, if the owner of intellectual property (in particular, patents or copyrights) refuses to work the property in the country within a certain period of time, a third party may apply for a compulsory license. The government issues such a license without the consent of the owner, so it is not subject to the same rules that apply to licensing and franchising.

E. LICENSING REGULATIONS

Grants of patents, trademarks, and copyrights create monopolies. In free-market countries, these grants run contrary to unfair competition laws.[129] In centrally planned economies, they run contrary to the notion of state ownership of the means of production. To balance the interests of consumers in free-market countries and the interests of the state in planned economy countries with the rights of intellectual property owners, most countries treat intellectual property rights as special exceptions to their general laws prohibiting monopolies. As such, the rights held by patent, trademark, and copyright owners are strictly construed and limited to the narrow confines of the grant. The U.S. Supreme Court, for example, has stated that the grant of a patent is

> . . . an exception to the general rule against monopolies and to the right to access to a free and open market. The far-reaching social and economic consequences of a patent, therefore, give the public a paramount interest in seeing that patent monopolies spring from backgrounds free from fraud or other inequitable conduct and that such monopolies are kept within their legitimate scope.[130]

Licensing arrangements involving statutory grants must, accordingly, be limited to the rights contained in the grant. Any attempt to go beyond the scope of the grant—such as trying to license an expired patent, trademark, or copyright—is a "misuse" of the grant and (depending on the country) either without effect or illegal.

---

[129]The conflict between intellectual property rights and unfair competition laws is not a new problem. As the U.S. District Court in SCM Corp. v. Xerox Corp., *Federal Supplement,* vol. 463, p. 996 (1978), pointed out: "Ever since the [English Court of] King's Bench considered a patent-antitrust conflict in 1602 in the first reported case on the subject [Darcy v. Allein, *English Reports,* vol. 77, p. 1260 (1602)] the issues arising in this field have yielded few clear or satisfying answers.

"Economic arguments could be made that these statutes have a common goal of maximizing wealth by facilitating the production of what consumers want at the lowest cost. . . . Whatever their economic congruency, there can be little doubt that these two sets of laws are juridically divergent."

[130]Walker Process Equipment, Inc. v. Food Machines & Chemical Corp., *United States Reports,* vol. 382, p. 177 (Supreme Ct., 1965).

Nonstatutory grants (in particular, know-how) do not qualify for the special exceptions granted to patents, trademarks, and copyrights. As such, any licensing of these rights has to comply with the appropriate unfair competition laws.

The propriety of states adopting rules to regulate the anticompetitive aspects of intellectual property licenses is now specifically recognized in international law. Article 40, paragraph 2, of the Agreement on Trade-Related Aspects of Intellectual Property Rights provides:

> Nothing in this Agreement shall prevent [World Trade Organization] members from specifying in their national legislation licensing practices or conditions that may in particular cases constitute an abuse of intellectual property rights having an adverse effect on competition in the relevant market. As provided above, a member may adopt, consistently with the other provisions of this Agreement, appropriate measures to prevent or control such practices, which may include for example exclusive grantback conditions, conditions preventing challenges to validity, and coercive package licensing, in the light of the relevant laws and regulations of that member.

In developing countries (including Argentina, Hungary, Mexico, Poland, Russia, and the members of the Andean Common Market), such anticompetition rules are commonly found in transfer-of-technology codes. In the developed free-market countries (e.g., Germany, France, the United Kingdom, and the United States), they are found in longstanding antimonopoly legislation. The United States' Sherman Antitrust Act, among the oldest laws prohibiting unfair competition, is a good example of this type of legislation. It provides:

> § 1. Every contract, combination in the form of trust or otherwise, or conspiracy, in restraint of trade or commerce among the several states, or with foreign nations, is hereby declared to be illegal. . . .
>
> § 2. Every person who shall monopolize, or attempt to monopolize, or combine or conspire with any other person or persons, to monopolize any part of the trade or commerce among the several states, or with foreign nations, shall be deemed guilty of a felony. . . . [131]

Similar provisions are found in Articles 81 and 82[132] of the European Union's European Community Treaty.[133] Unlike the Sherman Antitrust Act, however, the EC Treaty provisions contain an express exemption (Article 81(3)) that allows the European Commission to authorize arrangements that would otherwise violate the general prohibitions, either through block grants (that apply to a particular category of agreements) or on a case-by-case basis. The Commission may do so when the overall effect of a challenged activity is one that "contributes to improving the production or distribution of goods, or to promoting technical or economic

---

[131] *United States Code*, title 15, §§ 1 and 2.

[132] Articles 81 and 82 were previously Articles 85 and 86 prior to the renumbering of the Treaty Establishing the European Community agreed to by the Treaty of Amsterdam. For a table of equivalencies *see* Annex IV of the Treaty of Amsterdam at europa.eu.int/eur-lex/en/treaties/selected/livre550.html.

[133] European Union, Treaty Establishing the European Community, Article 81, provides:

1. The following shall be prohibited as incompatible with the common market: all arrangements between undertakings, decisions by associations of undertakings and concerted practices which may affect trade between Member States and which have as their object or effect the prevention, restriction or distortion of competition within the common market. . . .

2. Any agreement or decision prohibited pursuant to this Article shall be automatically void.

3. The provisions of paragraph 1 may, however, be declared inapplicable in the case of: any agreement or category of agreements between undertakings; any decision or category of decisions by associations of undertakings; any concerted practice or category of concerted practices; which contributes to improving the production or distribution of goods, or to promoting technical or economic progress, while allowing consumers a fair share of the resulting benefit, and which does not:

    (a) impose on the undertakings concerned restrictions which are not indispensable to the attainment of these objectives;

    (b) afford such undertakings the possibility of eliminating competition in respect of a substantial part of the products in question.

Article 82 provides: "Any abuse by one or more undertakings of a dominant position within the common market or in a substantial part of it shall be prohibited as incompatible with the common market in so far as it may affect trade between Member States. . . .'

rule of reason: Court-adopted rule that allows a reviewing court to consider the overall impact of a particular agreement on competition within its relevant market.

progress, while allowing consumers a fair share of the resulting benefit." The same result is achieved in the United States with the development of a court-made **rule of reason**. Except for certain agreements, such as horizontal price-fixing, which the courts regard as illegal *per se*,[134] the rule of reason requires courts to consider the overall impact of the particular agreement on competition within the relevant market. Courts, accordingly, must identify the pro-competitive effects of the agreement, and then weigh them against its anticompetitive effects. A common example involves the sale of a firm. In order to sell the firm, the seller may have to agree not to compete with the buyer by setting up a new business in the same area for a reasonable period of time. Such an agreement allows the seller to make a sale and the buyer to protect the goodwill it has purchased, and overall, it increases competition.[135]

Although it can be stated as a general proposition that (a) licenses granting statutory intellectual rights are enforceable exceptions to technology transfer codes and the unfair competition laws and (b) that licenses granting nonstatutory rights must comply with both, this is only a general statement. Countries differ in their application of these general rules. We will look, therefore, at several examples of how particular licensing clauses are regulated in different countries.

In considering the following licensing provisions and their corresponding regulations, one needs to keep in mind that they apply to different kinds of intellectual property in varying degrees. Export restrictions, for example, apply to all kinds of intellectual property (including copyrights, patents, trademarks, and know-how), whereas restrictions on research and development, as another example, apply—obviously—only to patents and know-how.

Territorial Restrictions

In almost every country, a restriction on the territorial scope granted in the license of a statutory right (i.e., a patent, trademark, or copyright) is treated as a normal incidence of that right. Article 24 of the 1919 Honduran Law on Patents provides a typical example:

> In the instrument of transfer an indication shall be given of whether . . . the transfer is effective in a certain area only or throughout the Republic.

Such restrictions, however, apply only to the immediate licensee. Attempts to limit the territory in which an article can be traded after it has left the hands of the licensee are universally condemned. The rationale underlying this is a doctrine known as "exhaustion-of-rights."

exhaustion-of-rights doctrine: Once a good made or sold under license is in circulation, the licensor has no further right to control its distribution.

Although the **exhaustion-of-rights doctrine** first appeared as a court-made rule in the United States and Germany,[136] the European Court of Justice has given the doctrine its broadest application and its most careful analysis. This is because the European Union is confronted with the problem of rationalizing the separate intellectual property laws of its member states with its own express goal of establishing the free movement of goods among those states. As the Court of Justice observed in *Parke, Davis v. Centrafarm*:

> The national rules relating to the protecting of industrial property have not yet been unified within the Community. In the absence of such unification, the national character of the protection of industrial property and the variations between the different legislative systems on this subject are capable of creating obstacles both to the free movement of the patented products and to competition within the common market.[137]

---

[134]Latin: "by itself" or "in itself"; "intrinsically."
[135]*See* National Society of Professional Engineers v. United States, *United States Reports,* vol. 435, p. 689 (Supreme Ct., 1978).
[136]The first statement of the rule by the U.S. Supreme Court was in Adams v. Burks, *United States Reports,* vol. 84, p. 453 (1873). In Continental T.V., Inc. v. GTE Sylvania, Inc., *id.,* vol. 433, p. 36 (1977), the Supreme Court set out the rule this way: "[U]nder the Sherman Act, it is unreasonable without more for a manufacturer to restrict and confine areas or persons with whom an article may be traded after the manufacturer has parted with dominion over it."
For a statement of the German rule, *see* Federal Cartel Office decision of May 5, 1960, *Wirtschaft und Wettbewerb, Entscheidungssammlung,* p. 251.
[137]Case 24/67, *European Court Reports,* vol. 1968, p. 71 (1968).

This rationalization problem is, in some respects, made more difficult by the EU's fundamental law—the European Community Treaty—which expressly recognizes the rights of the member states to regulate intellectual property rights. Article 30 of the EC Treaty provides:

> The provisions of Articles 28 and 29 [which establish the free movement of goods within the European Union] shall not preclude prohibitions or restrictions on imports, exports, or goods in transit justified on grounds of . . . the protection of industrial and commercial property. Such prohibitions or restrictions shall not, however, constitute a means of arbitrary discrimination or disguised restriction on trade between Member States.

To avoid the conflict between the rights of the Union and the rights of the member states, which Article 30 seems to create, the Court of Justice has taken the novel, although somewhat obvious step, of narrowly defining the "industrial and commercial property" rights retained by the member states. Thus, in the landmark case of *Terrapin v. Terranova* the Court stated:

> . . . whilst the Treaty does not affect the existence of rights recognized by the legislation of the Member States in matters of industrial and commercial property, yet the *exercise* of those rights may nevertheless, depending on the circumstances, be restricted by the prohibitions in the Treaty. Inasmuch as it provides an exception to one of the fundamental principles of the common market, Article 36 in fact admits exceptions to the free movement of goods only to the extent to which such exceptions are justified for the purposes of safeguarding the rights which constitute the specific subject-matter of the property.[138]

In other words, although the Court recognizes that the member states can create and grant rights in the "specific subject-matter" of intellectual property, when the "exercise" of those rights impacts on the Union, Union law will govern. Put yet another way, the rights created by the member states are "exhausted" whenever the protected goods move across the national boundaries of the member states.

The leading EU patent case dealing with the exhaustion-of-rights doctrine is *Centrafarm v. Sterling Drug.*[139] The case involved patents for a drug used in the treatment of urinary infections that were held by Sterling Drug, an American company, in the Netherlands and the United Kingdom. Sterling sued Centrafarm (a company famous in the annals of the Court of Justice as a parallel importer of pharmaceuticals) for infringement of the Dutch patent. Centrafarm's alleged impropriety was the importation into the Netherlands for sale of certain quantities of the patented drug that had been lawfully marketed in the United Kingdom by Sterling licensees. This was commercially attractive to Centrafarm because the goods were marketed in the United Kingdom under government price regulations for about half of what they sold for in the Netherlands.

The Court of Justice defined the rights that member states could grant to the owner of a patent. Thus, a patent is

> . . . the guarantee that the patentee, to reward the creative effort of the inventor, has the right to use an invention with the view to manufacturing industrial products and putting them into circulation for the first time, either directly or by the grant of licenses to third parties, as well as the right to oppose infringements.

By this definition, a patent's essential function is to reward and encourage creative effort. The reward comes from the grant of a monopoly, which allows the patent owner to manufacture the protected product and to put it into circulation for the first time. This monopoly may be exercised either directly or through licensees. It is a significant grant, because the patent owner is also given the corollary right of objecting to its infringement.

The patent owner's rights, however, are significantly limited by this definition. The monopoly consists only of manufacturing the protected products and putting them into circulation for

---

[138]Case 119/75, *id.,* vol. 1976, p. 1039 (1976).
[139]Case 15/74, *id.,* vol. 1974, p. 1147 (1974); *Common Market Law Reports,* vol. 1974, pt. 2, p. 480 (1974).

the *first time*. In other words, the patent owner may not restrict any subsequent circulation of the products.

Considering this limitation, the Court of Justice gave two examples of when a patent owner in one member state could restrict imports from another member state. One example is where a product is patentable in State A but not patentable in State B. If it is manufactured in State B by a third party without the consent of the State A patent owner, and then imported into State A, the patent owner may object. The other example is where the product is patented in both State A and State B, but the original owners of the two patents are persons who are legally and economically independent.[140] Either may object to the other's product being imported into its state.

In contrast to these two cases, the Court said that a patent owner would not be justified in opposing importation "where the product has been put onto the market in a legal manner, by the patentee himself or with his consent, in the member states from which it has been imported, in particular in the case of a proprietor of parallel patents." To hold otherwise, the Court said, would allow a patent owner to cordon off each member state into a separate national market—something that is contrary to the notion of the free movement of goods, which is basic to the EU common market. In conclusion, the Court noted:

> [T]he exercise, by a patentee, of the right which he enjoys under the legislation of a Member State to prohibit the sale, in that state, of a product protected by the patent which has been marketed in another Member State by the patentee or with his consent is incompatible with the rules of the EEC Treaty concerning the free movement of goods within the common market.

In *Centrafarm v. Winthrop,*[141] the Court applied the exhaustion-of-rights doctrine—with the same result—to a trademark infringement case. The Court has also applied the doctrine to a copyright case in *Deutsche Gramophone v. Metro*[142] and to a neighboring rights case in *Coditel v. Ciné Vog Films (No. 1).*[143] The EU Commission's Block Exemption for Know-how Licensing extends it to know-how licenses.[144]

Case 9–5 is a landmark European Union intellectual property case involving a German manufacturer of electronic equipment that had attempted to grant "absolute territorial protection" to its French licensee. The manufacturer did so by allowing the licensee to register in France a unique trademark that the manufacturer affixed to products it produced for sale in France and by promising not to deliver the products, even indirectly, to competitors of its licensee.

---

[140]The converse of this situation is the "common origin" doctrine, discussed below.
[141]Case 16/74, *European Court Reports,* vol. 1974, p. 1183 (1974).
[142]Case 78/70, *id.,* vol. 1971, p. 487 (1971).
[143]Case 62/79, *id.,* vol. 1980, p. 881 (1980). The particular case involved the unauthorized rebroadcast over a cable network of a film that had been broadcast over a different network in another member state.
[144]European Union, *Block Exemption for Know-How Licensing,* Articles 3(6), 3(7), 3(12), and 9(5) (1987).

Case 9–5   *Consten and Grundig v. Commission*

European Community,[145] Court of Justice, 1966. *European Community Reports*, Cases 56/64 and 58/64, p. 299 (1966).

Grundig, a German firm, manufactured radios, televisions, tape recorders, and other electronic equipment.

Consten, a French firm, was an electronics wholesaler. In 1957 the two entered into an exclusive distributorship contract that granted Consten the sole right to sell Grundig products in France. The contract contained a provision requiring Grundig to include in its other distributorship agreements a clause preventing Grundig

---
[145]The European Community became the European Union, the European Economic Community Treaty became the European Community Treaty, and the Court of Justice of the European Community became the European Court of Justice in November 1993.

products from being shipped to France. In return, Consten agreed to handle Grundig products exclusively and not deliver those products outside of France.

The Grundig products all carried the trademark GINT. Grundig consented to Consten registering the mark in France in Consten's name. The reason for doing this was so that Consten could use the French trademark law to keep other importers from bringing Grundig goods carrying the same mark into France. Grundig itself owned the GINT trademark in Germany, and others of its exclusive distributors owned the mark in other countries.

The European Economic Community came into being in 1958, and in 1962 the EEC Council promulgated Regulation 17 requiring the parties to agreements such as this to notify the Commission about them. Grundig did so.

About the same time, competitors of Consten were buying Grundig products from outside of France and importing them into France, where they were selling them at lower prices. Consten brought suit in the French courts against these competitors to enjoin their infringement of its GINT trademark.

The competitors informed the EEC Commission of the suit, and the Commission, after studying the agreement between Consten and Grundig, issued a decision addressed to the two firms holding that their agreement violated Article 85 (now Article 81[146]) of the EEC Treaty. Accordingly, the Commission forbade the firms from hindering competitors from importing Grundig products into France from other EEC member states. The decision was appealed to the EEC Court of Justice pursuant to Article 173 (now Article 230) of the EEC Treaty.

MAP 9-5 European Community (1966)

Article 85 of the EEC Treaty prohibits, among other things, agreements "which may affect trade between Member States and which have as their object or effect the prevention, restriction, or distortion of competition within the common market." Paragraph (2) declares such agreements "automatically void."

Consten, Grundig, and the Italian Government (which had intervened in the case) argued that the restrictive agreements addressed by Article 85 are "horizontal agreements" (i.e., contracts between competitors at the same level, such as those between two manufacturers or two distributors) and not "vertical agreements" (i.e., contracts between firms that are not competitors, such as those between a manufacturer and a wholesaler or a wholesaler and a retailer).

The two firms and the German government (which also had intervened) argued that the agreement did not restrict trade but actually improved trade between France and Germany. These parties also argued that the order issued by the Commission was too wide, in that it annulled the entire contract, not just those provisions that violated Article 85.

Finally the firms argued that the Commission's decision prohibiting Consten from using its trademark right to stop parallel imports from other EEC member states violated Article 222 of the EEC Treaty. Article 222 (now Article 295) declares that the Treaty "shall in no way prejudice the rules in Member States governing the system of property ownership."

GROUNDS OF JUDGMENT

The Complaints Concerning the Applicability of Article 85(1) to Sole Distribution Agreements

The applicants submit that the prohibition in Article 85(1) applies only to so-called horizontal agreements. The Italian Government submits furthermore that sole distributorship contracts do not constitute "agreements between undertakings" within the meaning of the provision, since the parties are not on a footing of equality. With regard to these contracts, freedom of competition may be protected only by virtue of Article 86 [now Article 82] of the Treaty.

Neither the wording of Article 85 nor that of Article 86 gives any ground for holding that distinct areas of application are to be assigned to each of the two articles according to the level of the economy in which all the contracting parties operate. Article 85 refers in a general way to all agreements which distort competition within the common market and does not lay down any distinction between these agreements based on whether they are made between competitors operating on the same

---

[146]European Community Treaty Articles 85, 86, 173, and 222 were renumbered as 81, 82, 230, and 295 by the Treaty of Amsterdam. For a table of equivalencies *see* Annex IV of the Treaty of Amsterdam at europa.eu.int/eur-lex/en/treaties/selected/livre550.html.

level in the economic process or between noncompeting persons operating at different levels. In principle, no distinction can be made where the Treaty does not make any distinction.

Furthermore, the possible application of Article 85 to a sole distributorship contract cannot be excluded merely because the grantor and the concessionaire are not competitors *inter se*[147] and not on a footing of equality. Competition may be distorted within the meaning of Article 85(1) not only by agreements which limit it as between the parties, but also by agreements which prevent or restrict the competition which might take place between one of them and third parties. For this purpose, it is irrelevant whether the parties to the agreement are or are not on a footing of equality as regards their position and function in the economy. This applies all the more since, by such an agreement, the parties might seek, by preventing or limiting the competition of third parties in respect of the products, to create or guarantee for their benefit an unjustified advantage at the expense of consumers, contrary to the general aims of Article 85(1).

Finally, an agreement between producer and distributor which might tend to restore the national divisions in trade between Member States might be such as to frustrate the most fundamental objectives of the Community. The Treaty, whose preamble and content aim at abolishing the barriers between states, and which in several provisions gives evidence of a stern attitude to their reappearance, could not allow undertakings to reconstruct such barriers.

The submissions set out above are consequently unfounded.

The Complaints Relating to the Concepts of "Agreements . . . Which May Affect Trade Between Member States"

The applicants and the German Government maintain that the Commission has relied on a mistaken interpretation of the concept of an agreement which may affect trade between Member States and has not shown that such trade would have been greater without the agreement in dispute.

The defendant replies that this requirement in Article 85(1) is fulfilled once trade between Member States develops, as a result of the agreement, differently from ways in which it would have done without the restriction resulting from the agreement, and once the influence of the agreement on market conditions reaches a certain degree. Such is the case here, according to the defendant, particularly in view of the impediments resulting within the Common Market from the disputed

agreement as regards the exporting and importing of Grundig products to and from France.

The concept of an agreement "which may affect trade between Member States" is intended to define, in the law governing cartels, the boundary between the areas respectively covered by Community law and national law. It is only to the extent to which the agreement may affect trade between Member States that the deterioration in competition falls under the prohibition of Community law contained in Article 85; otherwise, it escapes prohibition.

In this connection, what is particularly important is whether the agreement is capable of constituting a threat, either direct or indirect, actual or potential, to freedom of trade between Member States in a manner which might harm the attainment of the objectives of a single market between states. Thus the fact that the agreement encourages an increase, even a large one, in the volume of trade between states is not sufficient to exclude the possibility that the agreement might "affect" such trade in the above-mentioned manner. In the present case, the contract between Grundig and Consten, on the one hand by preventing undertakings other than Consten from importing Grundig products into France, and on the other hand by prohibiting Consten from re-exporting those products to other countries of the Common Market, indisputably affects trade between Member States. These limitations on the freedom of trade, as well as those which might ensue for third parties from the registration by Consten of the GINT trademark which Grundig places on all its products, are enough to satisfy the requirement in question.

Consequently, the complaints raised in this respect must be dismissed.

The Complaints Concerning the Criterion of Restriction on Competition

The applicants and the German Government maintain that, since the Commission restricted its examination solely to Grundig's products, the decision was based upon a false concept of competition, since this applies particularly to competition between similar products of different makes; the Commission before declaring Article 85(1) to be applicable, should, by basing itself upon the "rule of reason", have considered the economic effects of the disputes contract upon competition between the different makes. There is a presumption that vertical sole-distribution agreements are not harmful to competition, and in the present case there is nothing to invalidate that presumption. On the contrary, the contract in question has increased the competition between similar products of different makes.

[147Latin: "among or between themselves."]

The principle of freedom of competition concerns the various stages and manifestations of competition. Although competition between producers is generally more noticeable than between distributors of products of the same make, it does not thereby follow that an agreement tending to restrict the latter kind of competition should escape the prohibition of Article 85(1) merely because it might increase the former.

Besides, for the purpose of applying Article 85(1), there is no need to take account of the concrete effects of an agreement once it appears that it has as its object the prevention, restriction, or distortion of competition.

The Complaints Relating to the Extent of the Prohibition

The applicant Grundig and the German Government complain that the Commission did not exclude from the prohibition, in the operative part of the disputed decision, those clauses of the contract in respect of which there was found no effect capable of restricting competition, and that it thereby failed to define the infringement.

It is apparent from the statement of the reasons for the contested decision that the infringement is not to be found in the undertaking by Grundig not to make direct deliveries in France except to Consten. That infringement arises from the clauses which, added to this grant of exclusive rights, are intended to impede, relying upon national law, parallel imports of Grundig products into France by establishing absolute territorial protection in favor of the sole concessionaire.

The provision in Article 85(2) that agreements prohibited pursuant to Article 85(1) shall be automatically void applies only to those parts of the agreement which are subject to the prohibition, or to the agreement as a whole if those parts do not appear to be serviceable. The Commission should, therefore, either have confined itself to declaring that an infringement lay in parts only of the agreement, or else it should have set out the reason why those parts did not appear to be severable.

Article 1 of the contested decision must therefore be annulled, in so far as it renders void, without any valid reason, all the clauses of the agreement.

The Submissions Concerning the Finding of an Infringement in Respect of the Agreement on the GINT Trademark

The applicants complain that the Commission infringed Article 222 of the EEC Treaty and furthermore exceeded the limits of its powers by excluding, in its decision, any possibility of Consten's asserting its rights under national trademark law to oppose parallel imports.

Consten's right under the contract to be the exclusive user of the GINT trademark is intended to make it possible to place an obstacle in the way of parallel imports. Thus the agreement tends to restrict competition.

That agreement therefore is one which may be caught by the prohibition in Article 85(1). The prohibition would be ineffective if Consten could continue to use the trademark to achieve the same object as that pursued by the agreement which has been held to be unlawful.

Article 222 confines itself to stating that the "Treaty shall in no way prejudice the rules in Member States governing the system of property ownership." The injunction contained in the contested decision to refrain from using rights under national trademark law in order to set an obstacle in the way of parallel imports does not affect the grant of those rights but only limits their exercise to the extent necessary to give effect to Article 85(1). The power of the Commission rules on competition which have immediate effect and are binding on individuals.

Such a body of rules, by reason of its nature described above and its function, does not allow the improper use of rights under any national trademark law in order to frustrate the Community's law on cartels.

The above-mentioned submissions are therefore unfounded. ■

---

common origin doctrine: Owners of the same intellectual property right who acquired it from a common predecessor cannot restrict each other from using the right.

The European Court of Justice has devised another doctrine, related to the doctrine of exhaustion of rights, to promote the free movement of goods at the expense of trademark owners. This is the **common origin doctrine**, which was first announced in the case of *Van Zuylen v. Hag*, then revised and narrowed in *CNL-Sucal v. Hag*.

The *Van Zuylen* case was a trademark infringement action that arose as the result of the importation into Luxembourg of decaffeinated coffee manufactured in Germany by Hag AG and bearing the HAG trademark. In 1927, Hag AG had established a subsidiary in Belgium to which it assigned the rights to the HAG trademark for both Belgium and Luxembourg. After World War II, the Belgian government expropriated the subsidiary as enemy property and ultimately sold it to the Van Oevelen family, who, in 1971, assigned the trademark to Van Zuylen

Frères. Van Zuylen Frères was the owner of the mark at the time that Hag AG began its imports to Luxembourg. In sum, the case involved a trademark that had originally been the property of a common owner, but which was now owned in one member state by the original owner and in another state by a legally and economically unrelated company. The Court of Justice concluded that the Belgian expropriation of the subsidiary did not break the common origin of the HAG trademark. It therefore held that the parallel importation into Luxembourg had to be allowed. The Court stated:

> The exercise of a trademark right tends to contribute to the partitioning off of the markets and thus to affect the free movement of goods between Member States, and all the more so since—unlike other rights of industrial and commercial property—it is not subject to limitations in point of time.
>
> Accordingly, one cannot allow the holder of a trademark to rely upon the exclusiveness of a trademark right—which may be the consequence of the territorial limitation of national legislations—with a view to prohibiting the marketing in a Member State of goods legally produced in another Member State under an identical mark having the same origin. Such a prohibition, which would legitimize the isolation of national markets, would collide with one of the essential objects of the Treaty, which is to unite national markets in a single market.

The holding in the *Van Zuylen* case was later summarized by the Court in *Terrapin v. Terranova*. There the Court said that a trademark could not be used to prevent goods from being sold in the state granting the mark when the mark was "the result of the subdivision, either by voluntary act or *a result of public constraint*, of a trademark right which originally belonged to one and the same proprietor."[148]

In 1990, the Court overruled its decision in the *Van Zuylen* case. In *CNL-Sucal v. Hag*, the Court held that the expropriation of the HAG mark by Belgium after World War II had indeed broken the unity of the trademark and destroyed the common origin. As a consequence, there were now two separate marks, which enjoyed full protection in their respective territories. Both owners were now "able to prevent the importation and marketing in the Member State where the mark belongs to him, of products originating from the other owner."[149]

Although there is some authority for the proposition that the EU's common origin doctrine may apply to other forms of intellectual property, there are several good arguments for believing that it applies only to trademarks. In particular, the primary function of a trademark is to assure consumers of the place of origin of a product, while the primary function of patents and copyrights is the rewarding of creativity. Also, the subdivision of a market through the use of trademarks is a reasonably serious matter because a trademark is of an essentially permanent nature, whereas patents and copyrights are temporary monopolies.[150]

It is important to note that both the exhaustion-of-rights doctrine and the common origin doctrine apply only in cases involving the movement of goods between the member states of the European Union.[151] When protected products are manufactured outside the EU, they may not be imported into the EU without the express consent of the EU intellectual property owner. This was the circumstance in the *EMI v. CBS* cases.[152] Until 1917, the same company had owned the COLUMBIA trademark in Europe and the United States. By 1931, however,

---

[148]Case 119/76, *European Court Reports,* vol. 1976, p. 1039 (1976); *Common Market Law Reports,* vol. 2, p. 482 (1976).

[149]Case 10/89, *Common Market Law Reports,* vol. 3, p. 571 at 609 (1990).

[150]For additional reasons, *see* Derrick Wyatt and Alan Dashwood, *The Substantive Law of the EEC,* p. 499 (2nd ed., 1987).

[151]The exhaustion-of-rights doctrine and the common origin doctrine also do not apply in the European Free Trade Area, which is a free-trading group made up of the European Union, Iceland, Norway, and Switzerland. Case E2/97, Mag Instrument Inc. v. California Trading Company (EFTA Court of Justice 1997), posted at www.efta.int/docs/Court/Publications/Decision/1997/ao2–97.htm.

[152]Case 51/75, EMI Records v. CBS United Kingdom, *European Court Reports,* vol. 1976, p. 811 (1976); *Common Market Law Reports,* vol. 1976, pt. 2, p. 235 (1976); Case 86/75, EMI Records v. CBS Grammofon, *European Court Reports,* vol. 1976, p. 871 (1976); Case 96/75, EMI Records v. CBS Schallplatten, *id.,* vol. 1976, p. 913 (1976).

EMI acquired the European mark, and in 1938 CBS acquired the American mark. Because the trademarks were of a common origin, CBS attempted to take advantage of the common origin doctrine announced in *Van Zuylen v. Hag* to be able to sell its products in Europe. The Court rejected CBS's arguments, holding:

> [T]he exercise of a trademark right in order to prevent the marketing of products coming from a third country under an identical mark, even if this constitutes a measure having an effect equivalent to a quantitative restriction, does not affect the free movement of goods between Member States and thus does not come under the prohibitions set out in Article 30 [now Article 28] *et seq* of the Treaty.

Like the European Court of Justice, the courts in the United States have faced the problem of parallel imports of protected products that have been lawfully manufactured outside the United States—a problem known in the United States as **gray marketing**—and come to very similar results. See Case 9–2.

gray marketing: The domestic sale of products manufactured under a license that only grants a foreign licensee the right to sell the goods overseas.

Export Restrictions

Export restrictions limit partially, or entirely, the rights of a licensee to export goods from the territory where the licensee or its production facilities are located. Most countries, as a general rule, prohibit export restrictions.[153] This general rule, however, is often subject to many exceptions.

In some countries, restrictions will be tolerated if they limit exports to a country where (a) the licensor owns intellectual property rights and (b) the local laws allow the licensor to restrict foreign imports.[154] In other countries, export restrictions will be tolerated if the limitation applies to a territory where (a) the licensor is manufacturing or distributing the restricted goods or (b) the licensor has granted an exclusive license to a third party to manufacture or distribute the goods.[155]

In the United States, export restriction agreements between competitors (so called **horizontal competition agreements**) have been held to be *per se* violations of the Sherman Antitrust Act.[156] For example, in *United States v. National Lead Co.*, the U.S. Supreme Court found a worldwide patent pool covering an entire industry and dividing the whole world into exclusive territories to be illegal.[157] On the other hand, agreements between a seller and a buyer (**vertical competition agreements**) are not bad *per se* and will be tested by a "rule of reason."[158]

horizontal competition agreements: Agreements between competitors that have the effect of diminishing competition.

vertical competition agreements: Agreements between sellers and buyers.

In the European Union export restriction agreements that affect the movement of goods between EU member states violate the Union's European Community Treaty's unfair competition article (Article 81), whether they are reasonable or not.[159] Restrictions on exports to countries outside the Union, however, are prohibited only if they can be shown to have a direct

---

[153]E.g., India, Guidelines for Industries, Chap. 3, Article 9(v) (1988), provides: "To the fullest extent possible, there should be no restrictions on free exports to all countries." Similar provisions exist in Nigeria, the Philippines, Portugal, Spain, and Zambia.

[154]E.g., Brazil, Normative Act No. 015 of the National Institute of Industrial Property, Articles 2.5.2(b)(i), 3.5.2(c)(i), 4.5.2(d)(i), and 5.5.2(d)(i) (1975); Japan, Antimonopoly Act Guidelines for International Licensing Agreements, § 1.1(a) (1969); Mexico, Summary of the General Criteria for the Application of the Law Concerning Registration of the Transfer of Technology and the Use and Working of Patents, Trade Names and Trademarks (September 1974).

[155]E.g., Argentina, Law No. 21617 on the Transfer of Technology, Article 10(c) (August 12, 1972); Japan, Antimonopoly Act Guidelines for International Licensing Agreements, § 1.1(b) (1969); Mexico, Summary of the General Criteria for the Application of the Law Concerning Registration of the Transfer of Technology and the Use and Working of Patents, Trade Names and Trademarks (September 1974); Serbia and Montenegro, Law on Long-term Cooperation in Production, Commercial-technical Cooperation and the Awarding and Acquiring of Technology Between Organizations of Associated Labor and Foreign Persons, Article 37(10) (1978).

[156]United States v. Topco Associates, Inc., *United States Reports,* vol. 405, p. 596 (Supreme Ct., 1972); United States v. Sealey, Inc., *id.,* vol. 388, p. 350 (Supreme Ct., 1967).

[157]*Federal Supplement,* vol. 63, p. 513 (Dist. Ct. for S. Dist. of New York, 1945), affirmed *United States Reports,* vol. 332, p. 319 (Supreme Ct., 1947).

[158]For patent licenses, *see* Continental T.V., Inc. v. GTE Sylvania, Inc., *United States Reports,* vol. 433, p. 36 (1977); for trade secret licenses, *see* United States v. E.I. Du Pont de Nemours and Co., *Federal Supplement,* vol. 118, p. 41 (Dist. Ct. for Delaware, 1953), affirmed *United States Reports,* vol. 351, p. 377 (Supreme Ct., 1956); for trademarks, *see* United States v. Topco Associates, Inc., *id.,* vol. 405, p. 596 (Supreme Ct., 1972).

[159]*See,* for example, Kabelmetal/Luchaire, *Official Journal,* No. L 222, p. 34 (August 22, 1975) (Commission Decision).

effect on the member states. Such a case exists where, because of geographical proximity and the absence of tariff duties, the goods could easily be reimported from a third country into a member state. Otherwise, export restrictions that apply outside the Union are enforceable in the Union.[160]

Cartels

cartel: A combination of independent business firms organized to regulate the production, pricing, and marketing of goods by its members.

cross-licensing agreement: An agreement to exchange licenses.

patent pool: An agreement to share patents and other technology.

multiple licensing agreement: A contract for the licensing of industrial property rights to two or more licensees.

A **cartel** is an agreement between several business enterprises that is designed, among other things, to allocate markets, to fix prices, to promote the exchange of knowledge resulting from technical and scientific research, to exchange patent rights, or to standardize products. Arrangements of this sort are often called cross-licensing agreements, patent pools, and multiple licensing agreements.

A **cross-licensing agreement** is an arrangement between two parties to exchange licenses; that is, each party is both a licensor and a licensee. A **patent pool** is an agreement among several owners of related technology to "pool" their patents and other related technology. A **multiple licensing agreement** involves the licensing of technology to a number of recipients by a single licensor. In and of themselves, these agreements are not restrictive, but they may contain restrictive clauses. When they do, some countries prohibit them.

The European Union, for example, forbids cartel-type arrangements when they have as their purpose or effect the prevention, restriction, or distortion of competition between EU member states. Such arrangements may include agreements to allocate markets between competitors (i.e., "horizontal" market allocation), horizontal price fixing, and patent pools.[161] In its Block Exemption for Know-how Licensing, the EU Commission has indicated that it will not object to information exchanges and cross-licensing agreements between a single licensor and a single licensee that involve know-how, patents, and trademarks, so long as they do not have the effect of stifling competition. In particular, agreements to cross-license improvements and new applications are valid for up to seven years so long as licensees are not precluded from using their own improvements or licensing them to third parties.[162] On the other hand, cross-licensing agreements that involve any territorial restraint with respect to the manufacture, use, or marketing of goods are invalid.[163]

In the United States, cross-licensing and patent pooling are not unlawful unless they are used to divide up territories among competitors, exclude others from competing, or otherwise restrain trade.[164] Moreover, a rule known as the **bottleneck principle** may require the participants in an industry-wide patent exchange to grant reasonable access to any firm wishing to compete so that no firm will be disadvantaged and competition will not be impaired.[165]

bottleneck principle: Participants in an industry-wide patent pool must grant reasonable access to the pool to any firm wishing to compete so that no firm will be disadvantaged.

Japan provides much broader exemptions to its basic prohibition against cartels than do either the European Community or the United States. Thus, manufacturing cartels, which are designed to avoid economic depression to an industry through restrictions on production facilities, production quantities, or sales volumes, are valid.[166] Likewise, manufacturers' rationalization cartels aimed at improving technology, productivity, product quality, cost reduction, or any similar entrepreneurial rationalization scheme are also legal.[167] Other cartel-type arrangements are reviewed by the Japanese Fair Trade Commission using a rule-of-reason standard to determine if they have the effect of unreasonably restraining trade.[168]

---

[160]*See,* for example, Junghans, *id.,* No. L 30, p. 10 (February 2, 1977) (Commission Decision).
    The rule in Germany parallels that of the EU. Restrictions on exports to territories within Germany or to EU member states are unenforceable, but restrictions on exports to countries outside the EU are valid. *See Bundeskartellamt,* Decision of June 20, 1963, *Wirtschaft und Wettbewerb, Entscheidungssammlung,* p. 254 (1963).
[161]European Union, Block Exemption for Know-how Licensing, Articles 3(8) and 5.1(1).
[162]Licensees may, however, be restricted from disclosing secret know-how to third parties. *Id.,* Article 2.1(4).
[163]*Id.,* Articles 5.1(3) and 5.2.
[164]*See* United States v. National Lead Co., *Federal Supplement,* vol. 63, p. 513 (Dist. Ct. S. Dist. of New York, 1945), affirmed *United States Reports,* vol. 332, p. 319 (Supreme Ct., 1947); Zenith Radio Corp. v. Hazeltine Research, Inc., *id.,* vol. 395, p. 100 (Supreme Ct., 1969).
[165]Standard Oil Co. (Indiana) v. United States, *id.,* vol. 283, p. 163 (Supreme Ct., 1931).
[166]Law No. 54 on the Prohibition of Private Monopolies and the Preservation of Fair Trade, Articles 24-3.1, 24-3.2, and 24-3.3 (April 14, 1974).
[167]*Id.,* Article 24-4.1.
[168]*Id.,* Articles 24-3 and 24-4.

Exclusive Licenses

exclusive license: A license that restricts who may compete with the licensee.

Laws in several countries expressly state that the grant of a patent, trademark, or copyright gives the owner the right to confer either an **exclusive license** or a nonexclusive license.[169] In most other countries, both the government and the courts have held that such arrangements are implicitly proper.

Parties to agreements granting these rights need to be careful, however, in defining the terms they use. A licensee may receive *sole rights* (to the exclusion of all others, including the licensor), *exclusive rights* (preventing everyone except the licensor from competing), or *nonexclusive rights* (which allows the licensor to grant other licenses). Merely using these terms, however, may cause confusion because the terms are interpreted differently in different countries. For example, in the United States the term *exclusive rights* is generally held to mean that the licensor may not give a license to another licensee nor exploit the licensed property himself, unless he specifically reserves the right to do so.[170] In France, on the other hand, an exclusive license does not prevent the licensor from personally competing, unless the agreement specifically provides otherwise.[171]

The importance of fully and carefully defining the terms used in a licensing contract is illustrated by Case 9–6.

---

[169]E.g., Austria, Korea, and Zambia.

[170]*See* Cutter Laboratories, Inc. v. Lyophile-Cryochem Corp., *Federal Reports, Second Series,* vol. 179, p. 80 (Ninth Circuit Ct. of Appeals, 1949).

[171]Philippe Nouel, "Licensing in France," *International Licensing Agreements,* p. 158 (2nd ed., Götz M. Pollizen & Eugen Langen, eds., 1973).

Case 9–6   Ransome-Kuti v. Phonogram, Ltd.

Ghana, High Court at Accra, 1976.
Ghana Law Reports, vol. 1, p. 220 (1976).

JUDGE EDUSEI:

The plaintiff in this application is seeking an order of this court "restraining the defendant by itself, its agents, servants, and privies from publishing or causing to be published for distribution, sale, or use in Ghana, a musical tape entitled 'Everything Scatter' owned and produced by the plaintiff between May and October 1975."

The facts as revealed by the rival affidavits are not seriously in dispute. It is admitted by the defendants that the plaintiff created and composed a musical work entitled "Everything Scatter" in Nigeria, but by an agreement, Exhibit A, made between the plaintiff and Phonogram, Ltd. (Nigeria) dated 14 October 1975, the plaintiff assigned to Phonogram, Ltd. (Nigeria) the sole and exclusive right to produce or reproduce and sell the work on records and tapes as a single album as well as recordings on cassette tapes and cartridges all over the continent of Africa for a period of three years from

14 October 1975, in consideration of sums of money specified in the said agreement.

The plaintiff is contending that Phonogram, Ltd. (Nigeria) (hereinafter referred to as the Nigerian company) has no right whatsoever to delegate its duty of publishing to the defendants, and counsel for the plaintiff referred to the case of *Griffith v. Tower Publishing Co., Ltd.*,[172] where it was decided that a publishing agreement between an author and his publisher or firm of publishers is personal to the parties and cannot be assigned without the author's consent. In that case, the plaintiff agreed with the defendant-company, a firm of publishers, for the printing and selling of his three novels, but the publishers went into liquidation and were arranging for another company to publish the said novels. On application for an injunction to restrain the defendants and the receiver, the court said an injunction should go. It is clear from the judgment that the copyright in the novels remained in the plaintiff who was entitled to protect his interest in so far as the printing and selling of the novels were concerned. And, in the absence of any power in the defendants to assign their right and interest in the agreement, it is clear that they

---

[172]*All England Law Reports,* vol. 1895–99, p. 323.

could not without the consent of the author (the plaintiff) attempt to assign the publication of the novels to another company. Again, it seems that the right to assign any interest in the agreement was not reserved to either of the parties. There can be no doubt that this decision confirms the principle that such contracts are personal and on the facts of the case the decision in my view was correct.

In the case before me the parties entered into a formal agreement, Exhibit A, in which the parties include their successors-in-title and assigns. The opening words of the agreement, Exhibit A, presuppose that the right to assign the interest in the agreement is reserved to both parties unless there is a term to the contrary further down in Exhibit A. Again, by paragraph (5) of Exhibit A, the copyright in the musical work has passed to the Nigerian company for a period of three years during which the sole and exclusive right to produce or reproduce and sell the work in records and tapes over the continent of Africa is vested in the Nigerian company. The Nigerian company has licensed the defendants, a sister company in Ghana (part of Africa) to reproduce the said musical work in Ghana for them, and Section 10(5) of the *Copyright Act*, 1961 (Act No. 85), which permits the grant of licenses stipulates as follows, "A license to do an act falling within the copyright may be written or oral, or may be inferred from conduct, and may be revoked at any time." Also, Section 10(2) states:

An assignment or testamentary disposition may be limited so as to apply to only some of the acts which the owner of the copyright has the exclusive right to control or to a part only of the period of the copyright.

By virtue of Exhibit A, the plaintiff has no copyright in the said musical work to protect—at least for three years in Africa. Indeed, paragraph (6) of Exhibit A makes the position of the plaintiff clearer. It states:

The author [i.e., the plaintiff] further warrants that any records or works pressed or waxed on any other label . . . shall not be sold . . . in any part of the continent of Africa by the author, his agents, his representatives or any other person to whom the copyright shall be granted by the author outside the continent of Africa.

This quotation from Exhibit A means that the plaintiff is at liberty to grant to any other person outside the continent of Africa [the right] to reproduce the work on records and cassette tapes, but such records and cassette tapes cannot in any way be sold in Africa. In so far as the continent of Africa is concerned, the copyright in the musical work is vested in the Nigerian company. The Nigerian company—that has the copyright for a period of three years in Africa—has, in my opinion, every right to permit anyone in Africa under license to reproduce the work for that company.

. . . Since the copyright in the musical work is vested in the Nigerian company and the said company has given license to the defendant to reproduce the tape in this country which is part of the continent of Africa, I cannot see any infringement of the copyright by the defendants. It seems to me that I should be doing wrong if I decided that there has been an infringement in the face of Exhibit A and the facts in this case. . . .

The plaintiff's application was dismissed. ■

Sales and Distribution Arrangements

A sales or distribution arrangement limits a licensee's freedom to organize its distribution system independently of the licensor.

There are three basic approaches to the regulation of these agreements. One group of developing countries (e.g., Brazil, Serbia and Montenegro, and Zambia) prohibits any interference by the licensor in the licensee's distribution system.[173] A second group of developing and developed countries (e.g., Japan, Mexico, Nigeria, and Venezuela) prohibit only those provisions that give the licensor exclusive distribution rights.[174] Finally, a third group of generally developed countries (e.g., Germany, Portugal, Spain, the United States, and the European Community) only prohibit those exclusive sales arrangements that tend to allocate or monopolize markets.[175]

---

[173]For example, Zambia's Industrial Development Act, Article 16 (1977), provides: "A contract for the transfer of technology and expertise shall not contain any condition: . . . (c) Which restricts the manner of sale of products or the export of products to any country. . . ."

[174]For example, Venezuela's Decree No. 746 on Transfer of Technology Agreements, Article 1(e) (February 11, 1975), forbids any clause in a transfer of technology contract that "requires all or part of the goods produced to be sold to the supplier."

[175]*See*, for example, Elder-Beerman Stores Corp. v. Federated Dept. Stores, Inc., *Federal Reports, Second Series,* vol. 459, p. 138 (Sixth Circuit Ct. of Appeals, 1972); United States v. Imperial Chemical Industries, Ltd., *Federal Supplement,* vol. 105, p. 215 (Dist. Ct. for S. Dist. of New York, 1952).

Price-Fixing

price-fixing clause:
Provision requiring a licensee to sell products at a price set by the licensor.

A **price-fixing clause** requires a licensee to sell products at a price specified by the licensor. It may specify either maximum or minimum prices. It may be restricted to the technology or goods being licensed, or it may cover other products as well. It may apply only to the price charged by the licensee, or it may extend to the prices charged by retailers who purchase the goods from a wholesaler-licensee.

Price-fixing also arises in the context of cartels, particularly cross-licensing and patent pools.

Most countries—both developed and developing—prohibit all forms of price-fixing.[176] One exception is India, which allows a licensor to specify the price at which a licensee may sell a product manufactured using the licensor's technology or to which the licensor's trademark has been affixed (i.e., a vertical licensing arrangement).[177]

Noncompetition Clauses

noncompetition clause:
Provision forbidding a licensee from competing with the licensor.

Noncompetition clauses forbid a licensee from entering into agreements to acquire or distribute technologies or products that compete with ones furnished or designated by the licensor. Direct prohibitions may include an understanding that the licensee is not to manufacture or sell competing technologies, or that the licensee is to terminate the use of particular technologies or terminate the manufacture and distribution of particular products. Indirect prohibitions may require the licensee not to cooperate with a competing business or not to pay higher royalties for competing products.[178]

In general, noncompetition clauses are prohibited in all countries.[179] A few countries allow them under exceptional circumstances. The German Federal Cartel Office, for example, has sometimes granted an exemption to the German Act against Restraints on Competition when the restriction is narrowly drawn and when it is meant to prevent disclosure of confidential technical information.[180] In the United States, the courts have held that a clause prohibiting a trademark licensee from dealing in competing goods is not *per se* unlawful. Applying a rule of reason, the U.S. courts will consider the need to protect the mark, the need to avoid public confusion, and the impact of the restriction on competition.[181] Also, in connection with patent

---

[176]E.g., Argentina, Law No. 21617 on the Transfer of Technology, Article 10(i) (August 12, 1972); Brazil, Normative Act No. 015 of the National Institute of Industrial Property, Articles 2.5.2(b)(i) 3.5.2.(c)(i), 4.5.2(d)(i), and 5.5.2.(d)(i) (1975); Japan, Antimonopoly Act Guidelines for International Licensing Agreements, § 1.6 (1969); Mexico, Law on the Registration of the Transfer of Technology and the Use and Working of Patents, Trade Names, and Trade Marks, Article 7(xi) (December 29, 1972); Nigeria, Decree No. 70 Establishing the National Office of Industrial Property, Article 6.2.(j) (September 14, 1979); the Philippines, Regulation to Implement Article 5 of Presidential Decree No. 1520 establishing the Technology Board within the Ministry of Industry, Article 5.1(c) (October 10, 1978); Portugal, Foreign Investment Code (Legislative Decree No. 348/77, August 24, 1977), Article 28.1(f); Spain, Ministry of Industry Order Regulating the Entry of Contracts for the Transfer of Technology in the Register Established by Decree No. 2342 of September 21, 1973, § 3.6 (December 5, 1973); Serbia and Montenegro, Law on Long-Term Cooperation in Production, Commercial-Technical Cooperation and the Awarding and Acquiring of Technology between Organizations of Associated Labor and Foreign Persons, Article 37.9 (1978); European Union, Treaty Establishing the European Community, Article 81.1(a) (1957 as amended).

Price-fixing in the United States is *per se* illegal. Northern Pacific R. Co. v. United States, *United States Reports,* vol. 356, p. 1 (Supreme Ct., 1958); United States v. Trenton Potteries Co., *id.,* vol. 273, p. 392 (Supreme Ct., 1927).

[177]Monopolies and Restrictive Trade Practices Act No. 54, Article 39.3 (1969).

[178]A clause requiring a licensee to use its best efforts may sometimes work as an indirect noncompetition clause.

[179]A typical prohibition is Australia's Patents Act 1990 No. 83 of 1990, Article 144(1): "A condition in a contract relating to the sale or lease of, or a license to exploit, a patented invention is void if the effect of the condition would be: (a) to prohibit or restrict the buyer, lessee or licensee from using a product or process (whether patented or not) supplied or owned by a person other than the seller, lessor or licensor, or a nominee of the seller, lessor or licensor. . . ." The Australian Patents Act is posted on the Piper's Patent Attorneys' Web site at www.piperpat.co.nz/aulaw/aupatact.html.

Similar statutory prohibitions exist in Argentina, Austria, India, Japan, Mexico, Nigeria, the Philippines, Portugal, Serbia and Montenegro, Spain, the United Kingdom, and Zambia.

[180]E.g., Bundeskartellamt Decision of June 20, 1963, *Wirtschaft und Wettbewerb, Entscheidungssammlung,* p. 254 (1963).

[181]*See* American Motor Inns, Inc. v. Holiday Inns, Inc., *Federal Reporter, Second Series,* vol. 521, p. 1230 (Third Circuit Ct. of Appeals, 1975); Susser v. Carvel Corp., *id.,* vol. 332, p. 505 (Second Circuit Ct. of Appeals, 1964), *certoriari* denied, *United States Reports,* vol. 381, p. 125 (Supreme Ct., 1965); Denison Mattress Factory v. Spring-Air Co., *Federal Reports, Second Series,* vol. 308, p. 403 (Fifth Circuit Ct. of Appeals, 1962).

licenses, the U.S. courts have sometimes tolerated a noncompetition clause where the licensee has acquired an exclusive license.[182]

Challenges to Validity

No-challenge clauses forbid a licensee from challenging the validity of the statutory right granted by the licensor. The purpose of these clauses is to ensure that a licensee will comply with the agreed-to restrictions and payment obligations.

Only a few countries (e.g., Germany) permit no-challenge clauses generally.[183] Most consider such a clause in a patent or copyright license to be a restrictive trade practice. Many developing countries (e.g., Brazil, the Philippines, and Serbia and Montenegro) expressly condemn them in their transfer-of-technology codes.[184] Most developed countries (including the United States and the European Union) interpret their unfair competition laws as forbidding no-contest clauses in patent and copyright licenses.[185]

No-challenge clauses in trademark licenses are regarded in the same negative way by developing countries[186] and some developed countries. The European Union, accordingly, views such clauses as a violation of the unfair competition article (Article 81(1)) of the European Community Treaty.[187]

The United States, however, does not regard a no-contest clause in a trademark license as violating either its trademark laws or antitrust legislation.[188]

Tying Clauses

A **tying clause** is a provision that requires a licensee to acquire or use, separately from the technology wanted, additional goods (such as raw materials, intermediate products, machines, or additional technology) or designated personnel either from the licensor or from a source named by the licensor. In other words, the acquisition of these additional goods or services is a prerequisite to obtaining the technology license.

In general, tying clauses are illegal in virtually every country. Most countries, however, provide for exemptions in varying degrees. The most common exemption is granted on the grounds that a tie-in is necessary to protect quality standards or to protect the goodwill of a trademark.[189] Other exemptions (in a few countries) allow tie-ins if the licensee is not charged an excessive price,[190] if the licensee is free to terminate the tie-in arrangements at any

---

[182]*See* Carbo-Frost, Inc. v. Pure Carbonic, Inc., *Federal Reporter, Second Series,* vol. 103, p. 210 (Eighth Circuit Ct. of Appeals, 1964), certiorari denied, *United States Reports,* vol. 308, p. 569 (Supreme Ct., 1939); *see also* Wood v. Lucy, Lady Duff-Gordon, *North East Reporter,* vol. 118, p. 214 (New York Ct. of Appeals, 1917).

[183]Germany, Act against Restraints on Competition, Article 20.2(4).

[184]Brazil, Normative Act No. 015 of the National Institute of Industrial Property, Article 2.5.2 (1975); the Philippines, Regulation to Implement Article 5 of Presidential Decree No. 1520 establishing the Technology Board within the Ministry of Industry, Article 5.1.c.5 (October 10, 1978); Serbia and Montenegro, Law on Long-Term Cooperation in Production, Commercial-Technical Cooperation, and the Awarding and Acquiring of Technology between Organizations of Associated Labor and Foreign Persons, Article 37(4) (1978).

[185]*See* Lear, Inc. v. Adkins, *United States Reports,* vol. 395, p. 653 (Supreme Ct., 1969); AOIP/Beyard, *Official Journal,* No. L, p. 31 (January 13, 1976) (Commission Decision).

[186]E.g., Serbia and Montenegro's Law on Long-Term Cooperation in Production, Commercial-Technical Cooperation and the Awarding and Acquiring of Technology between Organizations of Associated Labor and Foreign Persons, Article 37(4) (1978), prohibits all no-contest clauses affecting rights in any form of industrial property.

[187]*See* Goodyear Italiana/Euram, *Official Journal,* No. L 38, p. 11 (February 12, 1975) (Commission Decision); but compare Penneys, *Official Journal,* No. L 60, p. 19 (March 2, 1978) (Commission Decision), in which the Commission held that a no-contest clause that ran for a period of only 5 years was not an appreciable restriction on competition.

[188]*See* Beer Nuts, Inc. v. Kings Nut Co., *Federal Reporter, Second Series,* vol. 477, p. 328, *certiorari* denied, *United States Reports,* vol. 414, p. 585 (Supreme Ct., 1973); Seven-Up Bottling Co. v. The Seven-Up Co., *Federal Supplement,* vol. 420, p. 1246 (Dist. Ct. for E. Dist. of Montana, 1976).

[189]E.g., India, Patents Act, Article 140.4(c) (1970); United Kingdom, Patents Act, Article 44.6 (1977); European Union, Block Exemption for Patent Licensing, Article 2(9).

In the United States, a tying clause was held to be justified to protect the licensor's goodwill in Dehydrating Process Co. v. A. O. Smith Corp., *Federal Reporter, Second Series,* vol. 292, p. 1 (1st Circuit Ct. of Appeals, 1961), *certiorari* denied, *United States Reports,* vol. 368, p. 931 (Supreme Ct., 1961), and when it was used to ensure that the product was manufactured according to the licensor's standards in Electric Pipe Line, Inc. v. Fluid Systems, Inc., *Federal Reporter, Second Series,* vol. 231, p. 370 (2nd Circuit Ct. of Appeals, 1956).

[190]E.g., Australia's Patents Act 1990 No. 83 of 1990, Article 144(2)(a); United Kingdom, Patents Act, Article 44.4(a) (1977).

time,[191] or if the licensee is allowed to terminate the clause as soon as a dependable local source of supply can be found.[192]

Quantity and Field-of-Use Restrictions

quantity restriction:
Provision in a license limiting the quantity of goods that may, or must, be produced.

field-of-use restrictions:
Provision limiting the fields in which goods acquired or produced under license may be used.

Countries regulate licensing arrangements with **quantity** and **field-of-use restrictions** in three ways. Developing countries (with transfer-of-technology codes) generally regard limitations on the quantity of goods that may, or must, be produced, or limits on the fields in which goods may be used or sold, as illegal. The prohibition in Article 16 of Zambia's Industrial Production Act of 1977 is a typical example:

> A contract for the transfer of technology and expertise shall not contain any condition: . . .
>
> (e) Which restricts the volume or structure of production;
> (f) Which limits the ways in which patents or other know-how may be used. . . .

Similar provisions exist in Brazil,[193] Mexico,[194] and the Philippines.[195]

A second group of countries, including Japan, the European Community, the United States, and most countries in the developed world, regard quantity and field-of-use restrictions as implicit elements in the statutory rights of a licensor. Section III of Japan's Antimonopoly Act Guidelines for International Licensing Agreements of 1969 is a representative example:

> In international licensing agreements on patent rights, etc., the following acts shall be regarded as the exercise of rights under the Patent Act or the Utility Model Act: . . .
>
> 3. To restrict the manufacture of patented goods to a limited field of technology or to restrict the sale thereof to a limited field of sales;
> 4. To restrict the use of patented processes to a limited field of technology;
> 5. To restrict the amount of output or the amount of sales of patented goods or to restrict the frequency of the use of patented processes; . . .

Most of these countries do not, however, allow licensors to impose quantity or field-of-use limitations on nonstatutory rights. When they relate to know-how and other contractually based rights, these provisions are typically held to violate unfair competition rules.[196] When they attempt to expand a statutory grant beyond its ordinary scope, such a license is treated as a misuse of the grant. For example, in *United States v. Studiengesellschaft Kohle, M.B.H.*, an American court found that a sales limit imposed on unpatented goods produced according to a patented process was a form of patent misuse.[197] One exception to this is the European Union's Block Exemption for Know-How Licensing, which expressly allows licensors to confine a licensee's exploitation of know-how to a specific field of application or market. However, restrictions on customers who may be supplied within a particular field of use or market, restrictions on quantities sold, or restrictions on supplying persons who would resell the product within the Union are all illegal.[198]

A third approach to quantity and field-of-use restrictions is found in Germany. There, restrictions on both statutory *and* nonstatutory rights—including limitations on the use of know-how and trade secrets—are expressly allowed. Article 20.1 of Germany's 1957 Act Against Restraints on Competition expressly states that "restrictions pertaining to the type, extent, quantity, territory, or period of exercise" of statutorily granted industrial property rights

---

[191]E.g., Australia's Patents Act 1990 No. 83 of 1990, Article 144(2)(b); United Kingdom, Patents Act, Article 44.4(b) (1977).

[192]E.g., Mexico, Law on the Registration of the Transfer of Technology and the Use and Working of Patents, Trade Names, and Trade Marks, Article 7(x) (December 29, 1972).

[193]Brazil, Normative Act No. 15 of the National Institute of Industrial Property, Article 2.5.2 (September 11, 1975).

[194]Mexico, Law on the Registration of the Transfer of Technology and the Use and Working of Patents, Trade Names and Trade Marks, Article 7 (December 29, 1972).

[195]Philippines, Regulation to Implement Article 5 of Presidential Decree No. 1520 establishing the Technology Board within the Ministry of Industry, Article 28.1 (October 10, 1978).

[196]*See* Continental T.V., Inc. v. GTE Sylvania, Inc., *United States Reports,* vol. 433, p. 36 (Supreme Ct., 1977).

[197]*Federal Supplement,* vol. 426, p. 143 (Dist. Court for the District of Columbia, 1976).

[198]European Union, Block Exemption for Know-how Licensing, Articles 2.1(10), 3(6), 3(7), 3(12), and 9.5 (1987).

are "within the scope" of the statutory grant itself, and therefore valid and enforceable. Article 21.1 states that the same rule applies as to agreements limiting the use of "legally unprotected inventions, manufacturing methods, instructions, technique-improving processes and secret plant-breeding methods."

Restrictions on Research and Development

Restrictions on research and development may relate to two different kinds of activities: (1) the research, adaptation, and improvement of the transferred technology or (2) the research and development of competing technologies. Both of these are condemned in almost all countries.[199] The one significant exception is the United States, where a restriction on research to adapt transferred technology will be tolerated if it serves to preserve a product's reputation or to protect the licensor from liability.[200] Also, if the restriction is comparable to a valid field-of-use restriction, it may also be justified.[201]

Quality Controls

quality control clause:
Provision requiring a licensee to meet quality standards or operate under quality controls set by a licensor.

Requirements that a licensor meet certain quality standards or comply with certain quality controls imposed by the licensor are almost uniformly accepted in all countries around the world. In particular, **quality control clauses** are justified where the trademark of the licensor is being applied to a product manufactured and/or distributed by the licensee.[202] They are also justified when they are imposed for the purpose of avoiding product liability.[203]

Quality control clauses will be prohibited, however, where they are used as a means of improperly tying in other products or services,[204] where they seek to make the licensee dependent on the licensor,[205] or where they seek to allocate trade territories.[206]

Grant-Back Provisions

grant-back provision:
Agreement that a technology licensee will transfer to the licensor any improvements, inventions, or know-how it acquires while using the technology.

A **grant-back provision** requires a technology recipient (that is, a patent or know-how recipient) to transfer back to the supplier any improvements, inventions, or special know-how that it acquires while using the technology. Such a provision may be unilateral or reciprocal, exclusive or nonexclusive. A unilateral grant-back provision requires one of the parties—usually the licensee—to transfer back new knowledge, whereas the reciprocal provision requires both to do so. Sometimes a reciprocity agreement will require both parties to exchange their developments (i.e., a true reciprocal exchange), but other times only one party will be required to transfer new knowledge, while the other is required merely to pay adequate compensation (i.e., a compensated unilateral exchange).

---

[199]A typical provision is found in Nigeria's Decree No. 70 Establishing the National Office of Industrial Property, Article 6.2(3) (September 14, 1979), which prohibits any transfer-of-technology provision "where limitations are imposed on technological research or development by the transferee."

[200]*See* Tripoli Co. v. Wella Corp., *Federal Reporter, Second Series,* vol. 452, p. 932 (Third Circuit Ct. of Appeals, 1970), *certiorari* denied, *United States Reports,* vol. 400, p. 831 (Supreme Ct., 1970).

[201]*See* Reliance Molded Plastics, Inc. v. Jiffy Products, *Federal Supplement,* vol. 215, p. 402 (Dist. Ct. for Dist. of New Jersey, 1963), affirmed without an opinion, *Federal Reporter, Second Series,* vol. 337, p. 857 (Third Circuit Ct. of Appeals, 1964).

[202]Germany, Act against Restraints on Competition, Article 20.2(1) (1957). United States, Lanham Trademark Act, para. 1127 (1976); European Union, Block Exemption for Patent Licensing, Article 2(9).

A leading U.S. case, Siegel v. Chicken Delight, Inc., *Federal Reporter, Second Series,* vol. 448, p. 51 (Ninth Circuit Ct. of Appeals, 1971), *certiorari* denied, *United States Reports,* vol. 405, p. 955 (Supreme Ct., 1972), observed: "For a licensor, through relaxation of quality control, to permit inferior products to be presented to the public under his licensed mark, might well constitute a misuse of the mark." An often-cited decision of the EU Commission, Campari, *Official Journal,* No. L 70, p. 69 (March 13, 1978), makes a similar observation.

[203]*See* Tripoli Co. v. Wella Corp., *Federal Reporter, Second Series,* vol. 452, p. 932 (Third Circuit Ct. of Appeals, 1970), *certiorari* denied, *United States Reports,* vol. 400, p. 831 (Supreme Ct., 1970).

[204]*Bericht der Bundeskartellamtes über seine Tätigkeit im Jahre 1974 sowie über Lage und Entwicklung auf seinem Ausgabengebeit,* p. 91.

[205]Nigeria, Decree No. 70 Establishing the National Office of Industrial Property, Article 6.2(o) (14 September 1979); Venezuela, Decree No. 746 on Transfer of Technology Agreements, Article 1(d) (February 11, 1975).

[206]E.g., Standard Oil v. United States, *United States Reports,* vol. 337, p. 293 (Supreme Ct., 1949).

An exclusive grant-back provision requires one of the parties—usually the licensee—to transfer any rights (i.e., patent or know-how rights) in the new development to the other party. A nonexclusive (or "sharing") provision would allow the parties to share these rights.

Most countries prohibit grant-back provisions that unilaterally require the licensee to transfer exclusive rights to the licensor. One exception is the United States, which permits such a provision so long as it has no anticompetitive effect.[207]

In contrast, most countries do not prohibit (and a few expressly allow) grant-back provisions that are reciprocal and nonexclusive—that is, provisions that require the parties to share the new knowledge. This is so for both "true" reciprocal exchanges (i.e., technology exchanged for technology) as well as compensated unilateral exchanges (i.e., technology exchanged for money).

Exhibit 9-3 summarizes the different approaches to grant-back provisions in several representative countries.

Restrictions That Apply after the Expiration of Intellectual Property Rights

Countries generally hold that payment obligations or restrictions based on statutory intellectual property rights must terminate when the statutory right expires.[208] The reason for this was stated succinctly by the U.S. Supreme Court in *Scott Paper Co. v. Marcalus Mfg. Co.*, a patent case:

> If a manufacturer or user could restrict himself, by express contract . . . from using the invention of an expired patent, he would deprive himself and the consuming public

EXHIBIT 9-3 Regulation of Grant-Back Provisions		
Types of Provisions	**Expressly Prohibited**	**Expressly Permitted**
Reciprocal exchange True reciprocal exchange (Technology for technology)		Argentina, Germany, Japan, Mexico
Compensated exchange (Technology for money)		Portugal, Serbia and Montenegro
Unilateral Exchange Exclusive (Transfer of all rights to one party)	Argentina, Japan, Mexico, Nigeria, Philippines, Spain, Venezuela, European Union	United States[a]
Nonexclusive (Sharing of rights with the other party)	Philippines	Brazil

[a]Permitted so long as there is no anticompetitive effect.

---

[207]*See* Transparent Wrap Machine Corp. v. Stokes and Smith Co., *United States Reports,* vol. 329, p. 637 (Supreme Ct., 1947). There the U.S. Supreme Court said a unilateral grant-back of exclusive rights to a licensor was not a *per se* violation of the antitrust laws and would be permitted so long as it had no anticompetitive effect beyond that inherent in patents or know-how. This decision was followed in Santa Fe Pomeroy, Inc. v. P. and Z. Co., *Federal Reporter, Second Series,* vol. 569, p. 1084 (Ninth Circuit Ct. of Appeals, 1978), where the evidence showed that the grant-back provision did not unduly restrain trade or suppress industry development. A grant-back provision was held illegal in United States v. Aluminum Co. of America, *Federal Supplement,* vol. 333, p. 410 (Dist. Ct. for S. Dist. of New York, 1950) because it tended to enhance the technological superiority of a company with monopoly or near monopoly power.

[208]As to payment obligations, most countries simply state that the obligations cease when the statutory right expires. Thus, Article 71 of Venezuela's Decree No. 2442 on the Treatment of Foreign Capital, Trademarks, Patents, Licenses and Royalties (1977) provides: "No payments shall be permissible by way of royalties or other charges in respect of the use of trademarks, processes, patents or industrial models for a period exceeding the period of validity of the industrial property rights recognized by the relevant legislative provision."

In the United Kingdom and many of its former colonies, including Australia and India, the obligations that arise under an intellectual property license will terminate at the time that the underlying statutory right expires and upon the licensee giving three months' notice to the licensor. *See* United Kingdom, Patents Act, Article 45(1) (1977); Australia's Patents Act No. 83 of 1990, Article 144(2)(b); India, Patents Act, Article 141(1) (1970).

As to restrictions on the free use of the protected technology after the expiration of the underlying statutory grant, countries commonly hold that it expires with the grant (e.g., Germany) or within a reasonable time after the grant (e.g., Brazil). *See* Germany, Act Against Restraints on Competition, Article 20.1 (1957); Brazil, Normative Act No. 015 of the National Institute of Industrial Property, Article 4.5.2(d)(vi) (1975).

of the advantage to be derived from his free use of the [patent] disclosures. . . . Hence, any attempted reservation or continuation in the patentee or those claiming under him of the patent monopoly, after the patent expires, whatever the legal device employed, runs counter to the policy and purpose of the patent laws.[209]

package licensing: The transfer of multiple statutory rights under a single license.

The principal problem that arises in connection with the expiration of statutory rights involves package licenses. **Package licensing** is the transfer of multiple statutory rights (often including multiple patents and multiple trademarks) under a single license. Generally, if the licensing agreement was entered into voluntarily by both sides and the payment obligations do not extend beyond that of the last-to-expire statutory right, these agreements will be enforceable. On the other hand, if the licensee was at an economic disadvantage and given only the option of taking or leaving the arrangement, it will commonly be found to be illegal as a form of statutory misuse. For example, in the American case of *McCullough Tool Co. v. Well Surveys, Inc.*, the court upheld a licensing arrangement under which the licensee agreed to pay level royalties on a package of patents, some of which were to expire during the period of the agreement. The court did so because the term of the license did not extend beyond the last-to-expire patent and because the licensee was not required to accept the package on a take-it-or-leave-it basis.[210] On the other hand, in *American Securit Co. v. Shatterproof Glass Corp.*, the court found that a package of patents, which the licensee was required to accept on a take-it-or-leave-it basis, was patent misuse.[211]

Concerning restrictions and payment obligations in connection with nonstatutory rights, in particular secret know-how, there are several differing approaches. In Germany, for example, a licensor may not enforce payment obligations or other restrictions once the know-how has lost its secret character or becomes economically worthless or technically outdated.[212] With respect to package licenses, a German licensee may bring suit to obtain an adjustment in the payment obligation or termination of the entire contract if some of the rights become worthless and the amount being paid is not reasonably related to the value of the remaining rights.[213]

In some developing countries, such as Brazil and Serbia and Montenegro, national legislation prohibits any restriction on the free use of know-how once a "reasonable" period has lapsed following the transfer of the technology. This is so even if secret know-how has not lost its secret character.[214] In other developing countries, including Zambia, the obligation to pay for the use of secret know-how will cease when it "becomes public knowledge otherwise than through the fault of the licensee."[215]

By contrast, in the United States, a licensee's agreement to pay for the use of secret know-how will remain in effect even after the secret becomes public knowledge, so long as the licensee's contractual obligation was "freely undertaken in arm's length negotiations."[216]

Restrictions That Apply After the Expiration of the Licensing Agreement

Licensing agreements may impose obligations on the licensee that continue even after the expiration of the license. Common examples include noncompetition agreements, limitations on the right to carry out research and development activities related to the technology transferred by the licensor, and, in particular, the obligation to keep secret and not make use of confidential information after the licensing arrangement expires.

The national regulations that apply to these kinds of arrangements can be categorized into three groups. One group of countries—including Germany and the United States—allows

---

[209]*United States Reports,* vol. 326, p. 29 (Supreme Ct., 1945).

[210]*Federal Reporter, Second Series,* vol. 343, p. 381 (Tenth Circuit Ct. of Appeals, 1965).

[211]*Id.,* vol. 268, p. 769 (Third Circuit Ct. of Appeals, 1959).

[212]*Bericht der Bundeskartellamtes über seine Tätigkeit im Jahre 1974 sowie über Lage und Entwicklung auf seinem Ausgabengebiet,* p. 90.

[213]*Id.,* p. 104, item 3.

[214]Brazil, Normative Act No. 015 of the National Institute of Industrial Property, Articles 4.5.2(d)(vi), 5.5.2(d)(vi) (1975); Serbia and Montenegro, Law on Long-Term Cooperation in Production, Commercial-Technical Cooperation and the Awarding and Acquiring of Technology between Organizations of Associated Labor and Foreign Persons, Article 37(5) (1978).

[215]Zambia, Industrial Development Act, Article 15(b) (1977).

[216]*See* Aronson v. Quick Point Pencil Co., *United States Reports,* vol. 440, p. 266 (Supreme Ct., 1979).

licensors to impose most types of reasonable restrictions. Continuing restrictions on the use of statutory rights (i.e., patents, trademarks, and copyrights) are valid, but only if the statutory rights have not expired. Restrictions on the use of secret know-how are valid as long as the know-how has not entered the public domain.[217] Noncompetition agreements must be "reasonable" to avoid conflict with unfair competition laws. In particular, they must (a) be "ancillary" to the license (that is, they must relate to the use of the subject matter of the license), (b) not be overly broad (i.e., they must relate only to matters in the license), and (c) be limited in duration and geographical scope.

A second group of countries, including India and the European Community, generally takes the same approach as the countries in the first group, except that they hold that a former licensee has a right to continue to use any acquired know-how (despite the expiration of the license) so long as the licensee pays reasonable compensation.[218]

The third group of countries—which includes Brazil, Mexico, the Philippines, Serbia and Montenegro, Venezuela, and Zambia—holds to the position that a former licensee is free to use or dispose of the statutory property rights or secret know-how once the licensing agreement terminates.[219]

F. COMPULSORY LICENSES

compulsory license: The grant, by state decree, of a license to use a statutory right when the owner has failed to work it.

As mentioned earlier, **compulsory licenses** are common in most countries of the world, especially in developing countries. They arise when the owner of intellectual property (in particular, patents or copyrights) refuses or is unable to work the property in a particular country within a certain period of time. In such a case, a third party may apply for a compulsory license, which will be issued by the government without the consent of the owner.[220]

Patents

The International Convention for the Protection of Industrial Property (the Paris Convention) recognizes the right of countries to "grant . . . compulsory licenses to prevent abuses of the exclusive rights conferred by the patent."[221] The WTO's Agreement on Trade-Related Aspects

---

[217]*See Bericht der Bundeskartellamtes über seine Tätigkeit im Jahre 1976 sowie über Lage und Entwicklung auf seinem Ausgabengebeit,* p. 107, for the German rules on statutory property rights and secret know-how. The U.S. rule on statutory property rights can be found in Scott Paper Co. v. Marcalus Mfg. Co., *United States Reports,* vol. 326, p. 249 (Supreme Ct., 1945); and the rule on secret know-how in Kewanee Oil Co. v. Bicron Corp., *id.,* vol. 416, p. 470 (1974).

[218]*See* India's Guidelines for Industries, Chap. 3, Article 9.ix (1976–1977). For the European Union's position *see* the decision of the European Commission in Kabelmetal/Luchaire, *Official Journal,* No. L 222, p. 34 (August 22, 1975).

[219]*See* Brazil, Normative Act No. 015 of the National Institute of Industrial Property, Articles 4.5.2(d)(vi), 5.2.(d)(vi), 6.5.2(b) (1975); Mexico, Law on the Registration of the Transfer of Technology and the Use and Working of Patents, Trade Names, and Trade Marks, Article 7(xi) (December 29, 1972); Philippines, Regulation to Implement Article 5 of Presidential Decree No. 1520 Establishing the Technology Board within the Ministry of Industry, Article 5.1(c)(1) (October 10, 1978); Venezuela, Decree No. 2442 on the Treatment of Foreign Capital, Trademarks, Patents, Licenses, and Royalties, Article 1 (1977); Serbia and Montenegro, Law on Long-Term Cooperation in Production, Commercial-Technical Cooperation and the Awarding and Acquiring of Technology between Organizations of Associated Labor and Foreign Persons, Article 37(5) (1978); Zambia, Industrial Development Act, Article 15(b) (1977).

[220]*See* Michael Scott, "Compulsory Licensing of Intellectual Property in International Transactions," *European Intellectual Property Review,* vol. 10, pp. 319–325 (1988).

[221]States with compulsory patent-licensing provisions include the member states of the African Intellectual Property Organization (Benin, Cameroon, Central African Empire, Chad, Congo, Ivory Coast, Mauritania, Niger, Senegal, Togo, and Upper Volta), Algeria, Australia, Austria, Bangladesh, Barbados, Bermuda, Bolivia, Brazil, Bulgaria, Canada, Chile, China, Columbia, the Czech Republic, Denmark, Ecuador, Egypt, El Salvador, Finland, France, Germany, Greece, Guatemala, Guyana, Honduras, Hungary, Iceland, India, Iraq, Israel, Italy, Japan, Jordan, Libya, Luxembourg, Malawi, Malta, Mexico, Monaco, Namibia, Nauru, the Netherlands, New Zealand, Nigeria, Norway, Pakistan, Paraguay, Peru, the Philippines, Portugal, Romania, Russia, Serbia and Montenegro, Slovakia, South Africa, South Korea, Spain, Sri Lanka, Sweden, Switzerland, Taiwan, Thailand, Turkey, the United Kingdom, Uruguay, Zambia, and Zimbabwe.

of Intellectual Property Rights similarly allows its member countries to grant "use of the subject matter of a patent without the authorization of the right holder"[222] provided that:

- such use may only be permitted if, prior to such use, the proposed user has made efforts to obtain authorization from the right holder on reasonable commercial terms and conditions and that such efforts have not been successful within a reasonable period of time. This requirement may be waived by a Member in the case of a national emergency or other circumstances of extreme urgency or in cases of public non-commercial use. In situations of national emergency or in other circumstances of extreme urgency, the right holder shall, nevertheless, be notified as soon as reasonably practicable. In the case of public noncommercial use, where the government or contractor, without making a patent search, knows or has demonstrable grounds to know that a valid patent is or will be used by or for the government, the right holder shall be informed promptly.[223]
- such use shall be non-exclusive.[224]
- such use shall be non-assignable.[225]
- any such use shall be authorized predominantly for the supply of the domestic market of the Member authorizing such use.[226]
- the right holder shall be paid adequate remuneration in the circumstances of each case, taking into account the economic value of the authorization.[227]

Reading 9–1 describes how compulsory licenses are sometimes used by countries to protect vital national interests.

---

[222]For an analysis of the TRIPS Agreements' compulsory license provisions and their application to pharmaceuticals *see* James Love, "Compulsory Licensing: Models For State Practice In Developing Countries, Access to Medicine and Compliance with the WTO TRIPS Accord," *Consumer Project on Technology* (Prepared for the United Nations Development Program, January 21, 2001) at www.cptech.org/ip/health/cl/recommendedstatepractice.html.
[223]Agreement on Trade-Related Aspects of Intellectual Property Rights, Article 31(b) (1994).
[224]*Id.* Article 31(d)
[225]*Id.* Article 31(e)
[226]*Id.* Article 31(f)
[227]*Id.* Article 31(h).

Reading 9–1   Compulsory Patent Licenses in the Fight Against AIDS

THE SOUTH AFRICAN EXPERIENCE

In its effort to fights a rampant HIV/AIDS epidemic, the South Africa parliament passed a Medicines and Related Substances Control Amendment Act of 1997 and a Medicines and Medical Devices Regulatory Act of 1998 authorizing the government's Health Minister to import generic versions of drugs, or license their domestic production, even if the drugs violated the South African patents of pharmaceutical companies. The parliament's legal justification for adopting the act was based on the rationale underlying compulsory licenses: to prevent a patent holder from abusing the exclusive rights conferred by the patent. In the case of medicines

to treat the HIV virus, South Africa's government claimed that the multinational pharmaceutical companies were abusing the privilege by charging excessive prices for the drugs.

The government argued also that it was faced by a national emergency. Of the 36 million people affected with HIV, 25 million live in sub-Saharan African and 10 percent of South Africa's 45 million people have the HIV virus.

The Pharmaceutical Manufacturers' Association of South Africa (PMA), joined by 39 pharmaceutical companies, promptly brought suit challenging the legislation and obtained an order that restrained the government from implementing the law until a full hearing could be

MAP 9-6 South Africa (2001)

EXHIBIT 9-4 Protestors Take to the Streets to Oppose the Drug Companies Suit Against South Africa (2001)

(Photo © M. Rhodes/BUSINESS D/CORBIS SYGMA.)

scheduled. According to Mirryena Deeb, head of PMA, "It's the arbitrariness and uncertainty we are fighting. It's got nothing to do with access" to HIV-drugs.[228] The case was eventually set for trial in March 2001.

The lawsuit stirred-up strong emotions. AIDS activists groups took to the streets and to the Internet to protest the pharmaceutical companies' efforts to protect their patent rights. Zackie Achmat, chairman of the Treatment Action Campaign, a South African AIDS activist organization, said: "This case is one of the most important things that is going to happen in Africa and for countries in Asia and Latin America."

Médecins Sans Frontières, the activist international doctors' organization, drafted and circulated a petition on the Internet asking the drug companies to drop their suit. Thousands of sympathizers signed it. Thousands more marched in parades in Europe and North America.

In the weeks before the case was set to go to trial the several pharmaceutical companies' offered to reduce the prices for their drugs. According to the South Africa government, the offers were insufficient: the reduced prices would still bankrupt its health budget.

"Those reductions are simply not enough," said Ellen 't Hoen, head of Médecins Sans Frontières' campaign for access to essential medicines. "Companies are gaining a lot in terms of goodwill and PR, but the effects on the ground are actually very, very little."[229]

At the request of PMA and the pharmaceutical companies, the trial date was postponed; and then on the new day set for the trial, PMA and the companies moved to have the case dismissed.

Kevin Watkins, a representative for the British aid group Oxfam, said "We have lost three years in the fight against AIDS, but it is a great victory for the people of South Africa and for the global campaign to make drugs more affordable."[230] Between 1998, when the suit was filed, and 2001, when the suit was dismissed, about 400,000 South Africans died of AIDS.

The PMA's Mirryena Deeb said the case was withdrawn because the government had agreed to consult the companies when it began to draft the regulations to implement the legislation. But South Africa's Health Minister, Manto Tshabalala-Msimang, denied that the government had agreed to any deals regarding the legislation.

DÉJÀ VU IN BRAZIL

At the time that South Africa was adopting legislation to authorize its Health Minister to take action against the AIDS epidemic, Brazil's Health Minister, José Serra, was taking action. With his government's backing, Serra authorized Brazilian drug companies to analyze patented drugs and to produce their own generic antiretroviral drugs.

The effort was a success. Far-Manguinhos Libratory, which had experience with producing drugs for diseases such as malaria that had largely vanished from developed countries, was able to determine the needed formulas. It began importing ingredients from Asia and producing a dozen antiretroviral drugs.

---

[228]CBS News, "AIDS Patents vs. Patients' Pleas," (March 4, 2001) at www.cbsnews.com/stories/2001/03/04/world/main276292.shtml.
[229]Id.
[230]BBC News, "S.A. Victory in Aids Drugs Case," (April 19, 2001) at news.bbc.co.uk/hi/english/world/africa/newsid_1285000/1285097.stm.

No. 9,279 of 14 May 1996; effective May 1997) and other related measures, which establish a "local working" requirement for the enjoyability of exclusive patent rights that can only be satisfied by the local production—and not the importation—of the patented subject matter.

Specifically, Brazil's "local working" requirement stipulates that a patent shall be subject to compulsory licensing if the subject matter of the patent is not "worked" in the territory of Brazil. Brazil then explicitly defines "failure to be worked" as "failure to manufacture or incomplete manufacture of the product," or "failure to make full use of the patented process." The United States considers that such a requirement is inconsistent with Brazil's obligations under Articles 27 and 28 of the TRIPS Agreement, and Article III of the GATT 1994.[232]

"For me it was a surprise that we had to face an international conflict on this issue," Brazil Heath Minister Serra said.[233] The Brazilian government responded with an advertising campaign in U.S. newspapers. One ad read: "Local manufacturing of many of the drugs used in the anti-AIDS cocktail permits Brazil to continue to control the spread of AIDS. The drug industry sees this as an act of war, we see it as an act of life."[234]

The pharmaceutical companies had long circulated the idea that developing countries were unable to establish effective drug treatment programs. Brazil's AIDS program effectively destroyed their contention.

Serra insisted that he respected intellectual property rights and patents. "The way out is to negotiate," he said. "To have a better reciprocal understanding. We hope the U.S. government will take into account our problems."

The pharmaceutical companies quickly responded, offering to cut prices on their drugs. "When (the pharmaceutical company) Merck told me they were lowering prices," said Serra, "we said we would forget about the compulsory licensing."[235]

But the question Serra remained: "What is the right price to compensate (drug companies for their investment?" "No one knows," he said. He wondered: "Is a profit margin of 1,000 percent necessary?"

As was the case in South Africa, nongovernmental organizations and human rights activists came to the defense of the Brazil. The case was not about patent rights, it was "most definitely about AIDS" they noted. "It challenges a key part of Serra's program: the free

MAP 9-7   Brazil (2001)

The drugs, distributed to 200,000 Brazilians with the HIV virus, had a dramatic impact: the mortality rate from AIDS was cut in half. Health Minister Serra said, "Brazil can only afford the producing expenditures because we won't pay market prices."[231] According to the Far-Manguinhos Lab, the drugs produced in Brazil are 79 percent cheaper than imported drugs.

Brazil's success was not appreciated by everyone. The pharmaceutical companies were less than pleased and they sought help from the United States government. In May 2000, the U.S. challenged Brazil in the World Trade Organization.

The U.S. "Request for Consultations" stated:

My authorities have instructed me to request consultations with the Government of Brazil pursuant to Article 4 of the Understanding on Rules and Procedures Governing the Settlement of Disputes (DSU), Article XXII of the General Agreement on Tariffs and Trade 1994 (GATT 1994) and Article 64 of the Agreement on Trade-Related Aspects of Intellectual Property Rights (TRIPS Agreement) (to the extent that it incorporates by reference Article XXII of GATT 1994), concerning those provisions of Brazil's 1996 industrial property law (Law

[231]Paulo Rebêlo, "AIDS Drugs: U.S. vs. the World," *Wired News* (May 31, 2001) at www.wired.com/news/print/0,1294,44175,00.html.

[232]Brazil—Measures Affecting Patent Protection, WT/DS199/1 G/L/385 IP/D/23 (June 8, 2000) at www.wto.int/.

[233]Trudy Rubin, "Brazil Battles AIDS and U.S. Resistance," *Philadelphia Inquirer* (June 24, 2001) at www.pewfellowships.org/gatekeeper/brazil/brazilbattles.html.

[234]Quoted in *id.*

[235]*Id.*

distribution of the anti-AIDS cocktail, which is only possible because Brazil makes generic knockoffs of several AIDS drugs at about a fourth of what they would cost in America."[236]

In April 2001, UN Secretary General Kofi Anan entered the fray, meeting with the CEOs and senior executives of six major pharmaceutical companies. In a statement released after the meeting he announced: "Encouraging the active participation of all partners in the fight against AIDS has become my personal priority." While noting that "the pharmaceutical industry is playing a crucial role," he stressed that the world needed to "combine incentive for research with access to medication for the poor."[237]

That same month, Brazil with the support of 20 other states submitted a resolution on "access to medication in the context of pandemics such as HIV/AIDS" to the United Nations Human Rights Commission. The resolution, adopted by a vote of 54 to 0, with one abstention,[238] declared that access to medications was a human right.[239] (The one abstaining country was the United States.)

Then in May 2001, the World Health Assembly adopted a resolution calling on the 191 member states of the World Health Organization to "cooperate constructively" to "increase access to medicines." The members states were urged to strengthen their "pharmaceutical policies . . . including those applicable to generic drugs and intellectual property regimes in order to further promote innovation and the development of domestic industries consistent with international law."[240]

Following its successes in the UNHRC and the WHA Brazil let it be known that it was willing to negotiate with the U.S. over the case before the WTO, as Health Minister Serra had earlier said. José Graça Lima, Brazil's Under-Secretary-General for Integration, Economic and Trade matters sent the following proposal to the U.S.:

I refer to the panel initiated by your Government questioning the compatibility of Article 68 of Brazil's Industrial Property Law (Law 9.279/96) with the TRIPS Agreement. In the view of Brazil, as you are aware, Article 68 is fully compatible with the TRIPS Agreement.

Nevertheless, in the spirit of the proposal made by Ambassador Robert Zoellick to Minister

Celso Lafer in their recent meeting in Geneva for a common endeavor to find a mutually satisfactory solution for the dispute, and following up on our recent conversation about the same subject in Washington D.C., on May 24, I would like to convey to you the following proposal.

Should the U.S. withdraw the WTO panel against Brazil concerning the interpretation of Article 68, the Brazilian Government would agree, in the event it deems necessary to apply Article 68 to grant compulsory license on patents held by the U.S. companies, to hold prior talks on the matter with the U.S. Government. These talks would be held within the scope of the U.S.-Brazil Consultative Mechanism, in a special session scheduled to discuss the subject.

I look forward to receiving your response to this proposal.[241]

The proposal certainly wasn't what the pharmaceutical companies or the U.S. government would have preferred, but it was essentially the same arrangement that the pharmaceutical companies had agreed to in South Africa. On July 5, 2001, the U.S. government agreed to withdraw its complaint before the WTO Peter Allgeier, the Deputy U.S. Trade Representative responded to Graça Lima:

As Ambassador Zoellick mentioned during his meeting with Minister Celso Lafer, we are interested in finding a mutually satisfactory solution to this dispute. Your letter conveyed a proposal that should lead to such a solution. I am pleased to report that my government will agree to terminate the WTO panel proceeding without prejudice concerning the interpretation of Article 68, based on your government's commitment to hold prior talks with the United States with sufficient advance notice to permit constructive discussions in the context of a special session of the U.S.-Brazil Consultative Mechanism, should Brazil deem it necessary to apply Article 68 to grant a compulsory license on patents held by U.S. companies. . . .

As Ambassador Zoellick noted during his meeting with Minister Lafer, the United States' concerns were never directed at your government's bold and effective program to combat HIV/AIDS. Our ability to find a mutually satisfactory solution to this

---

[236]*Id.*

[237]"The United Nations Secretary General to Lead the Fight Against HIV/AIDS," Joint Press Release UN/UNAIDS/WHO/19 (April 5, 2001) at www.who.int/inf-pr-2001/en/pr2001–19.html.

[238]United Nations Human Rights Commission, Declaration 2001/33 (April 23, 2001) at www.aids.gov.br/pdf/resolucao_comissao_dh.pdf.

[239]Commission on Human Rights, 57th Session, Summary of Resolutions and Decisions (Geneva, March 19 to April 27, 2001) at www.ishr.ch/About%20UN/Charter%20based%20bodies/CHR/57session.htm.

[240]54th World Health Assembly, Resolution on Global Response to AIDS (May 21, 2001) at www.mre.gov.br/projeto/proposta-i.htm.

[241]Brazil—Measures Affecting Patent Protection, WT/DS199/1 G/L/385 IP/D/23 Add.1 (July 19, 2001) at www.wto.int/.

WTO dispute will allow our conversation regarding this scourge to turn to our shared goal of defeating the HIV/AIDS virus.

We will make the necessary arrangements to notify the WTO Secretariat of our decision as soon as possible.[242]

POSTSCRIPT

In August of 2001, Brazil's Health Minister, José Serra, announced that his government had been unsuccessful in negotiating a reduction in the price for antiretroviral drug nelfinavir (sold under the brand name Viracept) with its German pharmaceutical company Roche and that Brazil would issue a compulsory license to the Far Manguinhos Laboratory for the drug's manufacture. Far Manguinhos was to produce the drug for 40 percent less than Roche's price.[243] Six days later, the Brazil and Roche resumed talks, and on August 31, they reached an agreement. Roche would sell the drug in Brazil at a 40 percent discount and Brazil would not issue the compulsory license.[244] ∎

---

[242]*Id.*

[243]Brazilian Ministry of Health, Press Office, National STD/AIDS Program, Official Notice: "Ministry of Health Announces Compulsory Licensing of Nelfinavir Patent" (August 22, 2001) at www.cptech.org/ip/health/c/brazil/nelf08222001.html.

[244]Roche press release, August 31, 2001 at www.roche.com/med-corp-detail-2001?id=689.

Copyrights

statutory copyright license: Authorizes a third party to use a copyrighted work for a fee stipulated in the statute.

compulsory copyright license: Compels a copyright owner to grant a license but allows the owner to negotiate the fee.

Two types of compulsory licensing apply to copyrights. A **statutory copyright license** authorizes third parties to use a copyrighted work in exchange for a fee, which is fixed either in the legislation itself or by a public or private agency authorized to fix, collect, and distribute license fees.[245] A **compulsory copyright license** compels a copyright owner to grant a license, but it allows the owner to negotiate the terms of the license (subject to the intervention of a court or administrative tribunal if the parties cannot agree).

The Berne Convention for the Protection of Literary and Artistic Works recognizes the right of countries to impose compulsory licenses for broadcasting and recording. This right is limited, however, by the proviso that compulsory licenses may "not in any circumstances be prejudicial to the moral rights of the author, nor to his right to obtain equitable remuneration which, in the absence of agreement, shall be fixed by competent authority."[246]

---

[245]Statutory licenses for the recording of musical works are provided, for example, in the United States, Copyright Act, § 115 (1976), and in the United Kingdom, Copyright Act, Article 12 (1956).

[246]Berne Convention for the Protection of Literary and Artistic Works, Article 11 bis, § 2 (broadcast rights) (1886). A similar provision relating to recording rights is in *id.*, Article 13(1).

Chapter Questions

1. Alvin, Bob, Calvin, Don, and Edgar are friends who enroll in a university course to study international business law. The textbook required for the course costs $50, which the five friends agree is expensive. They agree to chip in $10 each and buy one copy from a bookstore. They then take the copy to the local Discount Copy Store and make five copies of the complete book for $15 a copy. Then they return the book to the bookstore and get a refund of their original purchase price. Have the five friends done anything wrong? If so, what? Explain.

2. Elvira is an abstract painter of incredible talent, but of little notoriety. One of her paintings, entitled "Blue Lady 13," is a piece of intense power and sensuality. In 1990, she sold it to Mega Company for display in the main public entrance of the business's new headquarters building. Several art critics attending the opening of the building mistook the painting for a long lost work of Pablo Picasso. The critics wrote about the painting in their newspaper columns as though they had made a great discovery. When people began flooding into the Mega Building to see "Blue Lady 13," the directors of Mega were delighted. They even went so far as to put up a sign that said: "This painting, entitled 'La Dama Azul,' was probably painted by Pablo Picasso during his blue period, ca. 1913." Is there anything that Elvira can do? Explain.

3. The First-to-Market Computer Software Company owns the copyright to a highly successful spreadsheet program—Blossom 3-2-1—which has dominated the worldwide market for several years. Recently, Clone Software Co. devised a look-alike program that does everything that the Blossom 3-2-1 program does, except that the Clone sells for only one-tenth the price of the original. First-to-Market has sued Clone for copyright infringement. Clone defends itself by saying that the coding of its program is entirely different from that of Blossom 3-2-1 and that the only similarity between the programs is that the images that appear on the computer screen and the key sequences used to operate the program are identical. Has Clone infringed First-to-Market's copyright? Explain.

4. The Whopper Co. is a manufacturer of gumballs. The technology and know-how to do this are well-known in the scientific and engineering community in Whopper's home country, where gumballs have been popular with consumers for decades. Whopper decided recently to expand into Country X and to introduce gumballs to a market that has never seen them before. Before doing so, Whopper filed for a patent in Country X. The local patent office examined the application as to form (it was fine), searched the local records to determine if the technology was known locally (it was not), and then published notice of the application in the *Patent Gazette* for public comment. There was no public comment, and the patent was issued. Now, Bubble Co., a local Country X business, has begun manufacturing and selling gumballs in Country X that are identical to those being manufactured and sold by Whopper. Whopper brings suit for patent infringement. Bubble countersues to have Whopper's patent revoked. Who will win? Explain.

5. Matilda, who owns the trademark "Mr. Wiggles" for use on a line of children's toys in Country A, learns that Nina has applied to register the same mark for use on a line of similar toys in Country B. Will Matilda be successful in opposing Nina's application? Would it make a difference if "Mr. Wiggles" were a mark with worldwide fame? Explain.

6. Jacques Pierre manufactures and sells a line of perfume—*Le Peux*—in distinctively shaped containers that are instantly recognizable. May Jacques Pierre register the shape of the containers as a trademark? Explain. If not, how else might Jacques Pierre keep competitors from selling their perfumes in similar containers?

7. Barley Beer Co. owns the trademark "Super Suds" for use on bottled and canned beer in Country X. Barley has not used the mark in Country X for six years. Hops Beer Co. would like to use the mark, and it brings suit in the Country X courts to have Barley's trademark revoked. Will Hops succeed? Explain.

8. A Japanese firm, Omega Company, manufactures cassette tapes with the trademark TXX. Omega licensed Alpha Company to distribute and sell the tapes in Australia and Sigma Company to do the same in South Africa. The license with Sigma expired after three years, and Omega refused to renew the license. Sigma then began buying cassettes from Alpha in Australia in bulk quantities and importing them into South Africa. These tapes had no individual wrappers or labels and Sigma affixed both wrappers and labels with the TXX trademark on the cassettes, which it then sold throughout South Africa. Omega, which owns the TXX trademark in South Africa, has brought suit to enjoin Sigma from importing the cassettes into South Africa. Will Omega succeed? Would it make any difference if Omega's license with Alpha forbade Alpha from selling tapes for export to South Africa? Explain.

9. "Preventing the importation of gray goods legitimately manufactured outside the country is, in reality, injurious to consumers and contrary to basic principles of unfair competition laws." Comment.

10. The world's seven principal manufacturers of widgets have entered into an agreement to exchange with each other for a period of seven years all of their patents, petty patents, and know-how, and to enter into jointly funded research and development activities to improve widgets. Is this agreement enforceable? Explain. Would it matter if all of the participants were located in the European Union? Japan? The United States?

11. The Slinky Co. is a manufacturer of revealing bedroom apparel, especially negligees and pajamas, which it sells through franchised retail outlets that operate under its trade name. The franchisees are prohibited from handling any other line of clothing. One franchisee has challenged this particular provision in court, arguing that it is an invalid noncompetition clause. Will the franchisee be successful? Explain.

12. The Huge Company owns several patents that are essential both to the manufacture of xerographic copiers and to the manufacture of photographic developing machines. Huge Company's standard license agreement contains the following clauses:

    a. The licensee may use the technology only for the manufacture and sale of xerographic equipment.
    b. The licensee may sell the products made with this technology only in Country X.
    c. The licensee may not sell the products made with this technology to anyone intending to resell the goods in any other country.
    d. The licensee must grant to the licensor all technological improvements it makes in connection with the licensed technology. The licensee is expressly forbidden from applying for patents in its own name on any improvements to the licensed technology.
    e. The licensee may not undertake any research and development activities relating to the development of competing products or technologies.
    f. The licensee may not disclose to any other party any secret know-how provided by the licensor to the licensee.
    g. The licensee may not use any know-how or other knowledge learned from the licensor for a period of three years following the expiration of the license.
    h. The licensee may not use any of the licensor's patented technology for a period of three years following the expiration of the last patent.

    Comment on the validity of these clauses.

Review Problem

You are now the permanent head of the legal department of MegaBranch Industries (MBI). Congratulations. As a consequence, you now have direct responsibility for overseeing the legal transactions relating to MBI's most valuable assets: its intellectual property.

1. MBI owns a newsmagazine named *The Looking Glass* in State A. A television station in the capital city of State A has a morning "news" program that consists solely of a commentator reading stories from *The Looking Glass* over the air—some in their entirety, others excerpted. Can MBI sue the station for infringing its copyright in these stories? Would it make any difference if the station noted that the stories were all being read from *The Looking Glass?*
2. MBI produces and distributes university textbooks. Its salespeople give "review copies" of the texts to professors who they hope will adopt the text for use in their classes and, consequently, require their students to buy the texts. These copies are marked across the cover with the words "professional review copy, not for resale." One professor, Professor X, regularly sells all the review copies he gets from MBI to used-book buyers. May MBI sue him to get him to stop doing this?
3. On the inside cover of MBI's *The Looking Glass* is a statement authorizing other newspapers and journals to make brief quotations from the stories in the magazine. A competitor, *The Fog,* regularly takes advantage of this. Purposefully, however, it always misspells a word, deletes a word, or inserts an extra word or two, to change the entire meaning of the quotation. It does this to make *The Looking Glass* look bad. Can MBI do anything about this?
4. An MBI subsidiary in State B manufactures computer software. One of its programs is called "Tax Dodger." It allows an individual to prepare his or her State B income tax returns on a personal computer. The program is readily identifiable by its use of a lifelike human figure, called "Roger the Tax Dodger," that volunteers user-friendly information on how to keep one's taxes to a minimum. Recently, a competitor had its computer-programming department come up with a competing program that has a figure similar to Roger and for all intents and purposes "looks" and "feels" exactly like the Tax Dodger program. The competitor's program, however, was programmed in an entirely different way and in a different programming language. Can MBI and its subsidiary prevent the competitor from marketing this program?

5. An MBI subsidiary in State C has invented what it believes to be a better mousetrap. The "MBI-C mousetrap" consists of a small rectangular piece of cardboard onto which a piece of poisoned hard cheese is glued. Is this invention patentable?

6. Assuming that the MBI subsidiary in State C decides that it wants to patent its mousetrap in State C, what procedure does it need to follow? What does it need to do if it wants to obtain patents in other countries?

7. Assume the State C subsidiary gets a patent on its mousetrap in State C, but, after the term of the patent runs out, it has not recouped its development costs. Can it obtain an extension in the period of its patent? What must it show to do this?

8. MBI's logo is a stylized tree with many branches. The logo is used on all of MBI's trademarks, trade names, service marks, and the like, and is well known worldwide. MBI likes to think that the symbol tells customers they are getting a good product at a fair price. MBI has now discovered that a small clothing manufacturer is putting a label with the same logo on clothes it makes and sells in State D. State D is a small developing country with no trademark registration law and no local MBI subsidiary. Can MBI, nonetheless, obtain an injunction in a State D court to stop the local company from using its logo? Would it make any difference if MBI does not manufacture any articles of clothing?

9. The International Association of Toy Makers is holding its annual convention in the city where MBI has its main offices. They have asked you to give them a short talk describing the different international organizations and international treaties that protect both artistic and industrial property. Outline your talk.

10. MBI is one of a handful of firms that is involved in developing High Definition Television (HDTV). The development costs, however, are extraordinarily high. As a consequence, MBI would like to enter into a cross-licensing agreement with its principal competitors. The agreement would require each of the participants to share their know-how and any patents they develop but would forbid them from sharing either with anyone not a party to the agreement. Would this agreement violate any unfair competition laws?

11. MBI owns the patents and the secret know-how necessary to manufacture "wonder widgets." It is willing to license this technology to manufacturers in countries where there is no MBI subsidiary already making or selling these widgets. What terms should be included in the license?

12. One of MBI's competitors owns the patents in State G on a medical prosthetic device that makes it easier for people with certain disabilities to walk. It has not, however, made or sold any of the devices in State G for the last five years, nor has it been willing to license any local manufacturers to do so. An MBI subsidiary in State G would like to make and sell the devices there. Can the subsidiary do anything to force the competitor to give it a license?

CHAPTER

10 Sales

A. UNITED NATIONS CONVENTION ON CONTRACTS FOR THE INTERNATIONAL SALE OF GOODS

The 1980 *United Nations Convention on Contracts for the International Sale of Goods* (CISG) came into force January 1, 1988, climaxing more than 50 years of negotiations. CISG supersedes two earlier conventions, the *Convention Relating to a Uniform Law on the International Sale of Goods* (ULIS) and the *Convention Relating to a Uniform Law on the Formation of Contracts for the International Sale of Goods* (ULF), which were never widely adopted.

Support for ULIS and ULF was limited because they were drafted without the participation of the Third World or the Eastern bloc. CISG, on the other hand, is the work of more than 62 states and 8 international organizations. Adopted at a conference in Vienna in 1980, it incorporates rules from all the major legal systems. It has, accordingly, received widespread support from developed, developing, and communist countries. See Exhibit 10-1.

CISG is organized in four parts: Part I (Articles 1 to 13) contains the Convention's general provisions, including rules on the scope of its applications and rules of interpretation. Part II (Articles 14 to 24) governs the formation of contracts. Part III (Articles 25 to 88) governs the rights and obligations of buyers and sellers. Part IV (Articles 89 to 101) contains provisions for the ratification and the entry into force of the Convention.

Ratifying Country	Became a Party on	Ratifying Country	Became a Party on
Argentina	January 1, 1988	Lesotho	January 1, 1988
Australia	April 1, 1989	Lithuania	February 1, 1996
Austria	January 1, 1989	Lesotho	January 1, 1988
Belarus	November 1, 1990	Lithuania	February 1, 1996
Belgium	November 1, 1997	Luxembourg	February 1, 1998
Bosnia and Herzegovina	March 6, 1992	Mauritania	September 1, 2000
Bulgaria	August 1, 1991	Mexico	January 1, 1989
Burundi	October 1, 1999	Mongolia	January 1, 1999
Canada	May 1, 1992	Netherlands	January 1, 1992
Chile	March 1, 1991	New Zealand	October 1, 1995
China	January 1, 1988	Norway	August 1, 1989
Colombia	August 1, 2002	Peru	April 1, 2000
Croatia d	October 8, 1991	Poland	June 1, 1996
Cuba	December 1, 1995	Republic of Moldova	November 1, 1995
Czech Republic	January 1, 1993	Romania	June 1, 1992
Denmark	March 1, 1990	Russia	September 1, 1991
Ecuador	February 1, 1993	Saint Vincent & the Grenadines	October 1, 2001
Egypt	January 1, 1988	Singapore	March 1, 1996
Estonia	October 1, 1994	Slovakia	January 1, 1993
Finland	January 1, 1989	Slovenia	June 25, 1991
France	January 1, 1988	Spain	August 1, 1991
Georgia	September 1, 1995	Sweden	January 1, 1989
Germany	January 1, 1991	Switzerland	March 1, 1991
Greece	February 1, 1999	Syrian Arab Republic	January 1, 1988
Guinea	February 1, 1992	Uganda	March 1, 1993
Hungary	January 1, 1988	Ukraine	February 1, 1991
Iceland	June 1, 2002	United States	January 1, 1988
Iraq	April 1, 1991	Uruguay	February 1, 2000
Israel	February 1, 2003	Uzbekistan	December 1, 1997
Italy	January 1, 1988	Yugoslavia	April 27, 1992
Kyrgyzstan	June 1, 2000	Zambia	January 1, 1988
Latvia	August 1, 1998		

EXHIBIT 10-1   Parties to the United Nations Convention on Contracts for the International Sale of Goods

Source: United Nations Commission on International Trade Law (UNCITRAL), "Status of Conventions and Model Laws" (July 17, 2002) at www.uncitral.org/.

B. TRANSACTIONS COVERED IN CISG

international sale: A sale involving a buyer and seller with places of business in different states.

CISG applies to contracts for the **international sale** of goods—that is, the buyer and seller must have their places of business in different states.[1] In addition, either (a) both of the states must be contracting parties to the Convention or (b) the rules of private international law must "lead to the application of the law of a contracting state."[2]

---

[1] Contracts carried out entirely within one country's borders are governed by that country's laws. In the United States, the principal domestic law governing the sales of goods is the Uniform Commercial Code (UCC); in the United Kingdom, the Sale of Goods Acts (1893 and 1979) apply; in France, sales of goods are regulated by both the law of obligations in the Civil Code (*Code Civil*) of 1804 and the Code of Commerce (*Code de Commerce*) of 1807; in Germany, the law of obligations in the Civil Code (*Bürgerliches Gesetzbuch*) of 1896 applies.

[2] UN Convention on Contracts for the International Sale of Goods, Article 1 (1980), provides: "(1) This Convention applies to contracts of sale of goods between parties whose places of business are in different states: (a) when the states are contracting states; or (b) when the rules of private international law lead to the application of the law of a contracting state. (2) The fact that the parties have their places of business in different states is to be disregarded whenever this fact does not appear either from the contract or from any dealings between, or from information disclosed by, the parties at any time before or at the conclusion of the contract. (3) Neither the nationality of the parties nor the civil or commercial character of the parties or of the contract is to be taken into consideration in determining the application of this Convention."

CISG may apply even if the buyer's and seller's places of business are not in a contracting state. For example, assume that Seller has a place of business in State A (a noncontracting state) and Buyer a place of business in State B (also a noncontracting State). They enter into a contract in State C (which is a contracting state) and the Seller breaches performance in State C. Buyer brings an action in State B, whose choice-of-law rules point to the laws of State C as applying to the contract. Because State C is a contracting party and the transaction is international, CISG would apply.

This possibility—that the Convention could apply in situations where neither the seller nor the buyer had a place of business in a contracting state—was a cause of concern for some of the Convention's drafters. They feared that the choice-of-law rules might lead to the application of one state's laws for the formation of a contract and to another state's laws for its performance. This could mean that only parts of CISG might apply, when the Convention was meant to apply as a unified whole. As a consequence, the final provisions of the Convention allow a ratifying state, if it wishes, to declare that it will apply CISG only when the buyer and seller are both from contracting states.[3]

Opting In and Out

choice-of-law clause:
Contractual provision that identifies the law to be applied in the event of a dispute over the terms or the performance of the contract.

While either the contracting states or the choice-of-law rules may direct that CISG apply, the parties to a contract may exclude (i.e., they may opt out) or modify its application by a **choice-of-law clause**.[4] Whether they can use that same clause to exclude a domestic law and adopt CISG in its place (i.e., opt in) depends on the rules of the state where the case is heard.

Case 10–1 deals with the question of when the CISG applies and what parties to a contract must do to opt out of the Convention.

---

[3]*Id.,* Article 95 states: "Any state may declare at the time of the deposit of its instrument of ratification, acceptance, approval or accession that it will not be bound by subparagraph (1)(b) of Article 1 of this Convention." The United States, for one, has so declared.

[4]*Id.,* Article 6: "The parties may exclude the application of this Convention or, subject to Article 12, derogate from or vary the effect of any of its provisions."

Case 10–1   Asante Technologies, Inc. v. PMC-Sierra, Inc.

United States, District Court for the Northern District of California.
Federal Supplement, Second Series, vol. 164, p. 1142 (2001).

DISTRICT JUDGE JAMES WARE:

I. Introduction

This lawsuit arises out of a dispute involving the sale of electronic components. Plaintiff, Asante Technologies Inc., filed the action in the Superior Court for the State of California, Santa Clara County, on February 13, 2001. Defendant, PMC-Sierra, Inc., removed the action to this Court, asserting federal question jurisdiction pursuant to *United States Code*, title 28, section 1331. Specifically, Defendant asserts that Plaintiff's claims for breach of contract and breach of express warranty are governed by the United Nations Convention on Contracts for the International Sale of Goods ("CISG"). Plaintiff disputes jurisdiction and filed [a] Motion to Remand. . . .

II. Background

The Complaint in this action alleges claims based in tort and contract. Plaintiff contends that Defendant failed to provide it with electronic components meeting certain designated technical specifications. Defendant timely removed the action to this Court on March 16, 2001.

Plaintiff is a Delaware corporation having its primary place of business in Santa Clara County, California. Plaintiff produces network switchers, a type of electronic component used to connect multiple computers to one another and to the Internet. Plaintiff purchases

MAP 10-1   British Columbia and California (2001)

Determining Defendant's "place of business" with respect to its contract with Plaintiff is critical to the question of whether the Court has jurisdiction in this case.

Plaintiff's Complaint focuses on five purchase orders. Four of the five purchase orders were submitted to Defendant through Unique as directed by Defendant. However, Plaintiff does not dispute that one of the purchase orders, dated January 28, 2000, was sent by fax directly to Defendant in British Columbia, and that Defendant processed the order in British Columbia. Defendant shipped all orders to Plaintiff's headquarters in California. Upon delivery of the goods, Unique sent invoices to Plaintiff, at which time Plaintiff tendered payment to Unique either in California or in Nevada.

* * *

Plaintiff now requests this Court to remand this action back to the Superior Court of the County of Santa Clara pursuant to *United States Code*, title 28, section 1447(c), asserting lack of subject matter jurisdiction. . . .

III. Standards

A defendant may remove to federal court any civil action brought in a state court that originally could have been filed in federal court.[5] When a case originally filed in state court contains separate and independent federal and state law claims, the entire case may be removed to federal court.[6]

The determination of whether an action arises under federal law is guided by the "well-pleaded complaint" rule.[7] The rule provides that removal is proper when a federal question is presented on the face of the Complaint.[8] However, in areas where federal law completely preempts state law, even if the claims are purportedly based on state law, the claims are considered to have arisen under federal law. Defendant has the burden of establishing that removal is proper. . . .

The Convention on Contracts for the International Sale of Goods ("CISG") is an international treaty which has been signed and ratified by the United States and Canada, among other countries. The CISG was adopted for the purpose of establishing "substantive provisions of law to govern the formation of international sales contracts and the rights and obligations of the buyer and the seller."[9] The CISG applies "to contracts of sale of goods between parties whose places of business are in different States . . . when the States are Contracting States."[10]

component parts from a number of manufacturers. In particular, Plaintiff purchases application-specific integrated circuits ("ASICs"), which are considered the control center of its network switchers, from Defendant.

Defendant is also a Delaware corporation. Defendant asserts that, at all relevant times, its corporate headquarters, inside sales and marketing office, public relations department, principal warehouse, and most design and engineering functions were located in Burnaby, British Columbia, Canada. Defendant also maintains an office in Portland, Oregon, where many of its engineers are based. Defendant's products are sold in California through Unique Technologies, which is an authorized distributor of Defendant's products in North America. It is undisputed that Defendant directed Plaintiff to purchase Defendant's products through Unique, and that Defendant honored purchase orders solicited by Unique. Unique is located in California.

---

[5]*United States Code,* title 28, § 1441(a). . . .

[6]*Id.,* § 1441(c).

[7]Franchise Tax Board v. Construction Laborers Vacation Trust, *United States Reports,* vol. 463, p. 1 (Supreme Ct. 1983).

[8]*Id.* at p. 9.

[9]U.S. Ratification of 1980 United Nations Convention on Contracts for the International Sale of Goods: Official English Text, *United States Code,* title 15, App. at p. 52 (1997).

[10]*United States Code,* title 15, App. Article 1 (1)(a).

Article 10 of the CISG provides that "if a party has more than one place of business, the place of business is that which has the closest relationship to the contract and its performance."

IV. Discussion

Defendant asserts that this Court has jurisdiction to hear this case pursuant to *United States Code*, title 28, section 1331, which dictates that the "district courts shall have original jurisdiction of all civil actions arising under the Constitution, laws, or treaties of the United States." Specifically, Defendant contends that the contract claims at issue necessarily implicate the CISG, because the contract is between parties having their places of business in two nations which have adopted the CISG treaty....

A. Federal Jurisdiction Attaches to Claims Governed by the CISG

Although the general federal question statute, *United States Code*, title 28, § 1331(a), gives district courts original jurisdiction over every civil action that "arises under the ... treaties of the United States," an individual may only enforce a treaty's provisions when the treaty is self-executing, that is, when it expressly or impliedly creates a private right of action.[11] The parties do not dispute that the CISG properly creates a private right of action.[12] Therefore, if the CISG properly applies to this action, federal jurisdiction exists.

B. The Contract in Question Is Between Parties from Two Different Contracting States

The CISG only applies when a contract is "between parties whose places of business are in different States."[13] If this requirement is not satisfied, Defendant cannot claim jurisdiction under the CISG. It is undisputed that Plaintiff's place of business is Santa Clara County, California, U.S.A. It is further undisputed that during the relevant time period, Defendant's corporate headquarters, inside sales and marketing office, public relations department, principal warehouse, and most of its design and engineering functions were located in Burnaby, British Columbia, Canada. However, Plaintiff contends that, pursuant to Article 10 of the CISG, Defendant's "place of business" having the closest relationship to the contract at issue is the United States.

* * *

... Plaintiff [points] to the purchase orders submitted by Plaintiff to Unique Technologies, a nonexclusive distributor of Defendant's products. Plaintiff asserts that Unique acted in the United States as an agent of Defendant, and that Plaintiff's contacts with Unique establish Defendant's place of business in the U.S. for the purposes of this contract.

... Plaintiff provides no legal support for this proposition. To the contrary, a distributor of goods for resale is normally not treated as an agent of the manufacturer. Agency results "from the manifestation of consent by one person to another that the other shall act on his behalf and subject to his control, and consent by the other so to act."[14] Plaintiff has produced no evidence of consent by Defendant to be bound by the acts of Unique. To the contrary, Defendant cites the distributorship agreement with Unique, which expressly states that the contract does not "allow Distributor to create or assume any obligation on behalf of [Defendant] for any purpose whatsoever." Furthermore, while Unique may distribute Defendant's products, Plaintiff does not allege that Unique made any representations regarding technical specifications on behalf of Defendant. Indeed, Unique is not even mentioned in the Complaint. To the extent that representations were made regarding the technical specifications of the ASICs, and those specifications were not satisfied by the delivered goods, the relevant agreement is that between Plaintiff and Defendant. Accordingly, the Court finds that Unique is not an agent of Defendant in this dispute. Plaintiff's dealings with Unique do not establish Defendant's place of business in the United States.

* * *

C. The Effect of the Choice of Law Clauses

Plaintiff next argues that, even if the Parties are from two nations that have adopted the CISG, the choice of law provisions in the "Terms and Conditions" set forth by both Parties reflect the Parties' intent to "opt out" of application of the treaty.[15] Article 6 of the CISG provides that "the parties may exclude the application of the Convention or, subject to Article 12, derogate from or vary the effect of any of its provisions."[16] Defendant asserts that merely choosing the law of a jurisdiction is insufficient to opt

---

[11]*See* Tel-Oren v. Libyan Arab Republic, *Federal Reporter, Second Series,* vol. 726, p. 774 at p. 808 (District of Columbia Circuit Ct. of Appeals 1984) (Judge Bork concurring)....

[12]*See* Delchi Carrier v. Rotorex Corp., *Federal Reporter, Third Series,* vol. 71, p. 1024 at p. 1027–28 (2nd Circuit Ct. of Appeals 1995)....

[13]*United States Code,* title 15, App. Article 1(1)(a).

[14]Restatement, Second, of the Law of Agency, § 1 (1957).

[15]Plaintiff's Terms and Conditions provides "APPLICABLE LAW. The validity [and] performance of this [purchase] order shall be governed by the laws of the state shown on Buyer's address on this order." The buyer's address as shown on each of the Purchase Orders is San Jose, California.

Defendant's Terms and Conditions provides "APPLICABLE LAW: The contract between the parties is made, governed by, and shall be construed in accordance with the laws of the Province of British Columbia and the laws of Canada applicable therein, which shall be deemed to be the proper law hereof.... " It is undisputed that British Columbia has adopted the CISG.

[16]*United States Code,* title 15, App. Article 6.

out of the CISG, absent express exclusion of the CISG. The Court finds that the particular choice of law provisions in the "Terms and Conditions" of both parties are inadequate to effectuate an opt out of the CISG.

Although selection of a particular choice of law, such as "the California Commercial Code" or the "Uniform Commercial Code" could amount to implied exclusion of the CISG, the choice of law clauses at issue here do not evince a clear intent to opt out of the CISG. For example, Defendant's choice of applicable law adopts the law of British Columbia, and it is undisputed that the CISG is the law of British Columbia.[17] Furthermore, even Plaintiff's choice of applicable law generally adopts the "laws of" the State of California, and California is bound by the Supremacy Clause to the treaties of the United States.[18] Thus, under general California law, the CISG is applicable to contracts where the contracting parties are from different countries that have adopted the CISG. In the absence of clear language indicating that both contracting parties intended to opt out of the CISG, and in view of Defendant's Terms and Conditions which would apply the CISG, the Court rejects Plaintiff's contention that the choice of law provisions preclude the applicability of the CISG.

D. Federal Jurisdiction Based upon the CISG Does Not Violate the Well-Pleaded Complaint Rule The Court rejects Plaintiff's argument that removal is improper because of the well-pleaded complaint rule. The rule states that a cause of action arises under federal law only when the plaintiff's well-pleaded complaint raises issues of federal law.[19]

It is undisputed that the Complaint on its face does not refer to the CISG. However, Defendants argue that the preemptive force of the CISG converts the state breach of contract claim into a federal claim. Indeed, Congress may establish a federal law that so completely preempts a particular area of law that any civil complaint raising that select group of claims is necessarily federal in character.[20]

It appears that the issue of whether or not the CISG preempts state law is a matter of first impression. In the case of federal statutes, "the question of whether a certain action is preempted by federal law is one of con-

gressional intent. The purpose of Congress is the ultimate touchstone."[21] Transferring this analysis to the question of preemption by a treaty, the Court focuses on the intent of the treaty's contracting parties.[22]

In the case of the CISG treaty, this intent can be discerned from the introductory text, which states that "the adoption of uniform rules which govern contracts for the international sale of goods and take into account the different social, economic and legal systems would contribute to the removal of legal barriers in international trade and promote the development of international trade."[23] The CISG further recognizes the importance of "the development of international trade on the basis of equality and mutual benefit."[24] These objectives are reiterated in the President's Letter of Transmittal of the CISG to the Senate as well as the Secretary of State's Letter of Submittal of the CISG to the President.[25] The Secretary of State, George P. Shultz, noted:

> Sales transactions that cross international boundaries are subject to legal uncertainty—doubt as to which legal system will apply and the difficulty of coping with unfamiliar foreign law. The sales contract may specify which law will apply, but our sellers and buyers cannot expect that foreign trading partners will always agree on the applicability of United States law.... The Convention's approach provides an effective solution for this difficult problem. When a contract for an international sale of goods does not make clear what rule of law applies, the Convention provides uniform rules to govern the questions that arise in making and performance of the contract.[26]

The Court concludes that the expressly stated goal of developing uniform international contract law to promote international trade indicates the intent of the parties to the treaty to have the treaty preempt state law causes of action.

* * *

V. Conclusion

For the foregoing reasons, Plaintiff's Motion to Remand is DENIED.... ■

---

[17]International Sale of Goods Act, chap. 236, *Statutes of British Columbia,* vol. 1996, § 1 *et seq.*

[18]U.S. Constitution, Article 6, clause 2: "This Constitution, and the laws of the United States which shall be made in pursuance thereof; and all treaties made, or which shall be made, under the authority of the United States, shall be the supreme law of the land."

[19]Gully v. First National Bank, *United States Reports,* vol. 299, p. 109 (Supreme Ct.1936)....

[20]Metropolitan Life Ins. Co. v. Taylor, *id.,* vol. 481, p. 58 at p. 62 (Supreme Ct.1987)....

[21]Pilot Life Ins. Co. v. Dedeaux, *id.,* vol. 481, p. 41 at p. 45 (Supreme Ct.1987).

[22]*See* Husmann v. Trans World Airlines, Inc., *Federal Reporter, Third Series,* vol. 169, p. 1151 at p. 1153 (8th Circuit Ct. of Appeals 1999)....

[23]*United States Code,* title 15, App. 15 at p. 53.

[24]*Id.*

[25]*Id.,* at pp. 70–72.

[26]*Id.,* at p. 71.

Sales Defined

sale: The exchange of goods for an amount of money or its equivalent.

CISG does not directly define **sales**. Instead, it speaks of the seller's and buyer's obligations. The seller is to "deliver the goods, hand over any documents relating to them and transfer the property in the goods, as required by the contract and this Convention";[27] the buyer, in exchange, is to "pay the price."[28] Although not stated in a single article, this is the same definition found in many domestic laws, including the U.S. Uniform Commercial Code, which describes a sale as the "passing of title from the seller to the buyer for a price."[29]

Goods Defined

good: A movable tangible object. For the purposes of CISG, goods do not include things bought for personal use or at an auction or foreclosure sale, nor may they be oceangoing vessels or aircraft.

CISG also does not directly define **goods**. Instead, it defines those kinds of sales that are *not* governed by the Convention. Six specific categories are excluded. Three are based on the nature of the transaction, three on the kinds of goods. The excluded transactions are (1) "goods bought for personal, family, or household use"; (2) auction sales; and (3) sales "on execution or otherwise by authority of law." The excluded goods are (1) stocks, shares, investment securities, negotiable instruments, or money; (2) ships, vessels, hovercraft, or aircraft; and (3) electricity.[30]

The drafters adopted this list of exclusions on the assumption that the Convention applies only to goods that are movable and tangible. The nature of goods was made clearer in the French-language version of the 1964 *Convention Relating to a Uniform Law on the International Sale of Goods*, which used the phrase *objets mobiliers corporels.*[31] In CISG, however, the French version uses the term *marchandises.*[32] Regardless, legal usage internationally is consistent in its interpretation of the word *goods* (*marchandises*). Plus, many transactions, such as the sale of real property, are by their very nature domestic rather than international. The list of exclusions, therefore, only includes goods that the drafters felt were not already obviously excluded.[33]

Goods bought for personal, family, or household use are excluded for two reasons. First, a double standard could arise if different rules governed sales by local shopkeepers to foreigners. Second, many local laws protect consumers, and that protection would be lost if CISG applied. This exclusion does not apply, however, "unless" the seller "knew or ought to have known" that the goods were bought for personal use or consumption.

This "unless" clause is best illustrated by an example. Seller, a computer retailer, receives an order for a computer from Buyer, a resident of State B. The order is for a powerful, expensive computer of the sort commonly bought for use in business firms. When a dispute about the sale arises, Seller relies on CISG. Buyer then offers evidence that he bought the computer for his personal use as a hobbyist. In this example, the Seller should be able to show that he neither knew nor ought to have known that the computer was bought for personal use. The Convention would then apply.

Auction sales, sales on execution, and sales "otherwise by authority of law" are excluded because of the uniqueness of the transactions involved. Auction sales present problems in determining when the contract was formed. Executions and other kinds of forced sales do not involve the negotiation of terms by the parties. Special local laws govern these sales, and CISG does not disturb that arrangement.

Transactions in stocks, shares, investment securities, negotiable instruments, and money are excluded because a wide variety of local rules govern them, and the drafters could not agree on how to harmonize the rules in this Convention. However, the drafters did not exclude a long list of other similar assets, such as patent rights, copyrights, and trademarks, whose international sale is now governed by CISG.

---

[27]UN Convention on Contracts for the International Sale of Goods, Article 30.
[28]*Id.,* Article 54.
[29]Uniform Commercial Code, § 2-106.
[30]UN Convention on Contracts for the International Sale of Goods, Article 2 (1980).
[31]French: "tangible moveable objects."
[32]French: "goods," "wares," or "commodities."
[33]*See* John Honnold, *Uniform Law for International Sales under the 1980 United Nations Convention,* pp. 85–87 (1982), for a discussion of the drafters intent on the meaning of *goods.*

Sales of ships, vessels, hovercraft, aircraft, and electricity were also excluded from CISG because most domestic legal systems have special rules that apply to them.

Mixed Sales

A seller of goods often furnishes services when delivering a product to a buyer. For example, restaurants provide both food and service. Manufacturers that contract to produce goods are similarly providing both goods and services. Are these sales of goods or sales of services?

CISG looks upon mixed sales and services contracts—the restaurant example—as sales of goods, unless "the preponderant part of the obligations" of the seller "consists in the supply of labor or other services." One may assume that preponderant has its normal meaning of "more than half"; but whether this is measured by the cost, the sale price, or some other basis is something the Convention does not make clear.

Contracts for goods to be manufactured are treated by CISG as sales of goods unless the buyer "undertakes to supply a substantial part of the materials." Whereas "substantial" probably means less than half, how much less is unclear. The French-language version of the Convention suggests a possible test, as it uses the term "*une part essentielle.*"[34] Thus, if the buyer provides the components essential to the manufacture of a product—regardless of their size or value—the Convention would not apply.

C. CONTRACTUAL ISSUES EXCLUDED FROM THE COVERAGE OF CISG

Courts face a variety of issues in determining if a contract should be enforced or if a remedy should be granted when a contract is breached. CISG only deals with (a) the formation of the contract and (b) the remedies available to the buyer and seller. It specifically excludes questions about (a) the legality of the contract, (b) the competency of the parties, (c) the rights of third parties, and (d) liability for death or personal injury.[35]

Illegality and Incompetency

Domestic laws vary greatly in determining when a contract is illegal and when it is void or voidable because one or both of the parties are incompetent. Contraband, for example, cannot be legally sold. However, what constitutes contraband in one country may not in another; for example, alcohol, drugs, pornography, religious tracts, political tracts, and so on, may be treated differently from one country to the next. Similarly, the extent to which a contract can be avoided because it was fraudulently obtained varies greatly. Domestic rules on insanity, infancy, and other contractual disabilities are equally diverse.

The drafters of the Convention recognized that legality and competency are sensitive issues that reflect the mores and social values of particular cultures. To avoid a disagreement that might have jeopardized the adoption of CISG, these questions were left for settlement by domestic law.

Third-Party Claims and Personal Injuries

Equally diverse domestic laws apply to the matters of third-party claims and the liability of a seller for death or personal injury. Again, to avoid the possibility of a deadlock in the drafting of the Convention, the drafters left them out.

---

[34]French: "an essential part."

[35]UN Convention on Contracts for the International Sale of Goods, Article 4 (1980), provides: "This Convention governs only the formation of the contract of sale and the rights and obligations of the seller and the buyer arising from such a contract. In particular, except as otherwise expressly provided in this Convention, it is not concerned with: (a) the validity of the contract or any of its provisions or of any usage; (b) the effect which the contract may have on the property in the goods sold."

Article 5 states: "This Convention does not apply to the liability of the seller for death or personal injury caused by the goods to any person."

Preemption

preempt: To take precedence over.

To determine if CISG applies to a particular contractual issue, one must look to the Convention itself, and not domestic law. If the Convention does apply, domestic law is **preempted**. That is, the remedies provided in CISG are the only remedies available. This result is the consequence of the Convention's basic function: to establish uniform rules for international sales contracts.[36]

Preemption applies both in cases where domestic law calls the matter contractual and where it gives it some other name. Consider the following example. A seller delivers chemicals to a buyer that are defective. The chemicals spontaneously burst into flames, burning down the buyer's warehouse. In such a circumstance, some domestic law systems would impose a sanction in tort or delict that is commonly called product liability. To prove product liability, the injured buyer must typically show (a) that the goods failed to conform to the contract, (b) that the damage resulted from the defect, and (c) that the seller failed to exercise due care. Under CISG, however, a remedy is available if the goods failed to conform to the contract (Article 35) and damage resulted from the defect (Article 74). Despite the fact that local law requires a third proof element to establish product liability, this does not mean that a tort or delict remedy is available. The only permissible remedy is the one provided by CISG.

For reference, a summary comparison of CISG rules and the sale-of-goods rules in France and the United States is set out in Exhibit 10-2.

D. INTERPRETING CISG

The underlying goal of CISG is the creation of a uniform body of international commercial sales law. In deciding questions governed by the Convention, Article 7(2) directs a court to look to the following sources, in the following order: (1) the Convention, (2) the general principles on which the Convention is based, and (3) the rules of private international law.

The Convention

When the words of CISG itself require interpretation, Article 7(1) directs a court to consider (a) the international character of the Convention, (b) the need to promote uniformity in the Convention's application, and (c) the observance of good faith. Article 7(1), however, does not describe the sources the Court may—or must—use in making its interpretation.

plain meaning rule: A statute or treaty is to be interpreted only from the words contained within the statute or treaty.

On its face, CISG implies that a court may use only the **plain meaning** of the language in the Convention. The plain meaning rule is common to countries whose judicial practices follow those of England. In England, at least until very recently, courts may deduce the meaning of legislation only from the words contained in a statute.[37] In most other countries, however, including the United States and the civil law countries, the courts also look to a statute's legislative history—the ***travaux préparatoires***—to determine its intent. Additionally, when an international tribunal interprets a treaty, its legislative history is commonly used both to *confirm* the meaning derived from the treaty's terms and to *determine* the treaty's meaning when the terms are ambiguous or obscure.[38] Considering the widespread general use of *travaux*

travaux préparatoires: (French: "preparatory work.") The legislative history of a statute or treaty. That is, the negotiations leading up to its final drafting and adoption.

---

[36]*Id.,* Article 7(1).

[37]In 1980, the English House of Lords used legislative history in interpreting the Warsaw Convention's provisions on the liability of air carriers. In the landmark decision of Fothergill v. Monarch Airlines, *All England Law Reports,* vol. 1980, pt. 2, p. 696 (1980), a majority of opinions relied on the rules of interpretation in the Vienna Convention on the Law of Treaties (1969). Article 32 of that treaty expressly provides for the use of "the preparatory work of the treaty and the circumstances of its conclusion" in interpreting international conventions.

[38]Article 31(1) of the Vienna Convention on the Law of Treaties (1969) provides: "A treaty shall be interpreted in good faith in accordance with the ordinary meaning to be given to the terms of the treaty in their context and in the light of its object and purpose." Article 32 adds: "Recourse may be had to supplementary means of interpretation including the preparatory work of the treaty and the circumstances of its conclusion, in order to confirm the meaning resulting from the application of Article 31, or to determine the meaning when the interpretation according to Article 31: (a) leaves the meaning ambiguous or obscure; or (b) leads to a result which is manifestly absurd or unreasonable."

Contract Provision	French Civil Code and Code of Commerce	United States Uniform Commercial Code	United Nations Convention on Contracts for the International Sale of Goods
Sale is a passage of title for a price	Yes	Yes	Yes
Goods are movable and tangible things	Yes	Yes	Yes
Mixed sales and service transactions that predominantly involve the delivery of goods are governed by sales law provisions	Yes	Yes	Yes
Sales law applies only to merchants	No	No	Yes
A merchant is:	A person who engages in a defined list of commercial acts.	A person who deals in goods of the kind involved in a particular transaction, or who by his occupation holds himself out as having special knowledge or skill related to the sale, or who is represented by a merchant.	A person who has a place of business.
Parties must act in good faith	Yes	Yes	Yes
Unconscionable contracts are unenforceable	Yes	Yes	Yes
A sales contract must be memorialized in a writing signed by the party against whom it is being asserted.	Yes, if the party against whom the contract is being asserted is a nonmerchant and the price is €800 or more; no, if the party against whom the contract is being asserted is a merchant.	Yes, if the price is $500 or more; no, if both parties are merchants and one of the parties sends a written confirmation that is not promptly objected to.	No
Subjective intent of parties may be used to interpret contracts	Yes	No	Yes
Parol evidence is admissible to interpret written contracts the parties intended to be a final expression of their agreement.	Yes, if the party objecting is a merchant; no, if the party is a nonmerchant unless the parol evidence is supported by a written memorandum originating with the objecting party.	No	Yes

EXHIBIT 10-2 Comparative Summary of French, United States, and United Nations Convention Sale of Goods Provisions

A contract may be explained or interpreted by a course of performance, a course of dealing, and a usage of trade.	Yes	Yes	Yes
Terms that should not be left open are:	Price	Quantity	Price and quantity.
Firm offers can be made by:	Anyone	Merchants in a signed writing.	Merchants
If offeror does not specify a medium for acceptance, any reasonable medium may be used.	Yes	Yes	Yes
An offer may be revoked prior to an acceptance's	Receipt	Dispatch	Dispatch
Acceptance is effective upon	Receipt	Dispatch	Receipt
Acceptance is valid even if it contains additional terms.	No	Yes	No
Additional terms in an acceptance become proposals for addition that offeror may accept or reject.	No	Yes, when either party is a nonmerchant.	No
Additional terms become part of a contract unless promptly objected to by offeror.	No	Yes, if both parties are merchants.	No
Offeree who accepts by performance must notify the offeror within a reasonable time after beginning performance.	No	Yes	No
The scope of a specific performance decree is to:	Carry out any terms of the contract.	Deliver the goods.	Same as local law.
Place for delivery	(1) As specified in contract; (2) Location of goods at time of sale; (3) Seller's residence.	(1) As specified in contract; (2) Seller's business place; (3) Seller's residence; (4) Known location of goods.	(1)As specified in contract; (2) Carrier's business place; (3) Known location of goods.
Time for delivery	(1) As specified in contract.	(1) As specified in contract; (2) Reasonable time after contracting.	(1) As specified in contract; (2) Reasonable time after contracting.

(continued)

EXHIBIT 10-2   Continued

Conformity of goods (guarantees and warranties)	(1) Fit for ordinary purpose; (2) Fit for a particular purpose.	(1) Warranty of merchantability; (2) Warranty of fitness for a particular purpose.	(1) Fit for ordinary purpose; (2) Fit for a particular purpose.
Waiver of guarantees conformity requires use of specific words.	No	Yes	No
Waiver of guarantee of conformity must be made expressly.	Yes	Yes	No
Buyer must promptly notify seller of any nonconformity.	Yes	Yes	Yes
Seller may cure defects before delivery time.	Yes	Yes	Yes
Seller may cure defects after delivery time.	No	No	No
Time and place when buyer must pay is:	Delivery	Delivery	Delivery
Seller must make formal demand for payment.	Yes	No	No
Buyer must pay price once risk passes.	Yes	Yes	Yes
Risk passes when goods are delivered.	Yes	Yes	Yes
Risk passes for goods sent by carrier when the goods are identified to contract and delivered to carrier.	Yes	Yes	Yes
Remedies and damages are cumulative.	Yes	Yes	Yes
A period of grace is available to delay the granting of remedies.	Yes	No	No
Nonconforming party is entitled to *Nachfrist* notice	Yes	No	Yes
Buyers' remedies include price reduction.	Yes	No	Yes
General remedies include suspension of performance and anticipatory avoidance.	Yes	Yes	Yes
Injured party has duty to mitigate damages.	Yes	Yes	Yes
Excuse of *force majeure* is available.	Yes	Yes	Yes

EXHIBIT 10-2 Continued

préparatoires, it seems likely that most courts will turn to it in interpreting CISG's provisions, especially as the record of the Convention's preparation is now widely available.[39]

In addition to *travaux préparatoires*, courts in most countries use case law to interpret statutes and treaties.[40] At present, the number of cases that have interpreted CISG are few. Undoubtedly, this will change quickly. As it does, the courts will have to keep in mind the Convention's admonitions: that CISG is an international treaty, that its purpose is to establish uniform international rules, and that the courts are bound by the principle of good faith in interpreting the Convention. Because CISG is an international treaty, the courts of many countries will interpret it. The directive that it be interpreted to promote uniformity in its application compels courts to examine and follow the decisions of the courts in other contracting states. The requirement to use good faith means that courts must accept foreign decisions as precedents and depart from them only when they are clearly distinguishable, clearly erroneous, or no longer applicable to changed international circumstances.[41]

General Principles

general principles: Those principles underlying and common to a statutory scheme or treaty.

CISG calls for courts to look to the **general principles** on which the Convention is based when interpreting its provisions, but it gives no list of general principles. It is for the courts to divine those principles. The following two have been suggested: (1) A party to a contract has the duty to communicate information needed by the other party, and (2) parties have the obligation to mitigate damages resulting from a breach.[42] Both concepts appear, in varying forms, throughout the Convention.[43]

Although CISG does not give a list of general principles, it does set out the mechanism for determining them. They must be derived (as is the case for the suggestions listed above) from particular sections of the Convention, and then extended, by analogy, to the case at hand.[44] In choosing this particular mechanism, the drafters rejected the adoption of general principles derived from public or private international law, as well as from domestic law codes. This limitation on the sources that the courts may turn to in creating general principles was consciously made, and it reflects the drafters' concern for uniformity and consistency, both in the drafting and in the evolution of the Convention.

Rules of Private International Law

The rules of private international law are the third and final source for interpreting the Convention. They may be used, however, only when CISG itself does not directly settle a matter or when the matter cannot be resolved by the application of a general principle derived from the Convention itself.

---

[39]*See* John Honnold, *Uniform Law for International Sales under the 1980 United Nations Convention* (1982); and John Honnold, *Documentary History of the Uniform Law for International Sales* (1989).

[40]Scholarly writings (*doctrine*) are also widely relied on in civil law and the United States to interpret legislative materials. In England, and in the countries that derive their judicial practice from England, scholarly writing is generally given little weight. Because the Convention does not name the sources that courts are to use in its interpretation, this disparity will undoubtedly continue.

[41]The use of case law will present difficulties when different courts come to different conclusions based on similar facts. Absent the existence of a single appellate court to harmonize differing opinions, the principle of good faith imposes on every court that is hearing a dispute the obligation to harmonize its decision with those of other courts and, where there are conflicting precedents, to harmonize the precedents.

The principle of good faith that appears in CISG is apparently limited. The drafters meant that it be used only in interpreting the provisions of the Convention, and not as a loose or general obligation imposed on the parties. This is in contrast to its much broader application in the German Civil Code, § 242; the United States Uniform Commercial Code, § 1–203; and other code systems. However, one might note that the drafters of the German Civil Code also originally meant for good faith to be used in a similar limited way. Nevertheless, German judges ignored the drafters' intention because the principle proved to be a convenient tool for adding flexibility. One can also anticipate that courts used to a more liberal use of the concept will apply it in a similar liberal way when interpreting CISG.

[42]John Honnold, *Uniform Law for International Sales under the 1980 United Nations Convention,* pp. 131–132 (1982).

[43]The general duty to communicate is in the UN Convention on Contracts for the International Sale of Goods, Articles 19(2), 21(2), 26, 39(1), 48(2), 65, 71(3), 72(2), 79(4), and 88(1) (1980). The duty to mitigate is in *id.,* Articles 77, 85, and 86.

[44]*Id.,* Article 7(2), states: "Questions concerning matters governed by this Convention which are not expressly settled in it are to be settled in conformity with the general principles on which *it* is based. . . ." The mechanism is described

Private international law rules vary from country to country. Some states—notably in Central and Eastern Europe—have enacted private international law codes, whereas others—such as the English common law countries—rely on case law. This will undoubtedly produce inconsistent holdings. Nevertheless, these rules are much more harmonious internationally than other rules of domestic law, and adoption of their use represents a pragmatic decision by the authors of the Convention. By allowing courts to turn to the rules of private international law, the Convention avoids the possibility that courts will adopt interpretive aids on an entirely *ad hoc*[45] basis.

E. INTERPRETING SALES CONTRACTS

In determining if a contract has been made, in interpreting its terms, and in ascertaining if it has been performed as agreed, courts throughout the world look at the statements, the conduct, and the usages and practices of the parties, as well as the practices of the trade to which the contract relates. Article 8 of CISG establishes rules for interpreting the statements and conduct of the parties; Article 9 deals with usages and practices.

Statements and Conduct of the Parties

subjective intent approach: Rule that contracts should be interpreted according to the actual intent and understanding of the parties at the time they made their agreement.

A contract is sometimes said to be formed only when the parties have a "meeting of the minds" or a "common intent." This comes from the idea, commonly accepted in many civil law countries, that parties are only bound by a contract when they subject their "will" to its terms. Such a **subjective approach**, however, has its problems. If a dispute arises about the meaning of the contract, the parties are hardly impartial witnesses about what was in their minds at the time they made the contract. This shortcoming has led some courts, notably those in the common law countries, to reject completely the use of subjective intent in the interpretation of a contract. As Oliver Wendell Holmes, a noted American judge, once wrote: "The law has nothing to do with the actual state of the parties' minds. In contract, as elsewhere, it must go by the externals, and judge parties by their conduct."[46]

objective intent approach: Rule that contracts should be interpreted according to the understanding that a reasonable person would have had at the time the agreement was made.

Of course, the subjective intent of the parties is the best evidence for interpreting a contract—if it can be fairly ascertained—and CISG allows courts to turn to it first. Thus, courts are to use the subjective intent of a speaker, but only if "the other party knew or could not have been unaware" of the speaker's intent. When a speaker's intent is not clear, CISG directs the court to look at **objective intent**. In that case, a party's statements and other conduct "are to be interpreted according to the understanding that a reasonable person of the same kind as the other party would have had in the same circumstances."

Negotiations

negotiations: The preliminary discussions leading up to the adoption of an agreement.

When a court is to determine intent—be it the party's subjective intent or a reasonable person's objective understanding—Article 8(3) of CISG directs that "due consideration" be given "to all relevant circumstances," including (a) the **negotiations** leading up to the contract, (b) the practices that the parties have established between themselves, and (c) the parties' conduct after they agree to the contract.

common law parol evidence rule: When a contract describes itself as being complete and final, preliminary or informal agreements made prior to or at the same time the contract was made will be ignored when interpreting it.

The purpose of Article 8(3) is to do away with the technical rules that domestic courts sometimes use to interpret contracts. One notable example is the common law's **parol evidence rule**.[47] This rule forbids a court from considering any "prior" or any "contemporaneous oral understanding" when it is interpreting a writing that the parties intended as a "final expression of their agreement."[48] Article 8(3) specifically allows courts to consider the parties' preliminary negotiations when they interpret a contract.

---

in more detail in John Honnold, *Uniform Law for International Sales under the 1980 United Nations Convention*, p. 132 (1982).

[45]Latin: "for this." Something done for a specific purpose, circumstance, or case.

[46]Oliver W. Holmes, *The Common Law*, p. 242 (M. A. DeWolfe Howe, ed., 1963).

[47]CISG does not directly mention the parol evidence rule. To have done so, one commentator has suggested, "would have mystified jurists from legal systems that have no such rule." John Honnold, *Uniform Law for International Sales under the 1980 United Nations Convention*, p. 142 (1982).

[48]United States, Uniform Commercial Code, § 2-202.

Nevertheless, while Article 8(3) gives a court the flexibility to consider all relevant evidence, Article 6 allows the parties to "derogate from or vary the effect of" any of the provisions of the Convention. Thus, if the parties include a contract term (often called an "integration clause") that directs a court to ignore all prior or contemporaneous agreements, the court will have to give effect to that term. In other words, if the parties choose to adopt the parol evidence rule, they can do so. However, unless they specifically do so, the court will look at all the relevant circumstances of the case.

In addition to considering prior and contemporaneous conduct, CISG lets a court consider the parties' subsequent conduct. Again, this is contrary to the practice in some domestic tribunals.[49] CISG, however, does reflect the most widely followed practice, and, as is the case for parol evidence, the parties are free to insert a provision in their contract excluding its consideration.

In Case 10–2, a U.S. court analyzed the CISG provisions dealing with parol evidence.

---

[49]Lord Denning's criticism of the English practice is in Port Soudan Cotton Co. v. Chettiar and Sons, *Lloyd's Law Reports,* vol. 2, p. 5 at p. 11 (Ct. of Appeal, 1977).

Case 10–2   MCC Marble Ceramic v. Ceramica

United States, Eleventh Circuit Court of Appeals.
Federal Reporter, Third Series, vol. 144, p. 1384 (1998).[50]

CIRCUIT JUDGE BIRCH

This case requires us to determine whether a court must consider parol evidence in a contract dispute governed by the United Nations Convention on Contracts for the International Sale of Goods ("CISG"). The district court granted summary judgment on behalf of the defendant-appellee, relying on certain terms and provisions that appeared on the reverse of a pre-printed form contract for the sale of ceramic tiles. The plaintiff-appellant sought to rely on a number of affidavits that tended to show both that the parties had arrived at an oral contract before memorializing their agreement in writing and that they subjectively intended not to apply the terms on the reverse of the contract to their agreements. The magistrate judge held that the affidavits did not raise an issue of material fact and recommended that the district court grant summary judgment based on the terms of the contract. The district court agreed with the magistrate judge's reasoning and entered summary judgment in the defendant-appellee's favor. We REVERSE.

BACKGROUND

The plaintiff-appellant, MCC-Marble Ceramic, Inc. ("MCC"), is a Florida corporation engaged in the retail sale of tiles, and the defendant-appellee, Ceramica Nuova d'Agostino S.p.A. ("D'Agostino") is an Italian corporation engaged in the manufacture of ceramic tiles. In October 1990, MCC's president, Juan Carlos Monzon, met representatives of D'Agostino at a trade fair in Bologna, Italy, and negotiated an agreement to purchase ceramic tiles from D'Agostino based on samples he examined at the trade fair. Monzon, who spoke no Italian, communicated with Gianni Silingardi, then D'Agostino's commercial director, through a translator, Gianfranco Copelli, who was himself an agent of D'Agostino.[51] The parties apparently arrived at an oral agreement on the crucial terms of price, quality, quantity, delivery, and payment. The parties then recorded these terms on one of D'Agostino's standard, pre-printed order forms and Monzon signed the contract on MCC's behalf. According to MCC, the parties also entered into a requirements contract in February 1991, subject to which D'Agostino agreed to supply MCC with high grade ceramic tile at specific discounts as long as MCC purchased sufficient quantities of tile. MCC completed a

---

[50]This case is posted on the Internet at laws.findlaw.com/ 11th/974250OPNv2.html.
[51]Since this case is before us on summary judgment, we consider the facts in the light most favorable to MCC, the non-moving party, and grant MCC the benefit of every factual inference. *See* Welch v. Celotex Corp., 951 F.2d 1235, 1237 (11th Circuit Ct. of Appeals, 1992).

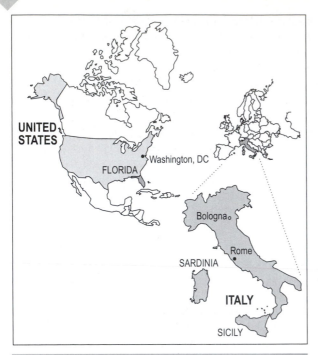

MAP 10-2 Italy and United States (1998)

number of additional order forms requesting tile deliveries pursuant to that agreement.

MCC brought suit against D'Agostino claiming a breach of the February 1991 requirements contract when D'Agostino failed to satisfy orders in April, May, and August of 1991. In addition to other defenses, D'Agostino responded that it was under no obligation to fill MCC's orders because MCC had defaulted on payment for previous shipments. In support of its position, D'Agostino relied on the pre-printed terms of the contracts that MCC had executed. The executed forms were printed in Italian and contained terms and conditions on both the front and reverse. According to an English translation of the October 1990 contract, the front of the order form contained the following language directly beneath Monzon's signature:

> [T]he buyer hereby states that he is aware of the sales conditions stated on the reverse and that he expressly approves of them with special reference to those numbered 1-2-3-4-5-6-7-8.

Clause 6(b), printed on the back of the form states:

> [D]efault or delay in payment within the time agreed upon gives D'Agostino the right to . . . suspend or

cancel the contract itself and to cancel possible other pending contracts and the buyer does not have the right to indemnification or damages.

D'Agostino also brought a number of counterclaims against MCC, seeking damages for MCC's alleged non-payment for deliveries of tile that D'Agostino had made between February 28, 1991, and July 4, 1991. MCC responded that the tile it had received was of a lower quality than contracted for, and that, pursuant to the CISG, MCC was entitled to reduce payment in proportion to the defects.[52] D'Agostino, however, noted that clause 4 on the reverse of the contract states, in pertinent part:

> Possible complaints for defects of the merchandise must be made in writing by means of a certified letter within and not later than 10 days after receipt of the merchandise. . . .

Although there is evidence to support MCC's claims that it complained about the quality of the deliveries it received, MCC never submitted any written complaints.

MCC did not dispute these underlying facts before the district court, but argued that the parties never intended the terms and conditions printed on the reverse of the order form to apply to their agreements. As evidence for this assertion, MCC submitted Monzon's affidavit, which claims that MCC had no subjective intent to be bound by those terms and that D'Agostino was aware of this intent. MCC also filed affidavits from Silingardi and Copelli, D'Agostino's representatives at the trade fair, which support Monzon's claim that the parties subjectively intended not to be bound by the terms on the reverse of the order form. The magistrate judge held that the affidavits, even if true, did not raise an issue of material fact regarding the interpretation or applicability of the terms of the written contracts and the district court accepted his recommendation to award summary judgment in D'Agostino's favor. MCC then filed this timely appeal.

DISCUSSION

We review a district court's grant of summary judgment *de novo*[53] and apply the same standards as the district court. Summary judgment is appropriate when the pleadings, depositions, and affidavits reveal that no gen-

---

[52]Article 50 of the CISG permits a buyer to reduce payment for nonconforming goods in proportion to the nonconformity under certain conditions. *See* CISG, art. 50.

[[53]Latin: "over again" or "anew." A *de novo* trial is one that is tried anew as if it had not been previously heard and as if no decision had been previously rendered.]

uine issue of material fact exists and the moving party is entitled to judgment as a matter of law.

The parties to this case agree that the CISG governs their dispute because the United States, where MCC has its place of business, and Italy, where D'Agostino has its place of business, are both States Party to the Convention.[54] Article 8 of the CISG governs the interpretation of international contracts for the sale of goods and forms the basis of MCC's appeal from the district court's grant of summary judgment in D'Agostino's favor.[55] MCC argues that the magistrate judge and the district court improperly ignored evidence that MCC submitted regarding the parties' subjective intent when they memorialized the terms of their agreement on D'Agostino's pre-printed form contract, and that the magistrate judge erred by applying the parol evidence rule in derogation of the CISG.

I. Subjective Intent Under the CISG

Contrary to what is familiar practice in United States courts, the CISG appears to permit a substantial inquiry into the parties' subjective intent, even if the parties did not engage in any objectively ascertainable means of registering this intent. Article 8(1) of the CISG instructs courts to interpret the "statements . . . and other conduct of a party . . . according to his intent" as long as the other party "knew or could not have been unaware" of that intent. The plain language of the Convention, therefore, requires an inquiry into a party's subjective intent as long as the other party to the contract was aware of that intent.

In this case, MCC has submitted three affidavits that discuss the purported subjective intent of the parties to the initial agreement concluded between MCC and D'Agostino in October 1990. All three affidavits discuss the preliminary negotiations and report that the parties arrived at an oral agreement for D'Agostino to supply quantities of a specific grade of ceramic tile to MCC at an agreed upon price. The affidavits state that the "oral agreement established the essential terms of

quality, quantity, description of goods, delivery, price and payment." The affidavits also note that the parties memorialized the terms of their oral agreement on a standard D'Agostino order form, but all three affiants contend that the parties *subjectively* intended not to be bound by the terms on the reverse of that form despite a provision directly below the signature line that expressly and specifically incorporated those terms.[56]

The terms on the reverse of the contract give D'Agostino the right to suspend or cancel all contracts in the event of a buyer's non-payment and require a buyer to make a written report of all defects within ten days. As the magistrate judge's report and recommendation makes clear, if these terms applied to the agreements between MCC and D'Agostino, summary judgment would be appropriate because MCC failed to make any written complaints about the quality of tile it received and D'Agostino has established MCC's non-payment of a number of invoices amounting to $108,389.40 and 102,053,846.00 Italian lira.

Article 8(1) of the CISG requires a court to consider this evidence of the parties' subjective intent. Contrary to the magistrate judge's report, which the district court endorsed and adopted, article 8(1) does not focus on interpreting the parties' statements alone. Although we agree with the magistrate judge's conclusion that no "interpretation" of the contract's *terms* could support MCC's position, article 8(1) also requires a court to consider subjective intent while interpreting the *conduct* of the parties. The CISG's language, therefore, requires courts to consider evidence of a party's subjective intent when signing a contract if the other party to the contract was aware of that intent at the time. This is precisely the type of evidence that MCC has provided through the Silingardi, Copelli, and Monzon affidavits, which discuss not only Monzon's intent as MCC's representative but also discuss the intent of D'Agostino's representatives and their knowledge that Monzon did not intend to agree to the terms on the reverse of the form contract. This acknowledgment that D'Agostino's representatives

---

[54]*See* CISG, art. 1

[55]Article 8 provides:

   (1) For the purposes of this Convention statements made by and other conduct of a party are to be interpreted according to his intent where the other party knew or could not have been unaware what that intent was.

   (2) If the preceding paragraph is not applicable, statements made by and conduct of a party are to be interpreted according to the understanding a reasonable person of the same kind as the other party would have had in the same circumstances.

   (3) In determining the intent of a party or the understanding a reasonable person would have had, due consideration is to be given to all relevant circumstances of the case including the negotiations, any practices which the parties have established between themselves, usages, and any subsequent conduct of the parties.

[56]MCC makes much of the fact that the written order form is entirely in Italian and that Monzon, who signed the contract on MCC's behalf directly below this provision incorporating the terms on the reverse of the form, neither spoke nor read Italian. This fact is of no assistance to MCC's position. We find it nothing short of astounding that an individual, purportedly experienced in commercial matters, would sign a contract in a foreign language and expect not to be bound simply because he could not comprehend its terms. We find nothing in the CISG that might counsel this type of reckless behavior and nothing that signals any retreat from the proposition that parties who sign contracts will be bound by them regardless of whether they have read them or understood them. *See* e.g., Samson Plastic Conduit and Pipe Corp. v. Battenfeld Extrusionstechnik GmBH, *Federal Supplement,* vol. 718, p. 886 at p., 890 (Dist. Ct. for Middle Dist. of Ala., 1989) ("A good and recurring illustration of the problem . . . involves a person who is . . . unfamiliar with the language in which a contract is written and who has signed a document which was not read to him. There is all but unanimous agreement that he is bound. . . .")

were aware of Monzon's subjective intent puts this case squarely within article 8(1) of the CISG, and therefore requires the court to consider MCC's evidence as it interprets the parties' conduct.[57]

II. Parol Evidence and the CISG

Given our determination that the magistrate judge and the district court should have considered MCC's affidavits regarding the parties' subjective intentions, we must address a question of first impression in this circuit: whether the parol evidence rule, which bars evidence of an earlier oral contract that contradicts or varies the terms of a subsequent or contemporaneous written contract,[58] plays any role in cases involving the CISG. We begin by observing that the parol evidence rule, contrary to its title, is a substantive rule of law, not a rule of evidence.[59] The rule does not purport to exclude a particular type of evidence as an "untrustworthy or undesirable" way of proving a fact, but prevents a litigant from attempting to show "the fact itself-the fact that the terms of the agreement are other than those in the writing."[60] As such, a federal district court cannot simply apply the parol evidence rule as a procedural matter—as it might if excluding a particular type of evidence under the Federal Rules of Evidence, which apply in federal court regardless of the source of the substantive rule of decision.[61]

The CISG itself contains no express statement on the role of parol evidence. It is clear, however, that the drafters of the CISG were comfortable with the concept of permitting parties to rely on oral contracts because they eschewed any statutes of fraud provision and expressly provided for the enforcement of oral contracts. Moreover, article 8(3) of the CISG expressly directs courts to give "due consideration . . . to all relevant circumstances of the case including the negotiations . . ." to

determine the intent of the parties. Given article 8(1)'s directive to use the intent of the parties to interpret their statements and conduct, article 8(3) is a clear instruction to admit and consider parol evidence regarding the negotiations to the extent they reveal the parties' subjective intent.

* * *

Our reading of article 8(3) as a rejection of the parol evidence rule . . . is in accordance with the great weight of academic commentary on the issue. As one scholar has explained:

> [T]he language of Article 8(3) that "due consideration is to be given to *all relevant* circumstances of the case" seems adequate to override any domestic rule that would bar a tribunal from considering the relevance of other agreements. . . . Article 8(3) relieves tribunals from domestic rules that might bar them from "considering" any evidence between the parties that is relevant. This added flexibility for interpretation is consistent with a growing body of opinion that the "parol evidence rule" has been an embarrassment for the administration of modern transactions.[62]

Indeed, only one commentator has made any serious attempt to reconcile the parol evidence rule with the CISG.[63] [That commentator] argues that the parol evidence rule often permits the admission of evidence discussed in article 8(3), and that the rule could be an appropriate way to discern what consideration is "due" under article 8(3) to evidence of a parol nature. He also argues that the parol evidence rule, by limiting the incentive for perjury and pleading prior understandings in bad faith, promotes good faith and uniformity in the interpretation of contracts and therefore is in harmony

---

[57]Without this crucial acknowledgment, we would interpret the contract and the parties' actions according to article 8(2), which directs courts to rely on objective evidence of the parties' intent. On the facts of this case it seems readily apparent that MCC's affidavits provide *no evidence* that Monzon's actions would have made his alleged subjective intent not to be bound by the terms of the contract known to "the understanding that a reasonable person . . . would have had in the same circumstances." CISG, art 8(2).

[58]The Uniform Commercial Code includes a version of the parol evidence rule applicable to contracts for the sale of goods in most states:
   Terms with respect to which the confirmatory memoranda of the parties agree or which are otherwise set forth in a writing intended by the parties as a final expression of their agreement with respect to such terms as are included therein may not be contradicted by evidence of any prior agreement or of a contemporaneous oral agreement but may be explained or supplemented
      (a) by course of dealing or usage of trade . . . or by course of performance . . . ; and
      (b) by evidence of consistent additional terms unless the court finds the writing to have been intended also as a complete and exclusive statement of the terms of the agreement.
   U.C.C. § 2–202.

[59]See E. Allen Farnsworth, *Farnsworth on Contracts*, vol. II, § 7.2 at p. 194 (1990).

[60]*Id.*

[61]*Confirm id.* § 7.2 at p. 196. An example demonstrates this point. The CISG provides that a contract for the sale of goods need not be in writing and that the parties may prove the contract "by any means, including witnesses." CISG, art. 11. Nevertheless, a party seeking to prove a contract in such a manner in federal court could not do so in a way that violated the rule against hearsay. See Federal Rules of Evidence, Rule 802 (barring hearsay evidence). A federal district court applies the Federal Rules of Evidence because these rules are considered procedural, regardless of the source of the law that governs the substantive decision. *Confirm Farnsworth on Contracts*, § 7.2 at p. 196 and n. 16 (citing cases).

[62]John O. Honnold, *Uniform Law for International Sales under the 1980 United Nations Convention*, § 110 at 170–71. (2d ed. 1991)

[63]*See* David H. Moore, "Note, The Parol Evidence Rule and the United Nations Convention on Contracts for the International Sale of Goods: Justifying Beijing Metals & Minerals Import/Export Corp. v. American Business Center, Inc.," *Brigham Young University Law Review,* vol. 1995, p. 1347 (1995).

with the principles of the CISG, as expressed in article 7. The answer to both these arguments, however, is the same: although jurisdictions in the United States have found the parol evidence rule helpful to promote good faith and uniformity in contract, as well as an appropriate answer to the question of how much consideration to give parol evidence, a wide number of other States Party to the CISG have rejected the rule in their domestic jurisdictions. One of the primary factors motivating the negotiation and adoption of the CISG was to provide parties to international contracts for the sale of goods with some degree of certainty as to the principles of law that would govern potential disputes and remove the previous doubt regarding which party's legal system might otherwise apply. Courts applying the CISG cannot, therefore, upset the parties' reliance on the Convention by substituting familiar principles of domestic law when the Convention requires a different result. We may only achieve the directives of good faith and uniformity in contracts under the CISG by interpreting and applying the plain language of article 8(3) as written and obeying its directive to consider this type of parol evidence.

This is not to say that parties to an international contract for the sale of goods cannot depend on written contracts or that parol evidence regarding subjective contractual intent need always prevent a party relying on a written agreement from securing summary judgment. To the contrary, most cases will not present a situation (as exists in this case) in which both parties to the contract acknowledge a subjective intent not to be bound by the terms of a pre-printed writing. In most cases, therefore, article 8(2) of the CISG will apply, and objective evidence will provide the basis for the court's decision. Consequently, a party to a contract governed by the CISG will not be able to avoid the terms of a contract and force a jury trial simply by submitting an affidavit which states that he or she did not have the subjective intent to be bound by the contract's terms. Moreover, to the extent parties wish to avoid parol evidence problems they can do so by including a merger clause in their agreement that extinguishes any and all prior agreements and understandings not expressed in the writing.

Considering MCC's affidavits in this case, however, we conclude that the magistrate judge and the district court improperly granted summary judgment in favor of D'Agostino. Although the affidavits are, as D'Agostino observes, relatively conclusory and unsupported by facts that would *objectively* establish MCC's intent not to be bound by the conditions on the reverse of the form, article 8(1) requires a court to consider evidence of a party's subjective intent when the other party was aware of it, and the Silingardi and Copelli affidavits provide that evidence. This is not to say that the affidavits are conclusive proof of what the parties intended. A reasonable finder

of fact, for example, could disregard testimony that purportedly sophisticated international merchants signed a contract without intending to be bound as simply too incredible to believe and hold MCC to the conditions printed on the reverse of the contract. Nevertheless, the affidavits raise an issue of material fact regarding the parties' intent to incorporate the provisions on the reverse of the form contract. If the finder of fact determines that the parties did not intend to rely on those provisions, then the more general provisions of the CISG will govern the outcome of the dispute.

MCC's affidavits, however, do not discuss all of the transactions and orders that MCC placed with D'Agostino. Each of the affidavits discusses the parties' subjective intent surrounding the initial order MCC placed with D'Agostino in October 1990. The Copelli affidavit also discusses a February 1991 requirements contract between the parties and reports that the parties subjectively did not intend the terms on the reverse of the D'Agostino order form to apply to that contract either. D'Agostino, however, submitted the affidavit of its chairman, Vincenzo Maselli, which describes at least three other orders from MCC on form contracts dated January 15, 1991, April 27, 1991, and May 4, 1991, in addition to the October 1990 contract. MCC's affidavits do not discuss the subjective intent of the parties to be bound by language in those contracts, and D'Agostino, therefore, argues that we should affirm summary judgment to the extent damages can be traced to those order forms. It is unclear from the record, however, whether all of these contracts contained the terms that appeared in the October 1990 contract. Moreover, because article 8 requires a court to consider any "practices which the parties have established between themselves, usages and any subsequent conduct of the parties" in interpreting contracts, CISG, art. 8(3), whether the parties intended to adhere to the ten day limit for complaints, as stated on the reverse of the initial contract, will have an impact on whether MCC was bound to adhere to the limit on subsequent deliveries. Since material issues of fact remain regarding the interpretation of the remaining contracts between MCC and D'Agostino, we cannot affirm any portion of the district court's summary judgment in D'Agostino's favor.

CONCLUSION

MCC asks us to reverse the district court's grant of summary judgment in favor of D'Agostino. The district court's decision rests on pre-printed contractual terms and conditions incorporated on the reverse of a standard order form that MCC's president signed on the company's behalf. Nevertheless, we conclude that the CISG, which governs international contracts for the sale of goods, precludes summary judgment in this case because MCC has raised an issue of material fact concerning the parties' subjective intent to be bound by the terms on the reverse of the pre-printed contract. The CISG also precludes the application of the parol evidence rule, which would otherwise bar the consideration of evidence concerning a prior or contemporaneously negotiated oral agreement. Accordingly, we REVERSE the district court's grant of summary judgment and REMAND this case for further proceedings consistent with this opinion. ∎

Practices and Usages

practice: The method of performance established between parties by their actions or conduct.

usage: The customary method of performing or acting that is followed by a particular group of people, such as people within a particular trade.

Both Article 8(3) and Article 9(1) of CISG state that parties are bound by "any **practices** which they have established between themselves." Article 9(1) also allows a court to consider any **usages** that the parties agreed to,[64] and Article 9(2) lets it consider "a usage of which the parties knew or ought to have known and which in international trade is widely known to, and regularly observed by parties to contracts of the type involved in the particular trade concerned."

Article 9(2) was a compromise between the capitalist and communist delegates who participated in the drafting of CISG. In the former Soviet bloc, certainty was more important than flexibility. Trade usages are not considered unless a contract specifically adopted them and they did not violate statutory rules. In the Western world, on the other hand, flexibility and freedom of contract are more important than certainty. In some circumstances, trade usages apply in the West even when they contradict a statutory provision or the contract is silent.[65] The delegates ultimately agreed to let a court consider international trade usages, but only if they are "widely known" and "regularly observed."

Form

Traditionally, many countries have required that a contract be in writing. The English Statute of Frauds of 1677 required a signed writing to enforce a wide variety of contracts, including contracts for the sale of goods.[66] This same requirement reappears in the U.K. Sale of Goods Act of 1893, the U.S. Uniform Sales Act of 1896, and more recently in the U.S. Uniform Commercial Code.[67] In 1954, however, the United Kingdom repealed the writing requirement when it revised its Sale of Goods Act,[68] and this revision was adopted by many former colonies that had inherited the British Act.[69]

In the civil law countries, the requirement that a contract be in writing generally does not apply to commercial transactions.[70] In socialist countries, on the other hand, the need for certainty both in interpreting and enforcing foreign trade contracts is of paramount concern. The laws of the former Soviet Union, for example, imposed strict writing and registration requirements on foreign trade contracts.[71]

Most of the delegates involved in the drafting of CISG were of the opinion that a writing requirement is inconsistent with modern commercial practice, especially in market economies where speed and informality characterize so many transactions. The Soviet delegates, however, insisted that a writing requirement is important for protecting their country's longtime pattern

---

[64]An example would be a provision that trade terms, such as FOB, CIF, and the like, must comply with the International Chamber of Commerce's *Incoterms.*

[65]*See* United States, Uniform Commercial Code, §§ 1-205 and 2-208.

[66]*Charles II,* Year 29, chap. 3, § 17.

[67]United States, Uniform Commercial Code, § 2-201.

[68]United Kingdom, Law Reform (Enforcement of Contracts) Act (1954).

[69]Including Australia and Canada. *See* Kenneth C. Sutton, "Formation of Contract: Unity in International Sales of Goods," *University of Western Ontario Law Review,* vol. 16, pp. 148–150 (1977).

[70]E.g., France, Civil Code, Article 1341; and *see* Stojan Cigoj, "International Sales, Formation of Contracts," *Netherlands International Law Review,* vol. 23, pp. 270–272 (1976), which surveys the rules of many countries.

[71]John Honnold, Uniform *Law for International Sales under the 1980 United Nations Convention,* p. 155 (1982).

International Sales Company 1234 Main Street Pullman, Washington 99163 U.S.A.	**Pro Forma** **I N V O I C E**	
Date: **July 1, 2003**	Invoice No.	**030701**
To: **Compañia Mundial, S.A.** **567 Avenida de Mayo** **Buenos Aires** **1103 Argentina**	Order No.	
	Shipped:	
	Payment:	

Identifying Marks & Nos.	Qty	Description	Unit Price	Amt.
		<u>**Widgets**</u> **As per specification and samples forwarded by air parcel on June 7, 2003.**	<u>**FOB**</u> **port of Seattle** **US$**	
	Each Each Each	**Type "A"** **Type "B"** **Type "C"**	**1.23** **4.56** **7.89**	
		Packing: Each in inner box; 144 per double export carton weighing 14 kg and measuring 25 x 25 x 10 cm. **Shipment within 30 days after receipt of your firm order and payment.** **Payment: Irrevocable Letter of Credit for 100% of invoice value payable at sight through Washington National Bank of Pullman.** **Minimum Order: 144 each per type.** **Offer Duration: Effective until August 15, 2003.**		
		International Sales Company *Jane Doe* Jane Doe, Pres.		

EXHIBIT 10-3   An Offer — Pro Forma Invoice

of making foreign trade contracts. The result of this disagreement was a compromise. First, Article 11 of the Convention states:

A contract of sale need not be concluded in or evidenced by writing and is not subject to any other requirements as to form. It may be proved by any means, including witnesses.

Article 96, however, authorizes a contracting state "whose legislation requires contracts of sale to be concluded in or evidenced by writing" to make a declaration at the time of ratification that Article 11 (and some other provisions of the Convention involving requirements of form) "does not apply where any party has his place of business in that state."[72]

F. FORMATION OF THE CONTRACT

A contract is formed, and the parties are bound by its provisions, when an offer to buy or sell a good is accepted.[73]

The Offer

offer: A proposal by one person to another indicating an intention to enter into a contract under specified terms.

An **offer** is a proposal addressed to specific persons indicating an intention by the offeror to be bound to the sale or purchase of particular goods for a price.[74] The pro forma invoice shown in Exhibit 10-3 (page 555) is an example of an offer commonly used in international trade. Should there be some doubt whether a communication is an offer or not, CISG directs a court to ascertain if the offeror communicated an *intention* to be bound. This can be determined from the general rules of interpretation in Article 8 of the Convention—that is, by looking at the offeror's proposal within its full context, including any negotiations, any practices between the parties, any usages, and any subsequent conduct. It can also be determined from the subsidiary rules contained in Article 14.

Definiteness

According to Article 14, a "proposal is sufficiently definite if it indicates the goods and expressly or implicitly fixes or makes provision for determining the quantity and price." In other words, an offer must describe the goods with sufficient clarity that the parties know what is being offered for sale, and it must also state the quantity and price.

The price provision in Article 14 has to be read together with Article 55, which was added to the Convention at the last minute, during the Diplomatic Conference that adopted CISG. The delegates to the Conference were concerned that Article 14, standing alone, could be confusing. For example, if a buyer needs a particular part for a machine to keep a production line operational, he may ask the seller to rush it to him without first agreeing to the price, assuming that the seller will charge the customary price. In such a circumstance, the seller would probably treat the buyer's request as an offer. However, if the seller was unaware of the urgency of the buyer's request, the seller might well disregard it, since the proposal does not fix a price. If the seller did so, would the buyer be entitled to a remedy under CISG? Probably not, since Article 14 suggests that it is the duty of the offeror (the buyer in this example) to communicate the means for fixing a price. On the other hand, if the seller shipped the part anyway, and the buyer changed his mind, would the seller have a remedy? Possibly, because the buyer originally subjectively intended to be bound, even though he did not objectively indicate this. Remember that Article 8 allows courts to rely on subjective intent in interpreting the terms of a contract.

---

[72]UN Convention on Contracts for the International Sale of Goods, Article 12 (1980), further describes the effect of a state making a declaration under Article 96: "Any provision of Article 11, Article 29 or Part II of this Convention that allows a contract of sale or its modification or termination by agreement or any offer, acceptance or other indication of intention to be made in any form other than in writing does not apply where any party has his place of business in a contracting state which has made a declaration under Article 96 of this Convention. The parties may not derogate from or vary the effect of this Article."

　　A few provisions of the Convention refer to the use of a writing. Article 21(2) refers to a "letter or other writing containing a late acceptance," and Article 29(2) states that a "contract in writing which contains a provision requiring any modification or termination by agreement to be in writing may not be otherwise modified or terminated by agreement." Neither of these requires that a writing be signed. Article 13 states that "for the purposes of this Convention 'writing' includes telegram and telex."

[73]*Id.,* Article 23.

[74]*Id.,* Article 14(1): "A proposal for concluding a contract addressed to one or more specific persons constitutes an offer if it is sufficiently definite and indicates the intention of the offeror to be bound in case of acceptance. A proposal is sufficiently definite if it indicates the goods and expressly or implicitly fixes or makes provision for determining the quantity and price."

To avoid any possible confusion, Article 55 was added to CISG. It provides:

> Where a contract has been validly concluded but does not expressly or implicitly fix or make provision for determining the price, the parties are considered in the absence of any indication to the contrary, to have impliedly made reference to the price generally charged at the time of the conclusion of the contract for such goods sold under comparable circumstances in the trade concerned.

Thus, even though an offer does not "expressly or implicitly" fix a price, it is still a valid offer. The offeror is assumed to have "impliedly made reference to the price generally charged."[75]

Specific Offerees

For a proposal to be an offer, it must be addressed to "one or more specific persons." Proposals made to the public are ordinarily intended to be nothing more than invitations to negotiate. For example, an advertisement in a newspaper for the sale of goods at a particular price might put the advertiser in the awkward position of having to deliver more goods than he has on hand because of heavier than expected demand, or of absorbing a substantial loss because of an increase in the cost of the goods between the time the advertisement was placed and the time it appeared. CISG, accordingly, adopts the rule that public offers are only invitations to negotiate "unless the contrary is clearly indicated."[76]

Effectiveness of an Offer

An offer becomes effective only after it reaches the offeree.[77] Thus, offers—including offers that promise that they are irrevocable—can be withdrawn prior to their reaching the offeree.[78]

Revocation

revocation: Cancellation by the offeror of an offer.

Offers that do not state that they are irrevocable can be **revoked** any time before the offeree *dispatches* an acceptance.[79] This rule is based on the famous English common law "post box" rule,[80] which limits the ability of the offeror to cancel an offer where the offeree has reasonably relied on it. Under the common law, the acceptance had to be returned using the same medium in which the offer was originally sent (e.g., a mailed offer had to be accepted by mail). Under CISG, the acceptance can be sent by any means.

Firm Offers

firm offer: An offer that the offeror promises to keep open for a fixed period of time.

Under traditional Anglo-American common law rules, the doctrine of consideration prevents an offeror from making an offer irrevocable. An option contract (i.e., one in which the offeree pays the offeror for the promise to keep the offer open) has to be used. The doctrine of consideration does not apply to CISG, however, and **firm offers** (i.e., ones where the offeror promises to keep the offer open for a fixed period) are enforceable. Most common law countries have modified the traditional rule, allowing offerees to enforce firm offers made by merchants if they are made in writing, signed by the offeror, and are effective for only a limited time period.[81] CISG goes further than this. The promise of irrevocability does not have to be signed,

---

[75]*Id.,* Article 55. If a contract fixes a price based on weight but does not specify the gross or net weight, Article 56 says that "in case of doubt it is to be determined by the net weight."

[76]*Id.,* Article 14(2).

[77]*Id.,* Article 24, defines when a communication reaches an addressee as follows: "For the purposes of this Part of the Convention, an offer, declaration of acceptance or any other indication of intention 'reaches' the addressee when it is made orally to him or delivered by any other means to him personally, to his place of business or mailing address or, if he does not have a place of business or mailing address, to his habitual residence."

[78]*Id.,* Article 15.

[79]*Id.,* Article 16(1).

[80]The "post box" rule applies in most Anglo-American common law countries, including England, Australia, Canada, New Zealand, and the United States. The original cases developing the rule are Adams v. Lindsell, *English Reports,* vol. 106, p. 250 (1818), and Dunlop v. Higgins, *English Reports,* vol. 9, p. 805 (House of Lords, 1848).

[81]*See* United States, Uniform Commercial Code, § 2–205.

Compañia Mundial, S.A.
567 Avenida de Mayo
Buenos Aires
1103 Argentina

PURCHASE ORDER

Date: **August 2, 2003**	No.	080203

To: **International Sales Company** **1234 Main Street** **Pullman, Washington** **99163** **U.S.A.**	Date Required:	**Sept. 15, 2003**
	Deliver to:	**Address above**
	Packing:	**Standard Export**
	Payment:	**Irrevocable Letter**

Identifying Marks & Nos.	Qty.	Description	Unit Price	Amt.
		<u>FOB Port of Seattle</u>	<u>US $</u>	<u>US $</u>
	Each	Type "A"	1.23	531.36
	Each	Type "B"	4.56	1313.28
	Each	Type "C"	7.89	<u>1136.16</u>
				2980.80

Packing: As per your offer sheet, each in cardboard inner box, 144 per double export carton weighing 14 kg and measuring 25 x 25 x 10 cm.
Shipment via M/V El Mar from port of Seattle to Buenos Aires
Payment: Irrevocable Letter of Credit for 100% of invoice value payable at sight through Banco del Sur, Buenos Aires, to Washington National Bank of Pullman.
Notify party: Agencia Rosas, 989 Calle de los Marineros, Buenos Aires, 1117 Argentina

Case Mark: | Cia Mundial |
Buenos Aires
Made in USA
C/No. _____

Accepted	Confirmed
_____	*Juan Valdez*
	J. Valdez, Gte.

EXHIBIT 10-4 An Acceptance—Purchase Order

does not have to be in writing, and there is no time limitation. A firm offer is enforceable if the offeror makes the offer irrevocable or if the offeree can reasonably rely on conduct that implies that the offer is firm.[82]

Acceptance

acceptance: Agreement to enter into a contract proposed by an offeror.

A contract comes into existence at the point in time an offer is accepted. **Acceptance** is a statement or conduct by the offeree indicating assent that is communicated to the offeror. The form or mode in which an offeree expresses assent is unlimited; however, the offeree must communicate his assent to the offeror.[83] The purchase order shown in Exhibit 10-4 (page 558) is an example of an acceptance commonly used in international trade.

Silence

Silence or inactivity does not, in and of itself, constitute acceptance. For example, if a seller sends a buyer an offer that says, "I know that this is such a good deal that I will assume that you have accepted unless I hear otherwise," the fact that the buyer does not respond will not create a contract. A different result would occur, however, if the seller were to send the buyer an invitation to negotiate that says, "Unless you hear otherwise from me within three days after I receive your order, I will deliver the widgets you need at $100 each." In such a case, the seller's silence would constitute an acceptance. In the first instance, the seller attempted to force acceptance on the buyer. In the second, the seller voluntarily assumed the duty to respond.

Time of Acceptance

Acceptance must be received by the offeror within the time period specified in the offer. If no time period is given, acceptance must be received within a "reasonable" time. If the offer is oral, the acceptance must be made immediately, unless the circumstances indicate otherwise.[84]

In devising the acceptance rule for CISG, the drafters opted for the receipt theory used in civil law countries. In common law countries, the dispatch or post box theory is used. The difference between the two relates to the allocation of risk when an acceptance is lost or delayed. For example, a buyer sends a seller an acceptance through the mail and the acceptance is lost. If the dispatch theory were applied, a contract would have come into existence at the time the acceptance was mailed, and the seller would be required to perform. Under the receipt rule adopted by CISG, however, no contract would exist, and the buyer would be left empty-handed. The reason the drafters chose the receipt rule was a perception that it more fairly allocates responsibility for loss or delay. Because it is the offeree who chooses the medium through which to send a response, it is the offeree who is better able to avoid the risk of loss or delay, and therefore CISG imposes responsibility for avoiding that risk on the offeree.[85]

In Case 10–3, the court was asked to determine if an offer had been made and if a contract came into effect at the time the offeror received the offeree's acceptance.

---

[82]UN Convention on Contracts for the International Sale of Goods, Article 16(2) (1980).
[83]*Id.*, Article 18(1).
[84]*Id.*, Article 18(2).
[85]*Id.*, Article 21(1), allows an offeror to treat a late acceptance as valid "if without delay the offeror orally so informs the offeree or dispatches a notice to that effect." Article 21(2) says that an offeror who receives a late acceptance under such circumstances that he can see that it was delayed in transmission must give the acceptance effect "unless, without delay, the offeror orally informs the offeree that he considers his offer as having lapsed or dispatches a notice to that effect."

Case 10–3   United Technologies International, Inc. v. Magyar Légi Közlekedési Vállalat   ⌒

Hungary, Metropolitan Court of Budapest, 1992.
Case No. 3.G.50.289/1991/32.[86]

Magyar Légi Közlekedési Vállalat (Málev Hungarian Airlines) planned to buy wide-bodied jet aircraft either from Boeing Aircraft Co. of the United States or Airbus Industries of Europe. It planned to buy the engines for these aircraft separately. After completing negotiations for engines with the Pratt & Whitney division of United Technologies International, Málev Hungarian Airlines reneged on going forward with the purchase. United Technologies International thereupon sued in the Metropolitan Court of Budapest to obtain a declaratory judgment holding that a valid contract existed between Pratt & Whitney and Málev.

JUDGE PISKOLTI:

* * *

The Offer

The plaintiff [Pratt & Whitney] delivered an offer to the defendant's [Málev Hungarian Airlines'] General Manager on December 14, 1990. This offer described Pratt & Whitney's financial assistance plans, product warranties, as well as the support services that it would provide for its PW4056 engine. The offer updated and amended an earlier offer made on November 9, 1990. It said that plaintiff was "pleased to submit this revised support services proposal in connection with Málev Hungarian Airlines' purchase of two 767-200ER aircraft, powered by Pratt & Whitney PW4056 engines (with an option to purchase a third such aircraft), and the purchase of one PW4056 spare engine (with an option to buy a second spare), all of which are scheduled to be delivered as stated in Attachment 1." . . . The plaintiff's offer also set out a complete technical description of the PW4000 series engines. . . .

Paragraph Y of the plaintiff's offer is entitled "Purchase Agreement." This states that the buyer agrees to buy, and the seller agrees to sell, four new PW4056 engines to be mounted on two 767-200ER aircraft according to the attached schedule. The buyer also is given an option to buy two more new PW4056 engines in the event that it exercises its option to buy an additional 767-200ER aircraft. Additionally, the buyer agrees to buy one PW4056 engine as a spare. . . . The plaintiff's Purchase Agreement also establishes a deadline of December 21, 1990, for the buyer to accept the offer. If the buyer needs additional information or assistance, it is encouraged to contact the plaintiff's legal and accounting staff. In this regard, the plaintiff's offer notes that the buyer's acceptance is conditional on the agreement being approved by the governments of both Hungary and the United States.

* * *

Extension of the Offer

In a separate document, also delivered to the defendant on December 14, 1990, the plaintiff offered to sell to the defendant its PW4152 or PW4156/A engines. Again, this offer updated and amended an earlier offer made on November 9, 1990. It also described the assistance the plaintiff would provide the defendant with respect to defendant's purchase of two A310-300 aircraft (with an option to buy a third) that were to be equipped either the two PW4152 or two PW4156/A engines (with the option to a third engine) according to the attached schedule. . . . Additionally, paragraph W of this offer, which is entitled "Spare Engine Price," states that the base price of a new PW4152 is $5,552,675 and the base price of a new PW4156/A engine is $5,847,675. Finally, once again, December 21, 1990, is set as the date by which the buyer must accept the plaintiff's offer.

* * *

The parties have stipulated that their relationship is governed by the United Nations Convention on Contracts for the International Sale of Goods (CISG).[87] According to CISG, Article 14(1), "a contract addressed

---

[86]Another English translation of this case is posted on the Internet at www.cisg.law.pace.edu/cisg/wais/db/cases2/920110h1.html.
[87]The Convention is in force in Hungary. *See* Law Decree No. 20 of 1987. [The Convention was also in force in the United States at the time of this dispute.]

MAP 10-3   Hungary (1992)

to one or more specific persons constitutes an offer if it is sufficiently definite and indicates the intention of the offeror to be bound in case of acceptance." Additionally, "[a] proposal is sufficiently definite if it indicates the goods and expressly or implicitly fixes or makes provision for determining the quantity and the price."

It is clear from the circumstances that the plaintiff's proposal was addressed to the defendant. What needs to be ascertained, first, is whether the offer sufficiently describes the goods involved. The first of the offers described above clearly states that the goods offered for sale are PW4056 and PW4060 engines and the second offer clearly states that goods offered are the PW4152 and PW4156/A engines. . . . The fact that the defendant has the right to choose between the listed engines, depending on whether it elects to buy the Boeing 767-200ER aircraft (which requires either the PW4056 or the PW4060 engine) or the Airbus A310-300 (which requires the PW4152 or the PW4156/A engine) does not effect the description of the goods. The offer gives the buyer the right to choose between offered engines. Such a unilateral right is common in . . . commercial practice and it does not make the description of the goods uncertain, as the defendant has argued. Contrary to the defendant's argument, the plaintiff's proposals unambiguously describe the goods offered to the defendant.

Defendant also argues that the plaintiff's proposals could not be construed to be offers because they do not establish the quantity of the goods involved [because the defendant is allowed to choose between taking two or

three engines]. This argument is also untenable. Again, the offer gives the unilateral right to the defendant to determine the quantity.

That is, the defendant is able to determine the quantity involved based on its choice as to the number of aircraft. . . . As the plaintiff has pointed out in oral argument, the plaintiff's proposal clearly indicates that the defendant intended to purchase at least two aircraft, whether they were made by Boeing or Airbus, and that the defendant had an option to purchase a third aircraft. If the defendant does not choose to exercise its option to buy a third aircraft, the quantity specified in the plaintiff's proposal is for four engines and one spare engine. If the defendant does choose to exercise its option, then quantity would be six engines and one spare.

The defendant's argument that the plaintiff's offers fails to state a price is also unfounded. The plaintiff's written offers (described above) state that the price of a PW4056 engine is $5,552,675 and the price of the PW4152 and PW4156/A engine is $5,847,675. . . .

Finally, the plaintiff's proposals include a schedule setting out the time for the delivery of the engines, so the defendant could not be uncertain as to this either.

In light of the above, it is clear that the plaintiff's proposal of December 14, 1990, is an offer. It clearly describes the goods, states the price and quantity, and sets out the time for delivery. Thus, the plaintiff's offer satisfies all of requirements of Article 14(1) of CISG.

The Acceptance

On December 21, 1990, the defendant sent a letter of acceptance to the plaintiff. This was within the deadline set by the plaintiff. In its letter of acceptance the defendant informed the plaintiff that it had chosen the PW4000 series engine for its fleet of wide-bodied aircraft. Moreover, it gave its reasons for doing so (namely, that its decision was based on a thorough technical and economic evaluation). . . .

The letter unambiguously states it accepts all of the terms and conditions set out in the plaintiff's proposal of December 14, 1990. It only asks that the letter be kept confidential until the parties can make a joint public announcement. . . .

. . . According to Article 18(1) of CISG, an acceptance is "[a] statement made by, or other conduct of, the offeree indicating assent to an offer is an acceptance." It is clear that the defendant's letter of acceptance is just that.

Article 19(1) of CISG adds that "[a] reply to an offer which purports to be an acceptance but contains additions, limitations, or other modifications is a rejection of the offer and constitutes a counter-offer." The request made by the defendant at the end of its letter of acceptance [to keep the letter confidential until a joint announcement could be made] cannot be construed as an addition, limitation, or other modification. It is not a counter-offer. This being so, the defendant's letter of acceptance is an acceptance. That being so, it had the effect of creating a contract between the plaintiff and defendant.

* * *

CISG, Article 23, provides that "[a] contract is concluded at the moment when an acceptance of an offer becomes effective in accordance with the provisions of this Convention." Accordingly, the present contract came into effect when the plaintiff received the defendant's letter of acceptance. In other words, the effect of the defendant's letter of acceptance agreeing to all of the terms of the plaintiff's offer was to create a contract between them.

* * *

[The Condition Requiring Government Approval]

. . . Section 215(1) of the Hungarian *Civil Code* states, that, if the conclusion of a contract requires the approval of a third person, or official approval, the contract will not come into force until the approval is obtained. . . . Section 228(1) of the *Civil Code* states that, if the parties agree to terms that makes a contract's entry into force dependent on an the occurrence of an uncertain future event (a condition precedent), the agreement will not come into force until the event occurs. And Section 228(2) provides that, if the parties provide for the termination of a contract upon the occurrence an uncertain future event (a condition subsequent), the contract will terminate upon the occurrence of that event.

Notably, there are no provisions of this sort to be found in the CISG. Accordingly, these provisions cannot be used in ascertaining the validity of the contract under consideration. . . .

While there are no provisions in CISG describing the effect of a condition, there is also nothing in the CISG that forbids the parties from agreeing to a condition. Thus, the provision in the plaintiff's offer that "Málev Hungarian Airlines' acceptance of this offer is conditional on the agreement being approved by the governments of both Hungary and the United States" is not ineffective. However, the exact nature of the provision's effect has to be determined in light of the CISG's directive that a contract comes into existence at the time that an acceptance is received by the offeror. The parties may not ignore this mandate, even though they are otherwise free to set the terms and conditions of their contract.

During the course of the oral hearings in this case, it became evident to the court that the plaintiff viewed the condition that it had included in the contract as a device for avoiding governmental interference . . . and not as a condition precedent to the creation of a contract. . . .

* * *

[Only after the plaintiff received the defendant's acceptance,] did it become clear to the plaintiff that the defendant, although owned by the State, was an independent company that did not require the State's approval to make decisions. The Hungarian Ministry of Transportation, Communication, and Construction eventually did make a declaration in connection with the contract at hand, but this was to assure the plaintiff that the defendant had the right to act on its own.

As for the approval required from the U.S. government, the plaintiff was only thinking in terms of obtaining the appropriate export license. . . .

In sum, the plaintiff intended, and the defendant agreed to, a condition subsequent. That is, to a condition that would terminate the contract. They did not agree to a condition precedent; a condition that must be fulfilled before a contract can come into effect.

Considering all of the above, it is the opinion of this court that the parties entered into a valid and enforceable contract. ■

Assent by Performance of an Act

If the offeror asks for performance of an act rather than the indication of acceptance, the acceptance is effective at the moment the act is performed. However, the offer, a trade usage, or the practice of the parties must make it clear that the offeree is not required to notify the offeror.[88] Consider the following example. A buyer sends a seller the following offer: "Ship me 100 widgets at your customary price for delivery on or before May 31." The seller responds by shipping the goods for delivery on May 30. The day after the goods are shipped, however, the buyer calls the seller and withdraws his offer. Can the buyer withdraw the offer?

---

[88]UN Convention on Contracts for the International Sale of Goods, Article 18(3) (1980).

The buyer might argue that Article 18(2) says that a contract only becomes effective when "the indication of assent *reaches* the offeror." Here, of course, the buyer would not have been aware of the acceptance until the goods arrived. The seller would, however, be able to rely on Article 18(3), which says that an offeree "may indicate assent by performing an act . . . without [giving] notice to the offeror." The seller shipped the goods precisely in the manner requested by the buyer, and the buyer's offer did not ask for notice of acceptance or even confirmation of shipment.

Withdrawal

Because an acceptance is normally not effective until the offeror receives it, an offeree may **withdraw** his acceptance any time before or simultaneous with its receipt.[89]

withdrawal: Cancellation by the offeree of an acceptance.

rejection: Refusal by an offeree to become a party to a proposed contract.

Rejection

A **rejection** becomes effective when it reaches the offeror.[90] If an offeree were to dispatch both a rejection and an acceptance at the same time, the one that reached the offeror first would be the one given effect.

Acceptance with Modifications

A seller sends an offer to a buyer. The buyer responds with an acceptance that modifies some of the terms in the offer. Is there a contract?

This scenario—commonly called the "Battle of the Forms"—occurs when merchants use preprinted forms both to make offers and to send back acceptances. The typed-in descriptions commonly match up; it is the "fine print" on the back of the forms, however, that contains differences.[91] Under CISG, if the inconsistencies are "material" the would-be acceptance is a counteroffer.[92] Article 19(3) states:

> Additional or different terms relating, among other things, to the price, payment, quality of the goods, place and time of delivery, extent of one party's liability to the other, or the settlement of disputes are considered to alter the terms of the offer materially.

Terms that are not material are considered to be proposals for addition that will become part of the contract unless the offeror promptly objects.[93]

Case 10–4 compares the way that CISG and the U.S. Uniform Commercial Code treat acceptances with additional terms.

---

[89]*Id.*, Article 22.
[90]*Id.*, Article 17.
[91]One businessperson wryly observed when responding to a survey on the use of forms that business would come to a halt if buyers and sellers "read the backsides of the other's forms." Quoted in John Honnold, *Uniform Law for International Sales under the 1980 United Nations Convention,* p. 166 (1982).
[92]UN Convention on Contracts for the International Sale of Goods, Article 19(1) (1980).
[93]*Id.*, Article 19(2). This CISG rule is based on legislation originally drafted in the Scandinavian countries. Article 19 is based on Article 6 of the Swedish Conclusion of Contracts Act (1915). The same act was adopted in Denmark in 1917, Norway in 1918, Finland in 1929, and Iceland in 1936. John Honnold, *Uniform Law for International Sales under the 1980 United Nations Convention,* p. 191 (1982).

Case 10–4   Filanto, SpA v. Chilewich International Corp.

United States, District Court, Southern District of New York.
Federal Supplement, vol. 789, p. 1229 (1992).

Filanto, SpA, the plaintiff, was an Italian corporation engaged in the manufacture and sale of footwear. Chilewich International Corp. (Chilewich), the

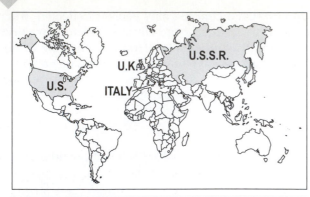

MAP 10-4   United States, United Kingdom, Union of Soviet Socialist Republics and Italy (1991)

defendant, was an export-import firm incorporated in New York.

On February 28, 1989, Chilewich's agent in the United Kingdom, Byerly Johnson, Ltd., signed a contract with the Soviet Union's Foreign Economic Association (known as Raznoexport) that obligated Byerly Johnson and Chilewich to deliver footwear to Raznoexport in what is now Russia. This contract (the Russian Contract) contained an arbitration clause that read, in part, as follows:

> *All disputes or differences which may arise out of or in connection with the present Contract are to be settled, jurisdiction of ordinary courts being excluded, by the Arbitration at the USSR Chamber of Commerce and Industry, Moscow, in accordance with the Regulations of the said Arbitration. [sic]*

In order to fulfill the Russian Contract, Chilewich and Byerly Johnson met with Filanto, who was then supplying them with footwear under various ongoing contracts. On July 27, 1989, Mr. Melvin Chilewich sent a letter to Mr. Antonio Filograna, Chief Executive Officer of Filanto, which summarized the negotiations at this meeting, and then stated:

> *Attached please find our contract to cover our purchase from you. Same is governed by the conditions which are enumerated in the standard contract with the Soviet buyers [the Russian Contract], copy of which is also enclosed.*

Filanto claims that it sent a reply on September 2, 1989, that excluded the arbitration provision of the Russian Contract and that requested Chilewich to accept Filanto's counteroffer. Chilewich claimed not to have received this correspondence.

On March 13, 1990, Chilewich sent Filanto a Memorandum Agreement to confirm that Filanto was to deliver

a total of 250,000 pairs of boots to Chilewich. This memo again referred to the arbitration provision in the Russian Contract. Filanto did not immediately respond and Chilewich proceeded to obtain a letter of credit in Filanto's favor in the sum of $2,595,600 on May 11, 1990.

On August 7, 1990, Filanto signed and returned the Memorandum Agreement. Filanto's cover letter, however, stated that it would not be bound by several provisions of the Russian Contract, including the arbitration provision and provision governing procedures for making claims.

Chilewich accepted delivery and paid Filanto for 100,000 boots on September 15, 1990. Then in January 1991, Chilewich accepted and paid for another 60,000 boots. However, because Chilewich claimed that some of these boots were defective, it never purchased the 90,000 boots that made up the balance of its original order. Filanto, as a consequence, filed a complaint in a United States federal trial court in New York on May 14, 1991, alleging breach of contract. Chilewich answered the complaint by asking the Court to stop the proceedings while the matter was arbitrated in the Soviet Union.

CHIEF JUDGE BRIEANT: . . .

. . . [The law] to be applied in this case is found in the *United Nations Convention on Contracts for the International Sale of Goods* (the "Sale of Goods Convention"). This Convention, ratified by the Senate in 1986, is a self-executing agreement which entered into force between the United States and other signatories, including Italy, on January 1, 1988. Although there is as yet virtually no U.S. case law interpreting the Sale of Goods Convention, it may safely be predicted that this will change: absent a choice-of-law provision, and with certain exclusions not here relevant, the Convention governs all contracts between parties with places of business in different nations, so long as both nations are signatories to the Convention. Since the contract alleged in this case most certainly was formed, if at all, after January 1, 1988, and since both the United States and Italy are signatories to the Convention, the Court will [apply] . . . the substantive international law of contracts embodied in the Sale of Goods Convention.[94]

Not surprisingly, the parties offer varying interpretations of the numerous letters and documents exchanged between them. The Court will briefly summarize their respective contentions.

Defendant Chilewich contends that the Memorandum Agreement dated March 13, which it signed and sent to Filanto was an offer. It then argues that Filanto's retention of the letter, along with its subsequent acceptance of Chilewich's performance under the

---
[94]United Nations Convention on Contracts for the International Sale of Goods (1980), Article 1 (1)(a).

Agreement—the furnishing of the May 11 letter of credit—estops it from denying its acceptance of the contract. Although phrased as an estoppel argument, this contention is better viewed as an acceptance by conduct argument, e.g., that in light of the parties' course of dealing, Filanto had a duty timely to inform Chilewich that it objected to the incorporation by reference of all the terms of the Russian Contract. Under this view, the return of the Memorandum Agreement, signed by Filanto, on August 7, 1990, along with the covering letter purporting to exclude parts of the Russian Contract, was ineffective as a matter of law as a rejection of the March 13 offer, because this occurred some five months after Filanto received the Memorandum Agreement and two months after Chilewich furnished the Letter of Credit. Instead, in Chilewich's view, this action was a proposal for modification of the March 13 Agreement. Chilewich rejected this proposal, by its letter of August 7 to Byerly Johnson, and the August 29 fax by Johnson to Italian Trading SRL, which communication Filanto acknowledges receiving. Accordingly, Filanto under this interpretation is bound by the written terms of the March 13 Memorandum Agreement; since that agreement incorporates by reference the Russian Contract containing the arbitration provision, Filanto is bound to arbitrate.

Plaintiff Filanto's interpretation of the evidence is rather different. While Filanto apparently agrees that the March 13 Memorandum Agreement was indeed an offer, it characterizes its August 7 return of the signed Memorandum Agreement with the covering letter as a counteroffer. While defendant contends that under *Uniform Commercial Code* § 2-207 this action would be viewed as an acceptance with a proposal for a material modification, the *Uniform Commercial Code*, as previously noted does not apply to this case, because the State Department undertook to fix something that was not broken by helping to create the Sale of Goods Convention which varies from the Uniform Commercial Code in many significant ways. Instead, under this analysis, Article 19(1) of the Sale of Goods Convention would apply. That section, as the Commentary to the Sale of Goods Convention notes, reverses the rule of *Uniform Commercial Code* § 2-207, and reverts to the common law rule that "A reply to an offer which purports to be an acceptance but contains additions, limitations or other modifications is a rejection of the offer and constitutes a counteroffer."[95] Although the Convention, like the *Uniform Commercial Code*, does state that nonmaterial

terms do become part of the contract unless objected to,[96] the Convention treats inclusion (or deletion) of an arbitration provision as "material."[97] The August 7 letter, therefore, was a counteroffer which, according to Filanto, Chilewich accepted by its letter dated September 27, 1990. Though that letter refers to and acknowledges the "contractual obligations" between the parties, it is doubtful whether it can be characterized as an acceptance.

Since the issue of whether and how a contract between these parties was formed is obviously related to the issue of whether Chilewich breached any contractual obligations, the Court will direct its analysis to whether there was objective conduct evidencing an intent to be bound with respect to the arbitration provision.

The Court is satisfied on this record that there was indeed an agreement to arbitrate between these parties.

There is simply no satisfactory explanation as to why Filanto failed to object to the incorporation by reference of the Russian Contract in a timely fashion. As noted above, Chilewich had in the meantime commenced its performance under the Agreement, and the Letter of Credit it furnished Filanto on May 11 itself mentioned the Russian Contract. An offeree who, knowing that the offeror has commenced performance, fails to notify the offeror of its objection to the terms of the contract within a reasonable time will, under certain circumstances, be deemed to have assented to those terms.[98] The Sale of Goods Convention itself recognizes this rule.

Article 18(1), provides that "A statement made by or other conduct of the offeree indicating assent to an offer is an acceptance". Although mere "silence or inactivity" does not constitute acceptance,[99] the Court may consider previous relations between the parties in assessing whether a party's conduct constituted acceptance.[100] In this case, in light of the extensive course of prior dealing between these parties, Filanto was certainly under a duty to alert Chilewich in timely fashion to its objections to the terms of the March 13 Memorandum Agreement—particularly since Chilewich had repeatedly referred it to the Russian Contract and Filanto had had a copy of that document for some time.

. . . [Filanto's letter of June 21, 1991, to Byerly Johnson], which responds to claims by Johnson that some of the boots that were supplied were defective, expressly relies on Section 9 of the Russian Contract—another section which Filanto had in its earlier correspondence

---

[95]*Id.,* Article 19(1).
[96]*Id.,* Article 19(2).
[97]*Id.,* Article 19(3).
[98]*Restatement (Second) of Contracts,* § 69 (1981).
[99]United Nations Convention on Contracts for the International Sale of Goods (1980), Article 18(1).
[100]*Id.,* Article 8(3).

purported to exclude. The Sale of Goods Convention specifically directs that "[i]n determining the intent of a party . . . due consideration is to be given to . . . any subsequent conduct of the parties."[101] In this case, as the letter postdates the partial performance of the contract, it is particularly strong evidence that Filanto recog-

nized itself to be bound by all the terms of the Russian Contract.

In light of these factors . . . the Court holds that Filanto is bound by the terms of the March 13 Memorandum Agreement, and so must arbitrate its dispute in Moscow. ■

---

[101]*Id.*

G. GENERAL STANDARDS OF PERFORMANCE

CISG imposes general standards of performance on both the buyer and seller. In general, both parties are entitled to get from their contract what they expect.[102] A party that fails to perform accordingly is in breach of contract. When one party breaches, the other party may avoid the contract or make a demand for specific performance.

Fundamental Breach

fundamental breach: A failure to perform that substantially deprives the other party of that which he was entitled to expect.

When one party substantially fails to deliver what the other reasonably anticipated receiving, there is a **fundamental breach** Article 25 defines a fundamental breach this way:

A breach of contract committed by one of the parties is fundamental if it results in such detriment to the other party as substantially to deprive him of what he is entitled to expect under the contract, unless the party in breach did not foresee and a reasonable person of the same kind in the same circumstances would not have foreseen such a result.

Avoidance

avoidance: Notification by a party that it is canceling a contract and returning everything already received.

If there has been a fundamental breach, one remedy available to the injured party is **avoidance** (i.e., notification by a party that it is canceling the contract). To be entitled to avoid a contract, however, the injured party must—in all cases—notify the other party[103] and be able to return any goods he has already received.[104]

When a party avoids, only the obligation to perform is affected. Avoidance does not cancel (a) any provision in the contract concerning the settlement of disputes (such as arbitration, choice-of-law, or choice-of-forum clauses) or (b) any other provisions governing the rights and duties of the parties "consequent upon the avoidance of the contract."[105]

Requests for Specific Performance

CISG authorizes an injured party to ask a court "to require performance" if the other party fails to carry out his obligations.[106] A court is not obliged to grant this request, however, unless the court can do so under its own domestic rules.[107]

specific performance: A court order directing a party to carry out the obligations it had contractually promised to do.

What constitutes **specific performance** varies from country to country, and the rule in CISG reflects the difficulties the drafters had in defining the concept. In common law countries, the concept is fairly narrow, referring to a court decree that compels a defendant to do a specific act, such as delivering goods. Disobeying the decree can be serious. It is treated as a "contempt of court" punishable by fine or imprisonment. In the civil law countries, the idea of "requiring

---

[102]UN Convention on Contracts for the International Sale of Goods, Articles 53 and 54 (1980).
[103]*Id.,* Article 26.
[104]*Id.,* Article 82.
[105]*Id.,* Article 81(1).
[106]*Id.,* Article 46, provides that "[t]he buyer may require performance by the seller of his obligations," and Article 62 states that "[t]he seller may require the buyer to pay the price, take delivery or perform his other obligations."
[107]*Id.,* Article 28.

performance" is much broader and includes such things as the buying of a substitute at the defaulting party's expense; but the sanctions are not as burdensome—a court may not impose a fine or throw a disobedient party into jail.[108]

The prerequisites that must be shown before a party can obtain specific performance also vary. The United Kingdom's Sale of Goods Act of 1893, which is widely followed in the common law world, states that a court, "if it thinks fit," may enter a decree requiring a party in breach of contract to deliver "specific or ascertained goods."[109] The difficulty of determining when goods are "specific or ascertained," however, is a problem that limits the application of this section. In the United States, the Uniform Commercial Code allows for decrees of specific performance that "a court may deem just," so long as "the goods are unique" or "in other proper circumstances."[110] In the civil law countries, a party is "entitled" to require performance. Civil judges do not have the discretion to deny a decree, as their common law brethren do, nor is the remedy limited by the nature of the goods involved.[111]

H. SELLER'S OBLIGATIONS

A seller is required to (a) deliver the goods, (b) hand over any documents relating to them, and (c) ensure that the goods conform with the contract.[112] If a contract fails to specify how this is done, CISG provides rules to fill in the gaps.

Place for Delivery

The place for delivery is the place agreed to in the contract; otherwise it is (a) the first carrier's place of business if the contract involves the carriage of goods or (b) the place where the parties knew the goods were located or were to be manufactured or produced.[113]

If the contract requires the seller to arrange for shipping but does not specify the carrier or the terms, the transportation selected must be "appropriate in the circumstances" and made "according to the usual terms for such transportation."[114] Also, if the seller is not required to arrange for insurance, "he must, at the buyer's request, provide him with all available information necessary to enable him to effect such insurance."[115]

In addition to providing insurance information when requested, the seller must, at the time he delivers the goods to a carrier, either (a) identify to the carrier both the goods and the buyer "by markings on the goods, by shipping documents or otherwise," or (b) "give the buyer notice of the consignment of the specifying goods."[116] Failure to comply with this requirement is a breach of the contract, and the seller will be liable for any damages that may result.[117]

Time for Delivery

The seller is to deliver the goods on the date fixed in the contract, or, if no date is fixed, within a reasonable time after the conclusion of the contract.[118] If a time period is provided, the seller may deliver at any time within that period, unless the contract expressly says that the buyer is to choose the time.[119]

---

[108]G. H. Treitel, "Remedies for Breach of Contract," *International Encyclopedia of Comparative Law,* vol. 7, chap. 16, § 9 (1976).
[109]United Kingdom, Sale of Goods Act, § 52 (1893).
[110]United States, Uniform Commercial Code, § 2-716(1).
[111]*See* Konrad Zweigert, in *Some Comparative Aspects of the Law Relating to Sale of Goods,* p. 5 (International Comparative Law Quarterly, Publication No. 9, 1964).
[112]UN Convention on Contracts for the International Sale of Goods, Article 30 (1980).
[113]*Id.,* Article 31.
[114]*Id.,* Article 32(2).
[115]*Id.,* Article 32(3).
[116]*Id.,* Article 32(1).
[117]*Id.,* Articles 45, 49, and 74.
[118]*Id.,* Article 33.
[119]*Id.,* Article 33(b).

The Turning Over of Documents

At the time and place for delivery, a seller must turn over any documents relating to the goods that the contract requires. If he does so early, he has the right to "cure any lack of conformity in the documents," so long as this does not cause the buyer "unreasonable inconvenience or unreasonable expense."[120]

Conformity of Goods

Article 35(1) of CISG states that the seller "must deliver goods which are of the quantity, quality, and description required by the contract and which are contained or packaged in the manner required by the contract." This provision is similar to many warranty provisions found in common law countries, with the notable exception that it does not use the terms *warranty* or *guarantee*.[121] This is important, because the seller's obligation (and the buyer's right) arises—and can be waived—without the use of these terms.

Determining Conformity

The rules for determining whether the goods conform are set out in Article 35(2).

Except where the parties have agreed otherwise, the goods do not conform with the contract unless they:

(a) are fit for the purposes for which goods of the same description would ordinarily be used;

(b) are fit for any particular purpose expressly or impliedly made known to the seller at the time of the conclusion of the contract, except where the circumstances show that the buyer did not rely, or that it was unreasonable for him to rely, on the seller's skill and judgment;

(c) possess the qualities of goods which the seller has held out to the buyer as a sample or model;

(d) are contained or packaged in the same manner usual for such goods or, where there is no such manner, in a manner adequate to preserve and protect the goods.

Third-Party Claims

Goods also do not conform if they are subject to third-party claims. Third-party claims include assertions of ownership,[122] and rights in intellectual property such as patents, copyrights, and trademarks.[123]

Waiver

Although the seller is obliged to produce goods that conform to the contract, the parties may (a) expressly excuse him from complying[124] or (b) impliedly excuse him if the buyer knew or "could not have been unaware" that the goods were nonconforming.[125] These rules are similar to the waiver provisions found in most common law countries, except—as mentioned earlier—there is no requirement to use any particular terms to make the waiver.[126] Moreover, unlike the practice in many civil law countries, a waiver can be implied from the buyer's conduct.[127]

The basic philosophy of the Convention—that the parties should determine the terms of their contract—compelled the drafters of CISG to adopt these waiver provisions. As noted

---

[120]*Id.*, Article 34.

[121]United States, Uniform Commercial Code, § 2-313 (express warranties) and § 2-314 (implied warranties). United Kingdom, Sale of Goods Act, § 14 (warranties) (1979).

[122]UN Convention on Contracts for the International Sale of Goods, Article 41 (1980).

[123]*Id.*, Article 42. Third-party claims to intellectual property will make goods nonconforming, but only if the claims exist in (a) the state where the goods are sold or (b) the state where the buyer has his or her place of business.

[124]*Id.*, Articles 35(3), 41, and 42.

[125]*Id.*, Articles 35(2) and 42.

[126]*Id.*, Articles 35(3), 41, and 42.

[127]*Id.*, Articles 35(2) and 42.

earlier, the parties under Article 6 may "derogate from or vary the effect of *any*" provision; and under Article 35(2), the Convention-defined obligation of the seller to produce conforming goods does not apply "where the parties have agreed otherwise."

Time for Examining Goods

The buyer has an obligation to examine the goods for defects "within as short a period as is practicable" after delivery. If the goods are shipped, the examination "may be deferred until after the goods have arrived at their destination"; and, if the buyer has to redirect or redispatch the goods while they are in transit, the examination "may be deferred until after the goods have arrived at the new destination," so long as the seller "knew or ought to have known of the possibility of such redirection or redispatch."[128]

Notice of Defect

In order for the buyer to avoid waiving his rights to require performance, he is obligated to inform the seller of any defects he discovers within a reasonable time after delivery. If the buyer discovers a defect at some later time, he must also promptly notify the seller in order to preserve his rights.[129] In any event, the seller will not be responsible for a defect that arises more than two years after delivery, unless (a) the seller knew or ought to have known of a nonconformity and did not disclose it to the buyer, or (b) the contract establishes a longer "period of guarantee."[130]

CISG does not describe specifically what the buyer has to do in notifying the seller of a defect, but the notice undoubtedly must be sufficient to inform the seller of the problem.

Curing Defects

If the seller delivers his goods early, he may correct or "cure" any defect up to the agreed-upon date for delivery, so long as this does not cause the buyer any unreasonable inconvenience or expense. Nevertheless, even if the seller does make a cure, the buyer retains the right to claim any damages that are provided for in CISG.

I. BUYER'S OBLIGATIONS

A buyer is required to (a) pay the price and (b) take delivery of the goods.[131] Again, as is the case for the seller's obligations, CISG's rules apply only when a contract fails to describe how this is done.

Payment of the Price

The buyer is obliged to take whatever preliminary steps are necessary "under the contract or any laws or regulations to enable payment to be made."[132] He is then to pay the price at the time and place designated in the contract. If no time is specified, the buyer is to pay when "the goods or the documents controlling their disposition" are delivered.[133]

Contrary to the practice in some civil law countries (of requiring the seller to make a formal demand for payment), the buyer has to pay "without the need for any request or compliance with any formality on the part of the seller."[134] However, unless the parties agree otherwise, the buyer does not have to pay until after he has had a chance to examine the goods.[135]

---

[128]*Id.*, Article 38(3).
[129]*Id.*, Article 39(1).
[130]*Id.*, Articles 39(2) and 40.
[131]*Id.*, Article 53.
[132]*Id.*, Article 54.
[133]*Id.*, Articles 58(1) and 58(2).
[134]*Id.*, Article 59. In France the request is called a *mise en demeure*, in Germany a *Mahnung. See* Konrad Zweigert and Hein Kötz, *An Introduction to Comparative Law,* vol. 2, pp. 164, 171 (Tony Weir, trans.,1977).
[135]UN Convention on Contracts for the International Sale of Goods, Article 58(3) (1980).

If the parties have not agreed to a place for payment but have agreed to a place for the delivery of either the goods or their controlling documents, then payment will be made at that place.[136] If they did not specify a place for delivery, then the buyer must pay at the seller's place of business.[137]

In Case 10–5, the court was asked to determine if the buyer had breached its obligation to make payment to the seller.

---

[136]*Id.,* Article 57(1)(b).
[137]*Id.,* Article 57(1)(a).

Case 10–5   The Natural Gas Case

Austria, Supreme Court, 1996.
Case No. 518/95.
Österreichische Zeitschrift für Rechtsvergleichung, vol. 1996, p. 248 (1996).

In the fall of 1990, the plaintiff, a German company, negotiated to buy natural gas from the defendant, an Austrian partnership. After a series of proposals and counterproposals, the plaintiff faxed the defendant on December 18, 1990, offering to buy 700 to 800 metric tons of propane gas from the defendant. The defendant responded the next morning that it could ship the propane from the United States for delivery to the plaintiff in Belgium for $376 per ton. At 2:16 P.M. on December 19, the plaintiff sent a confirming fax agreeing to this price and confirming the other terms of contract, including that the propane would be shipped by a tanker from the United States on January 2, 1991. Because the parties had not dealt with each other before, the plaintiff agreed to secure its purchase with a letter of credit. In the 2:16 P.M. fax, the plaintiff asked the defendant to identify the place in the United States where the gas would be loaded aboard a tanker, because the plaintiff's bank needed this information before it would issue a letter of credit. At 3:19 P.M. the defendant responded by fax stating that it was waiting to get the information from the United States as to the place of loading.

While this exchange of faxes was taking place, the parties were talking to each other on the telephone. The defendant wanted the plaintiff to order a larger quantity of propane to make the transaction more worth its time. The plaintiff, in response to this request, contacted a Dutch natural gas reseller that agreed to buy 3,000 tons of propane at $381 per ton. The plaintiff then increased its order by 3,000 tons.

On January 2, 1991, [not having heard if the propane had been loaded for shipment as the parties had agreed,]

the plaintiff sent a fax to the defendant asking to be notified of the place where the propane would be loaded. The next day the plaintiff sent another fax to tell the defendant that its bank would not process the letter of credit until the bank received the place of loading information.

On January 7, 1991, the defendant informed the plaintiff by fax that its United States supplier would not

MAP 10-5   Austria, Belgium, Germany, and the Netherlands (1991)

agree to let the propane gas be exported to Belgium, and therefore that the defendant could not deliver the propane.

The next day the plaintiff notified the defendant that, because of the defendant's breach, the Dutch natural gas reseller had had to make a substitute purchase at a price above what the defendant had promised. On January 15, 1991, the plaintiff sent a letter to the defendant forwarding the Dutch natural gas reseller's claim of $141,131 arising out of the substitute purchase. The defendant rejected this claim.

Later, after the Dutch natural gas reseller sued the plaintiff in a separate proceeding for $141,131, the plaintiff sued the defendant in this case both to cover the $141,131 compensation due the reseller and for the loss of its own profits of $15,000. The trial court held in favor of the plaintiff and the court of appeals affirmed its decision. The defendant then appealed to the Supreme Court.

DECISION OF THE COURT:

* * *

[The Breach]

[Following the making of the contract,] the plaintiff did not open a letter of credit and the plaintiff did not deliver the agreed goods (the natural gas).

The [United Nations Convention on Contracts for the International Sale of Goods (CISG),] Article 54, provides that "[t]he buyer's obligation to pay the price includes taking such steps and complying with such formalities as may be required under the contract or any laws and regulations to enable payment to be made." In light of this, a buyer in a sale of goods contract who has agreed to open a letter of credit must do so in a timely manner. Indeed, in the case at hand, only after the defendant had a claim against the bank was the defendant required to treat the letter of credit as open. In other words, because the buyer agreed to obtain a letter of credit, the buyer was obliged to do so before the seller was required to perform. And only after the buyer opened the letter of credit, was the buyer entitled to demand that the seller perform. . . .

In the case at hand, however, the plaintiff did not open the letter of credit because the defendant failed to notify it of the place where the natural gas would be loaded. And this was so, even though the defendant had expressly promised to do so in its fax of December 19, 1990. . . . The defendant cannot complain that the plaintiff did not fulfill its obligation [to open a letter of credit,] as the defendant's own obligation to notify the plaintiff as to the place where the goods were to be loaded had to happen first. The defendant knew that the plaintiff had to know the place of loading in order to

open the letter, and it was the defendant's failure to notify the plaintiff of the place of loading that led to the plaintiff's failure to open the letter of credit. [The defendant cannot now complain] that the plaintiff could have opened the letter of credit anyway, because the defendant had expressly agreed that it would notify the plaintiff of the place of loading. . . . In other words, the failure of the plaintiff to open the letter of credit was caused by the defendant's own failure to act. And, as stated in CISG, Article 80, "[a] party may not rely on a failure of the other party to perform, to the extent that such failure was caused by the first party's act or omission."

More significantly, the failure of the plaintiff to open a letter of credit was not the reason for the breach of this contract. As the lower courts have held, it was the defendant's failure to obtain the appropriate clearances . . . needed to export the propane gas to Belgium that was the cause of the breach. According to CISG, Article 30, "[t]he seller must deliver the goods, hand over any documents relating to them and transfer the property in the goods, as required by the contract. . . ." The defendant's argument (first made in this appeal) that it was the buyer that was obliged to obtain the appropriate authorization for the goods to be imported into Belgium is without merit. . . . A buyer is not obliged to ask a seller if there are any unusual restrictions that may keep the seller from performing. If the seller does not inform the buyer of such restrictions, the seller may reasonably assume that such circumstances do not exist. CISG, Article 41 says that "[t]he seller must deliver goods which are free from any right or claim of a third party" unless the buyer had agreed to accept such goods. If the seller's supplier will not allow the goods to be exported, then the goods are subject to a restriction. The buyer, of course, may agree to accept the goods anyway, but it doesn't have to. And, if the buyer doesn't agree to accept the goods, and the seller is then unable to deliver them because of the restriction, it is the seller that has breached the contract.

[Indemnification]

Because the seller breached the contract, the buyer is entitled to be fully indemnified for its losses. In other words, the non-breaching party is to be put in the position that it would have been had the breaching party performed as promised. The breaching party, moreover, does not have to be at fault or to have acted illegally to be liable in such a case.

[The parties sought to apply CISG, Articles 75 and 76 in ascertaining the damages due the plaintiff.]

The provisions in the CISG, Articles 75 and 76, deal with the awarding of damages when one party avoids the contract because of a breach by the other party. However, because there has been a breach, does not necessarily mean that there will be an avoidance. The CISG does not provide for avoidance as a matter of law, even if the non-breaching party is deprived of what it expected to receive.[138] Avoidance, under the CISG, can only come about by a unilateral declaration of the non-breaching party. Such a declaration, however, does not have to be in any particular form, nor (with the exception of certain cases set out in CISG, Article 49(2) which are inapplicable here) is it subject to any time limit.

The parties to this case argued over whether the declaration of avoidance described in CISG, Article 49(1), had to be made expressly or whether it could be implied from the non-breaching party's conduct. This argument, however, is irrelevant, because it is not the mere giving of notice that constitutes avoidance, but the non-breaching party's intention not to adhere to the contract that is important. This intention, moreover, must be clear to the breach party.

The findings of fact in the lower courts suggest that the plaintiff never actually notified the defendant that it was avoiding the contract. Indeed, the plaintiff never claimed that it had given such notice. Nor can one imply that such notice was given merely from the fact that the plaintiff gave the defendant a list of the losses suffered by its customer [the Dutch natural gas reseller].

Because the contract was not avoided, the damages [are not to be determined in accordance with CISG, Articles 75 and 76, but rather] are to be determined in accordance with CISG, Article 74. Article 74 applies to those cases when the damages come about because of delay in delivery or because of some defect in the goods.

[Loss of Profits]

When, as the case here, the non-breaching party is claiming a loss of profits from an expected resale of the goods to a third party, the loss of profits will only be considered if the breaching party had reason to know of this expected resale. Of course, when merchantable goods are sold to a merchant, the expected resale can be presumed. The defendant does not challenge this. Indeed, it has conceded that it knew that the plaintiff intended to resell the goods. [The plaintiff, accordingly, is entitled to the $15,000 claimed in lost profits.]

[Duty to Mitigate]

A non-breaching party may not claim damages, including a loss of profits, if it fails to make reasonable efforts to mitigate its losses. Such efforts are reasonable if a reasonable person in the position of the non-breaching party would have undertaken them in good faith.[139]

The defendant argues that the plaintiff breached this obligation. However, the burden of proving such a breach is on the defendant, and the defendant has failed to meet its burden. . . . It has not shown what the plaintiff did to breach this obligation, it has not shown that the plaintiff had other alternatives to what it did, nor has it shown how much the damages would have been lessened if the plaintiff had engaged in some alternative conduct. [In addition to lost profits, therefore, the plaintiff is entitled to recoup the $141,131 due the Dutch natural gas reseller.]

* * *

The decision of the Court of Appeals is affirmed. ■

---

[138]Articles 25 and 49.

[139]United Nations Convention on Contracts for the International Sale of Goods, Article 77, [which provides: "A party who relies on a breach of contract must take such measures as are reasonable in the circumstances to mitigate the loss, including loss of profit, resulting from the breach. If he fails to take such measures, the party in breach may claim a reduction in the damages in the amount by which the loss should have been mitigated."]

Taking Delivery

In connection with the taking of delivery, a buyer is obligated to cooperate with the seller to facilitate the transfer and to actually "take over the goods."[140] A buyer who fails to cooperate will be responsible for any resulting costs, and one who fails to take delivery assumes the risk for any damage to the goods after that time.[141]

J. THE PASSING OF RISK

passage of risk: The point in time when the buyer becomes responsible for losses to the goods.

The loss of goods through fire, theft, or other means can occur at any time: prior to delivery, during transit or inspection, or after delivery. The legal concept of **passage of risk** determines who is responsible for the loss. In most cases, the loss will be covered by insurance. Even

---

[140]UN Convention on Contracts for the International Sale of Goods, Article 60 (1980).

[141]*See id.,* Articles 66–70.

so, it is important to determine whether the buyer or seller is responsible for obtaining the insurance.

To begin with, "passage of risk" is defined as the shifting of responsibility for loss or damage from the seller to the buyer. This means that once the risk passes, the buyer must pay the agreed-upon price for the goods involved. The buyer must then absorb the cost of the loss or lodge a claim against his insurer. Only if he can show that the loss or damage was due to an act or omission of the seller is he excused from paying the price.[142]

Like most domestic sales codes, CISG allocates risks by considering the agreement of the parties and the means of delivery. Unlike some domestic laws, however, CISG's risk allocation is not affected by breach of contract.

Agreement of the Parties

CISG allows parties to allocate risk among themselves and to specify when the risk will pass between them.[143] The parties most commonly do so through the use of trade terms, such as Free on Board (abbreviated FOB) or Cost, Insurance, and Freight (CIF). Unlike most domestic sales laws,[144] CISG does not define any trade terms. The parties may use domestic trade terms or (in what is the most common practice) they may use the terms defined by the International Chamber of Commerce and known as Incoterms. Incoterms, which are described in more detail in Chapter 11, are well known and their use in international sales is encouraged by trade councils, courts, and international lawyers.

Means of Delivery

Goods may be transported by a carrier or delivered by the seller without being transported by a carrier.

Goods Transported by Carrier

CISG distinguishes between shipment, transshipment, in-transit, and destination contracts. No matter which of these contracts is used, however, the risk of loss will not pass until the goods are clearly identified to the contract by markings on the goods, shipping documents, notice given to the buyer, or otherwise.[145]

Shipment Contracts When a contract requires the seller to deliver the goods to a carrier for shipment and does not require the seller to deliver them to a particular place, the risk of loss passes when the goods are "handed over" to the first carrier.[146] For example, if the delivery term in a contract between a seller in Paris, France, and a buyer in Denver, Colorado, is "Free Carrier (FCA) Paris," the risk of loss will pass to the buyer when the seller delivers the goods to the trucking company in Paris that will transport them to the international carrier in Le Havre, France.

Transshipment Contracts If a contract requires the seller to deliver the goods to a carrier at a named place, the risk of loss passes to the buyer when the goods are handed over to the carrier at that place.[147] Thus, if the contract contains a "Free Alongside Ship (FAS) M/V *Ocean Trader*, Vancouver, British Columbia" delivery term, the seller in Calgary will bear the risk of loss until the goods are delivered alongside the M/V *Ocean Trader* at the port of Vancouver.

---

[142]*Id.*, Article 66. This rule is common to virtually all domestic sale-of-goods laws: e.g., United Kingdom, Sale of Goods Act, § 20(2) (1893); Federal Republic of Germany, Civil Code, § 447(2); United States, Uniform Commercial Code, § 2–501.

[143]UN Convention on Contracts for the International Sale of Goods, Article 6 (1980).

[144]Most, but not all, countries use trade terms. Japan, for example, has no established set of domestic trade terms.

[145]UN Convention on Contracts for the International Sale of Goods, Article 67(2) (1980).

The CISG rule for assigning risk when goods are shipped is the same rule found in many domestic codes: e.g., United States, Uniform Commercial Code, § 2–509; Federal Republic of Germany, Civil Code, §§ 446(1) and 447(1); Israel, Sales Law, § 22(b); Sweden, Sales Act, § 10; United Kindom, Sale of Goods Acts, § 20 (1893 and 1979).

[146]UN Convention on Contracts for the International Sale of Goods, Article 67(1) (1980).

[147]*Id.*, Article 67(1).

In-Transit Contracts   Sometimes goods are sold after they are already aboard a carrier. In such a case, the risk of loss passes to the buyer at the time the contract is concluded. However, if at the time the contract was made, the seller knew or ought to have known that goods had been lost or damaged and he did not disclose this to the buyer, the risk will remain with the seller.[148] For example, if the owner of crude oil being transported on a tanker from the Middle East to Houston, Texas, contracts to sell the oil to a buyer, the risk of loss will pass to the buyer at the time the contract is made. If, however, the seller knew that the oil had been contaminated and did not tell the buyer, the risk of loss will not pass.

Destination Contracts   When a contract requires the seller to arrange transportation to a named place of destination, the risk of loss passes to the buyer when the goods are handed over or placed at his disposal at that place.[149] A contract containing a "Delivered Duty Paid (DDP) Seattle, Washington" trade term, for example, would require a seller in Tokyo to bear the risk of transporting the goods to Seattle.

Goods Delivered without Being Transported

When goods are not shipped to the buyer, the risk of loss passes when the goods are handed over by the seller or otherwise put at the buyer's disposal.[150] The goods are not considered to be put at the buyer's disposal, however, until they are clearly identified to the contract.[151] An example of such a contract is one containing an "Ex Works (EXW) Seller's City" trade term.

Breach of Contract

Unlike the Uniform Commercial Code and some other domestic sales laws, the CISG rules on risk of loss are not concerned with breach of contract. That is, with the exception of in-transit contracts (in which risk passes at the time of contracting unless the seller knows or to ought to know that the goods are lost or damaged), the risk of loss passes to the buyer at the agreed-upon time and place of delivery.

K. REMEDIES

CISG provides for remedies that are (1) unique to the buyer, (2) unique to the seller, and (3) available to either party. Although the buyer's and seller's remedies relate to their specific needs, they are also interrelated, and anyone studying CISG's remedies must keep this in mind.

Buyer's Remedies

cumulative: Able to be joined or taken together.

The buyer's remedies are **cumulative**. That is to say, the right to recover damages is not lost if a buyer exercises any other available remedy.[152] They are also immediate. In other words, unlike the rules in some civil law countries, CISG forbids a court or arbitral tribunal from granting the seller a period of grace (*délai de grâce*) in which to comply with a buyer's demand for a remedy.[153]

The remedies that are unique to the buyer are (1) to compel specific performance, (2) to avoid the contract for fundamental breach or nondelivery, (3) to reduce the price, (4) to refuse

---

[148]*Id.,* Article 68.
[149]*Id.,* Article 69(2).
[150]*Id.,* Article 69(1).
[151]*Id.,* Article 69(3).
[152]*Id.,* Article 45(2). Until the 1940s, U.S. case law and the U.S. Uniform Sales Act (1906) required buyers to make an election. The idea was to make it difficult for buyers to rescind contracts for trivial purposes. The election-of-remedies rule was overturned with the adoption of § 2–711(1) of the Uniform Commercial Code.
[153]UN Convention on Contracts for the International Sale of Goods, Article 45(3) (1980). *See* G H. Treitel, "Remedies for Breach of Contract," in *International Encyclopedia of Comparative Law,* vol. 7, chap. 16, §§ 147–148 (1976), for a discussion of the French *délai de grâce.*

early delivery, and (5) to refuse excess quantities. Most of these remedies are common to virtually every legal system, but two—the right to set an additional time in which to perform and the right to reduce the price—are not. All are applicable whether the seller's breach affects the whole contract or only a part.

Specific Performance

As we have already seen, the availability of a decree of specific performance depends on the domestic rules applicable to the court hearing the suit. Assuming it is available, a buyer can ask that a seller either (a) deliver substitute goods or (b) make repairs. In either case, the buyer must first notify the seller that the goods are nonconforming, and, if he is asking for substitute goods, the nonconformity must amount to a fundamental breach. Also, the buyer cannot have avoided the contract or resorted to some other inconsistent remedy.[154]

Avoidance

***Nachfrist* notice:** The fixing by the buyer of an additional reasonable period of time in which the seller may perform.

CISG's provisions for avoidance by a buyer are patterned after German law, especially in the Convention's adoption of the German *Nachfrist*[155] **notice**. A comparative analysis of several different approaches to avoidance is given in Reading 10–1.

---

[154]UN Convention on Contracts for the International Sale of Goods, Article 46 (1980).
[155]German: "to fix an appointed time."

Reading 10–1 The Buyer's Right to Avoid the Contract

John Honnold, *Uniform Law for International Sales under the 1980 United Nations Convention*, pp. 307, 315–316 (1982).

THE PROBLEM OF AVOIDANCE IN DOMESTIC LAW

When does a breach of contract by one party release the other party from his contractual obligations? Attempts to answer this question have produced rules of domestic law of unusual technicality and uncertainty.

The common law initially found it difficult to release a party (Party A) from his promise because of breach by the other party (B), unless the promises of the two parties were linked by some verbal formula such as "A promises, *in exchange* for B's delivery of first-quality hemp, to pay. . . ." Late in the eighteenth century this technical approach was relaxed by the judicial creation of rules that performance by B could be a "condition" of A's duty of performance; under some of the case law, whether B's breach released A depended on questions of degree such as the seriousness of the breach.[156]

However, some of the more technical case law was frozen into statutory form in the (U.K.) *Sale of Goods Act* (1893). The buyer's right to reject (avoid the contract) could turn on various factors—whether the contract involved "specific goods, the property in which has passed to the buyer," whether the sale was "by description," or whether the buyer had "accepted" all, or even part, of the goods. . . .

The (U.S.) *Uniform Commercial Code* created a somewhat different set of distinctions. A buyer may reject goods if the "goods or the tender of delivery fail in any respect to conform to the contract" (UCC, § 2-601). However, if the buyer has "accepted" the goods (even without an opportunity to ascertain the defect) he may refuse to keep the goods only if a "nonconformity *substantially* impairs its value" (UCC, § 2-608). The Code

---

[156]An important contribution to this development was made by Lord Mansfield in Kingston v. Preston, *English Reports,* vol. 99, p. 437 (King's Bench, 1773). *See* William Searle Holdsworth, *History of English Law,* vol. 8, pp. 70–88 (2d ed., 1937); Arthur L. Corbin, "Conditions in the Law of Contract," *Yale Law Journal,* vol. 28, p. 739 (1919), reprinted in *Selected Essays in the Law of Contracts,* p. 871 (1939); Edwin W. Patterson, "Constructive Conditions in Contracts," *Columbia Law Review,* vol. 42, p. 903 (1942).

also applies this test of "substantial" impairment of value to contracts calling for delivery in separate lots or installments, even with respect to rejection of those goods that were defective (UCC, § 2-612). In an earlier study, this writer found these provisions to be casuistic and unresponsive to commercial practice and the significant interests of the parties.[157]

In France, the Code does not define the grounds for avoidance of a contract for breach, but erects procedural barriers by a general rule (pitted by exceptions) that a party must apply to the court for termination of his obligation to perform. Professor Treitel reports that in determining whether to grant this remedy the court will consider "various factors such as the defendant's degree of fault and the seriousness of the defect in performance."[158]

* * *

The notice avoidance approach of Articles 47 and 49(1)(b) of the Convention was inspired by a provision of German law that, on default by one party:

the other party may give him a reasonable period within which to perform his part with a declaration that he will refuse to accept the performance after the expiration of the period.

If performance is not made in due time, the person who gave the above notice (often termed a *Nachfrist*) may "withdraw from the contract."[159]

Other aspects of the German *Nachfrist* were not employed in the Convention. [For example,] . . . under the Convention when the seller commits a breach that is fundamental, the buyer may declare the contract avoided (Article 49(1)(b)) without giving the seller an "additional period of time of reasonable length." However, the opportunity by advance notice to clarify the situation for both parties has received widespread international approval; the basic utility of this legal tool was never seriously questioned in the UNCITRAL proceeding or at the Diplomatic Conference. ■

---

[157]John Honnold, "Buyer's Right of Rejection—A Study in the Impact of Codification on a Commercial Problem," *University of Pennsylvania Law Review,* vol. 97, p. 457 (1949). *See also* George L. Priest, "Breach and Remedy for the Tender of Nonconforming Goods under the UCC: An Economic Approach," *Harvard Law Review,* vol. 91, p. 960 (1978) (includes economic analysis of the UCC decisions).

[158]G. H. Treitel, "Remedies for Breach of Contract," *International Encyclopedia of Comparative Law,* vol. 7, Chap. 16, § 147 (1976). This helpful study includes references to developments under other systems, such as Quebec and Louisiana, that have been influenced by French law. *See* also Konrad Zweigert and Hein Kötz, *An Introduction to Comparative Law,* vol. 2, pp. 168–170 (trans. Tony Weir, 1977) (means of overcoming practical difficulties of French rule requiring court action).

[159]German (F.R.G.) Civil Code, § 326. G. H. Treitel, "Remedies for Breach of Contract," *International Encyclopedia of Comparative Law,* vol. 7, Chap. 16, §§ 149–151 (1976), on which the present discussion relies, helpfully discusses the above provision and similar provisions in other legal systems—e.g., Austrian Civil Code, § 918, Swiss Code of Obligations, § 107. Konrad Zweigert and Hein Kötz, *An Introduction to Comparative Law,* vol. 2, pp. 170, 178 (trans. Tony Weir, 1977) discusses comparable rules in England and Italy. The (U.S.) UCC does not explicitly establish an additional time notice comparable to *Nachfrist,* but the official Comments to UCC, § 2–309 commend the use of such notices to add certainty to the relationship between the parties (Comments 3 and 5).

Under CISG, a buyer may avoid a contract if either (a) the seller commits a fundamental breach or (b) the buyer gives the seller a *Nachfrist* notice and the seller rejects it or does not perform within the period it specifies.[160] A buyer's *Nachfrist* notice is the fixing of "an additional period of time of reasonable length for performance by the seller of his obligations."[161] The period must be definite and the obligation to perform within that period must be clear. Once the *Nachfrist* period has run, or once the fundamental breach becomes clear, the buyer has a reasonable time in which to avoid the contract.[162]

During the *Nachfrist* period, the seller is entitled to correct (i.e., "cure") the nonconformity at his own expense. Even if there has been a breach, the seller is entitled to make a cure, unless the circumstances—including the circumstance of the offer to make the cure—indicate that the breach is fundamental and the buyer chooses to avoid the contract.[163]

When a buyer's avoidance remedy may be applied is considered in Case 10–6.

---

[160]UN Convention on Contracts for the International Sale of Goods, Article 49(1) (1980).

[161]*Id.,* Article 47(1).

[162]*Id.,* Article 49(2): "[I]n cases where the seller has delivered the goods, the buyer loses the right to declare the contract avoided unless he does so: (a) in respect of late delivery, within a reasonable time after he has become aware that delivery has been made; (b) in respect of any breach other than late delivery, within a reasonable time: (i) after he knew or ought to have known of the breach; [or] (ii) after the expiration of any additional period of time fixed by the buyer . . . or after the seller has declared that he will not perform his obligations within such an additional period. . . ."

[163]*Id.,* Article 48.

Case 10–6   The Shoe Seller's Case

Germany, Court of Appeals, Frankfurt am Main, 1994.
Case 5 U 15/93.
Journal of Law & Commerce, vol. 14, p. 201 (1995).

The plaintiff, an Italian business, contracted in January 1991 to sell women's shoes to the defendant, a German businesswoman. The plaintiff-seller was late in making its delivery and the shoes did not completely conform to the original sample that had been shown to the defendant-buyer. Although the defendant accepted delivery, she refused to pay on two of the plaintiff's invoices. The plaintiff then brought suit in a German court to recover the amounts it had billed the defendant on its invoices. In the defendant's answer to the plaintiff's complaint, the defendant relied on the remedy of avoidance, maintaining that she was entitled to avoid the contract and be excused from any liability on the unpaid invoices because of (a) the plaintiff's late delivery and (b) the nonconformity of the goods. The court found in favor of the plaintiff and the defendant appealed.

JUDGMENT:

* * *

The sales contract entered into by the parties in January 1991 is governed by the *United Nations Convention on Contracts for the International Sale of Goods* (Convention or CISG) pursuant to Articles 1 and 100(2) of that Convention. Both Italy and Germany were then, and are now, parties to the CISG, the CISG having come into force in Germany on January 1, 1991, and in Italy on January 1, 1988.

The plaintiff's claim in this case is based upon two unpaid invoices . . . relating to the sale of women's shoes. The plaintiff seeks to recover from the defendant . . . the unpaid balance due on those invoices. The defendant does not contest the making of the contract, her acceptance of delivery of the shoes, or the amount of the purchase price.

A buyer is excused from paying the purchase price for goods if the buyer can avoid the contract[164] and, except for the obligation to pay any damages that may be due, the avoidance of a contract releases both parties from their contractual obligations.[165]

The defendant's contention that she may avoid the contract because the plaintiff was late in delivering the goods is not by itself a sufficient basis for her to avoid the contract. Avoidance in such a case is only allowed after a buyer [gives a seller a *Nachfrist* notice and] defines an additional fixed period of time in which the seller may make delivery.[166] Because the defendant did not do so, she may not avoid the contract on this basis.

The defendant's contention that she may avoid the contract because the goods were predominantly nonconforming is also lacking in merit. According to the Convention, the tender of nonconforming goods does not amount to a failure to make delivery, it is only a breach of contract. Such a breach, moreover, may or may

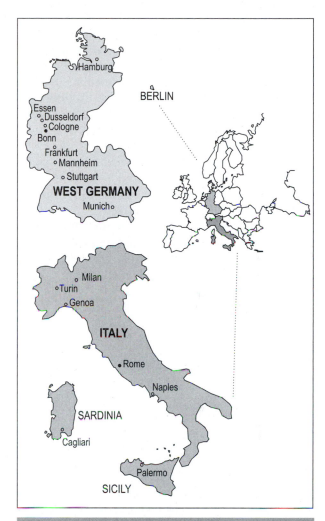

MAP 10-6   West Germany and Italy (1991)

---

[164]United Nations Convention on Contracts for the International Sale of Goods (1980), Article 49.
[165]*Id.,* Article 81(1).
[166]*Id.,* Articles 49(1)(b) and 47(1).

not be fundamental, and only in those cases in which the seller commits a fundamental breach of contract is the buyer entitled to use the remedy of avoidance.[167]

Germany's national sales law allows a buyer (with minor exceptions) to avoid a contract if the goods the seller delivers are defective. This is not so under the CISG. The CISG expects a buyer to accept deliveries of nonconforming goods [unless they are fundamentally nonconforming] and to invoke remedies other than avoidance (such as reduction of the price and damages) as compensation for the defects. For example, there would be no fundamental breach of contract [and no right to avoid the contract] in cases where the buyer is able to use some of the goods.[168]

Thus, if a buyer contends that there is a fundamental breach of contract because the goods delivered do not conform to the original sample the parties relied on in making their contract, the buyer must introduce evidence that (a) describes the exact nature of the defects and (b) shows that the goods cannot be used in any way. If a buyer does not do this, the court will be unable to determine if there was a fundamental breach.

In this case, the defendant only testified that . . . "[the shoes] were defectively made." She said that the materials had "defects," that the manufacture was "not uniform," that some of the shoes were "stitched together" while others were merely "folded," and overall that the shoes did not correspond to the original sample she had been shown. From this testimony it is not possible to determine the precise nature of the defects. More importantly, the defendant's evidence about how the shoes were different from the sample does not help us ascertain whether or not she could reasonably be expected to use the shoes.

In her allegations, the defendant . . . also complained that the shoes were made from a material called "S. Oro" rather than "Metallic Gold Leather" and that this caused the shoes to have heavy wrinkles rather than a smooth finish. Again, however, these allegations do not allow us to determine if the shoes—apart from their being made of different material and having a different appearance—were defective or unfit for use.

* * *

The Court of Appeals affirmed the decision in favor of the plaintiff. ■

---

[167]*Id.,* Article 49(1)(a).

[168]Ernst von Caemmerer and Peter Schlechtriem, eds., *Commentary on the Uniform UN Law of Sales—CISG,* Article 46, n. 64, Article 49, n. 27 (1990); Piltz, *International Sales Law,* § 5, n. 247 (1993).

Reduction in Price

reduction in price:
Remedy that allows a buyer to pay less for nonconforming goods in those cases where the buyer is not entitled to damages.

If a buyer is not entitled to damages when a seller delivers nonconforming goods, the buyer will be entitled to a **reduction in price**.[169] This remedy has its origins in the Roman law remedy of *actio quanti minoris,*[170] a remedy commonplace in civil law countries but generally unknown in the common law world. At the proceedings leading up to the adoption of CISG, many delegates argued that the price reduction remedy is little different from damages, and therefore served no real purpose. Nevertheless, most representatives from the civil law countries felt that it was different, and eventually it was incorporated in the Convention.

The price reduction remedy is different from damages because it applies to a very special situation. First, the buyer must have accepted goods that are nonconforming. Second, the seller must not be responsible for the nonconformity. An example of such a case is one where the goods were damaged by *force majeure*[171] or an act of nature. Consider the following situation. A seller in New Orleans agrees to deliver grade No. 1 corn to a buyer at the buyer's mill in Karachi for a price of $80,000. While the corn is in transit on the SS *Skipper,* a war breaks out and the ship is detained by one of the warring countries for three months. When the SS *Skipper* arrives in Karachi, the corn is moldy and graded only as No. 3. The buyer is happy to have the corn, even though it is moldy, because the war has interrupted all of its orders. Under the damage provisions of CISG, the buyer is not entitled to damages.[172] The buyer is, however, entitled to a price reduction.

---

[169]UN Convention on Contracts for the International Sale of Goods, Article 50 (1980).
[170]Latin: "action to determine the extent of a reduction."
[171]French: "superior force." An event or effect that cannot be reasonably anticipated or controlled.
[172]UN Convention on Contracts for the International Sale of Goods, Article 79 (1980).

The amount of the reduction is determined by a formula that looks at the relative price of conforming and nonconforming goods at the time of delivery. That is, "the buyer may reduce the price in the same proportion as the value that the goods actually delivered had at the time of delivery bears to the value that conforming goods would have had at that time."[173] In other words:

$$\text{Price Reduction} = [\text{Price}] - \left[\frac{\text{Price} \times \text{Value of goods as delivered}}{\text{Value of conforming goods at the time of delivery}} \right]$$

In our example, let us assume that the price for 25,000 bushels of No. 3 corn in Karachi at the time of delivery is $75,000 and the price for the same amount of No. 1 corn is $100,000. The original price ($80,000) will therefore be reduced by the ratio of the price of the No. 3 to the price of the No. 1 corn. Accordingly, the reduction will be $20,000 and the buyer will pay only $60,000.

Refusing Early Delivery and Excess Quantity

If the seller delivers early, the buyer is under no obligation to take delivery.[174] If the seller delivers more than the amount agreed upon, the buyer may also accept or reject the excess part. However, if the buyer does accept, he must pay for the excess goods at the contract rate.[175]

The Effect of Nonconformity in a Part of the Goods

Assume the following facts: A seller agrees to sell a buyer 1,000 bags of flour. At the time of delivery, 100 bags are vermin infested and totally unusable. May the buyer reject the 100 bags and accept the balance? May the buyer reject the entire contract?

As to the defective part, CISG provides that the buyer may seek specific performance, obtain a price reduction, or avoid that part of the contract. In doing so, however, he must comply with CISG's rules for those particular remedies.[176] As for avoiding the whole contract, a buyer may do so only if the partial delivery amounts to a fundamental breach of the whole.[177]

Seller's Remedies

The seller's remedies in CISG mirror those of the buyer. Like the buyer's remedies, the seller's remedies are both cumulative and immediate. That is, the right to recover damages is not lost if a seller exercises any other available remedy, and courts will not grant the buyer a grace period in which to perform.[178]

The remedies that are unique to the seller are (1) to compel specific performance, (2) to avoid the contract for a fundamental breach or failure to cure a defect, and (3) to obtain missing specifications. Again, each of these remedies is meant to mirror the buyer's remedies.

Specific Performance

Assuming that a decree of specific performance is available under local law, a seller may require a buyer to (a) take delivery and pay the contract price or (b) perform any other obligation required by the contract.[179]

This rather unusual remedy is included in the Convention primarily for symmetry, as a balance to the buyer's specific performance remedy. Its inclusion stresses the fact that CISG requires both parties to perform their obligations. However, because Article 28 of the Convention limits the availability of specific performance decrees to cases where the domestic court has powers to grant a similar decree, the likelihood that it will be used very often is small.

---

[173]*Id.*, Article 50.
[174]*Id.*, Article 52(1). The buyer, however, may have an obligation under Article 86 to take possession of the goods on behalf of the seller to prevent the seller from suffering injury.
[175]*Id.*, Article 52(2).
[176]*Id.*, Article 51(1).
[177]*Id.*, Article 51(2).
[178]*Id.*, Article 61.
[179]*Id.*, Article 62.

In common law countries, a suit to recover the full price from the buyer is not a form of "specific performance." Historically, specific performance was a decree issued by a court of equity. A suit to recover the price, normally called an action in "debt," was obtained from a different court, a court of law. An action in debt, moreover, was available only on a *quid pro quo*[180] basis. The seller could recover the price only for the things actually received by the buyer, and the buyer (at least in a court of law) could not be compelled to take delivery of the goods. This tradition survives in both the U.K. Sale of Goods Act of 1893 (§ 49) and the U.S. Uniform Commercial Code (§ 2-709), as well as in the statutes of other common law countries. The seller may recover the price, but only after "the property in the goods has passed to the buyer."[181]

Unlike the common law countries, the sales codes in civil law countries do have provisions that can require the buyer to take delivery and pay the full price. As a practical matter, however, they are seldom used.[182] Rather, when a buyer refuses to take delivery, the seller commonly resells the goods on the buyer's account and brings an action to recover any deficiency. Such a remedy for damages is also allowed under the Convention.[183]

Avoidance

The seller's avoidance remedy truly is the mirror image of the buyer's remedy. Like the buyer, the seller may avoid the contract only if there has been a fundamental breach or, following a *Nachfrist* notice, the buyer refuses to cure any defect in his performance.[184] The rules applying to fundamental breach and the *Nachfrist* notice, discussed earlier, apply here as well.

Missing Specifications

missing specifications: Remedy that allows a seller to ascertain specifications himself when the buyer fails to supply them as required by the contract or within a reasonable time after the seller requests them.

The **missing specifications** remedy applies to a special problem that can face sellers: obtaining specifications for goods that the buyer fails to supply. If the buyer does not produce the measurements that the seller needs by the date specified in the contract or within a reasonable time after the seller asks for them, CISG allows the seller to ascertain them himself "in accordance with the requirements of the buyer that may be known to him."[185] The seller must then inform the buyer of what he has done and set a reasonable time period for the buyer to supply different specifications. However, if the buyer does not respond, the seller's specifications become "binding."[186]

Remedies Available to Both Buyers and Sellers

The remedies available to both buyers and sellers are (1) suspension of performance, (2) avoidance in anticipation of a fundamental breach, (3) avoidance of an installment contract, and (4) damages.

Suspension of Performance

suspension of performance: Remedy available to either party when it becomes clear that the other party will not perform a substantial part of his obligation because of a serious deficiency in his ability to perform, his creditworthiness, his preparations for performing, or his performance.

CISG, Article 71, describes the remedy of **suspension of performance** as follows:

(1) A party may suspend the performance of his obligations if, after the conclusion of the contract, it becomes apparent that the other party will not perform a substantial part of his obligations as a result of: (a) a serious deficiency in his ability to perform or his creditworthiness; or (b) his conduct in preparing to perform or in performing the contract.

(2) If the seller has already dispatched the goods before the grounds described in the preceding paragraph become evident, he may prevent the handing over of the goods to the buyer even though the buyer holds a document which entitles him to obtain them. The present paragraph relates only to the rights in the goods as between the buyer and the seller.

---

[180]Latin: "something for something." One thing in return for another. In the traditional English common law, the giving of one valuable thing for another—called mutual consideration—was a necessary requirement for a contract to be valid.

[181]United Kingdom, Sale of Goods Act, § 49 (1893).

[182]*See* John Philip Dawson, "Specific Performance in France and Germany," *Michigan Law Review*, vol. 57, p. 495 (1959); and G. H. Treitel, "Remedies for Breach of Contract," in *International Encyclopedia of Comparative Law*, vol. 7, chap. 16, §§ 10–29, (1976).

[183]UN Convention on Contracts for the International Sale of Goods, Article 75 (1980).

[184]*Id.,* Article 64.

[185]*Id.,* Article 65(1).

[186]*Id.,* Article 65(2).

(3) A party suspending performance, whether before or after dispatch of the goods, must immediately give notice of the suspension to the other party and must continue with performance if the other party provides adequate assurance of his performance.

Paragraph (1) applies to threats of nonperformance, paragraph (2) to threats of nonpayment discovered after the goods are in transit, and paragraph (3) requires a suspending party to give notice and to resume his obligations under the contract if the other party provides adequate assurances of his capability to perform.

Paragraph (2) applies to a special set of circumstances. The threat that the buyer will not pay must be discovered after the goods are shipped but before they are handed over by the carrier, and the seller must not have retained control over the goods (for example, he may have turned over a negotiable bill of lading to the buyer).[187] In this situation, the seller can prevent the carrier from delivering the goods to the buyer. This right, however, "relates only to the rights in the goods as between the buyer and the seller." Should a third person acquire legal rights in the goods (e.g., as the holder in due course of a negotiable bill of lading), CISG will not apply.[188] Instead, the matter is left to domestic law; and, in most cases, the third party's right will prevail.

Anticipatory Avoidance

anticipatory avoidance: Remedy available to either party when it becomes clear that the other party will commit a fundamental breach.

Anticipatory avoidance is different from the avoidance remedies that apply specifically to buyers and sellers. Those remedies apply only *after* an offending party has committed a fundamental breach. The remedy provided in Article 72 arises as soon as "it is clear" that the other party "*will commit* a fundamental breach."

There seem to be only a few cases where this remedy can be invoked. These include (a) the specific goods promised to the buyer are wrongfully sold to a third party; (b) the seller's only employee capable of producing the goods dies or is fired; and (c) the seller's manufacturing plant is sold.[189] In most other cases the breach will already have occurred, or the circumstances will be such that a suspension of performance is the appropriate remedy.

If a party opts to anticipatorily avoid, CISG requires him, "if time allows," to notify the other party so that the latter can "provide adequate assurance of his performance."[190] In practice, this is worth doing, both to comply with the Convention's general requirement of "good faith," and to minimize any challenges to the use of the remedy.[191]

Avoidance of Installment Contracts

CISG's rule for avoiding installment contracts uses the same logic found in its other avoidance provisions. First, as to a particular installment, if there was a "fundamental breach with respect to *that* installment," then "the other party may declare the contract avoided with respect to *that* installment.[192] Second, if the breach of one installment gives a party "good grounds" to believe that a fundamental breach of later installments "*will occur*," then those later installments may be anticipatorily avoided.[193] Finally, if the installments are *interdependent*, a fundamental breach of one installment will allow a party to avoid the entire contract (past and future installments included).[194]

Damages

The basic rule on damages in CISG is common to both the civil law and common law worlds. Article 74 states:

Damages for breach of contract by one party consist of a sum equal to the loss, including loss of profit, suffered by the other party as a consequence of the breach. Such

---

[187]Similar provisions can be found in many domestic codes: e.g., United States, Uniform Commercial Code, § 2–704; Sweden, Sales Act, § 39; and United Kingdom, Sale of Goods Act, §§ 44–46 (1893 as amended in 1979).

[188]UN Convention on Contracts for the International Sale of Goods, Article 4(b) (1980).

[189]*See* James C. Gulotta Jr., "Anticipatory Breach—A Comparative Analysis," *Tulane Law Review,* vol. 50, p. 932 (1976).

[190]UN Convention on Contracts for the International Sale of Goods, Article 72(2) (1980).

[191]*See* John Honnold, *Uniform Law for International Sales under the 1980 United Nations Convention,* p. 402, n. 2 (1982).

[192]UN Convention on Contracts for the International Sale of Goods, Article 73(1) (1980).

[193]*Id.,* Article 73(2).

[194]*Id.,* Article 73(3).

damages may not exceed the loss which the party in breach foresaw or ought to have foreseen at the time of the conclusion of the contract, in the light of the facts and matters of which he then knew or ought to have known, as possible consequence of the breach of contract.

foreseeability test: A breaching party is liable only for those damages that he or she foresaw or ought to have foreseen.

This rule, that a breaching party is liable for any foreseeable damages, is derived from Section 1150 of the French Civil Code, which limits damages to those "which were foreseen or which could have been foreseen at the time of the contract." In England, the French law was referred to with favor in the landmark 1854 case of *Hadley v. Baxendale*, which established the **foreseeability** or "improbability" test as a common law rule.[195] A similar but slightly different test is followed in Germany and the Scandinavian countries.[196]

To calculate the damages, the Convention uses two different rules. First, if an avoiding party has entered into a good-faith substitute transaction—the buyer obtaining substitute goods or the seller reselling the goods to another party—then damages are measured by the difference between contract price and the price received in the substitute transaction.[197]

Alternatively, if the avoiding party did not enter into a substitute transaction, then the damages are calculated by taking the difference between the contract price and the current price at the time of avoidance.[198] The current price is defined as "the price prevailing at the place where delivery of the goods should have been made or, if there is not current price at that place, the price at such other places as serves as a reasonable substitute."[199]

mitigation: Obligation of a party claiming damages to keep the damages to a minimum.

No matter which of the two CISG damage rules applies, the party claiming damages is under an obligation to take reasonable measures "to **mitigate** the loss." If the claiming party fails to take such action, the other may seek a proportionate reduction in the damages.[200]

The CISG's damages provisions and its requirement that the injured party must mitigate damages are discussed in Case 10–7.

---

[195] *English Reports,* vol. 156, p. 145. The English rule was codified in the Sale of Goods Act, §§ 50(2), 51(2), and 53(2) (1893); however, the phrase "loss directly and naturally resulting in the ordinary course of events" is used rather than the word "foreseeable." The U.S. Uniform Commercial Code, § 2-715(2), speaks of "any loss resulting from general or particular requirements and needs of which the seller at the time of contracting had reason to know."

[196] G. H. Treitel, "Remedies for Breach of Contract," *International Encyclopedia of Comparative Law,* vol. 7, chap. 16, §§ 91–93 (1976), examines the extent to which the German concept of "adequate causation" approximates the "foreseeability" test. The Scandinavian countries' adoption of the German rule is discussed in Kurt Heller, "The Limits of Contractual Damages in the Scandinavian Law of Sales," *Scandinavian Studies,* vol. 10, pp. 40–79 (1978).

[197] UN Convention on Contracts for the International Sale of Goods, Article 75 (1980).

[198] *Id.,* Article 76(1).

[199] *Id.,* Article 76(2).

[200] *Id.,* Article 77. Related to the requirement of mitigation of damages is the requirement to preserve goods. Thus, a seller must preserve goods in his possession if the buyer is late taking delivery (Article 85), and a buyer must preserve goods in his possession if he intends to reject them (Article 86). In doing so, the goods can either be deposited in a warehouse at the expense of the other party (Article 87) or sold when the other party has unreasonably delayed in reclaiming them (Article 88).

Case 10–7   *Downs Investments Pty. Ltd. v.* *Perwaja Steel SDN BHD*

Australia, Supreme Court of Queensland.
Queensland Supreme Court Reports, vol. 2000, p. 421 (2000).

JUSTICE BRIAN W. AMBROSE:

The Plaintiff [Downs Investments Pty. Ltd.] continues this action commenced by Wanless Metal Industries Pty. Ltd. ("Wanless") to enforce its rights against Perwaja Steel SDN BHD ("Perwaja") under a contract between Wanless and Perwaja dated 7 May 1996 under which Wanless agreed to supply approximately 30,000 metric tons plus/minus ten percent of scrap steel at the price of U.S.$164 per metric ton C.N. F.F.O. Kemaman, Malaysia. Within that range the seller had the option to select the metric tonnage to be supplied and the quantity actually supplied was to be determined by a draft survey at the load port (or ports presumably) by a nominated company (or equivalent).

That contract also provided terms for the discharge of the scrap steel at Kemaman, Malaysia.

The contract provided that Perwaja would make payment for the material delivered in the following terms:

PAYMENT
By irrevocable Letter of Credit from A1 Bank in our favor payable, at sight, for 100% of the invoice value. The L/C is to be established, by 1 July. . . .

* * *

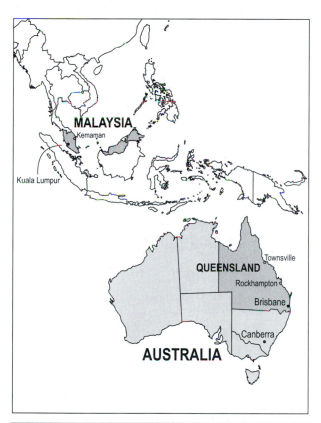

MAP 10-7   Australia and Malaysia (2000)

Documentation

Mr. Anderson gave evidence that the terms of the contract were negotiated between him and the purchasing officer of Perwaja, Rohani Basir. It was a standard form contract which had been used on previous occasions when Wanless sold scrap metal to Perwaja. . . .

After the contract had been signed by and on behalf of Wanless and Perwaja, Wanless's business management, rights, and obligations were acquired by the plain-

tiff. It is not in contest that the plaintiff in this case may enforce against Perwaja any rights which Wanless may have had against it as a result of any breach of contract on its part.

Shortly before the alleged breach by Perwaja of its contract with Wanless the structure and management of Perwaja was changed.

However at the time both of the making of the contract and its alleged breach by Perwaja, Mr. Anderson was the manager of Wanless.

At the time of the making of the contract Rohani Basir and Wan Ghani, the then managing director of Perwaja, were the officers of Perwaja authorized to negotiate the terms of and execute the contract in issue. However, at the time of the alleged breach of that contract by Perwaja, towards the end of July and early August 1996, both Rohani Basir and Wan Ghani had been removed from their former positions of authority with Perwaja in the course of the alteration in its management structure. After that restructuring exercise, the new management team involved Mr. Yunus and Datuk Abu. The case for the defendant was that under the new management structure a letter of credit could not be provided without the permission of an executive committee which had been established as part of the change of the management structure of Perwaja.

* * *

Wanless' agent in Malaysia was Mr. Teo. He attended discussions with Mr. Yunus and others between Mr. Anderson and Mr. Yunus and Datuk Abu.

At the stage of Perwaja's alleged wrongful repudiation of the contract in August 1996 the international price for the sale of that material had dropped by U.S.$20.50 per ton. So, had in fact Perwaja accepted the scrap steel at the contract price fixed in May, because of the drop in market value occurring over a period of about two months it would have had to pay U.S.$705,000.00 in excess of the then current market value. It emerged in the evidence that some members of the executive committee, which declined to permit the issue of the letter of credit requested by Wanless, expressed the view that Perwaja at that time had an excess supply of scrap metal of the sort that it had agreed to purchase from Wanless in May–June 1996.

Stated shortly, the case for Wanless is that it suffered a significant loss on the resale of the 30,000 metric tons of scrap steel it was ready, willing, and able to ship to Perwaja pursuant to the contract and a further sum of $343,163.47 arising from the necessity to sub-charter the vessel chartered to deliver the material to Perwaja.

Wanless claims that Perwaja repudiated the contract because it failed and indeed refused to provide a letter of credit as required by the contract and that it accepted that repudiation reserving its rights to recover its resulting loss.

It is the case for Wanless that the legislation relevant to determine the dispute between Wanless and Perwaja is the Queensland *Sale of Goods (Vienna Convention) Act* 1986.

It is the case for Wanless that Perwaja's failure to establish a letter of credit to cover the cost of the scrap metal under the contract before 9 August 1996 also amounted to a fundamental breach of the contract entitling Wanless to terminate it and recover its resulting loss. The provision of the letter of credit in the circumstances was an essential security for payment of the contract price by Perwaja when the scrap metal arrived at Kemaman by which time Wanless would have incurred significant costs. Obviously the obtaining of a letter of credit before loading commenced in Australia was designed to avoid any attempt by Perwaja to "renegotiate" its contractual obligations in circumstances in which Wanless would find itself in an impossible negotiating position.

* * *

[Discussion]

(1) Terms of Written Contract of 7 May 1996 as Varied to 9 August 1996   I accept the evidence of Neil Anderson, the purchasing officer of Wanless, that he negotiated a contract with Rohani Basir in Brisbane in April/May 1996. . . .

* * *

On 18 July 1996 Wanless sent to Basir of Perwaja a fax in the following terms:

REF: AUGUST SHIPMENT
Please find below our proposed loading schedule—

Bell Bay 19/8 to 23/8
Brisbane 27/8 to 31/8
Gladstone 1/9 to 4/9
Townsville 6/9/ to 10/9
ETA Kemaman 22/9

Accordingly we would request your opening the Letter of Credit for 30,000 ton +/- 10% with the following dates—

Issue—1st August
Expiry—30th September
Latest shipment—29th September

We understand that we will have to accept the cost for the extra 30 days on the L/C. Please advise amount.

Kind regards,
Neil Anderson
PS. Please remember also for L/C:

1.   SHIPMENT FROM AUSTRALIAN PORTS
2.   Cert of origin from Griffith or equiv."

Basir replied to that letter as assistant manager of the bulk purchase division on 22 July 1996. The reply reads as follows:

"We refer to your fax dated 18th July 1996.

We will establish L/C as per your request once you have confirmed the vessel of this contract. Thank you and regards."

* * *

It was on 29 or 30 July that Anderson and Teo together visited Datuk Abu. . . .

Mr. Anderson . . . produced all the documentary evidence . . . [related to the sale of the scrap metal]. Datuk Abu said that he was very sorry that this was not part of the handover notes between the previous management and that which he headed and that had he known that there was this outstanding contract he would have asked the officials from the Ministry of Finance to issue the letter of credit. He then discussed the changes in the management structure and said that he would have to go to an "executive committee" that was now running the company to ask for permission for the issue of the letter of credit. This executive committee comprised Datuk Abu and his brother, a representative from the Ministry of Finance and a chartered accountant.

Anderson told Datuk Abu that they had already committed and arranged for a ship to perform the contract and that it was not possible for them to cancel that charter. He advised that if the letter of credit did not issue Wanless would suffer very significant loss. To this Datuk Abu responded:

"Since you have already committed to a vessel perhaps you could ship the cargo first and we will pay you later or alternatively sell the shipment to another company."

He added:

"If you do it this way in future Perwaja will buy scrap metal from you under the new management."

Mr. Anderson said that he was sorry that he could not accede to that request having regard to the drop in prices that had occurred since the contract was made.

Datuk Abu said that he would like very much to help but it would be difficult and suggested that they come back and see him later because the decision was not his to make; the decision had to be made by the committee.

* * *

On the evening of 2 August 1996 Teo did make contact with Datuk Abu who informed him that he had brought the matter to the attention of the executive committee and one of the committee members objected that the committee could not proceed with the issuing of a letter of credit because the contract had not been made during the tenure of office of the present management. . . .

* * *

(2) Extent to Which Perwaja . . . Had Breached Any Essential Terms of the Contract . . .   Because the parties to the contract agreed that the law applying in Brisbane would define their contractual obligations, the Queensland *Sale of Goods (Vienna Convention) Act 1968* requires the application of the *United Nations Convention on Contracts for the International Sale of Goods 1980* to this contract.

Article 64 of the Convention provides—

(1) The seller may declare the contract avoided—

    (a) if the failure by the buyer to perform any of his obligations under the contract or this Convention amounts to a fundamental breach of contract; or

    (b) if the buyer does not within the additional period of time fixed by the seller in accordance with paragraph (1) of article 63 perform his obligations to pay the price or take delivery of the goods or if he declares that he will not do so within the period so fixed.

"Fundamental breach" is defined in article 25 of the Convention to mean a breach "that results in such detriment to the other party as substantially to deprive him of what he is entitled to expect under the contract unless the party in breach did not foresee and a reasonable person of the same kind in the same circumstances would not have foreseen such a result."

Article 72 provides—

(1) If prior to the date for performance of the contract it is clear that one of the parties will commit a fundamental breach of contract the other party may declare the contract avoided.

(2) If time allows, the party intending to declare the contract avoided must give reasonable notice to the other party in order to permit him to provide adequate assurance of his performance.

(3) The requirements of the preceding paragraph do not apply if the other party has declared that he will not perform his obligations.

Repudiation involves conduct on the part of one party to the contract which when viewed objectively is such "as to convey to a reasonable person in the situation of the other party repudiation or disavowal either of the contract as a whole or of a fundamental obligation under it."[201]

The refusal to establish a timely letter of credit was clearly a fundamental breach within the meaning of Article 25 and Article 64(1)(a) of the Convention. I refer to [John] Honnold, *Uniform Law for International Sales under the United Nations Convention*[202] and *Helen Kaminski Pty. Ltd. v. Marketing Australian Products, Inc.*[203] . . .

* * *

It is possible, if indeed not likely, that members of the committee in declining to meet the contractual obligations of Perwaja to provide the letter of credit to meet the cost of the scrap steel that was awaiting shipment to Kemaman from Australia were conscious of the fact that the contract price for that scrap steel was U.S. $705,000.00 in excess of its then current market value.

(3) Was Wanless Entitled to End the Contract with Perwaja and Recover Damages an the Ground of Perwaja's Repudiation and/or Non-Compliance with an Essential Term of the Contract?

* * *

In my view, the most likely explanation for the refusal of Perwaja to issue the letter of credit without delay was the resolution of the executive committee on 2 August 1996 that the management be authorized "to renegotiate and recommend appropriate action in relation to the supply of scrap" by Wanless.

In my view, Perwaja, by the officers who succeeded Rohani Basir and Wan Ghani in its management, clearly evinced an intention not to meet Perwaja's contractual obligation. It is clear when one reads the "PAYMENT" clause and the letter from Wanless to Perwaja of 18 July 1996 that the provision of the letter of credit prior to the commencement of loading of the shipment to Perwaja of scrap metal was an essential term of contract. It is clear in my view that Perwaja indicated that it did not intend to comply with that requirement. It is equally clear from the resolution of the committee meeting of 2 August 1996 that Perwaja proposed instead

---

[201] *See* Laurinda Pty Ltd v Capalaba Park Shopping Centre Pty. Ltd., *Commonwealth Law Reports,* vol. 166, p. 623 (Australia High Court 1989) per Justice Deane and Dawson.
[202] 2nd ed. at pp. 510, 511.
[203] *Lexis United States District Court Reports,* vol. 1997, No. 10630, *West Law Reports,* vol. 1997, No. 414137 (U.S. District Ct. S. District of New York 1997).

of meeting its contractual obligations with Wanless to embark upon a "renegotiation" of that contract—presumably in the light of the fall in the current market value of scrap steel.

* * *

In my judgment Wanless was entitled to avoid the contract and to recover the loss it suffered as a consequence of Perwaja's repudiation and/or non-compliance with an essential term of its contract with Wanless.

(4) Whether Wanless was Ready, Willing, and Able to Perform Its Obligations at Material Times Prior to Its Avoiding the Contract

* * *

The likelihood of Wanless not being able to fulfill its contractual obligations to supply 30,000 metric tons of scrap metal +/- 10 percent at the time it negotiated the chartering of a vessel to carry such steel from four ports in Australia to Kemaman in Malaysia, because it did not have enough steel to do so in my view is so remote for a scrap metal merchant with the years of experience of Wanless in selling scrap metal both within and outside Australia as to be rejected out of hand.

* * *

I am satisfied that in the months of August and September Wanless was ready, willing, and able to deliver to Perwaja at Kemaman 30,000 metric tons +/- 10 percent of scrap steel in accord with its contract so that delivery would be effected before the end of September 1996.

(5) Whether Wanless Is Entitled to Damages against Perwaja
It is clear that the repudiation of its contractual obligation by Perwaja caused very significant loss to Wanless.

Firstly it had chartered the "Dooyang Winner" for the sole purpose of meeting its contractual obligations with Perwaja. That vessel at the time Perwaja declined to provide letters of credit was in fact waiting to commence loading scrap steel at Bell Bay.

As a result of Perwaja's repudiation of its contractual obligations, Wanless found it necessary to sub-charter that boat, which resulted in financial losses.

In addition it found it necessary to sell both within Australia and outside Australia the scrap steel which it was holding to meet its contractual obligation to Perwaja. The sale outside Australia required scrap material to be unloaded in an Asian port, which required a vessel with a more shallow draught than the "Dooyang Winner". Clearly, in my view, Wanless is entitled to recover against Perwaja damages which it suffered as a consequence of Perwaja's repudiation of its contractual obligation.

Quantum of Damage

The Convention articles relevant to damages recoverable by Wanless for Perwaja's breach of contract are articles 74 and 75.

Article 74 provides—

Damages for breach of contract by one party consist of a sum equal to the loss including loss of profit suffered by the other party as a consequence of the breach. Such damages may not exceed the loss which the party in breach foresaw or ought to have foreseen at the time of the conclusion of the contract in the light of the facts and matters of which he then knew or ought to have known as a possible consequence of the breach of contract.

Article 75 provides, *inter alia:*

If the contract is avoided, and if in a reasonable manner and within a reasonable time after avoidance—the seller has resold the goods the party claiming damages may recover the difference between the contract price and the price in the substitute transaction as well as any further damages recoverable under Article 74.

It is clear on the evidence that Wanless sold 25,100 tons of the metal it was holding to fulfill its contract with Perwaja to Pernas at the then market rate of U.S.$143.50 per ton for delivery at Penang in Malaysia. It was necessary for Wanless to charter another vessel called "MV Handy Light" at approximately the same cost per ton to ship that material as the cost of chartering the "Dooyang Winner" which was unsuitable for that port. In any event I accept that the sub-charter of the "Dooyang Winner" as soon as possible was a reasonable step to minimize the damage incurred by Wanless in having such a large vessel standing by at the expense of Wanless and not being used for the purpose of shipping its scrap steel to Perwaja.

It was agreed between the parties with a view to shortening the evidence which would otherwise necessarily be called that the best estimate of the cost per ton for shipping 30,000 tons on the "Dooyang Winner" was $21.11 per ton. . . .

* * *

Wanless sold a further 5,000 tons to BHP by contracts made in August, September and October 1996 at a price of AU$156.75 per ton, i.e. AU$783,750.00. . . .

* * *

In the months of August, September, and October 1996 the average exchange rate for an Australian dollar and U.S. dollar was—AU$1.00 = U.S.$0.7917. Therefore, AU$783,750.00 equals U.S.$620,494.87.

* * *

It is not disputed by Perwaja that Wanless suffered a net loss of U.S.$343,163.47 as a result of chartering and rechartering the "Dooyang Winner".

This loss was clearly incurred as a consequence of Perwaja's breach of its obligation to establish the appropriate letter of credit. The incurring of a loss of this kind was clearly foreseeable and Perwaja must have known that its failure to establish a letter of credit as promised would result in Wanless being left with a chartered vessel at hand which could not be used for the purpose for which it had been chartered.

In my view once Wanless accepted Perwaja's repudiation of its obligations under the contract and terminated that contract it promptly took all steps reasonably necessary to mitigate the damages it suffered as a consequence of Perwaja's repudiation.

* * *

I assess the plaintiff's damages in U.S. dollars because that is the currency in which the parties expressed their contractual obligations—

Loss of profit on the substitute Pernas sale	U.S.$498,450.00
Loss of profit on the BHP substitute sale	U.S.$ 89,955.13
Loss resulting from rechartering "MV Dooyang Winner"	U.S.$343,163.47
	U.S.$931,568.60
Interest at 9 percent from 30/9/96 to 17/11/2000 [or] 4.16 yrs on U.S.$931,568.60	U.S.$348,779.28

I give judgment for the plaintiff in the sum of U.S.$1,280,347.80 ■

L. EXCUSES FOR NONPERFORMANCE

Two excuses are provided in CISG for a party's failure to perform. One is *force majeure;* the other is "dirty hands."

Force Majeure

A party is not liable for any damages resulting from his failure to perform if he can show (a) that his failure was "due to an impediment beyond his control," (b) that the impediment was not something he could have reasonably taken into account at the time of contracting, and (c) that he remains unable to overcome the impediment or its consequences.[204]

force majeure: (French: "superior force.") An event or effect that cannot be reasonably anticipated or controlled.

This excuse, commonly known as *force majeure*, is not only narrowly defined, it is also limited in its application.[205] It applies to situations—such as natural disasters, war, embargoes, strikes, breakdowns, and the bankruptcy of a supplier—that frustrate both the party attempting to perform and the party expecting performance. Because neither party is really at fault, the breaching party is excused from paying damages. He is not, however, exempted from the application of any other appropriate remedy (such as suspension of performance or avoidance).

A party seeking to use CISG's excuse of *force majeure* is under some additional limitations. First, he has a duty to promptly notify the other party of "the impediment and its effect on his ability to perform."[206] Second, if his claim is based on the failure of a third person to perform (such as a supplier), the third person must himself be able to claim the excuse.[207] Finally, the excuse may be used only as long as the underlying impediment continues in existence.[208]

In Case 10–8, the court was asked to determine if the seller was excused from performing because of "an impediment beyond his control."

---

[204]UN Convention on Contracts for the International Sale of Goods, Article 79(1) (1980).

[205]The CISG rule, based on civil law practice, is much broader, however, than the rule followed in common law countries. For example, in the United States, the Uniform Commercial Code, § 2-615, applies only to a seller and only in respect to two aspects of his performance: delay in delivery and nondelivery. For a comparison of the CISG provision with various domestic rules, *see* John Honnold, *Uniform Law for International Sales under the 1980 United Nations Convention,* pp. 425–427 (1982).

[206]UN Convention on Contracts for the International Sale of Goods, Article 79(4) (1980).

[207]*Id.,* Article 79(2).

[208]*Id.,* Article 79(3).

Case 10–8   Nuova Fucinati, SpA v. Fondmetall International, AB

Italy, Civil Court of Monza, 1993.
Il Foro italiano, vol. 1994, part 1, pp. 916–923 (1994);
Giurisprudenza italiana, vol. 1994, part 1, pp. 146–154.[209]

On February 3, 1988, plaintiff, Nuova Fucinati, SpA, of Monza, Italy, agreed to deliver 1,000 metric tons of chromite to defendant, Fondmetall International, A.B., of Goteborg, Sweden, between March 20, 1988, and April 10, 1998. When plaintiff failed to make delivery, defendant petitioned the Civil Court in Monza, Italy, for a decree of specific performance. On July 20, 1988, the Chief Judge of that court issued the requested decree.

On September 29, 1988, the plaintiff initiated this proceeding to have the original contract set aside on grounds of commercial impracticability. According to the plaintiff, the price of chromite had risen dramatically between the time of the contract and the time of delivery, beyond what could reasonably be anticipated, such that it was too costly for the plaintiff to perform without a price adjustment, which the defendant refused to accept.

The defendant argued that the United Nations Convention on Contracts for the International Sale of Goods (CISG) governed this contractual relationship and that CISG did not provide for the excuse of commercial impracticability.

OPINION:

* * *

The defendant argues that the contract should not be dissolved both as a matter of law [because CISG does not provide for the excuse of commercial impracticability] and because the plaintiff has not alleged facts sufficient to meet the requirements of Article 1467 of the Italian Civil Code [which defines commercial impracticability]. . . .

This is an international sale of goods contract, between an Italian corporation (the seller) and a Swedish corporation (the buyer). The first question we must resolve, therefore, is whether it is governed by *United Nations Convention on Contracts for the International Sale of Goods.*[210] This is not an insignificant question. If the Convention applies, the excuse that a seller may set aside an onerous contract on the grounds

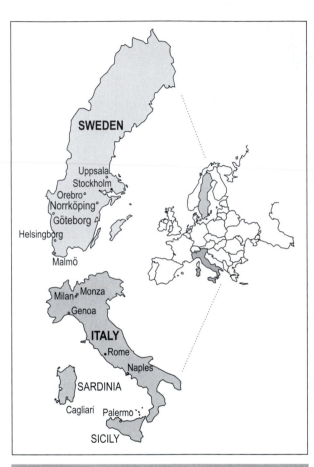

MAP 10-8   Italy and Sweden (1993)

of commercial impracticability does not seem to be available. If the Convention does not apply, then the Article 1467 of the [Italian] Civil Code will apply, and this article does allow a seller to set aside an onerous contract on the basis of commercial impracticability. . . .

[THE EXCUSE OF COMMERCIAL IMPRACTICABILITY]

Article 79 of CISG [which the defendant relies upon] provides:

A party is not liable for a failure to perform any of his obligations if he proves that the failure was due

---

[209]A summary of this case in Italian is posted on the Internet at soi.cnr.it/~crdcs/crdcs/it140193f.htm. Another English translation is posted at cisgw3.law.pace.edu/cases/ 930329i3.html.
[210]Italy ratified the Convention on December 11, 1985, by Law No. 765 and it came into force on January 1, 1988.

to an impediment beyond his control and that he could not reasonably be expected to have taken the impediment into account at the time of the conclusion of the contract. . . .

This article, however, is not concerned with the excuse of commercial impracticability. Rather, it deals with an intervening change in circumstances beyond the control of the breaching party, similar to the excuse of impossibility of performance that is to set out in Article 1463 of the Civil Code. The breaching party invokes it after breaching a contract as an excuse for not performing as required.

Indeed, the main remedy that the CISG grants to a non-breaching party[211] is the remedy of avoidance (or "dissolution" as it is called in the Civil Code), and this remedy can only be invoked *after* a contract has been breached. By comparison, the excuse of commercial impracticability is unrelated to a breach. [It is invoked by a seller *before* there has been a breach to avoid a contract that the seller can perform, but at great cost.] Thus, commercial impracticability does not fit within the general scheme of remedies or excuses set out in the CISG.

. . . This conclusion is confirmed by Article 4 of CISG, which states:

This Convention governs only the formation of the contract of sale and the rights and obligations of the seller and the buyer arising from such a contract. In particular, except as otherwise expressly provided in this Convention, it is not concerned with:

(a) the validity of the contract or of any of its provisions or of any usage; [or]
(b) the effect which the contract may have on the property in the goods sold.

Avoidance of a contract because of commercial impracticability would affect neither the validity of the contract nor the property in the goods (except indirectly, by avoiding the seller's obligation to deliver the goods and thereby keeping the goods from being identified to the contract).

[EFFECT OF THE CISG'S APPLICATION]

The CISG is a "special law." [That is, it governs a specific subject matter.] As a consequence, if it does apply in this case, it will preempt the more general provision set out in Article 1467 *et seq.* of the Civil Code.

[APPLICATION OF THE CISG]

The United Nations Convention came into force in Italy on January 1, 1988. This was before the contract was concluded on February 3, 1988. . . . However, the Convention did not come into force in Sweden until January 1, 1989 [after the contract was concluded]. . . .

Because of an express statement that the buyer added to its acceptance (that is, "law: Italian law shall apply"), the law governing this contract is Italian law. At the time of the contract, of course, the CISG was in effect in Italy and it therefore must be applied like any other law.

* * *

Article 1(1) of the CISG states:

This Convention applies to contracts of sale of goods between parties whose places of business are in different States:

(a) when the States are Contracting States; or
(b) when the rules of private international law lead to the application of the law of a Contracting State.

[The first of these possibilities, option (a), does not lead us to apply the CISG because Sweden was not a Contracting State at the time that the contract was concluded.]

The second possibility, option (b), [which directs us to apply the Italian rules of private international law,] does not lead us to apply the CISG [either]. The rules of private international law set out in Article 25 of the Introductory Provisions of the [Italian] *Civil Code* direct us to apply Swedish law. That is because the contract was concluded in Sweden.[212] However, the CISG was not in force in Sweden when the contract was made. So, again, the CISG cannot apply.

Therefore, because the "special law" (the CISG) does not apply, the "general law" (Article 1467 *et seq.* of the *Civil Code*) is not preempted, and it must be applied as the parties' directed that it should. As a consequence, the seller *can* invoke the excuse of commercial impracticability. . . .

[THE PLAINTIFF'S CLAIM]

The plaintiff asserted that it was entitled to invoke the excuse of commercial impracticability on the fact that, between February 3, 1988 (the date when the contract was concluded) and April (when the plaintiff asserts that the goods were to be delivered), the fair market price of chromite had increased by 43.71 percent. That is from 1,496 lira per kilogram to 2,150 lira per kilogram. This increase, even though proven by the plaintiff, is simply not enough to show that the plaintiff is excused from performing as a matter of commercial impracticability.

---

[211]Article 61 *et seq.* defines seller's remedies and Article 45 *et seq.* defines a buyer's remedies.
[212]Article 1326(1) of the Civil Code provides that the law of the State where a contract is made shall govern the interpretation and enforcement of the contract.

[Such an excuse is allowed only when performance is so economically burdensome that the seller would not have the resources to perform.]

The plaintiff's case was dismissed. Because it was obvious that the buyer had breached the contract, the Chief Judge's

order for specific performance was rescinded and the case was remanded to the examining magistrate for further inquiry into the defendant's claim for compensatory damages. ■

Dirty Hands

dirty hands: Maxim that a party whose actions cause the other party to breach may not complain.

The **dirty hands** excuse is based on a very simple premise, succinctly stated in CISG, Article 80:

> A party may not rely on a failure of the other party to perform, to the extent that such failure was caused by the first party's act or omission.

For example, if a seller agrees to deliver goods to a buyer at the buyer's warehouse, but the buyer's warehouse is locked and inaccessible at the time that the seller is supposed to make delivery, the buyer cannot complain that the seller failed to deliver on time.

Chapter Questions

1. Seller, whose place of business is in State A, and Buyer, whose place of business is in State B, enter into a contract that stipulates that the UN Convention on Contracts for the International Sale of Goods applies. Neither State A nor State B is a contracting state. Does the Convention apply?

2. Retailer in State A decides to go into the catalog sales business in State B. Both countries are parties to CISG. Retailer purchases a mailing list from Ace Credit Card Company. The list has the names and addresses of 500,000 persons owning Ace credit cards in State B, and Retailer uses this to prepare mailing labels. John Q. Public receives a catalog addressed to him personally from Retailer. The catalog describes various types of widgets and gives prices for each one. Has the Retailer made an offer to sell the widgets? If John accepts, will there be a binding contract?

3. On January 1, Seller sent a letter to Buyer offering to sell to Buyer 5,000 widgets for $25 apiece. The letter also stated: "This offer is binding and irrevocable until February 1." On January 5, prior to Buyer's receipt of the letter, Seller called Buyer on the telephone and left the following message on the answering machine at Buyer's place of business: "Ignore my letter of January 1. I have decided to withdraw the offer contained in it." On January 7, after listening to her answering machine and reading the letter that arrived that same day, Buyer sent Seller the following telegram: "I accept your offer of January 1." Is there a contract under CISG?

4. On December 1, Seller sent to Buyer an offer to sell 5,000 widgets to Buyer for $25 apiece. The offer stated: "The offer will remain open until December 31." On December 10, Buyer answered: "The price is too high, I don't accept your offer." Then, on December 15, Buyer changed his mind and sent a telegram stating: "I accept your December 1 offer after all." Seller replied: "Your acceptance is too late, since you already rejected the offer." In turn, Buyer answered: "The acceptance is good, since you promised to keep your offer open until December 31." Is there a contract under the CISG?

5. Buyer received a letter in her mail on January 1 offering to sell Buyer 5,000 widgets for $20 apiece. Seller's letter closed with the following statement: "I know that this offer is so attractive that I will assume that you accept it unless I hear otherwise by January 31." Buyer did not reply. Seller shipped the widgets on February 1. What are Buyer's responsibilities under CISG?

6. Seller and Buyer entered into a written contract for the manufacture by Seller of 10,000 widgets of a design specified by Buyer and set out in the contract. The contract also provided: "This contract may only be modified in a writing signed by both parties." Before Seller had begun work on the widgets, Buyer and Seller agreed by telephone to a change in

the specifications for 2,500 of the widgets. Seller then produced and delivered the 2,500 widgets as specified. Buyer refused to accept them because they did not conform to the specifications in the original contract. Assuming CISG applies, who breached?

7. Buyer and Seller entered into a contract governed by CISG for Seller to deliver a sophisticated computer to Buyer by January 1. Seller was late in delivering the machine, so Buyer wired Seller on January 2: "Anxious to take delivery of the computer. Hope that it arrives by February 1." Seller delivers the computer on February 5, but Buyer refuses to accept it and declares that the contract is avoided because Seller failed to hand over the computer before the February 1 date specified in the January 2 telegram. Both Buyer and Seller agree that there has not been a fundamental breach. Is Buyer able to avoid the contract under these circumstances?

8. Dealer in the United States owned a cargo of 10,000 barrels of oil that had been shipped from Mexico on January 1 for arrival in the United States on February 1. On January 15, Dealer informed Buyer that the oil was *en route* and they concluded a contract. On arrival, inspection showed that the oil had been contaminated by seawater at some indeterminate time during the voyage. Assuming CISG applies, who bears the risk?

9. Seller agreed to deliver three software programs to Buyer that are specially designed for Buyer's business. The first was to be delivered in January, the second in February, the third in March. The program delivered in January worked fine, but the one delivered in February was defective. It not only failed to function properly, it also made the other two programs effectively worthless. Seller was unable to correct the defect, and no suitable replacement could be found from another supplier. What CISG remedies are available to Buyer?

10. Seller contracted to deliver 1,000 barrels of oil to Buyer for $14,000. When the oil arrived, 975 barrels complied fully with the contract description. Twenty-five were contaminated and unacceptable. Oil in comparable barrels was available in the local market for a price of $18 a barrel in 25-barrel lots. Seller offered not to charge Buyer for the barrels. Is there a contract under CISG? If so, what payment is due Seller?

Review Problem

As the Senior Chief Assistant in the law department of MegaBranch Industries (MBI) you have been assigned to oversee the negotiation and signing of one of the largest contracts that MBI has ever been involved in. The MBI subsidiary that is most directly involved is located in a state that is a member of the UN Convention on Contracts for the International Sale of Goods (CISG). Three other firms are also going to be parties to the contract. One is located in another country that is a member of CISG; the other two are not. One of the latter is located in a state that has a civil law legal system; the other is located in a state that has a common law legal system.

1. What law will govern this contract? Can the parties agree that CISG will govern their relationship?
2. The contract involves the sale of goods (including parts and assembled products) as well as the supply of services. Can CISG regulate the entire contract? If not, what parts?
3. Should the parties agree that CISG will be the governing law, what aspects of the contract will be governed, nevertheless, by local law?
4. If the parties agree that CISG will be the governing law, how will the provisions of CISG be interpreted in the event there is some dispute about their meaning?
5. If some provision of the contract is unclear, how will it be interpreted?
6. Must the contract be in writing? Must it be under seal?
7. If one of the parties makes an offer and promises to keep it open for a period of 30 days, can it later change its mind and withdraw the offer?
8. When does an acceptance become effective? Does it matter if the acceptance calls for minor changes in the terms contained in the offer?
9. What criteria will be used to determine if a party has breached?
10. If a party does breach, can the other parties avoid their obligations to perform? Can all of the provisions of the contract—including the choice of law clause—be avoided?

11. If a party fails to perform, can a court intervene and order the party to perform? Are there any limits on what a court may order a party to do?
12. If nothing is said in the contract, where must the seller deliver the goods? When must delivery be made? Where and when must documents of title be turned over?
13. What must a buyer do to reject nonconforming goods?
14. When must the buyer make payment?
15. At what point in time will the buyer become liable for any accidental loss or damage suffered by the goods?
16. What duty does a party have to keep the damages caused by another party's breach to a minimum?
17. What must a seller do if it wishes to seek damages, avoid the contract, or obtain specific performance?
18. What must a buyer do if it wishes to seek damages, avoid the contract, or obtain specific performance?
19. What excuses are available to a breaching party to justify its nonperformance?

CHAPTER

11

Transportation

Chapter Outline

A. TRADE TERMS

trade terms:
Standardized terms used in sales contracts that describe the time, place, and manner for the transfer of goods from the seller to the buyer.

Sales contracts involving transportation customarily contain abbreviated terms describing the time and place where the buyer is to take delivery. These **trade terms**, such as free on board (FOB) and cost, insurance, and freight (CIF), may also define a variety of other matters, including the time and place of payment, the price, the time when the risk of loss shifts from the seller to the buyer, and the costs of freight and insurance.

The same trade abbreviations are widely used in both domestic and international transactions. Unfortunately, they have different meanings depending on the governing law.[1] In the United States, for example, the Uniform Commercial Code defines trade terms for domestic and export sales. In the United Kingdom, the terms are defined by reference to case law.[2] Virtually all domestic laws, however, allow the parties to define the terms themselves, or to incorporate definitions from foreign legislation or from a specific set of private rules. The United Nations Convention on Contracts for the International Sale of Goods similarly allows parties to incorporate trade terms of their choosing.[3]

Incoterms: Trade terms published by the International Chamber of Commerce.

The most widely used private trade terms are those published by the International Chamber of Commerce (ICC). Called **Incoterms**, they are well known throughout the world, and their use in international sales is encouraged by trade councils, courts, and international lawyers.[4] First

---

[1]*See Trade Terms,* an International Chamber of Commerce publication (Document No. 16, issued in 1955), which describes how 10 major trade terms are defined in 18 countries.
    Not all countries use trade terms, however. Japan, for example, has no established set of domestic trade terms. Hisashi Tanikawa, "Risk of Loss in Japanese Sales Transactions," *Washington Law Review,* vol. 42, p. 475 (1967).
[2]*See* D. Michael Day, *The Law of International Trade,* pp. 40–80 (1981).
[3]UN Convention on the International Sale of Goods, Article 6 (1980), provides: "The parties may exclude the application of this Convention, or . . . derogate from or vary the effect of any of its provisions."
[4]The National Foreign Trade Council in New York, which issued its own definitions, the *Revised American Foreign Trade Definitions,* in 1941, has since 1980 encouraged traders to use the Incoterms instead. *See* Paul H. Vishny, *Guide to International Commerce Law,* § 2-36 (1998).

published in 1936, the current version is *Incoterms 2000.*[5] Parties who adopt the Incoterms, or any other trade terms, should make sure they express their desire clearly. For example, a contract might refer to "FOB (*Incoterms 2000*)" or "CIF (U.S. Uniform Commercial Code)." Courts will otherwise apply the definitions used in their own jurisdictions.[6] Parties should also refrain from casually adopting any particular set of terms. The ICC's Incoterms, which are possibly the most complete of all such rules, are lengthy and deserve careful study. Finally, parties should be wary about making additions or varying the meaning of any particular term, except to the extent that it is allowed by the rules they adopt or by judicial decision. Courts are as apt to ignore a variation, or hold that the entire term is ineffective, as they are to apply it.[7]

The parties' failure to use any trade term at all can also produce unexpected results. Courts are then left to divine the parties' intent and to decide the case based on local commercial practice. Such a problem arose in Case 11–1.

---

[5]International Chamber of Commerce, *Incoterms 2000* (Publication No. 560, 2000). The Incoterms are currently revised every 10 years.
[6]Frederic Eisemann, "Incoterms and the British Export Trade," *Journal of Business Law,* vol. 1965, p. 119 (1965), doubts that Incoterms have become sufficiently accepted to constitute a trade usage or custom.
[7]Paul H. Vishny, *Guide to International Commerce Law,* § 2-37 (1998).

Case 11–1   *St. Paul Guardian Insurance Company v. Neuromed Medical Systems & Support, GmbH*

United States District Court for the Southern District of New York
LEXIS United States District Court Cases, no. 5096 (2002).

DISTRICT JUDGE SIDNEY H. STEIN:

Plaintiffs St. Paul Guardian Insurance Company and Travelers Property Casualty Insurance Company have brought this action as subrogees[8] of Shared Imaging, Inc., to recover $285,000 they paid to Shared Imaging for damage to a mobile magnetic resonance imaging system ("MRI") purchased by Shared Imaging from defendant Neuromed Medical Systems & Support GmbH ("Neuromed"). Neuromed has moved to dismiss the complaint. . . . [It contends that] the complaint fails to state a claim for relief. . . .

The crux of Neuromed's argument is that it had no further obligations regarding the risk of loss once it delivered the MRI to the vessel at the port of shipment due to a "CIF" clause included in the underlying contract. Plaintiffs respond that . . . the generally understood definition of the "CIF" term as defined by the International Chamber of

Commerce's publication, INCOTERMS 1990, is inapplicable here. . . .

Pursuant to the applicable German law—the U.N. Convention on Contracts for the International Sale of Goods—the "CIF" term in the contract operated to pass the risk of loss to Shared Imaging at the port of shipment, at which time, the parties agree, the MRI was undamaged and in good working order. Accordingly, Neuromed's motion to dismiss the complaint should be granted and the complaint dismissed.

BACKGROUND

Shared Imaging, an American corporation, and Neuromed, a German corporation, entered into a contract of sale for a Siemens Harmony 1.0 Tesla mobile MRI. Thereafter, both parties engaged various entities to transport, insure, and provide customs entry service for the MRI. Plaintiffs originally named those entities as defendants, but the action has been discontinued against them by agreement of the parties. Neuromed is the sole remaining defendant.

---

[8]Subrogees are persons who have been subrogated to the legal claim of another; that is, persons who have assumed the legal right to collect another's debt or damages.]

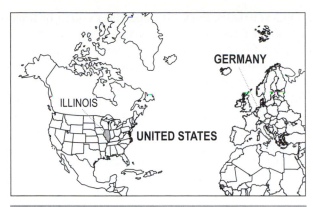

MAP 11-1   Germany and United States (2002)

According to the complaint, the MRI was loaded aboard the vessel "Atlantic Carrier" undamaged and in good working order. When it reached its destination of Calmut City, Illinois, it had been damaged and was in need of extensive repair, which led plaintiffs to conclude that the MRI had been damaged in transit.

The one page contract of sale contains nine headings, including: "Product," "Delivery Terms," "Payment Terms," "Disclaimer," and "Applicable Law." Under "Product" the contract provides, the "system will be delivered cold and fully functional." Under "Delivery Terms" it provides, "CIF New York Seaport, the buyer will arrange and pay for customs clearance as well as transport to Calmut City."

Under "Payment Terms" it states, "By money transfer to one of our accounts, with following payment terms: U.S. $93,000—downpayment to secure the system; U.S. $744,000—prior to shipping; U.S. $93,000—upon acceptance by Siemens of the MRI system within three business days after arrival in Calmut City." In addition, under "Disclaimer" it states, "system including all accessories and options remain the property of Neuromed till complete payment has been received." Preceding this clause is a handwritten note, allegedly initialed by Raymond Stachowiak of Shared Imaging, stating, "Acceptance subject to Inspection."

Discussion

Neuromed contends that because the delivery terms were "CIF New York Seaport," its contractual obligation, with regard to risk of loss or damage, ended when it delivered the MRI to the vessel at the port of shipment and therefore the action must be dismissed because plaintiffs have failed to state a claim for which relief can be granted. Plaintiffs respond that the generally accepted definition of the "CIF" term as defined in

INCOTERMS 1990, is inapplicable. Moreover, plaintiffs suggest that other provisions of the contract are inconsistent with the "CIF" term because Neuromed, pursuant to the contract, retained title subsequent to delivery to the vessel at the port of shipment and thus, Neuromed manifestly retained the risk of loss.

* * *

B. Applicable Law

* * *

The parties have each submitted relevant opinions of German legal experts and the Court has independently researched the applicable foreign law. On the basis of those submissions and analysis, the Court finds the expert opinion of Karl-Ulrich Werkmeister for the defendants to be an accurate statement of German law.

2. Applicable German Law   The parties concede that pursuant to German law, the UN Convention on Contracts for the International Sale of Goods ("CISG") governs this transaction because (1) both the U.S. and Germany are Contracting States to that Convention, and (2) neither party chose, by express provision in the contract, to opt out of the application of the CISG.[9]

The CISG aims to bring uniformity to international business transactions, using simple, non-nation specific language. To that end, it is comprised of rules applicable to the conclusion of contracts of sale of international goods. In its application regard is to be paid to comity and interpretations grounded in its underlying principles rather than in specific national conventions.[10]

Germany has been a Contracting State since 1991, and the CISG is an integral part of German law. Where parties, as here, designate a choice of law clause in their contract—selecting the law of a Contracting State without expressly excluding application of the CISG—German courts uphold application of the Convention as the law of the designated Contracting state. To hold otherwise would undermine the objectives of the Convention which Germany has agreed to uphold.

C. CISG, INCOTERMS and "CIF"   "CIF," which stands for "cost, insurance and freight," is a commercial trade term that is defined in INCOTERMS 1990, published by the International Chamber of Commerce ("ICC"). The aim of INCOTERMS, which stands for international commercial terms, is "to provide a set of international rules for the interpretation of the most commonly used trade terms in foreign trade." These "trade terms are used to allocate the costs of freight and

---

[9]*See* CISG, art. 1(1)(a) . . . ; Larry A. DiMatteo, *The Law of International Contracting*, p. 206 (2000).
[10]*See* CISG art. 7(1), (2). . . .

insurance" in addition to designating the point in time when the risk of loss passes to the purchaser. INCOTERMS are incorporated into the CISG through Article 9(2) which provides that,

> The parties are considered, unless otherwise agreed, to have impliedly made applicable to their contract or its formation a usage of which the parties knew or ought to have known and which in international trade is widely known to, and regularly observed by, parties to contracts of the type involved in the particular trade concerned.

At the time the contract was entered into, INCOTERMS 1990 was applicable. INCOTERMS define "CIF" (named port of destination) to mean the seller delivers when the goods pass "the ship's rail in the port of shipment." The seller is responsible for paying the cost, freight, and insurance coverage necessary to bring the goods to the named port of destination, but the risk of loss or damage to the goods passes from seller to buyer upon delivery to the port of shipment. Further, "CIF" requires the seller to obtain insurance only on minimum cover.

Plaintiffs' legal expert contends that INCOTERMS are inapplicable here because the contract fails to specifically incorporate them. Nonetheless, he cites and acknowledges that the German Supreme Court—the court of last resort in the Federal Republic of Germany for civil matters—concluded that a clause "fob" without specific reference to INCOTERMS was to be interpreted according to INCOTERMS "simply because the [INCOTERMS] include a clause 'fob.'"

Conceding that commercial practice attains the force of law under section 346 of the German Commercial Code, plaintiffs' expert concludes that the opinion of the BGH "amounts to saying that the [INCOTERMS] definitions in Germany have the force of law as trade custom." As encapsulated by defendant's legal expert, "It is accepted under German law that in case a contract refers to CIF-delivery, the parties refer to the INCOTERMS rules. . . ."

The use of the "CIF" term in the contract demonstrates that the parties "agreed to the detailed oriented [INCOTERMS] in order to enhance the Convention."[11] Thus, pursuant to CISG art. 9(2), INCOTERMS definitions should be applied to the contract despite the lack of an explicit INCOTERMS reference in the contract.

D. INCOTERMS, the CISG, and the Passage of Risk of Loss and Title Plaintiffs argue that Neuromed's explicit retention of title in the contract to the MRI machine modified the "CIF" term, such that Neuromed retained title and assumed the risk of loss. INCOTERMS, however, only address passage of risk, not transfer of title. Under the CISG, the passage of risk is likewise independent of the transfer of title.[12] Plaintiffs' legal expert mistakenly asserts that the moment of 'passing of risk' has not been defined in the CISG. Chapter IV of that Convention, entitled "Passing of Risk," explicitly defines the time at which risk passes from seller to buyer pursuant to Article 67(1),

> If the contract of sale involves carriage of the goods and seller is not bound to hand them over at a particular place, the risk passes to the buyer when the goods are handed over to the first carrier for transmission to the buyer in accordance with the contract of sale. If the seller is bound to hand the goods over to a carrier at a particular place, the risk does not pass to the buyer until the goods are handed over to the carrier at that place.

Pursuant to the CISG, "the risk passes without taking into account who owns the goods. The passing of ownership is not regulated by the CISG according to art. 4(b)."[13] Article 4(b) provides that the Convention is not concerned with "the effect which the contract may have on the property in the goods sold."[14] Moreover, according to Article 67(1), the passage of risk and transfer of title need not occur at the same time, as the seller's retention of "documents controlling the disposition of the goods does not affect the passage of risk."

Had the CISG been silent, as plaintiffs' expert claimed, the Court would have been required to turn to German law as a "gap filler." There again, plaintiffs' assertions falter. German law also recognizes passage of risk and transfer of title as two independent legal acts. In fact, it is standard "practice under German law to agree that the transfer of title will only occur upon payment of the entire purchase price, well after the date of passing of risk and after receipt of the goods by the buyer."[15] Support for this proposition of German law is cited by both experts. They each refer to section 447 of the German Civil Code, a provision dealing with long distance sales, providing in part—as translated by plaintiff's expert—that "the risk of loss passes to the buyer at the

---

[11]Neil Gary Oberman, "Transfer of Risk From Seller to Buyer in International Commercial Contracts: A Comparative Analysis of Risk Allocation Under CISG, UCC and INCOTERMS," at www.cisg.law.pace.edu/cisg/thesis/Oberman.html.

[12]*See* CISG art. 67(1).

[13]Annemieke Romein, "The Passing of Risk: A Comparison Between the Passing of Risk under the CISG and German Law" (Heidelberg, June 1999), at www.cisg.law.pace.edu/cisg/biblio/romein.html.

[14]CISG art. 4(b).

[15]Werkmeister's Reply Opinion at p. 7.

moment when the seller has handed the matter to the forwarder, the carrier or to the otherwise determined person or institution for the transport."[16]

Accordingly, pursuant to INCOTERMS, the CISG, and specific German law, Neuromed's retention of title did not thereby implicate retention of the risk of loss or damage.

* * *

Conclusion

For the foregoing reasons, Neuromed's motion to dismiss for failure to state a claim is granted and the complaint is dismissed. ■

---

[16]Strube's Opinion at p. 5.

A Note on the Incoterms

Because the ICC's Incoterms are the most commonly used trade terms, most of this discussion of trade terms will focus on them.

The 2000 revision makes few changes from the previous revision, *Incoterms 1990.*[17] The 1990 revision made several significant modifications to the earlier terms, reflecting changes both in technology and in shipping practices that occurred during the 1980s. According to the ICC, "The main reason for the 1990 revision of *Incoterms* was the desire to adapt terms to the increasing use of electronic data interchange (EDI)." The terms, accordingly, allow parties to transmit documents electronically, including negotiable bills of lading, so long as their contract specifically allows them to do so. The second major reason for the revision stemmed "from transportation techniques, particularly the unitization of cargo in containers, multimodal transport, and roll-on roll-off traffic with road vehicles and railway wagons in 'short sea' maritime transport." Older terms that applied to peculiar modes of land and air transport—such as free on rail (FOR), free on truck (FOT), and FOB airport—were eliminated and the "free carrier" term was expanded.

The Incoterms are classified into four groups arranged according to the parties' obligations. The "E" Group (i.e., ex works [EXW]) requires the buyer to take delivery of the goods at the buyer's premises. The "F" Group (i.e., free carrier [FCA], free alongside ship [FAS], and free on board) requires the seller to deliver goods to a carrier. The "C" Group (i.e., cost and freight [CFR]; cost, insurance, and freight [CIF]; carriage paid to [CPT]; and carriage and insurance paid to [CIP]) requires the seller to arrange and pay for carriage, but he does not assume the risk for loss or damage once the goods are delivered to the carrier. The "D" Group (i.e., delivered at frontier [DAF], delivered ex ship [DES], delivered ex quay [DEQ], delivered duty unpaid [DDU], and delivered duty paid [DDP]) requires the seller to bear all costs and risks of bringing the goods to the buyer's country.

Certain Incoterms apply only to particular forms of transport. FAS, FOB, CFR, CIF, DES, and DEQ apply only to sea and inland waterway transport. The other terms—EXW, FCA, CPT, CIP, DAF, DDU, and DDP—apply to any form of transport. These last are especially important when several different forms of transport (i.e., "multimodal" transport) are used to get goods to their destination. This arrangement of the Incoterms is summarized in Exhibit 11-1.

The most important Incoterms are discussed in the text. Other terms are defined in Exhibit 11-2.

"Free" Terms

free: When used in a trade term, it means that the seller has an obligation to deliver goods to a named place for transfer to a carrier.

Several of the common trade terms begin with the word **free** (e.g., free on board, free alongside, free carrier). "Free" means that the seller has an obligation to deliver the goods to a named place for transfer to a carrier. National laws sometimes treat the "free" terms as interchangeable, so

---

[17]International Chamber of Commerce, Pub. No. 460.

Any mode of transport	**EXW**	Ex Works (. . . named place)
	FCA	Free Carrier (. . . named place)
	CPT	Carriage Paid To (. . . named place of destination)
	CIP	Carriage and Insurance Paid To (. . . named place of destination)
	DAF	Delivered at Frontier (. . . named place)
	DDU	Delivered Duty Unpaid (. . . named place of destination)
	DDP	Delivered Duty Paid (. . . named place of destination)
Maritime and inland waterway transport only	**FAS**	Free alongside Ship (. . . named port of shipment)
	FOB	Free on Board (. . . named port of shipment)
	CFR	Cost and Freight (. . . named port of destination)
	CIF	Cost, Insurance, and Freight (. . . named port of destination)
	DES	Delivered Ex Ship (. . . named port of destination)
	DEQ	Delivered Ex Quay (. . . named port of destination)

EXHIBIT 11-1 Mode of Transport and the Appropriate Incoterm 2000

Source: Incoterms 2000 (International Chamber of Commerce, Pub. No. 560).

it is important for contracting parties to identify not only the term but also the set of rules that applies to their particular transaction.[18]

FOB—Free on Board

free on board: Seller fulfills his obligations to deliver when the goods have passed over the ship's rail at the named port of shipment.

Historically, **free on board,** as its name suggests, is a maritime trade term; and in most of the world its use remains limited to seaborne commerce. The ICC's *Incoterms 2000*, accordingly, uses it only in connection with the carriage of goods by sea. In common law countries, however, it is also used for inland carriage aboard any "vessel, car or other vehicle."[19]

The FOB (port of shipment) contract requires a seller to deliver goods on board a vessel that is to be designated by the buyer in a manner customary at the particular port. For example,

EXHIBIT 11-2 Incoterms 2000—Trade Terms

Term	Definition
Ex works	The seller fulfills his obligations to deliver when he has made the goods available at his premises.
Free carrier	The seller fulfills his obligations to deliver when he has handed over the goods, cleared for export, into the charge of the carrier named by the buyer at the named place or point.
Free alongside ship	The seller fulfills his obligations to deliver when the goods have been placed alongside the vessel on the quay or in lighters at the named port of shipment.
Free on board	The seller fulfills his obligations to deliver when the goods have passed over the ship's rail at the named port of shipment.
Cost and freight	The seller must pay the costs and freight necessary to bring the goods to the named port of destination, but the risk of loss of or damage to the goods, as well as any additional costs due to events occurring after the time the goods have been delivered on board the vessel, is transferred from the seller to the buyer when the goods pass the ship's rail in the port of shipment.
Cost, insurance, and freight	The seller has the same obligations as under the cost and freight term but with the addition that he has to procure marine insurance against the buyer's risk of loss of or damage to the goods during the carriage.

---

[18]In France, for example, the distinction between FOB and FAS is sometimes blurred. Frederic Eisemann, *Usages de la Vente Commerciale Internationale,* p. 83 (1972).

[19]United States, Uniform Commercial Code, § 2–319(1)(c). For the practice in the United Kingdom, *see* D. Michael Day, *The Law of International Trade,* p. 42 (1981).

Carriage paid to	The seller pays the freight for the carriage of the goods to the named destination. The risk of loss of or damage to the goods, as well as any additional costs due to events occurring after the time the goods have been delivered to the carrier, is transferred from the seller to the buyer when the goods have been delivered into the custody of the carrier.
Carriage and insurance paid to	The seller has the same obligations as under the carriage and freight term but with the addition that he has to procure cargo insurance against the buyer's risk of loss of or damage to the goods during the carriage.
Delivered at frontier	The seller fulfills his obligation to deliver when the goods have been made available, cleared for export, at the named point and place at the frontier, but before the customs border of the adjoining country.
Delivered ex ship	The seller fulfills his obligation to deliver when the goods have been made available to the buyer on board the ship, uncleared for import, at the named port of destination. The seller has to bear all the costs and risks involved in bringing the goods to the named port of destination.
Delivered ex quay (duty paid)	The seller fulfills his obligation to deliver when the goods have been made available to the buyer on the quay (wharf) at the named port of destination, cleared for importation. The seller has to bear all risks and costs including duties, taxes, and other charges of delivering the goods thereto.
Delivered duty unpaid	The seller fulfills his obligation to deliver when the goods have been made available at the named place in the country of importation. The seller has to bear the costs and risks involved in bringing the goods thereto (excluding duties, taxes, and other official charges payable upon importation) as well as the costs and risks of carrying out customs formalities. The buyer has to pay any additional costs and to bear any risks caused by his failure to clear the goods for importation in time.
Delivered duty paid	The seller fulfills his obligation to deliver when the goods have been made available at the named place in the country of importation. The seller has to bear the costs and risks, including duties, taxes, and other charges of delivering the goods cleared for importation.

EXHIBIT 11-2   Continued

Source: Incoterms 2000 (International Chamber of Commerce, Pub. No. 560).

FOB Singapore requires the buyer to name the ship that will accept delivery in Singapore, and the seller must deliver the goods on board the ship as required by the port rules in Singapore. The *Incoterms 2000* description of the parties' particular duties is set out in Exhibit 11-3.

The essence of an FOB contract is the notion that a seller is responsible for getting goods on board a ship designated by a buyer. What is meant by "on board" has been the issue in many cases and is described in detail in the Incoterms. Traditionally (and according to the Incoterms), goods are "on board" a ship the moment they cross its rail. A seller's responsibility, however, does not end at that point, unless the goods are also "appropriated to the contract"—that is, they are "clearly set aside or otherwise identified as the contract goods." Thus, the seller continues to be responsible for the goods even after the buyer's chosen ship takes control of the goods at the end of its cargo boom and begins to hoist the goods off the dock. Moreover, the seller may remain responsible for the goods even after they are loaded onto the ship, if they remain unidentified to the buyer's contract. This traditional rule is both applied and criticized in Case 11–2.

EXHIBIT 11-3   Incoterms 2000—Free on Board (. . . named port of shipment)

A. THE SELLER'S OBLIGATIONS:	B. THE BUYER'S OBLIGATIONS:
A1 Provision of goods in conformity with the contract	**B1 Payment of the price**
The seller must provide the goods and the commercial invoice, or its equivalent electronic message, in conformity with the contract of sale, and any other evidence of conformity which may be required by the contract.	The buyer must pay the price as provided in the contract of sale.

(continued)

A2 Licenses, authorizations, and formalities

The seller must obtain at his own risk and expense any export license or official authorization and carry out, where applicable, all customs formalities necessary for the exportation of the goods.

A3 Contracts of carriage and insurance

a) *Contract of Carriage*
   No obligation.
b) *Contract of Insurance*
   No obligation.

A4 Delivery

The seller must deliver the goods on the date or within the period at the named port of shipment and in the manner customary at the port on board the vessel nominated by the buyer.

A5 Transfer of risks

The seller must, subject to the provisions of B5, bear all risks of loss of or damage to the goods until such time as they shall have passed the ship's rail at the named port of shipment.

A6 Division of costs

The seller must, subject to the provisions of B6, pay
• all costs relating to the goods until such time as they have passed the ship's rail at the named port of of shipment; and
• where applicable, the costs of customs formalities necessary for exportation as well as all duties, taxes and other official charges payable upon export.

A7 Notice to the buyer

The seller must give the buyer sufficient notice that the goods have been delivered in accordance with A4.

B2 Licenses, authorizations, and formalities

The buyer must obtain at his own risk and expense any import license or other official authorization and carry out, where applicable, all customs formalities for the importation of the goods and, where necessary, for their transit through another country.

B3 Contracts of carriage and insurance

a) *Contract of carriage*
   The buyer must contract at his own expense for the carriage of the goods from the named port of shipment.
b) *Contract of insurance*
   No obligation.

B4 Taking delivery

The buyer must take delivery of the goods when they have been delivered in accordance with A4.

B5 Transfer of risks

The buyer must bear all risks of loss of or damage to the goods
• from the time they have passed the ship's rail at the named port of shipment; and
• from the agreed date or the expiry date of the agreed period for delivery which arise because he fails to give notice in accordance with B7, or because the vessel nominated by him fails to arrive on time, or is unable to take the goods, or closes for cargo earlier than the time notified in accordance with B7, provided, however, that the goods have been duly appropriated to the contract, that is to say, clearly set aside or otherwise identified as the contract goods.

B6 Division of costs

The buyer must pay
• all costs relating to the goods from the time they have passed the ship's rail at the named port of shipment; and
• any additional costs incurred, either because the vessel named by him has failed to arrive on time, or is unable to take the goods, or closes for cargo earlier than the time notified in accordance with B7, or because the buyer has failed to give appropriate notice in accordance with B7, provided, however, that the goods have been duly appropriated to the contract, that is to say, clearly set aside or otherwise identified as the contract goods; and
• where applicable, all duties, taxes, and other official charges as well as the costs of carrying out customs formalities payable upon import of the goods and for their transit through any country.

B7 Notice to the seller

The buyer must give the seller sufficient notice of the vessel name, loading point, and required delivery time.

EXHIBIT 11-3   Continued

A8 Proof of delivery, transport document, or equivalent electronic message

The seller must provide the buyer at the seller's expense with the usual proof of delivery in accordance with A4.

Unless the document referred to in the preceding paragraph is the transport document, the seller must render the buyer, at the latter's request, risk, and expense, every assistance in obtaining a transport document for the contract of carriage (for example, a negotiable bill of lading, a non-negotiable sea waybill, an inland waterway document, or a multimodal transport document).

Where the seller and the buyer have agreed to communicate electronically, the document referred to in the preceding paragraph may be replaced by an equivalent electronic data interchange (EDI) message.

A9 Checking—packaging—marking

The seller must pay the costs of those checking operations (such as checking quality, measuring, weighing, counting) which are necessary for the purpose of delivering the the goods in accordance with A4.

The seller must provide at his own expense packaging (unless it is usual for the particular trade to ship the goods of the contract description unpacked) which is required for the transport of the goods, to the extent that the circumstances relating to the transport (for example modalities, destination) are made known to the seller before the contract of sale is concluded. Packaging is to be marked appropriately.

A10 Other obligations

The seller must render the buyer at the latter's request, risk, and expense, every assistance in obtaining any documents or equivalent electronic messages (other than those mentioned in A8) issued or transmitted in the country of shipment and/or of origin which the buyer may require for the import of the goods, and, where necessary, for their transit through another country. The seller must provide the buyer, upon request, with the necessary information for procuring insurance.

B8 Proof of delivery, transport document, or equivalent electronic message

The buyer must accept the proof of delivery in accordance with A8.

B9 Inspection of goods

The buyer must pay the costs of pre-shipment inspection except when such inspection is mandated by the authorities of the country of export.

B10 Other applications

The buyer must pay all costs and charges incurred in obtaining the documents or equivalent electronic messages mentioned in A10 and reimburse those incurred by the seller in rendering his assistance in accordance therewith.

EXHIBIT 11-3   Continued

Source: Incoterms 2000 (International Chamber of Commerce, Pub. No. 560).

Case 11–2   Pyrene Co., Ltd. v. Scindia Navigation Co., Ltd.

England, Queen's Bench, 1954.
All England Law Reports, vol. 1954, pt. 2, p. 158 (1954).

In August, 1948, the plaintiffs entered into a contract with the Government of India, through the Indian Store

Department (known as I.S.D.), by which they agreed to sell a number of "Pyrene" airfield crash tenders, FOB London. In February, 1951, the plaintiffs notified I.S.D. that one of the tenders was ready for delivery. I.S.D., through its shipping agents, Bahr, Behrend & Co. (who were also freight brokers for the defendants), arranged for the tender to be shipped on the SS Jalazad, belonging to the defendants. In pursuance of instructions contained in a letter dated April 7, 1951, from I.S.D., the plaintiffs delivered the tender at the Royal Albert Dock in the Port of London for delivery to the defendants for loading. On April 16, 1951, the tender was put into a Port of London barge and delivered to the defendants alongside the Jalazad, and, while the defendants' stevedores were in the process of lifting it on board the ship by means of the ship's tackle and before it was across the ship's rail, it was, through the fault of the ship, dropped and damaged.

JUDGE DEVLIN:

. . . The damage to the tender cost £966 to repair and the plaintiffs sue for that sum. The defendants admit liability, but claim that the amount is limited under Article IV (5) of the Hague Rules. The limit stated in that rule is . . . £200. . . .

The fire tender was not the only piece of machinery supplied by the plaintiffs for shipment on board this ship, though it was the only piece that was damaged before shipment. A bill of lading had been prepared to cover the whole shipment, and it was issued to I.S.D. in due course but with the fire tender deleted from it. The bill of lading incorporated the Hague Rules and was subject to their provisions, as by the Carriage of Goods by Sea Act, 1924, § 3, it was bound to be. It is not disputed that, in this case, as in the vast majority of cases, the contract of carriage was actually created before the issue of the bill of lading which evidences its terms.

I think it is convenient to begin by considering the effect of the rules. For counsel for the plaintiffs contends that, even if a bill of lading covering the fire tender had been issued incorporating the rules, the holder of the bill would not be subject to immunity in respect of an accident occurring at this stage of the loading. If this is so, it disposes of the defendants' plea. If it is not so, I shall have to consider whether the rules affect the contract of affreightment when no bill of lading is issued, and whether the plaintiffs were a party to that or any similar contract. The argument of counsel for the plaintiffs turns on the meaning to be given to Article I(e) which defines "carriage for goods" as covering:

> the period from the time when the goods are loaded on to the time when they are discharged from the ship.

MAP 11-2 United Kingdom (1954)

Counsel says these goods never were loaded *on* to the ship. In a literal sense obviously they were not. But counsel does not rely on the literal sense; there are rules which could hardly be made intelligible if they began to operate only after the goods had been landed on deck. He treats the word "on" as having the same meaning as in "free on board"; goods are loaded on the ship as soon as they are put across the ship's rail, which the tender never was. . . . He relies on *Harris v. Best, Ryley & Co.*[20] and *Argonaut Navigation Co., Ltd., v. Ministry of Food, S.S. Argobec*[21] which lay down the rule that loading is a joint operation, the shipper's duty being to lift the cargo to the rail of the ship (I shall refer to that as the first stage of the loading) and the shipowners to take it on board and stow it (I shall refer to that as the second stage).

Counsel contends, therefore, that the accident occurred outside the period specified in Article I(e). So, he says Article IV (5) (which limits liability), and, indeed, all the other rules which regulate the rights and responsibilities of the shipowner, do not apply. . . .

In my judgment, this argument is fallacious, the cause of the fallacy, perhaps, lying in the supposition inherent in it that the rights and liabilities under the rules attach to a period of time. I think they attach to a contract or part of a contract. I say "part of a contract"

[20]*Law Times Reports,* vol. 68, p. 76 (1892).
[21]*All England Law Reports,* vol. 1949, pt. 1, p. 160 at p. 163 (King's Bench, 1949).

because a single contract may cover both inland and sea transport; and, in that case, the only part of it that falls within the rules is that which, to use the words in the definition of "contract of carriage" in Article I(b), "relates to the carriage of goods by sea." Even if "carriage of goods by sea" were given by definition the most restricted meaning possible—for example, the period of the voyage—the loading of the goods (by which I mean the whole operation of loading in both its stages and whichever side of the ship's rail) would still *relate* to the carriage on the voyage and so be within the "contract of carriage."

Article II is the crucial article which, for this purpose, has to be construed. It is this article that gives the carrier all his rights and immunities, including the right to limit his liability. . . .

But before I try to elucidate that, let me state my view of Article I(e). For, as I have said, though not dominant, it is not irrelevant; in construing "loading" in Article II you must have regard to similar expressions throughout the rules, Article I(e) included. In my judgment, no special significance need be given to the phrase "loaded on". It is not intended to specify a precise moment of time. . . . The function of Article I(e) is, I think, only to assist in the definition of contract of carriage. As I have already pointed out, there is excluded from that definition any part of a larger contract which relates, for example, to inland transport. It is natural to divide such a contract into periods, a period of inland transport, followed, perhaps, by a period of sea transport and then again by a period of inland transport. Discharging from rail at the port of loading may fall into the first period; loading on to the ship into the second. The reference to "when the goods are loaded on" in Article I(e) is not, I think, intended to do more than identify the first operation in the series which constitute the carriage of goods by sea, as "when they are discharged" denotes the last. The use of the rather loose word "cover," I think, supports this view.

. . . Article III(2), for example, provides: "the carrier shall properly and carefully load," etc. If "load" includes both stages, does that oblige the shipowner, whether he wants to or not, to undertake the whole of the loading? If so, it is a new idea to English lawyers, though, perhaps, more revolutionary in theory than in practice. But, if not, and "load" includes only the second stage, then should it not be given a similar meaning in Article II with the result that immunity extends only to the second stage? There is, however, a third interpretation to Article III(2). The phrase "shall properly and carefully load" may mean that the carrier shall load and that he shall do it

properly and carefully, or that he shall do whatever loading he does properly and carefully. The former interpretation, perhaps, fits the language more closely, but the latter may be more consistent with the object of the rules. Their object as it is put, I think, correctly in Carver's *Carriage of Goods by Sea*,[22] is to define, not the scope of the contract service, but the terms on which that service is to be performed. The extent to which the carrier has to undertake the loading of the vessel may depend not only on different systems of law but on the custom and practice of the port and the nature of the cargo. It is difficult to believe that the rules were intended to impose a universal rigidity in this respect, or to deny freedom of contract to the carrier. The carrier is practically bound to play some part in the loading and discharging, so that both operations are naturally included in those covered by the contract of carriage. But I see no reason why the rules should not leave the parties free to determine by their own contract the part which each has to play. On this view, the whole contract of carriage is subject to the rules, but the extent to which loading and discharging are brought within the carrier's obligations is left to the parties themselves to decide.

I reject the interpretation of loading in Article II as covering only the second stage of the operation. Such authority as there is against it. If loading under the rules does not begin before the ship's rail, by parity of reasoning discharging should end at the ship's rail; but so to hold would be contrary to the decision of Judge Roche in *Goodwin, Ferreira & Co., Ltd. v. Lamport & Holt, Ltd.*[23]

Since the shipowner in this case in fact undertook the whole operation of loading it is unnecessary to decide which of the other two interpretations is correct. I prefer the more elastic one, that which I have called the third. There appears to be no binding authority on the point. . . . However, it is sufficient for me to say that, . . . the division of loading into two parts is suited to more antiquated methods of loading than are now generally adopted and the ship's rail has lost much of its nineteenth century significance. Only the most enthusiastic lawyer could watch with satisfaction the spectacle of liabilities shifting uneasily as the cargo sways at the end of a derrick across a notional perpendicular projecting from the ship's rail.

. . . In my judgment, the plaintiffs are bound by the Hague Rules as embodied in the contract of carriage and, accordingly, can recover no more than £200. There will be judgment for them for that sum.

Judgment for the plaintiffs. ■

---

[22]At p. 186 (9th ed.).
[23]*Lloyd's Reports,* vol. 34, p. 192 (1929).

FAS—Free Alongside

The term **free alongside** or **free alongside ship** requires the seller to deliver goods to a named port alongside a vessel to be designated by the buyer and in a manner customary to the particular port.[24] "Alongside" has traditionally meant that the goods be within reach of a ship's lifting tackle. This may, as a consequence, require that the seller hire lighters to take the goods out to a ship in ports where this is the practice. In other respects, the requirements of an FAS term are the same as an FOB contract. The seller's responsibilities end upon delivery of the goods alongside.

CIF—Cost, Insurance, and Freight

The most important and commonly used shipping term is **cost, insurance, and freight**. The CIF term is preferred by buyers because it means that they have little to do with the goods until the goods arrive at a port of destination in their country. A CIF price quote also allows buyers to compare prices from suppliers around the world without having to take into consideration differing freight rates, since the seller pays the freight and insurance. Export-sellers are often under pressure from their governments to use domestic carriers and insurers, so they too like the term. On the other hand, sellers may not be able to find domestic carriers or insurers; and buyers, under pressure from governments that are also concerned about employing national carriers and insurers, may settle for an FOB contract.

In short, a CIF contract requires the seller to arrange for the carriage of goods by sea to a port of destination and to turn over to the buyer the documents necessary to obtain the goods from the carrier or to assert a claim against an insurer if the goods are lost or damaged. The three documents that the seller (as a minimum) has to provide—the invoice, the insurance policy, and the bill of lading—represent the three elements of the contract: cost, insurance, and freight. The seller's obligations are complete when the documents are tendered to the buyer. At that time, the buyer is obliged to pay the agreed-upon price.

The responsibilities of the parties to a CIF contract under *Incoterms 2000* are described in Exhibit 11-4.

CFR—Cost and Freight

The **cost and freight (port of destination)** term is the same as the CIF term except that the seller does not have to procure marine insurance against the risk of loss or damage to the goods during transit. Because the insurance required under a CIF contract only has to cover minimum conditions (the so-called FPA or free from particular average conditions), buyers wishing to purchase more extensive policies will want to use a CFR contract. The buyer's responsibilities under a CFR contract (known also as a C & F contract) are considered in Case 11–3.

EXHIBIT 11-4 Incoterms 2000—Cost, Insurance, and Freight (. . . named port of destination)

A. THE SELLER'S OBLIGATIONS:	B. THE BUYER'S OBLIGATIONS:
A1 Provision of goods in conformity with the contract	**B1 Payment of the price**
The seller must provide the goods and the commercial invoice, or its equivalent electronic message, in conformity with the contract of sale, and any other evidence of conformity which may be required by the contract.	The buyer must pay the price as provided in the contract of sale.
A2 Licenses, authorizations, and formalities	**B2 Licenses, authorizations, and formalities**
The seller must obtain at his own risk and expense any export license or official authorization and carry out, where applicable, all customs formalities necessary for the exportation of the goods.	The buyer must obtain at his own risk and expense any import license or other official authorization and carry out, where applicable, all customs formalities for the import of the goods and, where necessary, for their transit through any country.

---

[24]*Incoterms 2000*, p. 41 (International Chamber of Commerce, Pub. No. 560).

A3 Contracts of carriage and insurance

a) *Contract of Carriage*
   The seller must contract on usual terms at his own expense for the carriage of the goods to the named port of destination by the usual route in a seagoing vessel (or inland waterway vessel as the case may be) of the type normally used for the transport of the goods of the contract description.
b) *Contract of Insurance*
   The seller must obtain at his own expense cargo insurance as agreed in the contract, such that the buyer, or any other person having an insurable interest in the goods, shall be entitled to claim directly from the insurer and provide the buyer with the insurance policy or other evidence of insurance cover. The insurance shall be contracted with underwriters or an insurance company of good repute and, failing express agreement to the contrary, be in accordance with minimum cover of the Institute of Cargo Clauses (Institute of London Underwriters) or any similar set of clauses. The duration of insurance cover shall be in accordance with B.5 and B.4. When required by the buyer, the seller shall provide at the buyer's expense war, strikes, riots, and civil commotion risk insurance if procurable. The minimum insurance shall cover the price provided in the contract plus ten percent (i.e., 110%) and shall be provided in the currency of the contract.

A4 Delivery

The seller must deliver the goods on board the vessel named by the buyer at the named port of shipment on the date or within the period stipulated.

A5 Transfer of risks

The seller must, subject to the provisions of B5, bear all risks of loss of or damage to the goods until such time as they shall have passed the ship's rail at the named port of shipment.

A6 Division of costs

The seller must, subject to the provisions of B6, pay
- all costs relating to the goods until they have been delivered in accordance with A4; and
- the freight and all other costs resulting from A3 a), including costs of loading the goods on board; and
- any charges for unloading at the agreed port of discharge which were for the sellers account under the contract of carriage; and
- where applicable, the costs of customs formalities necessary for export as well as all duties, taxes and other charges payable upon export, and for their transit through any country if they were for the seller's account under the contract of carriage.

B3 Contracts of carriage and insurance

a) *Contract of Carriage*
   No obligation.
b) *Contract of Insurance*
   No obligation.

B4 Taking delivery

The buyer must accept delivery of the goods when they have been delivered in accordance with A4 and receive them from the carrier at the named port of destination.

B5 Transfer of risks

The buyer must bear all risks of loss of or damage to the goods from the time they have passed the ship's rail at the named port of shipment. The buyer must, should he fail to give notice in accordance with B7, bear all risks of loss of or the expiry date of the period fixed for shipment provided, however, that the goods have been duly appropriated to the contract, that is to say, clearly set aside or otherwise identified as the contract goods.

B6 Division of costs

The buyer must, subject to the provisions of A3, pay
- all costs relating to the goods from the time they have been delivered in accordance with A4; and
- costs and charges relating to the goods whilst in transit until their arrival at the port of destination, unless such costs and charges were for the seller's account under the contract of carriage; and
- unloading costs including lighterage and wharfage charges, unless such costs and charges were for the seller's account under the contract of carriage; and
- all the additional costs incurred if he fails to give notice in accordance with B7, for the goods from the agreed date or expiry date of the period fixed for shipment provided, however, that the goods have been duly appropriated to the contract, that is to say, clearly set aside or otherwise identified as the contract goods; and

(continued)

EXHIBIT 11-4 Continued

- where applicable, all duties, taxes, and other charges as well as the costs of carrying out customs formalities payable upon importation of the goods and, where necessary, for their transit through any country unless included within the cost of the contract of carriage.

A7 Notice to the buyer

The seller must give the buyer sufficient notice that the goods have been in accordance with A4 as well as any other notice required in order to allow the buyer to take measures which are normally necessary to enable him to take the goods.

A8 Proof of delivery, transport document, or equivalent electronic message

The seller must, at his own expense provide the buyer without delay the usual transport document for the agreed port of destination.

This document (for example, a negotiable bill of lading, a nonnegotiable sea waybill, an inland waterway document, or a multimodal transport document) must cover the contract goods, be dated within the period agreed for shipment, enable the buyer to claim the goods from the carrier at the port of destination, and, unless otherwise agreed, enable the buyer to sell the goods in transit by the transfer of the document to a subsequent buyer (the negotiable bill of lading) or by notification to the carrier.

When such a transport document is issued in several originals, a full set of originals must be presented to the buyer.

Where the seller and the buyer have agreed to communicate electronically, the document referred to in the preceding paragraph may be replaced by an equivalent electronic data interchange (EDI) message.

A9 Checking—packaging—marking

The seller must pay the costs of those checking operations (such as checking quality, measuring, weighing, counting) which are necessary for the purpose of delivering the goods in accordance with A4.

The seller must provide at his own expense packaging (unless it is usual for the particular trade to ship the goods of the contract description unpacked) which is required for the transport of the goods arranged by him. Packaging is to be marked appropriately.

A10 Other obligations

The seller must render the buyer at the latter's request, risk and expense, every assistance in obtaining any documents or equivalent electronic messages (other than those mentioned in A8) issued or transmitted in the country of shipment and/or of origin which the buyer may require for the import of the goods and, where necessary, for their transit through any country.

The seller must provide the buyer, upon request, with the necessary information for procuring any additional insurance.

B7 Notice to the seller

The buyer must, whenever he is entitled to determine the time for shipping the goods and/or the port of destination, give the seller sufficient notice thereof.

B8 Proof of delivery, transport document, or equivalent electronic message

The buyer must accept the transport document in accordance with A8 if it is in conformity with the contract.

B9 Inspection of goods

The buyer must pay the costs of any pre-shipment inspection except when such inspection is mandated by the authorities of the country of export.

B10 Other obligations

The buyer must pay all costs and charges incurred in obtaining the documents or equivalent electronic messages mentioned in A10 and reimburse those incurred by the seller in rendering his assistance in accordance therewith.

The buyer must provide the seller, upon request, with the necessary information for procuring insurance

---

EXHIBIT 11-4 Continued

Source: Incoterms 2000 (International Chamber of Commerce, Pub. No. 560).

Case 11–3   Phillips Puerto Rico Core, Inc. v. Tradax Petroleum, Ltd.

United States, Court of Appeals, Second Circuit, 1985.
Federal Reporter, Second Series, vol. 782, p. 314 (1985).

CIRCUIT JUDGE MANSFIELD: . . .

This convoluted maritime controversy had its origins in early September 1981 when Phillips, a corporation organized under Delaware law with its principal place of business in Puerto Rico, agreed to buy 25–30,000 metric tons of naphtha from Tradax, a corporation organized under Bermuda law, with its principal place of business in Switzerland. Tradax had just purchased the naphtha from another firm, Schlubach & Co., and the naphtha was located in Skikda, Algeria. The Tradax-Phillips contract, which was made by telephone and then confirmed by telex on September 3, 1981, specified that the sale was to be "C & F" (cost and freight) Guayama, Puerto Rico and that shipment was to be made between September 20–28, 1981. No dates for delivery were specified. The agreement incorporated the International Chamber of Commerce 1980 *Incoterms*, a set of standardized terms for international commercial contracts, which define a "C & F" contract as one in which the seller arranges and pays for the transport of the goods, but the buyer assumes title and risk of loss at the time of shipment. The contract was also to include Tradax's standard contract provisions "subject to [Phillips'] review and acceptance." These standard terms, including a *force majeure*[25] clause and an arbitration clause, were not recited in the telex but were subsequently mailed by Tradax to Phillips with a confirming letter and arrived several weeks later.

Soon after the original contract was entered into on September 8, 1981, a telex from Phillips to Tradax provided documentation and delivery instructions giving the destination in Puerto Rico and listing Phillips as consignee. The telex confirmed that "title and risk of loss to products shall pass to buyer at the time product reaches the vessel[']s flange at the load port." On September 16, Tradax nominated the Oxy Trader, an integrated tug barge, as the vessel for the journey, and after determining that the Trader would fit in the Puerto Rico berth and was available at the correct times, Phillips accepted the nomination.

The Trader arrived at Skikda for loading on the afternoon of September 20, 1981, and loading com-

MAP 11-3   *Algeria and Gibraltar (1981)*

menced the following day. The naphtha was completely loaded by the early morning of September 24 and at 1030 hours that morning the ship embarked. . . .

The Trader's voyage was cut short . . . when the ship was detained by the Coast Guard at Gibraltar for an inspection. Tradax relayed word of the delay to Phillips, which telexed back on October 1 that October 15 was the last acceptable delivery date. . . .

On October 7, Tradax received word that the Trader might have a latent defect . . . that the authorities were not letting the Trader proceed, and that the naphtha cargo would have to be transshipped. Tradax relayed this message to Phillips.

On October 9, Phillips telexed Tradax stating that it was "declar[ing] *force majeure*," that it would "not make any payments under the contract until the event of *force*

---

majeure abates," and that it was reserving the right to cancel the contract if delivery did not occur within 30 days. Tradax responded, reiterating its claim that its responsibility ended at the time of shipment and notifying Phillips that it would present the shipping documents for payment of the contract price the following day. Phillips again instructed its Puerto Rico office not to make payment if Tradax tendered the documents.

On October 13, a Tradax representative presented the shipping documents for payment at Phillips' Puerto Rico office. A Phillips employee examined the documents briefly—about 30 seconds according to Tradax's witness—and stated that they seemed to be in order but that he had been instructed not to pay. A telex back to Tradax that day reaffirmed Phillips' unwillingness to pay until the abatement of the claimed *force majeure*.

. . . [O]n November 9, Phillips informed Tradax that it was terminating the contract due to the "unseaworthiness" of the Trader, "discrepancies in the documents," and an "unreasonable delay" in performance. Although Phillips and Tradax representatives tried to negotiate a new contract by which Phillips would buy the naphtha on "delivery" terms, negotiations fell through when Tradax's management refused to accept that deal. The transshipment then began on November 13, with a bill of lading which left open the destination port. On November 19, Tradax informed Phillips that it would try to sell the naphtha on the open market and would hold Phillips liable for any damages. Tradax then sold the naphtha to a third party for $.88 per gallon, after first offering it to Phillips on condition that Tradax retain its right to claim in arbitration the difference between that price and the contract price. Tradax's total loss on the naphtha, compared to the contract price, was $911,710.31, plus incidental damages.

. . . On August 1, 1984, Judge Carter filed his decision in the case, finding Phillips liable to Tradax for $1,039,330.99 plus prejudgment interest from October 13, 1981. The court held that Phillips had anticipatorily breached the contract by declaring its unwillingness to pay because of *force majeure*. . . .

From this judgment Phillips appeals.

DISCUSSION

The 1980 *Incoterms* define a "C & F" contract as one in which:

[t]he seller must pay the costs and freight necessary to bring the goods to the named destination but the risk of loss of or damage to the goods, as well as of any cost increases, is transferred from the seller to the buyer when the goods pass the ship's rail in the port of shipment.

. . . As a "C & F" seller Tradax had two duties that are relevant here: to deliver the naphtha to an appropriate carrier with which it had contracted for shipment and to tender proper documents to Phillips. Phillips in return was contractually obliged to pay for the naphtha when presented with the shipping documents by Tradax. It is undisputed that after Tradax loaded the naphtha on the Oxy Trader and presented Phillips with the shipping documents on October 13, 1981, Phillips refused to pay for the cargo. If Tradax had adequately performed its contractual duties, Phillips' refusal to pay for the naphtha constituted a breach of the contract as of October 13, unless it was somehow excused from performing.

Phillips asserts several grounds for its failure to pay Tradax on October 13: (1) the existence of a "*force majeure*," (2) unreasonable delay in Tradax's performance, (3) discrepancies in Tradax's shipping documents, and (4) unsuitability (unseaworthiness) of the Oxy Trader. On the undisputed circumstances of this case, however, none of these theories suffice to excuse Phillips' failure to pay on Tradax's presentation of the documents.

Force Majeure

Phillips first relies on the *force majeure* clause among Tradax's standard contract terms, which were to be included in the contract "subject to [Phillips'] review and acceptance;" the contract, however, did not actually arrive at Phillips' office for review until after the Oxy Trader left port. The standard *force majeure* clause reads:

FORCE MAJEURE: In the event of any strike, fire or other event . . . preventing or delaying shipment or delivery of the goods by the seller . . . the unaffected party may cancel the unfulfilled balance of the contract. . . .

. . . We . . . look to the basic purpose of *force majeure* clauses, which is in general to relieve a party from its contractual duties when its performance has been prevented by a force beyond its control or when the purpose of the contract has been frustrated. . . . The burden of demonstrating *force majeure* is on the party seeking to have its performance excused, . . . and, as Judge Carter pointed out, the nonperforming party must demonstrate its efforts to perform its contractual duties despite the occurrence of the event that it claims constituted *force majeure*. . . .

With these principles in mind, we cannot agree that Phillips' performance was excused by its invocation of *force majeure*. Even if the detention of the ship by the Coast Guard constituted *force majeure*, and we are inclined to agree with Judge Carter that it did not, that detention did not frustrate the purpose of the contract or prevent Phillips from carrying out its obligation under the terms of the parties' contract to make payment. Indeed, to hold that the *force majeure* clause may be interpreted to excuse the buyer from that obligation, as Phillips urges, would be to wholly overturn the allocation of duties provided for in "C & F" sales. We do not find any evidence that the parties intended such a result.

. . . The *force majeure* clause thus did not alter the design of the "C & F" contract by requiring Tradax to assure delivery of the naphtha at the ultimate destination in Puerto Rico before it would be entitled to payment. The authorities Phillips cites in support of its contention that a "C & F" seller retains responsibility for events after the time of shipment are plainly distinguishable. The court in *Gatoil International Inc. v. Tradax Petroleum, Ltd.*[26] stated "tentative[ly]" that a "C & F" seller could be liable for having "wrongfully delay[ed] the actual delivery of the goods," in that case by instructing a ship to wait outside the harbor at the port of discharge. Here, in contrast, the absence of any such wrongful conduct on Tradax's part makes such deviation from the standard "C & F" division of responsibility inappropriate.

* * *

Defects in the Documents

There is equally little merit in Phillips' claim that it was excused from payment under the contract because Tradax tendered defective shipping documents. While it is true that in a sale by documents the seller's tender of the documents is judged very strictly, Phillips' objection to the documents here, as Judge Carter noted, "is an afterthought and must fail." Without having seen the shipping documents, Phillips twice instructed its agents that because of *force majeure*, they were not to pay Tradax when the latter presented the papers for payment. When Tradax presented the papers in Puerto Rico, a Phillips employee chose to give them only a cursory examination before stating that they seemed "okay," but that he had been instructed not to pay.

* * *

The Suitability of the Oxy Trader

Phillips was not relieved of its contractual obligation because of Tradax's selection of the Oxy Trader. The relevant provision in the 1980 Incoterms requires that a "C & F" seller contract for the carriage of the goods "in a seagoing vessel . . . of the type normally used for the transport of goods of the contract description." Although the Oxy Trader, an integrated tug barge, was of novel design in that the tug and the barge were married together, this feature did not disqualify the Trader as a ship that might "normally" be used for transport. A new design would not carry with it such a disqualification. Indeed, the status of the Trader as a ship normally used for transport was confirmed by the United States Coast Guard's certification of it for ocean transport and for carriage of comparable cargoes and by Phillips' own approval of the choice of the ship. Moreover, the Oxy Trader had safely sailed on transatlantic trips.

. . . The remaining claims raised on appeal need little discussion. . . . The judgment of the district court is affirmed. ■

---

[26]Commercial Ct., Queen's Bench Division, Slip Opinion at p. 24 (July 31, 1984); *Lloyd's Law Reports, Queen's Bench,* vol. 1985, pt. 1, p. 350 (1985).

DES—Delivered Ex Ship

delivered ex ship: Seller fulfills his obligation to deliver when the goods are made available to the buyer on board the ship, uncleared for import, at the named port of destination.

A **delivered ex ship**, or arrival, contract requires the seller to deliver goods to a buyer at an agreed-upon port of arrival. Lord Sumner, in *Yangtsze Insurance Association, Ltd. v. Lukmanjee*, described the seller's obligations under such a contract as follows:[27]

> In the case of a sale "ex ship," the seller has to cause delivery to be made to the buyer from a ship which has arrived at the port of delivery and has reached a place therein which is usual for the delivery of goods of the kind in question. The seller has therefore to pay the freight, or otherwise release the shipowner's lien and to furnish the buyer with an effectual direction to the ship to deliver. Until this is done, the buyer is not bound to pay for the goods.

This is very different from a CIF contract. Under the DES contract, the seller is not required to deliver documents to the buyer, but to deliver the goods. In practice, however, he

---

[27]*Law Reports, Appeal Cases,* vol. 1918, p. 585 at 589 (1918).

will probably provide the buyer with a delivery order or some other document that will enable the buyer to take possession from the ship, rather than appear in person to make delivery.

Also, the seller remains responsible for the goods until they are delivered. Thus, unlike the CIF term, the seller is not obliged to obtain insurance for the buyer's benefit. In the *Yangtsze Insurance* case, just quoted, timber to be delivered ex ship was off-loaded into the sea next to the carrier and consolidated into rafts for transfer ashore. However, before the transfer and delivery could be made, the timber was destroyed by bad weather. The English Court of Appeal observed that the risk for the loss of goods in an ex ship contract does not shift to the buyer until delivery is made. It consequently refused to hold that the insurance policy purchased by the seller for his own benefit could inure to the benefit of the buyer, because the buyer had yet to take delivery and therefore had no rights in the property.

FCA — Free Carrier

free carrier: Seller fulfills his obligations to deliver by handing over the goods, cleared for export, to a carrier named by the buyer.

The FCA term, which applies to any form of transport—maritime, inland waterways, air, rail, or truck—requires the seller to deliver goods to a particular carrier at a named terminal, depot, airport, or other place where the carrier operates. The costs of transportation and the risks for loss shift to the buyer at that time.[28]

EXW — Ex Works

ex works: Seller fulfills his obligations to deliver by making the goods available at his premises.

Under an **ex works** contract, a seller is obliged only to deliver the goods at his own place of business. All the costs connected with transportation are the responsibility of the buyer.

B. TRANSPORTATION

The following is a typical example of how goods are transported by sea from a seller in Country A to a buyer in Country B. Goods are picked up at the seller's place of business by an inland carrier and transported to a seaport for carriage abroad. The inland carrier will deposit the goods in a warehouse or port depository for examination by customs officials and for consolidation with other goods if the load is not large enough to occupy a ship by itself. A stevedore company or the ship's crew will load the goods. The crew will then stow the goods aboard ship, mark the goods with "leading" marks, and issue a bill of lading to the shipper. At a seaport in Country B, the ship will be directed by port authorities to tie up at a pier or to anchor at a moorage in the harbor. When the buyer produces the bill of lading, the ship's crew will unload the goods onto the dock or, if the ship is anchored out, into a lighter for transfer ashore. The crew or a stevedoring company will then deliver the goods to a customhouse or a bonded warehouse for inspection. Once customs has inspected the goods and their related documents, and collected any import taxes or duties, the goods will be released for entry into Country B. A local inland carrier will then transport the goods to the buyer's place of business.

When goods are transported by air, rail, or truck, much the same procedure is followed, except that the carrier will issue an air waybill or similar nonnegotiable receipt instead of a bill of lading, and the transfer of goods will more commonly be done by the carriers without the assistance of stevedores or other intermediaries.

freight forwarder: A firm that makes or assists in the making of shipping arrangements.

In making arrangements for the transportation of goods, the buyer and seller will deal with a variety of intermediaries, such as **freight forwarders**, warehousemen, port authorities, stevedores, and customhouse brokers. The most important of these agents for most shippers is the freight forwarder, or confirming house.[29] Unless a merchant has a large staff dedicated to making shipping arrangements, the use of a freight forwarder will save time and expense. Freight

---

[28]The 1990 revision of *Incoterms* expanded the coverage of the free carrier term, eliminating older terms, such as FOB airport, free on rail (FOR) and free on truck (FOT), were eliminated. FOR contracts required a seller to deliver goods to a railway carrier and pay all expenses up to that time, including the cost of packaging the goods for rail carriage. FOT contracts were the same as FOR contracts, except that the seller also had to pay for loading the goods on the railway's cars (or "trucks").

[29]The term "freight forwarder" is used in North America, while the terms "confirming house" or "export house" are used in the United Kingdom.

forwarders, for example, arrange three out of every four shipments moved across the New York docks.[30]

Freight forwarders are companies with specialized knowledge of international markets, finance, transport, customs, sales law, and other related matters. In most countries they are licensed by the government. In the United States, for example, inland freight forwarders are licensed by the Interstate Commerce Commission, air freight forwarders by the Civil Aeronautics Board, and ocean freight forwarders by the Federal Maritime Administration. Unlicensed brokers and agents also are commonly available who perform much more limited services (such as the booking of ocean freight or the handling of air cargo). A "full service" freight forwarder can help with or perform the following:

- Obtaining quotations on CIF and C & F contracts
- Determining the availability of ships and port facilities
- Estimating costs based on gross weight, cubic feet, value, description of the goods, and the port of destination
- Booking space
- Procuring export licenses
- Reviewing letter of credit terms
- Tracing inland shipments
- Preparing shipping documents, including export declarations
- Preparing and authenticating consular invoices
- Procuring certificates of origin from local Chambers of Commerce
- Purchasing insurance
- Presenting banking drafts and collecting payment

C. INLAND CARRIAGE

The first stage of transporting goods overseas almost always involves an inland carrier, either a trucking or rail company, which moves the seller's goods from the seller's place of business to a seaport or airport. Except for ex works contracts, it is common for the seller to arrange for inland carriage, with the inland carrier transferring the goods to a freight forwarder at a seaport or airport for the latter to arrange and oversee the shipment of the goods abroad.

In the absence of universal conventions, several regional agreements regulate transport by road and rail. In Europe, road transport is regulated by the 1956 Convention on the Contract for the International Carriage of Goods by Road *(Convention relative au contrat de transport international de merchandises par route or CMR)*[31] and rail transport is governed by the 1980 Convention Concerning International Carriage by Rail *(Convention relative aux transports international ferroviares or COTIF)*.[32] Similar agreements exist in other parts of the world, with the significant exception of North America.[33]

The *CMR* is representative of the conventions governing road transport. It applies whenever goods are shipped between two countries, at least one of which is a signatory of the

---

[30]Gerald H. Ullman, *The Ocean Freight Forwarder, The Exporter and the Law,* p. 2 (1967).

[31]The text of the *CMR* is posted on the Internet at www.unece.org/trans/conventn/cmr_e.pdf.

   The *CMR*'s member states as of August 2002 were Austria, Belarus, Belgium, Bosnia and Herzegovina, Bulgaria, Croatia, Czech Republic, Denmark, Estonia, Finland, France, Georgia, Germany, Greece, Hungary, Iran, Ireland, Italy, Kazakhstan, Kyrgyzstan, Latvia, Lithuania, Luxembourg, Moldova, Morocco, Netherlands, Norway, Poland, Portugal, Russia, Romania, Slovakia, Slovenia, Spain, Sweden, Switzerland, Tajikistan, Macedonia, Tunisia, Turkey, Turkmenistan, United Kingdom, Uzbekistan, and Yugoslavia. *Multilateral Treaties Deposited with the Secretary-General, Status as at 5 August 2002,* posted on the Internet at www.un.org/Depts/Treaty/final/ts2/newfiles/part_boo/xi_b-boo/xi_b_11.html.

[32]The text of the *COTIF* is posted on the Internet at www.unece.org/trade/cotif/Welcome.html.

   The member states as of August 2002 were Albania, Austria, Belgium, Bosnia, Bulgaria, Croatia, Denmark, Finland, France, Germany, Greece, Iran, Iraq, Ireland, Italy, Lebanon, Liechtenstein, Luxembourg, Macedonia, Morocco, Netherlands, Norway, Poland, Portugal, Romania, Slovakia, Slovenia, Spain, Sweden, Switzerland, Syria, Tunisia, Turkey, United Kingdom, and Yugoslavia. *See* InforMare at www.informare.it/dbase/convuk.htm.

[33]Paul H. Vishny, *Guide to International Commerce Law,* § 2-34 (1998).

Convention. The Convention requires a carrier to issue a consignment note. Unlike a bill of lading (including the bill of lading issued by inland carriers in the United States), the *CMR* consignment note is not a negotiable instrument. It is, nonetheless, *prima facie* evidence of the making of a transport contract and of the receipt and the condition of the goods. The Convention also grants the consignee the right to demand delivery of the goods in exchange for a receipt and to sue the carrier in his own name for any loss, damage, or delay for which the carrier is responsible. However, up until the time that the goods are turned over to the consignee, the shipper (consignor) has the right to order the carrier to stop them in transit, to change the place for delivery, or to order them delivered to a different consignee.

If a road carriage contract involves the use of multiple carriers, each carrier is treated as a party to the contract, and each is responsible for the entire transaction. Suits can be brought against the first or last carrier, or the carrier in possession at the time of the loss.

Carriers are liable for loss, damage, or delay up to the liability limit set by the Convention, so long as the consignment note states that carriage is governed by the *CMR*. The liability limit is 8.33 Special Drawing Rights (SDRs) per kilogram, unless the consignor declares a higher value and pays a surcharge. If the consignment note fails to include a reference to the *CMR*, the carrier will be liable for any resulting injury. In either case, the burden of proof rests on the carrier, which will be liable unless it can show that the loss, damage, or delay was caused by the consignor or the consignee, by an inherent defect in the goods, or "through circumstances which the carrier could not avoid and the consequences of which he was unable to prevent."[34] A consignee has to notify the carrier within seven days of delivery to assert a claim for loss or damages, and within 21 days to make a claim for losses resulting from delay.

The *COTIF*, which governs rail transport, contains in most respects the same provisions as the *CMR*. The carrier's liability for losses, however, is 17 SDRs per kilogram.[35]

D. CARRIAGE OF GOODS BY SEA

Most goods are transported by common carriers, that is, a carrier holding itself to carry goods for more than one party. Only a few shipments are large enough to require the shipper to hire an entire vessel. The contract to employ an entire vessel is known as a charterparty. We will return to charterparties after discussing common carriage.

Common Carriage

common carrier: A ship that carries goods for all persons who choose to employ it so long as there is room.

Where the owner or operator of a vessel is willing to carry goods for more than one person, the vessel is known as a *general ship* or **common carrier**.[36] Unlike private carriers, common carriers are the subject of extensive municipal legislation and international conventions.

conference line: An association of seagoing common carriers operating on established routes who have joined together to offer common freight rates.

Merchants who employ common carriers will find that there are three sorts. A **conference line** is an association of seagoing carriers who have joined together to offer common freight rates. **Independent lines** have their own rate schedules. **Tramp vessels** also have their own rate schedules, but unlike conference and independent lines, they do not operate on established schedules.

independent line: A seagoing common carrier operating over established routes with a stated rate schedule.

Exporters who agree to ship all or a large share of their cargoes with a conference line receive a discounted rate.[37] Independent lines, however, generally offer lower rates than a conference line's nondiscounted rates. In most countries, the tariffs of ocean carriers are not regu-

tramp vessel: A seagoing common carrier operating with a stated rate schedule but without established routes.

---

[34]CMR, article 17.2.

[35]The liability limit for personal injury to a passenger is 70,000 SDRs.

[36]The definition of "common carrier" has been the subject of much litigation. *See* Yung F. Chiang, "The Characterization of a Vessel as a Common or Private Carrier," *Tulane Law Review,* vol. 48, p. 299 (1974).

[37]Conference lines offer their regular customer rebates in two ways: (1) by a contract system in which the shipper signs a contract to use only conference ships and (2) by a system of deferred rebates of varying amounts that require the shipper to not use nonconference ships to send goods to the area in question for a period of time (commonly three or six months). Under the first of these arrangements the shipper is entitled to an immediate discount; under the second, the rebate is retained by the carrier until the shipper has met the condition of not using nonconference ships. Clive M. Schmitthoff, *Schmitthoff's Export Trade: The Law & Practice of International Trade,* p. 548 (8th ed., 1990).

International Sales Company
1234 Main Street
Pullman, Washington 99163
U.S.A.

INVOICE

Date:	**August 1, 2003**	Invoice No.	030701

		Order No.	080202

To:	**Compañia Mundial, S.A.** **567 Avenida de Mayo** **Buenos Aires** **1103 Argentina**	Shipped: **via M/V La Plata** **from Seattle, WA to** **Buenos Aires, Arg. on** **August 1, 2003**
		Payment: **L/C #099762** **dated August 1, 2003** **Banco del Sur,** **Buenos Aires, Arg.**

Identifying Marks & Numbers	Quantity	Description	Unit Price	Amount
			US $	US $
Cia	**432 ea**	**Type "A" Widgets**	**1.23**	**531.36**
Mundial	**288 ea**	**Type "B" Widgets**	**4.56**	**1313.28**
Buenos	**144 ea**	**Type "C" Widgets**	**7.89**	**1136.16**
Aires				
ARGENTINA		**TOTAL FOB PORT OF SEATTLE**		**2980.80**
Made				
in				
USA				

International Sales Company

Jane Doe

Jane Doe, Pres.

EXHIBIT 11-5   A Commercial Invoice

International Sales Company
1234 Main Street
Pullman, Washington 99163
U.S.A.

PACKING LIST

Date:	**August 1, 2003**	Invoice No.	030701

To: Compañia Mundial, S.A. 567 Avenida de Mayo Buenos Aires 1103 Argentina Notify: Agencia Rosas 987 Calle de los Marineros Buenos Aires 1117 Argentina	Order No. 080202
	Shipped: **via M/V La Plata from Seattle, WA to Buenos Aires, Arg. on August 1, 2003**
	Payment: **L/C #099762 dated August 1, 2003 Banco del Sur, Buenos Aires, Arg.**

Identifying Marks & Numbers	Quantity	Description	Net Weight	Gross Weight	Measurement Cu. Meters
Cia. Mundial Buenos Aires ARGENTINA Made in USA					
No. 1-3	432 ea	Type "A" Widgets	32 kg	42 kg	.006m^3
Ditto No. 4-5	288 ea	Type "B" Widgets	24 kg	28 kg	.004m^3
Ditto No. 6	144 ea	Type "C" Widgets	12 kg	14 kg	.002m^3
6 ctns			72 kg	84 kg	.012m^3

International Sales Company

Jane Doe

Jane Doe, Pres.

EXHIBIT 11-6 A Packing List

Seagoing Carrier Company
665 Dockside Drive
Seattle, Washington 98203
U.S.A.

DOCK RECEIPT

NOT NEGOTIABLE

Shipper: **International Sales Co. 1234 Main St, Pullman, WA 99163**

Vessel	Voyage Number	Flag	Port of Loading	Pier
La Plata	**03 W**	**Panama**	**Seattle**	**18**

PORT OF DISCHARGE (Where goods are to be delivered to consignee or on carrier)

Buenos Aires

For TRANSSHIPMENT (If goods are to be transshipped or forwarded at port of discharge)

PARTICULARS FURNISHED BY SHIPPER OF GOODS

Identifying Marks & Numbers	Number of Packages	Description	Gross Weight	Measurement Cu. Meters
Cia. Mundial Buenos Aires ARGENTINA Made in USA	**6**	**Widgets – Type "A", "B" and "C"** **ATTN: RECEIVING CLERK ONLY CLEAN DOCK RECEIPT ACCEPTED**	**84 kg**	**0.12m^3**

DIMENSIONS AND WEIGHT OF PACKAGES TO BE SHOWN ON REVERSE SIDE

RECEIVED THE ABOVE-DESCRIBED MERCHANDISE FOR SHIPMENT AS INDICATED HEREON, SUBJECT TO ALL CONDITIONS OF THE UNDERSIGNED'S USUAL FORM OF DOCK RECEIPT AND BILL OF LADING. COPIES OF THE UNDERSIGNED'S USUAL FORM OF DOCK RECEIPT AND BILL OF LADING MAY BE OBTAINED FROM THE MASTER OF THE VESSEL OR THE VESSEL'S AGENT.

LIGHTER TRUCK ————————————————

ARRIVED Date ——————— Time ———————

UNLOADED Date ——————— Time ———————

CHECKED BY ————————————————

PLACED   [ ] IN SHIP   [ ] ON DOCK

LOCATION ————————————————

Agent for Master

BY _____
Receiving Clerk

Date _____

EXHIBIT 11-7   A Dock Receipt

Seagoing Carrier Company
665 Dockside Drive
Seattle, Washington 98203
U.S.A.

BILL OF LADING

NOT NEGOTIABLE UNLESS
CONSIGNED TO ORDER

Shipper: **International Sales Co. 1234 Main St, Pullman, WA 99163**

Consignee: **To Order Banco del Sur, 17 Ave. Evita, Buenos Aires**

Address Arrival Notice to:	Also Notify:
Agencia Rosas	**Compañia Mundial, S.A.**
987 Calle Marineros	**567 Avenida de Mayo**
Buenos Aires	**Buenos Avenida**
1117 Argentina	**1103 Argentina**

Vessel	Voyage No.	Flag	Port of Loading
La Plata	**03 W**	**Panama**	**Seattle**

PARTICULARS FURNISHED BY SHIPPER OF GOODS

Identifying Marks & Numbers	Number of Packages	Description	Gross Weight	Measurement Cu. Meters
Cia. Mundial **Buenos Aires** **ARGENTINA** **Made in USA**	6	FINAL DESTINATION OF GOODS **BUENOS AIRES** **Widgets - Type "A", "B" and "C"** **FREIGHT COLLECT** **LADEN ABOARD**	**84 kg**	**0.12m^3**

THESE COMMODITIES LICENSED BY U.S. FOR ULTIMATE DESTINATION. DIVERSION CONTRARY TO U.S. LAW PROHIBITED.

Freight Payable at: **Buenos Aires**

Gross Weight	Measurements Cu. Meters	Rate	Ocean Freight	Receiving Charge	Delivery Charge	Total Charge	Total Prepaid	Total Collect
84 Kg	**0.12m^3**	**2.70**	**226.80**	**15.87**	**27.22**	**$269.89**		**$269.89**

Bill of Lading No. **582 63409**   Issued at **Seattle**   Date **Aug. 1, 2003**

WHEN VALIDATED, CARGO LADEN ON BOARD   DATED AT PORT OF LOADING SHOWN ABOVE
ON THE DATE APPEARING HEREON   Seagoing Carrier Company

Validation:

By _____
Agent - For the Master

EXHIBIT 11-8 A Bill of Lading

lated, and both conference and independent lines will commonly offer regular shippers substantial rebates. In the United States, however, ocean carriers have to file their tariffs with the Federal Maritime Commission, and American law forbids rebates.[38]

The Bill of Lading

A **bill of lading** is an instrument issued by an ocean carrier to a shipper with whom the carrier has entered into a contract for the carriage of goods.[39] The multilateral treaty governing bills of lading is the International Convention for the Unification of Certain Rules of Law Relating to Bills of Lading.[40] This treaty is known both as the 1921 Hague Rules—because they were originally proposed by the International Law Association at a meeting at The Hague in 1921—and the Brussels Convention of 1924—because they were recommended for adoption at a diplomatic conference held in Brussels in 1924. The Hague Rules were extensively revised in 1968 by a Brussels Protocol, and the amended 1968 version is known as the Hague-Visby Rules.[41] Most countries, including the United States, are parties to the 1921 Hague Rules.[42] A few, including France and the United Kingdom, have adopted the Hague-Visby amendments.[43] The domestic laws implementing these conventions are typically called Carriage of Goods by Sea acts.[44] In addition, many states have supplementary legislation that also governs bills of lading in both municipal and international settings.[45]

A bill of lading serves three purposes: First, it is a carrier's receipt for goods. Second, it is evidence of a contract of carriage. Finally, it is a document of title; that is, the person rightfully in possession of the bill is entitled to possess, use, and dispose of the goods that the bill represents.[46] A bill of lading and samples of the documents that a carrier collects in order to prepare a bill of lading are shown in Exhibits 11-5 through 11-8 on pages 613–616.

Receipt for Goods

A bill of lading describes the goods put on board a carrier, states the quantity, and their condition. The form itself is normally filled out in advance by the shipper; then, as the goods are loaded aboard the ship, the carrier's tally clerk will check to see that the goods loaded comply

---

[38]*United States Code,* Title 46, Appendix, § 1709, paras. (b)(1) and (b)(2).

[39]In the United States, a bill of lading is also issued by inland carriers. *See* Uniform Commercial Code, §§ 2–319 and 2–320.

[40]The text of the Hague Rules is posted on the Internet at www.austlii.edu.au/au/other/dfat/treaties/19560002.html.

[41]The text of the Hague Rules as modified by the Brussels Protocol (the Hague-Visby Rules) is posted on the Internet at www.jus.uio.no/lm/sea.carriage.hague.visby.rules.1968/doc.html and at www.admiraltylaw.com/statutes/hague.html. The Brussels Protocol itself is posted at www.austlii.edu.au/au/other/dfat/treaties/1993/23.html.

A United Nations Convention on the Carriage of Goods by Sea, drafted and signed in 1978 (the Hamburg Rules), came into force among 20 developing states in November 1992. As to those states, it modifies the Hague-Visby rules by establishing a single basis of liability for a carrier's breach of duty and it also governs "through transport," that is, shipments from the point of departure ashore through their final delivery inland via truck, rail, or plane. Because these rules also increase the liability of carriers, they have been ignored by all of the major maritime states. The text of the Hamburg Rules is posted at www.uncitral.org/english/texts/transport/hamburg.htm. As of August 2002, there were 26 states parties to the Hamburg Rules. *Multilateral Treaties Deposited with the Secretary-General, Status as at 5 August 2002,* www.un.org/Depts/Treaty/final/ts2/newfiles/part_boo/xi_d-boo/xi_d_3.html.

[42]The member states of the Hague Rules as of August 2002 were Algeria, Angola, Anguilla, Antigua and Barbuda, Argentina, Australia, Norfolk, Bahamas, Barbados, Belgium, Belize, Bolivia, Cameroon, Cape Verde, Cyprus, Croatia, Cuba, Dominican Republic, Ecuador, Egypt, Fiji, France, Gambia, Germany, Ghana, Goa, Greece, Grenada, Guyana, Guinea-Bissau, Hungary, Iran, Ireland, Israel, Ivory Coast, Jamaica, Kenya, Kiribati, Kuwait, Lebanon, Macao, Madagascar, Malaysia, Mauritius, Monaco, Mozambique, Nauru, Nigeria, Papua New Guinea, Paraguay, Peru, Poland, Portugal, Romania, Russian Federation , Sao Tomé and Principe, Sarawak, Senegal, Seychelles, Sierra-Leone, Singapore, Slovenia, Solomon Islands, Somalia, Spain, Sri-Lanka, St. Kitts and Nevis, St. Lucia, St. Vincent and the Grenadines, Switzerland, Syrian Arab Republic, Tanzania , Timor, Tonga, Trinidad and Tobago, Turkey, Tuvalu, United States, and Zaire. Comite Maritime International, *Status of Ratifications to Maritime Conventions* posted at www.comitemaritime.org/ratific/brus/bru05.html.

[43]The member states of the Hague-Visby Rules as of August 2002 were Belgium, Denmark, Ecuador, Egypt, Finland, France, Greece, Italy, Lebanon, Netherlands, Norway, Poland, Russia, Singapore, Sri-Lanka, Sweden, Switzerland, Syria, Tonga, and United Kingdom. *See id.* at www.comitemaritime.org/ratific/brus/bru06.html.

[44]The United Kingdom statute is the Carriage of Goods by Sea Act (1971) in *Statutes,* vol. 41, chap. 1312. The United States Carriage of Goods by Sea Act is codified in the *United States Code,* Title 46, § 1300 *et seq.*

[45]In the United States, the two other important acts are the Bill of Lading Act (Interstate and Foreign Commerce), in *United States Code,* Title 46, § 14306, and the Harter Act, in *United States Code,* Title 46, §§ 190–196. In the United Kingdom, the Bill of Lading Act (1855) in *Statutes,* vol. 31, Chap. 44 also applies.

[46]In re Marine Sulphur Queen, *Federal Reporter, Second Series,* vol. 460, p. 89 at p. 103 (Second Circuit Ct. of Appeals, 1972).

with the goods listed. The carrier, however, is responsible only to check for outward compliance—that is, that the labels comply and that the packages are not damaged. If all appears proper, the appropriate agent of the carrier will sign the bill and return it to the shipper.[47] Bills certifying that the goods have been properly loaded on board are known as "on board bills of lading," or **clean bills of lading**.

clean bill of lading: A bill of lading indicating that the goods have been properly loaded on board the carrier's ship.

Should there be a discrepancy between the goods loaded and the goods listed, the statement on the bill is considered *prima facie* evidence that the goods were received in the condition shown in any dispute between the shipper and the carrier.[48] Nevertheless, the carrier can, if it is able, introduce evidence to rebut this evidence. However, once the bill is endorsed and negotiated to a third party, this is no longer the case. An endorsee's knowledge of the goods is limited to what is on the bill of lading. For this reason, the Hague and Hague-Visby Rules hold that the bill is conclusive evidence as to the goods loaded once the bill has been negotiated in good faith to a third party. The carrier is then barred from introducing evidence to contradict the bill of lading.

claused bill of lading: A bill of lading indicating that some discrepancy exists between the goods loaded and the goods listed on the bill.

If, at the time the goods are being loaded, the carrier's tally clerk notes a discrepancy, a notation to this effect may be added to the bill of lading. Called a **claused bill of lading**, such bills are normally unacceptable to third parties, including a buyer of the goods under a CIF contract or a bank that has agreed to pay the seller under a documentary credit on receipt of the bill of lading and other documents. Such a notation, however, may be made on the bill only at the time the goods are loaded. Later notations will have no effect, and the bill will be treated as if it were "clean." The significance of clean and claused bills of lading is discussed in Case 11–4.

---

[47]The United States Carriage of Goods by Sea Act, *United States Code*, Title 46, § 1303(3), provides: "After receiving the goods into his charge the carrier, or the master or agent of the carrier, shall, on demand of the shipper, issue to the shipper a bill of lading showing among other things—

(a) The leading marks necessary for identification of the goods as the same are furnished in writing by the shipper before the loading of such goods starts, provided such marks are stamped or otherwise shown clearly upon the goods if uncovered, or on the cases or coverings in which such goods are contained, in such manner as should ordinarily remain legible until the end of the voyage.

(b) Either the number of packages or pieces, or the quantity or weight, as the case may be, as furnished in writing by the shipper.

(c) The apparent order and condition of the goods: Provided, that no carrier, master, or agent of the carrier, shall be bound to state or show in the bill of lading any marks, number, quantity, or weight which he has reasonable grounds for suspecting not accurately to represent the goods actually received, or which he has had no reasonable means of checking."

[48]*Id.,* § 1303(4), provides: "Such a bill of lading shall be prima facie evidence of the receipt by the carrier of the goods as described in accordance with paragraphs (3)(a), (b) and (c), of [§ 1303]. . . ."

Case 11–4 M. Golodetz & Co., Inc. v. Czarnikow-Rionda Co., Inc. (The Galitia)

England, Queen Bench's Division (1978).
All England Law Reports, vol. 1979, pt. 2, p. 726 (1979).[49]

The sellers contracted to sell to the buyers between 12,000 and 13,200 tons of sugar, C & F Bandarshapur, Iran. The contract provided, among other things, that payment was

to be made against a complete set of clean "on board" bills of lading evidencing that freight had been paid. After part of the consignment of sugar had been loaded, a fire broke out on the ship, as a result of which 200 tons of sugar were damaged and had to be discharged. The remainder of the consignment was loaded and carried to

---

[49]Affirmed by the Court of Appeal, Civil Division, *All England Law Reports,* vol. 1980, pt. 1, p. 501 (1980). The statement of facts is from the appellate report.

its destination. The sellers tendered two bills of lading to the buyers. The first was in respect to the 200 tons of sugar that had been lost and the second was in respect to the balance of the consignment. The first bill in its printed clauses acknowledged shipment of the goods in apparent good order and condition. In addition, however, it bore a typewritten note stating that the cargo covered by the bill had been discharged because it had been damaged by fire and/or water. The second bill was taken up and paid for by the buyers, but the first bill was rejected by them on the ground that it was not a "clean" bill of lading. The sellers claimed that the typewritten note did not prevent it being a clean bill of lading and that they were entitled to be paid the price of the 200 tons of sugar that had been lost.

JUDGE DONALDSON:

* * *

THE DISPUTE

The parties to this dispute are household names in the world trade in sugar. Both are based in New York. The sugar concerned was to be shipped from Kandla in India to Iran. The reason why the matter comes to the English Commercial Court is that the contract incorporated the rule of the Refined Sugar Association and provided for arbitration in London.

. . . The question at issue is, of course, who is to stand the loss in respect of the 200 tons of sugar which was destroyed by or as a consequence of the fire? The board of appeal of the Refined Sugar Association has held that the loss must fall on the sellers. The sellers now appeal.

* * *

The Sellers' Claim to the Price

Under the terms of the contract, the sellers are entitled to be paid the price on tender of "clean 'On Board' bills of lading evidencing freight having been paid." Counsel for the sellers submitted that this bill of lading qualified for this description, notwithstanding the notation recording that the sugar had been discharged fire damaged. . . . In his submission, the sellers, having tendered this bill of lading, were entitled to be paid the price. Alternatively, the sugar was at the risk of the buyers when it was destroyed and, that being so, the sellers were entitled to be paid the price whether or not they tendered this or any other bill of lading.

Counsel for the buyers challenged these submissions root and branch. In his submission, there were no less than eight reasons why the sellers were not entitled to be paid the price. It is, of course, for the sellers to make out their case, but in all the circumstances, it is convenient to consider whether they have done so in the context of counsel's objections.

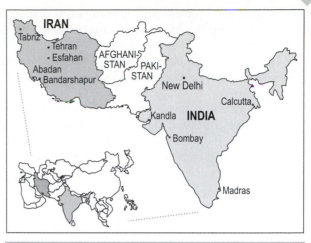

MAP 11-4   Iran and India (1978)

(a) That the Bill of Lading Was Not "Clean"

(i) The Practical Test   Counsel for the buyers submits that there are two possible tests to be applied, the practical and the legal. The practical test is whether a bill of lading in this form is acceptable to banks generally as being a "clean" bill of lading. Since 1962, virtually all banks have accepted the international rules set out in a document issued by the International Chamber of Commerce entitled *Uniform Customs and Practices for Documentary Credits* ("UCP Rules"). Rule 16 provides as follows:

> A clean shipping document is one which bears no superimposed clause or notation which expressly declares a defective condition of the goods and/or the packaging. Banks will refuse documents bearing such clauses or notations unless the credit expressly states clauses or notations which may be accepted.

This definition fails to specify the time with respect to which the notation speaks. The bill of lading and any notation speak *at* the date of issue, but they may speak *about* a state of affairs which then exist or about an earlier state of affairs or both. If the rule refers to notations about the state of affairs at the time of the issue of the bill of lading or, indeed, at any time after shipment of the 200 tons was completed, the bill of lading is not "clean" within the meaning of that word in the rule, for the notation clearly draws attention to the cargo being damaged. If, however, it refers to notations about the state of affairs on completion of shipment, the bill of lading is equally clearly clean for it shows that the goods were in apparent good order and condition on shipment and suggests only that they were damaged after shipment.

Counsel for the buyers draws attention to the fact that this bill of lading was rejected by two different banks. The first rejection was by the sellers' own bank when the bill of lading was tendered by the shippers under the FOB supply contract. The second rejection was by the buyers' subpurchasers bank when it was tendered to them by the buyers without prejudice to the rights of the parties as between sellers and buyers. On these facts, counsel for the buyers invites me to hold that this bill of lading is not a "clean" bill in commercial or practical terms.

Let me consider this "practical" test. The information as to what prompted the banks' action is somewhat sparse. . . .

. . . There is no contemporary note of why the banks refused to accept the documents, but there is a letter dated March 24, 1976, reading:

> Your draft and documents valued $183,732.00, payment for which was not effected because Bills of Lading showing the following clause Quote "Cargo covered by this Bill of Lading has been discharged at Kandla View damaged by fire and/or water used to extinguish fire for which general average declared" Unquote, whereas credit class of clean (unclaused) Bills of Lading.

It is not uninteresting that it was not the buyers' bank which rejected the documents, but the buyers themselves (by a letter of April 22nd, 1975, referred to in the [arbitration] award). Furthermore, although they gave as a reason the fact that the clause prejudiced their ability to negotiate the documents with their buyers, the letter of 24th March 1976 set out above suggests that the documents were only rejected by the subbuyers' bank some weeks later on May 13th, 1975. However, there may have been more than one rejection.

It is clear that the subbuyers' bank thought that a letter of credit incorporating the UCP rules and calling for "clean" bills of lading was only satisfied if the bills were wholly unclaused. This goes further than the UCP rules justify since they appear to take exception only to a "superimposed clause or notation which expressly declares a defective condition of the goods and/or the packaging," whatever that may mean.

There is, I think, more than one answer to this "practical test" objection. First, the contract . . . does not provide that the documents shall be such as to satisfy the UCP rules as to "clean" bills of lading. . . . Furthermore, if there is ambiguity as to the meaning of those rules, that ambiguity should, if possible, be resolved in a way which will result in the rules reflecting the position under general maritime and commercial law. So construed they add nothing to the legal test which I consider hereafter.

Second, the evidence does not disclose that banks generally would reject such a bill of lading as that relating to the 200 tons as not being a "clean" bill of lading or that, if they would do so, it would be for any better rea-

son than that they were applying what they though the UCP rules required.

Third, I am not satisfied that it is right to apply a practical test. . . . What is really being said here is that the very fact that the buyers and two banks rejected these documents proves that they are not "clean." This is a proposition which I decline to accept.

(ii) The Legal Test I, therefore, proceed to apply the legal test. As Judge Salmon remarked in *British Imex Industries, Ltd., v. Midland Bank, Ltd.*,[50] a "clean bill of lading" has never been exhaustively defined. I have been referred to a number of textbooks and authorities which support the proposition that a "clean" bill of lading is one in which there is nothing to qualify the admission that the goods were in apparent good order and condition and that the seller has no claim against the goods except in relation to freight. Some clearly regard the relevant time as being that of shipment. Some are silent as to what is the relevant time. None refers expressly to any time subsequent to shipment.

As between the shipowner and the shipper (including those claiming through the shippers as holders of the bill of lading) the crucial time is shipment. The shipowner's prime obligation is to deliver the goods at the contractual destination in the like good order and condition as when shipped. The cleanliness of the bill of lading may give rise to an estoppel and the terms of the bill of lading contract may exempt the shipowner from a breach of this obligation, but everything stems from the state of the goods as shipped. As between seller and CIF or C&F buyer, the property and risk normally pass on the negotiation of the bill of lading, but do so as from shipment. Thus, the fact that the ship and goods have been lost after shipment or that a liability to contribute in general average or salvage has arisen is no reason for refusing to take up and pay for the documents.

In these circumstances, it is not surprising that there appears to be no case in which the courts or the textbook writers have had to consider a bill of lading which records the fate of the goods subsequent to shipment and, indeed, I have never seen or heard of a bill of lading like that in the present case. Nor is it surprising that some of the judgments and textbooks do not in terms say that when reference is made to the condition of the goods what is meant is their condition on shipment.

However, I have no doubt that this is the position. The bill of lading with which I am concerned casts no doubt whatsoever on the condition of the goods at that time and does not assert that at that time the shipowner had any claim whatsoever against the goods. It follows that in my judgment this bill of lading, unusual though it is, passes the legal test of cleanliness.

---

[50]*All England Law Reports,* vol. 1958, pt. 1, p. 264 (Queen's Bench, 1958).

(b) The Bill of Lading Was Rightly Rejected as Being Unmerchantable   Counsel for the buyers submits that documents tendered under a C & F contract must be merchantable and that, in the context of a bill of lading, this may be a factor of cleanliness or an independent quality which is required. He seeks to support this proposition by reference to *Hansson v. Hamel & Horley, Ltd.*[51] in which Lord Sumner said:

> When documents are to be taken up the buyer is entitled to documents which substantially confer protective rights throughout. He is not buying a litigation, as Lord Trevethin (then Judge A. T. Lawrence) says in the *General Trade Co.'s Case.*[52] These documents have to be handled by banks, they have to be taken up or rejected promptly and without any opportunity for prolonged inquiry, they have to be such as can be re-tendered to subpurchasers, and it is essential that they should so conform to the accustomed shipping documents as to be reasonable and readily fit to pass current in commerce.

I need hardly say that I accept this proposition unreservedly. A tender of documents which, properly read and understood, calls for further enquiry or are such as to invite litigation is clearly a bad tender. But the operative words are "properly read and understood." I fully accept that the clause on this bill of lading makes it unusual, but properly read and understood it calls for no inquiry and it casts no doubt at all on the fact that the goods were shipped in apparent good order and condition or on the protection which anyone is entitled to expect when taking up such a document whether as a purchaser or as a lender on the security of the bill. . . .

The only ground for holding that the bill of lading was not "reasonably and readily fit to pass current in commerce" is that the form is unusual and that two banks and the buyers rejected it. If the buyers wanted bills of lading which were not only "clean," but also in "usual form," they should have contracted accordingly. They did not do so and I am not prepared to hold that the bill was unmerchantable. . . .

CONCLUSION

For the reasons which I have sought to express, I consider that this was a "clean" bill of lading and that the buyers should have accepted it and paid the price. In reaching this conclusion, I have, regretfully, to disagree with the decision of the board of appeal [of the Refined Sugar Association]. That decision seems to me to have been based solely on considerations of law. Had it been a conclusion based on trade practice and included, for example, a finding that a bill in this form was not acceptable in the trade, my decision would, of course, have been different.

. . . Accordingly, for the reasons which I have expressed, I answer the questions of law in favor of the sellers.

Order accordingly. Leave to appeal to the Court of Appeal. ∎

---

[51]*All England Law Reports,* vol. 1922, p. 237 at p. 241 (Ct. of Appeal, 1922).
[52]Re General Trading Co. & Van Stolk's Commissiehandel, *Commercial Cases,* vol. 16, p. 95 (1911).

Contract of Carriage

Between the shipper and the carrier the bill of lading is evidence of their contract of carriage. Either may rebut this by producing evidence of other terms. However, as is the case where the bill functions as a receipt, the bill becomes conclusive evidence of the terms of the contract of carriage once it is negotiated to a good-faith third party. Again, this is because the endorsee's knowledge of the terms of the contract of carriage is limited to what appears on the bill of lading.[53]

Document of Title

straight bill of lading: A bill of lading issued to a named consignee that is not negotiable.

order bill of lading: A bill of lading that is negotiable.

Two kinds of bills of lading need to be distinguished: the straight bill and the order bill. A **straight bill** is issued to a named consignee and is nonnegotiable. The transfer of a straight bill gives the transferee no greater rights than those of his transferor. An **order bill**, on the other hand, is negotiable and conveys greater rights. The holder of an order bill of lading, provided he has received it in good faith through due negotiation, has a claim to title and, by surrendering the bill, to delivery of the goods. In 1883, Lord Justice Bowen wrote what has become the time-honored definition of the order bill of lading:[54]

---

[53]In the Emilien Marie Case, *Law Journal Reports, Admiralty,* vol. 44, p. 9 (1875), the carrier issued three bills of lading to the shipper with the understanding that the last would apply only if there was enough of the perishable cargo left at the port of destination. The shipper nonetheless negotiated the bill to a third party who was unaware of the understanding. The court held that the endorsee was entitled to demand the full quantity.
[54]Sanders v. Maclean & Co., *Law Reports, Queen's Bench Division,* vol. 11, p. 327 at p. 341 (1883).

A cargo at sea while in the hands of the carrier is necessarily incapable of physical delivery. During this period of transit and voyage, the bill of lading by the law merchant is universally recognized as its symbol, and the endorsement and delivery of the bill of lading operates as a symbolical delivery of the cargo. Property in the goods passes by such endorsement and delivery of the bill of lading, whenever it is the intention of the parties that the property should pass, just as under similar circumstances the property would pass by an actual delivery of the goods. And for the purpose of passing such property in the goods and completing the title of the endorsee to full possession thereof, the bill of lading, until complete delivery of the cargo has been made on shore to someone rightfully claiming under it, remains in force as a symbol, and carries with it not only the full ownership of the goods, but also all rights created by the contract of carriage between the shipper and the shipowner. It is a key which in the hands of the rightful owner is intended to unlock the door of the warehouse, floating or fixed, in which the goods may chance to be.

Order bills, although they are negotiable instruments, should not be confused with bills of exchange (such as checks or trade acceptances). Maritime commercial practice is less developed than the law of commercial paper, and though both classes of instruments are related, they are also distinct.

Like bills of exchange, order bills of lading may be made out "to bearer" or "to the order" of a named party. Bearer instruments are transferred by delivery; order instruments by negotiation, that is, by endorsement and delivery. In practice, bills of lading are seldom made out to bearer, as they are documents of title that serve as the symbol or token of the goods described in the bill.

The negotiation of an order bill transfers title in the goods. This is what makes the bill valuable. Because the bill is "negotiable," so too are the goods. This enables the person named on the bill to transfer the goods while a ship is in transit. In other words, possession of the order bill is in most respects the same as possession of the goods. This was the holding in Case 11–5.

Case 11–5   Barclays Bank, Ltd. v. Commissioners of Customs and Excise

England, Queen's Bench Division, 1963.
Lloyd's Reports, vol. 1963, pt. 1, p. 81 (1963).

LORD JUSTICE DIPLOCK:

This case raises a short point of great importance to merchants, bankers, and other persons accustomed to dealing with bills of lading and documents of title by which symbolic delivery of the goods to which they relate may be made. The issue arises under a Sheriff's interpleader in which the plaintiffs, Barclays Bank, Ltd., whom I shall call "the Bank", claimed to be entitled to possession as pledgees of two consignments of washing machines shipped from Rotterdam to Cardiff in February and March, 1961, and seized in execution in September, 1961, on behalf of the defendants, Her Majesty's Customs and Excise, who are judgment creditors, while the goods were lying in a bonded warehouse at Cardiff docks. . . .

Bruitrix Electric Company, Ltd., whom I shall call "Bruitrix", in February, 1961, purchased from a Dutch supplier 100 cartons of washing machines, CIF Cardiff, delivery against acceptance of bills of exchange for £924 11s. 8d., payable 37 days after shipment. Barclays Bank, Ltd., were, in fact, also collecting agents for the shippers' bank, but that fact is immaterial. On February 15, 1961, the consignment was shipped under a bill of lading to order of shippers. It was shipped by Hudig & Pieters, of Rotterdam, Netherlands

. . . in and upon the . . . Motor Vessel *Echo* whereof [—the name is not inserted—] . . . is Master for the present voyage now lying in the Port of Rotterdam to be delivered at Cardiff. . . .

The goods were described as

. . . cartons washing machines . . . Freight Paid

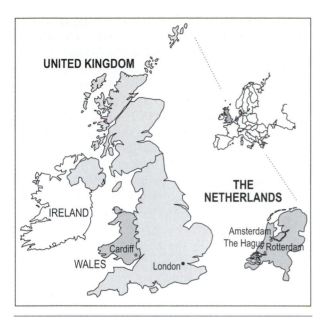

MAP 11-5   United Kingdom and the Netherlands (1963)

and then it says:

Notify address: Bruitrix Electric Co. Ltd., 1, Station Road, Hirwaun.

and by the bill of lading the shipowners, the Bristol Steam Navigation Company, Ltd., undertook to carry the goods and to deliver the same

. . . from the ship's deck (where the Shipowner's responsibility shall cease), at the Port of Cardiff . . . unto order of shippers or to his or their assigns. . . .

Suffice it to say, the documents came forward, the bill of exchange was accepted by Bruitrix, the bill of lading and invoice handed to Bruitrix in February, 1961. On February 18, 1961, the goods were discharged at Cardiff. They were put into a transit warehouse belonging to the British Transport Commission and there held to the order of Bristol Steam Navigation Company, Ltd., the shipowners. The outturn advice, issued by the British Transport Commission, show them as held on account of Bristol Steam Navigation Company, Ltd. No steps to obtain delivery or entry of customs clearance were taken by Bruitrix and the goods remained for the time being in the transit warehouse. . . .

On June 2, 1961, which is the crucial date for the purpose of this case, Bruitrix pledged the bills of lading with the Bank as security for advances made by the Bank on overdraft, and executed in respect of the deposit of the bills of lading, a memorandum of pledge. . . .

The bills of lading and apparently the invoices were deposited with the Bank by Bruitrix and remained in possession of the Bank at all material times until September, 1961. The shipowners were unaware of the Bank's interest in the bills of lading, or the goods, until early in July. In the meantime, the question of Custom's clearance became important. . . .

To resume the history of the matter, on August 22, 1961, the Customs and Excise recovered judgment against Bruitrix for £475 for arrears of purchase tax and upon Sept. 9, 1961, a writ of *fieri facias*[55] was issued to the Sheriff of Glamorgan. On Sept. 21, 1961, the Bank gave formal written notice of the pledge to the shipowners but, as I have already indicated, the shipowners had been aware of the Bank's interest in the matter since early in July before the goods were transferred from the transit shed to the bonded warehouse.

On September 26, the shipowners asked the Bank for payment of their charges, being charges which had accrued, I think, in most cases since July, but had accrued in respect of the warehousing and the removal from one warehouse to another. On September 29, the Sheriff entered into walking possession of the goods at 3 p.m. On September 28, the shipowners had issued delivery orders to the Bank upon presentation by the Bank to the shipowners of the bills of lading. The delivery orders were taken by the Bank to the British Transport Commission which issued dock warrants to the Bank in respect of the goods at 5 p.m. on September 29. The dock warrants are in fact by statute documents of title but at the time that they were issued the Sheriff had already taken walking possession of the goods on behalf of the Customs and Excise as judgment creditors.

Although I have dealt with the history after June 2, to show how the issue arises in this case, the question which I have to decide is whether on June 2, 1961, the bills of lading were still documents of title for the goods to which they related, so that effective pledge of the goods could be made by deposit of the bills of lading endorsed in blank with the Bank for security for money advanced to Bruitrix, or, put more broadly, whether the bills of lading were still documents of title to the goods by endorsement on delivery of which the rights and property in the goods would be transferred. If so, it is now conceded, first, that there was a valid pledge of the goods on June 2, 1961, and second, that nothing had happened after June 2, 1961, affecting the Bank's right as pledgees.

I find as facts, (1) that at all material times from the moment of their unloading at Cardiff docks until June 2, 1961, and, indeed, until September 29, 1961, the goods were in the physical possession of the British Transport Commission as warehousemen and held by the British Transport Commission as such warehousemen on behalf of and to the order of shipowners; (2) that at all material times the

---

[55]Latin: "cause it to be done." Judicial writ directing a sheriff to satisfy a judgment from a debtor's property.]

British Transport Commission would only have released physical possession of the goods or issued a dock warrant—that is a document of title—in respect thereof to a person named in and presenting a delivery order issued by the shipowners; (3) that the shipowners would at no material time have issued a delivery order authorizing the British Transport Commission to deliver possession of the goods to any person except upon the presentation by that person to the shipowners of a bill of lading relating to the goods either endorsed in blank or endorsed to the person presenting the bill of lading.

The contention of the Customs and Excise is that as soon as (1) a contract of carriage by sea is complete, or at any rate the contract of carriage evidenced by the bill of lading is complete, and (2), the bill of lading is in the hands of the person entitled to the property in, and possession of, the goods, and is in a form which would entitle him upon mere presentation to obtain delivery of the goods from the shipowner—that is endorsed to him or endorsed in blank—it ceases to be a document of title by delivery and endorsement of which the rights and property in the goods can be transferred. This is indeed a startling proposition of law which, if correct, would go far to destroy the value of a bill of lading as an instrument of overseas credit. It would mean that no bank could safely advance money on the security of a bill of lading without first making inquiries at the port of delivery, which may be at the other side of the world, as to whether the goods had been landed with the shipowner's lien, if any, discharged or released. It would also mean that no purchaser of goods could rely upon delivery and endorsement to him of the bill of lading as conferring upon him any title to the goods without making similar inquiries, for it would follow that once the goods had been landed and any lien of the shipowner released or discharged, the owner of the goods could divest himself of the property in them without reference to the bill of lading. It would also follow that the shipowner, once the goods had been landed in the absence of any lien, could not safely deliver the goods to the holder of the bill of lading upon presentation because the property in and right to possession of the goods, might have been transferred by the owner to some other person. To hold that this was the law would be to turn back the clock to 1794 before the acceptance by the Court of the special verdict of the Jury as to custom of merchants in the case of *Lickbarrow v. Mason*,[56] and which laid the foundation for the financing of overseas trade and the growth of commodity markets in the 19th century.

The contract for the carriage of goods by sea, which is evidenced by a bill of lading, is a combined contract of bailment and transportation under which the shipowner undertakes to accept possession of the goods from the shipper, to carry them to their contractual destination and there to surrender possession of them to the person who, under the terms of the contract, is entitled to obtain possession of them from the shipowners. Such a contract is not discharged by performance until the shipowner has actually surrendered possession (that is, has divested himself of all powers to control any physical dealing in the goods) to the person entitled under the terms of the contract to obtain possession of them.

So long as the contract is not discharged, the bill of lading, in my view, remains a document of title by endorsement and delivery of which the rights of property in the goods can be transferred. It is clear law that where a bill of lading or order is issued in respect of the contract of carriage by sea, the shipowner is not bound to surrender possession of the goods to any person whether named as consignee or not, except on production of the bill of lading. Until the bill of lading is produced to him, unless at any rate, its absence has been satisfactorily accounted for, he is entitled to retain possession of the goods and if he does part with possession he does so at his own risk if the person to whom he surrenders possession is not in fact entitled to the goods.

In the present case, the contract of carriage evidenced by the bills of lading, had not been discharged on June 2, 1961, when Bruitrix purported to pledge the goods to the Bank by deposit of the bills of lading as security for advancement of money to them. The goods were in the constructive possession of the shipowners being held in the physical possession of the British Transport Commission on behalf of and to the order of the shipowners who had power to control any physical dealing with them. No bill of lading had at that date been produced to the shipowners. The shipowners were under no obligation to surrender their constructive possession and control to deal with the goods, except on production of the bill of lading and had no intention of doing so. In those circumstances it seems to me beyond argument that the bills of lading were at all material times effective documents of title for the goods by deposit of which to the Bank a valid pledge of the goods for security on advances could be made. . . .

. . . Lord Justice Bowen says this

The law as to the endorsement of bills of lading is as clear as in my opinion the practice of all European merchants is thoroughly understood. A cargo at sea while in the hands of the carrier is necessarily incapable of physical delivery. During this period of transit and voyage, the bill of lading by the law merchant is universally recognized as its symbol, and the endorsement and delivery of the bill of lading operates as a symbolical delivery of the cargo. Property in the goods passes by such endorsement and delivery of the bill of lading, whenever it is the intention of the parties that the property should pass, just as under similar circumstances the property would pass by an actual delivery of the goods. And for the purpose of passing such property in the goods and completing the title of the endorsee to full possession thereof, the bill of lading, until complete delivery of the cargo has been made on shore to some one rightfully claiming under it, remains in force as a symbol, and carries with it not only the full ownership of the goods, but also all rights created by the contract of carriage between the shipper and the shipowner. It is a key which in the hands of a rightful owner is intended to unlock the door of the warehouse, floating or fixed, in which the goods may chance to be.

. . . In my opinion the pledge made on June 2, by deposit of the bill of lading was a valid pledge and as a consequence I think that I can give judgment for the plaintiffs in this case. ■

Unlike transferees of bills of exchange, a transferee who obtains an order bill of lading in good faith and for value paid is not a holder in due course who is entitled to claim the goods from the carrier "free of equities" or "free of personal defenses."[57] This is a significant difference. In practice, it means that should an order bill of lading be obtained by fraud and endorsed to a bona fide purchaser for value, the recipient will not acquire title to the goods described in the bill. On the other hand, if the same thing were to happen with a bill of exchange that was neither overdue nor dishonored, the recipient (who would be a holder in due course) would be entitled to the money or property described in that bill. Because of this difference, an order bill of lading is sometimes described as only a "quasi-negotiable" instrument.[58]

The definitional basis for this difference between bills of exchange and order bills of lading can be found in Lord Justice Bowen's description, quoted earlier. Even when a bill of lading is properly endorsed and delivered, title to the goods will pass only when the bill of lading is negotiated *with the intention* of transferring the goods. For example, a seller may endorse a bill of lading to his agent in the port where the goods are to be discharged so that the agent can deal directly with a particular buyer. Because the seller did not intend to pass title to the agent by his endorsement, title would not pass. If the agent were to fraudulently sell the bill to a third party, the third party would also not have title. In such a circumstance, the seller could order the carrier to deliver the goods only to the intended buyer, or if delivery had already been made to the third party, the seller could sue that person for conversion. This is so because the transferee of an order bill of lading acquires both the rights *and* the liabilities of his transferor.[59]

Bills of lading are also distinct from bills of exchange because they additionally represent a contract for carriage. Negotiation of an order bill of lading produces the unique result of a transfer of the right to enforce the underlying transportation agreement. For example, in the case of *The Albazero*, cargo was lost due to the alleged negligence of the carrier. The holders of the bill of lading were unable to sue because the statute of limitation set by the Hague Rules had run. Accordingly, the charterers, who were business affiliates of the holders, attempted to sue under the charterparty, which was not subject to the same statutory time limits. The British House of Lords held that the charterers could not sue. By endorsing the bill of lading, which also represented the contract of carriage, they had transferred all of their contractual rights to the transferee.[60]

---

[57]British practice uses the phrase "free of equities"; American practice uses "free of personal defenses." Both refer to a class of adverse claims that the person obliged to perform may assert against a holder, but not a holder in due course. Such equities or personal defenses include breach of contract, lack or failure of consideration, fraud in the inducement, some forms of illegality, mental incapacity, ordinary duress, discharge by payment or cancellation, and nondelivery.

[58]Leo D'Arcy, *Schmitthoff's Export Trade: The Law & Practice of International Trade,* p. 276 (10th ed. 2000).

[59]The rule was applied in a more roundabout way in Sewell v. Burdick, *Law Reports, Appeal Cases,* vol. 10, p. 74 (1884). There, a bank that was the holder of the bill of lading argued that it was not obligated to pay the cost for storing the goods after they were discharged from the carrier because the shipper had not intended to transfer title to it. The court agreed, noting that the shipper had given the bill of lading to the bank only as a pledge for a loan.

[60]*All England Law Reports,* vol. 1976, pt. 3, p. 129 (House of Lords, 1976).

Carrier's Duties Under a Bill of Lading

A carrier transporting goods under a bill of lading is required by the Hague and Hague-Visby Rules to exercise "due diligence" in:[61]

(a) Making the ship seaworthy.

(b) Properly manning, equipping, and supplying the ship.

(c) Making the holds, refrigerating, and cool chambers, and all other parts of the ship in which goods are carried, fit and safe for their reception, carriage, and preservation.

(d) Properly and carefully loading, handling, stowing, carrying, keeping, caring for, and discharging the goods carried.

Most courts strictly enforce this obligation. For example, in *Riverstone Meat Co. Pty., Ltd. v. Lancashire Shipping Co., Ltd.*, cargo was damaged by water due to the negligent work of a ship-fitter employed by a ship repair company. The court held that the carrier had failed to use due diligence in making the ship seaworthy.[62]

Carrier's Immunities

Both the Hague and Hague-Visby Rules exempt carriers from liability from damages that arise from any:[63]

(a) Act, neglect, or default of the master, mariner, pilot, or the servants of the carrier in the navigation or in the management of the ship;

(b) Fire, unless caused by the actual fault or privity of the carrier;

(c) Perils, dangers, and accidents of the sea or other navigable water;

(d) Act of God;

(e) Act of war;

(f) Act of public enemies;

(g) Arrest or restraint of princes, rulers, or people, or seizure under legal process;

(h) Quarantine restrictions;

(i) Act or omission of the shipper or owner of the goods, or his agent or representative;

(j) Strikes or lockouts or stoppage or restraint of labor from whatever cause, whether partial or general; provided that nothing herein contained shall be construed to relieve a carrier from responsibility for the carrier's own acts;

(k) Riots and civil commotions;

(l) Saving or attempting to save life or property at sea;

(m) Wastage in bulk or weight or any other loss or damage arising from inherent defect, quality, or vice of the goods;

(n) Insufficiency of packing;

(o) Insufficiency or inadequacy of marks;

(p) Latent defects not discoverable by due diligence; and

(q) Any other cause arising without the actual fault and privity of the carrier and without the fault or negligence of the agents or servants of the carrier, but the burden of proof shall be on the person claiming the benefit of this exception to show that neither the actual fault or privity of the carrier nor the fault or neglect of the agents or servants of the carrier contributed to the loss or damage.

These immunities are narrowly construed. If cargo is injured and the injury falls within one of the exemptions, the carrier will nonetheless be responsible if the underlying cause was the result of the carrier's failure to exercise due diligence in carrying out its fundamental duties. This point is illustrated in Case 11–6.

---

[61] International Convention for the Unification of Certain Rules of Law Relating to Bills of Lading, Article 3 (1924) (the 1921 Hague Rules); Brussels Protocol, Article 3 (1968) (the Hague-Visby Rules).

[62] *All England Law Reports,* vol. 1961, pt. 1, p. 495 (1961).

[63] International Convention for the Unification of Certain Rules of Law Relating to Bills of Lading, Article 4, (1924) (the 1921 Hague Rules); Brussels Protocol, Article 4, (1968) (the Hague-Visby Rules).

Case 11–6   Great China Metal Industries Co. Ltd. v. Malaysian International Shipping Corp.

High Court of Australia.
High Court of Australia Reports, vol. 1998, no. 65 (1998).

JUSTICES GAUDRON, GUMMOW AND HAYNE:

In 1989, 40 cases of aluminum can body stock in coils were consigned from Sydney to Keelung, Taiwan. The respondent issued a bill of lading dated 5 October 1989, acknowledging receipt of the goods in apparent good order and condition. The vessel named in the bill as the intended vessel was the *MV Bunga Seroja.*

The shipper named in the bill was Strang International Pty. Ltd. ("Strang") as agent for Comalco Aluminium Ltd. Strang packed the containers in which the cargo was shipped. The appellant was named in the bill as "the notify party" and property in the goods duly passed to it.

The bill provided that it should have effect subject to legislation giving effect to the Hague Rules. By the *Sea-Carriage of Goods Act 1924* (Commonwealth),[64] the Hague Rules applied to the carriage of the goods. The parties to the bill of lading were deemed by §§ 4(1) and 9(1) of that statute to have intended to contract according to the Hague Rules.

In the course of its passage across the Great Australian Bight, the vessel encountered heavy weather. That weather had been forecast before the vessel left port. Some of the goods were damaged.

Although, as will appear, it is not determinative of the outcome of the appeal, the question to which submissions primarily were directed is the meaning and effect of Art. IV rule 2(c) of the Hague Rules that:

"Neither the carrier nor the ship shall be responsible for loss or damage arising or resulting from—

* * *

(c) perils, dangers, and accidents of the sea or other navigable waters . . ."

The appellant contended that:

- this exception (the "perils of the sea" exception) does not apply if damage to cargo results from sea

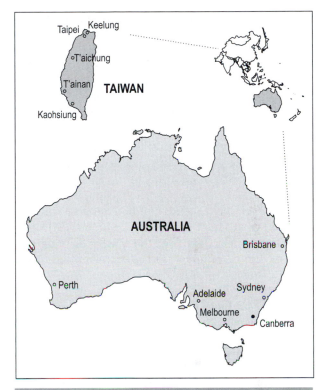

MAP 11-6   Australia and Taiwan (1998)

and weather conditions which could reasonably be foreseen and guarded against;

- the weather encountered by the *Bunga Seroja* was foreseen; and

- the statement of Judges Mason and Wilson in *Shipping Corporation of India Ltd. v Gamlen Chemical Co (A/Asia) Pty Ltd.*[65] that "sea and weather conditions which may reasonably be foreseen and guarded against may constitute a peril of the sea" is wrong and should not be followed.

The appellant pleaded that the respondent had failed to meet its responsibility under Art. III rule 1 of the Hague Rules to exercise, before and at the beginning of the voyage, due diligence to make the ship seaworthy; to properly man, equip, and supply the ship; and to make the holds and all other parts of the ship in which the goods were carried fit and safe for their reception,

---

[64]Section 4(1). This has now been replaced by the *Carriage of Goods by Sea Act 1991* (Commonwealth), which incorporates the Hague-Visby Rules.
[65]*Commonwealth Law Reports,* vol. 147, p. 142 at p. 166 (1980).

carriage, and preservation. It also pleaded failure by the respondent to properly and carefully load, handle, stow, carry, keep, care for, and discharge the goods carried (Art. III rule 2). By its defense, the respondent relied upon various immunities specified in Art. IV rule 2. In particular, the respondent pleaded that it was not responsible for any loss or damage to the goods arising or resulting from perils of the sea and that any damage to the goods resulted or occurred by reason of that matter.

The trial judge (Judge Carruthers) entered judgment for the respondent. His Honor concluded:

"In my view, the [respondent] has established to the requisite degree that the damage to the subject cargo was occasioned by perils of the sea. . . . In summary, the evidence satisfies me that, bearing in mind the anticipated weather conditions: (i) when the *Bunga Seroja* sailed from Burnie she was fit in all respects for the voyage; (ii) the [respondent] properly and carefully loaded, handled, stowed, carried, kept, and cared for the subject cargo; and (iii) there was no neglect or default of the master or other servants of the [respondent] in the management of the ship or cargo.

I am satisfied that the damage to the subject cargo was occasioned by perils of the sea, in that, the pounding of the ship by reason of the heavy weather caused the coils within the container to be dislodged and thereby sustain damage."

The New South Wales Court of Appeal dismissed an appeal. The appeal to this Court also should be dismissed.

* * *

In understanding the operation of the Hague Rules, there are three important considerations. The rules must be read as a whole, they must be read in the light of the history behind them, and they must be read as a set of rules devised by international agreement for use in contracts that could be governed by any of several different, sometimes radically different, legal systems. It is convenient to begin by touching upon some matters of history.

UNIFORM CONSTRUCTION

Because the Hague Rules are intended to apply widely in international trade, it is self-evidently desirable to strive for uniform construction of them. As has been said earlier, the rules seek to allocate risks between cargo and carrier interests and it follows that the allocation of those risks that is made when the rules are construed by national courts should, as far as possible, be uniform. Only then can insurance markets set premiums efficiently and the cost of double insurance be avoided.

In *Gamlen*, Judges Mason and Wilson note that:[66]

[t]here is a difference between the Anglo-Australian conception of "perils of the sea" and the United States-Canadian conception. According to the latter, 'perils of the sea' include losses to goods on board which are peculiar to the sea and "are of an extraordinary nature or arise from irresistible force or overwhelming power, and which cannot be guarded against by the ordinary exertions of human skill and prudence."[67] In the United Kingdom and Australia it is not necessary that the losses or the cause of the losses should be "extraordinary."[68] Consequently sea and weather conditions which may reasonably be foreseen and guarded against may constitute a peril of the sea.

When reference is made to occurrences identified as "extraordinary." the question arises as to the nature of the relativity which is contemplated. Thus it has been said that the events which occurred "may be considered extraordinary as compared with an even voyage upon a placid sea; and yet [they] may be an entirely ordinary occurrence as compared with transportation by sea generally."[69]

It may be that the difference between Anglo-Australian and American-Canadian construction of the "perils of the sea" exception is less than might appear from reference to cases such as *The Giulia*[70] or *The Rosalia*[71]—both decisions of the [United States] Second Circuit Court of Appeals. In *The Rosalia* a peril of the sea was described as "something so catastrophic as to triumph over those safeguards by which skillful and vigilant seamen usually bring ship and cargo to port in safety." More recent authority in the United States has, perhaps, placed less emphasis on whether what hap-

---

[66]*Id.*, at pp. 165–166.

[67]The Giulia, *Federal Reporter*, vol. 218, p. 744 (U.S. 2nd Circuit Ct. of Appeals, 1914), adopting Joseph Story, *Commentaries on the Law of Bailments: with Illustrations from the Civil and the Foreign Law*, § 512(a) (9th ed. 1878).

[68]Thomas G. Carver, *Carriage by Sea*, vol. 1, § 161, (12th ed., 1971); Skandia Insurance Co. Ltd. v. Skoljarev, *Commonwealth Law Reports*, vol. 142, p. 375 at pp. 386–387 (1979). . . .

[69]Clinchfield Fuel Co. v. Aetna Insurance Co., *South Eastern Reporter*, vol. 114, p. 543 at p. 546 (Supreme Ct. of South Carolina, 1922).

[70]*Federal Reporter*, vol. 218, p. 744 (U.S. 2nd Circuit Ct. of Appeals, 1914).

[71]*Id.*, vol. 264, p. 285 (U.S. 2nd Circuit Ct. of Appeals, 1920).

pened was extraordinary and catastrophic. But whether or not that is an accurate reflection of more recent developments, there is great force in what Judge Learned Hand said in *Philippine Sugar Centrals Agency v. Kokusai Kisen Kabushiki Kaisha:*[72]

> The phrase, "perils of the sea," has at times been treated as though its meaning were esoteric: Judge Hough's vivid language in *The Rosalia* . . . has perhaps given currency to the notion. That meant nothing more, however, than that the weather encountered must be too much for a well-found vessel to withstand . . . The standard of seaworthiness, like so many other legal standards, must always be uncertain, for the law cannot fix in advance those precautions in hull and gear which will be necessary to meet the manifold dangers of the sea. That Judge Hough meant no more than this in *The Rosalia* . . . is shown by his reference to the definition in *The Warren Adams*[73] . . . as the equivalent of what he said. That definition was as follows: "That term may be defined as denoting 'all marine casualties resulting from the violent action of the elements, as distinguished from their natural, silent influence.'" It would be too much to hope that *The Rosalia* . . . will not continue to be cited for more than this, but it would be gratifying if it were not.

* * *

. . . [A]s the Second Circuit Court of Appeals said of perils of the sea, in a marine insurance case, *New Zealand Insurance Co v. Hecht, Levis & Kahn:*[74]

> We may concede *arguendo*[75] that they cover only "extraordinary occurrences," . . . but if so, while they do not include those injuries which are the run of all voyages, they certainly do include occasional visitations of the violence of nature, like great storms, even though these are no more than should be expected.

Thus there are statements to be found in the United States authorities that a "perils of the sea" exception may apply even if the weather encountered was no more than expected.

Nor should statements made in the many English cases dealing with perils of the sea be read divorced from their context. Some can, we think, be seen as no more than decisions about particular facts. Others examine questions of onus of proof and concurrent causation, which do not arise in this case. Particular reference need be made to only two of the English cases — *The "Xantho"*[76] and *Hamilton, Fraser & Co v, Pandorf & Co.*[77] Both cases pre-dated the Hague Rules and concerned the construction of an exception in bills of lading in favor of "dangers and accidents of the seas." We mention *The "Xantho"* for the distinction drawn by Lord Herschell between perils of the sea and other losses of which the sea is the immediate cause. He said:

> I think it clear that the term "perils of the sea" does not cover every accident or casualty which may happen to the subject-matter of the insurance on the sea. It must be a peril "of" the sea. Again, it is well settled that it is not every loss or damage of which the sea is the immediate cause that is covered by these words. They do not protect, for example, against that natural and inevitable action of the winds and waves, which results in what may be described as wear and tear. There must be some casualty, something which could not be foreseen as one of the necessary incidents of the adventure.

The distinction drawn by his Lordship is important and must be borne in mind when considering the operation of the "perils of the sea" exception.

The second case, *Pandorf*, is worthy of note because it shows that there may be damage resulting from a peril of the sea despite there being no great catastrophic event. It was held, there, that a cargo was damaged by "dangers and accidents of the seas" when, during the voyage, rats gnawed a hole in a pipe thus allowing water into the hold. It is important to note, however, that it was admitted or proved that the ship was seaworthy and that the damage occurred without fault on the part of the crew. Those facts being accepted, what other explanation for the occurrence could be given save that it was a peril of the sea? If the decision appears strange to the modern eye, its oddity lies not in the conclusion reached but in the premises from which that conclusion proceeded: that the ship was seaworthy and that the loss was not caused by default of the crew. But we need not say whether those findings of fact would now be regarded as open.

Many other cases were mentioned in argument or can be found in the books. We think it desirable to touch briefly on only three other streams of authority.

---

[72]*Id.*, vol. 106, p. 32 at pp. 34–35 (U.S. 2nd Circuit Ct. of Appeals, 1939).
[73]*Id.*, vol. 74, p. 413 at p. 415 (U.S. 2nd Circuit Ct. of Appeals, 1896).
[74]*American Maritime Cases*, vol. 1941, p. 1188 at p. 1189 (1941) per Judges Learned Hand, Chase and Clarke.
[[75]Latin: "as a matter of argument." A statement made by way of argument or as a hypothetical.]
[76]*Law Reports, Appellate Cases*, vol. 12, p. 503 (1887).
[77]*Id.*, vol. 12, p. 518 (1887).

First, it seems that in German law, a peril of the sea need not be an extraordinary event and that a storm of a certain force is regarded as a peril of the sea.[78] Similarly, in French law a peril of the sea need not be "unforeseeable and insurmountable."[79] Finally, the Supreme Court of Canada held in *Goodfellow Lumber Sales v. Verreault*[80] that:

> . . . even if the loss is occasioned by perils of the sea, the ship owner is nevertheless liable if he failed to exercise due diligence to make the ship seaworthy at the beginning of the voyage and that unseaworthiness was a decisive cause of the loss.

How then are these disparate streams of authority to be brought together? In our view one must begin by recognizing that the inquiry is, in large part, a factual inquiry—is the carrier immune in respect of what otherwise would be its failure to discharge its responsibilities under Art. III because the loss or damage to the goods arose or resulted from a cause which brings the carrier within the immunity conferred by Art. IV, rule 2?

If cargo has been lost or damaged and if the vessel was seaworthy, properly manned, equipped, and supplied, what led to the loss or damage? Did it arise or result from want of proper stowing (Art. III rule 2)? Did it arise from the "act, neglect or default of the master. . . . or the servants of the carrier in the navigation, or in the management of the ship" (Art. IV rule 2(a))? Or, did it result from some other cause peculiar to the sea? The last is a peril of the sea.

In *Gamlen*, Judges Mason and Wilson said that "sea and weather conditions which may reasonably be foreseen and guarded against may constitute a peril of the sea." The fact that the sea and weather conditions that were encountered could reasonably be foreseen, or were actually forecast, may be important in deciding issues like an issue of alleged want of seaworthiness of the vessel, an alleged default of the master in navigation or management, or an alleged want of proper stowage. Similarly, the fact that the conditions encountered could have been guarded against may be very important, if not decisive, in considering those issues. (Their decision may then make it unnecessary to consider the "perils of the sea" exception.) But if it is necessary to consider the "perils of the sea" exception, the fact that the conditions that were encountered could reasonably be expected or were forecast should not be taken to conclude that question. To that extent we agree with what was said by Judges Mason and Wilson in *Gamlen*. Such an approach, even if it is different from the American and Canadian approach, better reflects the history of the rules, their international origins, and is the better construction of the rules as a whole.

THE PRESENT APPEAL

In the present case, the trial judge held that there was no breach of Art. III, rule 1 or rule 2. That is, the trial judge rejected the contentions that due diligence had not been exercised to make the ship seaworthy, to properly man, equip, and supply the ship and to "make the holds . . . and all other parts of the ship in which goods are carried, fit and safe for their reception, carriage and preservation." Indeed the trial judge found that in fact the vessel was fit in all respects for the voyage when it left port. Further, the trial judge rejected the contention that the carrier had not properly and carefully stowed the goods. It follows, as we have indicated earlier in these reasons, that the owner having failed to prove any breach of the carrier's responsibilities under Art. III, the applicability of the defense of perils of the sea within the meaning of paragraph (c) of Art. IV, rule 2, did not strictly arise. However, in the light of the findings made at the trial, the conclusion that the damage to the cargo was occasioned by perils of the sea was correct. The fact that the weather encountered had been forecast before the vessel left port does not deny that conclusion.

It was submitted by the appellant that the master should not have left port or should have diverted so as to avoid the weather which was forecast. The former contention appears not to have been made at trial. The latter was, but was rejected. The trial judge, having heard the evidence of experts called by both parties, said that he was "unable to conclude that any deficiencies in the conduct of the ship and her cargo by [the ship's master] have been demonstrated". There is no basis for departing from that finding. Once it was made, the trial judge's conclusion that there was no neglect or default of the master or other servants of the carrier in the management of the ship or cargo was inevitable. To the extent that the appellant now seeks to expand its contention to include the proposition that the vessel should not have left port, it is enough to say that, if the judge's finding does not meet the contention, it is a contention that could be made only with evidence to support it and there was none.

* * *

The failure of the submissions by the appellant makes it unnecessary to consider grounds urged in support of the decision of the Court of Appeal by the respondent in its Notice of Contention.

The appeal should be dismissed with costs. ∎

---

[78]General Motors Overseas Operation v SS Goettingen, *Federal Supplement,* vol. 225, p. 902 at pp. 904–905 (U.S. Dist. Ct. S. Dist. of N.Y., 1964).
[79]William Tetley, *Marine Cargo Claims,* p. 441 (3rd ed., 1988).
[80]*Supreme Court Reports,* vol. 1971 p. 522 at p. 528 (1971).

Liability Limits

Carriers have long attempted to set monetary limits on their liability in the event they are found liable for loss of or damage to a cargo. The permissible limits are now established by convention. The Hague Rules of 1921 limit a carrier's liability to (a) UK £100 per package or (b) UK £100 per unit when shipped in "customary freight units."[81]

One reason many nations had a strong interest in amending the Hague Rules in the 1960s was the belief that its monetary limits were inadequate. The limits were dramatically raised in the Hague-Visby Rules. Those rules set the limits at "10,000 gold francs per package or unit, or thirty gold francs per kilo of the gross weight of the goods lost or damaged, whichever is the higher."[82] This gold or "*Poincaré*" franc is not a unit of currency, but rather an amount of gold. At current conversion rates, it is equivalent to approximately U.S. $1 or U.K. £0.60.

The limits do not apply if the parties agree to higher amounts. They also do not apply if the carrier acted either (a) "with intent to cause damage" or (b) "recklessly and with knowledge that damage would probably result."[83]

The low limits set in the Hague Rules—which remain in effect in the United States—have forced shippers suing in American courts to suggest creative definitions for the terms "package" and "customary freight unit" as a way to obtain a respectable recovery. Courts, not unsympathetic to their plight, have sometimes adopted these suggestions. One such court produced the opinion in Case 11–7.

---

[81]International Convention for the Unification of Certain Rules of Law Relating to Bills of Lading, Article 4, § 5 (1924) (the 1921 Hague Rules). Article 9 provides: "Those contracting states in which the pound sterling is not a monetary unit reserve to themselves the right of translating the sums indicated in this convention in terms of pounds sterling into terms of their own monetary system in round figures."

[82]*Id.,* Article 4, § 5.

[83]*Id.,* and Brussels Protocol, Article 4, § 5 (1968) (the Hague-Visby Rules).

Case 11–7   *Croft & Scully Co. v. M/V Skulptor Vuchetich et al.*

United States, Court of Appeals, Fifth Circuit, 1982.
Federal Reporter, Second Series, vol. 664, p. 1277 (1982).

CIRCUIT JUDGE JOHN R. BROWN:

Appellant Croft & Scully Co. appeals from a decision by the District Court limiting to $500 its recovery in an incident where the parties stipulated negligence. . . .

Things Go Better with Coke

Croft & Scully contracted to ship 1755 cases of soft drink from Houston, Texas, to the middle eastern country of Kuwait. Apparently, Kuwaitis would like to be Peppers, too. Croft & Scully arranged to ship the soft drinks on board M/V *Skulptor Vuchetich*, which arrived in Houston December 8, 1977. Baltic Shipping Co., owner of *Skulptor*, dispatched a 20-foot steel container to Croft & Scully's warehouse in Wharton, Texas. Employees of the supplier loaded the 1755 cases, each containing 4 "6-packs" or 24 cartons, into the container, closed, and sealed it—a real Teem effort. The supplier then trucked the container to Goodpasture's yard, near the Houston Ship Channel, which Baltic had selected as convenient storage facility pending arrival of *Skulptor*.

During the Refreshing Pause between arrival of the container and arrival of *Skulptor*, the vessel's agent prepared a Bill of Lading, and hired Shippers Stevedoring, Inc., to load the soft drink container on board *Skulptor*.

Pepsi Cola Hits the Spot—On the Pavement

As one of the Stevedore's employees was lifting the container, with the use of a forklift, he negligently dropped it. By our calculations, 42,120 cans of soft drinks crashed to the ground, never a thirst to quench. In the Crush, the cans were damaged. The stevedore, no doubt, was in no mood to have a Coke and a smile.

Dr. Pepper at 10, 2, and § 1304

Croft & Scully sued Goodpasture, Shippers Stevedoring, and *Skulptor* and her owners to pick up the Tab for its damages. The District Court dismissed the suit as to Goodpasture because it had no agency relationship with Shippers Stevedoring. Relying upon a so-called Himalaya Clause in the Bill of Lading, it granted the remaining defendants' motion for summary judgment and, finding that the container constituted a "package" within the meaning of § 4(5) of [the *Carriage of Goods by Sea Act* (COGSA), which implements the Hague Rules in the United States,] limited Shippers Stevedoring's liability to $500. Croft & Scully appeals. Things Go Better on appeal, and we reverse and remand.

MAP 11-7   Texas (1982)

A Peek at the Himalaya Clause

Croft & Scully asserts that the Himalaya Clause limiting recovery to $500 violates public policy. That claim fails to make the grade, given our decision in *Brown & Root v. M/V Peisander*[84] upholding such a clause. Indeed, the conflict which we surmounted there does not even arise in this case. Clause 17 of the Bill of Lading makes clear provision for an increased valuation at a higher freight rate. A more unequivocal declaration, in fact, one could not find. As Croft & Scully could have availed itself of extra loss or damage protection, but chose not to, the District Court ruled that the Himalaya Clause applied.

Don't Judge the Package by Its Appearance

Even if liability is limited to $500 per package, Croft & Scully argues, the cardboard cases of soft drinks rather than the 20-foot container should constitute the relevant "package." Shippers Stevedoring responds with equal fervor that the container is the "package." Their argument, we think, given the recent decision in *Allstate Insurance Co. v. Inversiones Navieras Imparca*,[85] holds no water, carbonated or otherwise.

We begin by pointing out that COGSA does not apply by its own force and effect, since the incident occurred in the yard and not on the vessel. Rather the Bill of Lading incorporates COGSA. Thus, its provisions are merely terms of the contract of carriage which, like any other contractual terms, call out for judicial interpretation in case of dispute. . . .

The District Court further observed that the Fifth Circuit had not established a test to determine what constitutes a "package" under COGSA. Since the date of its order, this Court has formulated such a test in whose good hands the parties—and the District Court—must rest.

Allstate involved the loss of 341 cartons of stereo equipment. The shipper loaded the cartons inside a container, sealed it, and had its agent deliver it to the carrier. The carrier issued a Bill of Lading which described the contents both in number and in kind. When the container arrived in Venezuela, it was as empty as a can of soda on a hot summer day. The shipper sought recovery for its full damages, but the carrier relying on COGSA, sought shelter in the $500 limitation. Although the District Court concluded that the container was the COGSA package, the winds of judicial change Schwepped away the $500 shelter and exposed the carrier to full liability.

Judge Anderson, writing for the Court, after reviewing the history of COGSA and decisions in other Circuits, found that each stereo carton was a discrete "package." He based his decision on a case in the Second Circuit, *Mitsui & Co. v. American Export Lines*.[86] There Judge Friendly expressly rejected as unworkable and unsound the old "functional economics" test.[87] . . . Instead, relying on dicta in *Leather's Best, Inc. v. S.S. Mormaclynx*[88] he looked to see whether the carrier had clear, unequivocal notice of the container's contents:

---

[84]*Federal Reporter, Second Series,* vol. 648, p. 415 (Fifth Circuit Ct. of Appeals, 1981).

[85]*Id.,* vol. 646, p. 169 (Fifth Circuit Ct. of Appeals, 1981).

[86]*Id.,* vol. 636, p. 807 (Second Circuit Ct. of Appeals, 1981).

[87]That test, which lingered beyond its time as a Sprite disrupting the admiralty for some years, looks to see whether the goods as packaged prior to shipping were "functional," i.e., fit for shipping and transport individually as packed. It necessitated much judicial guessing work, and we are well rid of it.

[88]*Federal Reporter, Second Series,* vol. 800, p. 815 (Second Circuit Ct. of Appeals, 1971).

Clearly the goal of international uniformity is better served by the approach in *Leather's Best* that generally a container supplied by the carrier is not a COGSA package if its contents and the number of packages or units are disclosed. . . .

We find nothing in the Bill of Lading to indicate that the contracting parties intended some special meaning of the term "package." Since Croft & Scully included information about the contents of the container and their number, *Allstate* governs. Therefore, the District Court erred in granting summary judgment on the "package" issue.

Customary Freight Unit

Even if the container was not a COGSA "package," Shippers Stevedoring contends, the Court should uphold the $500 award because the container was a "customary freight unit" within the ambit of § 4(5) of COGSA, and thus the Himalaya Clause still applies. . . .

Caterpillar Americas Co. v. S/S Sea Roads[89] held that the "customary freight unit" was a tractor and its parts rather than hundredweight units, "regardless of the harshness or seemingly illogic of such result":

With respect to the words "customary freight unit," the authorities are conclusive that this phrase refers to the *unit upon which the charge for freight is computed* and not to the physical shipping unit. As thus construed, the statute gives the court the task of determining what unit was actually used by the carrier for computing the freight charge on the shipment in question. Under the statute the freight unit, if one exists, will control the question of limitation of liability, unless the freight unit employed was a mere

sham, and, therefore not a "customary" unit within the meaning of the statute. . . .

From these cases, we deduce that "customary freight unit" is a question of fact that will vary from contract to contract. Of particular importance in this as in any contractual dispute, then, is the parties' intent, as expressed in the Bill of Lading, applicable tariff, and perhaps elsewhere. . . .

Although Croft & Scully admitted that the freight charge was $2200, calculated on a "flat container rate," we do not know how the parties arrived at that rate. Does it depend upon the contents, weight, value, custom of the trade, applicable tariffs, if any, or other factors? The District Court must consider these questions on remand. If it finds that the container was a "customary freight unit," then the Court should reinstate the $500 limitation of liability. If not, then it should hold further proceedings to determine the amount of damages. We, of course, express no opinion concerning the outcome.

Recap

We affirm the District Court's dismissal of Goodpasture and its conclusion that the Himalaya Clause applies. We reverse its grant of summary judgment for Shippers Stevedoring and its finding that the steel container was a COGSA package. As the District Judge never reached the important factual question whether the container of soft drink cartons was a "customary freight unit," we remand for further inquiry into the facts and for consideration of the parties' intent, factors that will guide the trial Court in determining the meaning of that COGSA clause.

Affirmed in part, reversed in part and remanded. ◼

[89] *Federal Supplement,* vol. 231, p. 647 (Dist. Ct. S. Dist. of Florida, 1964), affirmed, *Federal Reporter, Second Series,* vol. 364, p. 829 (Fifth Circuit Ct. of Appeals, 1966).

Time Limitations

A claim for loss or damages must be instituted within one year after the goods were or should have been delivered.[90] The claim may be initiated by filing suit or commencing an arbitration proceeding.[91]

Third-Party Rights (Himalaya Clause)

The Hague and Hague-Visby Rules apply only to the carrier and the party or parties shipping goods under a bill of lading. Third parties who help in the transport of the goods but who are not parties to the carriage-of-goods contract contained in the bill of lading have no

[90] International Convention for the Unification of Certain Rules of Law Relating to Bills of Lading, Article 3, § 6 (1924) (the 1921 Hague Rules); Brussels Protocol, Article 3, § 6 (1968) (the Hague-Visby Rules).
[91] The Merak, *All England Law Reports,* vol. 1965, pt. 1, p. 230 (1965).

contractual right to claim the liability limits established by the conventions. Thus, officers, crew members, agents, and brokers who work for a carrier, as well as stevedores who commonly work for a unit of a shipping line, can be sued under local laws of tort or delict without the convention-imposed cap.

Himalaya Clause: A term in a bill of lading that purports to extend to third parties the carrier's liability limits established by the Hague and Hague-Visby Rules.

To extend the liability limits of the conventions to their employees, agents, and even independent contractors (such as stevedores), carriers have added a clause to their bills of lading, known as a **Himalaya Clause**, which entitles them to claim the protection of the Hague or the Hague-Visby Rules. These clauses are valid in the United States but generally unenforceable in the United Kingdom. Most U.K. courts refuse to enforce the Himalaya Clause because of a doctrine known as privity of contract, which says that only persons party to a contract may enforce its provisions.[92]

In the United States, on the other hand, the doctrine of privity is, at best, haphazardly enforced. As a consequence, most American courts allow the persons named in a Himalaya Clause to claim the rights it grants as third-party beneficiaries.[93]

E. CHARTERPARTIES

charterparty: A contract to hire an entire ship for a particular voyage or for a particular period of time.

A **charterparty** is a contract for the hire of an entire ship for a particular voyage or a set period of time. Oil, sugar, grain, ores, coal, and other bulk commodities are almost always shipped under such contracts.

The Hague and Hague-Visby Rules do not apply to charterparties, unless a bill of lading issued by the shipowner comes into the hands of a third party. The charterer and the owner are free to set the terms of their contract, and commonly they use standardized contracts drafted at various conferences and known by such code names as Baltime and Gencon. Interpretations and legal obligations vary from country to country, so a forum selection clause and a choice-of-law clause are common, and important, provisions.[94]

Voyage Charterparties

voyage charterparty: A contract to hire an entire ship for a particular voyage.

When a charterer employs a ship and its crew for the carriage of goods from one place to another, the charterer and shipowner have entered into a **voyage charterparty**. Under the terms most commonly used in such a contract, the owner agrees to provide the ship at a named port at a specified time and to carry the goods to the contract destination. The charterer agrees to provide a full cargo and to arrange for its loading at an agreed-upon time. If less than a full load is provided, the shipowner is entitled to charge **dead freight** for the amount of the deficiency. This dead-freight charge will be noted on the bill of lading issued by the shipowner and a holder who acquires the bill will be obliged to pay the charge before the ship will turn over the cargo.

dead freight: A charge imposed on a charterer when a chartered ship has less than a full load.

If the shipowner fails to arrive at the original port for loading at the specified time, the charterer will commonly be able to terminate the contract by virtue of a cancellation clause. The charterparty will also describe the number of **lay days** that the ship may be idle while goods are loaded or discharged. Because modern cargo ships are expensive and have a short working life, the charterparty will additionally describe damages, known as **demurrage**, that the shipowner can charge for every idle day that exceeds the agreed-upon lay days. The obligation

lay days: The days that a charterer may keep a chartered ship idle for the loading of goods.

demurrage: A charge made by a shipowner when a charterer keeps a ship idle for more than the agreed-upon lay days.

---

[92]In 1962, the Court of Appeal refused to enforce a Himalaya Clause in Scruttons, Ltd. v. Midland Silicones, Ltd., *All England Law Reports,* vol. 1962, pt. 1, p. 1 (1962). In 1975, the House of Lords in the case of New Zealand Shipping Co., Ltd. v. Satterthwaite, *All England Law Reports,* vol. 1974, pt. 1, p. 1015 (1974), said that there might be circumstances where stevedores could be treated as parties to a contract containing a Himalaya Clause. However, in 1980 the Privy Council reapplied the doctrine of privity and found the Himalaya Clause unenforceable in Port Jackson Stevedoring, Pty. Ltd. v. Salmond and Spraggon (Australia) Pty., *All England Law Reports,* vol. 1980, pt. 3, p. 257 (1980).

[93]Brown & Root v. M/V Peisander, *Federal Reporter, Second Series,* vol. 648, p. 415 (Fifth Circuit Ct. of Appeals, 1981).

[94]The law of charterparties is vast and its terminology peculiar. Reference to one of the standard texts on the subject is vital for a complete understanding. *See,* for example, J. Bes, *Chartering and Shipping Terms* (10th ed., 1977); Michael Wilford, Terrance Coghlin, and Nicholas Healy, *Time Charters* (2nd ed., 1982); Wharton Poor, *American Law of Charter Parties and Ocean Bills of Lading* (5th ed. supp. by R. Bauer, 1974); and Stewart C. Boyd, Andrew S. Burrows, and David Foxton, *Scrutton on Charterparties and Bills of Lading* (20th ed., 1996).

to pay the demurrage will be secured by a lien on the cargo, which any holder of the corresponding bill of lading will have to pay off before taking delivery.

Time Charterparties

time charterparty: A contract to hire an entire ship for a particular period of time.

Under a **time charterparty** the charterer engages the use of a vessel for a stated period of time. The charterer normally pays "hire" monthly, and the shipowner will be entitled to withdraw the ship from the charterer's use if a monthly installment is not paid promptly. Questions of demurrage and dead freight do not arise because the shipowner receives hire while the ship is loading and unloading and whether or not it is carrying a cargo.

The charterer has the right to direct the ship to proceed to wherever it is needed. Ordinarily, the only limitation on this right is the charterer's promise to engage only in lawful trades, to carry only lawful goods, and to only direct the vessel to safe ports. If the shipowner attempts to interfere with the charterer's use of the vessel, he will be in breach of the charterparty.

Charterparties and Bills of Lading

The contract of carriage between a charterer and a shipowner is the charterparty. The shipowner will commonly issue the charterer a bill of lading when goods are loaded on board; however, between the two of them, the bill will be only a receipt for goods and a document of title. Should the charterer transfer the bill, the position of the third-party endorsee will be different. The Hague or Hague-Visby Rules will apply, and the contract between the shipowner and the endorsee will be governed by the bill of lading. Of course, the bill of lading may incorporate the terms of the charterparty. In that case, the endorsee will be governed by its terms. To incorporate the terms of the charterparty, the bill of lading must do so clearly and unambiguously, and the terms of the charterparty must not conflict with any express terms of the bill of lading or (if they apply) the Hague or Hague-Visby Rules.

F. MARITIME LIENS

maritime lien: A charge or claim against a vessel or its cargo.

A lien is a charge or claim against property that exists to satisfy some debt or obligation. A **maritime lien** is a charge or claim against a vessel, its freight, or its cargo.[95] The main purpose of maritime liens is to ensure that a vessel can adequately obtain credit to properly outfit itself for a voyage.

In common law countries, a vessel is regarded as a juridical person separate and apart from its owner. Thus, a ship itself may be liable for the shipowner's breach of contract or for the crew's negligence, or even for damages caused without the shipowner's or crew's fault, as when port regulations require the ship to use a pilot and the pilot causes the injury. In sum, the owner is not essential to the existence of a lien against a ship. In civil law countries, on the other hand, a maritime lien (or "privilege") is a right in property, but the property is not independent of the owner. The lien, in essence, exists against the owner as a debtor.

res: (Latin: "a thing.") The vessel or cargo to which a maritime lien attaches.

The distinctive characteristic of maritime liens, whether defined by the common or the civil law, is that they do not require possession. They attach to the ***res*** (i.e., the vessel, freight, or cargo) and travel with it. They are also secret.[96] If a vessel is sold, the lien "goes with the ship," even if the new owner is unaware of its existence. In common law countries, the foreclosure of a maritime lien follows a peculiar procedure. The *res* is seized (if it is a vessel, it is "arrested")

---

[95] A *vessel* is practically any floating object capable of being propelled for the purpose of carrying goods, including any equipment or appurtenances on board. *Cargo* is the goods carried aboard a vessel. *Freight* is the sum of money paid for the carriage of cargo. Geoffrey H. Longnecker, "Development of the Law of Maritime Liens," *Tulane Law Review*, vol. 45, p. 574 (1971).

[96] In some civil law countries, however, shipbuilding liens (known as maritime mortgages) must be recorded with a government agency. Ivon d'Almeida Pires-Filho, "Priority of Maritime Liens in the Western Hemisphere: How Secure Is Your Claim?" *University of Miami Inter-American Law Review*, vol. 16, p. 507 (1985). The same is technically true in common law countries, because shipbuilding liens are not considered to be maritime transactions. *See* North Pacific S.S. Co. v. Hall Bros. Co., *United States Reports*, vol. 249, p. 119 (Supreme Ct., 1919).

without prior notice to the owner. An admiralty court takes custody, and a suit proceeds against the thing. If the lien-holder's claim succeeds, the *res* is sold, the proceeds are distributed among the various lien-holders, and the title to the property is transferred to the purchaser of the *res* free of all claims. In civil law countries, by comparison, the *res* is not regarded as something distinct from its owner. A foreclosure suit is initiated against the owner, and the *res* is then seized as a way to compel the owner to appear and furnish security before the *res* can be released.

When there are multiple lien-holders, the various claims must be ranked. A multilateral treaty, the 1926 International Convention for the Unification of Certain Rules Relating to Maritime Liens and Mortgages (known as the Brussels Convention), establishes a hierarchy among lien claims.[97] Although the Convention has not been widely adopted, its ranking of liens is representative of most municipal schemes.[98] Under the convention, claims are ranked as follows:

1. Judicial costs and other expenses
2. Seaman's wages
3. Salvage and general average
4. Tort claims
5. Repairs, supplies, and necessaries
6. Ship mortgages

Case 11–8 illustrates how courts go about applying this ranking.

---

[97]*League of Nations Treaty Series,* vol. 120, p. 187. The 1926 Convention was revised and updated in 1967. The text of the 1967 Convention is posted at www.admiraltylawguide.com/conven/liens1967.html.

[98]For a comparison of the 1926 Brussels Convention with the maritime lien laws of North and South America, *see* Ivon d'Almeida Pires-Filho, "Priority of Maritime Liens in the Western Hemisphere: How Secure Is Your Claim?" *University of Miami Inter-American Law Review,* vol. 16, p. 507 (1985).

Case 11–8   The Chinese Seamen's Foreign Technical Services Co. v. Soto Grande Shipping Corp., SA

People's Republic of China, Shanghai Maritime Court, 1987.
Journal of Maritime Law and Commerce, vol. 20, p. 217 (1989).[99]

THE FACTS

The plaintiff in this action was engaged in the provision of crewing services for vessels in maritime commerce. The defendant was the owner of the Panamanian M/V *Pomona.* The plaintiff and the defendant shipowner executed a crewing services contract on December 17, 1984, in Shanghai. The contract required the plaintiff to provide 25 seamen, including a master, officers, and crew, to serve for one year aboard the

Pomona. The defendant was to pay monthly wages of $20,833 to the plaintiff. On January 14, 1985, the plaintiff dispatched the 25 seamen to the vessel. By September 16, 1985, the plaintiff had received only two payments, totaling $21,455 for wages and $840.80 for ship's stores. The plaintiff claimed $225,283.05 in wage payments from the defendant shipowner.

THE SEIZURE AND SALE

On September 16, 1985, the plaintiff submitted to the Shanghai Maritime Court a petition for the seizure of the *Pomona.* The petition prayed for an order directing the shipowner to post security in the amount of U.S.$200,000, or alternatively, for an order directing the

---

[99]This decision was reported in the *Bulletin of the Supreme People's Court* (*Zhonghua Renmin Gongheguo Zuigao Renmin Fayuan Gongbao*), vol. 13, published March 20, 1988. The actual decision of the Shanghai Maritime Court is not available for public reference. Case files in Chinese courts are generally available for review only by court personnel and the attorneys for the parties. This summary was prepared by Todd L. Platek, Esq., Kirlin, Campbell & Keating, New York.

MAP 11-8   China (1987)

sale of the vessel. The court found that the petition was procedurally correct, that it alleged a claim for which seizure of foreign flag vessels is allowed under Chinese law, and that it set forth a reasonable basis for seizure. On September 28, the court therefore ordered the vessel's seizure.

Due to the failure of the shipowner to furnish security, the court ordered the sale of the *Pomona* in accordance with Article 93, clause 3 of the Law of Civil Procedure (For Trial Implementation) of the People's Republic of China.

Clause 3 . . . provides that if the property under legal custody cannot be held and maintained for a long period, the People's Court may compel a sale and deposit the proceeds in the court's registry. The *Pomona* was sold at public auction on October 18, 1985, and sales proceeds of $430,000 were generated and deposited in the court's registry. Simultaneously, the court published an official announcement that all creditors of the vessel should apply to register their claims within 30 days.

THE SUIT

On October 3, 1985, the plaintiff commenced suit in the Shanghai Maritime Court and sought, in addition to the above-mentioned back wages of the seamen, the fuel expenses which it had covered for the vessel, the cost of the vessel arrest, its legal fees, liquidated damages for breach of contract, and interest. The total amount of plaintiff's claim was $259,636.03.

The shipowner failed to file answering papers within the time limit prescribed by law. Although twice formally summoned by the court, the shipowner consistently failed to submit any legitimate reasons for its refusal to enter a formal appearance in the action.

Having given the defendant the requisite opportunity to be heard, the court conducted a trial of the action in the shipowner's absence.

THE RULINGS

The court ruled that the shipowner had breached the terms of the contract and should bear full responsibility for the consequences of its unfulfilled obligations. Following international custom and practice as well as Chinese law, the court ruled as follows:

1. The shipowner was required to compensate the plaintiff for crew wages in the amount of $190,149.24;
2. The shipowner was required to compensate the plaintiff for fuel expenses in the amount of $3,500.00;
3. The plaintiff's claims for other expenses were denied;
4. The shipowner was required to bear certain costs of litigation, including the filing fee ($1,176.87), the application fee for seizure of the vessel ($625), and miscellaneous litigation expenses ($139.90), totaling $1,941.77. Those expenses were to be deducted from the sales proceeds after the effective date of the ruling.

THE PRELIMINARY DISTRIBUTION OF THE SALES PROCEEDS

The order took effect after it was served upon the parties and the time for appeal had expired. In accordance with a recent Supreme People's Court directive entitled "Special Rules on the Payment of Claims Against Vessels Sold by Court Order," the court directed the convening of a meeting of creditors to engage in the liquidation of the debts arising out of this case. It publicly verified the sum of money available for distribution, the priority of claims, the nature and extent of each creditor's claim, and the methods of negotiating the creditors' claims. After marshalling the creditors' evidence and examining the value of the claims, the court certified four creditors' claims in addition to the plaintiff's judgment for crew wages. The additional claims certified by the court were the following:

1. A claim for seamen's wages in the sum of $171,840.26 put forward by the Chinese Seamen's Foreign Technical Services Company (CSFTSC) of the Shanghai Maritime Transport Bureau;
2. Claims totaling $23,292.18 for harbor usage, ship's stores and other items put forward by the Ningpo Branch of the China Ocean Shipping Agency (COSA);

3. A ship mortgage in the amount of $1,931,530.34 held by the National Westminster Bank, USA.

4. A claim asserted by the Repair Center of the Shanghai Shipbuilding Industry Corporation (SSIC) for repairs totaling $39,000.

The *Pomona* sales proceeds were applied first to litigation costs and certain . . . *custodia legis*[100] expenses. The costs and expenses paid in this manner consisted of the $1,941.77 in costs awarded to the plaintiff, $25,185.88 in claims and expenses arising from the sale of the vessel, and $3,500 for the diesel oil and lighterage expenses incurred by the plaintiff during the period of seizure. The remaining amount of U.S.$399,372.35 was augmented by $17,921.67 in interest earned while the sales proceeds were held in legal custody at the Bank of China. The fund available to creditors was thereby raised to U.S.$417,294.02.

The priority rules established by the aforementioned directive rank seamen's wages in the first priority class. The plaintiff's judgment for seamen's wages and the wage claim of the Shanghai CSFTSC, which together amounted to $361,989.50, were therefore paid first out of the remaining sales proceeds.

The second priority class established by the directive includes national taxes, harbor usage fees and other port expenses. The claim of the Ningpo COSA included items totalling $9,574.29, which fell within the second class. Those items were accordingly paid next.

There were no other claims in the first three priority classes established by the directive. The next highest claim was the mortgage held by the National Westminster Bank, which was listed between the fourth and fifth priority classes. The remaining claims of the Ningpo COSA, including claims for fuel and water supplied to the vessel, and the repair costs claimed by the Repair Center of SSIC, were deemed "other registered claims" within the meaning of the directive. They fell within the fifth priority class, below the mortgage. The balance of the sales proceeds, totalling $45,730.23 was therefore distributed to the mortgagee, and the remaining claims were left unpaid.

THE FINAL DISTRIBUTION OF SALES PROCEEDS

After another step in the deliberations, the Shanghai CSFTSC "reconsidered" the effect of the plaintiff's lead in this case and agreed to transfer $12,400.26 to the plaintiff from its own portion of the preliminary distribution. The Shanghai CSFTSC and the National Westminster Bank then "reconsidered" the actual losses of the Repair Center of SSIC Corporation and the Ningpo Branch of COSA, and agreed to allow them, from their portions of the preliminary distribution, "suitable amounts" to remedy their losses. In this way, the five claimants arrived at the following final distribution of payments:

- The plaintiff received $202,549.50;
- The Shanghai CSFTSC received $150,000;
- The Ningpo Branch of COSA received $15,274.29;
- The National Westminster Bank USA received $44,970.23;
- The Repair Center for SSIC Corporation received $4,500.00. ∎

[100Latin: "in the custody of the law." Refers to property held in the custody of a court.]

G. MARITIME INSURANCE

The trade terms the parties choose in their sales contract determine who is responsible for purchasing maritime insurance, and who benefits from it. However, even when the "risk of loss" shifts from the seller to the buyer, the seller continues to have an interest in seeing that the goods are insured. If the goods are lost and the buyer is either bankrupt or unwilling to pay, insurance may be the only basis for recovery available to the seller.

Should a party who is required to purchase insurance be involved in an isolated sale, he can purchase a special cargo policy covering the single sale. It is more common, however, for cargo to be covered by an open cargo policy. Such a policy is an open-ended contract that insures all the cargo of an exporter during a particular time period. All of the exporter's shipments, whether by truck, rail, air, or vessel, are covered. Parties involved in an isolated sale often arrange to have their goods covered by the open cargo policy of a freight forwarder or customhouse broker.

Perils

The perils covered by special and open cargo policies commonly include the following:

1. Loss or damage from the sea (e.g., weather, collision, stranding, sinking)
2. Fire
3. Jettison (i.e., the dumping of cargo in order to protect other property)
4. Forcible taking of the ship
5. Barratry (i.e., the fraudulent, criminal, or wrongful conduct of the captain or crew)
6. Explosion
7. Fumigation damage
8. Damage from loading, discharging, or transshipping cargo

The coverage of maritime insurance policies is examined in Case 11–9.

Case 11–9 Western Assurance Co. of Toronto v. Shaw

United States, Court of Appeals, Third Circuit, 1926.
Federal Reporter, Second Series, vol. 11, p. 495 (1926).

CIRCUIT JUDGE DAVIS:

This was an action to recover on a contract of maritime insurance against the Western Assurance Company for the total loss of the barge *Holly*, while moored at a wharf in Chester, Pennsylvania. She was insured "against the adventures and perils of the harbors, bays, sounds, seas, rivers," etc. She was loaded with three large boilers, weighing 60 tons each, which she was to take to Norfolk, Virginia. They were lying in the middle of the barge, lengthwise and end to end. On the night of December 18, 1919, she listed to the starboard and sank early the next morning. When she listed, the boilers rolled to starboard and caused or hastened her sinking.

The learned trial judge found that "the final plunge was due to the swell of a steamer breaking over the part of the deck, which served as a washboard and filling her," that this was a peril against which she was insured, and so decreed that the respondent pay for the loss sustained. The case is here on appeal.

The insurance company urged, as a defense in the District Court and here, that the libelant did not establish a loss by "perils of the seas" against which the company insured, and that the proximate cause of the loss was the unseaworthiness of the boat.

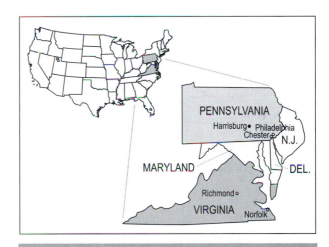

MAP 11-9   Pennsylvania and Virginia

In order to recover, it is necessary for the libelant to bring his claim for loss within the provisions of the policy and establish that the loss was caused by one of the perils against which the barge was insured. . . .

It is difficult to give a definition which will neither be too narrow nor too broad, of the phrase, "perils of the sea." In defining it, courts have used various expressions which cannot be easily reconciled. The learned trial judge defined a "peril of the sea" as "any threatening danger from the sea," the "operative cause," "the efficient cause," "the *causa causans*."[101] In an enlarged

[101]Latin: "the immediate cause."]

sense all losses from maritime adventures arise from perils of the sea, but such losses do not come under this phrase within the meaning of maritime insurance policies. "Perils of the sea" against which underwriters insure are confined to extraordinary occurrences, such as stress of weather, winds and waves, lightning, tempests, rocks, etc. . . .

If a loss arises from the ordinary circumstances or wear and tear of a voyage, the insurer is not liable because a seaworthy vessel is supposed to endure usual and customary occurrences. The words are therefore used to describe abnormal causes and extraordinary circumstances. . . .

The testimony by which libelant sought to establish that a steamer in fact passed which might have produced a swell is very unsatisfactory. By leading questions, Nicholein A. Delegeorgen, captain of the barge, was led to say that waves from a passing steamer caused the barge to roll. But, on the contrary, he said again and again that he did not see any boat or anything on the river at that time.

Assuming, however, that the swell from a passing steamer did cause the barge to roll, the further question arises: Was it a "peril of the sea," within the meaning of the policy? Was it an extraordinary, abnormal occurrence against which the insured could not protect himself with ordinary precaution? Or was it a normal, customary circumstance that may occur at Chester every day? The passing of steamers along the Delaware between the port of Philadelphia and the sea is a normal occurrence that may be expected at any time. It was not extraordinary or unusual. It does not seem to us that waves from a passing steamer washing against the shores of the Delaware are a "peril of the sea" against which the barge was insured. The following statement from the opinion of the learned trial judge indicated that he was inclined to this view, or at least had misgivings about the contrary conclusion:

It is difficult for any one to believe that a barge of a size and in condition to navigate the waters of the Delaware and Chesapeake Bays, in the lower reaches of which heavy weather and a nasty sea are often encountered, would be swamped by the swell from a passing steamer. If the latter fact was all which appeared, the mind would draw and would cling to the inference of unseaworthiness.

The respondent says that the barge was unseaworthy in respect to its loading and that this was the proximate cause of the loss. While the boilers rested on cradles or saddles, it is admitted that they had not been, as yet, shored or chocked at the sides, so as to keep them steady and from rolling. If they had been, the testimony tends to show, and we think does show, that they would have remained stationary when the barge rolled. If they had so remained, the barge would not have sunk.

The testimony conclusively establishes that to leave round boilers, such as the three loaded on the *Holly* were, unchocked and not shored over night is unsafe and improper stowage or loading. The boilers were loaded by the Sun Ship Building Company, and the captain of the barge asked the riggers, entrusted with the loading, to chock the boilers. They could not do so. The failure, therefore, to shore or chock the boilers, as safe and proper loading required, set in motion a train of consequences—the opening of seams, consequent leaking, the fastening of wire rope or cables to the boilers and wharf—that caused the sinking and occasioned the loss. It seems to us that there is no escape from the conclusion that there was "want of ordinary care and skill in loading" and that this resulted in an unseaworthy condition of the barge with respect thereto. . . .

The policy excepted from the risks insured against all claims arising "from the want of ordinary care and skill in loading and stowing the cargo." The proofs not only show that the claim does not come within the risks against which the barge was insured, but they clearly show that it arises from the want of ordinary care and skill in loading, and comes within the above exception.

Therefore the decree is reversed, with directions to the District Court to dismiss the libel, with costs. ■

Average Clauses

The loss of cargo can be either total or partial. Total loss is ordinarily governed by a "constructive loss" clause in a maritime insurance policy. This usually includes (a) losses exceeding one-half the value of the cargo or (b) losses where the cost of recovery exceeds the cargo's value.[102]

---

[102]Leslie J. Buglass, *Marine Insurance Claims; American Law and Practice,* p. 16 (2nd ed., 1972).

particular average: A loss to a ship or its cargo that is not to be shared in by contributions from all those interested, but is to be borne by the owner of the injured thing.

general average: A contribution by those jointly involved in a maritime venture to make good the loss by one of them for his voluntary sacrifice of a part of the ship or cargo to save the residue of the property and the lives on board, or for the extraordinary expenses necessarily incurred for the benefit and safety of all.

A partial loss is known in the marine insurance industry as a **particular average**. A "free from particular average" (FPA) policy provides the most limited recovery for partial losses. Such a policy ordinarily covers only losses from fire, stranding, sinking, or collision of the vessel. A "with average" (WA) policy provides more protection; however, it ordinarily contains a "franchise" clause that provides for payment only if the loss exceeds a specified minimum amount (the franchise amount). WA policies can also be purchased without a franchise clause.[103]

General average comes about in the carriage of goods at sea when, in order to avoid some threat to the whole venture, some expense has to be incurred, or some loss or damage is deliberately inflicted, in order to save the ship and its cargo. For example, a ship may run aground. In order to get it afloat, some of the cargo or some of the ship's supplies may have to be jettisoned, or salvage tugs may have to be hired. When this happens, everyone having an interest in the ship and its various cargoes will have benefited. Each must then contribute, in proportion to the value of their interest, to restoring the party who suffered the loss or damage or who incurred the expense. This is called a "general average" contribution.

Normally, marine insurance will cover each shipper's contribution. However, if insurance is not purchased or should a policy not cover general average, then the shipper must pay the contribution before the ship's crew will release the goods. Similarly, if a buyer has already paid for the goods and received a bill of lading, then the buyer (because the bill of lading will transfer the risk of loss to the buyer at that point) must come up with the contribution before the ship's crew will turn over the goods. In either case, the ship will have a lien claim against the goods, and, if the contribution is not paid, it may foreclose on the goods, sell them, and retain that portion of the sale price it receives to cover the cost of the contribution.

A person seeking to claim a general average contribution from other parties must show (a) that the loss was incurred to benefit everyone and (b) that the person making the claim was not responsible for causing the danger. For example, a shipping company cannot claim general average when it has hired tugs to refloat a ship that ran aground because of the captain's faulty navigation.

H. CARRIAGE OF GOODS BY AIR

The carriage of goods on aircraft is regulated by the 1929 Warsaw Convention (formally known as the Convention for the Unification of Certain Rules Relating to International Carriage by Air).[104] Four amendments to the Convention have been adopted and are now in force:[105] the

---

[103]W. Grunde, *Servicing World Markets: Administrative Procedures,* p. 61 (1979).

[104]The text of the Warsaw Convention is in *United Nations Treaty Series,* vol. 261, p. 421, and vol. 266, p. 444. A copy is posted at www.iasl.mcgill.ca/private.htm and at www.jus.uio.no/lm/air.carriage.warsaw.convention.1929/doc.html.

  The 150 states parties to the Warsaw Convention as of August 2002 were Afghanistan, Algeria, Angola, Argentina, Armenia, Australia, Austria, Azerbaijan, Bahamas, Bahrain, Bangladesh, Barbados, Belarus, Belgium, Benin, Bolivia, Bosnia and Herzegovina, Botswana, Brazil, Brunei Darussalam, Bulgaria, Burkina Faso, Cambodia, Cameroon, Canada, Cape Verde, Chile, China, Colombia, Comoros, Congo, Costa Rica, Croatia, Cuba, Cyprus, Czech Republic, Democratic Republic of the Congo, Denmark, Dominican Republic, Ecuador, Egypt, Equatorial Guinea, Estonia, Ethiopia, Fiji, Finland, France, Gabon, Germany, Ghana, Greece, Guatemala, Guinea, Honduras, Hungary, Iceland, India, Indonesia, Iran, Iraq, Ireland, Israel, Italy, Ivory Coast, Japan, Jordan, Kenya, Kuwait, Kyrgyzstan, Laos, Latvia, Lebanon, Lesotho, Liberia, Libya, Liechtenstein, Luxembourg, Macedonia, Madagascar, Malawi, Malaysia, Maldives, Mali, Malta, Mauritania, Mauritius, Mexico, Moldova, Mongolia, Morocco, Myanmar, Nauru, Nepal, Netherlands, New Zealand, Niger, Nigeria, North Korea, Norway, Oman, Pakistan, Panama, Papua New Guinea, Paraguay, Peru, Philippines, Poland, Portugal, Qatar, Romania, Russia, Rwanda, Saint Vincent and the Grenadines, Samoa, Saudi Arabia, Senegal, Seychelles, Sierra Leone, Singapore, Slovakia, Slovenia, Solomon Islands, South Africa, Spain, Sri Lanka, Sudan, Sweden, Switzerland, Syria, Togo, Tonga, Trinidad and Tobago, Tunisia, Turkey, Turkmenistan, Uganda, Ukraine, United Arab Emirates, United Kingdom, United Republic of Tanzania, United States, Uruguay, Uzbekistan, Vanuatu, Venezuela, Vietnam, Yemen, Yugoslavia , Zambia, and Zimbabwe. International Civil Aviation Organization Treaty Collection at www.icao.int/cgi/goto_leb.pl?icao/en/leb/treaty.htm.

[105]Montreal Protocol No. 3 of 1975 was also adopted but it is not yet in force. The text of Protocol No. 3 is at www.iasl.mcgill.ca/private.htm.

Hague Protocol of 1955,[106] Montreal Protocol No. 1,[107] Montreal Protocol No. 2,[108] and Montreal Protocol No. 4 of 1975.[109] As with inland carriage, the documents used in air carriage—the air waybills and consignment notes—are not documents of title.[110] This reflects the practical difference between air flight and ship transport. The bills and notes used in air transportation arrive with the goods rather than being sent separately.

At the heart of the Warsaw Convention is a definition of the **air waybill**. In states that are parties to the Convention—but not to Montreal Protocol No. 4—the bill must describe (a) the nature of the goods being shipped; (b) the method of packing and any marks or numbers; (c) the weight, quantity, volume, or dimensions of the goods; (d) the apparent condition of the goods and their packaging; and (e) a statement that the carriage is subject to the Convention's rules.[111] Montreal Protocol No. 4, which encourages carriers to use electronic records, requires only three things to appear on the paper waybill that accompanies a consignment of goods: (a) the places of departure and destination, (b) an intermediate stopping place in a different state (if the place of departure and destination are in the same state), and (c) the weight of the consignment.[112]

air waybill: An instrument issued by an air carrier to a shipper that serves as a receipt for goods and as evidence of the contract of carriage but is not a document of title for the goods.

[106]The text of the Hague Protocol is in *United Nations Treaty Series,* vol. 1963, p. 373, and is posted at *id.*

The Hague Protocol increased the liability limits for injuries to passengers and their baggage to 250,000 francs from the 20,000 francs set in the 1929 convention. Warsaw Convention (as amended by the Hague Protocol), Article 22.

States Parties to the Hague Protocol as of August 2002 were Afghanistan, Algeria, Angola, Argentina, Australia, Austria, Azerbaijan, Bahamas, Bahrain, Bangladesh, Belarus, Belgium, Benin, Bosnia and Herzegovina, Brazil, Bulgaria, Cambodia, Cameroon, Canada, Cape Verde, Chile, China, Colombia, Congo, Costa Rica, Côte d'Ivoire, Croatia, Cuba, Cyprus, Czech Republic, Denmark, Dominican Republic, Ecuador, Egypt, El Salvador, Estonia, Fiji(18), Finland, France, Gabon, Germany, Ghana, Greece, Grenada, Guatemala, Guinea, Hungary, Iceland, India, Iran , Iraq, Ireland, Israel, Italy, Japan, Jordan, Kenya, Kuwait, Kyrgyzstan, Laos , Latvia, Lebanon, Lesotho, Libya, Liechtenstein, Lithuania, Luxembourg, Macedonia, Madagascar, Malawi, Malaysia, Maldives, Mali, Mauritius, Mexico, Monaco, Morocco, Nauru, Nepal, Netherlands, New Zealand, Niger, Nigeria, North Korea, Norway, Oman, Pakistan, Panama, Papua New Guinea, Paraguay, Peru, Philippines, Poland, Portugal, Qatar, Republic of Korea, Republic of Moldova, Romania, Russian Federation, Rwanda, Saint Vincent and the Grenadines, Samoa, Saudi Arabia, Senegal, Seychelles, Singapore, Slovakia, Slovenia, Solomon Islands, South Africa, Spain, Sri Lanka, Sudan, Swaziland, Sweden, Switzerland, Syria, Togo, Tonga, Trinidad and Tobago, Tunisia, Turkey, Ukraine, United Arab Emirates, United Kingdom, Uzbekistan, Vanuatu, Venezuela, Vietnam, Yemen, Yugoslavia, Zambia, and Zimbabwe. International Civil Aviation Organization Treaty Collection at www.icao.int/icao/en/leb/ap1.htm.

[107]The text of Protocol No. 1 posted is at www.iasl.mcgill.ca/private.htm.

Protocol No. 1 limits a carrier's damages to 8,300 Special Drawing Rights for liability to passengers, to 17 Special Drawing Rights per kilogram for loss of baggage and cargo, and to 332 Special Drawing Rights for carry-on items.

States parties to Protocol No. 1 as of August 2002 were Argentina, Azerbaijan, Bahrain, Bosnia and Herzegovina, Brazil, Canada, Chile, Colombia, Croatia, Cuba, Cyprus, Denmark, Egypt, Estonia, Ethiopia, Finland, France, Ghana, Greece, Guatemala, Guinea, Honduras, Ireland, Israel, Italy, Jordan, Kenya, Kuwait, Lebanon, Macedonia, Mexico, Netherlands, New Zealand, Niger, Norway, Peru, Portugal, Slovenia, Spain, Sweden, Switzerland, Togo, Tunisia, United Kingdom, Uzbekistan, Venezuela, and Yugoslavia. International Civil Aviation Organization Treaty Collection at www.icao.int/icao/en/leb/ap1.htm.

[108]The text of Protocol No. 2 is at www.iasl.mcgill.ca/private.htm.

Protocol No. 2 limits a carrier's damages to 16,600 Special Drawing Rights for liability to passengers, to 17 Special Drawing Rights per kilogram for loss of baggage and cargo, and to 332 Special Drawing Rights for carry-on items.

States parties to Protocol No. 2 as of August 2002 were Argentina, Azerbaijan, Bahrain, Bosnia and Herzegovina, Brazil, Canada, Chile, Colombia, Croatia, Cuba, Cyprus, Denmark, Egypt, Estonia, Ethiopia, Finland, France, Ghana, Greece, Guatemala, Guinea, Honduras, Ireland, Israel, Italy, Jordan, Kenya, Kuwait, Lebanon, Macedonia, Mexico, Netherlands, New Zealand, Niger, Norway, Oman, Peru, Portugal, Slovenia, Spain, Sweden, Switzerland, Togo, Tunisia, United Kingdom, Uzbekistan, Venezuela, and Yugoslavia. International Civil Aviation Organization Treaty Collection at www.icao.int/icao/en/leb/ap2.htm.

[109]The text of Protocol No. 4 is at www.iasl.mcgill.ca/private.htm.

States parties to Protocol No. 4 as of August 2002 Argentina, Australia, Azerbaijan, Bahrain, Bosnia and Herzegovina, Brazil, Canada, Colombia, Croatia, Cyprus, Denmark, Ecuador, Egypt, Estonia, Ethiopia, Finland, Ghana, Greece, Guatemala, Guinea, Honduras, Hungary, Ireland, Israel, Italy, Japan, Jordan, Kenya, Kuwait, Lebanon, Macedonia, Mauritius, Nauru, Netherlands, New Zealand, Niger, Norway, Oman, Portugal, Singapore, Slovenia, Spain, Sweden, Switzerland, Togo, Turkey, United Arab Emirates, United Kingdom, United States, Uzbekistan, and Yugoslavia. International Civil Aviation Organization Treaty Collection at www.icao.int/icao/en/leb/mp4.htm.

Note: the states parties to the Montreal Protocol are automatically states parties to the Warsaw Convention as amended by the Hague Protocol. Montreal Protocol No. 4, Article XVII(2).

[110]Article 15(3) of the Convention as amended by the Hague Protocol, however, provides that "Nothing in this Convention prohibits the issue of a negotiable waybill."

[111]Warsaw Convention of 1929, Article 8.

[112]Warsaw Convention as amended by Montreal Protocol No. 4, Article 8.

The incentive the Convention offers carriers for including these required elements on a waybill is a limitation on liability. This is set at 17 Special Drawing Rights (SDRs) per kilogram.[113] This means that any provision in the waybill establishing a lower amount is void. Of course, a shipper may declare a higher value and pay the cost for insuring the excess.

The benefit to the shipper in using a Warsaw Convention air waybill is that the shipper does not have to prove that the carrier caused the injury to any lost, damaged, or delayed goods. The shipper has to make a claim within seven days when the bills are governed by the Warsaw Convention and 14 days if they are covered by the Amended Convention, but the burden is then on the carrier to prove that it did not take "all necessary measures" to avoid the loss, damage, or delay.[114]

In addition to regulating the carriage of goods, the two Warsaw Conventions also regulate the carriage of passengers. Again, the liability of the carrier is limited so long as the airline ticket contains a notice of the applicability of one of the Conventions. Whether the liability limits created by the Convention are exclusive is examined in Case 11–10.

---

[113]The Warsaw Convention of 1929 specifies a liability limit of 250 gold or "*Poincaré*" francs per kilogram (or approximately 200 SDRs per kilogram at current exchange rates).

[114]Lord Justice Greer in Grein v. Imperial Airways, Ltd., *Law Reports, King's Bench,* vol. 1937, pt. 1, p. 50 at p. 57 (1937), observed: "The effect of [the phrase 'all necessary measures'] is to put upon [the air carriers] the obligation of disproving negligence, leaving them liable for damages for negligence if they fail to disprove it." Under the Warsaw Convention of 1929, and as amended in 1955 by the Hague Protocol, a carrier may avoid all liability if it can show that the consignor was partly at fault. Montreal Protocol No. 4 changes this, establishing a system of comparative fault. If a percentage of loss or damage is attributable to both the consignor and the carrier, the air carrier will then be liable for its percentage share. Warsaw Convention as amended by Montreal Protocol No. 4, Article 21.

Case 11–10   Abnett v. British Airways Plc.

England, House of Lords, 1996.
All England Law Reports, vol. 1996, pt. 1, p. 193 (1996).

LORD HOPE OF CRAIGHEAD:

My Lords,
The question in these two appeals is whether the Warsaw Convention as amended at The Hague, 1955, as set out in the Schedule 1 to the *Carriage by Air Act 1961*, provides the exclusive cause of action and sole remedy for a passenger who claims against the carrier for loss, injury and damage sustained in the course of, or arising out of, international carriage by air.

In both cases claims were made against the respondents, British Airways Plc., by passengers who had been travelling on a scheduled international flight from the United Kingdom to Malaysia via Kuwait. The flight left London Heathrow for Kuala Lumpur on 1 August 1990. It landed in Kuwait for refueling on 2 August 1990, about five hours after Iraqi forces had begun to invade Kuwait at the commencement of what became known as the Gulf War. The passengers and crew were all taken prisoner by the Iraqis. They were detained initially at Kuwait Airport, then at Kuwait City, and thereafter in Baghdad. The appellants, who were subsequently released and returned to the United Kingdom, claimed damages against the respondents for the consequences of their captivity. Their claims for personal injury were made at common law, as it was accepted that they had no remedy in this regard under article 17 of the Convention. [This was because the appellants' injuries were not sustained on board or while embarking or disembarking from the respondent's aircraft, but while they were prisoners in Iraq.]

* * *

THE ISSUE

Although there are some differences of detail between the two actions . . . the issue of law which arises in both of these appeals is the same. It is whether the Warsaw Convention as amended at The Hague, 1955 provides the exclusive cause of action and remedy in respect of claims for loss, injury, and damage sustained in the course of, or arising out of, international carriage by air. If the answer to that question is in the affirmative, it is accepted that the claims which have been brought in each case for damages at common law for personal injury must be dismissed. . . .

* * *

MAP 11-10 Iraq and Kuwait (1987)

THE PROVISIONS OF THE CONVENTION

* * *

In Chapter I, Article 1(1) is in these terms:

(1) This Convention applies to all international carriage of persons, baggage, or cargo performed by aircraft for reward. It applies equally to gratuitous carriage by aircraft performed by an air transport undertaking.

* * *

The only other chapter which contains provisions relevant to this case is Chapter III, which is headed "Liability of the Carrier." The articles comprised in this chapter are those numbered from 17 to 30, of which the following is a brief summary. Article 17 is concerned with the carrier's liability for death or injury suffered by a passenger. Article 18 is concerned with the carrier's liability for destruction or loss of or damage to registered baggage or cargo. Article 19 provides that the carrier is liable for damage occasioned by delay in the carriage by air of passengers, baggage, or cargo. These provisions must be read together with Article 24, which provides that, in the cases covered by these articles, any action for damages, however founded, can only be brought subject to the conditions and limits set out in the Convention. Article 20 provides: "The carrier is not liable if he proves that he and his servants or agents have taken all necessary measures to avoid the damage or that it was impossible for him or them to take such measures." Article 21 deals with cases where the damage was caused or contributed to by the injured person's negligence. Article 22 makes provision for the limitation of the liability of the carrier for each passenger and for registered baggage and cargo, and Article 23 provides: "Any provision tending to relieve the carrier of liability or to fix a lower limit than that which is laid down by the Convention shall be null and void. . . ." Article 25 provides that these limits of liability shall not apply if the damage results from an act or omission of the carrier, his servants or agents done with intent to cause damage or recklessly. Article 25, 25A, 26 and 27 contain various ancillary provisions. Article 28, which deals with jurisdiction, restricts the places where an action for damages may be brought, and provides that "questions of procedure shall be governed by the law of the court seized of the case." Article 29 provides that the right to damages shall be extinguished if the action is not brought within two years. Lastly, Article 30 deals with the case where the carriage is to be performed by various successive carriers.

As I shall require examining the wording of Articles 17, 18, 23 and 24 more closely at a later stage, it is convenient now to set out the full terms of these articles. They are as follows:

Article 17:

The carrier is liable for damage sustained in the event of the death or wounding of a passenger or any other bodily injury suffered by a passenger, if the accident which caused the damage so sustained took place on board the aircraft or in the course of any of the operations of embarking or disembarking.

* * *

Article 23:

Any provision tending to relieve the carrier of liability or to fix a lower limit than that which is laid down in this Convention shall be null and void, but the nullity of any such provision does not involve the nullity of the whole contract, which shall remain subject to the provisions of this Convention.

Paragraph (1) of this article shall not apply to provisions governing loss or damage resulting from the inherent defect, quality or vice of the cargo carried.

Article 24:

In the cases covered by Articles 18 and 19 any action for damages, however founded, can only be brought subject to the conditions and limits set out in this Convention.

In the cases covered by Article 17 the provisions of the preceding paragraph also apply, without prejudice to the questions as to who are the persons who have the right to bring suit and what are their respective rights.

* * *

THE APPROACH TO CONSTRUCTION

I now turn to the material which we were invited to consider in reaching our decision as to how we should decide this issue. . . .

* * *

(VII) ANALYSIS OF THIS MATERIAL

. . . I turn therefore immediately to the Convention itself, which is the primary source to which we must look for a solution to the question we have to decide.

(a) The English Text of the Convention

I can confine myself to the English text, because all parties were agreed that . . . there was for present purposes no material difference between it and the French text.

The Convention describes itself as a "Convention for the Unification of Certain Rules relating to International Carriage by Air." The phrase "Unification of Certain Rules" tells us two things. The first, the aim of the Convention is to unify the rules to which it applies. If this aim is to be achieved, exceptions to these rules should not be permitted, except where the Convention itself provides for them. Second, the Convention is concerned with certain rules only, not with all the rules relating to international carriage by air. It does not purport to provide a code which is comprehensive of all the issues that may arise. It is a partial harmonization, directed to the particular issues with which it deals.

These issues are identified in the principal chapter headings, which are those to Chapters II, III, and IV—"Documents of Carriage," "Liability of the Carrier" and "Provisions Relating to Combined Carriage." Nothing is said in this Convention about the liability of passengers to the carrier, for example. Nor is anything said about the carrier's obligations of insurance, and in particular about compulsory insurance against third party risks. It is clear from the content and structure of the Convention that it is a partial harmonization only of the rules relating to international carriage by air. That is sufficient to give content to the phrase "Certain Rules." I do not find in that phrase an indication that, in regard to the issues with which the Convention does purport to deal, its provisions were intended to be other than comprehensive.

The principal search for indications of an intention one way or the other about exclusivity of provision in regard to the carrier's liability must be conducted within the provisions of Chapter III. . . . First, [however, it is worth noting that] Article 1(1) states that the Convention applies to "all international carriage of persons, baggage, or cargo performed by aircraft for reward." The word "all" is important, simply because it is so all embracing. It indicates that the framers of the Convention were looking to solutions, no doubt by a process of adjustment and compromise, which could be regarded as acceptable for universal application in all cases. . . .

* * *

Turning to Chapter III itself, the chapter heading expresses its subject matter in the words "Liability of the Carrier." In contrast to the title to the Convention itself, which uses the expression "Certain Rules," we find here a phrase which is unqualified. My understanding of the purpose of this chapter therefore, from what we have seen so far, is that it is designed to set out all the rules relating to the liability of the carrier which are to be applicable to all international carriage of persons, baggage or cargo by air to which the Convention applies.

* * *

Article 22 . . . is important, because it limits the liability of the carrier. It does so in terms which enable the limitation of liability to be applied generally to all cases where the carrier is liable in the carriage of persons and of registered baggage and cargo. Article 22(1) begins simply with the words "In the carriage of persons." Article 22(2)(*a*) begins with the words "In the carriage of registered baggage and of cargo." The intention which emerges from these words is that, unless he agrees otherwise by special contract—for which provision is made elsewhere in the article—the carrier can be assured that his liability to each passenger and for each package will not exceed the sums stated in the article. This has obvious implications for insurance by the carrier and for the cost of his undertaking as a whole. Article 22(4) makes provision for the award, in addition, of the whole or part of the costs of the litigation. But this is subject to the ability of the carrier to limit his liability for costs by an offer in writing to the plaintiff. The effect of these rules would, I think, be severely distorted if they could not be applied generally to all cases in which a claim is made against the carrier.

Articles 23 and 24 also are provisions which seem to have been designed to apply generally, and to indicate that the possibility of exceptions to the rules laid down in Chapter III was not being contemplated. Article 23 states that any provision tending to relieve the carrier of liability or to fix a lower limit than that which is laid down in the Convention shall be null and void. It then goes on to state that the nullity of any such provision does not involve the nullity of the whole contract, which is to remain subject to the provisions of the Convention. The generality of effect is to be found in the opening words, since the article applies to "any provision" which tends to relieve the carrier of liability or to fix a lower limit than that laid down by the Convention. I think that the purpose of this provision is clear. It is to protect the passenger or other person dealing with the carrier against provisions of the kind which it describes. Contracting out of liability in contracts of carriage is, of course, now widely regulated by statute. But no doubt in the early 1920's, when what became the Warsaw Convention was being negotiated, carriers engaged in international carriage by air were free to contract on whatever terms they cared to select, controlled only by the demands of the marketplace in which they were operating. To surrender freedom of contract on this issue was an important concession on the part of carriers, which made sense only in the context of the entire set of rules by which their conduct was to be regulated.

The counterpart of what was plainly a compromise is to be found in the following article, Article 24. This Article provides that in the cases covered by Articles 18 and 19 and by Article 17 respectively—these cases are dealt with separately in two different paragraphs—"any action of damages, however founded, can only be brought subject to the conditions and limits set" by the Convention. . . .

* * *

The structure of these two provisions seems to me therefore to be this. On the one hand the carrier surrenders his freedom to exclude or to limit his liability. On the other hand the passenger or other party to the contract is restricted in the claims which he can bring in an action of damages by the conditions and limits set out in the Convention. The idea that an action of damages may be brought by a passenger against the carrier outside the Convention in the cases covered by article 17—which is the issue in the present case—seems to be entirely contrary to the system which these two articles were designed to create.

* * *

(d) Decision by the Foreign Courts

Much of the discussion in both the Outer House and the Inner House in the Court of Session was taken up with a detailed examination of various cases on this topic from the United States of America. All the judges in that court were of the view however that, in the end, no clear guidance was available from this source to enable them to rely on this material in reaching their decision in the present case. Lord Marnoch observed that the Supreme Court had on two occasions in recent times found it either unnecessary or inappropriate to consider the question whether the Convention provided an exclusive course of action for injuries sustained during inter-

national air transportation: *Air France v. Saks*[115] and *Eastern Airlines Inc. v. Floyd.*[116] The result of his review was that there was no clear or very consistent line of reasoning in these cases to guide him in this area of international air law. Lord Mayfield said that it was impossible to draw any clear conclusion as to the state of U.S. law, and Lord Clyde expressed the same view, having observed earlier that it was pointless and perhaps impertinent to subject all these cases to critical analysis. Lord Allanbridge was able to find support in some of the cases for the view which he had already reached on his examination of the Convention. But in the end he agreed with the observations of Lord Justice Leggatt in [this case] in the Court of Appeal that, in view of the conflicting nature of these authorities and the fact that the Supreme Court had twice refrained from addressing the present problem, it was necessary to reach a conclusion in this case without any definite aid from the United States. As Lord Justice Leggatt said in his judgment, it appears that the point is not settled in the United States as between circuits and even in some instances within the same circuit. From his consideration of the cases cited to him he was not prepared to say where the preponderance of current opinion lies in the United States.

I do not think that I can usefully add much to these observations. . . .

* * *

CONCLUSION

I believe that the answer to the question raised in the present case is to be found in the objects and structure of the Convention. The language used and the subject matter with which it deals demonstrate that what was sought to be achieved was a uniform international code, which could be applied by the courts of all the High Contracting Parties without reference to the rules of their own domestic law. The Convention does not purport to deal with all matters relating to contracts of international carriage by air. But in those areas with which it deals—and the liability of the carrier is one of them—the code is intended to be uniform and to be exclusive also of any resort to the rules of domestic law.

* * *

For these reasons I would dismiss both appeals. ∎

---

[115] *United States Reports*, vol. 470, p. 392 (1985).
[116] *Id.*, vol. 499, p. 530 (1991).

Chapter Questions

1. Seller agreed to ship 10,000 tons of potatoes FOB Tacoma, Washington, to Buyer in Japan. Buyer designated the SS *Russet* to take delivery at pier 7 in Tacoma. On the agreed date for delivery, the Seller delivered the potatoes to pier 7, but the ship was not at the pier. Because another ship using the pier was slow in loading, the *Russet* had to anchor at a mooring buoy in the harbor and Seller had to arrange for a lighter to transport the potatoes in containers to the ship. The lighter tied up alongside the *Russet* and a cable from the ship's boom was attached to the first container. As the container began to cross the ship's rail the cable snapped. The container then fell on the rail, teetered back and forth for awhile, and finally crashed down the side of the ship and capsized the lighter. All of the potatoes were dumped into the sea. Buyer now sues Seller for failure to make delivery. Is Seller liable?

2. Suppose, in Question 1, the contract had been FAS Tacoma. Would Seller be liable?

3. Seller agreed to deliver 1,000 air conditioners to Buyer DES Port Moresby. The air conditioners were transported by ship to Port Moresby, where they were off-loaded to the customs shed for inspection. The ship then sent a cable to Buyer stating that the air conditioners were in the customs shed and that the ship was proceeding on its way. Before the Buyer could arrive to pay the customs duties and collect the air conditioners, the customs shed burned down, destroying all the air conditioners. Buyer sues Seller for failing to make delivery. Is Seller liable?

4. Suppose, in Question 3, the contract had been DEQ Port Moresby. Would Seller be liable?

5. Seller in Sydney, Australia, agreed to ship goods on or before December 31 under a CIF Sydney contract to Buyer in Honolulu. The seller was unable to assemble the goods for delivery in time to reach the ship in Sydney and had to transship the goods by rail to Melbourne, where the ship was taking on goods on January 3. Seller did load the goods aboard railway cars in Sydney on December 29 and received a bill of lading from the railway company on that date. Seller later obtained a bill of lading from the ship, and together with an invoice and a marine insurance policy, tendered both bills of lading to Buyer. Buyer refused to accept the documents or to pay Seller. Seller sues to enforce the contract. Will Seller win?

6. Seller in San Francisco agreed to ship goods to Buyer in London under a CIF San Francisco contract. After the goods were loaded aboard the ship, but before it departed from San Francisco, Seller tendered the documents required by the contract to Buyer and asked to be paid. Buyer refused, asserting that it had a right to inspect the goods upon their arrival in London, and that it did not have to pay until it did so and was satisfied that the goods were in compliance with the contract. Seller sues for immediate payment. Will Seller win?

7. Seller in Bombay sells 5,000 bales of cotton to Buyer, C & F (*Incoterms 1990*) Liverpool. Seller transports the cotton to the Bombay harbor and to the ship designated by Buyer, the SS *Allthumbs*. Due to an error in counting, there are only 4,987 bales loaded. The ship's bill of lading, however, shows a quantity of 5,000 bales. Seller then signs over the bill of lading to Buyer in exchange for payment in full for the cotton. When the *Allthumbs* arrives in Liverpool, the quantity error is discovered, and Buyer sues the ship for the lost value of the missing bales. Is the ship liable? Would it matter if the Seller admitted that the error was not the ship's fault, but that of the Seller?

8. The SS *Anxious* was transporting goods to several ports on the east coast of Africa, including Beira in Mozambique. While still several hundred miles at sea, the *Anxious* learned that rebel forces opposing the Mozambique government were attacking Beira. The ship, nonetheless, pulled into Beira and tied up at a pier. Immediately thereafter, it was struck by a mortar round. The goods in the ship's main cargo hold were destroyed. Is the ship liable for the loss?

9. Mr. Ess, the owner of the SS *Skimpy* and an American citizen, borrows money from MultiBank in London to outfit his ship, giving the bank a maritime lien. Mr. Ess sells the *Skimpy* to Mr. Tee, a Canadian. Mr. Tee is unaware of the lien, and unaware that Mr. Ess has defaulted on the loan. When the ship pulls into a British port the bank arranges for it to be arrested and sold to pay off the balance due on the loan. Can the bank do this?

Review Problem

As the Senior Chief Assistant in the law department of MegaBranch Industries (MBI), you are responsible for reviewing the transportation contracts made by MBI and its subsidiaries.

1. You are reviewing several proposed contracts with oceangoing carriers. The contracts contain a variety of *Incoterm* trade terms, including FOB, FAS, CIF, CFR, DES, FCA, and EXW As to each of these terms:
   a. When must the seller make delivery?
   b. What documentation must the seller provide to the buyer?
   c. What information must the buyer give the seller?
   d. Who is responsible for getting insurance?
   e. Who is responsible for hiring a carrier to transport the goods?
   f. When does the risk of loss shift from the seller to the buyer?

2. An MBI subsidiary in State A is shipping goods from its inland plant to a State-A port city where it has arranged for the goods to be loaded aboard an oceangoing carrier.
   a. Who should it contact to arrange the inland carriage?
   b. What kind of documentation should it provide to the inland carrier?
   c. What kind of documentation will the inland carrier provide it?
   d. What kind of liability limits apply to this carrier?

3. The MBI subsidiary in State A has its goods loaded aboard an oceangoing common carrier in a State-A port city for shipment abroad.
   a. What kind of documentation should the subsidiary provide this carrier?
   b. What kind of documentation will the carrier give the subsidiary?
   c. Should the bill of lading the carrier issues be a straight bill or an order bill?
   d. If the carrier issues a claused bill, what should the subsidiary do?
   e. What are the common carrier's responsibilities to MBI under the bill of lading? What are its immunities? What are its liability limits?
   f. Assuming that the bill of lading contains a Himalaya Clause, who benefits from this? As the shipper, should the subsidiary be happy about having this clause be a part of the bill of lading?

4. An MBI subsidiary in State B has arranged to hire a ship under a voyage charterparty. What are the rights and obligations of the subsidiary (i.e., the charterer)?

5. An MBI subsidiary in State C has arranged to hire a ship under a time charterparty. What are the rights and obligations of the subsidiary (i.e., the charterer)?

6. An MBI subsidiary in State D owns its own ship, the SS *Unlucky*. Unbeknownst to the subsidiary (or MBI), the master has a drinking problem and he runs the ship into the end of a pier in a port city in State E, causing damage to the pier, the ship, the ship's cargo, and several crew members. The master employed a local shipfitting firm to repair the ship but then never paid the firm. Now all the injured parties have brought suit in State E against the MBI subsidiary, and they all have asserted maritime liens against the SS *Unlucky*. What will happen in the suit against the subsidiary if it refuses to appear to defend itself? What will happen to the ship? Which of the claimants will be most likely to recover on its lien against the ship?

7. What kinds of risk does maritime insurance cover? What is an FPA policy? A WA policy?

8. An MBI subsidiary in Country F is shipping goods overseas by air. What documents does the subsidiary need to give the carrier? What kind of documents will it get in return? What liability limits apply to this carriage of goods?

9. The head of the MBI legal department was flying overseas on an international airline. The weather was perfectly clear and all went well until the plane was over the ocean. It was then struck by a freak lightning bolt that caused it to crash, killing everyone on board. What liability limits apply to the carrier? Would they be different if the crash had been due to pilot error?

CHAPTER

Financing

Chapter Outline

Introduction

International financing encompasses two kinds of activities: the financing of foreign trade and the underwriting of investments in foreign countries. The first of these, foreign trade financing, involves the underwriting, paying, and collecting of money for the purchase of goods and services. The second, the capitalization of foreign investments, involves the acquisition of debt and equity financing to establish or expand overseas business operations.

A. FINANCING FOREIGN TRADE

International traders need to be familiar with the kinds of documents, trade terms, and financing arrangements used in international sales.

The documents used in international sales are also used in domestic sales, but their use domestically is much less common. Most domestic sales are financed through open-account credit arrangements. That is, the buyer does not sign a formal debt instrument. Formalities are not needed because sellers only enter into sales after investigating the buyer's creditworthiness. By comparison, in international sales, buyers and sellers are separated both by distance and by the differing financial practices of their home countries. This means that it is difficult for the seller to determine the credit standing of a foreign buyer, and equally difficult for the buyer to reliably establish the foreign seller's integrity and reputation. To compensate for this, foreign traders use formal documents that serve to assure the parties that their sale will go forward as agreed. The most important of these documents are (a) the bill of lading, which is the transportation document and document of title described in Chapter 11; (b) bills of exchange and promissory notes, which are, respectively, orders to pay money and promises to pay money; and (c) the letter of credit, which is a third party's guarantee of a buyer's creditworthiness.

B. BILLS OF LADING

bill of lading: An instrument issued by a warehouseman or carrier to a shipper that serves as a receipt for goods shipped, as evidence of the contract of carriage, and as a document of title for the goods.

The essential document for all international sales is the **bill of lading**. As described in Chapter 11, the bill of lading is a document of title. That is, it represents the goods.

In international trade, goods shipped from one country to another may well be in the possession of a carrier or warehouseman for several weeks: from the time they are shipped to the time they are delivered. The bill of lading is important, therefore, because it lets the buyer and the seller (or their banks) exchange control over the goods while the goods are in the possession of the warehouseman or carrier. As one British judge once described it, the bill of lading is the "key" that permits its holder "to unlock the door of the warehouse, fixed or floating, in which the goods may chance to be."[1]

This ability to transfer title by the transfer of a bill of lading is central to the use of bills of exchange and letters of credit, the two basic financing and payment instruments used in international trade.

C. BILLS OF EXCHANGE

bill of exchange: A written, dated, and signed three-party instrument containing an unconditional order by a drawer that directs a drawee to pay a definite sum of money to a payee on demand or at a specified future date.

A **bill of exchange** (or draft as it is sometimes called) is a written, dated, and signed instrument that contains an unconditional order from the drawer that directs the drawee to pay a definite sum of money to a payee on demand or at a specified future date. It is a useful instrument because it allows one party (the drawer) to direct another (the drawee) to pay money either to himself, to his agent, or to a third party. Of course, the order is valid only if the drawee has an underlying obligation to pay money to the drawer. This can arise in situations where the drawee is holding money on account for the drawer (i.e., the drawee is a bank), where the drawer lent money to a drawee (i.e., the drawee is a borrower), or where the drawer has sold goods to the drawee and the drawee owes the sale price to the drawer (i.e., the drawee is a buyer).

In the first of these situations (where the drawee is a bank), the bill involved is known as a check. In the second situation (where the drawee is a borrower), the bill is called a note. The bills referred to in the third situation (where the drawee is a buyer) are called trade acceptances.

Bills of exchange are important devices for facilitating international trade because they are negotiable instruments. A person properly holding a negotiable instrument takes it free of most claims or defenses that the drawer might have that the underlying contract was improperly performed or that the instrument was improperly made. This freedom from the so-called "equities" or "personal defenses" of the drawer makes bills of exchange more readily salable, and therefore useful financial tools for raising money.

The Law Governing Bills of Exchange

Until the middle of the seventeenth century, bills of exchange were governed by a single international law, the *lex mercatoria*.[2] This law defined the bill of exchange as an instrument that allowed a *permutatio pecuniae presentis cum absenti* (an exchange of money by one who is present with one who is absent). Because the bill applied specifically to an exchange between *loci distantia* (distant places), it was exempt from the medieval Christian Church's prohibition against interest on loans. Because of this exemption, it rapidly became the key instrument of medieval banking.

---

[1]Saunders v. Maclean, *Law Reports, Queen's Bench Division,* vol. 11, p. 341 (1883).
[2]Latin: "law merchant." Common commercial rules and procedures used throughout Europe during the Renaissance.

In the seventeenth century, however, the rise of national laws brought about differences in the rules governing bills of exchange. The French bill of exchange came to be governed by the *Savary Code* of 1673, the *Perfect Tradesman*, and the works of Jousse. In Germany, the applicable law was the *Wechselrecht.* In England, the courts created a case law that reflected the practice in English banks.

At the end of the nineteenth century, the *lex mercatoria* was codified in England in the **Bills of Exchange Act** (BEA) of 1882. Today, the BEA continues in force in the United Kingdom and in virtually all of Britain's former colonies.

In 1896, in the United States, the National Conference on Commissioners of Uniform Laws drafted a Uniform Negotiable Instruments Law (UNIL), which was largely based on the BEA. By 1920, all of the American states had adopted the UNIL. Then, in the 1940s, the UNIL was modernized and integrated into the more comprehensive **Uniform Commercial Code** (UCC), which by 1950 had been adopted in all states except Louisiana.[3]

On the European continent, there were calls throughout the latter half of the nineteenth century for the creation of an international negotiable instruments law. Finally, in 1907, a conference convened at The Hague to draw up a convention. A draft was agreed to in 1912, but World War I interrupted ratification. The League of Nations then organized a series of conferences to update the 1912 draft. In 1930, three **Geneva Conventions on the Unification of the Law Relating to Bills of Exchange** (ULB) were signed.[4] The following year, two additional Geneva Conventions on Unification of the Law Relating to Checks (ULC) were also signed.[5] Within 15 years, the ULB and ULC had been ratified by most continental European countries, and today they serve as the standard laws governing bills of exchange and checks in virtually every nation,[6] with the exception of the Anglo-American common law countries.[7]

Although there are currently no uniform worldwide rules governing bills of exchange and promissory notes, there is a widely followed set of international rules governing the collection of checks:[8] the International Chamber of Commerce's Uniform Rules for Collections.[9] Most domestic laws allow banks to incorporate the ICC's Rules into their collection instructions, and this is the common practice for international collections worldwide.[10]

Types of Bills of Exchange

A bill of exchange is an unconditional written order. The party creating the bill (the drawer) orders another party (the drawee) to pay money, usually to a third party (a payee).

---

[3]The text of the Uniform Commercial Code is posted on the Legal Information Institute's Web site at www.law.cornell.edu/ucc/ucc.table.html.

[4]The three are the Convention Providing a Uniform Law for Bills of Exchange and Promissory Notes, the Convention for the Settlement of Certain Conflicts with Bills of Exchange and Promissory Notes, and the Convention on the Stamp Laws in Connection with Bills of Exchange and Promissory Notes.

[5]They are the Convention Providing a Uniform Law for Checks and the Convention for the Settlement of Certain Conflicts of Laws in Connection with Checks.

[6]For a brief history of negotiable instrument law in Europe, as well as the text of the ULB, *see* Frederick Wallace, *Introduction to European Commercial Law,* pp. 92–123 (1953).

[7]The differences between the Anglo-American rules and the Geneva conventions (which are fairly substantial) led to calls in the 1950s for the drafting of a new international convention with true international appeal. The call was taken up belatedly by the UN Commission on International Trade Law (UNCITRAL), which produced a final text in May 1988. In December of 1988, the UN General Assembly approved a resolution adopting the text and opened the convention—called the Convention on International Bills of Exchange and International Promissory Notes (CIBN)—for ratification. Although only 10 states must ratify the Convention before it will come into effect, as of 2002 only Guinea, Honduras, and Mexico had ratified the CIBN, and it seems unlikely that it will come into effect anytime soon. *See Multilateral Treaties Deposited with the Secretary-General: Status as at 12 November 2002,* posted on the Internet at www.un.org/Depts/Treaty/final/ts2/newfiles/part_boo/x_boo/x_12.html.

For a brief history and description of the CIBN, as well as the text, *see* "United Nations Convention on International Bills of Exchange and International Promissory Notes," *International Legal Materials,* vol. 28, pp. 170–211 (1989), with John Spagnole's "Introductory Note."

[8]Both the common law countries and the countries that follow the continental European practice have distinct rules governing bank deposits and the collection of checks. *See,* e.g., Article 4 of the UCC, entitled "Bank Deposits and Collections"; and the ULC.

[9]ICC Publication No. 522 (1996). The *Uniform Rules for Collection* was first published in 1956. The 1996 edition was the second revision. *See* the ICC Web site at www.iccwbo.org/iccpub/default.asp for information on this and other ICC publications.

[10]For example, UCC, § 4-102(3), states that the provisions in Article 4 (Bank Deposits and Collections) of the UCC may be varied by agreement, except that "no agreement can disclaim a bank's responsibility for its own lack of good faith or failure to exercise ordinary care."

Bills of Exchange Act: English act of 1882 regulating bills of exchange.

Uniform Commercial Code: Model United States act. Article 3 regulates negotiable instruments.

Geneva Conventions on the Unification of the Law Relating to Bills of Exchange: League of Nations–sponsored conventions signed at Geneva in 1930 that regulate negotiable instruments.

Common Law	ULB
1. In writing	1. In writing
2. Payable to order or to bearer	2. Payable to order or to bearer
	3. Contain the term *Bill of Exchange* or *Promissory Note*
	4. State the place where drawn
	5. State the place where payable
	6. Be dated

EXHIBIT 12-1 Form Requirements for Bills of Exchange and Promissory Notes

The form that a bill of exchange must take depends on the governing law. The common law requires only that a bill (or draft) be in writing and be payable either to order or to bearer.[11] The ULB adds to this the requirements that a bill (a) contain the term "bill of exchange" in the body and language of the check,[12] (b) state the place where the bill is drawn, (c) state the place where payment is to be made, and (d) be dated. These requirements are summarized in Exhibit 12-1.

Time and Sight Bills

time bill: Bill of exchange that is payable at a definite future time.

Bills may be either "time bills" or "sight bills." A **time bill** is payable at a definite future time. A **sight bill** (or demand bill) is payable when the holder presents it for payment or at a stated time after presentment. Exhibit 12-2 shows an example of a time bill.

sight bill: Bill of exchange that is payable at the time it is presented or at a stated time after presentment.

Trade Acceptances

A **trade acceptance** is the bill of exchange most commonly used in the sale of goods. On this bill, the seller of the goods is both the drawer and the payee. The bill orders the buyer—the drawee—to pay a specified sum of money.

trade acceptance: A bill of exchange on which the drawer and the payee are the same person.

The use of a trade acceptance is best illustrated with an example. SunnySales, Inc., in California has traditionally sold raisins to GuttenTag, GmBH, in Germany on terms that require GuttenTag to make payment in 90 days. This year, however, SunnySales needs cash. To get cash, it draws a trade acceptance that orders GuttenTag to pay $100,000 to the order of SunnySales 90 days later. SunnySales then presents the bill to GuttenTag. GuttenTag accepts by signing the bill on its face and returning the bill to SunnySales. GuttenTag's acceptance creates an enforceable promise to pay the bill when it comes due in 90 days.

EXHIBIT 12-2 Time Bill

```
November 22, 2002                                          $ 10,000.00
New York, NY

            Ninety days after above date    PAY TO THE ORDER OF
                            Bank of the River
                            100 Hudson Ave.
                            New York, NY 02167
        ------ Ten Thousand and 00/00 -------         Dollars
                for value received and charge the same to the account of

To: _____

    _____                    _____

    _____                    _____
    Drawer/Buyer                               Drawee/Seller
```

---

[11]UCC, § 3-104(2), provides: "A writing . . . is (a) a 'draft' ('bill of exchange') if it is an order; (b) a 'check' if it is drawn on a bank and payable on demand; (c) a 'certificate of deposit' if it is an acknowledgement by a bank of receipt of money with an engagement to repay it; (d) a 'note' if it is a promise other than a certificate of deposit."

[12]In the case of a promissory note, the term would be "promissory note," and, according to the ULC, a check requires the term "check."

101 Embarcadero
San Francisco, California

December 31, 2002

To: **GuttenTag GmBH**

On **Mar. 31, 2003**   PAY TO THE ORDER OF   **SunnySales, Inc.**

One Hundred Thousand and 00/100   DOLLARS **100,000.00**

The obligations of the drawee/acceptor of this bill arise out of the purchase of goods from the drawer. The drawee/acceptor may accept this bill payable at any bank or trust company in the United States which the drawee/acceptor may designate.

Accepted at   **Essen,Germany**   on   **December 31 2002**

Payable at   **Bank of the River**   **SunnySales, Inc.**

100 Hudson Ave

New York, NY 02167

Buyer's Signature   **GuttenTag, GmBH**

By Agent or Officer _____   by _____

EXHIBIT 12-3   Trade Acceptance

The advantage to SunnySales of having a trade acceptance is that it can sell the bill of exchange in the money market more easily than it can assign a $100,000 account receivable. A trade acceptance is shown in Exhibit 12-3.

check: A bill of exchange on which the drawee is a bank.

Checks

When the drawee of a bill of exchange is a bank, the bill is known as a **check**. Unlike other bills of exchange, checks are always payable on demand.[13] See Exhibit 12-4.

EXHIBIT 12-4   American Check/French Check

Nov. 22, 2002   11-95/980

PAY TO THE ORDER OF   **Sandra Smith** $ **100.00**

One Hundred and 00/100   DOLLARS

BANK OF THE RIVER
100 Hudson Ave.
New York, NY 02167
123456789-09876543

_____

Check

2 November   2002   at Paris, France

THIS CHECK IS TO BE
PAID TO THE ORDER OF   **Sandra Smith**   € **500.00**

Five Hundred and 00/100   EUROS

by the EX-PATRIOT BANK
at 100 Cours Albert 1er
75008 Paris, France
123456789-09876543

_____

---

[13]ULC, Article 28; UCC, § 3-104(2)(b).

D. PROMISSORY NOTES

promissory note: A written, dated, and signed two-party instrument containing an unconditional promise by a maker to pay a definite sum of money to a payee on demand or at a specified future date.

A written promise to pay a determinate sum of money made between two parties is a **promissory note**, or simply a note. The party who promises to pay is called the maker; the party who is to be paid is the payee. Exhibit 12-5 defines the different parties to bills of exchange and promissory notes.

The only difference between a promissory note and a bill of exchange is that the maker of a note promises to personally pay the payee, rather than ordering a third party to do so. Exhibit 12-6 shows examples of typical promissory notes.

The rules governing bills of exchange apply to promissory notes as well. The forms of both instruments are also alike. Thus, whereas the common law does not require that a note contain the words *promissory note*, the ULB does.

Notes are used in a variety of credit transactions and are commonly given the name of the transaction involved. For example, a "collateral note" is one secured by personal property; a "mortgage note" is secured by real property; an "installment note" is payable in installments.

certificate of deposit: A promissory note on which the maker is a bank.

When a bank is the maker promising to repay money it has received, plus interest, the promissory note is called a **certificate of deposit** (CD). CDs in amounts up to $100,000 are customarily called "small CDs"; those for $100,000 or more, "large CDs." Most large CDs, and some small CDs, are negotiable. Exhibit 12-7 shows a negotiable CD.

E. NEGOTIABILITY OF BILLS AND NOTES

Bills of exchange and promissory notes may be either negotiable or nonnegotiable. For trade to run smoothly, especially international trade, these instruments need to be negotiable—that is (generally speaking), as freely exchangeable as money. Indeed, so long as the form and content of the instruments are proper, the law guarantees the full transferability of the right to receive payment. If there is any limitation on this right, an instrument is said to be nonnegotiable.

EXHIBIT 12-5   Parties to Negotiable Instruments

Maker	The issuer of a promissory note
Drawer	The issuer of a bill of exchange
Drawee	The person ordered to pay a bill of exchange
Payee	The person to whom a bill or note is to be paid
Endorser	A payee who has signed (endorsed) and delivered a bill or note to an endorsee
Endorsee	A person who receives an endorsed bill or note from an endorser
Bearer	A person who has physical possession of a bill or note that is payable to anyone ("to bearer") or that has been endorsed without naming an endorsee (endorsed "in blank")
Holder	A person who has physical possession of a bill or note that was drawn, issued, or endorsed to him or her, or to his or her order, or to the bearer, or in blank
Holder in due course	Under common law (but not civil law), a person who acquires a bill or note for value, in good faith, and without notice that it is defective, overdue, or that any person has a claim to or defense against it
Acceptor	A drawee of a bill who, by signing the bill on its face, agrees to pay the bill when it is due
Accommodation party	A person who signs a bill or note to lend his or her credit to another party
Accommodation maker or aval	A person who signs a bill or note as a surety and comaker
Accommodation endorser	A person who endorses a bill or note as a guarantor of an endorsee

Nov. 22, 2002 $ __10,000.00__
New York, New York

_____ **Ninety days after above date** _____ for value received, the undersigned jointly and severally promise(s) to pay to the order of: BANK OF THE RIVER, at its offices at 100 Hudson Ave., New York, New York 02167,

_____ ----- Ten Thousand and 00/100 ----- _____ DOLLARS

with interest thereon from the date above at the rate of **-11-** percent per annum (computed on the basis of actual days and a year of 360 days) payable at maturity.

Officer: _____ **Jones** _____   _____
No. _____ **990-11-9999** _____   _____
                                         Makers

---

22 Nov. 2002   PROMISSORY NOTE   € __10,000.00__
Paris, France

_____ **Ninety days after above date** _____ for value received, the undersigned jointly and severally promise(s) to pay in French Francs this Promissory Note to the order of the EX-PATRIOT BANK at its offices at 100 Cours Albert 1er, 75008 Paris, France, at the official exchange rate on the date of maturity, the equivalent of

_____ ----- Ten Thousand and 00/100 ----- _____ EUROS

with interest thereon from the date above at the rate of **-11-** percent per annum (computed on the basis of actual days and a year of 360 days) payable at maturity.

Officer: _____ **Mitterand** _____   _____
No. _____ **1118-1-7932** _____   _____
                                          Makers

EXHIBIT 12-6 American Promissory Note/French Promissory Note

EXHIBIT 12-7 Certificate of Deposit

SMALLTOWN BANK   88-11/980   Number: _____ **99053**
901 Main St.   _____ **Jan. 1, 2002**
Pullman, Washington 99163   NEGOTIABLE CERTIFICATE OF DEPOSIT

THIS CERTIFIES to the deposit in this Bank the sum of
_____ **Ten Thousand and 00/100** _____ DOLLARS
which is payable to the order of _____ **Apples-R-Us, Inc.** _____ on the __**1st**__ day of
December 31, 2002 against presentation and surrender of this certificate, and bears interest at the rate of
__**6-3/4**__ percent per annum, computed (on the basis of actual days elapsed and a year of 360 days) to, and payable at, maturity. No payment may be made prior to, and no interest accrues after, that date. Payable at maturity in federal funds, and if desired, at the Major National Trust Company, New York.

THE SMALLTOWN BANK OF PULLMAN, WASHINGTON

By: _____
                                          Signature

To be negotiable, a bill or note must (a) be in the proper form and (b) contain a promise by the maker or drawer to make payment. The requirements for form were discussed earlier (see Exhibit 12-1). To meet the promissory requirements, a bill or note must do the following:

1. State an unconditional promise or order to pay
2. State a definite sum of money or a monetary unit of account
3. Be payable on demand or at a definite time
4. Be signed by the maker or drawer

Unconditional Promise or Order to Pay

A bill or note must contain a promise or an order to pay that is unconditional.

Promise or Order

A bill or note must contain an affirmative promise by the maker, or an order to a drawee, to be negotiable. The promise is inadequate if it is only implied.

For example, an "I.O.U." only acknowledges an obligation of indebtedness. Although it may imply an obligation to pay, it does not contain an affirmative undertaking to do so. It is not, therefore, a negotiable instrument.

The promissory notes shown in Exhibit 12-6 are different because they clearly state that the makers promise to pay the payees. Similarly, the bills of exchange shown in Exhibits 12-2, 12-3, and 12-4 each order a drawee to pay a payee.

Unconditionality

The promise or order to pay made in a bill or note cannot be conditioned upon the performance of some other obligation. The reason for this is basic to the concept of negotiability. If the holder of a bill or note had to determine whether a collateral promise had or had not been fulfilled, the utility of these instruments would be greatly reduced.

To illustrate, if Ivan promises to pay Pierre only if Pierre delivers goods to Ivan before July 4, anyone who might be interested in purchasing this promissory note would have to determine whether delivery was actually made. This would be both expensive and, if an error were made, risky. Thus, both the law and the pragmatic requirements of trade dictate that a bill or note containing a promise or order to pay that is conditioned on the performance of a collateral obligation is nonnegotiable.

Mere reference to some other agreement, however, does not make a bill or note nonnegotiable. It is common practice, in fact, to mention the underlying contract that caused the drawer or maker to issue the bill or note, either for record keeping or for informational purposes. Thus, statements that the bill or note arises out of a separate agreement, or that it is drawn under a letter of credit, or that the ability of the drawer or maker to perform is secured by a mortgage or a security interest do not affect negotiability.[14]

Definite Sum of Money or Monetary Unit of Account

A bill or note must be payable in money, which must be for a definite sum.

Money

money: A medium of exchange authorized or adopted by a domestic or foreign government and includes a monetary unit of account established by an intergovernmental organization or by agreement between two or more nations.

Both the common law and the ULB specify that the sum paid must be "money."[15] The common law defines money as "a medium of exchange authorized or adopted by a domestic or foreign government and includes a monetary unit of account established by an intergovernmental organization or by agreement between two or more nations."[16] The ULB provides that the "usages of the place of payment" determine the meaning and the value of money.[17]

In international practice, or usage, the parties to international bills and notes routinely define their monetary obligations by referring to monetary units of account (such as the

---

[14]*See* UCC, § 3-105(1).
[15]UCC, § 3-104(a); ULB, Article 1. Article 1 of the ULC contains the same provision for checks.
[16]UCC, § 1-201(24).
[17]ULB, Article 41.

International Monetary Fund's Special Drawing Right or the European Union's euro) or to an *ad hoc* basket of several foreign currencies (see Chapter 6). Both the common law and the ULB, accordingly, allow bills and notes to be payable in the currency of one country, of several countries, or a monetary unit of account defined by an IGO.

Definite Sum

The sum to be paid must be "certain" or "determinate."[18] In other words, the amount to be paid must be ascertainable from the bill or note itself without reference to an outside source. For example, a promissory note that provides for the payment of £1,000 plus interest of 10 percent per annum until the time it is cashed states a definite sum because the parties can figure out the amount that is due from the information provided on the face of the note.

Both of the principal negotiable instruments laws set out exceptions to this basic rule. Both allow the parties to define the sum to be paid in one currency (the money of account) while requiring payment to be made in another (the money of payment), even though this requires the parties to refer to exchange rates that are not embodied in the bill or note.[19] In addition, the common law allows for payments to be made in installments (the ULB does not).[20] Neither, however, permits the use of variable interest rates.[21]

Payable on Demand or at a Definite Time

For a bill or note to function reliably in commerce, the time when it is payable has to be ascertainable from its face.[22] The time requirement actually serves several functions. It tells the maker, drawee, accommodation maker, or acceptor when he is required to pay. It allows secondary parties, such as drawers, endorsers, and accommodation endorsers, to determine the date when their obligations arise. It establishes when the statute of limitations will run. And finally, with interest-bearing bills or notes, it defines the period for calculating the present value of the instrument.

Signed by the Maker or Drawer

signature: (From Latin: "*signare*," to mark.) The name of a person written by that person, or any distinctive mark meant to authenticate a writing.

Bills of exchange must be signed by the drawer, and promissory notes by their maker. For this purpose, a **signature** can be "any symbol executed or adopted by a party with present intention to authenticate a writing."[23] Signatures do not have to be put on bills or notes at any particular time. Bills and notes lacking a drawer's or maker's signature are simply incomplete, as Case 12–1 illustrates.

---

[18]UCC, § 3-106(1), uses the phrase "sum certain"; ULB, Article 1(1), uses "determinate sum."
[19]UCC, § 3-107(2); ULB, Article 41.
[20]UCC, § 3-106(1)(a); ULB, Article 5.
[21]UCC, § 3-106(1)(a); ULB, Article 5.
[22]So long as a final definite date for payment can be ascertained from the face of the instrument, this requirement is satisfied. The common law makes exceptions to this rule for acceleration clauses (which push forward the date when an instrument is payable in the event that an installment payment is missed), and the common law also allows for extension clauses (which let a maker or drawer postpone payment for a fixed time period). UCC, § 3-109(1)(c).
[23]UCC, § 1-201(39). No definition is given in the ULB, but commercial practice in Europe follows the common law usage.

Case 12–1   Constantaras v. Anagnostopoulos

South Africa, Witwatersrand Local Division, 1987.
South African Law Reports, vol. 1988, pt. 3, p. 769 (1988).

The defendant, Mr. Anagnostopoulos, signed several checks as an accommodation maker, or aval (that is, as a surety and coprincipal). A Mr. Evangelous Souloutas had drawn the checks, but Mr. Souloutas had not signed them at the time that the defendant put his signature on them. When the bank on which the checks were drawn refused to pay on two of the checks, each in the amount of

MAP 12-1   South Africa (1987)

4,200 rand, the holder, Mr. Constantaras, sought to obtain payment from Mr. Anagnostopoulos. When Mr. Anagnostopoulos refused to pay, Mr. Constantaras brought this suit.

JUDGE KRIEGLER:

* * *

I turn then to consider the . . . defense which was . . . that no liability *qua* aval arose because of the alleged sequence in which the defendant and Souloutas put their respective signatures on the check. Souloutas had allegedly not yet signed the checks as drawer when defendant, by his signature over the appropriate stamp, signified to the world at large and in particular to subsequent holders of the check, that he bound himself as surety and co-principal debtor for the obligations reflected on the face thereof. Therefore, so it was contended, defendant's signature was legally ineffectual.

Of course the argument was not as bluntly put as that. Its steps were the following. First, a contract of aval is unique in that it is a real undertaking of suretyship signified on and in respect of the obligation evidenced by a bill of exchange. That then entails, secondly, that the

document on which it is recorded must be a bill of exchange. Thirdly, one than goes to the definition in the *Bills of Exchange Act,* § 34 of 1964 to ascertain what a bill of exchange is. Reference is then made to the definitions in § 1 of the Act of the terms "bill" and "check," which in turn direct one to § 2. Subsections (1) and (2) of § 2 of the Act read as follows:

(1) A bill of exchange is an unconditional order in writing, addressed by one person to another, signed by the person giving it, requiring the person to whom it is addressed to pay on demand, or at a fixed or at a determinable future time, a sum certain in money to a specified person or his order, or to bearer.

(2) An instrument which does not comply with the requirements specified in subsection (1) or which orders any act to be done in addition to the payment of money, is not a bill.

The argument then focuses on the fifth characteristic of the bill as defined, namely that it is to be signed by the person giving it and, drawing support from subsection (2), [the defendant] argues that an unsigned check is not a bill. Therefore, so the argument concludes, the signature of an aval put on a check before the drawer has signed it is a nullity.

In my view the argument is fallacious. In the first instance it . . . [gives too much importance to] the heading to § 2, which reads "Definition of and requirements for a bill of exchange."[24] It is clear to me that the Legislature, in one and the same breath, defined a bill and listed the prerequisites for its validity. [It does not follow] . . . that an instrument, complete and regular in every other respect but lacking a signature, is some innominate[25] piece of paper, as Mr. Roos, for the defendant, would have it. It is simply a bill which, for lack of a signature, is inchoate,[26] e.g., an unsigned check.

The use of the term "an unsigned check" is common, not only in laymen's language but in a legal context. There are many examples of which this case is but one. The defendant admitted in paragraph 2 of his opposing affidavit that he signed "the checks, annexes A and B to the summons" and in paragraph 3.3 alleged that "not one of the checks . . . had been signed." To my mind there is nothing anomalous in that choice of language.

They were, indeed, unsigned checks. If one looks at the *Bills of Exchange Act* itself, there are several examples of similar use of language. Thus § 16(1) provides:

A bill may be accepted—(a) before it has been signed by the drawer. . . .

---

[24]"*Omskrywing van en vereistes vir'n wissel*" in the Afrikaans text. As to the propriety of referring to the heading of a section as an aid in interpretation, *see* L. C. Steyn, *Uitleg van Wette,* pp. 147, 148 (5th ed. 1974).

[25]From Latin *innominatus:* "unnamed" or "anonymous."]

[26]From Latin *inchoatus:* "has begun." It means "in its early stages of development" or "incipient."]

Clearly the notional lawgiver (in fact, the draftsman of § 18 of the United Kingdom progenitor of our § 16, namely in the Bills *of Exchange Act* 1882)[27] realized that a bill, before it has been signed by the drawer, is a bill capable of being accepted. So, too, the opening words of § 24(1) ("If a person signs a bill as drawer . . .") indicate that before the drawer has signed the instrument, it is a bill. The subtlety necessarily involved in regarding the document as something unknown and unnamed until the moment the drawer has put the last dot of his signature on it, is unrealistic, not consonant with commercial or legal parlance, and inconsistent with the very language of the Act.

* * *

Furthermore, the defendant unequivocally undertook specific obligations in the knowledge that the checks were as yet unsigned and, obviously, before they had been delivered he knew they had to be signed by the drawer and would be signed by him before they were delivered. Until delivery they would be inchoate (*see* § 88 of the Act), but once delivered the contract of the drawer would be concluded. *See* Denis V. Cowen,

The Law of Negotiable Instruments in South Africa.[28] The learned author . . . points out that:

> [t]here is no authority on the question whether the contract of aval is incomplete and revocable until delivery.

That question does not arise in the present case. Here the checks were delivered, as defendant intended them to be. In my opinion the defendant's obligations *qua* aval arose at the latest when the checks were delivered. They were delivered, bearing his signature, recording an obligation which he undertook to secure through his personal suretyship. The checks were delivered precisely as the defendant intended them to be. They signify to the payee and to any further holders of the checks that defendant stood surety for the obligations of the drawer. In my view, he is bound by that indication. It matters not that the drawer's signature had not yet been affixed when the aval signed on the reverse of the checks.

The defendant was ordered to pay the plaintiff 8,400 rand, plus interest. ■

---

[27]Victoria, Anno 45–46, Chap. 16.
[28]At p. 175 (4th ed. 1966).

F. THE NEGOTIATION AND TRANSFER OF BILLS AND NOTES

To satisfy commercial needs, bills and notes have to be freely transferable. Contract law governs the relationships between the original parties to a bill or note. Once a negotiable instrument circulates beyond the original parties, however, the laws governing negotiation come into play.

Assignment

assignment: The transfer of all or part of an assignor's contractual rights to an assignee.

The transfer of rights under a contract is called an **assignment**. When an assignment is made, the assignee acquires only those rights that the assignor possessed. Moreover, any objections to honoring the assigned obligations that could be raised against the assignor can also be raised against the assignee.

For example, Anna promises to deliver 10 widgets to Chekhov and Chekhov gives her an I.O.U. for $100. Anna promptly assigns the I.O.U. to Vanya, who several days later presents the I.O.U. to Chekhov, asking him to pay it. Anna, however, failed to deliver the promised widgets, so Chekhov refuses to pay the I.O.U. Because an I.O.U. is a nonnegotiable instrument (as mentioned earlier), Vanya can only be an assignee. He has no more rights in the I.O.U. than Anna had. As a consequence, Chekhov can use Anna's failure to make delivery of the widgets as an excuse (or "defense") for not paying Vanya. Vanya's only recourse is to return to Anna—if Anna can be found—and get back whatever money he may have paid for the I.O.U.

Bankers and merchants, who are well aware of the problems that arise in taking instruments by assignment, are not anxious to do so. They prefer to be paid in cash, or by a negotiable instrument—that is, by an instrument that is, for most purposes, the same as cash.

Negotiation

negotiation: The transfer of rights in an instrument, either by endorsement and delivery or merely by delivery, that entitles the holder to sue in his own name and to take the instrument free of some of the claims that persons obliged to pay on the instrument have against the transferor.

Negotiation is the transfer of a bill or note in such a way that the recipient becomes a holder. Unlike an assignee (who acquires only the rights of the assignor), a holder can acquire more

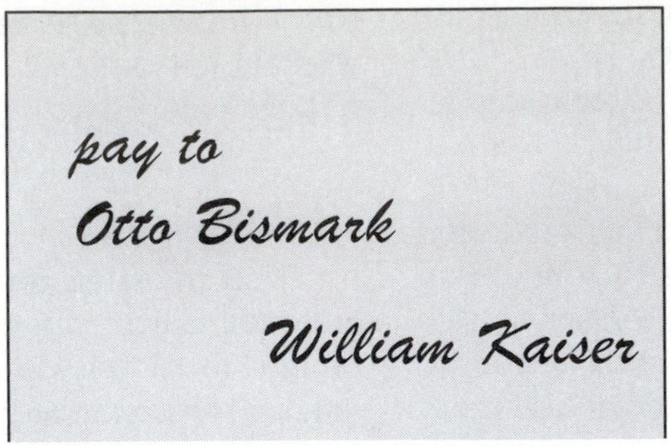

EXHIBIT 12-8 Special Endorsement

rights from the transferor than the transferor possessed. The rights that a holder acquires depend on the manner in which the instrument was negotiated and the governing law.

Negotiating Order Paper

order paper: A bill of exchange or promissory note that is payable to a named payee.

Order paper is a bill or note that either (a) contains the name of a payee capable of endorsing it, such as "pay to the order of Francisco Madero," or (b) contains as its last endorsement a so-called special endorsement—that is, for example, "pay to Otto Bismarck." (See Exhibit 12-8.) Order paper is negotiated by delivery and endorsement. That is, a bill payable to the order of Giulio Romano would be negotiated when Giulio signed the back and delivered it to a holder.

Negotiating Bearer Paper

bearer paper: A bill of exchange or promissory note that is payable to the bearer or to cash.

Bearer paper is an instrument that either (a) contains on its face an order to pay the bearer or to pay in cash or (b) contains as its last endorsement a so-called blank endorsement, that is, the signature of the payee or the signature of the last endorsee named in a special endorsement. (See Exhibit 12-9.) Bearer paper is negotiated by delivery alone.

The use of bearer paper is riskier than the use of order paper. If it is lost or stolen it must still be paid, as Case 12–2 points out.

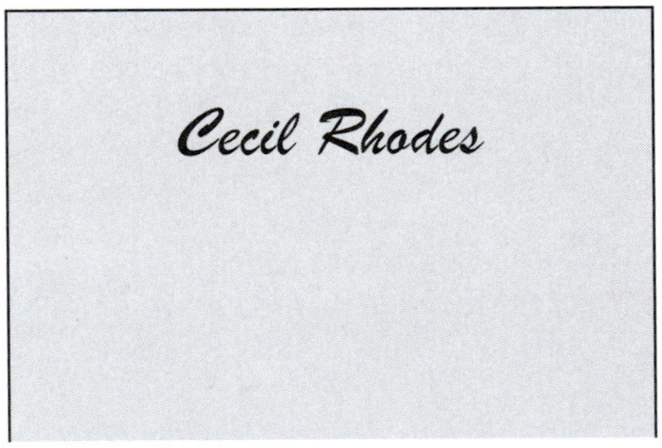

EXHIBIT 12-9 Blank Endorsement

Case 12–2   Miller v. Race

England, Court of King's Bench, 1758.
English Reports, vol. 97, p. 398.

William Finney owed 21 pounds and 10 shillings to Bernard Odenharty. Finney purchased a note in that amount from the Bank of England that was drawn upon

the bank itself and that was made payable to bearer. Finney then sent the bank's note to Odenharty in the mail on December 11, 1756. That night the mail was robbed, and the note in question, and several other notes, were carried off by the robber. On December 12, the note came into the possession of an innkeeper by the name of Miller.

of the argument turns upon comparing bank notes to what they do not resemble, *viz.* to goods, or to securities, or documents for debts.

Now they are not goods, not securities, nor documents for debts, nor are they so esteemed—but are treated as money, as cash, in the ordinary course and transaction of business, by the general consent of mankind; which gives them the credit and currency of money, to all intents and purposes. They are as much money as guineas themselves are; or any other current coin, that is used in common payments, as money or cash.

. . . Here, an innkeeper took it, bona fide, in his business from a person who made an appearance of a gentleman. Here is no pretense or suspicion of collusion with the robber—for this matter was strictly inquired and examined into at the trial—and it is so stated in the case, "that he took it for full and valuable consideration, in the usual course of business." Indeed, if there had been any collusion, or any circumstances of unfair dealing, the case had been much otherwise. If it had been a note for 1,000£ it might have been suspicious, but this was a small note for 21£ 10*s* only, and money was given in exchange for it.

. . . A bank note is constantly and universally, both at home and abroad, treated as money, as cash; and paid and received, as cash; and it is necessary, for the purposes of commerce, that their currency should be established and secured.

. . . No dispute ought to be made with the bearer of a cash note—in regard to commerce, and for the sake of credit—though it may be both reasonable and customary, to stay the payment, till inquiry can be made, whether the bearer of the note came by it fairly, or not.

Judgment for the plaintiff. ■

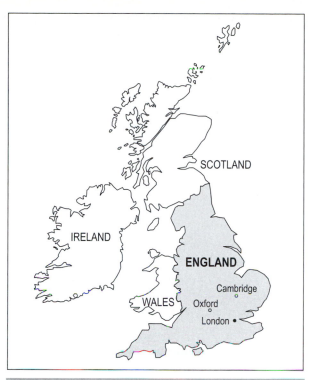

MAP 12-2 England (1758)

On December 13, having learned of the robbery, Finney applied to the Bank of England to stop payment on the note. The bank agreed to do so.

Shortly thereafter, Miller presented the note to the Bank of England for payment. The bank's clerk, who was named Race, refused either to pay the note or return it to Miller. Miller thereupon brought suit against Race to compel him to make payment.

At issue was the following question: "Whether, under the circumstances of this case, the plaintiff had a sufficient property in this bank note, to entitle him to recover in the present action."

LORD MANSFIELD:

* * *

[This case] has been very ingeniously argued by Sir Richard Lloyd for the defendant. But the whole fallacy

---

Converting Order to Bearer Paper and Bearer to Order Paper

Order paper can be converted to bearer paper by an endorsement in blank or by an endorsement to pay to the bearer. Bearer paper can be converted to order paper through the use of a special endorsement, such as "Pay to John Adams."

The manner in which a bill or note must be negotiated depends on its character at the time of negotiation. If it is order paper, it must be negotiated by delivery and endorsement; if it is bearer paper, by delivery alone. To illustrate: A note is made payable to Mustafa Kemal, who endorses it by signing his name on the back. The note can now be negotiated by delivery alone, and whoever receives it from Kemal can also negotiate by delivery alone. Any subsequent holder can, of course, add a special endorsement to convert the note back to order paper. For example, the note may come into the possession of Ali Jinnah, who could add the statement "pay Ahmad Khan," sign the note himself, and deliver it to Khan. Khan would then have to endorse it himself before he could negotiate the note.

Endorsements

endorsement: The act of a payee, drawee, accommodation party, or holder of a negotiable instrument in signing the back of the instrument, with or without qualifying words, to transfer rights in the instrument to another.

An **endorsement** is required to negotiate a bill or note that is in the form of order paper, and it may optionally be added to bearer paper. Endorsements are signatures, with or without additional statements, that are commonly written on the back of the instrument. There are four basic kinds: (a) special endorsements, (b) blank endorsements, (c) qualified endorsements, and (d) restrictive endorsements. The first two have already been described.

qualified endorsement: An endorsement in which the endorser does not guarantee that an instrument will be accepted and paid by the drawer or maker.

Qualified Endorsements   Normally, an endorser guarantees that the instrument will be accepted and paid by the drawee or maker. The endorser can avoid this guarantee, however, by making a **qualified endorsement**. Commonly, this is done by adding the words "without recourse."[29] Qualified endorsements are commonly used by persons acting in a representative capacity. For example, a lawyer may receive a check that is payable to him, which is really meant to be paid to a client. Because the lawyer is only endorsing the check to make it possible for the client to cash it, he should not have to make good on the check if it is later dishonored. By adding a qualified endorsement he will not have to do so. (See Exhibit 12-10.)

restrictive endorsement: An endorsement that restricts the rights of subsequent holders.

Restrictive Endorsements   **Restrictive endorsements** limit the rights of subsequent holders. There are several types, including conditional endorsements, endorsements for collection, endorsements prohibiting further endorsements, and agency endorsements. None of these, however, prevents the further transfer or negotiation of a bill or note.[30]

conditional endorsement: An endorsement that conditions payment on the occurrence of some event.

A **conditional endorsement** contains a statement that conditions payment on the occurrence of a specified event. (See Exhibit 12-11.) The effect of this endorsement is to make the bill or note a nonnegotiable instrument as to the endorser only. No subsequent holder has the right to enforce the payment against a conditional endorser until the condition is met.

endorsement for collection: An endorsement that makes the endorsee a collection agent for the endorser.

An **endorsement for collection** makes an endorsee (usually a bank) a collecting agent for the endorser. In common law countries such an endorsement is usually written as "for deposit only," "for collection only," or "pay any bank." In civil law countries, the phrases "value in collection" and "by procuration" are also commonly used.

The effect of an endorsement for collection is to put the instrument into the bank collection process. In common law countries, only a bank can become a holder once this endorsement has been added to a bill or note, unless the instrument is specially endorsed by a bank to a person who is not a bank.[31] Under the ULB, anyone can become a holder, but they can only endorse the instrument for the purpose of making collection.[32]

without recourse
Edgar A. Poe

EXHIBIT 12-10   Qualified Endorsement

---

[29]The words "without recourse" are required in the common law countries. UCC, § 3-417(3). No particular words are required in Europe. ULB, Article 15.
[30]UCC, § 3-206(1); ULB, Article 15.
[31]UCC, § 4-201(2).
[32]ULB, Article 18.

> *pay to Muhammad Ali on
> condition he deliver 1 pair
> of boxing gloves to me in
> 1 week
> Joe Frazier*

EXHIBIT 12-11
Conditional Endorsement

endorsement prohibiting further endorsements: An endorsement that states that the instrument may be paid only to a particular person.

An **endorsement prohibiting further endorsements** states that the instrument may be paid only to a particular person. An example is "Pay to Henrik Ibsen only." This endorsement is treated differently by the two main commercial law systems.

In common law countries, an endorsement prohibiting further endorsements is treated as if it were a special endorsement—that is, as though the example said, "Pay to Henrik Ibsen."[33] The ULB treats such an endorsement as if it were a qualified endorsement (e.g., "Pay to Henrik Ibsen, without recourse"); in other words, the endorser does not guarantee acceptance or payment.[34]

agency endorsement: An endorsement that requires the endorsee to pay the proceeds from the negotiation of the instrument to the endorser or a designated third party.

An **agency endorsement** requires the endorsee to pay the proceeds from the negotiation of a bill or note to the endorser or to some third party. In common law countries, such an endorsement is phrased as "Pay to Alexander Leslie, agent for Oliver Cromwell [*signed*] Oliver Cromwell" or "Pay to Alexander Leslie in Trust for Charles Tudor [*signed*] Oliver Cromwell." In civil law countries, the wording is "Pay to Maximilien Robespierre, for value in security [*signed*] Napoleon Bonaparte" or "Pay Maximilien Robespierre, for value in pledge to Louis Bourbon [*signed*] Napoleon Bonaparte."

Type of Endorsement	Example	Endorsee's Status	
		Common Law	**ULB**
Blank	[*signed*] Cecil Rhodes	Holder	Holder
Special	Pay to Otto Bismark, [*signed*] William Kaiser	Holder	Holder
Qualified	Pay to Jane Austen, without recourse, [*signed*] Edgar Poe	No rights against endorser	No rights against endorser
Conditional	Pay to Muhammad Ali on condition he deliver 1 pair of boxing gloves to me in 1 week, [*signed*] Joe Frazier	No rights against endorser until condition is met	No rights against endorser until condition is met
For collection	For collection only, [*signed*] Tom Dewey	Collecting agent for endorser	Collecting agent for endorser
Prohibiting further endorsements	Pay to Henrik Ibsen only, [*signed*] Hedda Gabler	Holder	No rights against endorser
Agency	Pay to Alexander Leslie, agent for Oliver Cromwell [*signed*] Oliver Cromwell	Collecting agent for endorser	Collecting agent for endorser

EXHIBIT 12-12   Effect of Different Endorsements under the Common Law and the ULB

---

[33]UCC, § 3-206(1).
[34]ULB, Article 15.

Under the common law and the ULB, an agency endorsee may properly negotiate the instrument only as directed. This restriction on rights, however, applies only to the immediate endorsee and not to any subsequent holder.[35]

Forged Endorsements

forgery: The false making or altering of a writing with the intent to defraud.

When an endorsement is **forged**, the question arises as to who should have to sue the forger; or, if the forger cannot be found, who has to assume the loss. There are several possible ways to answer this question. The one that makes most sense commercially (that is, the one that is most likely to encourage the free transfer and exchange of bills and notes) is to make the drawer or maker liable. This is the rule adopted by the ULB. The ULB makes a forged endorsement fully effective, and both the person taking an instrument with such an endorsement as well as all subsequent holders are entitled to payment.[36]

Another possibility is to impose liability on the person who was best able to prevent the forgery from happening. This is possibly the fairest rule, but it also encourages excessive and expensive litigation. It is the rule followed in most common law countries. As a general rule, the common law makes a forged endorsement ineffective, placing the burden for determining the validity of an endorsement on the endorsee taking an instrument from a forger. Case 12–3 illustrates this rule.

---

[35]UCC, § 3-206(1); ULB, Article 19.
[36]ULB, Article 7.

Case 12–3   Mair v. Bank of Nova Scotia

Court of Appeal of Eastern Caribbean States, Civil Division, 1983.
West Indian Reports, vol. 31, p. 186 (1983).

APPELLATE JUDGE BERRIDGE:

This is an appeal from a decision of Judge Robotham dated June 18, 1980, in which judgment was given for the respondent bank in respect of a claim by the appellant alleging negligence and breach of duty in the sum of $6,000 and interest, together with costs.

The brief facts of the case are that sometime in 1974 the appellant, an architect by profession, engaged one Barbara Hill of Barbados, herself an architect, to assist him in Antigua by doing specific architectural work. Hill took up her assignment with the appellant who gave her an advance of $6,000 payable by check drawn on the St John's, Antigua, branch of the Bank of Nova Scotia for work already done and to be done in the future. Shortly thereafter Hill returned to Barbados following differences which arose between her and the appellant and in respect of which there is litigation which is not before the court.

The check was dated January 16, 1974, and made payable to "Barbara Hill"; but it was altered on the face of it by the addition of the word "Associates" as payee, endorsed "Barbara Hill" and deposited at the branch of

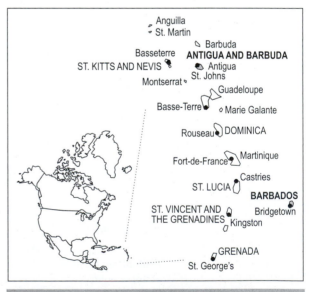

MAP 12-3 Antigua and Barbados (1983)

the respondent bank at Worthing, Christchurch, Barbados, on January 23, 1974, to the credit of "Barbara Hill Associates".

On January 29, 1974, the check was returned to the Antigua branch of the bank who deducted $6,000 from the appellant's account and in due course the canceled check was forwarded to the appellant who, by letter dated May 7, 1974, drew the bank's attention to the alteration and demanded reimbursement on the grounds that (i) it was negligent in not observing the alteration in which event it should not have paid, and (ii) it had not carried out his instructions. The bank refused to reimburse the appellant and as a consequence proceedings were instituted by the appellant.

* * *

In arguing the . . . appeal, counsel submitted that the alteration was a material alteration on the face of the instrument which [made it void] under Section 64 of the *Bills of Exchange Act* [of Antigua and Barbuda] the provisions of which are similar to, if not identical with, comparable legislation throughout the Commonwealth. Counsel further contended that (i) the mandate of the drawer of the check was not substantially carried out, (ii) the alteration was apparent, (iii) the bank was not a holder in due course, and (iv) the damage suffered was the debiting of the appellant's account with a payment to someone other than the payee stated by the appellant.

It is pertinent at this stage to set out the provisions of Section 64 of the *Bills of Exchange Act*, which reads as follows:

(1) Where a bill or acceptance is materially altered without the assent of all parties liable on the bill, the bill is avoided except as against a party who has himself made, authorized, or assented to the alteration, and subsequent endorsers. Provided that, where a bill has been materially altered, but the alteration is not apparent and the bill is in the hands of a holder in due course, such holder may avail himself of the bill as if it had not been altered, and may enforce payment of it according to its original tenor.

(2) In particular the following alterations are material, namely, any alteration of the date, the sum payable, the time of payment, the place of payment, and where a bill has been accepted generally, the addition of a place of payment without the acceptor's assent.

In *Vance v. Lowther*,[37] where an alteration related to the date of the check, it was held that it was material and invalidated the check; and that the circumstance that the plaintiff had not been guilty of negligence in taking it was immaterial. Baron[38] Pollock said:[39]

Any material alteration of a bill or note invalidates it, and the question is, what is the true principle on which the materiality must be determined. The county court judge seems to have thought that it was necessary to consider the surrounding circumstances in each case. In that I think he was wrong, and that we ought to look at the question of materiality with reference to the contract itself, and not with reference to the surrounding circumstances.

But it would be unreasonable if the alteration to an earlier date debarred the banker form debiting the customer, if paid after the original date.

Similar in a number of respects to the facts in the instant case are those in *Slingsby v. District Bank, Ltd.*[40] where words were inserted between the payee's name and the words "or order" and endorsed to conform with the designation of the payee as altered. It was held that the check had been materially altered within the body of Section 64 (1) of the Bills of Exchange Act and therefore the check had been avoided.

The materiality of the alteration being dependent upon its character and effect, it necessarily follows that if the mandate of the customer has been substantially complied with then the banker can charge the customer, the alteration notwithstanding. Authority for the foregoing is to be found in *Halsbury's Laws of England*.[41]

I am of the opinion that the check was materially altered without the assent of the appellant.

To constitute an apparent alteration within the meaning of the Bills of Exchange Act it should be apparent upon inspection of the bill that its text has undergone a change. The document itself must show that some revision of the text has taken place and its appearance must be consistent with the revision having occurred after completion or issue, although it may also be consistent with the revision having occurred before completion.[42]

An inspection of the check reveals that the alteration is obviously in a different handwriting from that in which the rest of the document was drawn and it should have been observed that it had undergone a change.

In regard to the difference between the rights of a "holder in due course" and a "holder" I can do no better than quote from the words of Lord Justice Denning in *Arab Bank, Ltd. v. Ross*:[43]

The difference between the rights of a "holder in due course" and those of a "holder" is that a holder in

[37]Law Reports, Exchequer's Division, vol. 1, p. 176 (1876).
[38]"Baron" is the title for the judges of the English Court of Exchequer.]
[39]*Id.*, at p. 178.
[40]*All England Law Reports*, vol. 1931, p. 143 (King's Bench, 1931).
[41]Vol. 2, p. 205, para. 380 (3rd ed.).
[42]Automobile Finance Co. of Australia, Ltd. v. Law, *Commonwealth Law Reports*, vol. 49, p. 1 (Australia, High Court, 1933) refers.
[43]*All England Law Reports*, vol. 1952, pt. 1, p. 709 at p. 717 (Court of Appeal, 1952).

due course may get a better title than the person from whom he took, whereas a holder gets no better title. In this regard a person who takes a bill, which is irregular on the face of it, is in the same position as a person who takes a bill which is overdue. He is a holder, but not a holder in due course. He does not receive the bill on its own intrinsic credit. He takes it on the credit of the person who gives it to him. He can sue in his own name but he takes it subject to the defects of title of prior parties: see Section 38 of the Act of 1882.

In the instant case the bank took the check which was irregular on the face of it. The bank was not a holder in due course and cannot [therefore] avail itself of the proviso to Section 64(1) of the *Bills of Exchange Act.*

On the question of damages, the appellant's claim is in contract. It is a well-established principle that whenever a party proves a breach of contract but no actual damage (as was contended by learned counsel for the bank) he recovers as a rule nominal damages only.

In the instant case the appellant claims that the damage suffered by him is the debiting of his bank account with an amount payable by check drawn by him to "Barbara Hill" and not "Barbara Hill Associates"; but, I am unable to perceive what damage the appellant has suffered on account of the alteration of the check.

. . . In the circumstances, I would allow the appeal and vary the order of the trial judge by entering judgment for the appellant in the sum of $5 nominal damages. . . . ∎

---

common law imposter rule: A person who pretends to be another so as to have a negotiable instrument drawn, made, or endorsed to that person may effectively endorse the pretended person's signature on the instrument.

common law fictitious payee rule: A person who solicits and obtains a negotiable instrument drawn or made to a fictitious person may effectively endorse the fictitious person's signature on the instrument.

There are two major exceptions to the general common law rule that a forged endorsement is ineffective. One is the **imposter rule**. This says that when a drawer, maker, or endorser draws, makes, or endorses an instrument to an imposter, the imposter's subsequent endorsement is effective. For example, a man walks into a shop, says that he is John Lender, a creditor of the shop owner, Pete Gullible, and asks to be paid. Gullible, believing the man to be his creditor, writes a check made out in favor of John Lender. The man then cashes the check at a nearby supermarket and disappears. Because the man was an *imposter*, the forged signature he put on the check is effective. Gullible cannot stop payment and his bank must negotiate the check when the supermarket presents it.

The second common law exception to the rule that a forged signature is ineffective is the **fictitious payee rule**. This says that when the instrument is issued in the name of a fictitious payee, the person purporting to be that payee can make an effective endorsement. To illustrate: A disgruntled employee, Ann Sly, tells her employer that he needs to sign a check that she has made out so that she can pay a supplier. He does so. Ann then forges the supplier's endorsement and cashes the check herself. In reality, the supplier (whether or not it really exists or was a fiction) has no claim against Sly's employer. The supplier's forged endorsement, however, is effective, and the employer must honor the check when an innocent holder presents it for payment.

The difficulty with the general common law rule is that the determination of whether one or the other of the two exceptions applies has to be made after the fact. In the meantime, the maker, drawer, or drawee can refuse to make payment, and the last holder will have to initiate suit against the dishonoring party to determine who is responsible for pressing the claim against the forger. The loser of that suit will, assuming the forger can be located, have to initiate a second suit to recoup the lost funds. This rule may assure employment for lawyers, but it does not promote the free transferability of negotiable instruments.

The liabilities of endorsers and drawers for forged instruments under the common law and the ULB are compared in Exhibit 12-13.

Limitations on the Excuses that Drawers and Makers Can Use to Avoid Paying Off a Bill or Note

The major disadvantage of taking a bill, note, or other contractual obligation by assignment is that the maker or drawer can raise a wide range of excuses for not having to pay off the instrument. The advantage of taking an instrument by negotiation is that many of these excuses are limited.[44]

---

[44]In the United States, the courts and statutory materials refer to "defenses" rather than excuses. In the United Kingdom, the phrase is "failure of equities." In the civil law countries, the terms "defenses," "justifications," and "excuses" are all used. Excuses will generally be used in this book.

EXHIBIT 12-13 Liability When a Negotiable Instrument Is Forged

Situation	Common Law	ULB
A stolen instrument is forged.	Immediate endorsee	Drawer
The forger is an imposter.	Drawer	Drawer
The forger endorses for a fictitious payee.	Drawer	Drawer

ULB holder: A person who acquires an instrument by negotiation.

The most extensive limitations imposed on the excuses of makers and drawers are those contained in the ULB. Anyone who acquires a bill or note by negotiation is a **holder** who is entitled to payment from the maker or drawer. There are only three excuses available to these parties. One is that the possessor is not a holder because he did not acquire title through an uninterrupted series of endorsements. For example, someone possessing an instrument that is payable on its face to one person but endorsed on the back by another could not be a holder.

ULB bad faith: Acquiring an instrument knowing that it was not properly negotiated to you.

The second excuse is that the holder acquired the instrument in bad faith. **Bad faith** includes such things as the actual theft of the instrument; having actual knowledge that the instrument is stolen, lost, or misplaced; or having actual knowledge that the payee, or some prior holder, is not properly entitled to payment.

ULB gross negligence: Acquiring an instrument in such a careless or reckless manner that one should have known that it was not properly negotiated.

The third excuse is that the holder acquired the instrument through **gross negligence**. This is essentially the same as bad faith, except that the holder does not have to have actual knowledge. He must, however, have acted in a truly careless manner in failing to detect some defect in the instrument or in the rights of the maker, drawer, or a prior holder.[45] These excuses are summarized in Exhibit 12-14.

In contrast to the ULB, the common law imposes very few limitations on the excuses that makers and drawers can use to get out of their obligation to pay off a bill or note. To cut short these excuses, a possessor must first (as is the case in the ULB) be a **holder**—that is, someone who acquired the bill or note through an uninterrupted series of endorsements. A person who is not a holder is not entitled to the instrument and must give it up.

common law holder: A person who acquires an instrument by negotiation.

common law holder in due course: A holder who acquires a negotiable instrument for value, in good faith, and without notice that it is overdue, that it has been dishonored, or that persons required to pay on it have some valid excuse for not doing so.

When the possessor of a bill or note is an ordinary holder, a maker or drawer can draw upon a lengthy list of excuses for not paying. (See Exhibit 12-15.) The list is narrowed, however, if the holder can prove that he is entitled to the additional status of a **holder in due course** (HDC).[46] An HDC is a holder who acquires an instrument (1) for value, (2) in good faith, and (3) without notice that it is overdue, that it has been dishonored, or that the maker, drawer, or a prior endorser has a valid excuse for not paying it off.[47] The requirement that an HDC has to give value for an instrument means that someone who receives an instrument as a gift or by inheritance can only be an ordinary holder. Good faith means that the holder cannot have known—or have reasonably suspected—that the instrument was defective.

Liabilities of Makers, Drawers, Drawees, Endorsers, and Accommodation Parties

Two kinds of liability are imposed on makers, drawers, and endorsers of bills and notes. One is liability "on the instrument"—that is, liability arising out of a signature. The other is "warranty" liability—that is, responsibility arising out of the implied guarantees a person makes at the time

EXHIBIT 12-14 ULB Excuses that Drawers and Makers Can Use to Avoid Paying Bills of Exchange and Promissory Notes

Person in Possession	Excuse
Not a holder	1. Not a holder
Holder	1. Acquired instrument in bad faith
	2. Acquired instrument through gross negligence

---

[45]ULB, Article 16.
[46]A holder has the burden of proving that he is a holder in due course. UCC, § 3-307(3).
[47]*Id.*, § 3-303.

EXHIBIT 12-15 Common Law Excuses That Drawers and Makers Can Use to Avoid Paying Bills of Exchange and Promissory Notes

Person in Possession	Excuse
Not a holder	Not a holder
Holder	Breach of contract (including breach of contract warranties)
	Lack or failure of consideration
	Fraud in the inducement
	Illegality, incapacity (other than minority), or duress, if the contract is voidable
	Previous payment of the instrument
	Unauthorized completion of an incomplete instrument
	Nondelivery of the instrument
Holder or holder in due course	Forgery
	Fraud in the execution
	Material alteration
	Discharge in bankruptcy
	Minority, if the contract is voidable
	Illegality, incapacity, or duress, if the contract is void

he transfers or presents a negotiable instrument. In neither case, it is important to note, is liability based on the underlying contract.

Liability on the Instrument

presentment: Production of an instrument to a party liable to pay on it for that party's acceptance (i.e., commitment to pay) or payment.

A person who signs an instrument has a contractual obligation to make payment. For makers, drawees, and accommodation parties, this obligation is "primary"; that is, they must make payment on **presentment** of the instrument. If it is other than a demand instrument, it must be presented on the day it is due. If it is a demand instrument, it must be presented within a reasonable time after it was signed.

Case 12–4   Far East Realty Investment, Inc. v. Court of Appeals et al.

The Philippines, Supreme Court, Second Division, 1988. *Supreme Court Reports Annotated, Second Series,* vol. 166, p. 256 (1988).

On September 13, 1960, Dy Hian Tat, Siy Chee, and Gaw Suy An went to the Manila office of Far East Realty Investment, Inc. (Far East) and obtained a loan in the sum of P4,500.00 (Philippine currency), which they needed in their business, and which they promised to pay, jointly and severally, in one month's time together with interest at the rate of 14 percent per annum. To assure Far East that it would be repaid, Dy Hian Tat drew a check on his account with China Banking Corporation (the bank), dated September 13, 1960, for P4,500.00, and Siy Chee and Gaw Suy An signed the check on its back as accommodation parties. The three men were to redeem the check

in one month's time by paying cash to Far East in the sum of P4,500.00; otherwise, Far East was to present the check for payment at the bank.

Almost four years later, on March 5, 1964, Far East presented the check to the bank for payment. The bank refused to pay as the account of Dy Hian Tat had been closed for some time. Far East then made a demand on the Dy Hian Tat, Siy Chee, and Gaw Suy An for repayment of their loan. When they refused to pay, Far East brought suit. The City Court of Manila ruled in favor of Far East, so Dy Hian Tat, Siy Chee, and Gaw Suy An appealed. The Court of First Instance of Manila also ruled in favor of Far East, but the Court of Appeals reversed, holding that Far East had not presented the check for payment within a reasonable time. Far East (the petitioner) then appealed to the Philippine Supreme Court.

MAP 12-4   Philippines (1988)

. . . Where the instrument is not payable on demand, presentment must be made on the day it falls due. Where it is payable on demand, presentment must be made within a reasonable time after issue, except that in the case of a bill of exchange, presentment for payment will be sufficient if made within a reasonable time after the last negotiation thereof.[48]

Notice may be given as soon as the instrument is dishonored, and, unless delay is excused, must be given within the time fixed by the law.[49]

No hard and fast demarcation line can be drawn between what may be considered as a reasonable or an unreasonable time, because "reasonable time" depends upon the peculiar facts and circumstances in each case.[50]

It is obvious in this case that presentment and notice of dishonor were not made within a reasonable time.

"Reasonable time" has been defined as so much time as is necessary under the circumstances for a reasonable prudent and diligent man to do, conveniently, what the contract or duty requires should be done, having a regard for the rights and possibility of loss, if any, to the other party.[51]

In the instant case, the check in question was issued on September 13, 1960, but was presented to the drawee bank only on March 5, 1964, and dishonored on the same date. After dishonor by the drawee bank, a formal notice of dishonor was made by the petitioner through a letter dated April 27, 1968. Under these circumstances, the petitioner undoubtedly failed to exercise prudence and diligence on what he ought to do as required by law. The petitioner likewise failed to show any justification for the unreasonable delay.

PREMISES CONSIDERED, the petition is DENIED and the decision of the Court of Appeals is AFFIRMED.

So Ordered. ◼

JUSTICE PARAS:

* * *

The main issue in this case is whether or not presentment for payment and notice of dishonor of the questioned check were made within reasonable time.

---

[48]Negotiable Instruments Law, § 71.
[49]*Id.*, § 102.
[50]Arturo M. Tolentino, *Commentaries and Jurisprudence on the Commercial Laws of the Philippines,* vol. 1, p. 327 (8th ed., 1986–1988).
[51]Citizens' Bank Bldg. v. L. & E. Wertheirmer, *South Western Reporter,* vol. 189, p. 361, at 362 (Arkansas Supreme Ct., 1917).

Liability on the instrument for drawers, endorsers, and accommodation endorsers is "secondary"; that is, they have to pay only if the maker, drawee, or accommodation maker fails to do so.

When a holder or transferee is unable to obtain payment from the maker, drawee, or accommodation maker, he must take three preliminary steps before he can seek recourse from the parties with secondary liability. First, the instrument has to be properly presented. That is, it must contain all necessary endorsements and it must be timely presented at the place required. Second, if the instrument is a bill of exchange, it must be **protested**. In other words, a

protest: Formal certification that a negotiable instrument was dishonored by a party liable for its payment.

formal certification of dishonor must be issued by "a person authorized to certify dishonor by the law of the place where the dishonor occurs."[52] In the United States, such a person is a notary public.[53] The certification has to show (a) who presented the instrument for payment, (b) the place where this was done, and (c) the reason given by the maker or drawee for refusing to make payment.[54]

The third requirement is to give notice to the parties with secondary liability. This is done, initially, by notifying the drawer (if the instrument is a bill) and the last endorser. At the same time, any other endorser whose address the holder is aware of must also be notified. In turn, any endorser who receives such a notice must—to maintain his rights against his immediate endorser—notify that person. In the United States, notice has to be given within three business days;[55] in Europe, the requirement is two business days.[56] Any form of notice is sufficient so long as it identifies the instrument and states that the instrument has been dishonored.[57]

Warranty Liability

The most dramatic difference between negotiable instrument law in the United States and in Europe (including the United Kingdom) shows up in connection with warranty liability. In Europe, liability can arise only on the instrument. That is, unless someone signs an instrument, he will have no liability for its payment. In sum, there is no warranty liability.

In the United States, by comparison, any person who transfers an instrument in exchange for consideration—which includes a transferor of bearer paper who does not endorse the instrument—makes five warranties, or implied guarantees, to his immediate transferee *and* to every subsequent holder who takes the instrument in good faith. These are as follows:

1. The transferor has good title to the instrument or is otherwise authorized to obtain payment or acceptance on behalf of one who does have good title.
2. All signatures are genuine or authorized.
3. The instrument has not been materially altered.
4. No defense of any party is good against the transferor.
5. The transferor has no knowledge of any insolvency proceedings against the maker, the acceptor, or the drawer of an unaccepted instrument.

The Role of Banks in Collecting and Paying Negotiable Instruments

Banks perform at least four functions in connection with the negotiation of bills and notes. First, they may issue instruments themselves, such as certified checks or certificates of deposit. Second, they may function as the drawee on a bill of exchange or as the acceptor of a bill or promissory note, assuming primary liability for payment. Third, they can act as an agent for a holder or transferee to make collection. Fourth, they can take an instrument as an endorsee, paying the endorser, and presenting the instrument for payment in their own right.

The significance of acting as an endorser rather than as an agent for collection—especially in connection with international transactions—is considered in Case 12–5.

---

[52]UCC, § 3-509(1).

[53]UCC, § 3-509(1). In the United States, protest is required only in connection with a bill of exchange (draft) "which appears to be drawn or payable outside of . . . the United States." UCC, § 3-501(3).

[54]UCC, § 3-509(2). If the maker or drawee could not be found, this fact can be substituted for the statement of the reason for refusal.

[55]Banks must give notice within one day. UCC, § 3-508(2).

[56]ULB, Article 44.

[57]UCC, § 3-508(3).

Case 12–5   Charles R. Allen, Inc. v. Island Cooperative Services Cooperative Association

United States, Supreme Court of South Carolina, 1959. *South Carolina Reports*, vol. 234, p. 537 (1959).

Island Cooperative Services Cooperative Associa- tion, Ltd. ("Island Coop"), a Canadian corporation, sold some seed potatoes to the Charleston County Wholesale Vegetable Market, Inc. ("Vegetable Market"), of Charles- ton, South Carolina, for a purchase price of $19,620. After the potatoes had been put aboard a ship in Charlottetown, Prince Edward Island, Canada, for shipment to Charles- ton, South Carolina, Island Coop prepared a draft (or bill of exchange) in the amount of $19,620 on February 7, 1955. Island Coop was the drawer, the Vegetable Market was the drawee, and the Bank of Nova Scotia's branch office at Charlottetown, Prince Edward Island, was the payee.

Island Coop offered this and several other drafts to the Bank of Nova Scotia at a discount, and the bank agreed to take them. Island Coop delivered the drafts to the Bank of Nova Scotia on February 7, 1955, accompa- nied by the following agreement:

1. The above bills, which represent amounts due to us for goods sold and delivered, are offered for discount. Our claims against Drawee are hereby transferred to you in the event of nonacceptance of any draft. The relative goods have already been shipped.
2. Credit Proceeds to Current A/C Savings A/C No. .

The Bank of Nova Scotia endorsed the draft drawn on the Vegetable Market and forwarded it through its cor- respondent, the Bank of New York, to the South Carolina National Bank of Charleston for collection. The Vege- table Market paid the South Carolina Bank the full $19,620 on February 14, 1955.

At the same time that this transaction was going on between Island Coop, the Vegetable Market, and the three banks, Charles R. Allen, Inc. ("Allen"), a South Carolina corporation, brought suit for breach of contract against Island Coop, and won. The judgment Allen received enti- tled it to attach Island Coop's assets in South Carolina.

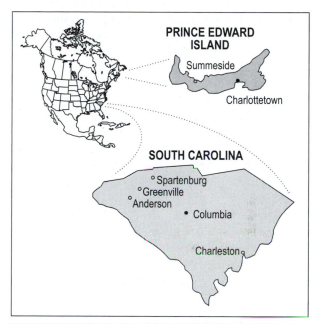

MAP 12-5   South Carolina and Prince Edward Island (1959)

Allen thereupon attached the $19,620 held in the South Carolina National Bank, claiming it was an asset of Island Coop. The Bank of Nova Scotia disagreed, and it promptly served a claim on Allen, stating that the pro- ceeds of the draft belonged to it.

The trial court held that the Bank of Nova Scotia had taken the draft as an agent for collection and not as a pur- chaser, and therefore Island Coop had been the owner of the proceeds of the draft. Accordingly, the trial court held that Allen's attachment was proper. The Bank of Nova Scotia appealed.

JUSTICE MOSS:

* * *

The basic question for determination in this case is whether the appellant, Bank of Nova Scotia, was the absolute owner of the proceeds of the draft at the time of the attachment of the funds by the respondent. If the appellant was the owner thereof, and Island Coop had no interest therein, then this action must fail. . . .

The appellant, in its claim to the proceeds of the draft here involved, asserted that under the laws of Canada that it had full and complete ownership and title to the draft and the proceeds thereof at the time of the attachment. The law of Canada has been proved to the effect that under the facts of this case surrounding the discount transaction as it took place in Canada, the Bank of Nova Scotia acquired under Canadian law an absolute title to and ownership of the draft in Canada at the time the draft was discounted on February 7, 1955. A consideration of the law of Canada and of the law of South Carolina, as applicable to factual situation here, leads us to the conclusion that the laws of Canada and South Carolina are in accord. The application of the laws of Canada or South Carolina requires us to reach the same conclusion. We will, therefore, as is contended for by the respondent, apply the law of South Carolina in this case.

It is the contention of the respondent that because the appellant had the right, in the event of nonpayment of the draft in question, to charge the dishonored draft back to the account of the depositor, that such showed that the appellant was a collecting agent and not the owner of the draft in question. This contention is contrary to the rule in this State. Likewise, the collection of interest upon the draft in question did not prevent the bank from becoming the sole owner thereof.

In the case of *Campbell v. Noble-Trotter Rice Milling Co., Inc.* (*Ex parte Calcasieu-Marine National Bank*) this Court completely answered these contentions when it said:[58]

According to the prevailing view, the rule as to the passing of title to commercial paper, deposited and credited as cash, applies, although the bank has the right to charge dishonored paper back to the depositor instead of proceeding against the maker.

And it has been held that an interest arrangement will not prevent a bank from becoming the sole owner of a draft. Thus, where the bank advances the full amount of a draft, it becomes the unconditional owner, though it is understood it will collect interest on the amount advanced, depending upon the time it takes for collection.

* * *

In the case of *Lawton v. Lower Main Street Bank*, it is said:[59]

. . . where an item is endorsed without restriction by a depositor, nothing appearing to indicate that it was received for collection, and it is at once passed to his credit by the bank, and he is permitted to check upon the account, he becomes the creditor of the bank, which, as the owner of the paper, is not the agent of the depositor in collecting it but collects on its own behalf. . . .

We think that under the authority of the case of *Campbell v. Noble-Trotter Rice Milling Co., Inc.* . . . the lower court must be reversed. The only factual difference between the present case and the *Campbell* case is that in the latter case the bank discounted a draft with a bill of lading attached, while here it discounted the draft only. This factual difference does not make the case inapplicable to the present situation.

In the *Campbell* case it appears that Noble-Trotter Rice Milling Co., Inc., a Louisiana corporation, drew a draft on Allen Bros. Milling Co., Columbia, South Carolina, which represented the purchase price of a shipment of rice. Attached to the draft was a bill of lading covering the shipment, an invoice thereof, and a certificate of insurance. This draft was made payable directly to the Calcasieu-Marine National Bank, located at Lake Charles, Louisiana, and was deposited . . . by the Rice Milling Company in that bank, where it maintained a regular account, and where it had been transacting business for years. The draft, according to the contention of the bank, was not entered for collection, but was treated as cash and was immediately and unconditionally placed to the credit of Rice Milling Co. and made subject to its check.

In due course, the draft, together with attached papers, was forwarded by the bank for collection to the First National Bank, Columbia, South Carolina, where it was paid by the drawee, Allen Bros. Milling Co. The day the draft was paid to the First National Bank of Columbia, South Carolina, the proceeds were attached by one M. P. Campbell for the satisfaction of an unliquidated demand against Noble-Trotter Rice Milling Co. The Louisiana bank intervened, claiming the proceeds of the draft by reason of its ownership thereof. Judgment was rendered in favor of Campbell and the case was appealed to this Court. The question for decision was whether the bank took the draft as owner thereof or as a mere collecting agent for the customer. This court held that the Louisiana bank was entitled to the proceeds of the draft in question. It was said that the determination of the question of title to commercial paper transferred to a bank, which credits it to the depositor's account, involves a question of intention. The Court then dis-

---

[58]*South Carolina Reports*, vol. 188, p. 212.
[59]*South Carolina Reports*, vol. 170, p. 334.

cussed how it may be shown that the bank became the owner of the commercial paper rather than a mere agent for collection, and it was expressly stated that the right accorded to a depositor to draw upon funds is especially material as showing an intention that title should pass to the bank. It was stated that another means of ascertaining the intention is a consideration of course of conduct or the ordinary course of business as disclosed by the evidence. It was also held that where there was a deposit of a draft in the ordinary course of banking business, whereby the depositor received from the bank an unconditional credit of the amount as cash against which the depositor had a right to draw, with nothing to qualify the effect of such act, such operated *prima facie* to transfer title of the draft to the bank.

Applying the rule set forth in *Campbell v. Noble-Trotter Rice Milling Co.* to the evidence in this case, and keeping in mind that the burden of proof was upon the respondent [who was the plaintiff in this case] to show ownership of the draft by Island Coop rather than by the Bank of Nova Scotia, we think that under the evidence the only conclusion that can be reached is that the respondent failed to carry the burden of proof. The evidence in behalf of the appellant is conclusive that it was the owner of the draft in question. Island Coop had been a customer of the appellant for a number of years, and over this period of time the bills of Island Coop had been discounted. The draft in question was handled by the discount department rather than by the collection department of said bank. The bank upon discounting the draft in question, placed it without restriction and unconditionally to the checking account of Island Coop and accorded to it the right to draw upon the funds, which said right was exercised. There is no evidence contradictory of these facts.

. . . We conclude, after a consideration of all the facts in this case, that under the applicable law thereto, that the title to the draft in question passed to the Bank of Nova Scotia, and that it is entitled to the proceeds now held in the custody of the South Carolina National Bank in Charleston, South Carolina.

* * *

Judgment reversed. ■

G. LETTERS OF CREDIT

Assume that a buyer purchases goods overseas. When must the buyer make payment? The seller, undoubtedly, would prefer to be paid in advance. The buyer, on the other hand, would like to make sure, before paying, that (a) the goods are actually shipped and that (b) the goods shipped meet his contractual specifications; and, in actuality, he would prefer (c) to take delivery before paying.

documents against payment: Term in a sales contract that provides for the seller to deliver shipping documents and title to a bank for release to the buyer after the buyer delivers to the bank a receipt from the seller verifying that the seller has received payment.

Depending on the relative bargaining power of the buyer and seller, any of these possible arrangements can be included as a term in the sales contract. If the seller is unable to determine the buyer's creditworthiness, he may insist upon "cash in advance." If the buyer wants to confirm that the goods have been shipped, the term **documents against payment** can be used. In such a case, the seller agrees to deliver a bill of lading to a bank in the buyer's country so that the buyer can confirm that the goods have been shipped. The bank is then to deliver the bill of lading (which is also title to the goods) to the buyer after the buyer delivers a receipt from the seller acknowledging that the seller has received payment. If the buyer insists upon taking delivery before making payment, a **documents against acceptance** term can be used. In this event, the buyer will instruct a bank in the seller's country to release payment only on the bank's receipt of an acknowledgement of delivery issued by the buyer.

documents against acceptance: Term in a sales contract that provides for the buyer to deliver payment to a bank for release to the seller after the seller delivers to the bank a receipt acknowledging that the buyer has accepted the goods.

None of these terms are used very often. In part, this is so because they imply that both sides distrust each other. To avoid this, contracting parties use a "letter of credit" (or "documentary credit" or "banker's credit" or, simply, a "credit").[60]

---

[60]"Letter of credit" is the term most often used in English-speaking countries. "Documentary credit," which is a literal translation of the French "crédit documentaire," and similar terms in other languages, is widely used in the rest of the world. It is the term preferred by the Paris-based International Chamber of Commerce.

letter of credit: An instrument issued by a bank or other person at the request of an account party that obliges the issuer to pay to a beneficiary a sum of money within a certain period of time upon the beneficiary's presentation of documents specified by the account party.

account party: The person who requests a bank or some other person to issue a letter of credit.

beneficiary: A person who is not a party to a contract who is designated by a party to receive the benefits of the contract.

A **letter of credit** is an instrument issued by a bank, or other person, at the request of a customer (called an **account party**). It is a conditional agreement between the issuer and the account party that is intended to benefit a third party. In accordance with this agreement, the issuer is obliged to pay a bill of exchange drawn by the account party, up to a certain sum of money, within a stated time period, and upon presentation by the **beneficiary** of documents designated by the account party.[61]

The function of the letter of credit in international sales transactions is to substitute the credit of a recognized international bank for that of the buyer. In such an undertaking, the buyer is the account party, the buyer's bank is the issuing bank, and the seller is the beneficiary. Exhibit 12-16 sets out the chronology of a typical letter of credit transaction. The mechanics and the reasons for using a letter of credit are described in the following oft-quoted passage of Lord Justice Scrutton, from the case of *Guaranty Trust Co. of New York v. Hannay & Co.*[62]

The enormous volume of sales of produce by a vendor in one country to a purchaser in another has led to the creation of an equally great financial system intervening between vendor and purchaser, and designed to enable commercial transactions to be carried out with the greatest money convenience to both parties. The vendor, to help the finance of his business, desires to get his purchase price as soon as possible after he has dispatched the goods to his purchaser; with this object he draws a bill of exchange for the price, attaches to the draft the documents of carriage and insurance of the

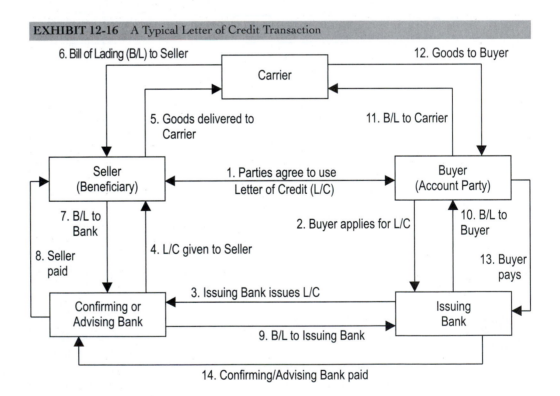

EXHIBIT 12-16 A Typical Letter of Credit Transaction

---

[61]The International Chamber of Commerce's *Uniform Customs and Practices for Documentary Credits* defines a documentary credit or letter of credit as "any arrangement, however named or described, whereby a bank (the issuing bank) acting at the request and in accordance with the instructions of a customer (the applicant for the credit) (i) is to make a payment to or to the order of a third party (the beneficiary) or is to pay or accept bills of exchange (drafts) drawn by the beneficiary, or (ii) authorizes another bank to effect such payment, or to pay, accept or negotiate such bills of exchange (drafts) against stipulated documents, provided that the terms and conditions of the credit are complied with."

[62]*Law Reports, King's Bench,* vol. 1918, pt. 2, p. 659 (1918).

goods sold and sometimes an invoice for the price, and discounts the bill—that is, sells the bill with documents attached to an exchange house.

The vendor thus gets his money before the purchaser would, in the ordinary course, pay; the exchange house duly presents the bill for acceptance, and has, until the bill is accepted, the security of a pledge of the documents attached and the goods they represent. The buyer on the other hand may not desire to pay the price till he has resold the goods. If the draft is drawn on him, the vendor or exchange house may not wish to part with the documents of title until the acceptance given by the purchaser is met at maturity. But if the purchaser can arrange that a bank of high standing shall accept the draft, the exchange house may be willing to part with the documents on receiving the acceptance of the bank. The exchange house will then have the promise of the bank to pay, which, if in the form of a bill of exchange, is negotiable and can be discounted at once. The bank will have the documents of title as security for its liability on the acceptance, and the purchaser can make arrangements to sell and deliver the goods.

Letters of credit exist in a wide variety of forms. The different types of credits are named and defined in Exhibit 12-17. Although they are defined separately, they are not necessarily

EXHIBIT 12-17 Types of Letters of Credit

Name	Description	Comments
Irrevocable	Cannot be altered without the beneficiary's express consent.	Preferred by beneficiaries because it provides the most security.
Revocable	Revocable by the issuing bank.	Disliked by beneficiaries because it provides the least security.
Confirmed	A second bank adds its endorsement to the credit, indicating that it too will make payment against the specified documents.	Gives the beneficiary additional assurance that payment will be made.
Negotiable	Permits the designated bills of exchange to be negotiated at any bank.	Only the issuing bank is obliged to pay. However, if another bank pays, it is assured by the issuing bank that it will be reimbursed.
Back to back	The buyer arranges for two credits: one to finance the purchase from the seller; a second, to be used by the seller, to finance a purchase from the seller's supplier.	Helps an exporter who may have difficulty obtaining local financing to make an export sale by facilitating the acquisition of supplies.
Transferable	Permits a beneficiary to transfer the credit to a second beneficiary.	Has the same advantages as a back-to-back credit, but only one credit has to be issued.
Revolving	A standing arrangement in which the buyer is allowed to replenish the credit after it is drawn down by a seller.	Used by large importers with a good credit record who import regularly from the same seller.
Clean	The beneficiary may obtain payment without presenting any documentation.	Used only where the buyer and issuer have a longstanding relationship with the seller.
Standby	A credit obtained by a seller naming the buyer as the beneficiary.	Used as a guarantee that the goods the seller delivers will perform as promised. If they do not, the buyer may return the goods and obtain reimbursement of the purchase price from the bank issuing this credit.
Sight bill	The buyer's bills of exchange will be paid when presented.	The default arrangement.
Time bill	The buyer's bills of exchange will be paid at a specified date or after a specified time.	Gives the buyer time in which to resell the goods before paying the seller.
Deferred payment	The seller agrees not to present a sight bill of exchange until after a specified period after the documents are presented.	Same as a time bill credit, except that the underlying bill is a sight bill.
Red clause	Advances are made to the seller before the seller presents the required documents.	A way to provide the seller with funds prior to shipment. It is beneficial to middlemen and dealers who require prefinancing.

mutually exclusive. Thus, for example, a letter of credit can be both clean and irrevocable (but not, of course, both revocable and irrevocable).

Governing Law

Uniform Customs and Practices for Documentary Credits: Model rules issued by the International Chamber of Commerce for regulating letters of credit.

Virtually all letters of credit are governed by the International Chamber of Commerce's **Uniform Customs and Practices for Documentary Credits** (UCP).[63] Although it is neither a treaty nor a legislative enactment, most banks incorporate the UCP in the terms of the credits they issue.

A few countries do have legislation governing letters of credit. In the United States, for example, Article 5 of the Uniform Commercial Code has been adopted in all 50 states. However, even where there is a statute, the UCP can still be made to apply by agreement of the parties. The UCC, again as an example, allows the parties to an agreement, including an agreement creating a letter of credit, to vary the statutory terms.[64]

Applying for a Letter of Credit

In most cases, a person who needs a letter of credit must apply to a bank with which he has an existing relationship. In all cases, a "Letter of Credit Application" must be completed (see Exhibit 12-18). The application is not an application for credit, but rather, a set of instructions telling the bank—which will be the issuing bank—what needs to be included in the letter of credit.[65] Of course, if the bank has not already extended a line of credit to the applicant, or if the applicant does not have sufficient funds on deposit in the bank to cover the face value of the credit, the bank may refuse to issue the letter.

The instructions the buyer needs to provide on the application include the following:

- The amount of the credit
- Whether the credit is revocable or irrevocable
- Whether the credit is transferable
- Whether the credit is to be made available by payment, deferred payment, acceptance, or negotiation
- How the credit is to be advised
- If there are bills of exchange involved, the party on whom they are drawn
- Details of the documents required as a prerequisite to making payment
- When the documents need to be delivered
- Whether partial shipments are prohibited
- Whether transshipment is prohibited
- The date and place at which the credit will expire

The Consequences of Not Obtaining a Letter of Credit

When a buyer and seller enter into a contract and the buyer agrees to obtain a letter of credit (or a seller agrees to obtain a standby letter of credit), the consequences of a failure to do so depends on whether the letter was (a) a condition precedent to the formation of the contract or (b) a condition for the performance of the contract. In the first case, there will be no contract, and consequently no breach. In the second, because the contract already exists, the failure to obtain a credit will be a breach that will entitle the injured party to sue for damages.

Lord Justice Denning examined the legal consequences that can flow from an ill-defined agreement to obtain a letter of credit in Case 12–6.

---

[63] 1993 Revision, ICC Publication No. 500 (effective January 1, 1994).

[64] UCC, § 1-102(3). Moreover, in Alabama, Arizona, Missouri, and New York the legislatures have adopted an amendment to the UCC that makes the Code ineffective whenever a letter of credit is subject, by its terms (even in part), to the UCP. *See,* e.g., NY UCC, § 5-102(4).

[65] Although the account party and the issuing bank will be parties to a contract, the applicant is not required to pay any consideration for the issuance, or even the modification, of a letter of credit. *See* UCC, § 5-105.

Applicant **The Importer, Ltd.** **76 Fleet Street** **London, England**	Issuing Bank **IMPORTERS BANK, PLC** **Lnd Branch, 13 Trenton** **Mews** **London, England**

Date of Application: **1 June 2002**	Date and place of expiration of the credit: **14 July 2002** **Buenos Aires, Argentina**

[**X**] Issue by (air) mail
[ ] Issue by air mail with brief advice by telegram or
    other written communication
[ ] Issue by telegram or other written communication
    (which shall be the operative credit instrument)
[ ] Transferable credit
	Beneficiary
	Compañia de Exportes, S.A.
	203 Avenida de las
	Americas
	Buenos Aires, Argentina

Confirmation of the credit to the beneficiary [**X**] Not requested [ ] Requested	Amount **£18,500 (eighteen thousand** **five hundred pounds** **sterling)**

[ ] Insurance will be covered by the applicant	

Partial Shipment [ ] Allowed [**X**] Not Allowed Transshipments [ ] Allowed [**X**] Not Allowed	Credit available with

Shipment/Dispatch/Delivery to **Buenos Aires** not later than **7 July 2002 for** **transportation to London**	by [ ] sight payment [**X**] acceptance [ ] negotiation [ ] deferred payment at against the documents detailed here [**X**] and beneficiary's draft at **sight** on **yourselves**

Goods (brief description without excessive detail) **10,000 pairs of woolen** **mittens @ £ 1.85/pair**	[ ] FOB [**X**] CIF **London** [ ] C&F [ ] Other terms

Commercial invoice and three (3) copies.
Full set of clean on board bills of lading to order and
blank endorsed, marked Freight Paid and Notify The
Importer, Ltd., 76 Fleet Street, London, England.
Insurance and certificate for invoice value plus 10%
covering marine and war risks and including all risks.
Certificates of Origin issued by a Chamber of Commerce
in three (3) copies evidencing that the goods are of
Argentine origin.
Packing lists in three (3) copies.

Documents to be presented within   **7**   days after date of issuance of the transport documents but within the validity of the credit.

Additional conditions

We request you to issue your IRREVOCABLE letter of credit for our account in accordance with the above instructions (marked with an X where appropriate). The credit shall be subject to the Uniform Customs and Practices for Documentary Credit (1993 Revision, Publication No. 500 of the International Chamber of Commerce, Paris, France), insofar as they are applicable. We authorize you to debit our account.

for The Importer, Ltd.

No.   994578-213

Treasurer

Name stamp and authorized signature of the applicant

EXHIBIT 12-18   Letter of Credit Application

Case 12–6   Trans Trust Sprl v. Danubian Trading Co., Ltd.

United Kingdom, England, Court of Appeal, 1952.
All England Law Reports, vol. 1952, pt. 1, p. 970 (1952).

In September 1950, a British seller agreed to sell one thousand tons of rolled steel sheets to a Belgian buyer for a price of 8,025 Belgian francs per 1,000 kilos and to deliver them FOB Antwerp in December 1950. To be able to carry out the contract, the British seller had arranged to buy the steel from an American company, S.A. Azur, which was a wholesaler for the manufacturer, S.A. Metallurgique d'Esperance Londoz.

The seller understood that the buyer was to arrange for a confirmed letter of credit with the Krediet Bank in Brussels, made out in favor of S.A. Azur, which would require the bank to pay cash upon the presentation of shipping documents. The buyer, however, did not arrange for the letter of credit and, when prompted to do so by the seller, sent the seller a letter on October 16, 1950, refusing to do so. The seller then sued the buyer, alleging that the contract it had with the buyer required the buyer to arrange for a letter to be opened and confirmed immediately, and that the buyer's failure to do so constituted a breach of contract. The buyer answered that the contract was conditional on a letter of credit being provided and that, if no such letter was provided, no obligation was to be assumed by the buyer.

The trial judge held that there had been a binding agreement between the parties, that a term of that agreement was that the buyer would see that a credit was opened immediately, and that the buyer was in breach of that agreement. The judge awarded the seller £3,214 5s. 8d. damages, which was the loss of profit suffered by the seller based on the difference between the price at which the seller had agreed to buy from S.A. Azur and the price which it would have received had the contract been performed.

LORD JUSTICE DENNING:

This is another case concerned with the modern practice whereby a buyer agrees to provide a banker's confirmed credit in favor of the seller. This credit is an irrevocable promise by a banker to pay money to the seller in return for the shipping documents. One reason for this practice is because the seller wishes to be assured in advance, not only that the buyer is in earnest, but also that he, the seller, will get his money when he delivers the goods. Another reason is because the seller often has expenses

to pay in connection with the goods and he wishes to use the credit to pay those expenses. He may, for instance, be himself a merchant, who is buying the goods from the growers or the manufacturers and has to pay for them before he can get delivery, and his own bank may only grant him facilities for the purpose if he has the backing of a letter of credit. The ability of the seller to carry out the transaction is, therefore, dependent on the buyer providing the letter of credit, and for this reason the seller stipulates that the credit should be provided at a specified time well in advance of the time for delivery of the goods.

What is the legal position of such a stipulation? Sometimes it is a condition precedent to the formation of a contract, that is, it is a condition which must be fulfilled before any contract is concluded at all. In those cases the stipulation "subject to the opening of a letter of credit" is rather like a stipulation "subject to contract." If no credit is provided, there is no contract between the parties. In other cases a contract is concluded and the stipulation for a credit is a condition which is an essential term of the contract. In those cases the provision of the credit is a condition precedent, not to the formation of a

MAP 12-6   United Kingdom and Belgium (1950)

contract, but to the obligation of the seller to deliver the goods. If the buyer fails to provide the credit, the seller can treat himself as discharged from any further performance of the contract and can sue the buyer for damages for not providing the credit.

The first question is: What was the nature of the stipulation in this case? When the buyers sent their order, they stated in writing on Sept. 25, 1950, that "a credit will be opened forthwith." It was suggested that the buyers were not making any firm promise on their own account, but were only passing on information which had been given to them by their American buyers. The judge did not accept that suggestion and I agree with him. The statement was a firm promise by the buyers by which they gave their personal assurance that a credit would be opened forthwith. At that time there were some discrepancies about gauges and dates of delivery which had to be cleared up, but these were all resolved at the meetings in Brussels, and there was then, as the judge found, a concluded contract by the sellers to sell, and the buyers to buy, the steel for December/January delivery, and it was a part of that contract that the buyers would be personally responsible for seeing that a credit should be opened forthwith. On those findings it is clear that the stipulation for a credit was not a condition precedent to the formation of any contract at all. It was a condition which was an essential term of a contract actually made. That condition was not fulfilled. The sellers extended the time for the credit, but it never came, not even after reasonable notice. The sellers were, therefore, discharged from any further performance on their side, and are entitled to claim damages.

But what is the measure of damages? That is the important question in the case. The price of the goods had steadily risen from the date of the contract onwards and the buyers say that the sellers could at any time have resold the goods for more than the contract price, and are, therefore, only entitled to nominal damages. If the claim of the sellers had been for damages for nonacceptance of goods or for repudiation of the obligation to take delivery, then the damages would, no doubt, be nominal. But it is none of those things. It is a claim for damages for not providing a letter of credit. The buyers say that, even so, the credit is only a way of paying the price, and that the damages recoverable on that score are only nominal because the seller could resell the goods at a profit. This argument . . . treats the obligation to provide a credit as the same thing as the obligation to pay the price. That is, I think, a mistake. A banker's confirmed credit is a different thing from payment. It is an assurance in advance that the seller will get paid. It is even more than that. It is a chose in action[66] which is of immediate benefit to the seller. It is irrevocably by the banker, and it is often expressly made transferable by the seller. The seller may be relying on it to get the goods himself. If it is not provided, the seller may be prevented from getting the goods at all. The damages he will then suffer will not, in fact, be nominal. Even if the market price of the goods has risen, he will not be able to take advantage of the rise because he will not have any goods to re-sell. His loss will be the profit which he would have made if the credit had been provided. Is he entitled to recover that loss? I think he is, if he can show that such a loss was at the time of the contract foreseeable by the buyer as the probable consequence of a breach. That was clearly the case here. The buyers knew that the sellers could not get the goods at all unless the credit was provided. The foreseeable loss was the loss of profit, no matter whether the market price of the goods went up or down. It is, therefore, the proper measure of damages. ◼

[66*Chose* is French for "a thing." A *chose in action* is a "thing in action." It is the right to bring an action, or suit, in a court of law to procure the return of a thing or the payment of a sum of money.]

Documentary Formalities

Although a letter of credit does not have to be in any particular form, it does need to be (a) in writing, (b) signed by the issuer, and (c) complete and precise.[67] A credit must also clearly

---

[67]UCC, § 5-104 provides: "(1) Except as otherwise required in subsection (1)(c) of Section 5-102 on scope, no particular form of phrasing is required for a credit. A credit must be in writing and signed by the issuer and a confirmation must be in writing and signed by the confirming bank. A modification of the terms of a credit or confirmation must be signed by the issuer or confirming bank.

"(2) A telegram may be a sufficient signed writing if it identifies its sender by an authorized authentication. The authentication may be in code and the authorized naming of the issuer in an advice of credit is a sufficient signing."

UCP, Article 5 provides: "Instructions for the issuance of credits, the credits themselves, instructions for any amendments thereto and the amendments themselves must be complete and precise. In order to guard against confusion and misunderstanding, banks should discourage any attempt to include excessive detail in the credit or in any amendment thereto."

indicate if it is irrevocable. Should there be any doubt, the credit will be interpreted as being revocable.[68] An example of an irrevocable letter of credit is shown in Exhibit 12-19.

Letters of credit must additionally indicate clearly when and how they are to be paid. That is, they must "clearly indicate whether they are available by sight payment, by deferred payment, by acceptance, or by negotiation."[69] Finally, they must also name the bank that is authorized to pay the credit, or to accept bills of exchange drawn in accordance with the letter, or to negotiate the credit.[70]

Advising and Confirming Letters of Credit

advising bank: A bank engaged by the issuer of a letter of credit to advise the beneficiary that it has a credit for delivery and to deliver the credit upon verification of the beneficiary's signature.

Once a bank issues a letter of credit, it will commonly deliver the credit to a correspondent bank located in the beneficiary's county, which will in turn deliver the credit to the beneficiary. The correspondent, formally known as an **advising bank**, assumes no liability for paying the letter of credit. Its only obligation is to the issuing bank, to ensure that the beneficiary is advised and the credit delivered, and to take "reasonable care to check the apparent authenticity of the credit."[71] It does this by comparing the signature on the credit with the authorized signatures it maintains on file.

An issuing bank may also request another bank to confirm an irrevocable letter of credit. A confirmation is an independent promise by a **confirming bank** that it will pay, accept, or negotiate a credit, as appropriate, when the documents specified in the credit are presented to it and the other terms and conditions of the credit have been complied with.[72] An example of a confirmation is shown in Exhibit 12-20.

confirming bank: A bank that makes an independent promise to pay, accept, or negotiate a letter of credit issued by another bank when the documents named in the credit are delivered to it.

A confirming bank is entitled to reimbursement from the issuing bank if the documents it receives are in order. If they are not, the confirming bank will be left with title to the goods in its own name, and it will have to assume the risk of liquidating them as best it can. A confirming bank also assumes the risk that the issuing bank or the account party may be unable to reimburse it. Again, it would retain title to the goods, so its losses may be partly offset by whatever price it gets from the sale of the goods.

The Obligations of Banks

An issuing bank, or any bank that pays, accepts, or negotiates a letter of credit, is obliged to "examine all documents with reasonable care to ascertain that they appear on their face in accordance with the terms and conditions of the credit."[73] If a paying, accepting, or negotiating bank believes the documents are irregular, it is required to pass them along to the issuing bank for the latter to determine whether it will honor or refuse them. The issuing bank must do so "on the basis of the documents alone."[74]

One should note that the issuing bank's obligations only relate to the appearance of the documents. So long as the documents appear regular on their face, the bank must pay. A bank is not to concern itself with matters "off the document," such as the condition of the goods, or even their existence.[75] This was emphasized in *Maurice O'Meara Co. v. National Park Bank of New York.* In that case, the issuing bank refused to pay on a letter of credit because it said that it had a reasonable doubt about the quality of goods (newspaper print) involved. The seller,

---

[68]UCP, Article 7 states: "(a) Credits may be either [i] revocable, or [ii] irrevocable. (b) All credits, therefore, should clearly indicate whether they are revocable or irrevocable. (c) In the absence of such indication the credit shall be deemed to be revocable."

[69]*Id.*, Article 11(a).

[70]*Id.*, Article 11(b).

[71]*Id.*, Article 8.

[72]*Id.*

[73]*Id.*, Article 15.

[74]*Id.*, Article 16(b).

[75]*Id.*, Article 17 provides: "Banks assume no liability or responsibility for the form, sufficiency, accuracy, genuineness, falsification, or legal effect of any documents, or for the general and/or particular conditions stipulated in the documents or superimposed thereon; nor do they assume any liability or responsibility for the description, quantity, condition, packing, delivery, value, or existence of the goods represented by any documents, or for the good faith or acts and/or omissions, solvency, performance, or standing of the consignor, the carriers, or the insurers of the goods, or any other person whomsoever."

IRREVOCABLE LETTER OF CREDIT Number **07889**	Issuing Bank IMPORTERS BANK PLC London Branch, 13 Trenton Mews London WC1, England
Place and date of issue **London, 15 June 2002**	Beneficiary **Compañia de Exportes, S.A.** **203 Avenida de las Americas** **Buenos Aires, 1109 Argentina**
Date and place of expiration of the credit **London, 14 July 2002, at the counters of the advising bank**	
	Amount **£18,500 (eighteen thousand five hundred pounds sterling)**
Applicant **The Importer, Ltd.** **76 Fleet Street** **London, England**	[ ] Insurance will be covered by applicant
Advising Bank **Banco del Sur** **47 Calle Corto** **Buenos Aires** **1117 Argentina**	Credit available with by [ ] sight payment [**X**] acceptance [ ] negotiation [ ] deferred payment at against the documents detailed here
Partial Shipment [ ] Allowed [**X**] Not Allowed Transshipments [ ] Allowed [**X**] Not Allowed	

Shipment/Dispatch/Taking in charge from/at
 Buenos Aires
 for transportation to:
 London
	[**X**] and beneficiary's draft at **sight**
	 on **Banco del Sur**
	         47 Calle Corto, Buenos
	         Aires, 1117 Argentina

SIGNED INVOICE IN THREE (3) COPIES certifying that the goods are in accordance with The Importer, Ltd.'s Order No. 0791 of 22 May 2002.

FULL SET OF CLEAN ON BOARD BILLS OF LADING to order and blank endorsed, marked Freight Paid and Notify The Importer, Ltd., 76 Fleet Street, London, England.

INSURANCE AND CERTIFICATE for invoice value plus 10% covering marine and war risks and including all risks.

CERTIFICATES OF ORIGIN issued by a Chamber of Commerce in three (3) copies evidencing that the goods are of Argentine origin.

Packing lists in TRIPLICATE.
covering woolen mittens, CIF, London.

Documents to be presented within   **7**   days after date of issuance of the transport documents but within the validity of the credit.

Additional conditions

We hereby issue this IRREVOCABLE letter of credit in your favor. It is subject to the Uniform Customs and Practices for Documentary Credit (1993 Revision, Publication No. 500 of the International Chamber of Commerce, Paris, France), insofar as they are applicable. The number and state of the credit and the name of our bank must be quoted in all drafts requested if the credit is available by negotiation, each presentation must be noted on the reverse of this advice by the bank where the credit is available.

IMPORTERS BANK PLC
London Branch

This document consist of   **1**   signed page(s)

EXHIBIT 12-19   An Irrevocable Letter of Credit

Notification of **IRREVOCABLE LETTER OF CREDIT**	Advising Bank Number **07889** **BANCO DEL SUR** 47 Calle Corto Buenos Aires, 1117 Argentina

Issuing Bank **Importers Bank, Plc.** **London Branch** **13 Trenton Mews** **London, England**	Reference Number of Advising Bank **1534**
	Place and date of notification **Buenos Aires, 17 June 2002**
Reference Number of Issuing Bank **07889**	Amount **£18,500 (eighteen thousand five hundred pounds sterling)**

Applicant **The Importer, Ltd.** **76 Fleet Street** **London, England**	Beneficiary **Compañia de Exportes, S.A.** **203 Avenida de las Americas** **Buenos Aires, Argentina**

We have been informed by our correspondent (the issuing bank above) that the letter of credit described above has been issued in your favor. Please find enclosed the advice intended for you.

PLEASE CHECK THE CREDIT TERMS CAREFULLY. If you do not agree with the terms and conditions or if you feel that you are unable to comply with any of the terms and conditions, please ARRANGE AN AMENDMENT OF THE CREDIT THROUGH YOUR CONTRACTING PARTY (the applicant for the credit).

[   ] This notification and the enclosed advice are sent to you without engagement on our part.

[**X**] As requested by our correspondent, we hereby confirm the credit described above.

BANCO DEL SUR

EXHIBIT 12-20 Confirmation of an Irrevocable Letter of Credit

who was forced to sell the goods at a loss, sued the bank. In its decision in favor of the seller, the court said:[76]

> [The letter of credit] . . . was in no way involved in or connected with, other than the presentation of the documents, the contract for the purchase and sale of the paper mentioned. That was a contract between buyer and seller, which in no way concerned the bank. The bank's obligation was to pay sight drafts when presented if accompanied by genuine documents specified in the letter of credit. If the paper when delivered did not correspond to what had been purchased, either in weight, kind, or quality, then the purchaser had his remedy against the seller for damages. . . . The bank was concerned only in the drafts and the documents accompanying them. This was the extent of its interest. If the drafts, when presented, were accompanied by the proper documents, then it was absolutely bound to make the payment under the letter of credit, irrespective of whether it knew, or had reason to believe, that the paper was not of the tensile strength contracted for. . . . It has never been held, so far as I am able to discover, that a bank has the right or is under an obligation to see that the description of the merchandise contained in the documents presented is correct.

The Rule of Strict Compliance

rule of strict compliance: A bank may reject a document submitted by a beneficiary seeking to obtain payment on a letter of credit when the document does not exactly comply with the description stated in the credit.

In determining whether the documents submitted by the beneficiary are in order, a bank is entitled to apply the so-called **rule of strict compliance**. In other words, a bank may reject documents that do not exactly comply with the terms specified in the letter of credit. For example, in the case of *Moralice (London), Ltd. v. E. D. and F. Man,* an English court held that an issuing bank had properly refused to pay on a letter of credit involving the shipment of 5,000 bags when the bill of lading the seller presented indicated that only 4,997 bags had been shipped.[77] Similarly, an American court, in the case of *Beyene v. Irving Trust Co.,* held that the misspelled name ("Soran" instead of "Sofan") of the person entitled to notice of the arrival of the goods being shipped was a material discrepancy that relieved a confirming bank from its duty to honor a letter of credit.[78]

Amendments

Discrepancies can come about in documents in a wide variety of ways, including typographical errors and simple mistakes. In cases where only a minor discrepancy exists, banks will commonly obtain a written waiver from the account party. If there is a major discrepancy or if the seller is unable to perform as originally agreed, the letter of credit can be amended. Amendments, however, require the approval of the issuing bank, the confirming bank (if there is one), and the beneficiary.[79]

Waiver

Should an issuing bank be notified of a discrepancy, it has "a reasonable time in which to examine the documents and to determine . . . whether to take up or to refuse the documents."[80] If it fails to act in a timely fashion or if it fails to return the documents to the person who presented them, "it is precluded from claiming that the documents are not in accordance with the terms and conditions of the credit."[81] In other words, failure to act is tantamount to an implied waiver.

Fraud

fraud: A knowing misrepresentation made with intent of causing another to rely upon it to the latter's detriment.

Suppose a bank is aware that the seller has perpetrated a **fraud** on the buyer. For example, suppose that a seller delivers mislabeled goods to a carrier to obtain the documents it needs to collect against a letter of credit. The documents themselves are obviously genuine. May the

---

[76]*New York Reports,* vol. 239, p. 386 (1925).
[77]*Lloyd's Reports,* vol. 2, p. 533 (1954).
[78]*Federal Reporter, Second Series,* vol. 762, p. 4 (2nd Circuit Ct. of Appeals, 1985).
[79]UCP, Article 10(d).
[80]*Id.,* Article 16(c).
[81]*Id.,* Article 16(e).

issuing bank pay the seller if it knows of this fraud? The answer is yes. The UCP states that "banks assume no liability or responsibility for the form, sufficiency, accuracy, genuineness, falsification or legal effect of any documents."[82]

The harder question is: May the bank refuse to pay on the credit when the underlying transaction is fraudulent? If the letter of credit is revocable, the answer is obviously yes. If the credit is irrevocable, the answer seems to be no. The UCP states that the obligation to pay on an irrevocable letter of credit "constitutes a *definite undertaking* of the issuing bank, provided that the stipulated documents are presented and the terms and conditions of the credit are complied with."[83] The UCP also states that "credits, by their nature, are separate transactions from the sales or other contracts on which they may be based and banks are in no way concerned with or bound by such contracts."[84] Read together, these two provisions suggest that the issuing bank must pay, regardless of any underlying fraud.

The suggestion in the UCP is supported by case law. In the case of *Discount Records, Ltd. v. Barclays Bank, Ltd.*, an English court was asked to enjoin payment of an irrevocable credit on an allegation of fraud. Judge Megarry refused, observing: "I would be slow to interfere with bankers' irrevocable credits, and not least in the sphere of international banking, unless a sufficiently good cause is shown; for interventions by the court that are too ready or too frequent might gravely impair the reliance which, quite properly, is placed on such credits."[85]

Nonetheless, Judge Megarry's decision and the UCP leave open the possibility that a court may intervene in exceptionally grievous circumstances. Case 12–7 is a famous example of just such a case.[86]

---

[82]*Id.*, Article 17.

[83]*Id.*, Article 10(a). The UCC takes a slightly different stand. UCC, § 5-114(2), provides: "Unless otherwise agreed when documents appear on their face to comply with the terms of a credit but a required document does not in fact conform to the warranties made on negotiation or transfer of a document of title (Section 7-507) or of a certificated security (Section 8-306) or is forged or fraudulent or there is fraud in the transaction:

"(a) the issuer must honor the draft or demand for payment if honor is demanded by a negotiating bank or other holder of the draft or demand which has taken the draft or demand under the credit and under circumstances which would make it a holder in due course (Section 3-302) and in an appropriate case would make it a person to whom a document of title has been duly negotiated (Section 7-502) or a bona fide purchaser of a certificated security (Section 8-302); and (b) in all other cases as against its customer, an issuer acting in good faith may honor the draft or demand for payment despite notification from the customer of fraud, forgery, or other defect not apparent on the face of the documents but a court of appropriate jurisdiction may enjoin such honor."

[84]UCP, Article 3. Similarly, Article 4 provides: "In credit operations all parties concerned deal in documents, and not in goods, services and/or other performances to which the documents relate."

[85]*All England Law Reports*, vol. 1975, pt. 1, p. 1075 (Chancery Division, 1974).

[86]A recent case examining the spread of the rule suggested in Discount Records, Ltd. v. Barclays Bank, Ltd. and set out in Sztejn v. J. Henry Schroeder Banking Corp. to most English-speaking jurisdiction is The Inflatable Toy Co. Pty Ltd. v. State Bank of New South Wales, *New South Wales Unreported Judgments* (1998), BC9405157 (Supreme Ct. of New South Wales, Equity Division, 1994).

Case 12–7   Sztejn v. J. Henry Schroeder Banking Corp.

United States, New York County Supreme Court, Special Term, 1941.
New York Supplement, Second Series, vol. 31, p. 631 (1941).

Transea Traders in India contracted to sell hog bristles to Sztejn, the plaintiff. At the request of Sztejn, the J. Henry Schroeder Banking Corp. (Schroeder), the defendant,

issued an irrevocable letter of credit in favor of Transea covering the shipment of the hog bristles and payable upon presentation of certain documents, including a maritime bill of lading. Transea allegedly filled 50 cases with cow hair and other rubbish and delivered these to the carrier in order to obtain the required bill of lading. This bill, along with the other required documents, and a draft payable to Transea, were presented to Schroeder by the

Chartered Bank of India, acting as an agent for Transea. Before Schroeder could pay on the credit, Sztejn brought this action against Schroeder to enjoin it from doing so. Schroeder asked the court to dismiss the case.

JUSTICE SHIENTAG:

One of the chief purposes of the letter of credit is to furnish the seller with a ready means of obtaining prompt payment for his merchandise. It would be most unfortunate interference with business transactions if a bank before honoring drafts drawn upon it was obliged or even allowed to go behind the documents, at the request of the buyer and enter into controversies between the buyer and the seller regarding the quality of the merchandise shipped. . . . Of course, the application of this doctrine presupposes that the documents accompanying the draft are genuine and conform in terms to the requirements of the letter of credit.

However, I believe that a different situation is presented in the instant action. This is not a controversy between the buyer and seller concerning a mere breach of warranty regarding the quality of the merchandise; on the present motion, it must be assumed that the seller has intentionally failed to ship any goods ordered by the buyer. In such a situation, where the seller's fraud has been called to the bank's attention before the drafts and documents have been presented for payment, the principle of independence of the bank's obligations under the letter of credit should not be extended to protect the unscrupulous seller. It is true that even though the documents are forged or fraudulent, if the issuing bank has already paid the draft before receiving notice of the seller's fraud, it will be protected if it exercised reasonable diligence before making such payment. However, in the instant action Schroeder has received notice of Transea's active fraud before it accepted or paid the draft. . . .

Although our courts have used broad language to the effect that a letter of credit is independent of the primary contract between the seller and buyer, that language was used in cases concerning alleged breaches of warranty; no case has been brought to my attention on this point involving an intentional fraud on the part of the seller which was brought to the bank's notice with

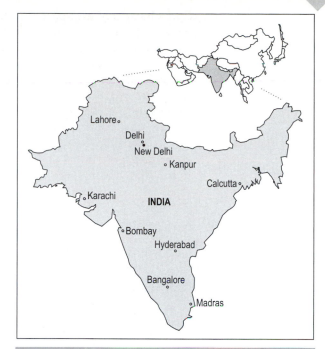

MAP 12-7   India (1941)

the request that it withhold payment of the draft on this account. The distinction between a breach of warranty and active fraud on the part of the seller is supported by authority and reason. As one court has stated: "Obviously, when the issuer of a letter of credit knows that a document, although correct in form, is, in point of fact, false or illegal, he cannot be called upon to recognize such a document as complying with the terms of a letter of credit." . . .

While the primary factor in the issuance of the letter of credit is the credit standing of the buyer, the security afforded by the merchandise is also taken into account. In fact, the letter of credit requires a bill of lading made out to the order of the bank and not the buyer. Although the bank is not interested in the exact detailed performance of the sales contract, it is vitally interested in assuring itself that there are some goods represented by the documents.

Accordingly, the defendant's motion to dismiss . . . is denied. ■

Fraud in the Collection Process

In addition to a fraud by the buyer, a collecting bank may also perpetrate fraud. To illustrate: X Company agrees to sell a large number of widgets to Y Corp., and Y Corp. arranges for Bank I to issue a letter of credit that requires X Company to present a bill of lading as a prerequisite to being paid. X Company is not able to deliver all of the widgets ordered and it has to alter the bill of lading in order for the bill to comply with the requirements of the letter of credit. X Company takes the letter of credit and the bill of lading to Bank C. X Company is a longtime customer of Bank C, and X Company owes Bank C substantial sums. Bank C realizes that if X Company does not collect on the letter of credit that X will be bankrupt and unable to pay any of its obligations. Bank C agrees to pay the letter of credit, even though it knows that X altered the bill of lading. But it does so only if X will agree to use the money to first pay off the loans it has from Bank C. X Company agrees. Bank C pays and X turns over the letter of credit and the bill of lading. Bank C, in turn, forwards the credit and the bill to Bank I, demanding to be reimbursed. In the case of *Pubali Bank v. City National Bank*, which involved a similar (but more complex) set of facts, the court held that the issuing bank did not have to pay. The court said that because the paying bank had participated in the fraud, it could "not hide behind the cloak" of a neutral collecting bank. The paying bank was therefore liable for the money it had paid out.[87]

Rights and Responsibilities of the Account Party

The account party's rights and obligations are based on two contracts: the underlying contract with the beneficiary (usually the seller) and the contract with the issuing bank relating to the letter of credit. Ordinary contract law determines the account party's rights under the first contract. International practice limits the account party's rights under the second contract.

The main limitation on an account party's rights under the contract with the issuing bank is the doctrine of privity. That is, because the account party is in privity (i.e., in a contractual relationship) only with the issuing bank, it can look only to the issuing bank for performance. In other words, it has no right to bring an action against the advising or confirming banks based on their contract with the issuing bank.

To illustrate, in the case of *Auto Servicio San Ignacio v. Compañia Anonima Venezolana de Navigación*, an account party sued a confirming bank for its negligence in failing to verify the authenticity of a bill of lading containing misleading information and in honoring the related letter of credit. Judge Schwarz dismissed the complaint, observing that the confirming bank owed a duty only to its customer, the issuing bank, and not to the issuing bank's customer, the account party, even though that party was involved in the underlying contract.[88]

Rights and Responsibilities of Beneficiaries

The right of beneficiaries to collect on letters of credit is based, not on contract, but on commercial practice. This is important, because it means that the beneficiary has no subsidiary contractual rights with respect to the letter of credit transaction. UCP, Article 6, puts it plainly: "A beneficiary can in no case avail himself of the contractual relationships existing between the banks or between the applicant for credit and the issuing bank."

Before a beneficiary is entitled to collect on a letter of credit, he must comply with the terms and conditions of the credit and present to the issuer (or the issuer's agent) the documents designated in the credit.[89] Commonly, these include

- a certificate of origin—to comply with customs requirements;
- an export license and/or a health inspection certificate—to show that the goods are approved for export;
- a certificate of inspection—to show that all of the goods have been shipped;
- a commercial invoice—to identify the shipment;
- a bill of lading—to show title to the goods; and
- a marine insurance policy.

As soon as a letter of credit is delivered to a beneficiary for advisement, he needs to examine it carefully to make sure that it reflects the underlying agreement he has with the account party. Changes can be made by amendment, but they need to be made promptly.[90]

---

[87]*Federal Reporter, Second Series,* vol. 676, p. 1326 (Ninth Circuit Ct. of Appeals, 1982).
[88]*Federal Supplement,* vol. 586, p. 259 (Dist. Ct. for E. Dist. of Louisiana, 1984).
[89]UCP, Article 10(a).
[90]*Id.,* Article 10(d).

standby letter of credit:
A letter of credit obtained by a buyer naming the seller as a beneficiary.

Standby Letters of Credit

To ensure that a seller will perform, a buyer can insist that the seller procure a **standby letter of credit**. Standby credits are most commonly used in situations where the seller is delivering a product that the buyer needs time to evaluate, such as a stand-alone factory or a computer installation. If the goods delivered do not perform as promised, the buyer may be left in the awkward position of absorbing the loss or suing the seller. To avoid this, the buyer may insist that the seller arrange for an irrevocable credit, one that will reimburse the buyer in the event that the goods do not perform.

H. FINANCING FOREIGN OPERATIONS

Multinational enterprises cannot always generate internally all of the funds they need for capital investment and operating expenses. To expand, to avoid cash flow problems, and for a variety of other reasons, they have to turn to the world's capital markets, and to governmental and intergovernmental investment and development programs.

Private Sources of Capital

As we discussed in Chapter 6, both equity and debt funding are available from the private sector to finance the operations of multinational ventures. **Equity funding** is generally available from stock exchanges, although it is not uncommon, especially for smaller firms, to raise funds privately. **Debt funding** is available in the multinational enterprise's home country, in its host countries, and now, more commonly, in a large number of so-called "capital-exporting" countries.[91]

equity funding:
Investments in the capital of a company.

debt funding: Loans to a person or company.

Governmental Sources of Capital

Both host and home governments provide capital for foreign investors.

Host Country Development Banks and Government Agencies

As discussed in Chapter 5, virtually every country—including less developed and developing nations—has an established bureaucracy that promotes local investment. Many have development banks that provide low-interest-rate, long-term loans to foreign investors. Morocco's Banque Nationale pur le Development Economique and Greece's National Investment Bank for Industrial Development are just two examples.

Information about investment opportunities in host countries is available from their embassies and consulates. A current list of embassies and consulates can be found in the *Europa Encyclopedia*. Most embassies and consulates also have Web sites.[92]

Home Country Import and Export Financing Agencies

Virtually every developed country has a variety of agencies that finance imports and exports. In the United States, for example, the U.S. Agency for International Development (AID) lends money directly to foreign governments to finance purchases from American exporters. As discussed in Chapter 2, the U.S. Overseas Private Investment Corporation (OPIC) provides loans, loan guarantees, and insurance to American firms to underwrite activities in developing countries. The U.S. Export-Import Bank promotes international trade by making loans to both American importers and foreign exporters.[93] And the U.S. Small Business Administration provides loans to American exporters.[94]

---

[91]WorldHot.com maintains links to 100 international capital venturers at www.worldhot.com/business/venturecapital/.

[92]For a list of embassy and consulate Web sites *see* www.embassyworld.com/embassy/directory.htm.

[93]Information about sources of export financing in the United States is available from the U.S. Department of Commerce's Commercial Service on the Internet at www.ita.doc.gov/uscs/.

    The United Nations also publishes *Business Development Online* on the Internet. It provides information on projects financed by the leading development banks, including the African, Asian, Caribbean, Inter-American, and North American development banks; the European Bank for Reconstruction and Development; and the World Bank. *See* www.devbusiness.com/.

[94]The Small Business Administration's international trade loans are described at www.sba.gov/financing/frinternational.html.

Regional and International Development Agencies

A number of regional development agencies promote investment within their regions. The African Development Bank,[95] the Asian Development Bank,[96] the Central American Bank for Economic Integration,[97] the European Bank for Reconstruction and Development,[98] the European Investment Bank,[99] and the Inter-American Development Bank[100] are the principal examples.

The world's development bank is the International Bank for Reconstruction and Development (IBRD), commonly called the World Bank.[101] The World Bank, together with its two subsidiary agencies, the International Development Association (IDA) and the International Finance Corporation (IFC), have a combined capital of more than $107 billion for investment, primarily in the less developed and the developing countries of the world.[102]

The World Bank and the IDA provide funds directly to governments. The IFC, on the other hand, provides funds to private companies.

I. COUNTERTRADE

countertrade: Any transaction linking exports and imports of goods or services in addition to, or in place of, a financial settlement.

Not all international trade involves the sale of goods or services for a monetary price. Often what is exchanged is not money, but goods or services. Such an exchange, when it is made in addition to, or in place of, a financial settlement, is known as a **countertrade**.

Contracting parties agree to countertrade for a number of reasons: when the buyer lacks commercial credit or a convertible currency; when the buyer wants to exploit a favorable market position to obtain better terms; or when a government purchaser seeks to protect or stimulate the output of domestic industries, or maintain the balance of its overseas trade. A number of transactions fit the definition of a countertrade, including:

- *Barter:* The exchange of a seller's goods or services for a buyer's goods or services.
- *Buyback:* An arrangement in which an exporter provides equipment or technology and the buyer uses it to produces goods that are used to pay for the equipment or technology.
- *Counter purchase:* A business deal in which the parties enter into two separate contracts specifying the goods or services to be delivered under the first contract and then the goods or services to be delivered under the second contract at a later date. Such an arrangement allows for performance of the first contract to go ahead when the performance of the second needs to be delayed. An example of a counter purchase is the delivery of goods in exchange for agricultural produce that is to be harvested at a later date.
- *Offset:* An agreement between a seller of high-priced items (such as military aircraft) and a government procurement agency in which the seller agrees to buy goods from the purchasing country to "offset" the negative effects of the large foreign purchase on the country's balance-of-payments account.
- *Production sharing:* A transaction, similar to a buyback, but used in mining and energy projects where the developer is paid out of a share of a mine or well's production.
- *Swap:* An agreement used when both parties (usually one of which is a government) face large debt burdens. It involves the exchange of a monetary debt for another form of debt, such as an equity share or an obligation to deliver products goods or services.
- *Tolling:* A foreign supplier employs a processor to process raw materials that the processor cannot afford to purchase. The supplier then sells the processed goods to a third party to pay for the processing.

A countertrade is agreed to by negotiation and contracting. The basic terms of a countertrade contract are the same as those for any other contract. They include: a description of the

---

[95]The African Development Bank's Web site is at www.afdb.org/.
[96]The Asian Development Bank's Web site is at www.adb.org.
[97]The Central American Bank for Economic Integration's Web site is at bcie.cabei.org.
[98]The European Bank for Reconstruction and Development's Web site is at www.ebrd.com/.
[99]The European Investment Bank's Web site is at www.eib.org.
[100]The Inter-American Development Bank's Web site is at www.iadb.org/.
[101]The World Bank Group's Web site is at www.worldbank.org/.
[102]*See* Frequently Asked Questions about the World Bank at www.worldbank.org/html/extdr/faq/ faqf98-47.htm.

goods or services, the time and place for performance, the price (if money is to be exchanged), guarantees and warranties, remedies in the event of a breach, the governing law, and agreement as to the settlement of disputes. The United Nations Commission on International Trade Law's (UNCITRAL's) *Legal Guide on International Countertrade Transactions* provides detailed guidance for entering into a countertrade contract.[103]

The next reading examines the benefits and shortcomings of countertrades.

_____

[103]The *Guide* is available in Arabic, Chinese, English, French, Russian, and Spanish at www.uncitral.org/english/texts/sales/countertrade.htm.

Reading 12–1 The Pros and Cons of Countertrade

Ross Davis, "A Deal With Strings Attached."
Financial Times, p. 8 (July 18, 2002).

When governments do international trade deals, what they buy is not always the chief consideration. As a recent U.S. Department of Commerce report to Congress explained: "Some governments readily admit that they are no longer concerned with the price or quality of the defense systems purchased but rather with the scope of the offset package offered.

"Recently, the Czech Republic announced that in competition for its jet fighter procurement, offset would be the deciding factor as opposed to technical and performance criteria and price." Such nuggets help explain why interest is taking off in offset—or countertrade, as this form of finance through reciprocal trade is also known.

According to Trade Partners U.K., a U.K. government agency that promotes British companies abroad, between 5 percent and 40 percent of world trade is countertrade-related, an indication of how substantial a part it now plays in international political and commercial transactions.

Countertrade is also growing. For example, it is spreading from arms and aerospace purchases to civil infrastructure projects. In a move likely to be followed by other Gulf states, the Kuwaiti Finance Ministry has begun requiring countertrade commitments from "all foreign companies, or national companies acting as agents for foreign companies" on civil-sector contracts of more than KD10 million (U.S.$33 million) with the Kuwaiti government.

There are five main strands of countertrade: barter; buyback; counter purchase; tolling; and offset, the biggest of the lot, which in turn divides into direct and indirect offsets. Two or more of the five may be stitched together to create a countertrade and if that is not complicated enough, the terms are sometimes used interchangeably.

Trading is heavy today. *Source:* © The New Yorker Collection from cartoonbank.com. All rights reserved.

In direct offset, the supplier agrees to incorporate materials, components, or sub-assemblies procured from the importer country. It is a way of promoting import substitution and local manufacture of defense or other equipment.

With indirect offset, suppliers enter into long-term cooperation and undertake to stimulate inward investment unconnected to the supply contract—again to support, increase, or diversify the local industrial base. These investments need not be made by the company winning the original contract and may be totally different in nature from the first sale.

Countertrade investments, the Kuwaitis say, promote and stimulate the private sector, attract modern technology, open up investment channels, help in training, and create jobs.

Poor countries also like countertrade, which casts them as "trade partners" of technologically and economically richer countries, rather than aid recipients. Countertrade contracts are also more reliable than pledges of aid.

Countertrade can also help to stifle domestic dissent, especially since South Africa raised its countertrade demands for military deals and is now asking—and getting—not Kuwaiti's 35 percent but 300 percent of the contract price in countertrade investments.

In late 1999, Mosiuoa Lekota, South Africa's Defense Minister, announced that the country was to spend R21.3 billion (then U.S.$3.5 billion—equivalent to half the education budget) on European-made helicopters, jets, Corvettes, and submarines—a move that raised eyebrows even within the ruling ANC. The deal was cut back by a third and the pill sweetened by screwing down the contracts—at a bad time for the arms industry—to a much bigger countertrade commitment than South Africa's normal requirement, which is 30 percent of any state arms purchase of more than U.S.$16 million. For example, a deal with Saab of Sweden and BAE of the U.K., for U.S.$2.5 billion of Hawk trainer jets and Gripen fighter jets, requires a total offset commitment, direct and indirect, of U.S.$8.7 billion, much of it in civil investment.

But countertrade is not universally loved. Some economists argue that, given half a chance, weapons contractors factor the cost of countertrade into the price of the contracts. South Africa's deal may be unique, since few companies could sell arms to South Africa during apartheid. As the first big arms deal in 30 years, it gives manufacturers the change to get a foot in the door—such as equity stakes in Denel, the state-owned arms conglomerate.

Opponents of countertrade say it is a restraint of free trade that costs jobs in the supplier nation. If the U.S. Department of Commerce and Congress are taking an interest in the offset game, it may be because U.S. companies have to comply with offset demands when selling arms abroad, while there is no similar requirement for foreign companies selling into the U.S., other than needing a U.S. presence.

BAE Systems, for example, is interested in acquiring TRW to build up its U.S. base. TRW had to sign up for an "industrial participation" deal with the British Ministry of Defense [MOD] when it won a contract to supply an ocean surveillance information system. Britain requires U.S. and other offshore arms suppliers to place defense and defense-related work in the U.K. on any deal of U.K. £10 million or more.

Indeed, although the U.K. has yet to go as far as the Czech Republic, the "industrial participation" element in a contract bid "contributes to the selection process," according to the MOD. Brinley Salzmann, of the British Defense Manufacturers Offset Group, which represents 62 companies doing business in 92 countries, says: "Our members have between £12 billion and £15 billion in offset obligations outstanding around the world, which equates to the total annual production turnover of the U.K. defense industry."

Expansion of countertrade to the civil sector, thinks John Burge, former head of countertrade at Dresdner Kleinwort Wasserstein, will be a problem for exporters that lack experience in this type of reciprocal trade.

"Other Gulf countries, to begin with, could follow the Kuwaitis; and that's going to be painful for a great number of civil-sector companies around the world who've long thought they don't have to worry about countertrade," says Mr. Burge. "Everybody will be in the same boat—the French, the Germans, the Italians, the Japanese, and the South Koreans—it's not easy finding solutions to countertrade requirements."

How complex some countertrade contracts can get is shown in one current Middle Eastern arms deal that requires the contractor to generate inward investments worth only 30 percent of the contract price within eight years. That may sound simple enough, but the investment has to be in an oil economy where investment in oil is not allowed—and where there is more money chasing permitted investments than the other way around.

As countertrade grows in importance, the British government is putting £250,000 into a new unit to advise novice companies. Baroness Symons, Minister for International Trade and Development, says it is "essential" for U.K. exporters to get to grips with countertrade.

"Many developing countries find it hard to buy much-needed goods or equipment due to a lack of foreign exchange," she says; in some countries, countertrade may be the only effective mechanism for doing business. ■

Chapter Questions

1. Identify the following instruments:
   a. A written promise by a bank to repay money received from a depositor.
   b. written promise to pay another a certain sum of money.
   c. An instrument drawn by one person ordering another to pay a third at a definite future time.
   d. An instrument drawn by one person ordering another to pay a third at presentment or at a stated time after presentment.

   e. An instrument drawn by person A ordering person B to pay person A.

   f. An instrument drawn by one person ordering a bank to pay a third person on demand.

   g. A written promise to pay another a certain sum of money that is secured by personal property.

   h. A written promise to pay another a certain sum of money that is secured by real property.

   i. A written promise to pay another a certain sum of money that is due in installments.

   j. An instrument that serves as a carrier's receipt for goods, evidence of a contract of carriage, and as a document of title.

2. The following instrument was written on a luncheonette napkin: "I, the undersigned, do acknowledge that I owe Vladimir Lenin ten thousand rubles, with interest, payable at Moscow out of the proceeds from the sale next month of my dacha in St. Petersburg. Payment is due on or before six months from this date. Signed at Berlin. *Otto von Bismarck.*" Is this instrument negotiable or nonnegotiable?

3. Muhammad Mussadegh purchased a store in Abadan from Reza Khan for 100,000 pounds sterling. To pay for the store, Mussadegh signed a promissory note that contained the following two clauses: (a) "On or before January 1, 1992, I promise to pay Reza Khan or bearer 100,000 pounds sterling in cash or deliver title to my house in Tehran, at the holder's option"; and (b) "The maker of this promissory note hereby reserves the right to extend the time of payment for six months; and the holder reserves the right to extend the time of payment indefinitely." What are the effects of these clauses on the negotiability of the note?

4. Ben Arnold has been an employee of Tom Jefferson for several years. During that time, Jefferson has relied on Arnold to prepare payroll checks, checks to pay suppliers, etc. Unknown to Jefferson, Arnold is a compulsive gambler who owes large sums of money to various underworld figures. Arnold, who has been threatened with death if he fails to pay on his debts, prepares a check payable to a nonexistent supplier. Jefferson innocently signs the check. Arnold then endorses the check with "Pay to Ben Arnold" and the supplier's name. Later, Arnold takes the check to his bank, endorses it in blank, deposits it in his personal checking account, and then, later still, withdraws the money and flees the country. Meanwhile, Arnold's bank sends the check through the collection process and Jefferson's bank pays the check. When Jefferson discovers that Arnold has abandoned his job and defrauded him of a large sum of money, he demands that Arnold's bank credit his account at his bank. Must Arnold's bank do so? Under the BEA or UCC? Under the ULB?

5. Ms. V, a wealthy art collector in Country W, is interested in buying a rare painting from Mr. Y in Country Z. Both parties agree that the price is to be determined by an independent appraiser. V informs Y that she will send her agent, X, with a check to collect the painting. V draws a check payable to Y, but leaves the amount blank. She gives the check to X and instructs him to deliver it to Y. Without authority, X fills in the amount for 1 million U.S. dollars and presents it to Y, who has, in the meantime, received the appraisal. The appraised price is $750,000. X tells Y that Ms. V had made the check out for $1 million to insure that it would exceed the appraisal price, and that V has instructed X to return with the painting and the difference in cash. Y gives X the painting and $250,000. X delivers the painting, but then disappears with the $250,000 in cash. When V discovers what has happened, she stops payment on her check and offers to pay Y $750,000 for the painting. Y insists that V must pay the check's full face value of $1 million. Is Y correct?

6. Doug Drawer makes out a check for $9 to Phil Payee. Phil cleverly alters the number 9 to a 90 and the written nine to a ninety, then cashes the check at a local convenience store. Must Doug (or Doug's bank) pay $90 to the store? Under the BEA or UCC? Under the ULB?

7. John Johnson, who works for a well-known parcel delivery service, delivered a large package to Pete Peterson, and had Pete sign what Pete believed was an acknowledgment of delivery. The package contained component stereo parts that Pete had ordered from a foreign supplier, and Pete was delighted to receive them. Pete did not give the matter a second thought until several months later when Donna Doe demanded payment of $5,000. Pete discovered that he had signed a three-month negotiable promissory note rather than the acknowledgment of a delivery, and that Donna had innocently purchased the note from John. Must Pete pay the note? Under the BEA or UCC? Under the ULB?

8. Cee Company in Canada agreed to sell 10,000 gallons of maple syrup to Dee Company in Denmark. Dee Company arranged for a letter of credit with its bank in Copenhagen. The credit required payment on the presentation of a bill of lading and an inspection certificate issued by a quality control company, Vigilance, Inc. of Toronto. Cee Company produced both the bill and the inspection certificate. The Copenhagen bank refused to pay because the inspection certificate stated that "based on a sample taken from 5 gallons, the maple syrup is of the kind ordered." The bank argued that the certificate, on its face, did not certify as to the regularity of the entire order. Was the bank correct in refusing payment?

9. Rousseau et Fils has signed a contract to buy 10,000 "new coffee percolators in the manufacturer's original packaging, with standard manufacturer's warranty," from Schwartz, GmBH. Schwartz agrees to ship the percolators CIF, and Rousseau agrees to make payment by means of an irrevocable letter of credit. Rousseau contacts Thermidor Bank, which issues a letter of credit promising to honor a promissory note payable to Schwartz when it is accompanied by an invoice and a clean, on board bill of lading for "10,000 new coffee percolators in the manufacturer's original packaging, with standard manufacturer's warranty." Rousseau learns from Weiss, a competitor of Schwartz, that even though Schwartz had obtained actual bills identifying the goods as "10,000 new coffee percolators in the manufacturer's original packaging, with standard manufacturer's warranty," the percolators were actually used and inoperable. Is there anything that Rousseau can do?

10. In Question 9, would it make any difference if Rousseau had positive proof that a fraud had been perpetrated?

11. In Question 9, would it make any difference if Schwartz's bank had confirmed the letter of credit and paid the promissory note before Rousseau learned of the supposedly defective shipment?

Review Problem

Following the tragic death of the head of the legal department at MegaBranch Industries (MBI), you have become the acting head. You are now responsible (at least for now) for all of the legal concerns of MBI and its many subsidiaries. Of immediate concern are the projects the last head of the department was working on.

1. An MBI subsidiary in State A had agreed to sell goods to a buyer in State B. The subsidiary has also agreed to provide financing in the form of a trade acceptance. It has asked you for instructions on how to draw up a negotiable trade acceptance.

2. An outside law firm employed by MBI recently received payment for a large judgment in favor of MBI. The check was made out to the law firm and it endorsed the check over to MBI. In doing so, the law firm added the qualifying words "without recourse" to its signature. What does this mean? Was it ethical for the law firm to do this?

3. An employee of an MBI subsidiary in State C stole several large promissory notes from the subsidiary's safe. The employee, who had access to the subsidiary's seal and the rubber stamp that makes the treasurer's signature, put the signature and the seal on each of the instruments as endorsements. The employee then negotiated the instruments to a local moneylender, who paid full value for them. The employee has disappeared. Must the maker (one of the subsidiary's largest customers) pay the moneylender on the note? If so, will the maker have any recourse against the subsidiary (which is the payee on the note)? If not, will the moneylender have any recourse against the subsidiary?

4. An MBI subsidiary in State D received payment from a buyer in the form of a negotiable certificate of deposit made out to "bearer." It turns out that the CD had been stolen. Can the subsidiary cash the CD anyway? If not, against whom will it have recourse?

5. A small MBI subsidiary in State E (MBI-E) has promised to buy goods from a seller, Local Enterprises, Ltd., in State F. The subsidiary has agreed to secure an irrevocable letter of credit that authorizes payment upon delivery of a clean bill of lading and all the usual export documents. The subsidiary has asked you for advice on how to apply for a letter of credit. What information should the subsidiary give the bank?

6. Since you helped MBI-E with its letter of credit arrangement with Local Enterprises, Ltd., Local delivered the required documents to a bank in State F that had confirmed the letter of credit. The bill of lading had a notation on it that the goods being shipped had been partially destroyed by water leakage after they were loaded on board the ship. Should the confirming bank pay the seller on the letter of credit? If it does, must the issuing bank reimburse the confirming bank? If so, does the MBI subsidiary have any recourse against either bank?

7. In the previous situation, assume that the water damage was done before the goods were loaded on the ship and this is noted on the bill of lading. Would this make any difference?

8. Assume, in the previous situation, that the seller had bribed the purser on the ship to issue a clean bill even though the goods had been damaged prior to their being loaded on the ship. Also, assume that both the confirming bank and the issuing bank know of this. What difference will this make?

9. MBI has offered to build a new hydroelectric dam for the government of State E. How can MBI and State E (a developing country) go about finding financing for this undertaking (which will cost several hundreds of millions of U.S. dollars)?

CHAPTER

13

Taxation

Chapter Outline

A. PURPOSES OF TAXATION

Taxation schemes are usually created for three basic purposes: to raise revenue for government; to encourage, regulate, or restrict local or foreign investment; or to protect consumers or local producers.

The most common rationale for adopting or changing a particular tax scheme is to improve revenues. For example, the multinational oil companies that developed the petroleum industry in the Middle East encouraged the local governments to impose a corporate income tax. Although this seems irrational at first blush, it was a sound financial move. The countries, rather than taking a percentage royalty on profits (which was the arrangement originally agreed to), imposed an income tax on profits at a slightly higher percentage. The result was an increase in income for both the companies and the countries. This was because the companies could use the taxes they paid to the Middle East countries to offset the taxes they paid to their home country governments. (Royalties, by contrast, cannot—in most countries—be used to offset corporate income taxes.) This meant that the companies paid fewer taxes at home and, even though they were paying more to the host countries, their after-tax profits were larger. A second example is the value-added tax (VAT), which generally produces greater revenues than a sales tax. Introduced less than 50 years ago, the VAT is now a key source of revenue in more than 120 countries.[1] (Income taxes, value-added taxes, and sales taxes will all be discussed in more detail in the following pages.)

By contrast, the most difficult tax scheme for governments to alter is one that protects local producers. Producers are commonly able to lobby the government to maintain a particular

---

[1] Liam Ebrill et al., *The Modern VAT*, p. xiv (2001).

scheme, even though it may run contrary to other governmental objectives. However, as Case 13–1 points out, the protection of local producers is not necessarily a frivolous rationale for a tax scheme, even in times of increased international trade.

Case 13–1   In re Natural Sweet Wines

European Community Commission v. France

European Community, Court of Justice, 1987.
Case 196/85, *Common Market Law Reports*, vol. 1988, pt. 2, p. 851 (1988).

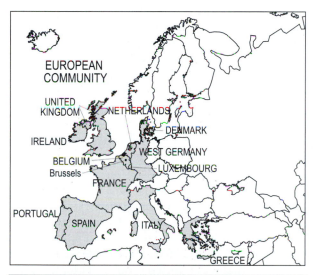

MAP 13-1   European Community (1985)

JUDGMENT

By an application lodged at the Court Registry on June 25, 1985, the Commission of the European Community brought an action under Article 169 [of the European Economic Community Treaty (EEC)[2]] for a declaration that by establishing and maintaining a system of differential taxation in respect of "natural sweet wines" and liqueur wines, the French Republic has failed to fulfill its obligations under Article 95 EEC.

The Commission, in essence, asserts that the provisions of the *Code Général des Impôts* (General Taxation Code, hereinafter referred to as "the Code") governing the consumption duty (*droit de consommation*) and circulation duty (*droit de circulation*) levied on liqueur wines and similar wines are not compatible with Arti-

cle 95 of the Treaty. Under the Code, liqueur wines and similar wines are generally subject to a consumption duty of 6,795 FF per hectoliter of pure alcohol and also to a circulation duty of 22 FF per hectoliter. However, certain such wines, namely natural sweet wines, are taxed at a rate of 2,545 FF and 54.80 FF, respectively. According to the Commission, the scheme is discriminatory inasmuch as it makes entitlement to preferential taxation subject to conditions which are less favorable to products imported from other member states than to comparable domestic (French) products.

Reference is made to the Report for the Hearing for the details of the French legislation in question, an account of the procedure and the submissions and arguments of the parties, which are mentioned or discussed hereinafter only in so far as is necessary for the reasoning of the Court.

CRITERION OF "TRADITIONAL AND CUSTOMARY PRODUCTION"

The Commission asserts that discrimination contrary to Article 95 of the Treaty arises from the fact that French legislation confines the preferential tax scheme to those liqueur wines whose production is "traditional and customary." Although it ostensibly applies without distinction to domestic products and to imports from other member states, that requirement can be fulfilled only by domestic products. Furthermore, the Commission claims that "traditional and customary production" is not an objective criterion since it leaves the authorities a margin of discretion in its application.

The French Government denies the existence of any discrimination. It contends that the concept of "traditional and customary production" has both a historical aspect, alluding to time-honored products closely associated with a particular locality, whose long ancestry is part of their fame, and a technical meaning, referring to oenological rules and practices which codify fair and traditional practices. Moreover, the concept is also used in

---

[2]In November 1993, the European Community became the European Union, the Court of Justice of the European Community became the European Court of Justice, the Commission of the European Community became the European Commission, and the European Economic Community Treaty became the European Community Treaty.]

Community legislation on the common organization of the market in wine.

It should first be pointed out that, as the Court has consistently held . . . at its present stage of development, Community law does not restrict the freedom of each member state to lay down tax arrangements which differentiate between certain products even products which are similar within the meaning of Article 95(1), on the basis of objective criteria, such as the nature of the raw materials used or the production processes employed. Such differentiation is compatible with Community law if it pursues objectives of economic policy which are themselves compatible with the requirements of the Treaty and its secondary law, and if the detailed rules are such as to avoid any form of discrimination, direct or indirect, in regard to imports from other member states or any form of protection of competing domestic products.

More specifically, the Court has held on several occasions that in the present state of Community law Article 95 EEC does not prohibit member states, in the pursuit of legitimate economic or social aims, from granting tax advantages, in the form of exemptions from or reduction of taxes, to certain types of spirits or to certain classes of producers, provided that such preferential systems are extended without discrimination to imported products conforming to the same conditions as preferred domestic products.

The above criteria are satisfied in this instance. With regard to the aims pursued by the contested tax scheme, the French Government explained during the oral procedure that natural sweet wines are made in regions characterized by low rainfall and relatively poor soil, in which the difficulty of growing other crops means that the local economy depends heavily on their production. The French Government maintains that the tax advantage enjoyed by those wines thus tends to offset the more severe conditions under which they are produced, in order to sustain the output of quality products which are of particular economic importance for certain regions of the Community. Such economic policies must be regarded as compatible with the requirements of Community law.

Furthermore, with regard to the extension of the preferential scheme to imported products, it must be concluded that the criterion of "traditional and customary production" applies without distinction to domestic and imported products. There is nothing in the evidence before the Court to suggest that the application of the scheme in fact gives preference to French wines at the expense of wines with the same characteristics from other member states. In particular, it has not been demonstrated that because of physical factors or patterns of production the tax advantage in question oper-

ates solely, or even preponderantly, to the benefit of the French product. It should be added that national provisions which cover both domestic and imported products without distinction cannot be regarded as contrary to Community law merely because they might lend themselves to discriminatory application, unless it is proved that they are actually applied in that way.

Consequently, the objection based on the fact that the benefit of the preferential tax scheme is confined to liqueur wines whose production is "traditional and customary" must be rejected.

REQUIREMENT OF CONTROLS IN THE MEMBER STATE OF EXPORTATION

The Commission further maintains that there is discrimination contrary to Article 95 of the Treaty inasmuch as wines imported from other member states qualify for the preferential tax scheme only if they are subject to controls in the member state of exportation which afford guarantees equivalent to those required of natural sweet wines produced in France. According to the Commission, that requirement has the effect of disqualifying products from other member states which make no provision for analogous controls, and is thus contrary to the principle that national legislation may not impose administrative procedures which cannot be complied with by producers in other member states.

The French Government contests the general thesis of the Commission. It contends that the Member State of importation is entitled to require evidence to enable it to ascertain whether imported products potentially qualifying for a preferential tax scheme do in fact fulfill the necessary conditions.

As the Court has consistently held . . . a member state may not deny a tax advantage to products from another member state on the basis of conditions laid down by its legislation which the imported products cannot fulfill by reason of their geographical situation or of the legislation of the state of production. That principle cannot, however, prevent a member state from making the availability of a tax advantage, whether for imported products or domestic ones, subject to proof that the conditions for granting it have been fulfilled, with the proviso that the evidentiary requirements may not be stricter in respect of imported products than they are for similar national products or disproportionate to the goal pursued, namely to eliminate the risk of fraud.

It follows that the Member State of importation is free to require evidence enabling it to ascertain that the imported products do indeed meet the standards laid down by its national legislation. Such evidence may be furnished, for example, by certificates issued by the authorities or other appropriate bodies of the Member State from which the products originate. Since a certificate such as that can only be issued on the basis of control procedures, the requirement of controls affording guarantees equivalent to those provided under French legislation may also be imposed on liqueur wines imported from other member states as a condition of their qualifying for the preferential tax scheme.

Nevertheless, if they are to be compatible with the principle of proportionality, such provisions must leave the exporting member state free to choose control methods and to designate the authority responsible for the controls, and they must not make recognition of equivalence dependent on the prior negotiation of an agreement between the national authorities concerned.

The evidence before the Court does not suggest that the French provisions in question are in breach of those overriding obligations. The Commission initially stated that the French authorities had decided to treat the wines known as "*Samos vin doux naturel grand cru*" (fine natural sweet wine of Samos) in the same way as natural sweet wines grown in France on the basis of an agreement concluded with the Greek authorities. How-

ever, the French Government denied the existence of such an agreement and explained that the sole purpose of contacting the Greek authorities in that connection had been to obtain the information needed by the French authorities in order to establish whether the conditions for allowing the tax advantage were actually fulfilled in that instance. Since the Commission has not adduced any evidence in support of its contentions to the contrary, it must be concluded that the allegations of an agreement have not been substantiated.

Consequently, the submission based on the fact the liqueur wines imported from other member states qualify for the preferential tax scheme only on condition that there is a system of controls affording equivalent guarantees must also be rejected.

. . . On those grounds, THE COURT, hereby:

1. Dismisses the application.
2. Orders the Commission of the European Community to pay the costs. ■

B. INCOME TAXES

income tax: Compulsory governmental levy on a person's income and profits.

schedular tax model: Imposes different flat taxes on different kinds of income.

global tax model: Imposes uniform (usually progressive) taxes on all types of income.

progressive tax: A tax in which the rate of taxation increases as income increases.

Worldwide, taxes on the income of individuals and the profits of companies are the most widely used basic taxes and the principal source of revenue for most countries. Two "models" may be used to describe (in abstract terms) how governments collect **income taxes**. The **schedular tax model** imposes taxes at flat rates on different sources of income. That is, a different flat rate will be imposed on different kinds of income, such as manufacturing, retail sales, agriculture, or employment income. The advantages of a schedular model include its simplicity in calculating taxes and its ability to encourage, or discourage, development of particular economic sectors within a country. The model has substantial shortcomings, however. It is regressive—that is, it imposes the same tax on the rich (those most able to afford the tax) as it does on the poor (those least able to afford it). It is also anti-entrepreneurial—that is, only the established and well-to-do are encouraged to expand and take risks.

The **global tax model**, imposes uniform rates on all sources of income. In other words, a taxpayer will pay taxes on the total of all income from all sources. Commonly, this is done on a progressive basis (see Exhibit 13-1), a **progressive tax** being one that increases as income increases.[3] For example, in Indonesia, individuals pay taxes as follows:[4]

- On the first 25,000,000 rupiahs   5%
- On the next 25,000,000 rupiahs   10%
- On the next 50,000,000 rupiahs   15%
- On the next 105,000,000 rupiahs   25%
- On income above 200,000,000 rupiahs   35%

---

[3]Normally, with a progressive tax, the higher rates apply only to each higher segment of income, as is the case for Indonesia in the example. However, if the entire amount of income is taxed at the highest rate the progressive tax is being applied according to the so-called "slab" principle. Kuwait, for example, applies income taxes on nonresidents companies at rates that vary from 5 to 55 percent on the total amount of their income. Thus, a nonresident company that earns 10,000 Kuwaiti dinars pays 5 percent or 500 dinars, while a nonresident company that earns 1,000,000 dinars pays 550,000 dinars in taxes.

[4]Unless indicated otherwise, the tax rates cited in this chapter are current as of January 1, 2001. They are from PriceWaterhouseCoopers, *Corporate Taxes 2001–2002: Worldwide Summaries* (2001) and PriceWaterhouseCoopers, *Individual Taxes 2001–2002: Worldwide Summaries* (2001).

Tax and Social Security Comparison Table (by Country)

Country	Tax Rates	Tax System — Global	Tax System — Schedular	Local Income Taxes	Social Security — Employee Contributions	Social Security — Monetary Ceiling on Employee Contribution	Social Security — Employer Contributions	Social Security — Monetary Ceiling on Employer Contribution	Capital Gains — Regular Rates	Capital Gains — Special Rates	Sources — Domestic	Sources — Worldwide	Foreign Tax Relief — Double Taxation Treaties	Foreign Tax Relief — Credit for Foreign Tax Payments	Foreign Tax Relief — Deduction for Foreign Tax Payments	Foreign Tax Relief — Exemption to Extent Subject to Foreign Tax
1. Antigua and Barbuda	None				3%		5%				•					
2. Argentina	9–35%	•			17%	•	32%					•		•		
3. Australia	17–47%	•			1.5%	•	8%	•	•	25%		•	•	•		
4. Austria	21–50%	•			17.7%		21.6%	•				•				
5. Azerbaijan	12–35%	•										•				
6. Bahamas	None															
7. Bahrain	None															
8. Barbados	25–40%	•			8%		9.8%					•				
9. Belgium	25–55%	•		0–8.5%	13%		34%	•		16.5%		•	•			
10. Bermuda	None						12%									
11. Bolivia	13%	•			12.5%	•					•					
12. Botswana	5–25%	•								5–25%		•	•	•		
13. Brazil	15–27.5%		•		8–11%	•						•				
14. Brunei	None															
15. Bulgaria	20–38%	•			6.4%	•	26.3%	•	•	20–38%		•	•	•		
16. Cambodia	5–20%	•										•	•			
17. Cameroon	10–60%	•		16–29%	2.8%	•	12–16.2%	•		20%		•				
18. Canada	17–29%	•			17%	•						•		•	•	
19. Cayman Islands	None															
20. Chile	5–45%	•			20%	•			•			•				
21. China	5–45%	•							•			•				
22. Colombia	20–35%	•			3.4–4.4%		8%			35%		•				
23. Congo (Zaire)	10–60%	•			3.5%		8%			40%	•					
24. Costa Rica	10–25%	•		9%				25%			•					
25. Croatia	15–35%	•		6–18%	20.6%		17%					•	•	•		
26. Cyprus	20–40%	•			6.3%	•	6.3%			20%		•	•	•		
27. Czech Republic	15–32%	•			12.5%	35%						•	•			

EXHIBIT 13-1 Income Taxes for Individuals in 115 Countries (2001)

#	Country					
28.	Denmark	27–35%	25–35%			25%
29.	Dominican Republic	15–25%		2.5%	7%	
30.	Ecuador	5–25%		9.4%		
31.	Egypt	20–32%		11–14%	24–26%	20–40%
32.	Estonia	26%			33%	
33.	Fiji	15–34%				
34.	Finland	14–37%	15–19.5%	1.5%		29%
35.	France	10.5–54%		18–23%	36–46%	26%
36.	Germany	22.9–53%		20.2%	20.2%	
37.	Ghana	5–30%		5%	12.5%	10%
38.	Greece	5–45%		15.9%		30%
39.	Guatemala	15–31%		4.8%	12%	10%
40.	Guyana	20–33.3%		4.8%	7.2%	20%
41.	Hong Kong	2–17%				
42.	Hungary	20–40%		11%	45%	20
43.	India	12.6–30%	Yes		3.7%	20–23.4%
44.	Indonesia	5–35%		2%		
45.	Iran	12–54%		7%	20	
46.	Ireland	20–42%		2–62%	8.5–12%	20–23%
47.	Israel	10–50%	0.9–4.9%	2.7–4.9%	4.9%	
48.	Italy	18–45%		10.9%	20.3–23.3%	12.5–27%
49.	Ivory Coast	1.5–10%		3.2%	4.8%	
50.	Jamaica	25%		4%	9%	7.5%
51.	Japan	10–37%	5–13%	13.6%	14.2%	
52.	Kazakhstan	5–30%			26%	
53.	Kenya	10–30%		5%	5%	10–25%
54.	Korea, South	10–40%	10%		5%	32%
55.	Kuwait	None				
56.	Laos	5–40%		4.5%		
57.	Latvia	25%		9%	26%	
58.	Liechtenstein	1.1–17.8%		4.4%	6.9%	
59.	Lithuania	33%		3%	28%	
60.	Luxembourg	6–46%		10.7%	10.6%	3–23%
61.	Malawi	16–38%		12%	13%	
62.	Malaysia	20–29%		10%	10%	0–30%
63.	Malta	15–35%		13%		
64.	Mauritius	15–25%		3%	8.5%	
65.	Mexico	3–40%		5.2%	20%	
66.	Monaco	None				
67.	Morocco	13–44%		yes		
68.	Mozambique	8–40%		3%	4%	18%

(continued)

Source: PriceWaterhouseCoopers, *Individual Taxes: Worldwide Summaries 2001–2002* (2001).

Country	Tax Rates	Tax System: Global	Tax System: Schedular	Local Income Taxes	Social Security: Employee Contributions	Social Security: Monetary Ceiling on Employee Contribution	Social Security: Employer Contributions	Social Security: Monetary Ceiling on Employer Contribution	Capital Gains: Regular Rates	Capital Gains: Special Rates	Sources: Domestic	Sources: Worldwide	Foreign Tax Relief: Double Taxation Treaties	Foreign Tax Relief: Credit for Foreign Tax Payments	Foreign Tax Relief: Deduction for Foreign Tax Payments	Foreign Tax Relief: Exemption to Extent Subject to Foreign Tax
69. Myanmar	3–30%	•								10%		•	•			
70. Namibia	18–36%	•			0.9%		0.9%					•				
71. Netherlands	3–52%	•			41.2%	•	8%	•		25%		•	•	•		
72. New Zealand	19.5–39%	•										•	•	•		
73. Nigeria	5–25%	•			3.5%	•	6.5%	•		10%		•	•			
74. Norway	13.5–19.5%	•			28%	7.8%	14.1%			28%		•	•		•	
75. Oman	None															
76. Pakistan	20–35%	•							•			•	•			
77. Panama	2–30%	•			8.5%		12.8–17.9%			•		•				
78. Papua New Guinea	25–47%	•								17%		•		•		
79. Paraguay	None				9.5%		16.5%									
80. Peru	15–20%				12–13%		9%		•							
81. Philippines	5–32%	•			2.7–3.5%	•	4.2–6%	•		0.5–10%		•	•	•		
82. Poland	19–40%	•			18.7%		20.4%	•		0–20%		•	•	•		
83. Portugal	12–40%				11%		23.8%									
84. Qatar	None															
85. Romania	18–40%	•			4%		30%			1%		•				
86. Russia	13–35%		•				35.6%					•	•	•		
87. St. Lucia	10–30%	•			5%	•	5%	•	•			•	•	•		
88. Saudi Arabia	None				5%		8–10%						•			
89. Senegal	14–50%		•				7%		•			•				

700

#	Country					
90.	Singapore	12–28%		20%	12%	
91.	Slovakia	12–42%		12%	38%	
92.	Slovenia	17–50%		22.1%	15.9%	30%
93.	Solomon Islands	11–40%		5%	7.5%	
94.	South Africa	34–45%	3–84%			
95.	Spain	15–39.6%		6.4%	30.7%	18%
96.	Sri Lanka	10–35%		8%	15%	10–25%
97.	Swaziland	12–39%				
98.	Sweden	31%	26–33%	7%	32.8%	30%
99.	Switzerland	0.8–13.2%	6.9–18%	6–6.5%	9.5%	
100.	Tahiti	None				
101.	Taiwan	6–40%				
102.	Tanzania	7.5–35%	1%	10%	10%	10%
103.	Thailand	5–37%		1.5%	1.5%	
104.	Trinidad and Tobago	28–35%		2–3%	4–6%	
105.	Turkey	15–45%		14%	19.5%	
106.	Uganda	10–30%		5%	15%	
107.	Ukraine	10–40%		3%	36.5%	
108.	United Kingdom	10–40%		7.6%	10%	
109.	United States	15–39.6%	0–12%	19.1–24.1%	7.7%	30%
110.	Uruguay	None			18.6%	
111.	Uzbekistan	12–36%				
112.	Venezuela	6–34%		4%	9–11%	
113.	Vietnam	10–50%		6%	17%	
114.	Zambia	10–30%		5%	8%	
115.	Zimbabwe	20–53.2%		3%	4.2%	20%

EXHIBIT 13-1 Continued

The global model, especially one with progressive income rates, has the advantages of not being regressive and not being anti-entrepreneurial. On the other hand, it will not encourage development in particular economic sectors.

Of these two models, the schedular model is seldom adopted in its pure form. At present, only Libya uses what can be called a predominantly schedular system, and that is only for income taxes paid by individuals. After personal allowances and other deductions are taken, Libya's individual tax rates are as follows:[5]

Real estate income (based on gross income less 20% for depreciation and maintenance):

- On the first 6,000 dinars   15%
- On the next 4,000 dinars   20%
- On income above 10,000 dinars   25%

Agricultural income: 5%

Commerce, industry, and crafts income (based on net income):

- On the first 12,000 dinars   20%
- On income above 12,000 dinars   35%

Professional income (based on net income—the first 2 years of earnings are exempt):

- On the first 16,000 dinars   20%
- On income above 16,000 dinars   35%

Wages and salaries (based on gross income):

- On the first 1,800 dinars   8%
- On the next 1,200 dinars   10%
- On the next 1,800 dinars   15%
- On the next 1,800 dinars   20%
- On the next 1,800 dinars   25%
- On income above 8,400 dinars   35%

Bank deposit interest income:

- On accounts of more than 5,000 dinars   20%

In contrast to the schedular model, the global model is more likely to be adopted in a relatively pure form. About one-third of the countries listed in the tables in this chapter impose a relatively straightforward global income tax on resident companies, and most (approximately 90 percent) impose a similar tax on resident individuals. Argentina, for example, imposes a flat rate of 35 percent on the net income of companies and a progressive rate, varying from 9 percent to 35 percent, on the net graduated income of individuals.

Some countries modify the global model by imposing different tax rates for particular industries or activities or by varying tax rates depending on how a company is owned or operated. Pakistan, for example, adjusts its company income tax rate by both activity and company form. Thus, it collects a flat 33 percent income tax from all companies, except privately held companies and banking companies. Privately held companies are taxed at 43 percent and banking companies at 58 percent.

C. TAXPAYERS

taxpayer: A person who must pay a tax.

Countries treat both individuals and juridical entities as **taxpayers**—that is, as separate legal entities that must pay taxes. Individuals, of course, are natural persons. Juridical entities—as discussed in Chapter 4—are fictions created by states.

---

[5]Coopers & Lybrand International Tax Network, *1998 International Tax Summaries: A Guide for Planning and Decisions,* p. L-19 (George J. Yost III, ed., 1998).

Company Taxpayers

The juridical entity most commonly subject to taxation is the company. Companies take many forms and a variety of names, but the most common are joint stock companies (or corporations), limited liability companies (or closely held corporations), limited liability partnerships, and general partnerships. (See chapter 4.)

The form that a company takes is important for determining its tax liability. Particular companies may be taxed either at (a) general company rates, (b) special company rates, or (c) individual rates. For example, in the United States, domestic corporations (both publicly traded and privately held) are taxed at general company rates, whereas partners in a partnership (whether a general or a limited partnership) are taxed as individuals. In Thailand, however, publicly traded corporations are taxed at the general company rate, and privately held corporations and limited liability partnerships are taxed at a higher special company rate. (See Exhibit 13-2.)

When a company organized in one country is obliged to pay taxes in another country, the taxing country will categorize the company according to its own rules. In many countries this is done by a central registrar (which is independent of the taxing agency) at the time the company begins doing business within the country. In the United Kingdom, the Registrar of Companies performs this task; in India and Korea it is done by the Central Bank; and in Portugal it is done by both the Commercial Registrar and the Portuguese Foreign Trade Institute. In other countries the taxing agency will determine the appropriate tax category at the time a company submits its tax return.

The categorization of companies is uniformly done by analogy: The central registrar or taxing agency looks for the domestic company that is most like the company to be categorized. In many countries this is done on an *ad hoc* basis—especially in less developed countries and in countries where all juridical entities (stock companies, limited liability companies, partnerships, trusts, etc.) are taxed as entities—but in other countries there are administrative guidelines for making this determination. The U.S. Internal Revenue Service, for example, uses the following factors to determine if a foreign company is equivalent to an American corporation: (1) Are there associates? (2) Is the business carried on for profit? (3) Does the company have continuity of life? (4) Is there centralized management? (5) Do the owners have limited liability? and (6) Are ownership interests freely transferable?[6]

Subordinate Business Structures

In addition to choosing a business form, an international company must also choose the subordinate business structure it will use to carry out its overseas operations. There are four possibilities: representative offices, agencies, branches, and subsidiaries.

representative office: A contact point where interested parties can obtain information about a company. It does not conduct business for the company.

A **representative office** is set up to promote imported products and to provide technical assistance to local importers and distributors. Such an office, however, may not engage directly in commercial activities, such as taking orders, making sales, or collecting debts.[7]

agent: An independent person or company with authority to act on behalf of another.

An **agent** is an individual or local company that acts on behalf of, and under the supervision of, a foreign firm. Unlike a representative office, an agent conducts business on behalf of the foreign firm (or principal), taking orders, making sales, and collecting debts.

branch: Unit or part of a company. It is not separately incorporated.

A **branch** is a unit of a foreign parent company that is normally set up to offer some expertise or service that is unavailable locally. It involves not only the placement of individuals in a particular locale but also the establishment of a facility, such as an assembly plant, mining operation, or service office. In essence, it is a large agency.

subsidiary: Company owned by a parent or a parent's holding company. Unlike a branch, it is separately incorporated.

A **subsidiary** is a locally established or incorporated company that is owned by a foreign parent but that is legally independent of it. Most countries allow foreign parents to maintain 100 percent ownership of a subsidiary, although many require that it be organized as a joint venture, with local citizens or domestic companies sharing in its control.

---

[6]U.S. Treasury Regulations, § 301.7701-1(a).
[7]Representative offices may be established in most countries, with Thailand being the only exception known to the author.

Tax data table — countries 1–30 (Antigua and Barbuda through Ecuador). Columns grouped under: Company Tax Rates; Company Tax Rates Vary By (Income, Activity, Ownership, Local Income Tax); Capital Gains (Not Taxed, Taxed at Regular Rates, Taxed at Special Rates); Sources from Which Income Is Taxed (Domestic, Worldwide); Foreign Branch Tax Rates; Tax on Repatriated Profits; Foreign Tax Relief (Double Taxation Treaties, Credit for Foreign Tax Payments, Deduction for Foreign Tax Payments, Reduced Rate on Foreign Source Income, Exemption to Extent Subject to Foreign Tax).

Country	Company Tax Rates	Vary By: Income	Vary By: Activity	Vary By: Ownership	Vary By: Local Income Tax	Cap Gains: Not Taxed	Cap Gains: Regular Rates	Cap Gains: Special Rates	Sources: Domestic	Sources: Worldwide	Foreign Branch Tax Rates	Tax on Repatriated Profits	Double Taxation Treaties	Credit for Foreign Tax Payments	Deduction for Foreign Tax Payments	Reduced Rate on Foreign Source Income	Exemption to Extent Subject to Foreign Tax
1. Antigua and Barbuda	40%					•				•	40%		•				
2. Argentina	35%						•			•	35%		•				
3. Australia	34%						•			•	34%		•				
4. Austria	34%						•			•	34%		•			•	
5. Azerbaijan	27%									•	10%	10%		•			
6. Bahamas	None					•					None						
7. Bahrain	None					•					None						
8. Barbados	5–40%	•	•				•			•	40%	10%	•				
9. Belgium	28.8–42.2%									•	28.8–42.2%		•			•	
10. Bermuda	None					•						None					
11. Bolivia	25%						•		•		25%						
12. Botswana	5–15%	•					•			•	25%						
13. Brazil	15–25%		•				•			•	15–25%			•			
14. Brunei	30%					•				•	30%			•			
15. Bulgaria	15–20%	•					•			•	15–20%						
16. Cambodia	5–20%		•				•			•	5–20%						
17. Cameroon	38.5%						•			•	38.5%			•			
18. Canada	22.1–29.1%		•		•		•			•	27.6–36.4%	None	•		•		
19. Cayman Islands	None					•											
20. Chile	15–35%	•			•			10–60%		•	35%						
21. China	30.9%				•					•	30.9%	7%	•	•	•		
22. Colombia	35%				•		•			•	35%						
23. Congo (Zaire)	40%				•				•		40%						
24. Costa Rica	10–20%					•			•		10–20%	15%					
25. Croatia	20%									•	20%						
26. Cyprus	20–25%				•			20%		•	20–25%		•				
27. Czech Republic	31%						•			•	31%		•		•		
28. Denmark	30%						•			•	30%		•				
29. Dominican Republic	25%						•			•	25%		•				
30. Ecuador	25–44.4%	•					•			•	25%		•		•		

EXHIBIT 13-2 Company Income Taxes in 115 Countries (2001)

#	Country			
31.	Egypt	34–42.5%		42–42.5%
32.	Estonia	35%	26–35%	35%
33.	Fiji	2–34%	2.5–30%	34%
34.	Finland	29%		29%
35.	France	38.6–39.6%		38.6–39.6%
36.	Germany	26.4%		26.4%
37.	Ghana	8–32.5%	10%	8–32.5%
38.	Greece	37.5%	20–30%	37.5%
39.	Guatemala	31%	10%	31%
40.	Guyana	35–45%		35–45%
41.	Hong Kong	16%		16%
42.	Hungary	18%		18%
43.	India	39.6%	20–22.6%	10–48%
44.	Indonesia	0.1–30%		0.1–30%
45.	Iran	12–54%		12–54%
46.	Ireland	10–25%	20%	10–25%
47.	Israel	36%		36%
48.	Italy	36%	19–36%	36%
49.	Ivory Coast	35%		35% 12%
50.	Jamaica	33.3%		33.3%
51.	Japan	22–30%		22–30%
52.	Kazakhstan	30%		30%
53.	Kenya	30%		37.5%
54.	Korea, South	16–28%	16–44%	16–28%
55.	Kuwait	None		5–55%
56.	Laos	10–45%		10–45%
57.	Latvia	25%		25%
58.	Liechtenstein	7.5–15%	1.2–35.6%	7.5–15%
59.	Lithuania	24%		24%
60.	Luxembourg	20–50%		30%
61.	Malawi	38%		43%
62.	Malaysia	28%		28%
63.	Malta	35%		35%
64.	Mauritius	15–25%		15–25%
65.	Mexico	17.5–35%		17.5–5.35%
66.	Monaco	33.3%		None
67.	Morocco	35–39.6%	25–70%	35–39.6% 10%
68.	Mozambique	10–35%		10–35%
69.	Myanmar	30%	10–40%	5–40%
70.	Namibia	35–55%		35–55%
71.	Netherlands	30–35%		30–35%
72.	New Zealand	33%		33%
73.	Nigeria	20–30%	10%	30%

(continued)

Source: PriceWaterhouseCoopers, *Corporate Taxes: Worldwide Summaries 2001–2002* (2001).

This table shows international corporate tax characteristics for countries numbered 74–98.

Country	Company Tax Rates	Income	Activity	Ownership	Local Income Tax	Not Taxed	Taxed at Regular Rates	Taxed at Special Rates	Domestic	Worldwide	Foreign Branch Tax Rates	Tax on Repatriated Profits	Double Taxation Treaties	Credit for Foreign Tax Payments	Deduction for Foreign Tax Payments	Reduced Rate on Foreign Source Income	Exemption to Extent Subject to Foreign Tax
74. Norway	28%	•			•		•			•	28%		•		•		
75. Oman	5–30%			•				25%		•	5–30%		•				
76. Pakistan	33–58%		•							•	33–58%		•				
77. Panama	30%							2–5%	•		30%						•
78. Papua New Guinea	20–50%	•	•	•			•			•	48%		•	•			
79. Paraguay	4–30%		•					30%		•	4–30%	5%					
80. Peru	20–30%								•		20–30%						
81. Philippines	32%			•	•			5–32%		•	32%	15%	•	•			
82. Poland	28%						•			•	28%		•	•			
83. Portugal	34%						•			•	34%		•	•			
84. Qatar	10–35%				•		•			•	10–35%		•				
85. Romania	25%						•			•	25%		•				
86. Russia	11%	•							•		11%		•				
87. St. Lucia	33.3%		•			•				•	33.3%		•	•	•		•
88. Saudi Arabia	25–30%						•			•	25–30%		•	•			
89. Senegal	35%						•			•	35%		•	•			
90. Singapore	25.5%					•				•	25.5%		•	•			
91. Slovakia	15–29%		•				•			•	29%		•	•			
92. Slovenia	25%		•		•			30%		•	25%		•	•			
93. Solomon Islands	30%		•			•				•	35%						
94. South Africa	15–35%						•		•		35%		•	•			
95. Spain	1–35%						•	0–25%		•	35–40%		•	•	•		
96. Sri Lanka	15–35%					•				•	35%	11.1%	•	•	•		
97. Swaziland	27–30%						•			•	27–30%		•	•			
98. Sweden	28%						•			•	28%		•	•			

99. Switzerland	8.5%	•			•	•	8.5%		•
100. Tahiti	35–50%	•	•		•	•	35–50%		•
101. Taiwan	15–25%				•	•	15–25%		•
102. Tanzania	35%		10%	•	•	•	30%		•
103. Thailand	30%			•	•	•	30%	10%	•
104. Trinidad and Tobago	15–50%	•		•	•	•	15–50%	10%	•
105. Turkey	33%			•	•	•	33%		•
106. Uganda	30%			•	•	•	30%		•
107. Ukraine	30%			•	•	•	30%		• •
108. United Kingdom	10–30%			•	•	•	30%		• •
109. United States	15–39%	•		•	•	•	15–39%	30%	•
110. Uruguay	30%	•			•	•	30%		•
111. Uzbekistan	26–35%			•	•	•	26%	10%	•
112. Venezuela	15–34%	•	25%	•	•	•	15–34%		•
113. Vietnam	10–32%	•		•	•	•	32%		•
114. Zambia	15–45%	•		•	•	•	15–45%		• •
115. Zimbabwe	30.9%		10–20%	•	•	•	30.9%	20%	•

EXHIBIT 13–2 Continued

For tax purposes, the representative office is the most advantageous of the subordinate business structures. Because it does not engage in any commercial activities within the host country, it is not subject to taxation. Such an entity, however, is frequently inadequate to meet other business requirements.

Agencies and branches are treated the same from a tax perspective. Because they are under the direct control of a foreign firm, they generally are subjected to less favorable administrative and tax treatment than either domestic companies or subsidiaries. Their principal advantage is the ease and low cost of obtaining local registration. Their disadvantages vary from country to country but can include (a) higher tax rates (see Exhibit 13-2); (b) the requirement to disclose the accounts of the entire company, either at the time of registration, during an audit, or as part of a civil or criminal suit (see the *In Re Sealed* case in Chapter 6);[8] (c) ineligibility for deductions, exemptions, incentives, or grants; (d) ineligibility to participate in some business activities;[9] (e) liability of the parent for the tax, contractual, and tortious obligations of the agency or branch; and (f) the attribution of funds earned by the parent from sales outside the country—or from sales facilitated by the presence of an independent representative office—to the local branch.

The tax laws of many countries encourage foreign investors to establish subsidiaries—especially joint ventures. Some of the advantages of setting up a subsidiary may include (a) lower tax rates (see Exhibit 13-2); (b) limited liability for the foreign parent; (c) the possibility of attracting local participation in the equity capital of the subsidiary company; (d) eligibility for the same deductions, exemptions, incentives, and grants offered to domestic companies; (e) the right to participate in the same activities as domestic companies; and (f) insulation of the parent company from audits by local authorities. The disadvantages may include (a) the higher costs of incorporation and operation, (b) the mandatory participation of local joint venturers, (c) the mandatory appointment of local citizens to hold some percentage of the seats on the board of directors, (d) more extensive audits than those imposed on branches, and (e) the filing of more detailed returns with the registrar of companies or the tax agency.

The distinguishing characteristic of a subsidiary is its separate legal status from the parent company. This insulates the parent from the tax, contract, and tort liabilities of the subsidiary. It also—as Case 13–2 shows—insulates the subsidiary from the obligations of the parent.

---

[8]Kenya, while permitting foreign parent companies to negotiate with its Tax Department as to the scope of a particular audit, can require the parent to disclose its entire accounts to the Registrar of Companies at the time it registers a branch. Coopers & Lybrand International Tax Network, *1998 International Tax Summaries: A Guide for Planning and Decisions,* p. K-19 (George J. Yost III, ed., 1998).

[9]For example, prior to Taiwan's accession to the World Trade Organization, an agency or branch of a foreign company could not engage in the following businesses: restaurants, consigned processing, investment, travel agencies, shipping agencies, leasing, container terminals, and construction and related activities. *Id.,* p. T-10.

Case 13–2 *Reiss and Company (Nigeria), Ltd. v. Federal Board of Inland Revenue*

Nigeria, Federal Revenue Court, 1977.
African Law Reports, Commercial Law Series, vol. 1977, pt. 2, p. 209 (1977).

Reiss & Co. (Nigeria), Ltd., was a joint stock company incorporated in Nigeria. Handelsvereeniging v/h Reiss & Co. (Amsterdam) was a private limited liability company incorporated in the Netherlands and a holder of 55 percent of the shares in Reiss & Co. (Nigeria), Ltd.

The Nigerian subsidiary served as an agent for the Dutch parent company, introducing Nigerian customers and forwarding orders for goods to be purchased by those customers from the parent. Once having introduced the customers and placed their orders, the

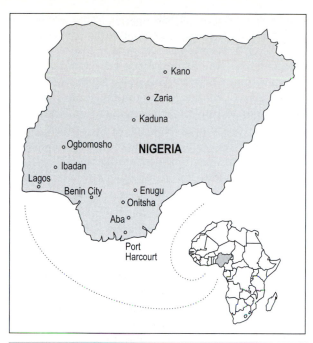

MAP 13-2 Nigeria (1977)

Nigerian company took no further part in the subsequent transactions. The Dutch company accepted or rejected the orders in Amsterdam, communicating that decision directly to the customers. Invoices for the price of the goods sold were sent directly to customers. Profits on these sales were 14 percent of the invoice price.

By an unwritten agreement, the Nigerian subsidiary was entitled to half of the profits (i.e., 7 percent of the sale price) on the transactions accepted by the parent as payment for its services. Upon receipt of payments from customers, the parent paid this amount to the Nigerian company.

The Nigerian company submitted tax returns in Nigeria for the years 1971/72 through 1974/75, showing income for half of the profits it was sharing with the Dutch parent. Nigeria's Federal Board of Inland Revenue made an additional assessment on a "best judgment" basis, assessing the Nigerian company for taxes on the entire amount of the profits paid to the Dutch company by its Nigerian customers.

After losing an appeal before the Board of Appeal Commissioners (which held that it was impossible to disentangle the accounts of the Nigerian subsidiary from its Dutch parent), Reiss & Co. (Nigeria), Ltd., appealed to Nigeria's Federal Revenue Court. The Nigerian company contended, among other things, that, although the Dutch company owned a majority of its shares, the Dutch parent did not control the subsidiary's affairs and that the two companies should have been treated entirely separately for tax purposes.

JUDGE KARIBI-WHYTE:

* * *

Whilst not disputing that the appellants are assessable to tax, counsel for the appellants contended that they are only assessable in respect of earned income and no more. Chief Williams [the appellants' counsel] pointed out that the circumstances in which Nigerian and overseas companies are assessable to tax are clearly stated in § 18 of the *Companies Income Tax Act* (1961). He argued that the appellants share the profits with Reiss & Co. (Amsterdam) and cannot be assessed to tax in respect of the whole.

In order to understand the situation, it is necessary to state the relationship between Reiss & Co. (Nigeria) and Reiss & Co. (Amsterdam) apart from the agency arrangement. In his evidence, the managing director of Reiss & Co. (Nigeria) stated on oath that the company's founder and principal shareholder is Reiss & Co. (Amsterdam). He said that the appellant company was incorporated on September 23rd, 1960. Mr. Jacob Dirk Moraal, assistant managing director of Reiss & Co. (Amsterdam) in his evidence on oath stated that Reiss & Co. (Amsterdam) owns 55 percent of the shares in Reiss & Co. (Nigeria). Notwithstanding this controlling shareholding, both witnesses stated in their evidence that Reiss & Co. (Amsterdam) does not control the affairs or management of the appellant company in any way. The services rendered under the agency agreement are paid out on the basis of a "gentlemen's agreement." There is no formal contract embodying the percentage due the appellants, although there is an understanding that 50 percent is due to the appellants.

It is vital in the circumstances to determine from where the source of income tax has accrued and to whom. Section 17(a) of the *Companies Income Tax Act* (1961) provides:

> The tax shall, subject to the provisions of this Act, be payable at the rate hereinafter specified for each year of assessment upon the profits of any company accruing in, derived from, brought into, or received in, Nigeria in respect of—
>
> (*a*) any trade or business for whatever period of time such trade or business may be carried on.

This enables profits of Nigerian companies to be assessed to tax wherever they have been made, if they are derived from, brought into or received in Nigeria. The profit must be made in a trade or business carried on by such company. Wherever such profits have arisen and whether or not they have been brought into or received in Nigeria they shall be deemed to accrue in Nigeria.[10]

---

[10]Section 18(1).

On the other hand, the situation with respect to a non-Nigerian company is different. Section 18(2) of the *Companies Income Tax Act* (1961) provides:

The profits of a company other than a Nigeria company from any trade or business shall be deemed to be derived from Nigeria to the extent to which such profits are not attributable to any part of the operations of the company carried on outside Nigeria.

The evidence that the appellant company is an intermediary of Reiss & Co. (Amsterdam) for the purposes of introducing Nigerian customers has not been controverted. There is no evidence that the appellant company does anything more with respect to such customers. This was clearly brought out by the evidence in chief and answers to cross-examination of the appellants' managing director. The assistant director of Reiss & Co. (Amsterdam) in his evidence gave a full description of the duties of the appellants and Reiss & Co. (Amsterdam) in respect of orders of customers. All the appellant company does is to take a pro forma invoice from the customer and send this to Reiss & Co. (Amsterdam). The deposit received by the appellants is refunded to the customer if Reiss & Co. (Amsterdam) rejects the order. Every other activity in respect of the transaction, and the financial obligations thereon are carried on in Amsterdam by Reiss & Co. (Amsterdam). Simply put, all operations relating to the transaction are carried on outside Nigeria by Reiss & Co. (Amsterdam). It therefore follows that it is not a trade or business carried on in Nigeria by a Nigerian company in accordance with § 18. Rather it is a trade or business carried on by a company other than a Nigerian company in Nigeria in accordance with § 18(2) of the *Companies Income Tax Act* (1961).

Considerable importance has been attached to and emphasis laid on the relationship between the appellants and Reiss & Co. (Amsterdam). It is in evidence that the appellant company was before September 23rd, 1960, only an overseas branch of Reiss & Co. (Amsterdam). Following the promulgation of the *Companies Decree* (1968), the Nigerian branch became incorporated as a separate legal entity with its own managing director and board of directors. There is, however, evidence before me that Reiss & Co. (Amsterdam) still has a controlling shareholding of 55 percent of the shares of the appellant company. There is no evidence before me of any actual control of affairs of the appellant company by Reiss & Co. (Amsterdam). The only evidence before me, which has remained uncontroverted, is the oral evidence of a sharing agreement in respect of commissions payable to the appellant company on the profits of business introduced to Reiss & Co. (Amsterdam). Although there is a considerable dark cloud of suspicion regarding the genuineness of this transaction, especially because the two companies were the same before the legal separation, the natural philosophical variety in the arrangement is more indicative of the arrangement generally understood of companies within the same group. The separate legal identity of the appellants and Reiss & Co. (Amsterdam), cannot be denied. . . . The respondent cannot impugn the legal situation successfully without adducing sufficient evidence to the contrary. It is not sufficient to allege that the profits in the transaction accrue to the appellants. It must be shown how they so accrue, notwithstanding the clear words of § 18(1) of the *Companies Income Tax Act* (1961).

In *F. L. Smidth & Co. v. Greenwood*[11] the facts were similar to this case. The appellants carried on business at Copenhagen in Denmark, as manufacturers of and dealers in cement-making and other allied machinery. All the partners were resident in Copenhagen where they had their head office. They had an employee in London, who was paid a salary and a bonus based on the profits of the entire turnover of the business. The appellants rented an office in London where the employee, whose duty was to ascertain the requirements of intending purchasers, inspect the proposed site of any proposed installation of machinery, and take samples of earth, used to report to the appellants in Copenhagen. Otherwise, the employee had no responsibility for the negotiation of contracts which were made directly with the appellants in Copenhagen. All machinery was sent FOB from Copenhagen. During the war, the appellants purchased parts of the machinery in the United Kingdom in order to complete installation or to carry out repairs. It was admitted that the appellants were liable to tax in respect of the profits arising from resale of the goods so purchased. It was held that, apart from the goods locally purchased and resold in the United Kingdom, the evidence before the Commission did not justify the conclusion of fact that the firm exercised a trade within the United Kingdom.

In the High Court, Judge Rowlatt gave a definition of where the trade or business is exercised, which is acceptable to me and was indeed accepted by the Court of Appeal and the House of Lords. He said . . . :

. . . [T]he real place where the trade is exercised is the place where the transactions forming the alleged business are closed, in the case of the selling business, by the sale of the commodity and profit thereby realized. It seems to me that is a clear and definite principle. Until the sale is effected, the trade is incomplete. Trading is buying or making and selling, and if I am right in supporting that one single place

---

[11] *Law Reports, King's Bench,* vol. 1920, pt. 3, p. 275 (1920); on appeal *Law Reports, King's Bench,* vol. 1921, pt. 3, p. 583 (1921); on further appeal, *Law Reports, Appeal Cases,* vol. 1922, pt. 1, p. 417 (Court of Appeal, 1922).

has to be treated as the place where the trade is exercised it seems to me that it must be where the profit-bearing transactions are closed.

. . . [This description] largely support[s] the agreed facts of the case before me, which is that the appellants company's only duty is to introduce customers to Reiss & Co. (Amsterdam). This function has been aptly described by Lord Herschell in *Grainger & Son v. Gough*[12] . . . as: ". . . only ancillary to the exercise of his trade in the country where he buys or makes stores, and sells his goods."

On examination of the facts, the appellant company in *F. L. Smidth & Co. v. Greenwood* was more involved in the transactions than were the appellants in this case.

It would seem from the cases referred to above as if the place of the conclusion of the contract of sale is of itself decisive of the test of the place where business is carried on. This is not so. As was said by Lord Justice Atkin in *Smidth's case* there is no exhaustive test as to what constitutes trading within or outside a place by a nonresident. Regard must be had to the whole circumstances of the case in order to see from the operations taking place where the profits in substance arise.

. . . The facts of *Mitchell v. Egyptian Hotels, Ltd.,*[13] a divided decision of the House of Lords, are very similar to the facts of the case before me if all the evidence necessary to establish the relationship between the appellants and Reiss & Co. (Amsterdam) has been adduced. . . . The facts of *Mitchell's case* are that the appellant company incorporated in England owned and carried on a hotel business in Egypt. In 1908, the company altered its articles of association by providing for a local board in Egypt to manage its Egyptian business including the hotel to the exclusion of any board of directors of the company itself. The local board was to exercise all the powers of the company in regard to the hotel. They were to retain all the profits made by the hotel and remit to England to the company only so much as was necessary to pay dividends to shareholders resident in England and for expenses incurred by the London board. The accounts of the company were kept in London, which recommended dividends and controlled the capital. The company was assessed tax upon the full amount of its profits, on the basis that the controlling power of the company remained with the London board. The assessment was upheld on appeal by the Revenue Commissioners, and Judge Horridge dismissed the appeal of the company to the High Court. His decision was reversed by the Court of Appeal. On a fur-

ther appeal to the House of Lords, the decision of the Court of Appeal was affirmed by the House being equally divided.

It was clear from the evidence that a considerable part of the essential management of the income-producing capital was in London. In affirming the decision of the Court of Appeal, Lord Parker of Weddington reviewed the facts and came to the conclusion that:

Under these circumstances it appears to me indisputable that no single act has been done in or directed from this country by way of participation in or furtherance of the trade or business of the company from which the profits or gains said to be chargeable to income tax since August 28, 1908, have arisen.[14]

On this reasoning his lordship came to the conclusion as follows:

In the absence of any act done or directed by any person resident here in participation or furtherance of the business operations in Egypt from which the profits and gains in question arose, I think your Lordships are bound to come to the conclusion that this trade or business was carried on wholly outside the United Kingdom.[15]

Lord Sumner agreed with this, but Earl Loreburn and Lord Parmoor held the contrary. The decision of the Court of Appeal was therefore affirmed.

I think the view of the Court of Appeal affirmed by this decision ought to be followed. I apply that decision as consistent with judicial authority and more in consonance with the express provisions of the enabling statutes. There is no doubt that the participation of the appellants in the profit earning business in Amsterdam is not significant. The appellant company can conveniently be regarded as a sleeping partner. . . . Again, from the evidence before me, there is nothing to show that any part of the transaction was carried on in this country. Apart from introducing customers who thereafter dealt directly with the principal, the appellant company has not featured again in any other important aspect of the transaction.

In *Grainger & Sons v. Gough*, one of the champagne cases, whose essential facts are fairly similar to the case before me, it was held that a foreign merchant who canvasses through agents in the United Kingdom for orders for the sale of his merchandise to customers in the United Kingdom, does not exercise a trade in the United Kingdom, within the meaning of the Income Tax Acts, so long as all contracts for the sale and all deliveries of merchandise are made in a foreign country.

[12]*Id.,* vol. 1896, p. 325 at p. 336 (Court of Appeal, 1896).
[13]*Id.,* vol. 1915, p. 1022 (Court of Appeal, 1915).
[14]*Id.,* at p. 1038.
[15]*Id.,* at p. 1039.

So in this case all the appellants did was to canvass for customers in Nigeria, as Grainger & Sons did to Louis Roederer, the French wine merchant in that case, who was held not to have exercised any trade in the United Kingdom. On my findings of fact on the evidence no trade or business was carried on in Nigeria either by the appellants or by Reiss & Co. (Amsterdam). This is because the acceptance of the orders is by Reiss & Co. (Amsterdam). The purchase of the goods is made outside Nigeria and the invoice is prepared outside Nigeria, and from there sent directly to the customer in Nigeria. Payment is made to Reiss & Co. (Amsterdam) in Amsterdam. That they are paid in Nigeria through Nigerian banks is a matter of convenience in accordance with modern commercial practice. The delivery is also made in Amsterdam, outside this country.

I am of the opinion that whenever profitable contracts are habitually made in this country, by or for foreigners, with persons in this country because they are to do something for or to supply something to those persons, such persons are exercising a profitable trade in the country even though everything to be done by them to fulfill the contract is done abroad. It is otherwise when the same result is achieved through an agent without coming into this country. It has been held in *Colquhoun v. Brooks*[16] that where there is resident in a country a sleeping partner with respect to a business carried on abroad, in the management of which he does not take part, such partner is only liable to be assessed on such parts of the profits as are remitted to him from abroad.

This accentuates the two different situations of trading in a country and carrying on a trade within the country. It would seem to me that Reiss & Co. (Amsterdam) in exporting goods to Nigerians or persons in Nigeria, through the appellant company, who only introduces customers to it, does not thereby carry on business in Nigeria. If, as I have held, Reiss & Co. (Amsterdam) does not carry on business in this country, I do not see how the activities of the appellant company, whose only association and participation on the transaction is to introduce customers, will amount to carrying on business. This is because the appellant company cannot be credited with what its principal cannot and does not do.

It follows, therefore, that all the profits shown in the invoices complained of were profits which were due to Reiss & Co. (Amsterdam) and not to the appellants. Counsel for the respondent contended that, the source of this income being Nigeria, the income was taxable. I cannot subscribe to that proposition. . . .

In *Mitchell v. Egyptian Hotels, Ltd.*, it was held that where the business of a company was wholly carried on abroad, it was not assessable to income tax. The facts of the case before me themselves exclude, by virtue of § 18(2) of the *Companies Income Tax* (1961), the possibility of imposing taxes on a foreign company not carrying on any trade or business within this country. Counsel for respondent has contended that the provisions of § 18(1) can be construed by virtue of the meaning of the word "deemed" used therein to include the profits of the foreign company. . . . I do not accept this view. The provisions of the two subsections of § 18 of the *Companies Income Tax* (1961) are intended to achieve similar objectives but with different subject matters and circumstances in contemplation. Where a Nigerian company is contemplated it is not allowable to transpose the situation and include a non-Nigerian company. If it was intended to apply the same standard it would have been necessary to place them in two different subsections. It could be observed that the expression "deemed" was also used in § 18(2) but in different circumstances. I am of the opinion that the construction contended for cannot be enlarged to bring foreign income earned by foreign companies operating entirely outside this country within the scope of § 18(1), as this is entirely within the provisions of § 18(2). . . .

* * *

The appeal of the appellants against the judgment of the Board of Appeal Commissioners is allowed. . . . The appellants are entitled to a refund of any tax assessed and paid on the agency commission in excess of the 7 percent commission due to the appellants by the agreement. . . . ■

---

[16]*All England Law Reports,* vol. 1886–1890, p. 1063 (Court of Appeal, 1889).

D. BASES OF INCOME TAXATION

National tax systems are based on (a) the nationality of the taxpayer, (b) the residence of the taxpayer, (c) the source of the taxpayer's income, or (d) some combination of these variables.

Nationality Principle

nationality principle: A state may tax the world-wide income of its nationals.

Countries that use the **nationality principle** tax their citizens or nationals on their worldwide income no matter where they may reside.[17] A citizen is an individual who is a member of a state or nation (usually a republic), who owes allegiance to it, and who is entitled to full civil rights. A national is an individual who owes allegiance and fealty to a sovereign. Domestic companies are sometimes treated as citizens or nationals of their home country.

In Case 13–3, the U.S. Supreme Court was asked whether the U.S. Constitution or international law is violated by a U.S. tax of the worldwide income of a citizen who resides and is permanently domiciled abroad, and who receives all of his income from outside the United States. The Court held that neither was violated.

---

[17]J. D. R. Adams and John Whaley, *The International Taxation of Multinational Enterprises in Developed Countries,* pp. 10–11 (1977).

Case 13–3   Cook v. Tait, United States Collector of Internal Revenue for the District of Maryland

United States, Supreme Court, 1924.
United States Reports, vol. 265, p. 47 (1924).

MR. JUSTICE MCKENNA delivered the opinion of the Court:

Action by plaintiff . . . to recover the sum of $298.34 as the first installment of an income tax paid, it is charged, under the threats and demands of Tait.

* * *

Plaintiff is a native citizen of the United States and was such when he took up his residence and became domiciled in the city of Mexico. A demand was made upon him by defendant . . . to make a return of his income for the purpose of taxation under the Revenue Laws of the United States. Plaintiff complied with the demand, but under protest, the income having been derived from property situated in the city of Mexico. . . .

The question in the case . . . is . . . whether Congress has power to impose a tax upon income received by a native citizen of the United States, who, at the time the income was received, was permanently resident and domiciled in the city of Mexico, the income being derived from real and personal property located in Mexico.

Plaintiff assigns against the power not only his rights under the Constitution of the United States, but under

international law; and, in support of the assignments, cites many cases. It will be observed that the foundation of the assignments is the fact that the citizen receiving the income, and the property of which it is the product, are outside the territorial limits of the United States. These two facts, the contention is, exclude the existence of the power to tax. . . . The contention is not justified, and that it is not justified is the necessary deduction of recent cases. In *United States v. Bennett*[18] the power of the United States to tax a foreign-built yacht owned and used during the taxing period outside of the United States, by a citizen domiciled in the United States, was sustained. The tax passed on was imposed by a tariff act, but necessarily the power does not depend upon the form by which it is exerted.

It will be observed that the case contained only one of the conditions of the present case,—the *property* taxed was outside of the United States. In *United States v. Goelet*[19] the yacht taxed was outside of the United States, but owned by a citizen of the United States who was "permanently resident and domiciled in a foreign country." It was decided that the yacht was not subject to the tax,—but this as a matter of construction. Pains were taken to say that the question of power was determined "wholly irrespective" of the owner's "permanent domicile in a foreign country." And the court put out of view

---

[18]*United States Reports,* vol. 232, p. 299.
[19]*Id.,* at p. 293.

MAP 13-3 Mexico (1924)

the *situs*[20] of the yacht. That the court had no doubt of the power to tax was illustrated by reference of the income tax laws of prior years and the express extension to those domiciled abroad. The illustration has pertinence to the case at bar, for the case at bar is concerned with an income tax, and the power to impose it.

We may make further exposition of the national power, as the case depends upon it. It was illustrated at once in *United States v. Bennett* by a contrast with the power of a state. It was pointed out that there were limitations upon the latter that were not on the national power. The taxing power of a state, it was decided, encountered at its borders the taxing power of other states and was limited by them. There was no such limitation, it was pointed out, upon the national power, and that the limitation upon the states affords, it was said, no ground for constructing a barrier around the United States, "shutting that government off from the exertion of powers which inherently belong to it by virtue of its sovereignty."

The contention was rejected that a citizen's property without the limit of the United States derives no benefit from the United States. The contention, it was said, came from the confusion of thought in "mistaking the scope and extent of the sovereign power of the United States as a nation, and its relations to its citizens and their relation to it." And that power, in its scope and extent, it was decided, is based on the presumption that government, by its very nature, benefits the citizen and his property wherever found, and that opposition to it holds on to citizenship while it "belittles and destroys its advantages and blessings by denying the possession by government of an essential power required to make citizenship completely beneficial." In other words, the principle was declared that the government, by its very nature, benefits the citizen and his property, wherever found, and therefore has the power to make the benefit complete. Or, to express it another way, the basis of the power to tax was not and cannot be made dependent upon the *situs* of the property in all cases, it being in or out of the United States, nor was not and cannot be made dependent upon the domicile of the citizen, that being out of the United States, but upon the relation as citizen to the United States, and the relation of the latter to him as citizen. The consequence of the relations is that the native citizen who is taxed may have domicile, and the property from which his income is derived may have *situs,* in a foreign country, and the tax be legal—the government has power to impose the tax.

The judgment of the trial court was affirmed. ■

[20Latin: The place where something is located.]

Residency Principle

residency principle:
A state may tax the worldwide income of persons residing within its territory.

According to the **residency principle**, a country taxes the worldwide income of persons legally resident within its territorial jurisdiction.[21]

Residence of Individuals

Generally, the residence of natural persons is determined by one of three tests. One test is objective: the length of time a person resides within the borders of a particular state; a second is subjective: the intent of the individual to make a place his or her permanent domicile or household; and the third is declarative: the individual obtains admission to a country as a resident.

India, Indonesia, Japan, Panama, Singapore, Taiwan, and Venezuela have all adopted a simple objective test (e.g., a stay within the country for an arbitrary period of time, most com-

---

[21]J. D. R. Adams and John Whaley, *The International Taxation of Multinational Enterprises in Developed Countries,* pp. 10–11 (1977).

monly a stay of at least six months).[22] Belgium uses a subjective test: It looks for a person's domicile or a principal home. Brazil uses a declarative test: Individuals with permanent visas are residents; individuals with temporary visas are nonresidents (unless they stay in the country for more than one year).

Many countries, however, use two or more of these tests in combination. Luxembourg, for example, treats an individual as a resident if he has a permanent home in the country or has been living in the country continuously for 6 months. Poland uses the same test. Mexico regards an individual who has established a home in Mexico as a resident unless the person has been outside the country for at least 183 days and can demonstrate residency in another country. Brazil, as already noted, treats both permanent visa holders and temporary visa holders who have been in the country for more than one year as residents.

Residence of Companies

The residence of companies is determined by two tests: (1) where the company was organized or (2) where the company is managed and controlled. In the United States, only the first is used. That is, corporations formed under the laws of any of the states or the federal government are regarded as residents. In the United Kingdom, its colonies, and former colonies, residence is determined solely by the place where the "central management and control" of the trade or business is exercised—the second test. In Germany, France, and most other civil law countries, both tests are applied. That is, a company is a resident if either its statutory seat or its center of management is within the country. Companies in civil law countries may, as a consequence, have dual residency.

The residency of a Bahaman company was the principal issue in Case 13–4.

---

[22]India: 182 days; Indonesia: 183 days; Japan: one year; Panama: 60 days; Singapore: 183 days; Taiwan: any 183 days in a calendar year; Venezuela: any 180 days, or, having been classified as a resident the previous year, any one day in the current year.

  Note: There are two categories of "nonresidents" in Taiwan. One who resides in the country for less than 90 days is liable for taxes only on income actually paid to the nonresident in Taiwan. One who resides in the country for more than 90 days but less than 183 days in a calendar year must pay taxes on income received from sources both within and without Taiwan so long as the services being reimbursed were rendered within Taiwan.

Case 13–4   Crown Forest Industries Ltd. v. Canada

Canada, Supreme Court
Supreme Court Reports, vol. 1995, part 2, p. 802 (1995).

JUSTICE IACOBUCCI—This appeal raises issues regarding the interpretation of international tax treaties.

The more specific question is whether Norsk Pacific Steamship Company Limited ("Norsk") is a "resident of a Contracting State"—in this case the United States—within the meaning of Article IV of the *Convention between Canada and the United States of America with respect to Taxes on Income and on Capital* (hereinafter the *Canada-United States Income Tax Convention (1980)*.[23] If it is, the amount of non-resident tax imposed

by Canada on Norsk and required to be withheld by Crown Forest Industries Limited ("Crown Forest") from the rent paid by it to Norsk for the lease of several maritime barges would be reduced by virtue of Article XII, paragraph 2 of the Convention from 25 percent to 10 percent. Article IV provides that a "resident of a Contracting State" is "any person [or entity] who, under the laws of that State, is liable to tax therein by reason of . . . domicile, residence, place of management, place of incorporation, or any other criterion of a similar nature".

* * *

---

[23]Enacted in law in Canada by the Canada-United States Tax Convention Act (1984), *Statues of Canada,* 1984, chap. 20.

I. BACKGROUND

In the 1987, 1988, and 1989 taxation years, Crown Forest paid rent to Norsk for the use of certain barges. These barges were used to transport wood chips to pulp mills, and goods from those mills to markets in Canada and the U.S. Norsk was incorporated in the Bahamas in 1962 but its only office and place of business has been in the United States, in the San Francisco area. At this office it, at all relevant times, employed approximately 19 people with a monthly payroll of about U.S. $75,000. Both Norsk and Crown Forest are owned by the same New Zealand corporation, Fletcher Challenge Limited.

For each of the years under review, the only income tax returns filed by Norsk with the United States Internal Revenue Service were entitled "Income Tax Return of a Foreign Corporation" (Form 1120F); however, Norsk has never filed income tax returns in Canada, the Bahamas, or any country other than the United States. To this end, Norsk is a foreign corporation for U.S. income tax purposes. Its primary source of income arises from the transportation of newsprint internationally.

In the relevant taxation years, Norsk paid no U.S. tax on the barge rental payments, claiming an exemption to which it was entitled as an international shipping company under § 883 of the U.S. *Internal Revenue Code*, 1986.

MAP 13-4 Canada, United States, and the Bahamas (1995)

This exemption accrued to Norsk owing to the fact that it had been incorporated in the Bahamas; given that the Bahamas has, in its income tax legislation, accorded a similar tax exemption to companies incorporated in the United States, these dual exemptions are reciprocal.

Crown Forest withheld 10 percent tax on the rental payments, on the footing that Norsk was a "resident of a Contracting State" for the purposes the *Canada-United States Income Tax Convention* (*1980*). For residents, the usual 25 percent rate of withholding tax paid by non-residents[24] is reduced to 10 percent by virtue of Article XII of the Convention. Although the Minister of National Revenue ("Minister") re-assessed Crown Forest at 25 percent, this finding was quashed by Judge Muldoon of the Federal Court Trial Division who found Norsk to be a resident of a contracting party (the United States). Judge Muldoon's decision was upheld by the Federal Court of Appeal, Judge Décary dissenting. The Minister appeals to this Court and is supported by the intervener, the Government of the United States of America, neither of which wishes Norsk to be considered a "resident" under the Convention.

* * *

IV. ISSUE ON APPEAL

Is Norsk a resident of one of the contracting parties to the Canada-United States Income Tax Convention (1980) pursuant to the following definition in Article IV thereof:

1. For the purposes of this Convention, the term "resident of a Contracting State" means any person who, under the laws of that State, is liable to tax therein by reason of his domicile, residence, place of management, place of incorporation, or any other criterion of a similar nature . . . ?

V. ANALYSIS

In interpreting a treaty, the paramount goal is to find the meaning of the words in question. This process involves looking to the language used and the intentions of the parties. Both upon the plain language reading of Article IV and through an interpretation of the goals and purposes of the Canada-United States Income Tax Convention (1980), I reach the same destination: to allow the appeal.

A. The Plain Language

At this stage of the analysis, the primary question to ask is why Norsk is liable to pay tax in the United States. If its liability is rooted in the fact that "it is engaged in a

---

[24]Pursuant to §. 212(1) of the Income Tax Act, *Statues of Canada*, 1970–71–72, chap. 63, as amended.

trade or business effectively connected with the U.S.", then it would seem that Norsk is not a "resident" of the United States under Article IV since "engaged in a trade or business" is not listed as a factor to trigger residency under that article. The only way residency could be found in such a situation would be to determine "engaged in a trade or business" to be a "similar criterion" under Article IV. On the other hand, if Norsk's tax liability in the U.S. emanates from the fact that its "place of management" is in the U.S., then it would appear, *prima facie*, that Norsk could satisfy the residency requirements under Article IV, since "place of management" is a sufficient condition of residence.

Article IV states that the term "resident" means "any person who, under the laws of [the contracting party in question], is liable to tax therein by reason of . . . domicile, residence, place of management, place of incorporation, or any other criterion of a similar nature." The courts below found Norsk's place of residence to be in the United States. At first blush, this seemingly disposes of the matter since such a finding appears to be sufficient to warrant a determination that Norsk is in fact a resident under the Convention.

Nevertheless, there is one important caveat. Under Article IV it must be shown that the liability to taxation operates *by reason of* one of the listed grounds. This connotes the existence of some sort of causal connection or, in the least, some relationship of proximity. In my opinion, the fact that Norsk's place of management is in the U.S. is not causally or even proximately connected to the basis of Norsk's tax liability in the U.S. Quite the contrary: in my mind, the reason why Norsk was liable to taxation in the U.S. was because of the income flowing from the business or trade it conducted that was connected to the United States.

I am supported in this conclusion by Judge Muldoon's summary of the findings of Ginsburg, the expert witnesses called by Crown Forest to testify:

> Norsk is liable to tax in the U.S.A. because it conducts a "trade or business which is effectively connected with the United States." . . . This latter expression is not identified in the *Internal Revenue Code* . . . but is determined by subjective factors according to common law. . . . The United States taxes foreign corporations on the basis of the continuous and continuing conduct of an active trade or business within the territorial jurisdiction of the U.S. and taxes the trade's or business's worldwide income "sourced" either within or outside of the U.S. . . . The fact that the foreign corporation's head office and place of management are in the U.S. are one factor—a principal factor—in determining whether it carries on a trade or business in the U.S. . . .

In fact, Ginsburg specifically testified:

In our opinion, the fact that Norsk was entitled to the benefit of this Section 883 exemption does not alter the fact that its income was effectively connected with a U.S. trade or business, and therefore it is "liable to tax" in the United States *by virtue of* its effectively connected U.S. trade or business. [Emphasis added.]

Norsk's tax liability thus derived from § 882 of the *Internal Revenue Code* which provides that a foreign corporation (such as Norsk) *engaged in a trade or business within the United States* shall be taxed in the same manner as a U.S. corporation *only on that portion of its taxable income which is effectively connected with the conduct of its U.S. trade or business*. In this respect, for a foreign corporation to be liable, under American law, to taxation in the U.S. it must meet two conditions: (1) it must be "engaged in trade or business in the United States", and (2) it must have income which is "effectively connected" to that trade or business. Clearly, a foreign corporation may have source income which is *not* effectively connected to its American operations; in that case, the U.S. would not have the jurisdiction to tax such income.

The place of management is only one factor in the determination of whether the first condition mentioned above is met. To this end, ascertaining that Norsk is a resident under the Convention because its place of management is in the United States erroneously amounts to elevating *a factor* used in determining its tax liability into *the actual grounds* for that tax liability. Place of management is one step removed from the true and immediate basis for tax liability.

* * *

In sum, I endorse the following excerpt of the judgment of Appellate Judge Décary [in his dissent]:

To say that Norsk, which is not liable to tax by reason of its place of management, is liable to tax by reason of a criterion of a similar nature because its place of management is one of the factors to be considered in determining the very reason of its liability to tax, i.e. the conduct of a business . . . , is to beg the question and try to enter through a door that has already been closed.

B. What Was the Intention of the Drafters of the Convention?

On a direct application of Article IV, I hold that Norsk is not a "resident." This conclusion is confirmed when undertaken with an eye to the intentions of the drafters of the Convention and to the goals of international taxation treaties. In other words, I do not believe that Norsk should be considered a resident under Article IV of the Convention nor that the designers of the Convention would have envisioned that it ought to benefit from the preferential tax treatment accorded to residents.

* * *

I accept the appellant and intervener [Government of the United States]'s submission that, since the application of the Convention is to be limited to taxpayers bearing full tax liability in one of the contracting parties, then Norsk cannot benefit from the Convention and is consequently not to be characterized as a resident under Article IV, paragraph 1. As shall become apparent in the discussion *infra,* the courts below departed from the historical *raison d'être* of international tax treaties when proposing that the *Canada-United States Income Tax Convention* (*1980*), covers taxpayers liable only to source taxation in one of the contracting parties.

At this point in the analysis, it is important to take a step backwards and isolate exactly whom the Convention was intended to benefit. The target group are Canadians working in the United States (or *vice versa*) and Canadian companies operating in the United States (again, or *vice versa*). It was deemed important, in order to promote international trade between Canada and the U.S., to spare such individuals and corporations double taxation (consequently promoting the equitable allocation of profits of enterprises doing business in both countries).[25] An ancillary goal would also be to mitigate the administrative complexities occasioned by having to file simultaneously income tax returns in two uncoordinated taxation systems.

* * *

In the case at bar, I underscore that there is no need to prevent double taxation because the U.S. has declined to tax Norsk's revenue. Although this does not affect Norsk's tax liability, the effect is still that Norsk is not required to pay any tax in the United States by virtue of the § 883(a) exemption, this exemption arising by virtue of a reciprocal arrangement between the U.S. and the Bahamas, where Norsk is incorporated. Further, it is unclear whether the specific rental income at issue is even, independent of the exemption, subject to taxation in the U.S. because, pursuant to § 864(c)(4) of the *Internal Revenue Code*, it might not be considered to be effectively connected with the conduct of Norsk's American trade or business. Allowing Norsk to benefit from the Convention in this case would actually lead to the avoidance of tax on the rental income because the liability for tax asserted by the Canadian authorities would be reduced notwithstanding that the United States chooses not to impose any tax thereon or does not even have the jurisdiction therefore.

The goal of the Convention is not to permit companies incorporated in a third party country (the Bahamas) to benefit from a reduced tax liability on source income merely by virtue of dealing with a Canadian company through an office situated in the United States. As far as I can see it, if there were any tax convention that Norsk would be able to benefit from, it is that concluded between the U.S. and the Bahamas. There is no reason to assume that, in the context of this case, Canada entered into a treaty with the United States with a view to ceding its taxing authority to a jurisdiction that is a stranger to the Convention, namely the Bahamas. As mentioned earlier, the reason Norsk benefited from the § 883 U.S. *Internal Revenue Code* tax exemption was because it was incorporated in the Bahamas which grants an equivalent exemption to U.S. corporations. It seems to me that both Norsk and the respondent are seeking to minimize their tax liability by picking and choosing the international tax regimes most immediately beneficial to them. Although there is nothing improper with such behavior, I certainly believe that it is not to be encouraged or promoted by judicial interpretation of existing agreements.

Nor do I believe it to have been within the intentions of the drafters of the Convention to permit a corporation (such as Norsk) who is liable for tax on a limited amount that is "sourced" to one of the contracting states—in this case only on income that is effectively connected to the United States—to avail itself of the benefits of the Convention even in respect of income which is not so connected and in respect of which the U.S. has no interest. Naturally, were Norsk to be a domestic corporation, it could properly benefit from the Convention since it would be subject to double taxation on the rental income in the U.S. (by virtue of its residency) as well as in Canada (by virtue of the "source" principle).

* * *

I now turn to another set of extrinsic materials, other international taxation conventions and general models thereof, in order to help illustrate and illuminate the intentions of the parties to the *Canada-United States Income Tax Convention* (*1980*). Articles 31 and 32 of the *Vienna Convention on the Law of Treaties* indicate that reference may be made to these types of extrinsic materials when interpreting international documents such as taxation conventions.

Of high persuasive value in terms of defining the parameters of the *Canada-United States Income Tax Convention* (*1980*) is the OECD *Model Double Taxation Convention on Income and on Capital* (1963, re-enacted

---

[25]*See* Preamble to the Convention; *see also* Utah Mines Ltd. v. The Queen, *Dominion Tax Cases,* vol. 92, p. 6194 (Federal Ct. of Appeals), and U.S. Senate (Foreign Relations Committee), *Tax Convention and Proposed Protocols with Canada,* at p. 2: "The principal purposes of the proposed income tax treaty between the United States and Canada are to reduce or eliminate double taxation of income earned by citizens and residents of either country from sources within the other country, and to prevent avoidance or evasion of income taxes of the two countries."

in 1977). As noted by the Court of Appeal, it served as the basis for the *Canada-United States Income Tax Convention* (*1980*) and also has world-wide recognition as a basic document of reference in the negotiation, application and interpretation of multilateral or bilateral tax conventions. . . .

* * *

The Commentaries to the OECD Model Convention as well as academic sources indicate that generally the domestic laws of the contracting states employ residence to apply on "full-tax liability."[26] So, too, does the American Law Institute, *Federal Income Tax Project—International Aspects of United States Income Taxation II—Proposals on United States Income Tax Treaties* (1992):[27]

Under the prevailing practice, a country entering into an income tax treaty extends the benefits of the treaty to a person or entity that is a "resident of (the other) Contracting State." "Residence," in turn, is defined in terms of taxing jurisdiction. A person or entity is considered resident in a country if that country asserts an unlimited right to tax his or its income—that is, a right based upon the taxpayer's personal connection with the country (as opposed to the source of the income or other income- or asset-related factors). The test of residence requires that the person or entity claiming treaty benefits be "fully taxable" in the residence country, in the sense of being fully subject to its plenary taxing jurisdiction.

Full tax liability is not satisfied in a case where an entity is liable to tax in a jurisdiction only on a part of its income.

* * *

It is for this reason that the trial judge's rhetorical conclusion ("if the negotiators of the Convention meant to exclude foreign corporations in the U.S., like Norsk, from the status of "resident of a Contracting State" (i.e., the U.S.A.) one wonders why they simply did not write into the Convention exactly what they allegedly meant to say") must be rejected. The extrinsic materials reveal that such explicit "writing-in" was simply not necessary. This analysis helps further rebut the respondent's other submission that, since in its tax treaties with other nations the U.S has chosen to utilize more restrictive language in terms of the definition of "resident", the intention of the U.S. in its agreement with Canada was not to limit the benefit of the Convention solely to those liable to taxation on world-wide income.

In sum, the intentions of the drafters of the Convention and the other extrinsic materials demonstrate that Norsk is not a resident under the Convention.

* * *

As a result, the courts below erred in limiting Crown Forest's non-resident withholding tax to 10 percent instead of 25 percent. Consequently, I would allow the appeal with costs throughout, set aside the judgment of the Federal Court of Appeal, and in substitution therefore restore the Minister's assessment of 25 percent withholding tax required of Crown Forest on rental payments to Norsk for the taxation years in question.

Appeal allowed. ■

---

[26]Paragraphs 3 and 8 to the Commentary to Article IV in Nathan Boidman, L. Frank Chopin and Alan W. Granwell, "Tax Effects for Canadians of the New U.S. Code and Treaty Residency Rules (Part Two)," *Tax Management International Journal*, vol. 14, p. 183, at pp. 184–85 (1985).
[27]At pp. 127–28.

Source Principle

source principle: A state may tax income derived from sources within its territory.

worldwide income: Income derived from all sources and from all parts of the world.

domestic income: Income derived from sources within a particular state.

Countries applying the **source principle** tax all income from sources within their territorial jurisdiction and generally exempt from taxation income accruing abroad.[28]

Of the 102 countries in Exhibit 13-1 that impose taxes on the worldwide income of domestic and resident taxpayers, all additionally impose taxes on the domestic income of nonresident taxpayers. (See Exhibit 13-3.) **Worldwide income**, of course, is income derived from any source, from any part of the world. **Domestic income** is income originating within a particular country.

Rules for Determining Domestic Income Sources

Domestic income is often described as income "accruing" or "deemed to be accruing" or, alternatively, "derived" or "deemed to be derived" from "sources" within a country.

---

[28]J. D. R. Adams and John Whaley, *The International Taxation of Multinational Enterprises in Developed Countries,* pp. 10–11 (1977).

Country	Basic Tax Rates		Withheld Amount is the Final Tax for its Category	Basic Withholding Rate*	Statutory Withholding Rate				Tax Treaty Withholding Rate			
	Non-resident Company	Non-resident Natural Person			Dividends to a Shareholder	Dividends to a Parent Company	Interest	Royalties	Dividends to a Shareholder	Dividends to a Parent Company	Interest	Royalties
1. Antigua and Barbuda	40%	45–55%					20–40%	25%				
2. Argentina	35%	35%	•	35%			15–35%	21–28%			10–20%	3–28%
3. Australia	34%	29–47%			30%	30%	10%	30%	10–25%	10–25%	10–25%	10–25%
4. Austria	27%	21–50%	•		25%	25%		20%	0–25%	0–25%		0–20%
5. Azerbaijan	27%	12–35%			15%	15%	10%	10%				
6. Bahamas	None	None										
7. Bahrain	None	None										
8. Barbados	40%	25–40%			15%	15%	15%	15%	0–15%	0–15%	5–15%	0–15%
9. Belgium	28–41%	25–55%			25%	25%	15%	15%	0–20%	0–20%	0–25%	0–25%
10. Bermuda	None	None										
11. Bolivia	25%	13%	•	12.5%	12.5%	12.5%	12.5%	12.5%	15%	15%	12–15%	12.5–15%
12. Botswana	10–15%	5–25%		15%	15%	15%	15%	15%	15–25%	15–25%	10–25%	10–25%
13. Brazil	15%	15–27.5%	•	15%			15%	15%				
14. Brunei	30%	None					20%					
15. Bulgaria	15–20%	20–38%		15%	15%`	15%	15%	15%	5–20%	5–20%	0–15%	0–20%
16. Cambodia	5–30%	5–20%			10–15%	10–15%	15%	15%				
17. Cameroon	38.5%	10–60%			15–25%	15–25%	16.5%	15%	5–25%	5–25%	10–15%	3–25%
18. Canada	35.1–44.6%	16–29%		25%	25%	25%	25%	25%	5–25%	5–25%	10–15%	3–25%
19. Cayman Islands	None	None										
20. Chile	35%	35%	•	20%					5–15%	5–15%	5–10%	6–25%
21. China	30%	5–45%	•	10%								
22. Colombia	35%	2–35%	•	39.6%	39.6%	39.6%	39.6%	39.6%				
23. Congo (Zaire)	40%	10–60%			20%	20%	20%	20%				
24. Costa Rica	10–30%	10–15%			15%	15%	15%	25%				
25. Croatia	20%	15–35%			15%	15%		15%				
26. Cyprus	20–25%	20–40%			20%	20%	20%	10%	0–25%	0–25%	0–20%	0–10%
27. Czech Republic	31%	15–32%			15%	15%	15%	1–25%	5–15%	5–15%	0–15%	0–25%
28. Denmark	30%	25%		28%	28%				0–5%	0–5%	0–25%	0–25%
29. Dominican Republic	25%	15–25%					25%	25%			18%	18%
30. Ecuador	25–44%	5–25%			33%	33%	33%	33%				

#	Country										
31.	Egypt	32–42.5%	20–32%			32%	32%				25%
32.	Estonia	35%	26%	0–26%	0–26%	26%	15%	0–15%	0.15%	0–10%	0–10%
33.	Fiji	2–34%	15–34%	15%	15%	15%	15%	15–20%	15–20%	10–15%	10–15%
34.	Finland	29%	35%	29%	29%	29%	29%	0–29%	0–29%	0–29%	0–29%
35.	France	33.3%	15–54%	25% •	25%	15%	15%	0–25%	0–25%	0–15%	0–33.3%
36.	Germany	25%	22.9–53%		20%	25%	25%	5–25%	5–25%	0–25%	5–25%
37.	Ghana	8–32.5%	5–30%	35%	10%	10%	15%				
38.	Greece	35–37.5%	5–31%	15–37.5%	15–37.5%	10–20%	5–47%	5–47%	5.47%	0.37.5%	5–10%
39.	Guatemala	31%	15–31%	10% •	10%	25%	25%				
40.	Guyana	35–45%	20–33.3%	15%	15%	0–10%	15%				
41.	Hong Kong	16%	2–17%	1.6–16%							
42.	Hungary	18%	20–40%	18%	18%	18%	18%	5–20%	5–20%	0–25%	0–40%
43.	India	29.6%	12.6–30%	20% •	20%	20–30%	20%	10–20%	10–20%	7.5–30%	10–30%
44.	Indonesia	2–30%	20% •	20%	20%	20%	20%	5–20%	5–20%	5–20%	5–20%
45.	Iran	12–54%									
46.	Ireland	20–25%	20–42%	20%	20%	20%	20%	0–20%	0–20%	0–20%	0–20%
47.	Israel	36%	10–50%	25%	25%	25%	25%	0–25%	5–25%	5–25%	0–15%
48.	Italy	36%	18–45%	27% •	27%	12.5–27%	30%	5–32.4%	5–32.4%	5–32.4%	0–30%
49.	Ivory Coast	35%	1.5–10%	12–18% •	12–18%	13.5–18%	25%				
50.	Jamaica	7.5–33%	25–33% •	25%	33%	33%	33%	0–22.5%	0.22.5%	7.5–15%	10–15%
51.	Japan	22–30%	20%	20%	0–20%	20%	20%	0–20%	0–20%	0–20%	0–20%
52.	Kazakhstan	30%	5–30% •	15%	15%	20%	20%	5–15%	5–15%	10–12.5%	10–15%
53.	Kenya	30–37.5	0–10% •	0–10%	20%	10%	10%	15%	15–20%		
54.	Korea, South	16–28%	25% •	25%	25%	25%	25%	0–25%	0–25%	0–15%	0–25%
55.	Kuwait	5–55%	None								
56.	Laos	10–45%	10%	10%	10%	5%	10%				
57.	Latvia	25%	25%	10%	10%	10%	5–15%	10%	0–15%	0–15%	
58.	Liechtenstein	7.5–20%	1.1–17.8%	4%	4%						
59.	Lithuania	24%	33%								
60.	Luxembourg	20–50%	6–46%	0–25%	0–25%	12%	5–15%	5–15%	2.5–15%	0–12.5%	
61.	Malawi	38%	16–38%	15% •	5–20%	5–20%					
62.	Malaysia	28%	20–29%	0–15%	10%	0–15%	0–10%				
63.	Malta	35%	15–35%	35% •	25%	35%	15–35%	15–35%	15–35%		
64.	Mauritius	15–25%	15–25%	15–35%							
65.	Mexico	15–35%	3–40%	5%	4.9–40%	15–40%	0–15%	0–15%	4–15%	10–15%	
66.	Monaco	33.3%	None								

(continued)

EXHIBIT 13-5 Income Taxes for Nonresidents in 115 Countries (2001)

* Applicable to all taxed income unless a different rate is indicated for a particular category.
Source: PriceWaterhouseCoopers, *Corporate Taxes: Worldwide Summaries 2001–2002* (2001); PriceWaterhouseCoopers, *Individual Taxes: Worldwide Summaries 2001–2002* (2001); PriceWaterhouseCoopers, *Corporate Taxes: Worldwide Summaries 2001–2002* (2001).

| Country | Basic Tax Rates | | Withheld Amount is the Final Tax for its Category | Basic Withholding Rate* | Statutory Withholding Rate | | | | Tax Treaty Withholding Rate | | | |
	Non-resident Company	Non-resident Natural Person			Dividends to a Shareholder	Dividends to a Parent Company	Interest	Royalties	Dividends to a Shareholder	Dividends to a Parent Company	Interest	Royalties
67. Morocco	35–39.5%	13–44%			10%	10%	10%	10%	5–10%	5–10%	10%	5–10%
68. Mozambique	25–35%	8–40						15%	8–15%	8–15%	8–10%	5–10%
69. Myanmar	30–35%	35%										
70. Namibia	35–55%	18–36%		25%	10%	10%		10.5%	5%	5%		
71. Netherlands	30–35%	3–52%			25%	25%	15%	15%	0–25%	0–25%		
72. New Zealand	33%	19.5–39%	•		30%	30%	15%		15%	15%	10–15%	10–15%
73. Nigeria	20–35%	5–25%		10%	10%	10%		10%				
74. Norway	28%	13.5–19.5%			25%	25%			0–25%	0–25%		
75. Oman	5–30%	None						10%				
76. Pakistan	33–58%	20–35%			10%	10%	10%	15%	5–15%	5–15%	0–30%	10–20%
77. Panama	30%	2–30%		15%	10–20%	10%	6%					
78. Papua New Guinea	30–50%	25–47%	•		0–17%	0–17%	15%	10–30%	15–17%	15–17%	10–15%	0–15%
79. Paraguay	4–30%	None			5%	5%	35%	35%				
80. Peru	20–30%	15–20%	•	30%			0–30%	15–30%				
81. Philippines	32%	5–32%		25–32%	25%	32%	0–30%	15–30%	15–20%	15–32%		
82. Poland	28%	19–40%			20%	20%	20%	20%	0–20%	0–20%	0–20%	0–20%
83. Portugal	34–37.4%	25%			25–30%	25–30%	20%	15%	15%	15%	10–15%	5–15%
84. Qatar	10–35%	None										
85. Romania	25%	18–40%			10%	10%	10%	15%				
86. Russia	35–43%	30%			30%	15%	15%	20%	0–15%	0–15%	0–15%	0–15%
87. St. Lucia	33.3%	10–30%						25%				
88. Saudi Arabia	25–45%	None										
89. Senegal	35%	14–50%		16%			20%	25%				
90. Singapore	25.5%	15–28%					15%	15%	0%	0%	0–15%	0–15%
91. Slovakia	15–29%	12–42%			15%	15%	15–25%	1–25%				
92. Slovenia	29%	17–50%			15%	15%	15%					
93. Solomon Islands	35%	11–40%	•		35%	35%	15%	15%				

94. South Africa	15–35%	34–45%									
95. Spain	1–35%	25%	•	25%	25%	25%	12%	5–15%	5–15%	0–15%	0–12%
96. Sri Lanka	15–35%	10–35%		15%	15%	20%	25%	10–15%	10–15%	10–15%	0–15%
97. Swaziland	30%	12–39%		12.5–15%	12.5–15%	10%	20%				0–10%
98. Sweden	28%	31%		30%	30%			0–30%	0–30%		0–25%
99. Switzerland	17–30%	0.8–13.2%	•	35%	35%	35%		0–25%	0–25%	0–15%	
100. Tahiti	35–50%	None					10%				
101. Taiwan	15–50%	20%		30%	20–25%	20%	20%	10–15%	10–15%	10–20%	10–15%
102. Tanzania	30%	7.5–35%		10%	10%	10%	15%	10–25%	10–25%	15–20%	15–30%
103. Thailand	30%	5–37%		10%	10%	15%	15%	10%	10%	3–15%	5–15%
104. Trinidad and Tobago	15–35%	28–35%		10%	10–15%	20%	20%	0–15%	0–15%	0–20%	0–20%
105. Turkey	30%	15–45%		5–15%	5–15%	16%	20–25%	10–30%	10–30%	5–12%	10–22%
106. Uganda	30%	10–30%		15%	15%	15%	15%	15%	15%	15%	15%
107. Ukraine	30%	20%		15%	15%	15–30%	15%	0–15%	0–15%	0–15%	0–15%
108. United Kingdom	10–30%	10–40%	30%	30%	30%	20%	22%			0–20%	0–22%
109. United States	15–39%	15–39.6%	30%			30%		5–30%	5–30%	0–30%	0–30%
110. Uruguay	30%	None		15%	15%	15%					
111. Uzbekistan	26–35%	12–36%		15%	15–34%	15%	20%	5–20%	5–20%	5–15%	0–20%
112. Venezuela	15–34%	6–34%	34%	34%	15–34%	5–34%	5–34%	5–15%	5–15%		
113. Vietnam	10–50%	10–50%		5–10%	5–10%	10%	10%	5–15%	5–15%	0–15%	5–15%
114. Zambia	15–45%	10–30%		10–15%	10–15%	10–15%	15%	0–20%	0–20%	0–30%	0–15%
115. Zimbabwe	30.9%	20–53.2%		15–20%	15–20%	10%	20%	15–20%	20%	10%	

EXHIBIT 13-3 Continued

Sometimes these terms are interpreted in the tax laws; other times administrative agencies are given discretion (often "wide" discretion) to interpret them.[29] Commonly, income that is accrued or derived from sources within a country will include three kinds: (1) income derived from property located within the country (including interest, dividends, fees, royalties, etc.), (2) income derived from any trade or profession carried on through any agency or branch within the country (with agriculture, mining, and manufacturing often being mentioned as examples), and (3) income derived from employment carried on within the country.

In Case 13–5, a court was asked to determine if interest income earned abroad was a source of domestic income.

_____

[29]Coopers & Lybrand International Tax Network, *1998 International Tax Summaries: A Guide for Planning and Decisions,* p. S-22 (George J. Yost III, ed., 1998).

Case 13–5   Bank of the Federated States of Micronesia v. Government of the Federated States of Micronesia

Federated States of Micronesia, Supreme Court, Trial Division, 1992.
Civil Action No. 1991-016.

DESIGNATED JUSTICE EDWARD C. KING:

This action has been filed by the Bank of the Federated States of Micronesia to challenge the assertion of the national government of the Federated States of Micronesia that the bank must pay FSM income taxes on income realized by the bank from funds invested in banks in Chicago and Honolulu in the United States.

The case is now before the Court on the bank's motion for summary judgment. The bank seeks a ruling that the bank's investments in Chicago and Honolulu are not business activities within the Federated States of Micronesia and therefore are not taxable under *Federated States of Micronesia Code*, title 54, § 141.

I. BACKGROUND

The parties have stipulated to the material facts in this case. The bank is a banking corporation organized and operating under the banking laws of the Federated States of Micronesia. Since the bank has full service branches in each state of the Federated States of Micronesia and does not engage in general banking activities elsewhere, there is no dispute that most revenues generated by the bank are subject to the national tax on gross revenues.

MAP 13-5   Micronesia (1992)

The dispute here concerns only the income realized from the bank's investment of excess funds in overnight loans or "fed funds" in accounts maintained by the bank with First Hawaiian Bank in Honolulu and with Boulevard Bank in Chicago.

Although interest from these investments in Chicago and Honolulu is reflected in the books and records of the bank, the bank has excluded that investment revenue for FSM income tax purposes on the theory that the revenue was derived from business outside the Federated States of Micronesia.

The government rejected the bank's interpretation and assessed taxes upon the bank's unreported investment income for the years 1987 through 1989. The bank has tendered the disputed amount to the Court for safekeeping and has filed this lawsuit to obtain a court ruling.

II. LEGAL ANALYSIS

The national income tax law does not seem to represent an effort to tax all income realized from all business activities of a business entity operating within the Federated States of Micronesia. The law does not contemplate taxation of business income generated outside of the Federated States of Micronesia.

"Business" under the FSM income tax law means "any . . . undertaking carried on for a pecuniary profit and include all activities . . . *carried on within the Federated States of Micronesia* for economic benefit either direct or indirect. . . . "[30] Limitation of this definition to activities carried on within the Federated States of Micronesia strongly implies that activities carried on elsewhere by a business functioning within the Federated States of Micronesia are not subject to FSM income tax.

The implication of section 112(1) is confirmed by *Federated States of Micronesia Code*, title 54, § 142, which provides a method of apportionment for the earnings of a business which "derives its gross revenue from business activities or undertakings both within and without the Federated States of Micronesia during the taxable year. . . . "[31]

Section 142(1) creates a presumption that all of the revenue of such a business was "derived from sources within the Federated States of Micronesia." However, the section goes on to provide a method for rebutting the presumption. "The business may file for an apportionment of the tax on a form prescribed by the Secretary and the tax shall be levied only on that portion which is earned in or derived from sources or transactions within the Federated States of Micronesia."[32]

The government has not questioned the procedures employed by the bank in seeking apportionment. The only question then is whether the investment income generated by the deposits of funds in Honolulu and Chicago is derived from "sources or transactions or parts of transactions" within the Federated States of Micronesia.

In rejecting the bank's request for apportionment, the government pointed out that the funds invested by the bank in Honolulu and Chicago have been obtained from depositors in the FSM. The government therefore asserted that the funds are derived from "sources of transactions" within the Federated States of Micronesia.

This approach, focusing on the source of funds used to generate the additional revenue, ignores the statutory scheme, which emphasizes the location of the business activity which generates the revenue in question. The fact that the funds invested flowed from sources and transactions within the Federated States of Micronesia does not alter the fact that the investment transactions themselves, which actually generated the new revenue sought to be taxed, took place outside of the Federated States of Micronesia. Those investments in Chicago and Honolulu were the source of this new revenue. Thus, the revenue is not subject to FSM income tax under the existing statute.

This result makes it unnecessary for the court to reach the other questions, relating to assessment of penalties, raised in the bank's motion for summary judgment.

III. CONCLUSION

The motion of plaintiff Bank of the Federated States of Micronesia for summary judgment is granted and declaratory judgment is granted in favor of the plaintiff. The funds tendered to the Court by the bank to be held while this case remains pending may be returned to the bank. ■

---

[30]*Federated States of Micronesia Code*, title 54, § 112(1)(emphasis added).
[31]*Id.*, § 142(1).
[32]*Id.*, § 142(2).

To determine if a trade or profession is "carried on" within a country, several countries' laws or regulatory rules provide a checklist of factors to be considered. These include (1) a fixed place of trade or business, (2) the manufacturing or assembly of a product, (3) the regular and continuous presence of employees, (4) the regular and continuous presence of after-sale support personnel, and (5) the active management of locally situated real estate.

To determine if particular income is "derived" from a trade or profession carried on within a country, the following factors are also commonly considered: (1) whether the gain was derived from assets used in the conduct of the trade or profession and (2) whether the activities of the trade or profession were a material factor in realizing the gain.

Deemed Income

Special rules often apply to **deem** where certain kinds of activities take place for tax purposes. The most important of these relates to sales transactions. Thus, a sale is usually "deemed to happen" where the buyer takes control or possession of the property. For example, the sale by a Costa Rican seller of 1,000 tons of bananas FOB London to a buyer in Poland would be deemed to have taken place in London. Similarly, the sale by an Egyptian of real property located in Uruguay to a Taiwanese would be deemed to have taken place in Uruguay. However, in some countries, a sale of personal property that is not in the ordinary course of business is deemed to have taken place in the taxpayer's country of residence.[33] Therefore, an American resident who speculates in stock sold on the Sidney Stock Exchange would have U.S.-source income on the sale of the stock.

Interrelationship of Taxation Bases

For countries that use more than one basis for determining taxation, one will be used as the ordinary, or default, rule and the other, or others, will be used as special or supplementary rules. The most common of the ordinary, or default, rules is the source principle. In such a case, nationality and residency are considered supplemental and subordinate rules that will either include or exclude the income of particular taxpayers, depending on the goals of the particular tax system.

Persons Immune from Taxation

The only foreign persons commonly able to escape taxes are foreign governments, diplomats, and international organizations. Governments can claim sovereign immunity. However, as we discussed in Chapter 3, sovereign, or state, immunity applies only to noncommercial transactions (i.e., transactions that do not involve the exercise of sovereign authority). Transactions of a commercial nature—such as the purchase or sale of goods or services, loans, guarantees, and employment contracts—are all potentially subject to taxation. Nevertheless, many countries choose not to tax foreign governments or to exempt them from certain types of taxation. For example, the U.S. Internal Revenue Code exempts "foreign governments," including "the integral parts [and] controlled entities of a foreign sovereign," from taxation on interest income, dividend income, and gains on sales of securities, and from branch profits taxes and withholding.[34] Income earned by foreign central banks from U.S. government obligations and from bank deposits is similarly exempt.[35]

Foreign diplomats are exempt from tax liability by the provisions of the Vienna Convention on Diplomatic Relations.[36] Embassy technical and support staff and consular officials are exempt only with respect to their employment in the embassy or consulate.[37] (See Chapter 3.)

The immunity of an international organization and its personnel from taxation does not exist as a matter of course in international law. Exemptions depend on (1) the instrument creating the organization, (2) agreements between the organization and the particular state, (3) the applicability of multilateral tax conventions, (4) local tax law,[38] and (5) the applicability of general principles of international private law.

---

[33]United States, Internal Revenue Code, § 865.

[34]*Id.*, § 892. United States, Internal Revenue Service Regulations, § 1.892T(a) defines foreign governments, foreign agencies and instrumentalities, and controlled entities. The latter must (a) be wholly owned and controlled by the government, either directly or through other controlled entities, (b) be organized under the laws of that government, (c) have no part of its earnings inure to any private person, and (d) turn over all of their assets to the government upon liquidation.

[35]United States, Internal Revenue Code, § 895.

[36]Vienna Convention on Diplomatic Relations (1961), Articles 34 and 36.

[37]*Id.*, Article 37; Vienna Convention of Consular Relations (1963), Article 31.

[38]United States, Internal Revenue Code, § 892 grants a blanket exemption to international organizations. Section 893 exempts the income of employees of international institutions, unless they are U.S. citizens.

E. INCOME

personal income: The earnings or profits made by individuals.

business income: The earnings or profits made by companies.

capital gains: Increases in the value of capital or other long-term investments.

Income Categories

Taxable income may be categorized as personal or business income or capital gains income. **Personal income** and **business income** are the earnings or profits made by individuals and businesses. **Capital gains** are the increases in value of the underlying capital owned or invested by individuals and businesses.

Many countries distinguish between personal or business income and capital gains income (see Exhibits 13-1 and 13-2). In some countries, capital gains—which are commonly calculated only at the time of the sale of capital assets—are taxed at a different (usually lower) rate; in other countries, taxpayers are given tax breaks on their capital gains depending on how long the assets are held or to what purpose the proceeds are put.[39] The main criticism of a capital gains tax is its implicit penalty on savings. Advocates look upon it as a social welfare measure. (The converse of these arguments is used when tax breaks are applied to capital gains.)

In contrast to those countries that impose taxes on capital gains at special rates, the great majority regard all sales of proceeds from a company as taxable at ordinary rates. In other words, all income derived from corporate assets is business income. In these countries, both capital gains and ordinary profits are treated as business income (see Exhibit 13-2).

Computation of Income

profit-and-loss statement method of computing income: Income is determined after offsetting allowable losses and deductions from all income received during an accounting period.

balance sheet method of computing income: Income is determined by calculating the difference in net worth at the beginning and end of an accounting period.

The income of employed persons is based on their salaries and wages. Income for self-employed persons and companies is calculated by one of two methods. The **profit-and-loss statement method** (where gross business income is offset by allowable losses and deductions) is used in the United States, the United Kingdom, Canada, Mexico, and the Philippines. Most of the rest of the world—including France, Germany, Italy, and the Netherlands—uses the **balance sheet method** (in which income is calculated as the difference between net worth at the beginning and the end of the accounting period). Countries using either of these methods make various adjustments to reflect local definitions of income. These typically include personal exemptions, deductions for expenses, and credits for double taxation.

Income Tax Rates

Of the 115 countries and territories listed in the tables in this chapter, only Bolivia, Estonia, Jamaica, Latvia, Lithuania, and Sweden impose flat rates on personal income. The 96 others that impose taxes (13 impose no personal income taxes at all) use a graduated scale of rates, some with a large number of gradations.

Flat rates are more commonly applied to company income, with nearly two-thirds of the countries listed in Exhibit 13-2 imposing them. About half of these countries have different flat rates for companies that are involved in particular industries or activities or that have a particular form of ownership, or both. Papua New Guinea, for example, imposes a flat rate of 25 percent but increases it to 30 percent for companies involved in natural gas and other mining operations, to 50 percent for companies engaged in petroleum mining operations.[40]

Countries imposing graduated rates on companies are more likely to use fewer gradations (two or three rates being the most common) when compared to the graduated rates they impose on individuals. Also, in comparison to individual rates, the lowest company rate is likely to be higher than the lowest individual rate, while the highest rate is likely to be lower than this highest individual rate.

Company tax rates are also sometimes different for foreign branches. Of the countries listed in Exhibit 13-2, 87 impose the same tax rates on domestic companies and foreign

---

[39]Y. Neeman, "General Report," *Cahiers de Droit Fiscal International,* vol. 61b, pp. 20–22 (National report on "The definition of capital gains in various countries," 1976).
[40]PriceWaterhouseCoopers, *Corporate Taxes 2001–2002: Worldwide Summaries,* p. 633 (2001).

branches; 7 impose higher rates on foreign branches; 9 use the highest rate they impose on domestic companies; 8 use a rate or rates that are intermediate between the highest and lowest domestic rates; and 3 impose rates that are both higher and lower rate than those for domestic companies.

Many developing countries also make other special adjustments. Countries suffering from high inflation rates adjust their taxes using various mechanisms, including inflation indexes, accounting adjustments, and secondary currencies.[41] Peru, for example, uses an official index (known as the Applicable Taxable Unit) to calculate individual liability to income tax.[42]

In several developing countries, income rates may also be adjusted if the country decides that an investor or company has failed to report a reasonable profit. In Case 13–6, Mobil Oil (Nigeria), Ltd., reported diminished income following the loss of its facilities in Eastern Nigeria to Biafran rebel attacks. Nigeria's Federal Board of Inland Revenue felt that Mobil's reported income was too low and it imposed a higher adjusted tax rate. Mobil appealed the case to Nigeria's Supreme Court.

---

[41]Paul H. Vishny, *Guide to International Commerce Law,* vol. 2, § 2.06, pp. 9–12 (1998).

[42]Coopers & Lybrand International Tax Network, *1998 International Tax Summaries: A Guide for Planning and Decisions,* p. P-53 (George J. Yost III, ed., 1998) and PriceWaterhouseCoopers, *Corporate Taxes 2001–2002: Worldwide Summaries,* p. 646 (2001).

Case 13–6   Mobil Oil (Nigeria), Ltd. v. Federal Board of Inland Revenue

Nigeria, Supreme Court, 1977.
African Law Reports, Commercial Law Series, vol. 1977, pt. 1, p. 1 (1977).

Mobil Oil (Nigeria), Ltd., submitted audited tax returns to Nigeria's Federal Board of Inland Revenue for the tax years of 1968 and 1969. Based on that return the Inland Revenue assessed, and Mobil paid, the amount of tax due.

In 1970, the Inland Revenue reexamined the company's accounts and informed Mobil that since its rate of profit for the years in question was lower than might have been expected, additional assessments were being made under Section 30A of Nigeria's Companies Income Tax Act (1961) on a percentage (15 percent) of Mobil's turnover for those years.

Mobil objected to this assessment, arguing that it had suffered losses in the Eastern Provinces of Nigeria that had been part of the secessionist Republic of Biafra. (Biafran leaders had declared it independent in July 1967. After a prolonged civil war, its leaders surrendered in January 1970.) The Federal Board then agreed to assess Mobil on a lower percentage of its turnover (10 percent).

Mobil, nevertheless, appealed to the Appeal Commissioners. It asserted that its audited accounts were accurate; that its profits, as revealed in those accounts, were in line with the prevailing conditions of the market;

and that the Inland Revenue was not entitled to make any additional assessments under Section 30A of Nigeria's Companies Income Tax Act (1961). Mobil also asserted that the Inland Revenue, having first accepted the company's audited return and having assessed the company on its assessable profits under Section 49(2)(a), was forbidden, by Section 60 of the Act, from imposing any additional assessments.

The Appeal Commissioners dismissed the appeal, holding that the assessed profits were less than what might have been reasonably expected. It also held that the original assessment under Section 49(2)(a) was not conclusive and that the Inland Revenue could collect additional taxes under Section 30A.

Mobil appealed to the Federal Revenue Court, which affirmed the decision of the Appeal Commissioners, and then to the Supreme Court. Mobil contended, among other things, that Section 60 of the Companies Income Tax Act (1961) permitted an additional assessment only if that did not "involve reopening any issue, on the same facts" and, since no new facts had been discovered, that Section 40 made the original assessment final and conclusive. The Inland Revenue answered this by arguing that under a proper interpretation of Section 60 an assessment could be reopened on the same facts, if new issues—such as whether the company's profits for the years in question were lower than might have reasonably been expected—were discovered.

JUSTICE BELLO:

* * *

There still remains the question as to whether the provisions of proviso (*b*) to Section 60 which authorizes the reopening of an assessment that has become final and conclusive under the main section are dependent upon the discovery of a new fact. The relevant part of the section is in these terms:

> Where no valid objection or appeal has been lodged within the time limited by Sections 53, 56, or 59 of this Act, as the case may be, against an assessment as regards the amount of the total profits assessed thereby, or where the amount of the total profits has been agreed to under subsection (3) of Section 53 of this Act, or where the amount of such total profits has been determined on objection, revision under the proviso to Subsection (3) of Section 53 of this Act, or on appeal, the assessments as made, agreed to, revised, or determined on appeal, as the case may be, shall be final and conclusive for all purposes of this Act as regards the amounts of such total profits. . . .
>
> Provided that: . . .
>
> (*b*) nothing in Section 53 or in Part XI of this Act shall prevent the Board from making any assessment or additional assessment for any year of assessment which does not involve reopening any issue, on the same facts, which has been determined for that year of assessment under Subsection (3) of 53 of this Act by agreement or otherwise or on appeal.

Chief Williams [counsel for Mobil Oil (Nigeria), Ltd.] conceded that notwithstanding the finality and conclusiveness of an assessment under the main section, the proviso permits the Board to make an additional assessment "which does not involve reopening any issue, on the same facts, which has been determined for that year of assessment under Subsection (3) of 53 of this Act by agreement or otherwise or on appeal." He contended that as the first assessment on the assessable profits of the company had been determined by agreement that assessment has therefore become final and conclusive and can only be reopened by virtue of the provisions of the proviso if there is a new fact. He concluded that since there is no new fact the finality and conclusiveness of the first assessment is absolute. In answer to this submission, Dr. Akintan [counsel for the Federal Board of Inland Revenue] contended that no new fact is needed to reopen an assessment.

It is pertinent to paraphrase the relevant provisions of Section 60 in order to highlight what is intended to be "final and conclusive" within the purview of the section. It may be read as follows:

> Where no valid objection or appeal has been lodged . . . against an assessment as regards the *amount of the total profits assessed* thereby, or where the *amount of the total profits* has been agreed to . . . or where *the amount of such total profits* has been determined on objection, revision . . . or on appeal . . . *shall be final and conclusive* for all purposes of this Act as regards *the amounts of such total profits . . . .* [Emphasis added.]

It is clear from the words of the section that the finality and conclusiveness of an assessment is restricted to the *amount of total profits* which has been agreed to or which has been determined on objection, revision or on appeal. It follows therefore that the *issue* in reaching such agreement or such determination is simply: What is the total profit of the company? The Act provides the means of resolving that *issue* which is the deduction from the turnover of the company of all its expenses, reliefs, and other matters in accordance with the provisions of Sections 27 to 38 inclusive of the Act. The amount arrived at from that exercise is *the total profit* of the company which will be final and conclusive if agreed to or determined.

Now to reiterate the facts of the case in hand: upon the returns submitted by the appellant company, the Board computed *the total profits* for the two years in question and assessed accordingly. The company agreed and paid. In the terms of Section 60 that assessment had become final and conclusive as regard *the total profits* made by the company for the years in question. Moreover, in terms of provision (*b*) to the section, *the issue* relating to that assessment, to wit: what were *the total profits* of the company for the two years, has been determined by agreement and cannot thereafter be reopened on the same facts.

It is not in dispute that the additional assessment under Section 30A was made on the same facts as the first assessment. The questions then are: What were *the issues* in making the assessment under Section 30A? Since *those issues* arose from the same facts, did they involve reopening the issue in the first assessment, which was: what were *the profits* of the company? If the answer to second question is in the affirmative, then the Board is prevented by the proviso from reopening it.

It seems that *the issues* in making the assessment under Section 30A are: Firstly, what were the total profits of the company? Secondly, were those total profits lower than might be expected? Thirdly, what fair and reasonable percentage of the turnover would the Board charge? The answer to first question has been agreed to in the first assessment and cannot therefore be reopened by virtue of the provisions of proviso. However, the second and third questions were *new issues* which did not arise at the time of making the first assessment and were not determined by agreement or otherwise at that time. Those two *new issues* subsequently arose after the Chief Inspector had made his discovery that the total profits of the company were lower than might be expected. Furthermore, neither of the *new issues* involved reopening the issue that had been determined in the first assessment. As a matter of fact, far from reopening the issue as to what were the total profits of the company, the Board partly relied on those total profits to make the additional assessment.

In our view the interpretation to be given to the provisions of proviso (*b*) to Section 60 of the Act is this: that the Board is prevented from making an assessment or additional assessment which may involve reopening any issue, on the same facts, which has been determined for that year of assessment; but the Board is not prevented from making an assessment or additional assessment not only on the discovery of new facts but also on the discovery of new issues which, though founded on the same facts, have not previously been determined. It seems to us that to construe the provisions so that it means that discovery of new facts is necessary in order to raise new issues for determination before making an additional assessment would defeat and frustrate the power of the Board under Section 50 of the Act, which power is expressly preserved by the proviso. A simple arithmetic error or error of law in making an assessment might never be corrected if such a construction were put on the proviso.

Accordingly, all the grounds of appeal argued relating to the liability of the appellant company for the additional assessment under Section 30A have failed.

The appeal was dismissed. ■

Integration of Company and Personal Income Taxes

Countries differ in the ways they attempt to integrate company taxes and personal income taxes through the device of company dividends. Various systems have been devised, but all impose taxes based on the following three factors: (1) who the taxpayer is (i.e., the company or the shareholder), (2) whether the dividends have been distributed or not, and (3) whether income from dividends is treated as ordinary income or as a separate class of income. Here are the most important of these systems.

classical system for integrating company and personal taxes: Company taxes are imposed on a company's earnings and personal taxes are imposed on distributed dividends.

The **classical system** of company taxation—which is used in most countries—imposes a tax on company earnings at the time they are received and on company dividends when they are distributed. That is, taxes are first imposed at ordinary company tax rates on the profits of a company. Later, when dividends are distributed, the recipients are taxed at ordinary personal income rates. The distributions are not deductible from the profits of the company, nor are the recipients entitled to a credit for the taxes already paid by the company. In other words, distributed profits are subject to both ordinary personal and ordinary company taxation, whereas undistributed profits are subject only to ordinary company taxes.

shareholder imputation system for integrating company and personal taxes: Shareholders are given credits for taxes paid by the company on distributed dividends.

The **shareholder imputation system** is similar to the classical system: Ordinary company taxes are imposed on all profits, and shareholders must pay ordinary personal income taxes on distributed dividends. Shareholders, however, are given a credit for the taxes paid by the company on distributed dividends, which they may use to offset their personal income tax obligation. The company tax is "imputed" to the shareholder.[43]

company deduction system for integrating company and personal taxes: Companies are allowed to deduct distributed dividends as business expenses.

The **company deduction system** is the converse of the shareholder imputation system. Companies are allowed to deduct distributed dividends as an operating expense before determining their company income (which they then pay at ordinary rates). Shareholders pay ordinary income taxes on the dividends they receive.

company two-rate system for integrating company and personal taxes: Companies pay higher rates on retained profits and lower rates on distributed profits.

The **company two-rate system** applies two rates of company taxes: a higher rate for undistributed profits and a lower rate for distributed profits. Distributed profits are taxed at a lower rate to compensate for the personal income tax to be paid by the shareholder (at the ordinary rate).[44]

---

[43]The shareholder imputation system is currently used in Canada, France, New Zealand, and Norway, among other countries.

[44]The company two-rate system is currently used in Germany, Japan, and Panama, among other countries.

shareholder two-rate system for integrating company and personal taxes: Shareholders pay lower tax rates on income from dividends.

The **shareholder two-rate system** imposes a lower personal tax rate for income received as dividends. Companies are taxed at the ordinary company rate.

The **shareholder exempt system** imposes no taxes on dividend income received by shareholders. Companies pay ordinary income taxes.

shareholder exempt system for integrating company and personal taxes: Shareholders pay no tax on income from dividends.

Other systems are generally variations on these. Fiji, for example, uses the imputation system, except that it allows shareholders to deduct from their income the taxes paid by the company, rather than giving them a credit against their tax obligation. Peru uses a company two-rate system, except that it charges companies a higher (rather than lower) rate on profits distributed as income.

full-integration system for integrating company and personal taxes: Shareholders pay taxes on all profits earned by a company, whether they are distributed or not. The company pays no taxes.

One unique system is the **full-integration system** This system imposes no company taxes; rather, all company profits, whether they are distributed or not, are deemed to be distributed to shareholders, and shareholders pay personal income taxes accordingly. This system, however, is not adopted as a general approach to taxation in any country. It has been adopted for smaller companies in a few countries, notably in the United States for S Companies and in Spain for small limited liability companies.

Two other factors that affect the amount of taxes collected by countries are (1) the nationality or residency of the shareholder and (2) the shareholder's personality (whether a natural or a juridical person). Thus, foreign shareholders may be subject to higher, or lower, personal income taxes on dividend income than nationals or residents. Similarly, many countries provide substantial tax breaks when the shareholder is a juridical person (i.e., a company). To illustrate, Portugal allows a holding company that owns more than 25 percent of a subsidiary to deduct 95 percent of the dividends it receives as a business expense. Sweden, on the other hand, exempts the subsidiary from paying taxes on any income distributed to a 25 percent holding company.

Other Tax-Generating Transactions

merger: The absorption of one firm by another.

When one company **merges** into another, countries vary in the way they tax both the surviving company and the former shareholders of the merged company. The surviving company is commonly taxed only on the increase in book value of the transferred assets.[45] In Germany, for example, a taxable gain arises if the value of the transferred assets exceeds book value.[46] In Japan, a taxable gain exists when the value of the assets entered on the books of the surviving company exceeds the total of the amount paid to the merged company's shareholders in cash, shares, and swapped property.[47]

Similarly, the shareholders of the merged company are usually taxed only if they make a capital gain at a later sale of the shares they receive from the surviving company. To illustrate: Shareholder A buys 1 share in Company X for $10 in 2001. In 2002, Company X merges into Company Y, and Shareholder A receives 1 share of Company Y in exchange for the Company X share. Shareholder A would have no tax obligation at this time. However, upon selling the share in 2003 for $12, Shareholder A would have a $2 capital gain and would be taxed accordingly. This is the rule in Belgium, France, Germany, Italy, the Netherlands, the United Kingdom, and the United States.[48] In countries that have no capital gains taxes, either the subsequent sale will be tax exempt (e.g., Costa Rica, Hong Kong, Hungary, Jamaica, Kenya, Malta, New Zealand, Poland, Portugal, South Africa, and Uganda) or shareholders of certain kinds of businesses will be subject to a special tax (e.g., Chile).[49]

consolidation: When two companies join to become parts of a new company.

Consolidations (or enterprise mergers), where two companies merge to form a new company, are generally tax-exempt transactions. As with mergers, the shareholders would be subject to capital gains only on a later sale of shares; and the new company will generally

---

[45]J. Van Hoorn Jr., "Taxation of Business Organizations," *International Encyclopedia of Comparative Law,* vol. 13, pp. 87–98 (1974).
[46]Paul H. Vishny, *Guide to International Commerce Law,* vol. 2, § 9.16, pp. 9-27 to 9-28 (2001).
[47]*Id.,* at p. 9-28.
[48]J. Van Hoorn Jr., "Taxation of Business Organizations," *International Encyclopedia of Comparative Law,* vol. 13, pp. 93–94 (1974).
[49]PriceWaterhouseCoopers, *Corporate Taxes 2001–2002: Worldwide Summaries passim* (2001).

have no tax obligations as long as the assets of the merged companies are carried over at their book value.[50]

Shareholders of companies that are liquidated (i.e., closed down) may incur tax liabilities. In most countries, the liquidating firm will be taxed on profits made from the sale of assets but otherwise will incur no further tax liability. Shareholders will normally be taxed at ordinary rates on the distribution of assets. A few countries impose no taxes on shareholders at the time of liquidation.[51]

Companies that retain income are sometimes subject to a levy on the accumulation that is not distributed. Australia, for example, imposes a tax when a company has an "insufficient distribution" of dividend income and other related income. Brazil imposes a tax on reserves or retained earnings until they are distributed or converted to capital. Japan imposes a tax on close or family-owned companies that do not distribute earnings. Venezuela imposes a tax surcharge on stock companies that fail to distribute at least 50 percent of their income.[52]

F. DOUBLE TAXATION

Taxpayers who earn income in two or more countries face the problem of dual taxation. That is, income earned in one country may be (and often is) taxed a second time in another country.

Systems for Relief from Double Taxation

double taxation: The payment of taxes on one source of income to two different states.

It is now the practice in virtually all countries to provide relief from **double taxation** either unilaterally or through a bilateral or multilateral treaty. Relief may take the form of an exemption, a credit, or a deduction.

exemption system for relieving dual taxation: Income is taxed in one state and exempted from taxation in another.

The **exemption system** provides for income that is subject to taxation in two or more states to be taxed in only one and exempted from tax in the others. Income may be exempted in either the host state (the state that is the source of income) or in the home state (the state where the taxpayer resides). Commonly, an exemption system exempts income that has been taxed in a host state from further taxation in the home state. To illustrate, assume that the Transnational Nickel Co. (TNC) is a resident company in the state of Alpha. TNC establishes a subsidiary in the state of Sigma. The subsidiary earns $1,000,000 in Sigma and pays a 30 percent tax on those earnings. The balance of the earnings is then paid to TNC. TNC, under an exemption system, would have no tax liability on that income in Alpha. This would be so, even if the income tax rate it would normally pay in Alpha is 40 percent or 20 percent.

credit system for relieving dual taxation: Tax paid in one state may be used as credit for tax due in another state.

The **credit system** allows the tax paid in one state to be used as a credit against a taxpayer's liability in another state. The credit will be in the form of a direct credit for an overseas branch or in the form of an indirect credit for a foreign subsidiary.

First, an example of a direct credit. Suppose that the International Business Co. (IBC) is a resident of the state of Beta, with a branch in the state of Omega. IBC has income in Beta of $1,000,000 and the subsidiary has an income of $100,000 in Omega. Assume that Beta has an income tax rate of 50 percent on the worldwide income of its residents' companies, while Omega has an income tax rate of 30 percent on foreign branch income. Omega will collect $30,000 from the subsidiary, which IBC may then use as a tax credit. IBC's taxes in Beta (before the credit is taken) will be 50 percent of $1,100,000 (the $1,000,000 of income earned in Beta plus the $100,000 earned in Omega), or $550,000. The tax credit of $30,000 will then be applied, bringing IBC's tax bill in Beta down to $520,000.

Note, in the preceding example, that the total tax bill paid by IBC amounts to $550,000, which is 50 percent of IBC's total worldwide income. The 50 percent rate is the same as the higher rate paid in the two countries.

Now, an example of an indirect credit. Assume that the Multinational Sales Co. (MSC), a company in the state of Gamma, has a subsidiary in the state of Lambda. The subsidiary earns

---

[50]J. Van Hoorn Jr., "Taxation of Business Organizations," *International Encyclopedia of Comparative Law,* vol. 13, pp. 90–94 (1974).
[51]*Id.,* pp. 84–87.
[52]Paul H. Vishny, *Guide to International Commerce Law,* vol. 2, § 9.17, pp. 9-28 to 9-29 (2001).

$100,000, which is subject to a 30 percent tax in Lambda, or $30,000. To determine the amount of taxes due on the $70,000 dividend paid by the subsidiary to MSC in Gamma, a four-step "grossing up" procedure will be followed.

First, the "deemed" amount of foreign taxes paid by the subsidiary to Lambda will be determined. This is the amount of foreign taxes paid multiplied by the ratio of dividends paid out to the after-tax earnings of the subsidiary.

$$Lambda\ Tax \times \frac{Dividends\ Paid}{After\text{-}Tax\ Earnings} = Taxes\ Deemed\ Paid$$

$$\$30,000 \times \frac{\$70,000}{\$70,000} = \$30,000$$

Second, the dividend is "grossed up" by adding to it the amount of "taxes deemed paid" that were just calculated.

$$Dividend + Taxes\ Deemed\ Paid = Taxable\ Income$$

$$\$70,000 + \$30,000 = \$100,000$$

Third, Gamma's taxes are determined before the credit is applied. Assume that Gamma has a 50 percent tax rate.

$$Taxable\ Income \times Tax\ Rate = Grossed\text{-}Up\ Tax$$

$$\$100,000 \times 50\% = \$50,000$$

Fourth, credit the "taxes deemed paid" to Lambda to the amount of the "grossed-up tax" to determine the actual taxes due to Gamma.

$$Grossed\text{-}Up\ Tax - Taxes\ Deemed\ Paid = Gamma\ Tax$$

$$\$50,000 - \$30,000 = \$20,000$$

Note, as with the direct credit example, the total taxes paid on the $100,000 of income earned by the subsidiary amount to $50,000, or 50 percent: the higher rate of the two countries.

deduction system for relieving dual taxation: Tax paid in one state may be deducted as an expense from the tax due in another state.

The **deduction system** allows a taxpayer to deduct the tax paid to one state from the profits liable to taxation in another state. To illustrate, assume that the Global Commerce Co. (GCC), a company located in the state of Theta, has a branch in the state of Kappa. The branch earns $100,000 and Kappa subjects it to a 40 percent foreign branch tax on the remission of profits to GCC, or $40,000. Theta allows GCC to deduct the tax paid by the branch to Kappa from the income earned overseas. Thus, GCC subtracts $40,000 from $100,000, leaving a taxable income of $60,000. This is then subject to Theta's tax. Assuming that the rate is 50 percent, GCC must pay Theta $30,000 in taxes. Note that the total tax bill in this example is $40,000 paid to Kappa and $30,000 paid to Theta, or $70,000.

Comparison of the Double Taxation Relief Systems

From the perspective of the taxpayer, the most advantageous of the systems of double taxation is the exemption system. By being exempt from tax liabilities in one state, the taxpayer is (generally speaking) subject to a lower overall tax bill. The least advantageous is the deduction system. Because it only allows the tax paid in one state to be deducted from gross income in the other state, the overall tax bill tends to be higher. The principal adverse feature of the credit system is that the taxpayer ends up paying whichever is the higher rate of the two taxing countries. In sum, for most taxpayers, the tax relief systems can be ranked as follows: exemption system—best, credit system—intermediate, deduction system—worst.

From the perspective of states concerned with raising tax revenues, the ranking would be the reverse of that for taxpayers. The exemption system raises the fewest revenues, the credit system an intermediate amount, and the deduction system the most. Taking in the most tax revenues, however, is not always the principal concern of countries. Host countries often want to entice foreign businesses to establish branch offices or local subsidiaries, and home countries want to encourage businesses and employees to repatriate profits and incomes earned abroad. As a consequence, the least used of all double taxation relief systems is the deduction system. The most popular—and almost universally applied system—is the credit system.

When asked to interpret double taxation treaties, a municipal court will take into consideration its state's objectives in granting this type of tax relief. Because home states are seeking to maximize the monies their nationals repatriate, and therefore maximize the tax revenues they can collect, courts in such states construe the relevant provisions in a tax treaty so as to favor the governmental tax-collecting agency. Host states, on the other hand, are looking to encourage foreign investment. Courts in host states, accordingly, generally interpret double taxation treaties in favor of the taxpayer. Case 13–7 provides an example of this.

Case 13–7   Director General of Inland Revenue v. Rothmans of Pall Mall (Malaysia) Bhd.

Malaysia, Supreme Court (Kuala Lumpur), 1988.
Malayan Law Journal, vol. 1989, pt. 1, p. 32 (1989).

JUSTICE WAN HAMZAH:

The question for determination by the Supreme Court in this appeal is whether Rothmans of Pall Mall (Malaysia) Bhd (the respondent company) is entitled, under the *Double Taxation Agreement* (1968) between Malaysia and Singapore, to double taxation relief in Malaysia for the Malaysian year of assessment [of] 1969 in respect of the Singapore income tax of $531,770.20 paid by the respondent company in Singapore on the profit for the period January 1, 1968 to June 30, 1968.

The following are the facts of the case. The respondent company was incorporated in Malaysia in 1961 and has a place of business at Petaling Jaya, Selangor. It had branch in Singapore which ceased business permanently on 30 June 1968. When the branch ceased business, the Singapore authorities assessed income tax on the respondent company for the Singapore year of assessment 1968 on the income of the branch for the period from January 1, 1968 to June 30, 1968 pursuant to the *Singapore Income Tax Act*. The income amounted to $1,329,433 and the income tax assessed thereon was $531,770.20. The respondent company paid it. There was no assessment of income tax on the respondent company for the Singapore year of assessment 1969. In Malaysia the income of the respondent company totaling $3,436,029 was charged to income tax of $1,546,214.40 for the Malaysian year of assessment 1969. This income included the same income of $1,329,433 of the branch in

MAP 13-6 Malaysia and Singapore (1988)

respect of which the respondent company paid in Singapore the income tax of $531,770.20 for the Singapore year of assessment 1968. The respondent company claimed from the Director General of Inland Revenue of Malaysia (the appellant) double taxation relief in the sum of $531,770.20 in respect of the income tax which it paid in Singapore, but the appellant disallowed it. The Special Commissioners dismissed the respondent company's appeal and affirmed that the respondent company was not entitled to the relief. The Special Commissioners stated as follows:

It has to be noted that the 1968 Agreement only provides the double taxation relief on the basis of the year of assessment, which is very clear and explicit and effect should be given to it. In the instant case, the Malaysia tax was for the year of assessment 1969, whereas there was no corresponding assessment raised by the Singapore tax authorities for the year of assessment 1969. As such, there was no way possible to apply the double taxation relief as advocated under the 1968 Agreement.

The respondent company's further appeal to the High Court was allowed, and the appellant now asks the Supreme Court to restore the order of the Special Commissioners.

The provisions of the *Double Taxation Agreement* (1968) which are relevant in this case are those contained in Article XVIII, paragraph 2(i), which reads as follows:

Subject to the provisions of the laws of Malaysia regarding the allowance as a credit against Malaysian tax of tax payable in any country other than Malaysia, Singapore tax payable whether directly or by deduction, in respect of income derived from Singapore, shall be allowed as a credit against Malaysian tax chargeable in respect of that income.

It should be noted that in paragraph 2(i) of Article XVIII, no reference is made to any year of assessment, so that it is immaterial and irrelevant which year of assessment the tax mentioned in that paragraph is in respect of. It is important to note the words "that income" at the end of that paragraph. These words specifically and expressly refer to the same "income derived from Singapore" referred to earlier in that paragraph. Thus, that paragraph means that Singapore tax payable in respect of certain income derived from Singapore shall be allowed as a credit against Malaysian tax assessed on that same income derived from Singapore, irrespective of which year of assessment that Singapore tax was assessed for and irrespective of which year of assessment that Malaysian tax was assessed for. In the present case, the Singapore income tax of $531,770.20 referred to above was assessed on the income of the respondent company's Singapore branch of $1,329,433. The Malaysian income tax of $1,546,214.40 referred to above includes income tax assessed on that same income of $1,329,433 of the branch. Therefore a credit of $531,770.20 representing the amount of that Singapore income tax should be given against that Malaysian income tax of $1,546,214.40 although that Singapore income tax was not in respect of the same year of assessment as that Malaysian income tax.

Therefore the decision of the High Court is correct. We dismiss this appeal with costs.

The appeal was dismissed. ■

G. TAX TREATIES

The problems presented by double taxation—as well as other problems that arise from tax incentives, tax avoidance, and tax evasion—can be dealt with unilaterally (that is, exclusively by one state) or through the use of reciprocal tax treaties. Although a few commentators have suggested that these problems can best be dealt with unilaterally,[53] most authorities hold that they can be better handled in treaties.[54]

Among the earliest advocates for the adoption of bilateral tax treaties was the League of Nations, which sponsored a group of experts who drafted several model tax treaties in the 1920s.[55] These draft treaties were later used by the Organization for Economic Cooperation and Development (OECD) in drafting its influential model treaty.[56] The OECD's **Model Convention for the Avoidance of Double Taxation with Respect to Taxes on Income and Capital** (OECD Model Tax Treaty) was issued first in 1963; it was revised and reissued most

OECD Model Convention for the Avoidance of Double Taxation with Respect to Taxes on Income and Capital: Model tax treaty promulgated by the Organization for Economic Cooperation and Development.

---

[53]Robert Hellawell, "The Home-Country Tax Credit," *Negotiating Foreign Investments: A Manual for the Third World,* vol. 1, para. 3.2C1 (Robert Hellawell and Don Wallace Jr., eds., 1982); Elizabeth A. Owens, "United States Income Tax Treaties: Their Role in Relieving Double Taxation," *Rutgers Law Review,* vol. 17, p. 428 (1963).

[54]T. Modibo Ocram, "Double Taxation and Transnational Investment: A Comparative Study," *The Transnational Lawyer,* vol. 2, p. 142 (1989); Klaus Vogel, "Double Tax Treaties and Their Interpretation," *International Tax and Business Law,* vol. 4, p. 10 (1986).

[55]*Report by the Government Experts on Double Taxation and Evasion of Taxation,* Annex I (League of Nations Doc. F.50.1923.II, 1923).

[56]The U.S. Model Income Tax Treaty, published by the U.S. Treasury Department in 1976, revised and reissued in 1981, withdrawn in 1991, and revised and reissued in 1996, is based on the 1995 revision of the OECD Model Convention. The U.S. Model Tax Treaty is posted on the Internet at www.ustreas.gov/taxpolicy/t0txmod2.html. The OECD Convention can be purchased on the Internet from the OECD online bookshop at www.oecd.org/bookshop.

recently in 1998.[57] Possibly because the OECD model is aimed primarily at resolving tax disputes between developed countries, the United Nations focused its efforts on formulating guidelines for treaties between developed and developing countries. Committees set up by the UN in 1968 and 1974 both advocated the drafting of a model bilateral convention that would contain as many standardized clauses as possible.[58] In 1980, the UN Secretariat acted on these recommendations, issuing a **Model Double Taxation Convention between Developed and Developing Countries** (UN Model Tax Treaty).[59]

Most tax treaties are bilateral agreements. Indeed, the UN's *ad hoc* Group of Experts on Tax Treaties between Developed and Developing Countries doubted in 1968 that any effort should be expended on developing multilateral agreements. Nevertheless, several multilateral agreements have been concluded, including the Double Taxation Agreement of 1966, entered into by the member states of the African and Malagasy Common Organization; the 1966 Convention for the Avoidance of Double Taxation, adopted by the member states of the Andean Common Market; and the 1972 Nordic Convention Regarding Mutual Assistance in Matters Relating to Tax, signed by Denmark, Finland, Iceland, Norway, and Sweden.

Some of the principal topics addressed in tax treaties—whether bilateral or multilateral—are (a) the persons and taxes covered by the treaty, (b) the basis (i.e., nationality, residence, or source) for imposing tax liability, (c) provisions for avoiding double taxation, and (d) provisions against tax avoidance and tax evasion.

Coverage of Tax Treaties

Most tax treaties mirror the coverage provisions of the OECD and UN model treaties (which themselves contain identical provisions). The taxes covered are income taxes, capital gains taxes, and taxes on net wealth. The persons covered are both natural persons and companies.[60]

Basis for Taxation

Both the OECD and the UN model tax treaties base taxation on the residency of persons within the contracting states. This was not always so. Some older treaties—including some League of Nations model treaties—based tax liability on citizenship. Today, with one notable exception, states do not insist upon taxing their nonresident citizens. The exception is the United States. In every tax treaty to which the United States is a party, without exception, the United States has refused to yield its right to tax the income of its citizens. The U.S. position is set out in Article 1 of the United States Model Income Tax Treaty, which provides:

> Notwithstanding any provision of the Convention . . . a Contracting State may tax . . . its citizens, as if this Convention had not come into effect. For this purpose the term "citizen" shall include a former citizen whose loss of citizenship had as one of its principal purposes the avoidance of income tax, but only for a period of 10 years following such loss.

The United States has said that its reason for retaining the right to tax citizens is based on the importance accorded citizenship in the United States. Economic factors, however, seem to be the predominant concern of the American government. By retaining the right to tax citizens, the United States can discourage wealthy Americans from setting up a permanent residence in a low-tax country and obtaining substantial tax relief because of a tax treaty provision.[61]

---

[57] The OECD Model Tax Treaty is posted at www.lemaitre.de/dba-e/OECDE2000.html and at www.intltaxlaw.com/TREATIES/OECD%20Model.pdf.

[58] United Nations, *Guidelines for Tax Treaties between Developed and Developing Countries* (UN Doc. ST/ESA/14, 1974).

[59] UN Doc. ST/ESA/102 (1980). The UN Model Tax Treaty is posted at www.law.wayne.edu/mcintyre/text/UN_Model-color.pdf and at www.law.nyu.edu/vannr/spring00/1980.pdf.

[60] OECD, Model Tax Treaty, Articles 2–3; UN, Model Tax Treaty, Articles 2–3.

[61] *See* Donald R. Whittaker, "An Examination of the OECD and UN Model Tax Treaties: History, Provisions and Application to U.S. Foreign Policy," *North Carolina Journal of International Law and Commercial Regulation,* vol. 8, p. 39 at p. 47 (1982–1983).

Aside from this one exception, residency is the key factor in determining the coverage of most tax treaties. It is typically established by domestic law—that is, by domicile, residence, place of management, or some similar rule. If individuals have dual residency, their tax status will then be determined by a series of tie-breaking rules set out in the treaty. The following are the rules from both the OECD and the UN model treaties:

1. An individual is normally a resident of the country in which he has "a permanent home available to him."

2. If an individual has a permanent home in both or neither of the counties, then his residence is in the country "with which his personal and economic relations are closest (center of vital interests)."

3. If a center of vital interest cannot be ascertained, residence is in the country of the individual's "habitual abode."

4. If an individual has a habitual abode in both or neither of the countries, then his residence is in the country of which he is a citizen or national.

5. If all of the foregoing fail to determine residence, then "the competent authorities of the contracting states shall settle the question by mutual agreement."[62]

Both treaties also have a tie-breaking rule for companies with dual residency. Treaty residence in such a case is determined by the place of "effective management" of the company.

Double Taxation Provisions

The provisions in most treaties—including the OECD and UN model treaties—for eliminating double taxation depend on three factors: (1) residency, (2) personality, and (3) type of income.

The general rule for avoiding double taxation relates to residency. That is, persons may be taxed only by the states of which they are residents.

The exceptions to this general rule relate to the taxpayer's personality and the types of income involved. The first of these exceptions pertains to the following persons: (a) persons providing independent or professional services, (b) employed persons, (c) companies, and (d) certain special persons.

Persons providing independent or professional services include individuals who carry on "independent scientific, literary, artistic, educational, or teaching activities," as well as self-employed "physicians, lawyers, engineers, architects, dentists, and accountants." Such persons may be taxed by a contracting state where they are not residents if they maintain a *fixed base* within that state. However, only the income attributable to the fixed base may be taxed.[63]

Nonresident employed persons may be taxed in a contracting state to the extent of the earnings they receive in that state. They are not to be taxed, however, if (a) they are present in that state for less than 183 days, (b) they are paid by a nonresident employer, and (c) the nonresident employer does not have a fixed base or permanent establishment within that state.[64] Case 13–8 illustrates how this works.

---

[62]OECD, Model Tax Treaty, Article 4; UN, Model Tax Treaty, Article 4.
[63]OECD, Model Tax Treaty, Article 14; UN, Model Tax Treaty, Article 14.
[64]OECD, Model Tax Treaty, Article 14; UN, Model Tax Treaty, Article 14.

Case 13–8   Johansson v. United States   ⟋⟍

United States, Court of Appeals, Fifth Circuit, 1964.
Federal Reporter, Second Series, vol. 336, p. 809 (1964).

Ingemar Johansson, a Swedish citizen, fought Floyd Patterson three times for the heavyweight boxing championship of the world, winning the title in 1959, but losing

it back to Patterson in 1960. Each of their matches was held in the United States. The U.S. government assessed Johansson taxes of approximately $1,000,000 on the resulting income. The government brought suit to collect the taxes, arguing that it was authorized by the Internal Revenue Code and not disallowed by a U.S. tax *convention with Switzerland, which Johansson claimed exempted him from taxation.*

CIRCUIT JUDGE RIVES:

* * *

. . . However, Johansson claims an exemption under the *Income Tax Convention* with Switzerland [of] May 24, 1951 . . . (effective September 27, 1951). Particular reliance is placed upon Article X(1), which provides:

An individual resident of Switzerland shall be exempt from United States Tax upon compensation for labor or personal services performed in the United States . . . if he is temporarily present in the United States for a period or periods not exceeding a total of 183 days during the taxable year, and . . .

(a) his compensation is received for such labor or personal services performed as an employee of, or under contract, with a resident or corporation or other entity of Switzerland. . . .

It is undisputed that Johansson was not present in the United States for more than 183 days in either of the tax years in question. But to bring himself within the purview of the treaty, Johansson had to establish (1) that he was a resident of Switzerland and (2) that he received the income in question as an employee of, or under contract with, a Swiss entity.

The term "resident" is nowhere defined in the Swiss treaty, but under article II(2) each country is authorized to apply its own definition to terms not expressly defined "unless the context otherwise requires." Johansson contends that, because of its position within the phrase "an individual resident of Switzerland," the term "resident" must be defined according to Swiss law. As conclusive proof that he comes within the Swiss definition of "resident" for tax purposes, he relies upon a determination by the Swiss tax authorities that he became a resident of Switzerland on December 1, 1959. Although the evidence on this point is ambiguous, the determination by the Swiss tax authorities may well have been based primarily upon Johansson's own declaration as to his residence in that country. . . . Be this as it may, we are not bound by the determination of the Swiss tax authorities. Article II(2) does no more than to provide the standard for defining the terms used in the rest of the treaty; application of that standard to particular facts remains, in this case, the job of the courts. There is no reason to decide whether the applicable standard for defining "resident" as used in the Swiss treaty is to be

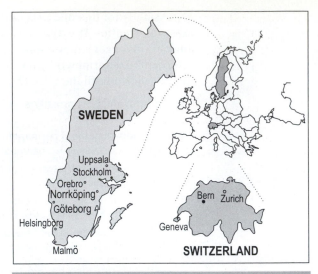

MAP 13-7 Sweden and Switzerland (1964)

found in Swiss or American law, for under both laws the criteria are the same.[65]

Applying this standard to the facts of the present case, the district court concluded that Johansson was not a resident of Switzerland during the period in question. This conclusion is fully supported by the evidence. In the year and a half between the date Johansson claims to have moved to Switzerland and March 13, 1961, the record shows that he spent only 79 days in that country as compared with 120 days in Sweden and 218 days in the United States. Except for his activities in the United States during this period, his social and economic ties remained predominantly with Sweden. Indeed, the summary of Johansson's ties with Switzerland presented in his brief to this Court cites only his maintenance of an apartment and bank account there, his self-declaration of residence, and two acts by the Swiss government that may well have been predicated upon his self-declaration of residence. . . .

Even if we were to find that the district court erred in determining that Johansson was not a resident of Switzerland, the tax exemption in the Swiss treaty does not apply unless Johansson received the income in question as an employee of or under contract with a Swiss entity. A contract of employment was entered into by Johansson in December 1959 with Scanart, SA, a Swiss corporation formed that very month. Scanart's sole employee and sole source of income is Johansson, who is entitled under the terms of the contract to seventy percent of Scanart's gross income, plus a pension fund. All expenses are to be paid by Scanart. During the period in question, Johansson conducted his affairs largely

---

[65]*Compare* Locher, statement of Dec. 29, 1962, in Commerce Clearing House, *Standard Federal Taxation Reports,* para. 6407, p. 71286 (1963) ("sojourn . . . with the intention to remain"), with *Treasury Regulations* § 1.871-2(b) ("intentions with regard to the length and nature of his stay").

independent of Scanart's sole director or its stockholders. The circumstances surrounding the formation of Scanart, the terms of the contract, and the conduct of the parties under the contract led the district court to find that:

> Scanart, SA, had no legitimate business purpose, but was a device which was used by Ingemar Johansson as a controlled depository and conduit by which he attempted to divert temporarily, his personal income, earned in the United States, so as to escape taxation thereon by the United States." . . .

As with the question of Johansson's residence, the record amply supports this finding.

Of course, the fact that Johansson was motivated in his actions by the desire to minimize his tax burden can in no way be taken to deprive him of an exemption to which an applicable treaty entitled him. . . . And in determining the applicability of a treaty, we recognize the necessity for liberal construction. . . . But "To say that we should give a broad and efficacious scope to a treaty does not mean that we must sweep with the Convention what are legally and traditionally recognized to be . . . taxpayers not clearly within its protections."[66] . . .

The primary objective of our treaty with Switzerland, as well as of those with more than twenty other countries, is the elimination of impediments to international commerce resulting from the double taxation of international transactions. The basic mechanism of these treaty arrangements is the establishment of standards for determining the single most appropriate locus for the taxation of any given transaction. Although some treaty provisions are inevitably the results of political compromise, the dominant criterion for determining the appropriate taxing locus is economic impact. Thus, as a general rule, the income from services is taxable where the services are rendered. Where, as here, services are performed in the United States and the compensation for them is drawn from the wealth of the United States, this is the country of primary economic impact and, consequently, the appropriate taxing locus.

There are, however, a number of prudential exceptions to the general "economic impact" rule. Among these is the view that a business enterprise engaged in international commerce ought not to be subject to taxation in every country in which it may transact some business. Although such an enterprise does draw upon the wealth of all the various countries with which it comes into contact, the over-all objective of encouraging international commerce, as well as the practical necessities of business planning, are better satisfied by a centralized regime of taxation at the enterprise's "business seat" or "permanent establishment." The "business seat" exception is found in Article III of the Swiss treaty.

Elements of this exception are also found in Article X. Typical of what have become known as "commercial traveler provisions" in international tax conventions, the article is designed to assure business establishments in each of the contracting states that they may freely send their agents and employees into the other contracting state without thereby subjecting those employees to the latter's taxes. Like Article III, it is an exception to the "economic impact" rule carved out in the interest of facilitating international trade. Where the practical reasons for the exception do not obtain, however, the general rule must apply. Thus, while Johansson may have brought himself within the words of the Swiss treaty by his "residence" in Switzerland and his "employment" by a "Swiss corporation," he has failed to establish any substantial reasons for deviating from the treaty's basic rule that income from services is taxable where the services were rendered. International trade will not be seriously encumbered by our refusal to grant special tax treatment to one only marginally, if at all, a Swiss resident and only technically, if at all, employed by a paper Swiss corporation. Therefore we affirm the district court's judgment that Johansson is liable for the taxes assessed against him in 1960 and 1961. . . . ■

---

[66]Maximov v. United States, *United States Reports*, vol. 373, p. 49 at p. 56 (Supreme Ct., 1963).

---

permanent establishment: A fixed place of business wherein a nonresident carries on commercial activity.

Nonresident companies may be taxed by a contracting state if they maintain a **permanent establishment** within that state. However, as is the case for income earned by professionals from a fixed base, only the income attributable to a company's permanent establishment may be taxed.[67]

Because of its importance for avoiding double taxation for companies, the phrase "permanent establishment" is defined at some length in most treaties. The OECD and the UN model treaties use the term to refer to a fixed place of business through which a nonresident carries

---

[67]OECD, Model Tax Treaty, Article 5; UN, Model Tax Treaty, Article 5.

on any commercial activity either wholly or partly. This includes, but is not limited to the following:[68]

a. Branch offices, factories, and workshops
b. Mines, oil and gas wells, quarries, and other places for extracting natural resources
c. Building sites, construction projects, and assembly projects that last for more than 12 months[69]

A permanent establishment does not, however, include any of the following:

a. The use of facilities to store, display, or deliver goods
b. The maintenance of a stock of goods or merchandise for the purpose of storage, display, delivery, or processing by another
c. The maintenance of a facility for purchasing goods or merchandise, for scientific research, or for collecting or disseminating information
d. The maintenance of a facility for advertising, marketing, or any other activity of a preparatory or auxiliary nature
e. The maintenance of a building site, construction project, or assembly project that lasts for 12 or fewer months
f. The carrying on of business through a broker, general commission agent, or any other agent of independent status acting in the ordinary course of business

force-of-attraction rule: Because a firm has a permanent establishment within a state, that state may tax all of the firm's income whether earned by the permanent establishment or not.

The OECD and the UN model treaties differ in their approach to determining the income that may be attributed to a permanent establishment. The UN model allows profits to be attributed from a wider range of sources than does the OECD model by following what is known as the **force-of-attraction rule**. This rule says that if a company in Country A has a permanent establishment in Country B, then Country B may tax not only the profits generated by the company through the permanent establishment but also any profits that come to the company from trade or business that is carried on in Country B independent of the permanent establishment.

There are also certain special persons, such as the estates of deceased individuals and personal trusts, who are subject to taxation by a contracting state. Although these persons are juridical entities similar to companies, they are not business entities. Because they exist to manage the assets of an individual (e.g., a deceased, or the beneficiary of a trust), the OECD and UN model treaties look to the residency of that individual in determining their residency.[70]

In addition to the exceptions relating to a taxpayer's personality, the general rule that states may tax only their residents is also limited by special rules relating to different types of property. These special rules pertain to (a) immovable property, (b) dividends, (c) royalties, and (d) capital gains.

Immovable property is treated in virtually all tax treaties by a long-standing rule: "Income from real property shall be taxable only in the State in which the property is situated."[71]

The taxation of company dividends varies among tax treaties. Older treaties allowed only the contracting state where the capital was invested (i.e., the "source" state) to tax the resulting dividends.[72] The OECD Model Tax Treaty takes a different approach. If a parent company in Country A owns more than a 25 percent share of a subsidiary in Country B, Country B may

---

[68]In 1984, the United Nations conducted a survey of member countries asking them to identify the differences between the UN Model Tax Treaty and the bilateral tax treaties they had entered into between 1977 and 1983. As to the definition of a permanent establishment, most respondents indicated few differences. It was not uncommon, however, for the following to also be included: storehouses, warehouses used for the storage of goods for other sales outlets, plantations and other establishments for the exploration of natural resources, and service establishments. *International Cooperation in Tax Matters: Report of the Ad Hoc Group of Experts on International Cooperation in Tax Matters*, p. 26 (UN Doc. ST/ESA/185, 1987).

[69]The 12-month period is the time set by the OECD Model Tax Treaty. The UN Model Tax Treaty shortens this to six months.

[70]OECD, Model Tax Treaty, Article 14; UN, Model Tax Treaty, Article 14.

[71]Model Bilateral Convention for the Prevention of the Double Taxation of Income (Mexico Draft), Article 2 (League of Nations Doc. C.88.M.88.1946.II.A, 1946); Model Bilateral Convention for the Prevention of the Double Taxation of Income and Property (London Draft), Article 2 (League of Nations Doc. C.88.M.88.1946.II.A, 1946); OECD, Model Tax Treaty, Article 11; UN, Model Tax Treaty, Article 11.

[72]E.g., Model Bilateral Convention for the Prevention of the Double Taxation of Income and Property (London Draft), Article 2 (League of Nations Doc. C.88.M.88.1946.II.A, 1946).

impose no greater than a 15 percent withholding tax on dividends remitted to the parent; and Country A may tax the dividends received by the parent.[73] The UN Model Tax Treaty approaches dividends in a fashion similar to the OECD treaty, except that it leaves open for negotiation between the contracting states the percentage ownership of the subsidiary and the percentage of withholding tax that a source country may impose.[74]

The UN Model Tax Treaty treats the taxation of interest the same way that it treats dividends.[75] The OECD treaty takes a different (and more traditional) approach. It allows the state where the recipient of the interest is a resident to impose taxes. Additionally, the source state may tax the same interest by imposing a withholding tax, but that tax is limited to a rate of 10 percent.[76] However, if the recipient carries on a business or trade in the source state through a permanent establishment or a fixed base, then these interest rules do not apply. Instead, the interest is treated as ordinary income attributable to a company or to a person providing independent or professional services.[77]

Royalties are also treated differently by the OECD and UN model treaties. Under the OECD treaty, they are to be taxed only in the state where the recipient is a resident (i.e., the home state).[78] Under the UN treaty, both the source state and the home state may tax royalties, but the contracting parties are to set a limit on the withholding rate that the source state may impose.[79]

The taxation of capital gains is treated similarly in both the OECD and UN treaties. Article 13 of the OECD Model Tax Treaty provides:

1. Gains derived by a resident of a contracting state from the alienation of immovable property . . . situated in the other contracting state may be taxed in that other state.
2. Gains from the alienation of movable property forming part of the business property of a permanent establishment which an enterprise of a contracting state has in the other contracting state or a movable property pertaining to a fixed base available to a resident of a contracting state in the other contracting state . . . may be taxed in that other state.
3. Gains from the alienation of ships or aircraft operated in international traffic, boats engaged in inland waterways transport, or movable property pertaining to the operation of such ships, aircraft, or boats, shall be taxable only in the Contracting State in which the place of effective management of the enterprise is situated.
4. Gains from the alienation of any property other than that referred to in paragraphs 1, 2, and 3, shall be taxed only in the contracting state of which the alienator is a resident.

H. TAX INCENTIVES

Host and home states both attempt to encourage international trade with their taxation schemes. Host states primarily encourage trade through local tax incentives; home states generally concentrate on relief from double taxation.

There are many forms of tax incentives. Some of the most important are

1. Income tax holidays for foreign investors.
2. Capital allowances, such as accelerated depreciation.
3. The carrying forward of allowances for income tax deductions.

[73]OECD, Model Tax Treaty, Article 10.
[74]UN, Model Tax Treaty, Article 10.
[75]*Id.*, Article 11.
[76]OECD, Model Tax Treaty, Article 11. *Compare* Model Bilateral Convention for the Prevention of the Double Taxation of Income and Property (London Draft), Article 9 (League of Nations Doc. C.88.M.88.1946.II.A, 1946).
[77]OECD, Model Tax Treaty, Article 4.
[78]*Id.*, Article 12.
[79]UN, Model Tax Treaty, Article 12.

4. Exemptions, deductions, or credits for:
    a. property taxes, including exemptions from mining taxes, forestry fees, and land levies.
    b. indirect taxes, including capital gains taxes, value added taxes, sales taxes, excise taxes, purchase taxes, etc.
    c. taxes paid on dividends to shareholders.
    d. social security and employment taxes.
    e. research and development costs.
    f. loans.

5. Import incentives, such as waivers or deductions from import duties on equipment, spare parts, and raw materials.

6. Export incentives, such as export subsidies, waivers of export tariffs, and the waiver of import duties for intermediate goods used in the manufacture of export goods.

7. The deferment of corporation registration fees and duties.

8. Tax exemptions for expatriate employees.

Tax incentives are generally meant to assist new industries during their first years, when they are subject to many start-up costs and to competition from existing competitors. Sometimes, host states are overly anxious to grant incentives. This can result in situations where a multinational enterprise (MNE) plays one potential host state off against another as the MNE looks for a profitable place to site a branch office or subsidiary.[80] It can also result in situations where the MNE does not benefit from the tax incentives. This happens where the home state does not recognize tax sparing.

Tax Sparing

tax sparing:
Recognition by a home state that tax incentives granted by a host state are equivalent to the payment of a tax to the host state.

Tax sparing entails the recognition by the home state of tax incentives granted by the host state as being equivalent to the payment of a tax. To illustrate the consequences of the absence of a tax-sparing provision in a home state, consider the following example. Transworld Co., a resident of the state of Sigma, has a branch office in the state of Omicron. The branch was set up in Omicron because Omicron (a developing country anxious for new industry) granted Transworld a 10-year holiday from the payment of its income taxes. Sigma, on the other hand, taxes Transworld on its worldwide income, and its double taxation relief provisions grant a credit only for taxes actually paid abroad. Because Transworld does not pay any taxes in Omicron, there is no creditable foreign tax. In effect, Transworld receives no benefit from Omicron's tax holiday. Instead, Sigma's taxing authority gets a windfall.

So that companies can benefit from host state tax incentives, home states must recognize tax sparing. Tax-sparing provisions commonly appear in tax treaties, especially in treaties between the United Kingdom and less developed countries, and between continental European countries and less developed countries. The United States does not recognize tax sparing.[81]

The Interaction of Tax Systems

For legislators writing national tax laws and business managers developing an international development strategy for their companies, it is vital to understand that double taxation, double taxation relief, tax incentives, and tax sparing, as well as the tax laws of home and host countries, all interact to form a matrix of international tax law. For every goal that may be achievable by tax legislation, there are always potentially adverse consequences, depending on the mechanism chosen. Exhibit 13-4 shows some examples.

---

[80]T. Modibo Ocran, "Double Taxation Treaties and Transnational Investment: A Comparative Study," *Transnational Lawyer,* vol. 2, p. 141 (1989).

[81]Robert Hellawell, "The Home-Country Tax Credit," *Negotiating Foreign Investments: A Manual for the Third World,* vol. 1, paras. 3.2D16 and 3.2D17 (Robert Hellawell and Don Wallace Jr., eds., 1982).

Goal	Mechanism	Consequence
Encourage investment	Lower taxes	Decreased tax revenue
Raise tax revenues	Raise taxes	Discourages investment
Encourage foreign investment	Allow foreign direct investment	Foreign ownership of local business
Encourage local ownership of business	Limit foreign direct investment	Discourages foreign investment
Restrict access to local markets	Tax foreign-owned subsidiaries	Discourages foreign investment
Encourage access to foreign markets	Reciprocal access to home markets	Loss of local jobs
Protect local jobs	Tax foreigners with access to local markets	Retaliatory loss of foreign markets

EXHIBIT 13-4   Adverse Consequences of Some Tax Mechanisms

I. TAX AVOIDANCE AND EVASION

Tax avoidance involves efforts by individuals and companies to take advantage of loopholes in the tax laws or, where some doubt exists as to the interpretation of a tax law, to benefit from that doubt. Tax evasion, by comparison, is the deliberate and illegal nonpayment of taxes. The former is legal, if sometimes only "technically" legal; the latter is illegal. The dividing line between the two, however, is seldom clear. Tax avoidance can easily become tax evasion, or vice versa.

In 1984, an *ad hoc* United Nations Group of Experts on International Cooperation in Tax Matters devised a list of examples of tax avoidance and tax evasion. That list is summarized in Exhibit 13-5.

Tax Avoidance

tax avoidance: Taking advantage of legal or arguably legal tax loopholes.

Tax avoidance provides some of the most difficult problems for tax authorities to counteract. Multinational enterprises frequently have armies of accountants ready to evaluate every possible loophole for its tax-saving potential and hordes of lawyers prepared to advocate the legitimacy of those that have maximum economic value to the company. Revenue agencies, on the other hand, especially in less developed and developing countries, often lack the manpower necessary to respond to the tax avoidance schemes devised by foreign multinationals. Moreover, a revenue agency in one country is frequently forbidden (by domestic constitutional and legal constraints) or limited (by jealousy, bureaucratic inertia, or the absence of an international accord) from sharing information with a sister agency in another country.

Despite these constraints, some countries (most notably the members of the Organization for Economic Cooperation and Development) have taken both individual and cooperative action to counter the most tax-costly forms of tax avoidance. These are generally grouped under the names of "tax havens," "transfer pricing," "treaty shopping," and "thin capitalization."

Tax Havens

tax haven: A state that imposes taxes that are substantially lower than those in other states.

Countries or territories that provide a refuge from taxes for (a) taxpayers themselves, (b) the taxpayers' income, or (c) the taxpayers' capital and other assets are known as **tax havens**. Commonly, tax havens not only impose few if any taxes, they also have secrecy laws that forbid foreign governments from obtaining information about the ownership of particular assets, as well as rules that allow for the full and complete transfer and exchange of currencies. The idea of offering either partial or complete exemption from taxation to foreigners is not a modern idea. In the Middle Ages, the city of London exempted merchants of the Hanseatic League from all its taxes. Flanders, in the fifteenth century, eliminated duties on most of its overseas trade. This (along with the absence of exchange restrictions on the repatriation of profits) attracted foreign merchants, especially English merchants who preferred to sell their wool in Flanders rather than pay England's high duties. The Netherlands, in the sixteenth,

Tax Avoidance Devices

Transformation of Income
  Transformation of ordinary income into capital gains
  Transformation of capital gains into ordinary income
  Transformation of payments for goods or services into interest-free or indefinite loans

Thin Capitalization
  Use of high ratio of loans to equity to achieve a tax advantage
  Use of investments in exchange for royalties or fees to achieve a tax advantage
  Transfer of legal ownership while retaining beneficial ownership
  Transfer of income or assets to a controlled company that is tax exempt
  Transfer of income or assets to a controlled company subject to lower tax rates

Transfer Pricing
  Transfer income to a branch or subsidiary in a low-tax country
  Transfer income to a branch or subsidiary in a country with a double-tax treaty
  Transfer income to a branch or subsidiary in a country with incentives or reliefs
  Allocate expenses to a branch or subsidiary in a high-tax country

Tax Evasion Devices

Failure to Provide Tax-Related Information
  Failure to file a return
  Failure to report all income or assets subject to tax

Misrepresentation of Items of Income
  Improper characterization of a gift of property as a sale
  Improper characterization of a gift of money as a loan
  Improper characterization of fees, interest, or royalties as dividends
  Improper characterization of the lease of equipment as a purchase

Misrepresentation of Items of Expense
  Allocation of inflated head-office expenses to branches
  Allocation of inflated parent-company expenses to subsidiaries
  Charging inflated fees for technical assistance and special services
  Overstatement of costs incurred in the implementation of turnkey projects

Material Concealment
  Concealment of imported or exported goods
  Concealment of wealth
  Concealment of transfer of money

Concealment through Falsification of Accounts
  Preparation of separate accounts
  False invoicing
  Inclusion of personal expenditure in company accounts under overhead
  Sales without invoicing
  Invoicing without sales
  Claiming false deductions

Flight of Taxpayer to Another Country
  Remuneration splitting
  Misrepresentation that services were performed abroad

Disguising Remuneration
  Disguising remuneration as reimbursement of expenses
  Disguising perquisites

EXHIBIT 13-5 Tax Avoidance and Tax Evasion Devices

Source: International Cooperation on Tax Matters: Guidelines for International Cooperation Against the Evasion and Avoidance of Taxes (with Special Reference to Taxes on Income, Profits, Capital and Capital Gains) (UN Doc. ST/ESA/142, 1984).

seventeenth, and eighteenth centuries, also imposed low duties and few restrictions. Each of these places became international commer-cial centers and thriving ports of trade. Today, many countries and territories—some that are commercial centers and others that aspire to be—continue to function as tax havens.

In the past several decades the scale on which individuals and companies have moved their operating bases to tax havens to obtain relief or refuge from political interference with their assets has grown dramatically. At the same time, this growth has been paralleled by an increase in the number of attempts to define and to curtail tax havens.

The term "tax haven," although in widespread use, has no internationally accepted definition. In part, this is because the concept is a relative one. One country with substantially lower tax rates on some (or all) taxable income may be considered a tax haven by a second country with substantially higher rates. It is also because the term has often been used pejoratively, so that countries with lower tax rates are unwilling to accept the "tax haven" label.

Several approaches to defining tax havens are used in national legislation. One is to make a list of countries that are regarded as tax havens. Germany, Australia, and Japan, for example, have compiled such lists. A second approach is to define tax havens quantitatively. Article 238A of the French General Tax Code, for example, describes a tax haven as a foreign state or territory that imposes "taxes on profits or income that are substantially lower than in France." What is meant by "substantially lower" is stated—albeit indirectly—in Article 81A:

> Salaries and wages received as remuneration for activities undertaken abroad by French nationals having their fiscal domicile in France who are sent abroad by an employer established in France are not subject to income tax when the taxpayer can prove that the remuneration concerned was in fact subject to income tax in the State where the activities are undertaken and that the foreign tax is equal to at least two-thirds of the tax he would have had to pay in France on the same tax basis.

The United Kingdom has taken a similar approach, defining a tax haven as one that imposes taxes on a company controlled by U.K. residents that are less than one-half of what the company would pay in the United Kingdom.

Other approaches involve neither making a list of nor defining tax havens. Canada, for example, has adopted a "functional" approach. Instead of enacting legislation directed particularly or exclusively at tax havens, it has adopted general legislation that effectively limits the usefulness of tax havens to Canadian taxpayers. The United States has taken a "transactional" approach, imposing restrictions on certain types of income (generally income from foreign holding companies controlled by Americans) and certain types of transactions (typically transactions with related persons) that commonly involve the use of tax havens.

Because individuals and companies do business in tax havens does not necessarily mean that they do so to escape high taxes. Some of the nontax reasons why individuals and firms may do business in a tax haven are the following: (1) to cater to the needs of the tax haven country itself; (2) to remain anonymous for reasons other than avoiding taxes (such as concealing one's identity for personal safety, or to avoid possible boycotts of one's products, or to conceal one's activities from competitors); (3) to protect a company or corporate group from nationalization, political unrest, revolution, or war; and (4) to avoid rules and regulations in a home country (such as national banking laws that dictate interest rate ceilings and set reserve requirements, company laws that prescribe particular management structures, or regulations that restrict foreign exchange).

Of course, many operations carried out in tax havens are tax motivated, or at least partly tax motivated. Many of these are legitimate forms of tax avoidance (as compared to tax evasion), conforming both to the laws in the tax haven country and the investor's home state. In such instances, of course, the possibility of minimizing one's taxes will depend not only on the tax relief offered by the tax haven country but also on the anti-tax haven laws in force in the home country. Some of the legitimate tax-motivated uses of tax havens are the following: (1) overall reduction of a person's tax burden; (2) deferral of tax payments on income from foreign sources until after it is repatriated to the home country so that profits can be accumulated without being depleted by tax payments; (3) minimizing taxes on certain types of income (such as investment income, income from shipping, etc.) that are covered by exceptions to the home country's anti-tax haven legislation; and (4) centralizing income in a tax haven country and repatriating it to the home country in a nontaxable form.

What might best be described as a model worldwide anti-tax haven law is the so-called "Subpart F" of the U.S. Internal Revenue Code.[82] Other countries with similar laws—including Canada, France, Germany, Japan, and the United Kingdom—have modeled their legislation on the American provisions. Several of these (France, Germany, Japan, and the United Kingdom) have, however, restricted the application of their laws to income derived from countries listed or defined as tax havens. As mentioned earlier, the U.S. rules are not limited to income derived from any particular country.[83]

The United States Subpart F rules apply to certain U.S. shareholders of Controlled Foreign Corporations (CFCs). A CFC is a foreign business entity equivalent to an American corporation that on any day of the entity's taxable year has more than 50 percent of all of its voting stock owned or controlled by U.S. shareholders. U.S. shareholders are "United States persons" (i.e., citizens, residents, domestic partnerships, corporations, estates, or trusts) who own more than 10 percent of the voting stock of the foreign business entity. Such shareholders are taxed on certain deemed income of the CFC whether or not it has been distributed. The deemed income includes (1) income from investments in the United States and (2) Subpart F income. Subpart F income is (1) income derived from the insurance of risks in the United States; (2) income earned by a foreign holding company;[84] (3) income earned from sales to a related company (i.e., one that controls the CFC, is controlled by the CFC, or is controlled by the persons who control the CFC); (4) income from services provided to a related company; (5) income derived from the use of an aircraft or vessel in foreign commerce; (6) income accrued from processing, transporting, or distributing oil or gas when these activities are located in a foreign country other than the country in which the oil or gas is extracted; (7) income produced from participation in an international boycott; and (8) the amounts of any illegal bribes, kickbacks, or other payments made to any official, employee, or agent of a government.[85]

Although the U.S. Subpart F Rules are intended to discourage U.S. corporations from reincorporating outside the United States to take advantage of lower corporate tax rates, a number of U.S. companies have done so anyway. Among the companies who have become U.S. "tax dodgers" are Accenture, Foster Wheeler, Global Crossing, Ingersoll-Rand, Stanley Works, and Tyco.[86]

In Reading 13–1, the Chairman and Chief Executive Officer of Stanley Works defends his company's decision to reincorporate in Bermuda.

---

[82]Sections 951–964, which constitute Subpart F of Part III of Subchapter N of Chapter 1 of Subtitle A of the Internal Revenue Code. These sections of the Internal Revenue Code are posted on the Internet at www4.law.cornell.edu/uscode/26/951.html.

[83]For a comparison of the anti-tax haven laws of Canada, France, Germany, Japan, the United Kingdom, and the United States, *see* Organization for Economic Cooperation and Development, *International Tax Avoidance and Evasion,* pp. 55–57 (1987).

As of November, 2000, the following countries had adopted legislation (in the years indicated) similar to the U.S. CFC legislation: Germany (1972); Canada (1972); Japan (1978); France (1980); United Kingdom (1984); New Zealand (1988); Sweden (1990); Australia (1990); Norway (1992); Finland (1995); Spain (1995); Indonesia (1995); Portugal (1995); Denmark (1995); Korea (1996); Hungary (1997); Mexico (1997); South Africa (1997); Estonia (2000); Italy (2000). Department of the Treasury, *The Deferral of Income Earned Through U.S. Controlled Foreign Corporations,* p. 58, n. 10 (2000) at www.ustreas.gov/taxpolicy/library/subpartf.pdf.

[84]The United States also has rules that impose taxes directly on the shareholders of Foreign Personal Holding Companies (FPHC). United States, Internal Revenue Code, §§ 551–556. These rules are similar to those that govern CFCs. Indeed, there is substantial overlap; and, to the extent there is overlap, the rules governing CFCs are applied. *Id.,* § 951(d).

[85]Taxpayer Relief Act of 1997, *United States Statues,* title 111, § 788 (1997) exempted from "deemed income" that income received from the active conduct of a banking, financing, or similar business.

[86]Daniel Gross, "Dodging the Costs of Corporate Citizenship." *Business 2.0* (March 27, 2002) at www.business2.com/articles/web/0,1653,39110,00.html.

Reading 13–1   Reincorporating Abroad to Minimize Taxes as an Act of Patriotism

John Trani, "The Offshore Patriots," *Financial Times*, p. 13 (June 5, 2002).

American manufacturers are under scrutiny, particularly those that operate in the international market.

Today, for example, my company, Stanley Works, will be one of the subjects of a [U.S.] House [of Representatives] ways and means committee hearing. At issue is our decision to do what so many companies have done: reincorporate offshore in order to take advantage of lower tax rates that are available elsewhere.

There is growing hostility directed towards companies that are seeking reincorporation. My own company has been labeled a traitor for its efforts to incorporate abroad, often known as corporate inversion. Given the immense pressure on Stanley and other companies not to take such action, it is worth making a few points about the realities U.S. companies face.

The first is that in today's global economy, numerous foreign competitors pay lower taxes on their worldwide operations. The U.S. tax rules place companies at a competitive disadvantage in the global marketplace. Companies that are not able to compete usually disappear or are acquired by stronger companies that are often incorporated outside the U.S. Accord-ing to a study by the National Foreign Trade Council almost 80 percent of all large acquisitions over the past four years involved foreign companies buying U.S. companies. This usually results in the loss of U.S. headquarters and U.S. jobs.

We believe that tax advantages play a big role in this phenomenon. Moreover, just recently two of our most important U.S. competitors, Ingersoll-Rand and Cooper Industries, reincorporated in Bermuda. In our view, our reincorporation in Bermuda is necessary in order for us to remain competitive and become a stronger, more successful company. It is our goal to keep our management in the U.S. and our headquarters in New Britain, Connecticut.

The second reality is that other U.S. companies may reincorporate offshore until Congress creates a tax system that does not put that at a disadvantage. There are several bills before Congress that aim to eliminate this type of transaction. Unfortunately, all of them deal with the issue in a piecemeal fashion. We would support legislation that is comprehensive—and wholeheartedly agree with the following statement issued by the U.S. Treasury in its May 17 [2002] press release: "Measures designed simply to halt inversion transactions may address the issues in the short run, but in the long run produce unintended and harmful effects for the U.S. economy."

However, we cannot afford to wait for Congress to act. Our competitors will not allow us to do so.

The third reality is that it is not necessarily unpatriotic, as so many are now alleging, for companies to reincorporate abroad. Some people believe that if Stanley lowers its tax rate, they as U.S. taxpayers will pay more. That is not our objective. In fact, the U.S. Treasury will generate more revenue in the short term because the transaction will create a capital gains tax for many shareholders.

In the long term, the issue is not about depriving the U.S. government of tax dollars. It is about reducing the company's global tax rate in order for it to grow and become stronger. We believe that the reorganization will also enhance out ability to expand internationally and potentially attract non-U.S. investors.

As for me, I believe in no taxation, with or without representation. *Source:* © 2002 The New Yorker Collection from cartoonbank.com. All rights reserved.

If Stanley is to be around for another 159 years, it must stay competitive in what has become a global marketplace for our products. Failing to take action to achieve that objective would be irresponsible, unethical and just not right. Becoming a stronger company allows us to preserve thousands of U.S. jobs and create new ones. Under these circumstances, we believe everyone will win, including the U.S. government. That is what real patriotism is all about.

Last, a word about the role of the chief executive officer in all of this. It hurts not to be able to keep old jobs. It hurts to make unpopular moves. And a chief executive who is arrogant about these actions will often lose out.

But the job of a leader is to face reality, distasteful though that may be. That is because a move that wins the popularity contest in the short run often drives the share price down in the long run and the CEO is forced to step down. When that happens, another CEO comes along and he or she has to make the same decisions anew. The more ethical way is to take action for the company as a whole rather than for the benefit of one or the other of its parts.

The unfortunate part of the story is when critics start to question management's character, as they have done with me. People may well be saying that Stanley has now become the poster child for the corporate inversion problem. Many say: "Why don't you back off and go home?" I do not think CEOs should back off when confronted with such challenges. To do so would be to take the easy path, rather than the right path. ■

Transfer Pricing

Consider two associated business establishments that are residents of different states. They may be loosely linked affiliates or close-knit elements of a multinational enterprise. In either case, they are under common ownership, and in both cases they **transfer** goods or merchandise back and forth between themselves. The price they set on the transfer of goods and services from one establishment to another is arbitrary. If the same taxing authority were taxing both establishments, the price would also be irrelevant, because the profit made by the overall enterprise would always be the same, and so would the taxes. However, if one enterprise is located in a low-tax country and the other in a high-tax country, this would not be the case. By charging the enterprise in the high-tax state a high price on transfers from the enterprise in the low-tax state, the first enterprise will have a lower profit and therefore less taxable income that is subject to taxation at high rates, whereas the second enterprise will have a higher profit and more taxable income to be taxed at low rates. The effect for the overall enterprise, of course, is a substantial tax saving.[87]

transfer pricing: A device used by affiliated companies to take advantage of differing tax rates in different countries. On transfers between the affiliates, a high price is charged to the affiliate in the high-tax state so that it will have a small profit; and a low price is charged to the affiliate in the low-tax state so that it will have a large profit. The result for the worldwide operation is a net tax savings.

arm's length principle: Transactions between affiliated firms must be carried on as if they were unrelated companies dealing at arm's length.

Tax authorities commonly approach this problem by assessing the profits earned by affiliated enterprises from international transactions between themselves on the basis of the **arm's length principle**. This principle has been widely accepted in domestic legislation, in model treaties (including the OECD and UN model treaties), and in most bilateral treaties for the avoidance of double taxation. The arm's length principle attributes to an affiliated establishment those profits that it would earn if it were a completely independent entity dealing with another affiliate as if the latter were a distinct and separate enterprise and both were operating under conditions and selling at prices prevailing in the regular market.

The arm's length principle lets tax authorities in the countries where affiliates are located determine the earnings of each affiliate as if it were an independent enterprise dealing with its associates at arm's length. This is true whether the affiliate is a branch, a subsidiary, or the head office.

Three methods for calculating an arm's length price are in common use. (1) The "comparable uncontrolled market price" method uses prices charged in comparable transactions between independent enterprises or between the concerned multinational enterprise and unrelated parties. This is often difficult to ascertain, either because comparable uncontrolled market prices are unavailable or because adjustments have to be made for a variety of factors, such

---

[87] A thorough discussion on transfer pricing can be found in Organization for Economic Cooperation and Development, *Transfer Pricing and Multinational Enterprises* (1979).

as shipping costs or differences in quantity or quality. When a comparable uncontrolled market price cannot be ascertained, taxing authorities use the "cost plus" or "resale minus" methods. (2) The cost plus method begins with the actual cost of goods, services, and the like, and then adds appropriate cost and profit markups. (3) The resale minus method starts with the final selling price and then deducts the appropriate markups for cost and profit. Of course, the complexities of business in the real world make it difficult to apply any of these three methods in its pure form. In practice, as a consequence, taxing authorities use a mixture of these and other methods.[88]

Another approach to countering transfer pricing is used in California (the taxing entity that originated the approach) and some 10 other states of the United States. It is known as the **unitary business rule**, and it taxes multinational enterprises on a percentage of their worldwide income, regardless of where it is earned or by whom.

unitary business rule: A state may tax a multinational enterprise on a share of its total worldwide income.

Instead of beginning with the local affiliated enterprise and adjusting its income so that it is treated as an independent arm's length entity, the unitary business rule begins with the worldwide enterprise and determines the share of income that it has earned locally. Because transfer pricing can distort the amount of profits earned locally, the unitary business rule does not compare local profits to worldwide profits. Instead, it uses three other factors to determine the share of income earned locally: property, payroll, and sales. The ratio between the local and worldwide figures for each of these is then used to adjust the total consolidated income of all the affiliates of the worldwide enterprise. The equation for this is as follows:

$$
\left[\left[\frac{\text{Taxpayer's property in state}}{\text{Taxpayer's and taxpayer's affiliates' worldwide property}} + \frac{\text{Payroll of taxpayer in state}}{\text{Taxpayer's and taxpayer's affiliates' worldwide payroll}} + \frac{\text{Sales of taxpayer in states}}{\text{Taxpayer's and taxpayer's affiliates' worldwide sales}}\right] \div 3\right] \times \begin{array}{c}\text{Consolidated}\\\text{worldwide}\\\text{taxable income}\\\text{of taxpayer}\\\text{and taxpayer's}\\\text{affiliated}\end{array} = \begin{array}{c}\text{Income}\\\text{deemed to}\\\text{be taxable}\\\text{by state}\end{array}
$$

The argument in favor of using this rule is the same as that for the arm's length rule: to give the local taxing authority a fairer (and purportedly larger) share of the income earned by multinational enterprises doing business within its territory. The arguments against the unitary business rule are (a) that it imposes a heavy accounting burden on the worldwide enterprise, which must determine figures for property, payroll, sales, and profits for every one of its worldwide affiliates by American accounting standards in addition to the accounting systems used in other countries; (b) that income is based on worldwide book value rather than taxable income determined after deductions, exemptions, and credits have been taken; and (c) that although it does not violate bilateral U.S. tax treaties (because U.S. tax treaties apply only to U.S. federal taxes), it does violate the Treaties of Friendship, Commerce and Navigation that the United States has entered into with many countries.[89]

Many of the United States' major trading partners oppose the unitary business rule, which they consider to be contrary to the international tax system.[90] In 1985, the U.S. administration proposed legislation to prevent unitary taxation by the American states, but the legislation was never adopted.[91] As a consequence, the individual states are free to impose their own taxes on enterprises operating within their boundaries—a freedom reaffirmed in several recent U.S. Supreme Court decisions, including Case 13–9.

---

[88]*International Cooperation in Tax Matters: Guidelines for International Cooperation against the Evasion and Avoidance of Taxes (with Special Reference to Taxes on Income, Profits, Capital and Capital Gains)*, p. 28 (UN Doc. ST/ESA/142, 1984).

[89]David R. Milton, "Worldwide Unitary Taxation: A Kaleidoscope of Inconsistencies and Double Taxation," *Journal of State Taxation*, vol. 3, pp. 17–18 (1984).

[90]*Id.*, p. 15.

[91]*International Legal Materials*, vol. 25, p. 750 (1986).

Case 13–9 Barclays Bank, PLC v. Franchise Tax Board of California

United States, Supreme Court, 1994.
United States Reports, vol. 512, p. 298 (1994); *International Legal Materials*, vol. 33, p. 909 (1994).[92]
JUSTICE GINSBURG Delivered the Opinion of the Court.

Eleven years ago, in *Container Corp. of America v. Franchise Tax Bd.*,[93] this Court upheld California's income-based corporate franchise tax, as applied to a multinational enterprise, against a comprehensive challenge made under the Due Process and Commerce Clause of the [United States] Federal *Constitution*. *Container Corp.* involved a corporate taxpayer domiciled and headquartered in the United States; in addition to its stateside components, the taxpayer had a number of overseas subsidiaries incorporated in the countries in which they operated. The Court's decision in *Container Corp.* did not address the constitutionality of California's taxing scheme as applied to "domestic corporations with foreign parents or [to] foreign corporations with either foreign parents or foreign subsidiaries."[94] In the consolidated cases before us,[95] we return to the taxing scheme earlier considered in *Container Corp.* and resolve matters left open in that case. The petitioner in [the first case], Barclays Bank, PLC (Barclays), is a United Kingdom corporation in the Barclays Group, a multinational banking enterprise. The petitioner in [the second case], Colgate-Palmolive Co. (Colgate), is the United States-based parent of a multinational manufacturing and sales enterprise. Each enterprise has operations in California. During the years here at issue, California determined the state corporate franchise tax due for these operations under a method known as "worldwide combined reporting." California's scheme first looked to the worldwide income of the multinational enterprise, and then attributed a portion of that income (equal to the average of the proportions of worldwide payroll, property, and sales located in California) to the California operations. The state imposed its tax on the income thus attributed to Barclays and Colgate's California business.

Barclays urges that California's tax system distinctively burdens foreign-based multinationals and results

MAP 13-8 California (1994)

in double international taxation, in violation of the Commerce and Due Process Clauses [of the United States Federal *Constitution*]. . . . We reject [this and other] arguments, and hold that the *Constitution* does not impede application of California's corporate franchise tax to Barclays and Colgate. Accordingly, we affirm the judgments of the California Court of Appeals [from which judgments this appeal was made].

I

A

The Due Process and Commerce Clauses of the *Constitution*, this Court has held, prevent states that impose an income-based tax on nonresidents from "tax[ing] value earned outside [the taxing state's] borders."[96] But when a business enterprise operates in more than one taxing

---

[92]This case is posted on the Internet at laws.findlaw.com/U.S./000/U10358.html.
[93]*United States Reports,* vol. 463, p. 159 (Supreme Ct., 1983).
[94]*Id.,* at p. 189, n. 26.
[[95]Barclays Bank, PLC v. Franchise Tax Board of California was consolidated with Colgate-Palmolive Company v. Franchise Tax Board of California.]
[96]ASARCO Inc. v. Idaho State Tax Comm'n, *United States Reports,* vol. 458, p. 307 at p. 315 (Supreme Ct., 1982).

jurisdiction, arriving at "precise territorial allocations of 'value' is often an elusive goal, both in theory and in practice."[97] Every method of allocation devised involves some degree of arbitrariness.[98]

One means of deriving locally taxable income, generally used by states that collect corporate income-based taxes, is the "unitary business" method. As explained in *Container Corp.*, unitary taxation "rejects geographical or transactional accounting," which is "subject to manipulation" and does not fully capture "the many subtle and largely unquantifiable transfers of value that take place among the components of a single enterprise."[99] The "unitary business/formula apportionment" method

> calculates the local tax base by first defining the scope of the "unitary business" of which the taxed enterprise's activities in the taxing jurisdiction form one part, and then apportioning the total income of that "unitary business" between the taxing jurisdiction and the rest of the world on the basis of a formula taking into account objective measures of the corporation's activities within and without the jurisdiction.[100]

During the income years at issue in these cases—1977 for Barclays, 1970–1973 for Colgate—California assessed its corporate franchise tax by employing a "worldwide combined reporting" method. California's scheme required the taxpayer to aggregate the income of all corporate entities composing the unitary business enterprise, including in the aggregation both affiliates operating abroad and those operating within the United States. Having defined the scope of the "unitary business" thus broadly, California used a long-accepted method of apportionment, commonly called the "three-factor" formula, to arrive at the amount of income attributable to the operations of the enterprise in California. Under the three-factor formula, California taxed a percentage of worldwide income equal to the arithmetic average of the proportions of worldwide payroll, property, and sales located inside the state.[101] Thus, if a unitary business had 8 percent of its payroll, 3 percent of its property, and 4 percent of its sales

in California, the state took the average—5 percent—and imposed its tax on that percentage of the business' total income.[102]

B

The corporate income tax imposed by the United States [federal government] employs a "separate accounting" method, a means of apportioning income among taxing sovereigns used by all major developed nations. In contrast to combined reporting, separate accounting treats each corporate entity discretely for the purpose of determining income tax liability.[103]

Separating accounting poses the risk that a conglomerate will manipulate transfers of value among its components to minimize its total tax liability. To guard against such manipulation, transactions between affiliated corporations must be scrutinized to ensure that they are reported on an "arm's length" basis, i.e., at a price reflecting their true market value.[104] Assuming that all transactions are assigned their arm's length values in the corporate accounts, a jurisdiction using separate accounting taxes corporations that operate within its borders only on the income those corporations recognize on their own books.[105]

At one time, a number of states [within the United States] used worldwide combined reporting, as California did during the years at issue. In recent years, such states, including California, have modified their systems at least to allow corporate election of some variant of an approach that confines combined reporting to the United States' "water's edge."[106] California's 1986 modification of its corporate franchise tax, effective in 1988,[107] made it nearly the last state to give way.[108]

California corporate taxpayers, under the state's water's edge alternative, may elect to limit their combined reporting group to corporations in the unitary business whose individual presence in the United States surpasses a certain threshold.[109] The 1986 amendment conditioned a corporate group's water's edge election on payment of a substantial fee, and allowed the California Franchise Tax Board (Tax Board) to disregard a water's edge election under certain circumstances. In 1993,

---

[97]Container Corp. of America v. Franchise Tax Bd., *id.*, vol. 463, p. 159 at p. 164 (Supreme Ct., 1983).

[98]*Id.*, at p. 182.

[99]*Id.*, at pp. 164–165.

[100]*Id.*, at p. 165.

[101]California Revenue and Tax Code Annotated, § 25128 (1992).

[102]In 1993, California modified the formula to double the weight of the sales factor. *Id.*, § 25128 (1994); *California Statutes,* Chap. 946, § 1 (1993).

[103]An affiliated group of domestic corporations may, however, elect to file a consolidated federal tax return in lieu of separate returns. *United States Code,* Title 26, § 1501.

[104]*See id.*, § 482.

[105]*See* Container Corp. of America v. Franchise Tax Bd., *United States Reports,* vol. 463, p. 159 at p. 185 (Supreme Ct., 1983).

[106]*See* Jerome R. Hellerstein and Walter Hellerstein, *State Taxation: Corporate Income and Franchise Taxes,* vol. 1, para. 8.16, pp. 8–187 (2nd ed., 1993).

[107]California Statutes, Chap. 660, § 6 (1986)

[108]Jerome R. Hellerstein and Walter Hellerstein, *State Taxation: Corporate Income and Franchise Taxes,* vol. 1, para. 8.16, pp. 8–187 (2nd ed., 1993).

[109]California Revenue and Tax Code Annotated, § 25110 (1992).

California again modified its corporate franchise tax statute, this time to allow domestic and foreign enterprises to elect water's edge treatment without payment of a fee and without the threat of disregard.[110] The new amendments became effective in January 1994.

C

The first of these consolidated cases . . . is a tax refund suit brought by two members of the Barclays Group, a multinational banking enterprise. Based in the United Kingdom, the Barclays Group includes more than 220 corporations doing business in some 60 nations. The two refund-seeking members of the Barclays corporate family did business in California and were therefore subject to California's franchise tax. Barclays Bank of California (Barcal), one of the two taxpayers, was a California banking corporation wholly owned by Barclays Bank International, Limited (BBI), the second taxpayer. BBI, a United Kingdom corporation, did business in the United Kingdom and in more than 33 other nations and territories.

In computing its California franchise tax based on 1997 income, Barcal reported only the income from its own operations. BBI reported income on the assumption that it participated in a unitary business composed of itself and its subsidiaries, but not its parent corporation and the parent's other subsidiaries. After auditing BBI's and Barcal's 1977 income year franchise tax returns, the Tax Board, respondent here, determined that both were part of a worldwide unitary business, the Barclays Group. Ultimately, the Board assessed additional tax liability of $1,678 for BBI and $152, 420 for Barcal.

Barcal and BBI paid the assessments and sued for refunds. . . .

The petitioner [in the second case], Colgate-Palmolive Co., is a Delaware corporation headquartered in New York. Colgate and its subsidiaries doing business in the United States engaged principally in the manufacture and distribution of household and personal hygiene products. In addition, Colgate owned some 75 corporations that operated entirely outside the United States; these foreign subsidiaries also engaged primarily in the manufacture and distribution of household and personal hygiene products. When Colgate filed California franchise tax returns based on 1970–1973 income, it reported the income earned from its foreign corporations on a separate accounting basis. Essentially, Colgate maintained that the [United States federal] *Constitution* compelled California to limit the reach of its unitary principle to the United States' water's edge. The Tax Board determined that Colgate's taxes should be computed on the basis of worldwide combined reporting, and assessed a four-year deficiency of $604,756. Colgate paid the tax and sued for a refund.

[Because the California courts ultimately upheld the unitary business tax method, the petitioners appealed to the United States Supreme Court.]

* * *

II

The Commerce Clause expressly gives Congress power "[t]o regulate Commerce with foreign Nations and among the several States."[111] It has long been understood, as well, to provide "protection from state legislation inimical to the national commerce [even] where Congress has not acted. . . . "[112] The Clause does not shield interstate (or foreign) commerce from its "fair share of the state tax burden."[113] Absent congressional approval, however, a state tax on such commerce will not survive Commerce Clause scrutiny if the taxpayer demonstrates that the tax either (1) applies to an activity lacking a substantial nexus to the taxing state; (2) is not fairly apportioned; (3) discriminates against interstate commerce; *or* (4) is not fairly related to the services provided by the state. [These factors were set out in, and are known as, the] *Complete Auto Transit, Inc. v. Brady*[114] [criteria].

In "the unique context of foreign commerce," a state's power is further constrained because of "the special need for federal uniformity."[115] "In international relations and with respect to foreign intercourse and trade the people of the United States act through a single government with unified and adequate national power."[116] A tax affecting *foreign* commerce therefore raises two concerns in addition to the four delineated in *Complete Auto*. The first is prompted by "the enhanced risk of multiple taxation."[117] The second relates to the Federal government's capacity to "speak with one voice when regulating commercial regulations with foreign governments."[118]

California's worldwide combined reporting system easily meets three of the four *Complete Auto* criteria.

---

[110]California Statutes, Chap. 31, § 53; Chap. 881, § 22 (1993). *See* California Revenue and Tax Code, § 25110 (1994).

[111]United States, *Constitution,* Article I, § 8, Clause 3.

[112]Southern Pacific Co. v. Arizona *ex rel.* Sullivan, *United States Reports,* vol. 325, p. 761 at p. 769 (Supreme Ct., 1945).

[113]Department of Revenue of Washington v. Association of Washington Stevedoring Cos., *id.,* vol. 435, p. 734 at p. 750 (Supreme Ct., 1978).

[114]*Id.,* vol. 430, p. 274 at p. 279 (Supreme Ct., 1977).

[115]Wardair Canada, Inc. v. Florida Dept. of Revenue, *id.,* vol. 477, p. 1 at p. 8 (Supreme Ct., 1986).

[116]Japan Line, Ltd. v. County of Los Angeles, *id.,* vol. 441, p. 434 at p. 448 (Supreme Court, 1979) quoting Board of Trustees v. United States, *id.,* vol. 289, p. 59 (Supreme Ct., 1933).

[117]Container Corp. of America v. Franchise Tax Bd., *id.,* vol. 463, p. 159 at p. 185 (1983).

[118]Japan Line, Ltd. v. County of Los Angeles, *id.,* vol. 441, p. 434 at p. 449 (Supreme Court, 1979) quoting Michelin Tire Corp. v. Wages, *id.,* vol. 423, p. 276 at p. 285 (Supreme Ct., 1976).

The nexus requirement is met by the business all three taxpayers—Barcal, BBI, and Colgate—did in California during the years in question.[119] The "fair apportionment" standard is also satisfied. Neither Barclays nor Colgate has demonstrated the lack of a "rational relationship between the income attributed to the state and the intrastate values of the enterprise";[120] nor have the petitioners shown that the income attributed to California is "out of all appropriate proportion to the business transacted by the [taxpayers]] in that state."[121] We note in this regard that, "if applied by every jurisdiction," California's method "would result in no more than all of unitary business' income being taxed."[122] And surely California has afforded Colgate and the Barclays taxpayers "protection, opportunities, and benefits" for which the state can exact a return.[123]

Barclays (but not Colgate) vigorously contends, however, that California's worldwide combined reporting scheme violates the antidiscrimination component of the *Complete Auto* test. Barclays maintains that a foreign-owner of a taxpayer filing a California tax return "is forced to convert its diverse financial and accounting records from around the world into the language, currency, and accounting principles of the United States" at "prohibitive" expense.[124] Domestic-owned taxpayers, by contrast, need not incur such expense because they "already keep most of their records in English, in United States currency, and in accord with United States accounting principles."[125] Barclays urges that imposing this "prohibitive administrative burden"[126] on foreign-owned enterprises gives a competitive advantage to their U.S.-owned counterparts and constitutes "economic protectionism" of the kind that this Court has often condemned.[127]

Compliance burdens, if disproportionately imposed on out-of-jurisdiction enterprises, may indeed be inconsonant with the Commerce Clause. . . . The factual predicate of Barclays' discrimination claim, however, is infirm.

Barclays points to provisions of California's implementing regulations setting out three discrete means for a taxpayer to fulfill its franchise tax reporting requirements. Each of these modes of compliance would require Barclays to gather and present much information not maintained by the unitary group in the ordinary course of business. California's regulations, however, also provide that the Tax Board "shall consider the effort and expense required to obtain the necessary information" and, in "appropriate cases, such as when the necessary data cannot be developed from financial records maintained in the regular course of business," may accept "reasonable approximations."[128] As the [California] Court of Appeal comprehended, in determining Barclays' 1977 worldwide income, Barclays and the Tax Board "used these [latter] provisions and [made] computations based on reasonable approximations,"[129] thus allowing Barclays to avoid the large compliance costs of which it complains. Barclays has not shown that California's provision for "reasonable approximations" systematically "overtaxes" foreign corporations generally or BBI or Barcal in particular.

In sum, Barclays has not demonstrated that California's tax system in fact operates to impose inordinate compliance burdens on foreign enterprises. Barclays' claim of unconstitutional discrimination against foreign commerce therefore fails.

III

* * *

B

We turn, finally, to the question ultimately and most energetically presented: Did California's worldwide combined reporting requirement, as applied to Barcal, BBI, and Colgate, "impair federal uniformity in an area where federal uniformity is essential,"[130] in particular, did the state's taxing scheme "preven[t] the Federal government from 'speaking with one voice' in international trade"?[131]

* * *

As in *Container Corp.* . . . we discern no "specific indications of congressional intent" to bar the state action here challenged. Our decision upholding California's franchise tax in *Container Corp.* left the ball in Congress' court; had Congress, the branch responsible

---

[119]*See* Mobil Oil Corp. v. Commissioner of Taxes of Vt., *id.,* vol. 445, p. 425 at pp. 436–437 (Supreme Ct., 1980).
[120]Container Corp. of America v. Franchise Tax Bd., *id.,* vol. 463, p. 159 at pp. 180–181 (1983).
[121]*Id.,* at p. 181.
[122]*Id.,* at p. 169.
[123]Wisconsin v. J. C. Penney Co., *id.,* vol. 311, p. 435 at p. 444 (1940).
[124]Brief for Petitioner in [Barclays case] at p. 44.
[125]*Id.,* at p. 45.
[126]*Id.,* at p. 43.
[127]*Id.,* at pp. 43–46.
[128]California Code of Regulations, Title 18, § 25137–6(e)(1) (1985).
[129]*California Appellate Reports, Fourth Series,* vol. 10, p. 1742 at p. 1756 (3rd Dist. Ct. of Appeal, 1992).
[130]Japan Line, Ltd. v. County of Los Angeles, *id.,* vol. 441, p. 434 at p. 448 (Supreme Court, 1979).
[131]*Id.,* at p. 453.

for the regulation of foreign commerce,[132] considered nationally uniform use of separate accounting "essential,"[133] it could have enacted legislation prohibiting the states from taxing corporate income based on the worldwide combined reporting method. In the 11 years that have elapsed since our decision in *Container Corp.*, Congress has failed to enact such legislation.

* * *

Given . . . Congress' willingness to tolerate states' worldwide combined reporting mandates . . . we cannot conclude that "the foreign policy of the United States—whose nuances . . . are much more the province of the Executive Branch and Congress than of this Court—is

[so] seriously threatened"[134] by Cali-fornia's practice as to warrant our intervention. This Court has no constitutional authority to make the policy judgments essential to regulating foreign commerce and conducting foreign affairs. Matters relating "to the conduct of foreign relations . . . are so exclusively entrusted to the political branches of government as to be largely immune from judicial inquiry or interference."[135] For this reason, Barclays' . . . argument that California's worldwide combined reporting requirement is unconstitutional . . . is directed to the wrong forum. . . .

* * *

Affirmed. ◼

---

[132]*See* United States, *Constitution*, Article I, § 8, Clause 3.
[133]Japan Line, Ltd. v. County of Los Angeles, *United States Reports,* vol. 441, p. 434 at p. 448 (Supreme Court, 1979).
[134]Container Corp. of America v. Franchise Tax Bd., *id.,* vol. 463, p. 159 at p. 196 (1983).
[135]Harisiades v. Shaughnessy, *id.,* vol. 342, p. 580 at p. 589 (Supreme Ct., 1952).

Treaty Shopping

treaty shopping: The selection of a state that has beneficial tax treaties as a place in which to set up a subsidiary.

Treaty shopping means that a taxpayer "shops" for countries with beneficial tax treaty provisions, then sets up subsidiary enterprises in those countries to take advantage of their treaties.

The expression "treaty shopping" was first used in congressional hearings on Offshore Tax Havens held in the United States in April 1971.[136] The tax problem it describes, however, has been around for quite some time. A 1945 tax treaty between the United States and the United Kingdom, for example, contains an "abuse" clause.[137] The OECD has been studying the problem since 1961; and it is discussed in the commentary to Article 1 of the OECD's 1977 Model Treaty.[138] A 1983 OECD Working Paper entitled "The Improper Use of Tax Conventions through Conduit Companies by Persons Not Entitled to Their Benefits" examines treaty shopping in depth, as does a 1987 United Nations report by the *ad hoc* Group of Experts on International Cooperation in Tax Matters.[139]

Treaty shopping involves two basic situations: the use of "direct conduit companies" and the use of "stepping-stone conduit companies." Both involve taxpayers who take advantage of tax treaties that were not meant to apply to them.

Direct Conduit Companies　Company A in State A has a subsidiary, Company B, in State B. When Company B remits dividends, interest, or royalties to Company A, State B withholds substantial taxes. To avoid these taxes, Company A shops around for a country, State C, that has a beneficial tax treaty with State A (i.e., a treaty that reduces or eliminates withholding taxes charged by State C when dividends, interest, or royalties are remitted to a company in State A) *and* State B (i.e., a treaty that reduces or eliminates withholding taxes charged by State B when dividends, interest, or royalties are remitted to a company in State A).

direct conduit company: A holding company is organized in a state that has beneficial tax provisions both with a state where a parent company is located and with a state where its subsidiary is located.

Having "shopped" and found State C, Company A will set up a subsidiary, Company C, in State C, and make it the parent of Company B. Company B will then remit its dividends, interest, or royalties to Company C (Company C serving as a **direct conduit company**). (See Exhibit 13-6.)

---

[136]David Rosenbloom, "Tax Treaty Abuse: Policies and Issues," *Law & Policy in International Business,* vol. 16, p. 783 (1983).
[137]Commerce Clearing House, *Tax Treaties,* vol. 2, § 8111.
[138]OECD, Model Tax Treaty, Article 1, note 9, commentary (1977).
[139]The OECD paper is reproduced in *International Tax Avoidance and Evasion,* pp. 87–106 (1987); the UN report is in *Contributions to International Cooperation in Tax Matters* (UN Doc. ST/ESA/203, 1988).

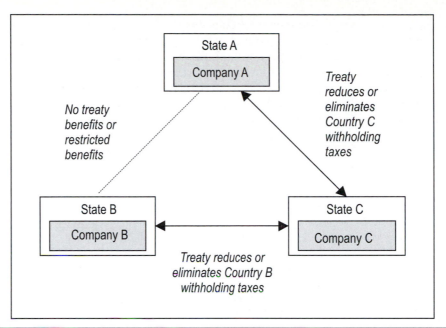

EXHIBIT 13-6   Treaty Shopping: Direct Conduit Companies

The major tax consequence of this arrangement is the elimination or reduction of the tax collected by State B. Indeed, neither State A nor State C have to be tax havens for Company A to have a tax advantage. The principal savings for Company A will be the difference between the tax imposed by State B on remittances to State A and the lower tax (or absence of tax) imposed on remittance to State C.

stepping-stone conduit companies: Holding companies are organized in states that have a mutually beneficial tax treaty—one of which also has a beneficial tax treaty with a state where a parent company is located, while the other also has a beneficial tax treaty with a state where the subsidiary is located.

tax sink: A state that imposes no income taxes.

Stepping-stone Conduit Companies   A **stepping-stone conduit companies** arrangement is similar to the direct conduit situation, except that a second intermediary country (State D) and company (Company D) has to be used to move profits from the source company (Company B) back to the parent (Company A). In this situation there is no tax treaty between State A and State C, and State C does impose taxes on profits earned by Company C. To remedy this, Company A shops for a second country, State D, to serve as a **tax sink**. To qualify as a tax sink, State D must impose no income taxes. In addition, State C must (because of a tax treaty or local legislation) allow its companies to deduct from their earnings any expenses paid to companies in State D.

Again, having "shopped" and found a tax sink in State D, Company A will set up a second subsidiary, Company D, in State D. Company D will be made an affiliate of Company C. Company D will grant Company C the technology licenses, the franchises, the loans, and so forth it needs to carry on its business. Company C will then pay Company D high fees, commissions, interest, and so forth, all of which Company C may deduct in State C from its income. Company C will, as a consequence, pay little or no income tax to State C. The income, having been transferred to Company D in State D, will then be remitted to Company A, free from the taxes of both State B and State C. (See Exhibit 13-7.)

Abuse   Most tax authorities consider treaty shopping to be improper. Three reasons are most commonly given for this: One, the states that signed a tax treaty meant for it to benefit only their residents and their states. Each gave up something in exchange for some benefit. If a person from a third state is allowed to take advantage of this, the principle of reciprocity is violated. Two, in granting benefits to residents of the other treaty state, the first state is assuming that those residents will be subject to the normal tax regime of the other state. Three, third states have little incentive to enter into tax treaties if their residents can take advantage of existing tax treaties.

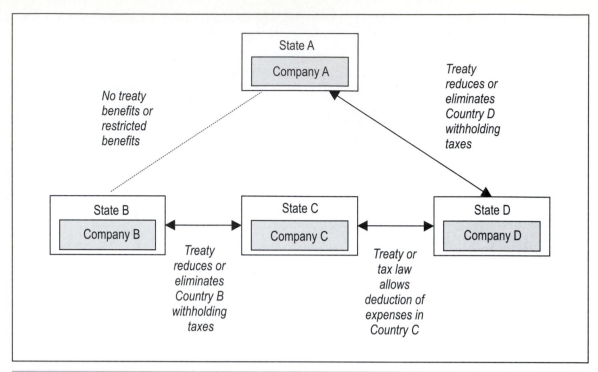

EXHIBIT 13-7 Treaty Shopping: Stepping-Stone Conduit Companies

Countermeasures The tax authorities opposed to treaty shopping have found solutions to the problem both in national legislation and through the use of specific anti-abuse provisions in tax treaties.

Only two countries have anti-abuse legislation: Switzerland and the United States. Switzerland enacted an anti-abuse ordinance in 1962 that suspends treaty benefits whenever a Swiss company makes a claim for a tax reduction that is abusive.[140] A claim is abusive (a) if a substantial part of a Swiss company's income is given to persons not entitled to treaty benefits, (b) if a substantial share of the Swiss company is held by nonresidents, (c) if the Swiss company is an agent of a nonresident, or (d) if the income is given to a Swiss family foundation or Swiss partnership in which nonresidents own a substantial portion.

The U.S. Tax Reform Act of 1986 introduced a national treaty abuse provision that limited treaty benefits to companies that are "qualified" residents of either the United States or the foreign country that was a signatory of the particular treaty.[141] Unqualified corporations are those with more than 50 percent of their stock in the hands of residents of third-party states, or that disburse more than 50 percent of their income to third-party residents.[142]

In countries that do not have specific anti-abuse legislation, the problem of treaty shopping is attacked using general principles of equity. Common law countries (including Australia, Canada, and the United Kingdom) use a "substance over form" approach. That is, their tax authorities attempt to determine if the movement of income between foreign affiliated companies is based on legitimate commercial reasons or if it is merely a sham set up in order to obtain treaty benefits. Civil law countries (including France and Germany) use an "abuse" approach.

---

[140]*Bundesratbesscluss betr. die ungerechtfertigte Inanspruchnahme von Doppelbesteuerungs abkommen* (December 14, 1962), *Eidgenössische Gesetzsammlung,* vol. 1962, p. 1622, amended by *Kreisschreiben der Eidgenössischen Steuerverwaltung* (December 31, 1962).

[141]United States, Internal Revenue Code, § 884.

[142]*Id.,* § 884(e)(B). Special provisions are made for publicly traded corporations. Regardless of the stock ownership of the corporation, they will be treated as qualified residents if their stock is traded regularly and primarily on an established securities market in the signatory foreign state.

In other words, their tax authorities ask whether a particular arrangement of companies constitutes an abuse, a misuse, or an improper use of a tax treaty.[143]

Tax Treaty Provisions   Anti-abuse provisions are becoming more common in bilateral tax treaties.[144] Several approaches are possible. Those that have appeared so far include

look-through approach: A company is entitled to tax treaty benefits only if it is owned completely by residents of the state in which it was organized.

exclusion approach: Holding companies and domestic companies that pay low taxes are not entitled to tax treaty benefits.

subject-to-tax approach: Tax treaty benefits are available only if income is subject to taxation in one or the other of the signatory states.

channel approach: Tax treaty benefits are denied if a share of a company's income is paid to a nonresident holding company.

bona fide approach: To be entitled to tax treaty benefits, a company must show that its structure and transactions are motivated by sound business reasons.

abstinence approach: Refusal by a state to enter into a tax treaty with a tax haven state.

thin capitalization: The intentional financing of a company with debt funding rather than equity funding.

1. The **look-through approach**. Treaty benefits are granted to a company only if it is owned completely or substantially by residents of the state in which it is organized. This is the most common approach and the one taken by the UN Model Tax Treaty and the 1981 United States Model Treaty.[145]

2. The **exclusion approach**. Low-taxed holding and domiciliary companies are excluded from treaty benefits.[146]

3. The **subject-to-tax approach.** Treaty benefits are based on the condition that income derived in one state must actually be subject to taxation in the other state. In other words, company income may not be exempt from taxation in both states.

4. The **channel approach**. This provision is primarily meant to address the stepping-stone arrangement. Treaty benefits are denied to a company if a certain percentage of its income is used to pay for charges made by individuals or companies who are not residents of one of the contracting states.

5. The **bona fide approach**. Affiliated companies are not entitled to treaty benefits unless they can demonstrate that the structure and the transactions of their business arrangements are motivated by sound commercial reasons. To qualify they must meet certain standards. These standards may address the motives for setting up the affiliated structure, the amount of business activity in an affiliate's state of residence, the amount of taxes paid in the state of residence, and whether or not the affiliate's shares are traded on an approved stock exchange.

6. The **abstinence approach**. Because tax haven countries often encourage treaty abuse, states opposed to it have simply abstained from entering into tax treaties with those countries. Liechtenstein, the Channel Islands, Monaco, and Panama, as a consequence, have no or only a few tax treaties.

Thin Capitalization   **Thin capitalization** is a term used to describe the situation where a company is purposely financed by loans rather than by equity capital. For example, a parent company may contribute money to a subsidiary in the form of loans, or it may contribute physical assets or technology, also in the form of loans. The result is a company with a high debt to equity (debt/equity) ratio.

The reason for thinly capitalizing a company relates to the fact that the tax treatment of interest differs from the treatment of dividends and other profit distributions. Interest is almost always deductible in determining taxable income, whereas dividends and other profit distributions—being part of that income—are not deductible. To illustrate: The Amalgamated Company has income of $100,000. If it pays out $25,000 in interest to creditors, it will have a net taxable income of $75,000. On the other hand, if it pays out that same $25,000 as dividends to shareholders, its net taxable income will remain as $100,000.

Thin capitalization is most commonly countered by national legislation rather than in tax treaties. The usual mechanism is to disallow the deduction of interest payments when the debt/equity exceeds a particular norm. In some countries, this is modified by allowing a

---

[143]Deloitte, Haskins & Sells International, *Treaty Shopping: An Emerging Tax Issue and its Present States in Various Countries,* p. 7 (1988).

[144]For a current survey of anti-abuse provisions in the bilateral treaties of 19 countries, *see* Deloitte, Haskins & Sells International, *Treaty Shopping: An Emerging Tax Issue and its Present States in Various Countries* (1988).

[145]UN, Model Tax Treaty, Article 16 (Alternative Draft published December 23, 1981); United States, Model Tax Treaty, Article 16 (1981 Draft).

[146]The treatment of holding and domiciliary companies in seven European countries is examined by Ned Shelton and Freddy de Petter in "Holding Companies: A Review of the New Luxembourg Rules and Six Other Countries," *European Taxation,* vol. 31, p. 63 (March/April 1991).

company to show that its debt/equity ratio is an "arm's length" ratio or that it is otherwise commercially reasonable.[147]

Tax Evasion

tax evasion: The intentional misrepresentation or concealment of a person's tax obligations.

The distinguishing feature of **tax evasion**, as compared to tax avoidance, is that it involves the willful and conscious misrepresentation or concealment of one's tax obligations or (rarely) the flight of a taxpayer to another country. Also, unlike tax avoidance, it is universally regarded as illegal.

Tax authorities are faced with several significant problems in trying to combat tax evasion internationally. First are the constitutional and political difficulties that many states face in helping a foreign tax authority collect taxes. Taxation is closely tied up with sovereignty, and to some extent a state abrogates its sovereignty by cooperating with a foreign tax authority. In addition, helping a foreign tax authority examine local records runs contrary to the right of privacy guaranteed by an ever-growing body of human rights legislation in many developed countries. The examination of local records is also at odds with the bank secrecy laws that are valued so highly in tax haven countries as tools for attracting foreign investment.

Second, the enforcement of foreign tax judgments puts burdens on local tax authorities and tax courts that they are often unprepared or unwilling to assume. Because the tax authorities in one state know little about the tax and legal system in a second state, they are commonly unable to reassure themselves that foreign taxes are equitable and that a taxpayer is being adequately protected from arbitrary treatment. Courts, similarly, are not always equipped to reach a just decision in enforcing a foreign tax judgment or to fairly determine that the documents provided by an applicant state are not flawed. By long tradition, both the local tax authorities and local courts have been quick to use the rule of *forum non conveniens*[148] as an excuse for ignoring foreign requests for tax information or for assistance in enforcing foreign tax judgments.

A third reason that local tax authorities have difficulty in helping their foreign colleagues in combating tax evasion has to do with purely practical problems. These include the lack of an adequate local library of foreign statutory and case materials, the problem of dealing with documents in foreign languages, and the difficulty of examining audits or other bookkeeping records maintained by an unfamiliar accounting system.

Despite these difficulties, taxing authorities are frequently successful in tracking down and prosecuting tax evaders. Case 13–10 is a case in point.

---

[147]*Contributions to International Cooperation in Tax Matters: Treaty Shopping, Thin Capitalization, Cooperation between Tax Authorities, Resolving International Tax Disputes,* pp. 24–27 (UN Doc. ST/ESA/203, 1988).
[148]*See* Chapter 3 for a discussion of the doctrine of *forum non conveniens.*

Case 13–10   Kalo v. Commissioner of Internal Revenue

United States, Sixth Circuit Court of Appeals, 1998. *United States Tax Cases* (CCH), vol. 98, pt. 2, para. 50,514; 81 (1998).

CIRCUIT JUDGE RONALD LEE GILMAN:

Circuit Judge. Jacob Kalo ("taxpayer") appeals the Tax Court's decision upholding the assessment by the Com-

missioner of Internal Revenue ("Commissioner") of penalties and interest for fraudulently failing to report income derived from interest-bearing foreign bank accounts. Since we find no error in the Tax Court's decision in this case, we AFFIRM.

I. Background

Taxpayer and his wife . . . (collectively "Kalos"), live in West Bloomfield, Michigan. He is an obstetrician and gynecologist whose patients often pay in cash for his medical services. Although a practicing physician, taxpayer does not carry medical malpractice insurance coverage. During the years 1986 through 1989, taxpayer was both a partner and an employee of Jacob Kalo, M.D. P.C. ("Kalo P.C."). Kalo P.C. operated five medical clinics in Michigan, including a clinic at 15650 E. Eight Mile Road in Detroit, Michigan ("East GYN Office"). Kalo P.C.'s business operations were in turmoil during the years 1986 through 1989 because of a legal dispute between taxpayer and his two former business partners. Taxpayer's business problems and his lack of malpractice insurance prompted him to hide a significant amount of money in foreign bank accounts.

To help him in making decisions concerning foreign investments, taxpayer consulted with an accountant and a financial advisor. The financial advisor provided financial services for taxpayer specifically tailored to foreign investment for nearly twelve years, including discussions concerning foreign interest rates and foreign investments. From these extensive dealings, the financial advisor formed the opinion that taxpayer had a better than average knowledge about foreign investments.

The Kalos filed joint income tax returns for the years 1986 through 1989. They held a number of overseas bank accounts during this period of time, particularly in Canada. For the years 1985 through 1988, taxpayer made numerous cash deposits into Canadian bank accounts, seven of which exceeded $10,000. Taxpayer, for example, deposited more than $230,000 in cash into a bank account at the Royal Bank of Canada during this three-year period. By 1989, the Kalos had deposited approximately $1 million with the Royal Bank of Canada and more than $3 million in all of their Canadian bank accounts combined.

The couple, however, neither disclosed the existence of these foreign bank accounts nor reported how much

interest income they received from them when they filed their original income tax returns. In fact, when answering Question 10 on Schedule B of their income tax returns, the couple specifically denied having any foreign bank accounts until the 1988 tax year. The total amount of interest income the Kalos failed to report for the years 1986 through 1989 was $309,322.

Beginning in 1990 and continuing into 1991, the Internal Revenue Service's Criminal Investigation Division ("CID") investigated the Kalos for possible income tax violations. Prodded by the efforts of the CID's investigation, the Kalos belatedly filed amended tax returns for the years 1986 through 1989. In these amended tax returns, the Kalos reported the previously undisclosed interest income from their foreign bank accounts and paid the additional taxes due.

As part of the investigation, CID special agents interviewed taxpayer on April 18, 1990. During the interview, the special agents asked taxpayer whether he had any money in foreign bank accounts. Taxpayer responded by telling the agents of a bank account in Israel that he first reported on his 1988 tax return, and that he might also have a bank account in Europe. When specifically questioned about Canadian bank accounts, taxpayer stated that the only bank account he held in Canada was a joint bank account shared with his father. At the time, this joint bank account held only $37. Taxpayer claimed that all the money in the joint bank account belonged to his father. In fact, taxpayer specifically told the special agents that he had nothing to do with this account because his father handled all of the banking transactions.

When questioned about business records for the East GYN Office, the special agents were informed by taxpayer that the state of Michigan had seized the business records during a Medicaid audit and had never returned them. In truth, the state of Michigan had never audited the business records, much less taken them. Instead, it was taxpayer who removed business records from the East GYN Office after the CID began its criminal investigation. In a further attempt to cover his tracks, taxpayer told one of his employees at the East GYN Office that if anyone asked about the records to say that the state of Michigan took the records during a Medicaid audit. In a subsequent interview with CID special agents, taxpayer indicated that the state of Michigan had returned the business records. The CID subpoenaed these records, along with records from the other Kalo P.C. clinics. Taxpayer, however, never produced the records subpoenaed.

In an interview with special agents on August 23, 1990, taxpayer stated that the East GYN Office never had a day where the cash receipts were more than $2,000. This statement was also false. On the following day, taxpayer asked two of his employees . . . to write letters to the CID stating that the daily cash flow at the

MAP 13-9 Michigan (1998)

clinic ranged from $40 to $800. Both employees refused, stating that those dollar amounts were false. Taxpayer nevertheless adhered to this dollar amount in subsequent discussions with the CID. Also during the August 23, 1990 interview, taxpayer informed the special agents that he believed that interest income was not taxable until withdrawn from a foreign bank because his accountant led him to believe this. When asked for his accountant's name, taxpayer's attorney interrupted and stated that it was not the accountant who gave this advice, but that his client heard or knew of it from someone else.

Taxpayer's accountant later testified that he never told taxpayer that the interest earned from foreign bank accounts was not taxable until withdrawn. In fact, when preparing the Kalos' tax returns for the years 1986 through 1989, the accountant specifically asked whether the couple had any foreign bank accounts. Taxpayer, however, never informed the accountant that the couple had any foreign bank accounts until the 1988 taxable year, when he told the accountant about the bank account in Israel. The accountant promptly reported the interest from the Israeli account on the Kalos' 1988 and 1989 income tax returns. Similarly, taxpayer never informed his financial advisor that he was receiving interest income from foreign bank accounts.

In light of the accountant's testimony, taxpayer refined his story and told the CID special agents that an unnamed bank official at an unnamed Canadian bank informed him that he did not have to pay taxes on the interest income. Proof was presented, however, that the policy of the Royal Bank of Canada is not to give advice to foreigners about the taxability of interest generated in their bank accounts.

On September 9, 1992, the United States Attorney filed an information charging taxpayer with four counts of willfully failing to disclose information on his income tax returns, a violation of 26 U.S.C. § 7203. On January 29, 1993, taxpayer pled guilty to one count of violating § 7203 for the 1987 tax year. The court sentenced taxpayer to 180 days of home confinement, one year of probation, and fined him $51,318.

On October 7, 1994, the Commissioner issued a notice of tax deficiencies against the Kalos for the 1986 tax year. The notice also assessed additions to and penalties on tax against the Kalos due to fraud for the tax years 1986 through 1989. The Commissioner later withdrew the deficiency assessment after the Kalos amended their income tax return for the 1986 tax year to reflect the underpayment in tax. On November 7, 1994, the Kalos filed a petition in Tax Court seeking a redetermination of the Commissioner's additions to and penalties on tax.

. . . During trial, counsel for the Kalos objected to the introduction of evidence related to the operation of the East GYN Office. Counsel asserted that the evidence was not relevant to a determination of fraud concerning foreign bank accounts. . . . The Commissioner responded by noting that "one of the indications of fraud [in this case] is that the monies that were in the foreign accounts were skimmed income [from the clinics]." The Tax Court overruled the objection and allowed the Commissioner to introduce evidence concerning taxpayer's management of the East GYN Office.

After the trial, the Tax Court issued its decision upholding the Commissioner's determinations of additions to and penalties on taxes due from taxpayer. Specifically, the Tax Court held that the Commissioner had proven by clear and convincing evidence that taxpayer underpaid his taxes for each year in question due to fraud. The Tax Court, however, disallowed the Commissioner's determinations against [taxpayer's spouse.]. The Tax Court's judgment was entered January 7, 1997. This appeal followed.

II. Analysis

* * *

. . . [T]axpayer contends that the Tax Court erred in finding that his failure to report interest income was due to fraud. The Tax Court's finding of fraud is a question of fact and will only be reversed if shown to be clearly erroneous. . . .

For the relevant period in question, former § 6653(B) [of the United States *Internal Revenue Code*] provided that "if any part of any underpayment . . . of tax . . . is due to fraud, there shall be added to the tax an amount equal to . . . 50 percent . . . of the underpayment." The Commissioner has the burden of proving by clear and convincing evidence that there was an underpayment of taxes and that some part of that underpayment was due to fraud. In the present case, it is uncontested that an underpayment of taxes occurred. The only remaining issue concerns taxpayer's alleged fraudulent intent.

A court may infer fraudulent intent by looking to various kinds of circumstantial evidence. Such "badges of fraud" include: (1) failure to file tax returns; (2) an understatement of income over an extended period; (3) failure to furnish the government with access to records; (4) failure to keep adequate books and records; (5) the sophistication of the taxpayer; (6) concealment of bank accounts; (7) giving implausible or inconsistent explanations of behavior; and (8) willingness to defraud another in a business transaction. While no single factor is necessarily conclusive, the combination of a number of these badges of fraud constitutes persuasive evidence of fraud.

The Tax Court found that taxpayer: (1) understated his income over a period of four years; (2) was relatively sophisticated with respect to issues concerning foreign investments; (3) attempted to conceal his activities with respect to his foreign bank accounts by giving false statements on his tax returns; (4) pled guilty to willfully failing to disclose information concerning his foreign bank accounts; and (5) misled authorities through evasion and obfuscation concerning the existence of the bank accounts and of business records pertinent to the CID's investigation. Since many badges of fraud were present, the Tax Court held that taxpayer's underpayment of interest income was due to fraud.

Taxpayer now claims that the Tax Court's findings of fact were clearly erroneous. Specifically, taxpayer claims that: (1) the Commissioner introduced no evidence that taxpayer was familiar with the tax laws; (2) his accountant lied when he testified that taxpayer failed to tell him about the foreign bank accounts; (3) the Tax Court failed to take into account that he reported interest income from his Israeli bank account for the years 1988 and 1989; (4) the Tax Court misconstrued his statements to the CID special agents concerning the Canadian bank accounts; and (5) the Tax Court failed to consider the fact that his true purpose in hiding the money in the foreign bank accounts was not to avoid paying taxes, but to hide his assets from potential malpractice claimants and former business partners.

Taxpayer's arguments are unpersuasive. First, and foremost, taxpayer's contention regarding his true purpose in opening the foreign bank accounts only serves to implicate another badge of fraud, i.e., taxpayer's willingness to defraud others in business transactions. We also find taxpayer's arguments regarding his accountant's testimony and the "true" nature of his statements to the CID agents equally unavailing. When presented with conflicting testimony, the Tax Court is free to resolve the conflict by judging the witnesses' credibility.

The fact that the Tax Court believed the testimony of the accountant and the CID agents over that of taxpayer does not make the Tax Court's decision clearly erroneous.[149] Furthermore, taxpayer's contention that the Tax Court did not adequately take into account his disclosure of the Israeli bank account is simply not supported by the record. The Tax Court explicitly acknowledged in its opinion that taxpayer had disclosed the existence of the Israeli bank account in his original income tax returns for 1988 and 1989. We cannot say that the Tax Court's refusal to give much weight to this "disclosure" was unjustified. Acknowledging the existence of this small bank account could just as easily be viewed as an attempt, albeit an unsuccessful one, to divert the Commissioner from investigating whether taxpayer had other foreign bank accounts with much larger balances.

Simply put, taxpayer's arguments go to the weight of the evidence presented and to the credibility of the witnesses who testified. "The Tax Court, like any other court, may disregard uncontradicted testimony by a taxpayer where it finds that testimony lacking in credibility, . . . or finds the testimony to be improbable, unreasonable or questionable."[150] Given taxpayer's inconsistent and implausible statements, his large understatement of income, his guilty plea for willfully failing to disclose information on his income tax returns, and his relative sophistication, the Tax Court did not err in finding that the Commissioner had established fraud.

III. Conclusion

For the foregoing reasons, we AFFIRM the Tax Court's decision in all respects. ■

---

[149]Conti v. Commissioner, *Federal Reporter, Third Series,* vol. 39, p. 658 at p. 664 (6th Circuit Ct. of Appeals 1994).
[150]*Id.,* at p. 664.

International Cooperation

The key to overcoming tax evasion in the international arena is cooperation. Although formal arrangements are still few, they are becoming more commonplace.

A few multilateral arrangements for the international exchange of information have been adopted. The 1972 Nordic Convention Regarding Mutual Assistance in Matters Relating to Tax is the most prominent. It provides for (1) exchanges of information automatically, on request, and spontaneously; (2) the presence of a tax official from one country at a tax investigation in another country when the investigation is of interest to both countries; and (3) one country to carry out a tax investigation or audit at the request of another.

The European Community adopted a tax collaboration directive in 1977 that is similar to the Nordic Convention.[151] Unlike the Nordic Convention, however, the EC directive places

---

[151]Council Directive 77/799/EEC of December 19, 1977. It has subsequently been amended by Directive 79/1070/EEC of December 6, 1979, and Council Directive 92/12/EEC of February 25, 1992. These directives are available on the Eur-Lex Web site at europa.eu.int/eur-lex/en/search/index.html.

several restrictions on the exchange of information between member states. First, a state does not have to provide the requested information if, under its own laws, it is not allowed to obtain that information for its own purposes. Second, a state may refuse to provide information that would disclose a commercial, industrial, or technical secret, or that would be contrary to the state's public policy. Third, a state does not have to provide information if the requesting state is unable to reciprocate (whether for practical or legal reasons) with equivalent information. Finally, a state receiving confidential information must treat it according to the stricter of the secrecy provisions of the states involved.

The Council of Europe and the Organization for Economic Cooperation and Development drafted a Convention on Mutual Administrative Assistance in Tax Matters in 1972 and it came into force in 1995.[152] This convention mirrors the provisions of the EC directive in most respects but adds a significant provision requiring contracting states to "take the necessary steps to recover tax claims of [a requesting] state as if they were its own tax claims."[153]

Bilateral tax cooperation agreements are much more common than multilateral agreements. Both the UN Model Tax Treaty and the OECD Model Tax Treaty have articles requiring the tax authorities of the contracting states to exchange information.[154] Both articles are similar to the European Community directive provisions, except that the tax information received by a state may be used only in connection with "taxes covered by the Convention." The EC directive, by comparison, allows information a state receives to be used for any "taxation purpose."

National Schemes for Combating Tax Evasion

Countries vary greatly in their abilities to combat tax evasion. Developed countries with large tax bureaucracies are often able to deploy a large number of investigators to undertake audits and other tax investigations, but not always. Less developed countries often have very small tax bureaucracies and consequently have greater difficulties in identifying and pursuing tax evaders.

tax amnesty: Onetime authorization for tax-payers to pay delinquent taxes and thereby avoid possible prosecution.

Frequently, both rich and poor countries have to turn to other devices. One of the most common is the **tax amnesty**. A tax amnesty allows delinquent taxpayers to pay all or part of their overdue taxes and thereby avoid possible prosecution. The goal of such amnesties is an increase in tax revenues, either through an immediate increase in funds collected or through a broadening of the tax base. The tax base is broadened when either new taxpayers are identified or previously unreported sources of income are identified.

J. OTHER FORMS OF TAXATION

From an international perspective, income taxes are the most important form of taxation. In most countries they are the principal source of government revenue. Also, unlike most other forms of taxation, many countries impose income taxes on worldwide income. Income taxes are not, however, the only source of government revenue and, in a few countries, other kinds of taxes are far more important.

Turnover Taxes

turnover tax: A tax paid when a good or a service is transferred from one person to another.

Next to income taxes, **turnover taxes** are the most important source of government revenue. The term *turnover tax*—which is not of English origin—is a translation of phrases such as the German "*Umsatzsteuer*," the French "*taxe sur le chiffre d'affaires*," and the Dutch "*omzetbelasting*." The term applies both to these taxes and to such levies as the "sales taxes" used in the United States, the "*impuestos a las ventas*" of Latin America, and the "value-added taxes" now commonly adopted around the world.

---

[152]The convention is posted on the Council of Europe's Web site at conventions.coe.int/treaty/en/Treaties/Html/127.htm.
  Currently there are nine states parties: Belgium, Denmark, Finland, Netherlands, Norway, Poland, Portugal, Sweden, and the United States. Council of Europe Treaty Office at *http://conventions.coe.int/*.
[153]Convention on Mutual Administrative Assistance in Tax Matters, Article 11.
[154]OECD, Model Tax Treaty, Article 26; UN, Model Tax Treaty, Article 26.

All these forms of turnover taxes are similar in that they are collected from persons other than those who are meant to bear the economic burden—that is, they are collected from manufacturers, wholesalers, retailers, etc., and not from consumers. For this reason they are generally referred to as "indirect" taxes. Because they increase the cost of goods and services, they are also sometimes known as "cost price increasing" or "cost" taxes.

Categories of Turnover Taxes

Turnover taxes may be either special or general. Special turnover taxes apply only to goods and services specifically listed in the tax law. Examples include taxes on gasoline sales and hotel rooms. General turnover taxes apply to all goods and services except for stated exclusions.

Turnover taxes may also be cumulative or noncumulative. Cumulative taxes are imposed on the total consideration paid, or the total value of goods sold or services provided at all or at several stages of the production or distribution process, without any credits or deductions for taxes paid at previous stages. To illustrate: A mining company extracts iron ore from the ground and sells it to a mill. The mining company must charge the mill a turnover tax. The mill then converts the ore into steel sheets and sells it to a manufacturing company. Again, the mill must charge a turnover tax. So, too, must the manufacturing company when it sells its finished products to a wholesaler. This is repeated again when the wholesaler sells it to the retailer, and when the retailer sells it to the consumer. Except for the original extractor of raw materials, every person in the chain is charged a turnover tax. Indeed, at each level the purchase price includes an increasing amount of tax—because tax is being paid on tax.

Noncumulative taxes take a variety of forms. The simplest is a single-stage tax—that is, a tax paid at only one point in the production or distribution process, with the preceding and subsequent transactions being tax free. Special turnover taxes are examples of a single-stage tax.

fractionalized production tax: Taxpayers pay taxes on goods they sell after deducting the taxes they paid on the materials and supplies.

value-added tax: Taxes are paid by a taxpayer only on the value added to a good.

Another kind of noncumulative tax is a **fractionalized production tax**. This tax system requires taxpayers to pay taxes on their sales of goods or services, but it allows them to deduct the tax they paid when purchasing raw materials or supplies. As a consequence, the taxpayer pays only a fraction of the total tax.

A sophisticated example of a fractionalized production tax is the **value-added tax** (VAT). The VAT "is a tax on turnover whose payment is split between all the economic stages that it covers, in the sense that at each of the stages that a product passes through, the tax is only levied on the value added to the product at that stage."[155]

Reading 13–2 attempts to provide a succinct definition of the VAT.

---

[155]Report of Subgroup C, *The EEC Reports on Tax Harmonization*, p. 54 (H. Thurston, trans., 1963).

Reading 13–2   Defining the Value-Added Tax

Liam Ebrill, Michael Keem, Jean-Paul Bodin, and Victoria Summers, *The Modern VAT*, pp. 1–4 (2001).

Value-Added Tax or VAT, first introduced less than 50 years ago, remained confined to a handful of countries until the late 1960s. Today, however, most countries [about 123] have a VAT, which raises, on average, 25 percent of their tax revenue. . . .

WHAT IS A VAT

Despite its name, the VAT is not generally intended to be a tax on value added as such: rather it is usually intended as a tax on consumption. Its essence is that it is charged at all stages of production, but with the provision of some mechanism enabling firms to offset the tax they have paid on their own purchase of goods and services against the tax they charge on their sales of goods and services.

Although this characteristic feature is very clear-cut, the VATs observed in practice show considerable diversity as regards, among other things, the range of inputs for which tax offsetting is available and the range of economic activity to which the tax applies (that is, the base of the tax). Some major countries (such as China) currently do not grant credits for taxes on capital goods purchases; moreover, of those that allow credits in respect of such purchases, some do not refund excess credits (any

MAP 13-10 Countries with VATs (2000)

systematic offsetting of tax charged on commodities purchased as inputs—except perhaps on capital goods—against that due on outputs.

This leaves scope for dispute, but does highlight what is taken here to be the key feature of the VAT: the tax is charged and collected throughout the production process, with provision for tax payable to be reduced by the tax paid in respect of purchases.

This definition is broad enough, for example, to encompass not only the dominant "invoice-credit" form of VAT (under which tax paid on inputs is offset by a means of a credit against tax due on output, tax paid being recorded by invoices issued by seller to buyer) but also the subtraction method (under which the offsetting is achieved implicitly, by charging tax on the difference between the values of output and inputs). . . .

The definition excludes, on the other hand, any scheme that allows crediting only in particular sectors of the economy, as well as sales taxes that grant credits only for inputs deemed to be physically incorporated into the output. "Ring" systems—under which tax that would otherwise be charged by one firm on sales to another is suspended for sales to a subset of firms with the "ring"—are also excluded, on the ground that it is an intrinsic feature of a VAT that tax is actually collected at intermediate stages of production. There is of course an issue of judgment as to when the exclusion from tax becomes so widespread that the tax ceases to be a VAT: the exclusion of services in some countries, for instance, is not taken to prevent a tax being labeled a VAT; the former Indian MODVAT, on the other hand, which offered crediting only of central excise taxes (rather than a broad-based output tax) is not regarded [by us] as being a VAT. More generally, it is immediately clear that VATs come in many different shapes and forms. ■

excess of tax paid on inputs over tax chargeable on outputs). Most countries exclude exports from the VAT, in the sense that tax is not charged on sales for export but tax paid on inputs is recoverable, although some (in the BRO[156] region, at least until recently) have systematically levied VAT on some exports. Some countries extend the VAT only to the manufacturing stage; others do not levy it on services.[157] Practice also varies in how tax offsetting is implemented: by far the most common method is through the use of invoices, but the same effect can be achieved on the basis of books of account. . . .

As a result of the diversity of practice, there can be disagreement as to whether a given tax is properly called a VAT or not.[158] For definiteness, though at the risk of creating the impression of an overly sharp dichotomy, we take a VAT to be:

A broad-based tax levied on commodity sales up to and including, at least, the manufacturing stage, with

---

[156]The Baltic countries, Russia, and other countries of the former Soviet Union.

[157]Bangladesh affords an example of the former, Pakistan an example of the latter.

[158]Malawi is a striking example. It was deemed by the Fiscal Affairs Department (FAD) of the IMF [International Monetary Fund] to have a VAT by 1999, though the tax did not extend to the retail stage. The adoption of a VAT—meaning extension to the retail stage—was then part of IMF program conditionality in 1996. In addition, many countries choose to call by some other name—a general sales tax, a goods and services tax—what is clearly a VAT. The label chosen is of no importance to this report.

The Impact of Turnover Taxes

Turnover taxes will always have an impact on national economies because they increase the price of goods and services to the consumer. Several effects may flow from this, one being a lower level of consumption. This may be beneficial if production has exceeded demand; it can be adverse, however, if it leads to demands for higher wages or if production has to be curtailed because the purchasing power of the ultimate consumer has been diminished. The possibility that a turnover tax will have adverse effects on production is aggravated if the tax has a differentiated rate structure, with exemptions and low, intermediate, and "luxury" tax rates. In this case, consumer demand can easily shift from one kind of product to another.

Other consequences of imposing turnover taxes depend on the kind of tax imposed. Single-level taxes imposed at the retail level are, as many tax administrators have found, difficult to apply. If they are imposed at the retail level (i.e., upon the delivery of goods to the final consumer), the tax must be collected from a large number of retailers, including many small entrepreneurs. Tax evasion—whether done negligently or intentionally—is prevalent and often impossible to combat.

Imposing single-level taxes at a stage earlier than the retail level produces other problems. For example, if the tax is imposed on the retailer who purchases goods from manufacturers or wholesalers, the retailer is faced with the potential problem of recovering the tax from its consumers. The retailer's profit margin will be reduced unless it can sell all of the goods on which it has paid taxes. Furthermore, unless the retailer can resell the goods immediately, it is, in effect, financing the state treasury on an interest-free basis until the goods are resold.

The escape route for the retailer in the previous example is vertical integration. That is, to integrate into a larger enterprise that can more easily absorb the tax cost. The result of this, of course, can be the distortion of free competition.

Cumulative turnover taxes have a similar impact. If the tax burden is increased with each turnover at every stage of production and distribution, there is a tendency to decrease the number of stages. Again, vertical integration is encouraged, along with its attendant diminution of competition.

To avoid the impetus toward vertical integration that is inherent in cumulative turnover taxes, several countries have devised schemes to make their tax systems neutral. These schemes in the main follow two methods. The first is to grant the benefits stemming from vertical integration to nonintegrated business. The second (which is the reverse of the first) is to take away the benefits of the vertically integrated business. This is done by treating internal transfers within the vertically integrated business as taxable transactions.

Since the 1950s, the most important development in improving turnover taxes has been the evolution of the value-added tax. As noted earlier, the VAT is a multistage tax that is imposed at all (or several) stages in the process of manufacturing and distributing goods or in the process of delivering services. However, tax paid at one stage is creditable against taxes payable at a subsequent stage. Only the final consumer is not entitled to a credit.

As originally adopted in France in 1954, the tax was not completely neutral.[159] This was because the VAT did not provide a full credit against the VAT paid at prior stages for certain transactions. Also, it did not apply to retail sales, which were subject to a local tax that could not be credited against the VAT. By the 1970s, however, these exceptions had been eliminated and a reasonably "pure" VAT exists not only in France but in the large number of other countries that have adopted it. (See Exhibit 13-8.)

"In its pure form the VAT is both completely noncumulative and entirely neutral in impact."[160] It avoids the main drawbacks of the cumulative turnover taxes because (assuming that one disregards the effect of profit) the total tax payable is the same no matter how many stages the goods or services pass through prior to reaching the consumer. To illustrate, assume that a product will be sold to the final consumer for $100. No matter whether the product goes directly from the manufacturer to the consumer or through several intermediary stages, so long as the final price is $100, a 10 percent "tax on the value added" will result in the same tax in either case.

Miscellaneous Taxes

In addition to income and value-added taxes, all countries impose a variety of other taxes. Some of the most common are (1) taxes on contributions to the capital stock of companies, (2) documentary stamp taxes for transfers of real estate, (3) documentary stamp taxes for transfers of securities, (4) net worth taxes, (5) import duties, (6) export duties, (7) excise taxes on certain products, and (8) payroll taxes.

---

[159]Law No. 54-404 *portant réforme fiscale* (April 10, 1954), *Journal Officiel de la République Française*, p. 3482 (April 11, 1954).

[160]J. Van Hoorn Jr., "Taxation of Business Organizations," *International Encyclopedia of Comparative Law*, vol. 13, chap. 11, p. 22 (1974).

Country	Type of Tax			Special Rates		No Tax on Exports
	VAT	Sales or Other	Basic Rate	Luxury	Low	
1. Antigua and Barbuda		•	2.5–7.5%			
2. Argentina	•		21%			•
3. Australia	•		10%			•
4. Austria	•		20%		10%	•
5. Azerbaijan	•		18%			•
6. Bahamas			None			•
7. Bahrain			None			•
8. Barbados	•		15%		7.5%	•
9. Belgium	•		21%		1%/6%/12%	•
10. Bermuda			None			•
11. Bolivia	•		13%			•
12. Botswana		•	10%			•
13. Brazil	•		11%	17%	9%	•
14. Brunei			None			•
15. Bulgaria	•		20%			•
16. Cambodia	•		10%			•
17. Cameroon	•		17%		8%	•
18. Canada	•		7%			•
19. Cayman Islands			None			•
20. Chile	•		18%			•
21. China	•		17%		13%	•
22. Colombia		•	16%	20%/35%/45%/60%		•
23. Congo (Zaire)		•	13%	15%/18%/25%	3%/6%	
24. Costa Rica		•	13%	10%–75%		
25. Croatia	•		22%			•
26. Cyprus	•		10%			•
27. Czech Republic	•		5%	22%		•
28. Denmark	•		25%			•
29. Dominican Republic	•		8%			•
30. Ecuador	•		12%			•
31. Egypt		•	10%		5%	•
32. Estonia	•		18%			•
33. Fiji	•		10%			•
34. Finland	•		22%		8%/17%	•
35. France	•		19.6%		2.1%/5.5%	•
36. Germany	•		16%		7%	•
37. Ghana	•		12.5%			
38. Greece	•		18%		4%/8%	•
39. Guatemala	•		10%			•
40. Guyana			None			•
41. Hong Kong			None			•
42. Hungary	•		25%		12%	•
43. India		•	Local			
44. Indonesia	•		10%	15%	5%	•
45. Iran			None			•
46. Ireland	•		20%		4.3%/12.5%	•
47. Israel	•		17%		8.5%	•
48. Italy	•		20%		4%/10%	•
49. Ivory Coast	•		20%			•
50. Jamaica	•		15%			•
51. Japan	•		5%			•
52. Kazakhstan	•		20%			•
53. Kenya	•		18%		16%	•
54. Korea	•		10%			•

EXHIBIT 13-8 Turnover Taxes in 115 Countries (2001)

Source: PriceWaterhouseCoopers, *Corporate Taxes: Worldwide Summaries 2001–2002* (2001) and online resources.

Country	Type of Tax			Special Rates		No Tax on Exports
	VAT	Sales or Other	Basic Rate	Luxury	Low	
55. Kuwait			None			•
56. Laos		•	5%/10%			
57. Latvia	•		18%			•
58. Liechtenstein	•		7.6%		2.4%	•
59. Lithuania	•		18%			•
60. Luxembourg	•		15%		3%/6%/12%	•
61. Malawi			None			•
62. Malaysia		•	5–25%			•
63. Malta	•		15%		5%	•
64. Mauritius	•		10%			•
65. Mexico	•		15%		10%	•
66. Monaco	•		20.6%		5%	•
67. Morocco	•		20%		7%	•
68. Mozambique	•		17%			•
69. Myanmar			None			•
70. Namibia	•		15%	30%		•
71. Netherlands	•		19%		6%	•
72. New Zealand	•		12.5%			•
73. Nigeria	•		5%			•
74. Norway	•		24%			•
75. Oman			None			•
76. Pakistan	•		15%			•
77. Panama	•		5%	10%		•
78. Papua New Guinea	•		10%			•
79. Paraguay	•		10%			•
80. Peru	•		8%			•
81. Philippines	•		10%			•
82. Poland	•		22%		7%	•
83. Portugal	•		17%		5%/12%	•
84. Qatar			None			•
85. Romania	•		19%			•
86. Russia	•		20%		10%	•
87. St. Lucia			None			•
88. Saudi Arabia			None			•
89. Senegal	•		20%		10%	•
90. Singapore	•		3%			•
91. Slovakia	•		23%		10%	•
92. Slovenia		•	20%	32%	3%/5%/10%	•
93. Solomon Islands	•		10%			•
94. South Africa	•		14%			•
95. Spain	•		16%		4%/7%	•
96. Sri Lanka	•		12.5%			•
97. Swaziland		•	12%	25%		•
98. Sweden	•		25%		12%/21%	•
99. Switzerland	•		7.6%		2.4%/3.6%	•
100. Tahiti	•		6%		2%/4%	•
101. Taiwan	•		5%		1%/2%	•
102. Tanzania	•		20%			•
103. Thailand	•		7%			•
104. Trinidad and Tobago	•		15%			•
105. Turkey	•		17%	25%/40%	1%/8%	•
106. Uganda	•		17%			•
107. Ukraine	•		20%			•

(continued)

EXHIBIT 13-8   Continued

Country	Type of Tax		Basic Rate	Special Rates		No Tax on Exports
	VAT	Sales or Other		Luxury	Low	
108. United Kingdom	•		17.5%		5%	•
109. United States		Local	0%–9.8%			
110. Uruguay	•		23%		14%	•
111. Uzbekistan	•		20%			•
112. Venezuela	•		14.5%			•
113. Vietnam		•	10%	20%	2%/3%/5%	•
114. Zambia	•		17.5%			•
115. Zimbabwe		•	15%	25%	5%	

EXHIBIT 13-8 Continued

Chapter Questions

1. You were a resident of Indonesia and earned 60,000,000 rupiahs during the tax year of 1990. Income from rents on an office building that you own was 30,000,000 rupiahs. Professional income from your work as an international tax lawyer was 30,000,000 rupiahs. Using the tax schedule for Indonesia from the text, determine the income tax you would have paid that year. Assume that you were entitled to no deductions, exemptions, or credits.

2. You were a resident of Libya and earned 40,000 dinars during the tax year of 1990. Income from rents on an office building that you own was 20,000 dinars. Professional income from your work as an international tax lawyer was 20,000 dinars. Using the tax schedule for Libya from the text, determine the income tax you would have paid that year. Assume that you were entitled to no deductions, exemptions, or credits.

3. Padre Co. is a multinational enterprise involved in selling cement mixers worldwide. It has established several subsidiaries in countries in Latin America. One subsidiary, Hijo Co., is located in Country X. Hijo is responsible for locating customers for Padre. Once the customer is put in touch with Padre, Hijo does nothing more. If the customer buys mixers, Padre pays Hijo 5 percent of the sales price as a finding fee. Payments by the customer are made directly to Padre at its home office in Topeka, Kansas, U.S.A. Padre itself does no business whatsoever in Country X, other than to pay Hijo its finding fees.

   During the current tax year, Padre sold U.S. $10,000,000 worth of cement mixers in Country X. It earned for itself (after paying Hijo $500,000) $1,500,000.

   Country X's Internal Revenue Agency (IRA) has assessed taxes on Hijo of $400,000, which is 20 percent (the appropriate tax rate) of $2,000,000. The IRA contends that Padre and Hijo are in reality one company and that Hijo's taxes are assessable on the total income of both Padre and Hijo. Is the IRA correct? Explain.

4. Assume that the 1980 *Convention between Canada and the United States of America with Respect to Taxes on Income and on Capital,* discussed in Case 13–4, applies to the following hypothetical situations.

   • The Free Rider Corporation, a Bahaman corporation, is engaged in business in the United States and earns $100 of "effectively connected income" (which is taxable in the U.S.) and $1,000,000 of foreign source "non-connected income" from Canada which is not taxable in the United States. Is the Free Rider exempt from paying taxes in Canada?

   • The Dude, Ltd., a United Kingdom corporation, that has been operating a Wyoming ranch for 50 years as its sole business, earns $100,000 annually in the United States. It also receives $100 in passive income from Canada on a small investment there. Is Dude, Ltd., exempt from paying taxes in the United States?

5. The Schizophrenic Co. was organized in the state of Delaware in the United States. All of its business is done in France. Its managerial offices are located in Luxembourg. Its board of directors holds its regular meeting in Luxembourg. The shareholders are all Swiss and they hold their annual meeting in Innsbruck, Austria. Of which country (countries) is Schizophrenic a resident for tax purposes? Explain.

6. Extracto Co. in Country A agrees to sell 1,000 tons of copper ore to Processo Co. in Country B. Assume that Country A has a 10 percent sales tax and a 20 percent income tax, while Country B has a 5 percent sales tax and a 15 percent income tax. Where should Processo Co. take delivery of the ore if it wishes to have the minimum amount of tax liability?

7. You owned 1,000 shares in Old Co., which you originally bought for £50 a share. Five years ago Old Co. merged into New Co., and you received 2,000 shares of New Co. stock in exchange for your Old Co. stock. This year you sold half of your shares of New Co. stock for £30 a share. Will the sale produce any income that is taxable? If so, how much?

8. The Amalgamated Manufacturing Company (AMC), a resident of State A, has a subsidiary, Bambino Retailing Co. (BRC), which is a resident of State B.

    In the current tax year, BRC earned $125,000 and remitted $100,000 in dividends (before paying withholding taxes) to AMC, retaining the $25,000 balance for itself.

    State B law imposes a tax of 10 percent on earned and undistributed income. According to the double taxation treaty between State A and State B, State B is to charge a 25 percent withholding tax on dividends remitted from a subsidiary in State B to a parent in State A.

    State A has a flat company income tax rate of 50 percent. State A's law also provides an indirect credit to companies in State A that receive income from subsidiaries in State B.

    Assuming no other exemptions, credits, or deductions, how much tax does BRC owe State B on its earnings? How much tax does AMC owe State A on the income remitted by BRC to it?

9. The Mother Construction Co. (MCC), a resident of State X, has a branch office in the western part of State Y. During the current tax year the branch earned £100,000. Also, during the current year, MCC undertook to build a highway in the eastern part of State Y. Because of the distance between the branch office and the construction site, the branch office was not involved in this project at all. The road was built in four months, and the construction site was abandoned after five months. MCC earned £250,000 from building the road.

    State X and State Y have entered into a double taxation treaty based on the UN Model Tax Treaty. On what income may State Y impose taxes? Explain.

10. Invento Co., a resident of State I, has just developed a new patent it wishes to license in State J. State I and State J have no tax treaties, however, and Invento would have to pay high taxes in both states if it remitted its royalty earnings directly from State J to State I.

    Invento has discovered that State K has double taxation treaties with both State J and State I. Royalties remitted to State K from State J are subject to no withholding taxes, nor are dividends remitted from State K to State I.

    Invento sets up a subsidiary in State K and it assigns its patents to the subsidiary. Royalties remitted by the licenses in State J are not taxed by State J. Dividends remitted by the subsidiary in State K are not taxed.

    State K is delighted to have Invento doing business in its territory through a subsidiary. State I is not affected one way or another. State J, however, is displeased at not being able to collect its taxes. Can State J do anything about this? If so, what?

11. Big Company, a multinational manufacturer of automotive parts, has 33 percent of its employees in California, pays 27 percent of its payroll in California, and sells 30 percent of its goods in California. On its books worldwide the Big Company earns a before-tax profit of $180 million. In California it actually loses about $3 million. Can California collect any income taxes from Big? Explain.

Review Problem

Because of the outstanding job you have done in MegaBranch Industry's (MBI's) legal department, you have been elected to MBI's Board of Directors. Partly because of your legal experience (and partly because you are the new person on the board), the board has named you to be the Chairperson of the Board's audit committee. As such, you are responsible for overseeing the firm's accountants and tax lawyers, who in turn are responsible for determining and paying the taxes for MBI and its subsidiaries. In addition, you are responsible for working with local and national governments to obtain the most advantageous tax arrangements for MBI.

1. State A is considering replacing its schedular income tax system with a global income tax. MBI manufactures electronic components and industrial chemicals in State A, and it presently pays a flat tax rate of 10 percent on income from profits from its electronics operations and 15 percent on its industrial chemical earnings. Under the proposed tax it would pay taxes at 10, 15, and 20 percent rates depending on the total amount of its overall earnings. Should MBI oppose this change? If so, what kind of arguments can it make in opposition?

2. MBI is thinking of doing business in State B. Initially, it would like to explore the opportunities available in State B; then, if these look promising, it would like to set up a distributorship there. Finally, if sales are good, it will set up a manufacturing plant. From a tax perspective, what kind of business structures should MBI use to do this?

3. Several members of the management of MBI's subsidiary in State C are U.S. citizens who earn salaries in excess of U.S. $150,000. May the United States impose income taxes on their salaries? If so, on what basis? May State C also tax them? If so, on what basis?

4. A subsidiary of MBI, MBI(X), was incorporated in State D, but it does most of its business in State E. Its manufacturing facilities are all located in State F, and its headquarters and managerial staff are located in State G. For tax purposes, in which state (or states) is MBI(X) a resident?

5. The MBI subsidiary in State H has agreed to sell goods to a buyer in State I. Although the subsidiary has a branch in State I, it manufactures its goods in State H; and it has agreed to deliver the goods to a carrier in State J, where the buyer will then legally take possession of the goods. Which of these states may tax the income earned by the subsidiary on this sale?

6. State A, which has now adopted a global income tax system, is considering whether it should tax capital gains at a lower rate than other income. Should MBI advocate this change? If so, what arguments can it make in favor of doing so?

7. State A is also considering changing from a "classical system" of integrating its taxes on company income and shareholder dividend income. What system would be most advantageous for MBI and its shareholders? Why?

8. State A is negotiating a double tax treaty with State J and its legislature has asked you to advise it on what kind of exemption system it should adopt. What will you advise? Why?

9. MBI is negotiating with State K (a developing country) to set up a subsidiary. What kind of tax incentives should MBI be looking to secure? What economic, political, and ethical considerations should MBI have in mind while it carries on these negotiations?

10. Assume that MBI's home country does not have a tax-sparing provision in any of its double taxation treaties or in its domestic tax law. If MBI is able to secure substantial tax incentives from State K for a subsidiary in that country, will this be of any benefit to MBI? Is there anything that MBI can do (including restructuring its organization in some way) to increase the benefits it might receive from the tax incentives?

11. The MBI subsidiary in State L is subject to a 20 percent net income tax. The subsidiary in State M is subject to a 5 percent net tax. Is there anything wrong with MBI structuring the prices charged by one subsidiary to another so that the subsidiary in State L makes few (if any) profits and the subsidiary in State M makes substantial profits?

12. MBI, which is incorporated and headquartered in a developed country, is considering whether or not to reincorporate in a tax haven to take advantage of the low corporate taxes there. Should it do so?

13. Assuming that MBI has restructured its transfer-pricing arrangements among its subsidiaries as suggested in the previous situation, what kind of measures can it expect that State L will take to counter this?

14. In setting up a new subsidiary in State M, how much of the start-up money should MBI provide to it in the form of loans (as compared to equity)?

15. A court in State N has ordered the local MBI subsidiary to turn over all of its financial records and all of the financial records of its parent (i.e., MBI). Can the court do this?

16. Assume that MBI's subsidiary in State O has been delinquent in paying some of its State O income taxes for the past few years and that State O has announced a tax amnesty. Are there any reasons why the subsidiary might not want to take advantage of this?

17. The legislature in MBI's home state is considering switching from a sales tax to a value-added tax. Should MBI support or oppose this change?

Credits for Readings and Cases

CHAPTER 1

Reading 1–1/p. 45   Samuel P. Huntington, "The Clash of Civilizations?" *Foreign Affairs,* vol. 72, no. 3, p. 22 (Summer 1993). © Council on Foreign Relations, Inc., 1993.

CHAPTER 3

Case 3–5/p. 145   *Attorney-General of the Government of Israel v. Eichmann,* Israel, District Court of Jerusalem, 1961. *International Law Reports,* vol. 36, p. 5 (1968) © *International Law Reports,* 1968.

Case 3–8/p. 159   *Abbott v. Republic of South Africa,* Spain, Constitutional Court, 1992, *International Law Reports,* vol. 113, p. 412 (1999). (Translation by T. F. K. Johnston). © *International Law Reports,* 1999.

CHAPTER 4

Reading 4–1/p. 207   Alison Maitland, "An Acid Test for Better Conduct in Business," *Financial Times* (August 12, 2001).

Case 4–8/p. 239   *Garden Contamination Case (No. 2),* Federal Republic of Germany, District Court (*Amtsgericht*) of Bonn, 1987. *International Law Reports,* vol. 80, p. 378 (1990). © *International Law Reports,* 1990.

CHAPTER 5

Reading 5–1/p. 248   Michael Skapinker, "How Monsanto Got Bruised in a Food Fight," *Financial Times* (March 7, 2002).

Case 5–1/p. 250   *Arab Republic of Egypt v. Southern Pacific Properties, Ltd. et al.,* France, Court of Appeals of Paris, 1984. *International Legal Materials,* vol. 23, p. 1048 (1984). (Translation by Emmanuel Gaillard). © The Society of International Law, *International Legal Materials,* 1984.

CHAPTER 6

Case 6–2/p. 309   Re Law Authorizing an Increase in the French Quota to the International Monetary Fund, France, Constitutional Council, 1978. *International Law Reports,* vol. 74, p. 685 (1987). ©*International Law Reports,* 1987.

Case 6–3/p. 313   *De Boer, Widow Moojen v. Ducro et al.,* France, Court of Appeal of Paris, 1961. *International Law Reports,* vol. 41, p. 46 (1963). © *International Law Reports,* 1963.

Reading 6–1/p. 332   Traute Wohlers-Scharf, *Arab and Islamic Banks: New Business Partners for Developing Countries,* p. 74 (1983). © 1983 by Organization for Economic Cooperation and Development.

Reading 6–2/p. 340   Jonathan M. Winer, "How to Clean up Dirty Money," *Financial Times* (March 22, 2002).

CHAPTER 7

Reading 7–1/p. 362   Judith Ann Maltz, "Behind the Screen at the WTO," *The Watertalk Forum,* December 5, 1999, at www.watertalk.org/forum/WTO-Seattle.html. Date accessed November 22, 2002.

Case 7–1/p. 369   *Finance Ministry v. Manifattura Lane Marzotto, SpA,* Italy, Court of Cassation (Joint Session), 1973. *International Law Reports,* vol. 77, p. 551 (1973). © *International Law Reports,* 1973.

CHAPTER 10

Reading 10–1/p. 573   John Honnold, *Uniform Law for International Sales under the 1980 United Nations Convention,* pp. 307, 315–316 (1982). © 1982 Kluwer Law & Tax.

CHAPTER 11

Case 11–8/p. 636   *The Chinese Seamen's Foreign Technical Services Co. v. Soto Grande Shipping Corp., SA,* People's Republic of China, Shanghai Maritime Court, 1987. *Journal of Maritime Law and Commerce,* vol. 20, p. 217 (1989). © Jefferson Law Book Co., Division of Anderson Publishing Co., and the author, Todd L. Platek, 1989.

CHAPTER 12

Reading 12–1/p. 689   Ross Davis, "A Deal With Strings Attached," *Financial Times* (July 18, 2002).

CHAPTER 13

Reading 13–1/p. 747   John Trani, "The Offshore Patriots," *Financial Times* (June 5, 2002).

Reading 13–2/p. 736   Liam Ebrill, Michael Keem, Jean-Paul Bodin, and Victoria Summers, *The Modern VAT,* pp. 1–4 (2001). © International Monetary Fund, 2001.

Case Index

Principal cases are in bold type

Key:

Arb.—Arbitration Tribunal
EFTA—European Free Trade Area
ICJ—International Court of Justice
ICSID—International Center for the Settlement on Investment Disputes
ILO—International Labor Organization Administrative Tribunal
ITLOS—International Tribunal for the Law of the Sea
PCA—Permanent Court of Arbitration
PCIJ—Permanent Court of International Justice
UAE—United Arab Emirates
UK—United Kingdom
US—United States
WTO—World Trade Organization

Statutory Index

Topical Index